Communications in Computer and Information Science 639

Commenced Publication in 2007
Founding and Former Series Editors:
Alfredo Cuzzocrea, Dominik Ślęzak, and Xiaokang Yang

More information about this series at http://www.springer.com/series/7899

Giedre Dregvaite · Robertas Damasevicius (Eds.)

Information and Software Technologies

22nd International Conference, ICIST 2016
Druskininkai, Lithuania, October 13–15, 2016
Proceedings

 Springer

Editors
Giedre Dregvaite
Kaunas University of Technology
Kaunas
Lithuania

Robertas Damasevicius
Kaunas University of Technology
Kaunas
Lithuania

ISSN 1865-0929   ISSN 1865-0937 (electronic)
Communications in Computer and Information Science
ISBN 978-3-319-46253-0   ISBN 978-3-319-46254-7 (eBook)
DOI 10.1007/978-3-319-46254-7

Library of Congress Control Number: 2016950911

Printed on acid-free paper

This Springer imprint is published by Springer Nature
The registered company is Springer International Publishing AG Switzerland

Preface

Information and Software Technologies contains papers presented at the 22nd International Conference on Information and Software Technologies, ICIST 2016, held in October 2016, in Druskininkai, Lithuania.

The papers presented in this volume address the topics of information systems, business intelligence for information and software systems, software engineering, and IT applications. The conference papers present original research results in methodologies for information systems development, conceptual modelling, ontologies, and databases, business processes and business rules, enterprise architecture and enterprise modelling, business intelligence for information and software systems, data mining and knowledge discovery, decision support systems, natural language processing and application of language technologies, knowledge-based system engineering, software engineering software and systems engineering methodologies, model-driven development, cloud computing, IT applications for teaching and learning, Internet of Things and smart environments, and wireless and mobile applications.

The conference included four keynote talks. Prof. Ajith Abraham of Machine Intelligence Research Labs, USA, delivered a keynote on "Cyber Physical Systems: Challenges from a Data Analysis Perspective." Prof. Sanjay Misra of Covenant University delivered a keynote on "Controlling Quality in Web Service." Prof. Christian Reimann of Dortmund University of Applied Sciences and Arts, Germany, delivered a keynote on "Software Agents and Services Process Improvement." Assoc. Prof. Tor-Morten Grønli Westerdals of Oslo School of Arts, Communication and Technology, Norway, presented a keynote on "Mobile Application Architecture and Design in the Era of Internet of Things."

The research part of the conference was organized in a number of special sessions:

1. Special Session on Intelligent Systems and Software Engineering Advances
2. Special Session on Intelligent Methods for Data Analysis and Computer-Aided Software Engineering
3. Special Session on Innovative Applications for Knowledge Transfer Support
4. Special Session on Information and Software Technologies for Intelligent Power Systems
5. Special Session on e-Health Information Systems
6. Special Session on Internet of Things in Mobility Applications
7. Special Session on Smart e-Learning Technologies and Applications
8. Special Session on Language Technologies

These special sessions provide the opportunity for researchers conducting research in specific areas to present their results in a more focused environment.

There were 158 submissions this year and 61 paper was selected for this publication, giving an acceptance rate of 39 %. The papers were reviewed and selected by the Program Committee consisting of 95 reviewers (supported by 85 additional reviewers) representing more than 99 academic institutions and 37 countries. Each submission was reviewed by at least two reviewers, while borderline papers were evaluated by three or more reviewers. We believe the selection of 62 accepted papers presented in this book is a good reflection of the latest research on the selected topics.

The participants of the conference were also encouraged to take part in the Industrial Tutorials session co-located with the conference for the sixth year in a row.

A conference would not be possible without the contribution of many people. Hence, we would like to thank particularly the general chair, Prof. E. Bareiša (Kaunas University of Technology), the session chairs and co-chairs, Prof. Carsten Wolff and Prof. Christian Reimann (Dortmund University of Applied Sciences and Arts), Adj. Prof. Pasi Kuvaja (University of Oulu), Prof. Irene Krebs (Brandenburg University of Technology Cottbus-Senftenberg), Prof. Justyna Patalas-Maliszewska (University of Zielona Góra), Prof. Rolf Engelbrecht (Germany), Assoc. Prof. Vytenis Punys (Kaunas University of Technology), Prof. Giedrius Vanagas (Lithuanian University of Health Sciences), Prof. Algirdas Pakštas (London Metropolitan University), Assoc. Prof. Vira Shendryk (Sumy State University), Dr. Marcin Woźniak (Silesian University of Technology), Prof. Emiliano Tramontana and Prof. Christian Napoli (University of Catania), Dr. Maria Dolores Alfonso Suárez (SIANI University Institute), Prof. Audrius Lopata (Vilnius University), Assoc. Prof. Danguolė Rutkauskienė (Kaunas University of Technology), Prof. Radu Adrian Vasiu (Politehnica University of Timisoara), Assoc. Prof. Jurgita Kapočiūtė-Dzikienė (Vytautas Magnus University), and Peter Dirix (University of Leuven).

We also thank the members of the Program Committee and all additional reviewers for providing thoughtful and knowledgeable reviews and ensuring the quality of papers accepted, as well as the local Organizing Committee for their great services and excellent organization of the conference.

The conference was made possible thanks to the support of the Faculty of Informatics, Kaunas University of Technology, and the Research Council of Lithuania, whose contribution is gratefully acknowledged.

As with the proceedings of the four previous ICIST conferences, the proceedings of the ICIST 2016 conference (in printed and electronic volumes) are published by Springer in their *Communications in Computer and Information Science* series. We are very proud of this continuing cooperation. We would like to express our sincere thanks to Leonie Kunz, Aliaksandr Birukou, and Ingrid Beyer, Springer, for their prompt and professional support throughout the entire project.

July 2016   Giedre Dregvaite
                                                              Robertas Damasevicius

Organization

The 22nd International Conference on Information and Software Technologies (ICIST 2016) was organized by Kaunas University of Technology and took place in Druskininkai, Lithuania (October 13–15, 2016).

General Chair

Eduardas Bareisa   Kaunas University of Technology, Lithuania

Local Organizing Committee

Giedre Dregvaite (*Chair*)   Kaunas University of Technology, Lithuania
Gintare Dzindzeletaite   Kaunas University of Technology, Lithuania
Lina Repsiene   Kaunas University of Technology, Lithuania
Romas Slezevicius   Kaunas University of Technology, Lithuania
Mindaugas Vasiljevas   Kaunas University of Technology, Lithuania

Special Section Chairs

Peter Dirix	University of Leuven, Belgium
Rolf Engelbrecht	ProRec Germany, Germany
Jurgita Kapočiūtė-Dzikienė	Vytautas Magnus University, Lithuania
Irene Krebs	University of Technology Cottbus, Germany
Pasi Kuvaja	University of Oulu, Finland
Audrius Lopata	Vilnius University, Lithuania
Christian Napoli	University of Catania, Italy
Algirdas Pakštas	London Metropolitan University, UK
Justyna Patalas-Maliszewska	University of Zielona Gora, Poland
Vytenis Punys	Kaunas University of Technology, Lithuania
Christian Reimann	Dortmund University of Applied Sciences and Arts, Germany
Danguole Rutkauskiene	Kaunas University of Technology, Lithuania
Vira Shendryk	Sumy State University, Ukraine
Maria Dolores Afonso Suárez	SIANI University Institute, Spain
Emiliano Tramontana	University of Catania, Italy
Giedrius Vanagas	Lithuanian University of Health Sciences, Lithuania
Radu Adrian Vasiu	Politehnica University of Timisoara, Romania
Carsten Wolff	Dortmund University of Applied Sciences and Arts, Germany
Marcin Woźniak	Silesian University of Technology, Poland

Program Committee

Jose Luis Herrero Agustin	University of Extremadura, Spain
Mehmet Aksit	University of Twente, The Netherlands
Liesbeth Augustinus	University of Leuven, Belgium
Eduard Babkin	National Research University, Russia
Marco Bajec	University of Ljubljana, Slovenia
Jorg Becker	University of Münster, Germany
Mokhtar Beldjehem	University of Otawa, Canada
Rimantas Butleris	Kaunas University of Technology, Lithuania
Albertas Caplinskas	Vilnius University, Lithuania
Nuno Castela	Polytechnic Institute of Castelo Branco, Portugal
Miloslava Cerna	University of Hradec Králové, Czech Republic
Paulo Rupino Cunha	University of Coimbra, Portugal
Valentina Dagienė	Vilnius University, Lithuania
Peter Dirix	University of Leuven, Belgium
da Silva Ana Paula Neves Ferreira	University of Coimbra, Portugal
Constantine Filote	Stefan cel Mare University of Suceava, Romania
John Gammack	College of Technological Innovation, United Arab Emirates
Jorge Garcia	University of Porto, Portugal
Efri Georgala	Nuance Communications, USA
Marisa Gil	Polytechnic University of Catalonia, Spain
Janis Grabis	Riga Technical University, Latvia
Tor-Morten Grønli	Brunel University, Norway
Saulius Gudas	Vilnius University, Lithuania
Sevinc Gulsecen	Istanbul University, Turkey
Karin Harbusch	University of Koblenz-Landau, Germany
Christian Hardmeier	Uppsala University, Sweden
Mirjana Ivanovic	University of Novi Sad, Serbia
Alvydas Jaliniauskas	SubscriberMail, A Harland Clarke Company, USA
Raimundas Jasinevicius	Kaunas University of Technology, Lithuania
Andras Javor	Budapest University of Technology and Economics, Hungary
Arnas Kaceniauskas	Vilnius Gediminas Technical University, Lithuania
Jurgita Kapočiūtė-Dzikienė	Vytautas Magnus University, Lithuania
Marite Kirikova	Riga Technical University, Latvia
Marek Krasinski	Wroclaw University of Economics, Poland
Irene Krebs	University of Technology Cottbus, Germany
Ondrej Krejcar	University of Hradec Králové, Czech Republic
Dalia Kriksciuniene	Vilnius University, Lithuania
Tomas Krilavicius	Vytautas Magnus University, Lithuania
Milena Krumova	Technical University of Sofia, Bulgaria
Olga Kurasova	Vilnius University, Lithuania
Linas Laibinis	Abo Akademi University, Finland

Peter Thanisch	University of Tampere, Finland
de Paolis Lucio Tommaso	University del Salento, Italy
Yuh-Min Tseng	National Changhua University of Education, Taiwan
Pascal Vaillant	IUT of Bobigny, France
Giedrius Vanagas	Lithuanian University of Health Sciences, Lithuania
Olegas Vasilecas	Vilnius Gediminas Technical University, Lithuania
Radu Adrian Vasiu	Politehnica University of Timisoara, Romania
Damjan Vavpotič	University of Ljubljana, Slovenia
Luigi Vladareanu	Romanian Academy Institute of Solid Mechanics, Romania
Benkt Wangler	Stockholm University, Sweden
Marcin Woźniak	Silesian University of Technology, Poland

Additional Reviewers

Salvatore Alaimo	University of Catania, Italy
Rimantas Barauskas	Kaunas University of Technology, Lithuania
Nabil Belala	University of Constantine, Algeria
Slobodan Beliga	University of Rijeka, Croatia
Solvita Bērziša	Riga Technical University, Latvia
Kristina Bespalova	Kaunas University of Technology, Lithuania
Darius Birvinskas	Kaunas University of Technology, Lithuania
Germanas Budnikas	Kaunas University of Technology, Lithuania
Renata Burbaite	Kaunas University of Technology, Lithuania
Rita Butkiene	Kaunas University of Technology, Lithuania
Lina Ceponiene	Kaunas University of Technology, Lithuania
Grzegorz Chmaj	University of Nevada, USA
Stanislaw Czapp	Gdansk University of Technology, Poland
Robertas Damasevicius	Kaunas University of Technology, Lithuania
Tomas Danikauskas	Kaunas University of Technology, Lithuania
Vilma Deltuvaite	Kaunas University of Technology, Lithuania
Vladimir Despotovic	University of Belgrade, Serbia
Borislav Djordjevic	Institute Mihailo Pupin, Serbia
Giedre Dregvaite	Kaunas University of Technology, Lithuania
Paweł Dworak	West Pomeranian University of Technology, Poland
Alessandro Filippeschi	PERCRO Perceptual Robotics Laboratory, Italy
Radek Fujdiak	Brno University of Technology, Czech Republic
Marcin Gabryel	Częstochowa University of Technology, Poland
Beata Gavurova	Technical University of Košice, Slovakia
Henrihs Gorskis	Riga Technical University, Latvia
Gintare Grigonyte	Stockholm University, Sweden
Daina Gudoniene	Kaunas University of Technology, Lithuania
Taflan Gündem	Bogaziçi University, Turkey
Prima Gustiene	Karlstad University, Sweden
Haryani Haron	University of Technology MARA, Malaysia

Robert Hoettger	Dortmund University of Applied Sciences and Arts, Germany
Jordan Hristov	University of Chemical Technology and Metallurgy, Bulgaria
Miloslav Hub	University of Pardubice, Czech Republic
Ali Isik	Mehmet Akif Ersoy University, Turkey
Nikša Jakovlević	University of Novi Sad, Serbia
Andrzej Jardzioch	West Pomeranian University of Technology Szczecin, Poland
Pavel Jirava	University of Pardubice, Czech Republic
Vacius Jusas	Kaunas University of Technology, Lithuania
Kestutis Kapocius	Kaunas University of Technology, Lithuania
Wojciech Kempa	Silesian University of Technology, Poland
Irina Kliziene	Kaunas University of Technology, Lithuania
Evgeniy Krastev	Sofia University St. Kliment Ohridsky, Bulgaria
Antonino Laudani	Roma Tre University, Italy
Antanas Lenkevicius	Kaunas University of Technology, Lithuania
Virginija Limanauskiene	Kaunas University of Technology, Lithuania
Reza Malekian	University of Pretoria, South Africa
Ka Lok Man	Xi'an Jiaotong-Liverpool University, China
Zbigniew Marszalek	Silesian University of Technology, Poland
Rytis Maskeliunas	Kaunas University of Technology, Lithuania
Ana Meštrović	University of Rijeka, Croatia
Wojciech Mitkowski	AGH University of Science and Technology, Poland
Vitaliy Mosiychuk	National Technical University of Ukraine, Ukraine
Tarik Mumcu	Yıldız Technical University, Turkey
Zenonas Navickas	Kaunas University of Technology, Lithuania
Lina Norbutaite	Kaunas University of Technology, Lithuania
Alius Noreika	Kaunas University of Technology, Lithuania
Jurij Novickij	Vilnius Gediminas Technical University, Lithuania
Bartosz Nowak	University of Warmia and Mazury, Poland
Robert Nowicki	Częstochowa University of Technology, Poland
Armantas Ostreika	Kaunas University of Technology, Lithuania
Iwona Paprocka	Silesian University of Technology, Poland
Martynas Patasius	Kaunas University of Technology, Lithuania
Petra Poulova	University of Hradec Králové, Czech Republic
Ralph Pridmore	Macquarie University, Australia
Vytenis Punys	Kaunas University of Technology, Lithuania
Eva Rakovska	University of Economics Bratislava, Slovakia
Kastytis Ratkevičius	Kaunas University of Technology, Lithuania
Samo Rauter	University of Ljubljana, Slovenia
Juha Roning	University of Oulu, Finland
Vytautas Rudžionis	Kaunas University of Technology, Lithuania
Grazia Lo Sciuto	University of Catania, Italy
Tomas Skersys	Kaunas University of Technology, Lithuania
Vita Speckauskiene	Lithuanian University of Health Sciences, Lithuania

Ranka Stanković	University of Belgrade, Serbia
Tõnu Tamme	University of Tartu, Estonia
Ilhan Tarimer	Muğla Sıtkı Koçman University, Turkey
Valentina Timcenko	Institute Mihailo Pupin, Serbia
Emiliano Tramontana	University of Catania, Italy
Tiberiu Tudorache	Polytechnic University of Bucharest, Romania
Volkan Tunali	Celal Bayar University, Turkey
Jonas Valantinas	Kaunas University of Technology, Lithuania
Marcin Zalasinski	Częstochowa University of Technology, Poland
Jan Zizka	Brno University of Technology, Czech Republic

Co-editors

| Robertas Damasevicius | Kaunas University of Technology, Lithuania |
| Giedre Dregvaite | Kaunas University of Technology, Lithuania |

Contents

**Information Systems: Special Session on Information and Software
Technologies for Intelligent Power Systems**

**Business Intelligence for Information and Software Systems: Special Session
on Intelligent Methods for Data Analysis and Computer
Aided Software Engineering**

**Software Engineering: Special Session on Intelligent Systems
and Software Engineering Advances**

**Information Technology Applications: Special Session on Smart
e-Learning Technologies and Applications**

**Information Technology Applications: Special Session
on Language Technologies**

Information Technology Applications: Special Session on Internet-of-Things in Mobility Applications

**Information Technology Applications: Regular Session on Information
Technology Applications**

Information Systems: Special Session on Innovative Applications for Knowledge Transfer Support

Modelling of Adequate Costs
of Utilities Services

Janis Zuters[1], Janis Valeinis[2], Girts Karnitis[1(✉)], and Edvins Karnitis[1]

[1] Faculty of Computing, University of Latvia, Riga, Latvia
{janis.zuters,girts.karnitis,edvins.karnitis}@lu.lv
[2] Faculty of Physics and Mathematics, University of Latvia, Riga, Latvia
janis.valeinis@lu.lv

Abstract. The paper propose methodology for benchmark modelling of adequate costs of utilities services, which is based on the data analysis of the factual cases (key performance indicators of utilities as the predictors). The proposed methodology was tested by modelling of Latvian water utilities with three tools: (1) a classical version of the multi-layer perceptron with error back-propagation training algorithm was sharpened up with task-specific monotony tests, (2) the fitting of the generalized additive model using the programming language R ensured the opportunity to evaluate the statistical significance and confidence bands of predictors, (3) the sequential iterative nonlinear regression process with minimizing mean squared error provided the notion of the impact of each predictor on the searched regularity. The quality of models is high: the adjusted determination coefficient is greater than 0.75, explained deviance exceeds 0.80, while the correlation between the respective modelled values exceeds even 0.95.

Keywords: Data analysis · Multi-layer perceptron · Generalized additive model · Nonlinear regression · Utility services

1   Introduction

Number of utilities services are and will be provided by monopolies due to the strong dependence on the infrastructure. Several of them are national wide monopolies (e.g., electricity and natural gas transmission operators), while the vast majority (in total dozens, even hundreds of utilities in any country) are local monopolies in a specific territory – water supply, district heating, sewerage and waste treatment services. National Regulatory Authorities (NRA) are monitoring operation of these utilities including the setting of adequate tariffs for services, which should be economically substantiated as well as provide sustainability of service and investment opportunities.

Assessment of the specific costs for monopoly services (€ per product unit) is one of the major regulatory functions; the essence of the methodologies usually is the aggregation of number of cost items (e.g., [1, 2]). The procedure is heavy and laborious. Large number (tens, even hundreds) of performance indicators (PI), which affect expenses of the utility (including those with a negligible impact), are used in various combinations and proportions as the cost drivers (e.g., [3–5]) – financial and economic

© Springer International Publishing Switzerland 2016
G. Dregvaite and R. Damasevicius (Eds.): ICIST 2016, CCIS 639, pp. 3–17, 2016.
DOI: 10.1007/978-3-319-46254-7_1

factors, indicators of product and service quality, infrastructure and consumption characteristics, environmental factors and consumer protection issues.

Whereas methodologies are based on the careful evaluation of all cost items, there is a need for detailed individual assessment of each position for each utility. Business models and account layouts of utilities are different; therefore, the comparative assessment of separate cost items and efficiency evaluation of utilities is impossible.

Low validity, compatibility and reliability of input data (the numerical values of the PIs) cause another problem (e.g., [6]). There is a lack of regulations on the material, human and other resources needed for an efficient (i.e., economically substantiated) service. The large number of utilities means a considerable diversity in the comprehension on the PIs. Huge number of PIs, which are used for tariff setting, is a strong administrative burden for utilities to provide all of them [7]. The information asymmetry gap between utilities and the NRA is large because of the local monopolism [8, 9]. In total adequacy of the applied tariffs becomes unconvincing; there is insufficient economic and hence legal justification of the tariffs.

The aim of current research is development of new methodology for determination of adequate service costs by synthesis of the general regularity using advanced benchmark modelling tools. It will significantly raise the tariffs credibility, reduce the administrative burden on utilities and increase the efficiency of the NRAs.

The methodology was developed and tested by benchmarked modelling of Latvian water utilities; methodological principles are applicable to other utilities sectors.

The structure of the paper is as follows. The next section shortly reviews related works. The key principles of the proposed methodology are described in Sect. 3. Section 4 analyses selection and review of input data, Sect. 5 – the peculiarities of usage of three modelling tools in our case. Modelled costs and their coincidence are presented in Sect. 6, while concluding remarks – in the final Sect. 7.

2   A Review of the Related Methods

Advanced methods have been introduced for management of the water sector in the last decades.

The benchmarking has been recognized as an efficient tool to compare various performance aspects as well to show the best practice [10]. Theoretical and applied studies have been carried out (e.g., [11, 12]), large number of PIs is benchmarked (e.g., [13]). Nevertheless any regulatory outcome, (e.g., for supervision of the sector or evaluation of total costs and tariff setting) has not achieved yet.

The modelling has already become popular and generally accepted method for the prediction of various water supply aspects to improve efficiency, safety and sustainability of the supply. Evaluation of the water markets (e.g., [14]) and analysis of costs (e.g., [15, 16]) are among modelled issues. We have used three modelling methods.

Artificial neural networks, including multi-layer perceptron (see, e.g., [17]), have been widely used as means for forecasting and modelling of natural, social and economic processes (e.g., [18–20]). In [21] a methodology is described to obtain neural network model for system evaluation in a similar manner to ours, using a validation set and good correlation as model quality criteria.

Generalized additive models have obtained large popularity among statisticians mainly due the nonparametric nature; they are blending properties of generalized linear models and additive models [22, 23]. Their main advantage is using appropriate smoothing methods to determine the best functional dependence form.

"Nonlinear regression is a powerful tool for fitting data to an equation to determine the values of one or more parameters" [24]. Many different equation forms can be applied to achieve the best description of regularities of input data. A sequential iterative man-machine optimization of the model is a characteristic peculiarity of the modelling process [e.g., 25].

3 Key Principles of the Methodology

The individual evaluation of any declared cost item (including the most marginal ones) causes the major problem – doubtful cost assessment (because of unreliable data and lack of any normative first of all) as well as unjustified administrative burden on utilities and long regulatory procedure. In fact, only total costs have to be evaluated; the existing widespread practice (that is near to the *due diligence* of companies) in fact is overregulation of utilities. Therefore, the assessment of the total specific costs has been put as the cornerstone of the proposed methodology.

Direct quantitative calculation of the adequate specific costs (i.e., efficiency and performance) of utilities is impossible. The alternative option is benchmarking of the declared specific costs of utilities, which really perform the same business (provision of identical services) under homogenous business conditions (in particular geographical area with similar environment and comparable socio-economic and business factors). Due to the analogous external impact factors, the benchmarking provides comparative assessment of utilities' performance, determination of the average values/utilities as well identification of the best performers and outsiders.

The internal structure, business model and operation of the utilities are irrelevant (*black box*); to find and to implement the optimal ones is the duty of companies' management. Consequently the utility can be formalized as the multiple-input (set Π of the n key PIs) single-output (specific costs C of the business at the certain set of the key PIs) converter with a variable transfer function, which is unambiguously defined by the concrete set of input PIs that characterizes specific features of the concrete business. Synthesis of the general transfer regularity will provide determination of the adequate specific costs for any concrete utility:

$$C = f(\Pi) = f\{PI_1, PI_2, PI_3 \ldots \ldots PI_n\}$$

Theoretical creation of the transfer regularity is impossible; therefore, the modelling is preferable. The sought general regularity can be synthesized from the practical/specific cases (declared data of utilities). An important task-oriented restriction is monotony of the regularity against any PI; the economic logic does not indicate any reason for some extremum.

To achieve the maximum coincidence of the synthesized regularity with practical cases, correlation of the modelled values with corresponding declared specific costs is used as the quality criterion during the creation of the model. We have applied also the adjusted determination coefficient R^2 and deviance explained for assessment of the quality of the synthesized models.

4 Input Data

One of the most popular information processing axioms (*garbage in, garbage out*) postulates that the quality of the input data strongly determines the quality of the output data. Especially it relates to our case; usage of huge number of unreliable and incompatible PIs actually is an irrational approach. To increase the accuracy of the actual values of PIs and thus to increase the quality of the model the input data set Π was limited by small number of key PIs, which:

- characterize the scale and specific features of the utility's business,
- are certainly, clearly and unambiguously defined,
- are quantitatively measurable and controllable,
- are primary operational indicators of everyday business that are well-known and widely used in the annual reports of utilities and their business accounting.

We used three kinds of PIs as cost drivers and predictors for modelling:

- the amount of authorized consumption A (in cubic meters) characterizes the variable costs; because of the existence of the non-revenue water (technological consumption and water losses), the water use efficiency E complements A by displaying share of produced water P that is supplied to authorized consumers:

$$E = A/P$$

- the total length of the pipe network L (in kilometers) characterizes fixed costs; the network concentration index H complements L showing the fragmentation of the total network L in s separate segments, which lengths are $L(m)$:

$$H = \sum_{m=1}^{s} (L(m)/L)^2$$

- the number of connections N (exit points of the utility's infrastructure) additionally characterizes costs related to the structure of the network (proportion of thin customer pipes) as well spending for consumer services.

Thus, the selected input dataset consists of five PIs:

$$\Pi = (A, E, L, H, N)$$

Nevertheless, the accuracy of PIs remains some challenge for the utilities; actually, it is clear that in any case part of the particular input datasets will stay in the risk zone. Therefore we took the opportunity to carry out the data analysis and to develop the model on the basis of the most reliable, *right* datasets instead of using the full data pack (see, e.g., [26, 27]); the obtained general regularity will be applicable to the remaining (*poor*) utilities too.

The coverage of the full ranges of declared data was the first criterion for selection of right data. To select other right datasets a formal analysis of declared data for 2014 (that were used for the creation of the model) and comparative analysis of declared data for 2012 ÷ 2014 were carried out. As the utilities of low confidence (poor cases) were considered those, which have declared, e.g.: identical PI values over several years or major changes of the PI during the year without some valid reason, impracticably large water efficiency or connection density, a very low consumption per connection, etc.

Practitioners of data analysis recommend including in the right dataset around 70 % of total datasets (see, e.g., [28]). In our case, we selected 60 % relatively more reliable utilities (38 of 63 utilities) to increase the trust in the used data.

Analyzing statistical properties of the chosen datasets (Fig. 1) we can see that there is an outlier, which strongly influences predictors A, L and N. There is clearly no linear dependency between the variables.

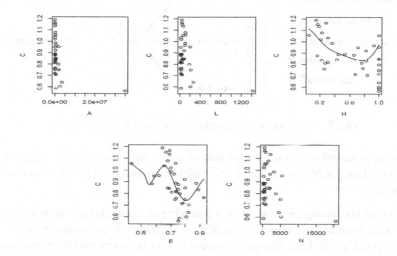

Fig. 1. Scatter plots for water costs C against the predictors. The curves are the local linear regression estimators for H and E variables.

Analysis of the input data shows a strong mutual correlation between basic PIs A and L (>0.9), while their correlation with specific costs C is low (<0.4) due to impact of H and E. On the one hand, it means high similarity of basic business conditions among small and large utilities that once again demonstrates the feasibility of creation of the model. On the other hand it puts some restriction – using the linear regression would lead to the so-called multicollinearity problem.

5 Modelling Methods

Three mutually independent modelling methods were applied to increase the truthfulness of results and to provide their cross checking.

5.1 Multi-layer Perceptron

We used a classical version of the multi-layer perceptron (MLP) with the error back-propagation training algorithm [17, 29]. In addition to standard procedures, to obtain the neural model we had to introduce techniques to cope with task-specific conditions: (a) relatively small amount of the training data, (b) insufficiently reliable training data and thus need for the evaluative aspect of the modelling, (c) the requirement for the resulting function to be monotone with regard to each of the input parameters.

The main challenge for the solution was combining the two counteractive goals: (a) modelling the cost function, (b) evaluating the actual costs via the obtained model. The main idea to accomplish this all was taking *external* and partly subjective quality assurance measures:

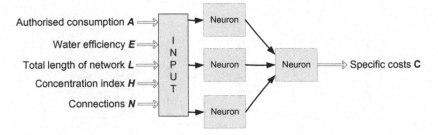

Fig. 2. Architecture of the task-specific multi-layer perceptron.

- training of neural network only on part of data – the most reliable (right) ones;
- applying task-specific monotony tests, which are non-typical for the neural network approach.

In the pre-processing phase we experimentally encountered that it is enough to have a MLP with three hidden neurons to achieve approximately maximum possible accuracy [29] (see Fig. 2). Each neuron (computing unit) is represented by a mathematical function, weights (or parameters) of which are set automatically via machine learning process. Additionally we made the input data normalization by sigmoid function because of very diverse scales of data values (see [17]).

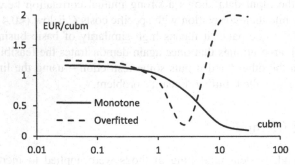

Fig. 3. A monotony test case: model suffering from overfitting and monotony recognized; E = 0, 5, L = 70 km, H = 1, N = 1000.

To avoid the effect of overfitting, a typical approach is using the cross-validation technique; however, it works best if extra data are available [30]. Due to specific conditions of the task, especially the relatively small amount of right data, we found this method as unreliable. To replace cross-validation we used a qualitative method by defining several specific monotony tests and applying them against the trained model. In terms of our approach, a monotony test is a sequence of generated data points with four out of five input parameters fixed, and the remaining one changing monotonously (e.g., C = f(A) at fixed E, L, H and N on Fig. 3).

Our task of the experimentation was to find the best (in terms of correlation, i.e. accuracy) neural network model from those with having passed all the monotony tests.

5.2   Generalized Additive Model

We applied a generalized additive model (GAM) to the water supply costs data using the programming language R. The GAM model uses the smooth extension of the generalized linear models, when the impact of all the predictors is analyzed by some smooth functions in a linear fashion [31].

Regarding our data, we have a multiple regression case, that is:

$$E(Y|X_1,\ldots,X_p) = f(X_1,\ldots,X_p) = f_0 + f_1(X_1) + \ldots + f_p(X_p)$$

$$= f_0 + \sum_{j=1}^{p} f_j(X_j)$$

where f_0 is a constant term, f_j is some unspecified regression function and p is the number of covariates or predictors. f_j is estimated nonparametrically by the smooth cubic spines as described above.

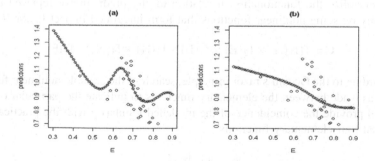

Fig. 4. A scatter plot of water efficiency E and the respective predictions of the water costs. A nonparametric local linear regression estimator has been added to both plots as a dotter curve. (a) no additional smoothing is introduced; (b) the additional smoothing is made choosing the parameter sp = 0.3.

For our case we have five predictors A, L, E, H and N, that is, $p = 5$. We implemented this model using the package *mgcv* in program R [32], which is arguably the most famous popular statistical program nowadays. We implemented the model using the following main r-code line:

$$b < -\text{gam}(y \sim s(A,k = kk) + s(H,k = kk) + s(L,k = kk) + s(E, k = kk,$$
$$sp = 0.3) + s(N,k = kk))$$

where the basis dimension kk was chosen to be equal to 8 and additional smoothing (controlled by the parameter $sp = 0.3$) was necessary for the covariate E. We chose the parameter kk in accordance to the procedure *choose.k*. Additional smoothing with the parameter $sp = 0.3$ does not change much the properties of the model (see Table 2). However, it makes economic consistency in sense that the costs decrease along the increase of the efficiency E (Fig. 4).

5.3 Nonlinear Regression Process

Although correlation of the basic PIs A and L with costs is low, the ratio A/L correlates with declared costs C much better (>0.65). This issue:

- conforms to the experience of water professionals – the ratio A/L provide the first relative notion (although the rough one) on specific costs of the water utility;
- shows the possibility to use the nonlinear regression process (NRP) to increase the coincidence of the searched regularity with declared costs.

Replenishment of the ratio by inclusion of other PIs E, H and N provides more precious attributing to the fixed and variable costs; then the sought regularity can be expressed as:

$$C = f(\Pi) = f(A, E, L, H, N)$$

where f is some nonlinear function of predictors A, E, L, H, N.

To generalize the functionality in relation to any predictor we replaced the proportionality by some nonlinear functions that form integrated impact factor *IF*:

$$C = f(f_1(A) \times f_2(E) \times f_3(L) \times f_4(H) \times f_5(N)) = f(\text{IF})$$

According to the Occam's razor principle, search of the suitable nonlinear functions $f_1 \div f_5$ was made between the elementary functions to indicate the particular ones that best of all provide the coincidence of the modelled regularity with the practical cases. We picked four elementary functions:

$$y_1 = a + b \times e^{cx}$$
$$y_2 = a + bx^c$$
$$y_3 = (a + bx)^c$$
$$y_4 = a \times \ln(bx) + c$$

The polynomial was not use because of the condition of the monotony.

Each function $f_1 \div f_5$ can be any of $y_1 \div y_4$ that gives us $4^5 = 1024$ different potential combinations. The best coincidence can be found by approximation of the parameters a, b, c for each function $f_1 \div f_5$ in each combination. We need to approximate in total 15 parameters in each of the 1024 cost functions to find the optimum.

To intensify the process, the model was created in several steps. At the first step we took two basic predictors A and L and created the impact factor in form:

$$IF = f_1(A) \times f_2(L)$$

All functions $y_1 \div y_4$ for both predictors was tested by approximation of parameters a, b, c to find optimum combination of functions and parameters. Correlation between IF and declared costs was used as the criterion for verification of the adequacy. On following steps we gradually tested functions $y_1 \div y_4$ for predictors E, H and N, more and more refined factor IF was developed. On the last step identically we searched for function f by maximal determination coefficient R^2 looking how regressed data fits are corresponding to the declared values.

6 Modelled Specific Costs

All modelled specific costs in comparison with the declared costs for 38 right cases are shown in Fig. 5; quality indicators of the models are presented in Table 1. The correlation between predictions and declared costs is strong. The coincidence of three synthesized regularities is high; there is an excellent correlation between the respective modelled values, while the mutual dispersions of modelled values for 84 % of utilities are below 10 % of respective declared values.

The GAM model ensures the opportunity to evaluate various statistical indicators. Figure 6 illustrates the confidence intervals for all the smooth functions estimated by the model. For the predictors E and H confidence intervals are very narrow, showing that the true function is close to the estimated one in the whole range of predictors and

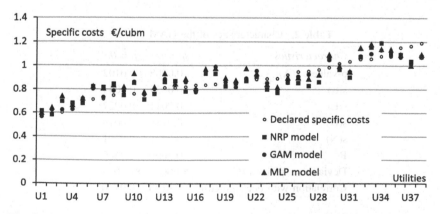

Fig. 5. Modelled specific costs of right 38 cases (utilities) arranged by declared costs.

the variance is small. On the contrary, for the predictors A, L and N the intervals are very large outside the value range, where are concentrated all utilities except the identified outlier (Fig. 1).

The statistical characteristics of the GAM model can be found in Table 2. First we can see that for the predictors A, L, E and H the smooth functions are significant according to the respective p-values (they are < 0.05). The smooth function for the factor N is not statistically significant at the 0.05 level.

Table 1. Quality indicators of the modelled costs

Characteristics		38 right	63 all
Correlation	MLP vs declared costs	0.88	0.56
	GAM vs declared costs	0.91	0.56
	NRP vs declared costs	0.88	0.59
	Integr. model vs declared costs	0.90	0.58
Mutual correlation	MLP vs GAM	0.97	0.96
	MLP vs NRP	0.97	0.96
	GAM vs NRP	0.96	0.95
Maximum mutual divergence (MLP, GAM, NRP)	<10 % of declared costs	32	52
	<15 % of declared costs	37	62
Divergence: integrated model vs declared costs	<10 % of model	30	31
	<15 % of model	38	39

The adjusted determination coefficient R^2 shows how much the variability in the data is explained by the model; it is more than 75 % (Table 2). The percentage deviance explained is another alternative measure for the fit of GAM model. It uses the residual deviance (RD) and null deviance (ND) by formula (RD-ND)/RD, where ND is the deviance for a model with just a constant term, while the RD is the deviance from the fitted model. In our case, the percentage deviance explained is greater than 0.82 (for details see [31]). All characteristics show that our model makes a good fit.

Table 2. Characteristics of the GAM model.

Characteristics	$sp = 0$	$sp = 0.3$
p-values: s(A)	0.0008	0.0102
s(L)	0.0025	0.0044
s(E)	0.0011	0.0027
s(H)	0.0185	0.0019
s(N)	0.3221	0.9791
R^2	0.7800	0.7680
Deviation explained (%)	84.00	82.80
Correlation with declared costs	0.9170	0.9100

In order to address the variability of the GAM fit the 95 % confidence bands are shown for all five smooth functions in Fig. 6. The presence of the outlier in three datasets (for predictors A, L and H) heavily influences the accuracy of the fit.

Figure 7 shows the behavior of residuals. It is desirable for a good model that the residuals are independent, normally distributed. We see in Fig. 7a from quantile-quantile plot that the straight line is a good fit for quantiles. Histogram Fig. 7c suggests the normality of the residuals. By the Shapiro-Wilk test in program R we found out that the respective p-value is 0.99, thus the normality is not rejected, say at the 0.05 level. The scatter plot of linear predictor versus residuals (Fig. 7b) shows that there are no patterns between them, thus the independence assumption might hold as well.

The NRP model makes it possible to track the real impact of each predictor on the quality of the model. Predictors A, L and E actually strongly affect costs over entire their range; it is well indicated by achieved correlation in various steps of the nonlinear regression process (Table 3). The network fragmentation affects the costs if H is less than 0.6; for very fragmented networks (H < 0.2) costs increase even by 20–30 %.

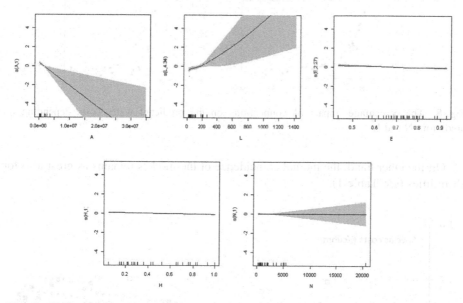

Fig. 6. 95 % confidence intervals for all five smoothing functions estimated by the model.

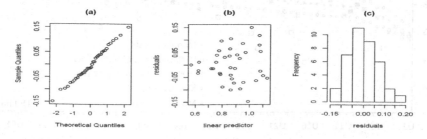

Fig. 7. Residual characteristics of the fitted GAM model to the water costs data.

Table 3. Achieved correlation depending on composition of the predictors

Set of predictors	{A, L}	{A, E, L}	{A, E, L, H}	{A, E, L, H, N}
Correlation	0.796	0.835	0.870	0.878

Direct overall impact of the predictor N on predicted water costs actually is negligible. Nevertheless, Fig. 8 shows quite significant impact on small networks (L < 30 km, N < 400); changes $\Delta C = f\{A, E, L, H\} - f\{A, E, L, H, N\}$, caused by including of the predictor N, can reach up to 10 % of specific costs.

Finally, we created an integrated model as the mean value of three samples (Fig. 9). Application of the synthesized regularities to the poor cases shows a huge difference between the coincidence with declared costs of right and poor cases (let us remain: the selection was made by formal data analysis criteria).

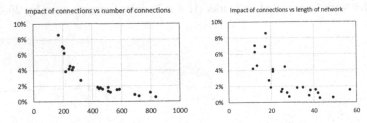

Fig. 8. The percentage impact of connections on the predicted water costs depending on predictors N and L.

On the other hand, the mutual coincidence of the models remains as great also for all utilities (see Table 1).

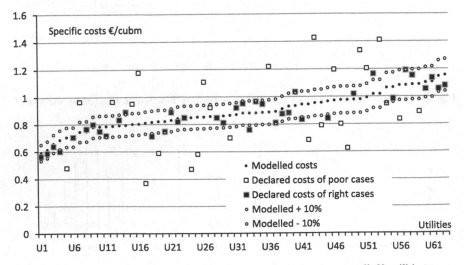

Fig. 9. The integrated model in comparison with declared costs; all 63 utilities.

7 Conclusions and Proposals

The adduced modelling results confirm expected benefits. There is high coincidence in the full costs range (i.e., in full range of real combinations of the PIs) of the three models created by mutually independent modelling tools. It clearly indicates quality and credibility of the models and proposed methodology, as well correctness of the selection of PIs. Actually any of the models can be used in practice.

The independence and normal distribution of residuals confirms the quality of the model. Existence of the outlier has not influenced modelling results. Data normalization in the MLP model and the modelling on the ratio A/L in the NLP model neutralizes this impact; nevertheless, both models are very identical with the GAM model.

The difference between right and poor cases indicates that grey subsidies of local governments (typical shareholders of utilities) on the one hand and inclusion of unjustified expenditures in the total costs on the other hand are the unsolved problems in the water sector. Sharp increase of the quality and reliability of the key PIs data is the principal task for continuation of the research.

The value of R^2 suggests that there could be another key PI, which inclusion in the input dataset is purposeful. Its identification and generalization of the proposed methodology for other utilities sectors are the next phases of development of the model.

Nevertheless, it is possible to start the gradual introduction of the methodology. The first phase would be the determination of the cost ceilings based on annual reports of utilities. Successful implementation of the previous phase will create the preconditions for a transition to the complete definition of the model-based specific costs and consequently tariff setting based on the key data of annual reports.

Thus, the general goals – setting of the substantiated tariffs, growing efficiency of utilities, reduction of the administrative burden on business and increase of the efficiency of the NRA will be achieved.

References

1. Public Utilities Commission of Latvia. Ūdenssaimniecības pakalpojumu tarifu aprēķināšanas metodika (in Latvian). http://likumi.lv/doc.php?id=209845
2. National Commission for Energy Control and Prices of Lithuania. Geriamojo vandens tiekimo ir nuoteku tvarkymo bei paviršiniu nuoteku tvarkymo paslaugu kainu nustatymo metodika (in Lithuanian). https://www.e-tar.lt/portal/lt/legalAct/4c3e62a08a9311e4a98a9f2247652cf4
3. Ziemele, J., Vigants, G., Vitolins, V., et al.: District heating systems performance analyses; heat energy tariff. Environ. Clim. Technol. **13**(1), 32–43 (2014). Scientific J. of RTU
4. Guerrini, A., Romano, G., Campadelli, B.: Factors affecting the performance of water utility companies. Int. J. Pub. Sect. Manage. **24**, 543–566 (2011)
5. Regulatory Implications of District Heating. https://www.yumpu.com/en/document/view/35150691/regulatory-implications-of-district-heating
6. European Commission. Costs for Municipal Waste management in the EU; Final Report to Directorate General Environment. http://ec.europa.eu/environment/waste/studies/eucostwaste_management.htm

7. Shinde, V.R., Hirayama, N., Mugita, A., Itoh, C.: Revising the existing performance indicator system for small water supply utilities in Japan. Urban Water J. **10**, 377–393 (2013)
8. Reynaud, A., Thomas, A.: Firm's profitability and regulation in water and network industries: an empirical analysis. Utilities Policy **24**, 48–58 (2013)
9. Marques, R.C., De Witte, K.: Towards a benchmarking paradigm in European water utilities. Public Money Manage. **30**, 42–48 (2010)
10. Berg, S.V.: Water Utility Benchmarking; Measurement, Methodologies, Performance Incentives. IWA Publishing, London (2010)
11. Marques, R.C., Simoes, P., Pires, J.S.: Performance benchmarking in utility regulation: the worldwide experience. Polish J. Environ. Stud. **20**, 125–132 (2011)
12. Dane, P., Schmitz, T.: A sharp improvement in the efficiency of Dutch water utilities: benchmarking of water supply in the Netherlands 1997–2007. Water Util. Manage. Int. **3**, 17–19 (2008)
13. Vilanova, M.R.N., Filho, P.M., Balestieri, J.A.P.: Performance measurement and indicators for water supply management: review and international cases. Renew. Sustain. Energy Rev. **43**, 1–12 (2015)
14. Calatrava, J.: Modelling water markets under uncertain water supply. Eur. Rev. Agric. Econ. **32**, 119–142 (2005)
15. Clark, R., Sivaganesan, M., Selvakumar, A., Sethi, V.: Cost models for water supply distribution systems. J. Water Resour. Plann. Manage. **128**, 312–321 (2002)
16. Malmsten, M., Lekkas, D.F.: Cost analysis of urban water supply and waste water treatment processes to support decisions and policy making: application to a number of Swedish communities. Desalin. Water Treat. **18**, 327–340 (2010)
17. Haykin, S.: Neural Networks and Learning Machines. Pearson Education Inc., Upper Saddle River (2009)
18. Shi, J., Wang, J., Macdonald, D.D.: Prediction of primary water stress corrosion crack growth rates in alloy 600 using artificial neural networks. Corros. Sci. **92**, 217–227 (2015)
19. Maier, H.R., Dandy, G.C.: Neural networks for the prediction and forecasting of water resources variables: a review of modelling issues and applications. Environ. Model Softw. **15**, 101–124 (2000)
20. Bini Verona, F., Ceraolo, M.: Use of neural networks for customer tariff exploitation by means of short-term load forecasting - prediction and system modelling. Neurocomputing **23**, 135–149 (1998)
21. Goncalves, F., Ramos, H.: Hybrid energy system evaluation in water supply systems: artificial neural network approach and methodology. J. Water Supply Res. Technol. **61**, 59–72 (2012)
22. Buja, A., Hastie, T., Tibshirani, R.: Linear smoothers and additive models. Ann. Stat. **17**, 453–510 (1989)
23. Hastie, T.J., Tibshirani, R.J.: Generalized Additive Models. Chapman & Hall/CRC, Boca Raton (1990)
24. Motulsky, H.J., Ransnas, L.A.: Fitting curves to data using nonlinear regression: a practical and nonmathematical review. FASEB J. **1**, 365–374 (1987)
25. Seber, G.A.F., Wild, C.F.: Nonlinear Regression. Wiley, Hoboken (2003)
26. Finlay, S.: Predictive Analysis, Data Mining and the Big Data; Myths. Misconceptions and Methods. Palgrave Macmillan, Basingstoke (2014)
27. Barzdins, J., Barzdins, G., Apsitis, K., Sarkans, U.: Towards efficient inductive synthesis of expressions from input/output examples. In: Jantke, K.P., Kobayashi, S., Tomita, E., Yokomori, T. (eds.) ALT 1993; Proceedings of the 4th International Workshop on Algorithmic Learning Theory, pp. 59–72. Springer, Heidelberg (1993)

28. Leek, J.: The Elements of Data Analytic Style. Leanpub, Victoria (2015)
29. Alpaydin, E.: Introduction to Machine Learning. The MIT Press, Cambridge (2010)
30. Mitchell, T.M.: Machine Learning. McGraw-Hill Companies Inc., Columbus (1997)
31. Wood, S.N.: Generalized Additive models: an introduction with R. Chapman & Hall/CRC, Boca Raton (2006)
32. Wood, S.N.: mgcv: mixed GAM computation vehicle with GCV/AIC/REML smoothness estimation; R package version 1.8-11 (2016). https://cran.r-project.org/web/packages/mgcv/mgcv.pdf

Views to Legal Information Systems and Legal Sublevels

Vytautas Čyras[1]([⊠]), Friedrich Lachmayer[2], and Erich Schweighofer[3]

[1] Faculty of Mathematics and Informatics, Vilnius University,
Naugarduko 24, 03225 Vilnius, Lithuania
vytautas.cyras@mif.vu.lt
[2] Faculty of Law, University of Innsbruck, Innrain 52, 6020 Innsbruck, Austria
friedrich.lachmayer@uibk.ac.at
[3] Faculty of Law, Centre for Computers and Law, University of Vienna,
Schottenbastei 10-16/2/5, 1010 Vienna, Austria
erich.schweighofer@univie.ac.at

Abstract. This paper concerns the legal system and legal documentation systems, as well as their interconnectedness and introduces the idea of legal sublevels. Examples of legal sublevels are legal terms, ontologies, annotations, commentaries, etc. A sublevel is treated as a representation level of the legal domain. In terms of software engineering, a sublevel can be defined as a level of infrastructural services for several domains. This paper is a kind of exploratory research; an abstract theory is being developed. A key question is "What are the sublevels in law and legal informatics?" We also examine the concept of view and project the core and peripheral areas around the legal system onto Schweighofer's 8 views/4 methods/4 syntheses model. We link the idea of sublevel with the notion of view.

Keywords: Interdisciplinarity · Legal data science · Legal documentation system · Legal meaning · Legal visualization · Visual navigation · View

1 Introduction

This paper is about (1) the legal system, (2) legal documentation and (3) their interconnectedness. A legal sublevel can be defined as a representation level of the legal system. Examples of legal sublevels are legal terms, thesauri, taxonomies, legal ontologies, annotations, commentaries, etc. Hans Kelsen, a prominent scholar of law, viewed legal terms from the standpoint of legal theory and denoted them 'legally indifferent substrate' (cf. Kelsen 1991, Chap. 16). Nowadays, particularly in the context of legal ontologies research (see e.g. Guarino et al. 2009), legal terms can be viewed from the standpoint of legal informatics and shared vocabularies.

From the standpoint of software engineering, a sublevel can be defined as a layer of infrastructural services for several domains (Fig. 1). The domains may be different representations of the legal system. Sublevels are horizontal layers and, therefore, contrast from vertical slices. A sublevel corresponds to a subsystem and leads to a framework that comprises horizontal and vertical interfaces. Sublevels can be compared

© Springer International Publishing Switzerland 2016
G. Dregvaite and R. Damasevicius (Eds.): ICIST 2016, CCIS 639, pp. 18–29, 2016.
DOI: 10.1007/978-3-319-46254-7_2

with horizontal layers of a more general matrix-shaped model, where vertical slices denote the branches of engineering such as aerospace engineering, automotive engineering, electrical engineering, chemical engineering, mechanical engineering, etc., and horizontal layers correspond to the features such as quality engineering, reliability engineering, safety engineering, etc.

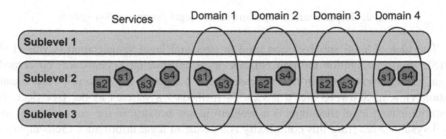

Fig. 1. A sublevel is defined as a layer of infrastructural services

Both systems – the legal system and the legal documentation system – have their own sublevels and metadata. The subject matter of this article can be split into two parts: sublevels in the law and sublevels in legal documentation. Section 2 introduces the granularity problem in legal documentation systems. Section 3 describes a shift from a legal hierarchy to a network. Section 4 links the idea of legal sublevels with the notion of view. We think about the sublevels in light of views in Schweighofer's 8 views/4 methods/4 syntheses model. Therefore we devote Sect. 5 to survey the notion of view. Further, Sect. 6 describes the Schweighofer's approach in more detail. Section 7 draws conclusions.

2 Granularity

We derive the idea of the legal sublevels from the granularity problem. Legal documentation does not reproduce a legal source one-to-one, and the granularity has to be taken into account (Fig. 2). A law does not need to be represented as a single document, e.g. a file in Word or PDF. Granularity raises the question, "What is the smallest entity?" In legal documentation, this question can have different answers: the whole text of a law, an article, a paragraph, a sentence, or even a word (legal term). In the Austrian Legal Information System (www.ris.bka.gv.at), a paragraph is the smallest entity. Smaller entities provide flexibility in legal information systems. A big document can be synthesized from its parts. However, making entities too small significantly increases the amount of metadata, because each entity type has its own metadata.

The granularity theme remains aside from the norm-institution relationship, but emerges in the law–legal informatics relationship. There are structures in the background that are independent from the norm-institution relationship, but that are important for the functioning of legal documentation, namely, for back-office software systems. The granularity could produce structures that differ from the current documentary structures.

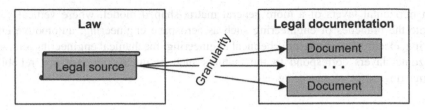

Fig. 2. Representing a legal source in a legal documentation system

The idea of legal sublevel was used in structural legal visualization (Čyras et al. 2015). Visual navigation through citizens' legal information systems was concerned. Legal visualization issues in law are assigned to a separate view, namely, the visualization view in Schweighofer's 8 views/4 methods/4 syntheses model (see Sect. 4). Communicating legal meanings is a problem in law because of the complexity of the legal system. Mastering this complexity is an issue in legal informatics (Schweighofer 2008). The concept of views is a means to master the complexity of a system and can be extended to the engineering of legal document systems.

3   A Shift from a Hierarchy to a Network

Our target is to explicate the network of legal sublevels. Constitution, law, statute and decision form a hierarchy; see Kelsen (1967, part V, especially Sect. 35). A hierarchical model of the legal system is presently too simple and strict. A network would be better suited (Fig. 3). Such a network would be partially hierarchical and contain horizontal links. In addition to explicit links, implicit links are important.

A network is a graph, and therefore, is a simple structure for reasoning in comparison with other formalizations such as formal logic. Paraphrasing Van Hoecke and Ost (1993, p. 1),[1] we see a task for legal informatics to transform the network of sublevels into a more "scientific" discipline by mathematical means.

The shift from a hierarchy also applies to legal document systems. Peripheral areas – sublevels – can be separated from the core, both in the legal system and in the document system (Fig. 4). We relate the idea of a network with the interdisciplinary approach and a pluralist epistemological perspective to legal science which is advocated by Van Hoecke and Ost (1993); see also Ost and van de Kerchove (1993).

Multi-stakeholder governance model. The idea of non-hierarchical relations is inherent in the multi-stakeholder governance model; cf. (Schweighofer 2015b, p. 53). The international players (or stakeholders) are states, international organizations, the business sector (companies, professional associations, funds) and non-state organizations (religions, NGOs, trade unions, think tanks). Global standards consist of "hard" law, e.g. legal instruments with binding force or "soft" law, e.g. quasi-legal instruments with or without a compliance mechanism but formally not legally binding.

---

[1] "Econometrics, for example, attempts to transform economic science into a more 'rigorous' and hence more 'scientific' discipline by mathematical means." Van Hoecke and Ost (1993).

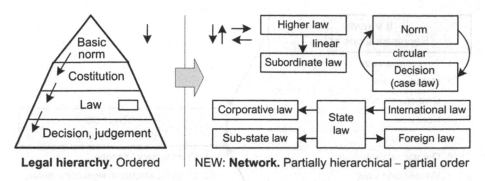

Legal hierarchy. Ordered | NEW: **Network.** Partially hierarchical – partial order

Fig. 3. A shift from a legal hierarchy to a network in the law

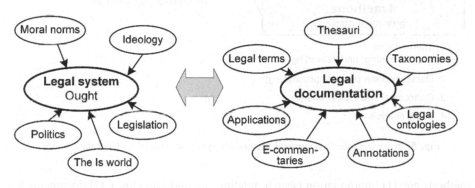

Fig. 4. Core-periphery subsystems around the legal system and the legal documentation system

The future "matrix of law" is discussed by Martin-Bariteau (2014), p. 11–18. He comments about Ost, although it has been 15 years since Ost's original predictive work, and points out the distinctions of law-making in the Information Society.

4   The 8 Views/4 Methods/4 Syntheses Approach in a Nutshell

Schweighofer's 8 views/4 methods/4 syntheses approach to legal data science (Schweighofer 2015a) is a methodological framework to investigate legal sublevels. He has structured newly developed methods for the representation, analysis and synthesis of legal materials as legal data science. His model describes the eight different representations of a legal system and four computer-supported methods of analysis, which lead to a synthesis, a consolidated and structured analysis of a legal domain, either (1) a commentary, an electronic legal handbook, or (2) a dynamic electronic legal commentary DynELC (Schweighofer 2011), or (3) a representation for citizens, or (4) a case-based synthesis (Fig. 5). The eight views (or representations of law) are: (1) text corpus, (2) metadata view, (3) citation network view, (4) user view, (5) logical view, (6) ontological view, (7) visualization view, and (8) argumentation view. The four

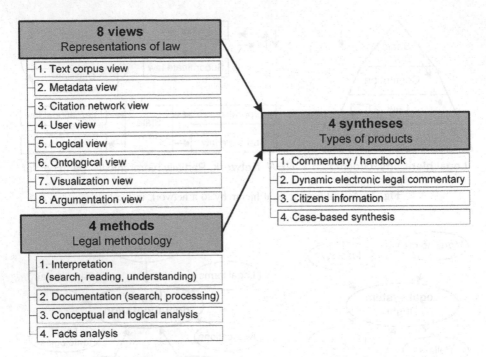

Fig. 5. Schweighofer's 8 views/4 methods/4 syntheses model to legal data science

methods are: (1) interpretation (search, reading and understanding), (2) documentation (search and processing), (3) structural analysis (conceptual and logical), and (4) fact analysis.

Schweighofer considers Lu and Conrad's "4 views theory" (2012, 2013) and extends it with four more views (representations of the law). It should be noted that in the knowledge representation of law, it is not solely about the documentation; each view represents further insights on the law itself (Schweighofer 2015a, p. 16).

5   The Notion of a View

Lu and Conrad (2012, 2013) view the system of legal documents from the standpoint of legal search engines. However, the legal system (in a broad sense) can also be viewed from other standpoints, e.g. a software engineer's or a legal philosopher's. Thus, different perspectives (a synonym for the term 'view') emerge.

Both the legal system and the legal documentation system are systems. They can be described from the outside and the inside. A system can be described from the outside as a black box: inputs, outputs and their relation. A system is described from the inside perspective by its elements and the relationships between them. Figure 6 can serve as such a description.

We will compare the concept of view in Lu and Conrad's 4 views and Schweighofer's 8 views with the concept of view in software engineering. The term 'view'

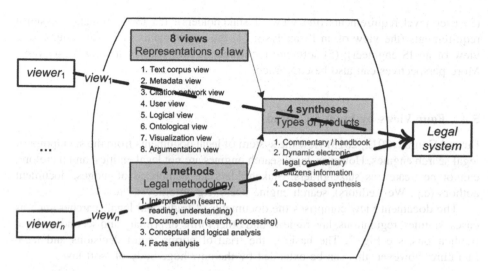

Fig. 6. Different perspectives of the legal system through a "lens", which comprises the 8 representations of law, the 4 methods and the 4 products

denotes a representation of the law in the works by Lu and Conrad, as well as Schweighofer. Each viewer looks through a "lens", which comprises the 8 representations of law, the 4 methods, and the 4 products (Fig. 6). Each viewer has his own perspective and projects the legal system onto the landscape of legal data science differently.

5.1   Views of an Enterprise System

Further, we consider an enterprise system in the role of a viewed object. Six views – the planner's, the owner's, the designer's, the builder's, the integrator's and the user's – are concerned in the Zachman framework (Sowa and Zachman 1992), which supposes that it is possible to manage an enterprise system using a multiperspective approach. Zachman's idea to decompose the system into a number of perspectives and focus areas serves as a theoretical basis for the *vision-driven approach* proposed by Čaplinskas (2009). Zachman decomposes each perspective into six focus areas to be answered: what (data)? how (function)? where (network)? who (people)? when (time)? and why (motive)? Čaplinskas calls it the H3W decomposition. The concept of views is driven by the separation of concerns principle.[2]

Five perspectives (views, levels) of the Čaplinskas' vision-driven methodological framework are: (1) business level requirements (the view of a business analyst);

---

[2] "The "separation of concerns" principle is realized by the concept of views. ...The separation of concerns principle refers to the description of different characteristics of a software system that may or may not relate to the later execution of those systems. The principle will be applied in the division of complex description of even small portions of software into hopefully better understanding partial descriptions – that we call views – that must later be superimposed to form a complete description." (Goedicke 1990, p. 5).

(2) user level requirements (the view of stakeholders); (3) IS (information system) requirements (the view of an IS analyst); (4) the requirements of IS subsystems (the view of an IS engineer); (5) software requirements (the view of a software analyst). More perspectives can also be concerned.

5.2   Four Views by Lu and Conrad

Lu and Conrad (2012, 2013) view the system of legal documents from the standpoint of legal search engines. However, legal search engines are not legal entities, and therefore, cannot be treated as stakeholders. Stakeholders are comprised of judges, document authors (e.g. West editors), search engine users (e.g. attorneys), etc.

The document view comprises the documents of traditional legal searches such as cases, statutes, regulations, law reviews and other forms of primary and secondary legal publications, see Fig. 7. The basis is the triad of norms, court decisions and legal literature; however, this can be extended by the now huge body of 'soft law'.

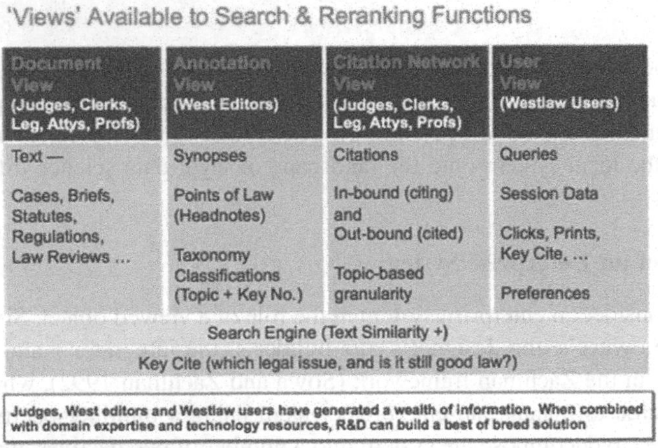

'Views' Available to Search & Reranking Functions

Document View (Judges, Clerks, Leg, Attys, Profs)	Annotation View (West Editors)	Citation Network View (Judges, Clerks, Leg, Attys, Profs)	User View (Westlaw Users)
Text —	Synopses	Citations	Queries
Cases, Briefs, Statutes, Regulations, Law Reviews ...	Points of Law (Headnotes)	In-bound (citing) and Out-bound (cited)	Session Data
	Taxonomy Classifications (Topic + Key No.)	Topic-based granularity	Clicks, Prints, Key Cite, ...
			Preferences

Search Engine (Text Similarity +)

Key Cite (which legal issue, and is it still good law?)

Judges, West editors and Westlaw users have generated a wealth of information. When combined with domain expertise and technology resources, R&D can build a best of breed solution

Fig. 7. The set of evidence (views) that can be used by modern legal search engines; see (Lu and Conrad 2013) at http://blog.law.cornell.edu/voxpop/2013/03/28/next-generation-legal-search-its-already-here/

The annotation view comprises "attorney-editor generated synopses, points of law (a.k.a. headnotes), and attorney-classifier assigned topical classifications that rely on a legal taxonomy such as West's Key Number System".[3] The annotation view is based on metadata, which can be formidable, e.g. EUR-Lex[4] metadata system. A sample headnote is shown in Fig. 8.

---

[3] West's Key Number System: http://info.legalsolutions.thomsonreuters.com/pdf/wln2/L-374484.pdf . This is a classification system for American law.

[4] Access to European Union law, http://eur-lex.europa.eu/.

The citation network view comprises out-bound (cited) sources and in-bound (citing) sources with respect to the document in question. The citations are very different: basis of the act, acts cited in the document, citations in the operative part of the judgment, document amending other documents, document is amended by other acts, etc.

⚮24 Aliens, Immigration, and Citizenship
  ⚮24V Denial of Admission and Removal
   ⚮24V(G) Judicial Review or Intervention
    ⚮24k396 Standard and Scope of Review
     ⚮24k403 Fact Questions
      ⚮24k403(2) k. Substantial evidence in general. Most Cited Cases

⚮24 Aliens, Immigration, and Citizenship ☑ KeyCite Citing
  ⚮24V Denial of Admission and Removal
   ⚮24V(G) Judicial Review or Intervention
    ⚮24k396 Standard and Scope of Review
     ⚮24k403 Fact Questions
      ⚮24k403(3) κ. Credibility. Most Cited Cases

Substantial evidence test, which is used in reviewing an immigration judge's (IJ's) factual findings and credibility determinations as to whether the government presented clear and convincing evidence of removal, is highly deferential and requires reversal of factual findings only if the evidence presented compels a contrary conclusion. Immigration and Nationality Act, § 212(a)(6)(C)(i), 8 U.S.C.A. § 1182(a) (6)(C)(i).

Fig. 8. An example of a headnote with its assigned key number (Lu and Conrad 2012)

The user view considers 'aggregated user behavior', for example, how often a document was opened, document popularity through citatory services, the jurisdiction in which a particular attorney-user practices, and the kinds of sources that a user has historically preferred. In contrast to data (documents) and metadata (citations, annotations), "the aggregated user behavior data represented in the user view is produced by the professional researchers who interact with the system."

6   Views in the Schweighofer's Approach

Schweighofer considers Lu and Conrad's "4 views theory" and extends it with 4 more views (representations of the law): the logical view, the ontological view, the visualization view, and the argumentation view. Further in this section we describe only the latter views. It should be noted that in the knowledge representation of law, it is not just about the documentation itself; each view represents further insights on the law itself (Schweighofer 2015a, p. 16).

6.1   The Logical View

The logical view is based on predicate logic. An example is implementing a big number of legal rules, e.g. rOWLer, a rule engine by Scharf (2016), which models legal norms with JAVA and OWL 2. Business rules management systems such as JBoss Enterprise BRMS is also a kind of a product. The logical view is restricted to "standard cases" (i.e. normal cases) leaving hard cases to the argumentation view.

The works by Monica Palmirani on modeling legal rules with LegalRuleML language are assigned to this view. LegalRuleML functionalities comprise modeling different types of rules, representing normative effects, defeasibility, correspondence between collections of rules in the formal model and natural language texts of legislation, alternative interpretations, etc. (Athan et al. 2015). Palmirani also contributes to making semantic Web the next step for the legal domain (Casanovas et al. 2016). Since 2005 she contributed to the Akoma Ntoso project that was devoted to access African parliamentary proceedings and currently followed by LegalRuleML (Palmirani 2012). Her contribution is related with the semantic Web and the law topic and also the text corpus view. These works produced an ontology for managing legislative text's evolution over time and its linguistic variants.

6.2 Ontological View

The ontological view considers legal ontologies, shared vocabularies, advanced thesauri, concepts and relations. A starting point of any legal ontology is the terminology of the law. Since the 19th century substantial preparatory work has been done in the concept jurisprudence. Reusing this work, the respective elements of the concepts have to be transposed into a computer-readable structure, e.g. header, definition, relations, presubsumption (relation between the normative concept of law and a factual element). In the 1990s, ontologies as a conceptualization of a domain have been recognized as a way to knowledge representation in the Semantic Web; cf. (Guarino et al. 2009). The main components of ontologies are terms that are connected with links such as upper/lower term, synonymy, antonymy, etc. (Peters et al. 2007). For example, the formalization of the norm graph concept is the starting phase in the approach of Oberle et al. (2012) to engineering compliant software.

6.3 The Legal Visualization View

The legal visualization view concerns the use of graphics, images and videos, cf. (Brunschwig 2014). The structural legal visualization (SLV) approach by Lachmayer concerns visualizing legal meanings (cf. Lachmayer 2002; Čyras et al. 2015).[5] These methods are human-oriented. The reason is that legal visualization is primarily a means of information visualization and serves humans. Therefore a challenge is computer-readable visualizations (i.e. computer-oriented) as well as computer-generated visualizations (human-oriented). Graphical notations should also support the formalization of the law similarly as UML supports software development.

6.4 The Legal Argumentation View

In recent years, the field of AI and Law has strongly concentrated on the formalization of arguments. This case-based reasoning approach started in the 1980s and culminated in Ashley's book (1990). Taking into account the dialectical nature of the legal process – thesis (plaintiff), antithesis (respondent), synthesis (judge) – a representation of possible arguments is important.

---

[5] See also www.legalvisualization.com and http://jusletter-it.weblaw.ch/visualisierung.html.

6.5   The 4 Methods and 4 Syntheses

We briefly describe the legal methods and the methods of synthesis.

Method 1 – Searching, Reading, Interpreting, Understanding. The basic methodology is to locate, read, interpret and understand the "legal stuff", taking into account the legal interpretation and reasoning methods in a dynamic world of concepts. The most significant ad-on of legal informatics is the revolution in legal search by the use of search engines. "Legal Googling" now belongs to the recognized methods.

Method 2 – Legal Documentation and Search. Due to the abundance of the material, legal documentation has become an independent method. However, this task is no longer done primarily by the users, but by the services of legal information providers.

Method 3 – Conceptual and Logical Analysis. Here the fundamental statement by John Sowa (2000) applies again: the terminology has to be developed and be brought into a convenient logical structure.

Method 4 – Factual Elements and Their Links to Law. In the practice of conflict resolution it is often argued about the existence of elements of the situation. Therefore it is helpful to make use of existing world ontologies. The automated generation of factual elements from pictures, videos, websites, intelligent forms, etc. is important. Successful practice can be found in tax law and e-Justice intelligent forms.

Synthesis 1 – Commentary/Handbook or Manual. Presently such handbooks are written traditionally. Due to the dynamics of the legal system, this task is getting difficult. Therefore authors favor a more documentary approach with extensive notes.

Synthesis 2 – Dynamic Electronic Legal Commentary (DynELC). The idea is simple – a change from the traditional to an electronic commentary. The 8 views and 4 methods are presented in a structured format and the basis for further analysis by legal experts is provided. The methods to be used: document categorization, multilingual thesaurus, citations, temporal relations, ranking, text summary, and multilingualism. The DynELC consists of a structured representation of the metadata and the text corpus. An advantage is taking into account the dynamics of the law.

Synthesis 3 – Citizens Information. Citizen-focused description of the legal system is provided. The focus is on authority structure and citizen's participation.

Synthesis 4 – Case-Based Synthesis. Contrary to a representation "legal system for all" a specific case is a standpoint. Relevant arguments and counter arguments are presented taking into account the claimant, the defendant or the judge.

7   Conclusions

The idea of core and periphery in law leads to the idea of legal sublevels. This idea contributes to the conceptualization of the legal domain from the technological view-point. Such conceptualization will contrast from the jurisprudential outlines of law, where the branches of law or the functions of law (legislative, executive and judicative) play the key role. Soft law in the information society challenges "black-letter" law. To represent data and services in the legal domain, a proper conceptualization is required. The views to a legal documentation system constitute a proper beginning.

The sublevels of legal information should be taken into account in the engineering of legal information systems (LISs). Explicating legal sublevels contributes to the evaluative synthesis of legal decisions. Thus, explicit visual navigation through a legal information system would support the wandering back and forth of the glance between the normative and the factual.

We tackle the granularity problem and take into account that legal documentation does not reproduce a legal source one-to-one. The periphery of the law can emerge in the core of legal document systems. Software engineers are the keypersons in the process of designing legal machines. To program institutional decision making, these engineers should interpret properly software requirements, which tackle the law.

The 8 views/4 methods/4 syntheses model is abstracted from decades of experience in the legal domain. This model is validated by numerous applications, some of which are cited in Sect. 6.

References

Ashley, K.D.: Modeling Legal Argument – Reasoning with Cases and Hypotheticals. Artificial Intelligence and Legal Reasoning. MIT Press, Cambridge (1990)

Athan, T., Governatori, G., Palmirani, M., Paschke, A., Wyner, A.: LegalRuleML: design principles and foundations. In: Faber, W., Paschke, A. (eds.) Reasoning Web 2015. LNCS, vol. 9203, pp. 151–188. Springer, Heidelberg (2015)

Brunschwig, C. R.: On visual law: visual legal communication practices and their scholarly exploration. In: Schweighofer, E., Handstanger, M., Hoffmann, H., Kummer, F., Primosch, E., Schefbeck, G., Withalm, G. (eds.) Zeichen und Zauber des Rechts. Editions Weblaw, Bern, pp. 899–933 (2014). http://ssrn.com/abstract=2405378

Casanovas, P., Palmirani, M., Peroni, S., van Engers, T., Vitali, F.: Special issue on the semantic web for the legal domain – guest editors' editorial: the next step. Semant. Web J. 7(3), 213–227 (2016). http://ssrn.com/abstract=2765912

Čaplinskas, A.: Requirements elicitation in the context of enterprise engineering a vision driven approach. Informatica 20(3), 343–368 (2009). http://www.mii.lt/informatica/pdf/INFO766.pdf

Čyras, V., Lachmayer, F., Lapin, K.: Structural legal visualization. Informatica 26(2), 199–219 (2015). http://www.mii.lt/informatica/pdf/INFO1059.pdf

Goedicke, M.: Paradigms of modular system development. In: Mitchell, R.J. (ed.) Managing Complexity in Software Engineering, IEE Computing Series 17, pp. 1–20. Peter Peregrinus, London (1990)

Guarino, N., Oberle, D., Staab, S.: What is an ontology? In: Staab, S., Studer, R. (eds.) Handbook on Ontologies, pp. 1–17. Springer, Heidelberg (2009). http://iaoa.org/isc2012/docs/Guarino2009_What_is_an_Ontology.pdf

Kelsen, H.: Pure Theory of Law, 2nd edn. University of California Press, Berkeley (1967). Knight, M. (trans.) (Reine Rechtslehre, 2. Auflage. Deuticke, Wien, 1960)

Kelsen, H.: General Theory of Norms. Clarendon Press, Oxford (1991). Hartney M. (trans.)

Lachmayer, F.: Visualization of abstract (Visualisierung des Abstrakten). In: Schweighofer, E., Menzel, T., Kreuzbauer, G. (eds.) IT Law and State (IT in Recht und Staat), Schriftenreihe Rechtsinformatik 6, pp. 309–317. Verlag Österreich, Vienna (2002)

Lu, Q., Conrad, J. G.: Bringing order to legal documents: an issue-based recommendation system via cluster association. In: Proceedings of the Fourth International Conference on Knowledge Engineering and Ontology Development (KEOD 2012), pp. 76–88. SciTePress, DL (2012)

Lu, Q., Conrad, J.G.: Next generation legal search – it's already here. voxpopulii blog, cornell legal information institute, 28 March 2013 (2013). http://blog.law.cornell.edu/voxpop/2013/03/28/next-generation-legal-search-its-already-here/

Martin-Bariteau, F.: The matrix of law: from paper, to word processing, to Wiki. Lex Electronica 19(1), 1–23 (2014). http://www.lex-electronica.org/docs/articles_331.pdf

Oberle, D., Drefs, F., Wacker, R., Baumann, C., Raabe, O.: Engineering compliant software: advising developers by automating legal reasoning. SCRIPTed 9(3), 280–313 (2012). http://script-ed.org/wp-content/uploads/2011/12/oberle.pdf

Ost, F., van de Kerchove, M.: Constructing the complexity of the law: towards a dialectic theory (1993). http://www.dhdi.free.fr/recherches/theoriedroit/articles/ostvdkcomplex.pdf

Palmirani, M.: Legislative XML: Principles and Technical Tools. Aracne, Rome (2012)

Peters, W., Sagri, M.-T., Tiscornia, D.: The structuring of legal knowledge in LOIS. Artif. Intell. Law 15(2), 117–135 (2007)

Scharf, J.: Artificial Intelligence and Law (Künstliche Intelligenz und Recht: Von der Wissensrepräsentation zur automatisierten Entscheidungsfindung). vol. 319 OCG Schriftenreihe books@ocg.at, OCG, Vienna (2016)

Schweighofer, E.: Reduktion von Komplexität. Durch Recht und IKT. In: Schweighofer, E., Geist, A., Heindl, G., Szücs, C. (eds.) Complexity Frontiers of Legal Informatics (Komplexitätsgrenzen der Rechtsinformatik), Proceedings of the 11th International Legal Informatics Symposium (IRIS 2008), pp. 42–47. Richard Boorberg Verlag, Stuttgart (2008)

Schweighofer, E.: Indexing as an ontological-based support for legal reasoning. In: Yearwood, J., Stranieri, A. (eds.) Technologies for Supporting Reasoning Communities and Collaborative Decision Making: Cooperative Approaches, pp. 213–236. IGI Global Publishers, Hershey (2011)

Schweighofer, E.: From information retrieval and artificial intelligence to legal data science. In: Schweighofer, E., Galindo, F., Cerbena, C. (eds.), Proceedings of MWAIL 2015, ICAIL Multilingual Workshop on AI & Law Research, held Within the 15th International Conference on Artificial Intelligence & Law (ICAIL 2015), pp. 13–23. OCG, Vienna (2015a)

Schweighofer, E.: Legal semantic web and participation. Democracia Digital e Governo Eletrônico 1(12), 50–65 (2015b). http://buscalegis.ufsc.br/revistas/index.php/observatoriodoegov/article/view/34400/

Sowa, J.F., Zachman, J.A.: Extending and formalizing the framework for information systems architecture. IBM Syst. J. 31(3), 590–616 (1992)

Sowa, J.F.: Knowledge Representation: Logical, Philosophical, and Computational Foundations. Brooks/Cole Thomson Learning, Pacific Grove (2000)

Van Hoecke, M., Ost, F.: Epistemological perspectives in jurisprudence. Ratio Juris 6(1), 30–47 (1993)

A Model of the Tacit Knowledge Transfer Support Tool: CKnow-Board

Justyna Patalas-Maliszewska[1(✉)] and Irene Krebs[2]

[1] University of Zielona Góra, Zielona Góra, Poland
J.Patalas@iizp.uz.zgora.pl
[2] Brandenburg University of Technology Cottbus-Senftenberg,
Cottbus, Germany
krebs@b-tu.de

Abstract. This article elaborates on the development of a dedicated Tacit Knowledge Transfer Support Tool for companies. The five main components of this tool are formulated: (1) Tacit Knowledge Source Identification; (2) Tacit Knowledge Source Determination using the FAHP (Fuzzy Analytic Hierarchy Process); (3) Tacit Knowledge Acquisition, (4) Tacit Knowledge Transformation, (5) A Tacit Knowledge Transfer Board. The proposed tool enables the identification of tacit knowledge in a company and the transformation of different types of knowledge into the form of explicit knowledge included in the Tacit Knowledge Transfer Board.

Keywords: Tacit knowledge · Transformation · Knowledge Transfer Support Tool

1 Introduction

Companies which operate in the knowledge economy need to improve their knowledge transfer (KT) processes in order to achieve adequate competitiveness. Knowledge is an intangible asset, and due to its specific characteristics, it is usually the most important resource for a company. However, it may also cause many difficulties, because the exploitation of knowledge typically relies strongly on the knowledge of workers within a company. Knowledge can be classified either as tacit or explicit. Explicit knowledge transfer can be realized by verbal explanation, documents and/or information systems [7] and tacit knowledge transfer can be supported by tools such as interviews, brainstorming, meetings, etc. [1] and also by methods such as blogs, wikis and internal networks [3, 5, 14]. Nonaka and Takeuchi [10] stated that tacit knowledge contained in the minds of employees determines the success of the company and explicit knowledge can exist on a continuum of tacit knowledge [9]. So, it is worth mentioning that the success of KT processes within a company depends on their acceptance by workers in the company involved in this process and on the tool that will support this process.

According to Alavi and Leidner [1], knowledge management tools (KMT) should support knowledge creation, storage/retrieval, transfer, and application within a company. To achieve a sufficient level of tacit knowledge transfer processes, and also of the conversion process of tacit knowledge into explicit knowledge, a dedicated Tacit

G. Dregvaite and R. Damasevicius (Eds.): ICIST 2016, CCIS 639, pp. 30–41, 2016.
DOI: 10.1007/978-3-319-46254-7_3

Knowledge Transfer Support Tool is needed in a company. According to Nevo and Chan [8], knowledge management tools should be adaptable, easy to use, fast to access and cost effective. So, we propose the CKnow-Board Tacit Knowledge Transfer Support Tool to support managers working in the field where the creation and transfer of tacit knowledge are highly critical, e.g. the IT industry. Typically, the most critical knowledge exploited in IT projects is based on a worker's competence and experience, so it is vital not to lose this knowledge when such workers cease to work for that company.

In this paper, we formulate the functionalities in the framework of the proposed CKnow-Board tool. The five main components of this tool are as follows: (1) Tacit Knowledge Source Identification; (2) Tacit Knowledge Source Determination using the FAHP (Fuzzy Analytic Hierarchy Process); (3) Tacit Knowledge Acquisition, (4) Tacit Knowledge Transformation, (5) A Tacit Knowledge Transfer Board. Through work based on the examples of IT companies we formulated the rules which determine the importance of tacit knowledge sources (of knowledge workers described by the personnel usefulness function), defined the tacit knowledge cores for IT companies and developed a mechanism to transform tacit knowledge into explicit knowledge.

The remainder of this paper is organized as follows: Sect. 2 presents the theoretical background of tacit knowledge transfer support tools and a conceptual model of the proposed CKnow-Board information system. Section 3 describes the methodology of the construction of CKnow-Board. Section 4 presents the implementation of CKnow-Board for an IT company. Section 5 discusses the implications of the results.

2 Tacit Knowledge Transfer Support Tools and a Conceptual Model of CKnow-Board

Knowledge is distinguished as tacit knowledge (related to worker in a company) and an explicit knowledge (contained in the documents, procedures, etc. of the company) [12]. Tacit knowledge, like explicit knowledge, should also be able to be reproduced and copied by others in a company [6]. So, the knowledge of key workers, even if they leave a firm to work for a competitor, should be acquired in a company.

According to Phang and Foong [15], ICTs are used in managing and transferring explicit knowledge within a company. Bigliardi et al. [2] identified expert systems, neural nets, fuzzy logic, genetic algorithms and intelligent agents as being support tools for the capture and codification of knowledge. Van Joolingenet et al. [19] states that ICT technologies support co-learning within a company, and also tacit knowledge processes. Among those tools which support tacit knowledge management within a company, it is also possible to list: knowledge maps, e-learning, web-blogs, social media, internal networks of practitioners (industry blogs), internal compendia of knowledge, video-conferencing, newsletters and corporate portals. However, ICT technologies alone are not sufficient for the management of tacit knowledge, due to the necessity of formulating knowledge gained from employees. Therefore, it is necessary to create a tool to acquire and transform the knowledge of workers within a company. Figure 1 shows the concept of a proposed Tacit Knowledge Transfer Support Tool: CKnow-Board, which consists of five components:

- C1: Tacit Knowledge Source Identification.
- C2: Tacit Knowledge Source Determination using the FAHP (Fuzzy Analytic Hierarchy Process).
- C3: Tacit Knowledge Acquisition.
- C4: Tacit Knowledge Transformation.
- C5: Explicit Knowledge Visualization: A Knowledge Transfer Board.

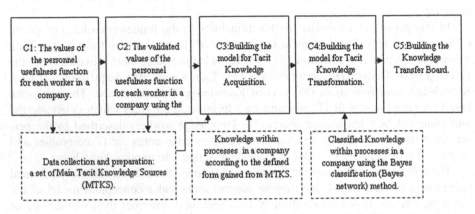

Fig. 1. A concept model of the Tacit Knowledge Transfer Support Tool: CKnow-Board; own elaboration.

The C1 component is implemented by using the personnel usefulness function [13], modified to the form:

$$F_n = f_1(GK) + f_2(PK) + f_3(A) + f_4(E) + f_5(I) \qquad (1)$$

where $n \in N$ and $1 \leq F_n \leq 25$ and $1 \leq f_1(GK) \leq 5$; $1 \leq f_2(PK) \leq 5$, $1 \leq f_3(A) \leq 5$, $1 \leq f_4(E) \leq 5$, $1 \leq f_5(I) \leq 5$,

- $f_1(GK)$-the general knowledge function for the n-th worker in a company, where $GK \in R$.
- $f_2(PK)$-the professional knowledge function for the n-th worker in a company, where $PK \in R$.
- $f_3(A)$-the professional abilities function for the n-th worker in a company, where $A \in R$.
- $f_4(E)$-the experience function for the n-th employee in a company, where E is a synthetic index of experience for the n-th employee in a company.
- $f_5(I)$-the capacity for innovation function for the n-th employee in a company, where I-synthetic index of patents for the n-th employee.

The values of the personnel usefulness function for each worker in a company (C1) will be obtained from workers through interviews/tests conducted at each element of this function according to the processes which are realized by the workers. Each worker completes a questionnaire. Using an algorithm to test solutions for each worker, it is possible to determine the value for the personnel usefulness function of the worker.

C2 is a structural synthesis of using the FAHP (Fuzzy Analytic Hierarchy Process) for validating the values of the personnel usefulness function to determinate the Main Tacit Knowledge Sources (MTKS) for each defined process in a company. Using the FAHP it is possible to determine the relative dominance of an element of the personnel usefulness function from which it is possible to assess these elements [4]. According to Nydick and Hill [11] a linguistic variable can be described by a fuzzy number $\tilde{a} = (l, m, u)$ of a triangular fuzzy membership function. The triangular fuzzy number $\tilde{a} = (l, m, u)$ is defined in the set $[l, u]$ and its membership function takes a value equal to 1 at point m. The fuzzy scale of preferences is also strictly defined by Nydick and Hill. The Main Tacit Knowledge Sources (MTKS) for each defined process will be chosen, if the validated value of the personnel usefulness function for a worker is more then 15.

To enable C3, CKnow-Board should include, for each defined process in a company, a special tool for acquiring the knowledge from the defined MTKS. Thus, it is necessary to introduce the Bayes algorithm to classify the obtained knowledge (C4) in order to create C5.

By integrating the components identified in Fig. 1, a model of the Tacit Knowledge Transfer Support Tool: CKnow-Board was developed.

3 A Model of the Information System: CKnow-Board

The proposed CKnow-Board tool will be used by workers in a company in order to store and then explicit their best knowledge needed to facilitate processes within a organization. Based on the approach of Roussey et al. [17] and [16], the methodology of the construction of CKnow-Board includes two steps: (1) Knowledge Identification, Acquisition and Transformation (2) Knowledge and Visualization (see Fig. 2).

In the defined model, Tacit Knowledge Main Sources (TKMS) are formalized using the personnel usefulness function [13] so it possible to find, according to [18] the relationship between workers (tacit knowledge) and the ICT tool.

Based on the steps involved in the methodology of the construction of the CKnow-Board system (outlined in Fig. 2), the Tacit Knowledge Transfer Support Tool: CKnow-Board was developed. A prototyping approach was applied for issues like interface design in the proposed TKMS.

4 CKnow-Board for IT Companies - A Case Study

According to the defined conceptual model of the Tacit Knowledge Transfer Support Tool: CKnow-Board (see Fig. 1), and the methodology of the construction of CKnow-Board (see Fig. 2) it is self-evident that the system is ideally suited to IT companies.

C1: Values of the personnel usefulness function for each worker in a company.

So, based on this case study the C1 component is implemented. In CKnow-Board each worker should select the processes that are carried out by this worker and if the

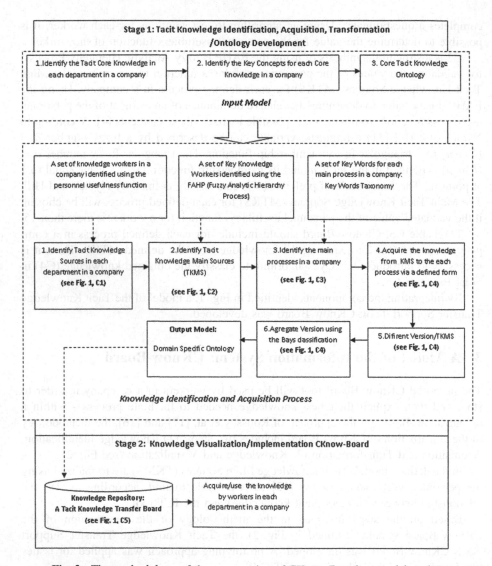

Fig. 2. The methodology of the construction of CKnow-Board; own elaboration.

processes are carried out more than 80 % of the time in a given month by a particular worker, then that particular process will be attributed to that particular worker (see Fig. 3):

An IT company typically consists of a number of departments: Production, Sales, Human Resources, Customer Services, Technical Support, Marketing, Finance, Research and Development. For each department in an IT company, the processes are defined (see Fig. 4):

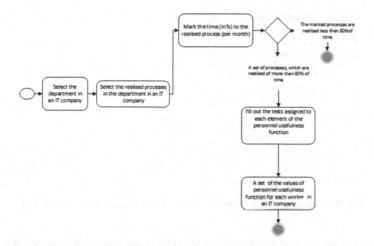

Fig. 3. The general procedure for building C1 of CKnow-Board; own elaboration.

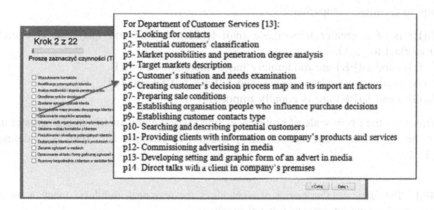

Fig. 4. The implementation of C1 of CKnow-Board; own elaboration.

If the worker is assigned to a defined process, then the answers will be checked and corrected by the managers of each department. Then the worker will be able to complete a specialized test assigned to each element of the personnel usefulness function. Then the value of the personnel usefulness function for this worker is possible to determine (see Fig. 5).

C2: The validated values of the personnel usefulness function for each worker in a company using the FAHP method.

The Main Tacit Knowledge Sources (MTKS) for each defined process in a company (C2) will be defined using the FAHP method. For each process, the weights of the elements of the personnel usefulness function: $f_1(GK)$, $f_2(PK)$, $f_3(A)$, $f_4(E)$, $f_5(I)$ will be different.

In our case study in IT companies, for the process: p1- Looking for contacts for the workers in the Department of Customer Services, the following assumptions are

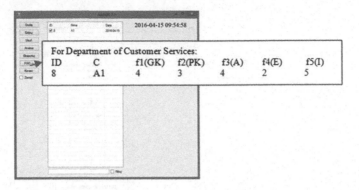

Fig. 5. The implementation of C1 of CKnow-Board; own elaboration.

defined – based on the research results of the pilot study among 30 owners/managers of Polish IT companies in the Lubuskie region (Poland) in the period May-October 2015, supported by project Nr: WND-POKL.08.02.01-08-013/12. Expert choice provides ratings to facilitate comparison:

- $f_4(E)$ is of a greater importance than $f_1(GK)$, $f_2(PK)$ and $f_5(I)$ and is equally important to $f_3(A)$.
- $f_1(GK)$ and $f_2(PK)$ are moderately more important than $f_5(I)$.
- $f_3(A)$ is of a greater importance than $f_1(GK)$, $f_2(PK)$ and $f_5(I)$.
- $f_1(GK)$ and $f_2(PK)$ are is equally important.

Based on the fuzzy scale of preferences, the fuzzy weights matrix of elements of the personnel usefulness function for the process: p1- Looking for contacts is defined (Table 1):

Table 1. The fuzzy weights matrix of elements of the personnel usefulness function for the process: p1- Looking for contacts (own elaboration)

	$f_1(GK)$	$f_2(PK)$	$f_3(A)$	$f_4(E)$	$f_5(I)$
$f_1(GK)$	(1, 1, 1)	(1, 1, 3)	(1/7, 1/5, 1/3)	(1/7, 1/5, 1/3)	(1, 3, 5)
$f_2(PK)$	(1, 1, 3)	(1, 1, 1)	(1/7, 1/5, 1/3)	(1/7, 1/5, 1/3)	(1, 3, 5)
$f_3(A)$	(3, 5, 7)	(3, 5, 7)	(1, 1, 1)	(1/3, 1, 1)	(1, 3, 5)
$f_4(E)$	(3, 5, 7)	(3, 5, 7)	(1, 1, 3)	(1, 1, 1)	(3, 5, 7)
$f_5(I)$	(1/5, 1/3, 1)	(1/5, 1/3, 1)	(1/5, 1/3, 1)	(1/7, 1/5, 1/3)	(1, 1, 1)

The geometric average of ratings for the elements of the personnel usefulness function, by the use of the FAHP method, takes the following value:

$$f_1(G\tilde{K}) = r_{\tilde{1}} = (\tilde{a}_{11} \otimes \tilde{a}_{12} \otimes \tilde{a}_{13} \otimes \tilde{a}_{14} \otimes \tilde{a}_{15} \otimes \tilde{a}_{16})^{\frac{1}{5}} = (0.4592; 0.6544; 1.1076) \quad (2)$$

$$f_2(P\tilde{K}) = r_{\tilde{2}} = (0.4592; 0.6544; 1.1076) \quad (3)$$

$$f_3(\tilde{A}) = \tilde{r}_3 = (1.2457; 2.3714; 3.0049) \tag{4}$$

$$f_4(\tilde{E}) = \tilde{r}_4 = (1.9332; 3.2719; 4.0039) \tag{5}$$

$$f_5(\tilde{I}) = \tilde{r}_5 = (0.2580; 0.3749; 0.8027) \tag{6}$$

Therefore we receive:

$$\tilde{r}_1 \oplus \tilde{r}_2 \oplus \tilde{r}_3 \oplus \tilde{r}_4 \oplus \tilde{r}_5 = (4.3552; 7.3271; 10.0267) \tag{7}$$

The weight of the f_1(GK) element of the personnel usefulness function is defined:

$$\tilde{w}_1 = \tilde{r}_1 \otimes (\tilde{r}_1 \oplus \tilde{r}_2 \oplus \tilde{r}_3 \oplus \tilde{r}_4 \oplus \tilde{r}_5)^{-1} = (0.0458; 0.0893; 0.2543) \tag{8}$$

And for the further elements:

$$\tilde{w}_3 = (0.1242; 0.3237; 0.6900) \tilde{w}_2 = (0.0458; 0.0893; 0.2543) \tag{9}$$

$$\tilde{w}_4 = (0.1928; 0.4466; 0.9193) \tag{10}$$

$$\tilde{w}_5 = (0.10257; 0.0512; 0.1843) \tag{11}$$

After the standardisation of the weights of each element, the values of the weights are estimated:

$$w_1 = 0.1042; w_2 = 0.1042; w_3 = 0.3045; w_4 = 0.4171; w_5 = 0.0699 \tag{12}$$

By the use of the FAHP method, the weights of the elements of the personnel usefulness function for the process: p1- Looking for contacts in an IT company for the workers in the department of Customer Services are assigned:

- The importance of the element: f_1(GK)– value: 0.1042.
- The importance of the criterion: f_2(PK)– value: 0.1042.
- The importance of the criterion: f_3(A)– value: 0.3045.
- The importance of the criterion: f_4(E) – value: 0.4171.
- The importance of the criterion: f_5(I)– value: 0.0699.

So, if the worker receives for each element in the personnel usefulness function the values: f_1(GK) = 4, f_2(PK) = 3, f_3(A) = 4, f_4(E) = 2, f_5(I) = 5 (see Fig. 5), then F = 18 (see Eq. 1) and then the validated value of the personnel usefulness function for this worker will be (see Eq. 13):

$$\begin{aligned} F' &= f_1(\text{GK}) \times 0.1042 + f_2(\text{PK}) \times 0.1042 + f_3(\text{A}) \times 0.3045 + f_4(\text{E}) \\ &\quad \times 0.4171 + f_5(\text{A}) \times 0.0699 \\ &= 3,1311 \end{aligned} \tag{13}$$

For each of the defined processes in each department in an IT company, an analysis of the importance of the elements of the personnel usefulness function is carried out. Based on the results, it is possible to define the set of Main Tacit Knowledge Sources (MTKS) for each defined process in a company.

C3: Building a model for Tacit Knowledge Acquisition.

A worker identified as MTKS is automatically assigned to the defined area of knowledge, which includes a set of assigned processes. Then the MTKS fills out the form, which will enable him/her to save his/her tacit knowledge in an explicit form of knowledge (see Fig. 6).

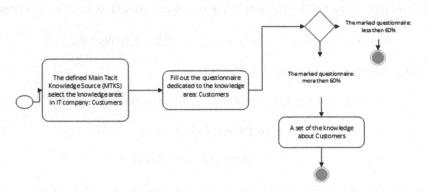

Fig. 6. The general procedure for the building of C3 of CKnow-Board; own elaboration.

C4: Building the model for Tacit Knowledge Transformation.

For the IT companies included in this study, the five main knowledge areas are defined as: (1) Customers, (2) New Technology/Software, (3) New Technology/ Hardware, (4) Competition, (5) Workers.

In this case study, a questionnaire was defined for an IT company which aims to acquire the tacit knowledge from the MTKS which can then be transferred to CKnow-Board. This questionnaire includes elements such as: e.g. x_1 - type of customer, x_2 – the values of realised projects, x_3 – the number of meetings with a customer per month, x_4 – the duration of a project, etc. Each element of this questionnaire has a set of defined answers (the set of values) which the MTKS must select and mark. Then these received values are classified using Bayes network in the Knowledge Transfer Board.

C5: Building the Knowledge Transfer Board.

To build the Bayes network, independent variables are defined (the answers selected by the MTKS), which correspond to the vertices of the "first" layer of the network. In our case study there are: x1 - types of customers, x2 – the values of realised projects, x3 – the number of meetings with a customer per month, x4 – the duration of a project. So, a model for Bayes network is defined also based on the research results of the pilot study among 30 owners/managers of Polish IT companies in the Lubuskie region (Poland) (the project Nr: WND-POKL.08.02.01-08-013/12):

- x_1 {x_{11} - a small company, x_{12} - a medium company, x_{13} - a large company}.
- $p(x_{11})$... $p(x_{13})$ - the probability of a particular type of a customer.
- x_2 {x_{21}- till 2000 euro, x_{22} – 2001–5000 euro, x_{23} – 5001–8000, x_{24} –8001–12000, x_{25} – 12001–20000 x_{26} – 20001–30000, x_{27} – more than 30001 euro}.
- $p(x_{21})$... $p(x_{27})$ - the probability of a particular values of a realized project
- x_3 {x_{31}- till 2, x_{32} – 3–5, x_{33} – 6–10, x_{34} – more than 11}.
- $p(x_{31})$... $p(x_{34})$ - the probability of a particular number of meetings with the customer per month.
- x_4 {x_{41}- till 1 month, x_{42} – 1–3 months, x_{43} – 4–6 months, x_{44} – 7-12 months, x_{45} – more than 12 months.
- $p(x_{41})$... $p(x_{45})$ - the probability of a particular duration of a project.

Based on previous rules, knowledge clusters about customers are defined. Variable A is defined as a cluster (Cluster1) and is dependent on a number of variables: x_1 - type of a customer, x_2 – the values of realized project, x_3 – the number of meetings with the customer per month, x_4 – duration of the project. Moreover, the classification of acquired knowledge from MTKS is dependent on variable A. The rules are defined for each of the five knowledge areas in an IT company. Based on the results from the use of the Bayes network, the Knowledge Transfer Board for the IT company for the knowledge area: Customers is formulated (see Fig. 7):

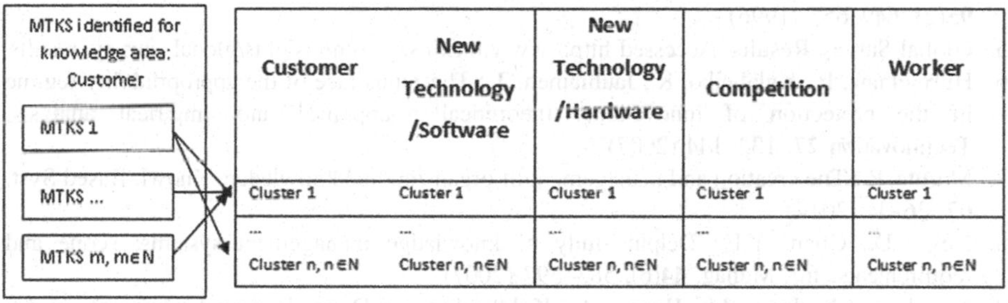

MTKS identified for knowledge area: Customer	Customer	New Technology /Software	New Technology /Hardware	Competition	Worker
MTKS 1					
MTKS ...	Cluster 1	Cluster 1	Cluster 1	Cluster 1	Cluster 1
	...	...	...	...	...
MTKS m, m∈N	Cluster n, n∈N	Cluster n, n∈N	Cluster n, n∈N	Cluster n, n∈N	Cluster n, n∈N

Fig. 7. The general structure for building C5 of CKnow-Board; own elaboration.

We receive a board in which the manager of an IT company can observe the activity of employees in the sharing of knowledge and the transferring of tacit knowledge, and in addition, we offer a Tacit Knowledge Transfer Support Tool for retaining the critical knowledge of other employees within the company.

So, the proposed tool enables the identification of tacit knowledge in a company and the transformation of different types of knowledge into the form of explicit knowledge included in the Tacit Knowledge Transfer Board.

5 Final Remarks

In this paper a model of a Tacit Knowledge Transfer Support Tool: CKnow-Board was illustrated. By using the proposed tool, critical tacit knowledge of workers should not be lost within a company and, moreover, should be retained in the form of explicit knowledge. By developing a model of this tool, we have tried to support the management of tacit knowledge within a company. The proposed tool is adaptable to the profile of a company.

The next step of the development of the CKnow-Board tool is the inclusion of all components to be implemented and introduced for IT companies. Then the software will be used by workers who will test if it is really simple to use [8]. Finally, tests of the effectiveness of the use of this tool will be carried out.

References

1. Alavi, M., Leidner, D.E.: Review: knowledge management and knowledge management systems: conceptual foundations and research issues. MIS Q. **25**, 107–136 (2001)
2. Bigliardi, B., Dormio, A.I., Galati, F.: ICTs and knowledge management: an Italian case study of a construction company. Meas. Bus. Excell. **14**(3), 16–29 (2010)
3. Bughin, J., Chui, M.: Evolution of the networked enterprise: McKinsey (2013). business_technology/evolution_of_the_networked_enterprise_mckinsey_3.0.pdf. Accessed 14 July 2014
4. Chang, D.-Y.: Application of the extent analysis method on fuzzy AHP. Eur. J. Oper. Res. **95**(2), 649–655 (1996)
5. Global Survey Results. Accessed http://www.mckinsey.com/insights/global_survey_results
6. Hurmelinna, P., Kyläheiko, K., Jauhiainen, T.: The Janus face of the appropriability regime in the protection of innovations: theoretical re-appraisal and empirical analysis. Technovation **27**, 133–144 (2007)
7. Maruta, R.: The creation and management of organizational knowledge. Knowl. Based Syst. **67**, 26–34 (2014)
8. Nevo, D., Chan, Y.E.: Delphi study of knowledge management systems: scope and requirements. Inf. Manag. **44**(6), 583–597 (2007)
9. Nonaka, I., Kodama, M., Hirose, A., Kohlbacher, F.: Dynamic fractal organizations for promoting knowledge-based transformation – a new paradigm for organizational theory. Eur. Manag. J. **2**(1), 137–146 (2014)
10. Nonaka, I., Takeuchi, H.: The knowledge-creating company: how Japanese companies create the dynamics of innovation. Oxford University Press, USA (1995)
11. Nydick, R.L., Hill, R.P.: Using the analytic hierarchy process to structure the supplier selection procedure. Int. J. Purch. Mater. Manag. **28**(2), 31–36 (1992)
12. Patalas-Maliszewska, J., Krebs, I.: Decision model for the use of the application for knowledge transfer support in manufacturing enterprises. In: Abramowicz, W. (ed.) BIS 2015 Workshops. LNBIP, vol. 228, pp. 48–55. Springer, Heidelberg (2015). doi:10.1007/978-3-319-26762-3_5
13. Patalas-Maliszewska, J.: Knowledge Worker Management: Value Assessment, Methods, and Application Tools. Springer, Heidelberg (2013)

14. Pfisterer, S., Streim, A., Hampe, K.: Arbeit 3.0. Arbeiten in der digitalen Welt (2013). Accessed http://www.bitkom.org/files/documents/Studie_Arbeit_
15. Phang, M.S., Foong, S.: Information Communication Technologies (ICTs) and knowledge sharing: the case of professional accountants in Malaysia. World J. Sci. Technol. Sustain. Dev. 7(1), 21–34 (2010)
16. Rialp, A.: El método del caso como técnica de investigación y su aplicación al estudio de la función directiva. In: IV Taller de Metodología ACEDE, Spain, 23–25 de abril 1998
17. Roussey, C., Pinet, F., Kang, M., Corcho. O.: An introduction to ontologies and ontology engineering. In: Ontologies in Urban Development Projects, pp. 9–38. Springer, London (2011)
18. Sure, Y., Staab, S., Studer, R.: On-to-knowledge methodology (OTKM). In: Handbook on Ontologies, pp. 117–132. Springer, Berlin (2004)
19. Van Joolingen, W.R., De Jong, T., Lazonder, A.W., Savelsbergh, E.R., Manlove, S.: Co-Lab: research and development of an online learning environment for collaborative scientific discovery learning. Comput. Hum. Behav. 21, 677–688 (2005)

A Model of an ERP-Based Knowledge Management System for Engineer-to-Order Enterprises

Sławomir Kłos[(⊠)]

Department of Computer Science and Production Management,
University of Zielona Góra, Zielona Góra, Poland
s.klos@iizp.uz.zgora.pl

Abstract. Today's enterprises require effective systems of knowledge management (KM) that guarantee proper know-how recording and processing in order to create innovative products and technologies. Part of a company's know-how is recorded in an enterprise resource planning (ERP) system database as data and information which could be transformed into knowledge. In this, paper, a model of a KM system for manufacturing companies that carry out engineer-to-order (ETO) production is proposed. The model is based on ERP systems and includes tools that enable data and information processing and its subsequent conversion into a form of knowledge. An analysis and understanding of the model may result in an improvement of innovation processes in high-tech manufacturing companies. The proposed model may additionally support the research and design activities of manufacturing enterprises. Illustrative examples are provided.

Keywords: Enterprise resource planning · Knowledge management · Innovation · Research and design · Engineer-to-order production

1 Introduction

An engineer-to-order (ETO) production approach is one in which a company designs and manufacturers a product based on very specific customer requirements. When an engineer-to-order manufacturing company signs a contract for a new product, it often has only a general concept based on customer assumptions for the functionality of the product. However, in the contract the most important information about total price, delivery time and guarantee should be included. It means that engineer-to-order companies can draw upon their own experiences when preparing a cost-effective and competitive contract. ETO production includes, for example, the manufacturing of production lines, machines, tools and equipment, etc. Such companies are typically based on the technical knowledge and competences of designers and technologists. A very important role in this kind of production is played by the research and design department which is responsible for the implementation of innovation via new products and technological development. In the area of production and services, an implementation of best practices and the permanent training of employees is of crucial

© Springer International Publishing Switzerland 2016
G. Dregvaite and R. Damasevicius (Eds.): ICIST 2016, CCIS 639, pp. 42–52, 2016.
DOI: 10.1007/978-3-319-46254-7_4

importance. To support the process of production and technological development, an effective KM system is required [5]. ERP systems can be a very important knowledge repository for each manufacturing enterprise. The data registered in an ERP database could be first transformed into information, and after interpretation, into knowledge about products and processes. The number of functional areas of a company included in an ERP and the lifetime of the system determine the size of a database (amount of data) and its resulting knowledge potential [7]. Effective KM is especially important for innovative engineer-to-order manufacturing companies which make high-tech proto-types of products or technologies whose research and design demand is relatively great. The research problem of this paper can be formulated as follows. Given is a manu-facturing enterprise that realises ETO production based on an ERP system. How can it effectively manage knowledge in the enterprise to support the development of inno-vative products or technologies using the ERP system.

In this paper, a model of a KM system dedicated to engineer-to-order companies is proposed. The model is based on an ERP system database in which both tacit and formal knowledge could be acquired. The model includes algorithms of processing information and transforming it into a form of knowledge.

2 ERP Systems in Engineer-to-Order Enterprises

Engineer-to-order production is dedicated to the manufacturing of short series or indi-vidual prototype products or technologies. The management system of this kind of pro-duction is mostly based on project management techniques. The ERP systems implemented in ETO companies not only support typical production and logistics pro-cesses, but also R&D or product developing processes. In Fig. 1, a framework of product development in engineer-to-order enterprises supported by an ERP system is presented. On the basis of customer requirements, a concept of a product is prepared. ETO com-panies have to closely cooperate with customers during new product development. Product concepts are based on economic limitations and technical assumptions specified by customers, these are often contradictory [6]. Producers are expected to offer high-tech solutions, low prices, relatively short times of product delivery and solid guarantee conditions. ETO companies often make prototypes that need to be preceded by scientific research (new materials, functionality, etc.). In ETO enterprises, the ERP system should support project management. On the basis of customer assumptions, the product design (costs, functions, variants, etc.) and technology is defined and registered as data in the ERP database. Since the form of the product is prepared together with the customer, the process of product development should be registered in the ERP database too (ideas, solutions, variants of design, bill of materials, technologies, etc.). Additionally, the negotiation process, variants of sales offers, delivery conditions and operating conditions are registered in the ERP database by the CRM system. During the manufacturing pro-cess, data about technological operations and quality control are also collected by the ERP system. Therefore, the database of ERP is not only a set of data, but also a very important knowledge repository about the processes and projects realized by a manufacturing company. For the KM process, it is highly important to transform data from the ERP database into know-how about products and processes carried out by the ETO company.

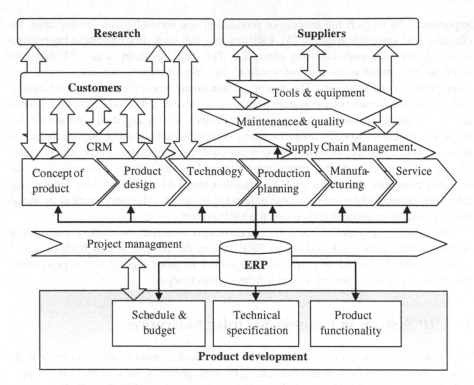

Fig. 1. A framework of product development in an ETO enterprise supported by an ERP system

ERP databases include a lot of data about both completed and ongoing projects. To create an effective system of KM, the data should be classified and interpreted (transformed into information). The method of access and indexation (tagging of information) is very important. To transform the information into a form of knowledge, the form of its presentation is also very important [8]. A part of the information could be presented as a best practices after verification by experts. Therefore, the methods and tools for information verification, and classification should be elaborated and implemented in a KM module of the ERP system. The methodology of the transformation of data into knowledge is proposed in Fig. 2.

In the first step of the proposed methodology, data analysis and interpretation should be performed. On the basis of data analysis, a set of information can be prepared. For example, in the area of product design, the following data can be analyzed: structure of products, average time of product module design, most problematic areas of product design (time-consuming), design errors, cards of design changes, etc. The interpretation of data enables the classification of modules (parts) of products according to labor intensity, the possibility of errors, reasons for changes in design, reasons for design errors, etc. Next, relationships between the data should be analyzed. For example, data from manufacturing related to reducibility are very important for the design department. Therefore, comparisons between assumed operation times and real

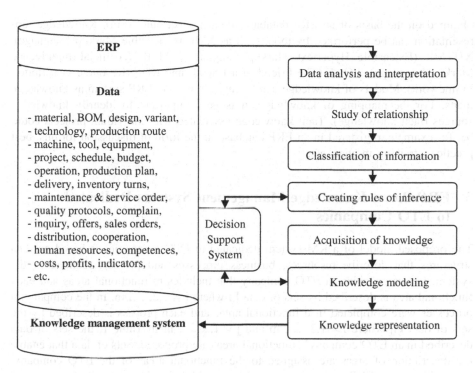

Fig. 2. The methodology of the transformation of data

operation times (registered in the manufacturing department could be crucial for processing guidelines for design.

In the next step, the classification of the information should be done. The information can be classified in different ways, for example – according to processes or functional areas (sales, design, technology, production, logistics, maintenance, etc.). To create an effective KM system, the most important information should be structured. The structure enables the systematization of the information and automated updates of the information downloaded from the ERP database and processes it into a useable form. The information could be used to support different decisions in an ETO company. To create an effective decision support system, rules of inference should be formulated. For example, some rules in the area of product design should identify any assumptions and limitations that may reduce production failures, manufacturing costs or operation times. Another example of a rule could be the application of hard-to-reach materials in the BOM. The rule can be formulated as follows: if material m_i is used in the construction of product P_j, the production plan should be shifted by t_k time because of delivery times. A decision support system is very useful for research and development project verification based on the rules of inference. The acquisition of knowledge includes the method of information collection (extraction from the ERP system) to create a basis of knowledge about products, or structural and situational knowledge about the system (ETO enterprises). The next step of the proposed methodology is the determination of knowledge representation. Knowledge will be obtained on the basis of an ERP database (data in electronic form). Knowledge representation can be performed by tools such as XML (eXtensible Markup Language), XHTML (Extensible Hypertext Markup Language), AIML (Artificial Intelligence Markup Language), FOAF (The Friend of a Friend) and RDF (Resource Description Framework). Models of knowledge can be registered in an ERP system as knowledge maps. For the mapping of knowledge, it is very important to identify knowledge sources (tacit knowledge). Tacit knowledge associated with individual projects could be, for example, registered in an ERP database in the form of discussion forums, best practices, training movies, etc.

3   ERP-Based Knowledge Management Systems Dedicated to ETO Companies

The proposed model of a KM system dedicated to ETO companies is based on data structures that describe resources, business processes and projects realized in the system. Let us consider an ETO company that includes m functional areas and each functional area is described by sets of data Fi where i = 1,2, …, m. In the company, n processes were completed in n functional areas and each process is described by the sets of data Pij where i = 1,2, …, m and j = 1,2, …, n. In Table 1, the sets of data described in an ETO company's functional areas are proposed. Sets of data that enable the description of areas are assigned to the functional areas of the ETO company. Depending on the ERP system, the sets of data could differ - but generally the proposed repository of data should enable a description of the functional areas of the ETO company. The number of functional areas could also be increased or reduced (for example marketing, tool management, logistics, services, etc.) but generally the proposed functional areas carry out the same functions. In the proposed model of data management in an ETO company, only operational departments are taken into consideration. On the basis of the methodology proposed in Fig. 2, ERP data analysis is required to create a KM system which can create useful information. For example: on the basis of a sales offer and sales order comparison, information about offer effectiveness could be obtained. Studying the relationships enables the construction and analysis of different ratios, for example the efficiency of employees, or OEE (overall effectiveness of equipment). In Table 1, the business processes realised in different functional areas are presented. The realized business processes result in the generation of data in functional areas of an ETO company. A model of a knowledge management system in an ETO company should include an algorithm of knowledge acquisition, a representation of knowledge and a modelling of knowledge on the basis of the data registered in the ERP system. The KM system supports the development processes of new products and technologies, operational decisions in functional areas, tactical and strategic decisions for the whole company and the training of workers, etc. On the basis of the structure of the functional areas, data sets and business processes presented in the Table 1, a model of an ERP-based KM system is proposed (Fig. 3).

Table 1. Data sets and processes of an ETO enterprise

Item	Functional area	Sets of data	Business proceses
F_1	Sales and distribution	F_{11} – sales inquiries, F_{12} – sales offers, F_{13} – sales orders, F_{14} – invoices, F_{15} – customers, F_{16} – shipments	P_{11} - market research. P_{12} - offers preparing, P_{13} - negotiations, P_{14} – product/project valuation, P_{15} – product/project delivery
F_2	Research & development	F_{21} – projects (products), F_{22} – innovations, F_{23} – patents, F_{24} – research results	P_{21} – prototyping products, P_{22} – research works, P_{23} – laboratory tests
F_3	Design & technology	F_{31} – materials, F_{32} – BOMs, F_{33} – products, F_{34} – variants, F_{35} – technologies, F_{36} – designs, F_{37} – calculations, F_{38} – production resources, F_{39} – maintenance manuals, F_{310} – guarantees	P_{31} – product design, P_{32} – material selection, P_{33} – technology design, P_{34} – cost analysis
F_4	Production planning and control	F_{41} – production plans, F_{42} – production abilities, F_{43} – production routes, F_{44} – priorities, F_{45} – subcontractors	P_{41} – production planning, P_{42} – balancing prod. capacity
F_5	Production and assembly	F_{51} – production orders, F_{52} – registered operations, F_{53} – subcontractor orders	P_{51} – production scheduling, P_{52} – production control, P_{53} – logistics management
F_6	Purchasing	F_{61} – purchasing orders, F_{62} – purchasing offers, F_{63} – material requirements. F_{64} – suppliers	P_{61} – MRP, P_{62} – validation of supplies, P_{63} – verification of offers, P_{63} – material ordering

(Continued)

Table 1. *(Continued)*

Item	Functional area	Sets of data	Business proceses
F_7	Material management and warehousing	F_{71} – material turnovers, F_{72} – inventory, F_{73} –structure of storage	P_{71} – registration of material flow, P_{72} – stocktaking, P_{73} – storage mapping
F_8	Maintenance & tools management	F_{81} – tools, F_{82} - equipments, F_{83} – maintenance orders, F_{84} – maintenance operations, F_{86} – service orders, F_{86} – spare parts	P_{81} – repairs, P_{82} – renovation, P_{83} – setups, P_{84} – services, P_{85} – design of tools, P_{86} – design of equipment
F_9	Quality control	F_{91} – quality of materials, F_{92} – quality of processes, F_{93} – quality of tools, F_{94} – quality of products	P_{91} – quality control, P_{92} – preparing procedures, P_{93} – implementing procedures

The KM system includes a data analyzer. The module is available in most ERP systems as a business intelligence (BI) functionality. On the basis of the data extracted from an ERP database, useful information can be created using the tool. For example, on the basis of data extracted from the F_{14} data set (invoices) – information about the lifecycle stage of each product can be delivered.

An analysis of the data should be performed by dedicated experts or knowledge engineers. An information classifier is a very important tool which can enable the systematization of information registered in an ERP database. For example, on the basis of material analyses (F_{31}), the set of data could be divided into many classification groups (steel materials: C-bars, T-bars, double T-bars, etc.). On the basis of the classified information, for example, a product configurator could be implemented to support the process of rapidly offering products. To analyze relationships among the ERP data, specialized tools such as BI, could also be used. For example a study of relationships among the production plans (F_{41}), maintenance orders (F_{83}), production orders (F_{51}) and material turnovers (F_{71}), enables the evaluation of the influence of the frequency of machine inspections and material delivery delays on the deadlines of production orders. The analysis of relationships can result in an elaboration of an advanced system of production planning and scheduling [3]. A time-series analysis of the quality control data of processes and products (F_{92}, F_{94}) and an implementation in

Shewharts charts can result in the creation of a new measurement methodology [1]. The data analysis, study of data relationships and the classification of information result in the creation of inference and decision rules.

The decision rules directly influence the realization of processes. Some examples of decision rules can be constructed as follows:

- if a customer has overdue payments $(F_{14}) > 30$ days then a new offer cannot be prepared (P_{12}),
- if inventory level (F_{72}) of material $M_x < Min_x$ $(F_{31})$where Min_x (minimum level of material x then order material M_x), (P_{63}),
- if a material M_x quality (F_{91}) is inconsistent with the specification (F_{31}) then the purchasing orders cannot be realized by supplier S_i (P_{63}).

The inference rules influence other data or enable the determination of some ratios, for example:

- if in the BOM material M_x is used (F_{31}) then technology T_y should be applied (F_{35}) to minimize manufacturing costs (F_{38}),
- if production variants V_y are applied (F_{34}) then production order (F_{51}) will be completed according to plan (F_{41}),
- if a production order (F_{51}) cannot be completed in time, then the production plan (F_{41}) will be verified.

The rules represent a form of knowledge. Knowledge acquisition involves the recording of inference and decision rules by knowledge engineers, but the rules are created by knowledge workers in various functional areas of the ETO company [4]. It is very important to associate experts and knowledge workers with functional areas and the processes carried out in the enterprise in order to create new knowledge about products, technical solutions and manufacturing technologies. To support knowledge acquisition, a knowledge map should be created. The map enables the identification of the intellectual potential of the company and on the basis of decision and inference rules which enable the modelling of knowledge. The knowledge obtained from experts and knowledge workers is saved in a form of rules and creates a knowledge base. The knowledge presentation may be in the form of best practices.

The procedure of knowledge management for new product development in an ETO enterprise is presented in Fig. 4. In the first step of the procedure, the product concept is elaborated on the basis of customer requirements and know-how about products. The product concept defines the assumptions and limitations of the scope of project. The realization of the next three steps is typical for project management (scope, schedule and budget).

The activities of new project development are supported by inference and decision rules created on the basis of sets of data extracted from an ERP database. A result of the procedure will be some variants of the product concepts (different variants of projects). Using the decision support system and decision analysis (for example based on the Analytical Hierarchy Processes methodology) the selection of the best solution is possible [2]. The evaluation criteria could be determined by customers or expert

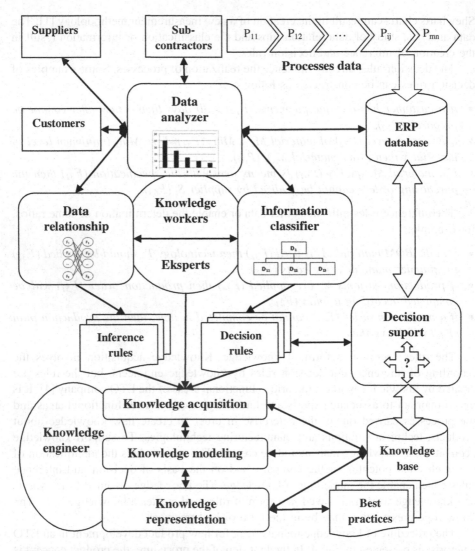

Fig. 3. A model of an ERP-based knowledge management system for an ETO enterprise

experience. Analogical procedures can be proposed for products, technology design, research methodology, maintenance and service procedures, etc. The proposed procedure of product development should be repeated for each new product. The knowledge about preparing a new project could be used for improving inference and decision rules.

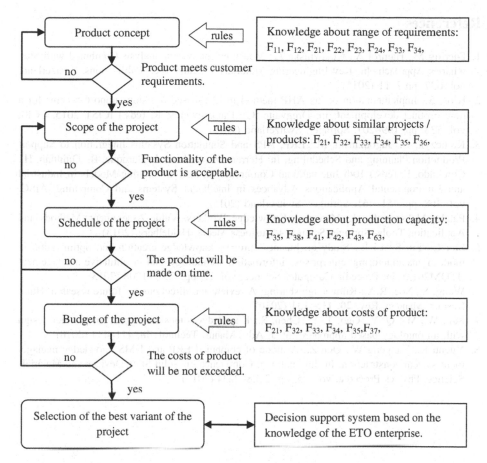

Fig. 4. The procedure of knowledge management for product development in an ETO enterprise

4 Conclusions

A lot of high-tech manufacturing enterprises work on the basis of ETO principles. For such companies, an effective knowledge management system is crucial for reducing the time of a new product development. Most companies use an ERP system to support business processes. An ERP database can be a very important knowledge repository. In this paper, a model of a knowledge management system dedicated to ETO enterprises is proposed. The model is based on the transformation of data from an ERP system using inference and decision rules into a form of knowledge. The procedure of knowledge management for product development is also proposed. An integral part of a knowledge management system is a module of decision support. Decision and inference rules should be created by experts or knowledge workers of an ETO company.

In further research, inference algorithms will be proposed that enable the automatic creation of inference and decision rules on the basis of the data sets of ERP data.

References

1. Diering M., Hamrol A., Kujawińska A.: Measurement system analysis Combined with She-what's Approach. In: Key Engineering Materials © Trans Tech Publications, Switzerland, vol. 637, pp 7–11 (2015)
2. Kłos, S.: Implementation of the AHP method in ERP-based decision support systems for a new product development. In: Dregvaite, G., Damasevicius, R. (eds.) ICIST 2015. CCIS, vol. 538, pp. 199–207. Springer, Switzerland (2015)
3. Krenczyk, D., Jagodzinski, M.: ERP, APS and Simulation Systems Integration to Support Production Planning and Scheduling. In: Herrero, Á., Sedano, J., Baruque, B., Quintián, H., Corchado, E. (eds.) 10th International Conference on Soft Computing Models in Industrial and Environmental Applications Advances in Intelligent Systems and Computing. AISC, vol. 368, pp. 451–461. Springer, Switzerland (2015)
4. Patalas-Maliszewska, J.: Managing Knowledge Workers: Value Assessment, Methods and Application Tools. Springer Science + Business Media, Heidelberg (2013)
5. Shu L., Liu S., Li L.: Study on business process knowledge creation and optimization in modern manufacturing enterprises, information technology and quantitative management (ITQM2013). In: Procedia Computer Science, vol. 17, pp. 1202–1208 (2013)
6. Wang, S., Noe, R.A.: Knowledge sharing: A review and directions for future research. Hum. Resour. Manage. Rev. **20**, 115–131 (2010)
7. Sun, W., Ma, Q.-Y., Gao, T.-Y., Chen, S.: Knowledge-intensive support for product design with an ontology-based approach. Int. J. Adv. Manuf. Technol. **48**, 421–434 (2010)
8. Yuena K., Yangeng W., Qun Z.: A mode of combined ERP and KMS knowledge management system construction. In: International Conference on Solid State Devices and Materials Science, Physics Procedia, vol. 25, pp. 2228–2234 (2012)

Cloud-Based Enterprise Information Systems: Determinants of Adoption in the Context of Organizations

Umut Şener$^{(\boxtimes)}$, Ebru Gökalp, and P. Erhan Eren

Department of Information Systems,
Informatics Institute, METU, Ankara, Turkey
{sumut,egokalp,ereren}@metu.edu.tr

Abstract. Cloud computing is growing at a very fast pace. Enterprise information systems (EISs) such as ERP, SCM, and CRM are used in organizations in order to increase customer satisfaction, operational excellence, and to decrease operational costs. Looking at the widespread literature available on both EIS and Cloud Computing, few researchers have examined the integration of both systems. While this area has not been fully investigated in the academia due to limited available literature, it has attracted significant interest from general practitioners. Accordingly, the Cloud-EIS can be considered as an important research problem. In this study, we attempt to investigate the factors influencing the usage and adoption of Cloud-EISs by considering Technology-Organization-Environment (TOE) framework as the basis to give directions to cloud service providers on how to design their products in order to increase adoption and usage. Analytic Hierarchy Process (AHP) is used in order to rank the determined factors. The results show that the most significant factors influencing the usage and adoption of Cloud-EISs are security & privacy, business activity- cloud EIS fitness, top management support, trust, and organization's IT resource.

Keywords: Cloud-based enterprise information systems adoption · Cloud computing · Enterprise information systems · Organizational adoption · Technology-Organization-Environment framework · Analytic Hierarchy Process

1 Introduction

With continuous advances in information technologies (IT), firms have been prompted to adopt innovation technologies in order to stay competitive and survive in the market place. In recent years, "cloud computing" have attracted many firms because of its benefits. Cloud computing is a relatively new technology that supports enterprises in using innovative IT at an affordable level of the operating cost [1]. The adoption of the cloud-based technologies have been spreading rapidly, owing to financial payback that reduces expenditures for existing applications [2]. It offers many services such as software, platforms, and infrastructure to enterprises.

As the world continues to transition into a global economy, enterprise information system (EIS), such as customer relationship management (CRM), supply chain

© Springer International Publishing Switzerland 2016
G. Dregvaite and R. Damasevicius (Eds.): ICIST 2016, CCIS 639, pp. 53–66, 2016.
DOI: 10.1007/978-3-319-46254-7_5

management (SCM), and enterprise resource planning (ERP) have been developed and widely adopted by organizations, in order to increase profit, improve business operations and maximize the service quality. Despite having significant benefits, traditional EIS can be clunky, costly, and complicated to implement for most organizations [3]. The cloud computing based EIS concept, which is referred to as "Cloud-EIS" in this paper, was recently introduced to improve such situations by offering competitive advantage to organizations through flexibility, scalability, and independence in IT infrastructure and capabilities.

Upon conducting an extensive literature search on both EIS and Cloud Computing, we have realized that very few researchers have investigated the integration of both systems. Accordingly, the purpose of this study is to determine factors affecting organization intention regarding Cloud-EIS applications in order to give guidance to Cloud-EIS service providers on how to design their products in order to increase customers' adoption of their services. Therefore, the research questions of the study are: How different types of factors affect organizational adoption of Cloud-EIS applications? What are the most significant factors influencing the usage and adoption of the Cloud-EIS?

The remainder of this study is structured as follows. The summary of the literature review is provided in Sect. 2. The proposed approach is presented in Sect. 3. The proposed research model is presented in Sect. 4. The ranking of the determinants is given in Sect. 5. Finally, the conclusion of the study is given.

2 Literature Review

2.1 Enterprise Information Systems

EIS refers to any kind of information systems that improve business operations by the integration of the functions of an enterprise. EIS offers a platform that enables enterprises to integrate and manage their business operations on a robust basis. Enterprises implement various EIS for their benefits, such as dealing with large volume of data, supporting complex business processes, and improving system quality.

ERP, an integrated software package which is composed of a set of functional modules such as production, sales, finance, and human resources, is adaptable to the specific needs of interested customers. As stated in [4], the adoption rate of ERP is rising, because of its major advantages, such as reduced managerial workload, reporting operations at a higher speed, real-time data handling, etc.

CRM system offers the infrastructure that enables sustainable and enhanced relationship building with customers. CRM is widely implemented by enterprises to have strengthened relationships with customers and improve their businesses [5].

SCM has been defined as "the integration of key business processes from end user through original suppliers that provides products, services, and information that add value for all stakeholders" [6]. As stated in [7], SCM keeps inventory cost at a minimum level and satisfies customer needs more quickly, with shorter lead times and replenishment through better collaboration with suppliers.

2.2   Cloud Computing

In the literature, there is no common or standard definition for "cloud computing" [8, 9]. Feuerlicht [10] defines "cloud computing" as follows: it involves the ability of the computing, data storage, and software services via internet. Cisco [11] points out that cloud computing is showing the capacity to offer services on demand, at lower cost than the existing options, with less complexity, better scalability, and wider availability.

2.3   Cloud-EIS

Until now, there is no standard definition of Cloud-EIS. As stated in [12], Cloud-EIS enables EIS to be provided through the Internet and available to a number of clients at much lower costs, by means of the flexibility and capability of Cloud Computing. As a result, it can be defined as a flexible, yet robust information system integrated with Cloud Computing, which enables enterprises to offer increasing levels of flexibility, and agility. The significant difference between Cloud EIS from On-Premise EIS is that users access services provided through the cloud and only relevant business modules could be bought on a pay-as-you-go basis without the need to purchase the entire EIS [13]. As stated in [14], Cloud-EIS is the fastest way to adopt new EIS and also a cost-effective approach to enable multiple users to access the same resource without upgrading a server or spending a lot of money for new IT infrastructure. Most firms have started to implement Cloud-EIS solutions to solve various problems encountered in the regular On-Premise EIS [15]. Cloud-EIS is a world-shattering transformation model especially for new start-ups that could not meet the expenses of pricy IT systems [16].

2.4   Theoretical Background

The literature review shows that the adoption of innovation technologies is significant in order to have competitive benefits such as increasing profits and improving business operations. There are many theories that incorporate the implementation of innovation technologies: diffusion of innovation (DOI) [17], technology acceptance model (TAM) [18], theory of planned behaviour (TPB) [19], unified theory of acceptance and use of technology (UTAUT) [20], and the TOE framework [21]. Whereas the TAM, TPB and UTAUT have been used for investigating the individual acceptance of a new technology, the DOI and TOE framework have been utilized to study the adoption of innovations at the organizational level. In the TOE framework, there are three contexts, that investigate the factors related to the technology, organization, and environment, and it provides a cohesive viewpoint regarding enterprises' inner and outer dynamics. As stated in [22], the TOE framework is reliable and applicable to numerous IT innovation fields. Therefore, the TOE framework is considered as an appropriate basis to investigate the organizational adoption of Cloud-EISs in this study.

Despite the limited number of studies available in the literature, there are many theories and researches that may contribute to the investigation of the significant determinants of the Cloud-EIS adoption.

3 Proposed Approach

The literature review of this study is conducted by following the systematic literature review proposed by Kitchenham [23]. The steps of the review are given in Table 1.

Table 1. The systematic review steps

Steps	Explanation
Starting point of the search	Technology-Organization-Environment (TOE) framework was selected as the starting point of the study
Search language	The search was performed in English
Search terms	The search strategy was performed around the terms "cloud computing", "cloud-based enterprise systems", "cloud-based enterprise information systems", "cloud enterprise systems" "software as a service", "saas", "acceptance", "adoption", "perception", "crm", "erp", "scm", etc
Databases	The search was performed on Scopus (www.scopus.com/search/form. url), Aisel (www.aisel.aisnet.org), and Web of Science (http://apps. webofknowledge.com/)
Checking the reference list	In Scopus, 276 articles were collected with the search terms, whereas the results were 568 articles in Aisel, and 105 in Web of Science, after entering the search terms. Additionally, references of these studies are re-viewed as well
Citation search	SSCI, SCI, and AIS index journals were selected in the results. Conference proceedings, series, meetings, and reviews are excluded
Management of results	A database was built in Microsoft Excel to manage the search results and findings
Selection of primary studies	Initial Exclusion: It is done by examining keywords, titles, and abstracts in order to understand the appropriateness of the studies before reading papers fully
	Date: The studies published before the year 2000 are excluded from the data-base After applying these steps, 139 studies remain
Study quality assessment	139 studies are reviewed and 52 studies of them investigate the adoption of the cloud-based solutions. 23 studies of them are mainly literature reviews or case studies conducted in the context of the domain and they do not contribute to the stage of defining the major factors that affect the adoption of Cloud EIS. Thus, the remaining 29 studies (primary studies) and the references of the primary studies are also reviewed
Data synthesis	Six experts who are PhD students in the domain of information systems analyzed and discussed which factors should be put into the research model. First, they judged independently and listed factors to put into the model. The inter-rater agreement was over the 85 %. Then in order to resolve conflicts, experts discussed conflicts in a meeting and they reached a consensus

As a result of the systematic review, 29 primary studies which explore the significant determinants of the cloud computing adoption, are referred as a baseline to build a research model of this study as listed in Table 2.

Table 2. Primary Cloud-EIS adoption studies

Contexts	Factors	Sources
Technology	Trust	[24–37]
	Relative Advantage	[26, 31, 32, 35, 38–41]
	Security & Privacy	[24, 26, 30, 33–36, 40, 42–45]
	Complexity	[31, 32, 38, 40]
	Customization	[25, 29, 33, 45]
Organization	Organizations' IT Resource	[24, 30, 38, 46, 47]
	Top Management Support	[25, 38, 41, 44, 47–50]
	Organization Size	[38, 41, 47]
	Business Activity-Cloud EIS Fitness	[51]
Environment	Competitive Pressure	[25–29, 41]
	Trading Partner Pressure	[28, 41]
	Government Policy & Regulations	[25, 38]
	Country-based Infrastructure	[33]

4 The Research Model

The most significant factors (constructs) that affect the adoption of Cloud-EIS are determined as: Relative Advantage, Complexity, Security & Privacy, Customization, Trust, Top Management Support, Organization Size, Organizations' IT Resource, Business Activity-Cloud EIS Fitness, Competitive Pressure, Trading Partner Pressure, Government Policy & Regulations, and Country based Infrastructure. As shown in Fig. 1, the constructs of the proposed research model are incorporated with the technological, organizational and environmental contexts of the TOE framework, and each factor has varying weights (W_i, i = 1..13) to affect the adoption.

Relative Advantage: Relative advantage refers to the "degree to which an innovation is perceived as being better than the idea it supersedes" [17]. According to Moore and Benbasat [52], the constructs of the perceived usefulness [18] and relative advantage [17] are obviously similar in the context of the innovation adoption. The definition of the perceived usefulness has been stated as "the prospective user's subjective probability that using a specific application system will increase his or her job performance within an organizational context" [18]. As stated in [39], perceived usefulness surely affects the users to adopt cloud-based solutions. A qualitative survey among SMEs in 2013 [14] states many relative advantages of the adoption of cloud-based solutions as follows: eliminating the cost of equipment maintenance, decreasing work load on network system, flexibility, simple administration, collaboration opportunities, improved automation and cost reduction by eliminating expenditure on the software licensing and installation with the pay-per-use model of the service. Wu [34] discovered that perceived usability is a key success factor of SaaS adoption.

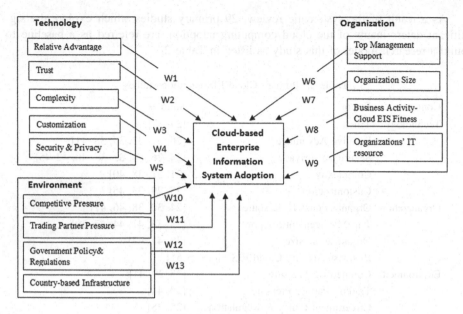

Fig. 1. Research model

Complexity: Complexity is the "degree to which an innovation is perceived to be relatively difficult to understand and use" [17]. As stated in [38], integrating business processes with the specialized cloud-based solution can be a significant issue for the enterprises that lack IT experts with a high level of technological skills. If the users spend less effort on learning and utilizing the functionality of the Cloud-EIS, they will be more willing to use the system.

Security & Privacy: Enterprises are more likely to adopt cloud-based enterprise solutions if the level of security and privacy are acceptable [40]. The main concerns are mostly related to confidentiality (unauthorized revelation of data) and integrity (unauthorized operation and destroying data) of the system [53]. As stated in [43], data confidentiality is a significant determinant to adopt cloud computing. The oppositions of cloud computing discuss the data security and privacy management [14]. Perceived security and safety can be a driver or an inhibitor within the case of the transition from on-premise IT to the cloud [54].

Customization: It has been found as a significant determinant to adopt Cloud-EIS in [33]. Customization refers to the flexibility and compatibility of the system to be adopted in the scope of this study. Rogers defined the compatibility as: "the degree to which the innovation fits with the potential adopter's existing values, previous practices, and current needs"[17]. As stated in [29], compatibility of the new system with the existing system is a significant determinant of using SaaS. In addition, SaaS business logic may not be suitable to the enterprise's activity requirements [33]. In that case, the enterprises may need to adjust the functionality of such system according to their business operations. Therefore, the flexibility of the system should also be considered.

Trust: It is described as the perception of trustfulness and investigated in terms of system performance, availability of the system, and possible risks related to the adoption. Firms are mainly concerned about the performance and availability risk to adopt SaaS [33]. A cloud vendor should specify the level of performance and availability of the new system through the Service Level Agreement (SLA) that guarantees clear understanding about services and responsibilities between the vendor and the user [55]. As stated in [56], personalized SLAs for clients, continuous communications with them and getting feedback regularly encourage the adoption of cloud computing.

Organizations' IT Resource: It refers to technological readiness of an organization and its on-premise IT resources in the developed research model. The technological readiness of organisations is related to technological infrastructure and IT human resources (HR) in the organization and it influences the adoption of new technology. As stated in [38], the availability of the HR with the required IT skills and experiences, and the compliance of the existing technological infrastructure (e.g., installed network equipment) with Cloud-EIS are significant determinants to adopt cloud solutions. As stated in [22, 46, 57], IT resource in the organization has vital importance to adopt new systems, because of providing essential hardware equipment, supporting application, networking and physical facilities. As stated in [58], the more advanced IT resources are, the easier it is to adopt SaaS to advance in business operations. It is proved in [26] that IT resource in the organizations strongly affects the adoption of SaaS.

Top Management Support: It is a significant organizational factor to adopt Cloud-EIS in organizations. Since the transition from on-premise IT operation to the cloud-based system is a strategic decision by itself, the executives' knowledge, and their positive/negative attitude toward the new system affect the decision on the adoption. If the top management is aware of the benefits of the cloud-based solutions, it is more likely to assign required resources for the adoption and encourage the employees to implement the new system [38]. The top manager of an organization regularly makes the final decision on IT strategy and investment [59], and the decision maker's knowledge about the benefits of the cloud computing adoption is an essential factor in the context of the adoption [50]. In addition, top management determines the extent to which cloud-based solutions are to be implemented [41].

Organization Size: It is stated in [14] that the organisation size is one of the most fundamental determinants of the innovator profile. Organization size is a significant determinant of the decision of adopting Cloud-EIS [41]. Large companies which have more resources have paybacks of firm size, since they can handle greater risks related to adopting new technology than smaller firms. Although small firms are more adaptable to the innovation, they are less willing to move into the cloud environment [60].

Business Activity-Cloud EIS Fitness: The decision to adopt cloud computing is affected by several factors, which are the business structures in organizations (e.g. primary and support activities), business strategy in general, existing principles, experience, work practice, and organizational requirements [51]. The compliance between Cloud-EIS and a firm's culture, value, and work practices is a significant determinant that affects the top manager's decision to adopt it [61]. As stated in [62], business process and data compatibility with the new system is the major difficulty for the adoption. Experts have stated during the interview conducted in [14], that cloud computing has the risk of noncompliance with the traditional organization philosophy which is conflicting to major features of cloud computing. In addition, having the culture of sharing and collaboration with colleagues and even with external clients are determinants of the SaaS adoption [26].

Competitive pressure: It refers to the level of pressure faced by the companies from competitors within the industry. As stated in [63], competitive pressure stimulates organizations to research and develop innovations to stay competitive. The organizations are prompted to adopt innovation technologies to compete and survive in the industry. Through implementing cloud-based solutions, enterprises can have significant advantages due to better market visibility, increased efficiency in business operations, and more accurate real-time data gathering [64].

Trading Partner Pressure: Some studies show that trading partner pressure is a significant factor to adopt Cloud-EIS [22, 28]. For example, a business partner in the supply chain may deploy an IT platform among the suppliers, manufacturers, wholesalers and retailers to cooperate efficiently. There are a number of studies [41, 46, 57] showing that trading partner pressure affects the adoption of IT applications.

Government Policy & Regulations: This factor refers to the support provided by the government authority to stimulate and control firms on adopting innovation technologies. Government policy and regulations profoundly impact firms' adoption of the SaaS [25]. The government should apply some policies to stimulate the development and implementation of the Cloud-EIS. Government policy and regulations and its preferential strategies can encourage or discourage the adoption of the Cloud-EIS. As stated in [57], present laws and regulations are critical in adoption of new technologies. Moreover, if the government mandates firms to comply with cloud-specific standards and protocols, firms will be more apt to adopt cloud computing[38].

Country-based Infrastructure: It is concerned with the enterprises to adopt Cloud-EIS. Especially, the bandwidth, reliability, and cost of the network connection, the Internet performance (e.g., latency limitations), and network technologies (e.g., deployment of fiber infrastructure) in a specific country may vary and affect the performance and availability of SaaS ERP solutions [33]. Thus, country-specific infrastructure is a significant factor to adopt Cloud-EIS.

5 Ranking of the Determinants

In order to determine the weights of the defined factors o the adoption of the cloud-EIS, a survey designed with Analytic Hierarchy Process (AHP) method has been distributed among 20 experts that are knowledgeable about the cloud computing and its adoption, 10 of them are PhD students and others are experts in the enterprises who directly interact with an EIS. Accordingly, the weights of the factors have been obtained by AHP method and the research model has been interpreted based on the weights of the factors.

5.1 Analytic Hierarchy Process (AHP)

Analytic Hierarchy Process (AHP) is a multi-criteria decision method that relies on the individuals's judgments resulting from a pairwise comparison of the factors. The AHP is easy to apply and efficient method for group decision making problem [65]. Since the decision on the adoption itself is multi-criteria decision making problem; the researchers have applied AHP to study Cloud Computing adoption [66].

Firstly, 13 most significant factors affecting the adoption of the Cloud-EIS are defined from the literature review. Then, the hierarchical structure of the factors is formed based on the TOE framework as seen from Table 2. And the AHP judgment matrix is constructed and the scale is determined as Saaty's Scale [65] which is from 1 to 9 numerical values, where a linguistic judgment of "equally important" is equal to 1, and a linguistic judgment of "extremely important" is equal to 9. Then, the surveys are distributed among participants. After receiving survey responses, the consistency of each response is checked. The responder is requested to revise his/her responses if there is inconsistency. Finally, the consistent surveys are collected and weights of the factors are calculated.

5.2 Weight Calculation and Normalization

After receiving the survey responses from 20 responders, the consistencies of them have been checked before calculating weights. Inconsistent responses have been discarded; however, there is no inconsistent response from 20 responders. The Consistency Ratio (CR) of each comparison item of the survey should not be greater than 10 % [67]. In this study, the CR does not exceed 9 %. The average CR of each comparison item is less than 5 %. The CRs of the Contexts, Technology, Organization and Environment are 3 %, 4.5 %, 4 %, 3 %, respectively.

Having checked the consistency ratio, the local weights of each construct are calculated. However, the local weight itself cannot show the comparison among all factors within the sub-level factors to ascertain the concealed meaning behind the scene. Thus, the global weight of the each factor should be calculated as multiplication of the local weight and its parent's weight. Finally, the normalization of the weights is conducted. The global weights are considered for prioritizing and interpreting factors (Table 3).

This research shows following substantial outcomes:

- "Technology" and "Organization" have an almost equal effect, where "Environment" has a relatively low effect on the decision on the adoption.
- The most significant factors are determined as "security & privacy", "business activity-Cloud EIS fitness", "top management support", "trust" and "organization's IT resource".

Table 3. The weights of the determinants

Contexts	Weight	i	Factor	Local weight	Global weight (W_i)	Normalized (%)	Priority
Technology	0.422	1	Relative Advantage	0.180	0.076	8 %	6
		2	Trust	0.243	0.103	10 %	4
		3	Complexity	0.078	0.033	3 %	13
		4	Customization	0.135	0.057	6 %	8
		5	Security & Privacy	0.364	0.154	15 %	1
Organization	0.405	6	Top Management Support	0.260	0.105	11 %	3
		7	Organization Size	0.176	0.071	7 %	7
		8	Business Activity-Cloud-EIS Fitness	0.319	0.129	13 %	2
		9	Organizations' IT Resource	0.245	0.099	10 %	5
Environment	0.173	10	Competitive Pressure	0.298	0.052	5 %	9
		11	Trading Partner Pressure	0.254	0.045	5 %	10
		12	Government Policy & Regulations	0.251	0.043	4 %	11
		13	Country-based Infrastructure	0.197	0.034	3 %	12

- Security & Privacy have been found as the most significant factor in the context of the "Technology". That means, a cloud provider should have a high level of security and privacy to resolve concerns regarding the cloud environment and to convince and appeal more customers to transition to Cloud-EIS.
- Business Activity-Cloud-EIS Fitness is defined as the fitness between Cloud-EIS and an organization's culture, value, and work practices, which is found as the second most important factor. If the business activity of the organization fits the Cloud EIS, such as if the enterprise has business processes which can be performed on cloud, and they are integrated and complicated, the adoption will be easier.
- Top management support is also seen as a significant organizational factor to adopt Cloud-EIS in organizations. Top managers should be aware of the paybacks of the cloud computing to encourage the adoption of Cloud-EIS. Free training on Cloud-EIS, demo presentations, and free use of the product in a certain period, and customer visits can be followed as a strategy to increase usage and to encourage adoption.
- Perceived trust towards cloud provider is a significant determinant. It is concluded that organizations are commonly concerned about the performance and availability of the cloud based system[33]. To reduce this concern and gain confidence, cloud service providers should specify the specifications related to system performance and availability in SLA [55]. Besides, arrangement of the customer-specific SLA,

and getting feedback with continuous and regular contact methods will provide an atmosphere of trust and encourage the use of Cloud-EIS [56].

- Organization IT Resource is the human resource with the required skills to transition to the cloud are more inclined to adopt Cloud-EIS. The compliance of on-premise infrastructure also affects the decision of the adoption.
- Complexity, country-based infrastructure, government policy & regulations and trading partner pressure are the most insignificant factors. Consequently, Cloud-EIS providers can assign lower priority to these factors while designing the product.

To understand whether there is a significant difference between sampling of the PhD students and Experts, we have conducted T-Test and it is observed that there is no significant difference between the responses of PhD students and experts from the companies. The responders have reached truly consensus on which factors are more significant than others.

6 Conclusion

In this study, it is aimed to investigate the most significant factors that affect the adoption of the Cloud-EIS. The study covers a literature review and development of a research model. Consequently, the ranking of the proposed determinants is performed based on AHP. An important contribution of this study is that it presents a systematic literature review on the adoption of the Cloud-EIS, which provides researchers and practitioners some insight on the importance of the factors influencing enterprises regarding the adoption of cloud-based solutions. The most significant factors (determinants) derived from the previous studies are presented in Table 2, together with the corresponding studies of each factor. Accordingly, the research model as depicted in Fig. 1 is developed based on the literature review and the theories related to IT innovation. It is structured within the three contexts of the TOE framework. Thereby, the determinants of the adoption of Cloud-EIS in the context of organization are investigated from the aspects of the TOE framework. Lastly, the ranking of the determinants of the adoption of Cloud-EIS is performed based on AHP. The most significant factors are determined as security & privacy, business activity-cloud EIS fitness, top management support, trust, and organization's IT resource.

References

1. Sultan, N.A.: Reaching for the "cloud": how SMEs can manage. Int. J. Inf. Manage. 31(3), 272–278 (2011)
2. Sandhu, R., Reich, J., Wolff, T., Krishnan, R., and Zachry, J., Towards a discipline of mission-aware cloud computing categories and subject descriptors, security, vol. Di, no. 13, pp. 13–17 (2010)
3. Buonanno, G., Faverio, P., Pigni, F., Ravarini, A., Sciuto, D., Tagliavini, M.: Factors affecting ERP system adoption: A comparative analysis between SMEs and large companies. J. Enterp. Inf. Manage. 18(4), 384–426 (2005)

4. Botta-Genoulaz, V., Millet, P.-A.: An investigation into the use of ERP systems in the service sector. Int. J. Prod. Econ. **99**(1-2), 202–221 (2006)
5. Suresh, H.: What is customer relationship management (CRM)? Supply Chain Planet (2004)
6. Lambert, D.M., Cooper, M.C., Pagh, J.D.: Supply chain management:implementation issues and research opportunities. Int. J. Logistics Manag. **9**(2), 1–19 (1998)
7. Daghfous, A., Barkhi, R.: The strategic management of information technology in UAE hotels: an exploratory study of TQM, SCM, and CRM implementations. Technovation **29** (9), 588–595 (2009)
8. Foster, I., Zhao, Y., Raicu, I., Lu, S.: Cloud computing and grid computing 360-degree compared. In: Grid Computing Environments Workshop 2008 (GCE 2008), pp. 1–10 (2008)
9. Sultan, N.: Cloud computing for education: a new dawn? Int. J. Inf. Manage. **30**(2), 109–116 (2010)
10. Feuerlicht, G.: Next generation SOA: can SOA survive cloud computing? In: Snášel, V., Szczepaniak, P.S., Abraham, A., Kacprzyk, J. (eds.) Advances in Intelligent Web Mastering-2. AISC, vol. 67, pp. 19–29. Springer, Heidelberg (2010)
11. Cisco, The Cisco powered network cloud: an exciting managed services opportunity, White Paper. Cisco Syst. (2009)
12. Salleh, S.M., Teoh, S.Y., Chan, C.: Cloud enterprise systems: a review of literature and its adoption. In: Pacis, p. 76 (2012)
13. Sharif, A.M.: It's written in the cloud: the hype and promise of cloud computing. J. Enterp. Inf. Manag. **23**(2), 131–134 (2010)
14. Nedbal, D., Stieninger, M., Erskine, M., Wagner, G.: The Adoption of Cloud Services in the Context of Organizations: An Examination of Drivers and Barriers (2014)
15. De Loo, I., Bots, J., Louwrink, E., Meeuwsen, D., van Moorsel, P., Rozel, C.: The effects of ERP-implementations on organizational benefits in small and medium-sized enterprises in the Netherlands. In: 8th International Conference on Enterprise Systems, Accounting and Logistics, pp. 11–12 (2011)
16. Beaubouef, B., Cloud Can Bring Out the Best of ERP | ERP the Right Way! on WordPress.com. https://gbeaubouef.wordpress.com/2011/11/23/cloud-erp-advantage/
17. Rogers, E.M.: Diffusion of Innovations. Free Press, New York (1995)
18. Davis, F.D.: Perceived usefulness, perceived ease of use, and user acceptance of information technology. MIS Q. **13**(3), 319–340 (1989)
19. Ajzen, I.: The theory of planned behaviour. Organ. Behav. Hum. Decis. Process. 50, 179–211 (1991). De Young, 509–526
20. Venkatesh, V., Morris, M.G., Davis, G.B., Davis, F.D.: User acceptance of information technology: toward a unified view. MIS Quart. **27**(3), 425–478 (2003)
21. Tornatzky, L., Fleischer, M.: The Process of Technology Innovation. Lexington Books, Lexington (2001). Trott, P.: The role of market research in the development of discontinuous new products. Eur. J. Innovation Manage. **4**, 117–125 (2001)
22. Oliveira, T., Martins, M.F.: Understanding e-business adoption across industries in European countries. Ind. Manag. Data Syst. **110**(9), 1337–1354 (2010)
23. Kitchenham, B.: Procedures for performing systematic reviews, vol. 33, pp. 1–26. Keele University, Keele (2004)
24. Seethamraju, R.: Adoption of software as a service (SaaS) enterprise resource planning (ERP) systems in small and medium sized enterprises (SMEs). Inf. Syst. Front. **17**(3), 475–492 (2015)
25. Mingxing, S., Long, P., Yafang, L.: A study on enterprise technology adoption of SaaS. In: Service Systems and Service Management (ICSSSM), pp. 1–6. IEEE (2015)
26. Safari, F., Safari, N., Hasanzadeh, A.: The adoption of SaaS: ranking the determinants. J. Enterp. Inf. Manage. **28**(3), 400–422 (2015)

27. Frisenvang, J., Pedersen, C.E., Svejvig, P.: The diffusion and adoption of a cloud-based enterprise system in danish municipalities. In: Business Technologies in Contemporary Organizations: Adoption, Assimilation, and Institutionalization, pp. 194–209 (2014)
28. Gangwar, H., Date, H., Ramaswamy, R.: Understanding determinants of cloud computing adoption using an integrated TAM-TOE model. J. Enterp. Inf. Manag. 28(1), 107–130 (2015)
29. Wu, Y., Cegielski, C.G., Hazen, B.T., Hall, D.J.: Cloud computing in support of supply chain information system infrastructure: understanding when to go to the cloud. J. Supply Chain Management 49(3), 25–41 (2013)
30. Milian, E.Z., Spinola, M.M., Gonçalves, R.F., Fleury, A.L.: An analysis of the advantages, challenges and obstacles of cloud computing adoption to an academic control system. In: Advances in Production Management Systems. Innovative and Knowledge-Based Production Management in a Global-Local World, pp. 564–571 (2014)
31. Le Thi Quynh, N., Heales, Jon, Xu, D.: Examing significant factors and risks affecting the willingness to adopt a cloud–based CRM. In: Nah, F.F.-H. (ed.) HCIB 2014. LNCS, vol. 8527, pp. 37–48. Springer, Heidelberg (2014)
32. Suhendra, A., Mutiara, A., Laily, I.: The factors of influencing acceptance of software as a service model, toward sales force automation system, on pharmaceutical company Indonesia. J. Theor. Appl. Inf. Technol. 47(2), 496–503 (2013)
33. Faasen, J., Seymour, L.F., Schuler, J.: SaaS ERP adoption intent: explaining the South African SME perspective. In: Poels, G. (ed.) CONFENIS 2012. LNBIP, vol. 139, pp. 35–47. Springer, Heidelberg (2013)
34. Wu, W.W.: Developing an explorative model for SaaS adoption. Expert Syst. Appl. 38(12), 15057–15064 (2011)
35. Kett, H., Kasper, H., Falkner, J., Weisbecker, A.: Trust factors for the usage of cloud computing in small and medium sized craft enterprises. In: Vanmechelen, K., Altmann, J., Rana, O.F. (eds.) GECON 2012. LNCS, vol. 7714, pp. 169–181. Springer, Heidelberg (2012)
36. Arinze, B., Anandarajan, M.: Factors that determine the adoption of cloud computing: a global perspective. In: Enterprise Information Systems and Advancing Business Solutions: Emerging Models: Emerging Models, pp. 210–223 (2012)
37. Fan, Y.W., Chen, C.D., Wu, C.C., Fang, Y.H.: The effect of status Quo Bias on cloud system adoption. J. Comput. Inf. Syst. 55(3), 55–64 (2015)
38. Oliveira, T., Thomas, M., Espadanal, M.: Assessing the determinants of cloud computing adoption: an analysis of the manufacturing and services sectors. Inf. Manag. 51(5), 497–510 (2014)
39. Tan, X., Kim, Y.: User acceptance of SaaS-based collaboration tools: a case of Google Docs. J. Enterp. Inf. Manage 28(3), 423–442 (2015)
40. Gupta, P., Seetharaman, A., Raj, J.R.: The usage and adoption of cloud computing by small and medium businesses. Int. J. Inform. Manage. 33(5), 861–874 (2013)
41. Low, C., Chen, Y., Wu, M.: Understanding the determinants of cloud computing adoption. Ind. Manage. Data Syst. 111(7), 1006–1023 (2011)
42. Saeed, I., Juell-Skielse, G., Uppström, E.: Cloud enterprise resource planning adoption: Motives & barriers. In: Advances in Enterprise Information Systems II, p. 429 (2012)
43. Yigitbasioglu, O.M.: External auditors' perceptions of cloud computing adoption in Australia. Int. J. Account. Inf. Syst. 18, 46–62 (2015)
44. Yigitbasioglu, O.: Modelling the intention to adopt cloud computing services: a transaction cost theory perspective. Aust. J. Inf. Syst. 18(3), 193–210 (2014)
45. Chowanetz, M., Pfarr, F., Winkelmann, A.: A model of critical success factors for software-as-a-service adoption. Manuf. Model. Manage. Control 7(1), 325–330 (2013)

46. Yang, Z., Sun, J., Zhang, Y., Wang, Y.: Understanding SaaS adoption from the perspective of organizational users: a tripod readiness model. Comput. Hum. Behav. **45**, 254–264 (2015)
47. Abdollahzadegan, A., Hussin, C, Razak, A., Moshfegh Gohary, M., Amini, M.: The organizational critical success factors for adopting cloud computing in SMEsJ. Inf. Syst. Res. Innov. (JISRI) **4**(1), 67−74 (2013)
48. Mezghani, K.: Switching toward cloud ERP: a research model to explain intentions. Int. J. Enterp. Inf. Syst. **10**(3), 46–61 (2014)
49. Yigitbasioglu, O.M.: The role of institutional pressures and top management support in the intention to adopt cloud computing solutions. J. Enterp. Inf. Manage. **28**(4), 579–594 (2015)
50. Tehrani, S.R., Shirazi, F.: Factors influencing the adoption of cloud computing by small and medium size enterprises (SMEs). In: Yamamoto, S. (ed.) HCI 2014, Part II. LNCS, vol. 8522, pp. 631–642. Springer, Heidelberg (2014)
51. Ratten, V.: Entrepreneurial and ethical adoption behaviour of cloud computing. J. High Technol. Manage. Res. **23**(2), 155–164 (2012)
52. Moore, G.C., Benbasat, I.: Development of an instrument to measure the perceptions of adopting an information technology innovation. IS Res. **2**(3), 192–222 (1991)
53. Barker, W.C.: Guide for mapping types of information and information systems to security categories. Netw. Secur. (2003)
54. Park, S.C., Ryoo, S.Y.: An empirical investigation of end-users' switching toward cloud computing: a two factor theory perspective. Comput. Hum. Behav. **29**(1), 160–170 (2013)
55. Linthicum, D.S.: Cloud Computing and SOA Convergence in Your Enterprise: A Step-by-Step Guide. Pearson Education, Upper Saddle River (2009)
56. Buyya, R., Yeo, C.S., Venugopal, S.: Market-oriented cloud computing: vision, hype, and reality for delivering it services as computing utilities. In: High Performance Computing and Communications, HPCC 2008, pp. 5–13. IEEE (2008)
57. Zhu, K., Kraemer, K.L., Dedrick, J.: Information technology payoff in e-business environments: An international perspective on value creation of e-business in the financial services industry. J. Manage. Inform. Syst. **21**(1), 17–54 (2004)
58. Xin, M., Levina, N.: Software-as-a-service model: elaborating client-side adoption factors. In: Proceedings of the 29th International Conference on Information Systems (2008)
59. Bradford, M., Florin, J.: Examining the role of innovation diffusion factors on the implementation success of enterprise resource planning systems. Int. J. Account. IS **4**(3), 205–225 (2003)
60. Lippert, S.K., Govindarajulu, C.: Technological, organizational, and environmental antecedents to web services adoption. Commun. IIMA **6**(1), 14 (2015)
61. Grandon, E.E., Pearson, J.M.: Electronic commerce adoption: an empirical study of small and medium US businesses. Inf. Manag. **42**(1), 197–216 (2004)
62. Armbrust, M., Fox, A., Griffith, R., Joseph, A.D., Katz, R., Konwinski, A., Zaharia, M.: A view of cloud computing. Commun. ACM **53**(4), 50–58 (2010)
63. Vives, X.: Innovation and competitive pressure. J. Industr. Econ. **56**(3), 419–469 (2008)
64. Misra, S.C., Mondal, A.: Identification of a company's suitability for the adoption of cloud computing and modelling its corresponding Return on Investment. Math. Comput. Model. **53**(3), 504–521 (2011)
65. Saaty, T.L.: The Analytic Hierarchy Process. McGraw-Hill, New York (1980)
66. Lee, S.G., Chae, S.H., Cho, K.M.: Drivers and inhibitors of SaaS adoption in Korea. Int. J. Inf. Manage. **33**(3), 429–440 (2013)
67. Saaty, T.L.: Decision making for leaders: the analytic hierarchy process for decisions in a complex world. RWS publications, Pittsburgh (1990)

Semi-supervised Learning Approach for Ontology Mapping Problem

Rima Linaburgyte[1,2(✉)] and Rimantas Butleris[1,2(✉)]

[1] Department of Information Systems, Kaunas University of Technology,
Studentu 50-313a, Kaunas, Lithuania
{rima.linaburgyte,rimantas.butleris}@ktu.lt
[2] Centre of Information Systems Design Technologies, Kaunas University of Technology,
K. Barsausko 59-A321, Kaunas, Lithuania

Abstract. The evolution of the Semantic Web depends on the growing number of ontologies it comprises. However, all ontologies have differences in structure and content because there is no unified standard for their design. To ensure interoperability and fluent information exchange, the correspondences between entities of different ontologies must be found and mapped. A lot of methods have already been proposed for matching heterogeneous ontologies, but they still have many shortcomings and require improvements. This paper suggests a novel semi-supervised machine learning method, which solves ontology mapping task as a classification problem with training set, comprised only of labeled positive examples. Negative examples are generated artificially using an entropy measure in order to build a more accurate Naive Bayesian classifier.

Keywords: Ontology mapping · PU learning · Entropy · Naive Bayesian classifier

1 Introduction

The Word Wide Web, known as the Web for short, has been undoubtedly one of the most important and indispensable means for knowledge sharing and decision making for almost three decades. If to explain the Web succinctly, it could be conceived as a set of documents, which are connected by the hyperlinks and easily reached via Internet access. Because of its current incredibly rapid development, an enormous amount of data is available. Fortunately, the keyword-based search engines, for example Google and Bing, are used in order to retrieve desirable webpages from a wide-ranging assortment. However, a bunch of serious problems such as an empty response to a query, a mismatch of terminology between queries and webpages or a retrieval of irrelevant documents, are inevitable during the search process. Although despite the successful retrieval, it would be necessary to select valuable information, which is normally spread over various documents, anyway. The main hindrance of such an inconvenient and inefficient way of knowledge exchange among people via computers rises from the missing capabilities of machine to recognize the meaning of the processed information. In other words, the content of current web does not contain structural information and

© Springer International Publishing Switzerland 2016
G. Dregvaite and R. Damasevicius (Eds.): ICIST 2016, CCIS 639, pp. 67–77, 2016.
DOI: 10.1007/978-3-319-46254-7_6

is only human-readable due to the fact, that predominant language, in which web pages are written, is HTML [1]. The objective of Semantic Web is to extend an existing web representing its content in machine-accessible form with well-defined meaning so that people and computers can work in cooperation easily [2]. Thus, all web pages with information on their content have to be annotated, formatted using standardized, expressive language and integrated through the use of ontologies to make them understandable to intelligent agents, i.e. pieces of software that work autonomously [2]. The ontologies convey the semantics of web recourses and enable search in the Web based on meaning rather than syntax. Basically, an ontology formally describes a specific domain of discourse including a finite list of significant concepts and relations between them. It provides a common terminology and a shared understanding of a domain, as well [3]. The effective use of ontologies in Semantic Web requires more advanced framework language. Web Ontology Language (OWL) fulfils all requirements for machine interpretability of web content because of its well-defined syntax, expressiveness, convenience of expression, formal semantics, compatibility with other existing standards, such as XML, RDF, RDFS, and support of reasoning tools [4, 5]. The Semantic Web is evolving with time, therefore an increasing number of ontologies comprise it. All ontologies have differences in structure and content because there is no unified standard for their design. Every actor is interested in the domain differently, has particular habits and knowledge, uses different tools. The main worry is that these and similar reasons lead to diverse forms of heterogeneity in ontologies and in the web, as well [6]. Theoretically, this phenomenon is called the semantic heterogeneity problem [7, 8]. In order to solve this problem and ensure interoperability in the Semantic Web, the correspondences between entities of different ontologies must be found and mapped [6]. In other words, ontology mapping is a process which is useful for ontology interaction and fluent information exchange between them.

A lot of methods have already been proposed for matching heterogeneous ontologies, but they still have many shortcomings and require improvements. Most of them exploit element-level techniques that map elements by analizing entities in isolation, ignoring their relationships with other entities, although structural information of an ontology plays an important role for the determination of the true semantics of corresponding entities [26]. Besides, the ontology mapping systems, which use a multi-strategy to establish corresponding matches, usually integrate the results of similarity measures linearly adding them multiplied by weights. Such methods do not show the influence to the final mapping result and require a lot of manual intervention, therefore they often lead to low quality matching. Some machine learning based approaches exist which strongly rely on instances, such as proposed in [27]. However, they are ineffective, if there are not enough instances provided. Another kind of machine learning based techniques demands for the sufficient amount of positive and negative examples. Due to these enumerated and other similar deficiencies of methods, the semantic heterogeneity problem remains under intensive research.

This paper suggests a piloting ontology mapping method which solves previously mentioned problems. Our method transforms ontology mapping task into PU learning problem, i.e. semi-supervised learning from positive and unlabeled examples. Here the examples are vectors, whose attributes are values of different similarity measures, calculated using various kinds of information from ontologies. The reason why negative instances are not needed to be labeled in order to build a more accurate classifier, is the fact, that negative examples are generated artificially using an entropy measure. Finally, the hidden positive examples are being identified in an unlabeled set with the assistance of the built Naive Bayesian classifier.

The rest of this paper is organized as follows. Section 2 overviews the related work. The proposed method for ontology mapping is introduced in Sect. 3. Section 4 presents experiment and its evaluation procedure. Conclusions and future work are described in Sect. 5.

2 Related Work

A lot of investigations have already been made in the field of ontology mapping, but due to the limitation of proposed solutions, this problem still remains controversial. All designed mapping discovery systems are based on the usage of multiple similarity measures. The comprehensive description of similarity functions, which have been exploited in order to measure similarity between entities of two heterogeneous ontologies, and their classifications is represented in [6]. The brief surveys of ontology mapping tools and systems are presented in [13, 14]. A few of them, such as OLA and H-Match, are described separately in [19, 20]. Because of a tremendous supply of mapping identification methods, it is worth to mention only those, which are especially related to the method of ours. The algorithm ASCO, which is described in detail in [15], identifies corresponding entities of ontologies using linguistic and structural similarity techniques. We have made slight corrections and exploited some computations of hierarchy similarity ideas, which integrate the information of lexical thesaurus, called WordNet. However, this algorithm combines all similarity strategies linearly adding them multiplied by weights. Due to selection of the best combination of weights, it is not very useful in practice and usually leads to low quality mapping.

Some machine learning based methods have been proposed in order to solve ontology mapping problem. The most considerable one is realized into mapping discovery system, called GLUE [16]. It also looks for the most similar entity in another ontology using probabilistic definitions of several distribution-based similarity measures. In [17], the ontology alignment approach combines calculated similarity measures and afterwards different supervised machine learning techniques are applied so as to select the best classifier. Ontology matching problem is dealt as a binary classification problem in [10, 18], as well. In both cases support vector machines are used as a classifier. Here the optimal separating hyperplane is constructed in a training set with similarity vectors, which are conceived as points in vector space. The labels of future examples are determined according to the side of a hyperplane they belong to. These three approaches differ only in usage of similarity measures, but all of them need the training set with labeled positive and negative instances.

The method, presented in this paper, is mostly based on [12], which prosecutes learning from positive and unlabeled examples in order to identify outliers in the text classification domain. It proposes to generate an artificial negative document so as to build more precise Naive Bayesian classifier without negative instances. We reformulated our ontology mapping task into PU learning problem too, treating that the training set consists only of positive examples, whereas the test set is considered as an unlabeled set with negative and hidden positive examples, which have to be identified as outliers by the designed classifier. For generation of a single negative example we use an entropy measure as in [21]. There are more PU learning based methods, such as [22–25], which use only a small positive training set for learning, but they are not as high-performing as in [12].

3 Proposed Technique

3.1 Construction of Feature Similarity Vectors

Ontology mapping is a process of finding correspondences between heterogeneous ontologies. Formally, ontology matching can be defined as a function $f(e_i^1) = e_j^2$, where $e_i^1 \in O_1, i = \overline{1, m_1}, m_1 \in N$ and $e_j^2 \in O_2, j = \overline{1, m_2}, m_2 \in N$ are entities of ontologies O_1 and O_2 respectively. The relations of equivalency are discovered through the measures of the similarity between entities [6]. However, the single measure of similarity for determination of corresponding entities is insufficient because of the diversity of ontology construction. Besides, most of the proposed ontology mapping approaches use only the element-level matching techniques, which map entities analyzing them in isolation, ignoring their relationships with other elements [26]. Therefore, the suggested method in this paper operates with various kinds of information from ontologies such as concepts, properties, instances, structure of taxonomy, etc. and uses g different strategies of measuring similarity to identify the appropriate matches [10]. The latter similarity measures are not described in details here because they are not the key points of this paper and each of them requires a great deal of discussion. Having applied k ($1 \le k \le g$) similarity metric to every pair of entities (e_i^1, e_j^2) from ontologies O_1 and O_2, the results can be written into a matrix [10]

$$M_{m_1 \times m_2}^k = \left[sim_k(e_i^1, e_j^2) \right]. \tag{1}$$

The values of each element of the matrix range over the unit interval of real numbers [0, 1] due to normalisation. It means that the bigger the value of similarity is, the more alike entities are. The most important task in ontology mapping is the aggregation of basic matchers in order to compute the compound similarity between entities and to define a new matching algorithm which could identify corresponding pairs of entities from two heterogeneous ontologies effectively. Thus, after execution of g different similarity strategies, the results can be combined into the $g \times m_1 \times m_2$ similarity rectangular. In other words, the rectangular is a combination of matrices $M_{m_1 \times m_2}^1, M_{m_1 \times m_2}^2, \cdots, M_{m_1 \times m_2}^g$. Then similarity vectors for each pair of entities (e_i^1, e_j^2) are obtained from the similarity rectangular. Formally, they could be expressed as $X_{ij} = \left(sim_1(e_i^1, e_j^2), sim_2(e_i^1, e_j^2), \cdots, sim_g(e_i^1, e_j^2) \right)$, where $sim_k(e_i^1, e_j^2)$ is calculated similarity between entities e_i^1, e_j^2 using k^{th} similarity strategy. All of these similarity vectors make up a similarity vector space R_g together and every similarity vector is a point in this space. Each point shows two possible mapping results, that match or do not match [10]. It is safe to say that each pair of entities with their similarity vector can be assigned to one of two possible classes with labels "positive" in the case of match and "negative" otherwise. Therefore, such ontology mapping problem can be solved in a manner of binary classification.

3.2 Ontology Mapping as a Binary Classification Problem

The aforementioned similarity vectors are concerned as feature vectors in this machine learning problem. The latter formalism of similarity vector can be rewritten into simpler form as follows $X_d = (x_{d1}, x_{d2}, \cdots, x_{dg})$, where $x_{dk} = sim_k(e_i^1, e_j^2)$, $d = \overline{1, m_1 m_2}$ and each vector element is called a feature or an atribute. Yet, the class label of one vector can not be determined directly. The simplest scenario will divide the available preclassified examples into two parts: the training set, from which the classifier is induced, and the testing set, on which it is evaluated. Practically speaking, a piece of feature vectors have to be labelled according to the class they get in. Having labelled vectors as positive or negative, they constitute a training set from which the machine induces a classifier – an algorithm capable of categorizing any test example into one of the two predefined classes: positive and negative. The goal is not to re-classify objects whose classes we already know, but label future examples, those classes, which are yet ignorant [11]. In this application, the attribute vectors are automatically calculated through execution of similarity strategies and labeled by an expert in order to form a training set. Whatever the source of the examples is, they are likely to suffer from imperfections whose essence and consequences the engineer has to understand and overcome [11]. Thus, saying formally, given a set of training data $Tr = \{(X_1, c_1), (X_2, c_2), \ldots, (X_n, c_n)\}$, where $X_d \in R_g, c_d \in C = \{+, -\}, d = \overline{1, n}$, a binary classification model could be built $t{:}X \to C$. The positive and negative classes are denoted by "+" and "−" respectively. There are a lot of options of machine learning methods, which could be applied to discover matches. At the present, researchers have already adjusted some well-known standard classification techniques in their mapping discovery systems. All of them require a set of positive and negative examples. Such classification methods are known as supervised learning because all training examples have pre-labeled classes. However, in practice it is often very difficult to get labeled negative examples. This happens because people usually keep only the data in which they are interested and do not label irrelevant data. In this case, an expert is concerned about corresponding entities between two ontologies. Therefore, an expert would look for mapping candidates, if the mapping problem was executed manually. One way or another, it is possible to train a classifier effectively without any negative examples. Semi-supervised learning is in its element developing classification algorithm using only a set of labeled positive examples P that we are interested in and a set of unlabeled examples U which contains both positive and negative examples.

3.3 Learning from Positive and Unlabelled Examples

Ontology mapping problem can be modeled as PU learning problem, treating all training data as the positive set P and the test set as the unlabeled set U. Then a classifier can be learned using PU learning algorithms to classify the test set to identify possible matches. Several innovative techniques have been proposed to solve the PU learning recently. In this paper one high-performing PU learning approach for text classification, called LGN (PU Learning by Generating Negative examples), was adjusted to solve our problem from the majority of well-known existing PU learning techniques, such as one-class SVM, Roc-SVM, S-EM, PEBL and so on, because of the fact that it had obtained better results [12]. This method was applied to detect unexpected instances in the unlabeled set before applying a traditional classifier. The unexpected examples were assumed to be the unclassifiable instances or outliers, which do not belong to any class in $c_1, c_2, \cdots, c_n$. Finally, the problem was restated into two-class classification problem, where the training set was renamed as P by changing every class label $c_i \in C$ to "+" (the positive class) and the test set was renamed as the unlabeled set U, which compounds both hidden positive instances and unexpected instances. Subsequently, using the information from P and U, artificial negative data was generated and applied to build a classifier whose purpose was to classify examples into two predefined classes "positive" and "negative". The latter class was composed of only the reliable unexpected instances [12].

In our problem, the training set Tr contains only the instances, which are labeled as "positive", i.e. the matching pairs of entities. We also renamed the training set Tr as the positive set P, which contains elements with labels "+". Then we renamed the test set T as the unlabeled set U with instances, whose labels are "−", despite the fact that there are many hidden positive instances in U. Then a classification function $t{:}X \rightarrow C, C = \{+, -\}$ is built and used as a classifier, which can identify negative instances in U. A significant problem is that there are not labeled negative examples for learning. Therefore, the problem becomes learning from positive and unlabeled examples or the so called PU learning for short. While tackling this problem, the negative data has to be generated using existing information. In our classification task, the examples are commonly represented by feature vectors $X_d = \left(x_{d1}, x_{d2}, \cdots, x_{dg}\right)$, where $x_{dk} = sim_k(e_i^1, e_j^2)$. Let x_+ be a positive feature value which defines the instances in P and x_- represent a negative feature value that characterizes negative instances in U. From a probabilistic viewpoint, if U was composed of a large proportion of positive examples, then the feature value x_+ would have similar distributions in both P and U, whereas the distributions of the feature value x_+ would be different in these sets. This difference can be used to generate a set of artificial negative instances N in order to train a classifier to identify negative instances in U accurately.

3.4 Generation of Negative Data

An artificial negative set contains reliable negative instances. A single artificial negative example A_N has to be generated in a manner that $Pr\left(x_+ | +\right) - Pr\left(x_+ | -\right) > 0$ for a positive attribute value x_+ and $Pr(x_-|+) - Pr(x_-|-) < 0$ for a negative attribute value x_-. An entropy can be used to assess if a feature value x_k in U has significantly different conditional probabilities in P and U [12]. The entropy is calculated as follows

$$E(x_k) = - \sum_{c \in \{+,-\}} Pr(x_k|c) * \log Pr(x_k|c). \tag{2}$$

An entropy defines the level of uncertainty. So, the bigger the entropy value of attribute is, the more likely that it has similar distributions in both sets. In other words, an entropy $E(x_-)$ is small for a negative attribute x_- when $Pr(x_-|-)$ is significantly larger than $Pr(x_-|+)$, whereas entropy $E(x_+)$ is large when $Pr(x_+|+)$ and $Pr(x_+|-)$ are alike. For the sake of such discrimination capability of entropy, it is possible to establish if a specific attribute belongs to the positive or negative class. The attributes of a negative example A_N are generated with their respective weights, which are calculated using entropy information as follows

$$q(x_k) = 1 - \frac{E(x_k)}{\max_{j=1,2,\cdots,g} E(x_k)}. \tag{3}$$

If $q(x_{dk}) = 0$, the distributions of attribute x_k are uniform in both sets P and U, therefore, it is not generated in A_N. Controversially, if $q(x_k) = 1$, it is most probably that x_k is negative attribute, that has to be generated for A_N, based on its distribution in U. In a few words, entropy value and weights of each attribute is calculated and its frequency in the negative example A_N is randomly generated using a Normal distribution according to computed weights. The algorithm of negative example construction is presented in [12] in detail.

3.5 Naive Bayesian Classifier

There are many machine learning methods but the Naive Bayesian classifier has been selected to assign examples to appropriate class. The essence of Naive Bayesian classification is the choice of the class with the highest probability of the given instance belonging to it [11]. The application of the Bayesian probabilistic theory in ontology mapping problem is explained in this section explicitly. So, it was mentioned previously, that the examples are described by vectors of attributes as follows $X_d = (x_{d1}, x_{d2}, \cdots, x_{dg})$. If c_i is the label of the i th class, and if X is the vector describing the instance we want to classify, the Bayes formula acquires the following form:

$$Pr(c_i|X) = \frac{Pr(X|c_i) * Pr(c_i)}{Pr(X)}. \tag{4}$$

Because of the dominator being the same for each class, the class that maximizes the numerator $Pr(X|c_i) * Pr(c_i)$ is chosen as a class of the example which is under consideration. Here $Pr(c_i)$ is estimated by the relative frequency of c_i in the training set.

$Pr(X|c_i)$ is the probability that a randomly selected representative of class c_i is described by vector X. If $Pr(x_jc_i)$ denotes the probability that the value of the j th attribute of an instance from class c_i is x_j, then the posterior probability, that a random representative of c_i is described by $X = (x_1, x_2, \cdots, x_g)$, is computed as follows: $Pr(X|c_i) = \prod_{j=1}^{g} Pr(x_j|c_i)$. An example will be assigned to the class with maximum numerator $\prod_{j=1}^{g} Pr(x_j|c_i) * Pr(c_i)$ [12].

However, it is important to highlight, that we have features, which assume values from continuous domains. Therefore, it is necessary to prosecute discretization in order to invoke the Naive Bayesian classifier.

3.6 Final Classifier

Eventually, having prepared data, i.e. the positive set P and the generated negative example A_N, it is possible to build a final classifier which could identify positive instances in the unlabeled set. The algorithm is presented in Fig. 1. A set PE stores positive instances identified in U. At the beginning, PE is an empty set (Step 1). In Step 2, the classifier Q is being built applying training set and single negative example A_N for calculating prior and conditional probabilities. The next Steps 3 and 4 show, that the constructed classifier Q is exploited so as to classify the test instances in U. In the Step 5, the instance X_j is being assigned to the class with maximum probability value [12]. Finally, the set PE which contains positive instances from unlabeled or test set U is obtained. Remaining instances belong to negative class. Those are the instances that refer to nonmatching pairs of the entities from two ontologies.

1. $PE = \emptyset$;
2.   Build a Naive Bayesian classifier Q with P and A_N;
3.   **for** each example $X_j \in U$
4.   Using Q to classify X_j using equation (4);
5.   **if** $(Pr(-|X_j) < Pr(+|X_j))$
6. $PE = PE \cup \{X_j\}$;
7.   **endif**
8.   **endfor**
9.   Output PE.

Fig. 1. Classification procedure

4   Experiment and Evaluation

Currently, the ontology mapping approach, proposed in this paper, is being verified with the real-world ontologies and experimental results are forthcoming. The data sets for testing have been taken from Ontology Alignment Evaluation Initiative (OAEI) campaign, which is responsible for assessing strengths and weaknesses of matching systems and comparing performance of methods [9]. Our approach is also being evaluated on four matching tasks from OAEI'2010 Benchmark dataset. These tasks are #301, #302, #303 and #304, which involve matching four real biography ontologies with one common ontology. In each matching task, there are more than 100 classes and properties in the ontologies as in [28].

Due to the fact that ontology mapping problem was finally converted into binary classification problem, the unified evaluation procedure will be applied in order to assess the proposed technique and compare it to another unique existing semi-supervised ontology mapping method, which is represented in [28]. Consequently, the experimental results will be presented as confusion matrix and measures of the performance of the classification function, such as recall and precision, will be calculated as follows:

$$Recall = \frac{TP}{TP + FN}, \tag{5}$$

$$Precision = \frac{TP}{TP + FP}, \tag{6}$$

where TP is a number of correctly identified positive examples, FN is a number of incorrectly identified negative examples and FP denotes the number of incorrectly identified positive examples.

F1 score is a combination of the aforementioned measures and is defined as a harmonic mean of precision and recall:

$$F1 = 2 * \frac{Precision * Recall}{Precision + Recall}. \tag{7}$$

5   Conclusions and Future Work

If we solved ontology mapping problem manually, we would probably focus only on the corresponding entity pairs without considering non-matching ones. Therefore, in this paper we propose a novel semi-supervised ontology mapping method, which requires only labeled positive examples. A single negative example is generated automatically from positive and unlabeled data in order to help to train a classifier. Our current experiment is being executed using Naive Bayesian classifier. Because of continuous attribute vectors, whose elements are values of similarity measures, the discretization process is performed, as well. In the future work, we plan to apply other machine learning approaches for classification and make it possible to employ the Naive Bayesian formula even in the case of continuous attributes.

References

1. Holzschlag, M.E.: 250 HTML and Web Design Secrets. Wiley, Indianapolis (2004)
2. Antoniou, G., van Harmelen, F.: A Semantic Web Primer. The MIT Press, Cambridge (2008)

3. Passin, T.B.: Explorer's Guide to the Semantic Web. Manning, Greenwich (2004)
4. Baader, F., Horrocks, I., Sattler, U.: Description logics as ontology languages for the semantic web. In: Hutter, D., Stephan, W. (eds.) Mechanizing Mathematical Reasoning. LNCS (LNAI), vol. 2605, pp. 228–248. Springer, Heidelberg (2005)
5. Antoniou, G., van Harmelen, F.: OWL: web ontology language. In: Handbook on Ontologies, pp. 91–110 (2009)
6. Euzenat, J., Shvaiko, P.: Ontology Matching. Springer, Heidelberg (2007)
7. Otero-Cerdeira, L., Rodriguez-Martinez, F.J., Gomez-Rodriguez, A.: Ontology matching: a literature review. Expert Syst. Appl. **42**, 949–971 (2015)
8. Euzenat, J., Shvaiko, P.: Ontology matching: state of the art and future challenges. IEEE Trans. Knowl. Data Eng. **25**, 158–176 (2013)
9. Ontology Alignment Evaluation Initiative. http://oaei.ontologymatching.org/
10. Liu, L., Yang, F., Zhang, P., Wu, J.Y., Hu, L.: SVM-based ontology mapping approach. Int. J. Autom. Comput. **9**, 306–314 (2012)
11. Kubat, M.: An Introduction to Machine Learning. Springer, Heidelberg (2015)
12. Li, X.L., Liu, B., Ng, S.K.: Learning to identify unexpected instances in the test set. In: IJCAI 2007 Proceedings of the 20th International Joint Conference on Artifical Intelligence, pp. 2802–2807. Morgan Kaufmann, San Francisco (2007)
13. Choi, N., Song, I.Y., Han, H.: A survey on ontology mapping. ACM SIGMOD Rec. **35**, 34–41 (2006)
14. Kalfoglou, Y.: Ontology mapping: the state of the art. Knowl. Eng. Rev. **18**, 1–31 (2003)
15. Thanh Le, B., Dieng-Kuntz, R., Gandon, F.: An ontology matching problems for building a corporate Semantic Web in a multi-communities organization. In: 6th International Conference on Enterprise Information Systems (ICEIS), pp. 236–243. Springer, Heidelberg (2004)
16. Doan, A., Madhavan, J., Domingos, P., Halevy, A.Y: Ontology matching: a machine learning approach. In: Handbook on Ontologies, pp. 385–404 (2004)
17. Nezdali, A.H., Shadgar, B., Osareh, A.: Ontology alignment using machine learning techniques. Int. J. Comput. Sci. Inf. Technol. **3**, 139–150 (2011)
18. Mao, M., Peng, Y., Spring, M.: Ontology mapping: as a binary classification problem. In: 4th International Conference on Semantics, Knowledge and Grid 2008 (SKG 2008), pp. 20–25. IEEE, New York (2008)
19. Euzenat, J., Valtchev, P.: Similarity-based ontology alignment for OWL-Lite. In: 16th European Conference on Artificial Intelligence (ECAI), pp. 333–337. IOS Press, Amsterdam (2004)
20. Castano, S., Ferrara, A., Montanelli, S.: Matching ontologies in open networked systems: techniques and applications. In: Spaccapietra, S., Atzeni, P., Chu, W.W., Catarci, T., Sycara, K. (eds.) Journal on Data Semantics V. LNCS, vol. 3870, pp. 25–63. Springer, Heidelberg (2006)
21. Daneshpazhouh, A., Sami, A.: Entropy-based outlier detection using semi-supervised approach with few positive examples. Pattern Recogn. Lett. **49**, 77–84 (2014)
22. Zhang, B., Zuo, W.: Reliable negative extracting based on kNN for learning from positive and unlabelled examples. J. Comput. **4**, 94–101 (2009)
23. Li, X., Liu, B.: Learning to classify texts using positive and unlabeled data. In: 18th International Joint Conference on Artificial Intelligence 2003 (IJCAI 2003), pp. 587–592. Morgan Kaufman, San Francisco (2003)
24. Wang, X., Xu, Z., Sha, C., Ester, M., Zhou, A.: Semi-supervised learning from only positive and unlabeled data using entropy. In: Chen, L., Tang, C., Yang, J., Gao, Y. (eds.) WAIM 2010. LNCS, vol. 6184, pp. 668–679. Springer, Heidelberg (2010)

25. Li, X.-L., Liu, B., Ng, S.-K.: Learning to classify documents with only a small positive training set. In: Kok, J.N., Koronacki, J., Lopez de Mantaras, R., Matwin, S., Mladenič, D., Skowron, A. (eds.) ECML 2007. LNCS (LNAI), vol. 4701, pp. 201–213. Springer, Heidelberg (2007)

26. Wang, Y., Liu, W., Bell, D.A.: A structure-based similarity spreading approach for ontology matching. In: Deshpande, A., Hunter, A. (eds.) SUM 2010. LNCS, vol. 6379, pp. 361–374. Springer, Heidelberg (2010)

27. Doan, A., Madhavan, J., Dhamankar, R., Domingos, P., Halevy, A.: Learning to match ontologies on the Semantic Web. Int. J. Very Large Data Bases (VLDB J.) **12**, 303–319 (2003)

28. Wang, Z.: A semi-supervised learning approach for ontology matching. In: Zhao, D., Du, J., Wang, H., Wang, P., Ji, D., Pan, J.Z. (eds.) CSWS 2014. CCIS, vol. 480, pp. 17–28. Springer, Heidelberg (2014)

Rule-Based Canonicalization of Arbitrary Tables in Spreadsheets

Alexey O. Shigarov$^{(\boxtimes)}$, Viacheslav V. Paramonov, Polina V. Belykh, and Alexander I. Bondarev

Matrosov Institute for System Dynamics and Control Theory of SB RAS, Irkutsk, Russia
shigarov@icc.ru
http://cells.icc.ru

Abstract. Arbitrary tables presented in spreadsheets can be an important data source in business intelligence. However, many of them have complex layouts that hinder the process of extracting, transforming, and loading their data in a database. The paper is devoted to the issues of rule-based data transformation from arbitrary tables presented in spreadsheets to a structured canonical form that can be loaded into a database by regular ETL-tools. We propose a system for canonicalization of arbitrary tables presented in spreadsheets as an implementation of our methodology for rule-based table analysis and interpretation. It enables the execution of rules expressed in our specialized rule language called CRL to recover implicit relationships in a table. Our experimental results show that particular CRL-programs can be developed for different sets of tables with similar features to automate table canonicalization with high accuracy.

Keywords: Unstructured data integration · Table understanding · Table analysis and interpretation · Spreadsheet data transformation

1 Introduction

A large number of data is presented as arbitrary tables in spreadsheets. Many of them are unstructured data [1]. They lack explicit semantics required to be interpreted by computer programs. At the same time, arbitrary tables can be a valuable data source for business intelligence. To be accessible for data analysis and visualization their data need to be extracted, transformed, and loaded into databases. However, if they have complex layouts of cells then the use of familiar ETL-tools is often not enough to automatically populate a database with their data.

The paper presents the rule-based data transformation from arbitrary tables presented in spreadsheets (Fig. 1) to the canonical form (Fig. 2) that can be loaded into a database by standard ETL-tools (Fig. 3). It consists in table analysis and interpretation for recovering cell-role pairs where a role is defined as an

© Springer International Publishing Switzerland 2016
G. Dregvaite and R. Damasevicius (Eds.): ICIST 2016, CCIS 639, pp. 78–91, 2016.
DOI: 10.1007/978-3-319-46254-7_7

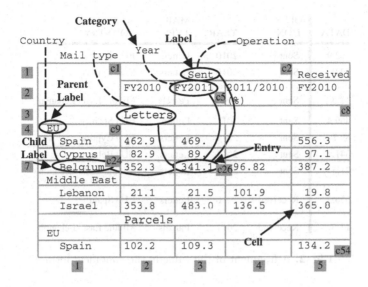

Fig. 1. An arbitrary table and its relationships

entry, label, or category, as well as entry-label, label-label, and label-category pairs.

Many methods for table analysis and interpretation were suggested in recent years. Some of them use extraction ontologies [11] or data frames [26] to bind natural language content of a table with their concepts. In a like manner Wang et al. [27] consider table understanding as associating a table with concepts in the general purpose knowledge taxonomy. Govindaraju et al. [14] combine table understanding and NLP techniques to extract relations from both text and tables. Astrakhantsev et al. [3] propose a method for data extraction from tables based on modeling user behavior. There are several methods [4,12] dealing with web-tables that fit in well with the relational form. The domain-independent methods [6,7,10,13,17–22] are based on the analysis and interpretation of spatial, style and textual information from tables instead of using external knowledge. These methods are generally designed for a few of widespread types of arbitrary tables.

The existing methods mostly deal with web-tables presented in HTML format. There are a few papers that are centered on tables presented in spreadsheets [2,5–8,10,16,19]. Erwig et al. [2,5] consider the issues of detecting errors in spreadsheets. Cunha et al. [8] focus on data normalization in spreadsheets. Hung et al. [15,16] propose the rule-based transformation of spreadsheet data into structured form using their original spreadsheet-like formula language called TranSheet. Chen and Cafarella [6,7] present a domain-independent method for extracting relational data from spreadsheets. Their method is designed for a widespread type of tables with a region of numeric values and two accompanied hierarchical regions of headings on the top and the left. The recent papers of

DATA	OPERA-TION	YEAR	MAIL TYPE	COUNTRY
462.9	Sent	2010	Letters	EU I Spain
82.9	Sent	2010	Letters	EU I Cyprus
...	...	...	...	...
12.3	Sent	2010	Parcels	Middle East I Lebanon
469.4	Sent	2011	Letters	EU I Spain
89.7	Sent	2011	Letters	EU I Cyprus
341.1	Sent	2011	Letters	EU I Belgium
21.5	Sent	2011	Letters	Middle East I Lebanon
...	...	...	...	...
556.3	Received	2010	Letters	EU I Spain
...	...	...	...	...
11.3	Received	2011	Parcels	Middle East I Lebanon

Fig. 2. A fragment of the table in the canonical form

Nagy, Embley, Seth and Krishnamoorthy [9,10,19,23] are devoted to the data transformation from web-tables converted into CSV files to a relational database.

We propose a system for canonicalization of arbitrary tables presented in spreadsheets as an implementation of our methodology for rule-based table analysis and interpretation [25]. It enables the execution of rules expressed in our specialized rule language called CRL [24] to recover missing relationships describing table semantics. CRL-rules map explicit features (layout, style, and text of cells) of an arbitrary table to its implicit semantic relationships. In contrast with the existing methods, our system is a tool for unstructured data integration. Instead of fixing one or more types of tables with typical structures, we propose to develop different declarative CRL-programs for particular sets of tables with similar features that can be both typical and specific. Our system supports relative cell addressing compared to the TranSheet [15,16]. In addition, we use the fixed canonical form instead of specifying a target schema.

2   Recovering Relationships in a Table

We use the terminology of the Wang's table model [28]: entries (data values), labels (headers), and categories (domains), Fig. 1. Our table model supports the following basic principles: (1) each cell can contain one or more entry, label and category values simultaneously, (2) an entry can be associated with only one label in each category, (3) each label must be associated with only one category, and (4) a category can be hierarchical. It is discussed more detail in [24,25].

Cells, entries, labels, and categories of a table are facts in the rule matching process. CRL-rules map explicit features of a table to its implicit relationships. The left hand side of a rule defines conditions using to query facts inserted into the working memory of a rule engine. Its right hand side contains actions that typically serve to generate new facts or to modify the existing facts.

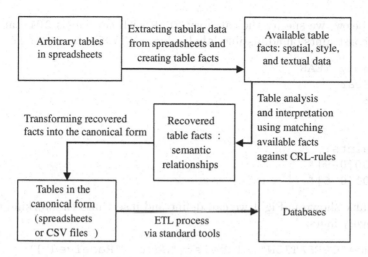

Fig. 3. Unstructured ETL for arbitrary tables in spreadsheets using CRL-rules

Input facts are formed from Excel cells of an arbitrary table. Each cell fact corresponds to an Excel cell of a table with slight modifications. It specifies four positions (`cl` — left column, `rt` — top row, `cr` — right column, and `rb` — bottom row), style characteristics (`style`), including a font (`style.font`), horizontal (`style.horzAlignment`) and vertical (`style.vertAlignment`) alignment, text rotation (`style.rotation`), background (`style.bgColor`) and foreground (`style.fgColor`) colors, border types and colors (`style.leftBorder`, `style.topBorder`, `style.rightBorder`, and `style.bottomBorder`), a primitive data type (`type`), an indent (`indent`), and its textual content (`text`).

For example, the table shown in Fig. 1 consists of 54 cells. Thus, the 54 cell facts `<cells>={c1,c2,...,c54}` are inserted into the working memory of a rule engine, including:

```
c1=(cl=1,rt=1,cr=1,rb=2,text=null)
c2=(cl=2,rt=1,cr=4,rb=1,text="Sent")
c5=(cl=3,rt=2,cr=3,rb=2,text="FY2010")
c8=(cl=1,rt=3,cr=5,rb=3,style.font.bold=true, text="Letters")
c9=(cl=1,rt=4,cr=1,rb=4,text="EU")
c24=(cl=1,rt=7,cl=1,rb=7,indent=4,text="Belgium")
c26=(cl=3,rt=7,cl=3,rb=7,type=Type.NUMERIC,text="341.1")
```

Moreover, an input can include category facts. A category can be specified as a set of its labels and constraints (regular expressions defining ranges of permissible labels) in YAML[1] format. Our YAML schema defines the following fields: a category name, list of label values, and list of constraints. Note that the current version of our system supports specifying only plain categories. In the

---

[1] http://yaml.org.

example below, we specify the category YEAR with two labels 2010 and 2011 and two constraints on admissible label values FY2000, ... , FY2016:

```
# category YEAR
name: Year
labels:
- 2010
- 2011
constraints:
- "FY200[0-9]"
- "FY201[0-6]"
```

For the table shown in Fig. 1 we can define and insert into the working memory four category facts:

```
d1=(name="OPERATION", labels={"Sent","Received"})
d2=(name="YEAR", constraints={"FY200[0-9]", "FY201[0-6]"})
d3=(name="MAIL_TYPE", labels={"Letters","Parcels"})
d4=(name="COUNTRY", labels={"Afghanistan",...,"Zimbabwe"})
```

All inserted facts are accessible through condition elements of a rule. A condition element enables to query facts of one of four types (cell, entry, label, or category) that satisfy constraints represented as Java-expressions. For example, the condition element <cell $c : c1 == 1> queries all cells located in the leftmost column (e.g. c1, c8, c9, c24), the other <cell $c : type==Type.NUMERIC> returns all cells with the NUMERIC type (e.g. c26).

Typically, CRL-rules can be separated into two groups designed for two functionally different stages: the first for recovering cell-role pairs where a role is defined as an entry, label, or category, and second for recovering entry-label, label-label, and label-category pairs.

The first group includes actions for generating entry and label facts from cell facts. Usually, a value of a created fact is a text of a cell, but it can also be a part or modification of the text. The cell becomes the provenance for the generated entry or label. For example, we can create the following label facts from the cells c2, c5, c8, c9, and c24 of the table shown in Fig. 1 respectively:

```
l1=(value="Sent", cell=c2), l2=(value="2011", cell=c5)
l3=(value="Letters", cell=c8), l4=(value="EU", cell=c9)
l5=(value="Belgium", cell=c24)
```

as well as the entry fact e1=(value="341.1", cell=c26) from the cell c26. Moreover, to simplify and generalize recovering relationships, rules of this stage often contain actions for splitting or merging cells, removing rows and columns, and modifying style and text content of cells.

The second group uses actions for associating entries, labels, and categories. A label can be associated with a category using either the corresponding category fact or specified name of the category. In the latter case, we look for the category by its name. If it exists, then the label is associated with it. Otherwise, we try to create it before categorizing. In our example (Fig. 1) we need to associate the labels with the categories as follows:

```
l1=(value="Sent", cell=c2, category=d1)
l2=(value="2011", cell=c5, category=d2)
l3=(value="Letters", cell=c8, category=d3)
l4=(value="EU", cell=c9, category=d4)
l5=(value="Belgium", cell=c24, category=d4)
```

Furthermore, two labels can be associated as parent and child. As the result, labels form trees to support hierarchical categories and compound values. All labels connected in a tree must be associated with the same category. In the case (Fig. 1) we relate the labels l4 and l5 as parent-child:

```
l4=(value="EU", cell=c9, category=d4, children={l5,...})
l5=(value="Belgium", cell=c24, category=d4, parent=l4)
```

It means that the compound value of the label l5 is "EU|Belgium".

In some cases, we can define that several labels relate to the same category, without knowing what the category is. For example, we may know that labels, which are located in the same row, relate to the same category. Instead of categorizing labels can be grouped in pairs. Each group of labels can be considered as an anonymous category. If one or more labels of a group are associated with a category then the remaining labels from the group also must be associated with the category. If no labels in a group are categorized then we create a category with the automatically generated name and associate all labels of this group with it.

An entry can be associated with a label using either the corresponding label fact or a specified value of the label from a designated category. In the latter case, we try to find this category among all accessible categories. If this category does not exist then we create it. After that, we look for the label with the specified value in the founded or created category. When there is no label, we create it, using this value. At last, the entry is associated with the founded or created label. Note that, this allows to generate labels independently of cells. In the example (Fig. 1) the entry e1 is associated with the labels l1, l2, l3, l4, and l5 i. e.

```
e1=(value="341.1", cell=c26, labels={l1,l2,l3,l4,l5})
```

As is mentioned above, any entry can be associated with only one label from each category. Moreover, this means that the label must belong to a category. If the added label is uncategorized then it is not associated with the entry at that moment. At first, it becomes a candidate that may be associated automatically with the entry only after it is categorized. Finally, all labels, which are not categorized or grouped in rule firing, are associated with a default category after that.

3   Generating a Canonical Table

Recovered relationships of a table enable generating its canonical form. We can consider the canonical form as a relational table. Its topmost row contains field (attribute) names. Each of the remaining rows is a record (tuple). It obligatorily includes the field named DATA that contains entries. Each recovered category becomes a separate field that contains its labels. Any record presents recovered relationships between an entry and one label in each category. Usually each record is unique within a canonical table.

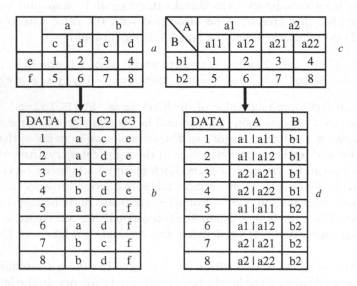

Fig. 4. Two arbitrary tables (a, c) and their canonical forms (b, d)

For example, as a result of analysis and interpretation of the table shown in Fig. 4, a the following relationships can be recovered:

```
<entries>={1,2,3,4,5,6,7,8}
<labels>={a,b,c,d,e,f}
<groups>={{a,b},{c,d},{e,f}}
<entry_label_pairs>={(1,a),(1,c),(1,e),(2,a),(2,d),(2,e),(3,b),
(3,c),(3,e),(4,b),(4,d),(4,e),(5,a),(5,c),(5,f),(6,a),(6,d),(6,f),
(7,b),(7,c),(7,f),(8,b),(8,d),(8,f)}
```

This example supposes that each group is an anonymous category. Thus, we generate three categories and associate them with the grouped labels as follows:

```
<categories>={C1,C2,C3}
<label_category_pairs>={(a,C1),(b,C1),(c,C2),(d,C2),(e,C3),(f,C3)}
```

Another example is the source table demonstrated in Fig. 4, c where we assume that 'A' and 'B' are category names, and the boxhead headings constitute hierarchy.

```
<entries>={1,2,3,4,5,6,7,8}
<labels>={a1,a11,a12,a2,a21,a22,b1,b2}
<categories>={A,B}
<entry_label_pairs>={(1,a11),(1,b1),(2,a12),(2,b1),(3,a21),
(3,b1),(4,a22),(4,b1),(5,a11),(5,b2),(6,a12),(6,b2),(7,a21),
(7,b2),(8,a22),(8,b2)}
<label_label_pairs>={(a11,a1),(a12,a1),(a21,a2),(a22,a2)}
<label_category_pairs>={(a1,A),(a11,A),(a12,A),(a2,A),(a21,A),
(a22,A),(b1,B),(b2,B)}
```

4 Implementation

We implement the proposed system for table canonicalization as shown in Fig. 5. First, we parse tabular data of a source spreadsheet in Excel format via "Apache POI"[2] library and generate cell facts from them. Optionally, categories specified in YAML format can also be loaded and presented as facts, using SnakeYAML[3] library for parsing YAML.

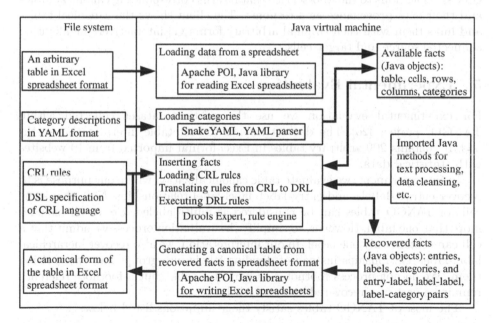

Fig. 5. Architecture of the system for rule-based canonicalization of arbitrary tables in spreadsheets

Our data structures for presenting table facts (cells, entries, labels, and categories) are Java classes developed in accordance with the naming conventions of

---

[2] http://poi.apache.org.
[3] http://snakeyaml.org.

JavaBeans[4] specification. This allows to use any rule engine implemented "JSR 94: Java Rule Engine API"[5] specification. Generated facts are instances of these classes. They are asserted in the working memory of the rule engine.

In the prototype we use Drools[6] rule engine. Rules for table analysis and interpretation can be expressed in either the Drools' native general-purpose DRL format or our domain-specific language, CRL. In case when loaded rules are presented in CRL they are translated to DRL format via Drools, using the DSL specification defining transformations from CRL to DRL constructs. Note that rules can use imported Java programs for text processing, data cleansing, or mathematical computations.

New facts (entries, labels, categories, and their relationships) are recovered in matching available facts against DRL-rules. Recovered facts provide generating canonical tables. The process ends with each canonical table being exported into Excel spreadsheet format, using "Apache POI" library.

The prototype of our system has been implemented as a command-line application[7] and web-service[8]. We have also developed a web-client for our web-service. It serves to transfer arbitrary tables in spreadsheets, rule sets, and category specifications to the web-service that returns corresponding canonical tables and their data provenance as a response. The client shows the canonical tables and links them with their original arbitrary forms via interactively highlighting connected source and target cells.

5   Experimental Evaluation

For experimental evaluation we use the existing dataset collected within TANGO[9] project [26]. The dataset intends to test table interpretation methods. It contains 200 arbitrary tables in Excel format imported from 10 websites with statistical data.

In the experiment, we evaluate table canonicalization where our purpose is to recover entries, labels, and entry-label, label-label relationships. Note that some cells of TANGO tables can be considered as multi-labeled, i.e. a cell includes more than one label. However, to simplify the evaluation process we admit that a cell can contain only one label. In our interpretation, we also recover hierarchical label-label relationships instead of dividing labels into groups and categorizing them. We do not process footnotes as part of a table, but a footnote reference remains a part of a recovered entry or label.

The most of TANGO tables satisfy the assumptions listed below:

- A table consists of four cell regions having different functions and separated by two invisible perpendicular lines as shown in Fig. 6, a: (1) each non-empty

---

[4] http://www.oracle.com/technetwork/java/javase/tech/spec-136004.html.
[5] http://jcp.org/en/jsr/detail?id=94.
[6] http://drools.org.
[7] Downloadable from https://github.com/shigarov/cells-ssdc.
[8] Accessible at http://cells.icc.ru:8080/ssdc.
[9] http://tango.byu.edu/data.

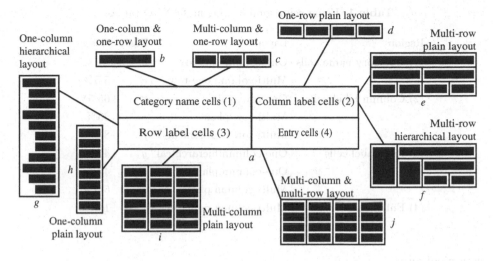

Fig. 6. Cell regions (a) and their layouts (b–j) in tables of TANGO dataset

cell of the top-left region contains a category name; (2) each non-empty cell of the top-right region contains a column label; (3) each non-empty cell of the bottom-left region contains a row label; (4) each non-empty cell of the bottom-right region contains an entry.

- Each cell region has one of the appropriate layouts as shown in Fig. 6 and enumerated in Table 1.
- If a cell located in a column contains a category name then all row labels produced from the rest of cells in this column belong to this category.
- Column labels can form a hierarchy (Fig. 6, e and f). If in the top right region a not empty cell c located on i-row spans several columns and not empty cells $c_1,\ldots,c_n$ are located in these columns on $i + 1$-row, then the cell c contains a parent label for labels produced from the cells $c_1,\ldots,c_n$.
- Row labels located in the leftmost column can form a hierarchy (Fig. 6, g). Three typographical ways can denote the presence of a label hierarchy: (1) each level of label nesting appends one additional indent equaled two spaces; (2) hyphen char ('-') at the beginning of a label indicates that the label is nested; (3) text highlighted by the bold font can signalize spanning label.
- An entry is either a number or special word (e.g. '#', 'F', '...', 'x', 'NA').

These assumptions are formally presented as a set of 16 CRL-rules combined into the CRL-program called TANGO-200.

To evaluate table canonicalization we use the following measures:

$$Completeness = \frac{\text{number of completely recovered tables}}{\text{number of all tables}}$$

where a table is completely recovered, when all entries, labels, entry-label pairs, and label-label pairs which are contained in its source form are included in its

Table 1. Using cell region layouts in TANGO tables

Region	Layout	Fig. 6	Cases
(1) Category name cells	One-column one-row	b	94.5%
	Multi-column one-row	c	5.5%
(2) Column label cells	One-row plain	d	65.5%
	Multi-row plain	e	26%
	Multi-row hierarchical	f	8.5%
(3) Row label cells	One-column hierarchical	g	47.5%
	One-column plain	h	47%
	Multi-column plain	i	5.5%
(4) Entry cells	Multi-column multi-row	j	100%

canonical form.

$$Preciseness = \frac{\text{number of precisely recovered tables}}{\text{number of all tables}}$$

where a table is precisely recovered, when all entries, labels, entry-label pairs, and label-label pairs which are included in its canonical form are contained in its source form.

The evaluation is carried out as follows. Two experts independently compare the source arbitrary tables with their canonical forms generated automatically. They referee that each table is processed successfully or not in terms of the completeness and preciseness. In case when two experts make opposite decisions on a table then the third expert makes a final decision. The experimental results are presented in Table 2.

The completeness is 87% and preciseness is 88.5% for TANGO-200 program. Among 200 tables of the dataset, total 33 are processed with errors, which reduce the completeness and preciseness. There are various causes of these errors, including the following: (1) ambiguity of text highlighting, e.g. the use of the bold font to emphasize a hierarchy of row labels or data aggregation, (2) absence of spatial or style features, when relationships are expressed by natural language only, and (3) messy layout and data of cells, e.g. two parts of a label can improperly be placed in two different cells. For the most part, errors appear in recovering label-label relationships between row labels located in the leftmost column with one-column hierarchical layout (Fig. 6, g), 28 of 33 cases, 85%.

Additionally, we evaluate our system for a subset of the dataset where we exclude all tables having one-column hierarchical layout of the bottom-left region (Fig. 6, g). Only 105 tables of the dataset belong to the subset. To process them, we use a subset of TANGO-200 rules where we remove 3 rules intended for recovering label-label relationships between row labels located in the leftmost column. The subset of 13 CRL-rules is combined into TANGO-SUB program. The experimental results for this case is also presented in Table 2.

Table 2. Experimental results

CRL-program	TANGO-200	TANGO-SUB
Total tables	200	105
Completely recovered tables	174	100
Precisely recovered tables	177	100
Completeness	87 %	95.2 %
Preciseness	88.5 %	95.2 %

The evaluation shows that particular CRL-programs can be developed for different sets of tables with similar features to automate table canonicalization with high accuracy. One set of rules can be suitable for processing a wide range of arbitrary tables. Furthermore, our experiment demonstrates that narrowing a table type, like from TANGO-200 to TANGO-SUB, can cause simplifying rules and increasing the completeness and preciseness in table canonicalization. The experimental results, including the generated canonical forms and the rule sets, are presented in more detail at address http://cells.icc.ru/pub/crl.

6 Conclusions and Further Work

The presented tools, system and rule language, are mainly designed for data integration. They can be applied to develop specialized ETL software where tagged arbitrary tables in spreadsheets, word documents, or web pages can be used as data sources. We expect that they are useful in business intelligence applications when data from a large number of arbitrary tables with similar features of their layout, style and text are required for populating a database.

We observe that arbitrary tables presented in spreadsheets can contain messy (not standardized) data. It seems to be interesting for the further work to integrate our tools with data cleansing techniques. The use of domain ontologies and global taxonomies (e.g. FreeBase, DBpedia, YAGO) is of special interest for recovering categories. In addition, the further work can be focused on developing table analysis and interpretation methods for widely used features, e.g. for automatically recovering a row label hierarchy in the leftmost column. We believe this can improve expressiveness and usefulness of our tools.

Acknowledgements. We thank Prof. George Nagy and all members of TANGO research group(http://tango.byu.edu) for providing and discussing the TANGO dataset for our experiments.

This work was financially supported by the Russian Foundation for Basic Research (Grant No. 15-37-20042 and 14-07-00166) and Council for Grants of the President of Russian Federation (Grant No. NSh-8081.2016.9). The presented web-service for table canonicalization is performed on resources of the Shared Equipment Center of Integrated information and computing network of Irkutsk Research and Educational Complex(http://net.icc.ru).

References

1. Unstructured information management architecture (UIMA) version 1.0 (2009). http://docs.oasis-open.org/uima/v1.0/uima-v1.0.html
2. Abraham, R., Erwig, M.: UCheck: A spreadsheet type checker for end users. J. Vis. Lang. Comput. **18**(1), 71–95 (2007)
3. Astrakhantsev, N., Turdakov, D., Vassilieva, N.: Semi-automatic data extraction from tables. In: Selected Papers of the 15th All-Russian Scientific Conference on Digital Libraries: Advanced Methods and Technologies, Digital Collections, pp. 14–20 (2013)
4. Cafarella, M.J., Halevy, A., Wang, D.Z., Wu, E., Zhang, Y.: WebTables: Exploring the power of tables on the web. Proc. VLDB Endow. **1**(1), 538–549 (2008)
5. Chambers, C., Erwig, M.: Automatic detection of dimension errors in spreadsheets. J. Vis. Lang. Comput. **20**(4), 269–283 (2009)
6. Chen, Z., Cafarella, M.: Automatic web spreadsheet data extraction. In: Proceedings 3rd International Workshop on Semantic Search Over the Web, pp. 1: 1–1: 8. ACM, New York, NY, USA (2013)
7. Chen, Z., Cafarella, M.: Lntegrating spreadsheet data via accurate and low-effort extraction. In: Proceedings of the 20th ACM SIGKDD International Conference on Knowledge Discovery and Data Mining, pp. 1126–1135. ACM, New York, NY, USA (2014)
8. Cunha, J., Saraiva, J.A., Visser, J.: From spreadsheets to relational databases and back. In: Proceedings ACM SIGPLAN Workshop on Partial Evaluation and Program Manipulation, pp. 179–188. ACM, New York, PEPM 2009, NY, USA (2009)
9. Embley, D.W., Krishnamoorthy, M.S., Nagy, G., Seth, S.: Converting heterogeneous statistical tables on the web to searchable databases. Int. J. Doc. Anal. Recogn. **19**, 1–20 (2016)
10. Embley, D.W., Seth, S., Nagy, G.: Transforming web tables to a relational database. In: Proceedings 22nd International Conference on Pattern Recognition, pp. 2781–2786. ICPR 2014, IEEE Comp. Soc., Washington, DC, USA (2014)
11. Embley, D., Tao, C., Liddle, S.: Automating the extraction of data from HTML tables with unknown structure. Data Knowl. Eng. **54**(1), 3–28 (2005)
12. Galkin, M., Mouromtsev, D., Auer, S.: Identifying web tables: Supporting a neglected type of content on the web. In: Proceedings of the 6th International Conference Knowledge Engineering and Semantic Web, Moscow, Russia. Communications in Computer and Information Science, vol. 518, pp. 48–62 (2015)
13. Gatterbauer, W., Bohunsky, P., Herzog, M., Krpl, B., Pollak, B.: Towards domain-independent information extraction from web tables. In: Proceedings 16th International Conference on World Wide Web, pp. 71–80. New York, US (2007)
14. Govindaraju, V., Zhang, C., Ré, C.: Understanding tables in context using standard NLP toolkits. In: Proceedings of the 51st Annual Meeting of the Association for Computational Linguistics, ACL. vol. 2: Short Papers, pp. 658–664 (2013)
15. Hung, V.: Spreadsheet-Based Complex Data Transformation. Ph.D. thesis, School of Computer Science and Engineering, University of New South Wales, Sydney, Australia (2011)
16. Hung, V., Benatallah, B., Saint-Paul, R.: Spreadsheet-based complex data transformation. In: Proceedings 20th ACM International Conference on Information and Knowledge Management, pp. 1749–1754. ACM, New York, CIKM 2011, NY, USA (2011)

17. Kim, Y.S., Lee, K.H.: Extracting logical structures from html tables. Comput. Stand. Interfaces **30**(5), 296–308 (2008)
18. Kudinov, P.Y.: Extracting statistics indicators from tables of basic structure. Pattern Recogn. Image Anal. **21**(4), 630–636 (2011)
19. Nagy, G., Embley, D., Seth, S.: End-to-end conversion of html tables for populating a relational database. In: Proceedings 11th IAPR International Workshop on Document Analysis Systems, pp. 222–226. IEEE Computer Society, Tours Loire Valley, France, April 2014
20. Pivk, A., Cimiano, P., Sure, Y.: From tables to frames. Web Semant. **3**(2–3), 132–146 (2005)
21. Pivk, A.: Thesis: Automatic ontology generation from web tabular structures. AI Commun. **19**(1), 83–85 (2006)
22. Pivk, A., Cimiano, P., Sure, Y., Gams, M., Rajkovič, V., Studer, R.: Transforming arbitrary tables into logical form with TARTAR. Data Knowl. Eng. **60**(3), 567–595 (2007)
23. Seth, S., Nagy, G.: Segmenting tables via indexing of value cells by table headers. In: 2013 12th International Conference on Document Analysis and Recognition (ICDAR), pp. 887–891, August 2013
24. Shigarov, A.: Rule-based table analysis and interpretation. In: Proceedings of the 21st International Conference on Information and Software Technologies. Communications in Computer and Information Science, vol. 538, pp. 175–186 (2015)
25. Shigarov, A.: Table understanding using a rule engine. Expert Syst. Appl. **42**(2), 929–937 (2015)
26. Tijerino, Y., Embley, D., Lonsdale, D., Ding, Y., Nagy, G.: Towards ontology generation from tables. World Wide Web: Int. Web Inf. Syst. **8**(3), 261–285 (2005)
27. Wang, J., Wang, H., Wang, Z., Zhu, K.Q.: Understanding tables on the web. In: Johannesson, P., Lee, M.L., Liddle, S.W., Opdahl, A.L., López, Ó.P. (eds.) ER 2015. LNCS, vol. 9381, pp. 141–155. Springer, Heidelberg (2012). doi:10.1007/978-3-642-34002-4_11
28. Wang, X.: Tabular Abstraction, Editing, and Formatting. Ph.D. thesis, University of Waterloo, Waterloo, Ontario, Canada (1996)

Information Systems: Special Session on e-Health Information Systems

Algorithm for Colorblindness Detection Sets Generation

Maciej Laskowski[(✉)]

Institute of Computer Science,
Lublin University of Technology, Lublin, Poland
m.laskowski@pollub.pl

Abstract. Currently there are numerous methods for detecting colorblindness. They differ in many aspects, e.g. the quality and accuracy of diagnosis, the spectrum of colors used during test or the ability of being reproduced on a mass scale. However, there is one thing that those methods do have in common – they are based on predefined, limited sets of color elements.

This paper presents the algorithm for generation of colorblindness detection sets – so called *quodlibets* – pairs of colors that are easily distinguishable by a person with normal color vision, but are hard (or impossible) to tell apart by a person with certain color vision disorder within defined timeframe. The discussed algorithm allow to generate many different *quodlibets*, which allow not only to detect certain types of colorblindness but also to estimate the strength of a color vision impairment.

Keywords: Colorblindness · Color vision disorders · Computer-aided diagnostic systems

1 Introduction

It is estimated that about 10 % of the whole human population is affected with some kind of color vision disorder, which is defined as the inability (or reduced ability) to distinguish between certain colors or shades under normal lighting condition [5]. There are several types of color vision disorder, differing from total color blindness (monochromacy), through dichromacy (where one out of three types of retinal cones are missing or strongly underdeveloped), up to reduced visible color spectrum – anomalous trichromacy, where the aforementioned types of retinal cones are underdeveloped or not working properly [12].

Colorblindness can be of genetic or acquired nature. In the first case, the majority of colorblindness types is caused by a faulty gene carried on the X chromosome (which results in higher percentage of colorblind males, since they have only one X chromosome), with an exception of tritan-type defects, which are encoded on chromosome 7 (which is gender-independent). In the second case, color vision disorders may be a result (or a symptom) of a disease, trauma (either to the optic nerve or brain) or exposure to certain chemicals (e.g. drugs) [10]. Acquired color vision disorders may be permanent or temporal.

© Springer International Publishing Switzerland 2016
G. Dregvaite and R. Damasevicius (Eds.): ICIST 2016, CCIS 639, pp. 95–106, 2016.
DOI: 10.1007/978-3-319-46254-7_8

Genetic types of colorblindness may be classified not only by the severity of color vision disorder, but also by the type of cone missing or not working properly. This classification is presented in Fig. 1. Table 1 presents the classification of acquired color vision disorders and their similarity to the genetic ones.

Due to the limitation of this paper and relative similarity of types between genetic and acquired types of color vision disorders, only the terms used for genetic types will be used from now on. The paper will also focus on dichromats and anomalous trichromats, as monochromacy is extremely rare and relatively easier to detect other kinds of color vision disorders.

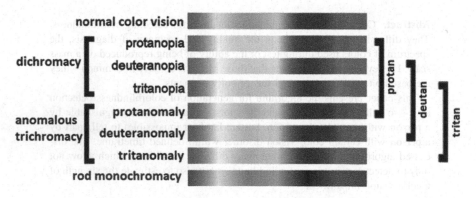

Fig. 1. Different approach to classification of genetic color vision disorders (Color figure online) (source: own work based on data from [3])

Table 1. The classification of acquired color vision disorders (source: [1])

Color vision disorder	Characteristics
Type 1	Similar to protan vision disorders
Type 2	Similar to deutan color vision disorders, less sensitive to shortwave light
Type 3a	Similar to tritan color vision disorders although with sensitivity shifted to shortwave light
Type 3b	Similar to tritan color vision disorders

2   Overview of Currently Used Colorblindness Detection Methods

Currently there are numerous methods for detecting color vision disorders. Those methods can be divided into four main groups:

- **arrangement,** in which the examinee has either to select a number of samples with color matching (or close to) to the one given by the examiner or to arrange the samples in a certain order (e.g. from the lightest to the darkest). Example: Farns-worth D-15 pane.

- **nominative**, where the examinee usually has to read and name the pattern which is noticeable for people with normal color vison, but difficult to see (in certain timeframe) or even unnoticeable by persons with certain color vision disorder. Example: Ishihara's pseudoisochromatic plates.
- **spectral,** which are based on the fact that certain color can be obtained by mixing two other colors, e.g. yellow light can be obtained by mixing green and red light in a certain ratio.
- **lamp,** which focus only on checking the examinee's ability to distinguish only certain signal colors (e.g. used in navy or aviation), not to determine the type of potential color vision disorder

While analyzing the colorblindness detection methods, one should keep in mind that some of them allow not only the detection of color vision impairment, but also the classification of certain type, while others focus only on determining whether the testee has the ability to distinguish certain colors. Moreover, those diagnostic methods do differ on many factors, the most important being:

- **sensitivity,** which measures the proportion of people who are correctly identified as having the condition (in discussed case – people with color vision disorders) to the whole tested group. Sensitivity is often referred to as true positive rate;
- **specificity,** which measures the proportion of people who are correctly identified as not having the condition (in discussed case – people with normal color vision) to the whole tested group;
- **difficulty level** – some methods require certain knowledge or abilities of examinee (therefore are not suitable for testing color vision in children) or examiner;
- **examination cost** – including equipment cost (purchase cost, cost per use and top accuracy period), staff cost, etc.
- **time cost** – including examination time as well as time needed for analysis of the results.

Table 2 present the short overview on most popular color vision diagnostic methods, concerning sensitivity, specificity and main limitations.

As it can be noticed in Table 2, none of the methods can serve as ultimate diagnostic tool, due to different limitations. However, there is one more limitation to be considered: each of the discussed methods use certain, predefined set of colors. This means that only a small percentage of all colors which are perceivable by human eye (about 10 million) is used. In some cases this may be an additional risk of getting false diagnosis, as examinee e.g. can just learn the correct order of pseudoisochromatic plates. This problem will be discussed further in next chapter.

Table 2. Short overview on most popular color vision diagnostic methods (source: [1–5, 12])

Type	Method	Sensitivity	Specificity	Main limitations
Nominative	Ishihara plates	50-96	89-100	Cannot detect tritan color vision disorders, minimal age: 6 years
Nominative	AOHRR plates, 4th ed.	83-100	33-96	Min. age 3 years
Arrangement	FM-100	100	83	Time consuming data analysis, not suitable for screening
Arrangement	D-15	30-60	100	Time consuming data analysis, not suitable for screening
Spectral	Nagel anomalosope	100	100	Cannot detect tritan color vision disorders, complicated diagnostic process, expensive equipment
Lamp	FALANT	25	100	Checks only the ability to distinguish certain colors

3 Diagnostic Sets of Colors – An Overview

Each diagnostic method uses different set of colors for testing purposes. The number of those colors can be greatly reduced – e.g. lamp methods usually use up to five different colors (however, one should keep in mind, that this method just check if the examinee is able to distinguish between certain navigational lights). Moreover, the finite number of colors may be the result of the research: for example Shinobu Ishihara used pastels to create the first set of his pseudoisochromatic plates, therefore using only the available colors. Figure 2 presents the palette of colors used for generating standard Ishihara plates and FM-100 color pane superimposed on sRGB color space (triangle) and CIE 1931 color space.

It should be emphasized that despite the development of technology, creating a computer version of "analog" colorblindness detection method is not a trivial task, mainly due to the problem of converting printed colors into on-screen representation (effectively conversion from CMYK to RGB). This process is influenced not only by the potential conversion errors, but also by errors due to hardware – e.g. scanners and quality of the diagnostic equipment (as the pigments wear off with time).

All of those factors confirm that there is a need of developing new, computer based algorithm for generating sets of colors for diagnostic purposed, which will be hardware-independent.

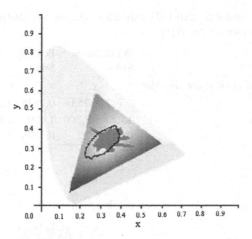

Fig. 2. Palette of colors used for generating standard Ishihara plates (gray area) and FM-100 color pane (black outline) superimposed on sRGB color space (triangle) and CIE 1931 color space (Color figure online) (source: [9])

4 The Algorithm

In order to generate sets of colors which allow detecting different types of color-blindness, the following algorithm is proposed. Algorithm generates pairs of colors, which are easily distinguishable by people with normal color vision and are hard (or impossible) to tell apart by people with certain color vision disorder within a defined timeframe. Those pairs are called quodlibets, from Latin *quod libet*, meaning *whatever you like*, as a colorblind person should not be able to tell the colors apart. Algorithm is used only for generating those color pairs, which should be used in some diagnostic method (e.g. arrangement method).

4.1 Confusion Lines

Confusion lines, also referred to as confusion axes, are intersecting lines (for each type of dichromacy) going through CIE 1931 color space. Colors placed on those lines are hard (or in case of severe color vision disorders – impossible) to distinguish by people with certain type of dichromacy [10]. Each type of dichromacy has a main confusion axis, which divides the color space into two halves, each with dominant hue (e.g. in case of protan defects, due to the red cone missing, one half is populated with colors with dominant green factor, while the other – with dominant blue factor).

It should be noticed, that sources differ on the coordinates of intersection point for each type of axes. Table 3 presents different coordinates as stated by Stiles and Wyszecki, as well as Pokorny and Smith. Figure 3 illustrates confusion axes within the CIE 1931 color space.

Table 3. x and y coordinates (in CIE 1931 chromacity diagram) of intersection points for each type of confusion axes (source: [8, 11])

Type of color vision disorder	Wyszecki & Stiles		Pokorny and Smith	
	x	y	x	y
Protan	0.747	0.253	0.7635	0.2365
Deutan	1.080	−0.800	1.400	−0.400
Tritan	0.171	0	0.1748	0

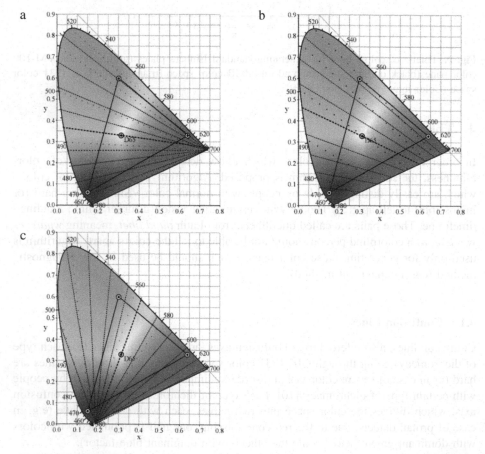

Fig. 3. CIE 1931 chromacity diagram with confusion lines for (a) protan, (b) deutan, (c) tritan color vision disorders. Confusion axes according to Wyszecki&Stiles are marked with dashed lines, according to Pokorny&Smith – with dotted lines. Main confusion line (according to Wyszecki&Stiles) is bolded. RGB color space and D65 illuminant are also marked. (Color figure online) (source: own work adapted from: [8, 11])

Confusion axes are also based on observations by Wright (Fig. 4a) and MacAdams (Fig. 4b), who designated the areas of visually equal color zones – in other words colors within those areas are perceived as the same by a person with normal color vision. However, it should be emphasized, that colors placed on a confusion axis should be distinguishable by such person.

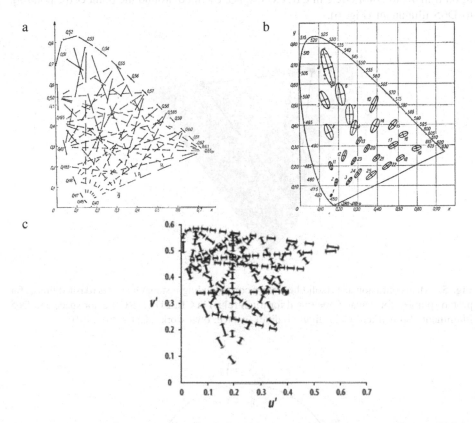

Fig. 4. (a) Perceptually equal colors in CIE 1931 chromacity diagram according to Wright (magnified 3 times) [13], (b) MacAdams ellipses (magnified 10 times) [13], (c) perceptually equal colors from (a) transferred to CIE LUV [13]

Confusion axes are usually shown on CIE 1931 chromacity diagram, which is not perceptually equal – in other words the distance between two colors does not collate with the difference in their perception. This fact can be observed by comparing Fig. 4a (showing visually equivalent color stimuli in CIE 1931 chromacity diagram) and Fig. 4c (which shows the same color stimuli in CIE LUV). The 1976 CIELUV color space is one attempt at providing a perceptually uniform color space. In this color space, the distance between two points is based on how different the two colors are in luminance, chroma, and hue.

By transferring confusion lines to CIE LUV (Fig. 5), an interesting observation can be made: the main confusion axis for protan disorders is perpendicular to main confusion line for tritan disorders. Additionally, by placing lines orthogonal to each confusion line (going through the illuminant point), it is possible to illustrate so called residual hues, which are perceived by dichromats in almost the same way as by persons with normal color vision [9].

The orthogonality of confusion lines and residual hues lines is more clearly visible upon transfer to color circle in CIE LUV space escribed around the point corresponding to D65 illuminant (Fig. 6).

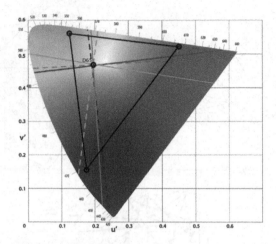

Fig. 5. Main confusion axes (solid lines) and corresponding residual hue axes (dashed lines). for protan (purple), for deutan (green) and for tritan (blue) in CIE LUV. sRGB color space and D65 illuminant also marked (Color figure online) (source: own work adapted from [9])

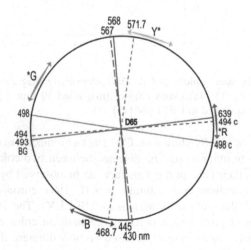

Fig. 6. Main confusion axes (solid lines) and corresponding residual hue axes (dashed lines) for protans (purple), deutans (green) and tritan (blue), transferred to color circle in CIE LUV space escribed around the point corresponding to D65 illuminant. (Color figure online) (source: [9])

4.2   Just Noticeable Difference

While discussing color perception, one should keep in mind that human eye has limited perception. This fact was illustrated in Fig. 4a–c. Just Noticeable Difference (JND) is a variable experimental parameter to determine the threshold T above which the observer (with normal color vision) reaches a desired level of confidence that two observed colors are different.

The color difference between two colors in CIE LUV can be computed as [7]:

$$\Delta E = \sqrt{(L_2 - L_1)^2 + (u_2 - u_1)^2 + (v_2 - v_1)^2} \tag{1.1}$$

The color difference follows this dependence [7]:

- $0 < \Delta E < 1$ – the observer (with standard color vision) is not able to notice the difference between colors
- $1 < \Delta E < 2$ – an experienced observer is able to notice the difference between colors
- $2 < \Delta E < 3.5$ – an inexperienced observer is able to notice the difference between colors
- $3.5 < \Delta E < 5$ – a significant difference between colors
- $5 < \Delta E$ – observer sees two completely different colors.

4.3   Algorithm Assumptions

Algorithm for generation of colorblindness detection sets is based on the following assumptions:

- There should be separate color set for detecting each type of dichromacy and each type of trichromacy
- Each set should consist of pairs of colors which are at least possible to be told apart by an inexperienced observer with normal color vision – $JND \in (1 < \Delta E < 2)$
- Developed pairs should be complementary in corresponding types of color vision disorders: e.g. people with protanomaly should be able to distinguish colors, which are perceived wrongly by people with protanopia.
- Each pair for detecting trichromacy should have a JND lower than pair for detecting dichromacy. Therefore quodlibets with $JND \in (1 < \Delta E < 1.5)$ will be used for detecting anomalous trichromacy while pairs with $JND \in (1.5 < \Delta E)$ will be used for detecting dichromacy.
- Differences in confusion axes definition should be taken into account while generating quodlibets.
- Pairs should be generated relatively randomly, so that testee cannot influence the results of examination by e.g. memorizing the order of elements used.

4.4   Algorithm

The algorithm consists of following steps:

1. A color vision disorder type (protan, deutan, tritan) is selected (e.g. by examiner);
2. Examiner selects if the quodlibets should be generated for testing dichromacy or anomalous trichromacy;
3. Examiner selects number of quodlibets to be generated;
4. A point on confusion axis corresponding to the selected color vision disorder is chosen randomly (confusion axis with coordinates by Wyszecki&Stiles is being used) in CIE LUV. This point A(u,v) represents the first color of a quodlibet;
5. Vector B($\pm$ a, $\pm$ b) is chosen randomly from the area defined by JND (based on point A) for the generated type of quodlibet. The considered area should also be placed within sRGB color space in order to be properly displayed on standard computer screen.
6. Second color is chosen by offsetting point A(u,v) by a vector B($\pm$ a, $\pm$ b). The color represented by point B(u $\pm$ a, v $\pm$ b) is the second color of a quodlibet;
7. The quodlibet is saved and scenario repeats from step 4 until sufficient number of color pairs is generated).

5   Example Quodlibets for Dichromats

Example quodlibets for each type of color vision disorders are presented in Table 4, with color values presented in RGB format. Additionally, to illustrate the potential difficulties of distinguishing colors in each quodlibets by a person with certain color

Table 4. Example quodlibets (source: own work)

Type of color vision disorder	Normal color vision		Color vision disorder - simulation	
	Color 1	Color 2	Color 1	Color 2
Protanopia	#344C51	#704E53		
Deuteranopia	#4CBCAB	#FA86BC		
Tritanopia	#DD607B	#DB6D00		

vision disorder, Vischeck simulation software was used. It should be noticed that due to its nature, colorblindness concerns subjective perceptions, so any kind of simulation should be perceived as illustrative only.

6 Conclusions and Future Work

The proposed algorithm allows in theory to generate almost any combination of color pairs which can be used for colorblindness detection. However, it should be noticed that colorblindness is a very individual vision disorder and the ability to distinguish between two colors may be different even among people who are e.g. deutans (suffering from deuteranopia). Therefore the quality of generated quodlibets should be verified experimentally.

The quodlibets generated by described algorithm may be used in any diagnostic method which allows user to compare with each other two color elements, e.g. arrangement method. Experimental results of implementing quodlibets into diagnostic process may be found in paper [6]. The results of those experiments seem promising, although still require some more research to be done.

There are several issues to be solved in the near future:

- What is the optimal value of JND to distinguish dichromat from anomalous trichromat?
- May this algorithm be used for generating control group (distinguishable by anyone) for quodlibets?

The described algorithm can serve as an basis and relatively cheap alternative to currently used colorblindness tests. Limiting generated color pairs to sRGB color spaces allows using quodlibets in any context, e.g. as a replacement of original colors in computer implementation of certain colorblindness detection method.

References

1. Birch, J.: Diagnosis of Defective Colour Vision. Elsevier, Amsterdam (2003)
2. Dain, S.J.: Clinical colour vision tests. Clin. Exp. Optom. **87**(4–5), 276–293 (2004)
3. Fluck, D.: Color Blindness Tests (2010). http://www.colblindor.com/2010/03/23/color_blindness_tests. Accessed
4. French, A.L., et al.: The evolution of colour vision testing. Aust. Orthoptic J. **40**(2), 7–15 (2008)
5. Gündogan, N.U., Durmazlar, N., Gümüş, K., Ozdemir, P.G., Altintaş, A.G., Durur, I., Acaroglu, G.: Projected color slides as a method for mass screening test for color vision deficiency (a preliminary study). Int. J. Neurosci. **115**(8), 1105–1117 (2005)
6. Khan, M.A., Joshi, D., Pawan, G.K.: Colour vision testing for selection of civil and military pilots in india: a comparative study of four different testing methods. Indian J. Aerosp. Med. **56**(2), 1–8 (2012)
7. Laskowski, M.: A comparative cost and accuracy analysis of selected colorblindness detection methods. Actual Probl. Econ. **3**(141), 327–333 (2013)

8. Laskowski, M.: Automation of colorblindness detection in computer-based screening test. In: Dregvaite, G., Damasevicius, R. (eds.) Information and Software Technologies. CCIS, vol. 538, pp. 45–56. Springer, Heidelberg (2015)

9. Mokrzycki, W., Tatol, M.: Color difference Delta E – a survey. Mach. Graph. Vis. **20**(4), 383–411 (2011)

10. Pokorny, J., Smith, V.C.: Color matching and color discrimination. In: Shevell, S.K. (red.) The Science of Color, 2nd edn. Optical Society of America, Oxford (2003)

11. Pridmore, R.W.: Orthogonal relations and color constancy in dichromatic colorblindness. PLoS ONE **9**(9), e107035 (2014). doi:10.1371/journal.pone.0107035

12. Spalding, J.A.B.: Confessions of a colour blind physician. Clin. Exp. Optom. **87**(4–5), 344–349 (2004)

13. Wyszecki, G., Stiles, W.S.: Color Science. Concepts and Methods, Quantitative Data and Formulae, 2nd edn. Wiley, New York (2000)

Analysis of Selected Elements of a Rower's Posture Using Motion Capture – a Case Study

Jerzy Montusiewicz[1(✉)], Jakub Smolka[1], Maria Skublewska-Paszkowska[1],
Edyta Lukasik[1], Katarzyna R. Baran[1], and Izabela Pszczola-Pasierbiewicz[2]

[1] Institute of Computer Science, Lublin University of Technology,
Nadbystrzycka St. 38D, 20-618 Lublin, Poland
{j.montusiewicz,jakub.smolka,maria.paszkowska,e.lukasik,
katarzyna.baran}@pollub.pl
[2] Department of Physical Education and Sport, Lublin University of Technology,
Lublin, Poland
i.pszczola-pasierbiewicz@pollub.pl

Abstract. The paper presents research on the motion capture of rowers practising on the Concept II Indoor Rower ergometer, using a motion capture device produced by the Vicon company, as well as a wireless heart rate monitor. The aim of the article is to analyse and assess the extent of variation of the angular position of the rower's back at different phases of rowing and in different degrees of fatigue. The back's position during rowing was recorded using three markers: one being a component of the Plug-in Gait model (T10) and two additional ones (marked as S1 and S2). The results obtained with the motion capture system allow to clearly identify the degree of training of the subjects studied, their fatigue and rowing technique on the basis of the analysis of changes in the inclination of the back in different positions of the successive phases of rowing.

Keywords: Motion capture · Ergometer rowing · Study of body motion · Spine angle

1 Introduction

It is hard in today's world of sport to imagine responsible coaching of players without introducing modern technologies in support of the process of training. One possible solution is to use methods of registration of the three-dimensional movement of an athlete's whole body and its individual components (arms, legs, head, individual joints, shoulders, etc.). Having a recording of the position of selected elements of the competitor's body at successive intervals of its motion allows precise analysis of the position of individual body parts. Registration of movement using passive optical motion capture system makes it possible to generate reference trajectories. Thus master players can be compared as to their movement with amateurs. It also allows to define qualitative and quantitative measures reflecting the relative positions of selected parts of the body of a single player. Detailed analysis of the designated trajectories, as well as other measures

© Springer International Publishing Switzerland 2016
G. Dregvaite and R. Damasevicius (Eds.): ICIST 2016, CCIS 639, pp. 107–118, 2016.
DOI: 10.1007/978-3-319-46254-7_9

used, permits the assessment of the player's fitness level from the point of view of the correctness of his or her motor technology, or so-called muscle memory.

In this study of rowers the optical Motion Capture (MC) system from Vicon was used to register three-dimensional movement. Moreover, a heart rate monitor was applied as well as an ergometer where the exercise was carried out. The entire study was conducted in the Laboratory of Motion Analysis and Interface Ergonomics of the Institute of Computer Science at the Lublin University of Technology, which was opened in 2014. The record of the signal from the heart rate monitor and the MC system allows to search for correlations between the biomechanical properties of specific players, their technical skills and individually permissible training load. The possibility of combining the results of the research will allow, among other things, to develop individual training plans for individual athletes.

The authors set themselves the research objective involving the correlation of the angular position of the back of the player in different phases of the cycle of rowing with his effort (exertion) while overcoming the subsequent declared distances to be covered.

It should be noted that the introduction of the test equipment allowing the digital three-dimensional mapping of the rowers' spatial movement leads to a significant increase in the accuracy of the data gathered as compared to traditional technologies such as a video or digital image. By using modern MC technology the obtained results are stored directly in the form of spatial coordinates, which allows immediate treatment. In previous solutions we had to perform a vectorisation, which has always been fraught with greater or lesser error of the conversion process from raster to vector image.

2   Overview of Similar Work

Propelling a boat with oars along a stretch of water is something other than rowing on an ergometer. Rowing ergometer is a sports discipline in which regional competitions and national championships are held, e.g. in the academic environment. Nevertheless water rowers very often, especially off season, use the ergometer to maintain the correct state of fitness. The differences between the kinematics of rowers exercising on a Concept II ergometer and real on-watering were examined in [9]. The results of studies of biomechanical parameters and the movement effectiveness and efficiency of legs and hands in rowers were presented in [1, 3, 11, 16]. Baudouin [2], without using MC, analysed the rower's posture on the boat and the location of the oars in various phases of rowing on the basis of theoretical models developed.

The biomechanical analysis of rowers is described in [4] (using an electromagnetic device), [21] (using acquisition systems) and in [13, 19] (with a wireless motion system based on accelerometers). The main aspects that deal with rowing simulation and Skills Professional Rowing Indoor Training (SPRINT) are presented in [7].

Cerne and others [5] used the optical system of Optotrak Certus (14 markers attached with wires to the recording station) to study the biomechanical parameters associated with the technique of rowing on a Concept II type ergometer. They took measurements of the trajectory of the ergometer rod, the rower's back tilt, speed and accuracy of rowing. In addition, they measured the length of the rowing cycle, the strength of rowing and the pressure exerted by the rower on the ergometer footrests. The study involved three groups of rowers: experienced, beginners and amateurs. The research program included measurements of three different samples: the rate of 20 strokes/min for 60 s, of 26 strokes/min and 34 strokes/min for 30 s. The authors showed that the movement of the rod and the angle of the trunk at the beginning of the ramp-up phase of experienced and novice rowers are constant and independent of the speed of rowing. In addition, the study showed that the technique of rowing of amateurs varies at different times of rowing.

In [20] Sforza and others investigated the relationship between anthropometry and rowing kinematics (similar to Panjkota in [15]). Using an optoelectronic system (21 markers affixed to the body of the rowers), at the sampling frequency of 120 Hz, they recorded the movements of professional rowers (men and women), rowing at the rate of 28 strokes/min. The results of the study showed that the average slope of the thoracic spine was 52° in the catch position and 120° in the finish position. Lamb [12] and Nolte [14] believe that trunk inclination is the most important parameter of body posture during the stroke.

Fothergill [8] studied the consolidation of appropriate behaviour in athletes rowing an ergometer built through a system that addressed real-time visual information on the technique of rowing. The measures used by the author are: force, efficiency, approximated similarity to ideal performance and consistency.

Jones et al. [10], using the Swedish MC system Qualisys, studied at the sampling frequency of 60 Hz the effect of rowers' lower limbs work on two different rowing ergometers: Concept II and RowPerfect. The test results indicated that the structure of the RowPerfect ergometer is better suited for recreational use than Concept II.

In [18] investigated the usefulness of the SPRINT training platform consisting of an ergometer and the virtual environment displayed on the monitor. In the mind of the authors the platform is useful to conduct training classes especially for beginners when it includes systems of capturing different measures defining the rower's effort and movements. This virtual environment was used to assess the technique (e.g. motion timing, spatial accuracy and intrapersonal coordination), energy (boat speed profiles, power output and oxygen consumption) or team coordination.

The authors use a laboratory stand which increases the possibility of mapping the movement of the rower through the use of more sophisticated biomechanical model consisting of 41 markers (compared to 14 in [5] and 21 in [15]). In addition to the parameters captured by the microprocessor installed in the ergometer recorded the rower's heart rate at different times of rowing. The authors studied the position of the subject's back in 4 different phases of the cycle of rowing: P1 – catch, P2 – leg drive, P3 – finish and P5 – body over (the terminology of [10]), which had not yet been performed. Moreover, the study was conducted after doing the subsequent partial distances, so one could indirectly determine the rower's fatigue resulting from his entry into the anaerobic stage of the exercise. Comparing the position of the back, heart rate, power and other performance parameters of a professional rower and an amateur made it possible to determine the state of their fatigue during rowing.

3   Description of the Test

Research on ergometer rowing was conducted in the Laboratory of Motion Analysis and Interface Ergonomics (LMAIE) of the Institute of Computer Science at the Lublin University of Technology. The test stand consisted of a 3D motion acquisition system, an ergometer with a system recording the device's parameters and a heart rate monitor.

The study used an optical system from Vicon built of 8 T40S type cameras operating in the near infrared (measuring frequency of 100 Hz), two reference Bonita video cameras and a Giganet hub collecting data to a desktop computer. To calibrate the system, data logging and primary processing, the Nexus software from Vicon was used, version 2.0 from 2014. The system records the movement of the markers placed on the body of a subject, provided that they are seen by at least two infrared cameras. Two additional reference cameras record video, which is essential when processing data and generating video files that contain an integrated video and biomechanical model of man.

The study used the world-renowned Concept II Indoor Rower ergometer. The built-in microprocessor system with a Performance Monitor 4 (PM 4) allows to control the effects of rowing in real time. As a result, the rower can observe the values displayed directly on the monitor and in part control his activities. The parameters displayed are: rate of rowing, distance travelled, work performed, exercise duration and power. In the ergometer used it is possible to regulate the amount of air flow through the structure, which is suitable for use by rowers of different gender, age, body weight and degree of fitness [6].

At the height of the rower's chest the Suunto Dual Comfort Belt is fitted with a device for measuring pulse. The measurement results are transmitted wirelessly to the Suunto Quest watch placed on the subject's hand and to the Movescount site, which allows for their proper processing. During training the watch, apart from the current value of the pulse, also shows additional information (e.g.: workout intensity or tips regarding the obtained flow velocity).

4   Research Methodology

The study of an ergometer rower is a performance test, allowing to conduct multiple analyses of the biomechanical parameters. The study used a procedure developed and presented in [22]. The pilot study conducted there allowed these authors to modify and better adapt it to current research. The procedure consists of 4 stages divided into several steps.

The optical MC system applied requires the placement on the subject's skin of retroreflective markers with a hypoallergenic bilateral tie. Many of them are put on specific bone tabs, the position of which may be slightly different in different people. Their proper location is very important and requires a lot of experience of the research team. At the beginning, the tape with the heart rate monitor is placed on the body. To place the markers the biomechanical Plug-in Gait Model [17] was used. According to it, 39 markers are placed on the rower's body, adding 2 more on the spine in order to better examine the subject's posture (Fig. 1b). Due to the fact that the heart rate monitor is positioned exactly at the point where there should be two markers, they are attached to the fixing band and the heart rate monitor. The Plug-in Gait Model, properly applied, can calculate a number of different measures of a biomechanical model, including angles, moments and forces in the joints of a subject.

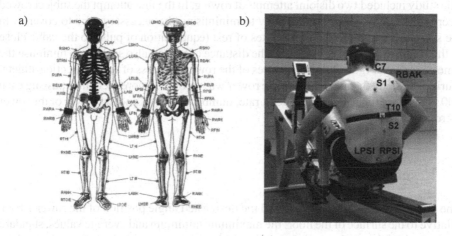

Fig. 1. Distribution of markers: (a) Plug-in Gait Model details [17]; (b) on the rower's back

The study involved two participants: a rower (age 29, weight 80.0 kg, height 182 cm) of the Academic Sports Association (AZS) and a non-rower (age 37, weight 78.5, height 185 cm). Participants in the experiment were briefed about the study and agreed to participate in it. The participants had a similar Rate of weight to height index (BMI): 22.94 kg/m^2 and 24.15 kg/m^2. These individuals presented a different level of motor skills and abilities to exercise and one of them was an amateur, while the other an AZS athlete.

Doing a preliminary test on a person rowing along the distance of 100 m helped to analyse the nature of the subject's exercise and make basic measurements. These included the estimated total time required for covering a specified distance (for different players this ranged from 20 to 25 s), the number of rowing cycles, (about 14) and the approximate duration of a single cycle (on average about 1.4 s). On this basis it was assumed that the optimum resolution value of the T40S cameras will be 100 Hz. At this frequency of recording a rower's motion the successive frames store the subject's position at intervals of about 2 cm. Such an accuracy of motion capture allows for carrying out quantitative analyses in future.

Due to the sensitivity of the T40S cameras to glare appearing in their area of operation, care must be taken to eliminate reflexes from both the rower's attire and the surfaces of the ergometer. The appearance of random artefacts that are not a reflection of markers placed on the body of the rower significantly impedes data processing. The motion registration process is carried out automatically, but the time of switching the system on and off is determined by the operator. The recordings are always associated with a particular player.

5   Implementation of Research

The study included two disjoint attempts at rowing. In the first attempt the subject rowed over a distance of 100 m with a view to minimising the necessary time to cover it. In the second attempt, after a few minutes of rest (equalisation of pulse to the value close to the original), the rower overcame the distance of 500 m, also seeking to minimise the time of rowing. Figure 3 shows pictures of the rowing process of an AZS section athlete. During the study the movement of the rower was recorded; moreover, after passing each 100 m distance the rowing time, heart rate, number of moves and the power of the rower were measured.

6   Results and Discussion

The quantitative assessment analysed the designated angle position of the rower's back relative to the surface of the floor: the maximum, minimum and average values, standard deviation and the total range of variation taking into account their successive positions in repeated cycles of rowing after successive hundred-metre distances.

Non-rower Case Study. Table 1 shows the data obtained from the ergometer and heart rate monitor with a single amateur rowing at distances of 100 and 500 m.

Table 1. Results of the ergometer and heart rate monitor at distances of 100 and 500 m for a non-rower

Distance [m]	Distance 100 m	Distance 500 m				
		100	200	300	400	500
Time [sec]	20.3	20.4	20.7	21.9	23.5	24.4
Tempo [sec/500 m]	101.5	103.5	109.5	117.5	122.0	129.5
Number of strokes [spm]	41	41	41	41	33	29
Power [W]	335	330	316	267	216	193
Heart rate at start [bpm]	109	132	174	184	187	189
Heart rate at end of [bpm]	172	174	184	187	189	189
Average heart rate [bpm]	138	132	174	184	187	189

Throughout the distance of 300 m the non-rower maintained a fixed number of strokes (41) generating a decreasing power (down from 335 W to 267 W, 19%). This indicates that the pulling phase is getting longer (apparent fatigue) with respect to the phase of return (which remains fast). With rowing for another 200 m the rate drops dramatically (down to 29 spm), which indicates entering the partly anaerobic stage of the exercise. From the moment overcoming the distance of 300 m the rate is clearly declining (the time to overcome the distance increases to 129.5 s at the end of the experiment, an increase of 25% in relation to the initial value). In the vicinity of the distance of 300 m the heartbeat, which was earlier rapidly increasing, stabilised at a submaximum level (184 bpm). Over further completed distances it increases slightly, since the player is no longer able to generate more power because of increasing fatigue.

In the process of rowing it is possible to isolate ramp-up time and exercise time. The preliminary studies indicate that the ramp-up time leading to achieving a rated speed of rowing/flow does not usually last longer than 2 cycles. When calculating the angles, the first two cycles were thus omitted in overcoming the total distance of both 100 and 500 m. To determine the position of the back of interest to us and its angles, the analysis of markers S1 and S2 was used. The values calculated for an amateur are shown in Table 2.

Table 2. Average values and standard deviations (SD) of the inclination angle of the non-rower's back over distances of 100 and 500 m

Distance [m]	P1[°] (±SD)	P2[°] (±SD)	P3[°] (±SD)	P5[°] (±SD)
single 100	94.18 (±4.15)	101.84 (±3.60)	120.12 (±4.24)	101.93 (±6.50)
[0–100]	91.53 (±7.52)	94.97 (±4.56)	118.49 (±4.31)	100.57 (±6.58)
[100–200]	96.80 (±4.29)	98.40 (±2.82)	122.47 (±2.32)	107.64 (±3.38)
[200–300]	90.18 (±2.62)	96.72 (±2.10)	116.34 (±4.80)	99.39 (±4.90)
[300–400]	85.36 (±3.48)	92.24 (±1.79)	112.82 (±4.78)	91.95 (±3.34)
[400–500]	81.97 (±2.73)	91.55 (±2.22)	112.34 (±4.33)	86.62 (±2.20)

A comparison of the average values of the inclination angle of the rower's back at a distance of 100 m in both research trials (Table 2) shows that the research was carried out correctly. After the first phase of rowing, the rest was long enough for the rower's body to recover. The difference between the measured values of the angles was not significant.

The range and the average values of the angles of the consecutive positions of the back for a non-rower over distances of 500 m are shown in Fig. 2. The symbol D100 stands for the distance [0–100], D200 – [100–200] and similarly the successive symbols.

Analysis of the angles of the back's position of a non-professional (Fig. 2) shows that for the distances greater than 200 m there is a clear tendency of change in the value of the determined angle for all recorded positions. The values of the angles of the back's inclination for the first 100 m distance are characterised by significantly higher values of the range of variation than for the subsequent 100 m stretches. For the P1 position it is even 27°, which represents 23% of the average.

This demonstrates the unconsolidated rowing technique during acceleration on the ergometer. The greatest volatility was observed for the P2 position (from 7° to 17°). The results obtained show that from the distance of 300 m there is a growing rower fatigue, described in the performance evaluation in Table 1. This fatigue is also manifested in significant changes in the angle of the back's position (Table 2), which indicates a crisis technique of rowing.

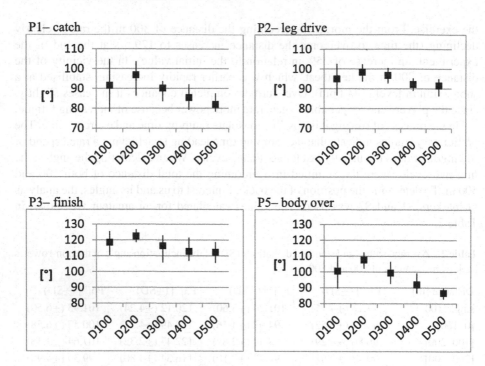

Fig. 2. The average values and ranges in degrees of the angle of the back's inclination for a non-rower over distances of 500 m

Rower Case Study. The microcomputer results of the ergometer and pulsometer (Table 3) obtained by a professional explicitly prove his better retraining than a non-rower's (e.g. for the distance of the first 100 m: generating higher power values by 90%, increased number of strokes by 44%, shorter time to overcome the distance of 19%).

Table 3. Results of the ergometer and heart rate monitor at distances of 100 and 500 m for a rower

Distance [m]	Distance 100 m	Distance 500 m				
		100	200	300	400	500
Time [sec]	16.4	16.8	16.4	16.7	17.5	18.5
Tempo [sec/500 m]	82	84	82	83.5	87.5	92.5
Number of strokes [spm]	59	50	48	50	48	49
Power [W]	635	591	635	601	522	442
Heart rate at start [bpm]	97	116	155	170	171	173
Heart rate at end of [bpm]	156	155	170	171	173	175
Average heart rate [bpm]	124	134	165	171	173	175

The calculated values of the inclination angle of the rower's back for different positions on the ergometer, based on the S1 and S2 markers, are shown in Table 4.

Table 4. Average values and standard deviations of the inclination angle of the rower's back over distances of 100 m and 500 m

Distance	P1[°] (±SD)	P2[°] (±SD)	P3[°] (±SD)	P5[°] (±SD)
Single 100	59.72 (±4.14)	91.61 (±2.18)	118.48 (±1.96)	78.39 (±1.16)
[0–100]	64.60 (±1.09)	91.29 (±1.14)	122.02 (±2.03)	79.66 (±1.22)
[100–200]	64.08 (±0.57)	91.46 (±0.95)	123.00 (±0.72)	80.81 (±0.96)
[200–300]	64.17 (±0.46)	91.33 (±1.14)	121.12 (±1.11)	80.37 (±0.89)
[300–400]	64.53 (±0.68)	93.90 (±1.45)	117.57 (±1.54)	80.37 (±1.08)
[400–500]	64.43 (±0.54)	92.58 (±1.33)	116.24 (±2.22)	80.57 (±2.76)

The calculated values of the inclination angle of the rower's back while overcoming the distance of 500 m (Table 4) and their small standard deviation (from 0.46 to 2.76) explicitly prove a correct and well-established technique of rowing. The highest SD values (from 1.09 to 2.03) are shown in the initial period (first 100 meters) when the player accelerates, and at the end of the distance (the last 100 meters), when fatigue sets in (from 0.54 to 2.76). In the remaining distance of 100 m to 400 m it is only from 0.46 to 1.54.

The angle values in successive positions over a distance of 100 m are shown in Fig. 3.

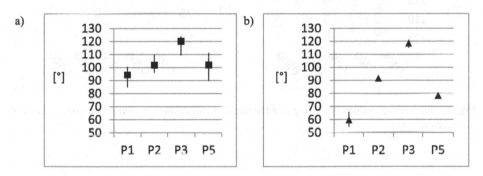

Fig. 3. The average values and ranges of the angle of the back's inclination over distances of 500 m for: a) a non-rower; b) rower

Comparison of the back's inclination angles over a distance of 100 m for a non-rower (■) and rower (▲) clearly shows the significance of differences in performance values in positions P1, P2 and P5. The average value of the inclination of the back for both players in position P3 (finish) differs slightly (120.12/118.48). The obtained result corresponds to the test carried out by Sforza [20], who stated that the angle can reach even 120°.

Figure 4 shows a comparison of the mean values of the back's inclination for highlighted items for the distance of 500 m for both players.

The results show that there are significant differences between the values of the angle of the back's inclination obtained by a rower and non-rower in all positions of the distances considered.

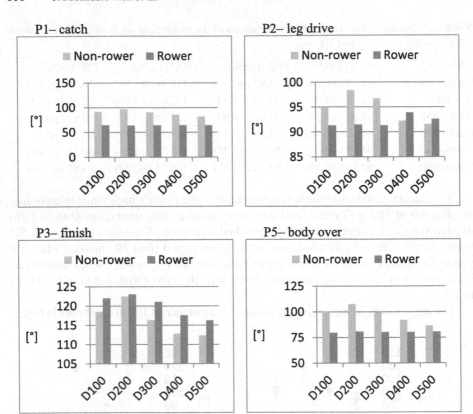

Fig. 4. The average values of the angle of the back's inclination for a non-rower and rower over distances of 500 m

The values of these angles in the case of a rower are stable or changing them is not significant for position P1 (64.08°–64.60°) and P5 (79.66°–80.81°). With regard to position P2 the differences are becoming significant at the distances (64.08°–64.60°) and P5 (79.66°–80.81°), reflecting the impact of rower fatigue setting in. In position P3 differences in the angle values for all distance numbers (D1-D5) were significant. The value of the inclination angle of the rower's back in position P1 is approximately 59.7° (Table 4) and is greater by 12° than the value given by Sforza [20]. The difference of the values obtained is presumably due to the fact that the cited study involved an experiment involving both men and women. In addition, the research was conducted at a twice smaller value of strokes made by a competitor 28 spm, compared to 59 spm in the present study.

Analysis of the results relating to a non-rower shows that in all positions of the subject and at all distances a change in the angle of the back's inclination was significant. Moreover, the resulting angle values were significantly different from those obtained a rower.

7 Summary

Motion capture using the eponymous MC method by Vicon, carried out according to the proposed scenario involving the calculation of the inclination angle of the subject's back in its various positions (P1 – catch, P2 – leg drive, P3 – finish, P5 – body over) at successively overcome partial distances (D1-D5) of a route measuring 500 m can clearly distinguish the degree of training of the subjects studied. For this purpose, the analysis of positions P1, P2 and P5 should be used.

Changes in the angle values of the inclination of the back for a non-rower are significant for all analysed positions (P1, P2, P3 and P5) at all partial distances and properly reflect a subject's state of fatigue and technical deficiencies in rowing.

Calculated values of the angle of the subject's back, obtained from the data recorded by the MC system properly correlate with the values from the ergometer and pulsometer microcomputer, which allows to draw valid conclusions on the rowing skills of the people trained. A non-rower's state of fatigue and entering the partly anaerobic stage of the exercise occurs after covering some 300 m of the route.

Future plans include research on a much more numerous group of rowers.

Acknowledgment. The research program titled "Optimization of training ergometer rowers based on the analysis of 3D motion data, EMG, ergometer and heart rate", realized in the Laboratory of Motion Analysis and Interface Ergonomics was approved by the Commission for Research Ethics, No. 7/2015 dated 12.11.2015.

References

1. Baker, J., Gal, J., Davies, B., Bailey, D., Morgan, R.: Power output of legs during high intensity cycle ergometry: influence of hand grip. J. Sci. Med. Sport 4(1), 10–18 (2001)
2. Baudouin, A., Hawkins, D.: A biomechanical review of factors affecting rowing performance. Br. J. Sports Med. **36**, 396–402 (2002)
3. Buckeridge, E., Hinslop, S., Bull, A., McGregor, A.: Kinematic asymmetries of the lower limbs during ergometer rowing. Med. Sci. Sport Exerc. **44**(11), 2147–2153 (2012)
4. Bull, M.J., McGregor, A.H.: Measuring spinal motion in rowers: the use of an electromagnetic device. Clin. Biomech. **15**, 772–776 (2000)
5. Cerne, T., Kamnik, R., Vesnicer, B., Gros, J.Z., Munih, M.: Differences between elite, junior and non-rowers in kinematic and kinetic parameters during ergometer rowing. Hum. Mov. Sci. **32**, 691–707 (2013)
6. The Concept II ergometer user guide
7. Filippeschi, A., Ruffaldi, E.: Boat dynamics and force rendering models for the SPRINT system. IEEE Trans. Hum. Mach. Syst. **43**(6), 631–642 (2013)
8. Fothergill, S.: Examining the effect of real-time visual feedback on the quality of rowing technique. Procedia Eng. **2**, 3083–3088 (2010)
9. Geng, R., Li, J.S., Gu, Y.: Biomechanical evaluation of two rowing training methods. Vibr. Struct. Eng. Meas. Book Ser. Appl. Mech. Mater. **105–107**, 283–285 (2012)
10. Jones, A., Allanson-Bailey, L., Jones, M.D., Holt, C.A.: An ergometer based study of the role of the upper limbs in the female rowing stroke. Procedia Eng. **2**, 2555–2561 (2010)

11. Kurihara, K.: Optical motion capture system with pan-tilt camera tracking and real-time data processing. In: ICRA, pp. 1241–1248 (2002)
12. Lamb, D.H.: A kinematic comparison of ergometer and on-water rowing. Am. J. Sports Med. **17**, 367–373 (1989)
13. Llosa, I., Vilajosana, X., Vilajosana, J.: Manuel marquès, design of a motion detector to monitor rowing performance based on wireless sensor networks. In: 2009 International Conference on Intelligent Networking and Collaborative Systems, pp. 397–400 (2009)
14. Nolte, V.: Rowing faster, pp. 125–140. Human Kinetics Inc., Champaign (2011)
15. Panjkota, A., Stancic, I., Supuk, T.: Outline of a qualitative analysis for the human motion in case of ergometer rowing. In: Rudas, I., Demiralp, M., Mastorakis, N. (eds.) WSEAS International Conference Mathematics and Computers in Science and Engineering Proceedings. no. 5. WSEAS (2009)
16. Pelz, P., Verge, A.: Validated biomechanical model for efficiency and speed of rowing. J. Biomech. **47**(13), 3415–3422 (2014)
17. Plug-in Gait Model. http://www.irc-web.co.jp/vicon_web/news_bn/PIGManualver1.pdf
18. Ruffaldi, E., Filippeschi, A.: Structuring a virtual environment for sport training: a case study on rowing technique. Robot. Auton. Syst. **61**(4), 390–397 (2013)
19. Ruffaldi, E., Peppoloni, L., Filippeschi, A.: Sensor fusion for complex articulated body tracking applied in rowing. Proc. Inst. Mech. Eng. Part P-J. Sports Eng. Technol. **229**(2), 92–102 (2015)
20. Sforza, C., Casiraghi, E., Lovecchio, N., Galante, D., Ferrario, V.F.: A Three-Dimensional Study of Body Motion During Ergometer Rowing. Open Sports Med. J. **6**, 22–28 (2012)
21. Schranza, G., Tomkinsona, T., Oldsa, N.: Daniella: three-dimensional anthropometric analysis: differences between elite australian rowers and the general population. J. Sports Sci. **28**(5), 459–469 (2010)
22. Skublewska-Paszkowska, M., Montusiewicz, J., Łukasik, E., Pszczoła-Pasierbiewicz, I., Baran, K.R., Smolka, J., Pueo, B.: Motion capture as a modern technology for analysing ergometer rowing. Adv. Sci. Technol. Res. J. **10**(29), 132–140 (2016)

Analysis of Pulmonary and Hemodynamic Parameters for the Weaning Process by Using Fuzzy Logic Based Technology

Ugur Kilic[1(✉)], Mehmet Tahir Gulluoglu[2], Hasan Guler[3], and Turgay Kaya[3]

[1] Department of Avionics, School of Civil Aviation,
Erzincan University, Erzincan, Turkey
ugr_2323@hotmail.com
[2] Electrical Electronics Engineering Department,
Harran University, Sanliurfa, Turkey
mtahir@harran.edu.tr
[3] Electrical Electronics Engineering Department,
Firat University, Elazig, Turkey
{hasanguler, tkaya}@firat.edu.tr

Abstract. This study aims to achieve accurate weaning process which is very important for patient under mechanical ventilation. The developed weaning algorithm was designed on LabVIEW software and fuzzy system designer part of LabVIEW software was used during to develop that algorithm. The developed weaning algorithm has six input parameters which are maximum inspiratory pressure (MIP), tidal volume on spontaneous breathing (TVS), minute ventilation (VE), heart rate, respiration per minute (RPM) and body temperature. 20 clinical scenarios were generated by using Monte-Carlo simulations and Gaussian distribution method to evaluate performance of the developed algorithm. An expert clinician was involved to this process to evaluate the each generated clinic scenario to determine weaning probability for the each patient. Student t-test for $p < 0.05$ was used to show statistical difference between the developed algorithm and clinician's evaluation. According to student t-test, there is no statistical difference for 98.2 % probability between the developed algorithm and the clinician's evaluation of weaning probability.

Keywords: Mechanical ventilation · Weaning · Fuzzy system · Student t-test · Gaussion distribution · LabVIEW

1 Introduction

Currently, patients who have respiratory failure are supported with device called as mechanical ventilator (MV). Weaning from mechanical ventilation is important level of mechanical ventilation process that starts with mechanical ventilation for the patient who needs mechanical support. So patients do not need any mechanical ventilation support, this ventilation support for breathing should be decreased gradually. In other words, work of breathing should be transmitted from mechanical ventilator to the

© Springer International Publishing Switzerland 2016
G. Dregvaite and R. Damasevicius (Eds.): ICIST 2016, CCIS 639, pp. 119–131, 2016.
DOI: 10.1007/978-3-319-46254-7_10

patient. However, problem of this process is prediction of starting time for weaning from mechanical ventilation. If this process cannot be predicted correctly and patient weans early from mechanical ventilation, time delay and reintubation occur in this process. If patient weans lately from mechanical ventilation, time delay occurs again and patient may be addicted to the mechanical ventilator [1–3]. Weaning from mechanical ventilation is very important process during mechanical ventilation. This process is part of mechanical ventilation and it constitutes 40 % of all process [4]. Most of patient who have respiratory failure wean incorrectly from mechanical ventilation [5, 6]. Because of that, patients who have respiratory failure spend much more time in intensive care units (ICU) to wean from mechanical ventilation. Prolonged ventilation process causes time delay and also patients who have respiratory failure may be addicted to the mechanical ventilator especially after 3 months [7–9]. Most of studies about mechanical ventilation are mostly related to improving mechanical ventilator using in ICU's during mechanical ventilation process. On the other hand, weaning from mechanical ventilation process, how to reduce the duration of mechanical ventilation and its causes such as mortality, morbidity and the increased intensive care cost are the main objectives of this study. Weaning process should be carried out by the expert clinician, so weaning failures could be pretended. Many researchers have attempted to reduce the duration of MV and have declared reducing the weaning time by their defined protocols [10–12]. In literature, there are many predictors which determine weaning probability. However there are three type of weaning predictors which are examining most of studies and giving most accurate results among all predictors. These are rapid shallow breathing index (RSBI), pressure time index (PTI) and Jabour' weaning index (JWI) [13–15]. Owing to its ease of calculation, RSBI is widely used to determine weaning probability. If this calculated value of RSBI is below the threshold of 100 (breaths/min)/L, RSBI predicts weaning success with a sensitivity of up to 97 %. But its calculation is inefficient to predict right weaning time and its success rate is 48 % for the patients who have respiratory failures. In addition, with prolonged mechanical ventilation process the sensitivity of RSBI decreases [16–20]. RSBI uses linear approach for the prediction of this process. Other predictors using in weaning process in literature require more detailed respiratory parameters which are difficult to use for this process such as average inspiratory muscle pressure per breath, negative inspiratory pressure, inspiratory time, total breath duration, peak airway pressure. These vital physiological parameters for patient under mechanical ventilation can be measured and interpreted by some advanced systems [21].

In literature, there is no universally accepted weaning protocol in ICU's, thus clinicians analyze parameters for all patients who have respiratory failure and also try to predict right time to start weaning process. But this approach causes time delay, the increased intensive care cost and also causes incorrect prediction of weaning time. In this study, it was attempted to develop a new LabVIEW-fuzzy based weaning protocol for weaning from mechanical ventilation. Main objective of the study is to eliminate disadvantages of the predictors used in literature and also try to find new method for weaning process which is universally accepted. The weaning algorithm was designed in LabVIEW and also fuzzy system designer toolkit of LabVIEW was used for this aim. The reason of preferring the LabVIEW program is its graphic based structure and the ease provided to user in constituting interface. In addition, fuzzy logic controller can be easily created by using fuzzy system designer toolkit on LabVIEW software. Fuzzy logic controller was used during this process and the reason why using of fuzzy controller is that fuzzy logic controller gave better results comparing to conventional methods [22]. Six vital parameters were used to determine weaning probability. Three of them such as MIP, TVS and VE were used to determine adequate pulmonary function and the other parameters such as heart rate, RPM and body temperature were used to determine hemodynamic stability. Then adequate pulmonary function and hemodynamic stability determined the percentage of weaning probability. For determining the percentage of weaning probability, 20 clinical scenarios for six parameters were generated randomly by using LabVIEW software based on Monte-Carlo simulations and Gaussian distribution method. The randomly generated clinical scenarios were used in developed algorithm which gave the result of prediction time. An expert clinician was involved to this process to design of fuzzy system rule tables and the all membership functions for each rule block. In addition, clinician evaluated the each scenario, independently to analyze developed system. Finally, student t-test was used to show statistical difference between the developed algorithm and the clinician's evaluation for each patient. According to the obtained results, there is no statistical difference for 98.2 % probability between developed algorithm and clinician's evaluation.

2   Materials and Methods

Clinicians working in ICUs try to achieve accurate weaning process so as to decrease time delay, the increased intensive care cost, mortality and morbidity. Because of the fact that there is no universally accepted weaning protocol in ICU's, clinicians analyze all parameters for all patients who have respiratory failure and also try to predict right time to start weaning process. But this approach causes time delay and also causes incorrect prediction of weaning time. Incorrect prediction of weaning time causes to increase clinician's workload in ICUs. Thus in most of the studies, this inaccurate prediction for weaning time is reduced. The schematic outline of the developed protocol is given in Fig. 1. MIP, TVS and VE were used to determine adequate pulmonary function and heart rate, RPM and body temperature were used to determine hemodynamic stability. These two systems were also used to determine the final percentage of weaning probability.

2.1   Design of Fuzzy System for Adequate Pulmonary Function

Fuzzy system for adequate pulmonary function has three input such as MIP, TVS and VE. The membership functions of fuzzy inputs and output are given in Figs. 2, 3, 4 and 5 and the rule table of the adequate pulmonary function is given in Table 1. Fuzzy system for adequate pulmonary function has four kind of membership functions which are Z, P, S and L type membership functions. Defuzzifier part of the system accepts a set one from each rule consequent and defuzzification method was selected as center of area to calculate output of the fuzzy system.

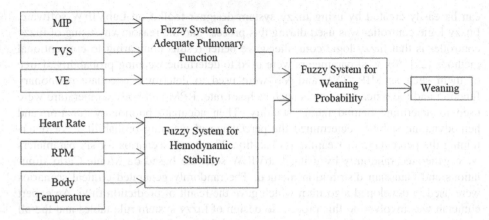

Fig. 1. The schematic outline of the developed algorithm

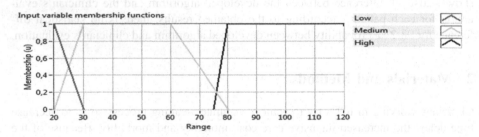

Fig. 2. MIP membership functions

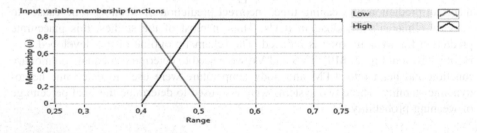

Fig. 3. TVS membership functions

An expert clinician involved in this study and the all rule table and the all membership functions were constituted with expert opinion and also have been asked to make determinations about range value of inputs. As previously described, fuzzy system for adequate pulmonary function has three input such as MIP, TVS and VE. MIP varies between 20 cmH$_2$O–120 cmH$_2$O, TVS varies between 0,25 L–0,75 L and VE varies between 5 L/min–20 L/min for patients who have respiratory failure. In addition, membership function rate of adequate pulmonary function varies between

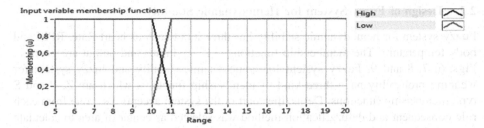

Fig. 4. VE membership functions

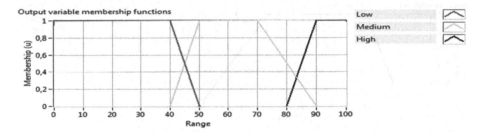

Fig. 5. Adequate pulmonary membership functions

Table 1. Rule table for adequate pulmonary function

MIP	TVS	VE	Adequate pulmonary function
Low	Low	Low	Low
Low	Low	High	Low
Low	High	High	Mcdium
Low	High	Low	Low
Medium	Low	Low	Low
Medium	Low	High	Medium
Medium	High	High	High
Medium	High	Low	Medium
High	Low	Low	Low
High	Low	High	High
High	High	High	High
High	High	Low	High

0–100 to determine adequate pulmonary function's output value. All input parameters data for each patient were generated randomly by using LabVIEW software based on Monte-Carlo simulations and Gaussian distribution method to evaluate performance of the developed algorithm.

2.2 Design of Fuzzy System for Hemodynamic Stability

Fuzzy system for hemodynamic stability has three input such as heart Rate, RPM and body temperature. The membership functions of fuzzy inputs and output are given in Figs. 6, 7, 8 and 9. Fuzzy system for hemodynamic stability and fuzzy system for weaning probability have three kind of membership functions which are Z, P and S type membership functions. Defuzzifier part of the system accepts a set one from each rule consequent and defuzzification method was selected as center of area to calculate output of the fuzzy system.

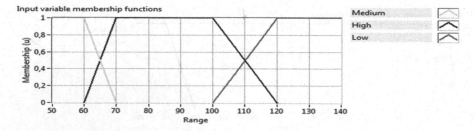

Fig. 6. Heart rate membership functions

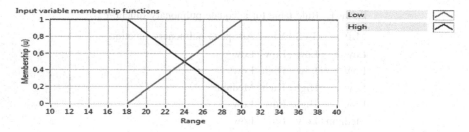

Fig. 7. RPM membership functions

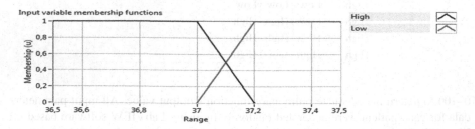

Fig. 8. Body temperature membership functions

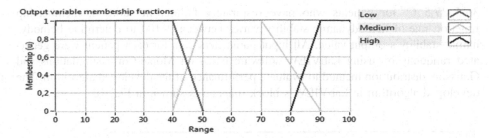

Fig. 9. Hemodynamic stability membership functions

The rule table of the hemodynamic stability is given in Table 2. In this study, Monte-Carlo simulation and Gaussian distribution method were used to generate random clinical scenarios. Gaussian distribution equation used in this algorithm is given in Eqs. 1–3 [23].

$$f\left(x; \mu; \sigma^2\right) = \frac{1}{\sigma\sqrt{2\pi}} * e^{\frac{-(x-\mu)^2}{2\sigma^2}} \tag{1}$$

$$z = \frac{x - \mu}{\sigma} \tag{2}$$

$$x = z\sigma + \mu \tag{3}$$

Where x is new data, z is standard normal distribution, μ is the mean value, σ^2 is the variance random value and σ is random value.

Table 2. Rule table for hemodynamic stability

Heart rate	RPM	Body temperature	Hemodynamic stability
Low	Low	Low	Low
Low	Low	High	Low
Low	High	Low	Low
Low	High	High	High
Medium	Low	Low	Low
Medium	Low	High	Medium
Medium	High	Low	Medium
Medium	High	High	High
High	Low	Low	Medium
High	Low	High	High
High	High	Low	High
High	High	High	High

As previously described, fuzzy system for hemodynamic stability has three input such as heart Rate, RPM and body temperature. Heart rate varies between 50–140 per minute, RPM varies between 10–40 per minute and body temperature varies between

36,5–37,5 C° for patients who have respiratory failure. In addition, membership function rate of hemodynamic stability varies between 0–100 to determine hemodynamic stability's output value. All input parameters data for each patient were generated randomly by using LabVIEW software based on Monte-Carlo simulations and Gaussian distribution method to evaluate performance of the developed algorithm. The developed algorithm in LabVIEW's block diagram is shown in Fig. 10.

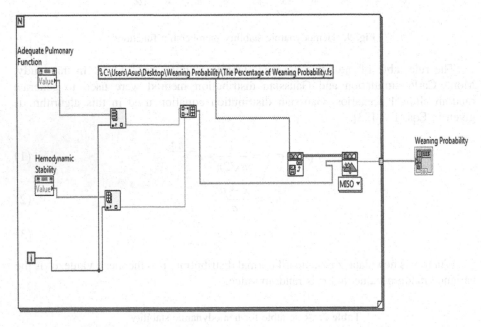

Fig. 10. The block diagram of the developed weaning algorithm

The output membership function of fuzzy system for weaning probability is given in Fig. 11 and the final rule table of fuzzy system for weaning probability is given in Table 3.

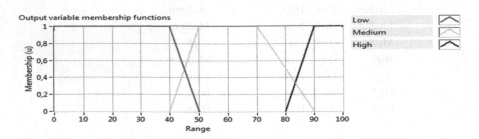

Fig. 11. Weaning probability membership functions

Table 3. Rule table for weaning probability

Adequate pulmonary function	Hemodynamic stability	Weaning probability
Low	Low	Low
Low	Medium	Low
Low	High	Medium
Medium	Low	Low
Medium	Medium	Medium
Medium	High	High
High	Low	Medium
High	Medium	High
High	High	High

The developed weaning algorithm that has six variables, and three rule blocks within two layers, has been designed and implemented over mathematical simulations and random clinical scenarios, to compare its behavior and performance in predicting the clinician's evaluation to weaning probability for patients who have respiratory failure. First rule block is adequate pulmonary function and MIP, TVS and VE are used as input to determine adequate pulmonary function's output value which varies between 0–100. Second rule block is hemodynamic stability and heart rate, RPM and body temperature are used as input to determine hemodynamic stability's output value which varies between 0–100. Third rule block is weaning probability and adequate pulmonary function's output value and hemodynamic stability's output value are used as input to determine weaning probability's output value which varies between 0–100.

3 Results

The developed algorithm gives the percentage of weaning probability for each of 20 patients according to the randomly generated clinical scenarios. In addition, clinician evaluated the each scenario and also clinician gave the percentage of weaning probability for each patients who have respiratory failure. Both of the results show success of the prediction time of weaning for the each patients. The results obtained from the developed algorithm and clinician's evaluation applied to student t-test for $p < 0.05$ and the obtained results are given in Table 4.

The Student's t-test was used to determine statistical difference, because it assesses whether the means of three groups are statistically different from each other. This test is appropriate for compare the means of two or more groups. Equations 4–6 were used to calculate the statistical difference between groups [24–27].

$$\bar{X} = \frac{\sum x}{n} \tag{4}$$

$$s^2 = \frac{\sum (x - \bar{x})^2}{n - 1} \tag{5}$$

Table 4. The obtained results from the developed weaning algorithm and clinician's evaluation

Patient data (P.D.)	The percentage of weaning probability (%)	The percentage of clinician's evaluation (%)
1st P.D.	94,234709	95
2nd P.D.	26,690792	25
3rd P.D.	32,889997	30
4th P.D.	45,453211	45
5th P.D.	32,465983	30
6th P.D.	22,593178	20
7th P.D.	44,197208	45
8th P.D.	32,644963	30
9th P.D.	41,588211	40
10th P.D.	62,853257	60
11th P.D.	87,459645	85
12th P.D.	82,358445	80
13th P.D.	75,665247	75
14th P.D.	28,487549	30
15th P.D.	70,596878	70
16th P.D.	61,861274	60
17th P.D.	96,996325	95
18th P.D.	50,322549	50
19th P.D.	63,988752	65
20th P.D.	70,167581	70

$$t = \frac{(\bar{x}_1 - \bar{x}_2)}{\sqrt{\frac{s_1^2}{n_1-1} + \frac{s_2^2}{n_2-1}}} \tag{6}$$

Where $\bar{x}$ is the arithmetic mean, S^2 is variance, t is the test formula, x is the investigated group and n is the number of data points in group. According to the results from the student t-test, there is no statistical difference for 98.2 % probability between the percentage of developed algorithm results and clinician evaluation for weaning probability.

4 Discussion

Patients who have respiratory failures need mechanical support during breathing. So patients do not need any mechanical ventilation support, this ventilation support should be decreased gradually. In other words, work of breathing should be transmitted from mechanical ventilator to the patient. Most of patients easily passes to spontaneous breathing. On the other hand, for some patients it is difficult to pass to spontaneous breating. Weaning process can take days or even weeks. Thus, some strategies need to be used during weaning process. If this process is carried out inaccurate and patient weans early or lately from mechanical ventilation; time delay, reintubation, addiction to mechanical ventilator, increased workload of clinician in ICU's and increased intensive care cost occur in this process. Thus, many biomedical researchers have tried to develop useful weaning protocol to predict right weaning time for the patients who have respiratory failure. In literature, there are many predictors which determine weaning probability. However there are three type of weaning predictors which are examining most of studies and giving most accurate results among all predictors and this predictors use linear approach. These predictors are rapid shallow breathing index (RSBI), pressure time index (PTI) and Jabour' weaning index (JWI). However, these predictors ignore many of the patients data which are very important for this process and also with prolonged mechanical ventilation sensitivity of this predictors decreases. For instance, RSBI is widely used to determine weaning probability, owing to its ease of calculation. However its calculation is inefficient to predict right weaning time and its success rate is 48 % for the patients who have respiratory failure. In addition, this predictors cannot be used in the ICUs because they have limited parameters to predict right weaning time and their prediction rate is very low. For more accurate results during this process, many of the parameters should be taken in considered.

Based on that there is no universally accepted weaning protocol in ICU's, it was tried to eliminate disadvantages of the predictors used in literature and tried to develop more accurate prediction algorithm in this paper. Fuzzy logic controller was used during this process and the reason why using of fuzzy controller is that fuzzy logic controller gave better results comparing to the conventional methods. Six vital parameters which are easy collected in ICU were used to determine weaning probability. Since the system has six parameters to predict weaning probability, some parameters were grouped. Otherwise, the fuzzy system would have 144 rules. However, after grouping, the all systems have 33 rules. MIP, TVS and VE were used to determine adequate pulmonary function, while heart rate, RPM and body temperature were used to determine hemodynamic stability. Finally, these two systems were used to determine weaning probability. 20 randomly clinical scenarios were generated by using LabVIEW software based on Monte-Carlo simulations and Gaussian distribution method to evaluate performance of the developed algorithm. These randomly generated patients data were applied to the fuzzy system by using LabVIEW software to evaluate performance of the developed algorithm. An expert clinician involved in this study and the all rule table and the all membership functions were constituted with expert opinion. In addition, clinician evaluated the each scenario and also clinician gave the percentage of weaning probability. Each randomly generated clinical scenario represented a patient in this study. The obtained results from the developed algorithm and clinician's evaluation applied to student t-test for $p < 0.05$ to show statistical difference. The results obtained from t-test, there is no statistical difference for 98.2 % probability between the developed algorithm and clinician's evaluation. As mentioned previously, an expert clinician involved in this study and evaluated the each scenario for each patient's input data. However, this approach normally causes to time delay, the increased intensive care cost, the increased workload of clinician in ICU's and incorrect prediction of weaning time. Hence, the main purpose of this study is to eliminate the all disadvantages of this approach.

Acknowledgements. This study is part of a project funded by FUBAP grant no. MF.13.21 and HUBAP grant no. 15130. The authors would like to thank Firat University Hospital-Anesthesia ICU doctors for their invaluable evaluations.

References

1. Hsu, J.C., Chen, Y.F., Du, Y.D., Huang, Y.F., Jiang, X., Chen, T.: Design of a clinical decision support for determining ventilator weaning using support vector machine. Int. J. Innovative Comput. Inf. Control **8**(1(B)), 933–952 (2012)
2. Brochard, L., Rauss, A., Benito, S., Conti, G., Mancebo, J., Rekik, N., Gasparetto, A., Lemaire, F.: Comparison of three methods of gradual withdrawal from ventilatory support during weaning from mechanical ventilation. Am. J. Respir. Crit. Care Med. **150**, 896–903 (1994)
3. Koyuncu, A., Yava, A., Kurkluoglu, M., Guler, A., Demirkilic, U.: Weaning from mechanical ventilation and nursing. Turk. J. Thorac. Cardiovasc. Surg. **19**(4), 671–681 (2011)
4. Esteban, A., Alia, I., Ibanez, J., et al.: Modes of mechanical ventilation and weaning. A national survey of Spanish hospitals. Chest **106**, 1188–1193 (1994)
5. Bates, J.H.T., Young, M.P.: Applying fuzzy logic to medical decision making in the intensive care unit. Am. J. Respir. Crit. Care Med. **167**, 948–952 (2003)
6. Eskandar, N., Apostolakos, M.J.: Weaning from mechanical ventilation. Crit. Care Clin. **23**(2), 263–274 (2007)
7. MacIntyre, N.R.: Evidence-based guidelines for weaning and discontinuing ventilatory support. Chest **120**, 375–396 (2001)
8. Esteban, A., Frutos, F., Tobin, M.J., Alia, I., Solsona, J.F., Valverdu, I., Fernandez, R., Cal, M.A.D.L., Benito, S., Tomas, R., Carriedo, D., Macias, S., Blanco, J.: A comparison of four methods of weaning patients from mechanical ventilation. N. Engl. J. Med. **332**, 345–350 (1995)
9. Krishnan, J.A., Moore, D., Robeson, C., Rand, C.S., Fessler, H.E.: A Prospective, controlled trial of a protocol-based strategy to discontinue mechanical ventilation. Am. J. Respir. Crit. Care Med. **169**, 673–678 (2004)
10. Guler, H., Ata, F.: Development of a fuzzy-based tidal volume algorithm for patients with respiratory distress. J. Fac. Eng. Archit. Gazi Univ. **29**(4), 699–706 (2014)
11. Bien, M.Y., Lin, Y.S., Shie, H.G., Yang, Y.L., Shih, C.H., Wang, J.H., Cheng, K.C.: Rapid Shallow Breathing Index and Its predictive accuracy measured under five different ventilatory strategies in the same patient group. Chin. J. Physiol. **53**(1), 1–10 (2010)
12. Yang, K.L., Tobin, M.J.: A prospective study of indexes predicting the outcome of trials of weaning from mechanical ventilation. N Engl. J. Med. **324**, 1445–1450 (1991)
13. Bien, M.Y., Hseu, S.S., Yien, H.W., Kuo, B.I., Lin, Y.T., Wang, J.H., Kou, Y.R.: Breathing pattern variability: a weaning predictor in postoperative patients recovering from systemic inflammatory response syndrome. Intensive Care Med. **30**(2), 241–247 (2004)
14. Vassilakopoulos, T., Zakynthinos, S., Roussos, C.: The tension-time index and the frequency/tidal volume ratio are the major pathophysiologic determinants of weaning failure and success. Am. J. Respir. Crit. Care Med. **158**(2), 378–385 (1998)
15. Bellemare, F., Grasino, A.: Effect of pressure and timing of contraction of the human diaphragm fatigue. J. Appl. Physiol. **53**, 1190–1195 (1982)

16. Nemoto, T., Hatzakis, G.E., Thorpe, C.W., Olivenstein, R., Dial, S., Bates, J.H.T.: Automatic control of pressure support mechanical ventilation using fuzzy logic. Am. J. Respir. Crit. Care Med. 160(2), 550–556 (1999)
17. Alia, I., Esteban, A.: Weaning from mechanical ventilation. Crit. Care 4(2), 72–80 (2000)
18. Butler, R., Keenan, S.P., Inman, K.J., Sibbald, W.J., Block, G.: Is there a preferred technique for weaning the difficult to wean patient? A systematic review of the literature. Crit. Care Med. 27(11), 2331–2336 (1999)
19. Ely, E.W., et al.: Effect on the duration of mechanical ventilation of identifying patients capable of breathing spontaneously. N Eng. J. Med. 335(25), 1864–1869 (1996)
20. Kilic, Y.A., Kilic, I.: A novel fuzzy logic inference system for decision support in weaning from mechanical ventilation. J. Med. Syst. 34(6), 1089–1095 (2010)
21. Wannenburg, J., Malekian, R.: Body sensor network for mobile health monitoring a diagnosis and anticipating system. IEEE Sens. J. 15(12), 6839–6852 (2015)
22. Wannenburg, J., Malekian, R.: Physical activity recognition from smartphone accelerometer data for user context awareness sensing. IEEE Trans. Syst. Man Cybern. Syst. PP(99), 1–8 (2016)
23. Kroese, D.P., Brereton, T., Taimre, T., Botev, Z.I.: Why the Monte Carlo method is so important today. WIREs Comput. Stat. 6, 386–392 (2014)
24. Guler, H., Turkoglu, I., Ata, F.: Designing intelligent mechanical ventilator and user interface using LabVIEW (R). Arab. J. Sci. Eng. 39(6), 4805–4813 (2014)
25. Guler, H., Ata, F.: Design of a fuzzy-labview-based mechanical ventilator. Comput. Syst. Sci. Eng. 29(3), 219–229 (2014)
26. Guler, H., Ata, F.: The comparison of manual and LabVIEW-based fuzzy control on mechanical ventilation. Proc. Inst. Mech. Eng. Part H-J. Eng. Med. 228(9), 916–925 (2014)
27. Guzel, S., Kaya, T., Guler, H.: LabVIEW -based analysis of EEG signals in determination of sleep stages. In: 23th Signal Processing and Communications Applications Conference (SIU), pp. 799–802 (2015)

Improving Business Processes in HIS by Adding Dynamicity

Diana Kalibatiene[1(✉)], Justas Trinkunas[1,2], Toma Rusinaite[1], and Olegas Vasilecas[1]

[1] Information Systems Research Laboratory, Vilnius Gediminas Technical University,
Vilnius, Lithuania
{diana.kalibatiene,justas.trinkumas,toma.rusinaite,
olegas.vasilecas}@vgtu.lt
[2] Information Systems Department, Informatics and Development Centre,
Vilnius University Hospital Santariskiu Klinikos, Vilnius, Lithuania

Abstract. Dynamic patient treatment (PT) processes are usually human-centric and often unique. Therefore, implemented PT processes into information system (IS) should be capable to adopt dynamically according to the real PT process changes at process instance runtime. Such processes are known as dynamic business processes (DBP). The problem of DBP modelling, simulation and execution has been actively investigated over the last few years, but existing approaches to DBP modelling, simulation and execution have been incomplete, i.e. they lack theory and/or a case study or both. Moreover, a question of implementation of the DBP modelling, execution and simulation is left without an answer. This paper presents a DBP modelling and simulation approach, which is realised in Hospital Santariskiu Klinikos and a PT process case study is conducted. The results obtained shows that the proposed approach and its implementation are suitable for DBP modelling and simulation in HIS (Health Information System).

Keywords: Process automation · Dynamic business process · Rules · Context · Hospital information system · HIS (Health Information System) · Treatment schema

1 Introduction

Business processes (BP) in hospital are changing due to changes in the environment of business systems, new treatment methods and new law enforcement. These changes should be implemented very fast because it is necessary to adapt in fast changing environment, maintain competitiveness and improve quality. Usually it requires a lot of resources (time, people, and finance) to implement new changes, because usually it is needed not only to reprogram the software, but also to change the BP components: activities (their contents, consistency and executors), business rules, decision nodes. It is desirable that the changes are implemented at the BP runtime in order to execute dynamic business processes (DBP).

© Springer International Publishing Switzerland 2016
G. Dregvaite and R. Damasevicius (Eds.): ICIST 2016, CCIS 639, pp. 132–147, 2016.
DOI: 10.1007/978-3-319-46254-7_11

Therefore, traditional approaches used to model, simulate and execute BP, like patient treatment (PT), are not flexible enough to cover the actual needs of the business. To fulfil this gap, we need an approach for DBP modelling and a tool.

As advocated in a number of papers, business rules and context-awareness, like in [1–3], are applicable for ensuring the dynamicity of BP. Therefore, existing approaches are reviewed in Sect. 2.

In our previous researches [4], we have proposed an approach for rules- and context-based DBP modelling and simulation. In this paper, we present the refined DBP modelling and simulation approach and adopt it to the PT process.

The rest of the paper is organized as follows. Section 2 presents related works on DBP and Health care IS. Section 3 presents our proposed requirements of DBP and approach for DBP modelling and simulation. Section 4 presents a case study of patient treatment HIS by using dynamic processes and rules. Section 5 concludes the paper.

2 Related Works

2.1 Concept of a Dynamic Business Process

Research related to DBP is becoming increasingly important for the past several years. However, concept of DBP still has no clear unified definition and authors, like [5–7], propose different definitions of a DBP depending on an application domain or authors emphasize different properties of the DBP. In our previous papers [4, 8–10], we have analyzed definitions of a DBP and proposed six requirements of a DBP. According to these requirements, DBP is a process, which supports changes to any process component (i.e. a condition, an activity, a sequence of activities, and participants), which is not predefined and could change at runtime according to the changes of a context or rules. The detailed analysis of proposed approaches and their implementations are presented in Table 1.

The analysis of some dynamic implementation solutions, presented in Table 1, showed that no one has proposed an approach and its implementation, which supports all features of a DBP, described in this section, i.e. the change of any BP component at runtime due to changes of the context.

In order to implement BP changes at runtime, Yoo et al. [17] proposed a rule-based dynamic schema modification and adaptation method to support dynamic business service integration. This method supports modification of schemas based on a set of user-definable rules and running instances' migration to the modified schemas at runtime. However, the two proposed solutions do not have a context processing component, which provides information about changes in the environment.

Hermosillo et al. [2, 5] proposed the use of CEVICHE (Complex Event processing for Context-adaptive processes in pervasive and Heterogeneous Environments) system framework, which combines the processing of complex events and events activated by changes in BP. However, the authors do not provide information about any real-life implementation, only some examples of code.

Table 1. Dynamicity of a BP ("+" – has this feature; "–"– has no this feature)

Authors/ approach, reference, year of publication	Change of a BP component			Has initial model	Implementation
	Change of an activity	Change of rules	Change of a context		
Adams et al. [11], 2006	–	–	+	+	Print screens, examples
Gartner [12], 2015	+	+	+	+	-
CEVICHE [2], 2010	+	–	+	+	Some examples of code
Kim et al. [13], 2007	+	+	+	+	Print screens, examples
Levina [14], 2012	+	+	+	+	Some textual description
Pucher [6], 2010	–	–	+	+	-
Rajabi and Lee [7], 2010	–	–	–	–	Some descriptions and examples
Weber et al. [15], 2013	+	+	–	+	Some examples
DYPROTO [16], 2011	–	+	–	+	Prototype, without examples
Yoo et al. [17], 2008	–	+	–	+	Some examples
PROVOP [18–20], 2008	+	+	+	+	Prototype, print screens, the automotive and healthcare industries

Another solution is DYPROTO tool [16]. This tool can delete old activities, insert new activities or dynamically implement activity loops. The tool has been developed on the ground of submitted Weber dynamic model. However, the main attention of the tool is to solve the correctness of problems that arise due to the dynamics [16].

According to the dynamicity supported in a BP, all the analysed papers (see Table 1) could be classified as follows:

1. Supporting *process variability*, like in a number of papers [20–23]. Here, a BP is divided in variable and non-variable segments. Non-variable segments stay constant in all cases. Variable segments vary according to the predefined rules. The proposed approaches differ in modelling and managing process variables. Moreover, as stated in [24], there is comparatively little tool support for analysing and constructing customizable process models.
2. Transforming a BP into a set of *event-condition-action* (ECA) rules or some variation of ECA rules, like in [25], and after event arises, check the condition and perform a consequent action. In [1] authors apply business rules for ensuring the dynamicity

of BP. However, the authors of [1] do not specify how they define, manage and adopt changes in a context. Moreover, all processes have a strictly defined sequence of activities and this sequence of activities can be changed according to the defined set of rules. There is no possibility to change existing and define new rules at BP runtime. However, in all analysed approaches authors use an initial BP model. As presented in [4, 8–10], a DBPis based on the idea that there is no initial process model, e.g. each activity for execution is selected according to the rules and a context. Therefore, there is a necessity for a new DBP approach.

2.2 Health Care IS

As argued in [26], healthcare organizations are facing the challenge of delivering personalized services to their patients in a cost-effective and efficient manner. Therefore, those organizations require advanced healthcare process support for covering both organizational procedures and knowledge-intensive, dynamic treatment processes to meet patients' needs. However, existing hospitals' IS are lack of flexibility. In this section, we review existing approaches on dynamic healthcare process implementation in healthcare organizations.

As presented in [26], existing approaches can be characterized along three dimensions, supported by IT. They are as follows:

- **Adaptation**, which is based on BP ability to cope with exceptional circumstances [27] and single BP instances, can be dynamically adapted to the real-world situation if required. For example, YAWL [28] provides support for the handling of expected exceptions, and ADEPT2 [29] enables the handling of exceptions through structural ad-hoc adaptations of single process instances (e.g., by adding, deleting or moving process activities at run-time). However, YAWL is based on workflow patterns [30, 31]. A number of disadvantages of YAWL are presented in [32].
- **Flexibility** is based on BP ability to execute based on a loosely or partially specified model, which is completed at runtime and may be unique to each process instance [33, 34]. For example, in DECLARE [33] and Alaska [35] allow defining process models in a way that allows individual instances to determine their own (unique) processes. In particular, declarative approaches allow for loosely specified process models by following a constraint-based approach. However, such loosely specified models raise a number of challenges including the flexible configuration of process models at design time or their constraint-based definition during runtime. Moreover, due to the high number of runtime choices, more sophisticated user support (e.g., recommender systems) becomes necessary.
- **Evolution**, which is based on the BP ability to change when the BP evolves, e.g., due to legal changes or process optimizations [36, 37]. Approaches like WASA2, ADEPT2 and WIDE allow process engineers to migrate such process instances to the new model version, while ensuring PAIS robustness and process consistency [26]. Moreover, pre-specified process models often have to be changed to cope with model design errors, technical problems or poor model quality.

Authors of [38] propose a navigation system to support dynamic changes of health-care process. However, it is based on templates, used for diagnosis. The clinical staff should be used to develop the initial hierarchical structure of a GPS and to identify relevant process activities. Moreover, the proposed approach needs more refinements.

Hermosillo et al. [5] proposed a CEVICHE framework, based on complex event processing and BP adaptation, to respond to the needs of the environment and apply it for healthcare process. However, as can be seen from Table 1, this framework does not support all BP changes. Moreover, the proposed framework has a weak implementation.

As can be summarized from the papers analysed above, DBP modelling, simulation an execution in healthcare domain lacks theory and/or a case study or both. Moreover, a question of implementation is not solved enough to meet needs of healthcare organizations and patients.

3   A Context and Rule Based Approach for DBPModelling and Execution in Healthcare Domain

3.1   Healthcare Process

In this section, we present a BPMN model for healthcare process, which is used as a basis to define requirements, concerned approach and its implementation.

In Figs. 1 and 2 the simplified and detailed models of dynamic treatment process (ambulatory care, inpatient and outpatient) is shown as follows.

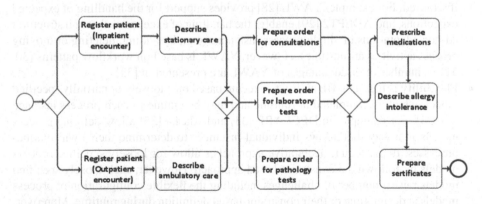

Fig. 1. Simplified process of stationary and ambulatory care

The process starts from an encounter (see definition http://hl7.org/fhir/). An encounter could be:

- inpatient – the patient is hospitalized and stays overnight (Fig. 1),
- outpatient – the patient is not hospitalized overnight (Fig. 1),
- ambulatory – the patient visits the practitioner in hospital (Fig. 2),
- virtual encounter – the patient gets health services without a visit (not presented here in the paper).

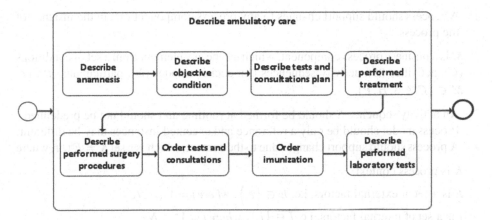

Fig. 2. Detailed description of ambulatory care

After the encounter the doctor assess the health status of the patient, if needed performs laboratory, radiological, instrumental, pathological and other investigations, if needed consults with other specialists and prescribes the medical treatment while patient is monitored at all the times. The treatment process is not the static one and has all dynamic characteristics. However, in most HIS only static processes are realized which causes many difficulties for the hospital personnel to achieve good results.

In Figs. 3 and 4, we have presented two instances of the ambulatory care process, which model is presented in Figs. 1 and 2. As can be seen from those figures (Figs. 3 and 4), instances of the ambulatory care process may be completely different. It depends on users' context.

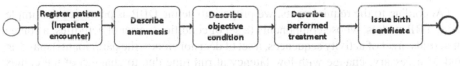

Fig. 3. Instance 1 of the ambulatory care process

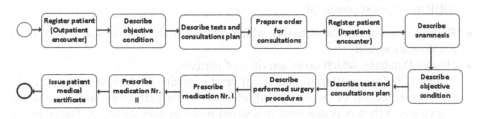

Fig. 4. Instance 2 of the ambulatory care process

3.2 A Context- and Rule- Based Approach for DBP Modelling and Execution in Healthcare Domain

According to the related works, here we compose a set of requirements for DBP:

1. A process should support changes to any process component (M) in the instance of the process.

- M is a business process component, which can be any element from a set of conditions (C), activities (A), activity sequences (S), decision nodes (H), participants (P), i.e. $M \in \{C, A, S, H, P\}$.

2. An activity sequence S should be formed at runtime and should not be predefined.
3. Process model should be only a reference and executed instances may be different.
4. A process should support changes due to the context, which is a set $K = E \cup I$, where

- K is process context.

- E is a set of external factors, i.e. $E \in \{e_j\}$, where $j = 1 \ldots N$.

- I is a set of internal factors, i.e. $I \in \{i_j\}$, where $j = 1 \ldots N$.

5. The term (T_K) of alteration of K should be shorter than the whole duration of the process (T_P), i.e. $T_K \ll T_P$.

- T_K is the term of alteration of context.
- T_P is the term of the process.

6. The process changes can be initiated by any performer role, at any time, with very low latency $(T_1 + T_2)$ compared with process term.

- T_1 is an interval from a moment in time when the necessity to perform a change in a process instance occurs until the implementation of the change is started.
- T_2 is time taken to implement the change.

According to the requirements, we propose to define DBP as processes that implement a BP models, whose components (a set of conditions, a set of activities, a content of activity, a set of activity sequences, a set of decision nodes, the participants) may vary and, if necessary, change with low latency at run time due to changes of the context (Fig. 5).

DBP model must consist of:

- Repository (context/rules/activity), which contains all the most topical C, A, S, H, P, K information, and
- History Database, which saves activities of perform.
  Primarily before starting to operate, it must evaluate K (context) and C (condition) for selection of A (activities) which is to be performed and execute the selected A. When A is executed it is saved in the history database. The steps are repeated again (evaluate K when C when select A, which to be carried out) until no A is found to be executed. If there was no A found for some time, then the process is counted as completed.

In Sect. 4, development of dynamic treatment processes in the hospital is described.

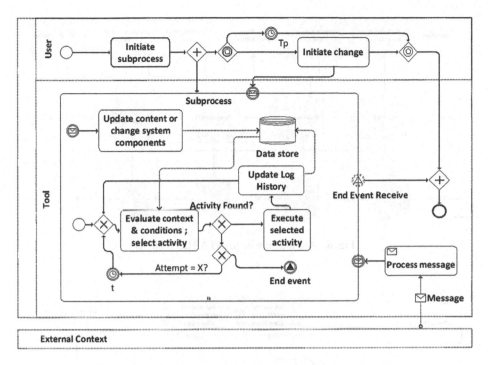

Fig. 5. A dynamic business process model

4   Description of Automated Medication Dispense System

Vilnius University Hospital Santariskiu Clinics is one of the major hospitals in Lithuania encompassing the provision of medical care in almost all key areas covering practical and scientific medicine, education of students, residents and physicians (www.santa.lt). The institution has developed HIS, which integrates electronic health record, laboratory, images and signals archives, staff and resource management, document management, and many other systems that are necessary for effective health care services. One of the goal of Santariskiu clinics is to develop paperless HIS while improving automation of all DBP.

SANTA-HIS (SANTA hospital information system) is composed of subsystems listed below. The main architecture of SANTA-HIS is described in Figs. 6 and 7, where Fig. 7 continues Fig. 6) as follows:

- SANTA-HIS core system (encounter, health records, orders, resources, documents, statistics, planning etc.),
- Automated medication dispense system,
- Instrumental, radiology, nuclear and other medicine investigation system,
- Laboratory system (haematology and general cytology, biochemistry, microbiology, clinical immunology, blood transfusion and molecular diagnostic laboratories),
- Pathology system,
- E-prescription system,
- Medication warehouse system.

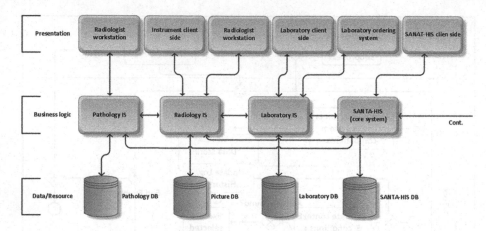

Fig. 6. Architecture of SANTA HIS (Part A)

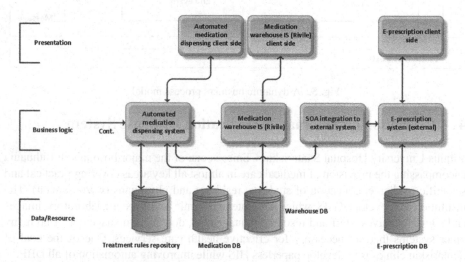

Fig. 7. Architecture of SANTA HIS (Part B)

Automated medication dispensing system is made of more than 300 treatment schemas and a number of different treatment rules. Treatment schemas and rules are configurable and saved in MS SQL server. The intelligent medication dispensing system dynamically provides list of medication, calculates doses of medication, date and time of medication dispenses according to patient data (age, sex, weight, height, laboratory results, stage of illness and other parameters) and provides other information for medical personnel.

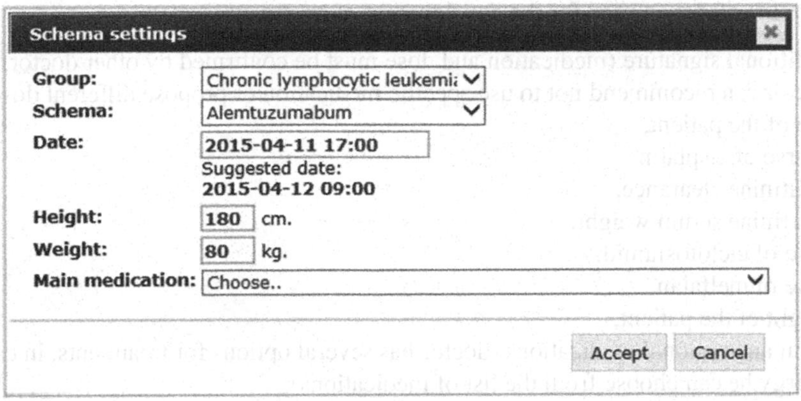

Fig. 8. Settings of treatment schema

An example of treatment schema is presented in Fig. 8. As can be seen form Fig. 8, Doctor needs to choose treatment schema, provide date when the treatment will begin and specify needed characteristics of the patient.

In Fig. 9, another dynamical treatment schema of the patient is shown. This schema is automatically made by the system according to the previously defined settings (the personal data of the patient is removed and is only visible for the doctor). In the first column of the table the list of medication is provided, in the next column – the dose of the medication, in the next columns dates and times of medication dispense is provided. The doctor can manually adapt treatment schema if needed according to the observation results of the patient.

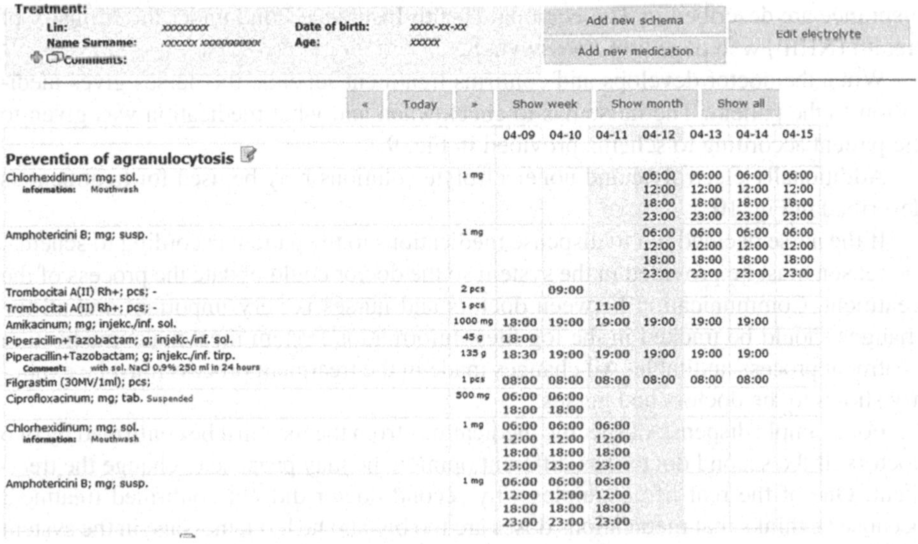

		04-09	04-10	04-11	04-12	04-13	04-14	04-15
Chlorhexidinum; mg; sol. information: Mouthwash	1 mg				06:00 12:00 18:00 23:00	06:00 12:00 18:00 23:00	06:00 12:00 18:00 23:00	06:00 12:00 18:00 23:00
Amphotericini B; mg; susp.	1 mg				06:00 12:00 18:00 23:00	06:00 12:00 18:00 23:00	06:00 12:00 18:00 23:00	06:00 12:00 18:00 23:00
Trombocitai A(II) Rh+; pcs; -	2 pcs		09:00					
Trombocitai A(II) Rh+; pcs; -	1 pcs			11:00				
Amikacinum; mg; injekc./inf. sol.	1000 mg	18:00	19:00	19:00	19:00	19:00	19:00	
Piperacillin+Tazobactam; g; injekc./inf. sol.	45 g	18:00						
Piperacillin+Tazobactam; g; injekc./inf. tirp. Comment: with sol. NaCl 0.9% 250 ml in 24 hours	135 g	18:30	19:00	19:00	19:00	19:00	19:00	
Filgrastim (30MV/1ml); pcs;	1 pcs	08:00	08:00	08:00	08:00	08:00	08:00	
Ciprofloxacinum; mg; tab. Suspended	500 mg	06:00 18:00	06:00 18:00					
Chlorhexidinum; mg; sol. information: Mouthwash	1 mg	06:00 12:00 18:00 23:00	06:00 12:00 18:00 23:00	06:00 12:00 18:00 23:00				
Amphotericini B; mg; susp.	1 mg	06:00 12:00 18:00 23:00	06:00 12:00 18:00 23:00	06:00 12:00 18:00 23:00				

Fig. 9. Medication treatment schema

The list ofcriteria used for the development of treatment process:

- additional signature (medication and dose must be confirmed by other doctor, other doctor can recommend not to use specific medication or propose different dose),
- age of the patient,
- course of cisplatin,
- creatinine clearance,
- creatinine serum weight,
- dose of ciclofosfamid,
- dose of melfalan,
- height of the patient,
- main and optional medications (doctor has several options for treatments, in case of allergy he can choose from the list of medications),
- sex of the patient.

Below several examples of self-explanatory formulas used for calculation of medication doses and development of dynamic treatment process are provided:

- if((Sqrt(height * weight/3600) * 1.4) > 2, "2", "Sqrt((height * weight)/3600) * 1.4")
- if(age < 66,"90 * Sqrt((height * weight)/3600)", "60 * Sqrt((height * weight)/3600)")
- 5*(((((140-age)*weight)*(if (sex = "male", "1.23", "1.04"))/creatinineClearance) + 25)
- if((5*(creatinineClearance +25)) > 420, 420, 5*(creatinineClearance +25))
- medication option 1|600*Sqrt((height * weight)/3600)
- medication option 2|if((Round(dose/0.5,0)/3) − Round((Round(dose/0.5,0)/3), 0) > 0.

Below in Table 2 we present five examples of rules, which are implemented in the system, and which are used to make decisions. Detailed rules of Compulsory health Insurance are described in The National Health Insurance Fund under the Ministry of Health (NHIF) web page http://www.vlk.lt.

When the doctor develops and confirms treatment schema, the nurses gives medication to the patient. The nurse has to check when and what medication was given to the patient according to schema provided in Fig. 9.

Additionally electrolyte and nonelectrolyte solutions may be used for treatment as described in Fig. 10.

If the nurse decided not to dispense medications to the patient according to schema, the reason must be provided in the system so the doctor could update the process of the treatment. Communication between doctors and nurses is very important and all the changes should be tracked in the log files. Information system must make medication treatment process auditable. All changes made in the treatment process must be explicitly shows to the doctors and nurses.

For example dispense of specific medications from the list must be confirmed by two doctors. If the second doctor has different opinion, he may propose to change the treatment. One of the real life examples why second doctor did not confirmed treatment because he thinks that medications doses are too big and he left a message in the system "it is sufficient dexamethasone 8 mg and 8 mg of ondansetron" for the patients treatment.

Table 2. Examples of rules, which are implemented in the system

Rule	Event	Condition	Action
R1: Check if person is insured by Compulsory Health insurance	Encounter	Person is insured by Compulsory Health Insurance	A person can receive medical treatment free of charge
		Person is not insured by Compulsory Health Insurance	A person cannot receive medical treatment free of charge
		If person has Lithuanian citizenship and the age is less than 18	A person can receive medical treatment free of charge
R2: Check if person is registered at a healthcare institution	Encounter	Patients is registered at a healthcare institution	Provide services of family physician
		Patients is not registered at a healthcare institution	Do not provide services of family physician
R3: Check if person is insured by European Health Insurance	Encounter	If European Health Insurance Card (EHIC) is presented	Urgent care shall be provided at the establishments belonging to the national healthcare system
		If European Health Insurance Card (EHIC) is not presented	Urgent care shall be provided and the invoice will be issued according to the provided services
R4: Check if ePrescription can be issued	Prescription of medicines	If encounter and main illness of the patient is registered in the system	Prescribe medicine
		If encounter and main illness of the patient is not registered in the system	Do not prescribe medicine
R5: Check if reimbursable medicines can be prescribed	Prescription of medicines	If medical indications for diseases, traumas and defects are in the list	Full price or part of a price can be reimbursed
		If medical indications for diseases, traumas and defects are not in the list	No reimbursement

The other feature of the integrated process system is that system automatically makes a record in medication warehouse system that medication was used for a patient using ATC code. Because of it person responsible for medication warehouse knows what medications will be used in near future, what medication exists in warehouse and what medication needs to be ordered. The main problem is that doctor prescribes generic medications to the patients but the nurse actually gives branded medication. To control such process without automated systems is nightmare for the hospitals personnel (Fig. 11).

Electrolyte and Nonelectrolyte Solutions		April		May			
		29d	30d	1d	2d	3d	4d
		→ ☑	→ ☑	→ ☑	→ ☑	→ ☑	→ ☑
NaCl 0,9%; ml; injekc./inf. sol.	1000	15:00	15:00	15:00	15:00	15:00	15:00
KCl 10%; ml; injekc./inf. sol.		10	10	10	10	10	10
MgSO4 25%; ml; injekc./inf. sol.		5	5	5	5	5	5
NaCl 10%; ml; injekc./inf.sol.		20	20	20	20	20	20
CaCl 10%; ml; injekc./inf.sol.		10	10	10	10	10	10
Glycophos; ml; injekc./inf.sol.		20	20	20	20	20	20

Fig. 10. Electrolyte and nonelectrolyte solutions

Medication	Dose	07:00 07:30 08:00 08:30 09:00 09:30 10:00 10:30 11:00 11:30 12:00 12:30 13:00 13:30
Valaciclovirum; mg; tab.	500mg	+
Omeprazolum; mg; tab.	20mg	+
NaCl 0,9%; ml; injekc./inf. sol.	1000ml	+ ... +
KCl 10%; ml; injekc./inf. sol.	10ml	↑ ... ↑
MgSO4 25%; ml; injekc./inf. sol.	5ml	↑ ... ↑
Furozemidum; mg; injekc./inf. sol.	10mg	+ ... +
Filgrastim (30MV/1ml); pcs;	1vnt	+
Amikacinum; mg; injekc./inf. sol.	1000mg	
Piperacillin+Tazobactam; g; injekc./inf. sol.	135g	
Comment: with sol. NaCl 0,9% 250 ml in 24 hours		
Chlorhexidinum; mg; sol.	1mg	+
Informacija: Mouthwash		
Amphotericini B; mg; susp.	1mg	+

Fig. 11. Dispense of medication

5 Conclusions and Future Work

The analysis of related works shows that the problem of process dynamics has been actively investigated over the last few years. However, existing approaches to DBP modelling, simulation and execution are limited and incomplete, i.e. they lack theory and/or a case study or both. Moreover, a question of implementation of the DBP modelling, execution and simulation is left without an answer.

In this paper we describe an approach for DBP modelling and simulation. The main idea of the approach is that during the simulation of activities each activity should be selected according to the context and rules. Consequently, the DBP has no strict activities and their sequence. In addition, we presented DBP requirements.

Experiment was made in hospital, where dynamic patient treatment process was developed and pilot testing of automated medication dispense system was accomplished. During these activities 12 treatment groups and more than 300 unique treatment schemas were developed, 2600 medication used in schemas (on average 8 medication per schema), 1400 settings for treatment schemas were configured, more than 900 unique patients were registered from the June of 2014 till the April of 2015, more than 90000 medications were given to the patients according to treatment schemas. After the analysis of experiment results we believe that automated dynamic medication dispense system will bring great benefit to doctors, nurses and patients of the hospital.

References

1. Mejia Bernal, J.F., Falcarin, P., Morisio, M., Dai, J.: Dynamic context-aware business process: a rule-based approach supported by pattern identification. In: The 2010 ACM Symposium on Applied Computing, pp. 470–474. ACM (2010)
2. Hermosillo, G., Seinturier, L., Duchien, L.: Using complex event processing for dynamic business process adaptation. In: IEEE SCC 2010, pp. 466–473. IEEE (2010)
3. Milanovic, M., Gasevic, D., Rocha, L.: Modeling flexible business processes with business rule patterns. In: IEEE EDOC 2011, pp. 65–74. IEEE (2011)
4. Trinkunas, J., Rusinaite, T., Vasilecas, O.: Research on improving dynamic business processes in HIS. In: Vogel, D., et al. (eds): ISD 2015. Department of Information Systems, Hong Kong (2015)
5. Hermosillo, G., Seinturier, L., Duchien, L.: Creating context-adaptive business processes. In: Maglio, P.P., Weske, M., Yang, J., Fantinato, M. (eds.) ICSOC 2010. LNCS, vol. 6470, pp. 228–242. Springer, Heidelberg (2010)
6. Pucher, M.J.: Agile-, AdHoc-, Dynamic-, Social-, or Adaptive BPM (2010). https://isismjpucher.wordpress.com/2010/03/30/dynamic-vs-adaptive-bpm/. Accessed 2 Feb 2015
7. Rajabi, B.A., Lee, S.P.: Modeling and analysis of change management in dynamic business process. Int. J. Comput. Electr. Eng. 2(1), 181 (2010)
8. Rusinaite, T., Kalibatiene, D., Vasilecas, O.: Requirements of dynamic business processes - a survey. In: AIEEE 2015, pp. 1–4. IEEE, New York (2015)
9. Rusinaite, T., Vasilecas, O., Kalibatiene, D.: A systematic literature review on dynamic business processes. Baltic J. Modern Comput. 4(2), 13–21 (2016)
10. Kalibatiene, D., Vasilecas, O., Savickas, T., Vysockis, T., Bobrovs, V.: A new approach on rule and context based dynamic business process simulation. Baltic J. Modern Comput. 4(2), 1–12 (2016)
11. Adams, M., ter Hofstede, A.H., Edmond, D., van der Aalst, W.M.: Worklets: a service-oriented implementation of dynamic flexibility in workflows. In: Meersman, R., Tari, Z. (eds.) OTM 2006. LNCS, vol. 4275, pp. 291–308. Springer, Heidelberg (2006)
12. Dynamic business process management (BPM). Gartner (2015). http://www.gartner.com/it-glossary/dynamic-business-process-management-bpm. Accessed 3 Feb 2015
13. Kim, D., Kim, M., Kim, H.: Dynamic business process management based on process change patterns. In: Proceedings of the Convergence Information Technology, pp. 1154–1161. IEEE (2007)
14. Levina, O.: Using business process simulation to assess the effect of business rules automation. In: BUSTECH 2012, pp. 61–66 (2012)
15. Weber, B., Reichert, M., Rinderle-Ma, S.: Change patterns and change support features–enhancing flexibility in process-aware information systems. Data Knowl. Eng. 66(3), 438–466 (2008)
16. Wörzberger, R., Heer, T.: DYPROTO - tools for dynamic business processes. Int. J. Bus. Process Integr. Manage. 5(4), 324–343 (2011)
17. Yoo, S., Roh, Y.H., Song, I.C., Jeon, J.H., Kim, M.H., et al.: Rule-based dynamic business process modification and adaptation. In: ICOIN 2008, pp. 1–5. IEEE (2008)

18. Hallerbach, A., Bauer, T., Reichert, M.: Managing process variants in the process lifecycle. In: TCoB 2008, pp. 31–40 (2008)
19. Hallerbach, A., Bauer, T., Reichert, M.: Guaranteeing soundness of configurable process variants in Provop. In: IEEE CEC 2009, pp. 98–105. IEEE Computer Society Press (2009)
20. Hallerbach, A., Bauer, T., Reichert, M.: Capturing variability in business process models: the provop approach. J. Softw. Maint. Evol. Res. Pract. **22**(6/7), 519–546 (2010)
21. van Eijndhoven, T., Iacob, M.E., Ponisio, M.L.: Achieving business process flexibility with business rules. In: IEEE EDOC 2008, pp. 95–104. IEEE, New York (2008)
22. Bui, D.V., Iacob, M.E., van Sinderen, M., Zarghami, A.: Achieving flexible process interoperability in the homecare domain through aspect-oriented service composition. In: van Sinderen, M., Oude Luttighuis, P., Folmer, E., Bosems, S. (eds.) IWEI 2013. LNBIP, vol. 144, pp. 50–64. Springer, Heidelberg (2013)
23. Yao, W., Basu, S., Li, J., Stephenson, B.: Modeling and configuration of process variants for on-boarding customers to IT outsourcing. In: IEEE SCC 2012, pp. 415–422. IEEE, New York (2012)
24. La Rosa, M., van der Aalst, W.M., Dumas, M., Milani, F.P.: Business process variability modeling: A survey. (2013)
25. Boukhebouze, M., Amghar, Y., Benharkat, A.N., Maamar, Z.: A rule-based approach to model and verify flexible business processes. Int. J. Bus. Process Integr. Manage. **5**(4), 287–307 (2011)
26. Reichert, M.: What BPM technology can do for healthcare process support. In: Peleg, M., Lavrač, N., Combi, C. (eds.) AIME 2011. LNCS, vol. 6747, pp. 2–13. Springer, Heidelberg (2011)
27. Reichert, M., Dadam, P.: ADEPTf lex – supporting dynamic changes of workflows without losing control. J. Intell. Inf. Syst. **10**, 93–129 (1998)
28. ter Hofstede, A.H.M., van der Aalst, W.M.P., Adams, M., Russell, N.: Modern Business Process Automation: YAWL and Its Support Environment. Springer, Heidelberg (2009)
29. Dadam, P., Reichert, M.: The ADEPT project: a decade of research and development for robust and flexible process support - challenges and achievements. Comput. Sci. Res. Dev. **23**, 81–97 (2009)
30. van der Aalst, W.M.P., Dumas, M., ter Hofstede, A.H.M., Wohed, P.: Pattern-based analysis of BPML (and WSCI). QUT Technical Report FIT-TR-2002-05. Queensland University of Technology, Brisbane (2002)
31. van der Aalst, W.M.P., ter Hofstede, A.H.M., Kiepuszewski, B., Barros, A.P.: Workflow patterns. QUT Technical Report, FIT-TR-2002-02. Queensland University of Technology, Brisbane (2002)
32. Börger, E.: Approaches to modeling business processes: a critical analysis of BPMN, workflow patterns and YAWL. Softw. Syst. Model. **11**(3), 305–318 (2012)
33. Pesic, M.: Constraint-based workflow management systems: shifting control to users. Ph.D. thesis, Eindhoven University of Technology (2008)
34. Sadiq, S., Sadiq, W., Orlowska, M.: A framework for constraint specification and validation in flexible workflows. Inf. Syst. **30**, 349–378 (2005)
35. Weber, B., Pinggera, J., Zugal, S., Wild, W.: Alaska simulator toolset for conducting controlled experiments on process flexibility. In: Soffer, P., Proper, E. (eds.) CAiSE Forum 2010. LNBIP, vol. 72, pp. 205–221. Springer, Heidelberg (2011)
36. Rinderle, S., Reichert, M., Dadam, P.: Flexible support of team processes by adaptive workflow systems. Distrib. Parallel Databases **16**, 91–116 (2004)

37. Casati, F., Ceri, S., Pernici, B., Pozzi, G.: Workflow evolution. Data Knowl. Eng. **24**, 211–238 (1998)
38. Reuter, C., Dadam, P., Rudolph, S., Deiters, W., Trillsch, S.: Guarded process spaces (GPS): a navigation system towards creation and dynamic change of healthcare processes from the end-user's perspective. In: Daniel, F., Barkaoui, K., Dustdar, S. (eds.) BPM Workshops 2011, Part II. LNBIP, vol. 100, pp. 237–248. Springer, Heidelberg (2012)

Information Systems: Special Session on Information and Software Technologies for Intelligent Power Systems

On Defining and Assessing of the Energy Balance and Operational Logic Within Hybrid Renewable Energy Systems

Algirdas Pakštas[1], Olha Shulyma[2(✉)], and Vira Shendryk[2]

[1] Institute of Mathematics and Informatics, Vilnius, Lithuania
a.pakstas@ieee.org
[2] Sumy State University, Sumy, Ukraine
{o.shulym, ve-shen}@opm.sumdu.edu.ua

Abstract. The paper is considering a problem of providing energy in small neighbourhoods consisting of the households and local industrial or commercial units (e.g. farms, workshops, offices). Such communities may benefit from the use of the Hybrid Renewable Energy Systems (HRES) harnessing solar and wind power, accumulating excess energy using Power Storage Banks and integrating to the External Power Grid (EPG). Phases of planning, design, installation and operation of HRESs are considered as interconnected complex tasks needing appropriate Requirement Analysis. Architecture and energy balance of the HRES are introduced where important role is devoted to the Energy Gateway Station. Characteristics of the exploiting of solar and wind potential energy and customer usage patterns in such communities are considered. Types of requests for energy use or its supply to EPG as well as principles of the operational logic of the HRES are introduced. Criteria for assessing of the effectiveness of HRES are briefly discussed.

Keywords: Renewable energy sources · Hybrid renewable energy system · System architecture · Energy balance · Operational logic · Energy potential assessment · Decision support system

1 Introduction

Present rate of all the energy consumption is growing very fast. Nowadays there is growing interest to development of the renewable energy sources (RES) in the energy supply chain. Various forms of RESs using solar and wind energy are proposed. Solar energy has a huge potential of $1.8 \times 10^{1}1$ MW [1], which is many times larger than total energy consumption of the world. Assessing of the wind energy potential is much more difficult and depends on the location. For example average wind speed in different countries onshore may vary from 1.8 to 4.3 m/s [2].

Current stage of development of the RESs in Ukraine was considered in [3]. The focus of our research is on defining general architecture and its operation rules for Hybrid RESs (HRES) having both renewable energy sources as well as access to the External Power Grid (EPG). Such HRESs will be used in small localities which are very sensitive to the costs of the energy. In such approach significant number of

© Springer International Publishing Switzerland 2016
G. Dregvaite and R. Damasevicius (Eds.): ICIST 2016, CCIS 639, pp. 151–160, 2016.
DOI: 10.1007/978-3-319-46254-7_12

consumers will produce energy for their own needs as well as may send surplus to the external grid. Such implementation decreases energy losses during transportation as generators are situated next to consumers.

Planning, design, installation and operation of HRESs are all complex tasks and shall be performed phase by phase and considered in total context from Request to Energy:

Planning(Request,Requirements,TP) =>

Design(Requirements,Drawings,TD) =>

Installation(Drawings,System,TI) =>

Operation(System,Energy,TO)

Here *Request* (formal or informal) is input to the *Planning* phase and has to be translated to the *Requirements* during *Planning Time TP. Design* phase is accepting *Requirements* and has to produce *Drawings* (a set of installation technical documentation) during *Design Time TD*. Similarly, *Installation* phase is producing working *System* during *Implementation Time TI*. Operating *System* is producing *Energy* during *Operation Time TO*.

Operation characteristics of the target HRES are pretty much defining steps of planning, design and installation. Thus, as in many other cases of dealing with complex systems, we have to start from the *Requirement Analysis*. Having clear targets defined in the requirements will allow to translate them to the operational parameters and this will enable modeling of the system with appropriate tools before starting of the design. Thus, it may be convenient to use Decision Support Systems (DSS), which can take on some the user's tasks. The architecture of such DSS is presented in [4].

The rest of the paper is organized as follows. Section 2 is presenting architecture and energy balance of the HRES in a small neighbourhood. Section 3 is devoted to characterization of the energy usage and generation in a small neighbourhood. Operational logic of the requests for energy use or supply is considered in Sect. 4. Section 5 is considering criteria for evaluation of the HRES. Conclusions are drawn in the Sect. 6 and followed by the discussion of the future work.

2   Architecture and Energy Balance of the HRES in a Small Neighbourhood

It is assumed that the legal entity operating HRES (*HRES Community)* is defining its operational goals, policies, etc. HRES Community is responsible for the costs incurred as a result of designing, installing and operating of the HRES as well as for obtaining, exploiting and sharing benefits/profits to its members.

Figure 1 depicts typical architecture of the HRES in a small neighbourhood comprising of the few households with possible commercial/industrial activities (farms, workshops, etc.). Here energy is generated using *sources* such as Photovoltaics (PV) elements (Solar Panels) installed on the roofs of the houses or nearby land (denoted as Es energy) and Wind Turbines installed where it is suitable (denoted as Ew

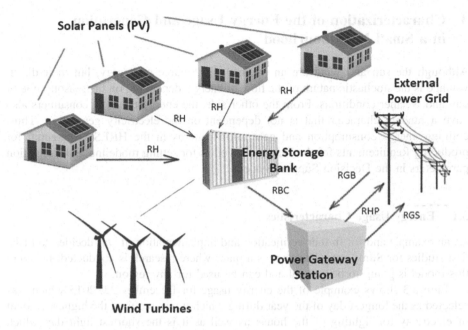

Fig. 1. Architecture of HRES in a small neighbourhood

energy). Energy is *stored* in the Energy Storage Bank (ESB) for the future use (denoted as Eb energy when used or Ebc when charged).

Additionally, HRES is connected to the External Power Grid (EPG) which can be serving as both a *source* of the additional purchased energy (denoted as Egp energy) and a *sink* to where surplus energy could be *supplied* and potentially *sold* for a certain *price* (denoted as Egs energy). EPG is assumed as *existing power network* belonging to the *EPG Operator*. It requires installing of the *Power Gateway Station (PGS)* which provides routing of the energy in and out of the HRES as required.

Total energy balance in the HRES is shown in Fig. 2. Here are defined energy requests as well as sources and parameters influencing need to purchase or opportunity to sell energy.

RH := SUM(1..N, Rhi)	-- Current ∑ of Rhi requests from N households
0 ≤ Es ≤ Esmax	-- Current solar energy Es is between 0 and Esmax
0 ≤ Ew ≤ Ewmax	-- Current wind energy Ew is between 0 and Ewmax
0 ≤ Ebmin ≤ Eb ≤ Ebmax	-- Current PSB capacity Eb is between Ebmin and Ebmax
Ea1 := Es + Ew	-- Current available solar and wind energy
Ea2 := Ea1 + Eb	-- Current available solar, wind and battery energy
Erp := RH —Ea	-- Current deficit of energy
Esale-max := Ea2 - RH	-- Current maximum energy for sale to EPG
0 ≤ Esale ≤ Esalemax ≤ Eo	-- Energy for sale to EPG is between 0 and Esalemax and is
	-- limited by maximum out line capacity Eo

Fig. 2. Total energy balance in the HRES

3 Characterization of the Energy Usage and Generation in a Small Neighbourhood

Although the sun and wind are an inexhaustible source of energy, but their disadvantage is the stochastic nature of the flow of energy, depending on the season, time of day and weather conditions. From the other side, the energy needs of consumers also have a random character that is not dependent on the electricity generation. Thus, defining energy consumption and generation patterns in the HRES is essential for producing Requirements for the Design as well as for setting modeling and simulation parameters in the Decision Support System.

3.1 Energy Usage Characteristics

As an example and for further verification and implementation, it was decided to make first studies for Sumy area, Ukraine, as a place where research is conducted. In future this model is going to be general and can be used for any region.

Figure 3 shows example of the energy usage for December 22, 2015 which was selected as the longest day of the year during which it was required the highest amount of electricity for lighting of the house as well as it is the shortest light day which directly affects output of the solar panels. Thus, this date is representing the worst operating conditions for PV sources and simultaneously the heaviest energy demand. These data are obtained from the local energy company Sumyoblenergo [5] and are representative for a typical private house in Sumy area, Ukraine. From this graph it is clear that used energy was fluctuating between minimum 3400 (at 04:00 and 05:00) and maximum 7350 (at 22:00) Watts and the average request from household was 5380 W.

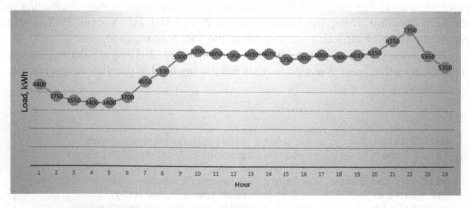

Fig. 3. Energy consumption during 22 December, 2015 in the private household in Sumy area

Power of electrical load required by the consumers is represented by the probability-statistical model which defines the daily schedule of the design load of the object for each day of the year P_{pi} as follows

$$P_{pi} = \overline{P_i} \times P_{max} \times (1 \pm \beta \times \sigma(P_i)) \times K_c \tag{1}$$

where $\overline{P_i}$ – the expectation of the load at the time i, P_{max} – maximum load, β – the reliability coefficient, σ – mean square deviation, and Kc – seasonality factor.

3.2 Energy Generation Characteristics

Suitability of the solar and wind energy sources very much depends on the *geographical location* and *climate conditions*. Energy generation depends on the following factors:

- Amount of the solar radiation in the given time of the day in the given day of the year in the given point on the Earth surface depending on sun position on the sky - defines daily cyclicity of the sun radiation and as a result *cyclicity* and *volume* of a power generated by the PV components;
- Weather and season conditions affecting amount of solar radiation and strength/direction of the wind – defines *variability* of generated energy;
- Total number and power of the individual generation components (PV panels/wind turbines) – defines *maximal possible outputs* in each time *t*;
- Periodical (planned) maintenance of the components (cleaning, tuning, servicing, replacing, etc.) – defines *periodical (planned) reduction* of the generated power;
- Occasional outages of the components requiring repairs or replacements – defines *unplanned reduction of the generated power.*

3.3 Assessment of the Solar and Wind Energy Potential

In [6] it is suggested top-down approach to estimate energy amount in the region which we apply for both solar and wind energy.

Available solar energy potential Esa is expressed as the physically available solar radiation on the earth's surface, which is influenced by various factors. The estimated potential is then reduced by considering technical limitations (e.g. conversion efficiency factors), which means taking into account the losses are associated with the conversion of solar irradiation to electric power or heat by state of the art technologies (Est). Additionally there are soft factors which may be modified over time and may vary regionally (e.g. acceptance of technology, legislation) and the potential is further reduced to realizable energy Esr. Thus,

$$\text{Esr} < \text{Est} < \text{Esa} \tag{2}$$

Estimated value of solar radiation available to PV panels is usually assumed for the region, but we are proposing to do more precise calculation and divide area to zones. For doing this it is necessary to obtain meteorological data based on hourly values inflow of solar radiation on an inclined surface and hourly values of ambient temperature.

The value of solar radiation Gtilt is considered as a function:

$$G_{tilt}(\varphi,\omega,\gamma,s,N) = (G_{dir}(\varphi,\omega,\gamma,s,N) + G_{dif}(\varphi,\omega,s,N)) \times (1-a+0,38 \times n) \times n \quad (3)$$

where *Gdir* – direct solar radiation, *Gdif*– diffuse solar radiation, φ – latitude location, ω – the angular displacement of the sun, depending on the time of day, s – platform tilt angle to the horizon, γ – plane azimuth angle, n – the value of cloudiness, a – coefficient depending on the type of terrain, N – the number of a day in year.

For each day in a year we use probability-statistical model to define the value of cloudiness which may produce geographical restrictions for the installation of solar energy systems and affect choosing suitable areas.

For estimation of exploitable solar potential it is planned to use data on parameters which are specific to the PV panel $E_s(t)$ at the time t:

$$E_s(t) = n_{pv} \times A \times G_{tilt}(t) \quad (4)$$

where A is a size of the area of solar panels, n_{pv} – efficiency coefficient specific to solar panel, *Gtilt(t)* – hourly values inflow of solar radiation on an inclined surface.

According to [7] n_{pv} depends on energy conversion efficiency of solar panel, energy conversion efficiency of maximum power point tracking system (MPPT), temperature coefficient of solar panels, solar panel temperature under standard measurement conditions and the actual temperature of the solar panel.

For identifying wind energy is used the following top down approach. At the first level, the potential energy is limited by all the physical geographical, socio geographical and land constraints which leads to the estimation of the theoretical energy. Here are used statistical models and interpolating techniques to determine the average wind speed as a basis to choose location. Also we determine the most common wind direction to give advices on installation specification of wind turbines.

The theoretical energy can be further limited by the characteristics of the commercially available wind turbines and the constraints of a wind farm.

Finally, the exploitable energy at the time t is defined as follows

$$Ew(t) = 0,5 \times \rho \times A \times C_p(\lambda) \times V_w(t)^3 \quad (5)$$

where ρ - air density, A – area size of rotor, $C_p(\lambda)$ – dependence coefficient of efficiency of selection wind power, which depends on the design features of wind turbines and its rapidity λ, and wind speed $V_w(t)$.

4   Operational Logic of the Requests for Energy Use or Supply

According to the suggested HRES architecture requests for energy use or supply within HRES or between HRES and EPG could be as follows:

- RH: requests from individual households to HRES for satisfying domestic/industrial use (i.e. total sum of the Rhi);
- RBC: from PSB to HRES/PGS/EPG for recharging;
- RHP: from HRES via PGS to EPG for purchasing Egp energy for satisfying domestic/industrial use (i.e. in a case of low Es + Ew/Es + Ew + Eb power);
- RGS: from the HRES via PGS to EPG for selling of the surplus energy;
- RGB: from the EPG via PGS to HRES for buying of the surplus energy.

We assume that power requests are coming as random sequences of events. Each type of request RHi/RHPi/RBCi/RGBi/RGSi in general is characterized by its discrete Time Ti, finite Time Length TLi, finite Energy Ei associated with the request (power volume), Priority Pi and Cost Ci.

$$RHi/RBCi/RHPi/RGSi/RGBi = (Ti, TLi, Ei, Pi, Ci) \qquad (6)$$

Operational logic of HRES is presented in Fig. 4. Here for simplicity are omitted instant discrete values of times, requested powers, priorities as well as costs and only generalized value of RH is used. Also, conditions such as "UNTIL Tx = 0" shall be understood as repeated generation of the request during specified period of time. Obviously, end users are not expected to generate their Rhi with attached time limit TL. It is rather a task for HRES control system to set suitable values for the TL intervals during which energy could be purchased from EPG. This means that in the situation when there is not enough Ea to satisfy total RH there could be generated repeated RPHi until either Ea or RH are changed and the need for purchasing is expired.

It is important to introduce the logic for purchasing and selling of the energy from/to EPG into the overall operating scheme of the HRES right from the design phase because adding it later to the live system could be problematic. As a temporary

```
REPEAT
GET(RH)                                 -- Get total energy request
IF (Eb ≤ Ebmin) OR                      -- If battery low OR
        ((Ebmin < Eb < Ebmax)           -- battery good
                AND (RH=0))             -- AND no other requests
        THEN (RBC(Ec,HRES);             -- then generate charging request
        RH := RH + Ec)                  -- and adjust total request RH
Ea := Ea1 – SOLD(EPG)                   -- Available power minus already sold
IF RH ≤ Ea THEN USE(Ea,RH)              -- If enough then use Ea to satisfy RH
IF RH > Ea THEN Ea := Ea + Eb           -- If not enough then add battery
IF RH ≤ Ea THEN USE(Ea,RH)              -- If enough then use Ea to satisfy RH
IF RH > Ea THEN RHP(RH-Ea,Tp,EPG)       -- If not enough then request RH-Ea
IF RHP(OK) THEN BUY(RH-Ea) UNTIL Tp=0   -- If OK then buy extra RH-Ea during Tp
IF Ea > RH THEN RGS(Ea–H,Ts,EPG)        -- If ∃ surplus then offer it to sell during Ts
IF RGS(OK) OR RGB                       -- If sell accepted or ∃ request for surplus
        THEN SELL(Ea–RH) UNTIL Ts=0     -- then sell surplus to EPG during Ts
IF CHARGING(FINISH) THEN RH:= RH–Ec     -- If charged then adjust total RH
UNTIL STOP
```

Fig. 4. Pseudocode for operational logic of the HRES

measure some fixed default prices can be allocated per energy unit (e.g. KWh) which can be later on assigned to the realistic floating market values.

5 Criteria for Evaluation of the HRES

Effectiveness of the system is usually evaluated by looking at its performance and cost. In the case of HRES it is suitable to use non-interrupted power supply to the customers, Deficiency of Power Supply Probability (DPSP) and Related Excess Power Generated (REPG) [7] as well as Cost Of Energy (COE) of a separate unit [8–10].

5.1 Evaluation of the Energy Efficiency of HRES

Minimizing of the DPSP and REPG are important targets which should be achieved by the efficient design.

The Deficiency of Power Supply Probability (DPSP) is defined as the sum of the deficit in power generated by HRES (i.e. sum of the requested extra energy) during the given time period as a ratio to the total sum of the energy requests RH:

$$DPSP = \sum\nolimits_{t=1}^{T} RHP(RH(t) - Ea(t)) \Big/ \sum\nolimits_{t=1}^{T} RH(t) \tag{7}$$

According to the operational logic (see Fig. 4), if energy generated by HRES exceeds required amount RH(t), then the excess energy is accumulated in the PSB until reaching its maximum value E_{Bmax}. After that these excesses can be sold or, if not sold, wasted.

The Relative Excess Power Generated by the HRES is defined as a ratio of the total excess power generated by the HRES in a given time period to that of the total sum of energy requests RH.

$$REPG = \sum\nolimits_{t=1}^{T} RGS(Ea(t) - RH(t)) \Big/ \sum\nolimits_{t=1}^{T} RH(t) \tag{8}$$

5.2 Cost Analysis of HRES

Approach to cost analysis of HRES elements and the system as a whole is suggested in [11–13]. The cost of 1 kWh of energy in the output of HRES for one separate object with a particular configuration of elements is the economic criterion which helps to determine system configuration.

The objective function of the optimum design problem is the minimization of COE. COE is an economic evaluation tool for the energy production in integrated system which includes all recurring and non-recurring costs over project lifetime. It is defined as the ratio of the total annualized cost of system (TAC) to the annual electricity production (TALE) by the system.

$$COE = TAC/TALE \tag{9}$$

In opposite to TALE (historical data), the annualized cost of system is the sum of the annualized capital cost (C_{cap}), the annualized replacement cost (C_{repl}), and the annualized maintenance cost (C_{maint}) of all components of system.

$$\text{TAC} = C_{cap} + C_{repl} + C_{maint} \tag{10}$$

Maintenance and replacement cost occur during the project life while capital cost occurs at the beginning of a project.

6 Conclusions and Future Work

A problem of defining and assessing of the energy balance and operational logic within HRESs harnessing solar and wind power for the use within small neighbourhood have been considered in this paper. Novel architecture of HRES, which is accumulating excess energy for the future usage as well as benefits from integration to the External Power Grid (EPG) via Energy Gateway Station is suggested. Total energy balance in the HRES is presented.

Characterization of the energy usage and generation in a small neighbourhood is performed with the focus on assessment of the solar and wind energy potential. Obtaining of data on energy usage in households (such as shown in Fig. 3) is important step for realistic modelling of the HRESs.

Five types of requests related to energy use or supply within HRES or between HRES and EPG are introduced: RH (from individual households for satisfying domestic/industrial power use), RBC (from PSB for recharging), RHP (from HRES to EPG for purchasing extra energy), RGS (from HRES to EPG for selling of the surplus energy) and RGB (from EPG to HRES for buying of the surplus energy). Operational logic of the HRES is presented in a form of pseudocode which is initial step towards formulating functional requirements. Finally, criteria for evaluation of the HRES are formulated and briefly discussed.

Future work requires the following steps:

- Development of the *Power Request and Supply Protocol (PRSP)* within HRES and between HRES and EPG via PGS.
- Detailization of the parameters used in the requests processed by the PRSP (i.e. Time Ti, finite Time Length TLi, finite Energy power volume Ei associated with the request, Priority Pi and Cost Ci).
- Detailization of the functions of the PGS and ESB Control System as relates to the PRSP.

References

1. Parida, B., Iniyan, S., Goic, R.: A review of solar photovoltaic technologies. Renew. Sustain. Energy Rev. **15**(3), 1625–1636 (2011)
2. Hoogwijk, M., Graus, W.: Global potential of renewable energy sources: a literature assessment. Background Report PECSNL072975. By order of REN21 - Renewable Energy Policy Network for the 21st Century (2008)
3. Shendryk, V., Shulyma, O., Parfenenko, Y.: The topicality and the peculiarities of the renewable energy sources integration into the ukrainian power grids and the heating system. In: González-Prida, V., Raman, A. (eds.) Promoting Sustainable Practices through Energy Engineering and Asset Management, pp. 162–192. Engineering Science Reference, Hershey (2015). doi:10.4018/978-1-4666-8222-1.ch007
4. Shulyma, O., Davidsson, P., Shendryk, V., Marchenko, A.: The architecture of an information system for the management of hybrid energy grids. Ann. Comput. Sci. Inform. Syst. **6**, 281–288 (2015)
5. Sumyoblenergo. https://www.soe.com.ua/
6. Angelis-Dimakis, A., Biberacher, M., Dominguez, J., Fiorese, G., Gadocha, S., Gnansounou, E., Guariso, G., Kartalidis, A., Panichelli, L., Pinedo, I., Robba, M.: Methods and tools to evaluate the availability of renewable energy sources. Renew. Sustain. Energy Rev. **15**(2), 1182–1200 (2011)
7. Kaabeche, A., Belhamel, M., Ibtiouen, R.: Techno-economic valuation and optimization of integrated photovoltaic/wind energy conversion system. Sol. Energy **85**(10), 2407–2420 (2011)
8. Belfkira, R., Zhang, L., Barakat, G.: Optimal sizing study of hybrid wind/PV/diesel power generation unit. Sol. Energy **85**(1), 100–110 (2011)
9. Ai, B., Yang, H., Shen, H., Liao, X.: Computer-aided design of PV/wind hybrid system. Renewable Energy **28**(10), 1491–1512 (2003)
10. Koutroulis, E., Kolokotsa, D., Potirakis, A., Kalaitzakis, K.: Methodology for optimal sizing of stand-alone photovoltaic/wind-generator systems using genetic algorithms. Sol. Energy **80**(9), 1072–1088 (2006)
11. Ismail, M.S., Moghavvemi, M., Mahlia, T.M.I.: Design of an optimized photovoltaic and microturbine hybrid power system for a remote small community: case study of Palestine. Energy Convers. Manage. **75**, 271–281 (2013)
12. Zhou, W., Lou, C., Li, Z., Lu, L., Yang, H.: Current status of research on optimum sizing of stand-alone hybrid solar–wind power generation systems. Appl. Energy **87**(2), 380–389 (2010)
13. Bilal, B.O., Sambou, V., Kébé, C.M.F., Ndiaye, P.A., Ndongo, M.: Methodology to size an optimal stand-alone PV/wind/diesel/battery system minimizing the levelized cost of energy and the CO_2 emissions. Energy Procedia **14**, 1636–1647 (2012)

Business Intelligence for Information and Software Systems: Special Session on Intelligent Methods for Data Analysis and Computer Aided Software Engineering

Predicting User Identity and Personality Traits from Mobile Sensor Data

Margit Antal[1(✉)], László Zsolt Szabó[1], and Győző Nemes[2]

[1] Faculty of Technical and Human Sciences, Sapientia University,
Soseaua Sighisoarei 1C, 540485 Tirgu Mures/Corunca, Romania
{manyi,lszabo}@ms.sapientia.ro
[2] Telekom, Bucharest, Romania
nemesgyozo@gmail.com

Abstract. Several types of information can be revealed from data provided by mobile sensors. In this study touchscreen and accelerometer data was collected from a group of 98 volunteers during filling in the Eysenck Personality Questionnaire on a tablet computer. Subjects performed swipes on the touchscreen in order to answer the questions. Touchscreen swipes have been already used for user authentication. We show that our constrained swipes contain enough user specific information to be utilized for the same task. Moreover, we have studied the predictability of personality traits such as extraversion, and neuroticism from the collected data. Extraversion was found to be the most reliably predictable personality trait.

Keywords: Mobile biometrics · Touchscreen · Personality traits · Eysenck personality questionnaire

1 Introduction

People use their mobile devices in a unique way. The way they hold and touch their devices can be sensed by the mobile's sensors (such as accelerometer or touchscreen). Several studies have used touchscreen swipes for continuous user authentication. Feng et al. [15] examined gesture based continuous user authentication for the first time, using horizontal and vertical swipes for user authentication. Zooming gestures were also investigated for the same purpose. Similar studies were performed by Li et al. [19] and Frank et al. [16], which resulted in the conclusion that user identity can be predicted with high accuracy based on a sequence of swipes. Bo et al. [2] added the micro-movement characteristics of the device (obtained from the accelerometer sensor) to the touchscreen data. In addition, Serwadda et al. [26] and Shahzad et al. [27] confirmed the requirement for several consecutive swipes in order to obtain a high accuracy in user authentication. Roy et al. [23] used Hidden Markov models on the dataset collected by Frank et al. and as a consequence improved the authentication performance obtained by the creators of the dataset. In this article we show to what extent personality traits of users can be predicted from touchscreen swipes.

© Springer International Publishing Switzerland 2016
G. Dregvaite and R. Damasevicius (Eds.): ICIST 2016, CCIS 639, pp. 163–173, 2016.
DOI: 10.1007/978-3-319-46254-7_13

Several studies have been conducted in order to reveal the relationship between the use of digital technology and personality traits of users. Phillips et al. [21] sought to identify personality traits associated with mobile phone games. Butt and Phillips reported that personality can predict the amount of mobile phone use [4]. Chittaranjan et al. [6,7] investigated the relationship between behavioural characteristics derived from rich smartphone data and self-reported personality traits, specifically an automatic method to infer the personality type of a user based on mobile phone usage was developed. de Montjoye et al. [20] provided the first evidence that personality traits could be reliably predicted from standard mobile phone logs. Again, personality traits were predicted from social media profiles such as Facebook or Twitter [1,9,22,28]. The use of Internet services and its relationship to personality traits was also investigated [18,29].

Eysenck Personality Questionnaire (EPQ) was developed and published in 1975 by Eysenck &Eysenck [12]. Afterwards, the addition of several improvements resulted in a revised version of the questionnaire (EPQ-R) [13], [11]. The EPQ-R has been translated into different languages and its validity demonstrated in several studies [5,10,14,24,25]. In our study we used the Hungarian 58-question Eysenck Personality Questionnaire. The participants completed the questionnaire on a mobile device, which was in our case a tablet computer.

Our first objective is to study whether user identity information can be revealed from such constrained swipes. The second objective is to examine how reliably personality traits can be predicted from the same data. We will reveal the significant differences in mobile usage data among people belonging to different personality types.

2   Materials and Methods

2.1   Participants and Materials

Ninety-eight participants (60 male, 38 female, aged 19–58) participated in the experiment. All participants completed the Hungarian 58-question Eysenck Personality Questionnaire in a controlled environment. Details of data acquisition are shown in Table 1. All information related to this research is available at http://www.ms.sapientia.ro/~manyi/personality.html

The questionnaire is used to assess four personality traits: Extraversion (E), Neuroticism (N), Psychoticism (P) and Social Desirability (L - Lie scale). The Lie scale measures to what extent subjects deliberately attempt to control their scores. This version of the Eysenck questionnaire consists of 16 questions related to Extraversion, 19 to Neuroticism, 15 to Psychoticism and 8 to the Lie-scale. On each scale the number of questions with corresponding answers were counted and then multiplied by 2 on evaluation purposes. This resulted in four integer numbers (denoted by E, N, P and L), one for each trait. For example, subjects obtained values between 0 and 32 on the extraversion scale. Subjects scoring below 16 may be considered introverted while those scoring above 16 may be regarded as extraverted.

Table 1. Details of data acquisition.

Information	Description
Number of subjects	98
Number of swipes	5684 (98 subjects x 58 questions)
Devices	5 identical Nexus 7 tablets
Number of swipes/question	1
Controlled acquisition	Yes
Age range	19-58 (average: 26.3)
Gender	60 male, 38 female

2.2 Procedure

Raw Data. Participants were instructed to answer all the 58 personality questions shown on a tablet by dragging a slider with their finger from the middle point to either left for a negative or right for a positive answer. Raw data recorded from sensors in each touch point during the drag operation are as follows (see Fig. 1): action code: $\{DOWN, MOVE, UP\}$; x, y coordinates; acceleration measured along x, y, z axes; pressure exerted on the screen; finger area - a normalized value of touch area in pixels; timestamp.

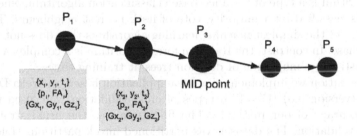

Fig. 1. Swipe consisting of five touch points. In each touch point the saved raw data are the following: x, y - touch point coordinates; t - timestamp; p - pressure; FA - Finger area; Gx, Gy, Gz - acceleration measured along the x, y and z axes

Some participants made more than one drag operation in order to answer the question, resulting in several swipes connected to a question. In these cases we always kept only the swipe that contained the most touch points.

Feature Extraction. For each swipe we computed a feature vector having nine features: average_velocity (av), acceleration_at_start (aas), midstroke_pressure (msp), midstroke_finger_area (msfa), mean_pressure (mp), mean_finger_area (mfa), meangx (mgx), meangy (mgy), meangz (mgz).

Let us consider a swipe consisting of n touch points: $Swipe = \{P_1, P_2, \ldots P_n\}$, where a touch point is defined as $P_i = (action_i, x_i, y_i, gx_i, gy_i, gz_i, p_i, fa_i, t_i)$ and $action_1 = DOWN$, $action_i = MOVE$ $i = 2 \ldots n - 1$, $action_n = UP$. The nine features were computed as follows:

$$av = \frac{\sum_{i=1}^{n-1} d(P_i, P_{i+1})}{t_n - t_1} \tag{1}$$

$$aas = \frac{1}{3} \sum_{i=1}^{3} \frac{v_{i+1} - v_i}{t_{i+1} - t_i}, v_{i+1} = \frac{d(P_{i+1}, P_i)}{t_{i+1} - t_i}, i > 0 \tag{2}$$

$$msp = p_{\lfloor \frac{n}{2} \rfloor}, msfa = fa_{\lfloor \frac{n}{2} \rfloor} \tag{3}$$

$$mp = \frac{1}{n} \sum_{i=1}^{n} p_i, mfa = \frac{1}{n} \sum_{i=1}^{n} fa_i \tag{4}$$

$$mgx = \frac{1}{n} \sum_{i=1}^{n} gx_i, mgy = \frac{1}{n} \sum_{i=1}^{n} gy_i, mgz = \frac{1}{n} \sum_{i=1}^{n} gz_i \tag{5}$$

Classification. Two well-known classification algorithms were used to evaluate our datasets: k-Nearest Neighbours (k-NN) and Random forest [3]. The k-NN algorithm is a type of instance-based classification algorithm, where a new instance is classified by a majority vote of its k nearest neighbours. The algorithm is one of the simplest machine learning algorithms that does not require a training phase. In contrast, the Random forest algorithm is a complex algorithm, which constructs a multitude of decision trees at training time.

For evaluation we implemented a Java application based on Weka Data mining tools (version 3.6) [17]. Two types of cross-validation were used to evaluate the accuracy of our methods. The first type was the usual stratified 10-fold cross-validation. The dataset was partitioned into k partitions (folds), then the classifier was trained using 9 partitions and tested with the remaining one. This was repeated 10 times for each partition. The second type is a variant of *leave-one-out cross-validation* of cross-validation, namely the *leave-one-user-out cross-validation*, introduced by Cornelius and Kotz [8]. In this case a classifier was trained using the whole dataset except one user's data and tested with the omitted user's data. The procedure was repeated for each user. This type of cross-validation tests the generality of the classifier, namely how it performs in the case of an unseen user [8].

Besides simple swipe classification we also evaluated the classification performance based on sequences of swipes. A sequence of swipes was classified using the following method. Let us denote N the number of classes and X the sequence of swipes to be classified:

$$X = \{x_1, x_2, \ldots, x_T\}, \qquad x_i \in R^D, \tag{6}$$

where T is the number of swipes and D is the dimension of the feature vector (in our case we used nine features). We computed for each swipe the prediction distribution (Eq. 7).

$$P_i = \{p_i^1, p_i^2, \ldots, p_i^N\}, p_i^k \in [0.1], k = 1 \ldots N, i = 1 \ldots T, \qquad (7)$$

where p_i^k is the probability that x_i belongs to class k (We used *distribution-ForInstance* function from Weka [17]).

This was followed by computing the average probability for each class and choosing the maximum one (Eq. 8).

$$Class(X) = \arg\max_{k=1}^{N} \left\{ \frac{\sum_{i=1}^{T} p_i^k}{T} \right\} \qquad (8)$$

Consequently, a sequence of swipes is classified as belonging to the kth class if the average probability for this class is the maximum one.

3   Results

3.1   Eysenck Personality Questionnaire Results

Table 2 presents the descriptive statistics of the personality trait scores of the 98 participants.

Table 2. EPQ results for the 98 participants, Means, Standard deviations (SD), Minimum, Maximum values and Medians for Extraverison, Neuroticism, Psychoticism and Lie scale traits.

Trait	Mean	SD	Min	Max	Median
Extraversion (E)	17.9	8.48	0	32	18
Neuroticism (N)	22.9	8.18	4	38	22
Psychoticism (P)	20.6	5.34	6	30	22
Lie scale (L)	5.39	2.79	0	12	6

Extraversion was negatively correlated with Neuroticism ($r = -0.33, p < 0.001$) and Psychoticism ($r = -0.23, p < 0.05$). Neuroticism was positively correlated with Psychoticism ($r = 0.33, p < 0.001$), while Lie scale was negatively correlated with Neuroticism ($r = -0.36, p < 0.001$) and positively correlated with Psychoticism ($r = 0.26, p < 0.01$).

3.2   User Classification Results

We performed user classification using 10-fold cross-validation for classifier evaluation. In this case we had 98 classes (the number of subjects) and 58 samples from each subject. Both k-NN and Random forest classifier were evaluated using 10-fold cross-validation. Measurements were repeated five times, each time increasing the length of the swipe sequence to be classified. Outstanding classification results were obtained in the case of Random forest classification algorithm, especially when using 5 swipes (98.8 % accuracy). The detailed results for k-NN and Random forest classifiers are shown in Table 3.

Table 3. User classification accuracies with standard deviation in parentheses. Measurements: 10-fold cross-validation. Swipe sequences of length: 1, 2, 3, 4, 5.

Classifier	#swipes				
	1	2	3	4	5
k-NN (k=1)	0.620 (0.018)	0.619 (0.018)	0.726 (0.026)	0.796 (0.034)	0.841 (0.023)
RF (T=100)	0.806 (0.016)	0.916 (0.008)	0.958 (0.006)	0.975 (0.008)	0.988 (0.005)

3.3   Personality Traits Classification Results

According to the EPQ evaluation procedure (using the Extroversion value obtained for each user), we can split the users into two classes: the more introverted $E1$ ($E < 16$) and the more extraverted class $E2$ ($E \geq 16$). Similarly, we split the dataset along the Neuroticism scale into a less neurotic $N1$ ($N < 19$) and a more neurotic class $N2$ ($N \geq 19$).

These splits resulted in two datasets. The only difference between these datasets is the class information. The population of classes for the two datasets are shown in Table 4.

Table 4. Datasets class information.

Name	Class:#users
E2dataset	E1:36, E2:62
N2dataset	N1:34, N2:64

We evaluated these datasets using the two types of cross-validations described in Sect. 2.2 and the results are presented in Table 5 and 6. In the case of leave-one-user-out cross-validation, classifiers were trained using data from 97 subjects (5626 instances) and tested by using data from a single user (58 instances). After repeating the same procedure for each of the 98 users, the mean and the standard deviation were computed.

Table 5. E and N classification accuracies with standard deviation in parentheses. Measurements: 10 runs, **10-fold cross-validation**. Swipe sequences of length: 1-5.

Classifier	#swipes				
	1	2	3	4	5
	E2dataset				
k-NN (k=1)	0.833 (0.013)	0.829 (0.022)	0.919 (0.014)	0.923 (0.015)	0.954 (0.005)
RF (T=100)	0.904 (0.012)	0.961 (0.007)	0.980 (0.008)	0.989 (0.007)	0.994 (0.005)
	N2dataset				
k-NN (k=1)	0.814 (0.011)	0.801 (0.012)	0.902 (0.015)	0.906 (0.015)	0.946 (0.016)
RF(T=100)	0.903 (0.010)	0.954 (0.008)	0.972 (0.010)	0.981 (0.011)	0.985 (0.008)

Table 6. E, N and EN classification accuracies with standard deviation in parentheses. Measurements: **leave one user out cross-validation.** Swipe sequences of length: 1-5.

Classifier	#swipes				
	1	2	3	4	5
	E2dataset				
k-NN (k=1)	0.582 (0.257)	0.547 (0.262)	0.597 (0.310)	0.579 (0.309)	0.612 (0.341)
RF (T=10)	0.605 (0.334)	0.612 (0.363)	0.620 (0.378)	0.629 (0.387)	0.629 (0.396)
	N2dataset				
k-NN (k=1)	0.527 (0.233)	0.469 (0.288)	0.525 (0.250)	0.490 (0.284)	0.523 (0.321)
RF(T=10)	0.535 (0.314)	0.550 (0.349)	0.556 (0.368)	0.558 (0.378)	0.558 (0.388)

As it can be seen in Table 5, high accuracies have been obtained for both datasets, especially in the case of Random forest classifier and using 5 swipes for classification. The best accuracy obtained was 90.4 % for one swipe and 99.4 % for five swipes, both obtained by the Random forest classifier and E2dataset.

Repeating the same measurements and using leave-one-user-out cross-validation resulted in dramatically dropped mean accuracies (see Table 5). Using Random forest classifier for the E2dataset the accuracies obtained varied from 60.5 % for one swipe to 62.9 % accuracy for five swipes. Nevertheless, the mean accuracy is low, 40 users out of 62 in the Extraversion class (E2dataset) are identified with high accuracy (over 80 %). The distribution of recognition accuracies for users is shown in Fig. 2. It can be seen that the classification accuracy is higher for the E2 class (more extraverted) than for the E1 class (more introverted).

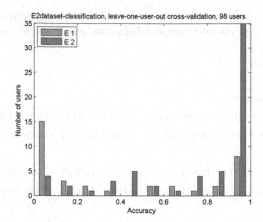

Fig. 2. E2dataset classification results for the 98 measurements (one swipe, **leave-one-user-out cross-validation**). Accuracy distribution among the two classes: E1 - more introverted and E2 - more extraverted.

3.4   Statistical Analysis

Statistical analysis was performed by using the *ttest2* function from MATLAB (The Mathworks, Inc., Natick, MA). The p value of 0.001 was considered significant.

The discriminatory capability of the features was tested using a two-tailed t-test for the difference of the mean values for class related feature sets individually, at a significance level of 0.001 and assuming equal variance. The mean values of 8 features out of 9 (except acceleration_at_start) differ significantly ($p < 0.001$) for the two classes of E2dataset. As for the N2dataset, significant differences in the mean were found only for two features, meangx and meangy.

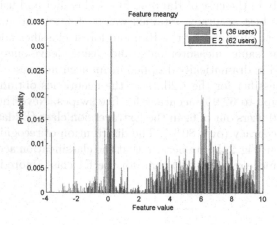

Fig. 3. E2dataset statistics. Sample probability distribution of the meangy feature for the classes in E2dataset.

Differences in device holding position can also be inferred from the sample probability distribution of the meangy feature for the classes in the E2dataset (Fig. 3). The mean values for meangy are 5.953 for class E1 and 3.979 for class E2, which is a consequence of the tendency in group E1 to hold the device more vertically. Lying the device on the table (meangy around 0) was mostly characteristic to the extraverted group.

4 Discussion

Several research papers have been dedicated to show that touchscreen swipes contain a high quantity of user specific information, therefore they may be used in authentication tasks. In this paper we have evaluated user classification based on information content obtained from constrained horizontal swipes. Among the two classifiers Random forest classifier provided the better accuracies for all test cases. However, accuracy for one swipe is not outstanding (80.6%), increasing the number of swipes to five resulted in 98.8% user classification accuracy.

Another question we have examined is whether personality traits can be reliably predicted from touchscreen swipes using machine learning methods. For this purpose two types of cross-validation measurement were used, namely 10-fold cross-validation and a leave-one-user-out cross-validation. While the first type of cross-validation shows how well a method is performing in the case of a particular known user, the second method shows how well an unseen user's data is classified according to a criterion (generalisation). We evaluated the two datasets (E2dataset, N2dataset) using binary classifiers. Our classifiers performed well for each dataset using the traditional 10-fold cross-validation (see Table 5). Moreover, the classification accuracies increased in the case where more than one swipe was used for classification.

In order to better reflect reality, we needed to predict the personality traits of an unseen user. This was achieved by using the leave-one-user-out cross-validation method. The results are shown in Table 6. We can see that the best results were obtained for the Extraversion trait, which can be predicted with approximately 60% accuracy. The huge differences between the two types of evaluation may be explained by taking into account the user identity classification results shown in Table 3. This clearly shows that swipes contain a large amount of information about user identity and this helps in recognising the personality traits of a user in the case of 10-fold cross-validation evaluation (in this case we used each user's data in the training set). However, when we classify the data of an unseen user (the case of leave-one-user-out cross-validation), the identity information is missing from the training data.

5 Conclusions

In this paper we have analysed user identity and personality related data contained in simple left-right swipes on a touchscreen of a mobile device. The mobile application we developed presents the user the Hungarian version of Eysenck's

Personality Questionnaire, containing 58 questions and it also records usage data for each answer. During our study 98 users completed the test using identical mobile devices. Despite using constrained swipes very good user classification accuracy was obtained by the Random forest classifier. We should mention that this good accuracy was obtained by using 5-swipe sequences (98.8 %).

From the collected data two datasets were created in order to analyse the predictability of users' personality traits across two dimensions: Extraversion and Neuroticism. These datasets were analysed with a 10-fold cross-validation and a leave-one-user-out cross-validation. Very high accuracies were obtained using the 10-fold cross-validation (over 99 % for 5 swipes), although this method cannot be used reliably to predict the personality traits of an unseen user based on our feature set. Only the leave-one-user-out cross-validation provides an effective method of predicting the personality traits of an unseen user. Results obtained by this method are slightly better than the chance level (62.9 % average accuracy for E2dataset and 5 swipes). However, the classification accuracy is over 80 % for two thirds of the more extroverted subjects. This may lead to some potentially promising future research.

Our conclusions are drawn taking into consideration the limitation imposed by having only 98 users with 58 samples/user in this study.

References

1. Back, M.D., Stopfer, J.M., Vazire, S., Gaddis, S., Schmukle, S.C., Egloff, B., Gosling, S.D.: Facebook profiles reflect actual personality, not self-idealization. Psychol. Sci. **21**(3), 372–374 (2010)
2. Bo, C., Zhang, L., Li, X.Y., Huang, Q., Wang, Y.: Silentsense: Silent user identification via touch and movement behavioral biometrics. In: Proceedings of the 19th Annual International Conference on Mobile Computing; Networking, pp. 187–190. MobiCom 2013, ACM (2013)
3. Breiman, L.: Random forests. Mach. Learn. **45**(1), 5–32 (2001)
4. Butt, S., Phillips, J.G.: Personality and self reported mobile phone use. Comput. Hum. Behav. **24**(2), 346–360 (2008)
5. Chico, E., Tous, J., Lorenzo-Seva, U., Vigil-Colet, A.: Spanish adaptation of dickman's impulsivity inventory: its relationship to eysenck's personality questionnaire. Pers. Individ. Differ. **35**(8), 1883–1892 (2003)
6. Chittaranjan, G., Blom, J., Gatica-Perez, D.: Who's who with big-five: Analyzing and classifying personality traits with smartphones. In: 2011 15th Annual International Symposium on Wearable Computers (ISWC), pp. 29–36. IEEE (2011)
7. Chittaranjan, G., Blom, J., Gatica-Perez, D.: Mining large-scale smartphone data for personality studies. Pers. Ubiquit. Comput. **17**(3), 433–450 (2013)
8. Cornelius, C.T., Kotz, D.F.: Recognizing whether sensors are on the same body. Pervasive Mobile Comput. **8**(6), 822–836 (2012)
9. Counts, S., Stecher, K.B.: Self-presentation of personality during online profile creation. In: ICWSM, pp. 191–194 (2009)
10. Dazzi, C.: The eysenck personality questionnaire-revised (epq-r): A confirmation of the factorial structure in the italian context. Pers. Individ. Differ. **50**(6), 790–794 (2011)

11. Eysenck, H.J., et al.: Manual of the eysenck personality scales (eps adult) (1991)
12. Eysenck, H.J., Eysenck, S.B.G.: Manual of the Eysenck Personality Questionnaire (junior and adult). Hodder and Stoughton, London (1975)
13. Eysenck, H., Eysenck, M.: A natural science approach (1985)
14. Eysenck, S.B., Barrett, P.T., Barnes, G.E.: A cross-cultural study of personality: Canada and england. Pers. Individ. Differ. **14**(1), 1–9 (1993)
15. Feng, T., Liu, Z., Kwon, K.A., Shi, W.: Continuous mobile authentication using touchscreen gestures. In: 2012 IEEE Conference on Technologies for Homeland Security (HST), pp. 451–456 (2012)
16. Frank, M., Biedert, R., Ma, E., Martinovic, I., Song, D.: Touchalytics: On the applicability of touchscreen input as a behavioral biometric for continuous authentication. Inf. Forensics Secur. IEEE Trans. **8**(1), 136–148 (2013)
17. Hall, M., Frank, E., Holmes, G., Pfahringer, B., Reutemann, P., Witten, I.H.: The weka data mining software: An update. SIGKDD Explor. Newsl. **11**(1), 10–18 (2009)
18. Hamburger, Y.A., Ben-Artzi, E.: The relationship between extraversion and neuroticism and the different uses of the internet. Comput. Human Behav. **16**(4), 441–449 (2000)
19. Li, L., Zhao, X., Xue, G.: Unobservable re-authentication for smartphones. In: NDSS. The Internet Society (2013)
20. de Montjoye, Y.A., Quoidbach, J., Robic, F., Pentland, A.S.: Predicting personality using novel mobile phone-based metrics. In: Social Computing, Behavioral-Cultural Modeling and Prediction, pp. 48–55. Springer (2013)
21. Phillips, J.G., Butt, S., Blaszczynski, A.: Personality and self-reported use of mobile phones for games. CyberPsychol. Behav. **9**(6), 753–758 (2006)
22. Ross, C., Orr, E.S., Sisic, M., Arseneault, J.M., Simmering, M.G., Orr, R.R.: Personality and motivations associated with facebook use. Comput. Hum. Behav. **25**(2), 578–586 (2009)
23. Roy, A., Halevi, T., Memon, N.: An hmm-based behavior modeling approach for continuous mobile authentication. In: 2014 IEEE International Conference on Acoustics, Speech and Signal Processing (ICASSP), pp. 3789–3793, May 2014
24. Ruch, W.: Die revidierte fassung des eysenck personality questionnaire und die konstruktion des deutschen epq-r bzw. epq-rk. Z. für Differ. Diagnostische Psychol. **20**, 1–14 (1999)
25. Sanderman, R., Eysenck, S., Arrindell, W.: Cross-cultural comparisons of personality: The netherlands and england. Psychol. Reports **69**(3f), 1091–1096 (1991)
26. Serwadda, A., Phoha, V., Wang, Z.: Which verifiers work?: A benchmark evaluation of touch-based authentication algorithms. In: 2013 IEEE Sixth International Conference on Biometrics: Theory, Applications and Systems (BTAS), pp. 1–8 (2013)
27. Shahzad, M., Liu, A.X., Samuel, A.: Secure unlocking of mobile touch screen devices by simple gestures: You can see it but you can not do it. In: Proceedings of the 19th Annual International Conference on Mobile Computing; Networking, pp. 39–50. ACM, New York, MobiCom 2013, NY, USA (2013)
28. Stecher, K.B., Counts, S.: Spontaneous inference of personality traits and effects on memory for online profiles. In: ICWSM, pp. 118–126 (2008)
29. Tosun, L.P., Lajunen, T.: Does internet use reflect your personality? relationship between eysenck's personality dimensions and internet use. Comput. Hum. Behav. **26**(2), 162–167 (2010)

Towards a Comprehensive Formal Model for Business Processes

Khalil Mecheraoui, Nabil Belala[✉], and Djamel Eddine Saïdouni

MISC Laboratory, University of Constantine 2 – Abdelhamid Mehri,
Constantine, Algeria
{mecheraoui,belala,saidouni}@misc-umc.org

Abstract. In order to enable enterprises to operate more effectively
and efficiently, providing a high reliability of the specification of business processes is an active research subject. However, the proposed
approaches use limited models. WS-BPEL (or BPEL for short) is the
most well known and used orchestration language describing the Web
services composition in form of business process. However, BPEL lacks
a formal semantics. This paper introduces High-Level Time Open Workflow Nets with Action Duration model (HL-DToN) which is an extension
of Time Petri Nets with Action Duration (DTPN) for tackling different
aspects of business processes as far as possible. We use this model either
to specify WS-BPEL processes or to directly specify business processes.

Keywords: Business processes · Open workflow model · Data modeling · Time constraints · Action durations · True-concurrency semantics ·
Formal specification

1 Introduction

To achieve its goals, an enterprise executes a collection of activities, sequentially or
in a concurrently, in a specific chronological and logical order, and possibly in different locations. This procedure, called *business process*, is designed to show how
and when the work is done with a beginning, an end, and identified inputs and
outputs. To improve business processes, Business Process Management (BPM) is
the key to align enterprises activities with the needs of their clients [1]. Therefore, there are some aspects to be considered in BPM such as time constraints,
data manipulation, and structural properties of business processes. Furthermore,
with the emergence of new information technologies, the enterprises want their
customers and partners to be able to access quickly and directly to their functionality. To achieve this, Web services are software systems designed to support
interoperability and carry out the business tasks over the web. However, as the
capability of completely separate Web services is limited, one have to create new
functionality by composing existing Web services in such way to interact together.
To achieve that, many languages that support the descriptions of orchestration
and choreography are proposed (e.g. [2–4] and [5]).

© Springer International Publishing Switzerland 2016
G. Dregvaite and R. Damasevicius (Eds.): ICIST 2016, CCIS 639, pp. 174–186, 2016.
DOI: 10.1007/978-3-319-46254-7_14

Web Services Business Process Execution Language (WS-BPEL) [5] is the most well known and used composition language which defines business processes by the orchestration of various partner interactions. However, WS-BPEL is defined informally in natural language. Thus, it lacks a formal semantics which allows a direct formal verification of well-functioning of web services. To solve this problem, one can specify business processes written in a WS-BPEL process through a formal model. Therefore, providing a formal semantics for BPEL (BPEL4WS 1.1 [6] or its revision WS-BPEL 2.0 [5]) is a research subject in several work using many approaches (e.g. [7–11]) based on various formal models. Nevertheless, many proposed approaches in the literature use limited models, either in terms of time characteristics, data modeling and manipulation, the composition and the interactions among processes; or in terms of the use of the interleaving semantics in low-level specification.

In this paper, we introduce and formalize *High-Level Time Open Workflow Nets with Action Duration* (HL-DToN). It is an extension of Time Petri Nets with Action Duration (DTPN) [12] which is proposed to deal with different aspects of business processes by adding an interface for inbound and outbound message exchange, and enabling representing and manipulating data. Furthermore, we consider both time constraints and action durations under a true-concurrency semantics to naturally express concurrent and parallel behaviors of processes. In fact, HL-DToN model can be considered as a convergence of the three models: DTPN, HLPN [13] and oWFN [14] in which we can specify WS-BPEL or directly specify business processes considering different aspects.

The remainder of this paper is organized as follows. First, we introduce in Sect. 2 some extensions of Petri nets. In Sect. 3, HL-DToN are introducted. Section 4 is devoted to show strengths of HL-DToN by providing two patterns for two activities of WS-BPEL 2.0. Finally, we give some conclusions and perspectives of our work.

2   Preliminaries

2.1   Petri Nets

Petri nets [15] are both formal and graphical modeling formalism, allowing the specification of distributed and concurrent systems by modeling states, events, conditions, synchronization, etc. Formally, $Q = (P, T, F, B)$ is a Petri net where P is a set of places, Tr is a set of transitions such that $P \cap Tr = \emptyset$. $B : P \times Tr \to \mathbb{N}$ is a backward incidence function such that $B(p_i, t_j)$ represents the arc weight from t_j to p_i and $F : P \times Tr \to \mathbb{N}$ is a forward incidence function such that $F(p_i, t_j)$ represents arc weight from p_i to t_j.

2.2   High Level Petri Nets

High-Level Petri Nets (HLPN) are defined in the international standard ISO/IEC 15909-1 [13] developed in 2004. This standard is mainly providing a glossary of

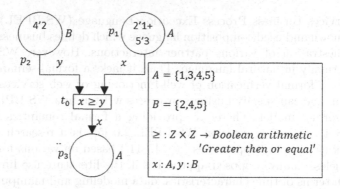

Fig. 1. An example of HLPNG

terms and abbreviations, the mathematical conventions needed for the definition of HLPN, the semantic model for HLPN, the formal definition for High-Level Petri Net Graph (HLPNG) which is the graphical form of HLPN, and the formal concepts of marking, enabling and transition rules.

A High-Level Petri Net Graph (HLPNG) includes a graph and a declaration part in which all the types, functions, constants and variables used for the graph are defined. Note that using HLPNG, we can find transition conditions (boolean expressions) associated with transitions, each place may contain a multiset of tokens, and over arcs we can find annotations (constants, variables and function images). An example of HLPNG is depicted in Fig. 1.

2.3 Workflow Nets

The workflow (workflow process) is the automation of a business process, in whole or part [16]. To model workflow processes, van der Aalst [17] defines the classical workflow net (WF-net) which is a special class of Petri nets satisfying two requirements. First, it has two special places: i and o. i is a source place, i.e., $°i = \emptyset$; and o is a final place, i.e., $o° = \emptyset$. A token in i corresponds to an instance that must be treated while a token in o corresponds to an instance that has been treated. Furthermore, for every node there exists a path from i to o which covers the node.

It is important to note that WF-nets ignore important aspects such as temporal characteristics of processes. Also, this model is unable to handle the interaction between workflow processes. Therefore, there are many extensions of WF-nets in the literature (see e.g. [14,18] and [19]).

Based on van der Aalst WF-nets and Timed Petri Nets of Jenner [20], Sbaï proposes a workflow net model handling the durations of tasks by associating with each transition an amount of time. This temporal extension is called *Time WF-nets* (TWF-nets) [18]. In this model, the tokens in an input place of a transition which can be fired t are removed by its firing, and the output places cannot be marked before the expiry of the duration associated to t. Thus, the

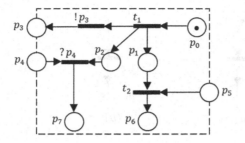

Fig. 2. Open workflow net

semantics of TWF-nets model is similar to the semantics of DTPN. We note that this model has weaknesses. For instance, it is not suitable for the composition of several processes.

In general, workflow processes are supposed to communicate with other processes. Therefore, in [14] the authors propose an open version of classical workflow nets named *open workflow nets* (oWFN). This open version is used to model workflow processes which communicate with other processes via communication channels (communication places). Graphically, a oWFN is surrounded by a dashed box, with the interface places. Also, a transition t connected to an input (resp. output) interface place p is labeled with $?p$ (resp. $!p$). Note that this open model ignores temporal characteristics of processes too. As an example, Fig. 2 shows an oWFN with three interface places (the input places p_4 and p_5 and the output place p_3), an initial place p_0, and two final places p_6 and p_7.

We know that in some real scenarios we cannot precisely determine the execution duration of an activity but it can be done in a time interval. In [19], the authors propose to adopt the Time Petri Nets of Merlin [21] to provide an extension of workflow nets called Time open Workflow Nets (ToWF-nets). In fact, this model associates two dates *min* and *max* with each transition of an open workflow net to define its interval. However, note that this model does not support data modeling and manipulation.

As we have seen, the different workflow nets presented above have weaknesses. Also, it is important to note that all these extensions are not based on a true-concurrency semantics.

2.4   Time Petri Nets with Action Duration

In [12], *Time Petri Nets with Action Duration* (DTPN), which can be considered as a generalization of Merlin's TPNs [21], T-TdPNs [22] and P-TdPN [23], are proposed. This model supports both time constraints and action durations under a true-concurrency semantics. A time constraint (temporal interval) associated to a transition t defines the firing interval in which t can be fired while an action duration indicates the duration of its corresponding action. A true-concurrency semantics was given for DTPN in terms of *Durational Action Timed Automata* (DATA) [24].

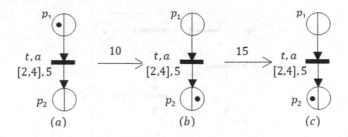

Fig. 3. Marking in DTPN

In DTPN, there are two sets of tokens, namely unavailable tokens (or *bound tokens*) and available tokens (or *free tokens*). Tokens are put on the right side of an output place of a transition t as long as the actions associated to this transition are running. We call these tokens unavailable tokens. An unavailable token becomes available at the end of the execution of the associated action. Hence, it is put at the left side. As an example, Fig. 3 describes a marked DTPN in which the token in the input place p_1 became available at the time 7.

Definition 1 (DTPN). *Let* $\mathbb{T}$ *be a non-negative temporal domain (like* $\mathbb{Q}^+$ *or* $\mathbb{R}^+$*) and* Act *be a finite set of actions, i.e. an alphabet[1]. A Time Petri Net with Action Duration (DTPN) on* $\mathbb{T}$ *and of support* Act *is a tuple* $N = (P, Tr, B, F, \lambda, SI, \Gamma)$ *such that*

- *$Q = (P, Tr, F, B)$ is a finite Petri net, i.e. $|P \cup Tr| \in \mathbb{N}$.;*
- *$\lambda : Tr \to Act \cup \{\tau\}$ is a labeling function of a DTPN. If $\lambda(t) \in Act$ then t is called observable or external;*
- *$SI : Tr \to \mathbb{T} \times \mathbb{T} \cup \infty$ is a function that associates to each transition a static firing interval;*
- *$\Gamma : Act \to \mathbb{T}$ is a function that associates to each action its static duration.*

In [12], a true-concurrency semantics is given to DTPN in terms of Durational Action Timed Automata.

3   High-Level Time Open Workflow Nets with Action Duration

3.1   Time Open Workflow Nets with Action Duration (DToN)

Given that workflow services are supposed to communicate with other work-flow services, and that time in workflow processes is very important and crucial to determine and control activities life cycle, we employ Time Petri Nets with Action Duration model in the context of workflow processes. We provide the

---

[1] Assuming that $\tau \notin Act$ (τ indicates *invisible* action, also known as silent or internal action).

formal model *Time Open Workflow Nets with Action Duration* (DToN) which is extended from DTPN as an open variant adapted to workflow. In fact, it is enriched with an interface for joining each DToN pattern with other DToN patterns to allow inbound and outbound message exchange. Specifically, it is enriched with communication places for asynchronous communication in which each communication place of a DToN pattern represents a channel to send (receive) messages to (from) other DToN patterns.

Definition 2 (DToN). *A Time Open Workflow Net with Action Duration is a Time Petri Net with Action Duration* $PN = (P, Tr, F, B, \lambda, SI, \Gamma)$ *with*

- *Two sets:* $P_{in}, P_{out} \subseteq P$ *such that* $\forall t \in Tr : B(p,t) = 0, \forall p \in P_{in}$ *and* $\forall t \in Tr : F(p,t) = 0, \forall p \in P_{out}$;
- *An initial marking* M_0 *and a set of final markings* Ω *such that* $\forall M \in \Omega : \nexists t \in Tr, M[t\rangle$ *and* $\forall M \in \Omega \cup \{M_0\} : M(p) = 0, \forall p \in P_{in} \cup P_{out}$.

According to Definition 2, the set of places P contains inner places and also two sets of special places that are P_{in} and P_{out}. These two sets represent respectively interface input places which are input places, not output, and interface output places which are output places, not input. Also, in DToN, two conditions must be met: no transition can be fired at any final marking, and in the initial and the final markings, the interface places should not be marked. Finally, note that DToN model considers both time constraints and action durations under a true-concurrency semantics.

Graphically, a DToN is surrounded by a dashed frame, with the interface places in which all interface places have a second label depicted outside the place. This latter is used for the composition or to show the purpose of the place. We note that initial and final places are always labeled respectively by *Initial* and *Final*. An example is shown in Fig. 4 which represents a DToN pattern named X and contains: two inner places p_1 and p_2, and four interface places on the dashed frame. Interface places are the initial place *Initial*, the final place *Final*, the interface output place α, and the interface input place β.

In order to compose open workflow nets, some approaches are provided. In [14] Massuthe, Reisig, and Schmidt propose the composition of two oWFN by

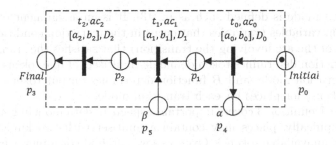

Fig. 4. DToN pattern X

sharing input and output elements in common, in which the composition of two oWFN A and B is an oWFN. Each input interface place of A must be joined with an output interface place of B and turns into an inner place if these two places have the same identifier, and vice-versa. However, it is important to note that this approach only supports the composition of two oWFN, no more. In [25], the authors propose the composition of Timed Open Workflow Nets (ToN) by adding a mediation net to deal with message mismatches in which the composition of two ToN A and B via a mediation net MN is called Mediation-Aided Composition of ToN (MToN).

In this paper, we propose a simple approach to compose DToN patterns. We model each process in a composition by a DToN pattern. All interface places have a second label (label 2) depicted outside the place in which the interface places of these several patterns, only which they have the same label $-$label $2-$, are joined without turning them into inner places. Except initial and final places because an initial place can generally be joined either with another initial place or with a final place (e.g. to sequentially compose patterns).

3.2   High-Level Time Open Workflow Nets with Action Duration

To model data flow and data manipulation based on the international standard ISO/IEC 15909-1 [13], we extend Time Open Workflow Nets with Action Duration to *High-Level Time Open Workflow Nets with Action Duration* (HL-DToN). This high-level model allows us to completely integrate data while such data can also be ignored by moving to DToN.

Definition 3. *A High-Level Time Open Workflow Nets with Action Duration is a tuple* $HN = (P, Tr, F, B, \lambda, SI, \Gamma, D, Type, M_0)$ *where*

- $N = (P, Tr, F, B, \lambda, SI, \Gamma)$ *is a DToN with* $F, B : TR \to \Phi PL^2$ *are the Pre and Post mappings with* $TR = \{(t, m) | t \in Tr, m \in Type(t)\}$ *and* $PL = \{(p, g) | p \in P, g \in Type(p)\}$;
- D *is a non-empty finite set of domains. Each element of* D *is called* type;
- $Type : P \cup Tr \to D$ *is a function used to assign types to places and to determine transition mode;*
- $M_0 \in \Phi PL$ *is a multiset called the* initial marking *of the net.*

Transition mode is defined such as in [13]. It is an assignment of values to the transition variables (variables that occur in the transition condition and the annotations of the arc involving the transition) that satisfies the transition condition. F function determines token demands (multisets of free tokens) on places for each transition mode, and B function determines output tokens (multisets of bound tokens) for places for each transition mode.

Note that Definition 3 covers important aspects of data modeling and manipulation. Graphically, places may contain a multiset with two kinds of tokens (available or unavailable tokens). Over arcs we can find constants, variables and

---

[2] ΦPL is the set of multisets over PL.

function images. Transitions can be associated with boolean expressions (transition conditions). Thus, a transition is annotated in this model by its name, a name of its associated action, a time interval (firing interval), a duration of execution, and a boolean expression (the transition condition).

Marking of HL-DToN. A marking M is a multiset of available and unavailable tokens of correct type for all places. Formally, $M \in \Phi PL$.

Enabling a Transition. A transition $t \in Tr$ is *enabled* in a transition mode $\hat{t}$ and a marking M iff

$$\forall p \in P, F_{\hat{t}}(p, t) \leq M(p)$$

Enabling free tokens are the free tokens resulting from evaluating input arc's expression in and with respect to a specific transition mode.

Firing Rule. Assuming that the firing interval of a transition t is $[min, max]$ and t is enabled in a transition mode at the time ϑ, t will be fired in the time interval $[\vartheta + min, \vartheta + max]$. When t is fired, its input arc enabling free tokens with respect to that mode are dropped from the left side of the input place (the available input place's marking) and the multiset of tokens of the evaluated output arc expression is added to the left side of the output place (the unavailable input place's marking).

Formally, The firing of $t \in Tr$ in transition mode $\hat{t}$ and marking M, results a new marking M' defined by:

$$\forall p \in P, M'(p) = M(p) - F_{\hat{t}}(p, t) + B_{\hat{t}}(p, t)$$

Now, we can make a comparison among Sect. 2 models and HL-DToN. Table 1 shows that HL-DToN overcomes the others. In each column, we use '+' for *yes* and '-' for *no*. The meaning of the column headers are as follows: A: supports the control of data flow using arc annotations and transition conditions. B: able to use complex structured data as tokens. C: adapted to workflow. D: suitable for the composition of several processes to handle the interaction between them. E: able to handle the duration of tasks. F: supports both time constraints and action durations under a true-concurrency semantics.

Table 1. Comparison of different formal models

	A	B	C	D	E	F		A	B	C	D	E	F
PN	−	−	−	−	−	−	oWFN	−	−	+	+	−	−
HLPN	+	+	−	−	−	−	ToWFN-net	−	−	+	+	+	−
WF-net	−	−	+	−	−	−	DTPN	−	−	−	−	+	+
TWF-net	−	−	+	−	+	−	HL-DToN	+	+	+	+	+	+

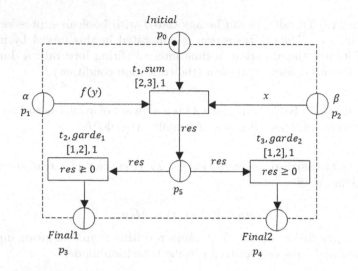

Fig. 5. Pattern for checking the result of $x + f(y)$

As example, we provide the HL-DToN pattern depicted in Fig. 5. This pattern is used to check if the result of $x + f(y)$ is negative or not. The control flow starts with an available token in the initial place p_0 and it ends either with an available token in the final place p_3 or in the final place p_4.

First, transition t_1 allows us to calculate the sum of x plus $f(y)$. The result of this sum is saved in the variable res. In the second step, this information is analyzed using both t_2 and t_3. Either the result is greater than or equal zero ($res \geq 0$) and therefore t_3 will be fired after a period between 1 and 2 units of time, or the result is negative and therefore t_2 will be fired after a period between 1 and 2 units of time. In the first case, p_4 will be marked by an available token after 1 unit of time. In the second case, p_3 will be marked by an available token after 1 unit of time.

4   An HL-DToN Semantics for WS-BPEL

WS-BPEL is the most used language to specify the behavior of business processes based on Web services. In our approach, which is similar to the one in [9], given that the construction of the WS-BPEL process is performed by the composition of its constructs, it is clear that each construct should be modeled, at least, by an HL-DToN pattern. This latter has an interface used to join this pattern with other patterns. The composition of all patterns forms an HL-DToN representing a formal semantics for the WS-BPEL process.

Thus, we must provide at least one pattern of each basic and structured activity, links, and the four handlers. In this paper, we provide two HL-DToN patterns. One for ⟨wait⟩ activity to specify a delay for a certain period of time,

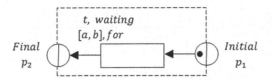

Fig. 6. A pattern for a ⟨wait⟩ activity

and the other for the activity ⟨forEach⟩ in the case of *parallel = yes*. Other patterns of the other activities can be found in [26].

⟨wait⟩ **Activity.** A ⟨wait⟩ activity is used to specify a delay for a certain period of time or until a certain deadline is reached [5].

The pattern of a ⟨wait⟩ activity to specify a delay of a certain period of time is given in Fig. 6. In this pattern, we represent the delay for a certain period by the duration of the action associated to transition t. It is clear that this transformation is very easy due to the existence of action durations associated to transitions in HL-DToN.

⟨forEach⟩ **Activity.** The ⟨forEach⟩ activity iterates its child scope activity exactly $N + 1$ times where N equals finalCounterValue minus startCounterValue. If *parallel=yes* then this is a parallel ⟨forEach⟩ where the $N + 1$ instances of the enclosed ⟨scope⟩ activity should occur in parallel [5].

The pattern of the activity ⟨forEach⟩ in the case of *parallel=yes* is depicted in Fig. 7. To simplify the pattern and such as they are defined in [9], we add the object variable and we use the variable X (in capital letter) representing a set of variables. Also, we use read arcs witch are unfolded to loops. Furthermore, it is important to note that this pattern represents the case in which the optional element ⟨completionCondition⟩[3] does not exist.

As depicted in Fig. 7, if the initial place is marked by an available token, the stored data in the object *Obj* will be read using two read arcs. Its values are saved in X and analyzed using t_1 and t_4. If an error[4] occurs ($EB = $ **true**), the error information will be saved in *error* and the interface place *failed* will be marked. This latter must be joined with the associated interface place on a pattern of a fault handler (labeled by *failed*). If there is not an error ($EB = $ **false**) and then the two places p_4 et p_5 become marked by available tokens, the two transitions t_2 and t_3 will be used respectively to evaluate the expressions in finalCounterValue and startCounterValue. Their two results will be respectively saved in *fcv* and *scv*. Thereafter, the transition conditions $fcv \geq scv$ (t_5) and $fcv \ngeq scv$ (t_6) must be evaluated[5]. If $fcv \geq scv$ (t_5), the two variables fcv and scv are used to calculate the arc weight from t_5 to the initial place (p_8) of

---

[3] It is used to force early termination of some of the children (in the parallel case) [5].
[4] For instance, because of a selection failure.
[5] In WS-BPEL, "if startCounterValue is greater than finalCounterValue, then the child ⟨scope⟩ activity must not be performed and the ⟨forEach⟩ activity is complete." [5].

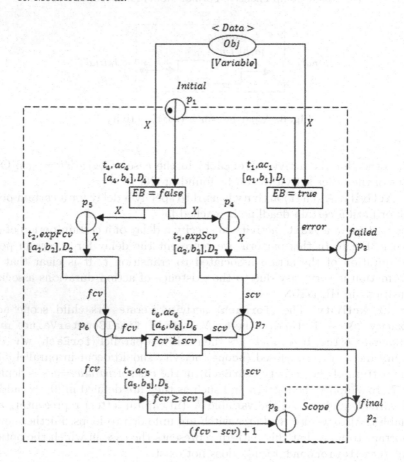

Fig. 7. Pattern for ⟨forEach⟩ activity in case of *parallel=yes*

the enclosed ⟨scope⟩. This allows us to iterate the child scope $N + 1$ times in parallel where N equals $(fcv - scv) + 1$ (this is thanks to DTPN semantics).

Finally, it is important to note that this approach differentiates from the already existing approaches by covering different characteristics of business processes. For instance, it covers the aspect of action duration and time constraints, unlike the other approaches.

5   Conclusion

In this paper, we introduced the formal model of High-Level Time Open Workflow Nets with Action Duration (HL-DToN) by which we do not only specify WS-BPEL processes but directly specify business processes as well. This model is able to enable inbound and outbound message exchange, to consider time constraints and action durations under a true-concurrency semantics, and also to cover important aspects of data modeling and manipulation.

Furthermore, a transformation of two WS-BPEL activities, featuring the advantages of the model, is presented. Actually, we provided a pattern of a ⟨wait⟩ activity that specifies a delay for a certain period of time, and a pattern for the activity ⟨forEach⟩ in the case of *parallel=yes*.

In the near future, we plan to express action durations using random variables as those present in some stochastic extensions of Petri nets. Also, we project to continue the transformation of WS-BPEL constructs using HL-DToN. Thereafter, we aim to extend the use of HL-DToN to verify qualitative and quantitative business processes properties.

References

1. Rogge-Solti, A., Kasneci, G.: Temporal anomaly detection in business processes. In: Sadiq, S., Soffer, P., Völzer, H. (eds.) BPM 2014. LNCS, vol. 8659, pp. 234–249. Springer, Heidelberg (2014). doi:10.1007/978-3-319-10172-9_15
2. Thatte, S.: XLANG: Web services for business process design. Microsoft Corporation (2001)
3. Leymann, F., et al.: Web services flow language (WSFL 1.0) (2001)
4. Kavantzas, N., et al.: Web services choreography description language version 1.0. W3C Candidate Recommendation **9**, 290–313 (2005)
5. OASIS Standard. WSBPEL Ver. 2.0 (2007). http://docs.oasis-open.org/wsbpel/2.0/OS/wsbpel-v2.0-OS.html
6. Andrews, T., et al.: Business Process Execution Language for Web services (2003)
7. Thivolle, D.: Langages modernes pour la modélisation et la vérification des systèmes asynchrones. Ph.D. thesis, Université de Grenoble and Université Polytechnique de Bucarest (2011)
8. Cavalli, A., et al.: Definition of the mapping from BPEL to WS-TEFSM. In: Livrable WEBMOV-FC-D2.3/T2.4 (2008)
9. Stahl, C.: A Petri net semantics for BPEL (2005)
10. Lohmann, N.: A feature-complete petri net semantics for WS-BPEL 2.0. In: Dumas, M., Heckel, R. (eds.) WS-FM 2007. LNCS, vol. 4937, pp. 77–91. Springer, Heidelberg (2008). doi:10.1007/978-3-540-79230-7_6
11. Abouzaid, F., Mullins, J.: A calculus for generation, verification and refinement of BPEL specifications. Electron. Notes Theor. Comput. Sci. **200**(3), 43–65 (2007)
12. Belala, N., et al.: Time petri nets with action duration: a true concurrency real-time model. Int. J. Embed. Real-Time Commun. Syst. (IJERTCS) **4**(2), 62–83 (2013)
13. ISO/JTC1/SC7/ WG19: International Standard ISO/IEC 15909: Software and Systems Engineering - High-level Petri Nets, Part 1: Concepts, Definitions and Graphical Notation (2004)
14. Reisig, W., Massuthe, P., Schmidt, K.: An Operating Guideline Approach to the SOA (2005)
15. Petri, C.: Kommunikation mit Automaten. Ph.D. thesis. Schriften des Instituts für instrumentelle Mathematik, University of Bonn, Germany (1962)
16. WFMC: Workflow management coalition terminology and glossary. Technical Report WFMC-TC-1011, Workflow Management Coalition, Brussels (1999)
17. van der Aalst, W.M.P.: Verification of workflow nets. In: Azéma, P., Balbo, G. (eds.) Application and Theory of Petri Nets 1997. LNCS, vol. 1248, pp. 407–426. Springer, Heidelberg (1997). doi:10.1007/3-540-63139-9_48

18. Sbaï, Z.: Contribution á la Modélisation et á la Vérification de Processus Workflow. Ph.D. thesis, Ecole Doctorale Informatique, Télécommunications et Electronique de paris. France (2010)
19. Sbaï, Z., Barkaoui, K., Boucheneb, H.: Compatibility analysis of time open workflow nets. In: PNSE 2014 - Petri Nets and Software Engineering (2014)
20. Jenner, L.: Further studies on timed testing of concurrent systems. Technical Report 4, Institute für Mathematik, Universität Augsburg (1998)
21. Merlin, P.M.: A study of the recoverability of computing systems. Ph.D. thesis. University of California, Irvine, USA (1974)
22. Ramchandani, C.: Analysis of asynchronous concurrent systems by timed Petri nets. PhD thesis, Massachusetts Institute of Technology, Cambridge, MA (1974)
23. Sifakis, J.: Use of petri nets for performance evaluation. Model. Perform. Eval. Comput. Syst. **4**, 75–93 (1977)
24. Saïdouni, D.E., Belala, N.: Actions duration in timed models. In: The International Arab Conference on Information Technology (2006)
25. Du, Y., et al.: Timed compatibility analysis of Web service composition: A modular approach based on Petri nets. Autom. Sci. Eng. **11**(2), 594–606 (2014)
26. Mecheraoui, K.: Spécification formelle des processus métiers par l'utilisation des réseaux de Petri temporellement temporisés. MSc Thesis, Ecole Nationale Supérieure d'Informatique (2015)

Adaptive Control of the Metalworking Technology Systems Operation Based on the Forecast of the Actual Resource of the Cutting Tool

Volodymyr Nahornyi[✉], Olga Aleksenko, and Natalia Fedotova

Sumy State University, Sumy, Ukraine
vnagornyi1989@gmail.com, aleksenko.olga@gmail.com,
fna_2000@mail.ru

Abstract. The article deals with the adaptive control algorithm of the metalworking industrial process systems operation, based on the comparison of the machining time of the part required by the process and the forecast of the actual resource of the tool. The forecast is carried out continuously during the entire period of the machining of the part by means of the specially developed for this software. The program implements the method of the parametric identification of the mathematical model of the sound trend, accompanying the metalworking process.

The sound is recorded via a microphone, which is installed near the cutting area. Incommensurability of the distance from the microphone to the source of the useful signal of cutting to the noise disturbance of the surrounding equipment operation, greatly reduce the distorting influence of this noise disturbance on the forecasting results. Contactless sound recording method allows also to avoid the drawbacks, the contact techniques of the vibrations measurements or the acoustic emission, traditionally used in the adaptive control.

The considered in the article adaptive control algorithm allows to use exhaustively the cutting properties of the tool and the operational capabilities of the machine, while ensuring the required quality of the manufacturing of a part.

Keywords: Adaptive control · Metalworking · Forecast of the resourse · Parametric identification · Sound trend · The mathematical model · The microphone · Noise disturbance

1 Introduction

The competitiveness of the modern industry depends directly on an optimal combination of the performance of its equipment and the cost of the products created on this equipment. The optimal combination of the performance and the cost is provided by the automation of the production process [1–3]. Metalworking industrial process systems occupy an important place among the industrial equipment.

For the metalworking industrial process systems, the automation provides computer control for the various machine tools operation. The CAM – systems (CAM from English Computer - Aided Manufacturing), carries out the most effective management

© Springer International Publishing Switzerland 2016
G. Dregvaite and R. Damasevicius (Eds.): ICIST 2016, CCIS 639, pp. 187–198, 2016.
DOI: 10.1007/978-3-319-46254-7_15

of the cutting process and its optimization, representing an automated system or module of an automated system for tools management of the machine tools with NC.

In these systems, the controller's parameters are changed after the change of the object's parameters, providing the constant behavior of the whole system, i.e., the adaptive control of the industrial process system operation is implemented. The adaptability (flexibility) is ensured by the fact that the programs which are placed in the controller's computer, implement the control algorithms focused on the choice of the optimal combinations of three control parameters of the metalworking process (depth, feed and cutting speed). The optimum is achieved by the determining of the extremum of the objective function that allows you to reach on this machine either maximum performance or low cost of the obtained part [4].

However, the main drawback of these algorithms is the implicit or explicit focus on the average data about the recourse of the cutting tool. This approach to the managing of the machine tool does not allow in the practice of the cutting to avoid sudden failure of the tool, which is inevitably accompanied by the appearance of the waste.

This is explained by the fact that the problem of the determining of the actual resource of the tool did not receive its workable solution that significantly reduces the efficiency of the functioning of the intensively developed at present intelligent systems for the industrial processes control.

The article discusses the algorithm for adaptive control of the work of cutting equipment, which is devoid of these disadvantages. The algorithm selects the optimum combination of cutting conditions because of comparing the required duration fabrication part with forecasts the actual resource of the tool. This allows timely adjustments to equipment operation to anticipate sudden failures tool and extending the period of its faultless operation. The probability of occurrence of the defect of manufactured parts is reduced at the same time, almost to zero.

This paper is organized as follows. Section 2 describes the previous work on the adaptive control and non-contact method of control of the machining industrial process system. In Sect. 3 the method of the forecasting of the resource of the cutting tool is considered. In Sect. 4, the algorithm of the adaptive control of the metalworking industrial process system operation is presented, which uses for the selection of the optimal combination of the control parameters the resource forecast of the tool. Conclusions are presented in Sect. 5.

2 Related Work and Method

At present, the work of the most automated machine tools subjects to the "hard" programming when the machining modes, are assigned according to the most loaded cutting conditions, which in the total time of the industrial process system take relatively small part [5–8]. For this reason, the main part of the cutting process takes place with the underutilization of the capacity of the cutting tool and the machine.

This is contrary to modern approaches to the organization of production, the aim of which is on the contrary to use exhaustively all the capabilities of the metalworking industrial process system provided by the developers of the machine and by the compilers of the industrial process. Following this rule allows increasing the productivity of metalworking, at the same time reducing its cost and deciding so the main task of the modern production - increasing its competitiveness.

Prevailing by the present time traditional algorithms of work of the adaptive control systems, despite their outward differences, have a common drawback - they all directly or indirectly based on the use of average (referential) data on the maximum permissible degree of tool wear and its resource. These algorithms do not allow creating a competitive production in practice.

This is because the reference information only with a certain probability characterizes the individual actual resource of the tool, which it has in the particular prevailing operating conditions. As a result, the existing control algorithms do not allow preempting the seemingly sudden damage of the tool and avoiding accompanying this defect of the part [9]. In order to combat a sudden tool failure, a compulsory tool change is provided, as a result, it be removed from the service beforehand, having a substantial reserve of the resource [10].

To solve this problem it was necessary to develop an algorithm of the adaptive control of the operation of the metalworking process system, which is radically different from the usual ones. The novelty of the algorithm is that for the first time in the history of the adaptive control of the cutting process, while selecting, it focuses on the forecast of the individual actual resource of the tool, which it has in the given operating conditions. The information about the resource is obtained by the operating computer processing of the initial data recorded during the continuous sound control operation of the industrial process systems [11].

Audio control is carried out by the contactless method of measurement using a microphone installed near the cutting area, which allows avoiding disadvantages of the contact techniques that are traditionally used in the adaptive control for the measurements such as vibrations or acoustic emission during the operation of the machine tool. The registration of these parameters takes place in the conditions of strong distorting effect of noise caused by the mechanical vibrations of the machine [12].

The distances from the microphone to the source of the useful signal of cutting and to the surrounding equipment, creating sound in the process of work, which can serve as a potential noise disturbance for the sound control, in practice, are incommensurable. The first distance is fractions of a centimeter, and the second, according to the rules of planning workshops and sanitary norms, is already measured in meters. This incommensurability of distances leads to the fact that the interference signal, according to the working in the acoustics "rule of six decibels" [13] undergoes a substantially greater compared with the useful signal, scattering on pathways from the source to the microphone.

The data obtained by measuring the sound come into the computing device (stationary, portable or embedded computer), where they, are analyzed to determine (forecast) the numerical values of the resource of the tool. The forecast of the resource is the main parameter, by which we are guided, in the performance of the adaptive control operation of the metalworking industrial process system.

3   Forecast of the Resource of the Tool

The task of the forecasting of the resource of the cutting tool has been solved as a result of the specially conducted for this researches, which showed, that a graph, showing the change of the sound level (Fig. 1), generated by the cutting process (trend of sound), is closely correlated with the tool wear curve [14].

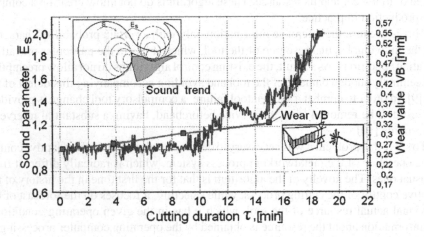

Fig. 1. The relation between the curve of the tool wear and sound trend accompanying the sharpening by the plate P25 of steel 12X18H10T for modes: $V = 33$ m/min, $S = 0,15$ mm/rev, $t = 1,0$ mm.

We get model sound trend, portraying him as a straight line connecting the two points M_0 (τ_0, E_{S0}) and M_{END} (T_{RES}, E_S^{max}). The first point $M0$ corresponds to the beginning of the cutting process, and the second – M_{END} denotes the time of failure (breakage) of the instrument T_{RES} (Fig. 2).

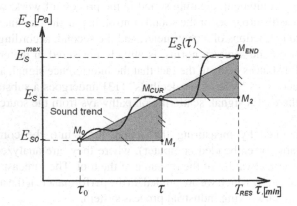

Fig. 2. Changing the sound level E_S (τ) during the cutting process and its trend

Apply on line point M_{CUR} (τ, E_S), describing the current time of the cutting process. Composed the following proportions, based on the similarity of triangles Δ M_0 M_1 M_{CUR} and Δ M_{CUR} M_2 M_{END}.

$$\frac{E_S - E_{S0}}{\tau - \tau_0} = \frac{E_S^{max} - E_S}{T_{RES} - \tau} \tag{1}$$

Resolve the proportion relative to the current value of a sound E_S

$$E_S = E_{S0} + \alpha E_{S0} \frac{\tau - \tau_0}{T_{RES} - \tau} \tag{2}$$

where $\alpha E_{S0} = E_S^{max} - E_S$.

Give the dimensionless form to expression (2) by deleting left and right parts on the value E_{S0} and erect a fraction located on the right side of the expression, in the degree of β

$$\overline{E_S^C} = 1 + \alpha \left(\frac{\tau - \tau_0}{T_{RES} - \tau} \right)^{\beta}, \tag{3}$$

where $\overline{E_S^C}$ - dimensionless parameter, τ_0, τ - respectively the initial (at the time of the first measurement) and the current duration of the cutting in minutes, T_{RES}, α, β – parameters of the model, determined in the process of it identification.

Expression (3) is a model of sound trend given for generality of the results to a dimensionless form. This model is the functions which usually are used for the approximation of the experimental data, the value of which can change dramatically over time [15, 16]. This property of the model provides its high sensitivity to the behavior of its parameters.

These parameters are determined in the process of parametric identification of the model on the results of monitoring the sound trend [17]. The identification is the minimization by the expression (4) divergences values $\overline{E_S^C}$, calculated using the given model, from the actually registered sound parameters $\overline{E_S^F}$

$$U = \sum_i^m \left[\overline{E_S^F} - \overline{E_S^C} \right]^2, \tag{4}$$

where $\overline{E_S^F} = \dfrac{E_S}{E_{S0}}$ – dimensionless parameter, equal to the ratio of the actually registered current value of the sound E_S to its value recorded during the first measurement E_{S0}, m – the number of measurements performed for all the time of the tool condition monitorin.

Defined as a result of the identification of the numerical value of the resource T_{RES} is used as the main parameter for the adaptive control the cutting process.

4   Algorithm of the Adaptive Control of the Industrial Metalworking System Operation

Viewed in the article the control algorithm consists in comparison of numerical tool life values T_{RES}, received by identification method, with a predetermined duration manufacturing of a detail. This duration, called the required machine time T_{TR}, spent on the production of the part, is determined from the following expression:

$$T_{TR} = \frac{L_D k_{PAS}}{f_0 n_0} \tag{5}$$

where L_D – is the length of the surface of the workpiece that is machined in a single pass, mm; k_{PAS} – the number of the passes of the tool, pieces; f_0 – is the initial feed rate, mm/rev; n_0 – is the initial value of revolutions, rev/min.

Initially assigned parameters f_0 and n_0 are optimum cutting modes for a given depth of the cut a_0, of the workpiece materials and the tool and the type of machining (roug, semi-finishing or finishing). The values of these parameters are scientifically proved, repeatedly confirmed by the practice of cutting and recorded in the appropriate reference and regulatory documents.

The adaptive control algorithm provides for the invariance of the initial modes as long as the following condition is being fulfilled: $T_{RES} \geq T_{TR}$. In case of the violation of this condition the cutting modes are subjected to the correction.

At the same time the newly appointed modes provide the lowest labor when fulfilling the following three rules:

– the full use of the cutting tool properties of the tool up to the point of the exhaustion of its actual resource, which the tool has under the given conditions of its operation;
– the use of all the operational capabilities of the machine tool;
– the observance of the required quality of the manufacturing of the part.

When fulfilling the first rule one is guided by the following relation between the resource of the tool T_{RES}, min. and the speed of its wear γ, mm/min:

$$T_{RES} = \frac{[VB]}{\gamma} \tag{6}$$

where $[VB]$ – is the maximum permissible value of the wear of the main tool back plane, mm, T_{RES} – value of the resource, which is a parameter of trend model (3) and determined by her identification, min.

The speed of the wear γ is proportional to the product of the pressing force and the speed of the reciprocal sliding motion [19]. For cutting this product is written as follows:

$$\gamma \approx P_{CUT} \cdot S, \tag{7}$$

where P_{CUT} – is the cutting force, N; S – is the cutting speed, m/min.

The adaptive control problem in this case is the change of the wear speed at the cost of the corresponding feed correction $f(\tau)$ and spindle rotations $n(\tau)$.

The control procedure in this case is reduced to the minimization of the value of the following objective function:

$$U = \left(\frac{T_{RES}}{T_{TR}} - \frac{\gamma_{TR}}{\gamma_0} \right)^2 \rightarrow min, \tag{8}$$

where γ_{TR} – is a variable speed of the tool wear, which is being tied in the process of the adaptive management of the cutting conditions, so that to complete the cutting process without the tool change; γ_0 - is the wear speed of the tool, actually realized at the initially assigned cutting modes (f_0 и n_0) under the current conditions of its operation.

Taking into account (7), the expression (8) has the following form:

$$U = \left(\frac{T_{RES}}{T_{TR}} - \frac{P^{TR}_{CUT} S_{TR}}{P^{INI}_{CUT} S_0} \right)^2 \rightarrow min \tag{9}$$

where P^{INI}_{CUT}, S_0 – respectively, the initial value of force and cutting speed, which corresponds to the initial cutting modes (a_0, f_0 and n_0), P^{TR}_{CUT}, S_{TR} – respectively, the value of power and cutting speed, which will provide the fulfillment of condition $T_{RES} \geq T_{TR}$ and allow to perform the processing of details.

The cutting force and the cutting modes are connected by the empirical dependence [20]:

$$P_{CUT} = 10 \cdot C_{CUT} a^x f^y S^n K_{CUT}, \tag{10}$$

where C_{CUT} – is a constant for a given type of the machining, work and tool materials; K_{CUT} – correction factor; x, y, n – the marks of the degree, characteristic for a given type of the machining, machined and tool materials.

Taking into account (10) under the condition of the constancy cutting depth ($a = const$) the objective function (9) takes the following form:

$$U = \left[\frac{T_{RES}}{T_{TR}} - \left(\frac{f(\tau)}{f_0} \right)^y \left(\frac{S(\tau)}{S_0} \right)^{n+1} \right]^2 \rightarrow min \tag{11}$$

where $f(\tau)$ and $S(\tau)$ – varying in the process of the adaptive management of cutting conditions.

To perform the second stated above adaptive control rule requiring the preservation of the constant within the certain limits of the dynamic loading of the machine, it is necessary to maintain the product of the controlled parameters $n(\tau) \cdot S(\tau)$ as close as possible from the product of their initial values $n_0 \cdot S_0$.

The implementation of the third rule provides the preservation in the process of the adaptive control the quality of the machining of the part, close to the initial, specified in the design of the process. The quality of the machining is known to be characterized by the precision of the geometry of the part and the cleanness (roughness) of the machined surface [20].

The accuracy of the geometry is determined by the wear value of the tool [21] and already is taken into account in the objective function (11). The roughness is measured according to the quantity of the parameter's tall R_Z, changing in the process of cutting proportionally to the square of the supply: $R_z \sim f^2$ [21].

This conditions can be accomplished by introducing into the objective function (11) an additional item:

$$U = \left[\frac{T_{RES}}{T_{TR}} - \left(\frac{f(\tau)}{f_0}\right)^y \left(\frac{S(\tau)}{S_0}\right)^{n+1}\right]^2 + \left[1 - \frac{f(\tau) \cdot n(\tau)}{f_0 \cdot n_0}\right]^2 \cdot \left[1 - \left(\frac{f(\tau)}{f_0}\right)^2\right]^2 \rightarrow min \quad (12)$$

Thus, the objective function (12) allows one to follow, in the process of the adaptive control, stated above rules requiring to withstand close to the initial the level of loading of the tool and the machine tool, as well as the quality of the part.

To test the effectiveness of the selection of required cutting conditions, performed by the objective function (12), it was conducted computer simulations. In the simulation modes were refined (recalculated by the formula (12)) is continuous during the entire cutting process.

In practice, the change mode is performed much less frequently, usually one - twice. The aim of regime changes is to reduce the load acting on the tool. Reducing the load increases the current resource instrument T_{RES}^{CUR} towards the starting value $T_{RES}^{INI}\left(T_{RES}^{CUR} > T_{RES}^{INI}\right)$. At the same time satisfies the following condition $T_{RES}^{CUR} > T_{PAS}$. The parameter T_{PAS} indicated the duration of the current tool passage. This provides a faultless completion of the passage and the timely replacement of the tool, which is in the pre-emergency condition.

Thus adaptive control algorithm, which is discussed in the article, is particularly effective in the production of lengthy details, where the tool breakage in the middle of the passage is not allowed.

Computer simulations were carried out applied to the kinematic scheme 16K20T1 lathe CNC machine. Kinematic масhine circuit has nine stages changing the spindle speed n in the range of 125 rev/min to 2000 rev/min, and feed f can change by 0.01 mm/rev, from 0.01 to 3.0 mm/rev, [22].

The machined material – is steel 40X, the tool material - hard alloy metal T15K6.

The initial cutting mode: $S_0 = 157$ m/min, $(n_0 = 500$ rev/min), $f_0 = 0,5$ mm/rev, $a_0 = 1,5$ mm.

The figures in the formula (10) are as follows: $n = -0,4$ (for P_x), -0.3 (for P_y), -0.15 (for P_z)); $x = 1,05$ (for P_x), 0.6 (for P_y), 0.9 (for P_z); $y = 0,2$ (for P_x), 0.8 (for P_y), 0.9 (for P_z) [23].

The diameter of the workpiece D_W was 100 mm, the diameter of part D_P was 20 mm, the length $-L_P = 280$ mm. The required length of cutting according to the process (initial machine time T_{TR}^{INI}) was 61 min.

The simulation results are presented in Figs. 3 and 4. It follows from Fig. 3 that at the beginning of the correction of the modes the forecast testified that the tool resource (starting value tool resource T_{RES}^{INI}) was less than the required machine time T_{TR}^{INI} (45 and 61 min, accordingly). Due to the correction (Fig. 4), we managed to reduce the wear speed $\gamma(\tau)$ to the level making 0.6–0.7 of its initial amount γ_0.

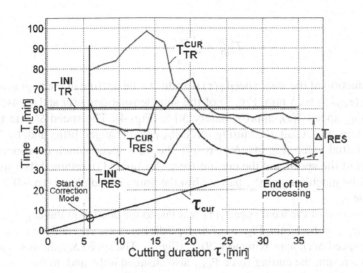

Fig. 3. The Forecast of the Initial T_{RES}^{INI} and the Current Resources of the Tool T_{RES}^{CUR}, As Well As the Initial T_{TR}^{INI} and Current required Machine Time T_{TR}^{CUR}

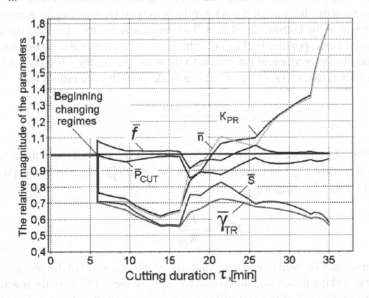

Fig. 4. The Change in the Process of the Adaptive Control of the Presented in dimensionless form Controlled Parameters $n(\tau)$ and $f(\tau)$, As Well As the Related With Them Values: Speed $S(\tau)$ and the Cutting Force P_{CUT}, Wear Speed $\gamma(\tau)$ and the Coefficient of the Performance Ratio K_{PR}

Due to this, the forecasted current resource of the tool T_{RES}^{CUR} (Fig. 3, formula (13)) increased, varying between 50–75 min around the Initial value of required machine time T_{TR}^{INI}, which is equal to 61 min. Current and initial values of forecasts tool resource related as follows:

$$T_{RES}^{CUR} = \frac{T_{RES}^{INI}}{\overline{\gamma}_{TR}} \tag{13}$$

The reduction of the wear speed $\gamma(\tau)$ was due to the decline in the beginning of the correction ($\tau_{KOP} = 6{,}25$ min, Fig. 3) of the spindle rotations $n(\tau)$ and, consequently, of the cutting speed $S(\tau)$, approximately 30 % (Fig. 4). The speed $S(\tau)$ in that case varied slightly, as a result, the cutting force P_{CUT} also changed little, and, to the lower side of its initial value (Fig. 4). As a result, the wear speed which is proportional to the product of the speed and the cutting force (formula (1)), retained its value in the process of the machining of the part within the limits stated above 0.6 – 0.7 from its initial value γ_0.

The reduction of the wear speed $\gamma(\tau)$ was due to the decline in the beginning of the correction ($\tau_{KOP} = 6{,}25$ min, Fig. 3) of the spindle rotations $n(\tau)$ and, consequently, of the cutting speed $S(\tau)$, approximately 30 % (Fig. 4). The speed $S(\tau)$ in that case varied slightly, as a result, the cutting force P_{CUT} also changed little, and, to the lower side of its initial value (Fig. 4). As a result, the wear speed which is proportional to the product of the speed and the cutting force (formula (1)), retained its value in the process of the machining of the part within the limits stated above 0.6–0.7 from its initial value. In the wake of rising of the duration of the machining of the part its diameter decreases, leading to the decrease of the cutting speed $S(\tau)$. To compensate for this decrease the rotations $n(\tau)$ increased correspondingly (Fig. 4), which led to forcing of the cutting modes and consequently to the increase of the productivity of the machining Changing of performance is characterized by the value of cutting mode performance ratio K_{PR}.

$$K_{PR} = \frac{f(\tau) \cdot n(\tau)}{f_0 \cdot n_0} \tag{14}$$

Changing of performance changes in large and in the smaller party the actual need of the machine time T_{TR}^{CUR} in relation to its initial value T_{TR}^{INI} (Fig. 3). These parameters are related in the following way:

$$T_{TR}^{CUR} = \frac{T_{TR}^{INI}}{K_{PR}} \tag{15}$$

The simulation showed that as a result of the adaptive control of the operation modes by the metalworking technological system we actually spent 35 min of the machine time T_{TR}^{CUR} for the machining of the part instead of the planned $T_{TR}^{INI} = 61$ min (Fig. 3). Thus, by reducing the wear speed, the tool had about 20 min of the resource reserve $\Delta T_{RES} (\Delta T_{RES} = T_{RES}^{CUR} - T_{TR}^{CUR})$ (Fig. 3). At the same time, the figure shows that in the absence of the adaptive control at the 35th minute of the machine operation the resource of the tool could have been exhausted and the machining of the part in the middle of its production could have been interrupted due to the tool breakage and possible defect of the part.

5   Conclusion

The competitiveness of the modern production is largely dependent on the efficient use of the metalworking processing equipment, which is the most significant part of the material resources of the enterprise. The effectiveness of the use of this type of equipment is provided by the intellectualization of the management processes of its operation, in particular, through the use of CAM-systems.

However, the implicit or explicit focus of such systems to use average data about the resource of the cutting tool significantly reduces the efficiency of the developed with their help algorithms of the adaptive control of the operation of various metal-working equipment.

According to this the algorithm of the adaptive control based on the forecast of individual actual resource of the cutting tool, described in this paper, may be useful for the developers of the control systems of the machine operation and for the practitioners using these systems.

The information about the actual resource of the tool in the practice of cutting tool allows to anticipate the failure and conduct a necessary correction of the mode of the part machining to extend the period of faultless use of the metalworking equipment.

As the modeling demonstrated the use of the forecast of the tool resource during the adaptive control and the selection of the mode as a result of the minimizing of the objective function, providing the stability of the dynamic loading of the tool or machine tool, as well as the maintaining the quality of the manufacturing of the part, allowed to complete the machining of the part without tool failure and defect of the part. At the same time the computer time, actually spent on the manufacturing of part has been reduced compared with the required, that is the key to improve the competitiveness of the enterprises wishing to apply considered in this article the adaptive control algorithm.

References

1. Solomentsev, Y.M., et al.: The Adaptive Control of the Technological Process, 536 p. Mechanical Engineering, Moscow (1980)
2. Degtyarev, Y.I.: Optimization Methods, 272 p. Sov.Radio, Moscow (1980)
3. Chistyakov, A.V., et al.: Optimization of Operational and Technological Processes in Mechanical Engineering, 228 p. Novocherk. state. tehn. Univ. Novocherkassk (1997)
4. Nikitina, L.G.: Adaptive machine control. In: Machine-building and life safety, number 3, pp. 61–64 (2011)
5. Mustafayev, G.A., Sidorchik, E.V.: Using adaptive control sensors to improve the quality of machining of parts on CNC machines. Young Sci. **9**, 60–62 (2013)
6. Sharabura, S.N., Shevchenko, V.V.: Adaptive control machining process parts on CNC system. In: Modern Scientific Research and Innovation, number 6 (2014). http://web.snauka.ru/issues/2014/06/34729. Accessed 20 Oct 2015

7. Postnov, V.V., Shafiq, A.A.: Development of an evolutionary model of cutting tool wear management process. Bull. Ufim's State Aviat. Tech. Univ. **11**(2), 139–145 (2008)
8. Yaruta, S.P., Usachev, P.A.: Development of adaptive control system for technological processes. J. FEN – Sci. **5**, 30–31 (2012)
9. Shorty, A.A., Shevchenko, V.V., Shorty, A.I.: Multivariable control of the cutting process. In: Modern scientific research and innovation, № 2 (2013). http://web.snauka.ru/issues/2013/02/21935. Accessed 22 Oct 2015
10. Bibik, V.L.: Methods of forecasting durability of cutting tools. In: Fundamental research, number 12, pp. 81–84 (2011). http://www.fundamental-research.ru/ru/article/view?id=28853. Accessed 02 Feb 2016
11. Nagorny V.V., Zaloga V.A.: Definition tool life and the degree of wear on the level of sound that accompanies the cutting process. In: Metalworking. St. Peterburg, № 2 (74), pp. 14–22 (2013)
12. Poduraev, V.N., Barzov, A.A., Gorelov, V.A.: Process Diagnostics Cutting Method of Acoustic Emission. 53 p. Mechanical Engineering, Moscow (1988)
13. Golyamina I. P.: Sound. In: Physical Encyclopedia. 754 p., Soviet entsiklopediya, Moscow (1988–1999)
14. Nagorny, V.V., Zaloga, V.A.: Prediction of the time a replacement of the cutting tool on the sound level generated by the cutting process. In: Proceedings of the III International Science-Practices and Conference Innovation, Quality and Service in Engineering and Technology, May 17–19, Kursk, pp. 107–111 (2012)
15. Crane, C.G., Ushakova, V.N.: Mathematical Analysis of Elementary Functions, 168 p. Fizmatgiz, Moscow (1963)
16. Gaskarov, D.V., Golinkevich, T.A.: Mozgalevskaya A.V.: Prediction of Technical-State and the Reliability of Electronic Equipment, 224 p. Sov. radio, Moscow (1974)
17. Nagorny, V.V., Zaloga, V.A.: Quality control of functioning of the technological system. In: Devices and Systems. Governance, Control, Diagnosis, number 7, pp. 39–45 (2014)
18. Golubkov, E.P.: Marketing Research, 379 p. Finpress, Moscow (1998)
19. Pronikov, A.C.: The Reliability of Machines. 592 p. Mechanical Engineering, Moscow (1978)
20. Krivoukhov, V.A., et al.: Cutting Metals, 471 p. Mashgiz, Moscow (1954)
21. Makarov A.D.: Wear and Cutting Tool Life. 264 p. Machine-building, Moscow (1966)
22. Lokteva, S.E.: Machines with Program Management, and Industrial Robots, 320 p. Mechanical Engineering, Moscow (1986)
23. Kosilova, A.G.: Manual Process Engineer, 496 p. Mechanical Engineering, Moscow (1985)

Dynamic Business Process Simulation - A Rule- and Context- Based Approach

Diana Kalibatiene[⊠] and Olegas Vasilecas

Vilnius Gediminas Technical University, Vilnius, Lithuania
{diana.kalibatiene,olegas.vasilecas}@vgtu.lt

Abstract. Business processes are dynamic by their nature, because of changes of their environment and customers' needs. Therefore, their supporting information systems should be dynamic as well. Although a number of approaches have been proposed to dynamic business process (DBP) modelling, there is lack of theory, implementation or both. This paper proposes a novel rule- and context- based approach of DBP modelling and simulation. The main idea of the approach is that the sequence of activities in a process depends on the environment, which is described as a context of a BP, and activities are selected according to the defined rules at BP instance runtime. The effectiveness of the proposed approach is evaluated with a simulation scenario, and the simulation results indicate that the proposed approach is suitable for DBP simulation.

Keywords: Dynamic business process · Business rule · Context · Simulation · Business process modelling

1 Introduction

Business processes (BP) are dynamic by their nature, because of changes of their environment and customers' needs. Therefore, their supporting information systems should be dynamic as well. Although a number of approaches have been proposed to dynamic business process (DBP) modelling, there is lack of theory, implementation or both. As analysis of the related works shows, nowadays tools and proposed methods allow for executing different configurations [1] or variants [2, 3] of a BP, or using templates for modifying sequence of activities in a BP, as in [4]. This means that the majority of existing approaches require strict specification of a BP, and unexpected sequences of BP activities cannot be included during a BP execution. Therefore, modelling and simulation of DBP is a challenging task.

This paper shortly describes existing DBP modelling approaches and their implementation. The main emphasize is placed on possibility to simulate DBP. Therefore, related works are reviewed and a rule- and context-based DBP modelling and simulation approach is presented. The rest of the paper is organized as follows. Section 2 presents related works on DBP. Section 3 presents an approach of DBP modelling and simulation. Section 4 describes a developed prototype and experiment results of ordering process simulation. Finally, Sect. 5 concludes the paper.

© Springer International Publishing Switzerland 2016
G. Dregvaite and R. Damasevicius (Eds.): ICIST 2016, CCIS 639, pp. 199–207, 2016.
DOI: 10.1007/978-3-319-46254-7_16

2 Related Works

In the research, we emphasize on DBP, where content and the sequence of activities depends on the environment of a BP and could be changed at BP instance runtime. I.e. according to [5], dynamic processes are designed to be highly adaptable, allowing participants to make rapid process adjustments at any time with low latency. A usual BP specification has static properties, like activities, sequence of activities, rules, etc., which are defined before BP instance execution and can be simply or cannot be modified at runtime.

According to [6], only 20 % of processes, which are internal processes, like not client-facing or standardized due to legal constraints (i.e. accounting processes, tax processes, some HR processes, etc.) processes, can be defined before their execution or simulation. The remaining 80 % processes contain actions or entire sub-processes, which are hard to conceptualize within an algorithm, since they depend on individual conditions of execution, or contain a large amount of variables that it is impossible to model them. Those processes are named as dynamic business processes (DBP).

Different approaches have been proposed to ensure dynamicity of a BP. According to the DBP implementation perspective, existing approaches can be classified as follows: (a) a BP has decision points, in which a human or an automated system decides what to do next according to the predefined rules; (b) a BP is divided in a variable and non-variable segments, like in [3, 7–11]; (c) a BP is transformed into a set of event-condition-action (ECA) rules or some variation of ECA rules, like in [7, 8]; and (d) goal-oriented BP. The last way of ensuring BP dynamicity allows achieving the highest level of dynamicity. E.g. a BP has no initial process model, each activity for execution is selected according to the rules and a context, the process is goal-oriented. For the BP with same goal different sets of activities occur, when different rules are applied and various contexts appear.

As proposed in [7, 12, 13], a *context-sensitive* BP is able to adapt the execution of its instances to the changing context [12]. According to [14, 15], a context of a BP is described by variables and rules. Moreover, a context can be external, i.e. describing a state of system environment, like user-context in [14, 15] or time, location, weather, legislation or performance requirements in [16], and internal, i.e. describing a state of system resources [17]. However, the existing approaches, like [7, 12, 13, 16], allow defining of one type of context, but not both. Still, in some application domains, only one type of context is important.

Authors, such as [18], suggest using *complex event processing* (CEP) or event-centric approach [19] to respond dynamically to the actual state of an environment. However, not all authors define the events, i.e. external or internal or both, to which their system reacts. Authors of [20] propose to extend the BPM engine with an Event Processing engine, which can obtain information about the events that happen outside and inside the BP, giving the system complete context-awareness when making decisions.

A number of authors use *business rules* to ensure BP dynamicity. In [21] the authors use rules to define the relationship between complex events and to filter the interesting ones, i.e. which should be processed further, in their proposed CEVICHE architecture. The authors of [22] use business rule patterns to enrich BP by possible cases and to increase BP flexibility. In [7] the authors propose decomposing a process into ECA (Event-Condition-Action) rule set and adapting process to the context data according those rules. However, the proposed rule-based approaches do not cover all aspects of a DBP, as was defined at the beginning of this section.

The results of the comparison of rule-based BP modelling and simulation tools (IBM Websphere (v.7.0 2014),[1] Simprocess (v 2015),[2] Simul8,[3] AccuProcess[4] and ARIS 9.7[5]), which are widely used for BP modelling and simulation, and presented in our previous research [23], shows that those are not suitable for simulation of DBP.

In our research, we are interested in *simulation*, since simulation is useful in [2, 9, 10]: improving activities; reducing costs of activities; using for "what-if" analysis; analyzing the correctness of a new model design; computing expected performance, etc.

Therefore, in the next section, we present a novel rule- and context- based DBP modelling and simulation approach.

3   A DBP Simulation Approach

Based on our research and related works, we present a DBP simulation approach (Fig. 1). The main steps of the approach are as follows.

At the beginning of simulation, it is necessary to define priorities through context and rules. This definition of priorities allows defining goal in some level. *Note* that this part is going to be extended in our future research. After that the flow passes to the Parallel Gateway, where two concurrent activities "*Analyze external and internal context*" (during which external and internal contexts are analyzed) and "*Analyze historical data of the process*" (during which historical data, consisting of logs and previous simulation results, of the process is analyzed) are performed. The result of the first activity is defined external and internal context. The result of the second activity is historical data of the similar instances. After the analysis results are obtained, it is determined what next should be done. There are two ways as follows: "*Simulate the existing suitable instance according to the context*" or "*Use rules to select activity from the non-simulated activities list*". In the first case, the most suitable existing instance of the process is chosen from historical data and simulated. The results of simulation, like simulated activities, simulation time and used resources, are saved in the Historical data storage. In the second case, activity for simulation is chosen according to the predefined rules and context. Here we may have three cases, as follows: (a) one activity – in this case the selected activity is simulated; (b) several activities – in this case collision solving is performed to select the activity with greater priority; and (c) no activities – in

---

[1] http://www-03.ibm.com/software/products/en/modeler-advanced.

[2] http://simprocess.com.

[3] http://www.simul8.com.

[4] http://bpmgeek.com/accuprocess-business-process-modeler.

[5] http://www.softwareag.com/corporate/products/new_releases/aris9/more_capabilities/default.asp.

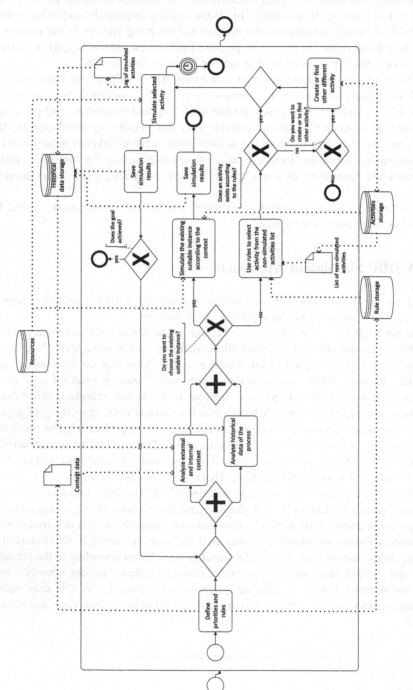

Fig. 1. A dynamic business process simulation approach

this case the simulation process is finished or we have to define a new activity or select another activity for simulation.

After that step, a chosen activity is simulated, and simulation results are saved in the Historical data storage. Then it is decided what to do. If the goal is achieved, the simulation is stopped. If the goal is not achieved, the simulation continues, as presented in the schema (see Fig. 1).

During the simulation, an activity uses resources. In our previous research, we have proposed a resource model for DBP simulation. For more see [24].

4 A Case Study

The proposed simulation approach was realized using Microsoft technologies. An implementation, named DRBPSimul, was developed and an experiment was carried out in Information Systems Research Laboratory (ISRL).[6]

An ordering process was chosen to demonstrate a DBP simulation. In Figs. 2 and 3, we present two instances of the same ordering process to show how instances could differ according to the changed context.

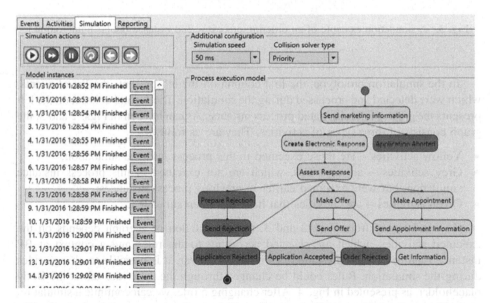

Fig. 2. A simulation example of an ordering process – 1st instance (Color figure online)

---

[6] Information Systems Research Laboratory, Institute of Applied Computer Science, Faculty of Fundamental Sciences, Vilnius Gediminas Technical University, http://fm.vgtu.lt/faculties/departments/institute-of-applied-computer-science/departaments/information-systems-research-laboratory/73139.

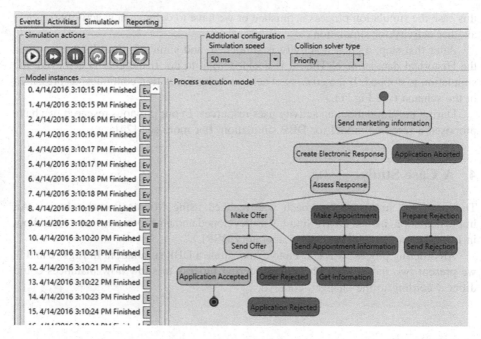

Fig. 3. A simulation example of an ordering process – 2nd instance (Color figure online)

In the simulation prototype, the first column on the left presents the list of events, which were detected and processed during the simulation. The second column on the left presents the graph of the simulated process instance. As can be seen in Figs. 2 and 3, the graph consists of three types of activities. They are as follows:

- Yellow activities – are those executed in this process instance simulation;
- Grey activities – are activities, which are not executed in this process instance simulation, but were executed earlier in previous process instances;
- Green activities – are activities that have just been simulated.

As can be seen from Figs. 2 and 3, the presentation of a graph depends on the executed activities, which are selected according to the rules and a context at BP instance runtime, as was presented in Fig. 1. Moreover, it is possible to change rules during the simulation. Rules could be changed through the Activities tab at the Body placeholder, as presented in Fig. 4. After changing a rule, we can continue a simulation of a BP instance to see how those changes affect the process instance.

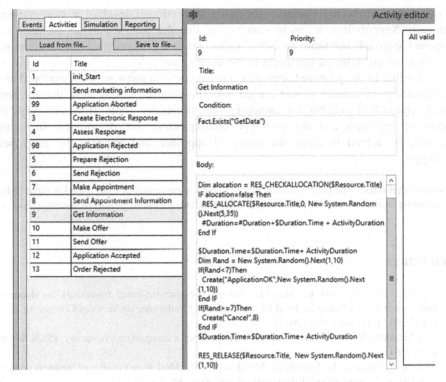

Fig. 4. An example of an activity "Get Information"

5   Conclusions and Future Works

The analysis of the related works on dynamic business process (DBP) modelling shows that there are a number of approaches to implement business process (BP) flexibility and dynamicity. However, the proposed approaches are limited in their ability to model DBP. Moreover, some of the approaches are limited in their application. Not all approaches are implemented as an execution or simulation tool.

In this paper, we proposed a new approach for DBP modelling and simulation, where dynamicity of BP ensured through rules and internal and external context. The main idea of the approach is that during the simulation of activities each activity should be selected according to the context and rules. Therefore, during the simulation of the same BP, instances could be different because of different rule set and different context. Moreover, rules and a context could be change during the simulation and those changes can be observed within the same BP instance immediately after changes come into force, e.g. activities and their sequence can be changed at runtime. Consequently, the DBP has no strict activities and their sequence.

Moreover, our proposed approach allows defining priorities through rules and context. This definition of priorities allows defining goal in some level. However, our research shows that this part should be analyzed in more details and should be extended in our future research to achieve the more sophisticated level of a goal-oriented approach. Nevertheless, it can be summarized that the main difference between our proposed approach and those analyzed is that ours is a goal-oriented, i.e. all activities for execution are selected according to the context and rules.

According to the proposed approach, a prototype of a software was developed and an experiment of simulation was carried out. The obtained results show that the proposed approach is suitable for modelling and simulating DBP. However, ways of improving approach and the prototype consequently were determined. In future research, we intend to refine the proposed approach and improve the developed prototype.

Acknowledgments. The authors would like to thank the personnel of ISRL (see Footnote 6) for participating in the rule- and context-based DBP simulation system prototype development.

References

1. Xiao, Z., Cao, D., You, C., Mei, H.: Towards a constraint-based framework for dynamic business process adaptation. In: IEEE International Conference on Services Computing 2011 (SCC 2011), pp. 685–692 (2011)
2. van der Aalst, W.M.: Business process management: a comprehensive survey. ISRN Softw. Eng. (2013)
3. Milani, F., Dumas, M., Ahmed, N., Matulevičius, R.: Modelling families of business process variants: a decomposition driven method. Inf. Syst. **56**, 55–72 (2016)
4. van Eijndhoven, T., Iacob, M.E., Ponisio, M.L.: Achieving business process flexibility with business rules. In: 12th International IEEE Enterprise Distributed Object Computing Conference (EDOC 2008), pp. 95–104. IEEE, New York (2008)
5. Dynamic BPM (business process management). WhatIs.com. http://whatis.techtarget.com/definition/dynamic-BPM-business-process-management
6. Szelagowski, M.: Static and Dynamic Processes. BPM Leader (2014). http://www.bpmleader.com/2014/08/28/static-and-dynamic-processes/
7. Mejia Bernal, J.F., Falcarin, P., Morisio, M., Dai, J.: Dynamic context-aware business process: a rule-based approach supported by pattern identification. In: 2010 ACM Symposium on Applied Computing, pp. 470–474. ACM (2010)
8. Boukhebouze, M., Amghar, Y., Benharkat, A.N., Maamar, Z.: A rule-based approach to model and verify flexible business processes. Int. J. Bus. Process. Integr. Manage. **5**(4), 287–307 (2011)
9. van der Aalst, W.M.: Business process simulation revisited. In: Barjis, J. (ed.) EOMAS 2010. LNBIP, vol. 63, pp. 1–14. Springer, Heidelberg (2010)
10. Kellner, M.I., Madachy, R.J., Raffo, D.M.: Software process simulation modeling: why? what? how? J. Syst. Softw. **46**(2), 91–105 (1999)
11. Santos, E., Castro, J., Sanchez, J., Pastor, O.: A goal-oriented approach for variability in BPMN. In: WER 2010 (2010)
12. Saidani, O., Nurcan, S.: Towards context aware business process modelling. In: 8th Workshop on Business Process Modeling, Development, and Support (BPMDS 2007), CAiSE, vol. 7. Springer (2007)

13. Nunes, V.T., Werner, C.M.L., Santoro, F.M.: Dynamic process adaptation: a context-aware approach. In: 15th International Conference on Computer Supported Cooperative Work in Design (CSCWD), pp. 97–104. IEEE (2011)

14. Bui, D.V., Iacob, M.E., van Sinderen, M., Zarghami, A.: Achieving flexible process interoperability in the homecare domain through aspect-oriented service composition. In: van Sinderen, M., Oude Luttighuis, P., Folmer, E., Bosems, S. (eds.) IWEI 2013. LNBIP, vol. 144, pp. 50–64. Springer, Heidelberg (2013)

15. Yao, W., Basu, S., Li, J., Stephenson, B.: Modeling and configuration of process variants for on-boarding customers to IT outsourcing. In: 9th International IEEE Conference on Services Computing (SCC 2012), pp. 415–422. IEEE, New York (2012)

16. Rosemann, M., Recker, J.C., Flender, C.: Contextualisation of business processes. Int. J. Bus. Process. Integr. Manage. 3(1), 47–60 (2008)

17. Hu, G., Wu, B., Chen, J.: Dynamic adaptation of business process based on context changes: a rule-oriented approach. In: Lomuscio, A.R., Nepal, S., Patrizi, F., Benatallah, B., Brandić, I. (eds.) ICSOC 2013. LNCS, vol. 8377, pp. 492–504. Springer, Heidelberg (2014)

18. Hermosillo, G., Seinturier, L., Duchien, L.: Creating context-adaptive business processes. In: Maglio, P.P., Weske, M., Yang, J., Fantinato, M. (eds.) ICSOC 2010. LNCS, vol. 6470, pp. 228–242. Springer, Heidelberg (2010)

19. Alexopoulou, N., Nikolaidou, M., Kanellis, P., Mantzana, V., Anagnostopoulos, D., Martakos, D.: Infusing agility in business processes through an event-centric approach. Int. J. Bus. Inf. Syst. 6(1), 58–78 (2010)

20. Chandy, K.M., Schulte, W.R.: Event Processing - Designing IT Systems for Agile Companies. McGraw-Hill (2009)

21. Hermosillo, G., Seinturier, L., Duchien, L.: Using complex event processing for dynamic business process adaptation. In: IEEE International Conference on Services Computing (SCC), pp. 466–473. IEEE (2010)

22. Milanovic, M., Gasevic, D., Rocha, L.: Modeling flexible business processes with business rule patterns. In: 15th IEEE International Enterprise Distributed Object Computing Conference (EDOC), pp. 65–74. IEEE (2011)

23. Kalibatiene, D., Vasilecas, O., Savickas, T., Vysockis, T., Bobrovs, V.: A new approach on rule and context based dynamic business process simulation. Baltic J. Modern Comput. XX (accepted, will be published)

24. Vasilecas O., Kalibatiene D., Rima A., Birzniece I., Rudzajs P.: A resource model for the rule-based dynamic business process modelling and simulation. In: 29th European Simulation and Modelling Conference (ESM 2015), pp. 36–41. Eurosis Publication (2015)

Research in High Frequency Trading and Pairs Selection Algorithm with Baltic Region Stocks

Mantas Vaitonis[✉] and Saulius Masteika

Faculty of Humanities, Vilnius University, Muitines 8, 44280 Kaunas, Lithuania
mantas.vaitonis@khf.stud.vu.lt, saulius.masteika@khf.vu.lt

Abstract. Pair trading is a popular strategy where a profit arises from pricing inefficiencies between stocks. The idea is simple: find two stocks that move together and take long/short positions when they diverge abnormally, hoping that the prices will converge in the future. During last few years high frequency trading in milliseconds or nanoseconds has drawn attention of not only to financial players but and to researchers and engineers. The main objective of this research is to check three different statistical arbitrage strategies using high frequency trading with 14 OMX Baltic market stocks and measure their efficiency and risks. One strategy used in this paper was first implemented by M.S Perlini, the other one by J.F. Caldeira and G.V. Moura and the last one was presented by D. Herlemont. Together with the strategies a pair selecting algorithm was presented. All three strategies were modified in order to be able to work with high frequency data. At the end of the research strategies where measured accordingly to the profit they did generate.

1 Introduction

The global financial crisis during 2007–2010 exposed the weak spots of financial market and the regulations that were supposed to protect the market participants. However, some market participants were able to make this crisis in their favor. Every investor understands that all markets come with great risks and uncertainties. However, many investors are able to use this risk to their advantage or are able to overcome all uncertainties. This is done by implementing technical analysis for buying stocks or the use of strategies that are based on market behavior. An example of a strategy which monitors market behavior would be pairs trading strategy that detects arbitrage opportunities in markets.

Algorithmic trading incorporates many different trading strategies including statistical arbitrage and pair trading, these strategies may be applied to various markets [16, 23–26]. Nath used simple pairs trading strategy with automatic extreme risk control using the entire universe of securities in the highly liquid secondary market for U.S. government debt [23]. Hendershott and Riordan tested the role of algorithmic traders in liquidity supply and demand in the 30 Deutscher Aktien Index stocks on the Deutsche Boerse. It was found that algorithmic traders consume liquidity when the bid-ask quotes are narrow and supply liquidity when it is wide [24]. Miao proposed a high frequency and pair trading system based on a market-neutral statistical arbitrage strategy using a two-stage correlation and co-integration approach. The proposed pairs trading system

© Springer International Publishing Switzerland 2016
G. Dregvaite and R. Damasevicius (Eds.): ICIST 2016, CCIS 639, pp. 208–217, 2016.
DOI: 10.1007/978-3-319-46254-7_17

was applied to equity trading in U.S. equity markets. It was concluded that, overall, the system exceeded the S&P500 index performance [16]. Cartea and Penalva analyzed the impact of HFT in financial markets. They found that the price impact of liquidity trades is higher in the presence of the HFT and is increasing with the size of the trade. However, authors argue that professional traders lose revenue in every trade intermediated by HFT [25]. The review of HFT strategies has revealed that market making HFT strategies contribute to market liquidity [7, 24, 26], and statistical arbitrage contribute to price discovery and market efficiency [4, 16, 23].

One of the most common statistical arbitrage strategies would be pairs trading [16]. Terms that defined this kind of strategies would vary from multivariate pairs trading, generalized pairs trading to statistical arbitrage. For simplicity we further consider all these strategies under the term of "statistical arbitrage pairs trading" or shorter, "pairs trading" [20], pairs trading can be traced to far more complex approaches [22]. The beginning of statistical arbitrage can be found with the start of the first hedge funds around 1950 [1] and since 1980 this type of strategy was widely used by professional traders and hedge funds [2]. The aim of pairs trading strategy is to find two financial instruments that move together and are correlated then open long position with one instrument and short the other, depending on the movement [3, 10]. In order to find two financial instruments that move together there should be an algorithm to select pairs. One of the methods is least square, which proves to be effective from the results shown in M.S. Perlini research and this method is procedure to determine the best fit line to data [21]. The profit for pair trading comes when the prices of two financial instruments converge and come back to their historical mean [4].

This paper is based on three different pairs trading strategies. One was implemented in Brazilian stock market using only low frequency data and was done by M.S. Perlini [4]. Second strategy was proposed by J.F. Calderia and G. V. Moura. Authors used their strategy in San Paul stock market with daily closing prices [5]. The last strategy was presented by D. Herlemont. Author did not implement its strategy to any market; however he did presented the detailed model of his pairs trading strategy [6]. Even though, all of the above mentioned authors did use pairs trading strategies, but they all are different and were tested only with low frequency information. The main differences of all three strategies are threshold parameter calculation, for defining trading opportunities and trading signals creation methods.

In this paper, the system related to market efficiency or price discovery and statistical arbitrage was chosen for a deeper analysis. Contribution of this paper lies in testing all three strategies with OMX Baltic market high frequency data, measure their efficiency. The main aim of this paper is to find the most effective pair trading strategy out of the proposed ones and to test the selected pair selection algorithm.

2   Pairs Trading in HFT

Based on information and statistical research, more than half of all trades made in the markets are done by high frequency traders and the number of these trades keeps increasing [7]. If one would like to trade using high frequency data it should be able to make decisions very fast. It means that trade signals would be created every millisecond or even nanosecond. Thus, this type of trading can be only done by computers and algorithms. High frequency trading typically refers to trading activity that employs extremely fast automated programs for generating, routing, canceling, and executing orders in electronic markets [13]. Reports, that were done by the one of market leaders shows the importance of understanding the algorithmic trading. As filed with the Securities and Exchange Commission, Virtu Financial, Inc. by 2014 was able to perform only with one day losing out of 1238 days using electronic trading strategies [8]. Research which was done by ESMA shows how big algorithmic trading is in European commodities market. Based on the report high frequency trading is responsible for about 24% of all trades made and it creates 43 % of all trading orders. High frequency trading makes 49% of all trading signals created in European commodities market [9, 17].

It is hard and expensive to receive high frequency data, thus not everyone is able to work with this kind of information. For this paper we use 14 stocks high frequency data form NASDAQ Baltics market. All the above mention strategies had to be adapted and modified to use high frequency information. One of the reasons to use this kind of data is that there are few researches done in academic level explaining the use of high frequency data with pairs trading strategies. The aim of the paper is to adapt all trading strategies for HFT. Secondly, it is necessary to find correlated pairs, before starting trading, thus this paper suggested the use of pairs selection algorithm. In 2010 NASDAQ OMX launched inet trading system across its seven markets in the Nordics and Baltics which allowed to trade using millisecond data. There is shortage of scientific evidence proving this system and technology efficiency in HFT trading in NASDAQ OMX. Thus, collaborating with NASDAQ OMX Vilnius it was decided to do primary experiments with HFT pairs trading. The main objective of this paper is to test all trading strategies in OMX Baltic market, find all correlated pairs and measure the performance of each strategy in order to find the most effective one.

As mentioned before this paper is based on three different pair's trading strategies, introduced by J.F. Caldeira, G.V. Moura, M.S. Perlini and D. Herlemont. Before starting to apply all these strategies it was necessary to modify them in order to fit author's needs. For this research all strategies were improved to work with millisecond data and were integrated with pair's selection algorithm.

2.1 Methodology of Pairs Trading Strategy

Statistical arbitrage pair's trading strategies are fairly simple, below is the proposed methodology of these strategies. The methodology consists of six steps, which are necessary to consider before applying any pairs trading strategy (Fig. 1):

During this research 14 OMX Baltic markets stocks are used to measure three strategies performance. These 14 stocks consist of different companies from Lithuania (AMG1L, APG1L, CTS1L, KNF1L, LDJ1L, LES1L, TEO1L), Estonia (SFG1T, TVEAT, OEG1T, TAL1T) and Latvia (GRD1R, GZE1R, OLF1R). It was chosen to use stocks from three different countries in order to show arbitrage opportunities that rises form working with different markets. All calculations and simulations are done in MATLAB environment.

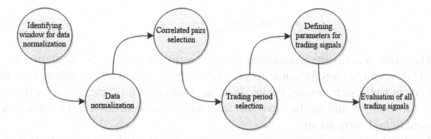

Fig. 1. Six steps of pairs trading strategy

Before starting to apply any of above mentioned trading strategies it is necessary to select two periods: training and data normalization with trading. When all data is ready to be sent to trading strategy we have to do training of it. The training period is the predefined period for computation of the training period. After training period is complete the trading period follows. Trading period uses the parameters from testing period which are measured against the trading period. Pairs are also parameters of the strategy, thus the trading starts with the pairs which were found during training period. All parameters calculated during training period are measured against the ones that are found during training, if parameters differ, they are changed accordingly. At the end of each trading period the operations that were opened are closed, and a new training period ending on the last observation of the previous trading period is initiated. Now pairs can be substituted and all parameters are re-estimated. This procedure continues in a rolling window fashion until the end of the sample [5]. Training period must not be too long, because strategy will over train and will not notice abnormal behavior in stock pricing [12, 13].

Second period defines data normalization and trading. The size of this window depends on how sensitive the strategy should be. The shorter period is the more sensitive trading strategy is used [12, 13]. The size for data normalization and trading is kept the same, because trading is only done within the normalized window. In our research we did define 1 min training period and 2 min window for data normalization and trading.

As shown in methodology second part is data normalization. This part consists of two steps:

1. Time stamps normalization;
2. Stocks prices normalization.

Time stamps normalization is needed because, different stocks has different time stamps. In other words if one stock has time stamp of 09:36:03,740 and the other has 09:36:03.745, it means both time stamps has to appear in each stock and they are filled with previous prices. This normalization is needed only for testing purposes of the strategy. [12, 13]

Stocks prices normalization is necessary in order to bring all prices to one size, in this way it is possible to compare stocks and find correlation more efficiently. High frequency data normalization is done as follows, for each price of stock $P(i,t)$ we calculate empirical mean $\mu(i,t)$ and standard deviation $\sigma(i,t)$ and then apply the following equation [4]:

$$p(i,t) = \frac{P(i,t) - \mu(i,t)}{\sigma(i,t)} \qquad (1)$$

The value p(i,t) is the normalized price of asset i at time t [4]. As shown in the Eq. (1) the method used for normalization is z-score. It would be possible to use other methods as well like min-max, decimal scaling, sliding window, etc., however the final result of trading would be the same, because we use normalization just for prices that are used to find correlations.

The third step after data normalization is to find correlated pair for each stock. The Least Squares is a procedure, requiring just some calculus and linear algebra, to determine what the "best fit" to the data and in our case which stock is best fit for other stock [21]. This method requires little resources of CPU and is time consuming, that means that the found pairs are calculated quickly, which is important for high frequency trading, thus it was selected for this research.

$$Qdist(i,j) = (x(i) - x(j))^3$$
$$N = min(Qdist) \qquad (2)$$

As show in the above equation we do calculate the difference in normalized stock prices of x(i) and x(j), which is then squared. It is done with all the stocks. In order to find the best pairs the algorithm needs to find pairs with minimal squared distance, which is done with second equation. In case when stock A is pair with stock B and stock B is pair with stock A, only the first pair is used in order to avoid multiple trading signals [4].

2.2 Proposed Pairs Trading Strategies

All HFT statistical arbitrage calculations and pair selection algorithm were implemented in MATLAB. Our data consist of 14 OMX Baltic market stocks. Period, which was used for testing is from 2014-10-01 till 2015-03-31. All information in the given data consists of millisecond timestamps. After normalization there were a total of 97032 records (Table 1).

After applying pair selection algorithm 52 unique pairs were found during the whole trading period. The above table shows top five highest frequency pairs, that are GRD1R with AMG1L were found 116 times, OEG1T with AMG1L – 106 times, TAL1T with AMG1L – 78 times, AMG1L with APG1L – 76 times and AMG1L with SFG1T – 72 times. These results may be taken in consideration when selectin correlated pairs for traders.

Table 1. Top five pairs

Pair		Times it was found
GRD1R	AMG1L	116
OEG1T	AMG1L	106
TAL1T	AMG1L	78
AMG1L	APG1L	76
AMG1L	SFG1T	72

After all pairs for the given trading window are found is time to create trading signals. For J.F. Caldeira and G.V. Moura trading strategy we need to find trading signals, it is done by calculating difference between prices of stock pairs [5]:

$$\varepsilon_t = P(i, t) - p(i, t) \tag{3}$$

Where ε_t is the difference at time t between stock $P(i,t)$ and $p(i,t)$. Then threshold z is founded [5]:

$$z_t = \frac{\varepsilon_t - \mu_t}{\sigma_t} \tag{4}$$

Where μ_ε is mean and σ_ε is standard deviation. When the threshold z_t is found, strategy can start looking for trading signals [5]:

Open long position, if $z_t < -2\sigma$;
Open short position, if $z_t > 2\sigma$;
Close short position, if $z_t < 0.75\sigma$;
Close long position, if $z_t > -0.50\sigma$ [5].

Based on these rules trading signals are created and long/short positions are placed accordingly. Every taken position is kept opened till threshold is reach or given time to keep positions open ends. During this experiment the maximum time to keep positions open was 2 min (Fig. 2).

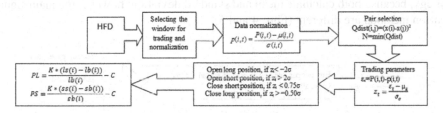

Fig. 2. J.F. Caldeira and G.V. Moura trading strategy

The second strategy was introduced by M. S. Perlini in Brazilian market. Same as before we must calculate the difference in stock prices and measure it against threshold **d** which is defined by trader. After that it is necessary to establish long or short position should be taken for given stock. If we have pair of two stocks A and B and one side of a pair price is $A(i,t)$ and the other $B(i,t)$ then when the value of $A(i,t)$ is higher than $B(i,t)$, then a short position is taken for stock $A(i,t)$, and a long position is made for the pair of stock $B(i,t)$, else do the opposite. Such position is kept till the value of the spread becomes smaller than the threshold d. Basic rules that do explain the strategy are below [4]:

while d > spread;
if $A(i,t)>B(i.t)$ then short $A(i,t)$ and long $B(i,t)$;
else long $A(i,t)$ and short $B(i,t)$ [4].

The main idea of this strategy is that when the distance between correlated stocks composing a pair is larger than threshold, there is a probability that such prices are going to converge in the future, and this logic can be explored for profit purposes [4] (Fig. 3).

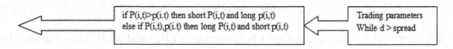

Fig. 3. M.S. Perlini trading strategy

The last strategy was proposed by D. Herlemont, the author did not implement his strategy to any market. D. Herlemont did work on theoretical pairs trading model, focused on its efficiency and was looking to find the right method for pair selection and correlation. Thus, for this research we did only use signal creation model [6].

The first step of D. Herlemont trading strategy is to calculate mean μ_t and standard deviation σ_t for given trading window. When all two criteria are found it is time to created trading signals, if difference between stock A and B pair prices is $<2* \sigma_t$:

If $A_t>B_t$, then open short position with A_t and long position with B_t;
If $A_t<B_t$, then open long position with P_t and short position with B_t [6]

Close all positions when difference between prices of A_t and $B_t < \mu_t$ or the period for keeping positions opened is reached [6].

In D. Herlemont strategy we can find similarities with J.F. Caldeira and G.V. Moura strategy, because both calculate mean and standard deviation; however the main signal creation methods are different (Figs. 4 and 5).

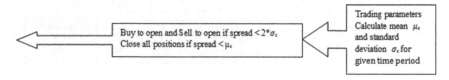

Fig. 4. D. Herlemonts trading strategy

During the research all main criteria were kept the same: training period – 1 min, trading and normalization period 2 min, period to keep positions opened – 2 min and trading cost per trade – 0. Due to the fact that research was done only to find the most effective trading strategy with best performance commissions were not taken in to consideration.

Previously all three strategies were tested by using low frequency information, which consists of day closing prices. Later when M.S. Perlini strategy was implemented in HFT of commodities future markets that showed it can be applied to high frequency information of milliseconds. Based on this research, it was possible to assume that all three strategies can be modified to work with high frequency information.

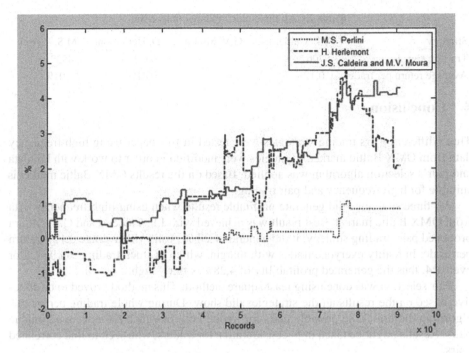

Fig. 5. Profit of all three strategies at the end of research

3   Results

At the end of the research all three strategies did show positive results. During whole trading period of six month every strategy did work with no days with loss. Least profitable strategy was M.S. Perlini, which did generate 0,69 % profit at the end of research. D. Herlemont was more profitable with 2,08 % and the most profitable and effective was J.F. Caldeira and G.V. Moura strategy with 4,28 of total profit. J.F. Caldeira and G.V. Moura strategy is more effective, due to fact it did generate less trading signals with better result, thus it did avoid unnecessary trading signals, that could ruin the strategy. This strategy proved to be as profitable as it did with high frequency gas futures [19] (Table 2).

Moreover, J.F. Caldeira and G.V. Moura strategy did generate better return per trade, which was 0,12 %. Due to the fact that this paper focused only on measuring strategies performance trading costs have not been taken in to account. If these strategies were applied to real markets with commissions, results may differ. However many markets, provides low or even no commissions for high frequency traders, because they bring liquidity to their market [11]. All this information must be taken in to account before applying any trading strategy to the real market.

Table 2. All three pairs trading comparison

Strategy	J.F. Caldeira and G.V. Moura	D. Herlemont	M.S. Perlini
Tradign signals	706	6434	4532
Average return per trade	0,12%	0,01%	0,01%

4   Conclusion

Three different pairs trading strategies were tested in this paper using high frequency data from OMX Baltic market. Strategies were modified in order to work with HF data and pair's selection algorithm was applied. Based on the results OMX Baltic market is suitable for high frequency and pair trading.

All three strategies did generate profitable results when using high frequency data from OMX Baltic market. Best result was achieved with J.F. Caldeira and G.V. Moura proposed pairs trading strategy, it did generate 4,28 % profit with average 0,12% return per trade. In reality everyone trades with margin, which in stock trading can be 1:2 or even 1:4, thus the generated profitability of 4,28% is fairly high.

Pair selection was done using least square method. This method proved to be effective based on the results all the strategies did show. During whole trading period this algorithm did find 1286 possible pairs for trading, out of which there were 52 unique pairs. Results might be taken in to consideration for traders, who seek to find correlated pairs.

Before starting to apply the most profitable strategy (J.F. Caldeira and M.V. Moura) out of this research to the real market it is necessary to consider some risks. It is very important to work with high frequency data as fast as possible with lowest latency – it depends on the hardware which is applied on the market and software which takes care of trades. Secondly, it is important to find if market does cover the commission, otherwise trader will have to pay for every trade he makes. High frequency traders bring liquidity to the market, thus it is possible that the market one will choose will cover the costs of trades.

Acknowledgements. We would also like to show our gratitude to the AB NASDAQ OMX Vilnius for providing with high frequency data of 14 OMX Baltic region stocks for this research.

References

1. Eichengreen, J.B.: Hedge funds and financial market dynamics. Intl. Monetary Fund. **4**, 83 (1998)
2. Madhavaram, G.R.: Statistical Arbitrage Using Pairs Trading With Support Vector Machine Learning, Saint Mary's University (2013)
3. Burton, G.M.: The efficient market hypothesis and its critics. J. Econo. Perspect. **17**(1), 59–82 (2003)
4. Perlin, M.S.: Evaluation of pairs-trading strategy at the brazilian financial market. J. Deriv. Hedge Funds **15**(2), 122–136 (2009)
5. Caldeira, J.F., Moura, G.V.: Selection of a portfolio of pairs based on cointegration: a statistical arbitrage strategy. Rev. Bras. de Financas **11**(1), 49–80 (2013)

6. Herlemont, D.: Pairs trading, convergence trading cointegration. Quant. Finan. **12**(9), 271–276 (2013)
7. Zubulake, P., Lee, S.: The High frequency game changer: how automated trading strategies have revolutionized the markets. Wiley, Boston (2011). Aite group
8. Cifu, D.A.: FORM S-1, Registration Statement Under The Securities Act Of 1933. Virtu Financial, Inc. (2014)
9. AFM. Authority for the Financial Markets, High frequency trading: The application of advanced trading technology in the European marketplace (2010). http://www.afm.nl/~/media/files/rapport/2010/hft-report-engels.ashx, Accessed February 20, 2014
10. Aldridge, I.: High-Frequency Trading: A Practical Guide to Algorithmic Strategies and Trading Systems, 2nd edn, p. 306. Wiley, Hoboken (2013)
11. Hagströmer, B., Norden, L.: The diversity of high-frequency traders. J. Fin. Markets **16**(4), 741–770 (2013)
12. Driaunys, K., Masteika, S., Sakalauskas, V., Vaitonis, M.: An algorithm-based statistical arbitrage high frequency trading system to forecast prices of natural gas futures. Transformations Bus. Econ. **13**(3), 96–109 (2014)
13. Masteika, S., Vaitonis, M.: Quantitative research in high frequency trading for natural gas futures market. In: Abramowicz, W., et al. (eds.) BIS 2015 Workshops. LNBIP, vol. 228, pp. 29–35. Springer, Heidelberg (2015). doi:10.1007/978-3-319-26762-3_3
14. Cvitanic, J., Kirilenko, A.: High Frequency Traders and Asset Prices (2010). Available at SSRN: http://ssrn.com/abstract=1569067 or http://dx.doi.org/10.2139/ssrn.1569067
15. Carrion, A.: Very fast money: High – frequency trading on the NASDAQ. J. Financ. Markets **16**(4), 680–711 (2013)
16. George, M.J.: high frequency and dynamic pairs trading based on statistical arbitrage using a two-stage correlation and cointegration approach. Int. J. Econ. Financ. **6**(3), 96–110 (2014)
17. Antoine, B., Cyrille, G., Carlos, A.R., Christian, W., Steffen, N.: High-frequency trading activity in EU equity markets. Economic Report. vol. 1 (2014)
18. Botos, B., Nagy, L., Ormos, M.: Pairs Trading Arbitrage Strategy in the Old and New EU Member States, ICFB (2014)
19. Vaitonis, M.: Porų prekybos strategijų taikymo gamtinių dujų rinkose tyrimas. Informacinės Technologijos, 117–120 (2015)
20. Krauss, C.: Statistical arbitrage pairs trading strategies: Review and outlook, IWQW Discussion Paper Series, No. 09/2015 (2015)
21. Miller, S.J.: The method of least squares, Mathematics Department Brown University (2006)
22. Vidyamurthy, G.: Pairs Trading – Quantitative Methods and Analysis, p. 210. John Wiley & Sons Inc., New Jersey (2004)
23. Nath, P.: High Frequency Pairs Trading with US Treasury Securities: Risks and Rewards for Hedge Funds (2003). SSEN: http://ssrn.com/abstract=565441
24. Hendershott, T., Riordan, R.: Algorithmic trading and the market for liquidity. J. Financ. Quant. Anal. **48**(4), 1001–1024 (2012)
25. Cartea, A., Penalva, J.: Where is the value in high frequency trading? Q. J. Financ. **2**(3), 1–46 (2012)
26. Menkveld, A.J.: High frequency trading and the new market makers. J. Financ. Markets **16**(4), 712–740 (2013)

Shared Resource Model for Allocating Resources to Activities in BP Simulation

Olegas Vasilecas, Kestutis Normantas, Toma Rusinaite,
Titas Savickas[✉], and Tadas Vysockis

Information Systems Research Laborary,
Vilnius Gediminas Technical University,
Sauletekio ave. 11, 10223 Vilnius, Lithuania
{Olegas.Vasilecas,Kestutis.Normantas,Toma.Rusinaite,
Titas.Savickas,Tadas.Vysockis}@vgtu.lt

Abstract. Resources shareability amongst simultaneous business process (BP) activities is one of the main issues in the BP simulation. Without realistic simulation of shared resources usage, it is difficult to obtain accurate BP performance measures. This paper presents an approach to model shareable resources and a set of rules to handle resources allocation and control their usage in the rule-based BP simulation. The presented model and set of constraints are formalized using the UML/OCL allowing validation of the proof of concept. The approach has been implemented in a prototype of BP simulation tool, and an example highlighting benefits of applying the approach in the BP simulation is presented.

Keywords: Business process simulation · Resource model · Shared resource

1 Introduction

Enterprises are surrounded by a competitive and dynamic environment forcing them to constantly revise and improve their business processes (BP). Therefore, a demand to simulate BP under different circumstances becomes crucial. Computer simulation, in general, has been in use since the 1960s and nowadays it is being applied in a wide range of domains to simulate system behaviour. Numerous methods and tools exist for BP simulation using which enterprises can gain insight into the current or a hypothetical situation and identify critical BP parts [10]. It is particularly important when starting up a new or optimizing an existing BP. Although BP simulation is widespread, in most cases the results of simulation are inconsistent with reality. The inaccuracy can be caused by the usage of oversimplified resource models and by not taking into the account that [18]:

1. resources involved in a simulation might be distributed over multiple processes, while a simulation model typically focuses on a single process;
2. resources (i.e., people) are not available all the time;
3. resources (i.e., people) do not work at a constant speed.

G. Dregvaite and R. Damasevicius (Eds.): ICIST 2016, CCIS 639, pp. 218–229, 2016.
DOI: 10.1007/978-3-319-46254-7_18

Unfortunately, resource allocation problem in business process simulation is not yet solved and there is no formal definition of shared resources in BP modelling as well as no approaches to simulate shared resources allocation to activities. An extensive resource model supporting definition of complex resources and their shareability among different process activities during simulation is required. There are many possible use cases requiring such model. Consider, for example, various containers for storing and distributing materials such as gases and liquids, or electricity generators in high-availability power systems – they are used simultaneously by multiple activities. The simulation of the shared resource allocation and usage enables advanced analysis and optimization of BP performance: assess resources utilization, identify the impact of resources availability on BP duration, and evaluate the effect of allocating resources to multiple activities.

To address these challenges, we propose an initial generic resource model suitable to define shareable resources and a set of constraints to control the states of a shared resource used by simultaneous activities during the rule-based BP simulation. The resource model allows definition of resources, specify their shareability parameters and model their states during simulation. The UML/OCL has been used to formalize the model and to enable model instance validation in the design phase. The proposed approach has been implemented in the prototype of BP simulation tool developed within the undergoing project [5]. To highlight the importance of the problem and show the benefits of this approach, we provide an example of BP simulation with and without the ability to simulate a usage of shareable resource.

The rest of the paper is organised as follows. Section 2 provides an overview of related works and specifies the problem. Section 3 presents an UML resource model for modelling and using shareable resources in the BP simulation. In addition, this section presents a set of OCL rules the resources must comply with and which define state transition constraints. An example of applying the approach in a simplified BP simulation and a discussion on results of that simulation are presented in the Sect. 4. Section 5 concludes the paper and provides a discussion on the further research.

2 Related Works

Resource allocation is a widely researched topic in various application domains. They all have common problems in resource modelling and shareability. In this section we will review how resources are understood and modelled, and how resource shareability problem is being solved.

Resources participate in processes by being allocated to activities [9] and they support or enable the execution of activities [15] making them a crucial aspect of BP simulation [10]. Some examples of widely used resources are Humans, Machines, Raw materials, Tools, etc. [1, 2, 6]. In respect to the physical consistence of resources, as stated by Taveter [8], they can be categorized into physical, abstract, and informational resources. Resources can be used, consumed, refined or produced [8]. Resources are generally in finite supply and their availability constrains execution of activities [15]. Authors of [19] provide model which characterizes resource availability. Although this model can be used for insights into resource utilization, it does not take into account shareable resources which might also have an effect on the availability. In addition, resources can be reusable, i.e. a human is performing an activity, or consumable, when the amount of available resource changes during activity execution. The capacity and amount of available resources are not always constant [16].

According to [14], resources from the standpoint of availability are classified into two classes: Capacitated-resources and Discrete-state-resources. There are other resource availability classifications. Authors of [16] propose to classify resources as follows: Capacitated, Discrete state and Renewable resources. Capacitated resources are divided into reusable and consumable subclasses. Renewable resources can be either atomic or aggregate. According to Smith et al. [15], resources are single or multi-capacitive. Bedrax-Weiss et al. [17] state that resources can be consumable, producible, replenishable or reusable. Of course, resources are not always available and, according to [11], resources can be subdivided into unschedulable and schedulable resource classes. Smith et al. [16] provide an ontology, which attempts to define how resources in general could be modelled, but their approach has not been applied to BP modelling and simulation.

The computation of resource utilization is one of the important roles of simulation in the BP modelling. This is because resource availability often determines the formation of queues and bottlenecks in the process flow [10]. Although there are works on resource allocation problems, in the context of BP modelling and simulation there is a lack of thorough BP simulation researches that focus on resource shareability problem.

To simulate resources, Pla et al. [3] propose Petri net modelling, which simulates workflows to identify possible delays caused by resource availability. The proposed approach uses two parameters – type and amount of available resources; however, it does not take into account how the availability changes and how resources are allocated to each of the activities in the workflow. In a more general approach, López-Grao et al. [7] present resource allocation algorithm, but the provided algorithm does not support concurrent usage of shared resources. There are also implemented system and applications used for resource allocation. For example, Podorozhny et al. [11], describe a prototype resource allocation and management system that makes effective use of resource models built with the formalism. They also describe and evaluate some experiences, however the provided prototype isn't adaptable to shared resource.

Resource sharing problem is applicable not only to simulation domains. Martin-Clouaire et al. [12] state that in biophysical systems, it is an important feature and provide concrete examples. A solution to share resources is provided in [13] but the solution presented is not sufficiently detailed.

Based on the review of the related literature, it can be observed that there is a lack of a methods allowing to analyse the behaviour of complex processes which use shared resources. Most of the reviewed approaches use simplified resource models due to focus on other areas, e.g. decision distributions, activity modelling, etc. Obviously, there is a need for an approach to a BP simulation supporting complex resource allocation [18]. Specifically, resource allocation and sharing between activities taking into account the availability and state of the resources appears to be the most impactful to the simulation results. More detailed resource model would facilitate results that are more precise and could be more accurate, than results obtained by traditional simulation methods.

3   Shared Resource Allocation Model

3.1   Resource Model

In this section, a generic resource model facilitating resource sharing and consumption is presented. We use the UML/OCL to formally define the model and to enable validation of its instances (that is, the shareable resources) using appropriate modelling tools before implementing it in the simulation tool. The proposed model is a part of ongoing research intended to define a model supporting a wide range of complex resource allocation scenarios. The Fig. 1 presents a fragment of the model highlighting the context considered in this paper: resources definition and allocation to BP activities.

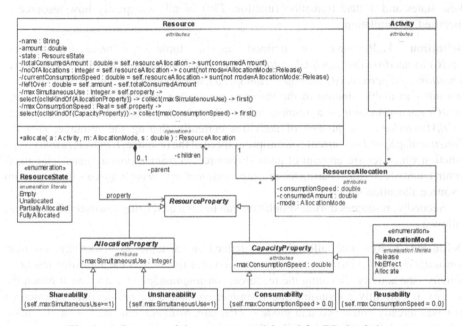

Fig. 1. A fragment of the resource model used for BP simulation.

The proposed model uses a concept of *ResourceProperty* to add flexibility in defining a resource. Possibility to share a resource among a set of activities at any given time is characterised by the property *AllocationProperty*. If a resource is shareable, it has the *Shareability* property and, in contrast, resources that cannot be shared among simultaneous activities are characterised by the *Unshareability* property and they can be allocated only to a single activity at a time. In addition, resources can be characterized by the means of the capacity (e.g. the total volume of the resource). If activities consume a resource, then it has the *Consumability* property, and contrarily, if they use a resource, then it has the *Reusability* property. A resource cannot be defined by a single property, either it is the *CapacityProperty*, or the *AllocationProperty*, both they must be defined for the resource at the same time to enable its allocation to activities. To ensure this rule, we define the following invariant:

```
context Resource
inv allowedProperties:
    let a : Integer = count(oclIsKindOf(AllocationProperty)),
      c : Integer = count(oclIsKindOf(CapacityProperty))
    in a > 0 and b > 0 implies a = 1 and b = 1
```

In order to manage resource allocation and release from activities, possible resource state transitions and constraints on them need to be defined.

3.2   Resource Allocation Rules

To define resource allocation rules, it is necessary to introduce definitions of resources, their states and a state transition function. First of all, we specify how resource is specified in simulation:

Definition 1. Resource is defined as a tuple $r = (name, amount, state, totalConsumedAmount, noOfAllocattions, curr - entConsumptionSpeed, leftOver, max-SimultaneousSpeed, maxConsump - tionSpeed)$, where *name* is a unique resource name, *amount* – available amount of the resource, *state* – one of states from *ResourceState*, *totalConsumedAmount* – a number of totally consumed amount of the resource, *noOfAllocattions* - a number of activities currently sharing the resource, *current-ConsumptionSpeed* – a current consumption speed of the resource, *leftOver(resource)* – a function which returns amount of unused resource, *maxSimultaneousSpeed* – the maximum count of activities sharing the resource and *maxConsumptionSpeed* – the maximum resource allocation speed.

Secondly, resources during simulation can be allocated using resource allocation as follows:

Definition 2. Resource allocation is defined as a tuple $m = (activity, resource, consumptionSpeed, consumedAmount, mode)$ where *resource* is the allocation resource, *activity* - the activity allocating the resource, *consumptionSpeed* is a speed at which the activity is currently consuming the resource, *consumedAmount*–amount of resource that was already consumed and $mode \in \{Release, NoEffect, Allocate\}$ – an allocation value which defines the state of the allocation.

Finally, a resource state transition is triggered by a resource allocation function:

Definition 3. The *allocation* function is defined as $A(activity, resource, Allocation - Mode, speed)$, where *Activity* is an activity which allocates the resource, *resource* – the resource to be allocated, $AllocationMode \in \{Release, NoEffect, Allocate\}$ and *speed* – is a resource allocation speed.

Having defined the general characteristics of a resource allocation, a set of rules for a resource state transitions can be specified.

A resource can be in several final states: *Unallocated* and *Empty*. The state *Unallocated* means that a resource is not assigned to any activity, but in a resource pool there is a certain amount of it. The state *Empty* means that the amount of a resource in a resource pool is equal to zero ($leftOver = 0$) and the resource is not used by any activity.

If *maxSimultaneousUse* = 1 then the state can only be changed to *FullyAllocated* from the *Unallocated* state. State *FullyAllocated* defines resources, which are fully in use. From this state, if a resource has *Reusability* property, then after the activity releases it, the resource is replenished back to the pool with the state *Unallocated*. Otherwise, the state becomes *Empty*. The resource state can become *PartiallyAllocated* when *maxSimultaneousUse* > 1 and *noOfAllocations* ≠ *maxSimultaneousUse*; it means that only shareable resources that are not fully distributed among activities can be in the state *PartiallyAllocated*. In case a resource is fully distributed, the state of a resource becomes *FullyAllocated* and when any activity releases the resource, the state returns to *PartiallyAllocated*. A transition from the state *PartiallyAllocated* to the state *Empty* of a resource is possible when the *leftOver* of the resource returns zero value; otherwise, the resource becomes *Unallocated*. If a resource state is *Empty* then it can be replenished and its state changes to *Unallocated* (Fig. 2).

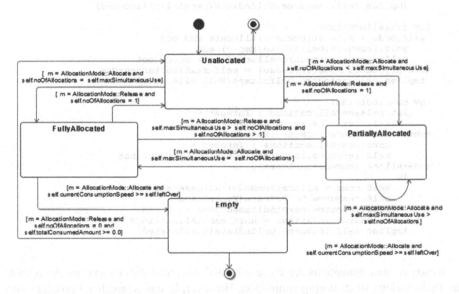

Fig. 2. Resource state transition model.

From the figure and explanations above it can be observed, that a Non-Shareable resource will never become in the state *PartiallyAllocated*. Moreover, a resource can be in the state *FullyAllocated* or *PartiallyAllocated* only if its previous state was *Unallocated* or *PartiallyAllocated*. Finally, the state *Unallocated* cannot be followed by the state *Empty*. Using formal descriptions, we can generate formal resource state transition rules in OCL as follows:

```
context Resource
inv resourceConsumption: self.amount >= r.resourceAllocation ->
sum(consumedAmount)

inv emptyResource: self.amount <> self.totalConsumedAmount implies
not self.OclInState(Empty)

context ResourceAllocation

inv partialAllocation:
    let releasedAllocations : Integer =
        self.resource.resourceAllocation ->
count(mode=AllocationMode::Release),
        unreleasedAllocations : Integer =
        self.resource.resourceAllocation -> count(not
mode=AllocationMode::Release),
    in
        self.mode = AllocationMode::Allocate and not
        self.resource.OclInState(Empty) and
        unreleasedAllocations - releasedAllocations <
self.resource.maxSimultaneousUse
    implies self.resource.OclInState(PartiallyAllocated)

inv fullAllocation:
  self.mode = AllocationMode::Allocate and not
    self.resource.OclInState(Empty) and
    self.resource.resourceAllocation -> count(not
mode=AllocationMode::Release) = self.maxSimultaneousUse
  implies self.resource.OclInState(FullyAllocated)

inv unallocation:
    let releasedAllocations : Integer =
        self.resource.resourceAllocation ->
count(mode=AllocationMode::Release),
        unreleasedAllocations : Integer =
        self.resource.resourceAllocation -> count(not
mode=AllocationMode::Release),
    in
        self.mode = AllocationMode::Release and not
        self.resource.OclInState(Empty) and
        self.resource.maxSimultaneousUse <> 0 and
        releasedAllocations = unreleasedAllocations
    implies self.resource.OclInState(Unallocated)
```

Resource state transitions are closely related with activities execution. An activity can be in various states during simulation. However, in this research we consider only three main states important for the resource model: Active, Passive and Paused. Active activities are being executed at the current moment, Passive activities are not conducted at the current moment, and Paused activities cannot be conducted at the current moment due to a lack of resources. The presented set of OCL constrains covers of these states.

It should be noted that the resource model presented in this section covers only shareable resources category. Other kinds of resources might require adaptations of state transition rules or model extensions; however, they are out of the scope of this paper and will be investigated in the further research. Nevertheless, the proposed model is suitable for shareable resource simulation as it is presented by experiments in the next section.

4 Experimental Results

In order to validate the feasibility of the proposed approach, we have implemented the resource model in the simulation engine [4]. This section presents an experiment of application of the approach in simulating shareable resources.

As an example, a simplified fire extinguishing process is presented in Fig. 3. In this BP, a hydrant is shareable resource that is used to refill fire trucks' tanks when they are out of water. The hydrant might be concurrently used by several fire trucks at the same time. Consider that the hydrant can be used by 2 fire trucks to refill their tanks and to stop the fire 8 tanks of water are required. A firefighting station has 6 fire trucks of the same tank's capacity. It is known that on average getting to that fireplace takes 10 min, emptying tank takes 15 min, and tank refill takes 30 min. The goal of simulation would be to identify an optimal number of fire trucks needed to be sent to extinguish the fire in the shortest time and to perform analysis on how resource shareability affects the results, i.e. what happens if a maximum possible count of activities sharing the resource is increased.

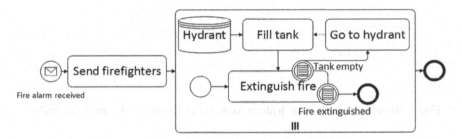

Fig. 3. Experimental fire extinguishment business process.

To show how resource status changes during the process execution an example can be used. Let's say, there are 2 fire trucks and a single hydrant that supports 2 allocations (*maxSimultaneousUse* = 2) at the same time. At the beginning the status of the hydrant is Unallocated because all fire trucks are full and do not need to fill the tank. When the first fire truck arrives to fill the tank, hydrant needs to be used to fill the tanks and its status changes into *PartiallyAllocated* because $0 < noOfAllocations < maxSimultaniuosUse$. When the second fire truck arrives, if the first one is still filling up the tank, then the hydrant status changes into *FullyAllocated* because $noOfAllocations = maxSimultaniuosUse$. When the first fire truck completes filling activity, the hydrant returns into state *PartialyAllocated* and, finally, when the second fire truck completes filling activity the hydrant become *Unallocated* because $noOfAllocations = 0$.

Typically, simulation tools cannot support shareable resources due to an over-simplified resource model [18]. In the given example, non-shareable hydrant means that all fire trucks sent to stop the fire might wait in the queue once they need to refill their tanks at the same time. It is obvious, that this scenario does not reflect the reality. To highlight the difference, we performed four simulations: one with the hydrant modelled as non-shareable resource, and the other three – as shareable with different number of trucks that the hydrant can be used by simultaneously. Each case consisted of 6 simulation runs with differing amount of fire trucks – ranging from 1 to 6 - sent to extinguish fire. To achieve consistent results and precise average of simulation run, 200 iterations were performed. The number of iterations in simulation was derived by observing average duration of the process. It was noticed that after 200 iterations the average duration becomes steady. Results of simulation runs using 4 fire trucks and hydrant modelled as non-shareable and shareable are presented in Figs. 4 and 5 respectively.

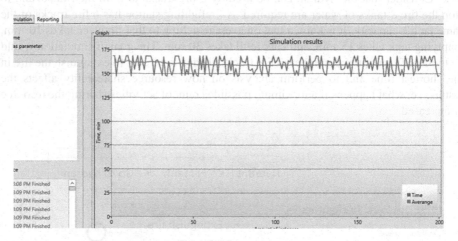

Fig. 4. Simulation results with hydrant modelled as non-shareable and 4 fire trucks.

When hydrant is modelled as non-shareable resource, the iteration times vary between 148 and 170 min. In contrast, when the hydrant is modelled as shareable resource, the iteration times vary between 52 and 90 min. It can be seen, that when hydrant is modelled as shareable, it's shared usage makes the process more efficient reducing the extinguishing time. In addition, higher time value dispersion makes the impact of hydrant sharing and fire truck queuing more apparent in the overall process.

Table 1 summarizes results obtained by all four cases. It can be observed, that the average time required to extinguish the fire is almost the same when there is a single fire truck sent. The reason for this is that the hydrant does not have to be shared when there is only a single fire truck and shareability does not have any impact. When there is more than one fire truck, the optimal number of truck decrease as the hydrant shareability increases. In each case of shareability, the optimum number of fire trucks is different. After reaching the optimum number of fire trucks, the average duration does not decrease or is within rounding error.

To conclude, this experiment showed the feasibility of the approach and highlighted the benefits of its application in simulation of BP, that is, the usage of a shareable resource concepts added more precision to simulation results and made simulation model closer to reality.

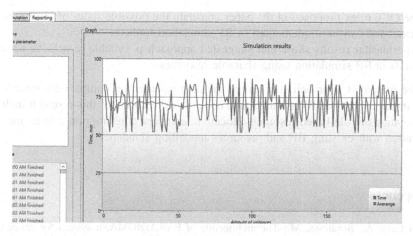

Fig. 5. Simulation results with hydrant modelled as shareable and 4 fire trucks.

Table 1. Average duration of the fire extinguishing process simulation for different resource types (rounded to nearest integer)

#	Number of trucks Results	1	2	3	4	5	6
1	Average time in minutes, without resource sharing	332	247	203	157	129	98
2	Average time in minutes, with resource sharing $v = 2$	332	157	148	129	99	67
3	Average time in minutes, with resource sharing $v = 3$	331	155	110	98	67	67
4	Average time in minutes, with resource sharing $v = 4$	330	156	113	68	68	66

5 Conclusions and Future Work

In this paper, a generic resource model supporting shareability of resources among simultaneous BP activities has been presented. The model was design using UML and it is supplemented with the resource state model and the state transition rules defined in OCL. The approach has been implemented in a prototype simulation tool and experiment has been conducted to showcase the feasibility and benefits of the approach. The main conclusions of the paper are as follows:

1. Review of related works revealed that the problem of resource shareability in the context of BP simulation has not received sufficient attention, although the problem is important and is widely researched in other domains.
2. The presented resource model is formally defined and enables definition of shared resources.

3. The OCL rules proposed in the paper constrain the possible states of resources, are formal and can be implemented in BP simulation tools.
4. Experimental results show that suggested approach is suitable to achieve accurate results in BP simulation using sharable resources.

The presented approach is a part of ongoing research on complex resource behaviour in the context of BP simulation. The further directions of this research includes investigation of rule-based resource allocation, complex consumption constraints, and integration with existing BP and resources modelling standards.

References

1. Di Leva, A., Sonnessa, M.: The architecture of PARADIGMA, a system for cooperative work in the medical domain. In: Proceedings of ICIT 2005 International Conference on Information Technology, pp. 31–38 (2005)
2. Di Leva, A., Berchi, R., Pescarmona, G., Sonnessa, M.: Analysis and Prototyping of Biological Systems: the Abstract Biological Process Model. Int. J. Inf. Technol. 2(3), 216–224 (2007)
3. Pla, A., Gay, P., Meléndez, J., López, B.: Petri net-based process monitoring: a workflow management system for process modelling and monitoring. J. Intell. Manuf. 25(3), 539–554 (2014)
4. Kalibatiene, D., Vasilecas, O., Rusinaite, T.: Implementing a rule-based dynamic business process modelling and simulation. In: 2015 Open Conference of Electrical, Electronic and Information Sciences (eStream), pp. 1–4. IEEE (2015)
5. DBPSim simulation tool, Vilnius Gediminias Technical University, Vilnius (2016). http://www.vgtu.lt/faculties/departments/institute-of-applied-computer-science/departaments/information-systems-research-laboratory/73139#tab-other-activity
6. Fadel, F.G., Fox, M.S., Gruninger, M.: A generic enterprise resource ontology. In: Proceedings of the Third Workshop on Enabling Technologies: Infrastructure for Collaborative Enterprises 1994, pp. 117–128. IEEE (1994)
7. López-Grao, J.P., Colom, J.M.: The resource allocation problem in software applications: a petri net perspective. In: ACSD/Petri Nets Workshops, pp. 219–233 (2010)
8. Taveter, K.: A multi-perspective methodology for agent-oriented business modelling and simulation, 244. Tallinn University of Technology Press (2004)
9. Tumay, K.: Business process simulation. In: Proceedings of the 27th Conference on Winter Simulation, pp. 55–60. IEEE Computer Society (1995)
10. Jansen-Vullers, M., Netjes, M.: Business process simulation–a tool survey. In: Workshop and Tutorial on Practical Use of Coloured Petri Nets and the CPN Tools, Aarhus, Denmark, pp. 1–20 (2006)
11. Podorozhny, R.M., Lerner, B.S., Osterweil, L.J.: A rigorous approach to resource management in activity coordination, 1003. University of Massachusetts, Amherst (1999)
12. Martin-Clouaire, R., Rellier, J.P.: A generic framework for simulating agricultural production systems. In: Modelling Nutrient Digestion and Utilisation in Farm Animals, pp. 13–21. Wageningen Academic Publishers (2011)
13. Martin-Clouaire, R., Rellier, J.P.: Dynamic resource allocation in a farm management simulation. In: 19th International Congress on Modelling and Simulation, Perth, Australia, pp. 808–814 (2011)

14. Arsovski, S., Arsovski, Z., Mirovic, Z.: The integrating role of simulation in modern manufacturing planning and scheduling. J. Mech. Eng. **55**(1), 33–44 (2009)
15. Smith, S.F., Cortellessa, G., Hildum, D.W., Ohler, C.M.: Using a scheduling domain ontology to compute user-oriented explanations. In: Castillo, L., Borrajo, D., Salido, M.A., Oddi, A. (eds) Planning, Scheduling and Constraint Satisfaction: From Theory to Practice, 117, pp. 179–188. IOS Press (2005)
16. Smith, S.F., Becker, M.A.: An ontology for constructing scheduling systems. In: Working Notes of 1997 AAAI Symposium on Ontological Engineering, pp. 120–127 (1997)
17. Bedrax-Weiss, T., McGann, C., Ramakrishnan, S.: Formalizing resources for planning. In: Proceedings of the ICAPS 2003 Workshop on PDDL, pp. 7–14 (2003)
18. van der Aalst, W.M.: Business process simulation revisited. In: Barjis, J. (ed.) EOMAS 2010. LNBIP, vol. 63, pp. 1–14. Springer, Heidelberg (2010)
19. van der Aalst, W.M.P., Nakatumba, J., Rozinat, A., Russell, N.: Business process simulation: how to get it right? In: International Handbook on Business Process Management 1, pp. 313–338. Springer, Berlin (2010)

Parallel Computing for Dimensionality Reduction

Jelena Zubova, Marius Liutvinavicius[(✉)], and Olga Kurasova

Vilnius University, Vilnius, Lithuania
{jelena.zubova,olga.kurasova}@mii.vu.lt,
marius.liutvinavicius@khf.vu.lt

Abstract. Big data analytics enables to uncover hidden and useful information for better decisions. Our research area covers big data visualization that is based on dimensionality reduction methods. It requires time and resource consuming processes, so in this paper we look for computing methods and environments that enable to execute the tasks and get results faster. In this research we use Random projection method to reduce the dimensions of the initial data. We investigate how parallel computing based on OpenMP and MPI technologies can increase the performance of these dimensionality reduction processes. The results show the significant improvement of performance when executing MPI code on computer cluster. However, the greater number of cores not always leads to higher speed.

Keywords: Parallel computing · Big data · Dimensionality reduction

1 Introduction

Big data analytics is the process of examining big data to uncover hidden and useful information for better decisions. It involves visual presentation of data that enables to see hidden relations between objects which cannot be detected using conventional data analysis methods. However big data visualization is a challenge for data analysts and researchers, because the methods and tools, applied to visualize ordinary data, become unsuitable for big data visualization. Ability to access big data provides many opportunities, but it also raises new challenges related with capabilities to handle such enormous amounts of data.

Our research area focuses on big data visualization that is based on dimensionality reduction methods. We seek to maximize the efficiency and speed of big data mining processes. Firstly, we look for the data visualization methods that are the most appropriate in certain conditions and can reveal the most information. Secondly we look for computing methods and environments that enable to execute the tasks and get results faster.

In this paper we investigate how parallel computing methods can increase the performance of dimensionality reduction processes. In this case we use Random projection method to reduce the dimensions of the initial data. It's complicated to process large data sets while using algorithm realized with serial code. Therefore we present how OpenMP and MPI parallel computing technologies can solve this problem.

© Springer International Publishing Switzerland 2016
G. Dregvaite and R. Damasevicius (Eds.): ICIST 2016, CCIS 639, pp. 230–241, 2016.
DOI: 10.1007/978-3-319-46254-7_19

In the second section of this paper we present related works that analysed OpenMP and MPI performance. In the third section we describe in detail these parallel computing methods and present the environments that enable them. We use these environments for our investigation process. In the fourth section we compare how fast Random projection method works in different cases: (1) sequential computing in personal computer, (2) OpenMP parallel computing in personal computer, (3) sequential computing on cluster, (4) MPI parallel computing on cluster.

2 Related Works

Jin and Jespersen [13] stated that the increasing number of cores in modern microprocessors is pushing the current high performance computing (HPC) systems into the petascale and exascale era. Authors presented case studies of the hybrid MPI + OpenMP programming approach applied to two pseudoapplication benchmarks and two real-world applications and demonstrated benefits of the hybrid approach for performance and resource usage on three multi-core based parallel systems. They also distinguished two primary limitations that impede a wider adoption of hybrid programming: no well-defined interaction between MPI processes and OpenMP threads, and limited performance of OpenMP.

According to Rabenseifner and Hager, etc. [14], most systems in high-performance computing feature a hierarchical hardware design: shared memory nodes with several multi-core CPUs are connected via a network infrastructure. Therefore parallel programming must combine distributed memory parallelization on the node interconnect with shared memory parallelization inside each node.

Mallon and Taboada [17] evaluated MPI performance against OpenMP. They found that MPI usually achieves good performance on shared memory, although OpenMP outperform it in some cases. OpenMP speedups are generally higher than those of MPI due to its direct shared memory access, which avoids memory copies as in MPI.

Mininni and Rosenberg [11] presented hybrid scheme that utilizes MPI for distributed memory parallelism and OpenMP for shared memory. They showed that the hybrid scheme achieves near ideal scalability up to 20000 compute cores with a maximum mean efficiency of 83 %. They also presented how to choose the optimal number of MPI processes and OpenMP threads in order to optimize code performance. Authors found that for large enough problems best scalability is got when the number of threads is 12 (one MPI process per compute node). On the other hand, the performance time is better when number of threads is 6, until the workload per MPI process is large enough.

Another one comparison between MPI and hybrid models was made by Cappello and Etiemble [15]. Authors claimed that superiority of one model depends on the level of shared memory model parallelization, the communication patterns and the memory access patterns. Their test results showed that a unified MPI approach is better for most of the benchmarks. The hybrid approach becomes better only when fast processors make the communication performance significant and the level of parallelization is sufficient.

Such claims were also confirmed by Chorley and Walker [16]. They found that the hybrid code spends less time carrying out communication than the pure MPI code, performing better communication at higher core counts. At low core counts the added overheads from OpenMP parallelization reduce the hybrid code performance, but the effects of these overheads lessen as the number of cores increases.

Rabenseifner and Hager, etc. [14] showed that machine topology has a significant impact on performance for all parallelization strategies and that topology awareness should be built into all applications in the future. Wolf and Mohr [12] presented a complete tracing-based solution for automatic performance analysis of MPI, OpenMP, or hybrid applications running on parallel computers.

Random projection method is based on matrix multiplication. Rifat Chowdhury [1] designed an algorithm using the libraries of OpenMP to compute Matrix Multiplication efficiently. As expected the speedup was close to the ideal 4 times using four cores of a processor to compute the final matrix instead of one. [1]

The researches of particularly parallel and distributed large data visualization were made by Wang and Chen et al. [18] and Dutra and Rodrigues et al. [19].

3   Parallel Computing Methods and Environments

In this paper we investigate the advantages of parallel computing versus sequential computing. Further in this section we present the OpenMP and MPI methodologies and software environments that enable them.

OpenMP. The OpenMP library is an API (Application Programming Interface) for writing shared memory parallel applications in programming languages such as C, C++ and Fortran. Table 1 presents vendors of OpenMP compilers [5].

Table 1. OpenMP compilers

Vendor/Source	Compilator
GNU	GCC
IBM	XL C/C++/Fortan
Oracle, Intel, PGI, Lahey/Fujitsu, PathScale, OpenUH, LLNL	C/C++/Fortan
Absoft Pro Fortan	Fortran
Microsoft	Visual Studio 2008-2010
Cray	Cray C/C++ and Fortran
Appentra Solutions, Texas Instruments	C

Source: http://openmp.org/wp/openmp-compilers/

This API consists of compiler directives, runtime routines, and environmental variables. Some advantages of OpenMP includes: good performance, portable, requires very little programming effort and allows the program to be parallelized incrementally. OpenMP is widely available and used, lightweight, and well suited for multi-core architectures. Data can be shared or private in the OpenMP memory model. When data is private it is visible to one thread only, when data is public it is global and visible to all threads. OpenMP divides tasks into threads. A thread is the smallest unit of a processing that can be scheduled by an operating system. The master thread assigns tasks unto worker threads. Afterwards, they execute the task in parallel using the multiple cores of a processor [1].

We chose Intel C++ compiler for its high performance. We used Intel Parallel Studio XE Cluster Edition (Fortran and C/C++) which includes high-performance compilers, libraries, parallel models, threading and vectorization advisor, VTune™ Amplifier performance profiler, memory/threading debugger. This edition includes standards based MPI Library, MPI communications profiling and analysis tool, MPI error checking and tuning tools. It can be successfully integrated in Microsoft Visual Studio (Windows), Eclipse (Linux* and OS X), XCode (OS X) [4].

MPI. MPI (Message-Passing Interface) is a message-passing library interface specification. MPI addresses primarily the message-passing parallel programming model, in which data is moved from the address space of one process to that of another process through cooperative operations on each process. MPI is a specification, not an implementation; there are multiple implementations of MPI [7].

MPI is not a language, and all MPI operations are expressed as functions, subroutines, or methods, according to the appropriate language bindings which, for C and Fortran, are part of the MPI standard [7].

Figure 1 shows typical structure of multi-socket multi-core SMP cluster and how pure MPI parallel programming model can be realized on it. In the pure MPI case there is one MPI process per core. Meanwhile OpenMP method uses distributed virtual shared memory.

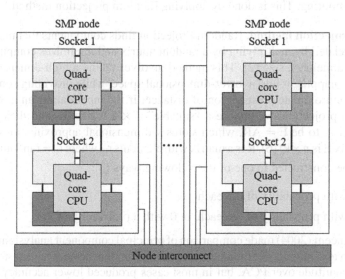

Fig. 1. MPI parallel programming on cluster

Originally, MPI was designed for distributed memory architectures, which were becoming increasingly popular at that time of 1980s – early 1990s. As architecture trends changed, shared memory SMPs were combined over networks creating hybrid distributed memory/shared memory systems. MPI implementers adapted their libraries to handle both types of underlying memory architectures seamlessly. Today, MPI runs on virtually any hardware platform: Distributed Memory, Shared Memory, Hybrid. All parallelism is explicit: the programmer is responsible for correctly identifying parallelism and implementing parallel algorithms using MPI constructs [10].

MPICH is a high performance and widely portable implementation of the MPI standard. MPICH and its derivatives form the most widely used implementations of MPI in the world. They are used exclusively on nine of the top 10 supercomputers (June 2015 ranking) [8].

The goal of MPICH is to provide an MPI implementation that efficiently supports different computation and communication platforms including commodity clusters (desktop systems, shared-memory systems, multi-core architectures), high-speed networks and proprietary high-end computing systems [8].

Microsoft MPI is a Microsoft implementation of the Message Passing Interface standard for developing and running parallel applications on the Windows platform. It enables to develop and run MPI applications without having to set up an HPC Pack cluster [9]. But in our case we use computer cluster with 120 cores and Linux operating system.

4   Research Methodology

Our aim is to compare the performance of sequential computing versus parallel OpenMP and MPI computing. This is done by applying Random projection method.

Random Projection method. Random Projection finds components that make projections uncorrelated by multiplying by a random matrix and minimizes computations for a particular dimension size [2]. This method involves taking a high-dimensional dataset and then mapping it into a lower-dimensional space, while providing some guarantees on the approximate preservation of distance. If the input data is an $n \times d$ matrix, then to do a projection, we choose a "suitable" $d \times k$ matrix R, and then define the projection of A to be $E = AR$, which stores k-dimensional approximations for our n points (matrix E is $n \times k$) [6]. R is a matrix with elements r_{ij}, where r_{ij} = random Gaussian. R can also be constructed in one of the following ways [2]:

- $r_{ij} = \pm 1$ with probability of 0.5 each
- $r_{ij} = \pm 1$ with probability of 1/6 each, or 0 with a probability of 2/3

Steve Vincent (2004) made comparison of principal component analysis and random projection in text mining. He found that in general Random projection is faster by many orders of magnitude over PCA, but in most cases produced lower accuracy. This lead to suggestion to use Random projection method if speed of processing is most important [2].

Serial code. Figure 2 presents the main schema of Random projection algorithm. Firstly, we declare 3 matrixes: $n \times d$ matrix1, $d \times k$ matrix2 and $n \times k$ matrix3. During the next step we initialize random integer values to all elements of matrix1. Then we assign values of 1 or -1 to matrix2 with probability 0,5 each. Finally, matrix1 and matrix2 are multiplied and the results are assigned to the elements of matrix3.

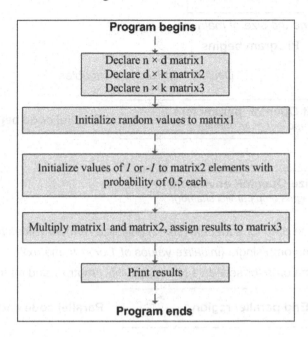

Fig. 2. Principal schema of Random projection algorithm

The code is written in C language. It is executed on personal computer with Intel Core i5-2450 M 2.5 GHz processor and 4 GB RAM. CodeBlocks with GNU GCC compiler are used to build and run the program. Only one thread is used to execute the program.

OpenMP parallel computing. In the second case we use OpenMP methodology to execute the program simultaneously on the several threads. In order to do this, we have to transform our initial serial code.

The algorithm for parallelization with OpenMP is presented in Fig. 3. We include *omp.h* file into the code. After declaring the matrixes and operating variables the number of threads is set. We use *#pragma omp for schedule ()* function for the initialization of the matrix1 and for multiplication of matrix1 and matrix2. This means that these parts of code are executed simultaneously on several threads. The function *#pragma omp single* allows executing the region of matrix2 initialization in sequential way. After the parallel code ends, the printing of results is executed in sequential way too.

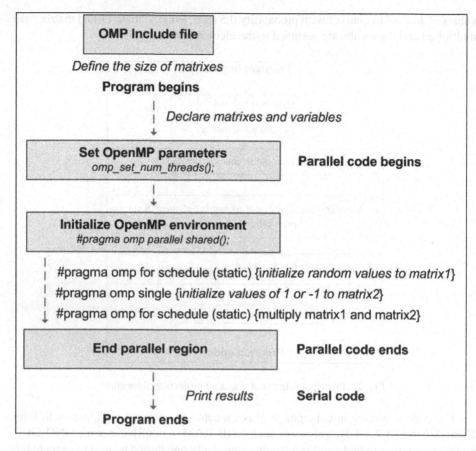

Fig. 3. Algorithm for parallelization with OpenMP

Intel Parallel Studio XE Cluster Edition integrated into Microsoft Visual Studio is used to execute the program.

Cluster based MPI parallel computing. In the last case we use MPI technology to execute the program on computer cluster. It runs on Linux operating system and consists of 120 cores.

The code is also modified accordingly to MPI requirements (Fig. 4). The program includes MPI library. All matrices and variables are declared in serial code region, but MPI environment is initialized by special functions before the parallel region begins. The program uses determined amount of threads. Whole multiplication task is divided into multiple operations that are simultaneously done by multiple threads. "Zero" thread handles incoming results from the remaining threads.

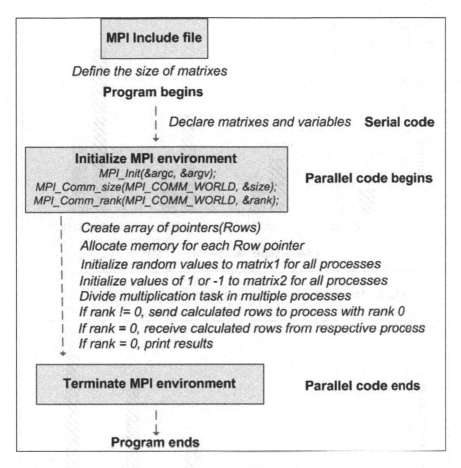

Fig. 4. Algorithm for parallelization with MPI

5   Research Results

In this section the results of applying Random projection method for various size matrixes by using different computing methods are presented. In all cases the number of initial dimensions is reduced twice.

Figure 5 presents the time of program execution that is needed to process relatively small matrixes. The results show that OpenMP code (using 4 cores) works 2 to 3 times faster than serial code (using 1 core). The difference increases with increasing the size of initial matrixes. By comparison, while executing MPI code on cluster (using 4 cores) the same tasks with small matrixes were performed from 100 to 1000 times faster versus OpenMP code executed in personal computer. The difference between MPI code and serial code (executed on personal computer) was even bigger.

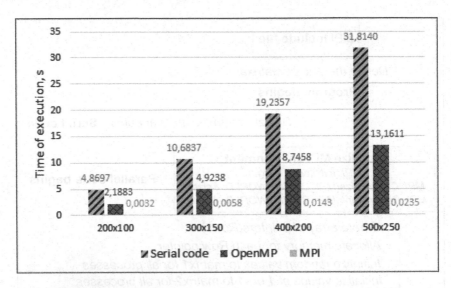

Fig. 5. The performance comparison of serial code, OpenMP and MPI

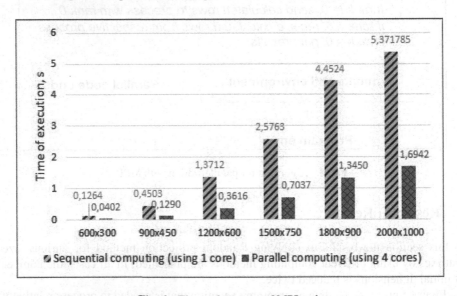

Fig. 6. The performance of MPI code

As it is not correct way to compare different methods in different environments, the larger matrixes were processed only on cluster. Another reason to do this was the fact that personal computer simply was unable to process larger matrixes. So to apply Random projection method for such data we needed to use computer cluster and MPI. There was one MPI process per core. Figure 6 shows that on cluster MPI code (using 4 cores) worked 3 to 4 times faster than the same code while using only 1 core. It's important to mention that when the size of matrix reached 1900 × 950 the sequential computing was unable to process the data.

It might seem that increasing the number of cores should increase the performance in all cases. But our results show that it's not always true.

Figure 7 shows that for different size matrixes to reduce the number of columns twice there is no significant performance improvement when using more cores than 20. The biggest effect is seen at the beginning of trying to increase the number of cores. Of course we can find cases when the best choice is 20 or even 100 cores.

Figure 8 presents the speedup ratio which shows how many times using the particular number of cores reduces the time of program execution in comparison with using the sequential computing. For example in the case of proceeding the 400 × 200 matrix the

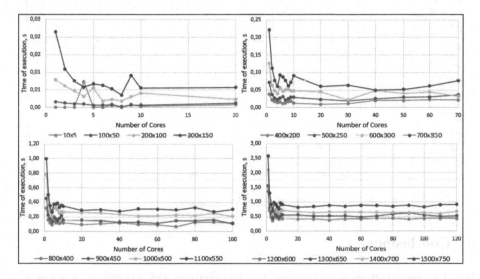

Fig. 7. The performance of MPI code with different number of cores

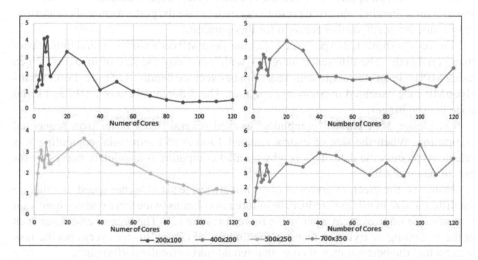

Fig. 8. Speedup ratio

best results were get while using 20 cores. For 500 × 250 matrix it was 30 cores, and for 700 × 350 it was 100 cores. So there is no one universal rule how to determine the best number of cores. It should be found for every specific case.

Figure 9 presents the parallel efficiency, which is the ratio of speedup ratio to number of cores. The results show that the smaller amount of cores is used, the more each of them is loaded. Therefore the efficiency ratio is decreasing while increasing the number of cores.

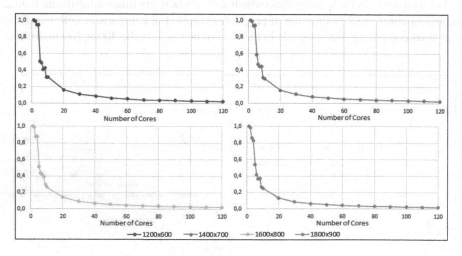

Fig. 9. Parallel efficiency

6   Conclusions

Big data visualization is a challenge for data analysts and researchers, because the methods and tools, applied to visualize ordinary data, become unsuitable for big data visualization. Parallel computing resources can increase the performance of dimensionality reduction methods that are used for this purpose.

The results show that in personal computer OpenMP code works several times faster than serial code. The difference increases with increasing the size of matrixes. When using MPI code on cluster the same tasks can be executed hundreds of times faster versus OpenMP code executed in personal computer. The difference between MPI and serial code is even bigger.

On cluster MPI parallel computing worked several times faster than sequential computing. When the size of matrix reached 1900 × 950 sequential computing was unable to process the data. This is why parallel computing is absolutely necessary for big amounts of data.

However, the greater number of cores not always leads to higher speed. In our case for different size matrixes to reduce the number of columns twice there was no significant performance improvement when using more cores than 20. The biggest effect was seen at the beginning of trying to increase the number of cores. But for every specific task we can find the best number of cores that would maximize the performance.

The research results suggest using MPI technology for further data visualization experiments in order to increase work efficiency.

References

1. Chowdhury, R.: Parallel Computing with OpenMP to solve matrix Multiplication. Uconn biogrid reu Summer 2010. Department of Computer Science & Engineering. University of Connecticut, Storrs, CT 06269
2. Dr. Domeniconi. Comparison of Principal Component Analysis and Random Projection in Text Mining. April 29, 2004. INFS 795
3. Fodor, I.K.: A survey of dimension reduction techniques. Center for Applied Scientific Computing, Lawrence Livermore National Laboratory, June 2002
4. Intel Parallel studio. https://software.intel.com/en-us/intel-parallel-studio-xe
5. OpenMP compilers. http://openmp.org/wp/openmp-compilers/
6. Menon, A.K.: Random projections and applications to dimensionality reduction. School of Information Technologies, The University of Sydney (2007)
7. MPI Technology. http://www.mpi-forum.org/docs/mpi-3.1/mpi31-report.pdf
8. MPICH Description. http://www.mpich.org/
9. Microsoft MPI. https://msdn.microsoft.com/en-us/library/windows/desktop/bb524831(v=vs.85).aspx
10. Message Passing Interface. https://computing.llnl.gov/tutorials/mpi/
11. Mininni, P.D., Rosenberg, D., Reddy, R., Pouquet, A.: A hybrid MPI-OpenMP scheme for scalable parallel pseudospectral computations for fluid Turbulence. Institute for Mathematics Applied to Geosciences (2010). arXiv:1003.4322
12. Wolf, F., Mohr, B.: Automatic performance analysis of hybrid MPI/OpenMP applications. J. Syst. Archit. **49**, 421–439 (2003)
13. Jin, H., Jespersen, D., et al.: High performance computing using MPI and OpenMP on multi-core parallel systems. Parallel Comput. **37**, 562–575 (2011)
14. Rabenseifner, R., Hager, G., etc.: Hybrid MPI/OpenMP parallel programming on clusters of multi-core SMP nodes. In: Conference, Proceedings of the 17th Euromicro International Conference on Parallel, Distributed and Network-Based Processing, PDP 2009, Weimar, Germany, 18-20 Febuary 2009
15. Cappello, F., Etiemble, D.: MPI versus MPI + OpenMP on the IBM SP for the NAS Benchmarks. In: ACM/IEEE 2000 Conference Supercomputing (2000)
16. Chorleya, M.J., Walkera, D.W.: Performance analysis of a hybrid MPI/OpenMP application on multi-core clusters. J. Comput. Sci. **1**(3), 168–174 (2010)
17. Mallon, D.A., Taboada, G.L. etc.: Performance evaluation of MPI, UPC and OpenMP on multicore architectures. In: Parallel and Distributed Processing Symposium, Proceedings (2004)
18. Wang, L., Chen, D., Deng, Z., Huang, F.: Large scale distributed visualization on computational Grids: a review. Comput. Electr. Eng. **37**(4), 403–416 (2011). Elsevier
19. Dutra, M., Rodrigues, P., Giraldi, G.A., Schulze, B.: Distributed visualization using VTK in grid environments. In: Seventh IEEE International Symposium on Cluster Computing and the Grid, pp. 381–388. IEEE (2007). ISBN: 0-7695-2833-3

Lessons Learned from Tool Integration
with OSLC

Andrea Leitner[1,2]([⊠]), Beate Herbst[2], and Roland Mathijssen[3]

[1] AVL List GmbH, Graz, Austria
andrea.leitner@avl.com
[2] Virtual Vehicle Research Center, Graz, Austria
{andrea.leitner,beate.herbst}@v2c2.at
[3] TNO-ESI, Eindhoven, The Netherlands
roland.mathijssen@tno.nl

Abstract. Today's embedded and cyber-physical systems are getting more connected and complex. One main challenge during development is the often loose coupling between engineering tools, which could lead to inconsistencies and errors due to the manual transfer and duplication of data. Open formats and specifications raise expectations for seamlessly integrated tool chains for systems engineering combining best-of-breed technologies and tools of different tool vendors.

The ARTEMIS JU project CRYSTAL aims for a harmonized inter-operability specification (IOS) incorporating various open specifications and standards such as OSLC (Open Services for Lifecycle Collaboration), ReqIF (Requirements Interchange Format) or FMI (Functional Mockup Interface) for supporting seamless model-based systems engineering.

This paper focuses on lifecycle integration using OSLC. We will report challenges we experienced in the implementation of an automotive and healthcare use case. The paper should support others in deciding if OSLC is an appropriate technology and to overcome common challenges in the implementation of OSLC adapters.

Keywords: Lifecycle integration · OSLC · Interoperability

1 Introduction

The processes of developing, deploying, governing, operating and maintaining modern safety-critical embedded systems is highly complex and requires specialized tools supporting different activities throughout the entire product lifecycle. OEMs and suppliers typically operate a large set of tools from different vendors often complemented by custom in-house solutions. The overall process can be effective and efficient only if it supports collaboration among all stakeholders and consequently interoperability between the tools they are using. Considering the ongoing outsourcing and globalization activities, interoperability and openness is getting even more crucial. In addition, the demand for supporting a large number of product variants further increases the complexity to be handled.

G. Dregvaite and R. Damasevicius (Eds.): ICIST 2016, CCIS 639, pp. 242–254, 2016.
DOI: 10.1007/978-3-319-46254-7_20

One approach for an integrated development environment are general all-in-one solutions delivered by one tool vendor. These solutions are of course perfectly integrated, but also have some drawbacks (e.g. monolithic data storage, proprietary interfaces, dependence on a specific tool vendor, etc.). Many companies have already established tools for their different engineering activities and the migration to an all-in-one solution is time consuming and expensive. Furthermore, all-in-one solutions often do not support all the required engineering activities. Point-to-point integrations are potential solutions that work well for a quite low number of integrations, but do not scale for more complex tool chains. An architecture based on an open specification as discussed in this paper and as suggested by the CRYSTAL [1] project enables the seamless integration of various domain-specific tools and will thus enable improved system development at lower cost, lower risk, less rework, and higher quality.

This paper focuses on lifecycle integration (traceability) as a major prerequisite for change impact analysis and a more holistic view on complex, distributed engineering data. Usually, data is stored in various independent databases which makes it difficult to answer questions such as "Has requirement x been implemented and tested successfully?". An important advantage of a standardized interoperability specification is the possibility to reuse tool interfaces i.e. replace a tool by a similar tool of a different vendor with little effort. This is one major driver of this paper: Consider a tier x supplier. Usually a supplier has several customers (e.g. different OEMs). Imagine that the supplier has to deliver a Matlab Simulink model for one customer. In another project, a different customer requests an ASCET model. Nevertheless, the supplier still wants to maintain one tool chain and just replace the modeling tool depending on the project setup. From a tool vendors perspective it is strategically important to keep the possibilities for interoperability as open as possible. A customer would not be happy to be forced to use a certain requirement management tool, just because the modeling tool only provides an interface to this tool. Customers appreciate it if a tool supports off-the-shelf integration for their preferred tool environment. Open Services for Lifecycle Collaboration [6] (OSLC) is a promising approach based on the linked data principles of the web. It is not trying to standardize the behavior or capabilities of a tool, instead it specifies a minimum amount of protocol and a small number of resource types to allow tools to work together relatively seamlessly. OSLC promotes the integration of data instead of the integration of tools. From this point of view, OSLC perfectly supports the idea of replacing tools. This paper will explain why this is not as easy as it seems by highlighting the challenges we experienced in the development of various tool integrations using OSLC.

This paper is structured as follows: Sect. 2 describes the most important concepts and related research activities. Section 3 points out some of the main challenges for the design of loosely coupled tool chains. Section 4 summarizes some important considerations when implementing an OSLC interface. Section 5 concerns the arising challenges when using OSLC queries and Sect. 6 includes a discussion and describes future work. Section 7 concludes the paper.

2   Background and Related Work

OSLC is an open community that creates specifications for integrating tools based on standardized and well-known web technologies such as Hypertext Transfer Protocol (HTTP), the Resource Description Framework [8] (RDF), and the Uniform Resource Identifier (URI). It makes use of the linked data principles defined by Tim Berners-Lee [5].

OSLC consists of a core specification [15] and a set of domain specifications. The core specification defines essential properties, behavior, and services that expand the W3C Linked Data concept [9]. Domain specifications are created and maintained by specific working groups in order to support a common vocabulary. These specifications include requirements management, change management, architecture management, and many more. OSLC follows a scenario-driven approach to ensure that the specifications only contain a minimal set of domain properties to have a stable standard which specifies just enough for realistic integration scenarios.

Saadatmand and Bucaioni [20] discuss the relationship between OSLC and systems engineering with the goal of promoting the application of systems engineering concepts and principles to tool integration. Their investigations are based on the observation that OSLC is completely aligned with the definition of a system which, in simplest terms, is a meaningful collection of elements and their relationships.

Aichernig et al. [10] report the application of OSLC to build a requirement-centered analysis and testing framework. Their goal is to supply a generic framework with standardized interfaces which supports the replacement of tools. The idea is to integrate existing tools in their methodology instead of developing new all-in-one solutions covering the entire workflow.

Zhang et al. [25] propose the use of an integration model for the description of the integration and as a base to generate the integration adapters. In a follow-up work [24], they refine their work by an extended notion of artifacts and roles.

In contrast to these works, we are focusing more on the design and implementation of the adapters themselves. Skoglund [22] has investigated in his master thesis a point-to-point integration using OSLC and has also identified some weaknesses, such as immature SDKs, lack of implementations, and so on. This is very similar to our observations. The Eclipse Lyo framework is a Java SDK, which provides a lot of implementations but is due to its complexity very complicated to use. We also have the feeling that there is not a huge community working on the improvement of the SDK (based on the Contribution Activity [3]). The status of the OSLC4Net SDK [19] is even worse. The SDK is still in Alpha status and has been updated the last time in 2013 (Fri Jul 26, 2013 - data accessed in May 2016). This indicates that OSLC is not as widely used as expected.

Seceleanu and Sapienza [21] introduce an orchestrator service, which was developed in the iFest [4] project. The developed framework aims to provide additional aspects which are not addressed by OSLC such as control/operational integration, model transformation, transactions, versioning, and licensing.

Biehl et al. [13] suggest the generation of adapters. Most of the issues we describe in this paper are applicable even if parts of the adapter can be generated.

3 Designing OSLC Adapters

Design challenges here cover the design of a single OSLC adapter as well as of an OSLC-based tool chain. Both are not independent from each other, because even when designing a tool adapter potential integration scenarios have to be kept in mind.

In both cases, a lot of decisions need to be taken, e.g. which data has to be provided/consumed, which domain specification should be used, what is the concrete workflow, and so on. We have identified three important questions (described below) which support the design process. Answering these questions requires a quite good understanding of the indented workflow.

Q1: Where do we need traceability links?

Establishing traceability links across tools is not easy. Thus, it is important to decide which links are really required. Defining questions which are relevant for the engineer has proven to be very helpful to get a clear understanding of the required integrations. Sample engineering questions are: "Which test cases have been used to validate a requirement?" or "Which values have been measured with a given calibration data set?". These questions already give a hint which data should be provided and which queries should be possible. A good approach is to elaborate this question together with the respective engineers. One major challenge is that engineers usually report their current way of working, which is influenced by the current tool capabilities. The most difficult part is to elaborate an optimized way of working based on possible capabilities. Talking to several persons usually results in various workflow descriptions depending on the concrete application scenario and the role of the user. It is important to get a common understanding of the indented workflow and the relations between data.

Q2: Which person/role or tool creates a link?

This is again closely related to the workflow. Assuming a user wants to link requirements to model elements: he most probably wants to select a model element and indicate that it implements certain requirements. So, the link creation should be done in the modeling tool. In another application scenario, requirements should be linked to calibration tasks. This means that the calibration engineer should calibrate an entity according to these requirements. From the requirements perspective, there is usually no need to know which requirements are linked to the calibration task. Linking the calibration task to requirements is better not done by the engineer, but e.g. by a project manager who is assigning the calibration task to a concrete engineer. It has shown to be useful to use sequence diagrams to describe the flow of data. Nevertheless, this diagram only shows part of the information. It is also important to make sure that the required data to establish a link is available by the tool that should establish the link and at the point in time when the link should be created.

Q3: How should links be managed?

Technically speaking, a link is a resource property which points to another resource, which is represented by its URI. The OSLC specification already provides several meaningful properties for general usage scenarios, but is not restricted to these properties. Additional properties can be defined using so called extended properties. But of course, the information provided in the extended property needs to be stored somewhere - so the tool needs to be able to handle them. Let's have a closer look at links using an example, where a requirement should be linked to a test case. We can see from the Requirements Management specification [14] that there is a property *oslc_rm:validatedBy*. This property can be used to point to a test case that validates this requirement. Using this property we have established a unidirectional link between the two resources. In this case, whenever the requirement is changed, some action is required to update the test case accordingly. But what happens if the test case is changed or deleted? Since there is no link from the test case back to the requirement, the test engineer will not be aware that there is a requirement which points to this test case. Deleting the test case will most probably lead to a dead link, and the requirement points to nowhere. If the test engineer knows that there should be a requirement linked to this test case, he can search through all the requirements if they point to this specific test case. Depending on the size of the requirements database, this can be very inefficient. Moreover, the test case could also be linked to other artifacts, which the engineer does not know. One potential solution is the introduction of a backlink from the test case to the requirement. This link type is also referred to as bidirectional link. From the OSLC QM specification [17], we can see that there is a property *oslc_qm:validates Requirement*, which can be used for this purpose. Now, the test case also contains a link to the validated requirement. This solution makes queries easier and avoids inconsistencies, because both sides know of each other. Nevertheless, this approach also has its disadvantages, because there is now no single point of information. First of all, links have to be set and updated in two resources at the same time to ensure the consistency. This means that write permissions are required in both tools and both tools need to be available. Summarized, OSLC provides an easy way to establish links, but it is not that easy to manage those links. All depicted examples show that multiple aspects need to be taken into account in the design-phase of an OSLC adapter. In our experience, the most time-consuming task of an OSLC implementation is the definition of a concrete usage scenario where all parties agree on. Without such a well defined scenario it is almost impossible to get a useful implementation.

3.1 Domain Selection

The next step is to select an appropriate domain specification. We distinguish four different cases here:

Matching domain specification exists. Selection of a domain specification is trivial when a dedicated domain specification exists (e.g. for requirements), but otherwise it can require strategic considerations.

One example are simulation models. OSLC provides the Architecture Management (AM) specification which makes it possible to expose models or model elements. This can be quite helpful for behavioral models, e.g. Simulink models, where a single part of the model can be directly related to a requirement. Here, AM makes perfect sense. But often physical, equation-based models are used for simulations and there we see no reason why to split them up in separate model elements, because requirements (especially non-functional ones) usually relate to the entire model. In case of pointing to a concrete model, an OSLC representation might be overhead, because just pointing to the file location might be enough. So, the intention of the model has an influence on the selection of the specification.

Proposing a new specification. We planned to implement a provider for calibration data management. There is nothing in the existing specifications which relates to this domain. The first idea was to propose a new specification, as calibration data is not tool or company specific. But soon we realized that it is quite hard to define a concrete use case, because there is not one main application scenario and there are only a few tools for calibration data management. This makes the definition of a data model almost impossible.

Using the core specification with extended properties. It is always an option to use the OSLC core specification and describe the OSLC Resources using the OSLC Extended Properties concept. This gives a lot of freedom, because almost everything can be expressed this way. The main drawback is that consumers have to be implemented especially for this provider since there is no defined common vocabulary.

Using an existing specification which might fit the most. Sometimes there is no matching specification. However, it is worth investigating the applicability of existing specifications. In our case, we ended up using the existing Asset Management specification [12] for calibration data. Nevertheless, this solution has the drawback that the semantics of the resources are not really clear. In this concrete case, Calibration Data Files are provided as Assets. For a consumer, there is no way to figure out that these Assets actually contain calibration data. But at least, it is possible to reuse existing Asset Management consumers with little effort.

4   Considerations for the Implementation of an OSLC Interface

Integration Type. There are three main approaches for the implementation of an OSLC interface as depicted in Fig. 1 [2]: native, plugin, or adapter. All have their pros and cons, but if the tool source code is not available and it is not possible to add a plug-in to the tool, an adapter is the sole solution. An adapter has the disadvantage that it is restricted by the capabilities of the tool API. If the tool API does not provide the possibility to create data, then it is not possible to implement a CreationFactory and thus it is not possible to fully comply to certain specifications. For the implementation of a provider all three approaches are feasible, but whenever possible a tight integration should be preferred. The implementation of a consumer as an adapter is not really advisable for a real integration, because a consumer needs to trigger actions which reflect the workflow. If the user wants to link a requirement to a test case, he must be able to select the test case and indicate that he wants to link it to a requirement. Triggering this action must be implemented in the consuming tool. This can be done best with a native integration. It is getting a bit more cumbersome with a plugin (depending on the plugin capabilities), but is almost impossible with an adapter approach. An adapter implementation of a consumer would mean a small additional tool which is consuming the tool internal data using the API. Then this tool internal data can be linked to the data provided by the provider. For a practical application, this is not a realistic implementation.

Flat Structure of OSLC Providers. Implementing a consumer which is capable of consuming data from various providers (implementing the same specification) can also be challenging. From a high-level perspective, a consumer just calls the services of the ServiceProvider in a standardized way by using HTTP requests. One main problem is that each tool has its own way of organizing data. For example, requirements in a requirements management tool are usually not organized in a flat structure. They are clustered in folders or any other hierarchical structure. This is true for other tools as well. The ServiceProvider is not reflecting the tools internal structure. Therefore, it is quite challenging to request the requirements from a specific folder in a standardized way. The same is true for the creation of a requirement. It depends on the implementation of the provider where in the internal data structure of the tool the requirement will be

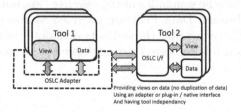

Fig. 1. Schematic overview of the different implementations

created. Some providers provide additional tool-specific properties to indicate the location and other tools provide their own solutions (see [18]). The only way of handling this problem is currently the use of Delegated UIs. Then the consuming person can browse the data and retrieve or create data at or from a specific location.

Efficient Provider implementations. In an OSLC provider, the tools internal data representation has to be transformed into an RDF representation. This can be considered as a temporary replication of data and could be done on the fly, whenever a consumer requests or updates information. This approach turns our to be inefficient, because the same transformations have to be done over and over again. On the other hand, the data can be transformed once when the OSLC provider is started, but this would mean that the OSLC provider and tool database are diverging quite fast. This means that for an efficient implementation an advanced strategy is required (e.g. using caching mechanisms), which considers the dynamics of the data.

Synchronizing Provider and Consumer. Inconsistencies between a provider and a consumer may occur in an OSLC update process (get - modify - update). If the server resource has been changed, a conflict occurs. To mitigate this problem, OSLC suggests the so called *Optimistic Collision Detection on Update*, which uses HTTPs ETags (entity tags) and If-Match-Headers. An ETag is a special unique identifier to be used in the header of a response. The If-Match request-header field is used to compare the calculated ETag of the current resource on the provider and the one sent by the consumer. If these values do not match, the user can be informed and can decide how to resolve the conflict. However, ETags and If-Match-Headers are not mandatory, but have been proven to be useful. We recommend this as a best practice.

5   Queries

One of the main reasons for traceability links is the need to answer questions about the relation of data from different data repositories. This makes queries an essential issue for a successful integration. A query URL is formed by appending a set of query parameters to a given base URL. The query result is normally requested by sending an HTTP GET request to the OSLC query URL. The OSLC query capabilities are designed to be a compromise between enough expressiveness to be useful to clients, but simple enough to be implemented with reasonable effort by tools. It is not required that an OSLC Service supports the OSLC Query Syntax. It may also support other query languages e.g. SQL or SPARQL. It is not obvious from the specification how to determine which query syntax is supported by a provider. The investigation of different sample queries revealed some issues of the current OSLC Query Syntax: A query to *get the id of all requirements in 'Project1' which have been validated by 'TestCase1'* can for instance be easily defined using the OSLC Query Language. The response of the RM Service Provider will include the IDs of all requirements which have been validated by 'TestCase1'. This query includes just one tool and thus could be done in a more efficient way without OSLC (e.g. SQL query). Observing another, more complex query where a user wants to *get all requirements which have been validated by user "Some User"*, shows that the limits of OSLC queries are reached quickly. We assume that a person who has created a test case which is linked to a requirement has validated the requirement. Here, the RM Service Provider needs to resolve the query. There are several possible implementations e.g. querying every requirement and extract the linked test case data (lot of communication overhead) or the consumer may perform a distributed query. All of them seem to have some restrictions. For the use of nested properties, the OSLC Query Syntax seems to be cumbersome and hard to implement. If a Service Provider supports OSLC Queries, it should implement the complete specification leading to a high implementation effort and overhead, especially because only parts of the specification seem to be useful. This poses the question, if it is useful to integrate the concept of nested queries into the query syntax. Moreover, it also makes sense to split the sample query into two queries, one for the QM and one for the RM provider. However, forwarding a query from a RM provider to a QM queryBase requires the QM Service Provider URI which is not mandatory (cardinality of the OSLC property is zero-or-many). The observation of a third query, where the consumer wants to *get the id of all requirements which have been validated by 'TestCase1'*, even showed that although this query seems to be quite similar to the first one it is not realizable. This time not only the requirements belonging to one specific project but all requirements of several project should be taken into account. The problem here is the fact that queries are only possible on a single Service Provider. Depending on the architecture (e.g. one Service Provider per project) it can be impossible to formulate a query over several projects or Service Providers, respectively. In summary, queries only seem to be useful for filtering data retrieved by a Service Provider. For more powerful queries, we suggest the use of a SPARQL (SPARQL Protocol and RDF Query Language) endpoint. Therefore the OSLC Tracked Resource Set (TRS) specification [23] can be used which allows a server to expose a set of resources in a way that allows clients to discover the exact set of resources as well as the delta to the last update. By additionally implementing the TRS specification for the respective tools, it is possible to set up, e.g. a triple store (RDF store) containing the required OSLC data, i.e. RDF representations. A triple store represents a specific kind of database for storing and retrieving RDF triples and can thus be used for SPARQL queries. Using this approach, it would be possible to support both queries. Nevertheless, it requires the implementation of an additional adapter (TRS adapter for each tool) and it requires to set up the respective data repository (triple store).

6   Discussion and Future Work

To show the reusability of interfaces, we have tried to consume data from various OSLC RM providers. Two OSLC RM consumers have been implemented

independently based on the Eclipse Lyo framework cq. sample code from the
IBM Rational CLM 2012 OSLC Workshop [11]. Both consumers should be able
to consume requirements, update them and create new ones via OSLC. Details
about one of the consumers can be found in Marko et al. [16]. The consumers
have been connected to four different RM providers, prototypes from the CRYS-
TAL project as well as commercially available ones. Furthermore, a consumer
has been connected to a similar RM provider (Doors NG), running on different servers on two different locations. None of the integrations worked really
straightforward without changes and also moving between apparently identical
RM tools required adaptations and showed issues in link stability (depicted in
Fig. 2). In the following, we will summarize the main problems:

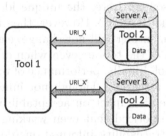

Moving a tool to another server should not impact links to data

Fig. 2. Issue of link stability

– Framework issues
  One provider has been implemented using OSLC4Net. Due to a bug in the
  framework, the RDF structure returned by the Service Provider Catalog was
  wrong. This was of course just an implementation issue, but it took us some
  time to figure out why the integration was not working.
– Additional information necessary
  In one integration, the creation of a new requirement did not work straight-
  away, because the tool requires a so called instanceShape for the creation. An
  instanceShape belongs to OSLCs resourceShapes, which are not mandatory
  according to the Core specification (Occurs: zero-or-many), but seem to be
  mandatory for this specific implementation.
– Wrong implementation of specification
  One used provider was sending the response in *text/xml* instead of the required
  application/rdf+xml format. Therefore the consumer could not parse the
  results via the Eclipse Lyo framework.
– Unclear specification
  Sometimes the specification is quite vague or the information is scattered over
  various documents. This makes it hard to find the required information.

A very important topic which has not even been touched in this paper is
the topic of security and access management. Especially when dealing with engineering data this can be a very tough topic. Security has to be considered for all

previously mentioned topics. When querying information it e.g. has to be clear which data a person is allowed to see or which data set a person is allowed to modify. Such aspects have to be considered across tools with different role models and authentication mechanisms. OSLC just bypasses this topic by referring to the use of standard web protocols for authentication (HTTP Basic Authentication/OAuth). Another issue which has not been mentioned is the creation of robust URIs. The URI should be used to unambiguously locate a resource. This requires a well thought out choice of the URL and the identifier. URIs need to be valid over a long period of time. After finishing a project, for example, it should be archived, i.e. copied to another server. If the server name has somehow been used for building the URI, this has to be considered before copying the data, otherwise the link information is lost. The same is true for the URN (Uniform Resource Name) of the resource. Here, the unique identifier used in the tool database could be a valuable choice [7]. However, then the tool or the standard has to guarantee that this identifier will not change, e.g. over different versions or different server locations of the tool or even when doing a backup/restore of the database to the same tool. Finally, performance of tool coupling using OSLC is a matter that may need attention. Though not immediately related to tool interoperability, it will have an impact on acceptability of OSLC in an industrial environment. We have noticed that even working with a limited amount of requirements, updating traceability information (deleting and adding some artifacts and updating links), can take minutes. This may partially be due to sub-optimal implementations and not yet using, however considering that in a real industrial environment the number of requirements will be much larger, this may lead to unacceptable long delays.

7 Conclusion

This paper does not represent an in-depth study of OSLC, but it should be understood as a collection of experiences from the application of OSLC the authors got from the CRYSTAL project. It should show where we currently see the main challenges in the design and implementation of OSLC interfaces. OSLC is focusing on interfaces and communication aspects. From a very high-level perspective these interfaces are reusable in different scenarios. However, OSLC does not cover an important aspect - the workflow. It has to be clear that many important aspects for the deployment of an OSLC enabled tool-chain are left to the user. Due to the flexibility of the specification, it is not easily possible to check the compliance of a tool to the specification nor to simply reuse interfaces in different application scenarios. This is not the intention and certainly not the expectation of OSLC and should be clear before starting to use it. We started with a wrong assumption and it took us quite some effort to realize that there are limitations. If it is a target to reuse interfaces in different scenarios, a more precise specification is required. Such a specification could be derived from the existing ones. Currently, the specifications contain many statements like "SHOULD implement" or "MAY implement". Taking clear decisions for these parts would make it a lot easier to provide compliance checks and improve the reusability of tool interfaces.

Acknowledgment. The research leading to these results has received partial funding from the European Union's Seventh Framework Program (FP7/2007-2013) for CRYS-TAL - Critical System Engineering Acceleration Joint Undertaking under grant agreement No 332830 and from Vinnova under DIARIENR 2012-04304. Further, the authors gratefully acknowledge financial support from FFG Austria for the project in which the above presented research results were achieved.

References

1. CRYSTAL Project Homepage. http://www.crystal-artemis.eu/. Accessed 19 May 2016
2. Different approaches to implementing OSLC support. http://openservices.net/resources/tutorials/integrating-products-with-oslc/implementing-an-oslc-provider/planning-out-a-partial-implementation-of-oslccm/. Accessed 19 May 2016
3. Eclipse Lyo Contribution Activity. https://projects.eclipse.org/projects/technology.lyo. Accessed 19 May 2016
4. iFest Project Homepage. www.artemis-ifest.eu/. Accessed 19 May 2016
5. Linked Data Principles Tim Berners-Lee. https://www.w3.org/DesignIssues/LinkedData.html. Accessed 19 May 2016
6. Open Services for Lifecycle Collaboration official homepage. http://openservices.net/. Accessed 19 May 2016
7. Purl DCMI Metadata Terms. http://purl.org/dc/terms/identifier. Accessed 19 May 2016
8. W3C Semantic Web - Resource Description Framework (RDF). http://www.w3.org/RDF/. Accessed 19 May 2016
9. W3C SemanticWeb - Linked Data. http://www.w3.org/standards/semanticweb/data. Accessed 19 May 2016
10. Aichernig, B., Hormaier, K., Lorber, F., Nickovic, D., Schlick, R., Simoneau, D., Tiran, S.: Integration of requirements engineering and test-case generationvia oslc. In: 2014 14th International Conference on Quality Software (QSIC), pp. 117–126, October 2014
11. Anderson, S.: IBM Rational CLM 2012 OSLC Workshop. IBM, Technical report (2012). https://jazz.net/wiki/pub/Main/OSLCWorkshopDownload/2012-11-26-OSLC-workshop.pdf
12. Anderson, S.: OSLC Asset Management 2.0 Specification. OSLC, Technical report, September 2012. http://open-services.net/wiki/asset-management/OSLC-Asset-Management-2.0-Specification
13. Biehl, M., El-Khoury, J., Torngren, M.: High-level specificationand code generation for service-oriented tool adapters. In: 2012 12th International Conference on Computational Science and Its Applications (ICCSA), pp. 35–42, June 2012
14. Green, I.: Open services for lifecycle collaboration requirements management specification version 2.0. OSLC, Technical report, September 2012. http://open-services.net/bin/view/Main/RmSpecificationV2
15. Johnson, D., Speicher, S.: Open services for lifecycle collaboration core specification version 2.0. OSLC, Technical report, February 2013. http://open-services.net/bin/view/Main/OslcCoreSpecification

16. Marko, N., Leitner, A., Herbst, B., Wallner, A.: Combining Xtext and OSLC for integrated model-based requirements engineering. In: 41st Euromicro Conference on Software Engineering and Advanced Applications, EUROMICRO-SEAA 2015, Madeira, Portugal, pp. 143–150, 26–28 August 2015
17. McMahan, P.: Open services for lifecycle collaboration quality management specification version 2.0. OSLC, Technical report, May 2011. http://open-services.net/bin/view/Main/QmSpecificationV2
18. Naranjo, R.: Folder support added to rrc 4.0 oslc-rm api implementation. Technical report, June 2012. https://rhnaranjo.wordpress.com/2012/06/25/folder-support-added-to-rrc-4-0-oslc-rm-api-implementation/
19. oslc4net, OSLC4Net - A .NET SDK for OSLC. https://oslc4net.codeplex.com/. Accessed 19 May 2016
20. Saadatmand, M., Bucaioni, A.: Oslc tool integration and systems engineering – the relationship between the two worlds. In: 2014 40th EUROMICRO Conference on Software Engineeringand Advanced Applications (SEAA), pp. 93–101, August 2014
21. Seceleanu, T., Sapienza, G.: A tool integration framework for sustainable embedded systems development. Computer **46**(11), 68–71 (2013)
22. Skoglund, D.: A standardized approach to tool integration. Master's thesis, Uppsala Universitet, Uppsala (2012). http://uu.diva-portal.org/smash/get/diva2:573987/FULLTEXT01.pdf
23. Speicher, S., Budinsky, F., Garg, V.: Open services for lifecycle collaboration tracked resource set specification version 2.0. OSLC, Technical report, January 2014. http://open-services.net/wiki/core/TrackedResourceSet-2.0/
24. Zhang, W., Møller-Pedersen, B.: Modeling of tool integration resources with oslc support. In: Proceedings of the 2nd International Conference on Model-Driven Engineering and Software Development, pp. 99–110 (2014)
25. Zhang, W., Møller-Pedersen, B., Biehl, M.: A light-weight tool integration approach - from a tool integration model to oslc integration services. In: Hammoudi, S., van Sinderen, M., Cordeiro, J., (eds.) ICSOFT, pp. 137–146. SciTePress (2012)

A Model-Driven Approach
to Adapt SysML Blocks

Hamida Bouaziz[✉], Samir Chouali, Ahmed Hammad, and Hassan Mountassir

FEMTO-ST Institute, University of Franche-Comté, Besançon, France
{hamida.bouaziz,schouali,ahammad,hmountas}@femto-st.fr

Abstract. Reusing and adapting existing components is the central topic of component-based development. The major differences between the existing approaches concern the models used to represent the components and the detail given to generate the adapters. In this paper, we present our approach which bases on the hierarchy to generate the adapters. Our components are modelled using SysML blocks and their interaction protocols are modelled using SysML Sequence Diagrams (SDs). We have used coloured Petri nets as formal model to define the adaptation rules, and we have based on meta-modelling and model transformation to implement these rules. We illustrate our approach through a case study.

Keywords: SysML blocks · Adaptation rules · Meta-modelling · Model transformation

1 Introduction

When assembling components developed separately, there is a high probability to confront the problem of mismatches. These mismatches can concern for example the name of services, as well as the order in which the component asks (resp. offers) for environment services (resp. its services). That is what justifies the introduction of third entities or components which are used to solve these mismatches. This kind of components are called 'adapters'. A big part of the works done in this field start from a formal specification of these components, which makes difficult the communication between the various stakeholder in CBD (Component-Based Development) projects. To tackle this problem and to make the communication easier, system engineering community proposes to use high level languages. This appears clearly through *SysML* [1], a language which is adopted by OMG, it is used to design systems that include software and hardware.

The System Modelling Language (SysML), through its diagrams, fosters the view point that takes the system as a set of components. In SysML, we call them blocks. A block is a modular unit of the system description. It may include both structural and behavioural features, such as properties and operations. To communicate with its environment, a block has a list of ports. These ports are

© Springer International Publishing Switzerland 2016
G. Dregvaite and R. Damasevicius (Eds.): ICIST 2016, CCIS 639, pp. 255–268, 2016.
DOI: 10.1007/978-3-319-46254-7_21

characterised by interfaces that present the offered and required services of the block. SysML also offers many diagrams to represent the structure, the behaviour and requirements of the blocks.

The privilege given to SysML doesn't mean that it will take the place of formal methods. But it replaces them at a level of system representation, where we need a high level specification of the system. We must mention that SysML lacks formal semantics which makes very interesting the introduction of formal methods in component adaptation domain to compute the adapters and their behaviour semantics. A combination of SysML and formal methods in the same approach is the solution that will tackle the lack of each of them. That is what Model Driven Engineering (MDE) tries to do through the introduction of model transformation approaches. In this paper, we propose to use SysML sequence diagrams to schedule the interactions of each block with its environment and we propose a transformation process to generate their equivalents of coloured Petri nets which are formal models that we consider more suitable for defining and generating adapters for blocks.

The major difference between the existing adaptation approaches concerns the detail given to generate the adapter. In [2], the authors give only an adaptation contract which is resumed in a specification of the correspondences between blocks services. This will have an impact on the generation of the adapter. The adapter will contain all the possible interaction scenarios of executing the reused components, it can contain scenarios which are not necessary for the cooperation of the reused components. However, in [3–5], the authors have enriched their adaptation contract by a specification of the adapter interactions by ordering the vectors of the adaptation contract using regular expressions. This requires that the developer, before making the specification of the adapter, must know very well the interactions of each component with its environment, and he must have an idea about the synchronous execution of the reused components. In this context, we ask the question about the detail that will be enough to generate adapters to make a set of components cooperate with respect of the intention behind their assembling?

In this context, we propose an incremental approach to develop systems by reusing and adapting components modelled using SysML, we base on coloured Petri nets as formal models to compute the adapter interactions. In our process, we do not give only the mapping rules between services like in [2], and we do not give the specification of the adapter as in the works already done in [3–5]. But, we give the interaction protocol of the composite block which will include the reused blocks. The specification of the composite block is built by the architect according to the interaction protocol of the system's part has already been designed, and in function of what the current composite block must perform to the system's part still to develop. The major difference comparing with our previous work [6], is that in this paper, we solve more problems such as the reordering of services calls, and we consider more types of correspondences between services.

In the remainder of this paper, in Sect. 2, we show our approach to adapt SysML blocks, in Sect. 3, we present the meta models of sequence diagrams, coloured Petri nets and adaptation contracts. In Sect. 4, we explain the rules to generate the adapter. In Sect. 5, we demonstrate our approach through a case study. Finally, in Sect. 6, we conclude and we give perspectives.

2 Our Approach

The goal of our approach consists on generating the adapter Ad for a set of blocks $\{B_i\}$ to meet the specification of their future parent block B (a composite block). In the context of our incremental approach, in the next step of adaptation, this block B will be adapted with other blocks to meet the specification of its parent. The interaction of each block with its environment is modelled using a SysML sequence diagram. Because sequence diagrams are not formal models, we have performed a transformation to obtain their equivalents of Coloured Petri Nets (CPNs). The formal semantic of CPNs allows us to reflect easily the adaptation contract on the interactions of the blocks to compute the interactions of the adapter.

Our approach of adaptation is based on meta-modelling and models transformation, where we base on 'ecore' models to represent the meta-models of formalisms that we use (Sequence diagrams, coloured Petri nets). The transformation is performed through the use of ATL [7] rules that allow to define the correspondences between source and target meta-models. To generate the adapter, we have introduced the meta-model of the adaptation contract, and we have based also on ATL rules to reflect the information present at the level of the contract model onto the coloured Petri nets of the reused blocks.

3 Meta-Modelling

3.1 Meta-Model of Sequence Diagrams

By intention to reuse existing modelling tools, we have used the sub-set of Papyrus [8] SysML meta-model and its graphical editor to draw the sequence diagrams. In Fig. 1, we represent the meta-model of sequence diagrams. The root is the class *Interaction*. So, each sequence diagrams is an instance of this class. Each interaction can include a set of life lines, a set of messages and a set of interaction fragments. The classes:

- **LifeLine:** represents the set of object which participates in the interaction.
- **Message:** each message has two ends; a send end and a receive end.
- **InteractionFragment:** is the super class of the classes: Interaction, CombinedFragment, InteractionOperand and OccurenceSpecification.
- **CombinedFragment:** each combined fragment includes a set of interaction operands, and it has its own interaction operator. The interaction operator takes a value of this list [alt, opt, break, loop, par, ...]
- **InteractionOperand:** each operand is associated to a combined fragment, and it can have a guard.

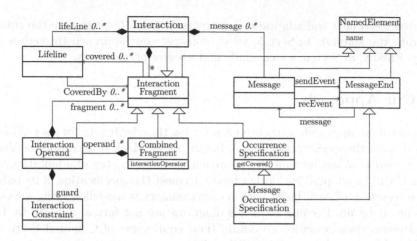

Fig. 1. Papyrus Meta-Model of SysML Sequence Diagram

- **MessageOccurenceSpecification:** Each event associated to the life line is represented as a message occurrence specification. It represents an extremity of a message. We can know the life line, to which the specification is associated, by executing the method *getCovered()* of the super class *Occurence-Specification*. We can also obtain the message started or finished at this specification, by navigating through the association *message* of the super class *MessageEnd*.

    The classes *MessageEnd*, *Message* and *InteractionFragment* inherit the class *NamedElement*.

3.2   Meta-Model of Coloured Petri Nets

Coloured Petri Nets (CPNs) preserve useful properties of Petri nets, and at the same time extend initial formalism to allow the distinction between tokens [9]. In CPNs, a token has a data value attached to it. This attached data value is called token colour. The Meta-model of coloured Petri nets is presented in Fig. 2. It contains the following classes:

- CPN: represents the root class, each instance of this class will include a set of places, a set of transitions, a set of input arcs (according to the transitions) and finally a set of output arcs (always according to the transitions).
- Place: each place has a name, a *colorSet* attribute which is a list that contains the set of colours of tokens that can be stored in this place. The attribute *nbrTokenPerColor* specifies the number of tokens of each colour.
- Transition: each instance of this class has a name that represents the action done at this stage of behaviour evolution. A transition is fired if the colour and the number of tokens mentioned at the level of each input arc is available in the place situated at the origin of this arc.

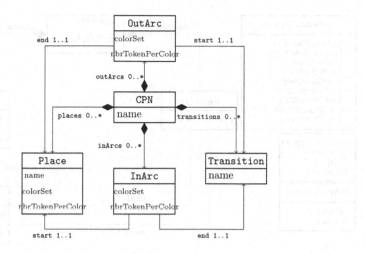

Fig. 2. Meta-Model of coloured Petri nets

- InArc: this class represents the set of arcs that starts at places and ends at transitions. To represent the colour of tokens consumed from source place to execute the transition located at the end of a given arc, we have defined the attribute *colorSet*. However, to specify the number of tokens of each colour ∈ *ColorSet*, we have used the attribute *nbrTokenPerColor*.
- OutArc: this class represents the set of arcs that starts at transitions and ends at places. The colours of tokens produced by executing the source transition of a given arc are recorded into the list *ColorSet*. To specify the number of produced tokens of each colour, we use the list *nbrTokenPerColor*.

3.3 Meta-Model of Adaptation Contracts

Our adaptation contract specifies the correspondences between blocks services. Its meta-model (see Fig. 3) contains the following classes:

- AdaptationContract: represents the root class. Each instance of this class includes a set of blocks and a set of vectors.
- Block: this class represents all the blocks which are concerned by the adaptation (Child blocks). It includes also the abstract block (Parent block) that represents the container of the reused blocks. Because we are interested by the correspondences between blocks services, we reduce the block features to the set of its required and provided services.
- Service: each service has a name and a type. The attribute *type* can take the value *Prov* or the value *Req*.
- Vector: each mapping vector establishes a link between the services of two blocks. According to its type, a vector can belong to one of these two sub-sets:
  - **a mapping vector between two reused blocks:** *OneReq2OneProv* (One required service to one provided service), *OneProv2ManyReq* (One

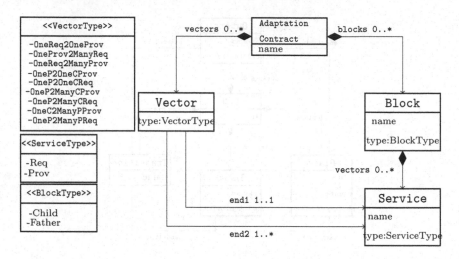

Fig. 3. Meta-Model of adaptation contracts

provided service to many required services), *OneReq2ManyProv* (One required service to many provided services).

- **a mapping vector between a reused block and its parent:** *OneP2OneCProv* (One provided service of the parent to one provided service of a child), *OneP2OneCReq* (One required service of the parent to one required service of a child), *OneP2ManyCProv* (One provided service of the parent to many provided services of a child), ...

So end1 represents the first extremity of the vector and end2 contains the services that correspond to the service end1.

To verify the contract validity, we have defined a set of OCL constraints. In the following, we give an example of an OCL constraint used in the class *Vector* to verify the extremities of a vector of type '*OneReq2OneProv*'.

```
/*contraints in the class Vector */
invariant verifysizeOfend2andTypeOfServicesOfAVectorOneReq2OneProv:
self.type=VectorType::OneReq2OneProv implies self.end1.type=TypeService::Req
and self.end2->size()=1 and self.end2->first().type=TypeService::Prov ;
```

4   Transformation from SD into CPN

In Fig. 4, we present the correspondences between sequence diagrams and coloured Petri nets (*!* represents a request of a service, and *?* represents a reception of this request).

To implement these correspondences, we have based on ATL rules that takes the meta-model of sequence diagrams as source of transformation and the meta-model of coloured Petri net as target. In the following we give the rules to transform the basic interaction of sequence diagrams into coloured Petri nets.

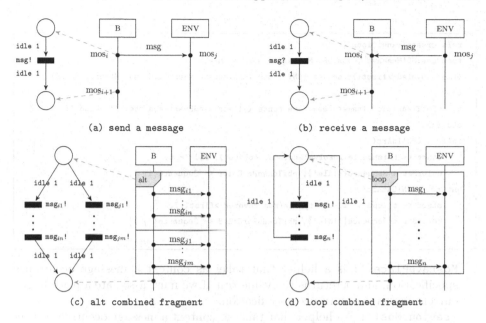

(a) send a message (b) receive a message

(c) alt combined fragment (d) loop combined fragment

Fig. 4. Transformation SD → CPN

The first rule *createCPN* allows to generate the CPN, the second rule *createStates* allows to create the states of the CPN, where the place associated to the first event on the life line of the block must contain a token *idle* which triggers the execution of the block interactions. Finally, the third rule *createTransitions* allows to create the transitions and the arcs that link the places and transitions.

```
rule createCPN {
from sd : SD!Interaction
to cpn : CPN!CPN ( name <- 'CPNBlocks',
    places <- CPN!Place.allInstances(), transitions <- CPN!Transition.allInstances(),
    inArcs <- CPN!InArc.allInstances(), outArcs <- CPN!OutArc.allInstances() )}
```

```
rule createStates {
from mos : SD!MessageOccurrenceSpecification
((mos.covered->first().name <> 'ENV') and (mos.MoshavePlace()))
to place : CPN!Place (
    colorSet <-if (mos.previousMos()=mos) then Sequence{'idle'} else Sequence{} endif,
    nbrTokenPerColor <- if (mos.previousMos()=mos) then Sequence{1} else Sequence{}
endif,
    name <- 'p'.concat(mos.covered->first().name).concat(mos.getCovered().coveredBy->
        select(e|e.oclIsTypeOf(SD!MessageOccurrenceSpecification))->indexOf(mos)) )}
```

```
rule createTransitions {
from mes:SD!Message , mos:SD! MessageOccurrenceSpecification
((mos.covered->first().name <> 'ENV') and (mos.message=mes) and (mos.MoshavePlace()))
to
t : CPN!Transition (name<- mes.name.concat(if mes.sendEvent=mos then '!' else '?'
endif)),
inArc : CPN!InArc(
    start <- thisModule.resolveTemp(mos, 'place'), end <- t,
    colorSet <-Sequence{'idle'}, nbrTokenPerColor <- Sequence{1} ),
outArc : CPN!OutArc(
    start <- t, end <- mos.nextplace(mos.covered->first()),
    colorSet <-Sequence{'idle'}, nbrTokenPerColor <- Sequence{1} )}
```

- **MoshavePlace()**: is a helper that takes as context a message occurrence specification, and it returns the value *true* if we must associate a place to the current message occurrence specification.
- **previousMos()**: is a helper that takes as context a message occurrence specification, and it returns the previous message occurrence specification.
- **nextplace(ln)**: is the helper that takes as context a message occurrence specification, and it returns the place associated to the next message occurrence specification on the life line *ln*.

5   Generating the Adaptor

To generate the adaptor, firstly we need to compute the global interaction of the reused blocks by gluing their CPNs according to the adaptation sub-contract that specifies the correspondences between the reused blocks. Thus, the CPNs of the reused blocks are glued using the *store* place and a set of transitions (which translate the adaptation contract). The store place will store the calls for services until the targeted blocks can receive these requests. In the following, through these rules, we explain how we glue them.

Rule 1: one-required-to-one-provided. This rule (presented in Fig. 5(a)) is applicable on vectors of type $OneReq2OneProv$: $\langle e_i, e_j \rangle$, where e_i =Bi:x! and e_j =Bj:{y?}. It specifies that the required service x of block B_i corresponds to the provided service y of block B_j. In this case, when the block B_i executes the transition $x!$, it generates the corresponding action y as a token, which will be consumed later by the block B_j, when it tries to execute the action y?

Rule 2: one-required-to-many-provided. This rule (presented in Fig. 5(b)) is applicable on vectors of type $OneReq2ManyProv$: $\langle e_i, e_j \rangle$, where e_i = Bi:x! and e_j = Bj:{y_1?, . . . , y_m?}. It specifies that the required service x of block B_i corresponds to the provided services $y_1, ..., y_m$ of block B_j. In this case, when the block B_i executes the transition $x!$, it generates the corresponding actions $y_1, ..., y_m$

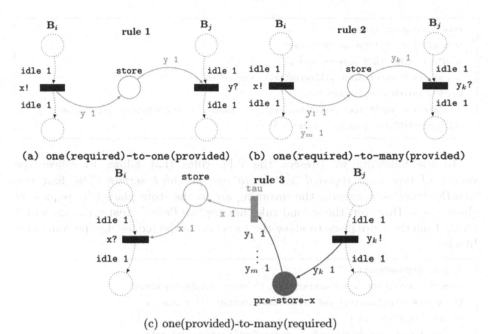

(a) one(required)-to-one(provided)   (b) one(required)-to-many(provided)

(c) one(provided)-to-many(required)

Fig. 5. Rules for synthesizing the reused blocks

as tokens, which will be consumed later by the block B_j when it tries to execute an action $y_k \in \{y_1,...,y_m\}$.

Rule 3: one-provided-to-many-required. It means that the block B_i can execute the service mentioned in '*one(provided)*' only after when the block B_j sends requests for all services specified in '*many(required)*'. This correspondence can be specified at the level of the adaptation contract by a vector: $\langle$ e_i, e_j $\rangle$, where e_i = Bi:x? and e_j = Bj:$\{y_1!,...,y_m!\}$. To represent this vector using CPNs, we apply the rule 3 (see Fig. 5(c)). So, we create a place '*pre-store-x*'. This place stores calls for the services that correspond to x. Then, we link all transitions labelled by $y_k!_{k=1..m}$ to the place '*pre-store-x*'. After, we must create a transition *tau* that has an incoming arc which starts from the place '*pre-store-x*'. This arc is labelled by $[y_k\ 1]_{k=1..m}$. We must also create an arc which starts from transition *tau* and ends at the *store* place, this arc must be labelled by '*x 1*'. Finally, to allow to the block B_i to execute the service x, we link the *store* state with the transition x?

The ATL grammar that implements these adaptation rules takes as entry the meta-model of CPNs and the meta-model of the adaptation contract, and it generates one CPN that represents the global interaction of the reused blocks. The grammar, at the first step, creates the new CPN and copies the places, the transitions, the in-arcs, the out-arcs, and creates the *store* place.

```
rule createStorePlace {
from contract : C!AdaptationContract
to GIR : outPN!CPN ( name <- 'GIR',
    places <- outPN!Place.allInstances(), transitions <-
outPN!Transition.allInstances(),
    inArcs <- outPN!InArc.allInstances(),      outArcs <- outPN!OutArc.allInstances() ),
store:outPN!Place( name <- 'store' ) }
```

In the following we present the ATL rules that allows to reflect the vector of type *one required service to one provided service*. The first one '*oneReq2oneProv1*' creates the incoming arc to the store place (the request of the service), However, the second rule '*oneReq2oneProv2*' creates the arc which starts from the store place to allow the reception of the request by the concerned block.

```
rule oneReq2oneProv1{
from contract:C!AdaptationContract, v : C!Vector, t:InPN!Transition
((v.type=#OneReq2OneProv) and (v.end1.name.concat('!')=t.name) )
to arc : outPN!OutArc (
    start <- t, end <- thisModule.resolveTemp(contract, 'store'),
    colorSet <- Sequence{v.end2->first().name}, nbrTokenPerColor <- Sequence{1} ) }
```
```
 rule oneReq2oneProv2 {
from contract:C!AdaptationContract, v : C!Vector, t:InPN!Transition
((v.type=#OneReq2OneProv) and (v.end2->first().name.concat('?')=t.name) )
to arc : outPN!InArc(
    start <- thisModule.resolveTemp(contract, 'store'), end <- t,
    colorSet <- Sequence{v.end2->first().name}, nbrTokenPerColor <- Sequence{1} ) }
```

To represent the exchange of requests between the blocks and their environment, we base on the mapping vectors that link the reused blocks and their parent block (vectors that represent the delegation relation between the parent and their children blocks), we have defined the correspondences using CPNs and we have implemented them using ATL. But due to the lack of space, we cannot present them in this paper.

Basing on the CPN that represents the interaction of the reused blocks according to the specification of their parent and the mapping between their services, we can generate the adapter. The adapter will play the role of a mirror between the reused sub-blocks $\{B_i\}$. So each call for a service by a sub-block B_i must be intercepted by the adapter, and each reception of a request for a service by a sub-block B_i must be preceded by a call for this service, this call must be emitted by the adapter. Thus, to generate the adapter, we base on the CPN synthesized in the last phase. We take this CPN, and we apply the mirror function on some transitions, we transform each call for a service $x!$ by a reused block B_i into a reception of this call, and each reception of a call for a service $x?$ by a reused block B_i must be transformed to an emission of this

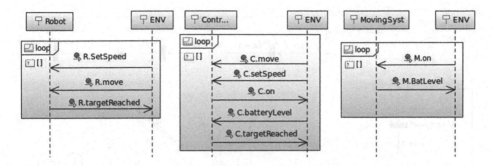

Fig. 6. Sequence diagrams of the robot, the controller and the moving system

call $x!$. Therefore this transformation concerns only the transitions of the reused blocks, because the adapter plays the role of mirror only between the reused sub-blocks. Concerning the relation between the adapter and the parent block, it is a delegation relation. So, the adapter delegates the parent to interact with the environment, that is why we do not need to inverse the actions done at the level of the parent transitions.

6 Case Study

We give an example of a simple robot which can receive a request to move with a given speed from a station, and it stops after reaching a goal. We consider that the robot that we want to construct and to integrate to our system, will have the interaction protocol given in Fig. 6. To build the robot, we have reused two blocks 'Controller' and 'MovingSystem', their interaction protocols modelled using SysML sequence diagrams in Fig. 6. To simplify we consider that the corresponding actions have the same name and we differentiate between them by

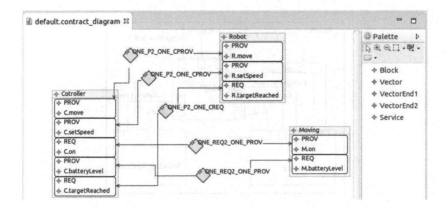

Fig. 7. The adaptation contract C

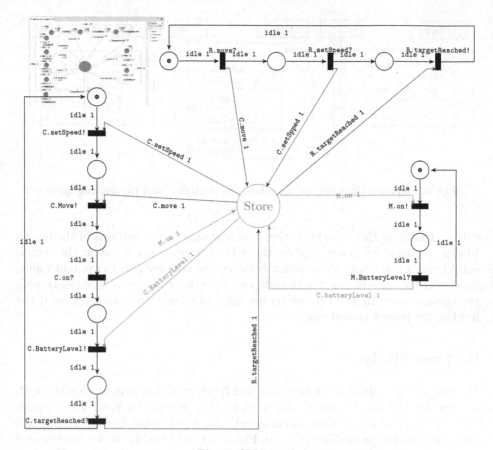

Fig. 8. CPN_adapter

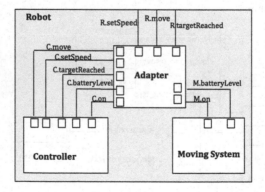

Fig. 9. Internal block diagram of the robot

adding the first letter of the block's name to each action. To obtain the interaction protocol of the adapter, we base on the adaptation contract modelled using our graphical editor in Fig. 7.

The CPN of the adapter is presented in Fig. 8. This adapter solves the problem of name mismatches between services of blocks, it restricts the interaction between blocks to the specification of their parent (the robot block) and reorders the call for services (*setSpeed* and *move*). To obtain the interaction protocol of the adapter, we need just to compute the reachability graph of its CPN using for example CPNtool [10]. In Fig. 9, we present the new internal structure of the robot block.

7   Conclusion

In this paper, we have presented a bottom-up model-driven approach to adapt SysML blocks. Our adaptation process takes a part of the system to develop, and generates an adapter for the SysML blocks which are reused to meet the specification of this part. We have based on SDs of SysML to model the interactions of each block. Due to the informal aspect of SysML, we have proposed to transform the SDs of blocks into CPNs, and we have implemented this transformation using ATL language. Now, we are working on the Acceleo templates that take our adapter and generate the input file for CPN tool, to discharge the user from redrawing the CPN of adapter to compute its reachability graph. In a future work, we plan to deal with the asynchronous aspect in the adaptation context.

References

1. OMG, OMG Systems Modeling Language (OMG SysML) Version 1.3 (2012). http://www.omg.org
2. Dahmani, D., Boukala, M.C., Mountassir, H.: A petri net approach for reusing and adapting components with atomic and non-atomic synchronisation. In: PNSE, Tunisia, Tunis, pp. 129–141 (2014)
3. Canal, C., Poizat, P., Salaün, G.: Adaptation de composants logiciels une approche automatisée basée sur des expressions régulières de vecteurs de synchronisation. In: CAL, pp. 31–39 (2006)
4. Canal, C., Poizat, P., Salaun, G.: Model-based adaptation of behavioral mismatching components. IEEE Trans. Softw. Eng. **34**(4), 546–563 (2008)
5. Mateescu, R., Poizat, P., Salaün, G.: Adaptation of service protocols using process algebra and on-the-fly reduction techniques. IEEE Trans. Softw. Eng. **38**(4), 755–777 (2012)
6. Bouaziz, H., Chouali, S., Hammad, A., Mountassir, H.: SysML blocks adaptation. In: Butler, M., Conchon, S., Zaïdi, F. (eds.) ICFEM 2015. LNCS, vol. 9407, pp. 417–433. Springer, Heidelberg (2015). doi:10.1007/978-3-319-25423-4_27
7. ATL: Atlas Transformation Language. https://eclipse.org/atl/

8. Papyrus. https://eclipse.org/papyrus/
9. Wade, N.: Colour. In: Nicholas, W. (ed.) Art and Illusionists. Vision, Illusion and Perception, vol. 1, pp. 207–226. Springer, Heidelberg (2016). doi:10.1007/978-3-319-25229-2_11
10. Cpn tool. http://cpntools.org/

BPMN Decision Footprint: Towards Decision Harmony Along BI Process

Riadh Ghlala[1,2(✉)], Zahra Kodia Aouina[1,3], and Lamjed Ben Said[1,4]

[1] SOIE Laboratory, High Institute of Management, Tunis, Tunisia
[2] Higher Institute of Technological Studies of Rades (ISETR), Rades, Tunisia
riadh.ghlala@isetr.rnu.tn
[3] High School of Commerce (ESC), Tunis, Tunisia
zahra.kodia@fshst.rnu.tn
[4] High Institute of Management (ISG), Tunis, Tunisia
lamjed.bensaid@isg.rnu.tn

Abstract. Nowadays, one of the companies challenges is to benefit from their Business Intelligence (BI) projects and not to see huge investments ruined. To address problems related to the modelling of these projects and the management of their life-cycle, Enterprise Architecture (EA) Frameworks are considered as an attractive alternative to strengthen the Business-IT alignment. Business Process Model and Notation (BPMN) represents a pillar of these Frameworks to minimize the gap between the expectations of managers and delivered technical solutions. The importance of decision-making in business process has led the Object Management Group (OMG) to announce its new standard: Decision Model and Notation (DMN). In this paper, we propose the BPMN Decision Footprint (BPMNDF), which is a coupling of a BPMN with a novel DMN version. This enhancement has an additional component as a repository of all decisions along the process, used in order to ensure the harmony of decision-making.

Keywords: Business intelligence project · BPMN decision footprint · Decision model and notation · Decision-making

1 Introduction

The last decade was characterized by the Business Intelligence (BI) revolution [1]. Therefore, companies are interested in BI projects investigation to develop IT solutions in order to help mangers make the best decisions at the right time. The innovativeness of BI Project requires a modelling approach to go beyond complexity and to overcome anomalies that sometimes reach the chaos. The range of proposed models has many gaps in terms of sensing, collecting, organizing, processing, and maintaining activities of a BI process [2], for this reason, Enterprise Architecture (EA) represents suitable Frameworks able to lead such kind of projects [3]. This approach ensures the synergy between, on one side the strategic vision of the company in terms of objectives and constraints, and

© Springer International Publishing Switzerland 2016
G. Dregvaite and R. Damasevicius (Eds.): ICIST 2016, CCIS 639, pp. 269–284, 2016.
DOI: 10.1007/978-3-319-46254-7_22

on the other side the computer vision with its three layers: (i) Applicative layer which implement communication and cooperation services, (ii) Data Access layer which focuses on model representation, purification and consolidation of data and query language, (iii) Infrastructure layer which manages software, hardware and networks. This approach is adopted using Frameworks like TOGAF, Zachman, FEAF and others.

When referring to these Frameworks, the objective of the first phase is to: (i) Develop the target business architecture that describes how the enterprise needs to operate in order to achieve the business goals and respond to the strategic drivers set out in the architecture vision, in a way that addresses the request for architecture work and stakeholder concerns, (ii) Identify candidate architecture roadmap components based upon gaps between the baseline and target business architectures [4]. To achieve these goals, several models can be used; the most important is the BPMN. Thanks to BPMN, a graphical notation for companies activities can be established [5,6] which helps manager and designer to be in harmony.

BPMN's mission is to represent all tasks of a business process, all connections between these tasks and decision-making to align the business layer with the IT layer. The importance of the decision-making in the business process had been for a long time a subject of research to provide more accurate representation of the real world. A brief study of decision-making history shows three important periods. Firstly, the origins of this interest started in the 80s with Expert Systems (ES), which is a modelling approach to provide a sophisticated software developed with a special programming language like Prolog, Lisp and Scheme. ES emulates the decision-making ability of a human expert [7], it applies an inference engine to deduce new facts from a knowledge base using a set of rules. Secondly, the beginning of the third millennium was branded in the field of modelling decision-making by concentrating on Business Rules (BR). This new trend is implemented with higher level languages derived from XML like RuleML [8], or based on Model-driven architecture (MDA) approach such as SBVR [9–12]. Unlike SE, BR based software are easily integrated into companies production environments [13]. Finally, the culmination of these efforts was the announcement of the DMN [14] by the OMG in 2013. This graphical representation of decision-making has become an indispensable complement of BPMN; it focuses on rationalizing the decision-making at every task, by gathering, modelling and integrating business rules in business process [15].

BI process present another challenge in decision-making throughout the process: it is not to be satisfied only with the streamlining of the decision in each task separately, but rather to ensure harmony between various decisions along the process [16]. The contribution of the DMN in terms of decision-making for the process is valuable. However, we consider that an important side attached to the decision-making is not explicitly mentioned. It is the harmony of the decision during the process.

In this paper, we propose our contribution called BPMNDF, which enriches DMN with a repository storing the decisions taken at each task in order to keep traceability and to ensure decision harmony along the process. This decision harmony improves rationality of decision-making. BPMNDF can help the designer to correlate his decisions, avoid choices that seem technically feasible but are really in conflict and therefore ensure harmony along the process.

This paper is structured as follows: Sect. 2 overviews the related work about decision-making and its relationship with business processes. In Sect. 3, we illustrate the specificity of BI process and the need to master decision-making. Section 4 presents our approach that is the BPMN Decision Footprint. In the Discussion section, we explain the contribution of BPMNDF in decision-making during BI process. Finally, we summarize the presented work and outline its extensions.

2 Related Works in BPMN Decision-Making

Decision-making takes an important place in the business process. Since a long time, several studies have focused on decision-making through control flow pattern-based reasoning, specially using gateways [17]. The mission was not obvious and designers were called in several cases to do acrobatics to model the decision such as the case of optional tasks [18] or the exceptional tasks [19]. Another investigative axis for improving decision-making in a business process is the collection, representation and integration of business rules [8]. Research in this domain have focused on the extraction of BR from the business layer and its automation while emphasizing the semantic aspect [9–12].

Merging two aspects in the same model, business processes and decision-making, was not a good choice. It led to a "spaghetti" representation, difficult to understand and maintain. Thus, extracting decision logic from process models was inevitable to ensure separation of decision-making from business process modelling [20]. To meet this need, DMN represents the final piece of the decision-making puzzle. It is proposed by the OMG to emerging standards in decision modelling [21]. Today, the majority of work is around the coupling BPMN/DMN for new engineering business processes or refactoring those already existing ones [22].

DMN is a BPMN add-in. It is structured in two distinct parts: (i) Decision Requirements Diagram containing the decision to study, business knowledge models, input data and Knowledge Source. (ii) Decision Logic which is represented by a decision table that can be converted into FEEL scripting language (Friendly Enough Expression Language) [21]. This table contains the rules with their input and output in addition to other technical details such as the hit policy. We can classify decisions handled by the DMN in several categories such as eligibility, validation, calculation, risk, fraud, etc. Decision-making by using DMN pushes towards defining roles and calls for specialization in construction of business processes. It also promotes agility and encourages the involvement of stakeholders in the process [22].

In summary, the OMG has filled a great need in business processes modelling. Its DMN standard replied to several questions about the decision-making and its relationship with the business process like the identification and description of the decision, the requirements specifications and the decomposition and refinement of the model [15]. Despite this improvement, the harmony of the decision-making along the process always remains a factor that is unheeded even by DMN. As mentioned in the introduction, our contribution called BPMNDF searching ensures this harmony.

3   Decision-Making in BI Process: The Necessity of Decision Harmony

3.1   BI Project Presentation

Business intelligence can be described as "a data-driven Decision Support System (DSS) that combines data gathering, data storage, and knowledge management with analysis to provide input to the decision process" [1]. Nowadays, we are noting at least three forms of BI projects:

- Corporate BI Project: whose mission has always been creation and periodic refresh of Enterprise Data Warehouse (EDW) with structured and semi-structured data. The EDW is a subject-oriented, non-volatile, integrated, time-variant collection of data [23] used with a batch analytical processing for a requirement reporting as shown in Fig. 1.
- Data Analytics Project: is a user-driven process of searching for specific items or patterns in a data set [24]. It is a popular discipline also known as self-service BI based on the in-memory processing.
- Big Data Project: was first introduced to the computing world by Roger Magoulas from OReilly media in 2005, in order to define a great amount of data that traditional data management techniques cannot manage and process due to the complexity and size of this data [25]. This definition leads automatically to a new generation of technologies, Frameworks and above all models and architectures for data ingestion, storage and processing.

In this paper, we will focus on the corporate BI project schematized in Fig. 1. BPMN can be considered as a useful paradigm to model this kind of complex project characterized by:

- Many tasks such as: building IT infrastructure, DW design & implementation and Extract Transform & Load (ETL) Data.
- Several actors like: manager, designer, DevOps, data integrator and data engineering & analysts.
- Multiple decisions like: hardware architecture policy, extraction strategy, data warehousing approach, slowly changing dimension and proactive caching.

Complexity of a BI project decreases chances of its success and induces to seek the causes of its failures.

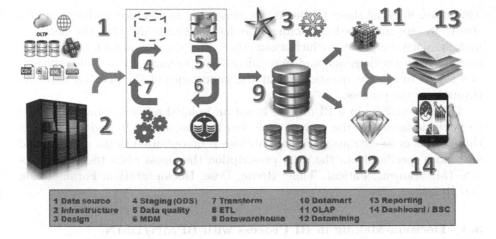

Fig. 1. Corporate BI project

3.2 Why BI Projects Fail?

Recently, Gartner noted a study that purported to show that "between 70 % and 80 % of BI projects fail." [26]. This study is a survey of 385 business technology professionals using business intelligence tools. Some of the problems cited as causing BI project failure are:

- Poor understanding of BI
- Poor data quality and integrity
- Incomplete requirements
- Lack of accountability
- Poor project team selection and training
- Using non suitable BI Tools
- Inability to pivot and anticipating change
- Performance considerations (Response time)

From these observations, we can deduce that:

1. The problem does not lie in choosing the tool but rather in the adaptation of the tool with specific scenarios, for example, a tool for in-memory processing is not necessarily beneficial with a multidimensional disk storage.
2. Inability to change is not due to a reluctance, incompetence or a lack of resources but rather to technical limitations imposed by previous choices. In fact, a non-pluggable infrastructure does not promote the scalability.
3. The tuning dilemma is a typical case in which the decision cannot be taken at a local level. However decision-making is necessarily an aggregation of several factors throughout the project [27]. Indeed, a fast analytical dashboard must be based on a small periodic extraction, high data retention and an in-memory processing.

Therefore, some of these problems are generated by decision-making. In this study, we are interested in factors that have relationship with the decision-making along the process: which means that every decision in each task is influenced by the previous one and may affect the upcoming other. This influence has led us to ask the question about the importance of the decision harmony throughout the process.

Decision-making in a BI process is not an isolated mission, which is limited to intrinsic factors of the current task, but it must be put in a global context that considers its extrinsic factors. This idea is materialized in the medical field and more specifically in the drug prescription that must obey the nine rights rule (Medicament, Patient, Time, Route, Dose, Documentation, Form, Action and Response) [28].

3.3   Decision-Making in BI Process with BPMN/DMN

A typical corporate BI project is composed of three phases: Integration, Analysis and Reporting. In the first phase, we are interested in the extraction, transform and data load. Every step in this phase presents many scenarios and therefore several decisions [29]. For example, the extraction can be continuous by using the high availability technics such as replication or it can be periodic by applying one of Slowly Changing Dimension (SCD) variant as shown in Fig. 2. Choosing between continuous and periodic scenario depends on activity dynamism. In the periodic alternative, upcoming decisions are sensitive, on the one side to data retention, granularity and design, on the other side to extraction periodicity as illustrated in Fig. 3.

The second phase can be an On Line Analytical Processing (OLAP) or a data analytics with a series of Datamining algorithms. Figure 4 presents another example in which we focus on OLAP cube building; therefore, we are called to make a strategic decision: a multidimensional (MOALP) or a relational (ROLAP) implementation. This choice is based on several factors such as: data volume, data processing, business requirement for time response and memory & storage configuration.

All these factors are essential to choose the OLAP option but note well that we did not take account of previous decisions in earlier tasks; such behaviour can obstruct our current choice. At the same time, we do not document our decision for the following tasks.

As shown in Fig. 1, Reporting is the last phase in a typical corporate BI project. Its mission is delivering reports, dashboard and/or balanced scorecard. The decision at this stage consists on privileging a near real time or a batch dashboard respectively for analytical or operational requirements as illustrated in Fig. 5. Consequently, decision depends on several parameters, the most important are: business activity, type of indicators, user profile and above all previous decisions.

Through these examples, we have tried to show that the decision-making at a task in the process includes all aspects attached to the current task but passes over the importance of the harmony with the previous.

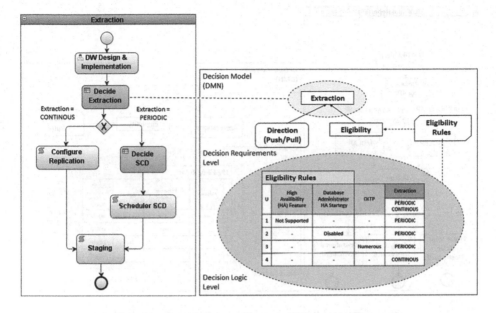

Fig. 2. BPMN/DMN modelling of extraction decision task

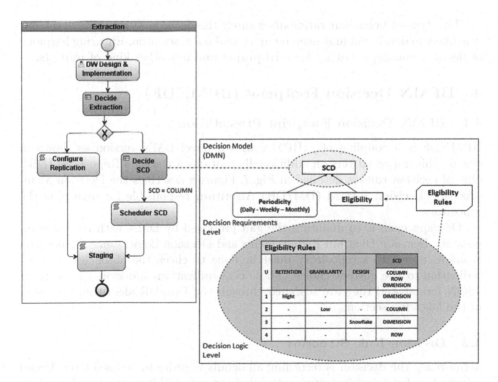

Fig. 3. BPMN/DMN modelling of SCD decision task

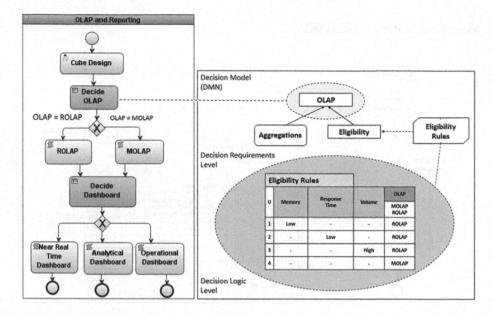

Fig. 4. BPMN/DMN modelling of OLAP Decision Task

This type of behaviour rationalizes surely the decision at a specific level, but it is likely to derail and may even be in a paradoxical scenario. Ensuring harmony of decision-making is crucial for a BI project and any other kind of projects.

4   BPMN Decision Footprint (BPMNDF)

4.1   BPMN Decision Footprint Presentation

BPMNDF is a coupling of a BPMN with a novel DMN version as shown in Fig. 6. This improved version additionally contains a Decision Repository (DR). One of decision rules is detailed in Fig. 7. Figure 8 describes the Decision Memorization/Decision Regard (DM/DR) Algorithm responsible for managing the repository.

Our approach is to maintain the gait proposed by DMN with its two components: Decision Diagram Requirements and Decision Logic. Once the decision is made, access to a repository must be done to check the absence of a cons-indication to the current choice. These cons-indications are stored in XML or JSON format and they are searched through the DM/DR algorithm presented in the following sections.

4.2   Decision Rule Structure

Memorizing the decision is recording all details in order to be used later. Useful information for a decision represents a decision rule and it is structured into four clauses:

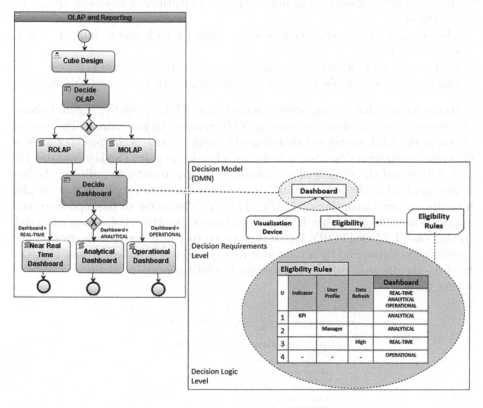

Fig. 5. BPMN/DMN modelling of Dashboard Decision Task

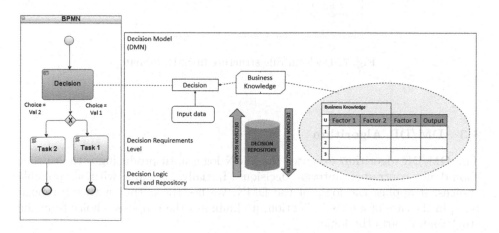

Fig. 6. BPMNDF

- Header: a description containing a sequential identifier, a label and optionally a comment.
- Choices: a list of possible choices with a flag for each one to indicate if it is selected or not.
- Factors: a list of factors that promoted or prohibited the choice.
- Blacklist: a list of probable upcoming decisions with prohibited choice.

Suitable formats for storing these data sets are XML or JSON. Figure 7 shows the structure of our decision rules in XML representation format. The factors clause in the XML document describing the decision rule is composed of a set of elements. Each item describes a factor as a key-value pair. The key contains the factor itself and the value will be assigned to 0 or 1 in order to indicate whether it was involved in the decision and the choice adopted or not. Note that we also introduce a new factor named REPOSITORY. The access to the repository and application of the algorithm DM/DR can impose an other choice than expected. In this case, REPOSITORY factor is assigned to 1 in order to indicate that the decision was influenced by an anterior task. In all cases, the algorithm DM/DR finalizes the decision rule by a potential blacklist containing choices to avoid in future tasks.

```xml
<?xml version="1.0" encoding="UTF-8"?>
<rules>
   <rule id="R1" label="Label 1" comment="Comment 1" >
      <choices>
         <choice value="Val 1" flag="0/1" />
         <choice value="Val 2" flag="0/1" />
      </choices>
      <factors>
         <factor value="Val 1" flag="0/1" />
         <factor value="Val 2" flag="0/1" />
         <factor value="REPOSITORY" flag="0/1"/>
      </factors>
      <blacklist>
         <decision label="Label M" choice="Val x" />
         <decision label="Label N" choice="Val y" />
      </blacklist>
   </rule>
</rules>
```

Fig. 7. Decision rule structure in XML format

4.3 DM/DR Algorithm

The DM/DR algorithm executes the DMN logic until producing a choice that should not contradict anterior decisions. Initially, it starts with all possible choices. It applies the logic of the DMN, verifies the output with the repository; in the case of a cons-indication, it eliminates the proposed choice from the stack and restarts the logic.

```
Input:
    Possible choices from Decision Table, which represents the
decision
    logic level in DMN
Output:
    The selected choice based on BPMNDF
    Updating the repository with a new decision rule
Begin
01.    Rule R = new Rule ()
02.    R.initialize ()
03.    Stack CH = R.choices
04.    String Choice
05.    Boolean Stop = False
06.    While not Stop or Empty (CH) do
07.        Choice ← Top (CH).Value
08.        If R.IsSuitable (Choice) Then
09.            If not R.Fetch (R.Blacklist, Choice) then
10.                R.ChangeChoicesFlag (Choice, 1)
11.                Stop ← True
12.            Else
13.                Pop (CH)
14.                R.ChangeFactorsFlag ("repository", 1)
15.            End If
16.        End If
17.    End while
18.    If Stop then
19.        R.GenerateBlacklist (Choice)
20.        R.Store ()
21.    End If
End
```

Fig. 8. DM/DR algorithm

- Initialize (): Initializes all factors and choices from DMN and all flags to 0
- IsSuitable (c): Applies the Decision Logic Level for a choice c to return a Boolean value
- Fetch (bl,v): Looks for the specified value v in the blacklist bl
- ChangeChoicesFlag (c,v): Affects the flag attribute of the indicated choice c with the specified value v
- ChangeFactorsFlag (f,v): Affects the flag attribute of the indicated factor f with the specified value v
- GenerateBlacklist (c): Predicts upcoming decisions with prohibited choices for a retained choice c
- Store (): Memorizes new decision rule in repository
- Empty (), Top () and Pop (): Universal data abstract type Stack methods

This algorithm does not cover all the scenarios that can occur when applying BPMNDF, such as the case of inability to adopt any of the choices provided because of the cons-indications in the repository. It has also a great challenge to implement the GenerateBlacklist method because of its predictive aspect. In these situations, recourse to an expert is unavoidable.

5   Discussion

In this section, we present the contribution of our BPMNDF approach through some illustrative examples of BI process tasks. In the first subsection, we present the rules generated by applying our BPMNDF approach; whereas, in the second subsection, we describe the impact of these decision rules on the progress of the project.

5.1   Decision-Making in BI Process with BPMNDF

In the first example (a) as shown in Fig. 9, we are dealing an extraction task; we note that the adopted choice is Periodic Extraction. This choice is due to the large number of transactions in the production system. The REPOSITORY factor is equal to 0, so the choice is adopted due to its intrinsic factor. The DM/DR Algorithm mentions a cons-indication on the choice ROLAP if we will have an OLAP decision. In the second example (b) also illustrated in Fig. 9, we handle a slowly changing dimension (SCD) task. The Column choice is adopted and it is due to the granularity factor. The REPOSITORY factor is also equal to 0, so the choice is due to its intrinsic factor. The DM/DR Algorithm mentions a cons-indication on the choice Analytical if we will have a Dashboard decision.

Example 1. (a). Rule Generated in Extraction Task	Example 2. (b). Rule Generated in SCD Task

`<?xml version="1.0" encoding="UTF-8"?>`
`<rules>`
  `<rule id="1" label="Extraction"`
    `comment="Periodic or Continous" >`
    `<choices>`
      `<choice value="Periodic" flag="1" />`
      `<choice value="Continous" flag="0" />`
    `</choices>`
    `<factors>`
      `<factor value="HA Feature" flag="0" />`
      `<factor value="HA Strategy" flag="0" />`
      `<factor value="OLTP" flag="1" />`
      `<factor value="REPOSITORY" flag="0"/>`
    `</factors>`
    `<blacklist>`
      `<decision label="OLAP" choice="ROLAP" />`
    `</blacklist>`
  `</rule>`
`</rules>`
	`<?xml version="1.0" encoding="UTF-8"?>`
	`<rules>`
	  `<rule id="3" label="SCD"`
	    `comment="Row, Column or Dimension" >`
	    `<choices>`
	      `<choice value="Row" flag="0" />`
	      `<choice value="Column" flag="1" />`
	      `<choice value="Dimension" flag="0" />`
	    `</choices>`
	    `<factors>`
	      `<factor value="Retention" flag="0" />`
	      `<factor value="Granularity" flag="1" />`
	      `<factor value="Design" flag="0" />`
	      `<factor value="REPOSITORY" flag="0"/>`
	    `</factors>`
	    `<blacklist>`
	      `<decision label="Dashboard" choice="Analytical" />`
	    `</blacklist>`
	  `</rule>`
	`</rules>`

Fig. 9. Examples of rules generation by DM/DR algorithm

5.2   Impact of Decision Harmony on the Decision-Making

In this second subsection, the idea is to discuss the behaviour of the designer in decision-making while considering OR NEGLECTING THE DECISION harmony. This contribution is presented through two examples describing two tasks in a BI process as shown respectively in Figs. 10 and 11: OLAP Decision Task and Dashboard Decision Task.

For example, in the OLAP task, as shown in Fig. 10, the choice adopted with BPMN/DMN modelling is ROLAP. It is due to intrinsic factors of this task. The choice seems technically feasible but is really conflicting an earlier decision that is the Periodic Extraction. When we apply BPMNDF, choice adopted is MOLAP; it is due to an extrinsic factor of the OLAP task. The adjusted choice is not the

Example 1. (a). Rule Generated in Extraction Task	Example 2. (b). Rule Generated in SCD Task

``
<?xml version="1.0" encoding="UTF-8"?>
<rules>
  <rule id="1" label="Extraction"
            comment="Periodic or Continous" >
    <choices>
      <choice value="Periodic" flag="1" />
      <choice value="Continous" flag="0" />
    </choices>
    <factors>
      <factor value="HA Feature" flag="0" />
      <factor value="HA Strategy" flag="0" />
      <factor value="OLTP" flag="1" />
      <factor value="REPOSITORY" flag="0"/>
    </factors>
    <blacklist>
      <decision label="OLAP" choice="ROLAP" />
    </blacklist>
  </rule>
</rules>
``
	``
	<?xml version="1.0" encoding="UTF-8"?>
	<rules>
	  <rule id="3" label="SCD"
	            comment="Row, Column or Dimension" >
	    <choices>
	      <choice value="Row" flag="0" />
	      <choice value="Column" flag="1" />
	      <choice value="Dimension" flag="0" />
	    </choices>
	    <factors>
	      <factor value="Retention" flag="0" />
	      <factor value="Granularity" flag="1" />
	      <factor value="Design" flag="0" />
	      <factor value="REPOSITORY" flag="0"/>
	    </factors>
	    <blacklist>
	      <decision label="Dashboard" choice="Analytical" />
	    </blacklist>
	  </rule>
	</rules>
	``

Fig. 10. Comparison between BPMN/DMN and BPMNDF modelling of OLAP Decision Task

best technical choice but is harmonized with an earlier decision, which is the Periodic Extraction.

Decision-making in the reporting task, as shown in Fig. 11, is very critical because, while adopting our BPMNDF approach, it is influenced by all decisions in the anterior tasks. Despite the technical feasibility of different types of dashboard (Real-Time, Analytical or Operational), the optimal solution in this

BPMN/DMN	BPMNDF

``
<?xml version="1.0" encoding="UTF-8"?>
<rules>
  <rule id="5" label="OLAP"
            comment="ROLAP or MOLAP" >
    <choices>
      <choice value="ROLAP" flag="1" />
      <choice value="MOLAP" flag="0" />
    </choices>
    <factors>
      <factor value="Memory" flag="0" />
      <factor value="Response Time" flag="1" />
      <factor value="Volume" flag="0" />
      <factor value="REPOSITORY" flag="0"/>
    </factors>
    <blacklist>
 	
    </blacklist>
  </rule>
</rules>
``
	``
	<?xml version="1.0" encoding="UTF-8"?>
	<rules>
	  <rule id="5" label="OLAP"
	            comment="ROLAP or MOLAP" >
	    <choices>
	      <choice value="ROLAP" flag="0" />
	      <choice value="MOLAP" flag="1" />
	    </choices>
	    <factors>
	      <factor value="Memory" flag="0" />
	      <factor value="Response Time" flag="1" />
	      <factor value="Volume" flag="0" />
	      <factor value="REPOSITORY" flag="1"/>
	    </factors>
	    <blacklist>
	      <decision label="Dashboard" choice="Real-Time"/>
	    </blacklist>
	  </rule>
	</rules>
	``

Fig. 11. Comparison between BPMN/DMN and BPMNDF Modelling of Dashboard Decision Task

example, that ensures harmony with the choices already made, is an Operational Dashboard. This choice is selected as a result of the elimination of both alternatives: Real-Time and Analytical Dashboards. The first alternative is eliminated according to the Periodic Extraction decision; however, the second alternative is eliminated because of the nature of the SCD.

Finally, these findings identified when leading a BI project allowed us to focus on the importance of harmonization of all decisions throughout the process. This concept is not limited to BI projects but it can be generalized to any kind of projects.

6   Conclusion and Future Works

In this paper, we argue that the decision-making in a business process management can be improved if we ensure the harmony between all decisions along the process. We present the problematic and we defend our approach through the example of a BI process. Indeed, without harmony in decision-making, such projects generally ends up failing despite all the efforts provided and the material and human resources deployed.

Our contribution is in the context of the OMGs works, especially their BPMN and DMN standards. We propose the BPMNDF, which is a coupling of BPMN with an enhancement for the DMN. This improvement is provided by a repository allowing memorisation in XML or JSON format of the whole of decisions taken during the process. The repository must be a stakeholder in decision-making. It handled with a DM/DR Algorithm to refer to the background of each task and predict possible scenarios for the upcoming other.

Our future work will be scheduled on three axes. First, the implementation of a Framework to apply the BPMNDF approach. The second step is to validate this approach with case studies in the industrial environment. The third axis is the improvement of this approach by addressing the two deficiencies of the DM/DR algorithm where we have to resort to an expert. Weighting factors and projects taxonomy may represent working tracks for potential solutions to these shortcomings.

References

1. Negash, S., Gray, P.: Business intelligence. Handbook on Decision Support Systems 2. International Handbooks Information System, pp. 175–193. Springer, Heidelberg (2008). ISBN 978-3-540-48715-9
2. Thamir, A., Theodoulidis, B.: Business intelligence maturity models: information management perspective. In: Dregvaite, G., Damasevicius, R. (eds.) ICIST 2015. CCIS, vol. 538, pp. 198–221. Springer, Heidelberg (2013). doi:10.1007/978-3-642-41947-8_18
3. Dokhanchi, A., Nazemi, E.: BISC: a framework for aligning business intelligence with corporate strategies based on enterprise architecture framework. Int. J. Enterp. Inf. Syst. 11(2), 90–106 (2015)

4. The Open Group Architecture Framework (TOGAF Version 9.1) Documentation. http://pubs.opengroup.org/architecture/togaf9-doc/arch/chap08.html
5. OMG. Business Process Modeling Notation Specification 2.0 (2011). http://www.omg.org/spec/BPMN/2.0/PDF/
6. Jankovic, M., Ljubicic, M., Anicic, N., Marjanovic, Z.: Enhancing BPMN 2.0 informational perspective to support interoperability for cross-organizational business processes. J. Comput. Sci. Inf. Syst. **12**(3), 1101–1120 (2015)
7. Hofmann, I., Meyer, U.: Expert systems and their applications: a survey. In: Popović, D. (ed.) Analysis and Control of Industrial Processes. Advances in System Analysis, pp. 23–33. Springer, Heidelberg (1991). ISBN 978-3-528-06340-5
8. Kluza, K., Nalepa, G.J.: Towards rule-oriented business process model generation. In: Proceedings of the Federated Conference on Computer Science and Information Systems, FedCSIS, Krakw, Poland, 8–11 September 2013, pp. 939–946 (2013)
9. Bajwa, I.S., Lee, M.G., Bordbar, B.: SBVR business rules generation from natural language specification. In: Artificial Intelligence for Business Agility. AAAI Spring Symposium Series (SS-11-03), pp. 2–8 (2011)
10. Tantan, O.C., Akoka, J.: Automated transformation of business rules into business processes. From SBVR to BPMN. In: Proceedings of the 26th International Conference on Software Engineering and Knowledge Engineering, SEKE, Vancouver, Canada, 1–3 July 2014, pp. 684–687 (2014)
11. Mickevičiūtė, E., Butleris, R.: Towards the combination of BPMN process models with SBVR business vocabularies and rules. In: Skersys, T., Butleris, R., Butkiene, R. (eds.) ICIST 2013. CCIS, vol. 403, pp. 114–121. Springer, Heidelberg (2013)
12. Skersys, T., Tutkute, L., Butleris, R.: The enrichment of BPMN business process model with SBVR business vocabulary and rules. J. Comput. Inf. Technol. **20**(3), 143–150 (2012)
13. Wang, W., Indulska, M., Sadiq, S.: Integrated modelling of business process models and business rules: a research agenda. In: Proceedings of the 25th Australasian Conference on Information Systems, ACIS, Auckland, New Zealand, 8–10 December 2014
14. OMG: Decision Model and Notation 1.0 (2015). http://www.omg.org/spec/DMN/1.0/PDF
15. Debevoise, T., Taylor, J., Sinur, J., Geneva, R.: The MicroGuide to Process and Decision Modeling in BPMN/DMN: Building More Effective Processes by Integrating Process Modeling with Decision Modeling. CreateSpace Independent Publishing Platform, North Charleston (2014)
16. Pourshahid, A., Johari, I., Richards, G., Amyot, D., Akhigbe, O.: A goal-oriented, business intelligence-supported decision-making methodology. Decis. Anal. **1**(1), 1–36 (2014). doi:10.1186/s40165-014-0009-8
17. Nazaruka, E., Ovchinnikova, V.: Specification of decision-making and control flow branching in topological functioning models of systems. In: Proceedings of the 10th International Conference on Evaluation of Novel Approaches to Software Engineering, ENASE, Barcelona, Spain, 29–30 April 2015, pp. 364–373 (2015)
18. Natschlager, C., Geist, V., Kossak, F., Freudenthaler, B.: Optional activities in process flows. In: Proceedings of Enterprise Modelling and Information Systems Architectures, EMISA, Vienna, Austria, 12–14 September 2012
19. Pourshahid, A., Johari, I., Richards, G., Amyot, D., Akhigbe, O.: Exception handling patterns for process modeling. IEEE Trans. Softw. Eng. **36**(2), 162–183 (2010)

20. Biard, T., LeMauff, A., Bigand, M., Bourey, J.P.: Separation of decision modeling from business process modeling using new "Decision Model and Notation" (DMN) for automating operational decision-making. In: Camarinha-Matos, L.M., Bénaben, F., Picard, W. (eds.) PRO-VE 2015. IFIP, vol. 463, pp. 489–496. Springer, Heidelberg (2015)

21. Taylor, J., Fish, A., Vincent, P.: Emerging Standards in Decision Modeling - An Introduction to Decision Model & Notation in iBPMS Intelligent BPM Systems: Impact and Opportunity. Future Strategies Inc., Brampton (2013). ISBN 978-0-9849764-6-1

22. Batoulis, K., Meyer, A., Bazhenova, E., Decker, G., Weske, M.: Extracting decision logic from process models. In: Nurcan, S., Soffer, P., Bajec, M., Eder, J. (eds.) CAiSE 2016. LNCS, vol. 9694, pp. 349–366. Springer, Heidelberg (2015). doi:10.1007/978-3-319-19069-3_22

23. Inmon, W.H.: Building the Data Warehouse. Wiley Computer Publishing, Chichester (2005). ISBN 978-0-471-08130-2

24. Vaisman, A., Zimányi, E.: Data analytics: exploiting the data warehouse. In: Vaisman, A., Zimányi, E. (eds.) Data Warehouse Systems, pp. 329–383. Springer, Heidelberg (2014)

25. Ularu, E.G., Puican, F.C., Apostu, A., Velican, M.: Perspectives on big data and big data analytics. Database Syst. J. 3(4), 3–14 (2012)

26. Hughes, R.: Agile Data Warehousing for the Enterprise: A Guide for Solution Architects and Project Leaders. Elsevier Science Publisher, North-Holland (2015). ISBN 978-0-12-396464-9

27. Poess, M., Nambiar, R.O.: Tuning servers, storage and database for energy efficient data warehouses. In: Proceedings of the IEEE 26th International Conference on Data Engineering, ICDE, Long Beach, California, USA, 1–6 March 2010, pp. 1006–1017 (2010)

28. Elliott, M., Liu, Y.: The nine rights of medication administration: an overview. Br. J. Nurs. 19(5), 300–305 (2010)

29. El Akkaoui, Z., Mazón, J.-N., Vaisman, A., Zimányi, E.: BPMN-based conceptual modeling of ETL processes. In: Proceedings of the 14th International Conference on Data Warehousing and Knowledge Discovery, DaWaK, Vienna, Austria, 3–6 September 2012, pp. 1–14 (2012)

A Cost-Aware and Workload-Based Index Advisor for Columnar In-Memory Databases

Martin Boissier[(✉)], Timo Djürken, Rainer Schlosser, and Martin Faust

Hasso Plattner Institute, Potsdam, Germany
{martin.boissier,timo.djurken,rainer.schlosser,martin.faust}@hpi.de
https://epic.hpi.de

Abstract. Optimal index configurations for in-memory databases differ significantly from configurations for their traditional disk-based counterparts. Operations like full column scans that have previously been prohibitively expensive in disk-based and row-oriented databases are now computationally feasible with columnar main memory-resident data structures and even outperform index-based accesses in many cases. Furthermore, index selection criteria are different for in-memory databases since maintenance costs are often lower while memory footprint considerations have become increasingly important.

In this paper, we introduce a workload-based and cost-aware index advisor tailored for columnar in-memory databases in mixed workload environments. We apply a memory traffic-driven model to estimate the efficiency of each index and to give a system-wide overview of the indices that are cost-ineffective with respect to their size and performance improvement. We also present our *Index Advisor Cockpit* applied to a real-world live production enterprise system of a Global 2000 company.

Keywords: Column store · Main memory · Index advisor · Live production system

1 Indices for Columnar In-Memory Databases

The evaluation of database indices typically boils down to three major aspects: (1) performance, (2) maintenance, and (3) storage costs. Indexing large database systems (particularly enterprise systems) is a thoroughly researched topic, especially for transactional enterprise workloads on row-oriented and disk-resident databases. However, recent hardware and software achievements introduced a completely new kind of database system into the field of enterprise systems: columnar in-memory databases. While in-memory databases have been used for decades for special purpose applications, modern servers with terabytes of DRAM allow storing entire enterprise systems completely in main memory. Furthermore, the same hardware developments as well as database research achievements made columnar databases – already established for analytical workloads – suitable for enterprise systems and their increasingly mixed workloads with transactional and analytical workloads on the same machine.

© Springer International Publishing Switzerland 2016
G. Dregvaite and R. Damasevicius (Eds.): ICIST 2016, CCIS 639, pp. 285–299, 2016.
DOI: 10.1007/978-3-319-46254-7_23

For these new database systems, previous assumptions about indices are no longer true in many cases. For example, indices on row-oriented databases basically always improve the read performance, because full table scans are prohibitively expensive on disk-based row stores. For columnar in-memory databases in contrast, scanning compressed columns outperforms accesses via an index in many cases (see Sect. 2.1).

The picture looks similar for maintenance costs. Columnar in-memory databases usually deploy a multi-level partition hierarchy with small write-optimized partitions handling modifying queries while the remaining tuples are stored in read-optimized partitions (e.g., SAP HANA [3], HYRISE [7], or HyPer [9]). Both partitions are then merged periodically in most systems. In HYRISE and SAP HANA, e.g., indices of read-optimized partitions are solely written when partitions are merged [4]. In this way, the maintenance overhead of indexing has significantly shifted.

Last but not least, storage cost considerations gained more importance. While disk-resident indices with buffer management can almost be considered as free of charge, their main memory-resident counterparts incur high costs since DRAM is still a comparatively expensive resource.

Consequently, the aspects with which an index evaluation is done have shifted notably with the recent rise of columnar in-memory databases. In this paper, we propose a workload-based index heuristic that focuses on performance through evaluating memory traffic and costs. We decided against an automated index evaluation and selection. Instead, we created a tool set that guides database administrators and gives thorough insights into the performance impact of each index and the added costs. We think this tool is of importance for several reasons: First, indices are still one of the major means of performance optimization for database administrators as indices can be added and removed relatively fast compared to other performance optimizations, such as application changes or data model adaptations. Second, automated index selection approaches still have not gained any relevance for real-world systems, as many situations still require the domain knowledge of human experts. One example are indices that are required to meet defined service level agreements (SLAs) but which might be both expensive and only adding little performance advantage, thus being a good candidate for removal in an automated system. As potential SLA violations can incur serious penalties, these indices have to be kept in the system. Third, existing index evaluations often fail to provide understandable and comparable results that can be interpreted without a deep understanding of the database implementation.

Throughout this paper, we make the following contributions:

- We reason why a memory traffic-based index evaluation provides a decent trade-off between precision and simplicity (Sect. 2).
- We argue that analyzing the database plan cache provides both thorough insights for the index evaluation on the basis of the actual workload while also making the analysis process simple and comparatively inexpensive, allowing to iteratively run analyses or react fast to sudden issues (Sect. 3).

- We present a simple and understandable but yet powerful *index coefficient* that simplifies the evaluation of particular indices as well as allowing to compare an index's performance-cost trade-offs (Sect. 4).
- We present exemplary results of our advisor applied on a live production enterprise resource planning system: the *index advisor cockpit*. This cockpit assists database administrators by analyzing the currently deployed indices and determining how much they are utilized under the current workload. Based on that information, the DBA can make an informed decision about which indices to keep, add, or remove from the system in order to improve performance or to reduce the memory footprint (Sect. 5).

2 Memory Traffic and Data Structures

Evaluating an index is a challenging task. First, an index's main characteristics performance and space consumption are often orthogonal. While it is trivial to calculate the space consumption, a thorough performance evaluation is often not feasible for large database systems. On the one hand, measuring the real-world performance is challenging as dynamically changing workloads often show high contention, which is hard to measure and simulate accurately. On the other hand, estimating an index's performance is hard since there is a multitude of factors involved. Manegold et al. studied cost models for operations in an in-memory database [11]. They found that a good model is hardly possible without exact knowledge about the underlying hardware (e.g., the cache sizes). Even worse, modern system architectures with multi-hop NUMA and highly contending mixed workloads add additional unknowns.

For our index evaluations, we decided to concentrate on memory traffic as the dominating factor in order to evaluate performance and completely disregard any low-level hardware aspects. With steadily improving processing power (e.g., 15-core CPUs, vectorized instructions, such as SSE/AVX, et cetera) memory access has become the main bottleneck and dominating cost factor in modern database systems [10]. Especially systems without NUMA-optimized physical partitioning to optimize local data access (compare Kissinger et al. [8]) suffer from NUMA effects, making memory traffic increasingly important for steadily growing NUMA architectures. Following Manegold, our model combines both logical costs and physical costs.

2.1 Data Structures

Throughout this paper, we describe data structures and explain our calculations in the context of HYRISE [7]. HYRISE is an open source[1] columnar in-memory database for mixed workloads (OLxP). It shares several concepts with SAP HANA [3], e.g., the main delta architecture, insert-only modifications, dictionary-encoded columns, and MVCC concurrency control.

In this paper, we focus on the following two data structures of HYRISE:

---

[1] HYRISE on Github: https://github.com/hyrise/hyrise.

Table 1. Symbols used in this paper

Symbol	Description
N_c	Length of column c
D_c	Length of the dictionary of column c
E_p	Execution count of plan p

Dictionary-Encoded Columns: HYRISE splits a table vertically into multiple columns. Each column consists of two data structures: a sorted dictionary that stores all distinct values of the column and an attribute vector that reflects the actual column. Instead of the actual values, the attribute vector stores the positional identifier (i.e., value ID) of the corresponding value in the dictionary. To reduce the memory footprint further, the attribute vector is fixed-width bit-packed [7].

Group-Key Indices: The group-key index is HYRISE's primary index structure [4]. The group-key index only indexes the main partition, which is read-only and is created periodically by merging the delta partition with it. Since the index is created/maintained during the merge phase as explained by Faust et al. [4], we do not consider maintenance costs of the group-key index throughout this paper.

The basic idea of the group-key index is to provide a mapping from dictionary values to all positions in the attribute vector that store this value. When creating a group-key index on a dictionary-encoded column, two structures will be created: Firstly, an Index Offset vector (IO) that contains the position in the Index Positions vector (IP) for each dictionary value. The IP vector contains all the positions in the attribute vector (AV) for each dictionary entry. An example is depicted in Fig. 1 with a column storing countries and the corresponding index offset vectors and index position vectors.

The IO vector has one entry for each dictionary entry and follows the same order. For each value in the dictionary, the IO vector contains the offset in the IP vector at which the list of positions for that specific value ID starts. The IP vector is a list of all attribute vector positions (or row IDs) where the attribute vector has a certain value. There is no implicit indicator for the value IDs, but instead the IO vector is used as an index for the IP.

In terms of memory consumption, the IP vector has N_c entries (Table 1) with a size of $\lceil \log_2(N_c) \rceil$ bits per entry as it points to a value in the attribute vector. The IO vector contains the same number of entries like the dictionary, i.e., D_c, and because it maps to the IP vector, each entry has a size of $\lceil \log_2(N_c) \rceil$ bits.

Thus, we denote MI_c as the total memory consumption of an index for column c:

$$MI_c = N_c \cdot \lceil \log_2(N_c) \rceil + D_c \cdot \lceil \log_2(N_c) \rceil \tag{1}$$

The actual benefit of indices is the fast lookup of values. When using an index to look up the value *"Hungary"*, the first step is to find the value ID

(a) Column   (b) Index

Fig. 1. Data structures for an indexed column storing countries. The two elements on the left show the default data structures in HYRISE to a table column: an (bit-packed) attribute vector that stores positional information referring to the (sorted) dictionary with all distinct column values. The two index structures on the right depict HYRISE's group-key index with an offset vector to find the row identifies in the position list.

in the dictionary. However, this step is also necessary when doing a regular column scan without an index, so this can be discarded when comparing the two approaches. The next step is to read the lower and upper bounds in the IO vector. With a complexity of $O(1)$ this step can also be safely ignored when analyzing the performance of an index look-up. The final step is reading the list of positions in the IP vector. Of course, the number of values to be read here depends on the value distribution in that column. However, on the assumption that the values are uniformly distributed, we need to read N_c/D_c entries. And since each entry in the IP vector has a size of $\lceil \log_2(N_c) \rceil$ the average amount of data that needs to be read is:

$$\frac{N_c \cdot \lceil \log_2(N_c) \rceil}{D_c} \tag{2}$$

In most cases, the memory to read using an index is significantly less than the memory traffic of a regular column scan. Figure 2 shows a direct comparison between IP vector look-up and attribute vector scan (which is basically reading $N_c \cdot \lceil \log_2(N_c) \rceil$ bits). The graph shows that an index results in reduced memory traffic if the dictionary contains at least nine dictionary values (assuming uniform distribution).

3   Workload Analyses

The value of an index depends to a large extend on the characteristics of the actual workload. As a result, we built our analyses on top of the database plan cache[2] of a live production system to obtain both thorough insights into the workload as well as an overview of the system-wide load. The plan cache is

---

[2] The Plan Cache of SAP HANA contains frequently executed query plans (including prepared SQL statements) as well as a number of monitoring statistics per plan, such as the aggregated execution count or the minimal/average/maximal run times.

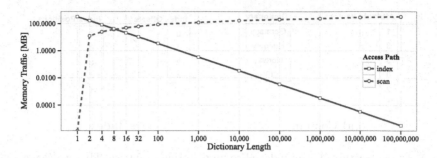

Fig. 2. Memory traffic for a single equi-predicate. Comparing scans on a dictionary-encoded and bit-packed column with index accesses using a group-key on a column with 100 million rows. For columns with less than nine distinct values, scanning a compressed column reads less memory from DRAM than an indexed access.

a standard component of every major database product (e.g., Microsoft SQL Server's *Plan Cache Object*, Oracle's *Optimizer Statistics*, IBM DB2's *Query engine Plan cache*) and can easily be exported and analyzed offline. Many index advisors require a complete copy of the running system in order to evoke the plan optimizer and evaluate indices. While these approaches are highly accurate, the costs of a second system copy are immense. Other advisors rely on static and simplified assumptions. We decided for a trade-off between both approaches and evaluate our cost-based index heuristics using the database plan cache of the production system. In this way, analyses can be executed offline on an export of the plan cache with minimal additional costs while still preserving a detailed view on the current workload of the system. With this setup, we gain the advantage of having different plan caches for different server nodes. In this way, each node can independently create the indices that yield the best performance for the workload. Especially systems that partition data along a time dimension see different workloads on server nodes storing recent data compared to server nodes storing historical data [13].

Comparing an index against the default selection mechanism of a database (i.e., column scanning) is helpful to obtain a first decent idea of the efficiency of an index. However, even the best index does not provide any advantages when the indexed column is never accessed during query execution. Even worse, for in-memory databases with limited DRAM resources a never or rarely used index wastes resources, because most in-memory databases deploy DRAM-resident indices to ensure optimal performance.

Consequently, we evaluate indices with their actual usage in the workload. The reason is simple: the later a selection on a column is executed in the query plan, the lower the advantages of an index are. We assume the traditional approach of query plan optimization. Here, first all selections on indexed columns are executed, then selections on non-indexed columns are performed. Both times the attributes are sorted by the selectivity of each attribute, beginning with the lowest selectivity (i.e., the smallest expected number of tuples to be returned).

While the costs of scanning increase linearly with the size of the vector, the costs for index accesses increase logarithmically. Let us consider a typical scan operation that is broken down into multiple chunks that are scanned in parallel on different cores. The higher the selectivity, the higher the probability that fewer blocks of the following attribute need to be evaluated. This simplified assumption is not always true. Even for selections with low selectivities there is the chance that all scanned blocks store qualifying tuples. However, for our model we assume that the first evaluated attribute is the one with the lowest selectivity and thus yields a smaller set of blocks including qualifying tuples.

In contrast, for the group-key index the position in the query plan does not matter. For every selection in the plan, the index will be accessed. In case that one or more selections have already been evaluated, the input position list from the previous operator will be merged with the result of the index access.

Consequently, we evaluate each attribute by looking at every query plan that executes a selection on that attribute and adapt the index coefficient depending on the selectivity of the attribute (i.e., the estimated position in the query plan).

4 Index Evaluation

In our model, the objective of an index is to reduce the memory traffic that is required in order to filter on an attribute. In this section, we present the *Index Coefficient* that quantifies the advantage of an index over the scan in respect to the required memory traffic and the *Index Cost Score* that puts the index memory traffic savings in relation with the index size.

4.1 Index Coefficient

It is an important index evaluation requirement that the coefficient is easy to understand and comparable. Thus, our index coefficient is a linear scalar representing the memory traffic saved by a particular index over the scan.

For example, index accesses on a particular attribute for the entire workload read on average 2 MB for a single equi-predicate to evaluate. The memory traffic for scan accesses on that attribute is 10 MB on average. In that example, the index coefficient would be 5×.

We decided for a two-phase approach for the evaluation of indices. In the first phase, the index is measured solely by comparing the index and its workload with the default non-index access (i.e., column scanning). The second phase adapts the coefficient according to the given workload to incorporate the frequency of potential accesses to the index and the order in the query plans. For simplicity, we will concentrate on single equi-predicates throughput this paper.

Columns are denoted by c while C denotes the set of all columns in the system. We consider a set of query plans P. For simplification and only assuming equi-predicates, a query plan p, $p \in P$, is characterized by a set of predicates on columns c, i.e., every plan p is a subset of C, $p \subseteq C$. Note, to evaluate the index coefficient for a given attribute c, it is sufficient to consider solely plans p that contain the column index c (i.e., evaluate a predicate on c).

As already mentioned, we do not aim for an automated index selection that finds the best index configuration for a system. We consider a given global status Z of the system that is characterized by values $z_c \in \{0, 1\}, c \in C$. z_c denotes whether column c is indexed (i.e., $z_c = 1$) or not (i.e., $z_c = 0$). The index coefficient for column c evaluates the effect of having an index over not having an index, where Z with the exception of z_c is stable.

We define the selectivity for single equi-predicates as follows, $c \in C$:

$$S_c = \frac{1}{D_c} \tag{3}$$

To compare the memory traffic for a predicate on a particular attribute c in a given plan p, we define function M for the binary case that c is not indexed (denoted by $^{(0)}$) or is indexed (denoted by $^{(1)}$). Please note that the indexed case does not incorporate the position in the query plan by multiplying the selectivities of previous selections as explained in Sect. 3.

$$M_{c,p}^{(0)} = \lceil log_2(D_c) \rceil \cdot N_c \cdot \prod_{\substack{i \in p \\ Z_i = 1}} S_i \cdot \prod_{\substack{j \in p \\ Z_j = 0 \\ S_j < S_c}} S_j$$

$$M_{c,p}^{(1)} = \lceil log_2(N_c) \rceil \cdot \lceil N_c/D_c \rceil \tag{4}$$

The next step is to calculate the memory traffic for a given workload (i.e., set P of query plans). Which set of query plans is considered depends on what aspects should be focused on. If the question is how efficient a particular index is for all queries selecting on that particular attribute, P should only include these relevant query plans. If the question is which indices of a particular table are the most/least efficient, P should include all query plans for that particular table. To obtain a system-wide overview and to determine the least efficient indices, P might even include all query plans. Whatever the focus is, the database administrator can simply adjust the current focus by defining what query plans to consider.

To denote the workload-adjusted traffic we define function MW for a given set of query plans P as follows (E_p denotes the execution count of plan p):

$$MW_c^{(0)} = \sum_{p \in P} M_{c,p}^{(0)} \cdot E_p$$

$$MW_c^{(1)} = \sum_{p \in P} M_{c,p}^{(1)} \cdot E_p \tag{5}$$

With these functions at hand we can finally calculate the index coefficient IC_c for a given column c that determines the relative memory benefit:

$$IC_c = \frac{MW_c^{(0)}}{MW_c^{(1)}} \tag{6}$$

4.2   Index Cost Score

So far, the index coefficient helps to calculate the expected memory transfer reduction when having an index on a particular column. Although scans are comparatively efficient on in-memory column stores and outperform index accesses in many cases, for most cases indices will have a better coefficient. But since every main memory-resident index increases the memory footprint and thus potentially also the overall system costs, we need to compare the relative index benefit against the costs of that particular index. In our case, the cost is the main memory-allocated space to store the index.

The *Index Cost Score* ICS_c puts the overall saved memory traffic for a given set of query plans P in relation to the cost of the index for a given column c (see Eq. (1) for the calculation of index size MI_c):

$$ICS_c = MW_c^{(0)} - MW_c^{(1)} - \alpha \cdot MI_c^{\beta} \tag{7}$$

We use two penalty parameters α and β. α is used to scale the index size accordingly to the size of the workload (i.e., the number of query plans and their execution counts), since the overall memory traffic reduction is relative to the size of the workload. The scaling parameter β is used to penalize large indices in a suitable way. Since performance gains and memory footprint reductions are usually orthogonal optimization objectives, α allows balancing the trade-off (also directly by the DBA in the front end to analyze the impact).

The model is well suited for dynamic programming approaches with which it is also possible to calculate (near) optimal index configurations with respect to given footprint constraints (see [12] for a such an approach). However, further use cases for the model are part of continued research.

5   Advisor Cockpit

In this section, we present the *Index Advisor Cockpit*. We also give a short overview of the production system we have run our analyses on. Then, we show exemplary screenshots of the HTML-based front end as well as a few insights from the analyzed real-world system.

Besides obvious requirements like accurate performance indicators and valuable insights for DBAs, we think a suitable user interface is crucial for any advisor tool. Nowadays, there is a vast array of tools for DBAs to control and monitor their databases. Unfortunately, many of them lack simple and easy understandable metrics that provide valuable insights without the need to fully understand the underlying database engines.

An easy to understand user interface is especially important for systems, such as enterprise systems. The analyzed SAP ERP installation consists of ∼112,000 tables with over 240,000 indices. We think our tool set with a workload-driven approach and a straightforward index evaluation model is a promising approach helping database administrators to handle such large systems.

5.1 Plan Cache Analysis

All data in this demo has been extracted from the live production enterprise system of a *Global 2000*[3] company:

- the uncompressed data amounts to over seven terabytes
- one of the most recent versions of an SAP ERP system including operational reporting on transactional data (i.e., OLxP)
- database system handles ~1.5 billion queries each day

For our analyses, we have exported the plan cache table as well as several statistic/administrative tables (e.g., column and index information of the system). The extracted plan cache included ~300,000 query plans, which account for ~5 billion query executions. All analyses shown here can also be executed directly on the production data. The computation overhead on the production is manageable, because most queries simply request data that has already been aggregated by the database system itself (e.g., overall plan executions of a particular query plan, average run times, et cetera).

An important capability of our tool set is the analysis of query plans that access logical database views. The inclusion of database views is increasingly important as modern enterprise systems use them, e.g., to ease the transition to new systems [13] and to disassemble sophisticated queries into multiple layers of logical views.

5.2 Table Information

The user has the opportunity to examine specific tables in detail. The *table detail page* displays details about the table in general, its columns and indices as well as information about primary key indices. To give the user a fast overview of the memory footprint of the table, the top of the page displays a graph about the overall memory footprint broken down in the table's elements (Fig. 3).

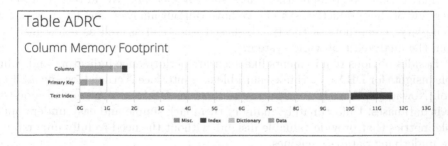

Fig. 3. Memory consumption overview for table ADRC, which stores customer address information. It is shown that text indices are responsible for most of the DRAM consumption of that – comparatively small – master data table.

---

[3] Global 2000: http://www.forbes.com/global2000/.

5.3 Index Information

Figure 4 shows two aspects of the index detail page. This page presents information about the currently viewed index, i.a., the ratio between all queries accessing the corresponding table and queries on the corresponding table that furthermore potentially access this index (see Fig. 4a). Most importantly, the user can analyze the index's ranking. In this example, the index ranks comparatively well with its rank 275 out of the 18,487 indices (see Fig. 4b) that have been ranked (we limited the ranking to indices that have been accessed at least once). Additionally, all factors used to calculate the coefficient are shown to ease understanding of the resulting coefficient. In this particular case, the evaluation of a single equi-predicate using a scan reads over 800 MB from DRAM, while an access via the index only reads threes Bytes from DRAM.

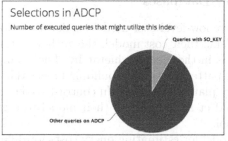

(a) Workload information.

(b) Index ranking.

Fig. 4. Index detail page: (a) ratio of queries on table ADCP that potentially access this particular index, (b) the ranking information.

5.4 Index Ranking and Issues

The *Index Ranking* page lists all indices that have been ranked according to their coefficient. The table can be searched and sorted. For each index, additional information, such as the column size, number of query executions and the source table are displayed as well.

The *Issues* page prepares two lists of indices that could be of interest to the database administrator. The first list displays all indices that are not used by the traced workload at all. That means that not even a single query with a selection on the indexed column has been found.

Secondly, a list of the least economical indices is provided for the user. Amongst these indices are typically indices that are automatically created by the ERP system, because they are advantageous for row stores. More importantly, for main memory column stores these indices are often wasting resources. Furthermore, they might even slow down the entire system in case the query optimizer does not recognize that scanning incurs a lower memory transfer.

Workload analyses have shown that over 5,000 indices in the system have not been accessed once during the recorded plan cache period. The footprint of these indices is 18.1 GB. We think this information is important for database administrators as those indices waste resources. Nevertheless, we do not propose to automatically remove these indices since even though they might be accesses rarely, they can still be necessary for a variety of reasons (e.g., to avoid SLA violations for certain processes).

6 Related Work

In this section, we briefly discuss related work in the areas of cost models for in-memory databases and index selection.

6.1 Cost Models for In-Memory Databases

Manegold et al. published an extensive low-level cost model for database operators for in-memory databases [11]. Using their cost model, the authors estimate the cost for accesses to different levels in the memory hierarchy. They compare the effects of different memory access patterns to create building blocks that can be used to estimate the costs of query plan alternatives. In contrast to our comparatively simple approach, Manegold et al. can adjust their model to a given hardware setup using a calibrator tool.

Schwalb et al. published a cost model for estimating query costs for different physical column organizations (e.g., uncompressed or bit-packed columns, sorted or unsorted dictionaries, et cetera) [15]. In contrast to Manegold et al., who focus on join operators, Schwalb et al. compare scan and lookup operators on different column layouts. Furthermore, the authors focus on mixed workload with the additional evaluation of inserts into read-optimized data structures. However, similar to Manegold et al. the work by Schwalb et al. does not investigate more complex systems with highly concurrent mixed workloads, which falsify several assumptions made throughout this work.

6.2 Index Selection

Finkelstein et al. worked on the topic of index selection as early as 1988 [5]. Similar to our solution, they analyzed the workload queries to gather information about how tables and their attributes are accessed. Based on these access statistics and the execution frequencies of workload queries, the authors try to find an optimal index configuration.

Another tool that allows the analysis of existing indices is *AutoAdmin* by Chaudhuri et al. [1]. AutoAdmin aims to be a multi-purpose tool set to analyze currently deployed indices, assist the database administrator in index selection and also perform what-if analysis for hypothetical indices. The tool integrates into the Microsoft SQL Server and gathers information about the workload during run time. This information can then be used to assess the benefits of the current indices, propose new (better) indices and do what-if analyses for theoretical changes to the current index setup.

The index selection approach by Finkelstein et al. has a clear focus on the workload similar the tools proposed in this paper, however, they focus on indices that are about to be created instead of evaluating the ones that are already in place. AutoAdmin, on the other hand, is much closer to what we are trying to achieve and offers workload-driven analysis of indices that are currently in place. However, since AutoAdmin is tightly integrated into the SQL Server, it only allows live analysis and no offline analysis.

The aforementioned approaches as well as most other approaches in this field are designed for traditional disk-based row stores. And since the index selection for columnar in-memory database differs considerably in many cases, those approaches cannot be simply adapted by changing expected access latencies and block sizes.

7   Future Work

There are several additional aspects we want to cover with our index coefficient and the index cost score. One aspect is the inclusion of additional data structures and approaching new hardware technologies, such as non-volatile memory (NVM). Another aspect is a declarative language than could narrow the gap between application requirements and the database.

7.1   Additional Data Structures

Besides the bit-packed and (sorted) dictionary-encoded columns and the group-key indices, we want to include additional data structures. On the one side, there are several alternatives to store columns, e.g., uncompressed columns as used in HyPer [6] or run-length encoded columns [14]. Both approaches have a significant impact on the expected memory traffic for a column scan. On the other side, we want to incorporate additional indices into our cost model, e.g., block indices [14] and compressed group-key indices (e.g., using *Golomb* or *Simple9* compression as used in SAP HANA).

7.2   New Storage Technologies

Upcoming non-volatile memory (NVM) promises to provide a persistent and byte-addressable DRAM alternative with larger capacities than DRAM. With the expected capacity increase of 5× at a lower price point and an expected latency orders of magnitudes better than PCIe-connected devices [2], NVM is a natural fit for index cost considerations. At the moment, data access to other storage tiers than DRAM is considered as too slow for applications with low latencies requirements. This is even the case when data is stored on high performance PCIe-connected NVMe NAND flash drives. However, the expected performance of NVM adds a new layer to the cost model for indices that provide performance advantages but are currently too large to be stored in DRAM.

While it is simple to add complexity to a cost model, let us emphasize that we explicitly decided for a model yielding results that are simple to interpret. We think that the main challenge will not be to find a cost model incorporating NVM, additional data structures and more. The main challenge will be to find a simple, yet powerful, and applicable cost model.

7.3   Declarative Languages for Business Requirements

As of now, one of the main tasks of a database administrator is to ensure that the database meets business requirements. Such requirements include highly prioritized processes, such as end-of-quarter closings or service-level agreements (SLAs). As already mentioned, we think that a completely automated index selection approach is not feasible for real-world systems since the database is not aware of external application requirements. We think a declarative language could narrow this gap. Using such a language, the application developer can define the requirements of the application, e.g., limits for certain processes that need to finish within a defined time frame. The language can be parsed and interpreted by the database to automatically optimize itself within the given constraints.

8   Conclusion

We presented a workload-aware heuristic to evaluate indices of columnar in-memory databases. The proposed model is cost-aware. This is increasingly important for main memory-resident indices that have a direct impact on the DRAM footprint and thus on the overall costs of a system.

The index coefficient is a straightforward linear scalar helping database administrators to understand and interpret the efficiency of a particular index without requiring a deep understanding of the implementation details of the database system. The coefficient ranking allows making informed decisions about the benefits and costs of an index configuration. We think that the presented heuristic with its focus on memory traffic is simple, but yet powerful.

Furthermore, we presented our *index advisor cockpit* applied on a production enterprise system of a Global 2000 enterprise. Particularly interesting was – as soon as the actual workload was incorporated – the unexpected high number of apparently unused indices that exist in a standard ERP installation and that waste main memory without further index tiering concepts. Furthermore, we determined indices that are no longer necessary with columnar data structures.

References

1. Chaudhuri, S., Narasayya, V.R.: Autoadmin 'what-if' index analysis utility. In: Proceedings ACM SIGMOD International Conference on Management of Data, SIGMOD 1998, Seattle, Washington, USA, pp. 367–378 (1998)

2. Dulloor, S., Roy, A., Zhao, Z., Sundaram, N., Satish, N., Sankaran, R., Jackson, J., Schwan, K.: Data tiering in heterogeneous memory systems. In: Proceedings of the Eleventh European Conference on Computer Systems, EuroSys 2016, London, United Kingdom, pp. 15: 1–15: 16, 18–21 April 2016
3. Färber, F., May, N., Lehner, W., Große, P., Müller, I., Rauhe, H., Dees, J.: The SAP HANA database - an architecture overview. IEEE Data Eng. Bull. **35**(1), 28–33 (2012)
4. Faust, M., Schwalb, D., Krüger, J., Plattner, H.: Fast lookups for in-memory column stores: group-key indices, lookup and maintenance. In: International Workshop on Accelerating Data Management Systems Using Modern Processor and Storage Architectures - ADMS 2012, pp. 13–22 (2012)
5. Finkelstein, S.J., Schkolnick, M., Tiberio, P.: Physical database design for relational databases. ACM Trans. Database Syst. **13**(1), 91–128 (1988)
6. Funke, F., Kemper, A., Neumann, T.: Compacting transactional data in hybrid OLTP & OLAP databases. PVLDB **5**(11), 1424–1435 (2012)
7. Grund, M., Krüger, J., Plattner, H., Zeier, A., Cudré-Mauroux, P., Madden, S.: HYRISE - a main memory hybrid storage engine. PVLDB **4**(2), 105–116 (2010)
8. Kissinger, T., Kiefer, T., Schlegel, B., Habich, D., Molka, D., Lehner, W.: ERIS: a NUMA-aware in-memory storage engine for analytical workload. In: International Workshop on Accelerating Data Management Systems Using Modern Processor and Storage Architectures - ADMS 2014, pp. 74–85 (2014)
9. Lang, H., Mühlbauer, T., Funke, F., Boncz, P., Neumann, T., Kemper, A.: Data blocks: hybrid OLTP and OLAP on compressed storage using both vectorization and compilation. In: International Conference on Management of Data, SIGMOD 2016, San Francisco, CA, USA (2016)
10. Manegold, S., Boncz, P.A., Kersten, M.L.: Optimizing database architecture for the new bottleneck: memory access. VLDB J. **9**(3), 231–246 (2000)
11. Manegold, S., Boncz, P.A., Kersten, M.L.: Generic database cost models for hierarchical memory systems. In: Proceedings of 28th International Conference on Very Large Data Bases, VLDB 2002, pp. 191–202 (2002)
12. Papadomolakis, S., Ailamaki, A.: An integer linear programming approach to database design. In: ICDE 2007, Istanbul, Turkey, pp. 442–449, 15–20 April 2007
13. Plattner, H.: The impact of columnar in-memory databases on enterprise systems. PVLDB **7**(13), 1722–1729 (2014)
14. Plattner, H., Zeier, A.: In-Memory Data Management: An Inflection Point for Enterprise Applications, 1st edn. Springer, Heidelberg (2011)
15. Schwalb, D., Faust, M., Krueger, J., Plattner, H.: Physical column organization in in-memory column stores. In: Gao, H., Kim, J., Sakurai, Y. (eds.) DASFAA 2016. LNCS, vol. 9645, pp. 48–63. Springer, Heidelberg (2013). doi:10. 1007/978-3-642-37450-0_4

S4J - Integrating SQL into Java at Compiler-Level

Keven Richly(✉), Martin Lorenz, and Sebastian Oergel

Hasso Plattner Institute, University of Potsdam,
Prof.-Dr.-Helmert-Str. 2-3, 14482 Potsdam, Germany
{keven.richly,martin.lorenz,sebastian.oergel}@hpi.de
http://hpi.de

Abstract. Object-oriented languages and relational database systems dominate the design of modern enterprise information systems. However, their interoperability has caused problems ever since. In this paper, we present an approach to integrate SQL into the Java programming language. The integration is done at compiler level, making SQL a first-class citizen of the programming language, including object-awareness, providing validation possibilities that cover e.g. query correctness and type compatibility. In contrast to existing solutions, these validations are carried out during compilation. To evaluate our approach, we implemented a standard business process (Order-To-Pay) using Hibernate, JDBC, and S4J. We compare each implementation in terms of query performance, code size, and code complexity. The evaluation shows that the integration of SQL into Java allows to reduce code size and complexity while maintaining an equal or better performance compared to competitive approaches.

Keywords: SQL · Object-relational impedance mismatch · Object-oriented data model · Java · Compiler integration

1 Introduction

Modern information system designs are dominated by object-oriented (OO) languages and relational databases. Both technologies have been proven effective in their respective area. Especially for enterprise applications, OO concepts allow system architects to develop complex domain models, which can be used to discuss and verify application logic and system design with domain experts. Relational databases form the backbone of almost all enterprise application's persistence layer. Relational algebra, and its impersonation in form of SQL, allows the simple storage and retrieval of database records and provides functionality to express complex business logic, e.g. analytics, at the same time. However, using object-oriented programming languages and relational databases in the same project is problematic. In object-orientation, we deal with objects and classes whereas relational algebra uses relations. The term *object-relational impedance mismatch* became a synonym for the problems that arise from the

© Springer International Publishing Switzerland 2016
G. Dregvaite and R. Damasevicius (Eds.): ICIST 2016, CCIS 639, pp. 300–315, 2016.
DOI: 10.1007/978-3-319-46254-7_24

inter-operation of OO languages and relational databases [9, 10]. Over the years, different solutions have been proposed to bridge the gap. Probably the most paradigm-shifting idea is NoSQL databases, whose data structures and data access methods promise to be more suitable to OO languages. However, the adoption of NoSQL for the majority of enterprise applications is rather unlikely, due to the complex requirements of such enterprise systems [12, 18]. Accepting the premise of using a relational storage mechanism, the traditional answer to effectively solving the impedance mismatch is to slave one model into the terms and approach of the other. Such type of solutions can be categorized into three groups: call level interfaces (CLIs) [8], object-relational mapper (ORM), and integrated query languages. Section 2 will elaborate on each group in detail. Integrating a database language directly into object-oriented programming languages is the most difficult approach, because the navigational model of OO languages is somewhat reluctant to the declarative nature of a database query language such as SQL. However, in this paper we want to show that the effort is worth the while.

The integration of SQL into the syntax of an object-oriented programming language such as Java, allows to enforce object awareness and type checking, which reduces the possibility of runtime errors significantly. Furthermore, we are able to use objects as input and output of database queries, which relieves the developer from writing boilerplate code to map generic database result sets to domain objects. By integrating SQL standard syntax into Java syntax, it is possible to leverage the unrestrained functionality of the SQL interface, which allows to perform efficient database queries, even for complex analytics. We implemented a prototype, which is available as open source project on GitHub[1]. To evaluate our approach we implemented a standard business process (Order-To-Pay) with JDBC, Hibernate, and S4J. This business process contains a number of characteristic database access patterns, reaching from simple transaction processing e.g., storing an order, all the way to complex analytics e.g., an available to promise check. Each implementation is compared in terms of code complexity, code size, and query performance. The results of our evaluation show that our approach to integrate SQL as a first-class citizen to the Java programming language, reduces code size and code complexity, while at the same time maintaining equal or better performance. Furthermore, we illustrate how meta data, taken from the underlying database model enables type checking at compile time, which allows to detect errors before runtime.

2 Related Work

There are various approaches to solve the object-rational impedance mismatch at different levels of abstraction. Object-relational mappers, which provide an OO interfaces for relational databases, are one of the most recognized approaches. Hibernate[2] is the most popular open source persistency framework for Java

---

[1] https://github.com/sebastianoe/s4j.
[2] http://hibernate.org.

and provides three different approaches – direct SQL strings, the Hibernate Query Language and the Criteria API – to realize the mapping [1]. Because some SQL expressions do not have equivalent representations the Criteria API does not expose the full expressiveness of pure SQL, which leads to analogous auto-generated SQL statements. Also Hibernate introduces a large amount of complexity due to third-party libraries and usually a high amount of manual XML configuration. A big advantage of Hibernate is the possibility to map query results directly to objects. However, this assignment of the result happens in an unchecked way. The automatic generation at runtime and the corresponding evaluation of the user-defined mapping configuration add potential overhead, which directly influences the application runtime by performing additional operations like the query translation. Additionally, generated queries can require more complex or even unnecessary database operations or the transfer of more data. The active record pattern [2] wraps database tables and views into classes, which also implement the corresponding accessor methods. Accordingly, an object instance represents a single row in the table. Thus, the objects that the active record pattern spawns are by trend more oriented on a relational structure than arbitrary business objects that ORMs typically cope with. Language Integrated Query (LINQ) [16] is an extension of Microsoft's .NET framework that adds native data access capabilities. The LINQ to SQL data provider internally translates LINQ queries into real SQL queries. Since plain SQL syntax is not supported and LINQ only mimics a subset of SQL, a direct integration of SQL as a first-class citizen into the programming languages does not happen. The full power of SQL is not directly provided and for an application programmer, it can become difficult to predict, which parts are executed on the application layer and are not transformed into SQL.

The Advanced Business Application Programming (ABAP) language [13] is a proprietary programming language developed by SAP. A component of ABAP is Open SQL, which is a set of ABAP commands that can be mapped to SQL commands. Thereby, SQL can be considered to be directly integrated into the ABAP language as a first-class citizen. Apart from the possibility to handle database query results as cursor data in ABAP applications, the so-called "Persistency Service" manages the connection between ABAP objects and the underlying relational data. Java Database Connectivity (JDBC) is a data access technology for Java, which implements the Call Level Interface (CLI) specification [11]. JDBC provides a standardized runtime API to query and update data from within Java applications. All SQL queries are string objects that are constructed and used at runtime, which allows the construction of dynamic SQL queries. Nevertheless, the handling of queries as strings introduces a high error-proneness, as all database interactions are only evaluated at runtime. SQLJ is a former approach to embed directly SQL statements into Java [17]. Due to the embedding into the language and not only using SQL queries as strings, the language processor can already check the correctness of a statement against a database schema before runtime. However, SQLJ could not be established in modern Java versions. The main reason is that an additional preprocessor, which transforms the SQLJ code

into valid Java code before compilation, realizes the language integration. Due
to the required preprocessing step SQLJ is hardly supported by standard IDEs,
Java tools and debuggers. SQL statements cannot be dynamically built up and
are static, as the preprocessor transforms the statements into JDBC statements
with fixed SQL strings.

3 The S4J Approach

The analysis of the existing solutions for relational data access from within OO
applications has shown that there is a large variety of possible solutions available.
Especially the direct integration of SQL into OO languages shows a multitude of
different problems. This section presents S4J, a concept to directly integrate SQL
in Java. SQL is well suited to be processed in its raw form by database engines,
which can use their optimizers to tune the query execution internally, in order
to achieve the maximum performance. For that reason such a direct integration
of SQL into an OO language as a first-class citizen is quite promising. The
nesting into the language core and the corresponding compiler tools allow new
possibilities for type safety checks and boilerplate code reduction.

3.1 Design and Specification

One of the most important aspects for the specification is the fact that pure SQL
can be used inside the Java code, as the usage of another kind of query language
should be avoided. On a conceptual level, the underlying Java language grammar, which is processed by the compiler, needs to be extended. At least one new
keyword needs to be added to the language specification in order to signalize the
compiler that an SQL statement is following. Integrated SQL queries should be
considered as special kinds of *Expression* elements in the grammar. Syntactically,
using SQL queries as expressions allows developers to use the queries at all places
where expressions are allowed, according to the Java grammar specification [4].
The direct integration into the Java language core allows a strong coupling of
the existing and the new language components. Semantically, embedded SQL
values should be able to replace entire code blocks of JDBC code, including the
required boilerplate code. The actual SQL queries are passed directly as SQL
expressions in the code, the database connection information are assumed to be
passed as a compiler option or simple configuration file. Listing 1.1 provides an
examplary S4J code snippet of the evaluation application.

```
1   public static Result edit(long id) {
2       Customer customer = SQL[
3           SELECT * FROM Customer WHERE id = $id$];
4
5       Form<Customer> customerForm =
6           Form.form(Customer.class).fill(customer);
7
8       return ok(edit.render(customerForm));
9   }
```

Listing 1.1. Examplary S4J code

Read Queries. The result of a read query is expected to be automatically mapped to the receiving Java object. Thereby, a *SELECT* query should always return the respective SQL result in a Java-friendly format that allows e.g. a direct assignment to a variable of a normal Java type. Queries that fetch data from the database should be parameterizable, taking normal Java expressions as parameters. A decoupling between the query and the actual parameter values can strongly decrease code readability. The validation functionality is required in order to make sure that a query result is even assignable to a Java type based on the form of the SQL result. S4J supports the type-aware assignment to primitive types (integer, string, etc.), self-defined types (i.e. own classes with complex data structures), lists of the previous mentioned types, maps of primitive types and *ResultSet* objects (i.e. the JDBC standard result pointer type).

DML Queries. In contrast to the previously described *SELECT* queries, DML queries don't return a direct SQL result but manipulate existing data. A more important aspect for DML statements are parameters as they are the input for the data manipulation. Similar to the parameters for the *SELECT* queries, normal Java expressions should be usable as parameters. However, a shortcut version that directly uses objects as parameters was considered to be useful. Such a solution would require again a mapping between the object attributes and the required SQL columns. As only single-table DML queries are supported, a potential object hierarchy might be ignored using the automatic object provisioning.

3.2   Implementation Aspects

All S4J implementations have been developed based on the OpenJDK 7 system, which is available as open source software. Only the compiler was modified. The actual virtual machine java was not changed. Thus, compiled programs with embedded SQL statements can be expected to run on any standard-conforming Java VM without any additional changes.

Integration into the Javac Process. The main idea of the SQL integration is to analyze the embedded SQL queries at compile time and to perform required validations on them. Afterwards, the embedded SQL code will be internally transformed to valid Java code by replacing the relevant code sectors with standard JDBC database access code. This method allows generating byte code that is executable by any Java VM. However, the user can directly embed SQL statements into the language. The compiler performs the required validations and transformations transparently to the user without changing the actual SQL query. The Java compilation process consists of a series of different steps that are involved in the transformation process from **.java* source files into byte code **.class* files, visualized in Fig. 1. Concerning the S4J implementation, some of these phases have to be modified. The most relevant modifications involve parsing phase and attribution phase. For the parsing phase, new keywords were

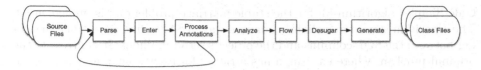

Fig. 1. javac compilation phases

added to the lexer and the parser was extended to include the S4J statements into the AST. In the attribution phase we added two additional steps. The first step is a type validation (i.e. make sure that the expected type and the S4J return type match). After a successful validation, the second new step is executed which generate the code to replaces the S4J statements by actual, checked standard Java code. Note that most of the other phases require some slight modifications but these are not directly relevant for the applied techniques.

Mapping of Query Results. A mapping of the query results is always necessary when the SQL query is a *SELECT* query and the expected return type is a complex object and not a primitive, respectively a list of primitives or a map. In these cases, the SQL result has potentially a multitude of result columns. A multiplicity of rows in the result is not relevant for a mapping as this only affects the question if the result represents a single instance or a list of those. Usually objects have multiple members of which some are publicly accessible. Objects, respectively their classes which store the SQL query results as a shortcut to avoid using a *ResultSet* cursor, generally don't have to be specially configured. This is a major difference to e.g. Hibernate where the models have to be previously defined via annotations or even via an explicit XML file. Using S4J, potentially every object can be used, as long as its structure follows the default Java Bean conventions [7]. As S4J follows a convention over configuration approach, the mapping is based on naming conventions. For a SQL result, all contained columns are considered to be part of the mapping. As the SQL result values should become part of the expected object, the public setter methods of the object are considered to be the target of the mapping. Thus, an ideal mapping links every SQL result column to an appropriate public setter method of the object. The setter method names are normalized in the further matching process to be comparable to the column names. This normalization includes the removal of the prefix of the method name. Further comparisons are handled in a case insensitive way.

As a naive approach, a simple name-based mapping would suffice. However, there are more criteria to respect for a more intelligent mapping. One is that the types of the columns match to the parameter types of the setter methods. Whereas the type information of the setter parameters are already available in the compilation phase of the matching, the types of the SQL columns have to be determined explicitly. To allow a more sophisticated matching including the application of specific rules and the support for nested objects, the

Gale-Shapley algorithm [3] for the stable marriage problem [5] is implemented. The algorithm is used in a slightly adapted way in S4J to find an optimal matching between the SQL columns and the object's setter methods. In contrast to the original problem, where each man has a rating for each woman and vice versa, the rating or votings are shared in the current case. This means that there is a rating for each potential pair. For each potential combination of columns and setters, an explicit rating is calculated. This is done by a *Voter* class, which accumulates potentially weighted votes that are given based on certain criteria. If e.g. the names of the setter and the columns are equal, a certain amount of votes is added to the final result. In contrast, if the types are incompatible, the final voting is automatically 0. Such a voting system should also include more complex conditions, e.g. for nested objects. If an object includes a property *id* and a reference to a nested object of another type, and this type also has an attribute with the name *id*, a column with the name *id* could potentially not be assigned unambiguously. However, as the compiler usually knows the base table or even the original table of a column (see Sect. 3.2), an additional criterion that considers the class and the table names can be used.

Using such criteria, a matrix that consists of votings for object setters and columns is created. The Gale-Shapley algorithm can then be used to calculate an optimal mapping. If the final mapping contains combinations with a rating of zero votings, these combinations are not considered for the final matching. Furthermore, the SQL query is considered to be incompatible to the expected type, if a mapping is empty. Often, the number of columns does not match the number of setter methods. In these cases, virtual dummy setters or columns are considered for the algorithm. Such dummy objects always get a rating of zero and are not included in the final matching. Introducing such virtual dummy setters or columns avoids having to cope with unequal sets. However, there are proposed solutions for this problem [15]. In case that a mapping is not successful due to e.g. non-matching or unknown column names, the developer can enforce a successful mapping by aliasing the corresponding column. Finally, the mapping algorithm (Fig. 2) provides a set of matching combinations of columns to be able to assign the correct values to the corresponding object members in the code generation. For the developer, this mapping seems to happen transparently. If no valid matching can be determined, the compilation fails.

SQL Parsing. By now, the SQL queries were only treated as raw strings. However, to further analyze these queries, they need to be parsed. In the S4J implementation, this is done by the *JSql* library[3] at compilation time. The compiler remains fully portable as the library is included in the final javac executable. The first task of the SQL parser is to validate the correctness of the SQL query. Although the parser supports a wide range of SQL dialects, obviously wrong queries lead to a failing compilation. Thus, erroneous SQL queries can be recognized early. The usage of shortcuts with e.g. objects as parameters requires a slight modification of the parser, respectively its underlying grammar, as these

---

[3] https://github.com/JSQLParser/JSqlParser.

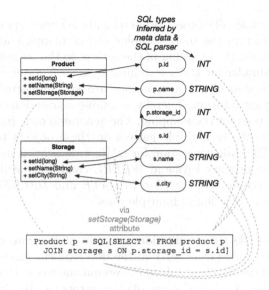

Fig. 2. S4J mapping of columns to attributes

shortcut constructs are not valid standard SQL. Additionally, parsing the query and its potential sub-queries allow a detailed, potentially recursive exploration of the final top-level query projections. Walking up from the deepest to the topmost recursion level, the base table, potential aliases and the types of the projections can be determined. To make this full query exploration possible, an additional data source is required, which allows the compiler to get meta data about the database's tables. Thus, even a star projection on a table can be resolved by looking up all the column names that the table includes. The types of the columns can be determined, which is essential for the mapping and validation processes. This additional information is stored by the S4J implementation "meta data repository" component. In order to get the database schema information, the compiler queries the database meta information during the compilation.

Parameterization. As previously mentioned, *SELECT* queries can be parameterized by directly inserting Java expressions into the query using a special delimiter. This parameter integration leads to a strong coupling between the parameters and the actual query, making the query potentially easier to understand. During the transformation phase, the parameter expressions are extracted and transformed into JDBC parameters. As the underlying database system is very generous with the parameter type, no further validation is performed. However, DML statement parameters require much more validations, as the parameters are the main data input source. These additionally required validations include e.g. a check if the parameters fill all key columns for an *INSERT* statement. At first, the required object content needs to be unwrapped. This happens based on the required columns, as e.g. *INSERT* queries can require only a subset of columns of one table. The object properties are accessed via bean-style getter methods. In contrast to the more complex object mapping algorithm for the query result matching, the mapping of the getters to the corresponding affected columns is much simpler for DML statements. As such statements usually only affect one table, nested object associations are not supported in the current version of the implementation. Thereby, a simple convention-oriented naming-based approach is used for the mapping. The generated code replaces the object parameters by potentially multiple getters on these objects to again retrieve primitive values. The code generation for DML statements is more complex and touches aspects like primary keys and *WHERE* conditions, which are automatically added with the key columns for *UPDATE* and *DELETE* statements to prevent an update or deletion of multiple rows.

Validations. Compile time validations are one of the core concepts of S4J. Uncovering SQL or code errors early in the development process can lead to a reduced effort and finally even reduced development costs. Due to the parsing of the queries during the compilation, obvious errors can be already recognized in this phase. More complex validations consider the typing and the embedding of the SQL queries with the help of the database meta data. Those validations mainly happen when the result of a query should be checked for its compatibility to the expected type. Thus, the validator always requires an expected Java type – either implicitly or explicitly provided – and an SQL query. Depending on the expected type, different kinds of validations are required. For primitive types and lists of those, the SQL result needs exactly one column and the column type must be compatible to the expected type. For more complex objects, the results of the mapping is taken as the primary validation criterion.

Maps as expected type get a special validation. In order for an SQL result to be compatible with a *Map* type, the SQL result must contain exactly two columns, which have to be compatible to the key and the value types of the map. As an additional criterion, the first column, which is mapped to the map's key, has to be guaranteed to be unique. Otherwise, the map cannot be a well-suited representation for the result. To validate that the first column only contains unique values, the column has to be explicitly declared as unique or be a primary column, or it must be the only column in a potential *GROUP BY* clause. DML-related validations are also based on the mappings that were performed before the actual validation, for complex object parameters. If no mapping was found, the object is considered to be incompatible.

4   Evaluation

Section 3 described requirements, design, and implementation of the S4J-approach. We explained how to enforce type-checking and object-awareness by integrating SQL syntax into the standard Java compiler. We compare S4J against a CLI (JDBC) and an ORM (Hibernate) implementation of a business process, called Order-To-Pay (OTP). The business process is depicted in Fig. 3.

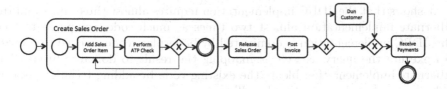

Fig. 3. BPMN Diagram of the Order-To-Pay Process

To reproduce our experiments and to understand the implementation details of that process, we made the implementation accessible on GitHub[4]. We chose this business process because its logic is fairly easy to understand and its activities include transactional as well as analytical aspects. Thus, an implementation of that process covers a variety of different database requests, ranging from simple entity lookup and storage to complex analytics, such as an available to promise check or dunning run. Based on these characteristic database requests, we compare each implementation based on the criteria code size, code complexity, and query performance. We briefly elaborate on each of the chosen criteria in Subsects. 4.1 through 4.3.

4.1   Code Size

We decided to incorporate code size as a criterion, because we wanted to understand how much code is needed to express a certain database access pattern in a particular technology. The unit, we measure code size is lines of code (LOC). We acknowledge the criticism that LOC may be inappropriate, because formatting preferences differ among programming languages and developers. However, we use Java as a single programming language and committed to reasonable formatting guidelines for all three implementations to the best of our knowledge. Furthermore, we only measure the code size of controller classes that contained database access code (for the Hibernate implementation, we disregard any configuration related code artifacts, i.e. XML-files or annotations). Table 1 contains the results of our measurements.

Table 1. Code Size Comparison in Lines of Code (LOC)

Controller	JDBC	Hibernate	S4J
CustomerController	203	101	56
InvoiceController	252	187	113
ProductController	126	67	38
SalesOrderControler	372	264	133
Overall	953	619	340

---

[4] https://github.com/sebastianoe/s4j-otp-demo.

It shows that the JDBC implementation requires almost three times and the Hibernate implementation almost two times as much code, compared to S4J. The JDBC implementation is dominated by boilerplate code, needed to prepare and execute the query as well as mapping the result to domain objects. The Hibernate implementation bloats the existing code by adding technical aspects such as session and transaction handling.

4.2   Code Complexity

Complementary to code size, we measure the code complexity of the different implementations. We chose two metrics to cover different aspects of code complexity. For one, we use the *cyclomatic complexity* [14] to understand the influence of the technology on the control flow of the program. Additionally, we use the Halstead metrics [6] to derive complexity based on the use of operands and operators. Table 2 shows a comparison of the cyclomatic complexity of two methods of the customer controller class. Method one represents a simple database look-up to retrieve a customer object from the database. Method two represents an implementation of days sales outstanding (DSO), which is an analytic function, commonly used by companies to calculate the average collection period of their customers. We argue that these two methods are suitable representatives for the different database access patterns that we observe in this business process.

Table 2. Comparison of Cyclomatic Complexity

Method	JDBC	Hibernate	S4J
CustomerLookup	3	1	1
DSO	3	2	1

The Halstead metrics that we measure include Halstead Length, Halstead Vocabulary, Halstead Volume, Halstead Difficulty, and Halstead Effort. For the Java programming language, the definition of what is an operand and what is an operator is ambiguous in the context of Halstead metrics. We consider identifiers, which are not reserved words (variable names, etc.), type names (int, float, etc.), and literals as operands. Consequently, we classify reserved keywords (for, return, etc.), operators ($+$, $-$, etc.), and punctuation signs (., ;, etc.) as operators. Table 3 presents an overview of the calculations of the Halstead metrics for the two methods CustomerLookup and DSO. Although Hibernate offers an OO navigational interface to define database queries, the expressiveness to define efficient queries is limited. Especially complex analytical queries are hard to express, relying solely on Hibernate's Criteria API. Also, we experienced the problem that the SQL, Hibernate generated from our Criteria API code, showed insufficient performance, especially for complex queries. That is why we decided to implement the DSO calculation using Hibernate's ability to

Table 3. Halstead Metrics for CustomerLookup and Days-Sales-Outstanding

Method	CustomerLookup			Days-Sales-Outstanding		
	JDBC	Hibernate	S4J	JDBC	Hibernate	S4J
Distinct no. operators	36	19	7	35	29	8
Total no. of operators	13	7	8	12	8	6
Distinct no. operands	61	23	8	57	48	13
Total no. of operands	70	27	10	62	52	14
Program vocabulary n	49	26	15	47	37	14
Program Length N	131	50	15	119	100	27
Halstead Length ^N	234.22	100.36	43.65	222.54	164.88	39.51
Volume V	735.53	235.02	70.32	661	520.95	102.8
Difficulty D	96.92	36.64	4.38	90.42	94.25	9.33
Effort E	71,289.54	8,611.88	307.67	59,765.06	49,099.10	959.45

execute standard SQL query, which is passed to the Hibernate framework as a string. So for Table 3, all metrics measurements for Hibernate are based on that design decision.

4.3 Query Performance

Following code size and code complexity, we also compare all three technologies in terms of performance. We distinguish between compile performance and runtime performance, whereas compile time tells us how long it takes to build the different code artifacts and runtime shows how much time the actual execution of a peace of code needs. It is rather uncommon to measure compile time, because in most cases the life cycle of a productive system starts with a single compilation and runs from that point until a new release is shipped. However, since our S4J approach interferes considerably into the inner workings of the JAVAC compiler,

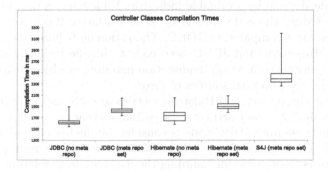

Fig. 4. Comparison of Compilation Performance

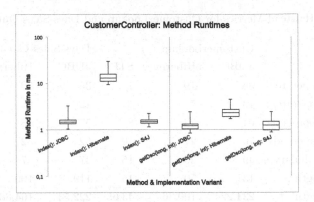

Fig. 5. Comparison of Runtime Performance

we incorporated this measure. Figure 4 depicts our measurements for compilation performance for all controller classes. We restricted our measurements to these classes, because only there, we use the S4J coding, which could impact the compile time performance. Complementary to compilation performance, we measure the actual query performance. To be consistent with the evaluation of code size and code complexity, we measured the same two methods (Customer-Lookup and DSO), using black box testing, whereas database and client program executed on the same machine, to minimize the impact of network latency on the measurements. Figure 5 depicts our measurements.

4.4   Discussion

In this project, we aimed at understanding the impact of the different database access technologies on non-functional requirements maintainability and performance. Maintainability is directly related to the size and the complexity of code artifacts. Although code size is only a weak indicator for complexity, we argue that based on our premise to commit to reasonable and consistent formatting rules and that all three technologies are evaluated within the same programming language, code size can be a valuable indicator. Table 1 shows that working with S4J allow to reduce the code volume by almost a factor 2 compared to Hibernate and a factor 3 compared to JDBC. The rationale behind that observation is that, both Hibernate and JDBC need code to handle technical aspects, e.g. session management, connection, transaction handling or object mapping. Both types of coding are potential sources of error.

Cyclomatic complexity and Halstead metrics are stronger indicators for the degree of complexity of code artifacts. Table 2 shows that control flow complexity of code artifacts running JDBC code is considerably higher compared to Hibernate and S4J. The rationale here is that JDBC queries simply return result sets. The developer is responsible for handling the mapping from relations to domain objects and possible data type conversions, which is error-prone and adds complexity. The control flow complexity of Hibernate is smaller compared to JDBC.

However, that is not entirely true. Hibernate exposes an OO navigational interface to access a databases. Especially analytics, potentially using complex joins are difficult to express using such an interface. Hibernate, similar to most ORMs provides additional interfaces such as Hibernate Query Language or access to the native JDBC CLI interface. We used this fallback solution for the implementation of the DSO method, which is why we see a higher cyclometic complexity for the calculation of the DSO in Hibernate.

Probably the most interesting set of complexity metrics are Halstead metrics. Table 3 shows a clear slope from JDBC down to S4J. We can see that S4J outperforms JDBC and Hibernate by far. We consider that observation as a clear indicator that the integration of SQL as a first-class citizen to the programming language, reduces program complexity significantly. Hibernate outperforms JDBC mainly, because its automated mapping process and navigational query definition interface abstracts from technical aspects of the underlying database, which allows to produces more maintainable code. However, especially complex analytical queries require the expressive power of SQL to define efficient database access. In those situations the features of Hibernate are bypassed. The effect can be seen in Table 3, where the complexity difference between JDBC and Hibernate is only marginal. Looking at the compile time performance, we can see a clear impact for the S4J approach. Collecting meta data from the repository increases compilation time around 22 %. This increase mainly results from the intensive data type checking, which is executed during compilation time. However, we consider this increase reasonable, given the fact that the gain of type safe query definition and automated mapping largely outweighs the penalty of a one time compilation phase. More interesting is the question of runtime performance. Figure 5 shows that JDBC and S4J are almost equal in query execution time. Hibernate in contrast falls short in terms of query performance. We see two reasons for that. First of all, the automated mapping and the convenience of an OO database interface do not come for free. The framework's code stack is deep and the number of runtime checks to determine possible mappings result in a performance decrease. The second reason is the navigational interface. Accessing the database is convenient, but it also introduces an indirection in the query definition process. Depending on the quality of the query translation, it is more than questionable that the ORM can guarantee an optimal declarative equivalent to the query that was defined with Hibernate's Criteria API. The impact of that problem might be small for simple queries, but it degrades with increasing complexity of the database access pattern. Many ORMs try to dilute this problem by introducing caches, buffers and complex fetching strategies, but the correct configuration of them is non-trivial and requires a deeper understanding of the overall query workload, data and domain object usage.

5 Future Work

The prototype that we present in this paper was developed to gain insights and an understanding, about the impact of integrating SQL into a modern object-oriented programming language like Java. There are still open questions and room for improvements. One drawback of our current solution is its inability to create SQL queries dynamically during runtime. It is common practice to construct and adapt SQL queries depending on programming parameters. Control flow structures a parameter values determine the final structure of the query that is issued to the database. We currently work on introducing query objects, which represent individual parts of a query. These query objects can be combined dynamically during runtime and type-checked during compile time.

6 Summary

In this paper, we propose a compiler-level integration of SQL into Java. Our approach enforces type checking and object awareness for database queries, which increases the robustness, readability, and efficiency of the database access layer and consequently of the overall application. The S4J approach was evaluated by comparing it with representatives of the group of call level interfaces (JDBC) and object relational mappers (Hibernate). The evaluation shows that the integration of the database access interface directly into the programming language allows to decrease code size and code complexity, while maintaining an equal or better performance. Finally, we discussed limitations and possible extensions of our approach. The project itself as well as the implementation of the OTP process are available as open source on GitHub and can be freely accessed to investigate the S4J implementation or to reproduce our experiments.

References

1. Bauer, C., King, G.: Java Persistance with Hibernate. Dreamtech Press (2006)
2. Fowler, M.: Patterns of Enterprise Application Architecture. Addison-Wesley Longman Publishing Co., Inc., Boston (2002)
3. Gale, D., Shapley, L.S.: College admissions and the stability of marriage. Am. Math. Monthly **69**(1), 9 (1962)
4. Gosling, J., Joy, B., Steele, G., Bracha, G.: The Java Language Specification, 3rd edn. Addison-Wesley Professional, Reading (2005)
5. Gusfield, D., Irving, R.W.: The Stable Marriage Problem: Structure and Algorithms, vol. 54. MIT Press, Cambridge (1989)
6. Halstead, M.H.: Elements of Software Science (Operating and Programming Systems Series). Elsevier Science Inc., New York (1977)
7. Hamilton, G.: JavaBeans, vol. 1. Sun Microsystems, Mountain View (1997)
8. Hamilton, J.: Java and jdbc: tools supporting data-centric business application development. In: Proceedings of the Fourth International Symposium on Assessment of Software Tools, pp. 121–138, May 1996
9. Ireland, C., Bowers, D., Newton, M., Waugh, K.: A classification of object-relational impedance mismatch. In: First International Conference on Advances in Databases, Knowledge, and Data Applications, 2009, pp. 36–43. IEEE (2009)
10. Keller, A.M., Jensen, R., Agarwal, S.: Persistence software: bridging object-oriented programming and relational databases (1993)
11. X/Open Company Limited: Data management: SQL call level interface (CLI) (1995)

12. Lombardo, S., Di Nitto, E., Ardagna, D.: Issues in handling complex data structures with nosql databases. In: 14th International Symposium on Symbolic and Numeric Algorithms for Scientific Computing, 2012, pp. 443–448. IEEE (2012)
13. Matzke, B.: ABAP: die Programmiersprache des SAP-Systems R/3. Pearson Deutschland GmbH (2002)
14. McCabe, T.: A complexity measure. IEEE Trans. Softw. Eng. **SE–2**(4), 308–320 (1976)
15. McVitie, D.G., Wilson, L.: Stable Marriage Assignment for Unequal Sets, pp. 295–309 (1970)
16. Meijer, E., Beckman, B., Bierman, G.: LINQ: reconciling object, relations and xml in the .NET framework. In: Proceedings of the 2006 ACM SIGMOD international conference on Management of data, p. 706. ACM (2006)
17. Melton, J., Eisenberg, A.: Understanding SQL and Java Together: a Guide to SQLJ, JDBC, and Related Technologies. Morgan Kaufmann, San Francisco (2000)
18. Mohan, C.: History repeats itself: sensible and NonsenSQL aspects of the NoSQL hoopla. In: Proceedings of the 16th International Conference on Extending Database Technology, pp. 11–16. ACM (2013)

Software Engineering: Special Session on Intelligent Systems and Software Engineering Advances

A New Estimator of the Mahalanobis Distance and its Application to Classification Error Rate Estimation

Mindaugas Gvardinskas[(✉)]

Department of System Analysis, Vytautas Magnus University,
Vileikos Street 8, 44404 Kaunas, Lithuania
m.gvardinskas@if.vdu.lt

Abstract. A well known category of classification error rate estimators is so called parametric error rate estimators. These estimators are typically expressed as functions of the training sample size, the dimensionality of the observation vector and the Mahalanobis distance between the classes. However, all parametric classification error rate estimators are biased and the main source of this bias is the estimate of the Mahalanobis distance. In this paper we propose a new Mahalanobis distance estimation method that is designed for use in parametric classification error rate estimators. Experiments with real world and synthetic data sets show that new estimator helps to reduce the bias of the most common parametric classification error rate estimators. Additionally, non-parametric classification error rate estimators, such as resubstitution, repeated 10-fold cross-validation and leave-one-out are outperformed (in terms of root-mean-square error) by parametric estimators that use new estimates of the Mahalanobis distance.

Keywords: Error estimation · Classification · Resubstitution · Cross-validation · Mahalanobis distance

1 Introduction

Conditional error rate is one of the most important characteristic of any classification rule. However, exact calculation of the conditional error rate requires prior knowledge about the underlying probability distribution, induction algorithm and sample size. In most cases, this information is unavailable and therefore classification error rate estimator must be used. A well known category of error estimation techniques is so called parametric classification error rate estimators. These estimators are typically designed for statistical classification techniques and are expressed as functions of the training sample size, the dimensionality of the observation vector and the Mahalanobis distance between the classes. A number of parametric error rate estimators have been proposed and evaluated over the years, mainly under the assumption of a homoscedastic (equal covariance matrices) normal model for the class-conditional distributions [11, 13, 14]. However, all parametric error rate estimators are highly biased and the main source of this bias is the estimate of Mahalanobis distance [11, 13]. In an attempt to remedy this problem investigators have proposed asymptotically unbiased estimate of the

© Springer International Publishing Switzerland 2016
G. Dregvaite and R. Damasevicius (Eds.): ICIST 2016, CCIS 639, pp. 319–331, 2016.
DOI: 10.1007/978-3-319-46254-7_25

Mahalanobis distance [11]. However, its effectiveness is limited, especially in small sample settings [13].

In this paper we propose a new Mahalanobis distance estimation method that is designed for use in parametric classification error rate estimators.

This paper is organized as follows. Section 2 presents basic definitions used throughout the paper and also, most common classification error rate estimation techniques. The new method is introduced in Sect. 3. Section 4 presents the results of our simulation study. Section 5 contains concluding remarks.

2 Methods Investigated

2.1 Basic Definitions

Consider two category classification problem where class label $y \in \{0, 1\}$, feature vector $\mathbf{x} \in R^n$ and a classifier is a function $f : R^n \rightarrow \{0, 1\}$. An induction algorithm builds a classifier from a set of $N = N_1 + N_2$ independent observations $D_N = \{(\mathbf{x}_1, y_1), \ldots, (\mathbf{x}_N, y_N)\}$ drawn from some distribution T. Formaly, it is a mapping $g : \{R^n \times \{0, 1\}\}^N \times R^n \rightarrow \{0, 1\}$. Here N_1 is the number of observations from the first class and N_2 is the number of observations from the second class. The performance of a classifier is measured by conditional probability of misclassification (conditional PMC):

$$\varepsilon_N = P(g(D_N, \mathbf{x}) \neq y) \tag{1}$$

This error is conditioned on one particular training set D_N and induction algorithm g. Another error rate is Bayes PMC. It is the minimum possible error rate which would result given complete knowledge of the class distributions. For the two category case Bayes error rate can be expressed as:

$$\varepsilon_{Bayes} = \int \min\{P_1 p_1(x), P_2 p_2(x)\} d\mathbf{x} \tag{2}$$

where P_1, P_2 are class prior probabilities and $p_1(x)$, $p_2(x)$ are class-conditional densities.

2.2 Fisher Linear Classifier

Fisher linear classifier is a well known and widely used statistical classification technique [3, 4, 6–8]. This classification rule is based on Anderson's W statistic, which can be defined as [13]:

$$W(\mathbf{x}) = \mathbf{V}^T \mathbf{x} + v_0 \tag{3}$$

where

$$\mathbf{V} = \hat{\Sigma}^{-1}(\hat{\mathbf{M}}_1 - \hat{\mathbf{M}}_2), \tag{4}$$

$$v_0 = -\frac{1}{2}(\hat{\mathbf{M}}_1 + \hat{\mathbf{M}}_2)^T \mathbf{V} \tag{5}$$

here $\hat{\Sigma}$ is a sample estimate of a common covariance matrix and $\hat{\Sigma}^{-1}$ is inverse of $\hat{\Sigma}$, $\hat{\mathbf{M}}_1$ and $\hat{\mathbf{M}}_2$ are the estimates of class mean vectors. The allocation rule is the following: allocate a new observation x to class 1 if

$$W(\mathbf{x}) > c \tag{6}$$

and to class 0, otherwise, where c is defined as $c = \ln\frac{P_1}{P_2}$.

2.3   The *L* and *LS* Methods

Both, *L* and *LS* methods are based on Lachenburch's approximations of expected classification error rate of the Fisher linear classifier. The *L* estimator is given by [11]

$$\hat{\varepsilon}_N^{(L)} = P_1\Phi\left\{-\frac{\frac{a_1}{2}\left(\hat{\delta}^2 - \frac{n(N_2-N_1)}{N_1N_2}\right)}{\sqrt{a_2\left(\hat{\delta}^2 + \frac{n(N_2+N_1)}{N_1N_2}\right)}}\right\} + P_2\Phi\left\{-\frac{\frac{a_1}{2}\left(\hat{\delta}^2 - \frac{n(N_1-N_2)}{N_1N_2}\right)}{\sqrt{a_2\left(\hat{\delta}^2 + \frac{n(N_2+N_1)}{N_1N_2}\right)}}\right\} \tag{7}$$

where

$$a_1 = \frac{N-2}{N-n-3} \tag{8}$$

$$a_2 = \frac{(N-3)(N-2)^2}{(N-n-2)(N-n-3)(N-n-5)} \tag{9}$$

Here Φ is a standard Gaussian cumulative distribution function and $\hat{\delta} = \sqrt{(\hat{\mathbf{M}}_1 - \hat{\mathbf{M}}_2)^T\hat{\Sigma}^{-1}(\hat{\mathbf{M}}_1 - \hat{\mathbf{M}}_2)}$ is an estimate of Mahalanobis distance δ. An estimate of the Mahalanobis distance $\hat{\delta}$ used in *L* estimator overestimates true Mahalanobis distance and this increases the bias of the above mentioned parametric error rate estimator. Corrected estimate of the Mahalanobis distance δ is given by [11]

$$\hat{\delta}_{DS} = \sqrt{\frac{N-n-3}{N-2}}\hat{\delta} \tag{10}$$

and corrected L estimator is obtained by replacing $\hat{\delta}$ with $\hat{\delta}_{DS}$. Comparative studies show that the bias of LS estimator is better than the bias of L estimator, however, L estimator is less variable [11].

2.4 The O and OS Methods

Okamoto's O estimator is based on theoretical expressions of expected classification error rate of the Fisher linear classifier and can be expressed as [19]

$$\hat{\varepsilon}_N^{(O)} = P_1\left(\Phi\{u\} + \phi\{u\}(\frac{a_1}{N_1} + \frac{a_2}{N_2} + \frac{a_3}{N-2})\right) + P_2\left(\Phi\{u\} + \phi\{u\}(\frac{a_2}{N_1} + \frac{a_1}{N_2} + \frac{a_3}{N-2})\right)$$

(11)

where

$$u = -\frac{\hat{\delta}}{2}$$

(12)

$$a_1 = -\frac{\hat{\delta}^{-2}}{2}\left(u^3 + (n-3)u - n\hat{\delta}\right)$$

(13)

$$a_2 = -\frac{\hat{\delta}^{-2}}{2}\left(u^3 + 2\hat{\delta}u^2 + \left(n - 3 + \hat{\delta}^2\right)u + (n-2)\hat{\delta}\right)$$

(14)

$$a_3 = -\frac{1}{4}\left(4u^3 + 4\hat{\delta}u^2 + \left(6n - 6 + \hat{\delta}^2\right)u + 2(n-1)\hat{\delta}\right)$$

(15)

The OS method is obtained by replacing $\hat{\delta}$ with $\hat{\delta}_{DS}$. It is known that O and OS methods have low variance, but large bias [11].

2.5 Deev's Parametric Classification Error Rate Estimators

Similar to most other parametric classification error rate estimators, Deev's estimators are based on theoretical expressions of expected error rate of the Fisher linear classifier. Deev's parametric classification error rate estimator can be expressed as [14]

$$\hat{\varepsilon}_N^{(DE)} = P_1\Phi\left\{-\frac{\hat{\delta}^2 - \lambda_1 + \lambda_2}{2\sqrt{\left(\hat{\delta}^2 + \lambda_1 + \lambda_2\right)\frac{N_1+N_2}{N_1+N_2-n}}}\right\} + P_2\Phi\left\{-\frac{\hat{\delta}^2 + \lambda_1 - \lambda_2}{2\sqrt{\left(\hat{\delta}^2 + \lambda_1 + \lambda_2\right)\frac{N_1+N_2}{N_1+N_2-n}}}\right\}$$

(16)

where $\lambda_1 = \frac{n}{N_1}$, $\lambda_2 = \frac{n}{N_2}$.

Corrected Deev's parametric classification error rate estimator is obtained by replacing $\hat{\delta}$ with $\hat{\delta}_{DS}$.

2.6   Resubstitution

Another commonly used error rate estimator, called the resubstitution estimator or the apparent error rate estimator was first proposed by Smith [17]. In this method, the whole data set is used as the training set and then reused as the test set. The resubstitution estimated error is defined as

$$\hat{\varepsilon}_N^{(R)} = \frac{1}{N} \sum_{i=1}^{N} |g(D_N, \mathbf{x}_i) - y_i| \qquad (17)$$

This method is known to have high bias, but low variance [2, 15].

2.7   Cross-Validation

It is one of the best known non-parametric classification error rate estimators. In k-fold cross-validation, the data set is randomly partitioned into k subsets of approximately equal size. Each subset is used as a test set and the remaining k-1 subsets are used as the training set. The cross-validation error estimate is defined as

$$\hat{\varepsilon}_N^{(CV)} = \frac{1}{N} \sum_{i=1}^{k} \sum_{j=1 \wedge (\mathbf{x}_j, y_j) \in D_i}^{N} |g(D_N \backslash D_i, \mathbf{x}_j) - y_j| \qquad (18)$$

where D_i is the i-th fold of the data set D_N, k is the number of folds and N is the size of D_N. Contrary to parametric classification error rate estimators, most variations of cross-validation have low bias [2, 10]. However, the main problem of cross-validation estimators is high variance [2].

2.8   Performance of Error Estimators

There are many measures of performance of an error estimator $\hat{\varepsilon}_N$, however, most popular measures are bias, deviation variance and root-mean-square error (RMS) [2, 5, 16]

$$Bias[\hat{\varepsilon}_N] = E[\hat{\varepsilon}_N] - E[\varepsilon_N] \qquad (19)$$

$$Var_{dev}[\hat{\varepsilon}_N] = Var(\hat{\varepsilon}_N - \varepsilon_N) = Var(\hat{\varepsilon}_N) + Var(\varepsilon_N) - 2Cov(\hat{\varepsilon}_N, \varepsilon_N) \qquad (20)$$

$$RMS[\hat{\varepsilon}_N] = \sqrt{E[(\varepsilon_N - \hat{\varepsilon}_N)^2]} = \sqrt{E[\varepsilon_N^2] + E[\hat{\varepsilon}_N^2] - 2E[\varepsilon_N \hat{\varepsilon}_N]} \qquad (21)$$

The bias measures whether, on average, the estimator overestimates or underestimates true conditional PMC, while deviation variance measures the variability of the estimator. Finally, root-mean-square error combines both, bias and the deviation variance into a single metric.

3 Proposed Method

As we have mentioned before, biased estimate of Mahalanobis distance can negatively affect the estimates of parametric classification error rate estimators. This situation can be improved by finding the unbiased estimate of Mahalanobis distance.

For the homoscedastic normal model for two classes with equal prior probabilities, Bayes error is given by [13]

$$\varepsilon_{Bayes} \approx \Phi\left\{-\frac{\delta}{2}\right\} \tag{22}$$

When true Bayes error is known, the unknown δ can be found from Eq. (22). However, in most cases, this error is also unknown. In order to find estimate of the Bayes error rate, we can form so-called combined classification error rate estimator [9, 16, 18]

$$\hat{\varepsilon}_{Bayes} = \omega\,\hat{\varepsilon}_N^{(1)} + (1-\omega)\,\hat{\varepsilon}_N^{(2)} \tag{23}$$

where $\hat{\varepsilon}_N^{(1)}$ and $\hat{\varepsilon}_N^{(2)}$ are error estimates, $\hat{\varepsilon}_N^{(1)} > \varepsilon_{Bayes}$, $\hat{\varepsilon}_N^{(2)} < \varepsilon_{Bayes}$ and $0 \le \omega \le 1$. Then, unbiased combined Bayes error rate estimator can be expressed as

$$Bias[\hat{\varepsilon}_{Bayes}] = \omega\,E[\hat{\varepsilon}_N^{(1)}] + (1-\omega)\,E[\hat{\varepsilon}_N^{(2)}] - \varepsilon_{Bayes} = 0 \tag{24}$$

Now, assume that estimator $\hat{\varepsilon}_N^{(1)}$ is repeated k-fold cross-validation. In each run, repeated k-fold cross-validation uses $N^* = N - N/k$ vectors for classifier training, therefore we can write that $E[\hat{\varepsilon}_N^{(1)}] \approx E[\varepsilon_{N^*}]$. Also, suppose that estimator $\hat{\varepsilon}_N^{(2)}$ is resubstitution and it uses N vectors to estimate resubstitution error. Now we can write that $E[\hat{\varepsilon}_N^{(2)}] = E[\varepsilon_N^R]$. Since $E[\varepsilon_{N^*}] > \varepsilon_{Bayes}$ and $E[\varepsilon_N^R] < \varepsilon_{Bayes}$[13], Eq. (24) can be rewritten as

$$Bias[\hat{\varepsilon}_{Bayes}] \approx \omega E[\varepsilon_{N^*}] + (1-\omega)E[\varepsilon_N^R] - \varepsilon_{Bayes} \approx 0 \tag{25}$$

From (25) we have that

$$\omega \approx \frac{\varepsilon_{Bayes} - E[\varepsilon_N^R]}{E[\varepsilon_{N^*}] - E[\varepsilon_N^R]} \tag{26}$$

Now, suppose that the following preconditions are met:

(1) Classifier deals with two multivariate Gaussian pattern classes;
(2) the covariance matrix is the same for all classes;
(3) class prior probabilities are equal;
(4) the training set has the same number of patterns from each class;
(5) Mahalanobis distance is constant;
(6) the dimensionality n is fixed and very large;
(7) both values, $N, N^* \to \infty$.

Then expected error of the Fisher linear classifier can be expressed as [13, 14]

$$E[\varepsilon_N] = \Phi\left\{-\frac{\delta}{2}\frac{1}{\sqrt{T_M T_\Sigma}}\right\} \qquad (27)$$

and expected resubstitution error can be expressed as

$$E[\varepsilon_N^R] \approx \Phi\left\{-\frac{\delta}{2}\sqrt{T_M T_\Sigma}\right\} \qquad (28)$$

where $T_M = 1 + \frac{4n}{\delta^2 N}$, $T_\Sigma = 1 + \frac{n}{N-n}$.

Finally, from (27) and (28) we get that the weight is

$$\omega \approx \lim_{\frac{n}{N}\to 0}\frac{\varepsilon_{Bayes} - E[\varepsilon_N^R]}{E[\varepsilon_{N^*}] - E[\varepsilon_N^R]} \approx \frac{1}{1 + \frac{N}{N^*}} \qquad (29)$$

The derivation of expression (29) is based on the Taylor series expansion of ε_{Bayes}, $E[\varepsilon_N^R]$ and $E[\varepsilon_{N^*}]$. Now, approximately unbiased estimator of the Bayes error rate can be defined as:

$$\hat{\varepsilon}_{Bayes}^{IM} = \frac{1}{r}\sum_{i=1}^{r}\left(\omega \cdot \hat{\varepsilon}_N^{(CV)} + (1 - \omega) \cdot \hat{\varepsilon}_N^{(R)}\right) \qquad (30)$$

where r is the number of repetitions. Finally, estimate $\hat{\delta}_{IM}$ of the Mahalanobis distance can be found by using $\hat{\varepsilon}_{Bayes}^{IM}$ and Eq. (22).

4 Simulation Study

4.1 Experimental Setup

In all experiments conducted in this study the following classification error rate estimators were used: resubstitution (resub), N-fold cross-validation or so-called leave-one-out (loo), repeated 10-fold cross-validation (rcv10) that averages 20 runs of 10-fold cross-validation, L-method (L), LS-method (LS), O method (O), OS method (OS),

Deev's estimator (DE), corrected Deev's estimator (DES), L method that use $\hat{\delta}_{IM}$ estimates of Mahalanobis distance (LIM), O method that use $\hat{\delta}_{IM}$ estimates (OIM) and Deev's estimator that use $\hat{\delta}_{IM}$ estimates $(DEIM)$. For the computation of $\hat{\delta}_{IM}$ estimates we use repeated 2-fold cross-validation (smallest variance among all cross-validation estimators) and resubstitution. In repeated 2-fold cross-validation the number of runs is set to 100 and this makes the number of designed classifiers equal to 200 (the same number of designed classifiers as in the case of repeated 10-fold cross-validation).

4.2 Synthetic Data

We use two data models to generate sample points. Data model 1 is a two-class Gaussian data model with equally likely classes, common covariance matrix and class means located at $\mathbf{M}_1 = (m, m, \ldots, m)^T$ and $\mathbf{M}_2 = (-m, -m, \ldots, -m)^T$. The elements of the common covariance matrix are equal to 0.1, except the main diagonal, where elements are equal to 1. Data model 2 is similar to model 1. The only difference is that different class prior probabilities are used. In model 2 we use $P_1 = 0.7$ and $P_2 = 0.3$. For each data model we choose five values of m such that Bayes error is from 0.05 to 0.25. Thus, in total, there are ten experimental conditions (ten experiments). Each Monte Carlo experiment is designed in the following way: first, 10000 independent samples of size $N = 60$ and dimensionality $n = 20$ are generated. Then, 10000 rules are derived by applying classification algorithm on each of 10000 samples. Finally, errors for all 10000 classifiers are estimated by various error estimation methods and corresponding conditional error rates are evaluated by utilizing the known underlying distribution of synthetic data.

Experimental results for data models 1–2 are displayed in Tables 1 and 2. The best bias, variance and RMS is marked in bold font for easier reading of the presented tables. Also, to better visualize the obtained results, RMS values from Tables 1 and 2 are additionally provided in Figs. 1 and 2. Our experiments show that the most biased error estimation methods are resubstitution, L-method, LS-method, O-method, OS-method, DE-method and DES-method while OIM-method, $DEIM$-method, LIM-method and repeated 10-fold cross-validation are moderately biased. The least biased error estimator is leave-one-out. However, leave-one-out has large variance. Experiments show that leave-one-out and repeated 10-fold cross-validation are more variable than resubstitution, L-method, LS-method, O-method, OS-method, DE-method, DES-method, OIM-method, $DEIM$-method and LIM-method. The experiments also show that parametric classification error rate estimators based on Okamoto's expressions of expected PMC generally are more variable than methods based on Deev's and Lachenburch's expressions of expected PMC. Also, we can see that performance (RMS) of classification error rate estimators depends on the Bayes error: when $\varepsilon_{Bayes} = 0.05$, the best error estimators are OS-method, DES-method and LS-method, however, when $\varepsilon_{Bayes} \geq 0.10$, the best error estimation methods are OIM-method, $DEIM$-method and LIM-method.

Table 1. Simulation results, data model 1.

		resub	loo	rcv10	O	DE	L	OS	DES	LS	OIM	DEIM	LIM
Bayes error 0.05	Bias	-0.0871	**0.0017**	0.0084	-0.0661	-0.0549	-0.0504	-0.0214	-0.0086	-0.0027	0.0287	0.0399	0.0465
	Variance	**7.1·10⁻⁴**	0.0025	0.0022	8.6·10⁻⁴	9.4·10⁻⁴	9.9·10⁻⁴	0.0014	0.0014	0.0015	0.0015	0.0013	0.0013
	RMS	0.0911	0.0497	0.0480	0.0723	0.0629	0.0594	0.0436	0.0388	**0.0384**	0.0479	0.0541	0.0592
Bayes error 0.10	Bias	-0.1276	**0.0020**	0.0094	-0.0897	-0.0770	-0.0711	-0.0300	-0.0196	-0.0131	0.0167	0.0232	0.0296
	Variance	**0.0014**	0.0037	0.0033	0.0017	0.0017	0.0018	0.0023	0.0021	0.0021	0.0024	0.0021	0.0020
	RMS	0.1330	0.0609	0.0583	0.0988	0.0874	0.0825	0.0567	0.0498	**0.0476**	0.0520	0.0509	0.0540
Bayes error 0.15	Bias	-0.1566	**0.0023**	0.0093	-0.1042	-0.0930	-0.0866	-0.0374	-0.0317	-0.0253	0.0035	0.0079	0.0138
	Variance	**0.0020**	0.0046	0.0040	0.0024	0.0023	0.0023	0.0029	0.0024	0.0024	0.0030	0.0025	0.0025
	RMS	0.1629	0.0676	0.0641	0.1153	0.1044	0.0988	0.0652	0.0584	0.0550	0.0549	**0.0507**	0.0514
Bayes error 0.20	Bias	-0.1792	0.0025	0.0088	-0.1144	-0.1065	-0.1001	-0.0447	-0.0449	-0.0390	**0.0014**	-0.0070	-0.0017
	Variance	0.0025	0.0053	0.0045	0.0030	0.0026	0.0026	0.0032	0.0025	**0.0024**	0.0037	0.0027	0.0027
	RMS	0.1861	0.0727	0.0679	0.1267	0.1180	0.1121	0.0719	0.0672	0.0630	0.0610	0.0528	**0.0517**
Bayes error 0.25	Bias	-0.1988	**0.0024**	0.0078	-0.1227	-0.1196	-0.1134	-0.0523	-0.0601	-0.0547	-0.0029	-0.0225	-0.0179
	Variance	0.0028	0.0058	0.0049	0.0033	0.0027	0.0027	0.0033	0.0024	**0.0023**	0.0047	0.0028	0.0027
	RMS	0.2058	0.0760	0.0701	0.1356	0.1304	0.1246	0.0780	0.0776	0.0731	0.0683	0.0571	**0.0547**

Table 2. Simulation results, data model 2.

		resub	loo	rcv10	O	DE	L	OS	DES	LS	OIM	DEIM	LIM
Bayes error 0.05	Bias	-0.0912	**0.0017**	0.0079	-0.0699	-0.0590	-0.0544	-0.0249	-0.0129	-0.0069	0.0228	0.0330	0.0396
	Variance	**8·10⁻⁴**	0.0025	0.0023	8.9·10⁻⁴	9.6·10⁻⁴	0.0010	0.0014	0.0014	0.0014	0.0014	0.0013	0.0013
	RMS	0.0955	0.0502	0.0482	0.0760	0.0666	0.0630	0.0452	0.0395	**0.0385**	0.0444	0.0490	0.0537
Bayes error 0.10	Bias	-0.1342	**0.0023**	0.0087	-0.0956	-0.0838	-0.0778	-0.0363	-0.0273	-0.0208	0.0068	0.0118	0.0183
	Variance	**0.0015**	0.0038	0.0033	0.0017	0.0017	0.0017	0.0022	0.0020	0.0020	0.0023	0.0019	0.0019
	RMS	0.1397	0.0617	0.0584	0.1043	0.0934	0.0883	0.0596	0.0524	0.0493	0.0485	**0.0456**	0.0475
Bayes error 0.15	Bias	-0.1646	0.0025	0.0081	-0.1120	-0.1024	-0.0959	-0.0468	-0.0431	-0.0368	-0.0059	-0.0080	**-0.0021**
	Variance	**0.0021**	0.0047	0.0040	0.0024	0.0022	0.0022	0.0027	0.0022	0.0022	0.0030	0.0023	0.0022
	RMS	0.1709	0.0687	0.0640	0.1223	0.1125	0.1068	0.0698	0.0640	0.0597	0.0549	0.0485	**0.0474**
Bayes error 0.20	Bias	-0.1895	**0.0028**	0.0066	-0.1249	-0.1197	-0.1133	-0.0579	-0.0617	-0.0559	-0.0165	-0.0286	-0.0234
	Variance	0.0026	0.0054	0.0045	0.0029	0.0024	0.0024	0.0029	**0.0022**	0.0022	0.0036	0.0024	0.0023
	RMS	0.1962	0.0734	0.0673	0.1360	0.1294	0.1235	0.0792	0.0777	0.0729	0.0620	0.0567	**0.0537**
Bayes error 0.25	Bias	-0.2121	**0.0026**	0.0041	-0.1367	-0.1380	-0.1321	-0.0703	-0.0839	-0.0788	-0.0255	-0.0520	-0.0475
	Variance	0.0029	0.0059	0.0048	0.0032	0.0024	0.0024	0.0030	0.0021	**0.0020**	0.0042	0.0023	0.0022
	RMS	0.2189	0.0769	0.0693	0.1478	0.1466	0.1408	0.0892	0.0954	0.0906	0.0698	0.0707	**0.0669**

4.3   Real Data

Real world experiments were conducted on four non Gaussian data sets (according to Mardia's and Henze-Zirkler tests):

Climate Model Simulation Crashes (CMS) data set [12]. This data set is composed of 540 instances and each instance is represented by 18 climate model input parameter values. The goal is to predict simulation outcomes (fail or succeed) from the input parameters. There are 46 instances classified as simulation crashes and 494 instances that are classified as not simulation crashes. Training/error estimation sample size is set to 50.

Spambase (Spam) data set [1]. This database is composed of 4601 instances of which 1813 are classified as spam and 2788 are classified as non-spam. The original data set contains 57 features, however, in order to avoid non-invertible singular

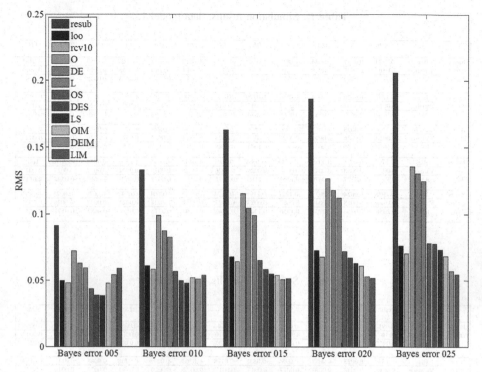

Fig. 1. RMS results, data model 1.

covariance matrix, the number of features is reduced to 20 (linear correlation based feature selection). Training/error estimation sample size is 80.

Magic Gamma Telescope (MGT) data set [1]. This data set is generated to simulate registration of high energy gamma particles in a ground-based atmospheric Cherenkov gamma telescope. The data set contains 19020 instances, of which 12332 are classified as signal and 6688 are classified as background. Each instance has 10 features. The size of the training/error estimation data set is 32.

Pima Indian Diabetes (PID) data [1]. It consists of 768 instances that are diabetes positive (268) or diabetes negative (500). The number of features is 8. Training/error estimation sample size is set to 32.

For each data set we perform 10000 runs, where in each run we randomly draw N instances from the original data set. These instances are used for classifier training/error estimation, while the remaining $N_{original} - N$ instances are used to calculate conditional PMC.

Table 3 displays experimental results based on real world data sets. The best bias, the best variance and the best RMS is marked in bold font for easier reading of the presented tables. Also, to better visualize the obtained results, RMS values from Table 3 are additionally provided in Fig. 3. Our experiments show that resubstitution, *L*-method, *LS*-method, *O*-method, *OS*-method, *DE*-method and *DES*- method are more biased than *OIM*-method, *DEIM*-method, *LIM*-method, leave-one-out and repeated

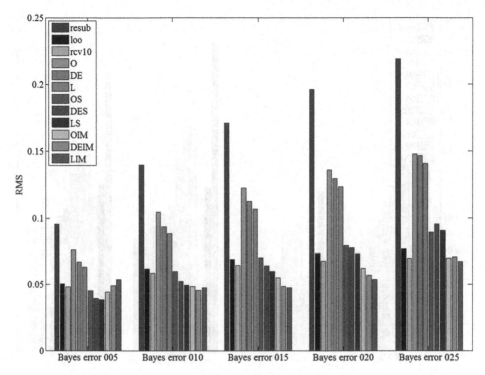

Fig. 2. RMS results, data model 2.

Table 3. Simulation results, real data.

		resub	loo	rcv10	O	DE	L	OS	DES	LS	OIM	DEIM	LIM
CMS	Bias	-0.1406	**0.0060**	$9\,10^{-4}$	0.1195	-0.1100	-0.1034	-0.0770	-0.0660	-0.0579	-0.0553	-0.0435	-0.0351
	Variance	0.0020	0.0050	0.0040	0.0018	0.0018	0.0019	0.0019	0.0020	0.0020	**0.0017**	0.0018	0.0018
	RMS	0.1474	0.0713	0.0631	0.1267	0.1180	0.1120	0.0886	0.0795	0.0731	0.0693	0.0605	**0.0548**
Spam	Bias	-0.0892	**$6.5\,10^{-4}$**	0.0051	-0.0655	-0.0589	-0.0554	-0.0245	-0.0191	-0.0154	0.0115	0.0152	0.0190
	Variance	**0.0011**	0.0022	0.0020	0.0018	0.0017	0.0018	0.0022	0.0020	0.0020	0.0016	0.0015	0.0015
	RMS	0.0954	0.0472	0.0447	0.0779	0.0721	0.0694	0.0525	0.0488	0.0476	0.0417	**0.0412**	0.0427
MGT	Bias	-0.1720	0.0056	0.0065	-0.1080	-0.1044	-0.0918	-0.0385	-0.0438	-0.0323	**-0.0038**	-0.0161	-0.0055
	Variance	0.0046	0.0096	0.0082	0.0060	0.0051	0.0050	0.0063	0.0049	0.0047	0.0070	0.0048	**0.0045**
	RMS	0.1849	0.0982	0.0910	0.1328	0.1265	0.1160	0.0882	0.0823	0.0756	0.0839	0.0708	**0.0675**
PID	Bias	-0.1481	0.0083	0.0078	-0.0898	-0.0899	-0.0797	-0.0379	-0.0434	-0.0341	**-0.0076**	-0.0195	-0.0109
	Variance	0.0055	0.0099	0.0085	0.0059	0.0050	0.0049	0.0058	0.0047	**0.0045**	0.0084	0.0056	0.0053
	RMS	0.1656	0.1000	0.0926	0.1182	0.1146	0.1062	0.0853	0.0809	0.0751	0.0920	0.0772	**0.0737**

10-fold cross-validation. Additionally, we can see that *OIM*-method is less biased than *DEIM*-method and *LIM*-method, however, it has higher variance. The experiments also show that *DEIM*-method and *LIM*-method generally outperform other error estimation techniques (in RMS sense). Also, we can see that parametric classification error rate estimators that use $\hat{\delta}$ and $\hat{\delta}_{DS}$ estimates perform worse than estimators that use $\hat{\delta}_{IM}$ estimates.

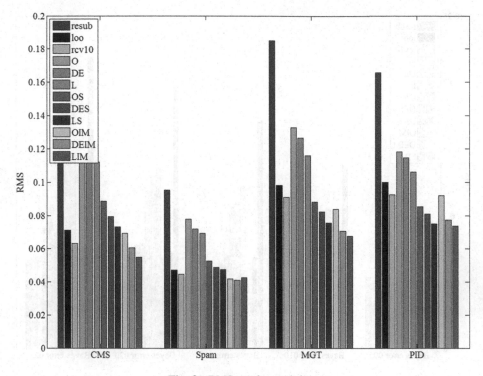

Fig. 3. RMS results, real data.

5   Conclusion

In this paper we have proposed a new estimator of the Mahalanobis distance that is designed for use in parametric classification error rate estimators. Similar to other asymptotically unbiased estimators of the Mahalanobis distance, this estimator assumes multivariate normality, however, it finds the estimates of the Mahalanobis distance indirectly, by calculating them from the Bayes error rate. Experiments with real world and synthetic data sets show that new estimator helps to reduce bias and RMS of O, L and Deev's parametric classification error rate estimators. Additionally, parametric classification error rate estimators that use new estimates, outperform corresponding methods based on $\hat{\delta}_{DS}$ estimates (in RMS sense).

References

1. Bache, K., Lichman, M.: UCI Machine Learning Repository. University of California, School of Information and Computer Science, Irvine, CA (2015). http://archive.ics.uci.edu/ml
2. Braga-Neto, U., Dougherty, E.: Is cross-validation valid for small sample microarray classification? Bioinform. **20**(3), 374–380 (2004)

3. Breukelen, M., Duin, R.P.V., Tax, D.M.J., Hartog, J.E.: Handwritten digit recognition by combined classifiers. Kybernetika **34**, 381–386 (1998)
4. Chen, Y., Wang, H., Zhang, J., Garty, G., Simaan, N., Yao, Y.L., Brenner, D.J.: Automated recognition of robotic manipulation failures in high-throughput biodosimetry tool. Expert Syst. Appl. **39**, 9602–9611 (2012)
5. Dougherty, E., Sima, C., Hua, J., Hanczar, B., Braga-Neto, U.: Performance of error estimators for classification. Curr. Bioinform. **5**(1), 53–67 (2010)
6. Duda, R., Hart, P., Stork, D.: Pattern Classification. Wiley, New York (2000)
7. Dudoit, S., Fridlyand, J., Speed, T.P.: Comparison of discrimination methods for the classification of tumors using gene expression data. J. Am. Stat. Assoc. **97**, 77–87 (2002)
8. Fisher, R.: The use of multiple measurements in taxonomic problems. Ann. Eugenics **7**, 179–188 (1936)
9. Gvardinskas, M.: Weighted classification error rate estimator for the euclidean distance classifier. In: Dregvaite, G., Damasevicius, R. (eds.) ICIST 2015. CCIS, vol. 538, pp. 343–355. Springer, Heidelberg (2015)
10. Kohavi, R.: A study of cross-validation and bootstrap for accuracy estimation and model selection. In: Proceedings of the Fourteenth International Joint Conference on Artificial Intelligence, pp. 1137–1143 (1995)
11. Lachenbruch, P., Mickey, R.: Estimation of error rates in discriminant analysis. Technometrics **10**(1), 1–11 (1968)
12. Lucas, D.D., Klein, R., Tannahill, J., Ivanova, D., Brandon, S., Domyancic, D., Zhang, Y.: Failure analysis of parameter-induced simulation crashes in climate models. Geoscientific Model Dev. **6**, 1157–1171 (2013)
13. Raudys, S.: Statistical and Neural Classifiers. An Integrated Approach to Design. Springer, London (2001)
14. Raudys, S., Young, D.M.: Results in statistical discriminant analysis: A review of the former soviet union literature. J. Multivar. Anal. **89**, 1–35 (2004)
15. Schiavo, R.A., Hand, D.J.: Ten more years of error rate research. Int. Stat. Rev. **68**(3), 295–310 (2000)
16. Sima, C., Dougherty, E.: Optimal convex error estimators for classification. Pattern Recogn. **39**(6), 1763–1780 (2006)
17. Smith, C.: Some examples of discrimination. Ann. Eugenics **18**, 272–282 (1947)
18. Toussaint, G., Sharpe, P.: An efficient method for estimating the probability of misclassification applied to a problem in medical diagnosis. Comput. Biol. Med. **4**, 269–278 (1975)
19. Wyman, F.J., Young, D.M., Turner, D.W.: A comparison of asymptotic error rate expansions for the sample linear discriminant function. Pattern Recogn. **23**(7), 775–783 (1990)

A Bag-of-Features Algorithm for Applications Using a NoSQL Database

Marcin Gabryel[(✉)]

Institute of Computational Intelligence, Częstochowa University of Technology,
Al. Armii Krajowej 36, 42-200 Częstochowa, Poland
marcin.gabryel@iisi.pcz.pl

Abstract. In this paper we present a Bag-of-Words (also known as a Bag-of-Features) method developed for the use of its implementation in NoSQL databases. When working with this algorithm special attention was brought to facilitating its implementation and reducing the number of computations to a minimum so as to use what the database engine has to offer to its maximum. The algorithm is presented using an example of image storing and retrieving. In this case it proves necessary to use an additional step of preprocessing, during which image characteristic features are retrieved and to use a clustering algorithm in order to create a dictionary. We present our own k-means algorithm which automatically selects the number of clusters. This algorithm does not comprise any computationally complicated classification algorithms, but it uses the majority vote method. This makes it possible to significantly simplify computations and use the Javascript language used in a common NoSQL database.

Keywords: NoSQL database · Image classification · Bag-of-Features · Modified k-means algorithm

1 Introduction

Relational databases enjoy a considerable popularity and have been used for a number of decades now. Their main advantages include durability of data storage, transaction processing, relational model, error handling and the SQL language. However, in distributed systems and in the case of data with different structure so-called NoSQL databases are used much more frequently. For Big Data processing special databases are developed, which work on special file systems supported for instance in Hadoop and dedicated frameworks for fast and parallel processing (e.g. MapReduce). NoSQL databases are different from commonly-used relational databases (RDBMS) in terms of the following aspects: not using the SQL language, not having to follow the ACID model (Atomicity, Consistency, Isolation, Durability), and also having no relationships and tables of a defined structure.

One of the tasks in which a NoSQL database can be used is effective browsing and searching a large number of images. NoSQL databases can successfully store enormous amounts of data including image data. In solving image processing and retrieval problems algorithms from different fields of computational intelligence are used [18, 22, 23, 25], in particular fuzzy systems [14, 15], rough neuro-fuzzy systems [16, 17, 26],

© Springer International Publishing Switzerland 2016
G. Dregvaite and R. Damasevicius (Eds.): ICIST 2016, CCIS 639, pp. 332–343, 2016.
DOI: 10.1007/978-3-319-46254-7_26

evolutionary algorithms [20, 24], swarm intelligence [27–29], mathematics [21, 30, 31], decision tree [19] and data mining [32, 33]. One of the most popular and widely spread algorithms used for indexation and image retrieval is the bag-of-words model (BoW) [4, 5], known also as a Bag-of-Features (BoF) or Bag-of-Visual-Words. This algorithm is based on a concept of text search methods within collections of documents. Single words are stored in dictionaries with emphasis on appearing in various documents. The BoW in a similar way creates dictionaries of characteristic features appearing in images. Additionally, the classification process enables during the search to determine what type of image class we are dealing with.

Practical aspects of the BoF algorithm implementation in image classification are rather rare in the literature. There are many modifications of this algorithm which, for example, use various image features [6–8] or various clustering and classification algorithms [9, 10], but there are no examples of practical applications of this algorithm. Most simulations and experiments are carried out with the use of OpenCV library, Matlab environment or multi-core processors. In practice direct usage of this particular kind of algorithms is connected with considerable computing capacities required when using classification algorithms and having no information concerning using data bases. The possibility of using a NoSQL database allows us to make a quite simple use of a number of computers to store large amount of data and do parallel computing. In most cases parallelism can be successfully carried out on a database which has been properly managed.

The article is divided into a few sections. Section 2 outlines the algorithms of which the whole image storing system. Section 3 presents the results of the experimental research testing the efficiency of the presented algorithms as well as the details connected with the NoSQL database being used for the implementation of this method. The conclusions in the last section present ideas concerning further improvement of the system efficiency.

2   Description of Algorithms

We are considering herein a set of given images $\mathbf{I}_i$, where $i = 1, \ldots, \mathbf{I}_M$ and M is the number of all images. Each image $\mathbf{I}_i$ has a class $c(\mathbf{I}_i)$ assigned to it, where $c(\mathbf{I}_i) \in \Omega$, $\Omega = \{\omega_1, \ldots, \omega_C\}$ is a set of all classes and C is the number of all classes. The images $\mathbf{I}_i$ make the initial data which will be stored in the NoSQL database and will be used to create a dictionary for the BoF method (see Sect. 2.3). K-means algorithm (see Sect. 2.2) groups characteristic features retrieved from an image concurrently reducing their number and creates words included in the dictionary. The modification of the k-means algorithm which we introduce allows for an automatic selection of the number of groups. Image characteristic features are obtained as a result of the operation of the SURF algorithm. (see Sect. 2.1).

2.1   SURF

SURF (Speeded Up Robust Features) is a robust local feature detector, first presented in [1]. It is partly inspired by the SIFT descriptor [2]. SURF gives description of an image by selecting its characteristic features. First, an integral image and filter approximation of block Hessian determinant is applied. Next, to detect interesting points, a special Hessian-matrix approximation is used. For features, orientation is based on information from circular region around the pixel. Then, a square region aligned to selected orientation is constructed and the SURF descriptor is extracted from it. It uses the sum of the Haar wavelet responses around an interest point. The local feature around the point is described by a 64-number vector $\mathbf{x} = [x_1, \ldots, x_{64}]$.

2.2   Modified k-Means Algorithm

The k-means algorithm is the most frequently used clustering algorithm used in the BoF. Its only drawback involves having to define the initial number of classes c. In this section we present an automatic selection mechanism of the number of classes during the operation of this algorithm. We have used the growing method used in the Growing Self-Organizing Map (GSOM) algorithm [3]. In that method a cluster is divided when the number of its data exceeds a certain threshold value Θ. Operation of the said algorithm starts with setting the threshold value Θ and defining two clusters ($c = 2$). In the subsequent steps the algorithm works as a classic k-means with the only difference being that at the end of each iteration the number of points belonging to each cluster $\tau_j, j = 1, \ldots, c$ is checked. If the number τ_j exceeds the threshold already set at Θ, then another cluster $c + 1$ is created. The algorithm is presented below in detail.

Let $\mathbf{X} = \mathbf{x}_1, \ldots, \mathbf{x}_n$ be a set of points in d-dimensional space, and $\mathbf{V} = \mathbf{v}_1, \ldots, \mathbf{v}_c$ be cluster centers, where n is the number of samples, $\mathbf{x}_i = [x_{i1}, \ldots, x_{id}]$, c is the number of clusters, and $\mathbf{v}_j = [v_{j1}, \ldots, v_{jd}]$.

1. Let the number of cluster $c = 2$. Determine Θ.
2. Randomly select c cluster centers $\mathbf{v}_j, j = 1, \ldots, c$, for example:

$$v_{ji} = rand\left(\min\left(x_{ij}\right), \max\left(x_{ij}\right)\right), \qquad (1)$$

where $rand(a, b)$ is a random number generated from the interval $[a; b]$.

3. Calculate the distance d_{ij} between each data point $\mathbf{x}_i$ and cluster centers $\mathbf{v}_j$:

$$d_{ij} = \| \mathbf{x}_i - \mathbf{v}_j \|, \qquad (2)$$

where $\| \cdot \|$ is a distance measure between two vectors (e.g. Euclidian or Manhattan distance).

4. Assign the data point x_i to the cluster center v_s whose distance from the cluster center is a minimum of all the cluster centers

$$x_i \in v_s \rightarrow d_{is} \leq d_{im}, \ m = 1, \ldots, c \qquad (3)$$

and increase counter of winnings $\tau_s = \tau_s + 1$.

5. Recalculate the new cluster center using:

$$v_i = \frac{1}{c_i} \Sigma_{j=1}^{c_i} x_j, \qquad (4)$$

where c_i represents the number of data points in i-th cluster.

6. If in the center s the number τ_s is greater than the threshold value Θ, create a new cluster, $c := c + 1$ and

$$v_c = x_{rand(j)}, \qquad (5)$$

where $rand(j)$ generates a random index of point x belonging to center v_s.

7. Remove clusters for which $\tau_s = 0$. Refresh the number of clusters c.
8. If no data point was reassigned, then stop; otherwise, repeat starting from step 3.

As a result of the algorithm operation we obtain c clusters with the centers in points $v_j, j = 1, \ldots, c$.

2.3 The Bag-of-Features Algorithm

The classic Bag-of-Features algorithm used in image classification most frequently uses classifiers (e.g. Support Vector Machine – SVM is used) during the stage when the decision is being made on the image class. The BoF comprises several stages:

1. Generate of characteristic features from images, which are most frequently saved in the form of number vectors.
2. Characteristic features are clustered and obtained clusters are treated as words, which create a dictionary.
3. Words (cluster centers) to which characteristic features of a given image belong make a histogram. Each element in the histogram specifies how many times a given word is present in the histogram.
4. The classifier is learnt to recognise histograms and to assign particular classes to them.

The points listed above show that it is possible to store three groups of data in a database, i.e. image characteristic features, centers of the clusters found, and histograms presenting membership of features in clusters. After a classifier has been learnt, it no longer needs to have access to the database.

A problem occurs when a query is made. The query image needs to have its features assigned to specific clusters in such way so as to create a histogram and to have it classified. This process requires a large number of computations given in formula (2). Thus the data-storing cluster centers need to be taken from the database. We can use this situation to our advantage and instead of using an ordinary query taking required data we can use the database engine in order to do computations and classification concurrently. A complex classifier (e.g. the abovementioned SVM) can be successfully replaced by the majority vote. We present below a BoF algorithm version which consists of two modules (one module – preparing data and the other – the classification process), which has been created in order to be able to use a NoSQL database.

The first of the BoF algorithm modules is supposed to prepare the database by creating a dictionary of characteristic features of sample images (to be used in the system learning process). This is carried out in a few steps presented below.

1. Starting operation of the algorithm generating image characteristic features. In our case we have used a well-known and fast SURF algorithm [1] which provides 64-number vectors $\mathbf{x}_i = [x_{i1}, \ldots, x_{id}]$ describing the surrounding of a characteristic point, where $i = 1, \ldots, L$, L – the total number of all characteristic points, d – the dimension of the vector describing a characteristic point ($d = 64$).

2. Starting operation of the k-means clustering algorithm. We have used the algorithm version presented in Sect. 2.2. As a result we obtain c clusters with the centers in points $\mathbf{v}_j$, $j = 1, \ldots, c$, which are treated as words in the BoF dictionary.

3. The value of the number of classes i of cluster j is calculated and defined as k_{ji}. This value is computed by counting the points $\mathbf{x}_n$ which belong to the center j provided that $\mathbf{x}_n \in \mathbf{I}$ and $c(\mathbf{I}) = \omega_i$:

$$k_{ji} = \sum_{n=1}^{L} \delta_{nj}(i), \ j = 1, \ldots, c, \ \ i = 1, \ldots, C, \tag{6}$$

Where

$$\delta_{nj}(i) = \begin{cases} 1 & \text{if } d_{nj} < d_{nm} \text{ for } \mathbf{x}_n \in \mathbf{I} \text{ and } c(\mathbf{I}) = \omega_i, \ m = 1, \ldots, c, \ j \neq m \\ 0 & \text{otherwise} \end{cases} \tag{7}$$

The variable $\delta_{nj}(i)$ is an indicator if a cluster $\mathbf{v}_j$ is the closest vector (a winner) for any sample $\mathbf{x}_n$ from an image $\mathbf{I}$ and $c(\mathbf{I}) = \omega_i$. Next, the values k_{ji} are normalised:

$$k_{ji} = \frac{k_{ji}}{\sum_{j=1,\ldots,c} k_{ji}} \tag{8}$$

4. Saving the values of centers $\mathbf{v}_j$ together with the information about the number of classes k_{ji} in the database.

The classification process, i.e. the process testing whether a given query image belongs to a particular class, requires that an additional pre-processing module be applied. This module is supposed to:

1. Use a feature extraction algorithm (the SURF algorithm – see Sect. 2.1) on query image $\mathbf{I}_q$ in order to obtain values of characteristic features $\mathbf{x}_i^q$, $i = 1, \ldots, L_q$, L_q – the number of obtained features.
2. Save points $\mathbf{x}^q$ in the database.
3. Assign points $\mathbf{x}^q$ to clusters in such way so as to compute values k_i^q. Computations are carried out as follows:

$$k_i^q = \Sigma_{n=1}^{L_q} \alpha_n(i), \; i = 1, \ldots, C \tag{9}$$

$$\alpha_n(i) = \begin{cases} k_{ji} & \text{if } d_{jn}^q \leq d_{mn}^q, \; j \neq m \\ 0 & \text{otherwise} \end{cases} \tag{10}$$

Where

$$d_{jn}^q = \| \mathbf{v}_j - \mathbf{x}_n^q \|, \; j = 1, \ldots, c \tag{11}$$

and

$$d_{mn}^q = \| \mathbf{v}_m - \mathbf{x}_n^q \|, \; m = 1, \ldots, c. \tag{12}$$

4. Assigning to class $c(\mathbf{I}_q)$ is done by the majority vote checking the maximum value k_i^q:

$$c(\mathbf{I}_q) = \text{argmax}_{i=1,\ldots,c} \; k_i^q \tag{13}$$

The algorithm facilitates an easy implementation by using only one SQL query. The algorithm's details and experimental research are presented in Sect. 3.

3 Experimental Research

In this section we present the results of the BoF algorithm discussed in Sect. 2.3 together with the modified k-means algorithm (outlined in Sect. 2.2). Practical application of the presented method in image classification with the use of the database needs two modules to be used:

– the module which is supposed to fill with the use of the Bag-of-Features algorithm the database with the cluster center values and also with the information on which class they belong to, i.e. creating the dictionary. The module creating the dictionary for the database should comprise the following steps:
  • preprocesing, i.e. extracting characteristic features from training images,
  • starting the operation of the *k*-means algorithm in order to perform clustering of the data and obtaining clusters with image characteristic features,
  • save the above data in the database;
– the module preparing for query image classification and saving its features in the database. It also comprises a few steps:
  • preprocesing, i.e. extracting characteristic features from a query image,
  • saving data in the database,
  • performing a query which will produce information on the class to which a particular image belongs.

Preprocessing algorithms were implemented in the Java language with the use JavaCV [11] library function. JavaCV is a library which adopts functions available in OpenCV [12] for the Java language needs. The research was performed on the Caltech 101 image database [13]. Six sample categories comprising motorbikes, car sides, revolvers, airplanes, leopards and wrenches were selected. Out of the remaining group of images, 20 % are randomly selected and marked as a set of testing images. During the operation of the SURF algorithm over 100,000 characteristic points are identified in the database for 180 images. The main value which is used to compute classification efficiency is a percentage of correctly classified images.

Three structures are used in data storing: learning image features, testing image features, and for values of the cluster centres. Structures are stored in collections:

– `train_images` and `eval_images` – collections storing the features values of learning and testing images have the following values:
    `imageId` – image identifier, file name,
    `classId` – image class,
    `pk1, pk2, ..., pk64` – values of the feature vector obtained as a result of the SURF algorithm operation.
– `centers_500` – the collection stores cluster centers and k_{ji} values (see formula (8)):
    `center_id` – cluster identification,
    `c1, c2, ..., c64` – cluster center values,
    `k1, ..., k6` – k_{ji} values for each of the class.

The script performing the query image classification comprises two stages. The `centers_temporary` collection is created during the first stage and it stores temporary results of computations checking membership of query image features in particular clusters. Particularly, values $\alpha_n(i)$ are computed here (according to formula (10)) and values k_{ji} from cluster j that are closest to the sample n are returned for all classes i. The script made for a commonly-used MongoDB database presents as follows:

```
db.centers_temporary.drop();
db.eval_images.find( { imageId : IMAGE_ID }, {_id:0}
).forEach(
  function( feature ) {
    var minDistance = { mm : -1 };
    db.centers_500.find().forEach(
      function( center ) {
        var oneDistance = { mm : 0,
          imageId : feature.imageId,
          class: [ center.k0, center.k1,
                   center.k2, center.k3,
                   center.k4, center.k5],
          cluster_id : center.cluster_id };
        oneDistance.mm =
          Math.abs(feature.pk0 - center.c0) +
          Math.abs(feature.pk1 - center.c1) +
          Math.abs(feature.pk2 - center.c2) +
          ...
          Math.abs(feature.pk63 - center.c63);
        if ( minDistance.mm > oneDistance.mm ||
             minDistance.mm == -1  ) {
          minDistance = oneDistance;
        }
      }
    );
    db.centers_temporary.insert( minDistance );
  }
);
```

The next step is to call the `mapReduce` function, which is supposed to compute for each class the k_i^q value (according to formula (9)) and to classify an image by applying the majority vote method according to (13):

```
db.centers_temporary.mapReduce(
  function() {
    classId = 0;
    for (var i=1; i<this.class.length; i++) {
      if (this.class[classId] < this.class[i]) {
        classId = i;
      }
    }
    emit( classId, this.class[classId] );
  },

  function (key, values) {
    return Array.sum( values );
  },
  {
    query: { imageId: IMAGE_ID },
    out: "outputResults"
  }
);
```

Table 1 presents the results of the operation of the algorithm for different Θ values (the parameter for the k-means method). The other columns present: Θ threshold value, the number of obtained clusters as a result of the operation of the k-means algorithm, and also the efficiency (given in percentages) of image recognition accuracy for the training and testing groups. As it can be noticed, the results proved best for $\theta = 50$ and $\theta = 100$. However, as far as the number of obtained clusters is concerned, value $\theta = 100$ proves to be the best choice under this research.

Table 1. Percentage efficiency of image classification for the presented algorithm in relation to θ threshold value.

Threshold Θ	Number of clusters	Train [%]	Test [%]
10000	38	45.50	46.85
5000	106	49.38	48.95
2000	852	60.49	53.84
1000	1958	68.61	63.63
500	3120	76.89	74.12
250	4077	80.77	73.42
100	7532	90.47	74.82
50	14591	94.70	74.82
25	28752	97.88	72.02
10	51915	99.83	71.32

4   Conclusions

In this paper we present a Bag-of-Features algorithm which we have developed. This algorithm works on the basis of a NoSQL database. We have presented the algorithm implementation on the example of image storage and classification. We have modified the classic Bag-of-Words algorithm so as to facilitate its implementation in a NoSQL database without compromising its efficiency. The tests which we have carried out show that the algorithm operates correctly, thus proving its efficiency. Although operation of the BoF algorithm cannot be compared to other image-recognition algorithms (e.g. a deep-learning network), it still proves efficient enough and simple in its implementation so that it can be successfully used in applications working on less sophisticated hardware. Better query efficiency can be achieved by means of reducing lengths of the vectors describing particular image features. The methods which reduce the number of dimensions can be used for this purpose and these methods, for instance, include the PCA algorithm, or some other completely different feature generating algorithms. Another possible procedure reducing the number of calculations is the exclusions of those clusters which are the least likely to affect unequivocally image class determination.

References

1. Bay, H., Tuytelaars, T., Van Gool, L.: SURF: speeded up robust features. In: Leonardis, A., Bischof, H., Pinz, A. (eds.) ECCV 2006, Part I. LNCS, vol. 3951, pp. 404–417. Springer, Heidelberg (2006)
2. Lowe, D.G.: Distinctive image features from scale-invariant keypoints. Int. J. Comput. Vision **60**(2), 91–110 (2004)
3. Fritzke, B.: Growing grid a self-organizing network with constant neighbourhood range and adaptation strength. Neural Process. Lett. **2**(5), 9–13 (1995)
4. Csurka, G., Dance, C.R., Fan, L., Willamowski, J., Bray, C.: Visual categorization with bags of keypoints. In: Workshop on Statistical Learning in Computer Vision, ECCV, pp. 1–22 (2004)
5. Liu, J.: Image retrieval based on bag-of-words model. CoRR abs/1304.5168 (2013). http://arxiv.org/abs/1304.5168
6. Lazebnik, S., Schmid, C., Ponce, J.: Beyond bags of features: spatial pyramid matching for recognizing natural scene categories. In: 2006 IEEE Computer Society Conference on Computer Vision and Pattern Recognition, vol. 2, pp. 2169–2178 (2006)
7. Li, W., Dong, P., Xiao, B., Zhou, L.: Object recognition based on the region of interest and optimal bag of words model. Neurocomputing **172**, 271–280 (2016)
8. Nanni, L., Melucci M.: Combination of projectors, standard texture descriptors and bag of features for classifying images. Neurocomputing **173**(P3), 1602–1614 (2016)
9. Gao, H., Dou, L., Chen, W., Sun, J.: Image classification with bag-of-words model based on improved sift algorithm. In: 2013 9th Asian Control Conference (ASCC), pp. 1–6 (2013)
10. Zhao, C., Li, X., Cang, Y.: Bisecting k-means clustering based face recognition using block-based bag of words model. Optik – Int. J. Light Electron Opt. **126**(19), 1761–1766 (2015)
11. Audet, S.: JavaCV (2016). http://bytedeco.org/. Accessed 1 Apr 2016

12. Bradski, G.: The OpenCV Library. Dr. Dobb's Journal of Software Tools (2000)
13. Fei-Fei, L., Fergus, R., Perona, P.: Learning generative visual models from few training examples: an incremental bayesian approach tested on 101 object categories. In: 2004 Conference on Computer Vision and Pattern Recognition Workshop, CVPRW 2004, p. 178, June 2004
14. Cpalka, K.: A new method for design and reduction of neuro-fuzzy classification systems. IEEE Trans. Neural Netw. **20**(4), 701–714 (2009)
15. Starczewski, J.T.: Centroid of triangular and gaussian type-2 fuzzy sets. Inf. Sci. **280**, 289–306 (2014)
16. Nowak, B.A., Nowicki, R.K., Starczewski, J.T., Marvuglia, A.: The learning of neuro-fuzzy classifier with fuzzy rough sets for imprecise datasets. In: Rutkowski, L., Korytkowski, M., Scherer, R., Tadeusiewicz, R., Zadeh, L.A., Zurada, J.M. (eds.) ICAISC 2014, Part I. LNCS, vol. 8467, pp. 256–266. Springer, Heidelberg (2014)
17. Nowicki, R.: Rough sets in the neuro-fuzzy architectures based on monotonic fuzzy implications. In: Rutkowski, L., Siekmann, J.H., Tadeusiewicz, R., Zadeh, L.A. (eds.) ICAISC 2004. LNCS (LNAI), vol. 3070, pp. 510–517. Springer, Heidelberg (2004)
18. Sakurai, S., Nishizawa, M.: A new approach for discovering top-k sequential patterns based on the variety of items. J. Artif. Intell. Soft Comput. Res. **5**(2), 141–153 (2015)
19. Tambouratzis, T., Souliou, D., Chalikias, M., Gregoriades, A.: Maximising accuracy and efficiency of traffic accident prediction combining information mining with computational intelligence approaches and decision trees. J. Artif. Intell. Soft Comput. Res. **4**(1), 31–42 (2014)
20. El-Samak, A.F., Ashour, W.: Optimization of traveling salesman problem using affinity propagation clustering and genetic algorithm. J. Artif. Intell. Soft Comput. Res. **5**(4), 239–245 (2015)
21. Woźniak, M., Kempa, W.M., Gabryel, M., Nowicki, R.K.: A finite-buffer queue with single vacation policy - analytical study with evolutionary positioning. Int. J. Appl. Math. Comput. Sci. **24**(4), 887–900 (2014)
22. Gabryel, M., Grycuk, R., Korytkowski, M., Holotyak, T.: Image indexing and retrieval using GSOM algorithm. In: Rutkowski, L., Korytkowski, M., Scherer, R., Tadeusiewicz, R., Zadeh, L.A., Zurada, J.M. (eds.) ICAISC 2015. LNCS, vol. 9119, pp. 706–714. Springer, Heidelberg (2015)
23. Grycuk, R., Gabryel, M., Korytkowski, M., Scherer, R., Voloshynovskiy, S.: From single image to list of objects based on edge and blob detection. In: Rutkowski, L., Korytkowski, M., Scherer, R., Tadeusiewicz, R., Zadeh, L.A., Zurada, J.M. (eds.) ICAISC 2014, Part II. LNCS, vol. 8468, pp. 605–615. Springer, Heidelberg (2014)
24. Gabryel, M., Woźniak, M., Damaševičius, R.: An application of differential evolution to positioning queueing systems. In: Rutkowski, L., Korytkowski, M., Scherer, R., Tadeusiewicz, R., Zadeh, L.A., Zurada, J.M. (eds.) ICAISC 2015. LNCS, vol. 9120, pp. 379–390. Springer, Heidelberg (2015)
25. Nowak, B.A., Nowicki, R.K., Woźniak, M., Napoli, C.: Multi-class nearest neighbour classifier for incomplete data handling. In: Rutkowski, L., Korytkowski, M., Scherer, R., Tadeusiewicz, R., Zadeh, L.A., Zurada, J.M. (eds.) ICAISC 2015. LNCS, vol. 9119, pp. 469–480. Springer, Heidelberg (2015)
26. Nowicki, R.K., Nowak, B.A., Woźniak, M.: Application of rough sets in k nearest neighbours algorithm for classification of incomplete samples. In: Kunifuji, S., Papadopoulos, G.A., Skulimowski, A.M.J., Kacprzyk, J. (eds.) KICSS 2014. AISC, vol. 416, pp. 243–257. Springer, Heidelberg (2016)

27. Połap, D., Woźniak, M., Napoli, C., Tramontana, E.: Real-time cloud-based game management system via cuckoo search algorithm. Int. J. Electron. Telecommun. **61**(4), 333–338 (2015)

28. Połap, D., Woźniak, M., Napoli, C., Tramontana, E.: Is swarm intelligence able to create mazes? Int. J. Electron. Telecommun. **61**(4), 305–310 (2015)

29. Woźniak, M., Gabryel, M., Nowicki, R.K., Nowak, B.A.: An application of firefly algorithm to position traffic in NoSQL database systems. In: Kunifuji, S., Papadopoulos, G.A., Skulimowski, A.M.J., Kacprzyk, J. (eds.) KICSS 2014. AISC, vol. 416, pp. 259–272. Springer, Heidelberg (2016)

30. Woźniak, M., Marszałek, Z., Gabryel, M., Nowicki, R.K.: Preprocessing large data sets by the use of quick sort algorithm. In: Skulimowski, A.M.J., Kacprzyk, J. (eds.) KICSS 2013. AISC, vol. 364, pp. 111–121. Springer, Heidelberg (2016)

31. Woźniak, M., Marszałek, Z., Gabryel, M., Nowicki, R.K.: Modified merge sort algorithm for large scale data sets. In: Rutkowski, L., Korytkowski, M., Scherer, R., Tadeusiewicz, R., Zadeh, L.A., Zurada, J.M. (eds.) ICAISC 2013, Part II. LNCS, vol. 7895, pp. 612–622. Springer, Heidelberg (2013)

32. Rutkowski, L., Jaworski, M., Pietruczuk, L., Duda, P.: Decision trees for mining data streams based on the Gaussian approximation. IEEE Trans. Knowl. Data Eng. **26**(1), 108–119 (2014)

33. Rutkowski, L., Jaworski, M., Pietruczuk, L., Duda, P.: A new method for data stream mining based on the misclassification error. IEEE Trans. Neural Networks Learn. Syst. **26**(5), 1048–1059 (2015)

Novel Recursive Fast Sort Algorithm

Zbigniew Marszałek[✉]

Institute of Mathematics, Silesian University of Technology, ul. Kaszubska 23,
44-100 Gliwice, Poland
Zbigniew.Marszalek@polsl.pl

Abstract. Sorting algorithms are important procedures to facilitate the order of data. In this paper, author describes new recursive version of fast sort algorithm for large data sets. Examination of the recursive fast sort algorithm performance was subject to performance tests, that showed validity. It is discussed, if non recursive version is faster than recursive.

Keywords: Computer algorithm · Data sorting · Data mining · Analysis of computer algorithms

1 Introduction

Computer Science is developing in recent years. Technological progress allows construction of faster and larger computers that store larger amounts of data. It means that we have to handle growing data sets, which need dedicated solutions for managing and optimal operating strategies [7, 8, 10, 11, 14, 34, 39]. Good example of these type are distributed and multi agent systems, where information is processed by several computing modules i.e. user oriented systems [18, 23, 24, 29, 30]. Similarly in large institutions information stock is growing and dedicated strategies help on efficient operations language operations [17, 20]; data-mining [21, 22, 26, 27] and requests management [12, 32, 35, 37]. Another aspect of efficient management is optimal energy balance, therefore here again dedicated solutions can be applied [1–3, 9, 13]. However special role in organizing information act sorting algorithms. To the date, many developed algorithms enabled sorting of large data sets [4, 5]. Sorting needs efficient memory management [6, 28, 38] and sometimes improved data handling structures [25, 31, 40]. Merge sort can be applied to both unsorted and partially sorted lists [15] and has wide possibility of applications [16]. However, still carried out work on their improvement and development of new versions for specific tasks is crucial. The improved triple marge, Fast Sort Algorithm (FSA) discussed in details in [19], for efficient sorting of large data sets is not recursive algorithm therefore further development was introduced. The paper presents new recursive version of this algorithm. Benchmark tests in comparison to first version have shown its effectiveness and improvements.

© Springer International Publishing Switzerland 2016
G. Dregvaite and R. Damasevicius (Eds.): ICIST 2016, CCIS 639, pp. 344–355, 2016.
DOI: 10.1007/978-3-319-46254-7_27

1.1   Related Work

Sorting is one of the most commonly used methods for scheduling information in business, economics and also in research. Experimental verification of methods for sorting different types of input data are presented in [33]. In [36] has been shown that the commonly used algorithms are sensitive to occur in practical situations. It is also important how the algorithm is written and whether it is a recursive form. Experimental tests allow to find the best solutions with the least possible computational complexity. The applicable method for large data sets is described in detail in [19]. In this article a novel recursive version of fast sorting algorithm is presented.

1.2   Sort Algorithms and Big Data Sets

Applications that use large data sets get them saved in the correct structure. This means that each client computer gets an application receipt of the information request from management system that stores them in a queue. Query management system processes them and sends back the results to the client computers. Figure 1 shows a simple information processing system. The processing of large data sets requires efficient methods that ensure speed and stability. The novel improved algorithm presented in the following sections has a low computational complexity and can present increased stability of Quality of Service (QoS). To compare methods are carried out benchmark tests to verify the time measured by the CPU (Central Processing Unit) and clock cycles (clock rate). It is a convenient way to compare algorithms.

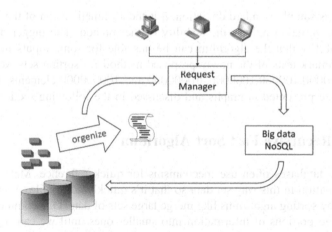

Fig. 1. Big data NoSQL system

1.3   Statistical Research on Algorithm Performance

The analysis for sorting time was carried out in 100 benchmark tests for each of the fixed dimension of the task on the input. A statistical average of n - element set of samples $a_1, \ldots, a_n$ is defined by the formula

$$\bar{a} = \frac{1}{n} \sum_{i=1}^{n} a_i$$

The standard deviation is the most commonly used measure of dispersion of statistical estimations and verification of statistical hypothesis based on the formula

$$\sigma = \sqrt{\frac{1}{(n-1)} \sum_{i=1}^{n} (a_i - \bar{a})^2}$$

where n is the number of elements in the sample, a_i is value of the random variable in the sample, $\bar{a}$ is the arithmetic mean of the sample. Analysis of the average durations of sorting algorithms for large data sets enables comparing them and find the most efficient algorithm. The standard deviation allows us to say how much sorting time is scattered around the average time. This does not mean, however, that the method having a low time complexity in the average time does not have input samples, for whom sorting time becomes polynomial as shown in [19, 33, 36].

Another measure of dispersion, which we can examine in the tests is the coefficient of variation. The coefficient of variation is very useful when you want to compare differences in some traits, i.e. the stability of the algorithm. This ratio is expressed by the formula

$$V = \frac{\sigma}{\bar{a}}$$

Where σ is sample standard deviation, $\bar{a}$ is the arithmetic mean of the sample. The coefficient of variation reflects the stability of the method. The bigger deviation the bigger probability that the algorithm can be unstable for some inputs in a statistical sense. Benchmark tests of the newly proposed method for sorting sets were taken for 100, 1000, 10000,100000,1000000, 10000000 and 100000000 elements on the input. The results are presented in graphs and discussed in the following sections.

2   Novel Recursive Fast Sort Algorithm

The NoSQL databases often use mechanisms for quick reference. Methods of organizing information in this way set data so that it's quickly accessible. A special role is played here by sorting algorithms like merge large sets of data. One common method is to divide large portions of information into smaller ones until we can organize them and combine them into one ordered sequence. In the proposed novel method, Recursive Fast Sort Algorithm (RFSA), a ternary division was used to improve efficiency sharing over three strings. Sharing is performed until we get three strings of single elements. Then the algorithm merges and passes them to the ternary divisions as consecutive substrings for merging. Relevant here is how to make the merge of three strings. This can be done i.e. as shown in [19] to select the smallest element and saving it merged within or act like [36] and merge the first two strings by writing the buffer, and then merge a third subsequence with buffer to store the result in a merged string. The second method is more efficient therefore it novel form was applied her. The whole process of sorting sequence of numbers is shown in Fig. 2.

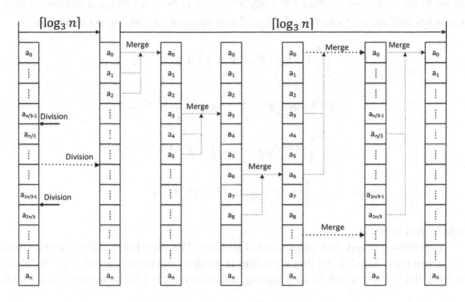

Fig. 2. Recursive Fast Sort algorithm

THEOREM 1. Recursive Fast Sort Algorithm has time complexity

$$T_{max} = \frac{5}{3}n \cdot \log_3 n - n + 1 \approx 1.05n \cdot \log_2 n - n + 1 \tag{1}$$

Proof. We are limiting deliberations to $n = 3^k$, where $k = 1, 2, \ldots$.

Inductive proof. For $k = 1$ the dimension of sorting sequence is $n = 3$. At the beginning algorithm merge two one elements strings into one string. Next it merges two elements string with one element string. We can marge two strings with u and v elements making $u + v - 1$ operations of comparisons. These operation for n – elements in the sequence is done within $\frac{5}{3}n - 2 = 3$ comparisons. To the formula (1), we get $\frac{5}{3}3 \cdot \log_3 3 - 3 + 1 = 3$. So for $k = 1$ the theorem is true.

We assume the truth of the theorem for k. Hence $n = 3^k$ and we can sort sequence doing no more comparisons than

$$\frac{5}{3}3^k \cdot \log_3 3^k - 3^k + 1 \tag{2}$$

We have to prove that for $k+1$ (the sequence is multiple by tree and $n = 3^{k+1}$) the statement $\frac{5}{3}3^{k+1} \cdot \log_3 3^{k+1} - 3^{k+1} + 1$ is true. In step $k+1$ we have tree sequences with 3^k elements. Each one of tree sequences, by the induction hypothesis, was sorted in no more compressions than $\frac{5}{3}3^k \cdot \log_3 3^k - 3^k + 1$. Now we merge 3 sequences of 3^k elements making no more than $5 \cdot 3^k - 2$ comparisons to sort. So estimating is:

$$\left(\frac{5}{3}3^k \cdot \log_3 3^k - 3^k + 1\right) + 5 \cdot 3^k - 2$$

$$\frac{5}{3}3^{k+1} \cdot \log_3 3^k - 3^{k+1} + 3 + \frac{5}{3} \cdot 3^{k+1} - 2$$

$$\frac{5}{3}3^{k+1}\left(\log_3 3^k + 1\right) - 3^{k+1} + 1$$

$$\frac{5}{3}3^{k+1} \cdot \log_3 3^{k+1} - 3^{k+1} + 1$$

which was to prove.

Presented method was implemented in C++. The algorithm is divided into parts shown in Figs. 3 and 4. Sorting algorithm is invoked by specifying the array, in which sorting index from which to start sorting and the number of items to sort is computed.

2.1 The Study of the Newly Proposed Recursive Method of Sorting

Performance analysis of presented method is based on benchmark tests for the algorithm implemented in C++ CLR in Visual Studio 2012 Ultimate on MS Windows Server 2008 R2. The study was conducted on 100 input samples randomly generated for each dimension of the task. Tests were carried out on quad core amd opteron processor 8356 8p. The purpose of the analysis and comparison is to check whether recursive sorting method is better than not recursive method of sorting large data sets. For the benchmark were applied input samples of 100, 1000, 10000, 100000, 1000000, 10000000 and 100000000 elements. Each sorting operation by examined methods was measured in time [ms] and CPU (Central Processing Unit) usage represented in tics of CPU clock (Table 1).

These results are averaged for 100 sorting samples. Benchmark comparison for FSA [1] and newly proposed in this paper RFSA are describe in Table 2 and Figs. 5 and 6.

Comparison of coefficient of variation for FSA and RFSA methods for large data sets is presented in Table 2.

Analyzing Table 2 we see that both algorithms are similar in statistical stability for large data sets. Some variations in stability of the algorithm for a small inputs are due to the fact that the system operation exceed the sorting algorithm. However as the size increases the coefficient of variation is stabilizing.

```
void merge(array<int>^ a ,int p, int m1, int m2, int
k)
{
   int p1=m1;
   int pb=0;
   int p0=p;
   int q1=p1;
   array<int> ^b = gcnew array<int>(k-p);
   int c0=m1-p;
   int c1=m2-m1;
   while(c0&&c1)
   {
   if(a[p0]<=a[p1])
      {
        b[pb]=a[p0++];
        c0--;
      }
      else
      {
        b[pb]=a[p1++];
        c1--;
      }
    pb++;
   }
   while(c0)
   {
               b[pb++]=a[p0++];
            c0--;
   }
   while(c1)
   {
               b[pb++]=a[p1++];
      c1--;
    }
    int pa=0;
    p0=p;
    int c2=k-m2;
    int q2=m2;
    while(pb&&c2)
    {
      if(b[pa]<=a[q2])
      {
        a[p0++]=b[pa++];
        pb--;
      }
      else
      {
        a[p0++]=a[q2++];
        c2--;
      }
    }
    while(pb)
    {
    a[p0++]=b[pa++];
    pb--;
    }
}
```

Fig. 3. Merge tree sequences method implemented in the distributed system

```
void fastr(array<int>^ a, int p, int k)
{
  if(p < k-1)
  {
    int m1 = (2*p+k) / 3;
    int m2 = (p+2*k) / 3;
    fastr(a,p, m1);
    fastr(a, m1, m2);
    fastr(a, m2, k);
    merge(a,  p, m1, m2, k);
  }
}
```

Fig. 4. Recursive Fast Sort method implemented in the distributed system

Table 1. Sorting results not recursive fast sort and recursive fast sort

Elements	Method – average time sorting for 100 samples			
	Fast Sort Algorithm – FSA		Recursive Fast Sort Algorithm – RFSA	
	[ms]	[ti]	[ms]	[ti]
100	1	225	1	258
1 000	1	429	1	756
10 000	4	5327	5	7650
100 000	34	53119	46	72248
1 000 000	459	715621	541	843242
10 000 000	5190	8089206	6090	9491823
100 000 000	58484	91155320	66903	104278520

Table 2. Coefficient of variation for FSA and newly proposed RFSA

Coefficient of variation		
Number of elements	FSA	RFSA
100	1,08953451690909	1,04539026796965
1 000	0,322597585191365	0,377073294410199
10 000	0,333717200082017	0,339903327318631
100 000	0,203695429333821	0,306555331381401
1 000 000	0,201304713734738	0,17129795522303
10 000 000	0,214803552944533	0,180969698905246
100 000 000	0,225844987448253	0,195340903908895

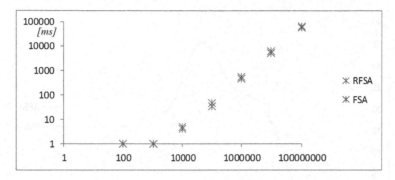

Fig. 5. Comparison of benchmark time [ms]

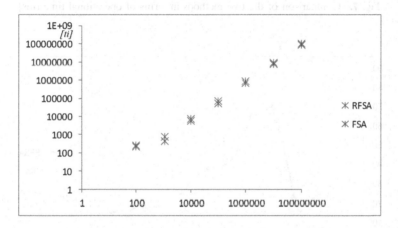

Fig. 6. Comparison of benchmark CPU operations [ti]

2.2 Analysis and Comparison of Sorting Time

Analysis and comparison will describe efficiency for sorting large data sets. Let us compare both methods assuming that the duration of the method is not recursive and let us examine if the duration of action is longer for the recursive method. The results are shown in the graphs Figs. 7 and 8.

The study shows that FSA operates in shorter time measuring tasks from 1 000 to 1 000 000. As size increases to infinity difference in the speed decreases to line, as asymptotically both methods have the same time complexity. The difference is that the RFSA method makes a recursive first division of tasks, and after the execution start merging, what improves sorting for large data sets.

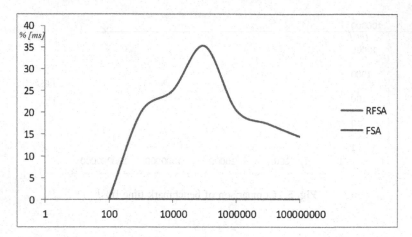

Fig. 7. Comparison of the two methods in terms of operational time [ms]

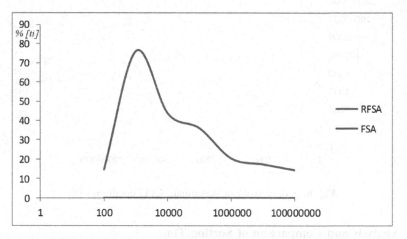

Fig. 8. Comparison of the two methods in CPU operations [ti]

3   Final Remarks

The article presented Recursive Fast Sort Algorithm for rapid sorting of large data sets. The tests demonstrate the stability of the method and confirm the theoretical time complexity. Both Recursive Fast Sort Algorithm and Fast Sort Algorithm can find practical application in NoSQL databases, however newly proposed method gives better effects in QoS in large distributed systems similar to multi-branch institutions.

References

1. Bonanno, F., Capizzi, G., Napoli, C.: Some remarks on the application of RNN and PRNN for the charge-discharge simulation of advanced lithium-ions battery energy storage. In: Power Electronics, Electrical Drives, Automation and Motion SPEEDAM 2012, pp. 941–945. IEEE (2012). doi:10.1109/SPEEDAM.2012.6264500

2. Capizzi, G., Bonanno, F., Tina, G.M.: Recurrent neural network-based modeling and simulation of lead-acid batteries charge-discharge. IEEE Trans. Energy Convers. **26**(2), 435–443 (2011). doi:10.1109/TEC.2010.2095015

3. Capizzi, G., Bonanno, F., Napoli, C.: Recurrent neural network-based control strategy for battery energy storage in generation systems with intermittent renewable energy sources. In: International Conference on Clean Electrical Power ICCEP 2011, pp. 336–340. IEEE (2011). doi:10.1109/ICCEP.2011.6036300

4. Carlsson, S., Levcopoulos, C., Petersson, O.: Sublinear merging and natural merge sort. In: Asano, T., Ibaraki, T., Imai, H., Nishizeki, T. (eds.) Algorithms. LNCS, vol. 450, pp. 251–260. Springer, Heidelberg (1990). doi:10.1007/3-540-52921-7_74

5. Cole, R.: Parallel merge sort. SIAM J. Comput. **17**(4), 770–785 (1988). doi:10.1137/0217049

6. Czerwinski, D.: Digital filter implementation in Hadoop data mining system. In: Gaj, P., Kwiecień, A., Stera, P. (eds.) Computer Networks. Communications in Computer and Information Science CN '2015, vol. 522, pp. 410–420. Springer, Switzerland (2015). doi:10.1007/978-3-319-07941-7_5

7. Czerwinski, D., Przylucki, S., Matejczuk, P.: Resource management in grid systems. In: Gaj, P., Stera, P. (eds.) Computer Networks. Communications in Computer and Information Science, vol. 291, pp. 101–110. Springer, Heidelberg (2012). doi:10.1007/978-3-642-31217-5_11

8. Czerwinski, D.: Numerical performance in the grid network relies on a grid appliance. In: Kwiecień, A., Gaj, P., Stera, P. (eds.) Computer Networks. Communications in Computer and Information Science CN 2011, vol. 160, pp. 214–223. Springer, Heidelberg (2012). doi:10.1007/978-3-642-21771-5_23

9. Damaševičius, R., Toldinas, J., Grigaravicius, G.: Modelling battery behaviour using chipset energy benchmarking. Elektronika Ir Elektrotechnika **19**(6), 117–120 (2013). doi:10.5755/j01.eee.19.6.4577

10. Gabryel, M.: The bag-of-features algorithm for practical applications using the MySQL database. In: Rutkowski, L., Korytkowski, M., Scherer, R., Tadeusiewicz, R., Zadeh, L.A., Zurada, J.M. (eds.) ICAISC 2016. LNCS, vol. 9693, pp. 635–646. Springer, Heidelberg (2016). doi:10.1007/978-3-319-39384-1_56

11. Gabryel, M., Grycuk, R., Korytkowski, M., Holotyak, T.: Image indexing and retrieval using GSOM algorithm. In: Rutkowski, L., Korytkowski, M., Scherer, R., Tadeusiewicz, R., Zadeh, L.A., Zurada, J.M. (eds.) ICAISC 2015. LNCS, vol. 9119, pp. 706–714. Springer, Heidelberg (2015). doi:10.1007/978-3-319-19324-3_63

12. Gabryel, M., Woźniak, M., Damaševičius, R.: An application of differential evolution to positioning queueing systems. In: Rutkowski, L., Korytkowski, M., Scherer, R., Tadeusiewicz, R., Zadeh, L.A., Zurada, J.M. (eds.) ICAISC 2015. LNCS, vol. 9120, pp. 379–390. Springer, Heidelberg (2015). doi:10.1007/978-3-319-19369-4_34

13. Gagliano, A., Nocera, F., Patania, F., Capizzi, G.: A case study of energy efficiency retrofit in social housing units. Energy Procedia **42**, 289–298 (2013)

14. Grycuk, R., Gabryel, M., Scherer, R., Voloshynovskiy, S.: Multi-layer architecture for storing visual data based on WCF and Microsoft SQL server database. In: Rutkowski, L., Korytkowski, M., Scherer, R., Tadeusiewicz, R., Zadeh, L.A., Zurada, J.M. (eds.) ICAISC 2015. LNCS, vol. 9119, pp. 715–726. Springer, Heidelberg (2015). doi:10.1007/978-3-319-19324-3_64

15. Gubias, L.J.: Sorting unsorted and partially sorted lists using the natural merge sort. Softw. Pract. Experience **11**(12), 1339–1340 (2006). doi:10.1002/spe.4380111211

16. Huang, B., Langston, M.: Practical in-place merging. Commun. ACM **31**(3), 348–352 (1988)

17. Karpovic, J., Krisciuniene, G., Ablonskis, L., Nemuraite, L.: The comprehensive mapping of semantics of business vocabulary and business rules (SBVR) to OWL 2 ontologies. Inf. Technol. Control **43**(3), 289–302 (2014). doi:10.5755/j01.itc.43.3.6651

18. Damaševičius, R., Vasiljevas, M., Salkevicius, J., Woźniak, M.: Human Activity Recognition in AAL Environments Using Random Projections. Comput. Math. Methods Med. **2016**, 4073584:1–4073584:17 (2016). doi:10.1155/2016/4073584. Hindawi Publishing Corporation

19. Marszałek, Z., Woźniak, G., Borowik, M., Wazirali, R., Napoli, C., Pappalardo, G., Tramontana, E.: Benchmark tests on improved merge for big data processing. In: Asia-Pacific Conference on Computer Aided System Engineering APCASE 2015, 14–16 July, Quito, Ecuador, pp. 96–101. IEEE (2015). doi:10.1109/APCASE.2015.24

20. Napoli, C., Tramontana, E., Lo Sciuto, G., Woźniak, M., Damaševičius, R., Borowik, G.: Authorship semantical identification using holomorphic Chebyshev projectors. In: Asia-Pacific Conference on Computer Aided System Engineering – APCASE 2015, 14–16 July, Quito, Ecuador, pp. 232-237. IEEE (2015) doi:10.1109/APCASE.2015.48

21. Nowak, B.A., Nowicki, R.K., Woźniak, M., Napoli, C.: Multi-class nearest neighbour classifier for incomplete data handling. In: Rutkowski, L., Korytkowski, M., Scherer, R., Tadeusiewicz, R., Zadeh, L.A., Zurada, J.M. (eds.) ICAISC 2015. LNCS, vol. 9119, pp. 469–480. Springer, Heidelberg (2015). doi:10.1007/978-3-319-19324-3_42

22. Nowicki, R., Nowak, B., Woźniak, M.: Application of rough sets in k nearest neighbours algorithm for classification of incomplete samples. In: Kunifuji, S., Papadopoulos, G.A., Skulimowski, A.M.J., Kacprzyk, J. (eds.) Knowledge, Information and Creativity Support Systems. Advances in Intelligent Systems and Computing KICSS 2014, vol. 416, pp. 243–257. Springer, Switzerland (2016). doi:10.1007/978-3-319-27478-2_17

23. Połap, D., Woźniak, M., Napoli, C., Tramontana, E.: Real-time cloud-based game management system via Cuckoo search algorithm. Int. J. Electron. Telecommun. **61**(4), 333–338 (2015). doi:10.1515/eletel-2015-0043

24. Połap, D., Woźniak, M., Napoli, C., Tramontana, E.: Is swarm intelligence able to create mazes? Int. J. Electron. Telecommun. **61**(4), 305–310 (2015). doi:10.1515/eletel-2015-0039

25. Rauh, A., Arce, G.: A fast weighted median algorithm based on quick select. In: Proceedings of the IEEE International Conference on Image Processing, pp. 105–108 (2010)

26. Rutkowski, L., Jaworski, M., Pietruczuk, L., Duda, P.: A new method for data stream mining based on the misclassification error. IEEE Trans. Neural Netw. Learn. Syst. **26**(5), 1048–1059 (2015). doi:10.1109/TNNLS.2014.2333557

27. Rutkowski, L., Jaworski, M., Pietruczuk, L., Duda, P.: The CART decision tree for mining data streams. Inf. Sci. **266**, 1–15 (2014). doi:10.1016/j.ins.2013.12.060

28. Salzberg, B.: Merging sorted runs using main memory. Acta Informatica **27**(3), 195–215 (1989). doi:10.1007/BF00572988

29. Napoli, C., Pappalardo, G., Tramontana, E.: A mathematical model for file fragment diffusion and a neural predictor to manage priority queues over BitTorrent. Appl. Math. Comput. Sci. **26**(1), 147–160 (2016)

30. Napoli, C., Pappalardo, G., Tramontana, E., Zappalà, G.: A cloud-distributed GPU architecture for pattern identification in segmented detectors big-data surveys. Comput. J. **59** (3), 338–352 (2016). Wegner, L., Teuhola, J. The external heap sort. IEEE Trans. Softw. Eng. 15 917-925 (1989)

31. Woźniak, M., Gabryel, M., Nowicki, R., Nowak, B.: An application of firefly algorithm to position traffic in NoSQL database systems. In: Kunifuji, S., Papadopoulos, G.A., Skulimowski, A.M.J., Kacprzyk, J. (eds.) Knowledge, Information and Creativity Support Systems. Advances in Intelligent Systems and Computing KICSS 2014, vol. 416, pp. 259–272. Springer, Switzerland (2016). doi:10.1007/978-3-319-27478-2_18

32. Woźniak, M., Marszałek, Z., Gabryel, M., Nowicki, R.: Preprocessing large data sets by the use of quick sort algorithm. In: Skulimowski, A.M.J., Kacprzyk, J. (eds.) Knowledge, Information and Creativity Support Systems: Recent Trends, Advances and Solutions. Advances in Intelligent Systems and Computing, vol. 364, pp. 111–121. Springer, Switzerland (2016). doi:10.1007/978-3-319-19090-7_9

33. Woźniak, M., Połap, D., Borowik, G., Napoli, C.: A first attempt to cloud-based user verification in distributed system. In: Asia-Pacific Conference on Computer Aided System Engineering – APCASE 2015, 14–16 July, Quito, Ecuador 2015, pp. 226-231. IEEE (2015). doi:10.1109/APCASE.2015.47

34. Woźniak, M., Kempa, W., Gabryel, M., Nowicki, R.: A finite-buffer queue with single vacation policy - analytical study with evolutionary positioning. Int. J. Appl. Math. Comput. Sci. **24**(4), 887–900 (2014). doi:10.2478/amcs-2014-0065

35. Woźniak, M., Marszałek, Z., Gabryel, M., Nowicki, R.K.: Modified merge sort algorithm for large scale data sets. In: Rutkowski, L., Korytkowski, M., Scherer, R., Tadeusiewicz, R., Zadeh, L.A., Zurada, J.M. (eds.) ICAISC 2013, Part II. LNCS, vol. 7895, pp. 612–622. Springer, Heidelberg (2013)

36. Woźniak, M.: On applying Cuckoo search algorithm to positioning GI/M/1/N finite-buffer queue with a single vacation policy. In: Proceedings of the 12th Mexican International Conference on Artificial Intelligence – MICAI 2013, 24–30 November, Mexico City, pp. 59-64. IEEE (2013). doi:10.1109/MICAI.2013.12

37. Zhang, W., Larson, P.A.: Dynamic memory adjustment for external mergesort. In: Proceedings of Very Large Data Bases Conference, pp. 376–385 (1997)

38. Zhang, W., Larson, P.A.: Buffering and read-ahead strategies for external mergesort. In: Proceedings of Very Large Data Bases Conference, pp. 523–533 (1998)

39. Zheng, L., Larson, P.A.: Speeding up external mergesort. IEEE Trans. Knowl. Data Eng. **8** (2), 322–332 (1996). doi:10.1109/69.494169

A Modified Electromagnetic-Like Mechanism for Rough Set Attribute Reduction

Majid Abdolrazzagh-Nezhad[1(✉)] and Shaghayegh Izadpanah[2]

[1] Department of Computer, Faculty of Engineering,
Bozorgmehr University of Qaenat, Qaen, Iran
abdolrazzagh@buqaen.ac.ir
[2] Department of Computer Engineering,
Faculty of Electronic and Computer Engineering,
Birjand University, Birjand, Iran
sh.izadpanah@birjand.ac.ir

Abstract. Reducing redundant attributes is the important issue in classification of data and knowledge discovery. This paper investigates a modified and adapted continuous optimization algorithm to solve a discrete optimization problem. To achieve this aim, a modified electromagnetic-like mechanism (MEM) is adapted to find the minimal attribute based on rough set for the first time. The procedure of MEM works based on the attraction-repulsion mechanism of electromagnetic theory, it memorizes and utilizes histories of the charges and the locations of points and the procedure also is able to escape from local optimal solutions. The MEM is adapted by a new discretization function and tested on well-known UCI datasets. Its experimental results show that proposed algorithm is able to find acceptable results when compared with the general draft of EM, GA and PSO algorithms.

Keywords: Electromagnetic-like mechanism · Attribute reduction · Rough set theory

1 Introduction

Data mining is the process of extracting patterns and knowledge. So research and propose new effective methods in this area are necessity of discovering knowledge in information age. Other side, with regard the fast growth of technology and the rapid rise of data, data mining involves various and huge data. This fact creates some problems such as big dimensional of attributes. Therefore, attribute reduction, as one of the preprocessing techniques for data mining process, is considered as a NP-hard problem which is proposed to solve big dimensional of attributes. Attribute reduction technique is able to eliminate irrelevant and redundant data by exploring minimal subset of original attribute set with minimum information loss and still keep the representations of original attributes [1, 2]. So it is motivation of rough set theory to discover patterns in inconsistent data [2]. Rough set theory [3] consists of mathematical tools to solve attribute reduction problems by discovering relation between conditional attributes and decision attribute.

© Springer International Publishing Switzerland 2016
G. Dregvaite and R. Damasevicius (Eds.): ICIST 2016, CCIS 639, pp. 356–368, 2016.
DOI: 10.1007/978-3-319-46254-7_28

Random generation method is one of the common methods to minimal the subset of the original attribute set in rough set theory [2]. The main disadvantage of this generation method is itself-consuming time and only suitable for small datasets. This fact fascinates many researchers to solve attribute reduction problems by applying some of meta-heuristic algorithms, such as genetic algorithm (GA) [4], accelerated genetic algorithm [5], particle swarm optimization (PSO) [6], scatter search (SR) [7], tabu search (TS) [8], ant colony optimization (ACO) [9], bee colony optimization (BCO) [10], firefly optimization (FO) [11], water drops algorithm (WDA) [12], bat algorithm (BA) [13] and simulated annealing (SA) [14]. Although, the previous literatures show the success of their proposed algorithms to solve attribute reduction (AR) in the rough set theory, there are significant disadvantages in these researches (See Table 1). These gaps were our motivation to adapting and modifying an effective meta-heuristic algorithm to fill up these disadvantages.

Table 1. Disadvantages of the priviouse applied algorithms for AR

Algorithm	Ref.	Disadvantages
GA	[4, 15, 16]	- Weakness in neighborhood search - Have no memory - search based on random techniques
PSO	[6, 17, 18]	- Difficulty in tuning the parameters of PSO for AR - Proposed continuous optimization problems and unsuitable for discrete problems such as AR
SR	[7]	- Failure in intensifying the search through the most promising regions of a neighborhood
TS	[8]	- Perfectly attracted to the big valley areas of solution space - Cannot explore through the whole solution space
ACO	[9, 19, 20]	- No centralized processor to guide ACO towards good solutions - Make up based on sequences of random decisions
BCO	[10]	- Premature convergence in the later search period - Accuracy of its minimal attributes is not desirable and needs to apply local search algorithms
SA	[14]	- Memory-less technique - Slowing convergence by high temperature, and dropping on local minimal by the low one

In the electromagnetic-like mechanism (EM), particles (solutions) with lower charges (better objective function values) attract others, while those with higher charges (worse objective function values) will repel. The general EM [21, 22] cannot directly handle the AR as a discrete optimization problem, because it has been designed for continuous optimization problems with bounded variables. This paper proposed a modified and adapted version of electromagnetic-like mechanism (MEM) to solve the AR in rough set theory, because it has strong advantages, solvable disadvantages. More importantly, it has not been applied for the AR up to now.

The rest of the paper is organized as follows. Section 2 describes the rough set theory. Section 3 discusses about the proposed methodology and explains the details of the modified version of electromagnetic-like mechanism. The proposed algorithm is implemented and its results compared with the state-of-the-art algorithms in Sect. 4. Finally, the conclusions and future work are discussed in Sect. 5.

2 Rough Set Attribute Reduction

Rough set theory (RST) [23] is mathematical technique for the patterns recognition in data reduction, decision rule generation and data significance evaluation. Attribute Reduction (AR) is an important issue in RST. The rough set attribute reduction (RSAR) offers a filter-based tool to gain the most informative attribute by removing all other attributes from the dataset with minimal information loss [24].

An information system is represented by $IS = (U, \mathbb{A})$, where U is a non-empty set of finite objects, which called the universe, and $\mathbb{A}$ is a non-empty set of attribute. A set V_a is the associated values to every attribute $a \in \mathbb{A}$. With regard to limited available information, objects of U maybe indiscernible. So the indiscernibility relation defines for a subset of attributes $P \subseteq \mathbb{A}$, by $IND(P)$ [25]:

$$IND(P) = \{(\kappa, \eta) \in U \times U \mid \forall a \in P, a(\kappa) = a(\eta)\} \tag{1}$$

Clearly, $IND(P)$ is an equivalence relation on U. The relation $IND(P)$, for $P \subseteq \mathbb{A}$, organizes a partition of U, which is denoted $U/IND(P)$. If $(\kappa, \eta) \in IND(P)$, then κ and η are indiscernible by attributes from P. The equivalence classes of the P-indiscernibility relation are denoted $[\kappa]_P$. So the indiscernibility relation is the mathematical basis of RST.

In RST, the lower and upper approximations consist of two basic operations [25]. For an arbitrary subset $\Omega \subseteq U$, the P-lower approximation of Ω, denoted as $\underline{P}\Omega$ is the set of all elements of U, which can be certainly classified as elements of Ω based on the attribute set P. The P-upper approximation of Ω, denoted as $\bar{P}\Omega$, is the set of elements of U, which can be possibly classified as elements of Ω based on the attribute set P. These definitions can be formulated as

$$\underline{P}\Omega = \{\kappa \mid [\kappa]_P \subseteq \Omega\} \tag{2}$$

$$\bar{P}\Omega = \left\{\kappa \mid [\kappa]_p \cap \Omega \neq \emptyset\right\} \tag{3}$$

Also, for subsets of attributes $P \subseteq \mathbb{A}$ and $Q \subseteq \mathbb{A}$, indiscernibility relations on U are $IND(P)$ and $IND(Q)$, respectively. The positive, negative and boundary regions of the partition $U/IND(Q)$ with respect to P can be defined as

$$POS_P(Q) = \cup_{\Omega \in U/IND(Q)} \underline{P}\Omega \tag{4}$$

$$NEG_P(Q) = U - \cup_{\Omega \in U/IND(Q)} \bar{P}\Omega \tag{5}$$

$$BND_P(Q) = \bigcup_{\Omega \in U/IND(Q)} \overline{P}\Omega - \bigcup_{\Omega \in U/IND(Q)} \underline{P}\Omega \tag{6}$$

The positive region, $POS_P(Q)$, is the set of all objective of U that can be uniquely classified to blocks of the partition $U/IND(Q)$ by means of the knowledge in attribute P. If a given set has a non-empty boundary region, it is rough set.

Generally, there are two approaches to find the RSAR such as dependency degree (positive regions) [25] and discernibility matrix [26]. In this paper, the dependency degree is considered to reduce the number of attributes as a cost function. So dependency can be defined in the following way. For subsets of attributes $P \subseteq A$ and $Q \subseteq A$, Q depends totally on P, if and only if $IND(Q) \subseteq IND(P)$. That means that the partition produced by Q is finer than the partition produced by P [25]. So the dependency degree of Q on P can be defined as:

$$\gamma_P(Q) = \frac{|POS_P(Q)|}{U} \tag{7}$$

Where $|.|$ is the cardinality of a set. If $\gamma_P(Q) = 1$, Q depends totally on P, if $0 < \gamma_P(Q) < 1$, Q depends partially on P, and if $\gamma_P(Q) = 0$, Q does not depend on P. In other words, Q depends totally on P, if all (some) objects of the universe U can be certainly classified to blocks of the partition $U/IND(Q)$, employing P.

In a decision system, $A = C \cup D$, where C is the set of condition attributes and D is the set of decision attributes. The quality of approximation of classification, which induced by D, is the dependency degree of C on D and denotes by $\gamma_C(D)$ [25]. Removing redundant attributes is the aim of attribute reduction, so that the reduced set offers the same quality of classification as the original. A reduct is defined for a subset $R \subseteq C$, if $\gamma_R(D) = \gamma_C(D)$. A given decision chart may consist of many attribute reducts. The set of all reducts is defined as

$$RED - \{R \subseteq C \mid \gamma_R(D) = \gamma_C(D) \land \forall B \subset R, \ \gamma_B(D) < \gamma_C(D)\} \tag{8}$$

The RSAT searches to achieve a reduct with minimal cardinality. So the objective function of RSAT is the minimal reduct and formulates as follow as:

$$\min_{R \subseteq C} |RED| = RED_{min} = \{R \in RED \mid \forall \ R' \in RED, \ |R| \leq |R'| \} \tag{9}$$

where $RED_{min} \subseteq RED$. The intersection of all reducts is called the core, the elements of which are those attributes that cannot be eliminated. The core is defined as

$$Core(C) = \cap RED \tag{10}$$

3 Modified Electromagnetic-Like Mechanism

The electromagnetic-like mechanism [21] (EM) was designed for the continuous optimization problems with bounded variables. The general EM cannot directly handle AR as a discrete optimization problem, because a point from the solution space of the AR, which shown a subset reduction of attributes, is represented by a binary array. One solution space in the iteration t is decoded in Fig. 1 that consist of 11 condition attributes ($\mathbb{C}$) and its reduction subset ($\mathbb{R}$) is $\{1, 2, 4, 7, 11\}$.

$$X_i^t \rightarrow \boxed{1\;|\;1\;|\;0\;|\;1\;|\;0\;|\;0\;|\;1\;|\;0\;|\;0\;|\;0\;|\;1}$$

Fig. 1. A sample point from the solution space of the AR in iteration t

The procedure of EM works based on the attraction-repulsion mechanism of electromagnetic theory. Birbil & Fang [21] has considered four phases for the general EM, as shown in Fig. 2. In this procedure, each candidate solution is considered as an electrically charged particle. The objective function value of each candidate solution assigns the charge of each particle and calculates the magnitude of attraction of the particles over the population.

They proposed the procedure of generation of initial bounded particles by **Algorithm 2** [p. 266, 21] as initial population. To exploit the local information for each particle, the procedure of local search was designed in **Algorithm 3** [pp. 266–267, 21]. Next, the charge of each particle and the total force applied on a particle via other ones were calculated based on *superposition principle* [27] by **Algorithm 4** in [pp. 268–269, 21]. As the last phase, Each sample particle is moved based on a vector reflecting the charge of the corresponding particle relative to the other particles in the population by **Algorithm 5** in [p. 269, 21].

To solve RSAR by the EM for the first time, a real bounded array such as $Y_i^t = \left(y_{i1}^t, y_{i2}^t, \ldots, y_{in}^t\right)$ is defined for the ith binary solution $X_i^t = \left(x_{i1}^t, x_{i2}^t, \ldots, x_{in}^t\right)$ in the iteration t that y_{ij}^t values continuously from $[0, 1]$. The binary array X_i^t is considered to calculate the dependency degree (Eq. 7) and fitness function (Eq. 11) that is designed based on the objective function (Eq. 9) of the RSAR and the real bounded array Y_i^t is utilized in the procedure of the EM.

```
Algorithm 1: Electromagnetism-like mechanism

Initialization
While termination criterion are not satisfied do
      Local search
      Computation of total forces
      Movement by total forces
End while
```

Fig. 2. Pseudo code of the general EM

Algorithm 2: Initialization

```
1:  for i = 1 to pop_size  do
2:        for j = 1 to n  do
3:            y_{ij}^0 ← U(0,1)
4:            x_{ij}^0 ← DF(y_{ij}^0)
5:        end for
6:        f(X_i^0) ← fitness(X_i^0)
7:  end for
8:  (Y_{best}^0, X_{best}^0) ← argmin{(Y_i^0, X_i^0, ), ∀i}
```

Fig. 3. Pseudo code of the initialization procedure

Algorithm 3: Local Search (LSITER, δ)

```
1: for i = 1 to δ × pop_size do
2:   Select Y_r^t from the population randomly    % no repeated
3:   Y ← Y_r^t
4:   for j = 1 to n  do
5:     counter ← 1
6:     λ_1 ← rand(0,1)
7:     While conter < LSITER do
8:        Select y_k from (y_1, ..., y_n) randomly    % no repeated
9:        λ_2 = rand(0,0.25)
10:       if (λ_1 > 0.5) and (y_k + λ_2 ≤ 1) then
11:          y_k ← y_k + λ_2
12:       else if (λ_1 > 0.5) and (y_k + λ_2 > 1) then
13:          y_k ← y_k − λ_2
14:       else if (λ_1 ≤ 0.5) and (0 ≤ y_k − λ_2) then
15:          y_k ← y_k − λ_2
16:       else if (λ_1 ≤ 0.5) and (0 > y_k − λ_2) then
17:          y_k ← y_k + λ_2
18:       end if
19:       Z = DF(Y)
20:       if fitness(Z) < f(X_r^t) then
21:          Y_r^t ← Y  and  f(X_r^t) ← fitness(z)  and  X_r^t ← Z
22:          counter ← LSITER − 1
23:       end if
24:       counter ← counter +
25:     end while
26:   end for
27: end for
28: (Y_{best}^t, X_{best}^t) ← argmin{(Y_i^t, X_i^t, ), ∀i}
```

Fig. 4. Pseudo code of the local search

Algorithm 4: Computation of total forces

1: for $i = 1$ to *pop_size*

2: $\qquad H_i^1 \leftarrow \dfrac{1}{\left|f(X_i^{t-1}) - f(X_i^t)\right|}$

3: $\qquad q_i^t \leftarrow exp\left(- H_i^1 \dfrac{f(X_i^t) - f(X_{Best}^t)}{\sum_{k=1}^{pop\_size}\left(f(X_i^t) - f(X_{Best}^t)\right)}\right)$

4: $\qquad F_i^t \leftarrow (0,0,\dots,0)$

5: end for

6: for $i = 1$ to *pop_size* do

7: $\qquad$ for $j = 1$ to *pop_size* do

8: $\qquad\qquad H_i^2 \leftarrow \dfrac{X_i^{t-1} - X_i^t}{\left\|X_i^{t-1} - X_i^t\right\|^2}$

9: $\qquad\qquad \alpha(t) \leftarrow \dfrac{1}{1 + \left(\frac{t}{0.5\,MaxIter}\right)^4}$

10: $\qquad\qquad$ if $f(X_j^t) < f(X_i^t)$ then

11: $\qquad\qquad\qquad F_i^t \leftarrow F_i^t + \alpha(t)H_i^2(X_j^t - X_i^t)\dfrac{q_i^t q_j^t}{\left\|x_j^t - x_i^t\right\|^2}$

12: $\qquad\qquad$ else

13: $\qquad\qquad\qquad F_i^t \leftarrow F_i^t + \alpha(t)H_i^2(X_j^t - X_i^t)\dfrac{q_i^t q_j^t}{\left\|x_j^t - x_i^t\right\|^2}$

14: $\qquad\qquad$ end if

15: $\qquad$ end for

16: end for

Fig. 5. Pseudo code of the computation of total forces

$$fitness(X_i^t) = \begin{cases} \sum_{j=1}^{n} x_{ij}^t & if\ \gamma_{X_{ij}^t}(\mathbb{D}) = \gamma_{\mathbb{C}}(\mathbb{D}) \\ \dfrac{n \times \left(\sum_{j=1}^{n} x_{ij}^t\right)}{\gamma_{X_{ij}^t}(\mathbb{D})} & if\ 0 < \gamma_{X_{ij}^t}(\mathbb{D}) < \gamma_{\mathbb{C}}(\mathbb{D}) \\ n \times \left(\sum_{j=1}^{n} x_{ij}^t\right) & if\ \gamma_{X_{ij}^t}(\mathbb{D}) = 0 \end{cases} \tag{11}$$

The arrays of X_i^t and Y_i^t are depended together by a new discretization function (DF), such that, any exchanges in values of Y_i^t cause one/some mutation in X_i^t. Due to exchanging elements of each points are not large in EM, the proposed DF is designed based on sensitive to small exchanges. So the DF is formulated as follow as:

$$x_{ij}^t = DF\left(y_{ij}^t\right) = \begin{cases} 1 & if\ 0.25 < y_{ij}^t \le 0.5 \quad or\ 0.75 < y_{ij}^t \le 1 \\ 0 & if\ 0 \le y_{ij}^t \le 0.25 \quad or\ 0.5 < y_{ij}^t \le 0.75 \end{cases} \tag{12}$$

Where t represents the number of iteration, $1 \le i \le pop\_size$, pop_size is the number of population and $1 \le j \le n$. So the procedures of initialization (**Algorithm 2**) and local search (**Algorithm 3**) are adapted to solve RSAR in Figs. 3 and 4.

Table 2. The Datasets utilized in the experiments

Data set	No. of Attributes	No. of Objects
Derm2	34	358
Derm	34	366
Exactly	13	1000
Exactly2	13	1000
Heart	13	294
M_of_N	13	1000
Mushroom	22	2000
Vote	16	300
WQ	38	521

Table 3. The parameters setting

Algorithm	Parameters
EM and MEM	$pop\_size = 20$, $MaxIter = 50$, $\delta = 0.25$, $LSITER = 4$
PSO	$swarm\_size = 20$, $MaxIter = 50$, $C_1 = C_2 = 1.05$, $Wt = [0.3, 1]$
GA	$pop\_size = 20$, $MaxIter = 50$, $R_C = 0.8$, $R_M = 0.2$

Calculating the charge and the total force for each particle are depend the information of the current iteration in the general EM and Birbil & Fang [21] do not have any memory to utilize the information of the previous iterations. To fill up this gap and improve the general EM, two memories are embedded to the computation of total forces. The first memory is considered to calculate the charge of the particle i that is called H_i^1 and it depends on the changes between the fitness function values of the particle i in iterations t and $t-1$. The second memory is calculated based on the normalized distances between the particle i in iterations t and $t-1$ that is named H_i^2. Also a descending nonlinear function such as $\alpha(t)$ is designed to control the impact of H_i^2 on calculating the total forces exerted on the particle i via other particles.

Table 4. The summarize and comparision of the performed algorithms

Data set	GA	PSO	EM	MEM
Derm2	$11^{(1)}\ 10^{(2)}\ 9^{(2)}$	$13^{(2)}\ 12^{(3)}$	$14^{(3)}12^{(2)}$	$11^{(2)}\ 10^{(1)}\ \mathbf{9}^{(2)}$
Derm	$10^{(4)}11^{(1)}$	$14^{(1)}13^{(2)}12^{(2)}$	$15^{(2)}14^{(2)}12^{(1)}$	$12^{(2)}\mathbf{10}^{(3)}$
Exactly	$6^{(4)}7^{(1)}$	$9^{(3)}8^{(1)}7^{(1)}$	$8^{(3)}6^{(2)}$	$7^{(1)}\mathbf{6}^{(4)}$
Exactly2	10	10	10	$11^{(2)}\mathbf{10}^{(3)}$
Heart	$\mathbf{9}^{(1)}10^{(4)}$	$12^{(1)}11^{(1)}10^{(3)}$	$13^{(3)}12^{(2)}$	10
M_of_N	$6^{(2)}7^{(3)}$	$8^{(3)}7^{(2)}$	$9^{(1)}8^{(1)}7^{(3)}$	$\mathbf{6}^{(4)}7^{(1)}$
Mushroom	$\mathbf{5}$	$8^{(1)}7^{(4)}$	$10^{(2)}8^{(1)}7^{(2)}$	$7^{(2)}6^{(3)}$
Vote	$\mathbf{8}^{(4)}12^{(1)}$	$13^{(2)}11^{(3)}$	$13^{(2)}11^{(3)}$	$12^{(2)}11^{(2)}9^{(1)}$
WQ	$\mathbf{13}^{(2)}15^{(2)}16^{(1)}$	$17^{(4)}16^{(1)}$	$18^{(3)}17^{(2)}$	$15^{(3)}\ 16^{(2)}$

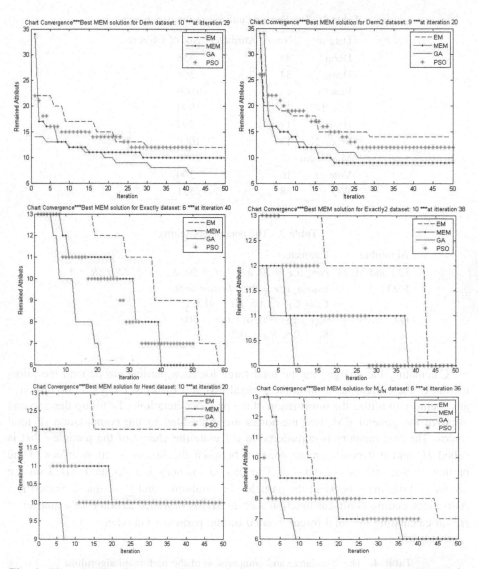

Fig. 6. The convergence cures of the performance algorithms on Derm, Derm2, Exactly, Exactly2, Heart and M_of_N datasets.

The procedure of the movement according to the total force, that was presented in **Algorithm 5** in [p. 269, 21], is utilized in the modified EM (MEM) without any serious change on its structure and only Eq. 13 is replaced with Eq. 14 [p. 269, Eq. 4, 21].

$$
x_{ij}^t = \begin{cases} x_{ij}^t + \lambda \frac{F_{ij}^t}{\|F_i^t\|} & \text{if } x_{ij}^t + \lambda \frac{F_{ij}^t}{\|F_i^t\|} \leq 1 \\ x_{ij}^t - \lambda \frac{F_{ij}^t}{\|F_i^t\|} & \text{if } x_{ij}^t + \lambda \frac{F_{ij}^t}{\|F_i^t\|} > 1 \end{cases} \tag{13}
$$

$$X_i^t = X_i^t + \lambda \frac{F_i^t}{\|F_i^t\|} (RNG) \qquad (14)$$

4   Experimental Results

The proposed algorithm MEM was programmed in MATLAB and simulations were performed on the Intel Core i50-2450 M, CPU 2.50 GHz. The experiments are carried out on nine well-known UCI datasets which are presented in Table 2. For each datasets, EM, MEM, PSO and GA MATLAB codes were run 5 times with different initial solutions that were generated randomly. The terminate condition was the number of iterations (*MaxIter*) when exceeds 50 for all preformed algorithms except run of EM for Mushroom and Exactly datasets that (*MaxIter*) set on 60 (Fig. 5).

Tuning parameters of EM and MEM were done based on performing these algorithms on a small size instance and parameters of PSO and GA were extracted from the previous literatures [4, 6, 9, 16–18], that these parameters setting are shown in Table 3.

The experimental results are summarized in Table 4 and the comparison of the performed results with GA, PSO and the general EM are provided for the benchmark

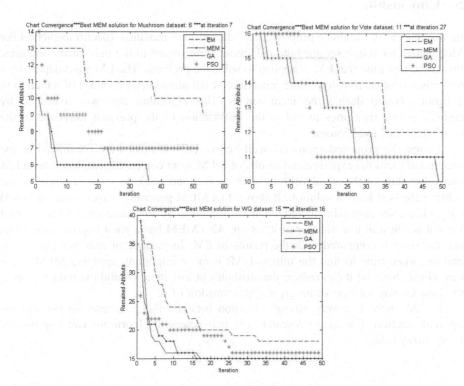

Fig. 7. The convergence cures of the performance algorithms on Mushroom, Vote and WQ datasets

datasets. The number of attributes in the minimal reducts obtained by each algorithms are represented in Table 4. The superscripts in parentheses show the number of runs that achieved the minimal reducts. The number of attribute without superscripts means that the method could obtain this number of attribute for all runs. With regard to comparison of results, which shown in Table 4, MEM has been successful to explore the solution space in finding the better solutions than the general EM and also the performance of MEM is achieved to the minimal number of reducts on five datasets from nine ones. However, MEM as a continuous optimization algorithm is less dependent on the parameters on exploring the search space.

The convergence curves of the above performed algorithms are shown in Figs. 6 and 7. The best solutions of MEM are obtained at iterations 29 for Derm, 20 for Derm2, 40 for Exactly, 38 for Exactly2, 20 for Heart, 36 for M_of_N, 7 for Mushroom, 27 for Vote and 16 for WQ. Because of the accidental nature of EM, these iteration numbers may be change in other experiments; but in comparison with other optimization algorithm like GA, PSO and EM, these show that, the speed convergence of MEM is a significant advantage and a comparable point with regard to the convergence curves. Therefore, utilizing MEM to find the minimal attribute reduction has been rationalized, since the processing time was more important than the accuracy of the minimal.

5 Conclusion

In this paper, the authors proposed an adapted and modified Electromagnetic-Like Mechanism for rough set attribute reduction. With regard to the published literatures, this is the first time that EM is applied to solve the problem. The EM was adapted by a new discretization function in the procedure of initialization and control of mutation in a limited bound during the local search. This algorithm also was improved by embedded two memories to utilize the information of the previous iterations in the computation of total forces.

To test the proposed approach, well-known UCI datasets were considered as the benchmarks and the experimental results of MEM were compared with the general EM and other state-of-the-art algorithms such as GA and PSO. In some datasets, it can achieve the best known solution. It shows that MEM generally (expect some data set) can achieve an approximate reduction of attributes by low difference with the best known solution in low number of iteration. Also MEM has a great improvement in its results, since it compared with the results of EM. In balance of accuracy and acceleration, when time to find the minimal AR is more important, applying MEM is the best chose; because it can reduce the attributes in low iteration and the reducted set is the best known solution or an great approximation of it.

In EM, there is a very strong affiliation between the parameter setting and the optimal solution. For future research, the parameters of algorithms can improve by using fuzzy rules.

References

1. Kantardzic, M.: Data Mining: Concepts, Models, Methods, and Algorithms. Wiley, New York (2011)
2. Thangavel, K., Pethalakshmi, A.: Dimensionality reduction based on rough set theory: a review. Appl. Soft Comput. **9**(1), 1–12 (2009)
3. Pawlak, Z.: Rough set theory and its applications to data analysis. Cybern. Syst. **29**(7), 661–688 (1998)
4. Dai, J.-H., Li, Y.-X.: Heuristic genetic algorithm for minimal reduction decision system based on rough set theory. In: Proceedings of 2002 International Conference on Machine Learning and Cybernetics. IEEE (2002)
5. Hedar, A.-R., Omar, M.A., Sewisy, A.A.: Rough sets attribute reduction using an accelerated genetic algorithm. In: 2015 16th IEEE/ACIS International Conference on Software Engineering, Artificial Intelligence, Networking and Parallel/Distributed Computing (SNPD). IEEE (2015)
6. Wang, X., et al.: Feature selection based on rough sets and particle swarm optimization. Pattern Recogn. Lett. **28**(4), 459–471 (2007)
7. Wang, J., et al.: Scatter search for rough set attribute reduction. In: CSO 2009 International Joint Conference on Computational Sciences and Optimization. IEEE (2009)
8. Hedar, A.-R., Wang, J., Fukushima, M.: Tabu search for attribute reduction in rough set theory. Soft. Comput. **12**(9), 909–918 (2008)
9. Chen, Y., Miao, D., Wang, R.: A rough set approach to feature selection based on ant colony optimization. Pattern Recogn. Lett. **31**(3), 226–233 (2010)
10. Suguna, N., Thanushkodi, K.G.: An independent rough set approach hybrid with artificial bee colony algorithm for dimensionality reduction. Am. J. Appl. Sci. **8**(3), 261 (2011)
11. Long, N.C., Meesad, P., Unger, H.: Attribute reduction based on rough sets and the discrete firefly algorithm. In: Boonkrong, S., Unger, H., Meesad, P. (eds.) Recent Advances in Information and Communication Technology. AISC, vol. 265, pp. 13–22. Springer, Heidelberg (2014)
12. Alijla, B.O., Peng, L.C., Khader, A.T., Al-Betar, M.A.: Intelligent water drops algorithm for rough set feature selection. In: Selamat, A., Nguyen, N.T., Haron, H. (eds.) ACIIDS 2013, Part II. LNCS, vol. 7803, pp. 356–365. Springer, Heidelberg (2013)
13. Emary, E., Yamany, W., Hassanien, A.E.: New approach for feature selection based on rough set and bat algorithm. In: 2014 9th International Conference on Computer Engineering & Systems (ICCES). IEEE (2014)
14. Abdullah, S., Golafshan, L., Nazri, M.Z.A.: Re-heat simulated annealing algorithm for rough set attribute reduction. Int. J. Phys. Sci. **6**(8), 2083–2089 (2011)
15. Lanzi, P.L.: Fast feature selection with genetic algorithms: a filter approach. In: IEEE International Conference on Evolutionary Computation. IEEE (1997)
16. Ślęzak, D., Wróblewski, J.: Order based genetic algorithms for the search of approximate entropy reducts. In: Wang, G., Liu, Q., Yao, Y., Skowron, A. (eds.) RSFDGrC 2003. LNCS, vol. 2639, pp. 308–311. Springer, Heidelberg (2003)
17. Ye, D., Chen, Z., Liao, J.: A new algorithm for minimum attribute reduction based on binary particle swarm optimization with vaccination. In: Zhou, Z.-H., Li, H., Yang, Q. (eds.) PAKDD 2007. LNCS (LNAI), vol. 4426, pp. 1029–1036. Springer, Heidelberg (2007)
18. Yue, B., Yao, W., Abraham, A., Liu, H.: A new rough set reduct algorithm based on particle swarm optimization. In: Mira, J., Álvarez, J.R. (eds.) IWINAC 2007. LNCS, vol. 4527, pp. 397–406. Springer, Heidelberg (2007)

19. Ke, L., Feng, Z., Ren, Z.: An efficient ant colony optimization approach to attribute reduction in rough set theory. Pattern Recogn. Lett. **29**(9), 1351–1357 (2008)
20. Deng, T. et al.: An improved ant colony optimization applied to attributes reduction. In: Cao, B., Zhang, C., Li, T., Fuzzy Information and Engineering. Advances in Soft Computing, vol. 54, pp. 1–6, Springer, Heidelberg (2009)
21. Birbil, Ş.İ., Fang, S.C.: An electromagnetism-like mechanism for global optimization. J. Glob. Optim. **25**(3), 263–282 (2003)
22. Birbil, Ş.İ., Fang, S.-C., Sheu, R.-L.: On the convergence of a population-based global optimization algorithm. J. Glob. Optim. **30**(2–3), 301–318 (2004)
23. Pawlak, Z., Skowron, A.: Rough sets and conflict analysis. In: Lu , J., Zhang , G., Ruan, D. (eds.) E-Service Intelligence 2007. Studies in Computational Intelligence, pp. 35–74. Springer, Heidelberg (2007)
24. Yao, Y., Zhao, Y.: Attribute reduction in decision-theoretic rough set models. Inf. Sci. **178**(17), 3356–3373 (2008)
25. Pawlak, Z.: Rough set approach to knowledge-based decision support. Eur. J. Oper. Res. **99**(1), 48–57 (1997)
26. Wang, J., Wang, J.: Reduction algorithms based on discernibility matrix: the ordered attributes method. J. Comput. Sci. Technol. **16**(6), 489–504 (2001)
27. Cowan, E.W.: Basic Electromagnetism. Academic Press, New York (1968)

Application of Real Ant Colony Optimization Algorithm to Solve Space Fractional Heat Conduction Inverse Problem

Rafał Brociek and Damian Słota[⊠]

Institute of Mathematics, Silesian University of Technology,
Kaszubska 23, 44-100 Gliwice, Poland
damian.slota@polsl.pl

Abstract. In this paper inverse problem for the space fractional heat conduction equation is investigated. In order to reconstruct the heat transfer coefficient, functional defining error of approximate solution is created. To minimize this functional the Real Ant Colony Optimization algorithm is used. The paper presents examples to illustrate the accuracy and stability of the presented algorithm.

Keywords: Intelligent algorithm · Inverse problem · Ant Colony Optimization algorithm · Space fractional heat conduction equation

1 Introduction

Inverse problems are some of the most important problems in mathematics and science. Solving inverse problems, we can determine the parameters of considered model, as well as the initial-boundary conditions. Such problems are widely used in control theory, signal processing and mechanics. In the case of differential equation of integer order, these problems have been widely described in the literature [1–8].

In papers [9–12] Murio dealt with the inverse problems for equations with fractional derivative. For example in paper [10] the mollification method was applied to solve inverse heat conduction problem with Caputo derivative, the heat flux was determined.

Also in the paper [13] the inverse diffusion problem was considered. The problem consists of determine the spatial coefficient and the order of the derivative. The authors prove that under certain conditions the solution of the problem is unique. The proof is done by transforming the solution to the solution of the wave equation. Also in the paper [14] the inverse problems of fractional order are considered. The inverse source problem is transformed into a first kind Volterra integral equation. Further, authors used a boundary element method and Tikhonov regularization to solve the Volterra integral equation of the first kind.

Paper [15] describes reconstruction of a spatially varying potential term in the one-dimensional time-fractional diffusion equation. Papers [16, 17] describe the time fractional inverse advection-dispersion problem. To solve this problems authors applied a new regularization method based on the solution given by the Fourier method. Similar problem formulated in the bounded domain is described in paper [18].

© Springer International Publishing Switzerland 2016
G. Dregvaite and R. Damasevicius (Eds.): ICIST 2016, CCIS 639, pp. 369–379, 2016.
DOI: 10.1007/978-3-319-46254-7_29

In this case kernel-based meshless method was applied. Xiong et al. [19] discuss the two-dimensional inverse problems for fractional diffusion equation.

Paper [20] describes the reconstruction of Robin boundary condition for heat conduction equation with fractional Caputo derivative. To find the heat transfer coefficient, occurring in the boundary condition of the third kind, the functional defining the error of approximate solution was minimized by using the Nelder-Mead method. Reconstruction of the diffusion coefficient and the order of fractional derivative for the equation with zero initial condition and the Dirichlet boundary condition is presented in paper [21].

Paper [22] describes numerical solution of direct problem in case of time fractional diffusion equation with homogeneous Dirichlet boundary condition. In paper [23] author presents numerical scheme for time fractional heat conduction equation with mixed boundary condition. Fractional derivative used in this case is Caputo derivative. Meerschaert in paper [24] describes numerical solution of space fractional diffusion equation with boundary condition of the first kind, and in paper [25] authors present finite difference method for two-dimensional fractional dispersion equation. In both papers, as the fractional derivative, the Riemann-Liouville derivative was used.

In this paper authors reconstruct the heat transfer coefficient occurring in the boundary condition of the third kind for the space fractional heat conduction equation. Fractional derivative with respect to spatial variable occurring in considered equation has been defined as the Riemann-Liouville derivative. Additional information for the considered inverse problem was given by the temperature measurements at selected points of the domain. The direct problem was solved by using the implicit finite difference method for space fractional heat conduction equation with mixed boundary conditions. To minimize functional defining the error of approximate solution the Real Ant Colony Optimization algorithm was used [26–28]. The algorithm has been adapted to parallel computing.

2   Formulation of the Problem

In this paper, we will consider the space fractional heat conduction equation

$$c\rho \frac{\partial u(x,t)}{\partial t} = \lambda(x) \frac{\partial u^\alpha(x,t)}{\partial x^\alpha} \tag{1}$$

defined in region

$$D = \{(x,t) : x \in [a,b], t \in [0,t^*)\}.$$

In this work, we use the terminology adopted in the case of classical heat conduction equation, despite the change of some units. By c, ρ, λ we denote the specific heat, the density and thermal conductivity, respectively. The initial condition is also added

$$u(x,0) = f(x), \qquad x \in [a,b], \tag{2}$$

as well as the Neumann and Robin boundary conditions

$$-\lambda(a)\frac{\partial u}{\partial x}(a,t) = q(t) \qquad t \in (0,t^*),$$ (3)

$$-\lambda(b)\frac{\partial u}{\partial x}(b,t) = h(t)(u(b,T) - u^\infty), \quad t \in (0,t^*),$$ (4)

where h is the heat transfer coefficient and u^∞ is the ambient temperature. Space fractional derivative occurring in Eq. (1) is interpreted in the sense of left-sided Riemann-Liouville derivative, which is defined by the formula [29]:

$$\frac{\partial^\alpha u(x,t)}{\partial x^\alpha} = \frac{1}{\Gamma(n-\alpha)}\frac{\partial^n}{\partial x^n}\int_a^x u(s,t)(x-s)^{n-1-\alpha}ds,$$ (5)

where Γ is the Gamma function, $\alpha \in (n-1,n]$. In case of $\alpha \in (1,2)$ Eq. (1) describes the phenomenon of super-diffusion, however for $\alpha = 2$ we get the classical heat conduction equation. In this paper we investigate case of $\alpha \in (1,2)$.

We assume that the heat transfer coefficient h, which is occurring in the boundary condition of the third kind, will be dependent on n parameters $a_i(i = 1,2,\ldots,n)$. Considered inverse problem will be consist of restore the parameters a_i (and therefore the boundary condition). Additional information is knowledge of temperature measurements at selected points inside the region D. Known values of the function u (input data for inverse problem) in the selected points (x_i,t_j) of the region D, we denote by

$$u(x_i,t_j) = \hat{U}_{ij}, \quad i = 1,2,\ldots,N_1, \quad j = 1,2,\ldots,N_2,$$ (6)

where N_1 is the number of sensors and N_2 denotes number of measurements at each sensor.

Solving the direct problem for fixed values of the coefficients a_i, we obtain a values approximating function u in selected points $(x_i,t_j) \in D$. These values will be denoted by $U_{ij}(h)$. Therefore based on this computation and input data, we create functional defining the error of approximate solution

$$J(h) = \sum_{i=1}^{N_1}\sum_{j=1}^{N_2}\left(U_{ij}(h) - \hat{U}_{ij}\right)^2.$$ (7)

By minimization of this functional we will reconstruct the heat transfer coefficient h.

3   Method of Solving

In this section, we describe the way to get approximate solution of space fractional heat conduction equation and Ant Colony Optimization algorithm.

Direct problem
For fixed value of heat transfer coefficient, we need to solve the direct problem, defined by the Eqs. (1)–(4). In order to do that, we used the implicit finite difference method. We built a grid of the form

$$S = \{(x_i, t_k) : x_i = a + i\Delta x, \ t_k = k\Delta t, \ i = 0, 1, \ldots, N, \ k = 0, 1, \ldots, M\}$$

where $N, M \in \mathbb{N}$ are sizes of grid with steps $\Delta x = (b-a)/N, \Delta t = t/M$.

Riemann-Liouville fractional derivative (5) is approximated using a Grünwald formula [26]:

$$\frac{\partial^\alpha u(x,t)}{\partial x^\alpha} = \frac{1}{\Gamma(-\alpha)} \lim_{N \to \infty} \frac{1}{r^\alpha} \sum_{j=0}^{N} \frac{\Gamma(j-\alpha)}{\Gamma(j+1)} u(x - (j-1)r, t), \tag{8}$$

where $= \frac{x-a}{N}$. Neumann boundary condition is approximated by

$$-\lambda_0 \frac{-U_2^{k+1} + 4U_1^{k+1} - 3U_0^{k+1}}{2\Delta x} = q^{k+1}, \tag{9}$$

and Robin boundary condition is approximated by

$$-\lambda_N \frac{U_{N+1}^{k+1} - U_{N-1}^{k+1}}{2\Delta x} = h^{k+1} \left(U_N^{k+1} - u^\infty \right). \tag{10}$$

In approximation (10), we considered additional node U_{N+1}. From (10) we obtain $U_{N+1}^{k+1} = -2\Delta x h^{k+1} \left(U_N^{k+1} - u^\infty \right) \lambda_N + U_{N-1}^{k+1}$ and these values will be use in (11). Using approximation of fractional derivative (8) and approximation of boundary conditions (9), (10), we obtain the following difference equations

$k = 0,1,2, \ldots, i = 1,2, \ldots, N$:

$$\frac{3\lambda_0}{2\Delta x} U_0^{k+1} - \frac{2\lambda_0}{\Delta x} U_1^{k+1} + \frac{\lambda_0}{2\Delta x} U_2^{k+1} = q^{k+1},$$

$$-\omega_{\alpha,0} \frac{\lambda_i \Delta t}{c\varrho(\Delta x)^\alpha} U_{i+1}^{k+1} + \left(1 - \omega_{\alpha,1} \frac{\lambda_i \Delta t}{c\varrho(\Delta x)^\alpha} \right) U_i^{k+1} \tag{11}$$

$$-\omega_{\alpha,2} \frac{\lambda_i \Delta t}{c\varrho(\Delta x)^\alpha} U_{i-1}^{k+1} - \frac{\lambda_i \Delta t}{c\varrho(\Delta x)^\alpha} \sum_{j}^{i+1} \omega_{\alpha,j} U_{i-j+1}^{k+1} = U_i^k,$$

where $U_i^k = u(x_i, t_k)$, $\lambda_i = \lambda(x_i)$ and

$$\omega_{\alpha,j} = \frac{\Gamma(j-\alpha)}{\Gamma(-\alpha)\Gamma(j+1)}. \tag{12}$$

Solving system of Eq. (11), we obtain approximate values of sought function u for grid points.

Inverse problem

To reconstruct the heat transfer coefficient, it is necessary to minimize functional (7). For this purpose, we used the parallel version of Real Ant Colony Optimization (ACO) algorithm [27]. Because it is a heuristic algorithm, so the calculation need to be repeated a certain number of times. In this paper, it will be ten times. In order to reduce computation time, we adapted algorithm for parallel computing. To describe the algorithm, we will use the following notation

F – minimized function, n – dimension (number of variables),
nT – number of threads, $M = nT \cdot p$ – number of ants,
I – number of iteration, L – number of pheromone spots,
q, ξ – parameters of the algorithm.
Now, we present the steps of the algorithm.

Initialization of the algorithm

1. Setting the input parameters of the algorithm L, M, I, nT, q, ξ.
2. Random generate L pheromone spots (solutions). Assigning them to set T_0 (starting archive).
3. Calculation of the minimized function F for each pheromone spot and organize the archive T_0 from best solution to worst.

Iterative process

4. Assigning probabilities to pheromone spots (solutions) according to the following formula

$$p_l = \frac{\omega_l}{\sum_{j=1}^{L} \omega_l} l = 1, 2, \ldots, L,$$

where weights ω_l are associated with l-th solution and expressed by the formula

$$\omega_l = \frac{1}{qL\sqrt{2\pi}} \cdot e^{\frac{-(l-1)^2}{2q^2 L^2}}.$$

5. Ant chooses a random l-th solution with probability p_l.
6. Ant transforms the j-th cordinate ($j = 1, 2, \ldots, n$) of l-th solution s_j^l sampling of proximity with the probability density function (Gaussian function)

$$g(x, \mu, \sigma) = \frac{1}{\sigma\sqrt{2\pi}} \cdot e^{\frac{-(x-\mu)^2}{2\sigma^2}}$$

where $\mu = s_j^l$, $\sigma = \frac{\xi}{L-1}\sum_{p=1}^{L} |s_p^l - s_j^l|$.

7. Repeat steps 5–6 for each ant. We obtain M new solutions (pheromone spots).
8. Dividing the new solutions on nT groups. Calculation of the minimized function F for each new solution (parallel computing).
9. Adding to the archive T_i new solutions, organize the archive by quality, removing M the worst solution.
10. Repeat steps 3–9 I times.

4 Numerical Results

We consider Eq. (1) with the following data $t^* = 500$, $x \in [0, 1]$, $c = 1000$, $\rho = 2680$, $\lambda = 240$, $u^\infty = 100$, $f(x) = 100x^2$, $q(t) = 0$ and

$$h(t) = 1400 \exp\left[\frac{t-45}{455}\ln\left(\frac{7}{4}\right)\right]$$

Heat transfer coefficient will be depend on four unknown parameters (which need to be reconstruct) in following form

$$h(t) = \begin{cases} a_1, & t \in [0, 100], \\ a_2, & t \in (100, 200], \\ a_3, & t \in (200, 350], \\ a_4, & t \in (350, 500]. \end{cases}$$

The exact values of sought parameters a1, a2, a3 and a4 are equal to 2000, 1400, 800 and 250, respectively.

As a result of solving the direct problem for exact heat transfer coefficient h, we obtain values of temperature at selected points in the grid of the domain D. Then, from these values, we select only those which correspond to the predetermined grid points (location of the thermocouple). These values simulate temperature measurements. We call it exact input data and denote by $\hat{U}_{ij}$. Grid used to generate these data was of the size 200×1000.

There is one measurement point $x_p = 0.18$ ($N_1 = 1$), the measurements from this point will be read every 1 s and 2 s ($N_2 = 501, 251$). In order to investigate the effect of measurement errors on the results of reconstruction and stability of the algorithm, the input data was perturbed by the pseudo-random error of sizes 1 and 2 %.

In the process of reconstruction the boundary condition (minimizing the functional), the direct problem was solved many times. The grid used for this purpose was a size of 150×500 and a different density than the grid used to generate the input data.

Minimum of functional (7) was searched using the ACO algorithm. This algorithm is heuristic, therefore it is required to repeat calculations a certain number of times. In this paper, we assumed that the calculations for each case will be repeated ten times. Algorithm was adapted for parallel computations (multithreads calculation), which significantly reduced the computational time. In ACO algorithm, we set following parameters

$$nT = 4, M = 12, L = 8, I = 30,$$

$$\alpha_1 \in [1800, 2300], \alpha_2 \in [1200, 1700],$$

$$\alpha_3 \in [500, 1000], \alpha_4 \in [100, 500].$$

Thus, the number of objective function calls is equal to 368.

Table 1 presents results of determining of a_1, a_2, a_3, a_4 depending on the size of disturbance input data at the measurement point $x_p = 0.18$ for measurements every 1 s and 2 s. Generally, the obtained results are quite good. Except error of the restoration parameter a_4, other errors do not exceed the input data errors. Maximal error of reconstruction parameter a_4 is 2.23 %, in case of other parameters errors do not exceed 0.91 %.

One of the main indicators of evaluating the obtained results are errors of reconstruction the temperature in the measurement point $x_p = 0.18$. Table 2 presents errors of this reconstruction in case of measurements every 1, and 2 s. Average errors of reconstructed temperature in measurement point are small. Relative average errors do not exceed 0.1 % in each case. The input errors are higher, then the average relative errors of temperature reconstruction slightly increases. These differences are minimal.

Table 1. Results of calculation in case of measurements every 1 s, 2 s ($\overline{a_i}$ – restored value of a_i, $\delta_{\overline{a_i}}$ - percentage relative error of a_i, σ - standard deviation (i = 1, 2, 3, 4))

Noise	$\overline{a_i}$	$\delta_{\overline{a_i}}$ [%]	σ	$\overline{a_i}$	$\delta_{\overline{a_i}}$ [%]	σ
every 1 s				every 2 s		
0 %	2003.22	0.17	7.78	2002.89	0.15	6.15
	1399.18	0.06	8.32	1400.90	0.07	7.33
	796.60	0.43	3.06	796.73	0.41	3.18
	245.11	1.96	3.34	245.35	1.86	2.34
1 %	2002.85	0.15	5.21	2003.34	0.17	2.41
	1398.24	0.13	3.93	1398.39	0.12	7.04
	797.16	0.36	1.56	795.59	0.56	2.81
	246.41	1.44	1.57	246.42	1.44	0.88
2 %	2004.94	0.25	2.13	2002.50	0.13	7.79
	1394.81	0.38	2.72	1401.83	0.14	4.62
	800.01	0.02	3.18	792.80	0.90	2.02
	244.44	2.23	3.72	245.08	1.97	3.52

Table 2. Errors of temperature reconstruction in measurement point $x_p = 0.18$ for measurements every 1, 2 s (Δ_{avg} - average absolute error, Δ_{max} - maximum absolute error, δ_{avg} - average relative error, δ_{max} - maximum relative error)

Noise	0 %	1 %	2 %	0 %	1 %	2 %
	every 1 s			every 2 s		
$\Delta_{avg}[K]$	0.0070	0.0113	0.0175	0.0097	0.0116	0.0278
$\Delta_{max}[K]$	0.0846	0.0846	0.0850	0.0846	0.0847	0.0845
$\delta_{avg}[\%]$	0.0424	0.0546	0.0663	0.0487	0.0524	0.0977
$\delta_{max}[\%]$	2.3406	2.3384	2.3508	2.3386	2.3413	2.3363

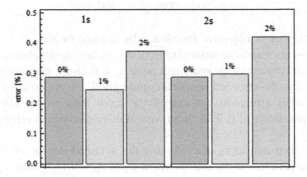

Fig. 1. Relative errors of reconstruction of the heat transfer coefficient for various perturbations of input data and for measurements every 1, 2 s

Figure 1 shows relative errors of reconstruction of heat transfer coefficient h for measurements every 1, 2 s. This error was calculated according to the formula

$$\delta_h = \frac{\| \hat{h}(t) - h(t) \|}{\| h(t) \|} \cdot 100[\%],$$

where $\hat{h}(t), h(t)$ are respectively reconstructed and exact heat transfer coefficient and $\| \cdot \|$ is norm defined by following formula

$$\|f(t)\| = \left(\int_0^{t^*} |f(t)|^2 \right)^{\frac{1}{2}}.$$

These errors are minimal and smaller than 0.42 %.

Figure 2 presents the distribution of errors of temperature reconstruction in measurement point $x_p = 0.18$ in case of measurements every 2 s. We can see that error of temperature reconstruction depend on perturbations of input data. The input errors are larger, the errors of reconstuction temperature increase. Generally temperature is reconstructed very well.

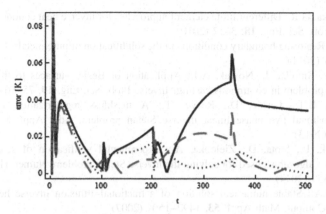

Fig. 2. Distribution of errors of temperature reconstruction in measurement point $x_p = 0.18$ for measurements every 2 s and for various perturbations of input data (0 % – dotted line, 1 % – dashed line, 2 % – solid line)

5 Conclusions

In this paper Real Ant Colony Optimization algorithm was used to solve heat conduction inverse problem of fractional order. Heat transfer coefficient occurring in Robin boundary condition was restored. In order to reconstruct it, functional defining error of approximate solution was minimized. Direct problem was solved using the finite difference method.

Obtained results are very good. Errors of reconstruction heat transfer coefficient in each case are less than 0.42 % and do not exceed the input data errors. More importantly, errors of reconstruction temperature at the measurement point are minimal, average relative errors are smaller than 0.1 %.

It is worth mentioning that the used algorithm can be easily adapted to parallel computing which allows to significantly reduce the computation time. Executing algorithm for the 4 threads, the computation performed nearly 3.8 times faster than without multithreading approach.

References

1. Hristov, J.: An inverse Stefan problem relevant to boilover: heat balance integral solutions and analysis. Therm. Sci. **11**, 141–160 (2007)
2. Hristov, J.: An approximate solution to the transient space-fractional diffusion equation: integral-balance approach, optimization problems and analyzes. Therm. Sci. (2016). doi:10. 2298/TSCI160113075HK
3. Hristov, J.: Transient heat diffusion with a non-singular fading memory from the Cattaneo constitutive equation with Jeffrey's kernel to the Caputo-Fabrizio time-fractional derivative. Therm. Sci. **20**, 765–770 (2016)

4. Leśniewska, G.R.: Different finite element approaches for inverse heat conduction problems. Inverse Prob. Sci. Eng. **18**, 3–17 (2010)
5. Słota, D.: Restoring boundary conditions in the solidification of pure metals. Comput. Struct. **89**, 48–54 (2011)
6. Nowak, I., Smołka, J., Nowak, A.J.: Application of Bezier surfaces to the 3-D inverse geometry problem in continuous casting. Inverse Prob. Sci. Eng. **19**, 75–86 (2011)
7. Johnsson, B.T., Lesnic, D., Reeve, T.: A meshless regularization method for a two-dimensional two phase linear inverse Stefan problem. Adv. Appl. Math. Mech. **5**, 825–845 (2013)
8. Hetmaniok, E., Słota, D., Zielonka, A.: Experimental verification of selected artificial intelligence algorithms used for solving the inverse Stefan problem. Numer. Heat Transfer B **66**, 343–359 (2014)
9. Murio, D.A.: Stable numerical solution of a fractional-diffusion inverse heat conduction problem. Comput. Math Appl. **53**, 1492–1501 (2007)
10. Murio, D.A.: Time fractional IHCP with Caputo fractional derivatives. Comput. Math Appl. **56**, 2371–2381 (2008)
11. Murio, D.A., Mejia, C.E.: Generalized time fractional IHCP with Caputo fractional derivatives. J. Phys. Conf. Ser. **135**, 012074 (8 pp.) (2008)
12. Murio, D.A.: Stable numerical evaluation of Grünwald-Letnikov fractional derivatives applied to a fractional IHCP. Inverse Prob. Sci. Eng. **17**, 229–243 (2009)
13. Miller, L., Yamamoto, M.: Coefficient inverse problem for a fractional diffusion equation. Inverse Probl. **8**, 075013 (8 pp.) (2013)
14. Wei, T., Zhang, Z.Q.: Reconstruction of time-dependent source term in time-fractional diffusion equation. Eng. Anal. Bound. Elem. **37**, 23–31 (2013)
15. Jin, B., Rundell, W.: An inverse problem for a one-dimensional time-fractional diffusion equation. Inverse Prob. **28**, 075010 (2012)
16. Zheng, G.H., Wei, T.: A new regularization method for the time fractional inverse advection-dispersion problem. SIAM J. Numer. Anal. **49**, 1972–1990 (2011)
17. Zheng, G.H., Wei, T.: A new regularization method for solving a time-fractional inverse diffusion problem. J. Math. Anal. Appl. **378**, 418–431 (2011)
18. Dou, F.F., Hon, Y.C.: Kernel-based approximation for Cauchy problem of the time-fractional diffusion equation. Eng. Anal. Bound. Elem. **36**, 1344–1352 (2012)
19. Xiong, X., Zhoua, Q., Hon, Y.C.: An inverse problem for fractional diffusion equation in 2-D dimensional case: stability analysis and regularization. J. Math. Anal. Appl. **393**, 185–199 (2012)
20. Brociek, R., Słota, D.: Reconstruction of the boundary condition for the heat conduction equation of fractional order. Therm. Sci. **19**, 35–42 (2015)
21. Bondarenko, A.N., Ivaschenko, D.S.: Numerical methods for solving invers problems for time fractional diffusion equation with variable coefficient. J. Inv. Ill-Posed Prob. **17**, 419–440 (2009)
22. Murio, D.: Implicit finite difference approximation for time fractional diffusion equations. Comput. Math Appl. **56**, 1138–1145 (2008)
23. Brociek, R.: Implicit finite difference method for time fractional diffusion equations with mixed boundary conditions. Zesz. Nauk. PŚ., Mat. Stosow. **4**, 73–87 (2014)
24. Meerschaert, M.M., Tadjeran, Ch.: Finite difference approximations for fractional advection-dispersion flow equations. J. Comput. Appl. Math. **172**, 65–77 (2006)
25. Meerschaert, M.M., Scheffler, H.P., Tadjeran, Ch.: Finite difference method for two-dimensional fractional dispersion equation. J. Comput. Phys. **211**, 249–261 (2006)
26. Dorigo, M., Stützle, T.: Ant Colony Optimization. MIT Press, Cambridge (2004)

27. Socha, K., Dorigo, M.: Ant Colony Optimization for continuous domains. Eur. J. Oper. Res. **185**, 1155–1173 (2008)
28. Brociek, R., Słota, D.: Application of intelligent algorithm to solve the fractional heat conduction inverse problem. Commun. Comput. Inf. Sci. **538**, 356–365 (2015)
29. Podlubny, I.: Fractional Differential Equations. Academic Press, San Diego (1999)

A New Classifier Based on the Dual Indiscernibility Matrix

Piotr Artiemjew[1], Bartosz A. Nowak[1(✉)], and Lech T. Polkowski[2]

[1] Department of Mathematical Methods in Computer Science,
University of Warmia and Mazury, ul. Sloneczna 54, 10-710 Olsztyn, Poland
{artem,bnowak}@matman.uwm.edu.pl
[2] Department of Computer Science,
Polish-Japanese Institute of Information Technology,
ul. Koszykowa 86, 02-008 Warsaw, Poland
polkow@pjwstk.edu.pl

Abstract. A new approach to classifier synthesis was proposed by Polkowski and in this work we propose an implementation of this idea. The idea is based on usage of a dual indiscernibility matrix which allows to determine for each test object in the data, pairs of training objects which cover in a sense the given test object. A family of pairs best covering the given object pass their decisions for majority voting on decision for the test object. We present results obtained by our classifier on standard data from UCI Repository and compare them with results obtained by means of k-NN and Bayes classifiers. The results are validated by multiple cross-validation. We find our classifier on par with k-NN and Bayes classifiers.

In this work Sect. 1, Introduction, gives basic definitions of the notions applied and proposed method, Sect. 2 brings forth results of experiments with real data from UCI Repository. The last Sect. 3 is devoted to a discussion of results and concluding remarks.

Keywords: Rough sets · Dual indiscernibility matrix · Pair classifier

1 Introduction

Classification is one of the most important tasks in Artificial Intelligence and has many applications, such as [18, 19]. Among paradigms worked out for Artificial Intelligence in the domain of Data Mining is the rough set theory, see [5, 6, 14]. This theory allows for generation of certain and possible decision/classifying rules along with minimal and irreducible rules, see [8, 9]. Those rules are generated by means of the discernibility matrix, see [11].

In [12] new notions were introduced into the field of rough set – based Data Mining, viz., relational separation of data, the dual indiscernibility matrix, and the idea of a new classifier, based on the notion of a neighborhood of an object, understood as a set of other objects which among themselves submit all attribute values for the given object, see also [1]. We use those notions in our present work. We begin with explanations of notions to be used in what follows.

© Springer International Publishing Switzerland 2016
G. Dregvaite and R. Damasevicius (Eds.): ICIST 2016, CCIS 639, pp. 380–391, 2016.
DOI: 10.1007/978-3-319-46254-7_30

1.1   Information/Decision Systems

Rough set theory, see [5–7], starts with the notion of an *information system* which is a triple $I = (U, A, val)$, where U is a set of objects, A - a set of attributes and $val : AxU \rightarrow V$, is a map which sends each pair (a, u), a in A, u in U, into the value $a(u)$. In case of a classification problem, the system I is augmented with the decision attributed and the task is to derive from the decision system $D = (U, A, val, d)$, a set of decision rules which would as best as possible classify yet unseen objects into decision classes.

1.2   The Dual Indiscernibility Matrix

Indiscernibility relation is the main tool in analysis of data by rough sets. For a set B of attributes, the relation $IND(B)$ is the set $\{(u, v) : u, v \in U, \forall a \in B \, a(u) = a(v)\}$. In [11], indiscernibility was exploited in construction of the discernibility matrix $IM, IM_{u,v} = \{a \in A : a(u) \neq a(v)\}]$, an instrumental notion in rough set-theoretical Data Mining, see, e.g., [2, 4, 8, 9]. The *dual indiscernibility matrix* (*DIM* for short) is defined as $DIM_{a,v} = \{u \in U : a(u) = v\}$.

DIM is useful in splitting the data set into two subsets: the kernel and the residuum, see [1, 12]. The kernel is a subset of data set with the property that each object in it has the set of its attribute values represented as a union of sets of attribute values of some other objects in the kernel, whereas the residuum consists of objects having at least one attribute value not met in any other object in data. Both the kernel and the residuum turned out to yield classification results fully comparable with those of the whole data set, see [1], showing the usefulness of *DIM*.

1.3   Neighborhoods, Partial Neighborhoods of Objects

For an object u in the data set U, we call a neighborhood of $u, N(u)$ in symbols, a set of objects in $U - (u)$ such that each attribute value $a(u)$ may be supplied by an object in $N(u)$. An algorithm was proposed in Polkowski [12], for assigning a decision value $d(t)$ to a test object *tst* by finding a set of minimal neighborhoods of *tst* in the training set *TRN*, voting for the decision $d(t)$ by each neighborhood and then voting by the ensemble of neighborhoods on the final value of $d(t)$, see [1].

A non-empty subset of a neighborhood of an object is called a *partial neighborhood* of that object. For complexity reasons, we are interested in partial neighborhoods of minimal cardinality, say 2, which cover as many as possible attribute values of the object.

For purpose of illustration, we include an exemplary information system in Table 1 from [1] along with *DIM* for it in Table 2. Objects in one-element cells of *DIM* belong in the residuum of the system in Table 1 and the remaining objects constitute the kernel of the system.

In Tables 3 and 4, we show, respectively, *DIM* for the residuum and *DIM* for the kernel. One can read off from *DIM* neighborhoods of objects, for instance, for the object number 4, a minimal neighborhood is {8, 10}, and {8} is a partial neighborhood

Table 1. Information system

Object	a_1	a_2	a_3	a_4	a_5	a_6
1	1	0	0	1	1	0
2	0	1	1	0	1	2
3	1	0	0	1	0	1
4	0	0	1	1	1	0
5	0	0	2	1	0	0
6	1	1	0	0	1	1
7	0	1	0	1	0	1
8	1	0	1	0	1	0
9	1	2	0	0	2	1
10	0	0	1	1	1	0

Table 2. The dual indiscernibility matrix

Value	a_1	a_2	a_3	a_4	a_5	a_6
0	$\{2,4,5,7,10\}$	$\{1,3,4,5,8,10\}$	$\{1,3,6,7,9\}$	$\{2,6,8,9\}$	$\{3,5,7,10\}$	$\{1,4,5,8,10\}$
1	$\{1,3,6,8,9\}$	$\{2,6,7\}$	$\{2,4,8,10\}$	$\{1,3,4,5,7,10\}$	$\{1,2,4,6,8\}$	$\{3,6,7,9\}$
2	$\emptyset$	$\{9\}$	$\{5\}$	$\emptyset$	$\{9\}$	$\{2\}$

Table 3. Data to remove

Value	a_1	a_2	a_3	a_4	a_5	a_6
0	$\{2,5\}$	$\{5\}$	$\{9\}$	$\{2,9\}$	$\{5\}$	$\{5\}$
1	$\{9\}$	$\{2\}$	$\{2\}$	$\{5\}$	$\{2\}$	$\{9\}$
2	$\emptyset$	$\{9\}$	$\{5\}$	$\emptyset$	$\{9\}$	$\{2\}$

Table 4. The dual indiscernibility matrix after deletion of the proper data – first level of reduction

Value	a_1	a_2	a_3	a_4	a_5	a_6
0	$\{4,7,10\}$	$\{1,3,4,8,10\}$	$\{1,3,6,7\}$	$\{6,8\}$	$\{3,7,10\}$	$\{1,4,8,10\}$
1	$\{1,3,6,8\}$	$\{6,7\}$	$\{4,8,10\}$	$\{1,3,4,7,10\}$	$\{1,4,6,8\}$	$\{3,6,7\}$

covering four out of six attribute values in the object 4 while $\{10\}$ is a partial neighborhood of the object 4 which covers five out of six attribute values in the object 4.

Let us notice that the system in Table 4 cannot be reduced further, i.e., its residuum is the empty set.

In this particular work the pair classifier is based on the original *DIM* without reduction. We have future plan to check the influence of this reduction on the quality of Pair classifier. In the next subsection we have detail description of our version of the Pair classifier.

1.4   The Pair Classifier

The Pair classifier can be compared to work of two physicians: they try to diagnose a single patient (*tst*). Each one has the same experience (*TRN*), and they have not met exactly the same case as the current patient (*tst* ∉ *TRN*). They consult each other and try to remind themselves two most similar cases which had in common as many symptoms with the current patient as possible. After each physician established decision, they agree that decision which base on the most similar case in their history is more appropriate. After that, they repeat the process, but they omit cases (two chosen cases in *TRN*) already mentioned.

For $TST = (U_{tst}, A, d)$ as a test decision system and $TRN = (U_{trn}, A, d)$ as a training decision system, the classification of objects from the test system (U_{tst}) based on training objects consists of the following steps:

(i) First of all, we search for maximal and minimal values of attributes on the training set in order to normalize the distance between descriptors. These values are marked as max_a and min_a, respectively, $a \in A$.

(ii) In the next step we create *DIM* from the training set (*TRN*), in this process we search for all distinct attribute values on objects in *TRN* and we collect them in the set *Val(TRN)*. For improvement of the speed of this process we can use [16].

We set two parameters, the first - ε describe indiscernibility ratio, useful in the process of classification based on the numerical attributes, and the second parameter is called *maxDeltaLevel*. Using the second parameter we can control size of the set of pairs useful in the classification process and their extent of covering. The *maxDeltaLevel* takes values from the set $\{0, 1, \ldots, |A| - 1\}$, ε is a value in the range $[0, 1)$. Detailed description of these parameters is given in the following part of the paper.

(iii) For a test object *tst* from U_{tst}, we compare the object with values in *DIM*. For all attributes and distinct values in *Val(TRN)*, we check which training objects have the same attribute values as the *tst* object. In *DIM*, it is reduced to the searching the row for the considered attribute for the respective value and recording the respective training objects. For symbolic attributes the comparison is based on the Hamming metric. In case of numerical values, a descriptor of *tst* object is indiscernible with the respective attribute of considered value from *DIM* when the following condition is fulfilled:

$$\frac{\left|a_i(tst) - val_j\right|}{max_{a_i} - min_{a_i}} < \varepsilon, \tag{1}$$

where $val_j \in Val(TRN)$ is the *j*-th distinctive value in *DIM*, *i* is the index of attribute. In this step we make the ranking of training objects, which best cover the *tst*.

(iv) In this step, we use the ranking found in (iii) to select the first pair for classification of *tst*. The first object $\left(trn_1^{first}\right)$ of the first pair is formed based on the training object with the best covering of *tst*, the second object $\left(trn_1^{second}\right)$ is the one which covers the most attributes not covered by the first object $\left(trn_1^{first}\right)$. In this way we get the pair

$$\left(trn_1^{first}, trn_1^{second}\right). \tag{2}$$

Level of covering of this pair we define as *level0,* and we remove objects from this pair from further consideration.

(v) We are searching for next pairs with covering not lesser than *level0 − maxDeltaLevel* and removing them respectively from further consideration. The result of this and previous step is the set of pairs

$$PAIRS = \{\left(trn_1^{first}, trn_1^{second}\right), \ldots, \left(trn_N^{first}, trn_N^{second}\right)\}, \tag{3}$$

where N is number of pairs.

(vi) In this step, we classify object *tst.* All pairs, separately, transfer to the final parameter of classification their own decision, and the most common is chosen as the final one. The decision made by particular pair is based on the real level of covering of objects, for instance, when in the pair $\left(trn_r^{first}, trn_r^{second}\right)$ the object trn_r^{first} covers more descriptors of *tst* than the object trn_r^{second} then, the decision forwarded to the final classifier is the class of object trn_r^{first}.

2   Results of Experiments

In this section we describe the experimental part of our work. We have carried out experiments with use of multiple Cross Validation 5 (CV-5) [3] method and we use the exemplary data from UCI Repository [10], the list of data is in the Table 5. The detailed

Table 5. The list of examined datasets

Name	Attr. type	Attr. no.	Obj. no.	Class no.
Adult	*categorical, integer*	15	48842	2
Australian credit	*categorical, integer, real*	15	690	2
Diabetes	*categorical, integer*	9	768	2
German credit	*categorical, integer*	21	1000	2
Heart disease	*categorical, real*	14	270	2
Hepatitis	*categorical, integer, real*	20	155	2
Congressional voting	*categorical*	17	435	2
Mushroom	*categorical*	23	8124	2
Nursery	*categorical*	9	12960	5
Soyabean large	*categorical*	36	307	19

Table 6. Rate of correctly classified samples from test set for k-NN, Naive Bayes classifier vs pair classifier, results for k-nn and Bayes are from [14]

Name	k-NN	Bayes	Pair, best	Pair, nil
Adult	0.841	0.864	0.853 *L1*	0.823
Australian credit	0.855	0.843	0.859 *L4,5*	0.859
Diabetes	0.631	0.652	0.721 *L0*	0.710
German credit	0.730	0.704	0.722 *L1*	0.721
Heart disease	0.837	0.829	0.822 *L1*	0.800
Hepatitis	0.890	0.845	0.892 *L0*	0.831
Congressional voting	0.938	0.927	0.928 *L0*	0.928
Mushroom	1.000	0.910	1.000 *L0*	1.000
Nursery	0.578	0.869	0.845 *L0*	0.845
Soyabean large	0.928	0.690	0.910 *L0*	0.910

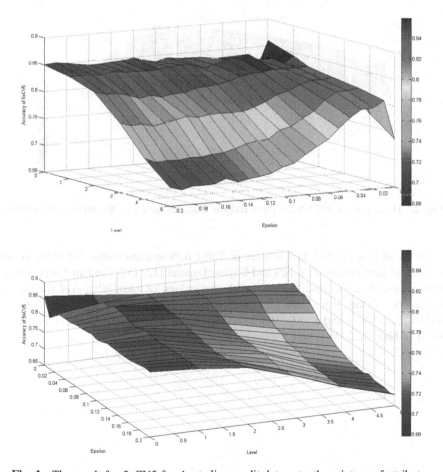

Fig. 1. The result for 5xCV5 for Australian credit data set - the mixture of attributes

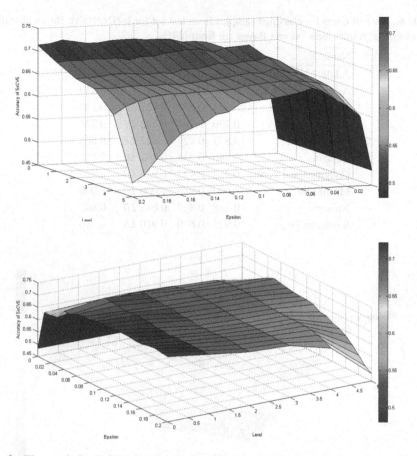

Fig. 2. The result for 5xCV5 for Pima Indians Diabetes data set - the mixture of attributes

results for all investigated data sets are in Table 6, where the results for Pair Classifier are given against results for k-NN and Bayes classifier [13, 15]. The Pair-best column in Table 6 describes the results along with the values of *maxDeltaLevel* for the best parameters of the pair classifier; in the column Pair-nil results are listed for *maxDeltaLevel* = 0 and $\varepsilon = 0$. We have visualized the selected results and they are shown in Figs. 1, 2, 3, 4, and 5.

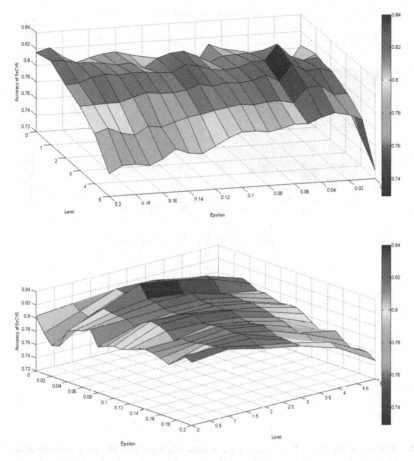

Fig. 3. The result for 5xCV5 for heart disease data set – the mixture of attributes

3   Discussion of Results and Conclusions

This section contains reflections about the obtained results, and the final conclusions.

3.1   Discussion of Results

The results of classification show the dependence of the indiscernibility ratio of descriptors on the accuracy of classification for the numerical data – see Fig. 3 (the top picture). We have obtained the best results for the parameters ε in the interval $[0, 0.1]$ and low values of *maxDeltaLevel*. Obviously, the quality of classification depends strictly on the type of data set (the internal logic). For selected data sets, the Pair classifier is fully comparable to the k-NN and Bayes classifiers, in some cases works

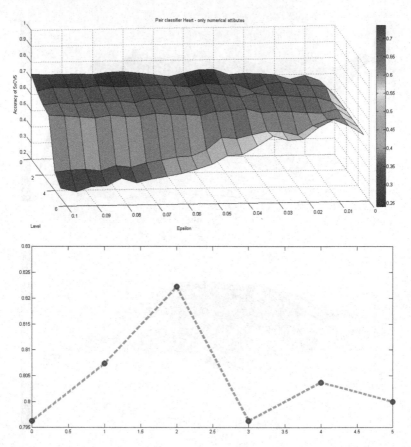

Fig. 4. The result for 5xCV5 for heart disease data set, top) NUMB- only numerical attributes, bottom) SYMB- only symbolical attributes (horizontal axis describe level and vertical accuracy of classification)

slightly worse or slightly better. Notable is the stability of Pair classifier: between k-NN and Bayes classifiers, it gives, as a rule, the value close to the better of the two. Lowering slightly the required level of covering (using greater value of *maxDeltaLevel*) by pairs, we can improve the quality of classification in some cases – see Figs. 1, 2, 3, 4 and 5 (bottom pictures). But when we continue the lowering of levels, the number of pairs in the classification process is too high, which may lead to a smaller accuracy of classification.

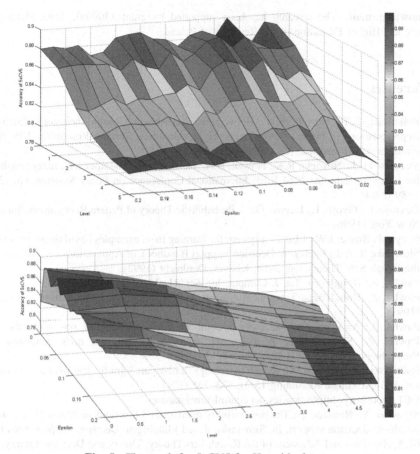

Fig. 5. The result for 5xCV5 for Hepatitis data set

3.2 Conclusions

In this work we have investigated the version of the pair based classifier, introduced after proposal by Polkowski in [1]. We have carried out experiments on the real data from the UCI Repository. The results show that classification quality of the new classification is fully comparable with the classic k-NN and Naive Bayes classifiers. The advantage of Pair classification is that we do not have to estimate here any parameter, because the basic - *level0* - is determined automatically and it depends on data. Additionally, the Pair classifier is based on *DIM* mechanism, which allows for an approximation of the decision system. We would like to check the effectiveness of Pair classifier on this approximated data in the next papers. Additionally, in the future works, we plan to extend the basic version of proposed classifier by focusing on the decision classes of the training data. We also plan to check the version based on the fuzzy sets and try to boost classification by using Boosting [17].

Acknowledgement. The research has been supported by grant 1309-802 from Ministry of Science and Higher Education of the Republic of Poland.

References

1. Polkowski, L.T., Nowak, B.A.: Betweeness, Lukasiewicz Rough Inclusions, Euclidean Representations in Information Systems, Hyper–Granules, Conflict Resolution. IOS Press, Fundamenta Informaticae XX (2016) (forthcoming)
2. Starczewski, J., Nowicki, R.K., Nowak, B.A.: Genetic fuzzy classifier with fuzzy rough sets for imprecise data. In: 2014 IEEE International Conference on Fuzzy Systems, pp. 1382–1389 (2014)
3. Devroye, L., Gyorfi, L., Lugosi, G.: A Probabilistic Theory of Pattern Recognition. Springer, New York (1996)
4. Grzymala-Busse, J.W.: LERS - a system for learning from examples based on rough sets. In: Słowiński, R. (ed.) Intelligent Decision Support Handbook of Applications and Advances of the Rough Sets Theory, pp. 3–18. Kluwer, Dordrecht (1992)
5. Pawlak, Z.: Rough sets. Int. J. Comput. Inf. Sci. **11**, 341–356 (1982)
6. Pawlak, Z.: Rough Sets: Theoretical Aspects of Reasoning about Data. Kluwer, Dordrecht (1991)
7. Pawlak, Z.: An inquiry into anatomy of conflicts. J. Inform. Sci. **109**, 65–78 (1998)
8. Pawlak, Z., Skowron, A.: A rough set approach for decision rules generation. In: Proceedings of IJCAI 1993 Workshop W12 (1993)
9. Polkowski, L., Skowron, A.: Rough mereology: a new paradigm for approximate reasoning. Int. J. Approximate Reasoning **15**(4), 333–365 (1997)
10. UCI Repository. http//www.ics.uci.edu/mlearn/databases
11. Skowron, A., Rauszer, C.: The discernibility matrices and functions in information systems, intelligent decision support. In: Slowinski, R. (ed.) Intelligent Decision Support: Handbook of Applications and Advances of the Rough Sets Theory. Theory and Decision Library, vol. 11, pp. 331–362. Springer, Dordrecht (1992)
12. Polkowski, L.: Betweenness, lukasiewicz rough inclusions, euclidean representations in information systems, hyper-granules, conflict resolution. In: Proceedings of the 24th International Workshop on Concurrency, Specification and Programming, pp 97–110. University of Rzeszow (2015). http://ceur-ws.org/Vol-1492/
13. Polkowski, L., Artiemjew, P.: Granular Computing in Decision Approximation: An Application of Rough Mereology. Intelligent Systems Reference Library, vol. 77. Springer, Heidelberg (2015)
14. Polkowski, L.: Rough Sets: Mathematical Foundations. Advances in Intelligent and Soft Computing. Springer/Physica-Verlag, Heidelberg (2002)
15. Nowak, B.A., Nowicki, R.K., Woźniak, M., Napoli, C.: Multi-class nearest neighbour classifier for incomplete data handling. In: Rutkowski, L., Korytkowski, M., Scherer, R., Tadeusiewicz, R., Zadeh, L.A., Zurada, J.M. (eds.). LNCS, vol. 9119, pp. 469–480. Springer, Heidelberg (2015)
16. Woźniak, M., Marszałek, Z., Gabryel, M., Nowicki, R.K.: Modified merge sort algorithm for large scale data sets. In: Rutkowski, L., Korytkowski, M., Scherer, R., Tadeusiewicz, R., Zadeh, L.A., Zurada, J.M. (eds.) ICAISC 2013, Part II. LNCS, vol. 7895, pp. 612–622. Springer, Heidelberg (2013)

17. Korytkowski, M., Nowicki, R., Rutkowski, L., Scherer, R.: AdaBoost ensemble of DCOG rough–neuro–fuzzy systems. In: Jędrzejowicz, P., Nguyen, N.T., Hoang, K. (eds.) ICCCI 2011, Part I. LNCS, vol. 6922, pp. 62–71. Springer, Heidelberg (2011)
18. Zalasiński, M., Cpałka, K.: New algorithm for on-line signature verification using characteristic hybrid partitions. In: Wilimowska, Z., Borzemski, L., Grzech, A., Świątek, J. (eds.) Information Systems Architecture and Technology: Proceedings of 36th International Conference on Information Systems Architecture and Technology – ISAT 2015 – Part IV. Advances in Intelligent Systems and Computing, vol. 432, pp. 147–157. Springer, Heidelberg (2016)
19. Drozda, P., Sopyła, K., Górecki, P.: Different orderings and visual sequence alignment algorithms for image classification. In: Rutkowski, L., Korytkowski, M., Scherer, R., Tadeusiewicz, R., Zadeh, L.A., Zurada, J.M. (eds.) ICAISC 2014, Part I. LNCS, vol. 8467, pp. 693–702. Springer, Heidelberg (2014)

Introduction to the Model of the Active Assistance System for Elder and Disabled People

Dawid Połap[✉] and Marcin Woźniak

Institute of Mathematics, Silesian University of Technology, Kaszubska 23,
44-100 Gliwice, Poland
dawid.polap@gmail.com, marcin.wozniak@polsl.pl

Abstract. In this article we present assumptions for development of novel model of active system that can assist elder and disabled people. In the following sections we discuss literature and propose a structure of decision support and data processing on levels: voice and speech processing, image processing based on proposed descriptors, routing and positioning. For these aspects pros and cons that can be faced in the development process are described with potential preventive actions.

Keywords: Automatic human support · Intelligent system · Human activity recognition · Ambient assisted living

1 Introduction

Automatic human support systems are designed to assist people that may need help in common activities, i.e. when elder people are talking with others, do shopping or just simply if they get lost in the city and want to get home or need to call for help in urgent situations. Similar support may be a valuable option for disabled people to help them in becoming independent and to gain confidence in rapidly changing environment. Mainly this type of support can be developed using sensors attached to body or other sensor methods to assist in continuous monitoring and processing of voice and speech, language and text, and GPS (*Global Positioning System*) based positioning according to current position in the city. Moreover considerably more developed support systems are also using additional sensors managed by intelligent healthcare applications for automatic measurements of life and physical activity to perform monitoring of elderly and disabled people.

Societies in all the countries varies in age, however in the developed parts of the World we can see rapid aging. According to WHO (*World Health Organization*) a number of aged people in the World shall increase up to 1 billion by the year 2030, and by the year 2050 people older than 60 years can reach over 25 % of the population. Similarly in these countries many disabled people want to take an active part in everyday life. Therefore these two groups are potential targets for these type of active assistance, since these people often suffer from age-related diseases or simply have weaker senses that may be actively supported by intelligent assistance systems. Ambient Assisted Living (AAL) developments can be divided into care-providing robots, surveillance applications, and man-machine interactions technology. However all them require

© Springer International Publishing Switzerland 2016
G. Dregvaite and R. Damasevicius (Eds.): ICIST 2016, CCIS 639, pp. 392–403, 2016.
DOI: 10.1007/978-3-319-46254-7_31

intelligent Human Activity Assistance (HAA) to support humans in common situations. Therefore sensor-based real-time assistance is extensively examined in recent years. In this article we would like to discuss an introduction to the development of novel model for this type of active human support.

1.1 Related Works

Human activity recognition and assistance are growing areas of computer implementations. We can present this topic from two sides: a computer designer that must implement a response to human action and also medical point of view where background for each behaviour and appropriate treatment and assistance are considered. In the developer point of view we can find aspects that consider usage of sensors and devices applied to recognize events. Medical attempt is concerned on medical reasons of each action and treatment that can support humans against consequences. Therefore in a system that can actively assist people we must built a bridge between these two to implement a reliable solution for various aspects using most efficient technology and methods.

Engineering aspects of HAA systems are based on activity recognition, which basics were discussed by Jain et al. [20]. Aggarwal and Ryoo presented extensive study of various activities that can be recognized using computer applications [1] and Aggarwal and Xia extended this approach to use 3D data for activity recognition [2]. Ziaeefrad and Beregevin [38] as well as Lara and Labrador [22] presented literature overview over semantic methods in human activity recognition. These methods gave attempt to proper classification based on categorization for various classes of similar activities, for which i.e. we can apply devoted vision-based techniques as presented in a survey by Poppe [30]. Since human activities have some patterns that are repeated in other situations we can create frameworks to cover these patterns as proposed by Govindaraju [16]. Similarly Suriani et al. proposed a catalogue of sudden event recognition possibilities [34] to divide them into classes of actions with possible ways of recognition. To each class a computer system must be trained to respond properly, it is a demanding process where various techniques of CI can be applied what was presented as a survey of various possibilities of human behaviour with corresponding computer recognitions by Turaga et al. [35].

Compendium of physical activities with extended descriptions and definitions was presented by Ainsworth et al. [3]. Medical aspects of behavioural biometrics with its usage for recognition purposes were discussed by Yampolskiy and Govindaraju [40]. The movements and actions of people differ with age but also depend on time of a day or weather conditions. Mathie et al. described daily movements and actions that can be classified with triaxial accelerometer [44], similar approach proposed Gupta et al. [17], while Cheung et al. described accelerometry aspects applicable into daily support of patients [10]. The knowledge about medical malfunctions and disorders must be processed to enable active and ad-hoc decision support, which discussion was given by Fleury et al. who proposed improved supervised method to classify living activities using prior knowledge [15]. Mainly the knowledge about activities and optimal way to use it for HAA systems is of paramount importance for development aspects.

There are various attempts to collect data for HAA systems. We can find several attempts to measure activities using wearable sensors, devoted electronic devices and use mobile technology to manage. Parkka et al. discussed wearable sensors and their usage in activity classification [46], while Lee et al. proposed devoted head pose estimations [23]. Artif et al. discussed monitoring of various activities by application of wearable sensors [4] and Atallah presented positioning of these systems [5]. We can find real applications of this type of devices. Ozdemir and Barshan discussed detection of falls, where wearable sensors can prevent humans and assist in emergency [29]. All applications depend on the technology that can be implemented and configured to support humans under given criterions.

One of very interesting trends in technology development in recent years is mobile technology. We can see growing amount of various smartphones and tablets that now have similar computing power as laptops. Therefore these devices can be efficiently use for HAA systems to support users each day. Capela et al. propose a set of conditions that can be used to select features for smartphone based systems for elderly and stroke patients [9]. Pei et al. discussed technical conditions, implementations and models of sensors for mobile technology [31], while Kwapisz et al. presented accelerometer for mobile phone technology [42]. Catalogues of this type of support can be found in work of Incel et al. [19]. Similarly to the devices we use each day we can also try to create entire environments that can support people. Hoque and Stankovic described a model of a system implemented in home [18]. Smart home technology is one of very promising for future developments. Home is a place where we want to be safe and therefore applications of intelligent systems to support activities and in case of emergency automatically call for help can be one of emerging topics in the following years. In this type of intelligent environmental support communication between all devices must be a priority aspect.

HAA system must be able to communicate with other services, i.e. to find a way back home or other destination pointed by user, call for help in emergency or provide some necessary information from internet services. Osmani et al. proposed pervasive healthcare assistance via remote control for medical centres [28]. Napoli et al. presented efficient model to manage and predict data queues for media transmission [25] and. proposed cloud-distributed architecture oriented on quality of service for pattern detections [26]. Cpałka et al. have proposed an approach for design of control systems based on genetic programming to solve complicated models [11], while Brociek and Słota proposed nature inspired methods for simulations of complicated mathematical models [6, 7].

Another aspect in HAA systems are proper language technologies that can assist daily actions, i.e. communication between passers-by or simply help people at work. To implement this kind of support we can use ontologies based programming proposed by Damasevicius et al. [12]. Other important aspects of assistance is processing of information from vision systems that can control surroundings and in case of danger inform user. To implement this kind of decision support we need to process input images using multi-layer compression discussed by Ferdowsi et al. [14] and fast classification method proposed by Korytkowski et al. [21]. Some of these techniques are also applicable in user verification. In each computer system we must identify user. This is necessary to adjust a system to his/her preferences and therefore more flexibly support them in various situations. However, identification must be simplified to help elder or disabled people identify themselves without any complicated passwords or sophisticated procedures. One od most promising technologies is to simply use biometrics that are unique for each one of us.

Drosou et al. introduced spatiotemporal activity analysis for biometric authentication, where information about user can be efficiently applied to identify them [13], what can be of great importance in case of elder or disabled people since this kind of identification in computer systems can help them in easier management of electronic devices.

Another important aspect to routing, since mainly HAA systems can be used to help on routing to destination. Okulewicz and Mandziuk presented efficient dynamic routing problem solving developed for vehicles [27], however this attempt after some modification to track routes for humans instead cars can be applied in HAA routing. Similarly we can also apply intelligent positioning technology proposed by Stateczny and Sielicka-Wlodarczyk [33, 37]. All these aspects of intelligent programming are possible for mobile devices used in daily life as presented by Zhu and Sheng [39], where mobile devices were reported to assist in motion and location support. Similar achievements reported Sohn et al. [48] for user independent mobile application for HAA support for mobility using GSM data. However elderly people can need some adjustment in this type of systems. There are some reasons to make these systems as simple as possible and therefore automatize as much as possible since elder people are not as much used for electronic devices as youth, therefore while development the main impact must be put on simplicity and intuitional usage. Yu et al. proposed adaptive technology approach for mobility support designed especially for elder people [41]. Martisius and Damasevicius discussed a prototype of real time man-machine interactions system [24], while Waledzik and Mandziuk proposed adaptive evaluation strategy for this type of interactions [36].

Each decision support methodology is based on knowledge transformation or devoted training method. HAA systems due to the specific design also demand training processes adopted to system assumptions and environmental conditions. Mannini and Sabatini discussed machine learning methods to classify physical activity [43]. Tran and Sorokin presented other approach based on metric learning technology [49], however any modelling of this kind of decision support is demanding since each of users may need different support due to various disorders. Therefore adaptation in this processes is of a paramount importance. Special constructions of input data and training sets may efficiently improve training processes. This novel initial data approaches may be based on activity dairy as proposed by Yang [50] or Zhan and Sawchuk [53]. However it is presently not evident how much this kind of approach can help.

Valuable information about users and their actions can be gathered from internet services and the way people use it. Budnikas proposed a model to discover possible aggression through online activities estimation [8]. There are some applications that support sensing of actions from social networks as reported by Miluzzo [45], however it is not evident if this kind of HAA support can be also applied for elderly and disabled people since users of social services are rather people under thirty. Therefore adaptation of smart internet techniques to fit interests of elder people will be definitely necessary. Shoaib et al. presented a survey of online activity applicable for mobile technology [32], what can start an extensive discussion which of them can be easily adapted to elder people habits. Similarly interesting propositions for user verification systems are presented by K. Cpalka et al. [51, 52]. This type of approach should be efficiently remodelled to assist elder and disabled people while searching www services and using online applications since HAA system can independently learn from the preferences of users as proposed by Siirtola and Roning [47] and therefore actively assist people in further actions.

All research and technological advances are important background to start a discussion over improved HAA systems. In this article, concluding from all the research, we want to discuss an introduction to the novel system of active assistance for elder and disabled people. To do this we present assumptions for the domain of human activity recognition, where mobile devices like smartphones or tablets connected to sensors and internet services can assist people in daily life: helping them to find a way to the shop or come home if they get lost somewhere in the city, assisting in contacts with other people to help on avoiding thefts or robbery, and also assisting in emergency situations when immediate contact with magicians or police will be necessary.

2   Introduction to the Model

In comparison to other systems we want to develop more user oriented software with flexible system design. Therefore we want make user choose modules to be installed into the system that can fit his/her criteria: frequency of using, useful functions, ease of use, active ad-hoc help, constant contact with selected people, and user oriented interface. Therefore in the proposed model of man-machine interactions for the HAA system we would like to consider four main aspects:

- Assist everyday motion by positioning and routing.
- Assist voice processing for easier communication and identification.
- Assist visual information processing for advisory purposes and identification.
- Constant network connection for communication, emergency, web browsing, knowledge acquisition and all above.

We have chosen these since elder and disabled people mainly need assistance to help them move from home to a destination where they must do some duties, i.e. when they must meet a doctor in clinic which they do not know and they need help on locating it, when they get lost somewhere and must find a way, or just to find faster way home. Voice processing is necessary, i.e. when they have problems with understanding other people or when they have some difficulties with speaking. Similarly voice processing is an option to be implemented a control method for the system and within identification procedure. Therefore it can be also used to protect them against danger, i.e. when they talk with a stranger the system may the system can warn of impending danger and advise precautions. Image processing can be used to identify places, help in positioning and routing when user can be shown important locations on the way to the destination and also this aspect can help in avoiding danger. Constant connection to networking services is necessary to perform all these mentioned above, but also to actively assist in any other situation. Using network connection users may communicate via voice communication systems to contact family or call for help in emergency situations. Moreover this connection can be necessary to plan the route to the destination, since the system may use GPS data but also find important locations (building, streets, parks, etc.) that the user will be passing by on the way. Other usage of networking services is to maintain constant connection with medical services responsible for activities evaluation and emergency prevention. These four HAA features can be modelled with necessary assumptions.

2.1 Model Assumptions

The assumptions of the model can help on evaluation of activities and active assistance according to taxonomies on various layers in the system. Various approaches to taxonomies of human activities can be found in the literature. Unfortunately almost all authors introduce and analyse various taxonomies from simple examples like lying, sitting, standing, walking to compositions of actions such as walk-to-stand. Similarly extensions to these are also given to cover transportation like riding, driving, bicycling and even daily activities like shopping, working, eating, etc. However according to our research most appropriate approaches applicable to the proposed introduction to the system model were proposed by the following Authors.

Lara et al. [22] divided human activities into groups: motion (walking, running, sitting, standing, stairs up/down, elevator up/down), transportation (riding a bus, cycling, driving), phoning (messaging, calling), daily activities (eating, drinking, working, watching TV, reading, cleaning), exercises, military (crawling, kneeling, etc.) and upper body activities (chewing, speaking, etc.). Fleury et al. [15] presented other classes: sleeping, meal/eating, dressing/undressing, resting (watching TV, listening to the music, reading a book, etc.), hygiene, communication. Capela et al. [17] identified meta-classes according to movements: large movements (mobile and immobile), small movements and transition states in-between movements. Atallah et al. [5] proposed classification based on energy expenditure: very low-level (sleeping, laying), low-level (eating, drinking, watching), medium level (walking, cleaning) high level (running, cycling) and transitional in-between states (walk-to-stand). Proposed system will be developed to assist people in contacts with others, help on street guiding, assist in emergency and help on knowledge acquisition in daily activities. Therefore to build classes of assisted activities we shall analyse diagram in Fig. 1.

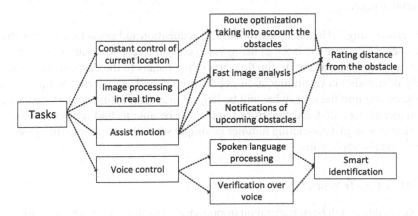

Fig. 1. Relation model for classified actions

We have extracted main classes for HAA system:

Voice processing: This includes assisting on voice processing from microphone in smartphone or tablet which will help to communicate with others. Therefore this module shall be designed to assist on voice identification and verification but also voice control of the system. These two aspects can assist users in daily activities helping them to manage the system which is very important for elder and disabled people.

Image processing: This includes processing images or video recordings taken by camera in smartphone or tablet. Using composed descriptors intelligent module will be able to verify some features important for authentication of people, i.e. to avoid thefts or to assist a user on the way to the destination.

Location positioning and routing: This includes active guiding module that will be connected to www services, i.e. google maps to control position and rout to the destination. Active connection to the web service will help on controlling route, suggesting appropriate means of travel and relocate the sure to other destination if user changes mind or in case of losing route contact family, friends, police or other services pointed by user.

Emergency actions: This includes active assistance in case of emergence, which can be divided between medical emergency, anti-criminal emergency and other. First type will be diagnosed using simple sensors attached to body to measure blood pressure and heart action which can be simply done using smart watch connected to the main module via bluetooth. In case of abnormal results of examinations the system will automatically inform user about changes and suggest contacting medics or family. Anti-criminal actions will be verified using speech processing module and image processing module. If the person voice will be verified as unwanted or the image verification can suggest potential criminal actions the system will automatically inform user about danger and suggest contacting police or other legal services as well as informing family about potential danger.

Internet browsing: This includes knowledge acquisition and extraction using web services. User can browse the internet using voice control to get necessary information, i.e. about opening hours at the destination, travelling means to the destination, contacting family or friends via communication applications. Similarly parallel to this a module will be positioning the user, what will be helpful in case of losing way. Position will be automatically recorded and therefore family will be able to find user on the way in a very simple way just contacting him/her or simply sending a request to the system from remote control application.

2.2 How Can It Work?

Simple operating will be of paramount importance. Therefore development of the system must be on light electronic devices that together compose efficient HAA system. Current technological development gave high computing powers to smartphone and tablets,

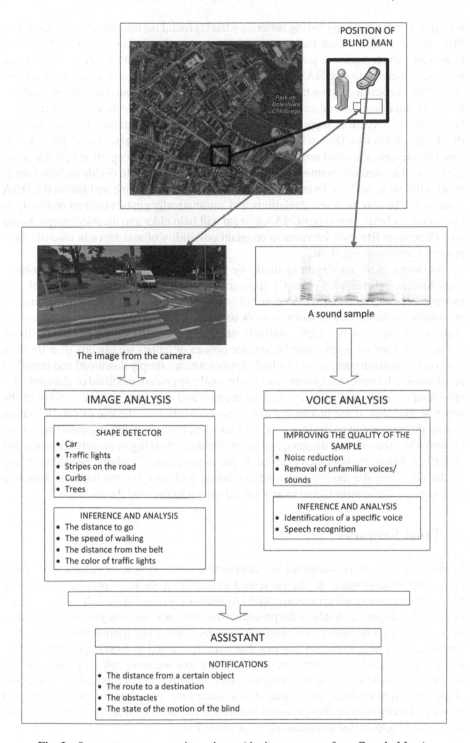

Fig. 2. Support system operation schema (the images come from Google Maps).

which now have also long lasting batteries what is crucial for usage over large distances. Moreover communication technology provides also simple connecting methods via bluetooth, which makes it possible to connect smartphone, tablet, camera and watch with pulsometer into one HAA system. These devices will be able to record activities and collect necessary data which can be analysed by implemented intelligent applications. Smartphones and tablets now are using multicore architectures therefore calculations run by Decision Support Applications (DSA) will not supress regular duties of the device. Therefore DSA will be able to verify voice or images, control route and in case of emergency contact user with appropriate responder. Recognition of daily activities as well as medical examinations will be useful for doctors to decide on better treatment adjusted to style of living. Moreover knowing daily routine and habits the HAA system will be able to detect deviations and automatically contact doctors or family to get necessary help. This type of HAA system will help elder and disabled people to run an independent life style however in constant possibility of assistance in case of emergency or abnormal situation.

As detectors for intelligent methods we plan to implement bio-inspired algorithms combined as hybrids with other CI approaches. This hybrids can give god results on image processing with fast detection and classification. Similarly these methods can help on routing to faster detect shortest ways to the destination. Technology used for the system development is widely available and therefore costs of the devices will not become a barrier for users, since i.e. mobile phones or tablets we can buy directly from telecommunication companies to which devices we can simply download and install an application. Moreover the system can also be easily upgraded, modified or changed with any other devices supporting connection method and operating system because of the separate modules of the processing and analysis. Moreover, the use of parallelization during the processing of the image and sound allows to reduce the response time of the system while the existing dangers, thereby reducing probability of occurrence unwanted situations. Sample schematic operation is presented in Fig. 2, where the system based on the data from the module of image and sound will interpret and transmit them to a person using the system (some examples are shown in the module assistant).

3   Final Remarks

In this article we have discussed an introduction to the system of elder and disabled people active assistance. In the presented introduction we have presented extensive literature discussion, which was necessary to discuss presented approaches to the similar systems development. Analysis the presented literature was necessary to extract the most important design features of the proposed system. Comparing approaches presented by others we were able to extract features that were mentioned as most important for elder and disabled people, and therefore for these features we were able to present crucial assumptions underlying the performance and reliability of the proposed system model along with simultaneous ease of use. At the same time, proposed for the implemented system CI methods will allow to assist users ensuring them with all the necessary information and support due to communication procedures.

Acknowledgments. Authors acknowledge contribution to this project of Operational Programme: "Knowledge, Education, Development" financed by the European Social Fund under grant application POWR.03.03.00-00-P001/15, contract no. MNiSW/2016/DIR/208/NN.

References

1. Aggarwal, J., Ryoo, M.: Human activity analysis: a review. ACM Comput. Surv. **43**, 1–43 (2011)
2. Aggarwal, J., Xia, L.: Human activity recognition from 3D data: a review. Pattern Recogn. Lett. **48**, 70–80 (2014)
3. Ainsworth, B., Haskell, W., Herrmann, S., Meckeset, N.: Compendium of physical activities: a second update of codes and MET values. Med. Sci. Sports Exerc. **43**(8), 1575–1581 (2011)
4. Arif, M., Kattan, A.: Physical activities monitoring using wearable acceleration sensors attached to the body. PLoS ONE **10**(7), e0130851 (2015)
5. Atallah, L., Lo, B., King, R., Yang, G.: Sensor positioning for activity recognition using wearable accelerometers. IEEE Trans. Biomed. Circ. Syst. **5**, 320–329 (2011)
6. Brociek, R., Słota, D.: Reconstruction of the boundary condition for the heat conduction equation of fractional order. Therm. Sci. **19**, 35–42 (2015)
7. Brociek, R., Słota, D.: Application of intelligent algorithm to solve the fractional heat conduction inverse problem. Commun. Comput. Inf. Sci. **538**, 356–365 (2015)
8. Budnikas, G.: A model for an aggression discovery through person online behavior. In: Saeed, K., Homenda, W. (eds.) CISIM 2015. LNCS, vol. 9339, pp. 305–315. Springer, Heidelberg (2015)
9. Capela, N., Lemaire, E., Baddour, N.: Feature selection for wearable smartphone-based human activity recognition with able bodied, elderly, and stroke patients. PLoS ONE **10**(4), e0124414 (2015)
10. Cheung, V., Gray, L., Karunanithi, M.: Review of accelerometry for determining daily activity among elderly patients. Arch. Phys. Med. Rehabil. **92**, 998–1014 (2011)
11. Cpałka, K., Łapa, K., Przybył, A.: A new approach to design of control systems using genetic programming. Inf. Technol. Control **44**(4), 433–442 (2015)
12. Damaševičius, R., Stuikys, V., Toldinas, J.: Domain ontology-based generative component design using feature diagrams and meta-programming technique. In: Proceedings of 2nd European Conference on Software Architecture ECSA 2008, pp. 338–341 (2008)
13. Drosou, A., Ioannidis, D., Moustakas, K., Tzovaras, D.: Spatiotemporal analysis of human activities for biometric authentication. Comput. Vis. Image Underst. **116**(3), 411–421 (2012)
14. Ferdowsi, S., Voloshynovskiy, S., Kostadinov, D., Korytkowski, M., Scherer, R.: Secure representation of images using multi-layer compression. In: Rutkowski, L., Korytkowski, M., Scherer, R., Tadeusiewicz, R., Zadeh, L.A., Zurada, J.M. (eds.) ICAISC 2015. LNCS, vol. 9119, pp. 696–705. Springer, Heidelberg (2015)
15. Fleury, A., Noury, N., Vacher, M.: Improving supervised classification of activities of daily living using prior knowledge. Int. J. E-Health Med. Commun. **2**(1), 17–34 (2011)
16. Govindaraju, V.: A generative framework to investigate the underlying patterns in human activities. In: Proceedings of the IEEE International Conference on Computer Vision Workshops, pp. 1472–1479 (2011)
17. Gupta, P., Dallas, T.: Feature selection and activity recognition system using a single triaxial accelerometer. IEEE Trans. Biomed. Eng. **61**(6), 1780–1786 (2014)
18. Hoque, E., Stankovic, J.: AALO: activity recognition in smart homes using Active Learning in the presence of Overlapped activities. In: PervasiveHealth, pp. 139–146 (2012)

19. Incel, O., Kose, M., Ersoy, C.: A review and taxonomy of activity recognition on mobile phones. BioNanoScience **3**, 145–171 (2013)
20. Jain, A., Ross, A., Prabhakar, S.: An introduction to biometric recognition. IEEE Trans. Circ. Syst. Video Technol. **14**, 4–20 (2004)
21. Korytkowski, M., Rutkowski, L., Scherer, R.: Fast image classification by boosting fuzzy classifiers. Inf. Sci. **327**, 175–182 (2016)
22. Lara, O., Labrador, M.: A survey on human activity recognition using wearable sensors. IEEE Commun. Surv. Tutorials **15**, 1192–1209 (2013)
23. Lee, D., Yang, M., Oh, S.: Fast and accurate head pose estimation via random projection forests. In: Proceedings of International Conference on Computer Vision (ICCV 2015), pp. 1958–1966 (2015)
24. Martišius, I., Damaševičius, R.: A prototype SSVEP based real time BCI gaming system. Comput. Intell. Neurosci. 2016 (2016)
25. Napoli, C., Pappalardo, G., Tramontana, E.: A mathematical model for file fragment diffusion and a neural predictor to manage priority queues over BitTorrent. Appl. Math. Comput. Sci. **26**(1), 147–160 (2016)
26. Napoli, C., Pappalardo, G., Tramontana, E., Zappalà, G.: A cloud-distributed GPU architecture for pattern identification in segmented detectors big-data surveys. Comput. J. **59**(3), 338–352 (2016)
27. Okulewicz, M., Mandziuk, J.: Two-phase multi-swarm PSO and the dynamic vehicle routing problem. In: Proceedings of the IEEE Symposium Series on Computational Intelligence, pp. 86–93 (2014)
28. Osmani, V., Balasubramaniam, S., Botvich, D.: Human activity recognition in pervasive health-care: supporting efficient remote collaboration. J. Netw. Comput. Appl. **31**(4), 628–655 (2008)
29. Özdemir, A., Barshan, B.: Detecting falls with wearable sensors using machine learning techniques. Sensors **14**(6), 10691–10708 (2014)
30. Poppe, R.: A survey on vision-based human action recognition. Image Vis. Comput. J. **28**, 976–990 (2010)
31. Pei, L., Guinness, R., Chen, R., Liu, J.: Human behavior cognition using smartphone sensors. Sensors **13**, 1402–1424 (2013)
32. Shoaib, M., Bosch, S., Incel, O., Scholten, H., Havinga, P.: A survey of online activity recognition using mobile phones. Sensors **15**(1), 2059–2085 (2015)
33. Stateczny, A., Wlodarczyk-Sielicka, M.: Self-organizing artificial neural networks into hydrographic big data reduction process. In: Kryszkiewicz, M., Cornelis, C., Ciucci, D., Medina-Moreno, J., Motoda, H., Raś, Z.W. (eds.) RSEISP 2014. LNCS, vol. 8537, pp. 335–342. Springer, Heidelberg (2014)
34. Suriani, N., Hussain, A., Zulkifley, M.: Sudden event recognition: a survey. Sensors **13**(8), 9966–9998 (2013)
35. Turaga, P., Chellappa, R., Subrahmanian, V., Udrea, O.: Machine recognition of human activities: a survey. IEEE Trans. Circ. Syst. Video Technol. **18**, 1473–1488 (2008)
36. Waledzik, K., Mandziuk, J.: An automatically generated evaluation function in general game playing. IEEE Trans. Comput. Intell. AI Games **6**(3), 258–270 (2014)
37. Wlodarczyk-Sielicka, M., Stateczny, A.: Selection of SOM parameters for the needs of clusterisation of data obtained by interferometric methods. In: Proceedings of 16th International Radar Symposium, Dresden, pp. 1129–1134 (2015)
38. Ziaeefard, M., Bergevin, R.: Semantic human activity recognition: a literature review. Pattern Recogn. **48**(8), 2329–2345 (2015)

39. Zhu, C., Sheng, W.: Motion- and location-based online human daily activity recognition. Pervasive Mob. Comput. **7**(2), 256–269 (2011)
40. Yampolskiy, R., Govindaraju, V.: Behavioural biometrics: a survey and classification. Int. J. Biometrics **1**(1), 81–113 (2008)
41. Yu, H., Spenko, M., Dubowsky, S.: An adaptive shared control system for an intelligent mobility aid for the elderly. Auton. Robots **15**, 53–66 (2003)
42. Kwapisz, J.R., Weiss, G., Moore, S.: Activity recognition using cell phone accelerometers. SIGKDD Explor. Newsl. **12**(2), 74–82 (2011)
43. Mannini, A., Sabatini, A.: Machine learning methods for classifying human physical activity from on-body accelerometers. Sensors **10**, 1154–1175 (2010)
44. Mathie, M., Celler, B., Lovell, N., Coster, A.: Classification of basic daily movements using a triaxial accelerometer. Med. Biol. Eng. Comput. **42**, 679–687 (2004)
45. Miluzzo, E., Lane, N., Fodor, K., Peterson, R.: Sensing meets mobile social networks: the design, implementation and evaluation of the cenceme application. In: Proceedings of the 6th ACM Conference on Embedded Network Sensor Systems, SenSys 2008, pp. 337–350 (2008)
46. Parkka, J., Ermes, M., Korpipaa, P., Mantyjarvi, J., Peltola, J.: Activity classification using realistic data from wearable sensors. IEEE Trans. Inf. Technol. Biomed. **10**, 119–128 (2006)
47. Siirtola, P., Roning, J.: Recognizing human activities user-independently on smartphones based on accelerometer data. Int. J. Interact. Multimedia Artif. Intell. **1**(5), 38–45 (2012)
48. Sohn, T., Varshavsky, A., LaMarca, A., Chen, M.Y., Choudhury, T., Smith, I., Consolvo, S., Hightower, J., Griswold, W.G., de Lara, E.: Mobility detection using everyday GSM traces. In: Dourish, P., Friday, A. (eds.) UbiComp 2006. LNCS, vol. 4206, pp. 212–224. Springer, Heidelberg (2006)
49. Tran, D., Sorokin, A.: Human activity recognition with metric learning. In: Forsyth, D., Torr, P., Zisserman, A. (eds.) ECCV 2008, Part I. LNCS, vol. 5302, pp. 548–561. Springer, Heidelberg (2008)
50. Yang, J.: Toward physical activity diary: motion recognition using simple acceleration features with mobile phones. In: Proceedings of the 1st International Workshop on Interactive Multimedia for Consumer Electronics, IMCE 2009, pp. 1–10 (2009)
51. Cpalka, K., Zalasinski, M., Rutkowski, L.: A new algorithm for identity verification based on the analysis of a handwritten dynamic signature. Appl. Soft Comput. **43**, 47–56 (2016)
52. Cpalka, K., Zalasinski, M.: On-line signature verification using vertical signature partitioning. Expert Syst. Appl. **41**(9), 4170–4180 (2014)
53. Zhang, M., Sawchuk, A.: USC-HAD: a daily activity dataset for ubiquitous activity recognition using wearable sensors. In: Proceedings of the 2012 ACM Conference on Ubiquitous Computing, pp. 1036–1043 (2012)

Novel Image Correction Method Based on Swarm Intelligence Approach

Marcin Woźniak[✉]

Institute of Mathematics, Silesian University of Technology,
Kaszubska 23, 44-100 Gliwice, Poland
marcin.wozniak@polsl.pl

Abstract. In the article an approach toward novel method for image features correction is proposed. For the input image developed swarm intelligence technique is applied to improve brightness, contrast, sharpen presentation and improve gamma correction. The following sections present proposed model of the correction techniques with applied swarm intelligence approach. Experimental results on a set of test images are presented with a discussion of achieved improvements.

Keywords: Image processing · Swarm algorithm

1 Introduction

Development in multimedia systems gives various opportunities for applications. We can see that modern societies and businesses use various multimedia techniques to improve production and efficiency of electronic devices. In the recent years various computer vision techniques are improved and constantly developed to achieve higher levels of image quality. Due to higher precision of recent screening and printing technologies we can work with images of much better digital quality than few years ago. Each new year brings development and further steps toward high definition crystal clear view where our eyes will be able to discover variety of details of the objects depicted in images.

Among newly developed techniques Computational Intelligence (CI) brings many interesting solutions that can be implemented in image processing and various fields of science. Techniques of CI are mainly based on observation of nature where we try to simulate actions of human brains in deduction processes, ability to learn from various contexts and adaptation of animal spices to environmental conditions. This approach is mainly based on constructing techniques that can simulate behavior of organisms while moving, living and developing in swarms. Since the simulation is based on implementation of multi individuals swarms that cooperate on the way to the destination we commonly call it a swarm intelligence. This type of CI technique has recently found many applications in simulation, optimization and image processing.

Brociek and Słota presented application of swarm intelligence in processes of heat conduction problems [4, 10] and related to them fractional equations [5]. Cpałka et al. has presented some results of application control systems design based on CI

© Springer International Publishing Switzerland 2016
G. Dregvaite and R. Damasevicius (Eds.): ICIST 2016, CCIS 639, pp. 404–413, 2016.
DOI: 10.1007/978-3-319-46254-7_32

approaches, while Okulewicz et al. have applied swarm intelligence to vehicle routing problems [17], Swiechowski et al. in games strategies managements where dedicated fitness conditions are important efficiency factors [21] and Walnedzik et al. in automated gaming systems [23]. Similarly we can find many applications of CI methods in decision support systems, where these algorithms are implemented to assist on evaluation. Damsasevicius presented application of intelligent methods to structural analysis of dna sequences [8]. Budnikas has shown that it also possible to detect various behaviors using information of users actions over internet applications [6], while Pranevicius et al. proposed to compose dedicated decision support based on intelligent modeling of applied rules [19]. Similarly Napoli presented extensive description of application of CI method to pattern identification [14] and bit torrent systems [15]. Stateczny et al. proposed dedicated CI architectures for hydrometric data analysis [20] and Wlodarczyk-Sielicka et al. discussed interferometric methods results clustered for decision support system [25]. Bhandari et al. discussed experimental results of wind driven optimization study by application of swarm methods to satellite image segmentation [3].

1.1 Related Works

Along with development in image processing technology CI methods find more and more applications in this field. Aydin has given an example of swarm method applied to edge detection [1]. Swarm intelligence techniques were also proposed in various applications devoted to edge detection of features in 2D images and their secure representation in various multi level compression methods as described by Ferdowsi et al. [9] and Tian et al. [22], Lakehal proposed swarm based feature extraction [13]. These methods can be also applied to the problem of image segmentation for further processing as discussed by Benatcha et al. [2] and Ouadfel [18]. Korytkowski et al. CI to image classification, and Keshtkar et al. gave an example of dental radiographs analysis using swarm intelligence [12]. These works gave interesting examples of swarm intelligence applied in various aspects of image processing.

In this article an approach to improve image features by application of swarm intelligence will be discussed. Proposed method is to give a novel approach to image correction techniques. In the implemented method, swarm of individuals is randomly placed over input image, than a mathematical model is introduced to simulate moves of these individuals over image in search of pixels that can be efficiently modify to increase quality of the image. Values of found pixels are stored in memory to be transformed at the end by application of proposed filtering method. To prove efficiency of this type of correction method some images from open test set (http://www.imageprocessing-place.com/root_files_V3/image_databases.htm) were used.

2 Applied Correction Model

Images used in multimedia systems are of various quality. Therefore to efficiently use them for processing purposes we need to correct them or improve quality of presentation. There are many methods to correct images or classify objects based on various techniques of CI. However mainly to use them we still need to perform complicated operations. Proposed in this article method is to show that swarm intelligence mixed with simple image correction operations are able to efficiently improve presentation quality. In this process simple modeling of basic image features with sharpening was introduced on pixels discovered by applied swarm technique, that is run over input image to discover pixels and their values that need to be corrected.

2.1 Pixels Values Adjustment

Brightness of pixel x_i is corrected applying basic operations on the pixel value

$$NewBrightness(x_i) = \alpha_1 \cdot Brightness(x_i) + \beta_1 \qquad (1)$$

where parameters α_1 and β_1 are introduced to control gain and bias of contrast and brightness. Contrast of pixel x_i is corrected applying basic operations on the pixel value

$$NewContrast(x_i) = \alpha_2 \cdot Contrast(x_i) + \beta_2 \qquad (2)$$

where parameters α_2 and β_2 are introduced to control gain and bias of contrast and brightness. For correction of brightness and contrast introduced parameters α_1, α_2, β_1, β_2 are introduced as statistical values for averaged pixels values measured in Swarm Detection Algorithm.

Filtering of pixel x_i is done applying filter matrix on the pixel Hue-Saturation-Brightness values

$$New(x_i) = [H(x_i), S(x_i), B(x_i)] \cdot \begin{bmatrix} -1 & -1 & -1 \\ -1 & 9 & -1 \\ -1 & -1 & -1 \end{bmatrix} \qquad (3)$$

therefore new values of these values are calculated increase the sharpness of objects shown in the processed picture. Further a gamma correction method for each pixel x_i is introduced by application of basic operation on the pixel Red-Green-Blue values

$$NewGamma(x_i) = 255 \cdot \left(\frac{Gamma(x_i)}{255} \right)^\gamma \qquad (4)$$

where parameter γ represents proportional change of these the color gamut values. These are commonly used in various image processing methods and sample implementations of these operations can be found i.e. at http://www.dfstudios.co.uk and http://docs.opencv.org. General algorithm that manages correction process for pixels found by applied Swarm Detection Algorithm is presented in Algorithm 1.

Start,
Compose a set of reference for the algorithm,
while *t   iterations* **do**
> Apply **Swarm Detection Algorithm** to collect data over input image,
> Save these values,
> Next *iteration t = t + 1*,

end
Average saved values,
Compare averaged values with original from input image,
Apply correction and filtering to values where difference between averaged and
original values is highest,
Stop.

Algorithm 1: Pixel Improvement Algorithm

2.2 Swarm Intelligence Approach

Swarm intelligence methods base on mapping various aspects from nature, where
swarms of insects or other organisms evolve or adapt to conditions of environment.
These processes are adapted to computer methods to serve as algorithms in intelligent
processing. In this article a swarm model id adopted to detect pixels with features to be
improved. This approach is similar to Mishra et al. where implemented swarm intelligence was help on image watermarking [16]. Other similar approach was proposed by
Wang et al. who discussed possible application of swarm intelligence for moving objects
detection [24]. In all these applications a swarm of individuals was modeled to move
over images to process selected features.

In this project is applied a swarm model based on behavior of flying insects attracted
by other members of the group. Movements of individuals are implemented to search
for pixels to be processed for improvements. The method describes behavior of insects
in natural conditions, so we can characterize their way of moving and attracting These
are modeled in numerical values to translate natural conditions into mathematical model,
however in most simple way. Therefore in applied swarm modeling following assumptions are applied:

- Individuals are unisex to enable free attraction modeling between all of them,
- Attractiveness is proportional to distance between individuals. Therefore it decreases
  with increasing distance between individuals,
- Similarly to natural conditions randomness is introduced as factor μ to each move of
  individuals.

Distance between individuals i and j in the swarm is positioned at points (pixels) x_i^t
and x_j^t over processed image is defined as Cartesian metric

$$distance_{ij}^t = ||x_i^t - x_j^t|| = \sqrt{\sum_{k=1}^{2} (x_{i,k}^t - x_{j,k}^t)^2}, \tag{5}$$

where x_i^t, x_j^t are positions over the picture with it's components $x_{j,k}^t$ representing spatial coordinates on each of the axes in iteration t.

In all the swarms or schools individuals keep together being attracted by others in a specific for each kind way. This attractiveness can be modeled in various ways, however in this application attractiveness is measured only according to the distance between individuals. This is introduced to simulate accumulation of insects in large groups. Therefore attractiveness between any two individuals x_i^t, and x_j^t is modeled to decreases with increasing distance, as a proportional in surrounding by formula

$$Attract_{ij}^t = \left| \frac{1}{1 - e^{distance_{ij}^t}} \right|, \tag{6}$$

where $distance_{ij}^t$ is calculated according to (5) in each iteration t.

Movement of individuals in the swarm is modeled on the distance to other individuals surrounding it (5) and attraction between them (6). Similarly to nature individuals that are closer see each other better and therefore attract more. In the swarm each individual i motion toward another individual j is modeled by formula

$$x_i^{t+1} = x_i^t + \mu \cdot (x_j^t - x_i^t) \cdot Attract_{ij}^t, \tag{7}$$

where x_i^t, x_j^t are positions over the picture, $Attract_{ij}^t$ is attraction between two individuals calculated using (6) and μ is randomness factor chosen at random to be responsible for randomization of motions in each iteration t.

These equations are used to simulate a swarm of individuals moving over input image to search for pixels to be processes for better quality, as presented in Algorithm 2.

Start,
Define number of *individuals* and *iterations* in the algorithm,
Define search conditions for the swarm,
Create at random initial swarm over input image,
$t = 0$,
while $t \leq iterations$ **do**
| Calculate distance between individuals using (5);
| Calculate attractiveness for individuals using (6),
| Randomize factor μ
| Move individuals in population using (7),
| Evaluate individuals in population,
| Select those with worst fitness and remember their positions and values of pixels,
| Next *iteration* $t = t + 1$,
end
Positions of selected individuals show values to be improved,
Stop.

Algorithm 2: Swarm Detection Algorithm

3   Research Results

In the research examinations proposed technique was implemented to process images from http://www.imageprocessingplace.com/root_files_V3/image_databases.htm. In Figs. 1, 2, 3, 4 and 5 we can see how the method works. In each of these figures original image and improved version are presented. Proposed method was applied to each of the input images. We can see that proposed method is valuable for color images as well as for gray scale images. Figure 1 presents correction of peppers in red and green colors where flashlight was reflected from the surface of peppers, however this made the situation more challenging for the method it was able to improve quality. Figure 2 presents another challenging task, where facial image was processed. This type of image is difficult for all correction methods since faces have many details which are hard for processing. Proposed method corrected the image making it more sharpen and therefore

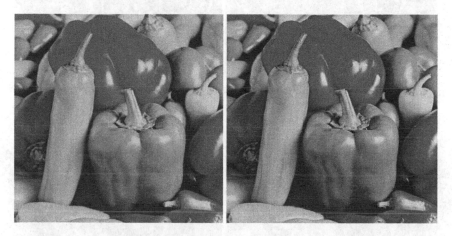

Fig. 1. On the left original image, on the right image after correction (Color figure online)

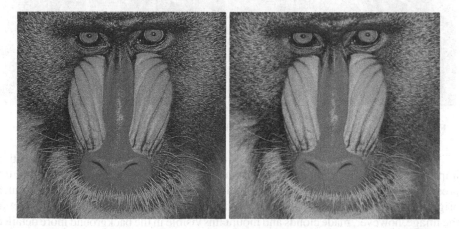

Fig. 2. On the left original image, on the right image after correction (Color figure online)

the face looks more natural. Another image presented in Fig. 3 presents a scene from gray scale movie, where the figure of a man and a woman are standing in a room with lots of furniture, decorations and other items. Correction of this image eliminated blur of some decorative elements and also sharpened both silhouettes.

Fig. 3. On the left original image, on the right image after correction

Fig. 4. On the left original image, on the right image after correction (Color figure online)

In Fig. 4 we can see correction of one of most common test images, where correction improved color gamut and therefore silhouette of woman looks more natural. Figure 5 presents correction of jet over clouds. In this case an image was transformed into much brighter, which unfortunately affected the deterioration of the natural look of the jet in the image, however, made clouds and mountains visible in the background more detailed and significantly increase the transparency of the whole presentation.

Fig. 5. On the left original image, on the right image after correction

3.1 Conclusions

Swarm of individuals moving over input image was able to collect information about processed images. These data was collected as knowledge about processed image and pixels values that can be corrected. After averaging these values were used by implemented adjustments to introduce new values of image pixels. These changes made processed images look more natural and reveal some details that were not properly presented in the classic image.

We can see that developed method is very efficient for gray scale images as well as for color images. Comparing results of improvements in Figs. 3 and 5 images after correction are more clear and objects are better visible. Similarly images in Figs. 2 and 4 were improved by better contrast and more natural look of the presentations. The method is also able to correct flash lighted images where flash of light is reflected from the objects.

4 Final Remarks

In this article a novel approach to image quality improvements was presented. In experimental research a set of images was presented to the developed method to improve brightness, contrast and sharpen input image along with applied gamma correction. Application of proposed method based on swarm intelligence application helped on processing input images to easily and reliably improve these feature. At the same time, CI methods allow to easily implement correction procedure over entire input image without complicated operations.

Research results presented in this paper show that proposed approach can be efficiently implemented in image processing systems. Therefore in the future research it is planned to use it as parallel method run with similar approaches over multiple image series to increase efficiency and make the processing even faster.

References

1. Aydin, D.: An efficient ant-based edge detector. T. Comput. Collective Intell. **1**, 39–55 (2010)
2. Benatcha, K., Koudil, M., Benkhelat, N., Boukir, Y.: ISA an algorithm for image segmentation using ants. In: Proceedings of IEEE International Symposium on Industrial Electronics, pp. 2503–2507 (2008)
3. Bhandari, A., Singh, V., Kumar, A., Singh, G.: Cuckoo search algorithm and wind driven optimization based study of satellite image segmentation for multilevel thresholding using kapurs entropy. Expert Syst. Appl. **41**(7), 3538–3560 (2014)
4. Brociek, R., Słota, D.: Reconstruction of the boundary condition for the heat conduction equation of fractional order. Thermal Sci. **19**, 35–42 (2015)
5. Brociek, R., Słota, D.: Application of intelligent algorithm to solve the fractional heat conduction inverse problem. Commun. Comput. Inf. Sci. **538**, 356–365 (2015)
6. Budnikas, G.: A model for an aggression discovery through person online behavior. In: Saeed, K., Homenda, W. (eds.) CISIM 2015. LNCS, vol. 9339, pp. 305–315. Springer, Heidelberg (2015). doi:10.1007/978-3-319-24369-6_25
7. Cpałka, K., Łapa, K., Przybył, A.: A new approach to design of control systems using genetic programming. Inf. Technol. Control **44**(4), 433–442 (2015)
8. Damaševičius, R.: Structural analysis of regulatory DNA sequences using grammar inference and support vector machine. Neurocomputing **73**(4–6), 633–638 (2010)
9. Ferdowsi, S., Voloshynovskiy, S., Kostadinov, D., Korytkowski, M., Scherer, R.: Secure representation of images using multi-layer compression. In: Rutkowski, L., Korytkowski, M., Scherer, R., Tadeusiewicz, R., Zadeh, L.A., Zurada, J.M. (eds.). LNCS, vol. 9119, pp. 696–705. Springer, Heidelberg (2015)
10. Hetmaniok, E., Słota, D., Zielonka, A.: Experimental verification of immune recruitment mechanism and clonal selection algorithm applied for solving the inverse problems of pure metal solidification. Int. Commun. Heat Mass Transf. **47**, 7–14 (2013)
11. Korytkowski, M., Rutkowski, L., Scherer, R.: Fast image classification by boosting fuzzy classifiers. Inf. Sci. **327**, 175–182 (2016)
12. Keshtkar, F., Gueaieb, W.: Segmentation of dental radiographs using a swarm intelligence approach. In: Proceedings of Canadian Conference Electrical and Computer Engineering, pp. 328–331 (2006)
13. Lakehal, E.: A swarm intelligence based approach for image feature extraction. In: Proceedings of International Conference on Multimedia Computing and Systems, pp. 31–35 (2009)
14. Napoli, C., Pappalardo, G., Tramontana, E.: A mathematical model for file fragment diffusion and a neural predictor to manage priority queues over BitTorrent. Appl. Math. Comput. Sci. **26**(1), 147–160 (2016)
15. Napoli, C., Pappalardo, G., Tramontana, E., Zappalà, G.: A cloud-distributed GPU architecture for pattern identification in segmented detectors big-data surveys. Comput. J. **59**(3), 338–352 (2016)
16. Mishra, A., Agarwal, C., Sharma, A., Bedi, P.: Optimized gray-scale image water- marking using DWT SVD and firefly algorithm. Expert Syst. Appl. **41**(17), 7858–7867 (2014)
17. Okulewicz, M., Mandziuk, J.: Two-phase multi-swarm PSO and the dynamic vehicle routing problem. In: Proceedings of the IEEE Symposium Series on Computational Intelligence, pp. 86–93 (2014)
18. Ouadfel, S., Batouche, M.: MRF-based image segmentation using ant colony system. Electron. Lett. Comput. Vis. Image Anal. **2**(2), 12–24 (2013)

19. Pranevicius, H., Kraujalis, T., Budnikas, G., Pilkauskas, V.: Fuzzy rule base generation using discretization of membership functions and neural network. Commun. Comput. Inf. Sci. **465**, 160–171 (2014)
20. Stateczny, A., Wlodarczyk-Sielicka, M.: Self-organizing artificial neural networks into hydrographic big data reduction process. In: Kryszkiewicz, M., Cornelis, C., Ciucci, D., Medina-Moreno, J., Motoda, H., Raś, Z.W. (eds.) RSEISP 2014. LNCS, vol. 8537, pp. 335–342. Springer, Heidelberg (2014)
21. Swiechowski, M., Mandziuk, J.: Self-adaptation of playing strategies in general game playing. IEEE Trans. Comput. Intell. AI Games **6**(4), 367–381 (2014)
22. Tian, J., Yu, W., Chen, L., Ma, L.: Image edge detection using variation-adaptive ant colony optimization. In: Nguyen, N.T. (ed.) Transactions on Computational Collective Intelligence V. LNCS, vol. 6910, pp. 27–40. Springer, Heidelberg (2011)
23. Waledzik, K., Mandziuk, J.: An automatically generated evaluation function in general game playing. IEEE Trans. Comput. Intell. AI Games **6**(3), 258–270 (2014)
24. Wang, Y., Wan, Q.: Detecting moving objects by ant colony system in a MAP-MRF framework. In: Proceedings of International Conference on E-Product E-Service and E-Entertainment, pp. 1–4 (2010)
25. Wlodarczyk-Sielicka, M., Stateczny, A.: Selection of SOM parameters for the needs of clusterisation of data obtained by interferometric methods. In: Proceedings of 16th International Radar Symposium, Dresden, pp. 1129–1134 (2015)

A Comparison of Mining Incomplete and Inconsistent Data

Patrick G. Clark[1], Cheng Gao[1], and Jerzy W. Grzymala-Busse[1,2(✉)]

[1] Department of Electrical Engineering and Computer Science,
University of Kansas, Lawrence, KS 66045, USA
patrick.g.clark@gmail.com, {cheng.gao,jerzy}@ku.edu
[2] Department of Expert Systems and Artificial Intelligence,
University of Information Technology and Management, 35-225 Rzeszow, Poland

Abstract. We present experimental results on a comparison of incompleteness and inconsistency. Our experiments were conducted on 141 data sets, including 71 incomplete data and 62 inconsistent, created from eight original numerical data sets. We used the Modified Learning from Examples Module version 2 (MLEM2) rule induction algorithm for data mining. Among eight types of data sets combined with three kinds of probabilistic approximations used in experiments, in 12 out of 24 combinations the error rate, computed as a result of ten-fold cross validation, was smaller for inconsistent data (two-tailed test, 5 % significance level). For one data set, combined with all three probabilistic approximations, the error rate was smaller for incomplete data. For remaining nine combinations the difference in performance was statistically insignificant. Thus, we may claim that there is some experimental evidence that incompleteness is generally worse than inconsistency for data mining.

Keywords: Incomplete data · Inconsistent data · Rough set theory · Probabilistic approximations · MLEM2 rule induction algorithm

1 Introduction

A complete data set, i.e., a data set having all attribute values specified, is consistent if for any two cases with the same attribute values, both cases belong to the same concept (class). Another definition of consistency is based on rough set theory: a complete data set is consistent if for any concept its lower and upper approximations are equal [9,10]. However, in some situations the data set being mined is either incomplete, some of the attribute values are missing; or inconsistent, there are cases that are indiscernable but belong to different concepts.

The main objective of our paper is to compare mining incomplete and inconsistent data in terms of an error rate computed as a result of ten-fold cross validation. Using eight numerical data sets, we discretized each of them and then converted to a symbolic and consistent data set with intervals as attribute

© Springer International Publishing Switzerland 2016
G. Dregvaite and R. Damasevicius (Eds.): ICIST 2016, CCIS 639, pp. 414–425, 2016.
DOI: 10.1007/978-3-319-46254-7_33

values. We then randomly replaced some of the intervals with symbols representing missing attribute values. This process was conducted incrementally, starting by randomly replacing 5 % of the intervals with missing attribute values, and then an additional 5 %, until a case occurred with all attribute values missing. The process was then attempted twice more with the maximum percentage and if again a case occurred with all attribute values missing, the process was terminated for that data set. The new data sets, with missing attribute values, were as close as possible to the original data sets, having the same number of attributes, cases, and concepts.

Additionally, any original data set was discretized with a controlled level of inconsistency, starting from about 5 %, with the same increment of about 5 %. Due to the nature of discretization, the levels of inconsistency were only approximately equal to 5 %, 10 %, etc. Our way of generation of inconsistent data preserved as much as possible the original data set. Again, the number of attributes, cases and concepts were not changed.

All such incomplete and inconsistent data sets were validated using the same setup, based on rule induction by the MLEM2 rule induction algorithm and the same system for ten-fold cross validation.

To the best of our knowledge, no research comparing incompleteness with inconsistency was ever undertaken. However, our results should be taken with a grain of salt since the measures of incompleteness and inconsistency are different. We measure both of them in the most natural way: for a data set, incompleteness is measured by the percentage of missing attribute values, or percentage of missing attribute values to the total number of cases in the data set. Inconsistency is measured by the level of inconsistency, i.e., percentage of conflicting cases to the number of cases. Yet the first measure is local, it is associated with the attribute-value pairs, while the second is global, it is computed by comparing entire cases. On the other hand, if we want to compare incompleteness with inconsistency, there is no better way than using these two measures.

In our experiments we used the idea of a probabilistic approximation, with a probability α, as an extension of the standard approximation, well known in rough set theory. For $\alpha = 1$, the probabilistic approximation is identical with the lower approximation; for very small α, it is identical with the upper approximation. Research on properties of probabilistic approximations was first reported in [12] and then was continued in many other papers, for example, [11,14–16].

Incomplete data sets are usually analyzed using special approximations such as singleton, subset and concept [4,5]. For incomplete data sets probabilistic approximations were used for the first time in [6]. The first experimental results using probabilistic approximations were published in [2]. In experiments reported in this paper, we used concept probabilistic approximations.

2   Incomplete Data

Data sets may be presented in the form of a decision table. An example of such a decision table is shown in Table 1. Rows of the decision table represent cases and columns represent variables. The set of all cases will be denoted by U. In Table 1, $U = \{1, 2, 3, 4, 5, 6, 7\}$. Independent variables are called attributes and a dependent variable is called a decision and is denoted by d. The set of all attributes will be denoted by A. In Table 1, $A = \{Age, Cholesterol, Weight\}$. The value for a case x and an attribute a will be denoted by $a(x)$.

Table 1. A data set with numerical attributes

Case	Attributes			Decision
	Age	Cholesterol	Weight	Risk
1	20	180	140	Low
2	60	200	180	Low
3	40	220	160	Low
4	50	200	180	Low
5	60	220	180	High
6	40	220	180	High
7	50	180	220	High

Table 2 presents an example of the discretized and consistent data set. All attribute values are intervals and as such are considered symbolic.

Table 2. A discretized, consistent data set

Case	Attributes			Decision
	Age	Cholesterol	Weight	Risk
1	20–45	180–210	140–170	Low
2	45–60	180–210	170–210	Low
3	20–45	210–220	140–170	Low
4	45–60	180–210	170–210	Low
5	45–60	210–220	170–210	High
6	20–45	210–220	170–210	High
7	45–60	180–210	210–220	High

Table 3 presents an example of an incomplete data set. In this paper, we use only one interpretation of missing attribute values, a lost value, denoted by "?" [8,13]. The percentage of missing attribute values is the total number of missing attribute values, equal to eight, divided by the total number of attribute values, equal to 21, i.e., the percentage of missing attribute values is 38.1 %.

Table 4 represent an inconsistent data set. This data set was created from the data set from Table 1. The numerical data set from Table 1 was discretized with 30 % level of inconsistency. Cases 3 and 6 are conflicting, so the level of inconsistency is $2/7 \approx 30$ %.

Table 3. An incomplete data set

Case	Attributes			Decision
	Age	Cholesterol	Weight	Risk
1	?	180–210	140–170	Low
2	45–60	?	170–210	Low
3	20–45	?	?	Low
4	45–60	180–210	170–210	Low
5	45–60	?	170–210	High
6	?	210–220	?	High
7	45–60	180–210	?	High

Table 4. An inconsistent data set

Case	Attributes			Decision
	Age	Cholesterol	Weight	Risk
1	20–45	180–210	140–210	Low
2	45–60	180–210	140–210	Low
3	20–45	210–220	140–210	Low
4	45–60	180–210	140–210	Low
5	45–60	210–220	140–210	High
6	20–45	210–220	140–210	High
7	45–60	180–210	210–220	High

A fundamental idea of rough set theory [9] is an indiscernibility relation, defined for complete data sets. Let B be a nonempty subset of the set A of all attributes. The indiscernibility relation $R(B)$ is a relation on U defined for $x, y \in U$ as defined by

$$(x, y) \in R(B) \text{ if and only if } \forall a \in B \ (a(x) = a(y))$$

The indiscernibility relation $R(B)$ is an equivalence relation. Equivalence classes of $R(B)$ are called *elementary sets* of B and are denoted by $[x]_B$. A subset of U is called *B-definable* if it is a union of elementary sets of B.

The set X of all cases defined by the same value of the decision d is called a *concept*. The set of all concepts is denoted by $\{d\}^*$. For example, a concept associated with the value *low* of the decision *Risk* is the set $\{1, 2, 3, 4\}$. The largest B-definable set contained in X is called the *B-lower approximation* of X, denoted by $\underline{appr}_B(X)$, and defined as follows

$$\cup\{[x]_B \mid [x]_B \subseteq X\}.$$

The smallest B-definable set containing X, denoted by $\overline{appr}_B(X)$ is called the *B-upper approximation* of X, and is defined by

$$\cup \{[x]_B \mid [x]_B \cap X \neq \emptyset\}.$$

For Table 4,

$$\underline{appr}_A(\{1, 2, 3, 4\}) = \{1, 2, 4\}$$

and

$$\overline{appr}_A(\{1, 2, 3, 4\}) = \{1, 2, 3, 4, 6\}.$$

The level of inconsistency may be defined as follows

$$1 - \frac{\sum_{X \in \{d\}^*} |\underline{appr}_A(X)|}{|U|},$$

where $|S|$ denotes the cardinality of the set S.

For a variable a and its value v, (a, v) is called a variable-value pair. A *block* of (a, v), denoted by $[(a, v)]$, is the set $\{x \in U \mid a(x) = v\}$ [3]. For incomplete decision tables the definition of a block of an attribute-value pair is modified in the following way.

If for an attribute a there exists a case x such that $a(x) = ?$, i.e., the corresponding value is lost, then the case x should not be included in any blocks $[(a, v)]$ for all values v of attribute a.

For the data set from Table 3 the blocks of attribute-value pairs are:

[(Age, 20–45)] = {3},
[(Age, 45–60)] = {2, 4, 5, 7},
[(Cholesterol, 180–210)] = {1, 4, 7},
[(Cholesterol, 210–220)] = {6},
[(Weight, 180–210)] = {1}, and
[(Weight, 170–220)] = {2, 4, 5}.

For a case $x \in U$ and $B \subseteq A$, the *characteristic set* $K_B(x)$ is defined as the intersection of the sets $K(x, a)$, for all $a \in B$, where the set $K(x, a)$ is defined in the following way:

– If $a(x)$ is specified, then $K(x, a)$ is the block $[(a, a(x))]$ of attribute a and its value $a(x)$,
– If $a(x) = ?$ then the set $K(x, a) = U$, where U is the set of all cases,

For Table 3 and $B = A$,

$K_A(1) = \{1\}$,
$K_A(2) = \{2, 4, 5\}$,
$K_A(3) = \{3\}$,
$K_A(4) = \{4\}$,
$K_A(5) = \{2, 4, 5\}$,
$K_A(6) = \{6\}$, and
$K_A(7) = \{4, 7\}$.

First we will quote some definitions from [7]. Let X be a subset of U. The B-*singleton lower approximation* of X, denoted by $\underline{appr}_B^{singleton}(X)$, is defined by

$$\{x \mid x \in U, K_B(x) \subseteq X\}.$$

The B-*singleton upper approximation* of X, denoted by $\overline{appr}_B^{singleton}(X)$, is defined by

$$\{x \mid x \in U, K_B(x) \cap X \neq \emptyset\}.$$

The B-*subset lower approximation* of X, denoted by $\underline{appr}_B^{subset}(X)$, is defined by

$$\cup \{K_B(x) \mid x \in U, K_B(x) \subseteq X\}.$$

The B-*subset upper approximation* of X, denoted by $\overline{appr}_B^{subset}(X)$, is defined by

$$\cup \{K_B(x) \mid x \in U, K_B(x) \cap X \neq \emptyset\}.$$

The B-*concept lower approximation* of X, denoted by $\underline{appr}_B^{concept}(X)$, is defined by

$$\cup \{K_B(x) \mid x \in X, K_B(x) \subseteq X\}.$$

The B-*concept upper approximation* of X, denoted by $\overline{appr}_B^{concept}(X)$, is defined by

$$\cup \{K_B(x) \mid x \in X, K_B(x) \cap X \neq \emptyset\} = \cup \{K_B(x) \mid x \in X\}.$$

For Table 3 and $X = \{5, 6, 7\}$, all A-singleton, A-subset and A-concept lower and upper approximations are:

$\underline{appr}_A^{singleton}(X) = \{6\}$,
$\overline{appr}_A^{singleton}(X) = \{2, 5, 6, 7\}$,
$\underline{appr}_A^{subset}(X) = \{6\}$,
$\overline{appr}_A^{subset}(X) = \{2, 4, 5, 6, 7\}$,
$\underline{appr}_A^{concept}(X) = \{6\}$,
$\overline{appr}_A^{concept}(X) = \{2, 4, 5, 6, 7\}$.

3 Probabilistic Approximations

Definitions of lower and upper approximations may be extended to the probabilistic approximations [6]. In our experiments we used only concept approximations, so we will cite the corresponding definition only for the concept approximation. A B-concept probabilistic approximation of the set X with the threshold α, $0 < \alpha \leq 1$, denoted by $appr_{\alpha,B}^{concept}(X)$, is defined by

$$\cup\{K_B(x) \mid x \in X, \; Pr(X \mid K_B(x)) \geq \alpha\},$$

where $Pr(X \mid K_B(x)) = \frac{|X \cap K_B(x)|}{|K_B(x)|}$ is the conditional probability of X given $K_B(x)$.

Since we are using only B-concept probabilistic approximations, for the sake of simplicity we will call them B-probabilistic approximations. Additionally, if $B = A$, B-probabilistic approximations will be called simply probabilistic approximations and will be denoted by $appr_\alpha(X)$.

Note that if $\alpha = 1$, the probabilistic approximation is equal to the concept lower approximation and if α is small, close to 0, in our experiments it is 0.001, the probabilistic approximation is equal to the concept upper approximation.

For Table 3 and the concept $X = \{5, 6, 7\}$, there exist the following distinct probabilistic approximations:

$$appr_{1.0}(X) = \{6\},$$
$$appr_{0.5}(X) = \{4, 6, 7\},$$
$$appr_{0.333}(X) = \{2, 4, 5, 6, 7\}.$$

A special probabilistic approximations with $\alpha = 0.5$ will be called *middle* approximations.

4   Experiments

Our experiments are based on eight data sets, all taken from the University of California at Irvine *Machine Learning Repository*. Essential information about these data sets is presented in Table 5. All eight data sets are numerical.

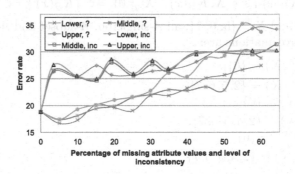

Fig. 1. Error rates for two series of data sets originated from the *Australian* data set. Incomplete data are denoted by "?", inconsistent data are denoted by "inc"

For any data set we created a series of incomplete data sets in the following way: first, the numerical data set was discretized using the agglomerative cluster analysis method [1]. Then we randomly replaced 5 % of specified attribute values by symbols of "?", denoting missing attribute values. After that, we replaced randomly and incrementally, with an increment equal to 5 %, new specified attribute values by symbols "?", preserving old ones. The process continued until we reached the point of having a case with all attribute values being "?"s. Then we returned to the one but last step and tried to add, randomly, 5 % of "?"s

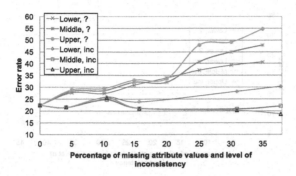

Fig. 2. Error rates for two series of data sets originated from the *Ecoli* data set. Incomplete data are denoted by "?", inconsistent data are denoted by "inc"

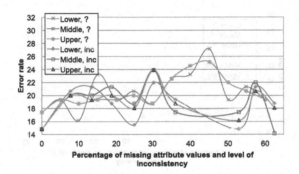

Fig. 3. Error rates for two series of data sets originated from the *Hepatitis* data set. Incomplete data are denoted by "?", inconsistent data are denoted by "inc"

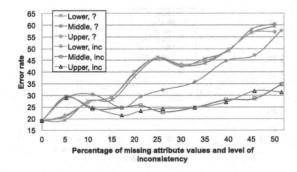

Fig. 4. Error rates for two series of data sets originated from the *Image Segmentation* data set. Incomplete data are denoted by "?", inconsistent data are denoted by "inc"

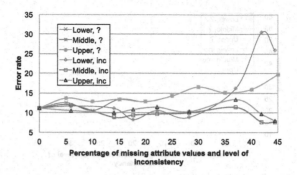

Fig. 5. Error rates for two series of data sets originated from the *Ionosphere* data set. Incomplete data are denoted by "?", inconsistent data are denoted by "inc"

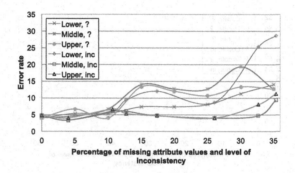

Fig. 6. Error rates for two series of data sets originated from the *Iris* data set. Incomplete data are denoted by "?", inconsistent data are denoted by "inc"

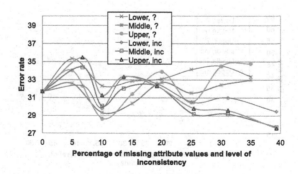

Fig. 7. Error rates for two series of data sets originated from the *Pima* data set. Incomplete data are denoted by "?", inconsistent data are denoted by "inc"

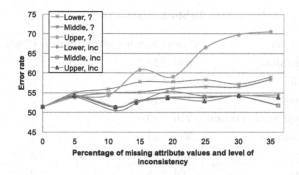

Fig. 8. Error rates for two series of data sets originated from the *Yeast* data set. Incomplete data are denoted by "?", inconsistent data are denoted by "inc"

again. If after three such attempts the result was still a case with "?"s as values for all attributes, the process was terminated. For example, for the *australian* data set such maximum for missing attribute values is 60 %.

For each original numerical data set, a series of inconsistent data sets was created by discretization, using the same agglomerative cluster analysis method as for the missing data sets. However, different levels of inconsistency were used as a stopping condition for discretization. Note that due to the nature of discretization, only some levels of inconsistency were possible to accomplish, so the levels of inconsistency are not as regular as percentage of missing attribute values. For example, for the *australian* data set these levels are 3.48, 9.71, 15.22 etc. instead of 5, 10, 15, as for the percentage of missing attribute values, though we tried to keep both series as close as possible.

Our experiments were conducted on 141 data sets, 71 among them were incomplete and 62 were inconsistent, 8 discretized and consistent data sets were used as special cases for both incomplete and inconsistent data sets.

For every data set we used three different probabilistic approximations for rule induction (lower, middle and upper). Thus we had 24 different approaches to rule induction. For rule induction we used the MLEM2 rule induction algorithm, a part of the Learning from Examples based on Rough Sets (LERS) data mining system [3].

For these 24 approaches we compared incomplete data with inconsistent ones for the same type of probabilistic approximations, using the Wilcoxon matched-pairs signed rank test, with 5 % level of significance, two-tailed test. Since we had 71 incomplete data sets and 62 inconsistent data sets, missing pairs were constructed by interpolation. Results of experiments rates for which there were no matching results, either incomplete or inconsistent, are not depicted in Figs. 1, 2, 3, 4, 5, 6, 7 and 8.

Results of our experiments, presented in Figs. 1, 2, 3, 4, 5, 6, 7 and 8, are: among 24 approaches, in 12 inconsistency was better (the error rate was smaller for inconsistent data). The *australian* data set was an exception, for all three probabilistic approximations the error rate was significantly smaller for incom-

Table 5. Data sets

Data set	Cases	Number of attributes	Concepts
Australian	690	14	2
Ecoli	336	8	8
Hepatitis	155	19	2
Image Segmentation	210	19	7
Ionosphere	351	34	2
Iris	150	4	3
Pima	768	8	2
Yeast	1484	8	9

plete data sets. For remaining nine approaches the difference between incompleteness and inconsistency was statistically insignificant.

In summary, there is evidence that inconsistency in data sets is less harmful for mining data than incompleteness, though more research is required.

5 Conclusions

As a results of our experiments, conducted on 141 data sets, including 71 incomplete data and 62 inconsistent, in 12 out of 24 combinations of the type of the original data set and a type of approximation, the error rate was smaller for inconsistent data. For one data set, combined with all three probabilistic approximations, the error rate was smaller for incomplete data. For remaining nine combinations the difference in performance was statistically insignificant. Thus, we may claim that there is some experimental evidence that incompleteness is generally worse than inconsistency for data mining.

References

1. Chmielewski, M.R., Grzymala-Busse, J.W.: Global discretization of continuous attributes as preprocessing for machine learning. Int. J. Approximate Reasoning 15(4), 319–331 (1996)
2. Clark, P.G., Grzymala-Busse, J.W.: Experiments on probabilistic approximations. In: Proceedings of the 2011 IEEE International Conference on Granular Computing, pp. 144–149 (2011)
3. Grzymala-Busse, J.W.: A new version of the rule induction system LERS. Fundamenta Informaticae 31, 27–39 (1997)
4. Grzymala-Busse, J.W.: Rough set strategies to data with missing attribute values. In: Notes of the Workshop on Foundations and New Directions of Data Mining, in conjunction with the Third International Conference on Data Mining, pp. 56–63 (2003)
5. Grzymala-Busse, J.W.: Data with missing attribute values: Generalization of indiscernibility relation and rule induction. Trans. Rough Sets 1, 78–95 (2004)

6. Grzymala-Busse, J.W.: Generalized parameterized approximations. In: Proceedings of the 6-th International Conference on Rough Sets and Knowledge Technology, pp. 136–145 (2011)
7. Grzymala-Busse, J.W., Rzasa, W.: Definability and other properties of approximations for generalized indiscernibility relations. Trans. Rough Sets 11, 14–39 (2010)
8. Grzymala-Busse, J.W., Wang, A.Y.: Modified algorithms LEM1 and LEM2 for rule induction from data with missing attribute values. In: Proceedings of the 5-th International Workshop on Rough Sets and Soft Computing in conjunction with the Third Joint Conference on Information Sciences, pp. 69–72 (1997)
9. Pawlak, Z.: Rough sets. Int. J. Comput. Inform. Sci. 11, 341–356 (1982)
10. Pawlak, Z.: Rough Sets. Theoretical Aspects of Reasoning about Data. Kluwer Academic Publishers, Dordrecht (1991)
11. Pawlak, Z., Skowron, A.: Rough sets: some extensions. Inf. Sci. 177, 28–40 (2007)
12. Pawlak, Z., Wong, S.K.M., Ziarko, W.: Rough sets: probabilistic versus deterministic approach. Int. J. Man Mach. Stud. 29, 81–95 (1988)
13. Stefanowski, J., Tsoukias, A.: Incomplete information tables and rough classification. Comput. Intell. 17(3), 545–566 (2001)
14. Yao, Y.Y.: Probabilistic rough set approximations. Int. J. Approximate Reasoning 49, 255–271 (2008)
15. Yao, Y.Y., Wong, S.K.M.: A decision theoretic framework for approximate concepts. Int. J. Man Mach. Stud. 37, 793–809 (1992)
16. Ziarko, W.: Probabilistic approach to rough sets. Int. J. Approximate Reasoning 49, 272–284 (2008)

Transient Solution for Queue-Size Distribution in a Certain Finite-Buffer Model with Server Working Vacations

Wojciech M. Kempa$^{(\boxtimes)}$ and Martyna Kobielnik

Faculty of Applied Mathematics, Institute of Mathematics,
Silesian University of Technology, 23 Kaszubska Street, 44-100 Gliwice, Poland
{wojciech.kempa,martyna.kobielnik}@polsl.pl

Abstract. A finite-buffer queueing model with Poisson arrivals and exponential processing times is investigated. Every time when the system empties, the server begins a generally distributed single working vacation period, during which the service is provided with another (slower) rate. After the completion of the vacation period the processing is being continued normally, with original speed. The next working vacation period is being initialized at the next time at which the system becomes empty, and so on. The system of Volterra-type integral equations for transient queue-size distribution, conditioned by the initial level of buffer saturation, is built. The solution of the corresponding system written for Laplace transforms is given in a compact-form using the linear algebraic approach and the corresponding result obtained for the ordinary model (without working vacation regime). Numerical examples are attached as well.

Keywords: Finite buffer · Poisson process · Queue size · Transient state · Working vacation

1 Introduction

Queueing models with finite buffer capacities are widely used in the analysis of real-life systems occurring in technical and economic sciences, and in transport and logistic problems, in which the phenomena of "queueing" of items [27, 28] (packets, calls, customers, jobs, etc.) and their losses due to buffer saturation can be observed. As it seems, particularly important are models in which different-type restrictions in access to the service station are implemented additionally. In practice, these restrictions are often a kind of energy saving mechanism (e.g., cyclic succession of listening and dormant modes in wireless networks, or switching off a machine in manufacturing process in the case of the traffic with low intensity), and are associated with temporary blocking the service of items despite their presence in the accumulation buffer. The scientific literature concerning such systems is already huge and still increasing. Servi and Finn proposed in [15] for the first time the model with the so called working vacation, in which the server, instead of total service stopping, offers the processing with another speed (usually lower). This model was originally motivated by a reconfigurable WDM (Wavelength-division multiplexing) optical access network in which a

© Springer International Publishing Switzerland 2016
G. Dregvaite and R. Damasevicius (Eds.): ICIST 2016, CCIS 639, pp. 426–440, 2016.
DOI: 10.1007/978-3-319-46254-7_34

single token cyclically visits each queue, operating at two different rates (faster and slower ones), but it can be successfully used in modelling many phenomena typical for, e.g. computer and telecommunication networks or manufacturing engineering. In particular, we can use it

- when the service station processes two types of packets with significantly different service speeds (e.g., different times of putting them in the link);
- in the case of temporary throughput reductions, due to parallel launching another application;
- in the situation of periodic reduction of the throughput of the production line (slower processing with lower power consumption).

As it is shown in [12, 29], a working vacation queueing system with two different processing rates can be successfully applied in modelling, e.g. the Ethernet Passive Optical Network (EPON), consisting of one optical line terminal (OLT), situated at the central office, and multiple optical network units (ONUs) situated at customer premises equipment (CPE), and a passive splitter/combiner. In EPON bi-directional transmissions are provided: in the downstream direction the OLT broadcasts to all ONUs and in the upstream direction (from ONUs to the OLT) the fiber channel is shared by all ONUs.

After the article [15] many papers were published on the analysis of stochastic characteristics of queueing models with working vacation mechanism. Working vacation models of GI/M/1 type are considered, e.g. in [2, 26] in the case of finite buffer capacity, and in [1, 13] for the infinite waiting room. Unfortunately, as one can see, most of the results relates only to the steady state of the system. Meanwhile, as it seems, in practice it is increasingly essential to investigate the system in the transient case. Such a study is of particular importance in the case of the observation the system shortly after its opening or applying new control mechanism. The high variability of the packet traffic (e.g., in the Internet) also can "force" the time-dependent analysis. In [18] the transient queue-size distribution for the infinite-sized M/M/1-type model with server working vacations is found. In [22] the study is extended for the multi-server case and multiple working vacation regime by using the matrix geometric method. Compact-form transient results for main stochastic characteristics of finite-buffer queues with different-type service restrictions can be found, e.g. in [7–10]. The case of infinite buffer is studied in [5, 6]. In [21] a processor-sharing model with limited total volume and probabilistic packet dropping is considered. In various data management systems (see [23]) we can find applications of queueing systems to enable faster requests management and therefore improved data mining (see e.g. [24, 25, 30, 31]).

The remaining part of the article is organized as follows. In the next Sect. 2 we give the precise description of the considered queueing model and state an auxiliary algebraic result which can be used in further analysis. Section 3 is devoted to the ordinary system (without server working vacation). The compact-form representation for the LT (=Laplace transform) of conditional transient queue-size distribution is derived there, and written by using the functional sequence recursively defined. In Sect. 4 we obtain the corresponding result for the original model with generally distributed working vacations, utilizing results from Sects. 2 and 3. In Sect. 5 numerical examples are attached and the last Sect. 6 contains a short summary and conclusions.

2 Model Description and Auxiliary Results

In the article we deal with the M/M/1/N-type queueing model with Poisson job arrivals with rate λ, exponential processing times with mean μ^{-1}, and finite capacity $N \geq 2$ ($N - 1$ places in the buffer queue and one place "in service"). Every time when the system empties the server begins a generally distributed single working vacation period, during which the processing of jobs is carried out with another (slower) rate $\mu^* < \mu$ (see Fig. 1 for the scheme of the system operation). We denote by $G(\cdot)$ the CDF (=cumulative distribution function) of the working vacation period duration. After finishing the vacation period the service process is being continued normally, with original speed. The next working vacation period is being initialized at the next time at which the queue becomes empty, and so on.

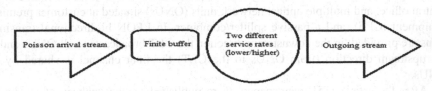

Fig. 1. Scheme of a single-server finite-buffer working vacation model with Poisson arrivals

The following theorem can be found in [11]:

Theorem 1. *Introduce two number sequences* $(\alpha_k), k \geq 0$, *and* $(\psi_k), k \geq 1$, *with the assumption* $\alpha_0 \neq 0$. *Each solution of the following system of linear equations with respect to* $x_n, n \geq 1$:

$$\sum_{k=-1}^{n-1} \alpha_{k+1} x_{n-k} - x_n = \psi_n, \quad n \geq 1, \tag{1}$$

can be written in the form

$$x_n = CR_n + \sum_{k=1}^{n} R_{n-k} \psi_k, \quad n \geq 1, \tag{2}$$

where C is a constant independent on n, and (R_k) *is connected with the sequence* (α_k) *by the following formula:*

$$\sum_{k=0}^{\infty} \theta^k R_k = \frac{1}{P_\alpha(\theta) - 1}, \text{ where } P_\alpha(\theta) = \sum_{k=-1}^{\infty} \theta^k \alpha_{k+1}, |\theta| < 1. \tag{3}$$

Moreover, in [11] it is proved that successive terms of the sequence (R_n) (called a potential) can be found recursively as follows:

$$R_0 = 0, R_1 = \alpha_0^{-1}, R_{k+1} = R_1\left(R_k - \sum_{i=0}^{k} \alpha_{i+1}R_{k-i}\right), \quad k \geq 1. \tag{4}$$

As it turns out, LTs of conditional queue-size distributions in the original system and in the ordinary one, satisfy systems of equations similar to (1). Hence, in solving these systems, we will use the formula (2), where the representation for C will be found from a boundary condition.

3 Conditional Transient Queue-Size Distribution in an Ordinary System

In this section we deal with the conditional queue-size distribution in the ordinary finite-buffer M/M/1/N-type model without working vacation discipline, corresponding to the original one, with λ and μ^* being the arrival intensity and service speed, respectively, and find the representation for its LT in terms of "input" system parameters, writing it in a specific way, by using a recursively defined sequence, called a potential. Similar result was obtained in [3] for the generally-distributed service time, however it is written in another form. It should be mentioned here that transient solutions for the M/M/1/N-type queue were also obtained in [19] (see also [14]) by using the technique of eigenvalues and eigenvectors, in [16] by applying Chebyshev polynomials, in [17] by utilizing matrix technique and in [20] via LTs. Introduce the following notation:

$$P_n^O(t, m) \stackrel{\text{def}}{=} P\{X^O(t) = m | X^O(0) = n\}, \quad 0 \leq m, n \leq N, \tag{5}$$

where $X^O(t)$ denotes the number of packets present in the ordinary system at time t. Since, due to exponential distributions of inter-arrival and service times, both arrival and service completion epochs are Markov moments, from the continuous version of the total probability formula written with respect to the first Markov moment after $t = 0$, we obtain the following system of integral equations:

$$P_0^O(t, m) = \lambda \int_0^t e^{-\lambda x} P_1^O(t - x, m)dx + e^{-\lambda t}\delta_{m,0}, \tag{6}$$

$$P_n^O(t, m) = \lambda \int_0^t e^{-(\lambda + \mu^*)x} P_{n+1}^O(t - x, m)dx$$
$$+ \mu^* \int_0^t e^{-(\lambda + \mu^*)x} P_{n-1}^O(t - x, m)dx \tag{7}$$
$$+ e^{-(\lambda + \mu^*)t}\delta_{m,n},$$

where $1 \leq n \leq N - 1$, and

$$P_N^O(t, m) = \lambda \int_0^t e^{-(\lambda + \mu^*)x} P_N^O(t - x, m) dx$$

$$+ \mu^* \int_0^t e^{-(\lambda + \mu^*)x} P_{N-1}^O(t - x, m) dx \tag{8}$$

$$+ e^{-(\lambda + \mu^*)t} \delta_{m,N},$$

where the notation $\delta_{i,j}$ stands for the Kronecker delta function. Let us comment (6)–(8) briefly. Indeed, the first summands on the right side of (7) and (8) relate to the case in which, as the first one, a jump of the arrival Poisson process occurs, while the second ones - to the situation in which the jump of the service process is observed as the first one. The last summands on the right side of (7) and (8) present the case in that there is no jump of the arrival and service processes before t. The formula (6), written for the case of the system being empty at the opening, is obvious. Defining

$$\tilde{p}_n^O(s, m) \overset{\text{def}}{=} \int_0^\infty e^{-st} P\{X^O(t) = m | X^O(0) = n\} dt, \quad \Re(s) > 0, \tag{9}$$

we obtain from (6)–(8) the following equations:

$$\tilde{p}_0^O(s, m) = \frac{\lambda}{\lambda + s} \tilde{p}_1^O(s, m) + \frac{\delta_{m,0}}{\lambda + s}, \tag{10}$$

$$\tilde{p}_n^O(s, m) = \frac{\lambda}{\lambda + \mu^* + s} \tilde{p}_{n+1}^O(s, m) + \frac{\mu^*}{\lambda + \mu^* + s} \tilde{p}_{n-1}^O(s, m) + \frac{\delta_{m,n}}{\lambda + \mu^* + s}, 1 \leq n \leq N - 1 \tag{11}$$

and

$$\tilde{p}_N^O(s, m) = \frac{\lambda}{\lambda + \mu^* + s} \tilde{p}_N^O(s, m) + \frac{\mu^*}{\lambda + \mu^* + s} \tilde{p}_{N-1}^O(s, m) + \frac{\delta_{m,N}}{\lambda + \mu^* + s}. \tag{12}$$

We will obtain the solution of the system (10)–(12) by applying the algebraic-type approach based on Theorem 1 that allows for writing the representation for $\tilde{p}_k^O(s, m)$ (at arbitrary k) via certain recursively-defined sequence (see (4)).

Let us note that, if we define

$$\alpha_0^*(s) = \frac{\lambda}{\lambda + \mu^* + s}, \alpha_1^*(s) = 0, \alpha_2^*(s) = \frac{\mu^*}{\lambda + \mu^* + s}, \alpha_k^*(s) = 0, \quad k \geq 3, \tag{13}$$

and, moreover,

$$\psi_n^*(s, m) = \phi_n^*(s, m) - D_n^*(s) \tilde{p}_0^O(s, m), \tag{14}$$

where

$$\phi_n^*(s,m) \overset{\text{def}}{=} -\frac{\delta_{m,n}}{\lambda + \mu^* + s}, \quad D_n^*(s) \overset{\text{def}}{=} \delta_{1,n}\alpha_2^*(s), \tag{15}$$

then the Eqs. (11) and (12) can be rewritten as

$$\sum_{k=-1}^{n-1} \alpha_{k+1}^*(s)\tilde{p}_{n-k}^O(s,m) - \tilde{p}_n^O(s,m) = \psi_n^*(s,m), \quad 1 \le n \le N-1, \tag{16}$$

and

$$\tilde{p}_N^O(s,m) = \left[1 - \alpha_0^*(s)\right]^{-1}\left[\alpha_2^*(s)\tilde{p}_{N-1}^O(s,m) - \phi_N^*(s,m)\right]. \tag{17}$$

Because (16) has the same form as (1) (now with α_k^* and ψ_n^* being functions of s and (s,m), respectively), then the following representation holds true (compare (2)):

$$\tilde{p}_n^O(s,m) = C^*(s,m)R_n^*(s) + \sum_{k=1}^{n} R_{n-k}^*(s)\psi_k^*(s,m), \quad n \ge 1, \tag{18}$$

where now (see (4) and refer to (13)) for $k \ge 1$

$$R_0^*(s) = 0, R_1^*(s) = \left[\alpha_0^*(s)\right]^{-1}, R_{k+1}^*(s) = R_1^*(s)\left(R_k^*(s) - \alpha_2^*(s)R_{k-1}^*(s)\right). \tag{19}$$

In order to find the explicit representation for $C^*(s,m)$, we will use the Eq. (17), treating it as a kind of boundary condition. Indeed, implementing (18) in (17), we obtain

$$\begin{aligned}
&\left[1 - \alpha_0^*(s)\right]\left[C^*(s,m)R_N^*(s) + \sum_{k=1}^{N} R_{N-k}^*(s)\left(\phi_k^*(s,m) - D_k^*(s)\tilde{p}_0^O(s,m)\right)\right] \\
&= \alpha_2^*(s)\left[C^*(s,m)R_{N-1}^*(s) + \sum_{k=1}^{N-1} R_{N-1-k}^*(s)\left(\phi_k^*(s,m) - D_k^*(s)\tilde{p}_0^O(s,m)\right)\right] \\
&\quad - \phi_N^*(s,m).
\end{aligned} \tag{20}$$

Observe that, taking in (18) $n = 1$, we have

$$\tilde{p}_1^O(s,m) = C^*(s,m)R_1^*(s) = C^*(s,m)\left[\alpha_0^*(s)\right]^{-1}. \tag{21}$$

Substituting now (21) into (10), we get

$$\tilde{p}_0^O(s,m) = A^*(s)C^*(s,m) + B^*(s,m), \tag{22}$$

where

$$A^*(s) \overset{\text{def}}{=} \frac{\lambda}{\lambda + s}\left[\alpha_0^*(s)\right]^{-1}, \quad B^*(s,m) \overset{\text{def}}{=} \frac{\delta_{m,0}}{\lambda + s}. \tag{23}$$

Inserting (22) into (20), we eliminate $C^*(s, m)$ in the following form:

$$C^*(s, m) = \frac{T^*(s, m)}{\Delta^*(s)}, \tag{24}$$

where we denote

$$\begin{aligned}
T^*(s, m) \overset{\text{def}}{=} \alpha_2^*(s) \sum_{k=1}^{N-1} R_{N-k-1}^*(s) \left[\phi_k^*(s, m) - D_k^*(s) B^*(s, m) \right] \\
- \left[1 - \alpha_0^*(s) \right] \sum_{k=1}^{N} R_{N-k}^*(s) \left[\phi_k^*(s, m) - D_k^*(s) B^*(s, m) \right] \\
- \phi_N^*(s, m)
\end{aligned} \tag{25}$$

and

$$\begin{aligned}
\Delta^*(s) \overset{\text{def}}{=} \left(1 - \alpha_0^*(s) \right) \left[R_N^*(s) - A^*(s) \sum_{k=1}^{N} R_{N-k}^*(s) D_k^*(s) \right] \\
+ \alpha_2^*(s) \left[A^*(s) \sum_{k=1}^{N-1} R_{N-1-k}^*(s) D_k^*(s) - R_{N-1}^*(s) \right].
\end{aligned} \tag{26}$$

Collecting the formulae (14), (18), (22) and (24), we can formulate the following:

Theorem 2. *The LT $\tilde{p}_n^O(s, m)$ of transient queue-size distribution in the ordinary M/M/1/N-type queue, conditioned by the number $0 \leq n \leq N$ of jobs present in the system initially, can be expressed in the following way:*

$$\tilde{p}_0^O(s, m) = A^*(s) \frac{T^*(s, m)}{\Delta^*(s)} + B^*(s, m), \tag{27}$$

$$\begin{aligned}
\tilde{p}_n^O(s, m) = \frac{T^*(s, m)}{\Delta^*(s)} R_n^*(s) \\
+ \sum_{k=1}^{N} R_{N-k}^*(s) \left[\phi_k^*(s, m) - D_k^*(s) \left(A^*(s) \frac{T^*(s, m)}{\Delta^*(s)} + B^*(s, m) \right) \right], \quad 1 \leq n \leq N,
\end{aligned} \tag{28}$$

where $\Re(s) > 0$ and $0 \leq m \leq N$, and the formulae for $\phi_k^*(s, m)$, $D_k^*(s)$, $R_k^*(s)$, $A^*(s)$, $B^*(s, m)$, $T^*(s, m)$ and $\Delta^*(s)$ are given in (15), (19), (23) (25) and (26), respectively.

4 Queue-Size Distribution in a Model with Working Vacations

Let us take into consideration the original model with generally-distributed server working vacation periods (each with a CDF $G(\cdot)$) during which the processing of jobs is offered with a slower rate $\mu^* < \mu$, where μ denotes the normal-mode service rate. Introduce the following notation:

$$P_n(t, m) \overset{\text{def}}{=} P\{X(t) = m | X(0) = n\}, \quad 0 \le m, n \le N, \tag{29}$$

where $X(t)$ denotes the number of packets present in the system with working vacations (original one) at time t. Assume, firstly, that the system starts its evolution being empty. So, at $t = 0$ the working vacation period begins. Observe, that the following equation is then satisfied:

$$P_0(t, m) = \sum_{k=0}^{N} \int_0^t P_0^O(x, k) P_k^O(t - x, m) dG(x) + [1 - G(t)] P_0^O(t, m). \tag{30}$$

Indeed, the first summand on the right side of (30) presents the situation in which the working vacation period completes at time $x < t$. Hence, at time x the system starts the operation in normal mode with $0 \le k \le N$ packets with probability $P_0^O(x, k)$. The second summand in (30) relates to the case in that the time epoch t is "inside" the working vacation period. If the number of packets equals $1 \le n \le N - 1$ initially, we similarly obtain

$$P_n(t, m) = \lambda \int_0^t e^{-(\lambda + \mu)x} P_{n+1}(t - x, m) dx + \mu \int_0^t e^{-(\lambda + \mu)x} P_{n-1}(t - x, m) dx + e^{-(\lambda + \mu)t} \delta_{m,n}. \tag{31}$$

Finally, $n = N$ we have

$$P_N(t, m) = \lambda \int_0^t e^{-(\lambda + \mu)x} P_N(t - x, m) dx + \mu \int_0^t e^{-(\lambda + \mu)x} P_{N-1}(t - x, m) dx + e^{-(\lambda + \mu)t} \delta_{m,N}. \tag{32}$$

The interpretation of (31) and (32) is the same as of (7) and (8). Defining

$$\tilde{p}_n(s, m) \overset{\text{def}}{=} \int_0^{\infty} e^{-st} P\{X(t) = m | X(0) = n\} dt, \quad \Re(s) > 0, \tag{33}$$

and, moreover (compare (13)–(15)),

$$\alpha_0(s) = \frac{\lambda}{\lambda + \mu + s}, \alpha_1(s) = 0, \alpha_2(s) = \frac{\mu}{\lambda + \mu + s}, \alpha_k(s) = 0, \quad k \ge 3, \tag{34}$$

and

$$\psi_n(s, m) = \phi_n(s, m) - D_n(s) \tilde{p}_0(s, m), \tag{35}$$

where

$$\phi_n(s,m) \overset{\text{def}}{=} -\frac{\delta_{m,n}}{\lambda+\mu+s}, D_n(s) \overset{\text{def}}{=} \delta_{1,n}\alpha_2(s), \tag{36}$$

we obtain from (30)–(32) the following system (see (10) ,(16) and (17)):

$$\tilde{p}_0(s,m) = \sum_{k=0}^{N} \tilde{p}_k(s,m) \int_0^{\infty} e^{-sx} P_0^O(x,k) dG(x) + \int_0^{\infty} e^{-st} P_0^O(t,m)[1-G(t)]dt, \tag{37}$$

$$\sum_{k=-1}^{n-1} \alpha_{k+1}(s)\tilde{p}_{n-k}(s,m) - \tilde{p}_n(s,m) = \psi_n(s,m), 1 \leq n \leq N-1, \tag{38}$$

and

$$\tilde{p}_N(s,m) = [1-\alpha_0(s)]^{-1}[\alpha_2(s)\tilde{p}_{N-1}(s,m) - \phi_N(s,m)]. \tag{39}$$

Since (38) has the same form as (1), then we can write (compare (18))

$$\tilde{p}_n(s,m) = C(s,m)R_n(s) + \sum_{k=1}^{n} R_{n-k}(s)\psi_k(s,m), \quad n \geq 1, \tag{40}$$

where here (see (19)) for $k \geq 1$

$$R_0(s) = 0, R_1(s) = [\alpha_0^*(s)]^{-1}, R_{k+1}(s) = R_1(s)(R_k(s) - \alpha_2(s)R_{k-1}(s)) \tag{41}$$

and the sequence $(\alpha_k(s))$ is defined in (34).

Let us note that, if we define

$$L_k(s) \overset{\text{def}}{=} \int_0^{\infty} e^{-st} P_0^O(t,k) dG(t) \tag{42}$$

and

$$M(s,m) \overset{\text{def}}{=} \int_0^{\infty} e^{-st} P_0^O(t,k)[1-G(t)]dt, \tag{43}$$

where $\Re(s) > 0$, then (37) can be rewritten in the following way:

$$\tilde{p}_0(s,m) = \sum_{k=0}^{N} \tilde{p}_k(s,m)L_k(s) + M(s,m). \tag{44}$$

Inserting now in (44), instead of $\tilde{p}_k(s,m)$, the right side of the representation (40), we obtain

$$\tilde{p}_0(s,m) = \tilde{p}_0(s,m)L_0(s)$$
$$+ \sum_{k=1}^{N} L_k(s) \left[C(s,m)R_k(s) + \sum_{i=1}^{k} R_{k-i}(s)(\phi_i(s,m) - D_i(s)\tilde{p}_0(s,m)) \right]$$
$$+ M(s,m),$$

(45)

and hence we get the following formula:

$$\tilde{p}_0(s,m) = A(s)C(s,m) + B(s,m),$$

(46)

where

$$A(s) \stackrel{\text{def}}{=} \left[1 - L_0(s) + \sum_{k=1}^{N} L_k(s) \sum_{i=1}^{k} R_{k-i}(s)D_i(s) \right]^{-1} \sum_{k=1}^{N} L_k(s)R_k(s)$$

(47)

and

$$B(s,m) \stackrel{\text{def}}{=} \left[1 - L_0(s) + \sum_{k=1}^{N} L_k(s) \sum_{i=1}^{k} R_{k-i}(s)D_i(s) \right]^{-1}$$
$$\left[\sum_{k=1}^{N} L_k(s) \sum_{i=1}^{k} R_{k-i}(s)\phi_i(s,m) + M(s,m) \right]$$

(48)

Having defined $A(s)$ and $B(s,m)$, we can execute successive steps of the procedure described for the ordinary system in (20)–(26) and formulate the following main theorem:

Theorem 3. *The LT $\tilde{p}_n(s,m)$ of time-dependent queue-size distribution in the M/M/1/N-type queue with working vacation mechanism, conditioned by the number $0 \le n \le N$ of jobs present in the system initially, can be written in the following way:*

$$\tilde{p}_0(s,m) = A(s)\frac{T(s,m)}{\Delta(s)} + B(s,m),$$

(49)

$$\tilde{p}_n(s,m) = \frac{T(s,m)}{\Delta(s)} R_n(s)$$
$$+ \sum_{k=1}^{N} R_{N-k}(s) \left[\phi_k(s,m) - D_k(s) \left(A(s)\frac{T(s,m)}{\Delta(s)} + B(s,m) \right) \right], \ 1 \le n \le N,$$

(50)

where $\Re(s) > 0$ and $0 \le m \le N$, and (compare (25) and (26))

$$T(s,m) \stackrel{\text{def}}{=} \alpha_2(s) \sum_{k=1}^{N-1} R_{N-1-k}(s)[\phi_k(s,m) - D_k(s)B(s,m)]$$
$$- [1 - \alpha_0(s)] \sum_{k=1}^{N} R_{N-k}(s)[\phi_k(s,m) - D_k(s)B(s,m)] - \phi_N(s,m),$$

(51)

$$\Delta(s) \overset{\text{def}}{=} (1 - \alpha_0(s)) \Big[R_N(s) - A(s) \sum_{k=1}^{N} R_{N-k}(s) D_k(s) \Big]$$
$$+ \alpha_2(s) \Big[A(s) \sum_{k=1}^{N-1} R_{N-1-k}(s) D_k(s) - R_{N-1}(s) \Big]. \tag{52}$$

Moreover, the formulae for $\phi_k(s,m), D_k(s), R_k(s), A(s)$ and $B(s,m)$ are given in (36), (41), (47) and (48), respectively.

Remark 1. *The formulae (49) and (50) allow for finding the LT of the queue-size distribution in the original system as functions of the appropriate distribution for the ordinary model (given in terms of LTs in (27) and (28)), by $L_k(s)$ and $M(s,m)$ defined in (42) and (43), respectively.*

Remark 2. *Having LTs of the probabilities $\tilde{p}_n(s,m)$, we can easily find the stationary queue-size distribution $\pi_0, \ldots, \pi_N$, by using the well-known Tauberian theorem, namely*

$$\pi_m = \lim_{t \to \infty} P\{X(t) = m\} = \lim_{s \downarrow 0} s \cdot \tilde{p}_n(s,m), \quad 0 \le m \le N, \tag{53}$$

where n can be chosen arbitrarily between 0 and N.

Remark 3. *In the case of exponentially distributed working vacation period with mean θ^{-1}, i.e. if $G(t) = 1 - e^{-\theta t}, t > 0$, we can evaluate $L_k(s)$ and $M(s,m)$ explicitly. Indeed, we obtain*

$$L_k(s) = \theta \tilde{p}_0^O(s + \theta, k), M(s,m) = \tilde{p}_0^O(s + \theta, m). \tag{54}$$

5 Numerical Examples

Let us consider a node of the wireless network in which packets of sizes 200 [B] arrive according to a Poisson process with intensity 600 [kb/s]. The normal throughput equals 800 [kb/s], but every time when the buffer empties the throughput is lower (500 [kb/s]) for a random exponential time with mean 0.1 [s]. Let us note that for such parameters the traffic load equals normally 0.75 and during the working vacation period 1.20 (so, in this case the link is overloaded). In Fig. 1 transient behaviour of probabilities $P\{X(t) = m \mid X(0) = 0\}$ is presented for $m = 0, 2$ and 4, where $N = 4$. In Fig. 2 transient behaviour of $P\{X(t) = 1 \mid X(0) = 0\}$ is visualized for different arrival rates: 200, 400 and 600 [kb/s], where the remaining system parameters are kept the same as in Fig. 1. As one can observe, for the lowest arrival rate, the time for the system stabilization is the shortest one. Figure 3 shows the behaviour of $P\{X(t) = 4 \mid X(0) = 0\}$ at arrival rate 400 [kb/s] and normal service speed 800 [kb/s], for three different processing speeds during the WV (= working vacation) period (the case 800 [kb/s] denotes, in fact, no working vacation) (Fig. 4).

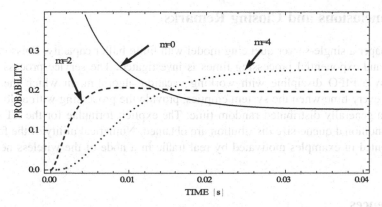

Fig. 2. Transient behaviour of $P\{X(t) = m \mid X(0) = 0\}$ for different values of m

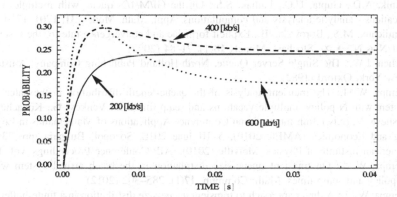

Fig. 3. Sensitivity of transient queue-size distribution on different arrival intensities

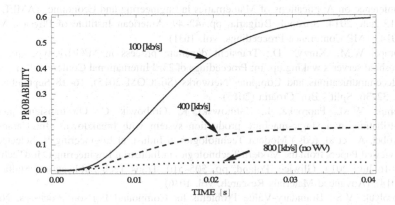

Fig. 4. Sensitivity of transient queue-size distribution on processing rates during WV

6 Conclusions and Closing Remarks

In the paper a single-server queueing model with finite buffer capacity, Poisson arrival stream and exponential processing times is investigated. The service process is governed by a FIFO discipline with working vacation algorithm, in which the service station, every time when the system empties, provide the processing with a slower rate during a generally distributed random time. The explicit formulae for the LT of transient conditional queue-size distribution are obtained. Numerical utility of the formulae is presented in examples motivated by real traffic in a node of the wireless network.

References

1. Baba, Y.: Analysis of a GI/M/1 queue with multiple working vacations. Oper. Res. Lett. **33**, 201–209 (2005)
2. Banik, A.D., Gupta, U.C., Pathak, S.S.: On the GI/M/1/N queue with multiple working vacations - analytic analysis and computations. Appl. Math. Model. **31**, 1701–1710 (2007)
3. Bratiichuk, M.S., Borowska, B.: Explicit formulae and convergence rate for the system $M^\alpha/$ G/1/N as N $\rightarrow \infty$. Stochast. Models **18**(1), 71–84 (2002)
4. Cohen, J.W.: The Single Server Queue. North-Holland Publishing Company, Amsterdam, New York, Oxford (1982)
5. Kempa, W.M.: The transient analysis of the queue-length distribution in the batch arrival system with N-policy, multiple vacations and setup times. In: Venkov, G., Kovacheva, R., Pasheva, V. (eds.) 36th International Conference Applications of Mathematics in Engineering and Economics (AMEE 2010), 5–10 June 2010, Sozopol, Bulgaria, pp. 235–242. American Institute of Physics, Melville (2010). (AIP Conference Proceedings, vol. 1293)
6. Kempa, W.M.: On transient queue-size distribution in the batch arrival system with the N-policy and setup times. Math. Commun. **17**(1), 285–302 (2012)
7. Kempa, W.M.: A direct approach to transient queue-size distribution in a finite-buffer queue with AQM. Appl. Math. Inf. Sci. **7**(3), 909–915 (2013)
8. Kempa, W.M.: On transient departure process in a finite-buffer queueing model with probabilistic packet dropping. In: Venkov, G., Pasheva, V. (eds.) 40th International Conference on Applications of Mathematics in Engineering and Economics (AMEE 2014), 8–13 June 2014, Sozopol, Bulgaria, pp. 42–49. American Institute of Physics, Melville (2014). (AIP Conference Proceedings, vol. 1631)
9. Kempa, W.M., Kurzyk, D.: Transient departure process in M/G/1/K-type queue with threshold server's waking up. In: Proceedings of 23rd International Conference on Software, Telecommunications and Computer Networks (SoftCOM 2015), 16–18 September 2015, pp. 32–36. Split - Bol, Croatia (2015)
10. Kempa, W.M., Paprocka, I., Kalinowski, K., Grabowik, C.: On transient queue-size distribution in a single-machine production system with breakdowns. In: Carausu, C., Wróbel, A., et al. (eds.) Modern Technologies in Industrial Engineering II. Selected, Peer Reviewed Papers from the Modern Technologies in Industrial Engineering (ModTech 2014), 13–16 July 2014, Gliwice, Poland, pp. 505–510. Trans Tech Publications, Staffa-Zurich (2014). (Advanced Materials Research, vol. 1036)
11. Korolyuk, V.S.: Boundary-Value Problems for Compound Poisson Processes. Naukova Dumka, Kiev (1975)

12. Li, J.-H., Liu, W.-Q., Tian, N.-S.: Steady-state analysis of a discrete-time batch arrival queue with working vacations. Perform. Eval. **67**, 897–912 (2010)

13. Li, J., Tian, N.: Performance analysis of a GI/M/1 queue with single working vacation. Appl. Math. Comput. **217**, 4960–4971 (2011)

14. Morse, P.M.: Queues, Inventories and Maintenance. Wiley, New York (1958)

15. Servi, L.D., Finn, S.G.: M/M/1 queues with working vacations. Perform. Eval. **50**, 41–52 (2002)

16. Sharma, O.P., Gupta, U.C.: Transient behaviour of an M/M/1/N queue. Stochast. Process. Appl. **13**, 327–331 (1982)

17. Sharma, O.P., Maheswar, M.V.R.: Transient behaviour of a simple queue with discouraged arrivals. Optimization **27**, 283–291 (1993)

18. Sudhesh, R., Raj, L.F.: Computational analysis of stationary and transient distribution of single server queue with working vacation. In: Krishna, P., Babu, M., Ariwa, E. (eds.) ObCom 2011, Part I. CCIS, vol. 269, pp. 480–489. Springer, Heidelberg (2012)

19. Takacs, L.: Introduction to the Theory of Queues. Oxford University Press, New York (1960)

20. Tarabia, A.M.K.: Transient analysis of M/M/1/N queue - an alternative approach. Tamkang J. Sci. Eng. **3**(4), 263–266 (2000)

21. Tikhonenko, O., Kempa, W.M.: Queueing system with processor sharing and limited memory under control of the AQM mechanism. Autom. Remote Control **76**(10), 1784–1796 (2015)

22. Vijayashree, K.V., Janani, B.: Transient analysis of an M/M/c queue subject to multiple exponential working vacation. Appl. Math. Sci. **9**(74), 3669–3677 (2015)

23. Woźniak, M., Gabryel, M., Nowicki, R.K., Nowak, B.: An application of firefly algorithm to position traffic in NoSQL database systems. In: Kunifuji, S., Papadopoulos, G.A., Skulimowski, A.M.J., Kacprzyk, J. (eds.) KICSS 2014. AISC, vol. 416, pp. 259–272. Springer, Heidelberg (2016). doi:10.1007/978-3-319-27478-2-18. ISSN 2194-5357

24. Woźniak, M., Marszałek, Z., Gabryel, M., Nowicki, R.K.: Preprocessing large data sets by the use of quick sort algorithm. In: Skulimowski, A.M.J., Kacprzyk, J. (eds.) KICSS 2013. AISC, vol. 364, pp. 111–121. Springer, Switzerland (2016). doi:10.1007/978-3-319-19090-7-9. ISSN 2194-5357

25. Woźniak, M., Marszałek, Z., Gabryel, M., Nowicki, R.K.: Modified merge sort algorithm for large scale data sets. In: Rutkowski, L., Korytkowski, M., Scherer, R., Tadeusiewicz, R., Zadeh, L.A., Zurada, J.M. (eds.) ICAISC 2013, Part II. LNCS, vol. 7895, pp. 612–622. Springer, Heidelberg (2013). doi:10.1007/978-3-642-38610-7-56

26. Zhang, M., Hou, Z.: Steady state analysis of the GI/M/1/N queue with a variant of multiple working vacations. Comput. Ind. Eng. **61**, 1296–1301 (2011)

27. Damaševičius, R., Vasiljevas, M., Šalkevičius, J., Woźniak, M.: Human activity recognition in AAL environments using random projections. Comput. Math. Methods Med. **2016**, Article ID 4073584, 17 p. (2016). doi:10.1155/2016/4073584

28. Capizzi, G., Lo Sciuto, G., Wozniak, M., Damaševičius, R.: A clustering based system for automated oil spill detection by satellite remote sensing. In: Rutkowski, L., Korytkowski, M., Scherer, R., Tadeusiewicz, R., Zadeh, L.A., Zurada, J.M. (eds.) ICAISC 2016. LNCS, vol. 9693, pp. 613–623. Springer, Heidelberg (2016). doi:10.1007/978-3-319-39384-1_54

29. Kempa, W.M., Wozniak, M., Nowicki, R.K., Gabryel, M., Damaševičius, R.: Transient solution for queueing delay distribution in the GI/M/1/K-type mode with "queued" waking up and balking. In: Rutkowski, L., Korytkowski, M., Scherer, R., Tadeusiewicz, R., Zadeh, L.A., Zurada, J.M. (eds.) ICAISC 2016. LNCS, vol. 9693, pp. 340–351. Springer, Heidelberg (2016). doi:10.1007/978-3-319-39384-1_29

30. Połap, D., Woźniak, M., Napoli, C., Tramontana, E.: Real-time cloud-based game management system via cuckoo search algorithm. Int. J. Electron. Telecommun. **61**(4), 333–338 (2015). doi:10.1515/eletel-2015-0043. De Gruyter Open Ltd
31. Połap, D., Woźniak, M., Napoli, C., Tramontana, E.: Is swarm intelligence able to create mazes? Int. J. Electron. Telecommun. **61**(4), 305–310 (2015). doi:10.1515/eletel-2015-0039. De Gruyter Open Ltd

Importance of Neighborhood Parameters During Clustering of Bathymetric Data Using Neural Network

Marta Wlodarczyk-Sielicka[✉]

Institute of Geoinformatics, Maritime University of Szczecin,
ul. Waly Chrobrego 1-2, Szczecin, Poland
m.wlodarczyk@am.szczecin.pl

Abstract. The main component, which has a significant impact on safety of navigation, is the information about depth of a water area. The commonly used solution for depths measurement is usage the echosounders. One of the problems associated with bathymetric measurements is recording a large number of data. The fundamental objective of the author's research is the implementation of a new reduction method for geodata to be used for the creation of bathymetric map. The main purpose of new reduction algorithm is that, the position of point and the depth value at this point will not be an interpolated value. In the article, author focused on importance of neighborhood parameters during clustering of bathymetric data using neural network (self-organizing map) – it is the first stage of the new method. During the use of Kohonen's algorithm, the author focused on two parameters: topology and initial neighborhood size. During the test, several populations were created with number of clusters equal 25 for data collected from the area of 625 square meters (dataset contains of 28911 XYZ points). In the next step, statistics were calculated and results were presented in two forms: tabular form and as spatial visualization. The final step was their comprehensive analysis.

Keywords: Bathymetry · Data processing · Clustering · Artificial neural network

1 Introduction

The main component, which has a significant impact on safety of navigation, is the information about depth of a water area. Relevant acquisition, data processing procedures and visualization of bathymetric data rest on hydrographer. During hydrographic operations connected to determining the surface of sea bottom or the localization of underwater target, plural factors have to be taken into consideration. Processing of bathymetric data is realized in several stages and its simplified scheme is presented on Fig. 1.

One of the problems associated with bathymetric measurements is recording a large number of data, as well as various types of interference. At the beginning, the following values of corrections are taken into account: properties of water on the area, submersion of echosounder transducer head, offsets input in the measurement devices and errors

© Springer International Publishing Switzerland 2016
G. Dregvaite and R. Damasevicius (Eds.): ICIST 2016, CCIS 639, pp. 441–452, 2016.
DOI: 10.1007/978-3-319-46254-7_35

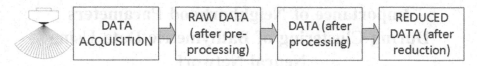

Fig. 1. Simplified scheme of bathymetric data processing.

related with the mean of sound velocity in water. They have great significance for the accuracy of the measurements. Next, using predefined data processing filters, hydrographer performs the initial data filtration. It is a process dependent on the current measurement session. Values assigned to each filter have to be applied with caution, after an analysis of the measurement conditions and the expected outcomes. The subsequent step is to process the data. Initially, the raw data are converted into 'swath' files (files working as a framework for the grid). There are four fundamental types of filters used to process the data: the amplitude filter, the limit filter, the across and along track filter. In the next step, the data are reduced. Data reduction is a procedure meant to decrease the size of the data set, in order to make them easier and more effective for the purposes of the analysis. During the reduction of bathymetric data, regularly spaced GRID is created – the output data are interpolated values. In hydrographic systems it can be distinguished the following methods to generate the grid: mean (select an average depth value), weighted mean (adapts amplitude values to give higher weighting to data samples which are higher in amplitude, when calculating the mean depth value), minimum (select the shallowest value), maximum (select the deepest value). In the last step data are presented on the final hydrographic products, i.e., bathymetric maps, such as: the reporting site plan, BENC (Bathymetric Electronic Navigational Chart) and PENC (Port Electronic Navigational Chart). For all of the above mentioned stages: appropriate collecting, processing and presentation of bathymetric data, a hydrographer is responsible. Notice that this is a long and laborious process.

2   Acquisition of Bathymetric Data

The techniques rules for collecting bathymetric data depend mainly on the nature of water area, its dimension and local characteristics. The commonly used solution for depths measurement is usage the echosounders – devices, which operation procedures are based on underwater acoustics principles. The echosounder is an equipment used to measure the vertical distance between its head and the sea bottom, or a structure situated on the sea bottom, using an acoustic wave. The determination of depths is reached by calculating the time difference between the moment of transmitting and receiving the sound wave after its reflection from the seabed bottom or other object. In order to acquire a full information about depth, the hydrographer, also, needs to know the sound velocity and the directions in which the impulse was sent and from which it returns. The survey of angle depends on the type of echosounder. The simples model is single-beam echosounder (SBES). It works by emitting a narrow acoustic signal beam from its transducer vertically downwards. In order to extend the productivity and effectiveness of the surveys, multibeam echosounder (MBES) should be used. The transducer of MBES

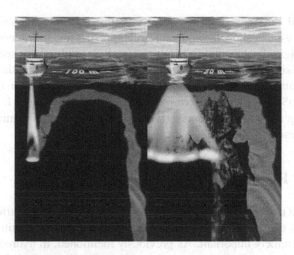

Fig. 2. The comparison SBES and MBES swaths [2].

sends several signal beams in multiple directions arranged into wide swath [1]. It permits for obtaining a much wider coverage of the seafloor, by increasing the width of the exploring domain. The schematic comparison of coverage of both measuring systems are presented in Fig. 2.

A particular modification of MBES is the interferometric bathymetric system. The value of depth is obtained not only by the measurement of difference of time, but also is based on surveying the difference between phases of the acoustic wave computed by the sensors installed within the transducer. The impulse emitted from the transducer head has a very wide angle profile across and the very narrow along. Due to the highly wide angle of survey, it allows to simultaneously gather vertical and horizontal data. Furthermore, the amplitude of the returning signal is also measured and a sonar image is received [3]. Table 1 presents a comparison of exemplary operational parameters of bathymetric measuring systems (relied on technical specifications).

Table 1. Comparison of operational parameters of bathymetric surveying systems [4]

	Example of SBES system: EA400	Example of MBES system: EM3002	Example of interferometric system: GeoSwath Plus
Operational frequency	38/210 kHz	300 kHz	250 kHz
Viewing angle	13/7°	200°	240°
Maximum coverage for depth = 10 m calculated for depth 10 m	2.2 m/1.2 m	8 × depth 80 m	12 × depth 120 m
Depth resolution	5/1 cm	1 cm	0.3 cm

SBES spatial data cover only a narrow portion of the sea bottom. MBES and interferometric systems allow to produce resolutions of a few (transverse resolution) by a few dozen (longitudinal resolution) centimeters. It depends on the speed of the vessel during the acquisition and frequency of the transducer. In case of shallow water surveying, interferometric systems are better in use than MBES. For the objective of the test, the GeoSwath Plus interferometric system has been used. It is a part of the hydrographic equipment of the survey vessel Hydrograf XXI, administrated by the Maritime University of Szczecin.

3 Proposed Reduction Method

Bathymetric data obtained by multibeam echosounder or interferometric system consist of very large set of measurement points. Information about the minimum depths in a given area is extremely important. As previously mentioned, in hydrographic systems, during the reduction of the data, regularly spaced GRID is created. Existing methods use interpolated values, so it is necessary to look for new solutions. The position of the measuring point and the depth value at this point should not be an interpolated value. The fundamental objective of the author's research is the implementation of a new reduction method for geodata (XYZ points: longitude, latitude and depth) to be used for the creation of bathymetric map [5, 6]. Due to the safety of the navigation, it is very important to preserve points of minimum depths. The main purpose of new reduction algorithm is that, the position of point and the depth at this point will not be an interpolated value. The clustering of geodata is the first stage of the search method and the second stage is the generalization of bathymetric data. Scheme of proposed reduction method is shown in Fig. 3.

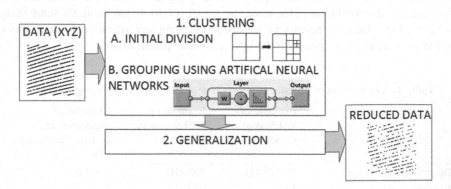

Fig. 3. Scheme of proposed reduction method.

The first stage consists of two steps. In the first step, the area will be divided into a grid of squares. The maximum level of generalization of the grid will be founded and its size will be determined. Depth differences in each square will be checked. If they are larger than predetermined tolerance, the square will be divided into four smaller squares. In the second step of data clustering, artificial neural networks will be used. The authors decided to use artificial intelligence methods during the processing of bathymetric data because it is novel approach to such issues. In the article, author focused only on this part of new method.

Clustering is a partition of data into groups, called cluster, of similar features. Each cluster consists of features that are similar between themselves and dissimilar to objects of other groups [7]. The author's goal is to sort a set of XYZ points into clusters and then represent each group by a single point with minimum depth depending on the compilation scale.

4   Artificial Neural Network

Artificial neural networks (ANNs) are a family of models inspired by biological neural networks. They can be treated as a some type of data structure, which modifies in the course of the learning process adapting to the kind of issue to be solved [8]. Subject concerning ANNs is part of the interdisciplinary field of research associated with electronics, applied mathematics, statistics, medicine and others [9–13]. ANNs are also very often used for navigation purposes, for example, during a sea bottom shape modelling [14, 15], target tracking [16] or comparative navigation [17].

One type of ANNs is self-organizing map (SOM), sometimes called a Kohonen network. In the case of Kohonen networks learning there is no relationship between input signals and the output of the network. The rivalry between neurons provides the basis for updating values assigned to weights. It can be assumed that c is the amount of clusters, x is the input vector, p is the number of samples, w is the weight vector and connected with the node l.

$$x = (x_1, x_2, x_3, \ldots, x_p)'$$ (1)

$$w_l = (w_{l1}, w_{l2}, w_{l3}, \ldots, w_{lp})'$$ (2)

Several samples of the training data set are presented to the network in random order. While neurons rivalling, the one nearest to the input sources is a winner for the input data set. The extent of adaptation depends on the distance of the neuron from the input data. The node l is shifted some proportion of the distance between it and the training simple. This proportion is depended on the learning rate. For several objects i, the distance between the weight vector and the input signal is estimated. After the start of the competition the node l with the nearest distance is the winner. Then, the weights of the winner are updated using the learning rule (4).

The weight vector for the lth node in the sth step of training can be described as w_l^s and the input vector for the ith training simple can be presented as X_i. After several epochs, a training simple is selected and the index q of the winning node is defined:

$$q = \underset{l}{argmin} \left\| w_l^s - X_i \right\|$$ (3)

The Kohonen updated rule is as follows [18]:

$$w_q^{s+1} = w_q^s(1 - \alpha^s) + X_i\alpha^s = w_q^s + \alpha^s\left(X_i - w_q^s\right) \tag{4}$$

where α^s is the learning rate for the sth step of training.

Figure 4 illustrates conceptually how neural networks generate self-organizing maps.

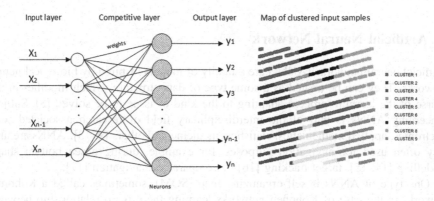

Fig. 4. Explanatory diagram of a Kohonen network.

In Matlab software, SOMs take the following variables: neuron distance function, row vector of dimension sizes, number of epochs for initial covering of the input space, layer topology function and initial neighborhood size. In this article the author focused on two parameters: topology and initial neighborhood size.

The neurons of SOM are organized originally in locations according to a topology function, which can form the neurons in a rectangular grid, hexagonal pattern, or random topology. All types of topology function are presented in Fig. 5.

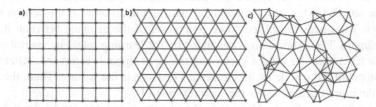

Fig. 5. Topologies: (a) rectangular grid, (b) hexagonal pattern, (c) random pattern.

The initial neighborhood size contains the indicators for all of the neurons that lie within a distance of the winning neuron. The neighborhood is gradually reduced from a maximum size of neighborhood down to 1, where it remains from then on.

5   Experiment

For the research purposes, Matlab software developed by MathWorks was used and for the clustering issues the self-organizing feature map was applied. During the use of Kohonen's algorithm, the author focused on two parameters: topology and initial neighborhood size. During the test, several populations were created with number of clusters equal 25 for data collected from the area of 625 square meters. In the next step, statistics were calculated and results were presented in two forms: tabular form and as spatial visualization. The final step was their comprehensive analysis.

5.1   The Scope of the Test Area

Very high density of data is the primary restriction of neural network usage. It is impossible to train the network from whole dataset obtained by hydrographic system using standard computer. In order to solve this problem, author separated primary dataset into smaller subsets, which could be tested separately. Test data was gathered within Szczecin Port and it is presented in Fig. 6. For collecting data, the vessel Hydrograf XXI, with the GeoSwath Plus 250 kHz system and supplementary equipment (GPS/RTK, satellite compass, motion sensor) hydrographic equipment were used. The measurement profiles were carried out due to maintain 100 % coverage of the measured body of water.

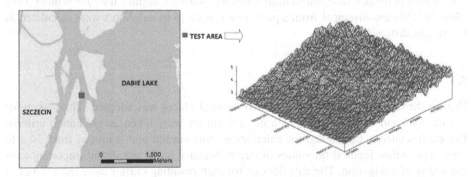

Fig. 6. Testing area.

As mentioned before, test data contain depth measurements from the area of 625 square meters. Tested dataset contains of 28911 points with three attributes: latitude, longitude and depth. The positions of points are given by the Universal Transverse Mercator coordinate system, which is an international locational reference system. The minimum depth within this area is 2.54 m and maximum depth is 5.36 m.

5.2   Selected Parameters

During the test, several populations were created with number of clusters equal 25 – the numbers of rows and columns was set to 5×5. The author tested the following scenarios of selected parameters:

- grid topology and:
  - initial neighborhood size equal to 1 (further referred to as A1);
  - initial neighborhood size equal to 3 (further referred to as A3);
  - initial neighborhood size equal to 5 (further referred to as A5);
  - initial neighborhood size equal to 10 (further referred to as A10);
- hexagonal topology and:
  - initial neighborhood size equal to 1 (further referred to as B1);
  - initial neighborhood size equal to 3 (further referred to as B3);
  - initial neighborhood size equal to 5 (further referred to as B5);
  - initial neighborhood size equal to 10 (further referred to as B10);
- random topology and:
  - initial neighborhood size equal to 1 (further referred to as C1);
  - initial neighborhood size equal to 3 (further referred to as C3);
  - initial neighborhood size equal to 5 (further referred to as C5);
  - initial neighborhood size equal to 10 (further referred to as C10).

Based on previous studies, during each trainings, the number of epochs was set at 200 [19]. The number of training steps for initial coverage of the input space was set at 100, which is default function in used software. Network applies the rule Winner Take Most (WTM) and distances from a particular neuron to its neighbors were calculated as Euclidean distance.

5.3   Results

During the research, the precision of two decimal places was adopted. Time taken for calculations and distribution of data in each cluster were taken as evaluation criteria. For each scenario, time taken for calculations was similar and it ranged from 14 s to 16 s. The author focused on values of depth, because it has significant importance for the safety of navigation. The calculations for each resulting cluster included number of samples, minimum depth, maximum depth, depth range (it is the difference between the maximum and minimum depth in the cluster) and mean values of depth. Additionally standard deviation of the sampling distribution was calculated. The most important value – minimum values of depth in each cluster are at a similar level for each scenario. For C1 the biggest differences in depth range could be observed. Using initial neighborhood size equal to 1 for each topology, spatial distribution of data is the most noticeable, which is shown in Fig. 7.

In case of use the hexagonal topology the results for each scenario (B1, B3, B5 and B10) are almost the same. Table 2 presents the results for hexagonal topology and initial neighborhood size equal to 5.

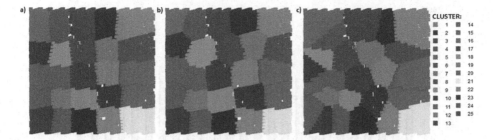

Fig. 7. Clusters received for: (a) A1, (b) B1, (c) C1.

Table 2. Comparison of statistics for B5 scenario.

Cluster	1	2	3	4	5	6	7	8	9	10	11	12	13
NoPa	823	1166	1022	885	1199	604	981	1019	1149	1330	1006	1248	1101
Min[b] [m]	3.88	3.59	3.19	2.82	2.54	4.02	3.93	3.27	2.99	2.8	4.1	3.57	3.51
Max[c] [m]	5.22	4.97	4.39	3.8	3.42	5.23	5.04	4.66	4.12	3.54	5.26	4.94	4.46
Ran[d] [m]	1.34	1.38	1.2	0.98	0.88	1.21	1.11	1.39	1.13	0.74	1.16	1.37	0.95
Mean[e] [m]	4.59	4.32	3.84	3.35	2.98	4.66	4.45	4.11	3.53	3.11	4.68	4.33	3.9
SD[f]	0.24	0.22	0.21	0.15	0.11	0.23	0.2	0.19	0.17	0.12	0.21	0.19	0.17

Cluster	14	15	16	17	18	19	20	21	22	23	24	25
NoP[a]	1301	1406	917	1143	1051	1287	1613	1207	1067	1141	1477	1768
Min[b] [m]	3.1	2.83	4.13	3.83	3.46	3.32	3.01	4.11	3.88	3.7	3.28	3.13
Max[c] [m]	3.89	3.65	5.36	4.98	4.57	3.99	3.71	5.29	5.02	4.68	4.19	3.76
Ran[d] [m]	0.79	0.82	1.23	1.15	1.11	0.67	0.7	1.18	1.14	0.98	0.91	0.63
Mean[e] [m]	3.53	3.18	4.72	4.44	3.98	3.61	3.28	4.68	4.43	4.1	3.75	3.43
SD[f]	0.12	0.12	0.22	0.19	0.16	0.11	0.11	0.19	0.19	0.16	0.12	0.11

a. Number of samples in each cluster b. Minimum value of depth c. Maximum value of depth d. Depth range
e. Mean value of depth f. Standard deviation.

Although, the statistics are the same for B1, B3, B5 and B10, it should be noted that the distribution of points in surface is slightly different. However, the most important are the smallest values of depth, which are the same for each scenario. The hexagonal topology is default topology in used software and it can be said that the obtained results are constant.

When using rectangular grid, the major differences in number of points are in cluster designated as 5. The difference is with 573 measurement points in cluster. Distribution of the number of samples in each cluster for grid topology is shown in Fig. 8.

The horizontal axis represents the number of clusters and the vertical axis shows the number of bathymetric data points. Using grid topology, should pay attention to the fact that A3 and A5 receive the same results.

The most varied results for each scenario were obtained with random topology. Distribution of the samples number for random topology is shown in Fig. 5.

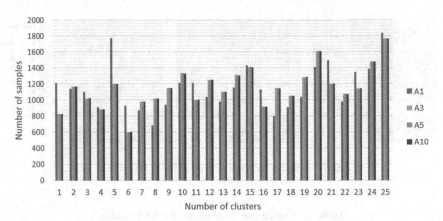

Fig. 8. Distribution of the number of samples in each cluster for grid topology.

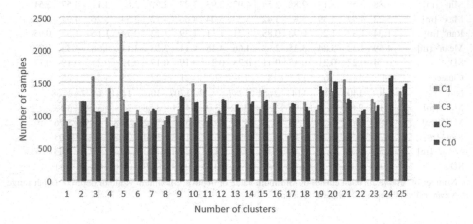

Fig. 9. Distribution of the number of samples in each cluster for random topology.

The biggest difference in number of samples are also in cluster designated as 5 (between C1 and C5) – it is equal to 1192 points in cluster. Spatial distribution of data for random topology is shown in Fig. 10. The results obtained by scenario C5 and C10 are the most similar (Fig. 9).

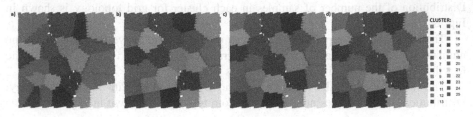

Fig. 10. Clusters received for: (a) C1, (b) C3, (c) C5, (d) C10.

Attention should be paid to the inclination of the bottom and the size of cluster associated with it. The amount of points in cluster has a close connection with the size of cluster. So, if depth range is wide, cluster size should be small – in the case of a large slope of the bottom, more points should be plotted on the bathymetric map. This condition is the best conform with the results obtained for hexagonal topology.

6 Summary

The main goal of author was to create a new reduction method for large dataset of bathymetric points. The main criterion is the legibility of the bathymetric map. Self-organizing maps have the ability to group bathymetric data into clusters. All statistics related to the depth (it has significant importance for the safety of navigation) were taken into account and the results in particular clusters were compared. The value of the minimum depth in each cluster are very similar. In case of use the hexagonal topology, the results for each scenario were almost the same. If depth range is wide, cluster size should be small. This condition is the best conform with the results obtained for hexagonal topology. In the case of the use of 25 clusters initial neighborhood size equal to 5 gives satisfactory results. With more clusters the greater neighborhood size should be selected. After analysis of the above outcomes, the best results were obtained using the hexagonal topology. The next step in the research will be testing areas characterized by varying slope of bottom.

References

1. IHO Manual on Hydrography 1st (edn.) May 2005 (Correction to February 2011). Publication C-13. IHO, Monaco (2011)
2. Norton, A.: How can we "see" the seafloor beneath the ocean waves? http://feedthe datamonster.com/home/2014/7/7/how-can-we-see-the-seafloor-beneath-the-ocean-waves
3. User Guide GeoSwath Plus Operational Manual, GeoAcoustics (2009)
4. Włodarczyk-Sielicka, M., Bodus-Olkowska, I., Stateczny, A.: Application of geodatabase dedicated for bathymetric data during the production of electronic navigational charts for inland shipping. Zeszyty Naukowe Akademii Morskiej w Szczecinie 35(107), 168–173 (2013). ISSN 2392-0378
5. Wlodarczyk-Sielicka, M., Stateczny, A.: Clustering bathymetric data for electronic navigational charts. J. Navigation (2016). doi:10.1017/S0373463316000035
6. Wlodarczyk-Sielicka, M., Stateczny, A.: Selection of SOM parameters for the needs of clusterisation of data obtained by interferometric methods. In: Rohling, H. (ed.) Proceedings of 16th International Radar Symposium (IRS), International Radar Symposium Proceedings, pp. 1129–1134. IEEE, Dresden (2015). doi:10.1109/IRS.2015.7226268
7. Gupta, N.S., Agrawal, B.S., Chauhan, R.M.: Survey on clustering techniques of data mining. Am. Int. J. Res. Sci. Technol. Eng. Math. 9(3), 206–211 (2015). (2328-3491) ISSN 2328-3580
8. Osowski, S.: Sieci neuronowe do przetwarzania informacji, Oficyna Wydawnicza Politechniki Warszawskiej (2013). ISBN 9788372076154

9. Woźniak, M., Połap, D., Kośmider, L., Napoli, C., Tramontana, E.: A novel approach toward X-ray images classifier. In: Proceedings of the IEEE Symposium Series on Computational Intelligence – SSCI 2015, 8-10 December 2015, Cape Town, Republic of South Africa, pp. 1635–1641. IEEE (2015). doi:10.1109/SSCI.2015.230

10. Napoli, C., Tramontana, E., Woźniak, M.: Enhancing environmental surveillance against organised crime with radial basis neural networks. In: Proceedings of the Symposium Series on Computational Intelligence – SSCI 2015, 8-10 December 2015, Cape Town, Republic of South Africa, pp. 1476-1483. Institute IEEE (2015) doi:10.1109/SSCI.2015.209

11. Capizzi, G., Lo Sciuto, G., Napoli, C., Tramontana, E., Woźniak, M.: Automatic classification of the Oranges defects based on co-occurrence matrix and probabilistic neural networks. In: Federated Conference on Computer Science and Information Systems – FedCSIS 2015, 13-16 September 2015, Łódź, Poland, pp. 861-867. IEEE (2015). doi:10. 15439/2015F258

12. Woźniak, M., Napoli, C., Tramontana, E., Capizzi, G., Lo Sciuto, G., Nowicki, R.K., Starczewski, J.T.: A multiscale image compressor with RBFNN and discrete wavelet decomposition. In: IEEE International Joint Conference on Neural Networks – IJCNN 2015, 12-17 July 2015 Killarney, Ireland, pp. 1219-1225. IEEE (2015). doi:10.1109/IJCNN.2015. 7280461

13. Woźniak, M., Połap, D., Nowicki, R.K., Napoli, C., Pappalardo, G., Tramontana, E.: Novel approach toward medical signals classifier. In: IEEE International Joint Conference on Neural Networks – IJCNN 2015, 12-17 July 2015, Killarney, Ireland, pp. 1924-1930. IEEE (2015). doi:10.1109/IJCNN.2015.7280556

14. Lubczonek, J., Stateczny, A.: Concept of neural model of the sea bottom surface. In: Rutkowski, L., Kacprzyk, J. Neural Networks and Soft Computing. ASC, pp. 861–866. Springer, Heidelberg (2003). doi:10.1007/978-3-7908-1902-1_135

15. Stateczny, A.: The neural method of sea bottom shape modelling for the spatial maritime information system. In: Brebbia, C.A., Olivella, J.: Maritime Engineering and Ports II. Water Studies Series, vol. 9, pp. 251–259, Barcelona 2000. doi:10.2495/PORTS000221

16. Stateczny, A., Kazimierski, W.: A comparison of the target tracking in marine navigational radars by means of GRNN filter and numerical filter. 2008 IEEE Radar Conference, vols. 1–4, pp. 1994-1997, Rome 2008. doi:10.1109/RADAR.2008.4721044

17. Stateczny, A.: Artificial neural networks for comparative navigation. In: Rutkowski, L., Siekmann, J.H., Tadeusiewicz, R., Zadeh, L.A. (eds.) ICAISC 2004. LNCS (LNAI), vol. 3070, pp. 1187–1192. Springer, Heidelberg (2004)

18. Mignot, S., Lima, J.: Comparing SOM neural network with Fuzzy c-means, K-Means and traditional hierarchical clustering algorithms. Eur. J. Oper. Res. **174**, 1742–1759 (2006)

19. Stateczny, A., Wlodarczyk-Sielicka, M.: Self-organizing artificial neural networks into hydrographic big data reduction process. In: Kryszkiewicz, M., Cornelis, C., Ciucci, D., Medina-Moreno, J., Motoda, H., Raś, Z.W. (eds.) RSEISP 2014. LNCS, vol. 8537, pp. 335–342. Springer, Heidelberg (2014)

A Cloud Oriented Support for Motion Detection in Video Surveillance Systems Using Computational Intelligence

Christian Napoli[✉] and Emiliano Tramontana

Department of Mathematics and Informatics, University of Catania,
Viale Andrea Doria 6, 95125 Catania, Italy
{napoli, tramontana}@dmi.unict.it

Abstract. This paper proposes a cloud-oriented architecture for video analysis and motion detection. The core algorithm as been based on a typical computational intelligence method called Firefly Algorithm jointly with a Sobel filter in order to reduce the analysis complexity and the required computational effort. The developed system is completely self sufficient and highly scalable and expandable on demand. To achieve this result the developed architecture has beed accurately engineered by means of design patterns and structured as a layered application. Therefore the developed computational core is able to manage high level interfaces for the cloud environment as well as to take advantage of hardware level optimizations in order to maximize its performance and make it suitable for real time analysis of continuous video streams coming from multiple sources.

Keywords: Cloud computing · High performance computing · Artificial intelligence · Image and video processing · Modularity · Software design

1 Introduction

The first decade of twenty-first century has witnessed a great market expansion for video surveillance systems while many technological advances have contributed to offer both cheap solutions for home customers and highly dedicated devices for big investors. Video surveillance systems constitute an important topic for both the market and the customers interested in personal security as well as law enforcement in commercial or institutional facilities, or more specific purposes such as military applications, satellite imagery systems for urban security, traffic monitoring, hydro-geological risk and emergency management, homeland protection, etc.... (Lee et al. 2000). While the number of surveillance systems has been growing a limited number of options have been presented concerning the analysis of the data coming from such devices. The usefulness of such kind of data is related to human interpretation. In most of the cases, it is neither possible nor affordable to employ a large workforce with the unique purpose of reviewing or investigate video content, especially if such a content is generated by means of a full-coverage 24-hour round cycle of video recording, sometime from multiple sources and related closed circuit cameras. In the recent years,

© Springer International Publishing Switzerland 2016
G. Dregvaite and R. Damasevicius (Eds.): ICIST 2016, CCIS 639, pp. 453–463, 2016.
DOI: 10.1007/978-3-319-46254-7_36

the need for human operators in order to review and control video surveillance devices has strongly limited both the effectiveness and applicability of such systems. In facts while such systems continue to undergo a constant technological evolution, their applicability in terms of land and time coverage, number of cameras and data acquisition parameters, is strongly dependent by the availability of human personnel. Moreover it is not possible to count on the reliability of a human operator if it is required to focus on steady video recordings for a prolonged time. Extended video surveillance systems, or applications that require a round-the-clock coverage from many video sources, also require a more sophisticated analysis method and cannot rely only on the human judgment. Motion detection is a main issue for automatic video surveillance, while static camera record the same image for extended period of times, important information (e.g. forensically relevant, signaling a modification of the environments, etc.) manifest after a sudden change of the scene which can be identified as motion. Robust detection of moving objects in video streams is a significant issue for video surveillance. One of the most conventional approaches is background subtraction (Tian et al. 2005; Mittal et al. 2004), probabilistic approaches (Napoli et al. 2015), mathematical models such as the co-occurrence matrix method (Capizzi et al. 2015). On the other hand such techniques are generally expensive in terms of required computational time when used to recognize and follow object motion, therefore are not suitable for real time recognition. In this paper a video security systems support is proposed in order to offer a fully automated, fully scalable, online and real-time analysis of video streams coming from multiple sources. This goal is achieved by means of a 2D image recognition algorithm (Starczewski et al. 2016) jointly with a fully parallel support, which uses both the performance of an *OpenMP* paradigm for multicore programming, as well as the versatility of the cloud. 2D image recognition is a non-trivial task, which requires both the application of Evolutionary Computation methods combined and image processing oriented approaches.

2 Automated Video Analysis

A digital video consists in a temporal sequence $V(t)$ of frames. Neglecting the color composition (e.g. for a gray-scale video, or after a dedicated preprocessing phase), each frame is constituted by a 2D image $I(t)$ consisting of pixels in a certain status. Status is determined not only by the position of the related pixel, but also by means of a set of properties such as brightness, saturation, color, sharpness, etc.... These properties are interpreted by our vision system in order to recognize the objects appearing in a video and the related motion. Therefore any computational intelligence approach should use such properties to identify object motions. Once each video frame has been isolated it is interpreted as a 2D image I, or trivially as a pixel matrix. To each pixel corresponds a pair of coordinates $x_i = (x_i, y_i) = (x_{i,1}, x_{i2})$ to take into consideration in order to collect spatial information about the object motion when analyzing a frame sequence. The human brain capability to recognize motion and locate it on video can be emulated computationally in order to obtain a computational intelligence based recognition system. The main goal of such a system is to locate those motion-related areas, which, now on, will be called key-areas. In other words, the goal is to recognize object motions in the same manner of our eyes when looking for areas in the picture that show a sudden change of their graphical content. In order to develop a very fast and easily implementable approach, in this work the algorithm extrapolates the edges of the object in a video frame and then it follows their motion. Hence Sobel filter is applied in order to preprocess the video frames highlighting edges. The resulting output is then passed to a Firefly Algorithm based feature extractor. These features can then be classified and interpreted finding differences among successive sets of frames, therefore identifying acts of motion and related time lapse. Finally the moving object is identified and singularly followed along the video. In this manner it is possible to obtain short video sequences which can be easily reviewed by an operator in a short time, moreover the obtained sequences automatically extract the interesting portion for each frame, helping the operator to focus on each interesting event (e.g., identify a suspect, send an alarm, manage an emergency situation, etc.). Finally the proposed architecture should cope with a constant flux of video streams, therefore a paramount concern regards the scalability and versatility. For this reason the architecture is constituted by cloud services, which can be instantiated on demand. This approach makes it possible to constantly scale-up or scale-down the overall system in order to suite every scenario independently by the organization and topology of the data producers (e.g. video cameras) and consumers (e.g. operators). In the following section the adopted cloud architecture is explained.

3 The Cloud Architecture

Cloud computing infrastructures can provide resources, i.e. VMs, on demand (Armbrust et al. 2010). For example, a commercial cloud, such as Amazon EC2/S3, allows users to have resources and pay for the duration of their usage (Jackson et al. 2010). Moreover, virtualization enables users to properly configure and run the desired services on VMs especially created for them. Generally, a properly configured image for a VM can be booted; alternatively, moving services and running scripts onto it can configure a standard VM. The proposed solution uses the ability to have properly configured VMs on demand, according to the needed computing power. The Fig. 1

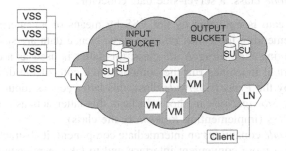

Fig. 1. The presented cloud architecture: VSS indicates the video surveillance systems (data producers), LN is a login node, SU is a storage unit, VM is a virtual machine.

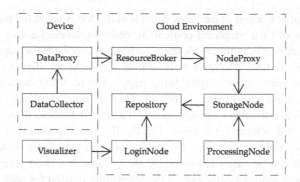

Fig. 2. An UML diagram representing the most important class implemented for the proposed architecture and the related dependencies.

shows our cloud architecture, designed to collect video streams produced by several video surveillance sources (VSS), then uploaded to an input bucket on the cloud delegating several storage units (SU) for the task. The uploaded data location and replica is transparent and organized by a cloud hypervisor, therefore the VSS needs only to be interfaced with a login node (LN). The client, in order to collect and view the analyzed data, depends only on a login node; this latter provides access to an output bucket where the elaborated data are stored. The presented architecture is designed in order to be modular and robust to changes, and such properties have been achieved thanks to *design patterns*, i.e. software solutions that have been proven successful to solve recurrent problems in the field of object-oriented programming (Gamma et al. 1994; Napoli and Tramontana, 2015).

Therefore the developed architecture (Fig. 2) is mainly derived by a typical *Resource Broker* design pattern (Buschmann et al. 1996) by means of the following components:

- The *DataCollector* class: a client-side data collector
- The *DataProxy* class: a client-side proxy
- The *ResourceBroker* class: the broker itself
- The *NodeProxy* class: a server-side proxy
- The *StorageNode* class: a server-side data collector

The video stream is uploaded by the VSS by means of an intermediate software component implementing the *DataCollector* class. Hence data are stored on the input bucket, implementing the *StorageNode* class, this latter is used as a data interchange manager. The virtual machines run the computational core of the developed systems which is colled by the *ProcessingNode* class, this latter gets as input the unprocessed data invoking the *StorageNode* methods, in facts this latter acts as a mediator for the data repository class (implementing *Repository* the class).

The *StorageNode* constitutes an intermediate component; it abstracts the *Repository* object to provide a more convenient interface and to take responsibility for the communication management which is an unrelated concern for the *Repository* class. Moreover in this manner the *Repository* class need not know the virtual machines, as well as the related status and topologies, on the other hand it remains directly accessible for a visualizer-side login node (implementing the *LoginNode* class). Finally the elaboration results can be collected and visualized by a human operator with dedicated software implementing the *Visualizer* class.

4 The Processing Nodes

The processing nodes use several software layers in order to concurrently manage different aspects of the data stream and related computations. Therefore the processing node component is constituted by separate processes, for communication, i.e. to receive/send status data and commands from/to other components located on storage nodes. Since the cloud environment takes advantage of a high level abstraction by means of Object Oriented Programming (Booch et al. 2007). For this reason the processing node interface is in Java, therefore it requires a Java Virtual Machine to run and interact with the other software components both locally and cloud based (see Fig. 3). On the other hand the purpose of this work is to provide the end user with a fast and responsive real time application for motion recognition in video streams, therefore, while the object oriented modules are ideal for communication and synchronization management within the cloud environment, for the processing stage, which is the real core of the developed architecture, an hardware oriented approach has been found more suitable in order to exploit all the computational power of multicore nodes. In order to achieve such goals, the developed application takes advantage of an *OpenMP* parallel executable and cannot be treated as an object oriented system. Hence in this work Java Native Interface has been used to make it possible for the object oriented layer to use and interact with the low level developed for the analysis and computations. In the following section the analysis algorithm will be presented.

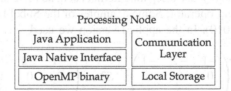

Fig. 3. The layer structure of the core application running on the Processing Nodes

5 Partitioning, Preprocessing and Filtering Phase

The first step of the processing pipeline is trivial but essential, since it regards data partitioning. The incoming video stream is uploaded by means of a login node to a set of storage unit that are part of a distributed file systems. Since the cloud services take care of the management and synchronizations regarding such storage units, we can describe their overall function as an *input bucket*. On this *input bucket* data are stored, replicated and partitioned, so that for each data (e.g. a portion of a video stream coming from one of the VSS) at least three replicas are maintained. In this manner corruption issues as well as sudden resource unavailability problems are avoided. Each processing node obtains a portion of the input dataset called *work unit*. For each work unit, then, a first preprocessing step splits each video in a sequence of pairs composed by a frame and a unique id identifying its temporal index and the source. Each frame is then elaborated independently, for this reason, to avoid a complex notation, we will simply focus on one frame, or image, that will be denoted **I**. The successive step takes care of the extrapolation of image edges for further analysis by implementing a Sobel filter. Sobel filter evaluates directional gradient of the luminosity values of the 2D input image. Then, according to computed values, it reveals the edges of the depicted objects as the pixels with high gradient value. These points are characterized by sharp-cut variations of luminosity (e.g. the sudden variation of luminosity for a well-lit object on a dark background provides the bright edge of the object itself). This information is preprocessed in black and white image, where applied FA can efficiently search for objects. For the presented solution, Sobel shape recognition in gray scale 2D input images is obtained by an edge detection approach using a derivative preprocessin, for more details see (Canny, 1986) and (Anusha, 2012). Applied Sobel operator approximates the two dimensional gradient of a luminance function by a convolution with an integer filter applied along the axial directions. Some basic versions of the filter are also discussed in (Pratt, 2001; Gonzalez, 2002) and (Parker, 2010). Sobel operator is a kind of orthogonal gradient operator in local (or differential) form. For a continuous function $F : R^2 \rightarrow R$ and a given point $\mathbf{x} = (x_1, x_2)$ the gradient can be expressed as $\vec{\nabla} f$ so that

$$df = \vec{\nabla} f \cdot d\mathbf{x} = [\partial_1 f, \partial_2 f] \cdot [dx_1, dx_2],$$

where partial derivatives ∂_1 and ∂_2 are computed for each pixel location. In the applied method, an approximation is achieved as a convolution of kernels for a small area of neighbor pixels. $\partial_1 f$ and $\partial_2 f$ use a separate kernel each, so there are two applied kernels combined into a gradient operator. Some examples of the Sobel kernel can be found in (Pratt, 2001; Parker, 2010). In the applied version we used

$$S1 = \begin{pmatrix} -1 & -2 & -1 \\ 0 & 0 & 0 \\ 1 & 2 & 1 \end{pmatrix}, \quad S2 = \begin{pmatrix} -1 & -2 & -1 \\ 0 & 0 & 0 \\ 1 & 2 & 1 \end{pmatrix}.$$

as kernels. The kernels *S1* and *S2* are applied because one of them has a maximum response for the vertical edge and the other has a maximum response for the horizontal edge of the input object. Therefore, in the applied method, the maximum value of the two convolutions is used as the output bit of each 2D input image point. As a result, we get an image of the edge amplitude. In order to obtain the edges of an image **I**, starting by its associated luminance intensity matrix I, for every pixel $\mathbf{x}_i = (x_{i,1}, x_{i,2})$ of the image we compute the following functions

$$g_1(\mathbf{x}_i) = g_1(x_{i,1}, x_{i,2}) = \sum_{m=1}^{3}\sum_{n=1}^{3} S1_{mn} \cdot I(x_{i,1} + m - 2, x_{i,2} + n - 2),$$

$$g_2(\mathbf{x}_i) = g_2(x_{i,1}, x_{i,2}) = \sum_{m=1}^{3}\sum_{n=1}^{3} S1_{mn} \cdot I(x_{i,1} + m - 2, x_{i,2} + n - 2),$$

$$g(\mathbf{x}_i) = g(x_{i,1}, x_{i,2}) = g_1^2(\mathbf{x}_{i,1}) + g_2^2(\mathbf{x}_{i,1}),$$

where $S1_{ij}$, $S2_{ij}$, g_1 and g_2 are taken form the classical Sobel approach. Once the values of the functions are obtained for each pixel, the edges are defined as the pixels in the subset of points $E \subset I$ so that

$$\forall x_i \in \varepsilon \Rightarrow \begin{cases} g(\mathbf{x}_i) & > & 4\langle g^2 \rangle \\ g_1(\mathbf{x}_i) & > & g_2(\mathbf{x}_i) \\ g(\mathbf{x}_i) & \geq & g(x_{i,1}, x_{i,2} - 1) \\ g(\mathbf{x}_i) & \geq & g(x_{i,1}, x_{i,2} + 1) \end{cases} \vee \begin{cases} g(\mathbf{x}_i) & > & 4\langle g^2 \rangle \\ g_1(\mathbf{x}_i) & > & g_2(\mathbf{x}_i) \\ g(\mathbf{x}_i) & \geq & g(x_{i,1} - 1, x_{i,2}) \\ g(\mathbf{x}_i) & \geq & g(x_{i,1} + 1, x_{i,2}) \end{cases},$$

basing on the g_1, g_2 and g computed for each pixel $\mathbf{x}_i$ in $\mathbf{I}$. When a sobel filter is applied to 2D input image $\mathbf{I}$, a new indexed image is depicted as a plain representation of the points of $E \subset \mathbf{I}$, as defined previously. The indexed image coordinate system is a representation of $\mathbf{I}$, whereby all the values are zeros, except for the coordinates of the points in E which are ones. Such a representation is lossy since it carries only a logical representation of the set E. In order to obtain ad advanced identification of the edges retaining partial information, such as the values of the functions, Sobel filter is unsuitable in the described form. Therefore for each point of $\mathbf{I}$, instead of obtaining E, we used the value of $g(\mathbf{x}_i)$ and its square root

$$\widetilde{g}(\mathbf{x}_i) = \sqrt{g(\mathbf{x}_i)} = \sqrt{g_1^2(\mathbf{x}_i) + g_2^2(\mathbf{x}_i)}.$$

By using the devised equations, edges become blurred, however they are more suitable for the application of firefly algorithm since higher values are obtained with respect to the other points of $\mathbf{I}$. Finally, we filter a 2D image, which is then processed by firefly algorithm to recognize the objects. The bright patterns, then, can become the shapes key-points for the evolutionary computing methods that can now be applied to the problem of shape detection and recognition. In the following section a brief introduction to the applied Firefly Algorithm is given.

6 The Applied Firefly Algorithm

The applied firefly algorithm (FA) describes fireflies characterized by specific features modeled with numerical values: way of flashing, specific way of moving and specific perception of other individuals. This algorithm also models the natural environment conditions and the related light absorption coefficient. The FA is based on the following assumptions:

1. All fireflies are unisex; therefore one individual can be attracted to any other firefly regardless of gender.
2. Attractiveness is proportional to brightness. Thus, for every two fireflies the less clear flashing one will move toward the brighter one.
3. Attractiveness is proportional to brightness and decreases with increasing distance between individuals.
4. If there is no clearer and more visible firefly within the range, then each one will move randomly.
5. Firefly and pixel (2D image point) are considered the same in FA algorithm.
6. Distance between any two fireflies situated at different points are determined by means of a Cartesian metric

Each firefly perceives light intensity emitted from another firefly, on the other hand the perceived light intensity decreases as much as the distance increases between two fireflies.

Media absorbs natural light, so attractiveness also varies depending on absorption and distance between them. It follows that the attractiveness between two different fireflies decreases with the distance since it is proportional to perceived light intensity. Individual movement is based on conditioned distance to the individuals surrounding it. A firefly will go to the most attractive one, measuring intensity of flicker over the distance between them. In the given model, the natural identification of individuals and their attractiveness depends on light intensity and distance separating them. In nature fireflies that are closer not only see themselves better, but also are more attractive to each other. Using these features in the model, calculations remap the natural behavior of fireflies. A firefly motions toward a more attractive and brighter individual using information about the overall population. To understand more about the Firefly Algorithm please refer to (Napoli et al. 2014a, b; Polap et al. 2015; Wozniak et al. 2015a, b, c; Wozniak et al. 2016a, b).

7 Object Motion Detection and Extraction

In the previous section the applied firefly algorithm (FA) has been introduced as developed in (Napoli et al. 2014a, b; Wozniak et al. 2015a, b, c), moreover in the presented approach the FA is applied to images that have been filtered by means of a Sobel filter, in this manner the algorithm localizes the pixels constituting the object edges. This latter result is reached by distributing almost homogeneously the fireflies on the edges, which constitute the special areas of our interest in order to detect motion. In facts we expect that, when a motion act takes place, two different frames will present different objects (with different edges) or a different edges location.

It should be highlighted that this definition of motion can be applied also to original images without any filtering. In facts the Sobel filter has been applied to the The images, not just for motion detection purposes, but because taking into account only the edges of the objects dramatically decreases the number of pixels to consider for our analysis with great advantages in terms of performances. As said before, when the FA is applied to the image, a limited number of pixels is selected (namely the pixels where the simulated fireflies will stop), and such pixels are located almost homogeneously (for statistical reasons) along the object edges. At this point the number of special pixels found by the FA in each row or each column is counted (see the following image). Hence, after the special pixels have been located, two numerical vectors are extracted representing the vertical count (number of pixels in each row) and the horizontal count (the number of pixels in each column). last step regard the comparison of set of vectors related to images with the same source and a determined temporal index. In other words basing on the number of special pixels localized by the FA for each row and column of an image at a certain time t_0, we are interested to know if, at a successive time $t_0 + \Delta t$, such counts differ. If the difference between two images is greater than a fixed threshold, then an act of motion has been found. Finally, it is possible to extract the exact image area where an act of motion is causing such a difference and follow it, frame by frame, trough time. When the extracted areas are joined, a smaller video is then obtained which can be passed as output to a human operator for visualization (see Fig. 4).

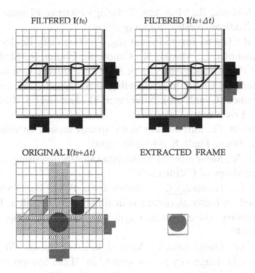

Fig. 4. The frame extraction procedure for motion detection

8   Conclusions

In this paper we presented a cloud-oriented architecture to process a constant flux of video streams. The platform has been designed to grant both scalability and versatility also for a large number of video sources. Our solution has put a high relevance on the modularity issues, hence the proposed components are loosely coupled and each one of them takes care of a relatively small concern, since the devised design is based on design patterns such as Broker and Mediator. The scalability of the approach is granted by the possibility to instantiate the cloud services on demand, which are accessible by means of an ad-hoc resource broker. Therefore, with this approach makes it possible to constantly scale-up or scale-down the overall system in order to suite every scenario independently by the organization and topology of the data producers and consumers.

References

Anusha, G., Prasad, T., Narayana, D.: Implementation of SOBEL edge detection on FPGA. Int. J. Comput. Trends and Technol. **3**(3), 472–475 (2012)

Armbrust, M., et al.: A view of cloud computing. Comm. ACM **53**, 50–58 (2010)

Booch, G., Maksimchuk, R.A.: Object-Oriented Analysis and Design with Applications. Addison- Wesley, Reading (2007)

Buschmann, F., Meunier, R., Rohnert, H., Sommerlad, P., Stal, M.: Pattern-oriented Software Architecture, vol. 1. Wiley, New York (1996)

Canny, J.: A computational approach to edge detection. IEEE Trans. Pattern Anal. Mach. Intell. **6**, 679–698 (1986)

Capizzi, G., Lo Sciuto, G., Napoli, C., Tramontana, E., and Wozniak, M.: Automatic classification of fruit defects based on co-occurrence matrix and neural networks. In: IEEE Federated Conference on Computer Science and Information Systems (FedCSIS), pp. 861–867 (2015)

Gamma, E., Helm, R., Johnson, R., Vlissiders, J.: Design Patterns: Elements of Reusable Object-Oriented Software. Addison-Wesley, Reading (1994)

Gonzalez, R., Woods, R.: Digital Image Processing. Prentice Hall, Englewood Cliffs (2002)

Jackson, K.R., Ramakrishnan, L., Muriki, K., Canon, S., Cholia, S., Shalf, J., Wasserman, H. J. and Wright, N.J.: Performance Analysis of High Performance Computing Applications on the Amazon Web Services Cloud. In: Proceeding International Conference Cloud Computing Technology and Science (CloudCom), November 30–December 3 2010, Indianapolis, USA, pp. 159–168. IEEE, Los Alamos (2010)

Lee, L., Romano, R., Stein, G.: Introduction to the special section on video surveillance. IEEE Trans. Pattern Anal. Mach. Intell. **8**, 740–745 (2000)

Mittal, A., and Paragios, N.: Motion-based background subtraction using adaptive kernel density estimation. In: Proceedings of CVPR (2004)

Napoli, C., Pappalardo, G., Tramontana, E., Borowik, G., Polap, D., Wozniak, M.: Toward 2D image classifier based on firefly algorithm with simplified sobel filter. In: IEEE Asia-Pacific Conference on Computer Aided System Engineering (APCASE), pp. 1–8 (2014a). doi:10.1109/APCASE.2015.40

Napoli, C., Pappalardo, G., Tramontana, E., Marszalek, Z., Polap, D., Wozniak, M.: Simplified firefly algorithm for 2D image key-points search. In: IEEE Symposium on Computational Intelligence for Human-like Intelligence (CIHLI), pp. 1–8 (2014b). doi:10.1109/CIHLI.2014.7013395

Napoli, C., Pappalardo, G., Tramontana, E., Nowicki, R.K., Starczewski, J.T., Woźniak, M.: Toward work groups classification based on probabilistic neural network approach. In: Rutkowski, L., Korytkowski, M., Scherer, R., Tadeusiewicz, R., Zadeh, L.A., Zurada, J.M. (eds.) AISC 2015. LNCS, vol. 9119, pp. 79–89. Springer, Heidelberg (2015)

Napoli, C., Tramontana, E.: An object-oriented neural network toolbox based on design patterns. In: International Conference on Information and Software Technologies, pp. 388–399 (2015)

Parker, J.: Algorithms for Image Processing and Computer Vision. John Wiley & Sons, Inc., New York (2010)

Polap, D., Wozniak, M., Napoli, C., Tramontana, E., and Damasevicius, R.: Is the colony of ants able to recognize graphic objects?. In International Conference on Information and Software Technologies, pp. 376–387 (2015). doi:10.1007/978-3-319-24770-0_33

Pratt, W.: Digital Image Processing: PIKS Inside, 3rd edn. John Wiley & Sons, Inc., New York (2001)

Starczewski, J.T., Pabiasz, S., Vladymyrska, N., Marvuglia, A., Napoli, C., Wozniak, M.: Self organizing maps for 3D face understanding. In: Rutkowski, L., Korytkowski, M., Scherer, R., Tadeusiewicz, R., Zadeh, L.A., Zurada, J.M. (eds.) ICAISC 2016. LNCS, vol. 9693, pp. 210–217. Springer, Heidelberg (2016). doi:10.1007/978-3-319-39384-1_19

Tian, Y.L., Lu, M., Hampapur, A.: Robust and efficient foreground analysis for real-time video surveillance. In: IEEE Computer Society Conference on Computer Vision and Pattern Recognition (CVPR 2005), pp. 1182–1187 (2005)

Wozniak, M., Gabryel, M., Nowicki, R.K., Nowak, B.: An application of firefly algorithm to position traffic in NoSQL database systems. In: Kunifuji, S., Papadopoulos, G.A., Skulimowski, A.M.J., Kacprzyk, J. (eds.) KICSS 2014. AISC, vol. 416, pp. 259–272 (2016a)

Wozniak, M., Marszalek, Z., Gabryel, M., Nowicki, R.K.: Preprocessing large data sets by the use of quick sort algorithm. In: Skulimowski, A.M.J., Kacprzyk, J. (eds.) KICSS 2013. AISC, vol. 364, pp. 111–121 (2016b)

Wozniak, M., Napoli, C., Tramontana, E., and Capizzi, G.: A multiscale image compressor with RBFNN and Discrete Wavelet decomposition. In: IEEE International Joint Conference on Neural Networks (IJCNN), pp. 1–7 (2015a). doi:10.1109/IJCNN.2015.7280461

Woźniak, M., Połap, D., Gabryel, M., Nowicki, R.K., Napoli, C., Tramontana, E.: Can we process 2D images using artificial bee colony? In: Rutkowski, L., Korytkowski, M., Scherer, R., Tadeusiewicz, R., Zadeh, L.A., Zurada, J.M. (eds.). LNCS, vol. 9119, pp. 660–671. Springer, Heidelberg (2015b)

Wozniak, M., Polap, D., Nowicki, R.K., Napoli, C., Pappalardo, G., Tramontana, E.: Novel approach toward medical signals classifier. In: IEEE International Joint Conference on Neural Networks (IJCNN), pp. 1–7 (2015c)

Study on Transient Queueing Delay
in a Single-Channel Queueing Model
with Setup and Closedown Times

Wojciech M. Kempa[1(✉)], Iwona Paprocka[2], Krzysztof Kalinowski[2],
Cezary Grabowik[2], and Damian Krenczyk[2]

[1] Faculty of Applied Mathematics, Institute of Mathematics, Silesian University
of Technology, 23 Kaszubska Street, 44-100 Gliwice, Poland
wojciech.kempa@polsl.pl
[2] Faculty of Mechanical Engineering, Institute of Engineering Processes
Automation and Integrated Manufacturing Systems,
Silesian University of Technology, 18A Konarskiego Street,
44-100 Gliwice, Poland
{iwona.paprocka,krzysztof.kalinowski,cezary.grabowik,
damian.krenczyk}@polsl.pl

Abstract. A single-channel queueing model with finite buffer capacity, Poisson
arrival stream and generally distributed processing times is considered. After
each busy period the service station is being switched off but this operation
requires a randomly distributed closedown time. Similarly, after the idle time,
the first service in a new busy period is preceded by a random setup time, during
which the processing is still suspended and the server achieves full readiness for
the service process. A system of integral equations for transient conditional
queueing delay distribution is derived, by using the idea of embedded Markov
chain and the formula of total probability. The solution of the corresponding
system written for Laplace transforms is obtained via the linear algebraic
technique. Numerical examples are attached as well.

Keywords: Closedown time · Finite buffer · Queueing delay · Setup time ·
Transient state

1 Introduction and Preliminaries

As it is commonly known, different-type real problems occurring in telecommunication
and computer networks, in manufacturing processes, in transport and logistics, tracking
systems and similar can be efficiently modelled by using appropriate queueing models
(e.g. see [18, 19]). Systems with one or more mechanisms limiting the access to the
service station seem to be of special importance. One of such mechanisms are server
setup and closedown times, occurring at the beginning and at the end of each busy
period of the system, respectively. Indeed, due to the energy saving strategy, the server
is being switched off when there are no customers present, and is being switched on
when a job arrives into the empty system. Switching off requires a time, usually
random, as, similarly, switching on during which the service station achieves full

G. Dregvaite and R. Damasevicius (Eds.): ICIST 2016, CCIS 639, pp. 464–475, 2016.
DOI: 10.1007/978-3-319-46254-7_37

readiness for processing. In the paper we deal with a single-channel queueing model with finite buffer capacity and the service process organized according to the FIFO service discipline, in which generally distributed closedown and setup times are implemented. The considered model has potential practical applications, e.g. in SVC (switched virtual connection) modelling, where the setup time corresponds to the time for building a new SVC by using the signalling procedure, and the closedown time stands for the deactivation timer during which the SVC resource (as, e.g. routing information or the bandwidth frequency) is reserved anticipating more packets from the same flow (see [12]).

One of the crucial operating characteristics in each queueing model is queueing delay, i.e. the time the potentially entering customer needs to wait until the start its processing. In the paper, using the technique based on the idea of embedded Markov chain, the total probability law and linear algebra, we obtain a compact-form representation for the LT (=Laplace transform) of the queueing delay conditional CDF (=cumulative distribution function).

As it is easy to note, in the literature most results for stochastic features of different-kind queueing systems are obtained for the stationary case, when the system is stable. However, transient (time-dependent) analysis is often desired or even necessary, e.g. due to high volatility of the arrival process (as it can be observed in the TCP/IP traffic) or in the case of large traffic in distributed systems [21, 22] or server breakdowns, when the stochastic stabilization of the system is longer or more difficult.

In [3] the M/G/1-type vacation queueing system with server breakdowns, setup and closedown times, in which the length of the vacation period is controlled either by the number of arrivals during the vacation period, or by a timer is investigated. The study on a batch-arrival queue with multiple vacation policy and server setup and closedown times in the stationary case can be found in [1]. Results for models with group arrivals are also presented in [4, 10, 20]. In [11] a discrete-time model is analyzed, where the mixed-type mechanism of a multiple vacation policy combined with setup/closedown periods is implemented. The case of a multi-server queue is investigated in [2]. Transient results for infinite-buffer systems with server setup times can be found in [5, 6]. Analytical solution for time-dependent queue-size distribution in the queueing model with finite buffer capacity and machine setup and closedown times is derived in [7] (similar technique is also applied in [8]). Evolutionary algorithms are used in [13, 14] for the analysis of a finite-buffer queue with temporary unavailable server. In various data management systems (see [15]) we can find applications of queueing systems to enable faster requests management and therefore improved data mining (see e.g. [16, 17]).

The remaining part of the article is organized as follows. In the next Sect. 2 we give a precise mathematical description of the considered queueing model. In Sect. 3 we derive a system of integral equations for conditional CDF of transient queueing delay. In Sect. 4 we obtain the corresponding system for LTs and write it in a specific form. Section 5 contains main result: the closed-form representation for the LT of conditional CDF of queueing delay and the last Sect. 7 gives a short conclusion.

2 System Description

In the paper we deal with a single-server queueing model with a reliable service station and finite capacity of the buffer for jobs waiting for service. Assume that the arrival process of jobs (packets, customers, calls, etc.) is described by a Poisson process with intensity λ, while the processing time of each one is generally distributed random variable with a CDF $F(\cdot)$. A number of jobs simultaneously present in the system is bounded by a non-random value N, i.e. we have a buffer with $N - 1$ places and one place in service station. Initially, at time $t = 0$, a buffer may contain a number of jobs waiting for service. Every time when the system becomes empty (a service of a job finishes and there are no waiting jobs in the buffer), the service station initializes a randomly distributed closedown time with a CDF $C(\cdot)$. If at the completion epoch of a closedown time a buffer contains at least one job waiting for service, the processing begins immediately, otherwise the server waits in the standby mode for the first arrival. The first processing after the idle period is always preceded by a setup time, duration of which is a random variable with a CDF $S(\cdot)$. Moreover, if a job enters the system during the closedown time, after its completion epoch the server immediately begins the setup time and next the processing. As it was mentioned in the previous section, the closedown time is needed for a server to switch off according to energy saving strategy. Similarly, the setup time is needed for a server to achieve full operational readiness after the idle period. Successive jobs are being processed according to the FIFO service discipline. Moreover, if the arriving job find the buffer being saturated, it is lost. We assume that the delay of the customer being lost equals 0.

3 Integral Equations for Conditional CDF of Queueing Delay

Let $v(t)$ be the (virtual) queueing delay at time t, i.e. the waiting time of a job entering the system exactly at time t. Introduce the conditional CDF of $v(t)$ in the following way:

$$V_n(t, x) \stackrel{\text{def}}{=} P\{v(t) < x \mid X(0) = n\}, 0 \le n \le N, t > 0, x > 0, \tag{1}$$

where $X(0)$ denotes the number of jobs present in the system at the opening.

Assume, firstly, that the system is empty at the start epoch $t = 0$. In such a case we treat this epoch as a time at which the last processing completes in a busy period, so, in consequence, a closedown time begins. In fact, one can distinguish eight different mutually excluding possibilities:

1. the first jobs arrives during the closedown time, and both the closedown and setup times finishes before time t (denote this random event by E_1);
2. the first job enters during the closedown time but that period completes after t (E_2);
3. the first job occurs during the closedown time and the time t is "inside" the following setup time (E_3);
4. the first job arrives after the closedown time but before t, and the setup time finishes before t (E_4);

5. the first job enters after the closedown time but before t, and the setup time ends after t (E_5);
6. the first jobs arrives after t, but the closedown time "closes" before t, so at the first arrival epoch the setup time begins (E_6);
7. the first job arrives after t but still "inside" the closedown time (E_7);
8. the first jobs joins the system after t and after the closedown time that "contains" the time t (E_8).

Introducing the following notation:

$$V_{0,i}(t,x) \stackrel{def}{=} P\{(v(t)<x)\} \cap E_i \mid X(0) = 0\}, 1 \le i \le 8, \qquad (2)$$

we can write the following representations:

$$V_{0,1}(t,x) = \int_{u=0}^{t} dC(u) \int_{v=0}^{t-u} dS(v) \int_{y=0}^{u} \left[\sum_{k=0}^{N-2} \frac{[\lambda(u+v-y)]^k}{k!} e^{-\lambda(u+v-y)} V_{k+1}(t-u-v,x) \right.$$
$$\left. + V_N(t-u-v,x) \sum_{k=N-1}^{\infty} \frac{[\lambda(u+v-y)]^k}{k!} e^{-\lambda(u+v-y)} \right] \lambda e^{-\lambda y} dy;$$

$$\qquad (3)$$

$$V_{0,2}(t,x) = \int_{u=t}^{\infty} dC(u) \int_{y=0}^{t} \lambda e^{-\lambda y} \sum_{k=0}^{N-2} \frac{[\lambda(t-y)]^k}{k!} e^{-\lambda(t-y)} dy \int_{v=0}^{\infty} F^{(k+1)*}(x-v-u+t) dS(v); \qquad (4)$$

$$V_{0,3}(t,x) = \int_{u=0}^{t} dC(u) \int_{y=0}^{u} \lambda e^{-\lambda y} \sum_{k=0}^{N-2} \frac{[\lambda(t-y)]^k}{k!} e^{-\lambda(t-y)} dy \int_{v=t-u}^{\infty} F^{(k+1)*}(x-v-u+t) dS(v); \qquad (5)$$

$$V_{0,4}(t,x) = \int_{u=0}^{t} dC(u) \int_{y=u}^{t} \lambda e^{-\lambda y} dy \int_{v=0}^{t-y} \left[\sum_{k=0}^{N-2} \frac{(\lambda v)^k}{k!} e^{-\lambda v} V_{k+1}(t-y-v,x) \right.$$
$$\left. + V_N(t-y-v,x) \sum_{k=N-1}^{\infty} \frac{(\lambda v)^k}{k!} e^{-\lambda v} \right] dS(v); \qquad (6)$$

$$V_{0,5}(t,x) = \int_{u=0}^{t} dC(u) \int_{y=u}^{t} \lambda e^{-\lambda y} \sum_{k=0}^{N-2} \frac{[\lambda(t-y)]^k}{k!} e^{-\lambda(t-y)} dy \int_{v=t-y}^{\infty} F^{(k+1)*}(x-y-v+t) dS(v); \qquad (7)$$

$$V_{0,6}(t,x) = C(t) \int_{t}^{\infty} \lambda e^{-\lambda y} S(x-y+t) dy; \qquad (8)$$

$$V_{0,7}(t,x) = \int\limits_{t}^{\infty} S(x - u + t)\left(e^{-\lambda t} - e^{-\lambda u}\right) dC(u); \tag{9}$$

and

$$V_{0,8}(t,x) = \int\limits_{u=t}^{\infty} dC(u) \int\limits_{y=u}^{\infty} \lambda e^{-\lambda y} S(x - y + t) dy. \tag{10}$$

In the formulae above $F^{j*}(\cdot)$ stands for the j-fold Stieltjes convolution of the CDF $F(\cdot)$ with itself.

Let us comment briefly some of the formulae (3)–(10). The first summands on the right sides of (3) and (6) refer to the situation in which there is at least one free place in the buffer at the completion epoch of the setup time, while the second one to the case in which the buffer becomes saturated during the setup time. In (4) and (7) the sum is taken only for $k = N-2$. Indeed, in the case t is "inside" the period during which the service is suspended (the closedown or the setup time) and the buffer becomes saturated before t, the "virtual" jobs occurring exactly at time t is lost.

Now, let us analyze the case where at $t = 0$ the buffer contains at least one job, i.e. the level of buffer saturation equals n, where $1 \leq n \leq N$. Since successive service completion epochs are Markov moments in the evolution of the system, then, applying the continuous version of the total probability law with respect to the first service completion epoch after the start of the system, the following system of integral equations can be written:

$$\begin{aligned}
V_n(t,x) = {}& \sum_{k=0}^{N-n-1} \int\limits_{0}^{t} V_{n+k-1}(t - y, x) \frac{(\lambda y)^k}{k!} e^{-\lambda y} dF(y) \\
&+ \sum_{k=N-n}^{\infty} \int\limits_{0}^{t} V_{N-1}(t - y, x) \frac{(\lambda y)^k}{k!} e^{-\lambda y} dF(y) \\
&+ \sum_{k=0}^{N-n-1} \frac{(\lambda t)^k}{k!} e^{-\lambda t} \int\limits_{t}^{\infty} F^{(n+k-1)*}(x - y + t) dF(y),
\end{aligned} \tag{11}$$

where $1 \leq n \leq N$. Indeed, the first term on the right side of (11) relates to the situation in which the buffer is not full before the first processing completion epoch, while the second one describes the case in which the buffer becomes saturated before the first departure moment. The last summand refers to the situation in which the first service completes after time t.

4   System of Equations for LTs of Delay Conditional CDFs

In this section we derive the system of equations for LTs of conditional CDFs of the queueing delay in the considered model and write it in a specific form. Thus, let us introduce the following notation:

$$\tilde{v}_n(s,x) \overset{\text{def}}{=} \int_0^\infty e^{-st} V_n(t,x)dt = \int_0^\infty e^{-st} P\{v(t) < x | X(0) = n\}dt, \quad \Re(s) > 0,$$

$$x > 0, \ 0 \leq n \leq N. \tag{12}$$

Moreover, due to the fact that $\tilde{v}_0(s,x) = \sum_{i=1}^{8} \int_0^\infty e^{-st} V_{0,i}(t,x)dt$, then just by virtue of the Eqs. (3)–(10), we obtain

$$\tilde{v}_0(s,x) = \sum_{k=0}^{N-2} \tilde{v}_{k+1}(s,x)\alpha_k(s) + \tilde{v}_N(s,x) \sum_{k=N-1}^{\infty} \alpha_k(s) + \beta(s,x), \tag{13}$$

where

$$\begin{aligned}
\alpha_k(s) &\overset{\text{def}}{=} \frac{\lambda^{k+1}}{(k+1)!} \int_{u=0}^{\infty} e^{-(\lambda+s)u} dC(u) \int_{v=0}^{\infty} e^{-(\lambda+s)v} \left[(v+u)^{k+1} - v^{k+1}\right] dS(v) \\
&\quad + \frac{\lambda}{\lambda+s} \tilde{c}(\lambda+s) \int_0^{\infty} e^{-(\lambda+s)v} \frac{(\lambda v)^k}{k!} dS(v);
\end{aligned} \tag{14}$$

$$\tilde{c}(s) \overset{\text{def}}{=} \int_0^{\infty} e^{-st} dC(t); \tag{15}$$

$$\begin{aligned}
\beta(s,x) &\overset{\text{def}}{=} \int_{t=0}^{\infty} e^{-(\lambda+s)t} \sum_{k=0}^{N-2} \frac{\lambda^{k+1}}{(k+1)!} \Bigg\{ \left[t^{k+1} - (t-u)^{k+1}\right] \int_{u=0}^{t} dC(u) \int_{v=t-u}^{\infty} F^{(k+1)*}(x - v - u + t)dS(v) \\
&\quad + t^{k+1} \int_{u=t}^{\infty} dC(u) \int_{v=0}^{\infty} F^{(k+1)*}(x - v - u + t)dS(v) \Bigg\} dt \\
&\quad + \int_{t=0}^{\infty} e^{-st} dt \int_{u=0}^{t} dC(u) \int_{y=u}^{t} \lambda e^{-\lambda y} \sum_{k=0}^{N-2} \frac{[\lambda(t-y)]^k}{k!} e^{-\lambda(t-y)} dy \int_{v=t-y}^{\infty} F^{(k+1)*}(x - y - v + t)dS(v) \\
&\quad + \int_{t=0}^{\infty} e^{-st} C(t) dt \int_{y=t}^{\infty} \lambda e^{-\lambda y} S(x - y + t) dy \\
&\quad + \int_{t=0}^{\infty} e^{-st} dt \int_{u=t}^{\infty} S(x - u + t)(e^{-\lambda t} - e^{-\lambda u}) dC(u) \\
&\quad + \int_{t=0}^{\infty} e^{-st} dt \int_{y=t}^{\infty} \lambda e^{-\lambda y} S(x - y + t)[C(y) - C(t)] dy.
\end{aligned} \tag{16}$$

In the similar manner, by defining the following functional sequences:

$$a_k(s) \overset{\text{def}}{=} \int_0^{\infty} e^{-(\lambda+s)t} \frac{(\lambda t)^k}{k!} dF(t), \tag{17}$$

$$\phi_n(s,x) \stackrel{\text{def}}{=} \int_{t=0}^{\infty} e^{-(\lambda+s)t} \sum_{k=0}^{N-n-1} \frac{(\lambda t)^k}{k!} dt \int_{y=t}^{\infty} F^{(n+k-1)*}(x-y+t)dF(y), \qquad (18)$$

we obtain from (11) the following system of equations:

$$\tilde{v}_n(s,x) = \sum_{k=0}^{N-n-1} a_k(s)\tilde{v}_{n+k-1}(s,x) + \tilde{v}_{N-1}(s,x) \sum_{k=N-n}^{\infty} a_k(s) + \phi_n(s,x), \qquad (19)$$

where $1 \le n \le N$. Let us apply to (13) and (19) the following substitution:

$$\tilde{\omega}_n(s,x) \stackrel{\text{def}}{=} \tilde{v}_{N-n}(s,x) \qquad (20)$$

Now, the representations (13) and (19) can be rewritten as follows:

$$\tilde{\omega}_N(s,x) = \sum_{k=1}^{N-1} \tilde{\omega}_k(s,x)\alpha_{N-k-1}(s) + \tilde{\omega}_0(s,x) \sum_{k=N-1}^{\infty} \alpha_k(s) + \beta(s,x), \qquad (21)$$

and

$$\sum_{k=-1}^{n} a_{k+1}(s)\tilde{\omega}_{n-k}(s,x) - \tilde{\omega}_n(s,x) = \Delta_n(s,x), 0 \le n \le N-1, \qquad (22)$$

where

$$\Delta_n(s,x) \stackrel{\text{def}}{=} a_{n+1}(s)\tilde{\omega}_0(s,x) - \tilde{\omega}_1(s,x) \sum_{k=n+1}^{\infty} a_k(s) - \phi_{N-n}(s,x). \qquad (23)$$

5   Transient Solution for LT of CDF of Queueing Delay

The system of equations of type (22) but with infinite number of equations, namely written for $n \ge 0$, was investigated in [9]. It was proved there that each its solution can be written in the form (we give here the representation for functional sequences, however, in [9], the equations with coefficients given by ordinary number sequences are considered):

$$\tilde{\omega}_n(s,x) = R_{n+1}(s)K(s,x) + \sum_{k=0}^{n} R_{n-k}(s)\Delta_k(s,x), \qquad n \ge 0, \qquad (24)$$

where $K(s,x)$ is independent on n, and successive terms of the functional sequence $R_k(s), k \ge 0$, can be found recursively from coefficients $a_k(s), k \ge 0$, of the system as follows:

$$R_0(s) = 0, R_1(s) = a_0^{-1}(s), R_{k+1}(s) = R_1(s)\left(R_k(s) - \sum_{i=0}^{k} a_{i+1}(s)R_{k-i}(s)\right), \quad k \geq 1.$$

(25)

Obviously, if we find closed-form representations for $\tilde{\omega}_0(s,x)$ and $\tilde{\omega}_1(s,x)$, which are present in the formula (23) for $\Delta_n(s,x)$, and the formula for $K(s,x)$, it will be possible to state a representation for $\tilde{\omega}_n(s,m)$ for arbitrary n, basing on (24).

Taking $n = 0$ in (24), we obtain

$$K(s,x) = a_0(s)\tilde{\omega}_0(s,x).$$

(26)

Similarly, substituting $n = 0$ into (22) and referring to (23), we have

$$\tilde{\omega}_1(s,x) = \frac{1}{\sum_{k=0}^{\infty} a_k(s)}[\tilde{\omega}_0(s,x) - \phi_N(s,x)] = \frac{\tilde{\omega}_0(s,x) - \phi_N(s,x)}{f(s)},$$

(27)

where

$$f(s) \stackrel{\text{def}}{=} \int_0^{\infty} e^{-st} dF(t), \Re(s) > 0.$$

(28)

In order to find the formula for $\tilde{\omega}_0(s,x)$ we must compare the right sides of (21), being in fact a kind of a boundary condition, and (24) taken for $n = N$. Executing necessary calculations, we obtain

$$\tilde{\omega}_0(s,x) = \tilde{v}_N(s,x) = \frac{\beta(s,m) + \gamma(s,x)}{H_N(s) - \sum_{k=1}^{N-1} \alpha_{N-k-1}(s)H_k(s) - \sum_{k=N-1}^{\infty} \alpha_k(s)},$$

(29)

where

$$\gamma(s,x) \stackrel{\text{def}}{=} \sum_{k=0}^{N} R_{N-k}(s)\left[(f(s))^{-1}\phi_N(s,x)\sum_{i=k+1}^{\infty} a_i(s) - \phi_{N-k}(s,x)\right]$$
$$+ \sum_{k=1}^{N-1} \alpha_{N-k-1}(s)\sum_{i=0}^{k} R_{k-i}(s)\left[(f(s))^{-1}\phi_N(s,x)\sum_{j=i+1}^{\infty} a_j(s) - \phi_{N-i}(s,x)\right]$$

(30)

and

$$H_k(s) \stackrel{\text{def}}{=} R_{k+1}(s)a_0(s) + \sum_{i=0}^{k} R_{k-i}(s)\left[a_{i+1}(s) - (f(s))^{-1}\sum_{j=i+1}^{\infty} a_j(s)\right].$$

(31)

After collecting the formulae (23)–(31), we can state the following main theorem:

Theorem 1. *The representations for the LT $\tilde{v}_n(s,x)$ of conditional CDF of the queueing delay in the M/G/1/N-type finite-buffer model with generally distributed setup and closedown times are following:*

$$\tilde{v}_n(s,x) = R_{N-n+1}(s)a_0(s)q_N(s) + \sum_{k=0}^{N-n} R_{N-n-k}(s)$$

$$\left[a_{k+1}(s)\tilde{v}_N(s,x) - (f(s))^{-1}(\tilde{v}_N(s,x) - \phi_N(s,x)) \sum_{i=k+1}^{\infty} a_i(s) - \phi_{N-n}(s,x) \right],$$

(32)

where $0 \leq n \leq N - 1$, and

$$\tilde{v}_N(s,x) = \frac{\beta(s,m) + \gamma(s,x)}{H_N(s) - \sum_{k=1}^{N-1} \alpha_{N-k-1}(s)H_k(s) - \sum_{k=N-1}^{\infty} \alpha_k(s)},$$

(33)

where the formulae for $\beta(s,x), a_k(s), \phi_k(s,x), R_k(s), f(s)$ and $\gamma(s,x)$ are given in (16), (17), (18), (25), (28) and (30), respectively.

6 Computational Examples

Let us consider the stream of packets of sizes 400 [B] arriving to the node of a network with buffer capacity 50 packets. The arrival stream is governed by a Poisson process with intensity 600 [kb/s], while the throughput of the output link is 800 [kb/s], so the traffic load equals 0.75. The mechanism of the node setup/closedown times is implemented. Three different situations of exponentially distributed setup and closedown times are investigated (see Table 1).

Table 1. Three different variants for the relationship between setup and closedown times

Variant	Mean setup time	Mean closedown time
SET < CLO	0.050 [s]	0.100 [s]
SET > CLO	0.100 [s]	0.050 [s]
SET = CLO	0.067 [s]	0.067 [s]

In Fig. 1 the behavior of the waiting time distribution in the stable system is shown for all considered cases. It is easy to note that for SET < CLO the probability of long waiting times for the arriving packets is relatively smallest one. In Fig. 2 the case of the arrival intensity 768 kb/s is considered (now the traffic load equals 0.96, so the system is close to the critical loading). Let us observe that in such a case the probability of waiting time less than e.g. 0.1 [s] is relatively large (equals approximately 0.4–0.5), while for the system less loaded equals even about 0.8.

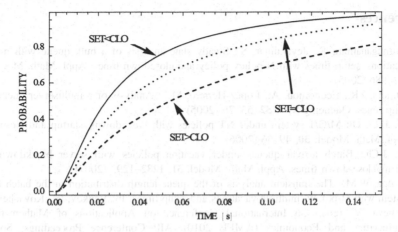

Fig. 1. Waiting time distribution for the stable system with traffic load 0.75

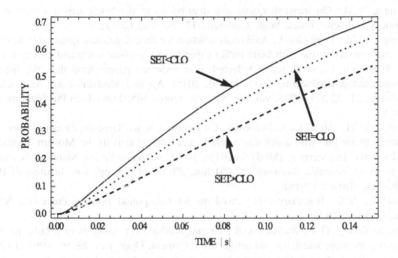

Fig. 2. Waiting time distribution for the stable system with traffic load 0.96

7 Conclusion

In the paper a single-channel queueing model with finite buffer capacity and server setup-closedown times is considered. The arrival process is governed by a single Poisson stream while the processing times are generally distributed random variables. By using the analytical approach based on the concept of embedded Markov chain, total probability law and linear algebra a closed-form representation for the LT of conditional CDF of the queueing delay is obtained. The final formulae are written in terms of "input" system characteristics and certain functional sequence, defined recursively, connected with them. Numerical examples, illustrating theoretical results, are attached.

References

1. Arumuganathan, R., Jeyakumar, S.: Steady state analysis of a bulk queue with multiple vacations, setup times with N-policy policy and closedown times. Appl. Math. Model. **29**, 972–986 (2005)
2. Artalejo, J.R., Economou, A., Lopez-Herrero, M.J.: Analysis of a multiserver queue with setup times. Queueing Syst. **52**, 53–76 (2005)
3. Ke, J.-C.: On M/G/1 system under NT policies with breakdowns, startup and closedown. Appl. Math. Model. **30**, 49–66 (2006)
4. Ke, J-Ch.: Batch arrival queues under vacation policies with server breakdowns and startup/close-down times. Appl. Math. Model. **31**, 1282–1292 (2007)
5. Kempa, W.M.: The transient analysis of the queue-length distribution in the batch arrival system with N-policy, multiple vacations and setup times. In: Venkov, G., Kovacheva, R., Pasheva, V. (eds.) 36 International Conference on Applications of Mathematics in Engineering and Economics (AMEE 2010). AIP Conference Proceedings, Sozopol, Bulgaria, 5–10 June 2010, Melville, American Institute of Physics, vol. 1293, pp. 235–242 (2010)
6. Kempa, W.M.: On transient queue-size distribution in the batch arrival system with the N-policy and setup times. Math. Commun. **17**, 285–302 (2012)
7. Kempa, W.M., Paprocka, I.: Analytical solution for time-dependent queue-size behavior in the manufacturing line with finite buffer capacity and machine setup and closedown times. In: Slatineanu, L., et al. (eds.) Selected, peer reviewed papers from the 19th Innovative Manufacturing Engineering 2015 (IManE 2015). Applied Mechanics and Materials, Iasi, Romania, 21–22 May 2015, vol. 809/810, pp. 1360–1365. Trans Tech Publications, Zurich (2015)
8. Kempa, W.M., Paprocka, I., Grabowik, C., Kalinowski, K.: Time-dependent solution for the manufacturing line with unreliable machine and batched arrivals. In: Modern Technologies in Industrial Engineering (ModTech2015). IOP Conference Series, Materials Science and Engineering, Mamaia, Romania, 17–20 June 2015, vol. 95, pp. 1–6. Institute of Physics Publishing, Bristol (2015)
9. Korolyuk, V.S.: Boundary-value Problems for Compound Poisson Processes. Naukova Dumka, Kiev (1975)
10. Krishna Reddy, G.V., Nadarajan, R., Arumuganathan, R.: Analysis of a bulk queue with N-policy multiple vacations and setup times. Comput. Oper. Res. **25**, 957–967 (1998)
11. Moreno, P.: A discrete-time single-server queueing system under multiple vacations and setup-closedown times. Stochast. Anal. Appl. **27**, 221–239 (2009)
12. Niu, Z., Takahashi, Y.: A finite-capacity queue with exhaustive vacation/close-down/setup times and Markovian arrival processes. Queueing Syst. **31**, 1–23 (1999)
13. Woźniak, M., Gabryel, M., Nowicki, R.K., Nowak, B.: An Application of firefly algorithm to position traffic in NoSQL database systems. Adv. Intell. Syst. Comput. (AISC) **416**, 259–272 (2016). doi:10.1007/978-3-319-27478-2-18
14. Woźniak, M., Kempa, W.M., Gabryel, M., Nowicki, R.: A finite-buffer queue with a single vacation policy: an analytical study with evolutionary positioning. Int. J. Appl. Math. Comput. Sci. **24**, 887–900 (2014)
15. Woźniak, M., Kempa, W.M., Gabryel, M., Nowicki, R.K., Shao, Z.: On applying evolutionary computation methods to optimization of vacation cycle costs in finite-buffer queue. In: Rutkowski, L., Korytkowski, M., Scherer, R., Tadeusiewicz, R., Zadeh, L.A., Zurada, J.M. (eds.) ICAISC 2014, Part I. LNCS, vol. 8467, pp. 480–491. Springer, Heidelberg (2014)

16. Woźniak, M., Marszałek, Z., Gabryel, M., Nowicki, R.K.: Preprocessing large data sets by the use of quick sort algorithm. Adv. Intell. Syst. Comput. (AISC) **364**, 111–121 (2016). doi:10.1007/978-3-319-19090-7-9

17. Woźniak, M., Marszałek, Z., Gabryel, M., Nowicki, R.K.: Modified merge sort algorithm for large scale data sets. In: Rutkowski, L., Korytkowski, M., Scherer, R., Tadeusiewicz, R., Zadeh, L.A., Zurada, J.M. (eds.) ICAISC 2013, Part II. LNCS, vol. 7895, pp. 612–622. Springer, Heidelberg (2013)

18. Damaševičius, R., Vasiljevas, M., Šalkevičius, J., Woźniak, M.: Human activity recognition in aal environments using random projections. Comput. Math. Methods Med. **2016**, 17 (2016). doi:10.1155/2016/4073584. Article ID 4073584

19. Capizzi, G., Lo Sciuto, G., Wozniak, M., Damaševičius, R.: A clustering based system for automated oil spill detection by satellite remote sensing. In: Rutkowski, L., Korytkowski, M., Scherer, R., Tadeusiewicz, R., Zadeh, L.A., Zurada, J.M. (eds.) ICAISC 2016. LNCS, vol. 9693, pp. 613–623. Springer, Heidelberg (2016). doi:10.1007/978-3-319-39384-1_54

20. Kempa, W.M., Wozniak, M., Nowicki, R.K., Gabryel, M., Damaševičius, R.: Transient solution for queueing delay distribution in the GI/M/1/K-type mode with "Queued" waking up and balking. In: Rutkowski, L., Korytkowski, M., Scherer, R., Tadeusiewicz, R., Zadeh, L.A., Zurada, J.M. (eds.) ICAISC 2016. LNCS, vol. 9693, pp. 340–351. Springer, Heidelberg (2016). doi:10.1007/978-3-319-39384-1_29

21. Połap, D., Woźniak, M., Napoli, C., Tramontana, E.: Real-time cloud-based game management system via cuckoo search algorithm. Int. J. Electron. Telecommun. **61**(4), 333–338 (2015). doi:10.1515/eletel-2015-0043. De Gruyter Open Ltd.

22. Połap, D., Woźniak, M., Napoli, C., Tramontana, E.: Is swarm intelligence able to create mazes? Int. J. Electron. Telecommun. **61**(4), 305–310 (2015). doi:10.1515/eletel-2015-0039. De Gruyter Open Ltd.

Information Technology Applications: Special Session on Smart e-Learning Technologies and Applications

On Suitability Index to Create Optimal Personalised Learning Packages

Eugenijus Kurilovas[1,2(✉)], Julija Kurilova[1], and Tomas Andruskevic[3]

[1] Vilnius University Institute of Mathematics and Informatics, Vilnius, Lithuania
jevgenij.kurilov@mii.vu.lt, saragosa21@gmail.com
[2] Vilnius Gediminas Technical University, Vilnius, Lithuania
jevgenij.kurilov@vgtu.lt
[3] Vilnius University Faculty of Mathematics and Informatics, Vilnius, Lithuania
tomas.andruskevic@mif.vu.lt

Abstract. The paper aims to present a novel probabilistic method to creating personalised learning packages. The method is based on learning components' suitability to students needs according to their learning styles. In the paper, the authors use Felder-Silverman Learning Styles Model and an example of Inquiry Based Learning (IBL) method. Expert evaluation method based on trapezoidal fuzzy numbers is applied in the research to obtain numerical values of suitability of learning styles and learning activities. Personalised learning packages should consist of learning components (learning objects, learning activities and learning environments) that are optimal (i.e. the most suitable) to particular students according to their learning styles. "Optimal" means "having the highest suitability index". Original probabilistic method is applied to establish not only students' learning styles but also probabilistic suitability of learning activities to students' learning styles. An example of personalised learning package using IBL activities is presented in more detail.

Keywords: Learning styles · Learning packages · Probabilistic method · Suitability index · Expert evaluation

1 Introduction

The aim of the paper is to present a novel probabilistic method to creating personalised learning packages. The method is based on learning components' suitability to students needs according to their learning styles (LS). Expert evaluation method based on application of trapezoidal fuzzy numbers is applied in the paper. Personalised learning packages should consist of smaller learning components (learning objects, learning activities and environments) that should be optimal (i.e. the most suitable) to particular students according to their LS.

The main research question of the paper is whether there is a methodology to create optimal personalised learning packages, and, if so, what should this methodology be based on. The answer is that such methodology should be based on analysis of learning components' suitability indexes to students' personal needs.

G. Dregvaite and R. Damasevicius (Eds.): ICIST 2016, CCIS 639, pp. 479–490, 2016.
DOI: 10.1007/978-3-319-46254-7_38

Suitability Index presented in the paper is the main value used to establish the preference list of learning components according to their suitability level to students' LS. It is based on probabilistic model of students' LS and ratings (values) of learning components' suitability to particular students according to their LS.

The rest of the paper is organised as follows: related research is presented in the following Section, research methodology is presented in Sect. 3, Sect. 4 presents research results, and Sect. 5 concludes the paper.

2   Related Research

2.1   Learning Personalisation

Learning personalisation became very popular topic in scientific literature during the last years [2, 6, 14, 21, 25, 26, 36, 38, 39]. Research topic on creating full learning packages (units) and smaller learning components that should be optimal (i.e. the most suitable) to particular students based on expert evaluation techniques has also become highly demanded, and there are some relevant methods and techniques proposed in the area [19, 20, 27, 37].

The overview of literature shows that there has not been a concrete definition of personalisation so far. The main idea is to reach an abstract common goal: to provide users with what they want or need without expecting them to ask for it explicitly [29]. From the educational point of view, personalisation attempts to provide for an individual tailored products, services, information, etc. A more technical standpoint to personalisation is linked with the modelling of Web objects (products and pages) and subjects (users), their categorisation, organising them to achieve the desired personalisation. According to Sampson [31], personalisation provides training programmes that are customised to individual learners, based on an analysis of the learners' objectives, current status of skills/knowledge, LS preferences, as well as constant monitoring of progress. The concept of personalised learning becomes increasingly popular. It advocates that instruction should not be restricted by time, place or any other barriers, and should be tailored to the continuously modified individual learner's requirements, abilities, preferences, background knowledge, interests, skills, etc. The personalised learning concept signifies a radical departure in educational theory and technology, from "traditional" interactive learning environments to personalised learning environments.

According to [32], some of the most prominent characteristics of this shift can be summarised as follows: (1) while "traditional" learning environments adopt the one-to-many learning mode, personalised learning environments are based on the one-to-one or many-to-one learning concept (i.e. one, or many tutors for one learner); (2) traditional learning environments usually pose a number of constraints in relation to the learning setting; personalised learning environments, on the other hand, facilitate learning independent of time, location etc.; (3) traditional learning environments are usually being designed for the "average learner"; while, in personalised learning environments, the learning material and sequencing, learning style, learning media etc., depend on the individual learner's characteristics, i.e. background, interests, skills, preferences etc.; (4) in traditional learning environments, the curriculum, learning units etc., are determined by the tutor, while in personalised learning settings, they are based on the learner's requirements (self-directed learning).

2.2 The Educational Perspective

According to [34], the concept of personalised learning builds mainly on the cognitive and constructivist theories of learning. Instructional principles of cognitive theories argue for active involvement by learners, emphasis on the structure and organisation of knowledge, and linking new knowledge to learner's prior cognitive structures. Constructivist instructional theory, on the other hand, implies that instructional designers determine which instructional methods and strategies will help learners to actively explore topics and advance their thinking. Learners are encouraged to develop their own understanding of knowledge [22].

Several research efforts have been devoted in the identification of the dimensions of individual differences. One of the most prominent research areas in this context concerns the learning styles and learning differences theory, which implies that how much individuals learn has more to do with whether the educational experience is geared towards their particular style of learning. LS are strategies, or regular mental behaviours, habitually applied by an individual to learning, particularly deliberate educational learning, and built on her/his underlying potentials. Learners are different from each other, and teaching should respond by creating different instruction for different kinds of learning. Learners also differ from each other in more subject-specific aptitudes of learning, e.g. some being better at verbal than numerical things, others vice versa [22].

There are numerous methodologies and tools that attempt to categorise learners according to differences in learning and cognitive styles. The most well-known of these efforts include Felder and Silverman LS Model [7]; Multiple Intelligences [8]; Grasha-Riechmann Student LS Scales [9]; Honey & Mumford LS [10]; the Myers-Briggs Type Indicator [15]; Kolb LS Theory [16]; and Auditory, Visual, Tactile/Kinaesthetic LS [33]. According to [32], in order for these methodologies and tools to be effectively applied, we need to be able to (1) accurately classify each learner according to a selected taxonomy of individual differences, and (2) determine which are the characteristics of the learning environment that are appropriate for this category of learners.

2.3 The Technological Perspective

Several notions are used to define personalised virtual learning environments.

According to [32], intelligent learning environments are capable of automatically adapting to the individual learner, and therefore constitute the most promising technological approach towards the realisation of the personalised learning concept. An intelligent learning environment is capable of automatically, dynamically, and continuously adapting to the learning context, which is defined by the learner characteristics, the type of educational material being exchanged etc.

According to [3], Adaptive Educational Hypermedia is a relatively new direction of research within the area of adaptive and user model-based educational applications

Adaptive Educational Hypermedia systems build a model of the individual user/learner, and apply it for adaptation to that user.

There are several works performed in the area. They are presented in [22], e.g. research on Intelligent Adaptive Learning Environments, on adaptivity features to a regular learning management system to support creation of advanced eLessons, and on diagnosing students' LS in an educational hypermedia system.

2.4 Application of Expert Evaluation Techniques in Education

With the aim of developing an evaluation method to evaluate creative products in science and technology class, Lu et al. [28] study constructed a set of criteria with data collected from teachers and students. The analytic hierarchy process (AHP), a multiple criteria decision-making tool for single rater, was selected for the purpose of weighting and evaluating students' products. However, the traditional AHP used one rater's pair-wise comparisons; its subjectivity and complexity limit its applications in school. For solving this problem, the [28] study developed an advanced technique, called direct-rating AHP (DR-AHP), to extend the applicability of the traditional AHP. The DR-AHP is used to obtain weights or preferences for criteria/alternatives by a process of directly ranking criteria/alternatives by single/multi rater(s), checking consistency, and developing a rank vector matrix.

Renzulli and Gaesser [30] consider that research over the past several decades supports an expanded system for gifted student identification. Most researchers and practitioners agree that isolated IQ or achievement score is no longer enough. In [27], the authors discuss the critical issue of having a cohesive relationship between the identification process and education programming for high ability students. The authors claim that conception or definition issue should be consistent with the types of services for which students are being identified.

In Wu et al. [40] study, the multiple criteria decision-making approach was adopted to construct an objective and effective analytical model of critical factors influencing college students' creativity. The fuzzy Delphi method was first employed to screen the critical influential factors (criteria/sub-criteria) categorised by four dimensions: "Individual qualities", "Family background", "School element", and "Community", which are synthesised from the literature review and in consultation with experts from relevant fields in Taiwan. Then, the fuzzy analytic hierarchy process (FAHP) method was applied in [40] to calculate the relative weights of the selected critical criteria/sub-criteria that impact creativity for college students.

In this paper, a novel research methodology is proposed to personalise learning.

3   Research Methodology

According to [22], learning software and all learning process should be personalised according to the main characteristics/needs of the learners. Learners have different needs and characteristics i.e. prior knowledge, intellectual level, interests, goals, cognitive traits (working memory capacity, inductive reasoning ability, and associative learning skills), learning behavioural type (according to his/her self-regulation level), and, finally, learning styles.

According to [24], future high-quality and effective education means personalisation plus intelligence. Learning personalisation means creating and implementing personalised learning packages (units) based on recommender system suitable for particular learners according to their personal needs. Educational intelligence means application of intelligent (smart) technologies and methods enabling personalised learning to improve learning quality and efficiency.

According to [13], (a) pedagogical change is necessary to improve learning outcomes for students, and (b) the main success factors in implementing personalised learning packages are: (1) identification of students' LS; (2) identification and application of suitable learning activities, methods, learning objects, tools and apps according to students' LS; and (3) use of proper sets and sequences of learning methods while implementing learning packages.

In personalised learning, first of all, integrated learner profile/model should be implemented, based on e.g. Felder & Silverman Learning Styles Model (FSLSM) [7]. Dedicated psychological questionnaires (e.g. Soloman and Felder's Index of LS questionnaire [35]) should be applied here. After that, one should integrate the rest features in the learner profile (knowledge, interests, goals, cognitive traits, learning behavioural type etc.). After that, ontologies-based personalised recommender system should be created to suggest learning components (learning objects, activities and methods, environments, tools, apps etc.) suitable to particular learners according to their profiles [22, 24].

Thus, personalised learning packages could be created for particular learners. A number of intelligent (smart) technologies should be applied to implement this approach, e.g. ontologies, recommender systems, intelligent agents, decision support systems to evaluate quality and suitability of the learning components, personal learning environments etc. [24].

In order to propose psychologically, pedagogically, mathematically, and technologically sound methodology to creating and evaluating the whole personalised learning package, several approaches, concepts and methods are applied in the paper as follows. They are: (1) the concept of learning package/unit developed in [17, 18]; (2) learning personalisation method based on application of intelligent technologies [24]; (3) a stochastic approach for automatic and dynamic modelling of students' learning styles proposed in [4]; (4) personalised learning objects' recommendation method [5, 22], and (5) personalised learning activities recommendation method based on expert evaluation techniques proposed in [12].

4   Research Results

4.1   Probabilistic Model of Learning Styles

According to [17], learning activities (LAs) are one of the core structural elements of the 'learning workflow' model for learning design. They form the link between the roles and the learning objects (LOs) and services in the learning environment. The activities describe a role they have to undertake within a specified environment composed of LOs and services. Activities take place in a so-called 'environment', which is a structured collection of LOs, services, and sub-environments. LO is referred here as any digital resource that can be reused to support learning [17]. Virtual Learning Environment (VLE) is referred here as a single piece of software, accessed via standard Web browser, which provides an integrated online learning environment [17]. Therefore, we can conclude that learning package (unit) could consist of LAs, LOs and learning environment referred here as services package. This kind of services package in e-learning theory is commonly known as VLE. Thus, we can divide the whole learning package/unit into three components, namely LAs, LOs and VLE [17].

Kurilovas and Zilnskiene [17, 18] argue that, from technological point of view, one can divide the learning software (in our case LOs, LAs and VLE) quality criteria into 'internal quality' and 'quality in use' criteria. 'Internal quality' is a descriptive characteristic that describes the quality of software independently from any particular context of its use, while 'quality in use' is evaluative characteristic of software obtained by making a judgment based on the criteria that determine the worthiness of software for a particular project or user [18].

LOs and VLE quality criteria (incl. personalisation) and evaluation methods are quite widely analysed in scientific literature [5, 20, 23]. Conversely, LA quality criteria and personalisation features are analysed insufficiently.

In this paper, Felder-Silverman LS Model (FSLSM) [7] is applied to create and evaluate personalised LS. FSLSM is known as the most suitable for engineering education and e-learning. FSLSM classifies students according to where they fit on 4 scales pertaining to the ways they receive and process information (dimensions) as follows:

- By Information type: Sensory (SEN) vs Intuitive (INT);
- By Sensory channel: Visual (VIS) vs Verbal (VER);
- By Information processing: Active (ACT) vs Reflective (REF), and
- By Understanding: Sequential (SEQ) vs Global (GLO).

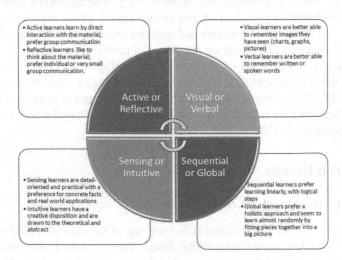

Fig. 1. FSLSM dimensions.

Probabilistic model of learning styles according to FSLSM is presented in [4]. It is based on the results of filling in Soloman and Felder Index of LS questionnaire [35] by students. Every student should fill in this questionnaire consisting of 44 questions, 11 questions for each of 4 aforementioned FSLSM dimensions (i.e. ways the students receive and process information). Students' preferences are considered as probabilities in the four-dimensional FSLSM (Fig. 1).

Due to the probabilistic nature of LS in the FSLSM, Dorca et al. [4] approach is based on probabilistic LS combinations. Each LS combination is a 4-tuple composed by one preference from each FSLSM dimension. Students' probable LS are stored in student profile/model as values of the interval [0,1]. Those values represent probabilities of preference in each of FSLSM dimension. Therefore, students' LS are stored as probability distributions considering each FSLSM learning dimension. Considering this kind of model, students' LS are stored in their profiles/models according to Definition 1:

Definition 1: $LS = \{(PR_{SEN} = x; PR_{INT} = 1 - x), (PR_{VIS} = y; PR_{VER} = 1 - y), (PR_{ACT} = z; PR_{REF} = 1 - z), (PR_{SEQ} = v, PR_{GLO} = 1 - v)\}$, where

PR_{SEN} is the probability of the student's preference for the Sensory LS; PR_{INT} is the probability of the student's preference for the Intuitive LS;
PR_{VIS} is the probability of the student's preference for the Visual LS; PR_{VER} is the probability of the student's preference for the Verbal LS;
PR_{ACT} is the probability of the student's preference for the Active LS; PR_{REF} is the probability of the student's preference for the Reflective LS; and
PR_{SEQ} is the probability of the student's preference for the Sequential LS; and PR_{GLO} is the probability of the student's preference for the Global LS.
Consequently, $PR_{SEN} + PR_{INT} = 1$; $PR_{VIS} + PR_{VER} = 1$; $PR_{ACT} + PR_{REF} = 1$; $PR_{SEQ} + PR_{GLO} = 1$. Calculations of probabilities should be done according to Formula 1:

$$PR_i = \frac{A_i}{11} \tag{1}$$

The Formula (1) divides by 11 the number of favourable answers to LS (A_i), considering that Index of LS [35] has 11 questions for each FSLSM dimension, totalling 44 questions. In (1), i represent a LS in FSLSM dimension, and A_i represent the number of favourable answers to a LS. PR_i is a probability of preference to a LS by the student in a FSLSM dimension, according to aforementioned Definition 1.

An example would be if a student answers 7 questions favourable to the Sensory LS, and 4 questions favourable to the Intuitive LS: $PR_{SEN} = 7 / 11 = 0.64$, and $PRI_{INT} = 4/11 = 0.36$, and further on to all dimensions of FSLSM. Thus, one could obtain e.g. the following LS initially stored in his/her student profile/model:

Table 1. Example of LS initially stored in the student profile/model.

Learning styles							
By Information type		By Sensory channel		By Information processing		By Understanding	
SEN	INT	VIS	VER	ACT	REF	SEQ	GLO
0.64	0.36	0.82	0.18	0.73	0.27	0.45	0.55

4.2 Learning Activities and Learning Styles Suitability Index

Since the aim of the paper is not only to present probabilistic model to establish students' LS but also to create probabilistic method to obtain suitability of learning components of the learning packages to particular students' according their LS, Inquiry-Based Learning (IBL) activity is used as an example.

IBL activity and sub-activities are presented in [12] based on [1]. According to [1, 12], IBL activity consists of a number of sub-activities as follows: A1: Orienting and asking questions; A2: Hypothesis generation; A3: Planning; A4: Investigation; A5: Analysis and interpretation; A6: Model exploration and creation; A7: Conclusion and evaluation; A8: Communication and justifying; A9: Prediction; and A10: Discover relationships.

According to [12] research methodology, in order to interrelate FSLSM and IBL activities, a special questionnaire was created for Lithuanian teachers-experts in the area. The questionnaire was created using FSLSM [7] and IBL activities and sub-activities vocabulary according to [1]. The experts have been asked to fill in the questionnaire in terms of establishing suitability of proposed IBL activities and sub-activities to students' LS according to FSLSM. The level of suitability have been proposed to express in linguistic variables 'bad', 'poor', 'fair', 'good' and 'excellent'. After teachers experts had filled in the questionnaire, the authors have mapped linguistic variables into non-fuzzy values using trapezoidal fuzzy numbers as presented in [19]. In [12], the Table of suitability of IBL activities and sub-activities to FSLSM is presented. IBL activities are divided into sub-activities, and all those sub-activities are evaluated by the experts in terms of their suitability to students' LS. Expert evaluation method is applied here. Suitability ratings obtained in [12] mean the aggregated level of suitability of particular IBL sub-activities to particular learning style.

If one should multiply these suitability ratings by probabilities of particular students' LS according to Table 1, he/she should obtain probabilistic ratings/values of suitability of particular IBL sub-activities to particular student's (i.e. Active) LS according to Formula 2:

$$PRV_{ACT} = PR_{ACT} * V_{ACT} \qquad (2)$$

This Formula should be applied for each IBL sub-activity analysed in [12], where PRV_{ACT} means probabilistic value (level) of suitability of particular IBL sub-activity to particular student according to his/her preference to Activist LS, PR_{ACT} means probabilistic value of the student's preference to Activist LS (e.g. 0.73 according to Table 1), and V_{ACT} means the value of suitability of particular IBL sub-activity to Activist LS (according to [12]).

Accordingly, one could calculate all probabilistic values (PRVs) of suitability of all IBL sub-activities to all students according whose data is stored in the student profile/model. In all cases, one should obtain PRVs as values of the interval [0,1].

Thus, according to Formula (2),

$PRV_{ACT} = 0.73 * 0.86 = 0.63$ for IBL sub-activity A1.1 (Observe phenomena), $PRV_{GLO} = 0.55 * 0.79 = 0.43$ for IBL sub-activity A2.1 (Select and complete hypotheses), $PRV_{VIS} = 0.82 * 0.88 = 0.72$ for IBL sub-activity A3.2 (Equipment and actions), $PRV_{INT} = 0.36 * 0.86 = 0.31$ for IBL sub-activity A4.1 (Explore) etc.

The higher PRV the higher is the student's preference to particular IBL sub-activity, and vice versa.

Accordingly, PRVs mean the indexes of particular learning component's suitability to particular student. These Suitability Indexes should be included in the recommender system, and all learning components should be linked to particular students according to those Suitability Indexes. The higher Suitability Index the better the learning component fits particular student's needs.

Thus, optimal learning package (i.e. learning package of the highest quality) for particular student means a methodological sequence of learning components (LAs, LOs to be learnt and VLE) having the highest Suitability Indexes. The level of students' competences, i.e. knowledge/understanding, skills and attitudes/values directly depends on the level of application of optimal learning packages in real pedagogical practice.

Thus, in order to create a probabilistic model for a whole personalised learning package consisting of suitable learning components optimal to particular students according to their profiles, one should apply Formula 1, appropriate Table 1, and Formula 2 for all aforementioned components of the learning packages.

Thus, pedagogically and technologically sound vocabularies/standards for learning components, such as IEEE LOM [11] for LOs and [1] for LAs such as IBL or Problem-Based Learning [22] should be prepared and stored in the recommender system. Furthermore, collective intelligence of experts and students (see e.g. top-down vs bottom-up evaluation approach [20]) should be used to evaluate suitability of learning components to particular learner needs [12].

Finally, evaluation of created learning packages should be performed by applying multiple criteria decision making methods as proposed e.g. in [17, 18, 20].

5 Conclusion

Future high-quality and effective education means personalisation plus intelligence. Learning personalisation means creating and implementing personalised learning packages based on recommender system suitable for particular learners according to their personal needs. Educational intelligence means application of intelligent (smart) technologies and methods enabling personalised learning to improve learning quality and efficiency. In personalised learning, first of all, integrated learner profile/model should be implemented. After that, ontologies-based personalised recommender system should be created to suggest learning components suitable to particular learners according to their profiles. Thus, personalised learning packages could be created for particular learners according to their profiles. A number of intelligent (smart) technologies should be applied to implement this approach, e.g. ontologies, recommender systems, intelligent agents, expert evaluation techniques etc.

In the paper, probabilistic method to create the whole personalised learning packages consisting of suitable learning components optimal to particular students according to their learning styles is proposed. The method is based on students' probabilistic learning styles and expert evaluation of suitability of different learning components to students' learning styles. Thus, the indexes of particular learning component's suitability to particular students could be calculated. The main limitation of the paper is that the only example of the learning components, i.e. inquiry-based learning activities, was analysed in terms of its suitability to learners.

All learning components in the recommender system should be linked to particular students according to their Suitability Indexes. The higher Suitability Index the better the learning component fits particular student's needs. The optimal learning package (i.e. learning package of the highest quality) for particular student means a methodological sequence of learning components with the highest Suitability Indexes. The level of students' competences, i.e. knowledge/understanding, skills and attitudes/values directly depends on the level of application of optimal learning packages in real pedagogical practice.

For this purpose, pedagogically and technologically sound vocabularies of learning components should be created and stored in the recommender system. Furthermore, collective intelligence of experts and students should be used to evaluate suitability of learning components to particular learner needs.

References

1. Bell, T., Urhahne, D., Schanze, S., Ploetzner, R.: Collaborative inquiry learning: models, tools and challenges. Int. J. Sci. Educ. **32**(3), 349–377 (2010)
2. Bobed, C., Bobillo, F., Ilarri, S., Mena, E.: Answering continuous description logic queries: managing static and volatile knowledge in ontologies. Int. J. Seman. Web Inf. Syst. **10**(3), 1–44 (2014)
3. Brusilovsky, P., Eklund, J., Schwarz, E.: Web-based education for all: a tool for development adaptive courseware. Comput. Netw. ISDN Syst. **30**(1–7), 291–300 (1998)
4. Dorca, F.A., Lima, L.V., Fernandes, M.A., Lopes, C.R.: A stochastic approach for automatic and dynamic modeling of students' learning styles in adaptive educational systems. Inf. Educ. **11**(2), 191–212 (2012)
5. Dorca, F.A., Araujo, R.D., de Carvalho, V.C., Resende, D.T., Cattelan, R.G.: An automatic and dynamic approach for personalized recommendation of learning objects considering students learning styles: an experimental analysis. Inf. Educ. **15**(1), 45–62 (2016)
6. Ermilov, T., Khalili, A., Auer, S.: Ubiquitous semantic applications: a systematic literature review. Int. J. Seman. Web Inf. Syst. **10**(1), 66–99 (2014)
7. Felder, R.M., Silverman, L.K.: learning and teaching styles in engineering education. Eng. Educ. **78**(7), 674–681 (1988)
8. Gardner, H.: Intelligence Reframed: Multiple Intelligences for the 21st Century, Basic Books (1999)
9. Grasha, A.: Teaching with Style. Alliance Publishers (1996)
10. Honey, P., Mumford, A.: The learning Styles Helper's Guide. Peter Honey Publications Ltd., Maidenhead (2000)
11. IEEE LOM (Learning Object Metadata). IEEE Learning Technology Standards Committee. http://ltsc.ieee.org/wg12/index.html

12. Jasute, E., Kubilinskiene, S., Juskeviciene, A., Kurilovas, E.: Personalised learning methods and activities for computer engineering education. Int. J. Eng. Educ. **32**(3), 1078–1086 (2016)
13. Juskeviciene, A., Jasute, E., Kurilovas, E., Mamcenko, J.: Application of 1:1 mobile learning scenarios in computer engineering education. Int. J. Eng. Educ. **32**(3), 1087–1096 (2016)
14. Juškevičienė, A., Kurilovas, E.: On recommending web 2.0 tools to personalise learning. Inf. Educ. **13**(1), 17–30 (2014)
15. Keirsey, D.: Please Understand Me II: Temperament Character Intelligence. Prometheus Nemesis Books (1998)
16. Kolb, D.A.: LSI Learning- Style Inventory, McBer & Company (1985)
17. Kurilovas, E., Zilinskiene, I.: Evaluation of quality of personalised learning scenarios: an improved MCEQLS AHP method. Int. J. Eng. Educ. **28**(6), 1309–1315 (2012)
18. Kurilovas, E., Zilinskiene, I.: New MCEQLS AHP method for evaluating quality of learning scenarios. Technol. Econ. Dev. Econ. **19**(1), 78–92 (2013)
19. Kurilovas, E., Serikoviene, S.: New MCEQLS TFN method for evaluating quality and reusability of learning objects. Technol. Econ. Dev. Econ. **19**(4), 706–723 (2013)
20. Kurilovas, E., Serikoviene, S., Vuorikari, R.: Expert centred vs learner centred approach for evaluating quality and reusability of learning objects. Comput. Hum. Behav. **30**, 526–534 (2014)
21. Kurilovas, E., Zilinskiene, I., Dagiene, V.: Recommending suitable learning scenarios according to learners' preferences: an improved swarm based approach. Comput. Hum. Behav. **30**, 550–557 (2014)
22. Kurilovas, E., Kubilinskiene, S., Dagiene, V.: Web 3.0 – based personalisation of learning objects in virtual learning environments. Comput. Hum. Behav. **30**, 654–662 (2014)
23. Kurilovas, E., Juskeviciene, A., Kubilinskiene, S., Serikoviene, S.: Several semantic web approaches to improving the adaptation quality of virtual learning environments. J. Univers. Comput. Sci. **20**(10), 1418–1432 (2014)
24. Kurilovas, E.: Application of intelligent technologies in computer engineering education. keynote paper. In: Proceedings of IFIP WC3 Working Conference "A New Culture of Learning: Computing and Next Generations". Vilnius, Lithuania, 1–3 July, 2015, pp. 15–26 (2015)
25. Kurilovas, E., Zilinskiene, I., Dagiene, V.: Recommending suitable learning paths according to learners' preferences: experimental research results. Comput. Hum. Behav. **51**, 945–951 (2015)
26. Kurilovas, E., Juskeviciene, A.: Creation of web 2.0 tools ontology to improve learning. Comput. Hum. Behav. **51**, 1380–1386 (2015)
27. Kurilovas, E., Vinogradova, I., Kubilinskiene, S.: New MCEQLS Fuzzy AHP methodology for evaluating learning repositories: a tool for technological development of economy. Technol. Econ. Dev. Econ. **22**(1), 142–155 (2016)
28. Lu, Y.L., Lian, I.B., Lien, C.J.: The application of the analytic hierarchy process for evaluating creative products in science class and its modification for educational evaluation. Int. J. Sci. Math. Educ. **13**(2), S413–S435 (2015)
29. Mulvenna, M.D., Anand, S.S., Buchner, A.G.: Personalization on the Net using Web Mining: Introduction. Commun. ACM **43**(8), 122–125 (2000)
30. Renzulli, J.S., Gaesser, A.H.: A multi criteria system for the identification of high achieving and creative/productive giftedness. Rev. de Educ. **368**, 96–131 (2015)
31. Sampson, D.: Current and future research and technology developments in e-Learning. Ind. High. Educ. J. **16**(4), (2002)
32. Sampson, D., Karagiannidis, C.: Kinshuk: personalised learning: educational, technological and standardisation perspective. Interact. Educ. Multimedia **4**, 24–39 (2002)

33. Sarasin, L.: Learning Style Perspectives: Impact in the Classroom. Atwood Publishing, Madison (1998)
34. Schunk, D.: Learning Theories: An Educational Perspective. Prentice Hall, Englewood Cliffs (1996)
35. Soloman, B.A., Felder, R.M.: Index of Learning Styles Questionnaire. http://www.engr. ncsu.edu/learningstyles/ilsweb.html
36. Spodniakova Pfefferova, M.: Computer simulations and their influence on students' understanding of oscillatory motion. informatics in. Education **14**(2), 279–289 (2015)
37. Spruit, M.R., Adriana, T.: quantifying education quality in secondary schools. Int. J. Knowl. Soc. Res. **6**(1), 55–86 (2015)
38. Troussas, C., Virvou, M., Alepis, E.: Collaborative learning: group interaction in an intelligent mobile-assessed multiple language learning system. Inf. Educ. **13**(2), 279–292 (2014)
39. Wallden, S., Makinen, E.: Educational data mining and problem-based learning. Inf. Educ. **13**(1), 141–156 (2014)
40. Wu, H.Y., Wu, H.S., Chen, I.S., Chen, H.C.: Exploring the critical influential factors of creativity for college students: a multiple criteria decision-making approach. Thinking Skills Creativity **11**, 1–21 (2014)

Technological Challenges for Learning Objects in MOOCs Design

Daina Gudonienė[1](✉), Rūta Dapkūnaitė[1], Danguolė Rutkauskienė[1],
Vytautas Štuikys[1], and Svitlana Kalashnikova[2]

[1] Kaunas University of Technology, Studentu Str. 50, 51392 Kaunas, Lithuania
{daina.gudoniene, ruta.dapkunaite,
danguole.rutkauskiene}@ktu.lt
[2] National Academy of Pedagogical Sciences of Ukraine,
Artema 52-D, Kyiv 04053, Ukraine
svit.ukr@ukr.net

Abstract. The paper presents discussion on the technological challenges for learning objects (LO) and massive open online courses (MOOCs) design. Research results will suggest to educators the model for modernization or design new educational content by using ICT tools and environments. New approach will be suggested for different LO design online in the learning objects repository, which one is developed for LO exchange, sharing and assuring reusability function of the educational content.

Keywords: Learning objects · MOOCs · Technological model · Original learning objects · Personal library

1 Introduction

Openness is one of the main aspects in education. Open Educational Resources (OER) are teaching, learning, and research resources that reside in the public domain or been released under copyright, that permits their free use and reusability. Open educational resources include full courses, course materials, modules, textbooks, streaming videos, tests, software, and any other tools, materials, or techniques used to support access to knowledge.

Open Educational Resources (OER) are important learning materials with the potential to facilitate the expansion of learning worldwide. The flexibility, both technological and legal, afforded by openly licensed content is an important precondition for supporting the educational use of content. Open standards support the deployment of learning objects as OER on a wide variety of different devices.

The problem still available that there are no repository for LO design, uploading, and the OER distributed in a big number of data basis. There is a request from academic community to have different LO in one data basis or semantically chosen and connected with the newly designed Lo any etc. content.

The research will introduce to academic community new ways of education, new model for OER, MOOCs etc. online courses improvement semantically by already

© Springer International Publishing Switzerland 2016
G. Dregvaite and R. Damasevicius (Eds.): ICIST 2016, CCIS 639, pp. 491–498, 2016.
DOI: 10.1007/978-3-319-46254-7_39

existing OER in the different world repositories. The paper presents research methodology, overview on the related works, learning objects design model for MOOCs and the experimental results.

2 Research Methodology

The conducted literature analysis enable to formulate the conception and to predict the guidance for implementation of MOOC technological model (TM) in accordance with the project's tasks and requirements. At the provisional stage, the formulated problems in the outcome of analysis are analysed and adjusted, i.e. the selection of course and MOOC platform; localization and personalization of the course; adaptation of the course and self-adaptation; material visualisation; feedback planning; evaluation and self-value; pedagogical and technological support to all previously listed problems solving.

MOOC technological model (TM) proposed in this study is based on the visualisation and variability of educational content. Such a model have to be based not only on content variations, that the student could choose the material for his/her self-adaptation, but also on learning in the field of variability.

The assumptions are starting circumstance of the research. The key assumptions are:

1. Pedagogical aspects of MOOC paradigm; the scenarios are formulated and described.
2. MOOC technological platform, which consists of learning environment, is already selected.
3. Technological facility of the platform is known.
4. MOOC course is selected. It consists of a set of open-access learning objects (LO). LO - is an educational content or any learning objects of low or medium granulated degree.
5. The profile of consumers is defined.

With the assumptions, researchers started analysing already existing data to find out the ways for the implementation of the research based on new technological challenges.

3 Related Works

The term Massive Open Online Course (MOOC) was used in 2008 by Dave Cormier to describe a course 'Constructivism and Connective Knowledge' run by George Siemens and Stephen Downes (Cormier 2008). Massive Open Online Courses (MOOCs) are free and open to the general public (Elizabeth L. Burd & Shamus P. Smith & Sorel Reisman 2014). As Conole (2015) marked, MOOCs have expanded significally in recent years and are challenging traditional educational free-paying offerings. Recently, MOOCs reached a new milestone for enrollment in a single run. FutureLearn's course Understanding IELTS: Techniques for English Language Tests launched in May, 2015 with over 400,000 learners from over 150 countries (Nazeeri F., Moore J., Benjamin N. 2015).

As Burd, et al. (2014) emphasized, MOOCs are online educational materials delivered via an electronic medium and offered freely and openly to learners, in other words - MOOC is an online educational resource aimed at largescale interactive participation via the Internet. What is more, MOOCs are available and open to anyone, hence potentially appealing to massive numbers of students and they are often typically under open access agreements and commonly have no application process. As Conole (2015) noticed MOOCs provide an alternative to campus-based courses, and emphasise the power of harnessing a global, distributed community of peers for learning.

However, it is also clear that many different kinds of course are labelled as MOOCs. An early distinction was made on the basis of pedagogy (JON ROSEWELL; Darco Jansen, 2014). Siemens (2012) used the terms cMOOC and xMOOC to contrast two forms of pedagogy. Siemens (2012) labelled the early courses, rooted in principles of connectivist learning that emphasise creation, creativity, autonomy and social networked learning, as cMOOCs. In cMOOCc participants collaborate on join projects, acting as both teachers and students (Bell 2012; Kizilcec et al. 2013). Siemens (2012) have suggested that the courses that had begun to appear on platforms such as Coursera and edX were based on a transmission model of teaching and learning would be called xMOOCs. In xMOOCs students are more passive like in large, lecture-based courses (Alraimi et al. 2015; Baturay 2015).

As Rosewel and Jansen (2014) remarked, questions about the quality of the MOOC experience were beginning to be widely asked in 2013. The concern over quality in MOOCs was coupled with a concern over high drop-out rates. As Rosewel. J. and Jansen D. (2014) stressed, MOOCs may attract participants with widely different cultures, motives and intentions, and the expectations and behaviour of MOOC students may therefore be quite different to fee-paying students studying for qualifications. It may be that some students are achieving their goals by simply 'browsing' in a MOOC without participating in assessments (Koller et al. 2013). Clow (2013) suggests that, although MOOCs are structured as non-formal courses, they are no more successful at engaging students than are informal learning communities (Rosewel. J. and Jansen D. 2014). What is more, Rosewel and Jansen (2014) stressed that MOOCs are usually branded by an Higher Education institution, and so the institution takes on a reputational risk unless quality is maintained. MOOCs are authored and taught by Higher Education staff. Material is often derived from existing credit-bearing courses, or is positioned as providing an access route to credit-bearing curriculum.

As mentioned above, MOOC technological model is based on the visualisation and variability of educational content, in general - learning object (LO) or objects. Learning object (LO) is one of the main courses elements. Mostly the definitions of learning objects, regard Lori Lockyer, et al. (2009), focus on flexibility, independence and reusability of content to offer a high degree of control to both, instructors and students. Different LO could be used from different national and international repositories. Some essential kind of LO in the picture below (Fig. 1).

The learning content or courses designed or redesigned from already existing LO or OER could be used many times and will assure the reusability and wide world access.

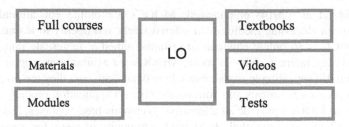

Fig. 1. LO for educational content.

4   LO Design Model for MOOCs

Conole (2015) has stressed that designing for learning is arguably one of the key challenges facing education today. Learning Design aims to help bridge the gap and guide teachers in the design practice and to help teachers think beyond content to the activities learners will engage with and the learner experience. Conole (2015) noticed, that digital technologies offer a plethora of ways in which learners can interact with rich multimedia resources and ways in which they can communicate and collaborate with peers.

The researchers are working on the model for learning objects design where learning objects model has ontology for learning material, test activity, metadata, copyrights information, relation to similar material. It is important to emphasize that there are several assumptions while creating new model, i.e. pedagogical aspects and scenarios of MOOC paradigm are already formulated and described, MOOC technological platform, which consists of learning environment, is chosen, technological options of the platform are known, MOOC course is chosen.

To begin with, the main requirements of technological model (TM): the model has to meet re-use requirements, Model has to describe LO structure and functionality, that it would fit for any LO (given from a set); Model has to meet the conditions of integrity and composition; Model should be based on and support the concept of variance for both the process – visualisation of LO, presentation and management; Model has to describe the structure of the LO, that it would not contradict would not create difficulties in the implementation of key attributes of MOOC paradigm (individuality of learning, communication and discussion, self-control, etc.); the integration process of Model in the infrastructure of MOOC should not be complicated.

The model in technological way has to support the conditions of process management, like reading, visualising, changing, commenting, feedback, transferring to the internal structure of MOOC platform, also it should has technological conditions for the external communication. The model has to ensure the technical realization of the above mentioned tasks, his integration and realization have to be supported by the accessible tools. The model has to be verified by inspecting at least few variations.

The purpose – to adapt an available platform of MOOC and its installed course for individual learning, i.e. to create an individualized learning environment. Such environments consist of:

(1) Personal library (PL) with the original learning objects (OLO) and adapted ALO;
(2) Tools that support adaptation;
(3) Tools that support PL.

In the simplest case, personal library (PL) could be a catalogue with few file levels that would be supported by standard OS tools. What is the difference between OLO and ALO? The main assumption is that the OLO could hardly meet the individual requirements of student. For instant, OLO is prepared in foreign language, while the student learns in his/her native language. Or maybe the structural level (granulation) is too low or high in the given OLO and the student would like to change it. So it is unlikely that OLO would be projected in the way that would meet individual requirements of the student. Consequently, OLO structural complement and modification, without changing the main functionality of OLO, is predicted.

In general, the basis of suggested TM is made of the student's personal library (PL) with adaptive LO (ALO) for the MOOC course. The technological model should be interpreted in such a way, that it would satisfy a wide spectrum of users.

5   Experimental Results

To realize this method the additional instrument was required - an external language for adoptable content to be summarized and specified. Original learning objects (OLO) will be treated as the goal (object-oriented) language. Then an external language, by whose instructions the OLO text is adopted, will be meta-language. As it is not appropriated to keep the specific meta-language, so the basic instructions (functions) of pseudo-code, which will perform meta-language functions, are given below. This action is based on the theoretical and practical provision, that any programming language can be used as meta-language, applying meta-programming paradigm to create the specifications.

The basic constructions are these:

<operation> (ascription":="),
if type alternative and
for (while) type cycle.
General description of pseudo-code:
<operation>::=<left side name>=<right side name>|<phrase>
<if-alternative>::=if <modification condition> then do <modification instructions> end
or
<if-alternative>::=if <modification condition> then do <modification instructions> end
                                            else do <modification instructions> end
<while-cycle>::= while <end of modification condition> do
                                    <modification instructions> end

The example of summarized structure. Please assume, that we do have three options of the same OLO: OLO1, OLO2, OLO3. These listed names are the OLO metadata of learning object, which characterizes the appropriate LO option. According to the metadata, the homogeneous logic equation is generated (automatic visualisation).

$$Y = X1 \wedge X2;$$
$$Y = X1 \vee X2;$$

$$Y = X1 \wedge X2 \wedge X3;$$
$$Y = X1 \vee X2 \vee X3;$$

$$Y = X1 \wedge X2 \wedge X3 \wedge X4$$
$$Y = X1 \vee X2 \vee X3 \vee X4$$

$$Z = X1 \wedge X2;$$
$$Z = X1 \vee X2;$$

$$Z = X1 \wedge X2 \wedge X3;$$
$$Z = X1 \vee X2 \vee X3;$$

$$Z = X1 \wedge X2 \wedge X3 \wedge X4$$
$$Z = X1 \vee X2 \vee X3 \vee X4$$

```php
<?php
//here is interface of SLO
$P1 = V; //PH-High Priority
$P2 = 3; //PI-Intermediate Priority
$P3 = Y; //PL-Low Priority
```

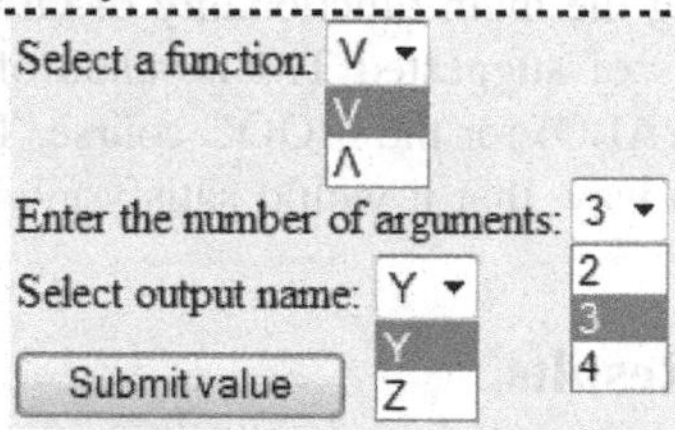

Select a function: V ▾
| V |
| ∧ |

Enter the number of arguments: 3 ▾

Select output name: Y ▾

| 2 |
| 3 |
| 4 |

Submit value

| Y |
| Z |

```php
//here is meta-body (MB) of SLO
echo "$P3 = X"."1";
for($i=2; $i<=$P2; $i++)
echo " $P1 X".$i;
?>
```

Fig. 2. Generative LO to generate the homogeneous logical equation (Stuikys 2010)

Of all possible visualisation options, the equation is automatically generated by the user's selection (see graphical interface menu Fig. 2). PHP processor will generate highlighted homogeneous logical equation. The generator matches the search in the library (if all options would be placed in it).

The generalized LO specification can describe the visualisation of the content. In that case the specification, combined with meta-language processor, is the generator of specific content.

The generalized LO specification can describe not only the visualisation of the content, but also student's actions with the visualised content. In this case, not only the content is generated, but also the learning is proceeding and the learning assessment is delivered (Fig. 3).

Learning objects design and reusability is very important for any educational content. There are a lot of good quality LO but this is still a problem to find out semantically from the other repositories and to use it for newly designed as an extra material with similar content (Fig. 4).

The developed repository (OER.ndma.lt) gives as a possibility to design the content and to leave it in the open repository for sharing as open educational resource. And this is directly related with the future education.

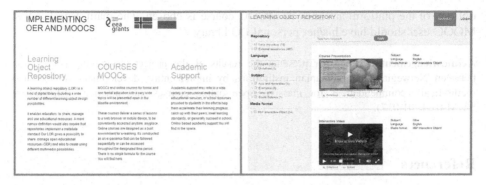

Fig. 3. LO design repository (oer.ndma.lt).

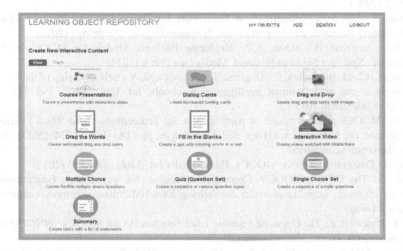

Fig. 4. LO design tools and environment.

6   Conclusions

Learning objects design online by using different templates will help to academic community to save time and to assure the reusability, what is very important for any educational content. There are a lot of good quality LO but this is still a problem to find out semantically from the other repositories and to use it for newly designed as an extra material with similar content.

It is important to know, that to assure the challenges for MOOCs - the interactivity, design LO, engagement, reusability and semantical extra content from existing LO - are needed.

There are several assumptions while creating new model, i.e. pedagogical aspects and scenarios of MOOC paradigm are already formulated and described, MOOC technological platform, which consists of learning environment, is chosen, technological options of the platform are known, MOOC course is chosen. The main aspect is that MOOC user should have his/her personal LO library.

Acknowledgements. The paper presents the results of the project "Promoting cooperation between Norwegian and Lithuanian institutions by implementing development strategy and methodical recommendations for massive open online courses into practice" (EEE-LT08-ŠMM-01-K-01-017).

References

Agostinho, S., Bennett, S., Harper, B., Lockyer, L.: Handbook of Research on Learning Design and Learning Objects: Issues, Applications, and Technologies. Educational IS&T Books, vols. 2 (2009)

Benjamin, N., Moore, J., Nazeeri, F.: A Framework for Online Learning Revenue Models at Universities: Research and Opportunities. ExtensionEngine, Cambridge (2015)

Burd, E.L., Reisman, S., Smith, S.P.: Exploring Business Models for MOOCs in Higher Education. Springer Science+Business Media New York (2014)

Carneiro, A., Child, R., Cullen, C., Dagienė, J., Juškevičienė, V.: Self-assessing of the emotional intelligence and organizational intelligence in schools. Inf. Educ. **14**(2), 199–217 (2015). doi:10.15388/infedu.2015.12

Clow, D.: MOOCs and the funnel of participation. In: Proceedings of the Third International Conference on Learning Analytics and Knowledge, pp. 185–189. ACM (2013). Source: http://oro.open.ac.uk/36657

Conole, G.: Designing effective MOOCs. Educ. Media Int. **52**(4), 239–252 (2015)

Cormier, D.: The CCK08 MOOC – Connectivism course, 1/4 way. Dave's Educational Blog (2008). Source: http://davecormier.com/edblog/2008/10/02/the-cck08-mooc-connectivism-course-14-way/

Darco, J., Rosewell, J.: The OpenupEd quality label: benchmarks for MOOCs. INNOQUAL: Int. J. Innov. Qual. Learn. **2**(3), 88–100 (2014)

Siemens, G.: MOOCs are really a platform. Elearnspace (2012). Source: http://www.elearnspace.org/blog/2012/07/25/moocs-are-really-a-platform/

Štuikys, V.: Smart Learning Objects for Smart Education in Computer Science. Springer, New York (2015)

Affective Engagement to Virtual and Live Lectures

Judita Kasperiuniene[1,2(✉)], Meet Jariwala[1], Egidijus Vaskevicius[1],
and Saulius Satkauskas[1]

[1] Vytautas Magnus University, Kaunas, Lithuania
judita.kasperiuniene@vdu.lt
[2] Aleksandras Stulginskis University, Kaunas, Lithuania

Abstract. Affective engagement to university lectures needs external stimulation. This paper presents an empirical study on student's engagement change to live and virtual lectures with complex, picture, video and human body movement stimuli. Each experiment lasted 30 min and was divided into 5 periods (10-5-5-5-5 min each). At the end of each period different stimuli were exposed: human interrupted the lecture; instructor presented slides; video materials; and intensive body movements. Stimuli and study materials for the live and virtual avatar- based lectures were developed following the same experiment lecture model. Avatar was created and animated with CrazyTalk software. Experimenting group consisted of 10 students, age 20–24, 4 females and 6 males. Changes of attention to lecture materials were measured using triple indicators: affective regulation monitored during all the lecture period with Muse portable headband device; cognitive self-regulation was measured before the lecture using questionnaire technique; behavioral regulation was observed using video recording through the entire lecture period. The highest concentration, attentiveness and active engagement was observed during the avatar-based lecture and complex human stimuli, while in live lecture all the stimuli activated approximately the same response. Image stimuli activated different reactions: in a live lecture it slightly tweaked student attentiveness, while in avatar-based lecture attentiveness was lowered. Reactions to video stimuli in both experimental groups were opposite as for image stimuli. These research results can prompt instructors how to construct training materials and implement additional stimuli grabbing student's attention. We recommend mixing video and live lectures and using stimuli evoking and strengthening active engagements.

Keywords: Affective engagement · Virtual lecture · Biodata collection · MUSE brain-sensing headband · Student attention span

1 Introduction

Affective engagement to lecture challenges university students [1–3]. Correlation between lecture attendance, early revisions of study materials and academic achievements is identified [5]; virtual lectures impact on exam performance researched [4, 10]; using gamification techniques [6], attention to reference materials is raised, online participation and proactivity is stimulated [7, 8]. It is researched that students' attention to the live instructor's, audio and video materials declines after first 10–15 min from the

© Springer International Publishing Switzerland 2016
G. Dregvaite and R. Damasevicius (Eds.): ICIST 2016, CCIS 639, pp. 499–508, 2016.
DOI: 10.1007/978-3-319-46254-7_40

start [11]. The use of various stimuli retrieving students' attention to the lecture materials has achieved much importance in the modern university [12]. Animated avatars of instructor in a virtual learning environment as online manifestation of teacher's self in virtual worlds were designed seeking to enhance virtual student-instructor interaction [9, 21, 24] and assisted in keeping temporal students attention and affective engagement to learning texts. Lecture engagement is a multi-dimensional construct composed of behavioral, emotional, and cognitive components [17]. Indicators of lecture engagement are divided into four groups: affective (belonging to school and school connectedness), cognitive (self-regulation, relevance of school to future aspirations, goal setting), behavioral (attendance, participation, behavioral incidents) and academic [13].

Affective engagement is defined through electroencephalographic monitoring of human brain activity. Alpha-band oscillations (9 to 13 Hz) reflected the temporal structure of cognitive learning processes, which may be described as 'knowledge-based consciousness. Alpha activity enabled 'semantic orientation' via controlled access to information stored in a complex knowledge system of the learner [18]. Researchers argued [14, 15] that alpha-band power could increase over cortical areas responsible for processing potentially distracting information and these attention-related sustained focus increases in alpha power occur prior to the arrival of an anticipated stimulus. Beta waves (12 to 30 Hz) represented the attentive state and occurred during the heightened state of awareness [16].

The model of physiology of emotions [25] considered that emotions are spread along two main axes: arousal and valence. An emotion can be defined according to how "positive" or "negative" it is felt (valence), and how much of activation it corresponds to (arousal). Although scholars argue that 2D model of emotions do not describe all the emotional states [26], such representation offers a great deal of simplicity. Emotional human mind states such as valence, arousal and dominance are detected from alpha and beta wave activity [20–22]. The model of learning in 3D virtual learning environments described engagement as one of learning benefits [23, 24, 27].

In this study affective students' engagement to a live and avatar-based video lecture was measured. Two hypotheses were raised: (1) student's attention span during virtual lecture is higher than in a live lecture with the same educational content and (2) the human- based stimuli evoke more active engagement to a virtual lecture than fully artificially created stimuli such as images or videos were conducted.

2 Methods

The experiment was organized using traditional live lecture (auditorium style) as a model of passive learning with the instructor. It is a common university practice that traditional live lecture lasts 45 min. We experimented with 30 min lecture. Straight before the lecture the self-control capacity state was measured using questionnaire technique. The lecture was conveyed in English (not-native language of the students) seeking to add additional longitudinal stimuli which lasted during all the lecture period. Entire lecture was video-recorded and observed later for interpretations. During the entire lecture brain sensing headband Muse [28] monitored participants' brain activity, which varied from calm states to neutral and active conditions. Taking into account that student's attention during the lecture starts to decrease after the first 10-15 min from the starting point; various stimuli were showed to the participants. We used 10-5-5-5-5 min model of lecture stimuli appearance. During the first lecture period (A to B in Fig. 1) no any stimuli appeared. The first period without any specific stimuli lasted 10 min and was twice longer than next periods. 10-5-5-5-5 min strategy of stimulus appearance was chosen letting the experiment participant to adapt to the brain monitoring device and to the lecture in foreign language. First stimulus- human (late student) entering the class- appeared after 10 min from the lecture start and interrupted instructors talk (point B in Fig. 1). The human interruption lasted approximately 1 min. Second stimulus – instructor starting to show lecture slides (picture stimulus) – appeared after 15 min from the lecture start (point C in Fig. 1). 5 static slides were shown to the learner one at a time in succession. The same time instructor explained the slides. The lecture period with the slides lasted approximatelly 1 min. Third stimulus – instructor showing and explaining the video materials– appeared after 20 min from the lecture start and lasted for 1 min (point D in Fig. 1.). The fourth stimulus – human body movements during the lecture (instructor started to make various body, hands movements and face mimics) appeared after 25 min from the lecture start (point E in Fig. 1) and lasted for approximately 1 min.

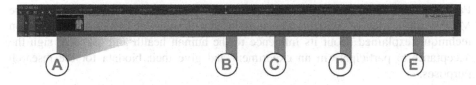

Fig. 1. The model of experiment-lecture

Two types of lectures were planned using the same experiment lecture model – first: live lecture in an auditorium, instructor standing in front of the class and reading the lecture; second: virtual avatar- based lecture (Fig. 2).

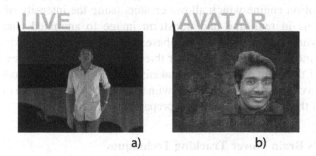

Fig. 2. Types of experiment lectures: (a) live lecture; (b) avatar-based video lecture

For the virtual avatar- based lecture the avatar of instructor was computer-modeled. The virtual lecture followed the same 10-5-5-5-5 model of lecture stimuli.

2.1 Participants

Research participants were university students, adults, ages ranged from 20 to 24, 4 female and 6 male. Each participant was randomly selected to one of the two experiment groups: live lecture group or virtual avatar-based lecture group. Experiment participants were evaluated for self-regulation before the lecture start using questionnaire for self-regulation. While in a lecture concentration and stress levels were monitored using the electroencephalography data extracted from the Muse headband.

2.2 Procedure

University students' attention in a lecture was measured using triple indicators: affective regulation during the lecture was monitored using Muse headband; cognitive (self-regulation) was measured using self-regulation questionnaire and behavioral regulation was observed using video recording of the experiment participant. The questionnaire of self-regulation was adapted from the state self-control capacity scale [18].

2.3 Ethical Considerations

Participants were informed about the experiment procedure and instructed about the Muse headband device. Students were introduced with wearable EEG biodata collection technique, explained about its influence to the human health and asked to sign the acceptance to participate in an experiment and give their biodata for the research purposes.

2.4 Design of an Avatar-Based Instructor

CrazyTalk^TM animation software from Reallusion, Inc. was used to create and animate the instructors' avatar. We chose CrazyTalk facial animation tool because of its potential to operate with recorded voice and text animating facial images [19]. CrazyTalk software has an auto motion engine which allows creators using the intensity of their voice to drive animations in real-time and transform image to animated character. Virtual avatar's face which appears in an avatar-based lecture was created taking real instructor's face as a model. To create an avatar three steps technique was developed: first, a digital photo of the human lecturer was taken; second - using a 3D modeling software a model of the avatar was created; third - with a CrazyTalk lip-sync the model using the audio file from the recorded lecture was prepared.

2.5 Student's Brain Power Tracking Techniques

Many EEG tests require attaching sensors to the head; the sensors are connected to a computer via wires. Dry EEG electrodes and simple wireless headsets offer partial but comfortable devices to wear for extended time-periods providing for the collection of large-time-extended data [29]. Muse device is a thin and light headband that was placed across the student's forehead and tucked behind ears during all the experiment. It uses

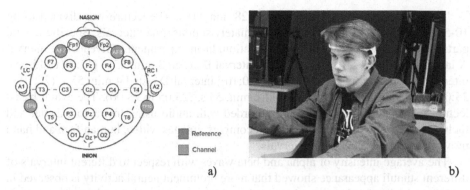

Fig. 3. (a) Muse electrode locations by 10-20 international standards [28]; (b) Student research participant with Muse headband in a classroom

seven electroencephalographic (EEG) sensors along the human scalp and data is collected via four channels (two on the forehead and two behind the ears, remaining are reference sensors). 7 sensors montage enables estimation of hemispheric asymmetries (with an emphasis on the pre-frontal lobe) and thus facilitates brain-state discrimination that depends on asymmetry, such as emotional valence (positive vs. negative emotions). For this research Muse headband was chosen because of dry EEG electrodes technology (TP9, AF7, AF8, TP10 dry; 3 electrode electrical reference FPz (CMS/DRL) and its compatibility to connect with monitoring system through Bluetooth. Muse headband utilizes minimal number of sensors to be more portable and unobtrusive (Fig. 3).

Moreover, Muse provides functions to filter the raw brain waves including the power frequency automatically, which helps increase the signal-noise ratio [29]. The device performed robust on-board digital signal processing to filter out noise and compute Fast Fourier Transforms (FFT) in real time [30]. The engagement was measured using a proprietary algorithm from Muse.

During all the experimenting period live EEG data was plotted and researcher had the possibility to monitor the biodata collection process. The frequencies of recorded signals vary from 1 to 50 Hz. Using Muse headband raw EEG and accelerometer data were collected; processed brain features, including typical EEG power-bands (delta, theta, alpha, beta, and gamma), raw power spectrum, and muscle activity measured. Muse fully processed data that yielded: beta/alpha ratio (focus vs relax) which will allow measuring the concentration or relaxation during the lecture period. Behavioral engagement was observed using lecture observation and video recording technique.

3 Data Analysis and Results

For the data collection and analysis MUSE software developer kit (SDK) and the additional tools coded by researchers were used. It allowed quantification of beta and alpha waves during each task. An analysis of variances was used to compare concentration, attentiveness, and active engagement, distraction and relaxation levels between research participant groups.

The experiment (live lecture) lasted 28 min. 00 s. The lecture was divided using 10-5-5-5-5 min's scheme into 5 approximately similar time intervals. Specific lecture parts (intervals) were taken into consideration. In an experiment of live lecture interval A lasted 12 min. 00 s. (0:00 to 12:00); interval B lasted 3 min. 35 s. (12:00 to 15:35); interval C lasted 4 min. 35 s. (15:35 to 20:10); interval D lasted 4 min. 55 s. (20:10 to 25:05); and the final interval E lasted 2 min. 55 s. (25:05 to 28:00). The avatar based lecture was made from live lecture recorded with audio using instructors avatar and including the same four stimuli (human complex, images, video, human face and hand movements) at the same time intervals.

The average intensity of alpha and beta waves with respect to different intervals of different stimuli appearance showed that more prominent neural activity is observed in students who listerned to virtual avatar-based lectures compared to those who participated in live lectures.

Students felt more distracted and relaxed during the experiment lectures without any stimuli; stimuli activated the participants. The most evoking was the first stimuli (point B in Fig. 4) because of the two reasons – this was the first stimuli that appeared to the participants and the only one stimuli which was complex, including human face, body movement (visual stimuli) and voice (audio stimuli). Students reactions to image (point C in Fig. 4) or video stimuli (point D in Fig. 4) was approximatelly the same and less than to human complex stimuli (point B in Fig. 4) or instructors body movement (point E in Fig. 4).

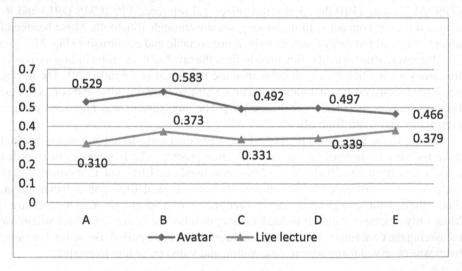

Fig. 4. Relative alpha wave power (Bel) in avatar-based and live lectures during experimenting time intervals.

Students were more concentrated and more attentive to the avatar based lecture than to the live instructors talk in an auditorium. Students watching the avatar-based lecture responded more eminently to stimuli than in a live lecture (Fig. 5).

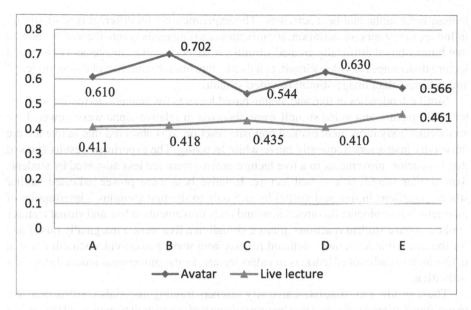

Fig. 5. Relative beta wave power (Bel) in avatar-based and live lectures during experimenting time intervals.

The highest concentration, attentiveness and active engagement was observed during the avatar-based lecture with complex human stimuli, while in a live lecture all the stimuli activated approximatelly the same students responses (point B in Fig. 5). Image stimuli activated different reactions (point C in Fig. 5): in a live lecture it slightly tweaked students attentiveness (beta change from 0.411 till 0.418) while in avatar-based lecture the observed response was lowering (beta change from 0.702 till 0.544). Reactions to video stimuli were opposite concerning to image stimuli (point D in Fig. 5): video stimuli in an avatar-based lecture call more active engagement (beta change from 0.554 till 0.630) while in a live lecture suppressed engagement (beta change from 0.435 till 0.410). Conditionally highest lecture engagement was observed in live lecture with human body movement stimuli (point E in Fig. 5). Similar stimuli appearing in an avatar-based lecture raised conditionally low response.

Results of all the lecture measurement showed that virtual avatar-based lectures activated relatively greater level of concentration, attentiveness and active engagement compared to live lectures.

4   Implications

Active students' engagement to the university lectures challenges instructors and professors. This research showed that virtual lecture forms such as avatar-based lectures activated learner engagement to the lecture materials. The hypothesis that students attention span during avatar-based video lecture is conditionally higher than in a live lecture with the same audio materials was proved through electroencephalographic monitoring of human brain alpha and beta activities. The experimenting on different type of stimuli influence to learner concentration, attentiveness and engagement into the lecture showed that human based artificially created stimuli evoke more active engagement to a virtual lecture than images or video stimuli. In a live lecture human stimuli evokes less students' attentiveness than image-stimuli or video stimuli.

Similar tendencies in live and avatar-based lectures for human interrupting instructors talk, picture and video stimuli were observed in relative alpha wave power. Live and virtual body movement evoked opposite reaction. It is observed that in live lecture university instructors frequently move while lecturing. The experiment results showed that instructor' movements in a live lecture environment are less answered by students than similar stimuli in a virtual lecture. Relative beta wave power indicated similar student reactions in live and virtual lecture only to the first stimulus – interruption of instructor's monologue. Pictures, video and body movements in live and virtual lectures evoked inverse student reactions: picture stimuli in a live lecture marginally raised and for the avatar-based lecture - deflated relative beta wave power; video stimuli deflated in live lecture and evoked learners in video-lecture; avatar movements reduced student's activation.

These results can stimulate university teachers training materials construction. We recommend mixing video and live lectures; using various stimuli to evoke and strengthen learners' concentration and active engagements to learning materials.

5   Study Limitations and Future Research

Our research has some limitations. The live lecture was read only to one student at a time because of biodata collection techniques and technical equipment. Because of that we avoided additional unexpected stimuli and constructed the pure environment which may limit our results.

In order to deepen understanding students' affective engagement during virtual and live lectures future research may be focused to larger experimental group and extended EEG measurements. The experiment can be reiterated using other EEG portable device (e.g. Emotiv Epoc) seeking for additional data validity.

References

1. Traphagan, T., Kucsera, J.V., Kishi, K.: Impact of class lecture webcasting on attendance and learning. Educ. Technol. Res. Dev. **58**(1), 19–37 (2010)
2. Bati, A.H., Mandiracioglu, A., Orgun, F., Govsa, F.: Why do students miss lectures? A study of lecture attendance amongst students of health science. Nurse Educ. Today **33**(6), 596–601 (2013)
3. Yeung, A., Raju, S., Sharma, M.D.: Investigating student preferences of online lecture recordings and lecture attendance in a large first year psychology course. In: Proceedings of The Australian Conference on Science and Mathematics Education (formerly UniServe Science Conference) (2016)

4. Bos, N., Groeneveld, C., Bruggen, J., Brand-Gruwel, S.: The use of recorded lectures in education and the impact on lecture attendance and exam performance. Br. J. Educ. Technol. **41**(2), 271–286 (2015)
5. Abdulghani, H.M., Al-Drees, A.A., Khalil, M.S., Ahmad, F., Ponnamperuma, G.G., Amin, Z.: What factors determine academic achievement in high achieving undergraduate medical students? Qual. Study Med. Teach. **36**(sup1), S43–S48 (2014)
6. Barata, G., Gama, S., Jorge, J., Gonçalves, D.: Improving participation and learning with gamification. In: Proceedings of the First International Conference on Gameful Design, Research, and Applications, pp. 10–17. ACM (2013)
7. Clarke, J.: Augmented reality, multimodal literacy and mobile technology: An experiment in teacher engagement. In: QScience Proceedings (2013)
8. Wu, H.K., Lee, S.W.Y., Chang, H.Y., Liang, J.C.: Current status, opportunities and challenges of augmented reality in education. Comput. Educ. **62**, 41–49 (2013)
9. Mat-jizat, J.E., Osman, J., Yahaya, R., Samsudin, N.: The use of augmented reality (AR) among tertiary level students: perception and experience. Aust. J. Sustain. Bus. Soc. **2**(1), 42–49 (2016)
10. O'Callaghan, F.V., Neumann, D.L., Jones, L., Creed, P.A.: The use of lecture recordings in higher education: A review of institutional, student, and lecturer issues. Educ. Inf. Technol. 1–17 (2015)
11. Wilson, K., Korn, J.H.: Attention during lectures: Beyond ten minutes. Teach. Psychol. **34**(2), 85–89 (2007)
12. Farley, J., Risko, E.F., Kingstone, A.: Everyday attention and lecture retention: the effects of time, fidgeting, and mind wandering. Front. Psychol. **4**(619), 1–9 (2013). 10-3389
13. Park, S., Holloway, S.D., Arendtsz, A., Bempechat, J., Li, J.: What makes students engaged in learning? A time-use study of within-and between-individual predictors of emotional engagement in low-performing high schools. J. Youth Adolesc. **41**(3), 390–401 (2012)
14. Klimesch, W.: Alpha-band oscillations, attention, and controlled access to stored information. Trends Cogn. Sci. **16**(12), 606–617 (2012)
15. Foxe, J.J., Snyder, A.C.: The role of alpha-band brain oscillations as a sensory suppression mechanism during selective attention. Front. Psychol. **2**(154), 1–13 (2011)
16. Desai, R., Tailor, A., Bhatt, T.: Effects of yoga on brain waves and structural activation: A review. Complement. Ther. Clin. Pract. **21**(2), 112–118 (2015)
17. Wang, M.T., Eccles, J.S.: Adolescent behavioral, emotional, and cognitive engagement trajectories in school and their differential relations to educational success. J. Res. Adolesc. **22**(1), 31–39 (2012)
18. Christian, M.S., Ellis, A.P.: Examining the effects of sleep deprivation on workplace deviance: a self-regulatory perspective. Acad. Manage. J. **54**(5), 913–934 (2011)
19. Gurvitch, R., Lund, J.: Animated video clips: Learning in the current generation. J. Physic. Educ. Recreation Dance **85**(5), 8–17 (2014)
20. Ramirez, R., Vamvakousis, Z.: Detecting emotion from EEG signals using the emotive epoc device. In: Zanzotto, F.M., Tsumoto, S., Taatgen, N., Yao, Y. (eds.) BI 2012. LNCS, vol. 7670, pp. 175–184. Springer, Heidelberg (2012)
21. Liu, Y., Sourina, O., Nguyen, M.K.: Real-time EEG-based human emotion recognition and visualization. In: 2010 International Conference on Cyberworlds (CW), pp. 262–269. IEEE, October 2010
22. Liao, L.D., Chen, C.Y., Wang, I.J., Chen, S.F., Li, S.Y., Chen, B.W., Lin, C.T.: Gaming control using a wearable and wireless EEG-based brain-computer interface device with novel dry foam-based sensors. J. Neuroengineering Rehabil. **9**(1), 1–11 (2012)

23. Merchant, Z., Goetz, E.T., Cifuentes, L., Keeney-Kennicutt, W., Davis, T.J.: Effectiveness of virtual reality-based instruction on students' learning outcomes in K-12 and higher education: A meta-analysis. Comput. Educ. **70**, 29–40 (2014)

24. Dalgarno, B., Lee, M.J.: What are the learning affordances of 3-D virtual environments? Br. J. Educ. Technol. **41**(1), 10–32 (2010)

25. Lane, R.D., Chua, P.M., Dolan, R.J.: Common effects of emotional valence, arousal and attention on neural activation during visual processing of pictures. Neuropsychologia **37**(9), 989–997 (1999)

26. Fontaine, J.R., Scherer, K.R., Roesch, E.B., Ellsworth, P.C.: The world of emotions is not two-dimensional. Psychol. Sci. **18**(12), 1050–1057 (2007)

27. Mensia technologies. http://www.mensiatech.com/emotions-mensia/, 7 June 2016

28. Muse™ headband development and technical specifications. http://developer.choosemuse.com/, Accessed 20 June 2016

29. Li, Z., Xu, J., Zhu, T.: Prediction of Brain States of Concentration and Relaxation in Real Time with Portable Electroencephalographs (2015). arXiv preprint arXiv:1509.07642

30. Karydis, T., Aguiar, F., Foster, S.L., Mershin, A.: Self-calibrating protocols enhance wearable EEG diagnostics and consumer applications. In: Proceedings of the 8th ACM International Conference on Pervasive Technologies Related to Assistive Environments, p. 96. ACM, July 2015

Information Technology Applications: Special Session on Language Technologies

Topic Classification Problem Solving
for Morphologically Complex Languages

Jurgita Kapočiūtė-Dzikienė$^{(\boxtimes)}$ and Tomas Krilavičius

Vytautas Magnus University, K. Donelaičio 58, 44248 Kaunas, Lithuania
{j.kapociute-dzikiene,t.krilavicius}@vdu.lt

Abstract. In this paper we are presenting a topic classification task for the morphologically complex Lithuanian and Russian languages, using popular supervised machine learning techniques. In our research we experimentally investigated two text classification methods and a big variety of feature types covering different levels of abstraction: character, lexical, and morpho-syntactic. In order to have comparable results for the both languages, we kept experimental conditions as similar as possible: the datasets were composed of the normative texts, taken from the news portals; contained similar topics; and had the same number of texts in each topic.

The best results (~ 0.86 of the accuracy) were achieved with the Support Vector Machine method and the token lemmas as a feature representation type. The character feature type capturing relevant patterns of the complex inflectional morphology without any external morphological tools was the second best. Since these findings hold for the both Lithuanian and Russian languages, we assume, they should hold for the entire group of the Baltic and Slavic languages.

Keywords: Topic classification · Supervised machine learning · Character · Lexical and morpho-syntactic feature types · Lithuanian and Russian languages

1 Introduction

The increased availability of electronic text documents and users' demands to access them in a flexible way encouraged researchers to search for the solutions how to organize those documents in the appropriate manner. It influenced that an automatic Text Classification (assigning documents to predefined categories) has become an important research topic used in many very different applications, e.g., topic classification, genre classification, opinion mining, authorship attribution, etc.

The topic classification task (grouping text documents according to their topics) which receives rather little attention recently was widely researched in the past. Refined methods and external morpho-syntactic tools, huge amounts of annotated text corpora, and other resources allowed solving this problem for the English language with a very high accuracy. However, the topic classification research recommendations are often the language (or the language group)-dependent, thus hardly transferable and adjustable for the other languages (or groups of languages) due to differences in their characteristics. Thus some technique achieving very high accuracy on the English language can perform extremely poor on, e.g., the particular Baltic or Slavic language, having

© Springer International Publishing Switzerland 2016
G. Dregvaite and R. Damasevicius (Eds.): ICIST 2016, CCIS 639, pp. 511–524, 2016.
DOI: 10.1007/978-3-319-46254-7_41

complex morphology (which reflects to a big variety of inflection forms), relatively free word-order in a sentence, rich vocabulary, and word derivation system.

For some Baltic and Slavic languages the topic classification task has already been solved (e.g., Lithuanian [18], Russian [1], Czech [14], etc.), but for some of them one of the most investigated areas of the Computational Linguistics is still under development. Since both Baltic and Slavic languages are from the same Indo-European family branch and share similar characteristics, we assume, it is possible to formulate recommendations beneficial for the whole group of these languages. However, to draw such recommendations from the existing research works is rather difficult: described experiments are hardly comparable due to the different applied methods, used topics, dataset sizes, language types, etc.

There are too many Baltic and Slavic languages to explore thoroughly them all, therefore in this research we are at least focusing on the Lithuanian and Russian languages, representing the Baltic and Slavic languages, respectively. By keeping as equal experimental conditions as possible for the both languages (in terms of applied methods, used topics, dataset sizes, and language types) we explore how the language-independent text classification techniques can be enhanced with the language-dependent, mostly focusing on a selection of the appropriate feature representation types. For this reason we test very different feature representation types covering various levels of abstraction (character, lexical, and morpho-syntactic) and, where necessary, employing available external tools (lemmatizers, morphological analyzers, and part-of-speech taggers).

2   Related Work

An automatic topic classification task can be solved using two main paradigms: knowledge engineering and machine learning (ML). The knowledge engineering requires human-expert intervention for manual construction of rules capable to take all classification decisions. Probably the most famous example of this type is the CON-STRUE categorization system [13] which assigns indexing terms to news stories according to their content. Despite the rule-based approaches mostly achieve very efficient results, they require considerable amount of human work (especially having a big diversity in the texts) and are hardly adjustable to the new domains or applications. ML has an advantage over knowledge engineering: it does not require the manual construction of rules, because rules (defined as a classifier) are built automatically by observing and generalizing the characteristics of given texts. In this paper we focus on the most accurate group of ML methods, in particular, supervised ML (for review see [20]) requiring the representative texts labeled with the thematic categories from a predefined closed-set of options used for the classifier creation. In our research we narrow down the area of the text classification techniques [34] to the single-labeled (having texts assigned to not more than one category each), multi-class (having more than two pre-defined categories), and flat (having no hierarchical structures) classification only.

For the long time in the past there was no consensus which supervised ML method is the best for the topic classification. The comparative analysis in [17] revealed that Support Vector Machine (SVM) and k-Nearest Neighbor (k-NN) are the top-notch classifiers, followed by Decision Trees (DTs) or Naïve Bayes (NB); moreover, SVM was even slightly better than k-NN. In [6] research SVM is the most accurate technique followed by DTs, and then by NB. Similar results were obtained in [42], where SVM and k-NN were ranked as the best classifiers. However, in [9], on the contrary, DTs (in particular C4.5) are significantly superior to SVM. Despite some controversial findings SVM has become the most popular technique for the topic classification. The comparative experiments with the different SVM's parameters revealed that the linear kernel function produces better results compared to polynomial or radial [42] on the English language. But the different kernel functions had no significant impact on the German [22] and Russian texts (except for the cost parameter) [1]. Despite domination of the SVM method, Bayesian methods maintained their popularity and are often selected as the baseline approaches. In particular, NB with a Multinomial model (NBM) is a popular choice compared to NB (with a Bernoulli model) because it is more adjusted to deal with the larger feature sets [25].

Topic classification results may also be affected by different feature set sizes, feature selection methods, preprocessing techniques, or feature representation types. Probably the most popular attempt to increase the text classification performance was based on the assumption that all irrelevant and noisy features degrading the classification speed and also accuracy should be omitted (review of the feature selection methods is in [16]). Despite that the feature set size and the ranking method has always been an issue, some conclusions can be drawn. For example, NB outperforms NBM on the smaller feature sets, but underperform on the larger [25]; SVM applied on the larger feature sets of the Arabic texts outperforms NB, k-NN, and Rocchio, but Rocchio gives the best results on the smaller [11]. Nevertheless, some experiments claim that in the text classification are only a few irrelevant features [17] and SVM is the least sensitive technique to the different feature selection methods [31] which performance cannot be beaten even using all available features [7].

Despite the language-dependent pre-processing as stemming or lemmatization is recommended for the morphologically complex languages, stemming enhanced the text classification results of NB, SVM, k-NN and had especially strong positive impact on DTs (C4.5) even on the English texts [29]. But on the contrary, it had no influence on the Dutch texts with NB [10] and even dropped down the SVM's classification accuracy on the Arabic [40]; lemmatization yielded worse results on the German texts [22]. However, the language itself is not the only factor determining the demand of stemming or lemmatization: the accuracy of applied external linguistic tools is especially important.

Probably the most crucial language-dependent factor is a feature representation type. Despite the most common type on the English texts remains simple bag-of-words interpretation, more sophisticated types also demonstrate improvements. The offered redundancy measure helped to select the most informative token bigrams and to achieve better results compared to the bag-of-words on NB and SVM [3]; the lexical analyzer determined the most important token bigrams which demonstrated positive impact with Mutual Information and NB [38]; syntactically related word pairs (verb + each of its arguments, noun + each of its modifiers) with SVM and DTs achieved better results over bag-of-words [27]. The character level n-grams are also very popular in the topic classification: they are robust to typing errors and can perform the particular intrinsic stemming function. E.g., the character trigrams with the Dice similarity measure and k-NN gave the best results on the Arabic texts [19]; the character tetra-grams with the Dot product similarity measure and k-NN were the best for Farsi [2]. Besides, the character n-grams give superior classification results on the English and competitive results on such languages as Chinese and Japanese compared to the bag-of-words [28].

Hence, the topic classification task has been examined from the very different perspectives. However, now we will focus on the works done for the Baltic and Slavic languages (excluding knowledge engineering approaches). The research done on the Czech news agency texts showed that Maximal Entropy (ME) and SVM classifiers outperform NB, part-of-speech tagging improves the results, but lemmatization plays only a marginal role [14]. In the multi-label task (where the main focus was on the transformation methods) the performed classification experiments demonstrated ME's and SVM's superiority over NB [15]; and linear SVM's with sublinear tf-idf vector space model superiority over NB [21]. The comparison of methods (NB, ranking method based on the frequency profiles, and k-NN), feature types (words, token n-grams, character n-grams), and pre-processing techniques (stemming and lemmatization) done on the Polish Wikipedia articles revealed that NB with the character n-grams (from bigrams to 5-grams) is the best, but stemming and lemmatization has no positive effect [41]. The binary topic detection (in domain, out-of-domain) on the web pages in Slovak is done by comparing documents (represented as vector space models with term weighting for the key phrases) based on the calculated values of the distance/similarity measures [37]. Another method for the Slovak language calculates the distance between the tested document's profile and profiles of the domain categories based on the normalized and non-normalized frequencies of the word-level character n-grams [39]. The Slovenian websites covering different topics are organized into topic ontology: authors tested two text representation methods (based on the bag-of-words with tf-idf and the String kernels, cutting text into sequences of characters regardless of word boundaries) in combination with linear SVM. String kernels significantly outperformed bag-of-words, besides it demonstrated advantage with unbalanced class distribution and eliminated the need for stemming and lemmatization [8]. The topic classification done separately on the Croatian and English parallel newspaper corpus with linear SVM and two text pre-processing methods (document-level character n-grams and the morphological normalization) revealed that n-grams can substitute morphological normalization. Besides, classification results on the English language were much better than on Croatian [35]. The authors in [43] considered the effect of the stemmer on the keywords and key phrases (for themes) extraction using the Bulgarian news web site (with an accent on political topics). They tested unsupervised and supervised (NBM, Perceptron and MIRA algorithms for classification) techniques with tf-idf scores for the candidates and made the following conclusions: unsupervised techniques are not significantly influenced by the stemmer; if a candidate length in tokens is added as a feature, the supervised approach outperforms unsupervised; the best results were achieved with NBM using tf-idf, positional offset (pos), candidate length (len) in tokens and conjunctions tf-idf&pos and tf-idf&len. Similar experiments on the Bulgarian language, but solving multi-label classification task were carried out in [44]. The comparative analysis of NB, k-NN, DTs, Neural Networks, and Ensemble of classifiers done on the Macedonian news documents using tf-idf scores on the bag-of-words revealed that the best results are achieved with the Ensemble of classifiers [32]. The classification of the Russian legal texts was performed with SVM using tf-idf on the token lemmas. These experiments revealed that none of other SVM parameters except for the cost parameter influenced significantly classification performance. Besides the results were compared with the proposed machine learning method which was used to construct DNF rules. The model created by DNF did not significantly outperform SVM, but it was easy interpretable by humans [1]. The topic classification done on the Lithuanian forum posts and political texts with SVM proved that the document-level character n-grams outperform bag-of-words and token lemmas [18].

As it can be seen from the related research works, the topic classification results are obtained under very different experimental conditions. Besides, we could not find any comparative research done for more than one Baltic or Slavic language. Due to all these reasons it is hard to make resumptive conclusions about more than one language. Consequently in our work we are going to solve this problem by running experiments under the same experimental conditions on the datasets of at least two languages (in particular, Lithuanian and Russian), comparing the results and, if possible, making generalized conclusions which, we assume, should hold for the whole group of Baltic and Slavic languages.

3   Topic Classification Framework

In essence, the topic classification task can be formally described as follows.

Let D be a document space containing text documents $d_1, d_2, ..., d_n = \{d_i\}$. Let $D^L \in D$ be a training dataset.

Let C be a closed-set of topics (defined as classes) $c_1, c_2, ..., c_m = \{c_j\}$ with m > 2 (multi-class classification case).

Let any d_i be labeled with one class c_j only (single-label classification case): $\langle d_i, c_j \in D^L$.

Let function φ determine the hidden logic how each d_i is assigned to c_j, i.e., φ : $D \rightarrow C$. The goal is: using $\{\langle d_i, c_j\}$ to train a classifier and to create a function φ' (defined as a model) which could approximate φ as precisely as possible.

3.1   Datasets Description

Datasets for both Lithuanian and Russian languages were composed of the text documents (articles) harvested from the Internet news' portals delfi.lt and gazeta.ru, respectively. Lithuanian articles cover the period from 2002 to 2011; Russian – from 2002 to 2014. All classes in the datasets corresponds categories by which articles are grouped in the news portals, thus we only accepted offered grouping without considerations.

During the pre-processing all meta-information (dates when articles were uploaded, authors of those articles, titles of pictures, and names of their photographers) was

Table 1. Statistics about the Lithuanian dataset. *Numb. of tokens* determines a number of words and digits; *Numb. of types* – a number of distinct tokens; *Numb. of lemmas* – a number of lemmas; *Avg. numb. of tokens in doc* – average document length in *tokens*.

Class	Numb. of texts	Numb. of tokens	Numb. of types	Numb. of lemmas	Avg. numb. of tokens in doc
Auto	500	117,804	20,891	9,959	235.61
Basketball	500	140,000	17,764	10,596	280.00
Beauty & health	500	227,634	42,575	17,955	455.27
Business	500	151,952	23,724	10,141	303.90
Career	500	339,608	53,404	20,048	679.22
In Lithuania	500	223,020	36,699	15,371	446.04
Life	500	175,201	41,904	18,793	350.40
Science	500	227,431	41,792	18,089	454.86
Stories	500	456,537	75,095	30,477	913.07
Technologies	500	192,538	32,924	13,948	385.08
Overall	5,000	2,251,725	187,034	71,205	450.35

Table 2. Statistics about the Russian dataset. For the notations see the caption of Table 1.

Class	Numb. of texts	Numb. of tokens	Numb. of types	Numb. of lemmas	Avg. numb. of tokens in doc
Auto	500	356,912	49,979	25,732	713.82
Business	500	305,233	38,832	20,432	610.47
Culture	500	391,654	72,770	40,467	783.31
Health	500	313,809	38,560	20,761	627.62
Politics	500	352,307	45,832	23,500	704.61
Reality	500	395,477	47,739	24,185	790.95
Science	500	404,800	59,217	31,586	809.60
Social	500	353,408	49,946	25,630	706.82
Sport	500	222,117	34,612	20,122	444.23
Tech zone	500	389,637	47,002	25,455	779.27
Overall	5,0000	3,485,354	213,513	129,893	697.07

removed. Both datasets were composed of 10 closely resembling categories (see statistics about the Lithuanian and Russian datasets in Tables 1 and 2, respectively) and balanced to avoid strong domination of the largest categories.

3.2 Text Classification Methods

Available text documents with the attached class labels narrowed down the area of the machine learning methods to supervised methods. We investigated the following techniques:

- Support Vector Machine – SVM (introduced in [4]) is a discriminative instance-based approach, which has been considered as the most popular for text classification in the resent years due to the following reasons. Firstly, SVM is the least sensitive technique to the feature selection, besides, its performance can be hardly beaten even using all available features [7]. It is especially important knowing that in the text classification there are only very few irrelevant features [17]. Secondly, SVM has mechanisms to cope effectively with the high dimensional feature spaces and sparseness of the feature vectors. E.g., if not performing any feature selection on the bag-of-words, the method would have to cope with > 187 thousand and > 213 thousand features (see the overall number of types in the Lithuanian and Russian datasets in Tables 1 and 2, respectively). The feature vectors would be very sparse as well, i.e., having less than ~ 450 and ~ 697 non-zero feature values (see the overall average length of the document in the Lithuanian and Russian datasets in Tables 1 and 2, respectively). Thirdly, SVM does not perform aggressive feature selection (when creating the model) which may result in a loss of information; and is robust when dealing with the heterogeneous use of features (when the instances sharing the same class do not share any common features).
- Naïve Bayes Multinomial – NBM (introduced in [23]) is a generative profile-based approach, adjusted to deal with the textual data and the large feature sets (for more details see [25]). The NB assumption about the feature independence allows parameters of each feature to be learned separately; the method performs especially well when the number of features having equal significance is large. Overall, NBM is selected mostly due to its simplicity, rapid processing, and low data storage resources. Besides, this Bayesian method is often used as the baseline approach for the comparison reasons.

However, it is important to notice that the choice of the classification algorithm is not more important than the choice of the appropriate feature type, especially dealing with the morphologically complex languages.

3.3   Feature Types

Since the accuracy of our classification tasks mostly depends on the correctly selected feature type, we explored the impact of the various individual and compound feature types covering character, lexical, and morpho-syntactic levels of abstraction:

- *chrN_dl* is a character feature type, representing document-level character n-grams (with $N = [2, 7]$ in our experiments). N-grams are successions of N characters sliding within the limits of the whole text document (one character at the time) including whitespaces but without punctuation marks. E.g., *chr6_dl* on the phrase *topic classification* would produce the following n-grams (where whitespaces are replaced with "_"): *topic, opic_c, pic_cl, ic_cla, c_clas, _class, classi, lassif*, etc.
- *chrN_wl* is a character feature type, representing word-level character n-grams (with $N = [2, 7]$): successions of N characters sliding within the limits of each word. E.g., *chr6_dl* on the same phrase would produce: *topic, classi, lassif, assifi, ssific*, etc.

- *lexN* is a most popular content-specific lexical feature type, which involves word tokens (bag-of-words) (with $N = 1$) or token n-grams (including all lower order n-grams up to N) (with $N = [2, 3]$). E.g., *lex1* on the phrase *text document classification* would produce *text*, *document*, and *classification*; *lex2* would produce isolated words *text*, *document*, *classification* plus pairs *text document*, and *document classification*; *lex3* would produce isolated words, their pairs, and the triplet *text document classification*.
- *lemN* is a content-specific lexical feature type which involves lemmas based on the word tokens (with $N = 1$) or their n-grams (with $N = [2, 3]$). The Lithuanian texts were lemmatized with the morphological analyzer-lemmatizer *Lemuoklis*[1] [5, 45] reaching 94 % of the accuracy on the normative texts [30]. This tool solves morphological disambiguation problems in the sentences, performs lemmatization, coarse-grained (determining main part-of-speech tags such as noun, verb, adjective, etc.) and fine-grained part-of-speech tagging (as cases, genders, numbers, tenses, moods, persons, etc.). The Russian texts were lemmatized with the TreeTagger[2] [33] which can also annotate texts with the part-of-speeches, i.e., morpho-syntactic descriptions [36] with already encoded fine-grained information. During the lemmatization all recognized generic words were transformed into the lower-case and all numbers were replaced with a special placeholder.
- *posN* is a content-free morphological feature type involving all part-of-speech information (coarse-grained and fine-grained) based on the word tokens ($N = 1$) or token n-grams (with $N = [2, 3]$ in our experiments).
- *lexposN*, *lemposN* are the aggregated feature types concatenating every *lex* with its *pos*, every *lem* with its *pos*, respectively. These types involve unigrams ($N = 1$) or n-grams (with $N = [2, 3]$ in our experiments). E.g., *lexpos1* on the phrase *interesting task* would produce two unigrams: *interesting_ADJ_fg*, *task_NOUN_fg* (where *fg* stands for the other related fine-grained morphological information).

4 Experimental Setup and Results

Our experiments involved investigation of two classifiers (presented in Sect. 3.2) and the various feature types (Sect. 3.3) on the Lithuanian and Russian datasets (Sect. 3.1). The random ($\Sigma P^2 (c_j)$) and majority (max $P (c_j)$) baselines gave the same value equal to 0.1 (due to the datasets balancing).

We used implementations of SVM and NBM from the WEKA 3.6 machine learning toolkit [12].[3] All parameters were set to their default values, expect for SVM, where tuning gave the best results with the polynomial kernel on the few control experiments. The feature selection was not performed.

All experiments were carried out with the stratified 10-fold cross validation and evaluated using accuracy and f-score. Obtained results are reported in Table 3. To

---

[1] http://tekstynas.vdu.lt/page.xhtml?id=morphological-annotator.

[2] http://www.cis.uni-muenchen.de/~schmid/tools/TreeTagger/.

[3] http://www.cs.waikato.ac.nz/ml/weka/.

Table 3. The results obtained on the Lithuanian and Russian datasets are sorted descending according to the *accruacy*. The cells in grey represent feature types for which difference in the *accuracy* is not statistically significant from the best obtained.

Lithuanian						Russian					
NBM			SVM			NBM			SVM		
feature type	acc.	f-score	feature type	acc.	f-score	feature type	acc.	f-score	feature type	acc.	f-score
lem1	0.837	0.836	*lem1*	0.858	0.859	*lem1*	0.801	0.803	*lem1*	0.860	0.860
lem2	0.835	0.835	*lem2*	0.855	0.856	*lem2*	0.796	0.797	*chr3_wl*	0.850	0.849
lem3	0.835	0.835	*lem3*	0.855	0.856	*chr3_wl*	0.793	0.794	*lem2*	0.849	0.849
chr3_wl	0.805	0.805	*chr2_dl*	0.849	0.849	*lem3*	0.790	0.791	*lem3*	0.849	0.849
chr6_wl	0.804	0.801	*chr3_wl*	0.839	0.840	*chr5_wl*	0.784	0.784	*chr2_dl*	0.848	0.848
chr4_wl	0.803	0.801	*chr3_dl*	0.838	0.839	*lex1*	0.784	0.786	*chr3_dl*	0.847	0.846
lempos1	0.803	0.801	*chr2_wl*	0.837	0.838	*chr6_wl*	0.782	0.782	*chr2_wl*	0.839	0.839
chr5_wl	0.801	0.798	*chr7_wl*	0.826	0.827	*chr4_wl*	0.780	0.781	*chr4_wl*	0.832	0.831
lex1	0.800	0.798	*chr4_dl*	0.824	0.825	*chr7_wl*	0.776	0.776	*chr5_wl*	0.823	0.823
chr7_wl	0.799	0.796	*lempos1*	0.821	0.822	*chr3_dl*	0.775	0.776	*chr6_wl*	0.823	0.822
chr3_dl	0.795	0.795	*chr6_wl*	0.821	0.822	*lempos1*	0.774	0.776	*lex1*	0.822	0.822
lex2	0.792	0.790	*lempos2*	0.818	0.820	*lexpos1*	0.767	0.769	*chr4_dl*	0.820	0.820
lex3	0.792	0.790	*chr4_wl*	0.816	0.817	*lex2*	0.765	0.765	*lempos1*	0.815	0.814
lexpos1	0.790	0.787	*lempos3*	0.816	0.818	*chr6_dl*	0.762	0.762	*lexpos1*	0.813	0.813
lempos2	0.789	0.786	*lex1*	0.814	0.815	*chr4_dl*	0.755	0.756	*chr7_wl*	0.811	0.810
lempos3	0.788	0.785	*chr5_wl*	0.813	0.815	*chr5_dl*	0.755	0.755	*chr6_dl*	0.809	0.809
lexpos2	0.785	0.783	*chr6_dl*	0.810	0.811	*chr7_dl*	0.750	0.750	*chr5_dl*	0.809	0.809
lexpos3	0.784	0.782	*lexpos1*	0.809	0.811	*lex3*	0.747	0.746	*lex2*	0.807	0.807
chr4_dl	0.781	0.779	*chr5_dl*	0.807	0.808	*chr2_wl*	0.743	0.744	*lex3*	0.803	0.803
chr5_dl	0.775	0.773	*chr7_dl*	0.802	0.804	*lempos2*	0.739	0.738	*chr7_dl*	0.798	0.798
chr6_dl	0.773	0.771	*lex2*	0.801	0.803	*lexpos2*	0.737	0.735	*lempos2*	0.795	0.795
chr2_wl	0.771	0.770	*lex3*	0.801	0.803	*lempos3*	0.710	0.706	*lempos3*	0.793	0.793
chr7_dl	0.769	0.766	*lexpos2*	0.798	0.800	*lexpos3*	0.709	0.706	*lexpos2*	0.787	0.786
chr2_dl	0.764	0.764	*lexpos3*	0.797	0.800	*chr2_dl*	0.708	0.705	*lexpos3*	0.784	0.783
pos3	0.640	0.634	*pos3*	0.632	0.633	*pos2*	0.639	0.631	*pos2*	0.696	0.695
pos1	0.625	0.615	*pos2*	0.627	0.628	*pos3*	0.628	0.619	*pos3*	0.691	0.690
pos2	0.620	0.613	*pos1*	0.526	0.524	*pos1*	0.564	0.558	*pos1*	0.626	0.626

determine if the differences between the results are statistically significant we performed McNemar test [26] with one degree of freedom at the significance level $\alpha = 0.05$.

5 Discussion

Zooming into the classification results in Table 3 allows us to report the following statements.

All obtained results are reasonable, because exceed random and majority baselines.

SVM is superior to NBM for the both languages. Our experiments once again prove SVM's robustness to deal with the textual data, huge feature sets, and sparse feature vectors that is especially important for the vocabulary and morphologically rich languages as Lithuanian and Russian.

However, the most important findings of this research are related with the analysis of the various feature representation types. Undoubtedly the best feature type for both languages is unigrams based on the token lemmas (*lem1*). The lemmatization of the Lithuanian and Russian texts decreased the number of types by ~ 62 % and ~ 39 %, respectively. Due to the high accuracy of these lemmatization tools on the normative texts (effectively coping with the different inflection forms) feature vectors became less sparse and it led to the creation of more robust models. Due to the same reason the most popular feature type (bag-of-words, i.e., *lex1*) for the English language is only in the middle of the whole list for the morphologically complex Lithuanian and Russian (except for NBM on the Russian dataset). The worst feature type is based on the part-of-speech information solely. However, longer patterns (*pos2*, *pos3*) (containing at least little bit extra information) outperform unigrams (*pos1*). These results are not surprising, but play an important starting point function (showing the accuracy which can be achieved without any contextual information). The lexical features used in aggregation with the part-of-speech tags (*lexpos*, *lempos*) are worse than used alone. It simply claims the fact that only the contextual information plays the major role in topic classification tasks. Moreover, all longer patterns (with $N \geq 2$) used with the lexical information alone or in aggregation with the part-of-speech tags underperform shorter patterns (with $N = 1$). It claims the fact that in the topic classification key words are informative enough: i.e., the key phrases added to the key words are already redundant and increase the sparseness of the feature vectors.

Although marginally the best results are obtained with the lemma information, character features should not be underestimated: i.e., they are among the best types for the both languages (except for NBM on the Lithuanian dataset). The high accuracy of the character features is the most likely due to the different inflective endings which are captured intrinsically, without referring to any external tools. Especially that the external tools (as lemmatizers) for some Baltic or Slavic languages are not available or, if available, are not very accurate. Besides, when dealing with the non-normative texts lemmatizers are not effective enough, therefore features based on the lemma information are easily outperformed by the character feature types (as in [18]). However, it is still difficult to draw the conclusion which character feature type in terms of the order (*N*) and the level (document or word) is the best for both languages. This issue still requires more thorough investigation on the selected Baltic or Slavic language.

We made an error analysis of the best results achieved with SVM and *lem1* on both Lithuanian and Russian datasets. The *Basketball* topic was classified the best, *Life* – the worst on the Lithuanian dataset. The *Life* topic is a very general topic, therefore it's confusions with *Beauty and health* or *Stories* can be logically explained. E.g., for the person working in the beauty and health business it becomes a part of his/her life; different stories are from his/her life as well. The *Sport* was classified the best, *Science* – the worst on the Russian dataset. The *Science* topic is confused with *Health* very often, which is again not very surprising, due the number articles about the scientific achievements in the medicine. In essence, all confusions can be logically explained, especially having in mind that even for the humans sometimes are rather difficult to make the correct topic assignment to some text.

Inspired by the results described in [24] (where the legislative text documents are classified effectively according to their title) we ran several control topic classification experiments, based on the titles of the articles only, but keeping all other experimental conditions the same. The best results were achieved with NBM and *leml* for both languages, which proved the robustness of NBM to deal with the smaller datasets. Since the titles contain less contextual information compared to the whole articles (including those titles), the accuracies were much lower. The best results are ~ 0.639 and ~ 0.371 of the accuracy on the Lithuanian and Russian datasets, respectively. Moreover, the Russian titles were ~ 2 tokens shorter (~ 4.43 tokens) compared to the Lithuanian (~ 6.36 tokens) resulting in even lower accuracy.

6 Conclusions and Future Research

The main contribution of this research is a comparative study of methods and feature types on the vocabulary and morphologically rich Lithuanian and Russian languages.

The datasets representing different languages were composed of normative texts, similar categories and the same number of instances to maintain as equal experimental conditions as possible. Afterwards we explored the impact of two classification techniques (Support Vector Machine and Naïve Bayes Multinomial) and the various individual and compound feature representation types (27 in total) covering different levels of abstraction: character, lexical, and morpho-syntactic.

The best results –in particular, ~ 0.858 and ~ 0.860 of accuracy on the Lithuanian and Russian datasets, respectively– were achieved with the Support Vector Machine method and the token lemmas as the feature representation type. The character feature types were the second best for the both languages and would be the best if morphological tools would be absent or not very accurate.

Since the same findings about the methods and feature types hold for both Lithuanian and Russian languages we anticipate these findings should hold for the other similar languages from the Baltic and Slavic branch.

In the future research we are planning to experiment with more languages and with different language types (including non-normative texts) to test if this hypothesis still holds.

Acknowledgments. This research is funded by ESFA (DADA, VP1-3.1-ŠMM-10-V-02-025).

References

1. Ageev, M.S., Dobrov, B.V., Lukashevich, N.V., Sidorov, A.V.: Experimental search/classification algorithms and comparison with the "basic line". In: All-Russian Scientific Conference (RCDL 2004), pp. 62–89 (2004). (in Russian)
2. Bina, B., Ahmadi, M.H., Rahgozar, M.: Farsi text classification using N-Grams and Knn algorithm a comparative study. In: Proceedings of the International Conference on Data Mining (DMIN 2008), pp. 385–390 (2008)

3. Boulis, C., Ostendorf, M.: Text classification by augmenting the bag-of-words representation with redundancy-compensated bigrams. In: Proceedings of the SIAM International Conference on Data Mining at the Workshop on Feature Selection in Data Mining, (SIAM-FSDM 2005) (2005)
4. Cortes, C., Vapnik, V.: Support-vector networks. Mach. Learn. 20(3), 273–297 (1995)
5. Daudaravičius, V., Rimkutė, E., Utka, A.: Morphological annotation of the Lithuanian corpus. In: Proceedings of the Workshop on Balto-Slavonic Natural Language Processing: Information Extraction and Enabling Technologies (ACL 2007), pp. 94–99 (2007)
6. Dumais, S., Platt, J., Heckerman, D., Sahami, M.: Inductive learning algorithms and representations for text categorization. In: Proceedings of the 7th International Conference on Information and Knowledge Management, pp. 148–155 (1998)
7. Forman, G., Guyon, I., Elisseeff, A.: An extensive empirical study of feature selection metrics for text classification. J. Mach. Learn. Res. 3, 1289–1305 (2003)
8. Fortuna, B., Mladenič, D.: Using string kernels for classification of slovenian web documents. In: Proceedings of From Data and Information Analysis to Knowledge Engineering, pp. 358–365 (2005)
9. Gabrilovich, E., Markovitch, S.: Text categorization with many redundant features: using aggressive feature selection to make SVMs competitive with C4.5. In: Proceedings of the 21st International Conference on Machine Learning, pp. 321–328 (2004)
10. Gaustad, T., Bouma, G.: Accurate stemming of dutch for text classification. In: Proceedings of the Computational Linguistics in the Netherlands, pp. 104–117 (2002)
11. Gharib, T.F., Habib, M.B., Fayed, Z.T.: Arabic text classification using support vector machines. Int. J. Comput. Appl. 16(4), 192–199 (2009)
12. Hall, M., Frank, E., Holmes, G., Pfahringer, B., Reutemann, P., Witten, I.H.: The WEKA data mining software: an update. SIGKDD Explor. 11(1), 10–18 (2009)
13. Hayes, P.J., Weinstein, S.P.: CONSTRUE/TIS: a system for content-based indexing of a database of news stories. In: Proceedings of the 2nd Conference on Innovative Applications of Artificial Intelligence (IAAI-90), pp. 49–64 (1990)
14. Hrala, M., Král, P.: Evaluation of the document classification approaches. In: Proceedings of the 8th International Conference on Computer Recognition Systems, pp. 877–885 (2013)
15. Hrala, M., Král, P.: Multi-label document classification in Czech. In: Proceedings of 16th International Conference on Text, Speech, and Dialogue, pp. 343–351 (2013)
16. Ikonomakis, M., Kotsiantis, S., Tampakas, V.: Text classification using machine learning techniques. WSEAS Trans. Comput. 8(4), 966–974 (2005)
17. Joachims, T.: Text categorization with support vector machines: learning with many relevant features. In: Proceedings of ECML-98, 10th European Conference on Machine Learning 1398, pp. 137–142 (1998)
18. Kapočiūtė-Dzikienė, J., Vaassen, F., Daelemans, W., Krupavičius, A.: Improving topic classification for highly inflective languages. In: Proceedings of the 24th International Conference on Computational Linguistics (COLING 2012), pp. 1393–1410 (2012)
19. Khreisat, K.: Arabic text classification using N-gram frequency statistics: a comparative study. In: Proceedings of International Conference on Data Mining (DMIN 2006), pp. 78–82 (2006)
20. Kotsiantis, S.B.: Supervised machine learning: a review of classification techniques. Informatica 31, 249–268 (2007)
21. Lehečka, J., Švec, J.: Improving multi-label document classification of Czech news articles. In: Proceedings of the 18th International Conference on Text, Speech and Dialogue, pp. 307–315 (2015)
22. Leopold, E., Kindermann, J.: Text categorization with support vector machines. how to represent texts in input space? Mach. Learn. 46(1–3), 423–444 (2002)

23. Lewis, D.D, Gale, W.A.: A sequential algorithm for training text classifiers. In: Proceedings of the 17th Annual International ACM-SIGIR Conference on Research and Development in Information Retrieval (SIGIR-94), pp. 3–12 (1994)

24. Mackutė-Varoneckienė, A., Krilavičius, T., Morkevičius, V., Medelis, Ž.: Automatic Classification of Lithuanian Parliament Bills. Technical report No. 2014-CS-01, Baltic Institute of Advanced Technology, Vilnius, Lithuania, p. 6 (2014)

25. McCallum, A., Nigam, K.: A comparison of event models for Naive Bayes text classification. In: Proceedings of AAAI-98 Workshop on Learning for Text Categorization, pp. 41–48 (1998)

26. McNemar, Q.M.: Note on the sampling error of the difference between correlated proportions or percentages. Psychometrika 12(2), 153–157 (1947)

27. Nastase, V., Sayyad, J., Caropreso, M.F.: Using Dependency Relations for Text Classification. Technical report TR-2007-12, University of Ottawa, Ottawa, Canada, p. 13 (2007)

28. Peng, F., Schuurmans, D., Wang, S.: Language and task independent text categorization with simple language models. In: Proceedings of the 2003 Conference of the North American Chapter of the Association for Computational Linguistics on Human Language Technology (NAACL 2003), vol. 1, pp. 110–117 (2003)

29. Radovanović, Miloš, Ivanović, Mirjana: Document representations for classification of short web-page descriptions. In: Tjoa, A.Min, Trujillo, Juan (eds.) DaWaK 2006. LNCS, vol. 4081, pp. 544–553. Springer, Heidelberg (2006)

30. Rimkutė, E., Daudaravičius, V.: Morphological annotation of the Lithuanian corpus. Kalbų studijos 11, 30–35 (2007). (in Lithuanian)

31. Rogati, M., Yang, Y.: High-performing feature selection for text classification. In: Proceedings of the 11th International Conference on Information and Knowledge Management (CIKM 2002), pp. 659–661 (2002)

32. Saveski, M., Trajkovski I., Pehcevski J.: Classification of macedonian news articles. In: Proceedings of the Conference on Information Technologies for Young Researchers, pp. 1–5 (2011)

33. Schmid, H.: Probabilistic part-of-speech tagging using decision trees. In: Proceedings of International Conference on New Methods in Language Processing (1994)

34. Sebastiani, F.: Machine learning in automated text categorization. ACM Comput. Surv. 34, 1–47 (2002)

35. Šilić, A., Chauchat, J.H., Bašić, B.D., Morin, A.: N-Grams and morphological normalization in text classification: a comparison on a Croatian-English parallel corpus. In: Proceedings of the 13th Portuguese Conference on Artificial Intelligence, pp. 671–682 (2007)

36. Sokyrko, A.B., Toldova, C.J.: Comparison of the effectiveness of two methods by removing the lexical and morphological ambiguity in the Russian language (hidden Markov model and syntactic parser) (2005). Technical report at http://www.aot.ru/docs/RusCorporaHMM.htm, (in Russian)

37. Stas, J., Zlacky, D., Hladek, D., Juhar, J.: Categorization of unorganized text corpora for better domain-specific language modeling. Adv. Electr. Electron. Eng. 11(5), 398–403 (2013)

38. Tan, C.M., Yuan-Fang, W., Chan-Do, L.: The use of bigrams to enhance text categorization. Inf. Process. Manage. 38(4), 529–546 (2002)

39. Tóth, J., Kondelová, A., Rozinaj, G.: Advanced text categorization methods with statistical approach. Electrorevue 4(2), 40–44 (2013)

40. Wahbeh, A., Al-Kabi, M., Al-Radaideh, Q.A., Al-Shawakfa, E.M., Alsmadi, I.: The effect of stemming on arabic text classification: an empirical study. Int. J. Inf. Retrieval Res. 1(3), 54–70 (2011)

41. Westa, Mateusz, Szymański, Julian, Krawczyk, Henryk: Text classifiers for automatic articles categorization. In: Rutkowski, Leszek, Korytkowski, Marcin, Scherer, Rafał, Tadeusiewicz, Ryszard, Zadeh, Lotfi A., Zurada, Jacek M. (eds.) ICAISC 2012, Part II. LNCS, vol. 7268, pp. 196–204. Springer, Heidelberg (2012)
42. Yang, Y., Liu, X.: A re-examination of text categorization methods. In: Proceedings of the 22nd Annual International ACM SIGIR Conference on Research and Development in Information Retrieval, pp. 42–49 (1999)
43. Zhikov, V., Nikolova, I., Tolosi, L., Ivanov, Y., Georgiev, G.: Theme extraction in bulgarian: experiments in supervised and unsupervised settings. In: Proceedings of CLoBL 2012: Workshop on Computational Linguistics and Natural Language Processing of Balkan Languages (2012)
44. Zhikov, V., Nikolova, I., Tolosi, L., Ivanov, Y., Popov, B., Georgiev, G.: Enhancing social news media in bulgarian with natural language processing. INFOtheca 2(13), 6–18 (2012)
45. Zinkevičius, V.: Morphological Analysis with Lemuoklis. Darbai ir dienos 24, 246–273 (2000). (in Lithuanian)

Vector Space Representations of Documents in Classifying Finnish Social Media Texts

Viljami Venekoski[✉], Samir Puuska, and Jouko Vankka

National Defence University, 00861 Helsinki, Finland
viljami.venekoski@mil.fi

Abstract. Computational analysis of linguistic data requires that texts are transformed into numeric representations. The aim of this research is to evaluate different methods for building vector representations of text documents from social media. The methods are compared in respect to their performance in a classification task. Namely, traditional count-based term frequency-inverse document frequency (TFIDF) is compared to the semantic distributed word embedding representations. Unlike previous research, we investigate document representations in the context of morphologically rich Finnish. Based on the results, we suggest a framework for building vector space representations of texts in social media, applicable to language technologies for morphologically rich languages. In the current study, lemmatization of tokens increased classification accuracy, while lexical filtering generally hindered performance. Finally, we report that distributed embeddings and TFIDF perform at comparable levels with our data.

Keywords: Natural language processing · Vector space models · Distributed embeddings · word2vec · TFIDF · Classification · Social media

1 Introduction

The vast amount of linguistic data constantly accumulating in online social media yields valuable information to many organization. Researches, corporations and the intelligence community alike can benefit from technologies designed to effectively analyze such data. Advances in natural language processing make text mining a more feasible task than ever before. However, the traditional natural language processing (NLP) methods can struggle with social media texts as these tend to be fragmentary and have different morpho-syntactic structure in comparison to more formal literary texts.

Language technologies benefit from transforming linguistic data into a more easily computable format than mere strings. The choice of representation is crucial to any linguistic analysis. Representational models need not be constructed from the entirety of data. Excluding a portion of tokens can enhance the performance of an NLP application such as a classifier. Feature reduction is a crucial step in avoiding the curse of dimensionality, and consequently, needs to be considered in order to achieve a successful document classification framework.

© Springer International Publishing Switzerland 2016
G. Dregvaite and R. Damasevicius (Eds.): ICIST 2016, CCIS 639, pp. 525–535, 2016.
DOI: 10.1007/978-3-319-46254-7_42

Following Baroni et al. [1], two types of representational vector space models for texts can be distinguished: context-counting and context-predicting models. Out of the former, the term frequency-inverse document frequency (TFIDF) weighting approach [2] has been arguably the most widely used vector space representation of text documents. Recently, the context-predicting models such as distributed word embeddings have risen in popularity. Notably, the neural network -based embeddings are able to capture semantic properties of words and can thus be better suited for language technologies where information on semantics ought to be beneficial, such as those related to information retrieval or knowledge discovery. Overall, the research comparing the two types of vector space models remains mixed [1,3].

The aim of this paper is to evaluate distributed embeddings against the traditional count-based TFIDF method. The methods for building document representations are evaluated in regards to differences in performance in a classification task. We focus on social media texts since there is much interest in efficient language technologies for that context [4]. Further, vector representations have previously struggled with the sparseness of social media texts, especially in the case morphologically rich languages such as Finnish. Thus, we address these isssues by evaluating the effects of lemmatization and Part of Speech filtering. Figure 1 illustrates an overview of the steps in the classification pipeline utilized in this study. It is demonstrated that lemmatization of input can provide improvements in classifier performance. We also find that Part of Speech filters do not benefit classification to a considerable degree, and can in fact hinder performance. Finally, we see that TFIDF and embedding-based representations achieve comparable classification performance with a 100 000 document corpus of Finnish social media text.

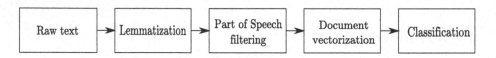

Fig. 1. The general classification pipeline of the study.

1.1   Related Work

In this paper, we evaluate only some of the proposed methods for building document representations. Three methods are examined: TFIDF, naïve doc2vec, and Paragraph Vector. TFIDF weighting was used as a baseline 'count' method but other similar approaches have been utilized extensively [1]. Other 'predict-models' such as Latent Drichilet Allocation [5] or Latent Semantic Indexing [6] are not evaluated here due to the fact that recent research [1,7,8] indicates that the utilized word2vec embeddings of Mikolov et al. [9] surpass the former approaches in performance.

There are numerous methods for constructing document representations from word embeddings. For instance, de Boom et al. [10] present an importance factor weighting approach, which is akin to POS filtering and lemmatization heuristics utilized in this paper, albeit a more sophisticated approach. Liu et al. [11] propose a 'topical word embedding' representation for individual documents where latent topic models are used to assign topics to all individual words, and subsequently, document embeddings are learned based on word and their associated topics. Our choice to include topic tags in building the Paragraph Vector models incorporates a similar principle.

Recently, embedding-based approaches to document classification have been presented. For instance, Taddy [12] proposes a classifier based on inversion of Bayes' rule on class likelihood of word vectors in a given document. Kusner et al. [13] present a method for computing similarities between documents based on earth mover's distance and a similarity-based implementation for a k-Nearest Neighbors classifier. Such solutions tailored for embedding representations may yield better classification scores than general purpose classifiers.

Only one previous study [14] has utilized distributed embeddings with Finnish. Applying language technologies to a morphologically complex language such as Finnish can be a non-trivial task particularly when the tools have been developed primarily for the analysis of English data [15]. Our research is first to investigate the usefulness of Finnish word embeddings in classification, and also the first to use the Suomi24 Corpus [16].

2 Document Representations

2.1 Term Frequency-Inverse Document Frequency

Term frequency-inverse document frequency weighting approach [2] is a widely applied method for representing text documents. First, a vocabulary is built from all the unique words that appear in the corpus. Given a vocabulary size n, documents are represented with an n-dimensional feature vector. The features or vector elements are assigned based on the frequency of the word in the document, and importantly, weighted based on the word's frequency in the whole corpus. Thus, words which appear in numerous documents contribute relatively little to the feature vectors while the contribution of uncommon words is increased.

In regards to classification, the method essentially relies on overlap of words in documents belonging to the same class [13]. However, sufficient overlap may not always exist, particularly in social media texts. Further, the features of TFIDF vectors do not reflect semantic similarities between individual words in the documents, merely the relative frequencies of tokens [10]. Despite its conceptual limitations, the TFIDF method generally performs at satisfactory levels in NLP tasks like document classification.

2.2 Distributed Word Embeddings

Distributed word embeddings are neural network -based vector space models which aim to learn words and their distributions across contexts. Their aim is to learn to predict the most likely word given a context, or vice versa, using a non-linear hidden layer. In the output layer, words are represented as d-dimensional feature vectors, where d is a model parameter which is usually assigned a value between 100–500. Together they form an embedding matrix $X \in \mathbb{R}^{d \times n}$ where n is the number of words in the vocabulary. As predicted by the distributional hypothesis in linguistics [17], learning distribution of words' contexts translates into learning semantic properties of the words. Recent research indicates that distributed embedding vectors can act as universal semantic feature extractors which can be utilized particularly well in semantic classification of texts [18].

We used the word2vec software [9,19] to create word embeddings, implemented in Python via the Gensim package [20]. Specifically, we utilized the Skip-gram architecture where the word vectors are built with a model which tries to learn maximum probability of a context given a word. Based on [1,3] and initial tests, the model was constructed with the following hyperparameters: negative sampling 10, feature vector size 400, window size 5, and minimum frequency of tokens set at 10. Approximately one fifth of the Suomi24 Corpus was used to construct the embeddings, encompassing more than 12 million unique messages and altogether 541 897 534 tokens.

2.3 Naïve Document Vectors

The word2vec embeddings have been proven to work very well as representations for individual words [1,21] but utilizing embeddings on sentence or document level is a more complex task. Presumably, sentences can be represented analogously to word representations – as n-dimensional feature vectors. However, there is no evidently superior method for constructing feature vectors from multi-word sentences.

A simple method is to compute a document's average word vector by taking the arithmetic mean of individual word vectors for words which occur in a given document (henceforth called naïve doc2vec or Nd2v). Consequently, such a method makes the implicit assumption that the semantic content of a sentence is equal to the average of semantic content of words. Note that as the distributed word embeddings of word2vec allow for any linear operations on the vectors, the methods discussed in this paper do not reflect all the possible ways in which one could, in principle, construct document vectors.

2.4 Paragraph Vectors

The principle used in building word2vec embeddings can equally be used to build vector representations of documents. The Paragraph Vector (PV) method [7] represents documents analogously to words in an embedding space. The PV method incorporates the document index as a contextual element in the context window alongside words. Thus, words within a document are associated with the document at the learning stage. Given a novel document d_j, the previously learned word embeddings for the words w_j in d_j can be utilized to predict the most likely vector representation for their common context, i.e., the document d_j.

Furthermore, it is possible to associate other tags with the embeddings being learned, such as a topic.

As with word embeddings, we first experimented with different hyperparameter settings. The chosen hyperparameters were: feature size 300, minimum token frequency of 5, window size 10, and hierarchical softmax. We utilized the Distributed Memory model instead of the Continuous Bag of Words model (see [7]). We also used the topic of a document as a contextual element in learning the embeddings (see [11]). As with word2vec models, the Paragraph Vectors were also built in Python using the Gensim package [20].

3   Preprocessing Documents

3.1   Normalizing Word Forms via Lemmatization

Most of the previous NLP research has been conducted with English or Chinese. Compared to these languages, Finnish has very rich morphology. Much of the grammatical information in Finnish is conveyed via inflectional morphemes, specifically, suffixes [22]. For instance, there are as much as 12 000 inflected forms for each verb. Due to morphological richness, the vocabulary sizes of Finnish corpora tend to be greater than, e.g., in equivalent English corpora [23]. If models are built from tokens as they appear in corpora, curse of dimensionality can become detrimental to vector space models. Normalizing the word forms can greatly reduce the number of vocabulary entries, and thus the dimensionality. However, some research indicates that word form normalization may have no significant effect [24] or even a negative effect on classification accuracy [25], also in morphologically rich languages [26].

The two main methods for word form normalization are stemming and lemmatization [26]. For Finnish, lemmatization functions significantly better than stemming [27]. Lemmatization is the process of identifying the base form for each inflected form. Homographic tokens present a further need for disambiguating what is the correct lemma referent for a token with alternative interpretations given its morphological form. For instance, the token *puheluilta* is a homograph for the inflected forms *puhelu+i+lta* (in English, call+PL+ABL, lit. *from the calls*), *puhe|lu+i+lta* (speech.SG.NOM|bone+PL+ABL, lit. *from the speech bones*) or *puhelu|ilta* (call.SG.NOM|night.SG.NOM, lit. *a call night*). Lemmatizers aim to predict the correct base form given the token's context.

Semantic information is lost when inflectional morphemes are removed. However, the information from morphemes may be irrelevant in regards to classification of documents. We hypothesize that document representations built from lemmatized tokens should yield better performance with classifiers compared to non-lemmatized versions. In the current study, the words were lemmatized with the open source Finnish-dep-parser software [28]. According to the authors, the parser estimates the correct lemma with 91.8 % accuracy. Lemmatized as well as non-lemmatized documents were used to build document representations.

3.2   Part of Speech Filtering

Document vectors can be constructed by selecting only some of the words as features contributing to the document vector. The most common methods are removal of punctuation and stop words, and lexical filters. Alternatively, the weights of elements corresponding to specific tokens can be adjusted in order to diminish the tokens' contribution. The purpose of filters is to prune the documents from irrelevant tokens and reduce semantic noise. For instance, Salvetti et al. [29] implemented a Part-of-Speech (POS) filter and hypernymy based generalization filter in an opinion polarity classifier of movie reviews. Both filters improved the classifier performance compared to a no-filter alternative, the POS filter improving classification accuracy the most. Research on Czech [24] – a morphologically rich language – indicates that POS filtering can result in substantial increase in classification accuracy, but only when the appropriate POS tags are removed.

We evaluated the effect of POS filtering by comparing results between classifiers using document representations built from POS filtered data to those using representations built from unfiltered data. We examined which POS tags should be retained to achieve best classifier performance. The POS tags were attained from the morphological analysis of Finnish-dep-parser, which is reported to estimate the correct POS with 94.4% accuracy [28].

4   Document Classification

4.1   Data

To evaluate the different document representations in social media context, we used data from the Suomi24 Corpus [16]. The corpus comprised of user posts on a popular Finnish internet forum between the years 2001–2015. In total, the corpus contains approximately 50 million unique messages. Each message in the corpus was associated with topics, and thus, no manual annotation to classes was required. There is great variably between individual posts as the average length of documents is 45 tokens while the standard deviation is 65 tokens. The messages are assumed to be semantically varied between topics, albeit only to an extent. The users may not always start threads in relevant topic sections and the conversations can be off-topic, which makes the data semantically noisy and the classes non-orthogonal. However, naturalistic conversations are semantically dynamic. Furthermore, text mining often relies on automatically labelled data while manually labelled golden standards are not available, and this data suits testing the document representations for such settings.

For the purposes of the current research, we included all the messages from five topic sections of the corpus – a total of appr. 12 million messages. An equal number of messages was chosen from each topic in order not to bias the classifiers towards specific topics by having an uneven amount of training data. The topics were labelled 'Travelling', 'Youth', 'Sports and Exercise', 'Vehicles and Traffic' and 'Society'. We did not include documents which contained only special characters or numbers, or those that had less than 2 tokens. All characters were changed to lower case. Further, we removed urls and email addresses from the documents alongside numbers and non-punctuation special characters.

4.2 Classifier

A multiclass Support Vector Machine (SVM) classifier was used as the classifier based on initial results and its suitability for classifying embedding-based document representations [30]. SVM separates two classes in the feature space with widest possible margin, and in the multiclass approach, a combination of multiple binary classifiers are used. The class whose classifier produces the highest output function value is chosen as the correct class. In our multiclass classifier, a one-versus-one max-wins method was used.

4.3 Evaluation of Performance

To evaluate classifier performance with different document representation, we calculated the standard classification performance metrics – recall, precision and F_1 [31]. We experimented with different set sizes but saw no significant increase in performance in other representations beside TFIDF with very large test sets. Thus, we chose to continue investigation with a 100 000 document test set for all methods to ease the computation time for more demanding representational models. 10-fold cross-validation was performed on the dataset and the differences in relevant values were compared using a two sample t tests with 95 % confidence level [32]. All the differences reported below were statistically significant ($p <$ 0.001).

5   Results

The document representations made via TFIDF, naïve doc2vec and Paragraph Vector methods were compared in categorical classification task. SVM classifier was used with all of the representations. In Table 1, results are reported for lemmatized (*lem*) and non-lemmatized data for each document representation, and for lemmatized POS filtered data (*POSf*) using the best POS filter.

The Nd2v representation with lemmatized and POS filtered input achieves the best classification scores. The difference to TFIDF and PV is statistically significant but only approximately 0.05 % points. Lemmatization results in notable increases in scores for TFIDF and Nd2v (appr. 4 %-points), and a lesser but significant increase for PV.

Based on the aforementioned research, Part of Speech filtering was expected to improve classification scores. The effects of different POS filters were evaluated by comparing the F_1 scores of the classifier when classifying document representations which were built from words with specified POS tags. We examined documents comprising of nouns (N) and additionally all configurations of verbs (V), adjectives (A) and adverbs (D). The results are reported in Fig. 2.

Table 1. Performance of different document representations in classification task.

Representation	Recall	Precision	F_1
TFIDF	0.73568	0.73374	0.73402
lem+TFIDF	0.77428	0.77170	0.77212
lem+POSf+TFIDF	0.77745	0.77322	0.77389
Nd2v	0.74068	0.73955	0.73884
lem+Nd2v	0.77727	0.77479	0.77481
lem+POSf+Nd2v	**0.78154**	**0.77859**	**0.77885**
PV	0.75112	0.75028	0.75027
lem+PV	0.77342	0.77192	0.77206
lem+POSf+PV	0.77984	0.77802	0.77829

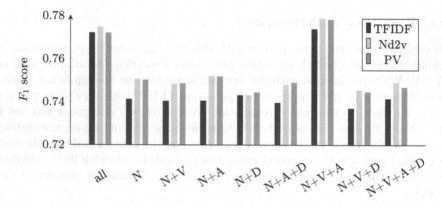

Fig. 2. Effect of different POS filters on F_1 score. The letters on the x-axis indicate which POS tagged words were utilized to construct the document vectors, when N = nouns, V = verbs, A = adjectives, D = adverbs.

Removing words with specific POS tags before constructing document representations appears to affect classification negatively. Most POS filtered documents achieve F_1 scores approximately 2 % points lower compared to documents with all original words. TFIDF in particular exhibits the greatest performance losses. Documents built from nouns, adjectives and adverbs improved the F_1 score compared to a no-filter alternative but only marginally.

6   Discussion

We examined different vector representations of social media text documents. The representations were tested in a topical classification task, where the methods achieved arguably sufficient performance. The performance of distributed embedding models did not yield significantly better results than the TFIDF method. We saw, however, a significant increase in performance when we used lemmatized documents compared to non-lemmatized alternatives. This indicates that lemmatization should be considered when working with language technologies in Finnish or other morphologically rich languages.

Lexical filtering based on POS tags was evaluated. Contrary to certain previous studies [24,29,33] yet in line with others [25,26], we mostly observed decreases in classification scores when POS filtering was used. While a filter which retained nouns, verbs and adjectives yielded slightly better scores, the improvement was marginal. This suggest that a POS filter may not provide to be useful in classification framework for Finnish documents. If used, it should be evaluated against a no-filter baseline to ensure whether it is beneficial to the task at hand.

Despite similar levels of classifier performance, the embedding-based representations may be more suitable for some text mining related tasks. As semantic representations, they allow a more efficient and reliable way of discovering relationships and similarities between documents particularly when the relationships are not known a priori. Where word2vec embeddings have consistently been demonstrated to retain semantic properties of words [1,21,34], the Paragraph Vector method has recently been shown to achieve the same with longer documents [8]. Accurate semantic representations and similarity estimates can be utilized in, e.g., commercial applications like user recommendations, or by the intelligence community in discovering unknown risks and entities. The classification task here should not be taken as an assessment of semantic reliability of vector representations – it merely functions as a baseline language technology task and enables comparisons between different representational approaches. Our results indicate that embedding representations are a potential alternative to tasks where count-based approaches are insufficient.

In respect to classification, the semantic accuracy of document representations is irrelevant as long as classifiers perform sufficiently well. Our results indicate that the simple method of averaging of word embeddings within a document (Nd2v) provided good scores on classification, although the method may be semantically questionable. The semantic reliability of embeddings should be evaluated in tasks which explicitly require assessing the semantic similarity of input units [34], such as information retrieval or in correlational studies with human similarity judgements. We would like to encourage future research directed towards systematic evaluation of different methods for constructing document and sentence level representations from distributed embeddings, as well as more exhaustive reviews of the usability of different vector representations.

References

1. Baroni, M., Dinu, G., Kruszewski, G.: Don't count, predict! A systematic comparison of context-counting vs. context-predicting semantic vectors. In: ACL (1). pp. 238–247 (2014)
2. Jones, K.S.: A statistical interpretation of term specificity and its application in retrieval. J. Documentation 28(1), 11–21 (1972)

3. Levy, O., Goldberg, Y., Dagan, I.: Improving distributional similarity with lessons learned from word embeddings. Trans. Assoc. Comput. Linguist. **3**, 211–225 (2015)
4. Friedman, C., Rindflesch, T.C., Corn, M.: Natural language processing: state of the art and prospects for significant progress, a workshop sponsored by the National Library of Medicine. J. Biomed. Inf. **46**(5), 765–773 (2013)
5. Blei, D.M., Ng, A.Y., Jordan, M.I.: Latent Dirichlet allocation. J. Mach. Learn. Res. **3**, 993–1022 (2003)
6. Deerwester, S., Dumais, S.T., Furnas, G.W., Landauer, T.K., Harshman, R.: Indexing by latent semantic analysis. J. Am. Soc. Inf. Sci. **41**(6), 391 (1990)
7. Le, Q.V., Mikolov, T.: Distributed representations of sentences and documents. arXiv preprint (2014). http://arxiv.org/pdf/1405.4053.pdf
8. Dai, A.M., Olah, C., Le, Q.V.: Document embedding with paragraph vectors. arXiv preprint arXiv:1507.07998 (2015)
9. Mikolov, T., Chen, K., Corrado, G., Dean, J.: Efficient estimation of word representations in vector space. arXiv preprint (2013). http://arxiv.org/pdf/1301.3781.pdf
10. De Boom, C., Van Canneyt, S., Bohez, S., Demeester, T., Dhoedt, B.: Learning semantic similarity for very short texts. arXiv preprint arXiv:1512.00765 (2015)
11. Liu, Y., Liu, Z., Chua, T.S., Sun, M.: Topical word embeddings. In: Proceedings of the Twenty-Ninth AAAI Conference on Artificial Intelligence, pp. 2418–2424 (2015)
12. Taddy, M.: Document classification by inversion of distributed language representations. arXiv preprint (2015). http://arxiv.org/pdf/1504.07295.pdf
13. Kusner, M., Sun, Y., Kolkin, N., Weinberger, K.Q.: From word embeddings to document distances. In: Proceedings of the 32nd International Conference on Machine Learning (ICML-2015), pp. 957–966 (2015)
14. Kanerva, J., Ginter, F.: Post-hoc manipulations of vector space models with application to semantic role labeling. In: Proceedings of the 2nd Workshop on Continuous Vector Space Models and their Compositionality (CVSC) at EACL 2014, pp. 1–10 (2014). https://aclweb.org/anthology/W/W14/W14-1501.pdf
15. Tsarfaty, R., Seddah, D., Kübler, S., Nivre, J.: Parsing morphologically rich languages: introduction to the special issue. Comput. Linguistics **39**(1), 15–22 (2013)
16. The Suomi24 Corpus (2015). http://urn.fi/urn:nbn:fi:lb-2015040801. 14 May 2015 Version
17. Harris, Z.S.: Distributional structure. Word **10**(2–3), 146–162 (1954)
18. Kim, Y.: Convolutional neural networks for sentence classification. In: Proceedings of the 2014 Conference on Empirical Methods in Natural Language Processing (EMNLP), pp. 1746–1751. Association for Computational Linguistics (2014)
19. Mikolov, T., Sutskever, I., Chen, K., Corrado, G., Dean, J.: Distributed representations of words and phrases and their compositionality. In: Advances in Neural Information Processing Systems, pp. 3111–3119 (2013)
20. Řehůřek, R., Sojka, P.: Software framework for topic modelling with large corpora. In: Proceedings of the LREC 2010 Workshop on New Challenges for NLP Frameworks, pp. 45–50. ELRA, Valletta, May 2010. http://is.muni.cz/publication/884893/en
21. Mikolov, T., Yih, W.t., Zweig, G.: Linguistic regularities in continuous space word representations. In: Proceedings of the HLT-NAACL, pp. 746–751 (2013)
22. Hakulinen, A., Vilkuna, M., Korhonen, R., Koivisto, V., Heinonen, T.R., Alho, I.: Ison suomen kielioppi [Great Grammar of Finnish]. Suomalaisen Kirjallisuuden Seura, Helsinki, Finland, online (edn.) (2004). http://scripta.kotus.fi/visk

23. Enarvi, S., Kurimo, M.: Studies on training text selection for conversational Finish language modeling. In: Proceedings of the 10th International Workshop on Spoken Language Translation (IWSLT 2013), pp. 256–263 (2013)
24. Hrala, M., Král, P.: Evaluation of the document classification approaches. In: Burduk, R., Jackowski, K., Kurzynski, M., Wozniak, M., Zolnierek, A. (eds.) CORES 2013. AISC, vol. 226, pp. 877–885. Springer, Switzerland (2013)
25. Khoo, A., Marom, Y., Albrecht, D.: Experiments with sentence classification. In: Proceedings of the 2006 Australasian Language Technology Workshop, pp. 18–25 (2006)
26. Toman, M., Tesar, R., Jezek, K.: Influence of word normalization on text classification. Proc. InSciT **4**, 354–358 (2006)
27. Korenius, T., Laurikkala, J., Järvelin, K., Juhola, M.: Stemming and lemmatization in the clustering of Finnish text documents. In: Proceedings of the Thirteenth ACM International Conference on Information and Knowledge Management, pp. 625–633. ACM (2004)
28. Haverinen, K., Nyblom, J., Viljanen, T., Laippala, V., Kohonen, S., Missilä, A., Ojala, S., Salakoski, T., Ginter, F.: Building the essential resources for Finnish: the Turku Dependency Treebank. Lang. Resour. Eval. **48**(3), 493–531 (2013)
29. Salvetti, F., Lewis, S., Reichenbach, C.: Automatic opinion polarity classification of movie reviews. Colorado Res. Linguist. **17**(1) (2004)
30. Joachims, Thorsten: Text categorization with Support Vector Machines: learning with many relevant features. In: Nédellec, Claire, Rouveirol, Céline (eds.) ECML 1998. LNCS, vol. 1398, pp. 137–142. Springer, Heidelberg (1998). doi:10.1007/BFb0026683
31. van Rijsbergen, C.J.: Information Retrieval, 2nd edn. Butterworth-Heinemann, Newton, MA, USA (1979)
32. Dietterich, T.G.: Approximate statistical tests for comparing supervised classification learning algorithms. Neural Comput. **10**(7), 1895–1923 (1998)
33. Qin, S., Song, J., Zhang, P., Tan, Y.: Feature selection for text classification based on part of speech filter and synonym merge. In: Proceedings of the 2015 12th International Conference on Fuzzy Systems and Knowledge Discovery (FSKD), pp. 681–685. IEEE (2015)
34. Hill, F., Reichart, R., Korhonen, A.: SimLex-999: evaluating semantic models with (genuine) similarity estimation. Computational Linguist. **41**(4), 665–695 (2015)

Text Type Differentiation Based on the Structural Properties of Language Networks

Sanda Martinčić-Ipšić$^{(\boxtimes)}$, Tanja Miličić, and Ana Meštrović

Department of Informatics, University of Rijeka,
Radmile Matejčić 2, 51000 Rijeka, Croatia
{smarti,tmilicic,amestrovic}@uniri.hr

Abstract. In this paper co-occurrence language network measures from literature and legal texts are compared on the global and on the local scale. Our dataset consists of four legal texts and four short novellas both written in English. For each text we construct one directed and weighted network, where weight of a link between two nodes represents overall co-occurrence frequencies of the corresponding words. We choose four literature-law pairs of texts with approximately the same number of different words for comparison. The aim of this experiment was to investigate how complex network measures operate in different structures of texts and which of them are sensitive to different text types. Our results show that on the global scale only average strength is the measure that exhibit some uniform behaviour due to the differences in textual complexity. In general, global measures may not be well suited to discriminate between mentioned genres of texts. However, local perspective rank plots of in and out selectivity (average node strength) indicate that there are more noticeable structural differences between legal texts and literature.

1 Introduction

Human language is one of the major transitions in evolution and forms the basis for the complexity of human society and culture. It allows us to express indefinite number of ideas by combining a discrete set of linguistic units (e.g. words, morphemes, syllables). Today, with the growth of the networking platforms and social media, the amount of the available documents is getting bigger every day. This lead to development of statistical natural language methods for wide variety of applications, among which is text classification. The task of text classification (assigning documents to predefined categories) is used in several domains including opinion mining, type classification, authorship attribution, topic classification, etc. This task is usually performed by representing documents as a word-vectors using the bag-of-words representation and applying some classification algorithms on these vectors [1]. With this approach documents are represented with frequencies of words that occur in them and classification tasks are dependent on their context. This way the underlying structure of documents is ignored. That may be a problem because the structure is crucial for the case of

© Springer International Publishing Switzerland 2016
G. Dregvaite and R. Damasevicius (Eds.): ICIST 2016, CCIS 639, pp. 536–548, 2016.
DOI: 10.1007/978-3-319-46254-7_43

text type classification. Since documents of different types can be written on the same topic, that is they can have a lot of words in common and may be classified together even though they should not be. More disadvantages of bag-of-words model lie in high number of features and sparse feature vectors. For example if we have to classify thousands of documents we could end up with millions of n-gram features where only a few hundreds of them are present in each document. We believe that this particularities could be avoided when representing documents in a form of a graph.

In recent years we have witnessed a growth of interest in modeling and analyzing language with complex networks (graphs) [2]. In the language complex networks linguistic units can be represented as nodes while their linguistic interactions define associations, or edges, between them. When dealing with such system that is so complex and multi-faced in its nature one cannot rely on a single type of model thus researchers have developed and analyzed various language network models such as semantic [3], syntactic [4], syllables networks [5,6], word co-occurrence networks [7,8] or multilayer language networks [9]. All of this studies show that language networks display features that are present in classical examples of complex networks. That means that starting from a given text we can construct different types of relationships among linguistic units, and thus analyze text in more abstract way that is not dependent on textual context.

In this paper we analyze topological features of language networks in order to find which network measure can best discriminate between two text types (literature and legislation). This work extends our previous research [10] by experimenting with different language and text types as well as introducing new complex networks measures that have not yet been analyzed on language networks such as efficiency and generalized centrality measure as defined in [11].

The rest of the paper is organized as follows. Section 2 reviews part of related work on language network analysis of different structures and types of texts. The key measures used in this experiment as well as basic definition of graph are presented in Sect. 3, with the experimental evaluation presented in Sect. 4. Section 5 concludes the paper.

2   Related Work

In this section, we briefly review the related work devoted to the stylistic classification and analysis of the texts within the complex networks. Results of these studies show that parameters of language networks may be potential indicators of different text types.

Amancio *et al.* [12] studied changes in writing style from books published over several centuries (from 1590 to 1922) by analyzing the metrics from complex networks. The obtained metrics, when analyzed with multivariate techniques, were able to identify periods of major literary movements. The most important measure was the asymmetry in the distribution of the average shortest path length. Next in [13] Amancio *et al.* used network measures and pattern recognition methods to investigate differences in original texts and their simplified versions.

They examined how values of local measures vary within the simplification process, which words have the same topological feature in the network, and used multivariate analysis to distinguish complex texts from their simplified versions. They showed that node strength, shortest paths, diversity and hierarchical measures can distinct between original and simplified texts. More recently, the same group of authors have also investigated the ability of network measures to classify informative and imaginative documents [14]. The most prominent measures were symmetry and accessibility. In the study of Antiqueira *et al.* [15] texts on the same topic produced by high-school students in Portuguese were represented as word co-occurrence networks. Texts were analyzed by human judges using three types of scores. It is shown that these scores are strongly correlated with particular parameters of their network models. Masucci and Rodgers [16] analyzed the difference between the statistical properties of original and shuffled networks and introduced node selectivity as a measure that can distinguish the difference. In [17] these results are confirmed for the Croatian language as well. In [18] authors analyzed statistical and network properties of literary and scientific texts written in English and Polish. They showed that the majority of the studied networks from literary texts revealed the scale-free structure, while that wasn't always true for scientific texts. They also showed that there exists some differences in node degree distributions between prose and poetry.

However, there has been no comprehensive study dedicated to find network measure that could possibly be sensitive to different text types except our previous research [10] on comparison of networks generated from literature and blogs. This initial attempt showed that calculated global network measures are not precise enough to distinguish texts from literature and blogs. The only measure that showed noticeable difference was node selectivity quantified by in-selectivity and out-selectivity rank plots. Here we extend the study of the potential of selectivity by introducing the generalized selectivity measure for text type differentiation.

3 Preliminaries

In this section we present some of the definitions and properties on the global and local scale associated with networks [19]. Local measures are calculated for each individual node and they can be of a great value in analyzing the role played by individuals in the network. On the other hand, analysis on the global scale can summarize the overall architecture of the given network. In this paper, we interchange the terminology of a graph and a network.

A graph $G = (V, E)$ is a set of nodes V and a set of edges $E = \{(i,j)|i,j \in V\}$ between the nodes. The number of nodes is $N = |V|$ and the number of edges $K = |E|$. In a directed graph each edge has a direction from one node to another. This type of graph has various types of components including weakly and strongly connected components. A node is part of strongly connected component if it has a directed path to the component and another from the component. On the other hand, two nodes are in the same weakly connected component if they are connected by one or more paths through the network, where they are allowed to go in either direction along any edge. In weighted graphs every edge has an associated weight $w \in R_0^+$ which reflects the strength of connection between the nodes.

Density of a network is a measure of network cohesion defined as the number of observed links divided by the number of total possible edges:

$$D = \frac{K}{N(N-1)} \tag{1}$$

A basic property of the nodes in G is their degree. In the case of directed networks every node is associated with an in-degree and out-degree. The out-degree and in-degree of node i, denoted by $k_i^{in/out}$, is the number of its in and out nearest neighbors. The average degree of the directed network is defined as:

$$\langle K \rangle = \frac{K}{N} \tag{2}$$

Network is said to show assortative mixing by degree if nodes tend to be connected to other nodes with similar degree. If opposite is true than we say that network show disassortative mixing by degree [23]. The assortativity coefficient r is defined as the Pearson correlation coefficient of the degrees of nodes at either ends of an edge.

$$r = \frac{\sum_{jk} jk(e_{jk} - q_j q_k)}{\sigma_q^2} \tag{3}$$

where e_{jk} refers to the joint probability distribution of the remaining degrees of the two nodes j and k, q_k is the distribution of the remaining degrees and σ_q^2 is maximal value of function for perfectly assortative network.

Degree has generally been extended to the node strength in weighted networks. The in-strength and out-strength $s_i^{in/out}$ of the node i is the sum of its ingoing and outgoing edge weights, that is:

$$s_i^{in/out} = \sum_j w_{ij/ji} \tag{4}$$

where w is weighted adjacency matrix in which $w_{ij/ji}$ represents the weight of link. Next we can define the average strength or selectivity as:

$$e_i^{in/out} = \frac{s_i^{in/out}}{k_i^{in/out}} \tag{5}$$

Opsahl et al. [11] introduced centrality measure that considers both degree and strength and uses a tuning parameter α which determines importance of the number of edges compared to edge weights. Here we call it generalized selectivity and in experimental results, we test performance with different values of parameter α.

$$C_{D-in/out}^{w\alpha} = k_i^{in/out} \times \left(\frac{s_i^{in/out}}{k_i^{in/out}}\right)^\alpha = k_i^{in/out} \times \left(e_i^{in/out}\right)^\alpha, \qquad \alpha > 0 \tag{6}$$

The clustering coefficient is a measure which defines the presence of loops of order three. It can be defined as:

$$C_i = \frac{e_{ij}}{k_i(k_i - 1)} \tag{7}$$

where e_{ij} represents the number of pairs of neighbors of i that are connected. And the average clustering coefficient of a network is defined as:

$$C = \frac{1}{N} \sum_i c_i. \tag{8}$$

Average shortest path length is:

$$L = \frac{1}{N(N - 1)} \sum_{i \neq j} d_{ij} \tag{9}$$

where d_{ij} is a shortest path between nodes i and j.

Efficiency measure was first defined by Latora and Marchiori in [20, 21] where they introduce it as a property which can show how efficiently information is exchanging over the network.

$$E_{glob}(G) = \frac{1}{N(N - 1)} \sum_{i \neq j \in G} \frac{1}{d_{ij}} \tag{10}$$

Since efficiency is also defined for disconnected graphs we can analyze the local properties of G. Local efficiency is defined as the average efficiency of the local subgraphs:

$$E_{loc} = \frac{1}{N} \sum_{i \in G} E_{glob}(G_i), \qquad i \notin G_i \tag{11}$$

where G_i is the subgraph of the neighbors of i. We note that efficiency have previously been estimated on diverse real world systems; however, there has been no previous application of these economical small metrics to human language network analysis.

4   Experimental Evaluation

4.1   Dataset

Our dataset consists of eight texts divided into two categories of four legal texts and four short novellas both written in English. Literature texts are taken from Project Gutenberg [22] and they include: "Metamorphosis" by Franz Kafka, "The Bet" and "Gooseberries" by Anton Chekhov and "Through the Looking-Glass" by Lewis Carroll. While legal text include: "Uniform Commercial Code", "Staff Regulations", "U.S. Constitution" and "Code of Federal Regulations" which are taken from web page of Legal Information Institute. Table 1 shows statistics about number of words by each category.

Table 1. Number of words by each text and category

Text	Number of words	Number of different words
Metamorphosis	22375	2599
The Bet	2866	876
Gooseberries	4017	1087
Through the Looking-Glass	30554	3034
Total	59812	7596
Uniform Commercial Code	40915	2486
Staff Regulations	4473	907
U.S. Constitution	4375	843
Code of Federal Regulations	42662	3115
Total	92425	7351

4.2 Network Construction

Network construction and analysis was implemented with the Python programming language using NetworkX software package developed for the creation, manipulation, and study of the structure, dynamics, and functions of complex networks. [24]. Additionally we use LaNCoA, a Python toolkit for language networks construction and analysis [26]. For the visualization we used Gephi software [25]. Networks are constructed in a way that words represent nodes which are in turn joined by an edge if they are adjacent in a text between punctuation marks (period, semicolon, comma, colon, parentheses, square brackets, exclamation point and question mark).

In the preprocessing step we only removed special symbols (e.g. §), we did not eliminate stop words nor used lemmatization or stemming. By this approach we can capture relations of linguistic units (words) in original language use. All networks are generated as directed and weighted, where weight of a link between two nodes represents overall co-occurrence frequencies of the corresponding words, while direction represents the ordering of linguistic units in a co-occurrence pair. Figure 1 show simple network constructed from the given text.

4.3 Results

Global Measures. The measures of the networks on the global scale are presented in Table 2. We select four literature-law pairs of texts with approximately the same number of different words for comparison. For the purpose of calculating clustering coefficient and efficiency graphs were converted to undirected, and all other measures were calculated for directed graphs.

Average clustering coefficient is low in both categories and exhibit no substantial deviations. Clustering coefficient has, as it is explained in [27], a positive effect on assortativity while branching has a negative effect. In other words,

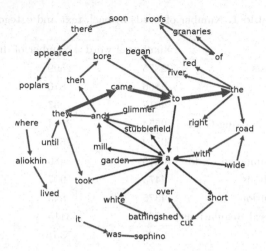

Fig. 1. Example network constructed from following text: "They took a short cut over a stubble-field and then bore to the right, until they came to the road. Soon there appeared poplars, a garden, the red roofs of granaries; the river began to glimmer and they came to a wide road with a mill and a white bathing-shed. It was Sophino, where Aliokhin lived." (Color figure online)

Table 2. Comparison of global measures

Measures	Texts							
	Metamorphosis	Uniform Commercial Code	The Bet	Staff Regulations	Gooseberries	U.S. Constitution	Through the Looking-Glass	Code of Federal Regulations
Number of words	22375	40915	2866	4473	4017	4375	30554	42662
Number of nodes (N)	2599	2486	876	907	1087	843	3034	3115
Number of edges (K)	11274	11282	1927	2131	2603	2237	12812	12810
Average degree $\langle K \rangle$	4.34	4.54	2.20	2.35	2.4	2.65	4.22	4.11
Average strength	15.19	28.32	5.64	8.61	6.2	9.02	15.96	23.43
Average clustering coefficient	0.33	0.39	0.17	0.21	0.19	0.28	0.28	0.30
Average shortest path length (L)	2.96	2.87	3.10	3.22	2.83	2.99	2.80	2.73
Global efficiency	0.32	0.28	0.29	0.29	0.3	0.3	0.31	0.26
Local efficiency	0.20	0.16	0.1	0.11	0.12	0.15	0.16	0.15
Density	0.0017	0.0018	0.0025	0.0026	0.0022	0.0032	0.0014	0.0013
Strongly connected components	385	315	222	176	311	176	631	639
Weakly connected components	1	7	5	4	7	2	3	14
Assortativity	−0.29	−0.31	−0.25	−0.28	−0.29	−0.31	−0.28	−0.28

graphs with high clustering coefficient are usually assortative and vice versa. That is also confirmed in our experiment since all networks are dissortative with low clustering coefficient. In dissortative networks nodes with high degree tend to be connected with nodes with low degree (e.g. stop words are connected to open class words like nouns, verbs and adjectives). A measure that plays a role similar to clustering coefficient is local efficiency, it tells how efficient is the communication between first neighbors of i when i is removed. In our experiment E_{loc} stays low (≤ 0.2), indicating a poor local behavior which means that removing one word will dramatically affect the connection between the previous and the next word. E_{glob} is relatively high, it is slightly lower than the best possible values obtained for random graphs in [20].

Although there are some differences between global measures for legal texts and literature they may not be well-suited to discriminate between two categories. Only average strength is higher for legal texts in all four pairs, which was expected from the statistics shown in Table 1 where we can see that legal texts need almost twice as much words for construction of the networks that are approximately the same size as the literature ones.

Local Measures. Comparison on the local scale was analyzed by plotting the local measurements extracted from two categories, node by node, so each distinguish measurement leads to rank plot on a log-log scale. Nodes colored in red represent legal texts while the black color is used for literature. Fig. 2 shows distributions of local clustering coefficient. No noticeable difference emerge when we compared two types of texts but we can see that nodes from legal texts are slightly above the ones from literature. That can be explained with the fact that literature texts have much richer vocabulary and thus nodes in their networks have less probability that their first neighbors will be connected to each other.

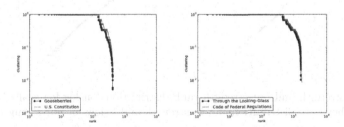

Fig. 2. Clustering coefficient rank distributions on log-log scale for two pairs of texts. (Color figure online)

Figures 3 and 4 present degree and strength rank distributions for two literature-law pairs. They, as well, exhibit no substantial deviations but it is clear that degree values of legal texts are slightly below values calculated from literature texts and opposite is exposed for strength measure.

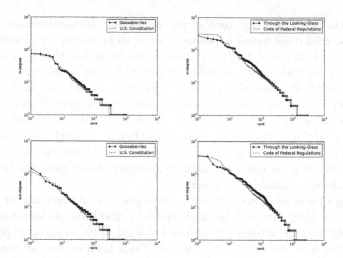

Fig. 3. In-degree and out-degree rank distributions on log-log scale for two pairs of texts. Above are distributions for in-degree and below for out-degree.

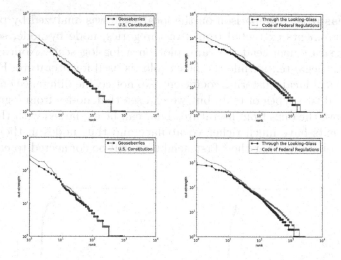

Fig. 4. In-strength and out-strength rank distributions on log-log scale for two pairs of texts. Above are distributions for in-strength and below for out-strength.

Node selectivity indicate words that have exclusive relation with other words and form morphological structures [7]. In Fig. 5 we show the distributions for the in-selectivity, and in Fig. 6 for the out-selectivity of the nodes. We can see that nodes in legal texts have higher values of selectivity measure in comparison with literature texts. This can be explained with the fact that legal texts have lots of repetitions of common bigrams (sequences of two adjacent words), when

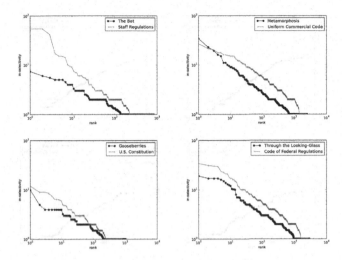

Fig. 5. In-selectivity rank distributions on log-log scale for all four pairs of texts. In each example legal texts have higher values of in-selectivity compared to literature texts.

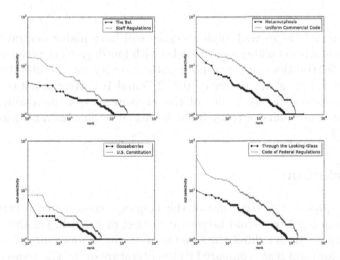

Fig. 6. Out-selectivity rank distributions on log-log scale for all four pairs of texts. As well as for in-selectivity legal texts have higher values of the measure.

in literature authors tend to use much wider vocabulary to avoid that kind of repetitions.

Motivated with this results we decided to try similar centrality measure that considers both weight and degree of a node. In [11] authors defined generalized degree centrality measure as a product of the node degree and its average weight (selectivity) adjusted by the tuning parameter α. Depending on α parameter nodes will gain different values of the measure, that is if parameter is set

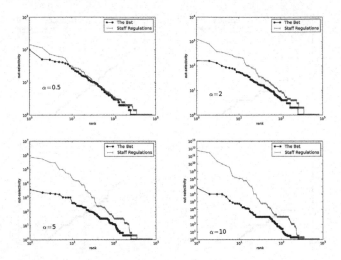

Fig. 7. Generalized out-selectivity rank distributions on log-log scale for one literature-law pair of texts. The α parameter introduced in Eq. 6 is set to 0.5, 2, 5 and 10 respectively.

between 0 and 1 nodes with higher degree will have higher centrality and vice versa, if parameter is higher than 1 nodes with low degree are preferred. Figure 7 shows the distributions of generalised out-selectivity for one literature-law pair for different values of parameter α (0.5, 2, 5 and 10). We can notice that nodes in law text expose higher values of the measure as α is increasing, the same happens for other pairs of texts. That is caused by low average degree in legal texts (Fig. 3).

5   Conclusion

This study probes the structure of the language co-occurrence networks constructed from legal texts and literature written in English. On the global scale only average strength exhibit the same relations in all four pairs of texts, that is it is higher for legal texts compared to the literature ones. The compared degree, strength and clustering coefficient rank distributions show no substantial deviations in legal texts and literature. However, our results show that the in and out selectivity, as well as in and out generalized selectivity from legal texts are constantly above selectivity values calculated from literature. Selectivity measure tends to indicate words that have exclusive relation with other words and since legal documents are known to use predefined terminology, common bigrams and trigrams, phrasal verbs more often than in literature they have higher values of the measure. Furthermore, as parameter α in generalized selectivity is increasing legal texts expose higher values while opposite is true for literature texts. We obtained the same results on comparison of the Croatian language networks from literature and blogs [10].

Obtained results imply that the node selectivity is a measure suitable for differentiation between two different text types (literature and legislation). The node selectivity and generalized node selectivity can be also exploited for keyword extraction task [28] and selectivity can be potentially considered as a measure for capturing the aspect of quality of texts. In future work we plan to investigate the complex network properties for text classification on larger scale. We will try to find other network measures which could possibly discriminate different text types for more than two categories and with larger amount of documents.

References

1. Sebastiani, F.: Machine learning in automated text categorization. ACM Comput. Surv. (CSUR) **34**(1), 1–47 (2002)
2. Cong, J., Liu, H.: Approaching human language with complex networks. Phys. Life Rev. **11**(4), 598–618 (2014)
3. Borge-Holthoefer, J., Arenas, A.: Semantic networks: structure and dynamics. Entropy **12**(5), 1264–1302 (2010)
4. Cancho, R.F.I., Solé, R.V., Köhler, R.: Patterns in syntactic dependency networks. Phys. Rev. E **69**(5), 051915 (2004)
5. Soares, M.M., Corso, G., Lucena, L.: The network of syllables in portuguese. Phys. A Stat. Mech. Appl. **355**(2), 678–684 (2005)
6. Ban, K., Ivakic, I., Meštrović, A.: A preliminary study of croatian language syllable networks. In: 2013 36th International Convention on Information & Communication Technology Electronics & Microelectronics (MIPRO), pp. 1296–1300. IEEE (2013)
7. Solé, R.V., Corominas-Murtra, B., Valverde, S., Steels, L.: Language networks: their structure, function, and evolution. Complexity **15**(6), 20–26 (2010)
8. Margan, D., Martinčić-Ipšić, S., Meštrović, A.: Preliminary report on the structure of Croatian linguistic co-occurrence networks. In: 5th International Conference on Information Technologies and Information Society (ITIS), pp. 89–96 (2013)
9. Ban Kirigin, T., Meštrović, A., Martinčić-Ipšić, S.: Towards a formal model of language networks. In: Dregvaite, G., Damasevicius, R. (eds.) ICIST 2015. CCIS, vol. 538, pp. 469–479. Springer, Heidelberg (2015). doi:10.1007/978-3-319-24770-0_40
10. Šišović, S., Martinčić-Ipšić, S., Meštrović, A.: Comparison of the language networks from literature and blogs. In: 2014 37th International Convention on Information and Communication Technology, Electronics and Microelectronics (MIPRO), pp. 1603–1608. IEEE (2014)
11. Opsahl, T., Agneessens, F., Skvoretz, J.: Node centrality in weighted networks: generalizing degree and shortest paths. Soc. Netw. **32**(3), 245–251 (2010)
12. Amancio, D.R., Oliveira Jr., O.N., da Fontoura Costa, L.: Identification of literary movements using complex networks to represent texts. New J. Phys. **14**(4), 043029 (2012)
13. Amancio, D.R., Aluisio, S.M., Oliveira Jr., O.N., da Fontoura Costa, L.: Complex networks analysis of language complexity. arXiv preprint arXiv:1302.4490 (2013)
14. de Arruda, H.F., da Fontoura Costa, L., Amancio, D.R.: Classifying informative, imaginative prose using complex networks. arXiv preprint arXiv: 1507.07826 (2015)

15. Antiqueira, L., Nunes, M.G.V., Oliveira Jr., O.N., da Fontoura Costa, L.: Strong correlations between text quality and complex networks features. Phys. A: Stat. Mech. Appl. **373**, 811–820 (2007)
16. Masucci, A., Rodgers, G.: Differences between normal and shuffled texts: structural properties of weighted networks. Adv. Complex Syst. **12**(01), 113–129 (2009)
17. Margan, D., Meštrović, A., Martinčić-Ipšić, S.: Complex networks measures for differentiation between normal and shuffled Croatian texts. In: 37th International IEEE Convention on Information and Communication Technology, Electronics and Microelectronics (MIPRO), pp. 1598–1602 (2014)
18. Grabska-Gradzińska, I., Kulig, A., Kwapień, J., Drożdż, S.: Complex network analysis of literary and scientific texts. Int. J. Mod. Phys. C **23**(07), 1250051 (2012)
19. Newman, M.E.J.: Networks, an introduction (2010)
20. Latora, V., Marchiori, M.: Efficient behavior of small-world networks. Physical Rev. Lett. **87**(19), 198701 (2001)
21. Latora, V., Marchiori, M.: Economic small-world behavior in weighted networks. The Eur. Phys. J. B-Condens. Matter Complex Syst. **32**(2), 249–263 (2003)
22. Project gutenberg. https://www.gutenberg.org/
23. Newman, M.E.J.: Assortative mixing in networks. Phys. Rev. Lett. **89**(20), 208701 (2002)
24. Schult, D.A., Swart, P.: Exploring network structure, dynamics, and function using networkx. In: Proceedings of the 7th Python in Science Conferences (SciPy 2008), vol. 2008, pp. 11–16 (2008)
25. Bastian, M., Heymann, S., Jacomy, M., et al.: Gephi: an open source software for exploring and manipulating networks. ICWSM **8**, 361–362 (2009)
26. Margan, D., Meštrović, A., LaNCoA: a python toolkit for language networks construction and analysis. In: 38th International IEEE Convention on Information and Communication Technology, Electronics and Microelectronics (MIPRO), pp. 1961–1966 (2015)
27. Noldus, R., Van Mieghem, P.: Assortativity in complex networks. J. Complex Netw. **3**(4), 507–542 (2015). http://dx.doi.org/10.1093/comnet/cnv005
28. Beliga, S., Meštrović, A., Martinčić-Ipšić, S.: Selectivity-Based Keyword Extraction Method. Int. J. Semant. Inf. Syst. (IJSWIS) **12**(3) (2016, accepted)

Running Out of Words: How Similar User Stories Can Help to Elaborate Individual Natural Language Requirement Descriptions

Frederik S. Bäumer[✉] and Michaela Geierhos

Heinz Nixdorf Institute, University of Paderborn,
Fürstenallee 11, 33102 Paderborn, Germany
{frederik.simon.baeumer,michaela.geierhos}@hni.upb.de

Abstract. While requirements focus on how the user interacts with the system, user stories concentrate on the purpose of software features. But in practice, functional requirements are also described in user stories. For this reason, requirements clarification is needed, especially when they are written in natural language and do not stick to any templates (e.g., "as an X, I want Y so that Z ..."). However, there is a lot of implicit knowledge that is not expressed in words. As a result, natural language requirements descriptions may suffer from incompleteness. Existing approaches try to formalize natural language or focus only on entirely missing and not on deficient requirements. In this paper, we therefore present an approach to detect knowledge gaps in user-generated software requirements for interactive requirement clarification: We provide tailored suggestions to the users in order to get more precise descriptions. For this purpose, we identify not fully instantiated predicate argument structures in requirements written in natural language and use context information to realize what was meant by the user.

Keywords: Natural language requirements clarification · Syntactically incomplete requirements · Compensatory user stories

1 Introduction

What user stories almost never capture are non-functional requirements such as performance and security. Since users can imagine for what purposes they want to apply a certain software, they describe which functions are therefor required. This also means that they make implicit assumptions for a particular application field. Nevertheless, it is desired to know why users define certain requirements and who they are, but it is even more crucial to fully understand what they want. For that reason, we develop interactive requirement clarification techniques in the Collaborative Research Center "On-The-Fly Computing"[1] to meet user needs. Besides consistency, clarity and verifiability [13,16], requirements

---

[1] Refer to http://sfb901.uni-paderborn.de for more information.

© Springer International Publishing Switzerland 2016
G. Dregvaite and R. Damasevicius (Eds.): ICIST 2016, CCIS 639, pp. 549–558, 2016.
DOI: 10.1007/978-3-319-46254-7_44

completeness is one of the fundamental aspects of software quality. Although the notion of completeness is widely discussed, there is a broad consensus on the negative impact of incomplete requirements for a software tool [11] or the entire project [19,28]. However, users are encouraged to express their individual demands in natural language (NL) during the requirement elicitation process [9]. Since the complexity and limitlessness of NL make the automated requirements extraction process very difficult, we want to improve the requirements clarification step by filling individual knowledge gaps. We therefore define incompleteness as missing information in user-generated requirements necessary for a feasible implementation. For incompleteness recognition, we search for predicates with non-instantiated, but mandatory, arguments. Therefore, our system analyzes unrestricted NL requirements descriptions and provides suggestions how to elaborate the user's suboptimal software specifications as far as possible.

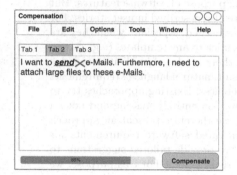

Fig. 1. Previous approach

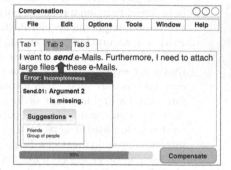

Fig. 2. Current approach

For this purpose, we rely on similar user stories and publisher's software descriptions to detect and fill gaps in requirements specifications. However, it is not sufficient to only point out the incomplete predicate argument structure of a sentence (cf. Fig. 1) because we cannot expect users to understand what is exactly missing and to compensate the incomplete specification on their own. For this reason, at least the error type (here: incompleteness) and the position of the error source in the input sentence have to be labeled and suggestions how to complement the missing argument must be provided (cf. Fig. 2). Thus, users are hint at the particular case of incompleteness and can select one of the given suggestions to refine their original requirement(s).

This paper is organized as follows: In Sect. 2, we provide a brief overview of related work before we describe by means of a concrete example how similar user stories can help to fill knowledge gaps in NL requirements descriptions (cf. Sect. 3). Finally, we conclude in Sect. 4.

2   Current State of Research

The term of *incomplete requirements* often refers to the complete absence of requirements within a requirements documentation. Here, we focus on existing but incomplete requirements, which we call *incomplete individual requirements* [9]. In general, the preparation of checklists for request types as well as the application of "project-specific requirement completeness guidelines and/or standards" is recommended for hand-crafted requirements gathering [9]. Other approaches for the identification (and compensation) of incompleteness are often based on third-party reviews and are therefore affected by subjectivity, limited views, and even again inconsistency [22,31]. Especially, the perception of completeness can widely vary due to explicit and implicit assumptions [1]. Furthermore, there are other approaches that can detect various hidden faults in requirements descriptions, such as ambiguity and incompleteness [6,14,15]. For example, Tjong and Berry (2013) as well as Bajwa et al. (2012) consider several forms of ambiguity in addition to incompleteness [2,29].

Especially NL requirements descriptions suffer from incompleteness if not all required arguments of a predicate are given. For example, "send" is a three-place predicate because it requires the agent ("sender"), the theme ("sent") and the beneficiary argument ("sent-to"). If the beneficiary is not specified here, it is unknown whether one or more recipients are possible. But how many arguments does any predicate require? This information is provided by linguistic resources like FrameNet [3] to enable automatic recognition of incompleteness [17,18] and its compensation [20]. For instance, RAT (Requirements Analysis Tool) can deal with incomplete (i.e. missing arguments of predicates) and missing NL requirements [30]. It therefore uses glossaries, controlled syntax and domain-specific ontologies. Another application is RESI (Requirements Engineering Specification Improver), which can point out linguistic errors in requirements by means of process words and ontologies. For the compensation, RESI starts a dialogue with the user and gives further information about missing arguments.

Since it remains unclear when some state of completeness will be reached [9], Ferrari et al. (2014) developed the Completeness Assistant for Requirements (CAR), which is a tool to measure the completeness of requirements specifications by aligning mentioned requirements to descriptions in transcripts [8]. Here, completeness is reached when all concepts and dependencies mentioned in the additional input documents are covered by the user's statement. This approach extracts terms and their dependencies from the existing document sources in order to create a kind of benchmark but without any use of external linguistic resources (e.g. ontologies).

Incompleteness occurs not only on the requester side (user requirements) but also on the provider side (specifications) in software projects. The reasons therefor range from knowledge gaps on the requester side to conscious omission of information due to non-disclosure agreements on the provider side [25,26]. Even the perception of (in)completeness can vary due to explicit and implicit assumptions [1]. Previous work in the On-The-Fly (OTF) context considered incomplete requirements as far as only (semi-)formal specifications were

supported as input format [23,26]. Geierhos et al. (2015) consider NL requirements and discuss an approach based on domain-based similarity search to compensate missing information. Their goal is to allow unrestricted requirements
descriptions and to support the user by a "how to complete" feature [10]. Here,
NL requirements descriptions that are unique in form and content are reduced to
their main semantic cues and stored in templates for matching purposes (between
requests and the provider's offers). Another way of reducing incompleteness is the
transformation of NL requirements into formal specifications [7,27], which goes
along with information loss due to the restrictions of the formal language [10].

3   Approach

We divide our approach into two steps: (1) detection and (2) compensation.
Based on the results of the *Predicate Argument Analysis* (cf. Fig. 3), we are able
to detect non-instantiated arguments and can then provide gap-filling suggestions taken from the collected user stories (*Similarity Search*).

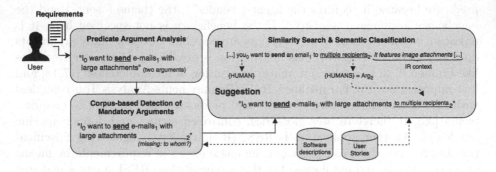

Fig. 3. Compensation of NL requirements descriptions

3.1   Similar User Stories

We assume our input to be at least one sentence[2] without further restrictions.
For that reason, we probably have to deal with spelling or grammatical errors.
Furthermore, we expect modality expressed by auxiliaries like "want", which
is important for ranking the requirements according to user's priority. In the
course of time, more and more NL requirements descriptions are provided by
users, so that we can compare new requests to older ones in our data set. But
the bottleneck is at the beginning, when the very first user writes down some
requirements. We therefore collected a seed of 319 user stories from the Web in
order to face this cold start problem.

---

[2] E.g.,"I *want* to *send* mails with large attachments."

3.2   Natural Language Processing

Since NL requirements descriptions vary in quality and scope, further processing is necessary: (1) end-of-sentence (EOS) detection, (2) filtering, (3) lemmatization, and (4) POS tagging. We perform text cleansing on the plain text because character encoding may be error-prone due to acquisition and/or storage process. Furthermore, HTML tags need to be removed because they may interrupt subsequent processing steps such as the EOS detection. Here, the EOS detection is even more challenging because requirements descriptions often contain enumerations. We therefor use the LingPipe Toolkit[3] that provides better results than other EOS approaches, such as Splitta [12] or CoreNLP [21], on our data. We thereby detected false-positive sentences with strong variance from the average sentence length. That occurs, for example, if numbers of an enumeration are recognized as whole sentences ("4."). Moreover, we used typical abbreviations featuring the end of a sentence (e.g. "etc."), multiple punctuation marks or semicolons in order to detect EOS errors.

Furthermore, we limit the recognition of a predicate argument structure to the scope of a sentence. Then we separate the off-topic sentences from the on-topic ones [5], which we lemmatize and parse. We therefor apply the requirements extraction approach by Dollmann (2016) because it focuses on user-generated content (UGC) [5]. Especially the morpho-syntactic output information is needed to search the PropBank [24] for the valence of a specific predicate (here: "send").

3.3   Semantic Role Labeling

The detection of incompleteness is conducted during the *Predicate Argument Analysis* (cf. Fig. 3). For each sentence, a semantic role labeler (SRL)[4] assigns iteratively semantic roles such as agent, theme, beneficiary represented by $Arg_0, ..., Arg_n$ to the arguments of a recognized predicate. In order to identify the different arguments, we use PropBank [24]. PropBank contains verbal propositions and their arguments. For the predicate *send* ("send.01"), we can obtain three possible arguments: "sender" (Arg_0), "sent" (Arg_1), "sent-to" (Arg_2). By matching this information to our sample input sentence given in Sect. 3.1, the third argument position Arg_2 ("sent-to") remains non-instantiated (cf. Fig. 3).

In this case, it is irrelevant to whom (in person) the e-mail should be sent. However, the number of recipients matters for the functionality of the software application: addressing a single person or a group of people. Since we cannot expect the user to specify a concrete number of addressees (e.g. "to a group of 4 persons"), it is sufficient to distinguish the number (i.e., between plural, e.g. "to my friends" and singular, e.g. "to Peter"). Of course, it is not helpful to only point out the user's mistake without providing concrete suggestions.

Based on the user stories, it would be possible to fill the gap with argument candidates such as "to my friends" or "to Peter". But if we suggested the users

---

[3] http://www.alias-i.com/lingpipe/.
[4] Curator's SRL [4] was selected because of its convincing results on UGC texts.

to elaborate their NL requirements description by replacing the undefined recipient with, for example, "Peter", this would be quite confusing. For this reason, we have to learn different variants for recipients, which will later be classified according to their semantic type (e.g. human being).

Since the recognition quality of existing SRL solutions varies greatly, we have a small number of annotated sentences, with which we can test the suggested approach independently of the SRL quality.

3.4 Context-Sensitive Classification

Semantically grouped argument candidates enable an intuitive user guidance. We therefore gathered 77,649 unique software descriptions and their corresponding reviews from download.com. Each record contains information about the rating, platform, publisher, version and the (sub-)category the software application belongs to (e.g. "communication → e-mail"). Then we applied both NLP (3.2) and SRL (3.3) on the texts. Since we are planing to integrate WordNet[5] and BabelNet[6] for word sense disambiguation in future versions of our system, we already considered this in the XML scheme (Fig. 4):

```
<predicate sense="send.01">
<sentence text="You can send highly customized messages and get the best
results of your campaigns." sid="10" tid="8141" alias="email">
<arguments>
<arg id="A1" babelnet="bn:00054523n" wordnet="06263820">highly cus-
tomized messages</arg>
<arg id="A0" babelnet="bn:01663932n" wordnet="">you</arg>
</arguments>
</sentence> [...]
</predicate>
```

Fig. 4. Snippet of the annotated corpus

According to the *Predicate Argument Analysis*, *send* only occurred in 5.7 % of all texts, but it appeared in 36.3 % of all e-mail app descriptions (2,088), where Arg_2 was non-instantiated in 60.1 % of these texts. Without any additional filtering, we receive a very long frequency list of possible argument candidates for the predicate *send* per category (cf. Table 1).

3.5 Similarity Search

Information retrieval (IR) is used for the *Similarity Search* component. Here, we call a user story similar to the (new) user input when (a) both share the

---

[5] https://wordnet.princeton.edu.

[6] http://babelnet.org.

Table 1. Possible instances for Arg_2 of *send*

Arg_2	Text	Category
sent-to	"to colleagues"	e-mail
sent-to	"to all costumers"	e-mail
sent-to	"to the (...) mailing list"	e-mail
sent-to	"to a specified address"	e-mail

same predicate (i.e. identical meaning), (b) only the user input is incomplete in terms of missing arguments, and (c) both refer to the same category (i.e. context consistency). The latter is extremely important because only context-sensitive similarity search can lead to precise results. We therefore adapted our IR index as shown in Table 2.

Table 2. Apache Solr schema

Field	Processing	Notes
Sentence	Tokenization, stemming	Main sentence
Context	Tokenization, stemming	Sentence before and after the main sentence
Predicate	Stemming	Example: "sending"
Sense	–	Example: "send.01"
Arguments	Tokenization, stemming	Example: "to friends"

In our sample sentence, the predicate *send* can also be used in the sense of faxing (Arg_1 = fax). This may change the possible instantiations for Arg_2 because a standard fax is not sent to "a mailing list" or to "multiple addresses" like an e-mail. For the technical implementation, we use Apache Solr[7] as search engine framework. We query the indexed user stories by the new user inputs, where the occurrence of predicate and argument(s) is higher-weighted. That way, similar user story candidates can be found in order to provide adequate suggestions for initially non-instantiated arguments.

3.6   Ranking of Argument Suggestions

Table 3 shows the top three suggestions for our sample input in Sect. 3.1 that are provided to the user based on the above described approach. But why is "multiple recipients" on first place? Having a look on the most similar user story to this input sentence, we retrieve the following annotated text as result of the *Predicate Argument Analysis*:

---

[7] Solr is an open source enterprise search platform built on Apache Lucene. Please refer to http://lucene.apache.org/solr/ for more information.

Table 3. Suggestions for Arg_2 of "send.01"

#	Argument Arg_2	Semantic type
1	"Multiple recipients"	Human
2	"All your customers"	Human
3	"Multiple addresses"	Abstract

"[...] you_{Arg_0} want to $send_{S_{01}}$ an $email_{Arg_1}$ to $multiple\ recipients_{Arg_2}$. It features multi $[image]_{IR_0}$ $[attachments]_{IR_1}$ [...]"

Here, three possible arguments for *send* in the first sense were identified because of keywords such as "image" and "attachments" which specify the meaning of *send* in the surrounding context.

4 Conclusion

Our approach is also able to semantically group argument candidates (e.g. suggestion no. 1 and no. 2 in Table 3 are typed as *human*). Thus, the user gets one more helpful hint that he or she only has to specify some kind of human being as Arg_2. The semantic typing is based on DELA[8] considering semantic classes such as human, animal, abstract, concrete, which is sufficient for our purposes right now. But we are working on the integration of the ConceptNet 5 Ontology[9] for a more detailed semantic classification. That way, we provide a better ranking of auto-completion candidates for the individual knowledge gaps by sorting the different argument instances grouped per semantic type.

When running out of words, users provide incomplete NL requirements descriptions containing lots of implicit knowledge. In order to assist them with words, we developed a gap-filling matching approach based on similar user stories. With regard to the requested software domain, context-sensitive solutions for the instantiation of argument positions of the user input are suggested.

Acknowledgments. This work was partially supported by the German Research Foundation (DFG) within the Collaborative Research Centre On-The-Fly Computing (SFB 901).

References

1. Albayrak, Ö, Kurtoglu, H., Biaki, M.: Incomplete software requirements and assumptions made by software engineers. In: Proceedings of the 9th Asia-Pacific Software Engineering Conference, pp. 333–339, December 2009

---

[8] http://infolingu.univ-mlv.fr/DonneesLinguistiques/Dictionnaires/dela-en-public.zip.

[9] http://conceptnet5.media.mit.edu.

2. Bajwa, I.S., Lee, M., Bordbar, B.: Resolving syntactic ambiguities in natural language specification of constraints. In: Gelbukh, A. (ed.) CICLing 2012. LNCS, vol. 7181, pp. 178–187. Springer, Heidelberg (2012). doi:10.1007/978-3-642-28604-9_15

3. Baker, C.F., Fillmore, C.J., Lowe, J.B., FrameNet, T.B.: The Berkeley FrameNet project. In: COLING-ACL 1998: Proceedings of the Conference, Montreal, Canada, pp. 86–90 (1998)

4. Clarke, J., Srikumar, V., Sammons, M., Roth, D.: An NLP curator (or: how ILearned to stop worrying and love NLP pipelines). In: Language Resources and Evaluation Journal, pp. 3276–3283 (2012)

5. Dollmann, M.: Frag die Anwender: Extraktion und Klassifikation von funktionalen Anforderungen aus User-Generated-Content. Master's thesis, University of Paderborn (2016)

6. Fabbrini, F., Fusani, M., Gnesi, S., Lami, G.: The linguistic approach to the natural language requirements quality: benefit of the use of an automatic tool. In: Proceedings of the 26th Annual NASA Goddard Software Engineering Workshop, Greenbelt, MD, USA, pp. 97–105, November 2001

7. Fatwanto, A.: Software requirements specification analysis using natural language processing technique. In: Proceedings of the International Conference on Quality in Research QiR 2013, Yogyakarta, pp. 105–110, June 2013

8. Ferrari, A., dell' Orletta, F., Spagnolo, G.O., Gnesi, S.: Measuring and improving the completeness of natural language requirements. In: Salinesi, C., Weerd, I. (eds.) REFSQ 2014. LNCS, vol. 8396, pp. 23–38. Springer, Heidelberg (2014). doi:10.1007/978-3-319-05843-6_3

9. Firesmith, D.G.: Are your requirements complete? J. Object Technol. 4(2), 27–43 (2005)

10. Geierhos, M., Schulze, S., Bäumer, F.S.: What did you mean? Facing the Challenges of User-generated Software Requirements. In: Loiseau, S., Filipe, J., Duval, B., van den Herik, J. (eds.) Proceedings of the 7th International Conference on Agents and Artificial Intelligence. Special Session on Partiality, Underspecification, and Natural Language Processing (PUaNLP 2015), pp. 277 283. SCITEPRESS - Science and Technology Publications, Lissabon, Portugal (2015)

11. Ghazarian, A.: A case study of defect introduction mechanisms. In: Eck, P., Gordijn, J., Wieringa, R. (eds.) CAiSE 2009. LNCS, vol. 5565, pp. 156–170. Springer, Heidelberg (2009). doi:10.1007/978-3-642-02144-2_16

12. Gillick, D.: Sentence boundary detection, the problem with the U.S. In: Proceedings of Human Language Technologies: The 2009 Annual Conference of the North American Chapter of the ACL, Companion Volume: Short Papers, NAACL-Short 2009, pp. 241–244. ACL, Stroudsburg (2009)

13. Grande, M.: 100 Minuten für Anforderungsmanagement - Kompaktes Wissen nicht nur für Projektleiter und Entwickler. Vieweg+Teubner Verlag/Springer Fachmedien, Wiesbaden (2011)

14. Huertas, C., Juárez-Ramírez, R.: NLARE, a natural language processing tool for automatic requirements evaluation. In: Proceedings of the CUBE International Information Technology Conference, CUBE 2012, pp. 371–378. ACM, New York (2012)

15. Huertas, C., Juárez-Ramírez, R.: Towards assessing the quality of functional requirements using English/Spanish controlled languages and context free grammar. In: Proceedings of the 3rd International Conference on Digital Information and Communication Technology and its Applications (DICTAP 2013), pp. 234–241. SDIWC, July 2013

16. IEEE. IEEE Std 830–1998 - Recommended Practice for Software Requirements Specifications. Institute of Electrical and Electronics Engineers, New York, USA (1998)
17. Kaiya, H., Saeki, M.: Analysis, ontology based requirements: lightweight semantic processing approach. In: Proceedings of the 5th International Conference on Quality Software, pp. 223–230, September 2005
18. Kaiya, H., Saeki, M.: Using domain ontology as domain knowledge for requirements elicitation. In: 14th IEEE International Requirements Engineering Conference, pp. 189–198, September 2006
19. Kamata, M.I., Tamai, T.: How does requirements quality relate to project success or failure? In: Proceedings of the 15th IEEE International Requirements Engineering Conference, pp. 69–78, October 2007
20. Körner, S.J.: RECAA - Werkzeugunterstützung in der Anforderungserhebung. PhD thesis, Karlsruher Institut für Technologie (KIT), Karlsruhe, February 2014
21. Manning, C.D., Surdeanu, M., Bauer, J., Finkel, J., Bethard, S.J., McClosky, D.: The stanford CoreNLP natural language processing toolkit. In: Association for Computational Linguistics (ACL) System Demonstrations, pp. 55–60 (2014)
22. Menzel, I., Mueller, M., Gross, A., Doerr, J.: An experimental comparison regarding the completeness of functional requirements specifications. In: Proceedings of the 18th IEEE International Requirements Engineering Conference, pp. 15–24, September 2010
23. Naeem, M., Heckel, R., Orejas, F., Hermann, F.: Incremental service composition based on partial matching of visual contracts. In: Rosenblum, D.S., Taentzer, G. (eds.) FASE 2010. LNCS, vol. 6013, pp. 123–138. Springer, Heidelberg (2010). doi:10.1007/978-3-642-12029-9_9
24. Palmer, M., Gildea, D., Kingsbury, P.: The proposition bank: an annotated corpus of semantic roles. Comput. Linguist. **31**(1), 71–106 (2005)
25. Platenius, M.C.: Fuzzy service matching in on-the-fly computing. In: Proceedings of the 2013 9th Joint Meeting on Foundations of Software Engineering, ESEC/FSE 2013, pp. 715–718. ACM, New York (2013)
26. Platenius, M.C., Arifulina, S., Petrlic, R., Schäfer, W.: Matching of incomplete service specifications exemplified by privacy policy matching. In: Ortiz, G., Tran, C. (eds.) ESOCC 2014. CCIS, vol. 508, pp. 6–17. Springer, Heidelberg (2015). doi:10.1007/978-3-319-14886-1_2
27. Saeki, M., Horai, H., Enomoto, H.: Software development process from natural language specification. In: Proceedings of the 11th International Conference on Software Engineering, ICSE 1989, pp. 64–73. ACM, New York (1989)
28. Standish Group International. The CHAOS Report (1994, 1995). https://www.standishgroup.com/sample_research_files/chaos_report_1994.pdf. Accessed 14 Feb 2016
29. Tjong, S.F., Berry, D.M.: The design of SREE — a prototype potential ambiguity finder for requirements specifications and lessons learned. In: Doerr, J., Opdahl, A.L. (eds.) REFSQ 2013. LNCS, vol. 7830, pp. 80–95. Springer, Heidelberg (2013). doi:10.1007/978-3-642-37422-7_6
30. Verma, K., Kass, A.: Requirements analysis tool: a tool for automatically analyzing software requirements documents. In: Sheth, A., Staab, S., Dean, M., Paolucci, M., Maynard, D., Finin, T., Thirunarayan, K. (eds.) ISWC 2008. LNCS, vol. 5318, pp. 751–763. Springer, Heidelberg (2008). doi:10.1007/978-3-540-88564-1_48
31. Yadav, S.B., Bravoco, R.R., Chatfield, A.T., Rajkumar, T.M.: Comparison of analysis techniques for information requirement determination. Commun. ACM **31**(9), 1090–1097 (1988)

Link Prediction on Tweets' Content

Sanda Martinčić-Ipšić[(✉)], Edvin Močibob, and Ana Meštrović

Department of Informatics, University of Rijeka,
Radmile Matejčić 2, 51000 Rijeka, Croatia
{smarti,emocibob,amestrovic}@inf.uniri.hr

Abstract. In this paper we test various weighted local similarity network measures for predicting the future content of tweets. Our aim is to determine the most suitable measure for predicting new content in tweets and subsequently explore the spreading positively and negatively oriented content on Twitter. The tweets in the English language were collected via the Twitter API depending on their content. That is, we searched for the tweets containing specific predefined keywords from different domains - positive or negative. From the gathered tweets the weighted complex network of words is formed, where nodes represent words and a link between two nodes exists if these two words co-occur in the same tweet, while the weight denotes the co-occurrence frequency. For the link prediction task we study five local similarity network measures commonly used in unweighted networks (Common Neighbors, Jaccard Coefficient, Preferential Attachment, Adamic Adar and Resource Allocation Index) which we have adapted to weighted networks. Finally, we evaluated all the modified measures in terms of the precision of predicted links. The obtained results suggest that the Weighted Resource Allocation Index has the best potential for the prediction of content in tweets.

1 Introduction

Twitter is a popular online social network created in 2006 that enables a user to send publicly visible messages called "tweets". One of the main characteristics that distinguishes Twitter from other online social networks is the limit on the length of a tweet - a maximum of 140 characters. Therefore Twitter is often categorized as a micro-blogging platform [1].

Due to its popularity, user-base size and vast amounts of tweets, Twitter has been studied in the context of person-to-person relations [2], sentiment analysis [8], user influence [3], economic predictions [4], predictions of political elections [5], conversational practices [6] and trends discovery [7].

The link prediction of Twitter data is currently in the focus of many studies and it refers to inferring the most likely future relationships (links) between nodes in the complex network. In this context nodes can represent Twitter objects (e.g. users, hashtags, retweets, words) and links can represent their relations or interactions. Link prediction in social media is generally utilized for recommender systems, for the prediction of information propagation [17] or for sentiment analysis

© Springer International Publishing Switzerland 2016
G. Dregvaite and R. Damasevicius (Eds.): ICIST 2016, CCIS 639, pp. 559–567, 2016.
DOI: 10.1007/978-3-319-46254-7_45

[18,19]. This can lead to the better understanding of the interplay of users' sentiments and social relationships. There are number of reported research in which link prediction is exploited for the purpose of predicting political opinions and the results of elections. In [18,19] authors propose prediction models for the US elections based upon the revealed sentiment in Twitter messages. A similar approach is used in [21] to predict the results of the UK 2015 General Election. In [17] the authors predict the popularity of messages measured by the number of future retweets and thus reveal what can influence the propagation on information on Twitter.

There are also reports about how link prediction is related to similarities in complex networks: similarities among users [20], similarities among users' interests [22] or sentiment homophily [16] derived from the complex network topology. In [23] the authors analyze how community structure may improve the link prediction task. They define two new measures based on communities and compare their performances to the local similarity measures. In [24] the authors provide an approach to predict future links by applying the Covariance Matrix Adaptation Evolution Strategy (CMA-ES) to optimize weights based on neighborhood and node similarity indices. This method is suitable for predicting future followers on social networks.

Our research is aimed in another direction since we are focused on the content of tweets and not on Twitter as a social network. Our goal is to analyse measures for predicting the future spread of content represented by words (or keywords used to express an opinion). This could be of special interest for the prediction of information propagation and, in particular, opinion propagation. In our approach we use link prediction to analyse the positive and negative content propagation on Twitter. We analyse the potential of five link prediction measures based on the local similarities: Common Neighbors (CN), Jaccard Coefficient (JC), Preferential Attachment (PA), Adamic Adar (AA) and Resource Allocation Index (RA). For the purpose of predicting links in weighted networks, we adapt some of the existing measures in undirected networks so that they can applied in weighted networks. Weighted Common Neighbors measure was already defined for weighted networks in [9], while for other four measures we define their weighted variants: Weighted Jaccard Coefficient, Weighted Preferential Attachment, Weighted Adamic Adar and Weighted Resource Allocation Index. Each of these measures has its own regularity and in this study we experimentally test which measure is the most suitable for the purpose of predicting future linking in tweets' content.

In the second Section we present the local similarity indices and evaluation measures used in our research. In the third Section we describe how we construct the tweet networks. The results and discussion are given in the fourth Section. Finally, the fifth Section contains the conclusions and directions for further research.

2   Link Prediction in Complex Networks

A complex network is a graph with non-trivial topological features (e.g. high clustering coefficient, low distances, heavy-tailed degree distribution, etc.). It can be represented by a graph G, defined as a pair of two sets $G = (V, E)$; the first set V consisting of vertices and the second set E consisting of edges. N as the number of vertices in V and K as the number of edges in E. In the domain of network analysis, the vertices are referred to as nodes and the edges are called links.

In weighted complex networks every link connecting two nodes u and v has an associated weight w_{uv}. A node degree is the number of links directly connected (or incident) to that node. The set of nodes incident to a node v is denoted as $\Gamma(v)$. The strength of a node v, denoted as s_v, is simply the sum of weights of all links incident to v.

There are various approaches for the link prediction task based upon similarity indices [25]. In this approach each pair of nodes, u and v, is assigned a score s_{uv}, which is directly defined as the similarity between nodes u and v. In our approach we use local similarity indices described as follows.

In Weighted Common Neighbors [9], weights of links connecting u and v to their common neighbors are calculated as follows:

$$CN(u,v) = \sum_{z \in \Gamma(u) \cap z \in \Gamma(v)} w_{uz} + w_{vz}. \tag{1}$$

Weighted Jaccards Coefficient, adapted from [10], which divides the weighted Common Neighbors value for u and v by the summed weights of all links incident to u and/or v:

$$JC(u,v) = \frac{\sum_{z \in \Gamma(u) \cap z \in \Gamma(v)} w_{uz} + w_{vz}}{\sum_{a \in \Gamma(u)} w_{au} + \sum_{b \in \Gamma(v)} w_{bv}}. \tag{2}$$

Weighted Preferential Attachment adapted from [10]:

$$PA(u,v) = \sum_{a \in \Gamma(u)} w_{au} * \sum_{b \in \Gamma(v)} w_{bv}. \tag{3}$$

Weighted Adamic-Adar adapted from [10]:

$$AA(u,v) = \sum_{z \in \Gamma(u) \cap z \in \Gamma(v)} \frac{w_{uz} + w_{vz}}{\log \left(1 + \sum_{c \in \Gamma(z)} w_{zc}\right)}. \tag{4}$$

Weighted Resource Allocation Index where s_z is the node strength of z:

$$RA(u,v) = \sum_{z \in \Gamma(u) \cap z \in \Gamma(v)} \frac{1}{s_z}. \tag{5}$$

Lastly, we present the link prediction precision as the ratio between the number of correctly predicted links and the total number of predicted links.

That is, we divide the number of true positives ($|TP|$) by the number of true and false positives ($|TP| + |FP|$) [11]

$$P = \frac{|TP|}{|TP| + |FP|}. \tag{6}$$

3   Construction of Networks

The first step in constructing networks is the collection of data. Initially, we searched for four sets of tweets in the English language according to the following criteria: (a) tweets associated to recent immigrant and war related events; (b) tweets containing negatively polarized words (e.g. anger, fear, ...); (c) tweets associated to house pets and (d) tweets containing positively polarized words (e.g. joy, happiness, ...). The subset of positive and negative polarized words is extracted from the sentiment lexicon in [12]. From now on we will refer to the networks built from their respective sets as: (a) emo-net^a, (b) emo-net^b, (c) emo-net^c and (d) emo-net^d.

For the data collection process we use Python in combination with the Python Twitter Tools package, which provides an easy-to-use interface for the official Twitter API. In the API request arguments we specified we are searching for a mix of recent and popular tweets in the English language. We scraped about 10,000 tweets for each of the four different queries, resulting in a dataset of 39,882 tweets. It is worth mentioning that the official Twitter API documentation states that the language detection is based on the "best-effort" principle [13].

In the preparation of the text (tweets) our first step was to eliminate the stopwords[1], and from the remaining text we computed the 100 most frequent words for each of the four subsets. We selected the top 100 words as the reasonable list which provides the best trade-off between computation time and link prediction results. Note that the former computation was case-insensitive and we used the list of English stopwords presented at http://www.ranks.nl/stopwords.

From the remaining words (top 100) of preprocessed tweets extended with the set of explicit keywords used to retrieve the tweets (e.g. joy, puppy, anger,...) in four datasets we formed the nodes of the networks. A link between two nodes (words) is established if these two words appear together in the same tweet. The weight on the link represents word co-occurrence frequencies, in other words, the number of tweets in which two high-frequency words from the top 100 list co-occurred. This makes the generated networks weighted and undirected. Hence, based on the high-frequency words, we constructed four different networks for each of the four data sets (two from the datasets with negative polarity (a) and (b) and two from the datasets with positive polarity (c) and (d)). For the purpose of evaluation, we removed a certain percentage of links from each network (25 %, 50 % and 75 %). More precisely, we built 16 distinct networks from the four

---

[1] Stopwords are a list of the most common, short function words that do not carry strong semantic properties, but are needed for the syntax of a language (pronouns, prepositions, conjunctions, abbreviations, ...).

datasets: the first network was built from 25 % of the data, the second from 50 %, the third from 75 % and the fourth from 100 % of the data in one dataset. With such a partitioning of the data we obtained three train networks (25 %, 50 % and 75 %) and one test network (100 %). We will denote these networks, respectively, as emo-net$_1^x$, emo-net$_2^x$, emo-net$_3^x$ and emo-net$_4^x$, where $x \in \{a, b, c, d\}$. This means we, as previously mentioned, constructed a total of 16 different networks, four per collected dataset.

Some other used Python packages not previously mentioned are NetworkX [14] and LaNCoA [15]. The first one is a popular Python tool for creating and manipulating complex networks. It also provides a rich collection of functions for studying complex networks on various levels. The LaNCoA toolkit provides procedures for the construction and analysis of complex language networks.

4   Results

In order to determine which measure has the best potential to predict co-occurrence of words in future tweets, we evaluated five link prediction measures in terms of precision (Eq. 6). We tested the accuracy of each measure using snap-shots of networks constructed by removing links. More precisely, we calculated the precisions for emo-net$_1^x$ (25 % of data), emo-net$_2^x$ (50 % of data) and emo-net$_3^x$ (75 % of data) against emo-net$_4^x$ (100 % of data).

Tables 1, 2, 3, 4 and 5 present the link prediction precisions for the defined weighted measures of Common Neighbors, Jaccard Coefficient, Preferential Attachment, Adamic Adar and Resource Allocation Index respectively according to the weigh-ted adaptation as defined above. If we compare the obtained results The Weighted Preferential Attachment measure performs the most modest, because in the general, it has the lowest prediction precision. It is the only measure with prediction precisions less than 10 % for the emo-net$_3^x$ networks. In contrast, the Weighted Resource Allocation Index has the prediction precisions for all emo-net$_3^x$ networks above 25 %. Also, if we explore the emo-net$_1^x$ and emo-net$_2^x$ networks' properties, the Weighted Resource Allocation Index outperforms all other measures. Therefore, for the collected data the Weighted Resource Allocation Index exposed the best precision while the Weighted Preferential Attachment was the least successful in predicting future links. The performance of the rest of the measures fall in between these two.

Moreover, in Tables 1, 2, 3, 4 and 5 we can also notice a trend of decreasing precisions along the emo-net$_1^x$, emo-net$_2^x$ and emo-net$_3^x$ networks. That is, for a given measure and data set (emo-net$_4^x$, $x \in \{a, b, c, d\}$) the emo-net$_1^x$ networks will have the highest prediction precisions, while the emo-net$_3^x$ will have the lowest. This behavior is expected since we calculated the precisions for emo-net$_1^x$, emo-net$_2^x$ and emo-net$_3^x$ against emo-net$_4^x$ (100 % of data). Since emo-net$_1^x$ networks are created from only 25 % of the data, they do not contain many links. Hence, many probable links are left out form the emo-net$_1^x$ network. Note that at the same time the most probable links are the most likely to be predicted. The link prediction measures are in fact generally most successful in predicting

Table 1. Prediction precision based on the Weighted Common Neighbors measure

Network	emo-net^a	emo-net^b	emo-net^c	emo-net^d
(25 %) emo-net$_1$	54.12 %	62.69 %	40.9 %	43.03 %
(50 %) emo-net$_2$	37.71 %	45.35 %	30.36 %	26.17 %
(75 %) emo-net$_3$	28.49 %	27.49 %	18.4 %	13.45 %

Table 2. Prediction precision based on the Weighted Jaccard Coefficient measure

Network	emo-net^a	emo-net^b	emo-net^c	emo-net^d
(25 %) emo-net$_1$	56.73 %	68.37 %	57.47 %	69.67 %
(50 %) emo-net$_2$	38.14 %	53.32 %	44.1 %	51.7 %
(75 %) emo-net$_3$	12.85 %	32.16 %	30.06 %	32.75 %

highly-probable links. With more data in emo-net$_2^x$ and emo-net$_3^x$ the majority of highly-probable links are already included in the network, therefore the prediction measure is expected to predict less-probable links, which causes the drop in the prediction precision.

Another perspective on the presented results in Tables 1, 2, 3, 4 and 5 is the differentiation of polarity of tweet domains. As already mentioned, the emo-net^a and emo-net^b networks were constructed from tweets with "negative" aspects, while emo-net^c and emo-net^d were constructed from tweets with "positive" aspects. We can observe no conclusive trends in that regard, because the prediction precisions vary between "positive" and "negative" networks, i.e. neither type gave generally better prediction results. The only exposed differences are on a local level when exploring specific measures. In that spirit, e.g. the Weighted Common Neighbors and the Weighted Preferential Attachment measures raised better prediction precisions for "positive" networks. However, no general conclusion should be drawn since for example the Weighted Resource Allocation Index performed better for emo-net^d than for emo-net^a networks. This remains an open question which we plan to investigate in the future.

Table 3. Prediction precision based on the Weighted Preferential Attachment measure

Network	emo-net^a	emo-net^b	emo-net^c	emo-net^d
(25 %) emo-net$_1$	48.59 %	51.63 %	24.33 %	20.57 %
(50 %) emo-net$_2$	24.79 %	23.45 %	7.95 %	11.49 %
(75 %) emo-net$_3$	18.99 %	8.77 %	3.07 %	5.85 %

Table 4. Prediction precision based on the Weighted Adamic-Adar measure

Network	emo-net^a	emo-net^b	emo-net^c	emo-net^d
(25 %) emo-net$_1$	54.72 %	64.52 %	44.96 %	45.69 %
(50 %) emo-net$_2$	39.62 %	47.79 %	33.25 %	30.64 %
(75 %) emo-net$_3$	29.05 %	30.41 %	20.25 %	15.2 %

Table 5. Prediction precision based on the Weighted Resource Allocation Index measure

Network	emo-net^a	emo-net^b	emo-net^c	emo-net^d
(25 %) emo-net$_1$	61.24 %	73.46 %	63.15 %	73.93 %
(50 %) emo-net$_2$	44.49 %	59.51 %	53.01 %	56.6 %
(75 %) emo-net$_3$	25.14 %	36.84 %	33.13 %	35.67 %

5   Conclusion

In this work we analysed different link prediction approaches based on the local measures on networks constructed from the content of tweets. The main goal of this analysis is to find which measure perform better in the task of predicting the future linking of keywords in the content of tweets. The results of this preliminary research will be further used for predicting the propagation of opinion in social networks.

For this first study we selected five measures: Common Neighbors, Jaccard Coefficient, Preferential Attachment, Adamic Adar and Resource Allocation Index. These measures are generally defined for unweighted networks (except Common Neighbors for which there is weighted variant). Therefore, we adapted each measure to be applicable in weighted networks as Weighted Jaccard Coefficient, Weighted Preferential Attachment, Weighted Adamic Adar and Weighted Resource Allocation Index.

We constructed four networks from collected tweets; two using keywords with negative polarity and another two using keywords with positive polarity. For the purpose of evaluation, for each dataset we constructed three more networks as snapshots constructed from 25 %, 50 %, 75 % of the data. Then we performed evaluation in terms of precision where we used 100 % of data as the test set. The results show that the Weighted Resource Allocation Index is potentially the best-suited measure for the proposed task.

Next we plan to include more weighted and unweighted measures in the study and possibly define new similarity measures that are appropriate for the prediction of keyword linking in tweets. Furthermore, the best measures will be included in the general approach for predicting the propagation of opinion. We also plan to consider different evaluation metrics.

References

1. Twitter - Wikipedia, the free encyclopedia. 20-Feb-2016. https://en.wikipedia.org/wiki/Twitter. Accessed 21 Feb 2016
2. Huberman, B.A., Romero, D.M., Wu, F.: Social networks that matter: Twitter under the microscope. arXiv:0812.1045 [physics] (2008)
3. Cha, M., Haddadi, H., Benevenuto, F., Gummadi, P.K.: Measuring user influence in twitter: the million follower fallacy. In: ICWSM, vol. 10, pp. 10–17 (2010)
4. Bollen, J., Mao, H., Zeng, X.J.: Twitter mood predicts the stock market. J. Comput. Sci. **2**(1), 1–8 (2011)
5. Tumasjan, A., Sprenger, T.O., Sandner, P.G., Welpe, I.M.: Predicting elections with twitter: what 140 characters reveal about political sentiment. In: Fourth International AAAI Conference on Weblogs and Social Media (2010)
6. Boyd, D., Golder, S., Lotan, G.: Tweet, tweet, retweet: conversational aspects of retweeting on twitter. In: 2010 43rd Hawaii International Conference on System Sciences (HICSS), pp. 1–10 (2010)
7. Mathioudakis, M., Koudas, N.: TwitterMonitor: trend detection over the twitter stream. In: Proceedings of the 2010 ACM SIGMOD International Conference on Management of Data, pp. 1155–1158 (2010)
8. Go, A., Bhayani, R., Huang, L.: Twitter sentiment classification using distant supervision. CS224N Project. Report **1**, 12 (2009)
9. Lu, L., Zhou, T.: Role of Weak Ties in Link Prediction of Complex Networks. arXiv:0907.1728 [cs] (2009)
10. De Sá, H.R., Prudêncio, R.B.: Supervised link prediction in weighted networks. In: The 2011 International Joint Conference on Neural Networks (IJCNN), pp. 2281–2288 (2011)
11. Yang, Y., Lichtenwalter, R.N., Chawla, N.V.: Evaluating link prediction methods. Knowl. Inf. Syst. **45**(3), 751–782 (2015)
12. Baccianella, S., Esuli, A., Sebastiani, F.: SentiWordNet 3.0: an enhanced lexical resource for sentiment analysis and opinion mining. In: LREC, pp. 2200–2204 (2010)
13. GET search/tweets — Twitter Developers. https://dev.twitter.com/rest/reference/get/search/tweets. Accessed 21 Feb 2016
14. Schult, D.A., Swart, P.: Exploring network structure, dynamics, and function using NetworkX. In: Proceedings of the 7th Python in Science Conferences (SciPy 2008), pp. 11–16 (2008)
15. Margan, D., Meštrović, A.: LaNCoA: a python toolkit for language networks construction and analysis. In: International Convention on Information and Communication Technology, Electronics and Microelectronics (MIPRO), pp. 1628–1633 (2015)
16. Yuan, G., Murukannaiah, P.K., Zhang, Z., Singh, M.P.: Exploiting sentiment homophily for link prediction. In: Proceedings of the 8th ACM Conference on Recommender Systems, pp. 17–24 (2014)
17. Hong, L., Dan, O., Davison, B.D.: Predicting popular messages in twitter. In: Proceedings of the 20th International Conference Companion on World Wide Web, pp. 57–58
18. Shi, L., Agarwal, N., Agrawal, A., Garg, R., Spoelstra, J.: Predicting US primary elections with Twitter (2012)
19. Tumasjan, A., Sprenger, T.O., Sandner, P.G., Welpe, I.M.: Predicting elections with twitter: what 140 characters reveal about political sentiment. In: ICWSM, vol. 10, pp. 178–185

20. Liben-Nowel, D., Kleinberg, J.: The link prediction problem for social networks. In: Proceedings of the CKIM, pp. 556–559 (2003)
21. Burnap, P., Gibson, R., Sloan, L., Southern, R., Williams, M.: 140 characters to victory?: Using Twitter to predict the UK 2015 General Election. arXiv:1505.01511 [physics] (2015)
22. Singla, P., Richardson, M.: Yes, there is a correlation: from social networks to personal behavior on the Web. In: Proceedings of the 17th International Conference on World Wide Web, pp. 655–664 (2008)
23. Valverde-Rebaza, J., de Andrade Lopes, A.: Exploiting behaviors of communities of twitter users for link prediction. Soc. Netw. Anal. Mining 3(4), 1063–1074 (2013)
24. Bliss, C.A., Frank, M.R., Danforth, C.M., Dodds, P.S.: An evolutionary algorithm approach to link prediction in dynamic social networks. J. Comput. Sci. 5(5), 750–764 (2011)
25. Lu, L., Zhou, T.: Link prediction in complex networks: a survey. Phys. A 390(6), 1150–1170 (2011)

Polyphon: An Algorithm for Phonetic String Matching in Russian Language

Viacheslav V. Paramonov[(⊠)], Alexey O. Shigarov,
Gennagy M. Ruzhnikov, and Polina V. Belykh

Matrosov Institute for System Dynamics and Control Theory of Siberian Branch
of Russian, Academy of Sciences (ISDCT SB RAS), Irkutsk, Russia
{slv,shigarov,rugnikov,polina}@icc.ru

Abstract. Data cleansing is the crucial matter in business intelligence. We propose a new phonetic algorithm to string matching in Russian language without transliteration from Cyrillic to Latin characters. It is based on the rules of sounds formation in Russian language. Additionally, we consider an extended algorithm for matching of Cyrillic strings where phonetic code letters are presented as primes, and the code of a string is the sum of these numbers. Experimental results show that our algorithms allow accurately matching phonetically similar strings in Russian language.

Keywords: Phonetic algorithms · String matching · Language · Classifiers

1 Introduction

Often, data integration as an important part of the business intelligence encounter messy data, including typos, misspelling strings, and repeated words. These problems require preliminary data cleansing which consists of many aspects such as detection and correction of spelling errors, missing data, incorrect values, and logical inconsistencies [1, 2]. One of the important tasks of data cleansing is to associate source values (natural language strings) with target thesauruses and qualifiers. In this task, phonetic algorithms [3] can be used to match phonetically similar strings.

The coding of strings (words) in phonetic algorithms is based on their pronunciation, but not on their spelling. Substantially, the familiar phonetic algorithms (e.g. Soundex, Metaphone, Double Metaphone, and Caverphone) are intended to find and match specific names which are written in Latin. In the case of text processing in the languages with rich morphology, e.g. Russian, there is a need to adapt phonetic algorithms to their features [4].

This paper introduces the method of detection and correction of Russian language spelling errors in data normalization processes. The proposed algorithm is based on matching analysis of phonetic coded strings.

Russian language belongs to East-Slavic language group. It is used by more than 250 million speakers [5]. The main aim of this research is to develop an algorithm of phonetic coding of words for Russian language.

© Springer International Publishing Switzerland 2016
G. Dregvaite and R. Damasevicius (Eds.): ICIST 2016, CCIS 639, pp. 568–579, 2016.
DOI: 10.1007/978-3-319-46254-7_46

A phonetic algorithm seeks to identify words according to similarities in their pronunciation [6]. The common purpose of phonetic algorithms is detection of the words similarity according to their phonetic resemblance. The most typical application of phonetic algorithms is intended for the surnames comparison [4].

Most of the existing phonetic algorithms are developed for English language [6]. Some of them support other languages partially [4, 6]. However, in our literature review, we were not able to find any research concerning with phonetic algorithms for Russian language where Cyrillic symbols are used. Implementation of phonetic algorithms for languages of this kind is usually implemented by transliterating Cyrillic characters to Latin. This approach lead to ignoring language phonetic features [4]. The aim of the research is to develop a phonetic algorithm that takes into accounts the rules of phonetic coding in the Russian language and analyses their applicability to the Russian language and possibility of their extending to other languages of East-Slavic language group such as Belorussian and Ukrainian.

Phonetic coded string matching is useful for eliminating errors occurring in typing processes of text values that might be compared with classifiers. The examples of qualifiers are KLADR (Russia' address database) [7], IPNI (International Plant Names Index) [8], ICD X (International Statistical Classification of Diseases and Related Health Problems 10th Revision) [9] etc.

It worth mentioning that data input is often accompanied by spelling errors occurring in words. It is done unintentionally in most cases but it leads to data incorrectness and complicates further processing. The rate errors in data entry process by an operator is about 5 % [10].

The first part of this paper considers phonetic spelling errors. The second part introduces phonetic algorithms for data cleansing tasks. Thirdly, the a phonetic algorithm for Russian language, Polyphon, is described. The last part describes data preparation for the algorithm testing and test results.

2 Phonetic Algorithms for Data Cleansing Tasks

2.1 Phonetic Spelling Errors

Spelling errors in Russian language words could be classified in following groups [11]:

- morphological – a uniform graphic symbol of morphemes by the letter i.e. a person tries to write all audible sounds by letters [12];
- phonologic – preservation of writing of phonemes spelling regardless the word of change;
- phonetic – words written as they are heard;
- traditional (historic) – writing by "tradition" i.e. as it was written in old times or as in the language which it is borrowed from.

Most of spelling errors in Russian are associated with phonetic norms. The type of mistakes generally depends on the level of one's education [13]. For example, elementary school students make mistakes because they write words as heard. High school students are more prone to hypercorrection errors. As the literacy level of a person does not improve after school graduation, adult persons also make hypercorrection errors. However, in general, many spelling mistakes are simply typos or associated with phonetic words representation.

Table 1. Share of most various spelling patterns in total number of mistakes

Place	Spelling pattern type	Share (in %)
1	Mixing of "и"-"e" in unstressed syllable	27.3
2	Mixing "a"-"o" in unstressed syllable	25.3
3	Separate writing instead of solid word writing	9.4
4	Solid word writing instead of the separate	8.8
5	Writing of one letter instead of the doubled	6.6
6	Mixture deaf and ringing letters	3.6
7	Vowels after hissing sounds and ц	2.7
8	Excess doubling of letters	2.6
9	Absence of ь character	1.3
10	Writing of the superfluous ъ character	0.6

It is noted in [13] that phonetic spelling principle is the most natural and efficient. Therefore phonetic algorithms would be useful for similar strings matching. Table 1 represents Russian language general spelling errors. It is a simplified table from [13]. Thus, these kinds of spelling errors make nearly 90 % of all errors. Other spelling errors are represented by mixing of some vowels, concordant, letter sequences or dividing (special) letters "ь" and "ъ". Forming rules that allow to find words matching with due regard to errors type help to find and eliminate errors in words.

Here and in other examples Russian language words will be presented in transliteration according to [14] and shown in square brackets "[]" characters. This notation is aimed to help understanding of text for persons who are not familiar with the Cyrillic characters.

2.2 Textual Data Cleansing

We typically deal with nouns and adjectives in singular and nominative form in data cleansing. Therefore, it is reasonable to apply fuzzy string comparison methods and phonetic algorithms. Fuzzy string comparison algorithms aid to determine level of string similarity. Phonetic algorithms help to clarify identity of similar words.

(1) **Fuzzy string comparison**

We assume that the first stage of data cleansing in case of qualifiers linked data is a fuzzy string comparison. The duplicating values (words) in lexeme are not considered. There are many lexemes processes realization for East-Slavic group languages. Samples of words normalization are shown in Table 2.

Table 2. Lexeme words normalization sample

Lexemes	Words in normalized form	Language
GENERAL DOVATOR STREETS	"DOVAT" "GENERAL" "STREET"	English
УЛИЦЫ ГЕНЕРАЛА ДОВАТОРА [ULITSY GENERALA DOVATORA]	ГЕНЕРА ДОВАТОР УЛИЦ [GENERA DOVATOR ULITS]	Russian
ВУЛИЦ ГЕНЕРАЛА ДОВАТОРА	ВУЛИЦ ГЕНЕРА ДОВАТОР [VULITS GENERA DOVATOR]	Ukrainian
ВУЛIЦЫ ГЕНЕРАЛА ДАВАТАРА	ВУЛIЦ ГЕНЕРА ДАВАТАР [VULITS GENERA DOVATOR]	Belorussian

Algorithms for fuzzy string comparison are applied to estimate similarity of normalized lexemes. If the measure of similarity with predetermined values by operator is not 0, then phonetic algorithms are applied to achieve the precise result.

One of the popular methods of substring search in the text is fuzzy string search. These kind of algorithms use for orthography check and for text search. The well-known search engines as Yandex (http://yandex.com) and Google (http://google.com) both use fuzzy search algorithms [15, 16]. The common idea of these algorithms is as following: by a given word it is possible to find in a text or in a dictionary all words which is matching the given word (or starting with it) in view of k possible differences.

Fuzzy string comparison is used in word and expression search. This kind of algorithms is language independent (e.g. with non-Hieroglyphic characters).

Phonetic Algorithms. Phonetic algorithms are used for estimation of word similarity according to their phonetic forms. This coding depends on pronunciation particularities but not on orthographic rules. The word is phonetically similar to the matching codes.

This kind of algorithms allow to find typos related to changing places of two adjacent letters and typos based on sound similarities. We suggest that the following categories of errors are allocated to estimate overall performance of phonetic algorithms:

- First category – errors associated with incorrect writing (morphological errors).
- Second category – various typographical errors (misprints, typos).
- Third category – errors related to incorrect rule usage (hypercorrection [13] errors).

There are many phonetic algorithms, which use Latin characters or English language rules and some local dialects of it while particularities of Cyrillic letters in East-Slavic group languages and their sounds are not taken into account. Using well-known phonetic algorithms for Russian language texts usually results in transliteration of Cyrillic letters to Latin. Transliterated words do not always have an unique record. For example, such name as "АНТОН ЧЕХОВ" ["ANTON CHEKHOV"] has been variously transliterated as TSJECHOF, TSJECHOW, TJEKHOW, CHEKHOV, CHEKHOW etc. Further addition of the word suffix will complicate transliteration.

Appling phonetic codes allow increasing the word comparison quality in the case of the incorrect writing [17]. All phonetic algorithms use words coding. Changing of noun case and form, for example, leads to ineffective use of phonetic algorithms. However, such changes are not significant in our case. Therefore, phonetic algorithms are most suitable for word comparison with reference books or dictionaries. Phonetic algorithms are used expediently for the solution of issues of comparison word with their meanings in reference books or dictionaries (classifiers).

3   Phonetic Algorithms for Russian Language

3.1   Polyphon: Russian Language Phonetic Algorithms Adaptation

The common phonetic algorithms originally are intended for English language. They can be applied to non-Latin characters after transliteration, e.g. from Cyrillic letters to Latin ones. There are many ways to transliterate some letters. For example, we can transliterate the Ukrainian word « вчора » (yesterday) as "vchera", "vchora", "fchora". In addition, misspellings in East Slavic languages with Cyrillic letters generally differ from these in English or German texts due to dissimilar rules of pronunciation and writing in different languages. However, it is unable to consider language phonetic features of letter sequences for each language in transliteration. Thus, the most known phonetic algorithms are not so effective for texts with non-Latin characters.

The proposed algorithm Polyphon uses word transformation according rules of Russian language and its phonetic particularities. It transforms words to codes as well as others phonetic algorithms. The codes matching define words phonetic similarity. The algorithm allows to get a more accurate phonetic code for conformable strings according phonetic rules of Russian language. The stages of algorithm are:

– substitution of Latin letters which are similar to Russian with Russian letters;
– removal of all non-Russian characters from the string;
– removal dividers (special characters) from string;
– transformation of doubled characters into one;
– transformation of character sequences.

Details of Polyphon Algorithm. Some letters in Russian alphabet have equivalent in writing with Latin. These are letters: а **[a]** ~ a, е **[e]** ~ e, о **[o]** ~ o, с **[es]** ~ c, х **[kha]** ~ x. Some letters equal in capital letters only: В **[ve]** ~ B, М **[em]** ~ M, Н **[en]** ~ H. Sometimes these letters are substituted (incidentally or purposely) when text typing. Thereunder such Latin characters replace by corresponding Russian. It is preparatory stage of the algorithm.

There are some dividers – special letters "ь" ("soft" sign), "ъ" ("hard" sing) presented in Russian language. They are not pronounced and used for giving softness or hardness for consonants respectively. For this reason, there is no need to consider these characters.

The developed phonetic algorithm Polyphon operates with Russian language letters only. The initial operation is to remove all characters, which are not in the Russian alphabet.

The following stage is transformation of letters repeated in a row. Doubled letters will transform to one e.g. "xx" to "x". It is not always possible to define double letters in hearing. Consequently, we carry out these transformations for rule of generalization.

Table 3. Processing a set of words

Standard value	Code	Fuzzy phonetic equivalents
ГЕНЕРАЛА ДОВАТОРА [GENERALA DOVATORA]	154	ДОВАТОРА ГЕНЕРАЛА [DOVATORA GENERALA] ГЕНЕРАЛА ДОВАТОРА [GENERALA DOVATORA] ГЕНИРАЛА ДАВАТОРА [GENIRALA DOVATORA]

Table 4. Replacement of some letters

Letters	А, Е, Ё, И,О, Ы, Э, Я	Б	В	Г	Д	З	Щ	Ж	М	Ю
Modification result	А	П	Ф	К	Т	С	Ш	Ш	Н	У

Table 5. Letters sequence conversion

Sequence	АКА	АН	ЗЧ	ЛНЦ	ЛФСТФ	НАТ	НТЦ	НТ
result	АФА	Н	Ш	НЦ	ЛСТФ	Н	НЦ	Н
Sequence	НТА	НТК	НТС	НТСК	НТШ	ОКО	ПАЛ	РТЧ
result	НА	НК	НС	НСК	НШ	ОФО	ПЛ	РЧ
Sequence	РТЦ	СП	ТСЯ	СТЛ	СТН	СЧ	СШ	ТАТ
Result	РЦ	СФ	Ц	СЛ	СН	Ш	Ш	Т
Sequence	ТСА	ТАФ	ТС	ТЦ	ТЧ	ФАК	ФСТФ	ШЧ
Result	Ц	ТФ	ТЦ	Ц	Ч	ФК	СТФ	Ш

It is taken into account that phonetic code depends on the sound that can correspond with some letters or their sequences. Some different letters or their combinations have different sounds. Accordingly, Polyphon codes letters by sounds as heard. The ways of the replacement are provided in Table 3. The aim of the proposed phonetic algorithm is to generalize letters and sounds combinations [18]. The reason of generalization is based on idea that some sounds form letter sequences according their stress position. Such deviations from norms are common in social and territorial dialects in Russia [19].

There is a reduction of vowels occurring in Russian language when a word has 3 or more syllables. Vowels at the beginning and the end of the word are remained. Therefore in a word which contains 3 and more syllables the algorithm will remove all vowels in the middle of the word. The basis of splitting a word into syllables is the number of vowels in the word. Some vowels may be placed in the word with an error. We assume that if there are more than 4 consonants they will form 2 syllables.

The next stage is the substitution of the sequences of letters taking into account the changes made in Table 4. Examples of letters sequence substitution are presented in

Table 5. Often a combination of letters leads to different sound. The data from [18] was used as a basis for these combinations.

The result of word transformation is a phonetic code where consecutive same letters are replaced, for example: "телегаммааппарат" [**telegrammaapparat**] – "тэлэ-гамаапарат" [**telegramaaparat**].

We extended the Polyphon application to using phonetic code as primes. Firstly, all repeated letters are deleted from the string. Therefore, one letter presented in the string one time only. Each letter has a prime numerical code according to Table 6. The resulting code is the sum of primes. Usage of the sum of primes guarantees that strings with different letters will have different codes. This algorithm extension uses fuzzy phonetic comparison.

3.2   Fuzzy Phonetic Comparison

The word represented in phonetic code can be shown as a sum of primes. In this way, it is possible to use fuzzy phonetic comparison to extend the area of algorithm applicability. The algorithm facilities process phrase treatment when the word order can be broken. The example of such phrases is given in Table 6. It is possible to eliminate typos related to shift of letters also. Example of these typos is "компьютер" [**comp'yuter**] –"компьюетр" [**comp'yuetr**].

It is necessary to remove all duplicating letters from phrase except one code word by primes. The resulting code of the word will be the sum of letter coding. If the resulting code of two words is identical to the meaning, so the words are phonetically similar.

The essence of the algorithm is modification of words, processing a certain number of letters and summation of their codes. The algorithm for phonetic words coding is offered that considers phonetic particularities of Russian language.

Table 6. Letters coding

letter	А	П	К	Л	М	Н	Р	С	Т
code	2	3	5	7	11	13	17	19	23
letter	У	Ф	Х	Ц	Ч	Щ	Э	Я	
code	29	31	37	41	43	47	53	59	

4   Experimental Testing of Polyphon Algorithm

4.1   Description of Experiment

We perform the following experiment as to efficiency and accuracy of the proposed algorithm:

The experiment consists of several stages:

– data preparation: to generate a data set of words with mistakes;
– testing of phonetic algorithms;
– comparison with existing algorithms.

The basis for testing – words from Ozhegov' explanatory dictionary [20]. The words without their description were used for the experiment. Some words are identical because a word could have more than one meaning. The initial amount of words for error introduction is 11601.

The method for errors generation was developed. The errors, which expressed in words, reflect the phonetic phenomena and processes of Russian language. First category errors consider such processes as:

- **position changes** – the phonetic rule at the end of the word (devocalization of a paired consonant on the end of the word) and reduction (a qualitative reduction is letters substitution e.g. "о" [o] and "и" [i], "е" [e] to "и" [i], etc. in a weak position).

  We used a positional stunning and voicing of consonants. Voiced pair stunned at the end of words and before voiceless consonants. (мозг {ск}[**mozg {sk}**], параход {т} [**parahod {t}**]). Voiceless consonants converts to voiced consonants every time, in the case when their location before voiced (сдать {здать} [**sdat' {zdat'}**]). The exception is the unpaired voiced consonants and "в" character. In the diaeresis process one sound is removed out and a different sound appears (сердце {с'эрцъ} [**serdtse {s'ertc'}**], солнце {сонцэ} [**solntse {solntce}**]). The fusion process is merging of consonants (жарится моется [**zharitsya – moetsya**] – жарит(ц)а [**zharit(c)ya**], мыться [**myt'sya**] – мы(ц)а [**my(tc)a**]).

- **assimilation and dissimilation processes** - devocalization and vocalization of concordats in the word. The phenomenon of assimilation is the similarity of sounds, i.e. (ножка {шк} [**nozhka {shk}**], отдать {дд} [**otdat' {dd}**], сдоба {зд} [**sdoba {zd}**], косьба {зьб} [**kos'ba {z'b}**]).

  The basis for this category of errors is Russian language it is orthography errors in unstressed vowels and "ь", "ъ".

  Wrong writing of "ь" for assimilation softness of consonants in combinations зд(*) [**zd**], -ст(*) [**st**],-зн(*) [**zn**],-тн(*) [**tn**],-сн(*) [**ch**],-ст(*) [**st**],-нн(*) [**nn**], -нч(*) [**nch**], -нщ(*) [**nsh**], - нт(*) [**nt**], -дн(*) [**dn**], where (*) is vowel е [e], ё [jo], ю [yu], я [ya], и [i]. (гвозьди [**gvozdi**], есьть [**es't'**], жизьнь [**zhizh'n'**], защитьник [**zash'itnik**], лисьтья [**list'ya**], раньнего [**ran'ego**], сеньтябрь [**sentyabr'**], утреньнюю [**utren'yuyu**], шерсьть [**shers't'**], коньчились [**konchilis'**], опусьтели [**opus'teli**], отьнес [**otnes**], песьня [**pes'nya**], полдьнью [**pold'nyu**]). The submission of "ь" instead of "ъ" in words with "ь" before vowels "е", "ё", "ю", "я", "и". (бьют [**b'yut**] – бъют [**byut**]) and (сьезд [**s'ezd**]) on the contrary was considered as well.

  Errors of incorrect « не » [**ne**] and « ни » [**ni**] writing were not considered. Errors of letters mixing and their shift are not generated.

The software use all words and tries entering errors of each type into the word if it is possible. The number of generated words, which contain errors, is 50196.

The resulting document has two columns – original "correct" word and the same word with phonetic error(s). Examples of words with mistakes are shown in Table 7.

Table 7. Example of words with mistakes

Original word	Word with mistak(es)
АВАНЗАЛ [AVANZAL]	АВВАНЗАЛ [AVVANZAL]
	АВАНЗЗАЛ [AVANZZAL]
	ЕВАНЗАЛ [EVANZAL]
	АВАНЗАЛЛ [AVANZALL]
	АВААНЗАЛ [AVAANZAL]
	АВАНЗАЛ [AVANZAL]
	АВАННЗАЛ [AVANNZAL]
	ААВАНЗАЛ [AAVANZAL]
	АВАНЗААЛ [AVANZAAL]

Table 8. Algorithms comparison results

Algorithm	Matches of phonetic codes (in %)	Time (in milliseconds)
Proposed algorithm	95.12	2003
Proposed algorithm (fuzzy phonetic comparison)	98.8	1623
Soundex	90.24	1096
Metaphone	90.29	870
Double Metaphone	96.15	1451
Caverphone	90.41	9770
NYSIIS	75.97	1517
DaitchMokotoffSoundex	96.84 %	1763

4.2 Algorithm Testing and Comparison

The proposed algorithm is applied to a prepared set of test data. As a result we have an accurate verification of all words from a reference. We compare such phonetic algorithms as Soundex, Metaphone, Caverphone, Daitch-Mokotoff Soundex (implemented in Java language package org.apache.commons.codec.language). These algorithms use English alphabet characters only as in the Russian standard of transliteration GOST R 52535.1-2006 [14].

The results of testing is obtained by the Polyphon algorithm, Double Metaphone, Caverphone and Daitch-Mokotoff Soundex are shown in Table 8. Note that strings which were shown as different in Double Metaphone, Caverphone and Daitch-Mokotoff Soundex are displayed as equal in the proposed algorithm. Moreover, the algorithm has been tested on single words only.

A part of information about a word might be lost by any phonetic algorithm which can lead to wrong comparisons. Word transformation with the suggested approach allows comparing word according to their possible phonetic transformation. The suggested approach permits to compare words accurately. Unrecognized words represent words with several types of mistakes, including reduction.

Table 9. The results of estimating the accuracy for the word matching.

Range of code coincidences	Number of ambiguous cases
More than 100	0
from 10 to 100	608
from 5 to 9	2056
from 3 to 4	10034
1	37496
0	2

We also estimate the accuracy for the word matching as follows. We match in pairs each misspelled word with each reference word from Ozhegov' dictionary. If their codes are identical then we increment the number of code coincidences with the misspelled word. The experimental results are shown in Table 9. For example, the misspelled word "литие" [litie] and the five reference words "ладо" [lado], "литье" [lit'e], "летие" [letie], "лето" [leto], and "леди" [ledi] have the same code "лата" [lata]. It means that we have one ambiguous case of the word matching in the range from 5 to 9. The experimental results demonstrate the high rate of accuracy for the word matching.

5 Conclusions

In this paper, we presented the algorithm for phonetic word comparison including fuzzy phonetic comparison option. This algorithm can be used not only for surnames but also for establishing corresponds of the word meaning to the qualifier entry. The described approach is useful for data integration process. The proposed methods can be applied into data cleaning tools for Russian text processing. Accurate data clean-up is of help for integrating data from different sources.

The proposed approach is based on Russian language phonetic rules. Phonetic coding is more exact in comparison with the algorithms based on transliteration. We suggest that our algorithm could be used not only for surnames but for establishing compliance of word meaning to qualifiers. Letters transformation rules allow it to be used for languages similar to the Russian language, such as Belorussian, Ukrainian.

Phonetic fuzzy string coding allows to process a large number of similar words. As for further work, in order to improve the effectiveness of the proposed algorithm, fuzzy string comparison methods need to be included.

Acknowledgments. The reported study was supported in part by RFBR (grants 15-37-20042, 15-47-04348, 16-07-00411, and 16-57-44034); Council for Grants of the President of Russian Foundation (grant NSh-8081.2016.9). Experiments were performed on the resources of the Shared Equipment Centre of Integrated information and computing network of Irkutsk Research and Educational Complex (http://net.icc.ru).

References

1. Müller, H., Freytag, J.-Ch.: Problems, Methods, and Challenges in Comprehensive Data Cleansing, pp 5–12. Berlin University (2003)
2. Maletic, J., Marcus, A.: DataCleansing: A Prelude to Knowledge Discovery. Data Mining and Knowledge Discovery Handbook, pp. 19–32. Springer, Heidelberg (2010)
3. Zobel, J., Dart, Ph: Finding approximate matches in large lexicons. Softw. Pract. Exp. **25**(3), 331–345 (1995)
4. Zahoransky, D., Polasek I.: Text search of surnames in some slavic and other morphologically rich languages using rule based phonetic algorithms. In: Processing, IEEE/ACM Trans on Audio, Speech, and Language (T-ASL), pp. 553–563. IEEE (2015)
5. Cubberley, P.: Russian A Linguistic Introduction, p. 369. Cambridge press, New York (2002)
6. Parmar, V.P., Kumbharana, C.K.: Study existing various phonetic algorithms and designing and development of a working model for the new developed algorithm and comparison by implementing it with existing algorithm(s). Int. J. Comput. Appl. **98**(19), 45–49 (2014). (0975 – 8887)
7. Russia' address classifiactior. Tax Service of Russia (Классификатор адресов России (КЛАДР)). http://www.gnivc.ru/inf_provision/classifiers_reference/kladr/ (in Russian)
8. The International Plant Names Index (IPNI). http://www.ipni.org/
9. International Statistical Classification of Diseases and Related Health Problems 10th Revision. http://apps.who.int/classifications/icd10/browse/2016/en
10. Orr, K.: Data quality and systems theory. Commun. ACM **41**(2), 66–71 (1998)
11. Skripnik, Ya.N., Smolenskaya, T.M.: Phonetic of modern Russian language: study book. (Скрипник Я.Н., Смоленская Т.М. Фонетика современного русского языка: Учебное пособие / Под ред. Я.Н. Скрипник.) Stavropol, 152p (2010). (in Russian)
12. Valgina, N.S., Rozental, D.E., Fomina M.I.: Modern Russian language: Textbook (Валгина Н.С., Розенталь Д.Э., Фомина М.И. Современный русский язык: Учебник) 6th edition Moscow: Logos. 2002 – 528 p (in Russian)
13. Osipov, B.I., Galushinskaya, L.G., Popkov, V.V.: Phonetic and hypercorrection errors in written assignments of pupils of 3-11 classes of high school (Фонетические и гиперические ошибки в письменных работах учащихся 3–11-х классов средней школы). Russian Language journal. # 15, 2002 (in Russian). http://rus.1september.ru/article. php?ID=200201501
14. GOST R 52535.1-2006. Identification cards. Machine readable travel documents. Part 1 Machine Readable Passports. National Standard of the Russian Federation (ГОСТ Р 52535.1-2006. Карты идентификационные. Машиносчитываемые дорожные документы. Часть 1. Машиносчитываемые паспорта. Национальный стандарт Российской Федерации). Moscow, Russia, 18 p (2006). (in Russian)
15. Brin, S., Page, L.: The anatomy of a large-scale hypertextual Web search engine. Comput. Netw. ISDN Syst. **30**(1), 107–117 (1998)
16. Haveliwala, T.: Efficient computation of pagerank. Technical Report 1999-31. Stanford University (1999). http://dbpubs.stanford.edu/pub/1999-31
17. The Soundex Indexing System. National archives. http://www.archives.gov/research/census/soundex.html
18. Ivanova, T.F.: New orthoepic dictionary of Russian. Pronunciation. Accent. Grammatical forms (Иванова Т.Ф. Новый орфоэпический словарь русского языка. Произношение. Ударение. Грамматические формы) Second edititon. – Russian language-Media, 893 p. (2005) (in Russian)

19. Zhirmunsky, V.: National Language and social dialects (Жирмкнский В. Национальный язык и социальные диалекты).Moscow: The state publisher of fiction, 300 p. (1936). (in Russian)
20. Ozhegov, S.I.: Dictionary of Russian language. About 53000 words. (Словарь русского языка: Ок. 53 000 слов) / Editor Skvortsova L.I. Edition 24, Moscow: Oniks, World and education, 1200 p. (2007). (in Russian)

Automatic Detection of Nominal Events in Hungarian Texts with Dependency Parsing and WordNet

Zoltán Subecz[✉]

Technical, Agricultural and Economic Analysis Department,
College of Szolnok, Szolnok, Hungary
subecz@szolf.hu

Abstract. Besides named entity recognition, the detection of events in natural language is an important area of Information Extraction. The detection and analysis of events in natural language texts play an important role in several NLP applications such as summarization and question answering. Most events are denoted by verbs in texts and the verbs usually denote events. But other parts of speech (e.g. noun, participle) can also denote events. In our work we deal with the detection of nominal events. In this study we introduce a machine learning-based approach with a rich feature set that can automatically detect nominal events in Hungarian texts based on dependency parsing and WordNet. Additional methods were also applied beside the features, which improved the results and decreased running time. To our best knowledge, ours is the first result for *detecting nominal events* in Hungarian natural language texts, with dependency parsing and WordNet. Having evaluated them on test databases, our algorithms achieve competitive results as compared to the current English and other language results.

Keywords: Information extraction · Event detection · Nominal event detection · WordNet · Dependency parsing

1 Introduction

The detection of events in natural language is an important area of Information Extraction, besides named entity detection [7]. The detection and analysis of events in natural language texts plays an important role in several NLP applications such as summarization and question answering. Finding and analyzing events in a text, the way they relate to each other in time, is crucial to extract the detailed contents of a text.

Most events belong to verbs in texts and the verbs usually denote events. But other parts of speech (e.g. noun, participle) can also denote events. In our work we dealt with the detection of *nominal events* (nouns and nominalizations).

There are words (e.g. *írás* writing) that denote events in some sentences, but non-events in others, so the context of the words should be analyzed. In this study

© Springer International Publishing Switzerland 2016
G. Dregvaite and R. Damasevicius (Eds.): ICIST 2016, CCIS 639, pp. 580–592, 2016.
DOI: 10.1007/978-3-319-46254-7_47

we introduce a machine learning-based approach with a rich feature set that can automatically detect nominal events in Hungarian texts with dependency parser and WordNet. Our systems input is a token-level labeled training corpus. The models candidates are nouns. In several cases the candidate has a sub-tree in the dependency tree.

A classifier based upon a rich feature set was applied. Additional methods were used besides the features that improved the results and decreased running time. Our model was tested on five domains of the Szeged Corpus [4].

For English texts *constituency-based* syntactic parsers are used for preprocessing, because the English language is strongly configurational, where most of the sentence level syntactical information is expressed by word order. Conversely, Hungarian is a morphologically rich language with free word order. *Dependency parsers* are very useful for morphologically rich languages with free word order, like Hungarian, because they facilitate finding relations between non-neighboring but coherent words. Therefore, we used a *dependency parser* for our Hungarian texts.

In our system we applied the *Hungarian WordNet* [9] for the semantic characterization of the examined words. Since several meanings may belong to one word form in WordNet, we performed *word sense disambiguation* (WSD) among the particular senses with the *Lesk algorithm* [7].

To our best knowledge, ours is the first result for *detection of nominal events in Hungarian* natural language texts, with dependency parser and WordNet. Having evaluated them on test databases, our algorithms achieve competitive results as compared to the current English and other language results.

2   Related Work

EVITA [12] was one of the first event recognition tools. It recognizes events by combining linguistic and statistical techniques. It uses manually encoded rules based on linguistic information as main features. It also uses WorldNet classes to those rules for nominal event recognition. For sense disambiguation of nouns, it utilizes a Bayesian classifier.

Boguraev and Ando [2] presented a machine-learning based approach for automatic event annotation. They set out the task as a classification problem, and used a robust risk minimization (RRM) classifier to solve it. They used lexical and morphological attributes and syntactic chunk types in bi- and trigram windows as features.

Bethard and Martin [1] developed a system, STEP, for event recognition. They adopted syntactic and semantic features, and formulated the event recognition task as classification in the word-chunking paradigm. They used a rich set of features: textual, morphological, syntactic dependency and some selected WordNet classes. They implemented a Support Vector Machine (SVM) model based on those features.

Llorens et al. [8] presented an evaluation on event recognition. They added semantic roles to features, and built the Conditional Random Field (CRF) model to recognize events.

Jeong and Myaeng [6] used a dependency parser, but investigated the relation only between the candidate noun and the direct verb. They used combined features, applying them for verb + relation type pairs. They used WordNet, but without word sense disambiguation. They applied the MaxEnt classification algorithm with the following feature sets: basic, lexical, semantic, and dependency-based features. They weighted the features with Kullback-Leibler divergence.

For Italian texts Caselli et al. [3] dealt only with deverbal events. They used the Weka decision tree classifier. They investigated the argument structure of the candidate, the aspectual modifiers and the POS code of the 3-3 words before and after the candidate.

For Spanish texts Peris et al. [10] treated only deverbal events. For classification the Weka decision tree classifier was applied and an external nominal lexicon was utilized. They used a dependency parser, but investigated only the relation between the candidate and the direct verb. They employed the argument structure of the candidate.

For German texts Gorzitze and Padó [5] used a bootstrapping method for event recognition. They searched for temporal expressions and aspectual verbs near the candidate. They investigated the relation type between the candidate and the verb and used a rule-based dependency parser.

For Hungarian text Subecz [13] detected events, but he *dealt only with verbal and infinitival events.* He used the following feature set: surface, lexical, morphological, syntactic, WordNet and frequency features. Beside these features he applied rule based methods too.

3   Events, Nominal Events

Most events belong to verbs in texts and the verbs usually denote events. But other parts of speech (e.g. noun, participle) can also denote events. In our work we dealt with the detection of *nominal events* (nouns and nominalizations). Some examples for nominal events: *futás* (running), *építés* (building), *írás* (writing), *háború* (war), *ünnep* (feast).

Nominal events have two main groups: deverbal and non-deverbal nouns. Deverbal nouns: *írás* (writing), *futás* (running). Non-deverbal nouns: *háború* (war), *ünnep* (feast). The deverbal nouns have two main types: events and results. These nouns are often ambiguous. These are events in some sentences and results in other sentences.

For example the noun *writing* is an event in the following sentence: *The writing began at 5 o clock.* But it is a result in the following sentence: *We have read the writing.* Because of the ambiguity, the words analysis is not sufficient, the context must be analyzed too.

Annotation example: *Élvezem az* **utazást**, *különösen nagyon eltérő helyekre.* (I enjoy **traveling**, especially to very different places.) annotation: 3;utazást; deverbal.

4   Environment

One part of the Szeged Corpus [4] was used in our application from the following domains: *business and financial news, fictions and compositions of pupils, computer texts, newspaper articles, legal texts.* For training and evaluating 10 fold cross validation was used. The texts were annotated by two linguists. The inter-annotator agreement was Kappa = 0.7.

The *Weka*[1] data mining suite were employed for machine learning. For linguistic preprocessing segmentation, morphological analysis, POS-tagging and dependency parsing we applied the *Magyarlanc* 2.0 program package [14]. The Magyarlanc package creates morphological analyses, but the *HunMorph*[2] package age creates more detailed analysis in some cases, so this was also used. Thus two morphological parsers were applied.

As we can see at the related works, dependency parsing was used by other studies too. But they examined only the candidate and the direct parent and children in the dependency tree. We examined also the relation between the candidate and the further verbs in the tree. The models candidates are the nouns. In several cases the candidate has a sub-tree in the dependency tree.

In our system we applied the *Hungarian WordNet* [9] for the semantic characterization of the examined nouns. The semantic relations of the WordNet hypernym hierarchy were used.

Sentences make up a *dependency tree* on the basis of the syntactic relations between words. The trees topmost element is the *Root*. The sentences words are in the trees *nodes*, the *syntactic relationships* between the words are represented by the *edges*. If the candidate consists of several words, then these words compose a *sub-tree* within the main tree. The sub-tree is attached to the main tree by its *head word*.

Statistical data: The examined corpus contains 10,000 sentences. Number of candidates (nouns): 48,388. Number of positive candidates (event nouns): 7,626. Deverbal candidates: 5,325, positive deverbal candidates: 4,169. Non-deverbal candidates: 43,063, positive non-deverbal candidates: 3,457.

5   Classification

We applied *binary classification* for the problem. *Decision tree* (J48) and *Support Vector Machine* (SVM) algorithms of the *Weka* data mining suite were used. The sentences' nouns were the candidates. These are nodes of the dependency tree. For dependency parsing we applied the *Magyarlanc* program package.

5.1   Feature Set

We assigned features for the candidates on the training and evaluation set. Our method applied a rich feature set. The commonly used features of the event

---

[1] www.cs.waikato.ac.nz/ml/weka.
[2] mokk.bme.hu/resources/hunmorph.

detection tasks were also employed. Besides them, our feature set was extended with new ones. The *new features* were selected according to the characteristics of the *Hungarian language*. For the features the *dependency tree* and the *Wordnet* were also used. The main feature groups were divided into smaller groups, since the effect of features belonging to one such group was also investigated. *The following groups were the new ones* (these had not been applied in the previous studies of event detection): *two morphological parsers together, dependency tree 1–2, bag of words 1–3, WordNet 2–4.*

Surface features: *Bigrams and Trigrams*: The character bigrams and trigrams at the end of the examined words. *PositionInSentence*: The sequential number of the candidate in the sentence. *UpperCaseLetterInsideSentence*: The nouns, not at the beginning of the sentence, with uppercase letter at start, are usually named entities. Thus this feature can indicate non-eventive nature.

Morphological features-1: Since the Hungarian language has rich morphology, several morphology-based features were defined. For this group the morphological parser of the Magyarlanc package were used. We utilized the MSD codes (morphological coding system) of the event candidates for the following morphological features: *type, mood, case, tense, person of possessor, number, definiteness. Lemma*: the candidates lemma. *Deverbal*: whether the candidate is derived from a verb. *PrevPOS, SubPOS*: the POS codes of the previous and the subsequent words. *NearestVerbLemmaInSentence*: The lemma of the verb nearest to the candidate in the sentence. *Stem*: the deverbal candidates stem.

Morphological features-2: The HunMorph morphological parser was applied in this group. *DeverbalHunMorph*: whether the noun is derived from a verb. *DeverbalSuffix*: The derivational suffix of a deverbal noun. *StemHunMorph*: the deverbal candidates stem.

Morphological features-3: The morphological parsers give several parsing possibilities for ambiguous words. The derivational and inflectional suffixes of the candidate were given in this group for both parsers separately

Dependency tree features-1: These features were extracted from the dependency tree. *EdgeType*: The relationship between the candidate and the word above it in the tree (Example: SUBJ, OBJ, COORD). *EdgeTypeNE*: Whether the label (EdgeType) is named entity (NE). The relationship type is NE between the words of multiword named entities. This can suggest that the candidate is non-event. *LemmaAbove*: The lemma of the parent word of the candidate in the tree. *VerbLemmaAbove*: The lemma of the parent verb of the candidate (if any). *DirectVerbConnectionEdgeType*: The dependency label between the candidate and its parent verb (if any) (Example: SUBJ, OBJ). *NearestVerbLemmaAboveCandidate* and *NearestVerbAboveCandidateDistance*: The lemma of the nearest verb above the candidate in the tree and the distance between the verb and the candidate. *CandidateSubTreeTokenNumbers*: The number of nodes belonging to the candidates sub-tree. *WordAboveCandidateEdgeType*: The dependency label between the parent word of the candidate and its parent word. (Example: TLOCY) A temporal expression belonging to the candidate is usually above the candidate in the tree and its dependency label indicates that it is a temporal expression. The presence of a temporal expression above the candidate can indicate its eventive character.

Dependency tree features-2: If there is a verb above the candidate in the dependency tree, but the connection is not direct, the path between the candidate and the verb was characterized in detail. *POSPath*: The parts of speech of the nodes between the candidate and the verb were written one after the other. For example: $C\uparrow S\uparrow V\uparrow C\uparrow V\uparrow V$. *LemmaPath*: The lemmas between the candidate and the verb were written in a sequence. For example: napoztatás↑és↑törölgetés↑hajszártó↑megszárít. *EdgeTypePath*: The sequence of the dependency labels between the candidate and the verb. Example: OBL↑COORD↑SUBJ↑COORD↑CONJ↑.

Bag of words features-1: The bag of words (BoW) model was used for the characterization of word groups. *CandidateSubTreeLemmasBoWAverage*: The candidates usually have a sub-tree. This feature characterizes not only the subtrees headword but also the other words of the sub-tree. The lemmas of the sub-tree were represented with the bag of words model. First, we calculated for each lemma in the training set the probability of the particular lemma belonging to a positive candidates sub-tree. Second, for each candidate we calculated the average of these probabilities of the lemmas of the candidates sub-tree. A high average value indicates that the lemmas of the candidates sub-tree are important as eventiveness is concerned. *CandidateSubTreeLemmasBoWMax*: Similar to the previous feature, but at the second step for each candidate we chose the maximum of these probabilities that belong to the lemmas of the candidates sub-tree. A high maximum probability indicates that there is at least one lemma in the candidates sub-tree which is highly important as eventiveness is concerned. *LemmasUnderCandidateBoWAverage* and *LemmasUnder-CandidateBoWMax*: Similar to the previous features, but in this case not all of the lemmas of the candidates sub-tree were investigated, but only those lemmas of the sub-tree that are children of the candidate in the bag of words model. *EdgeTypesUnderCandidateBoWAverage* and *EdgeTypesUnderCandidateBoWMax*: Similar to the previous ones, the dependency labels between the candidate and the lemmas of the candidates children were represented with bag of words. *LemmaBetweenCandidateVerbBoWAverage* and *LemmaBetweenCandidateVerbBoW-Max*: For these features the lemmas between the candidate and the nearest verb above the candidate got into the bag of words.

Bag of words features-2: For these features the lemmas were represented in the bag of words from the sentence, not from the dependency tree. *WindowN-LemmasBoWAverage* and *WindowNLemmasBoWMax*: The lemmas before and after the candidate in N size window in the sentence were characterized with a bag of word model, using $N = 3$ and $N = 5$.

WordNet features: For these features the semantic relations of the WordNet [9] hypernym hierarchy were used. Since several meanings may belong to a word form in the WordNet, we performed *word sense disambiguation* (WSD) among the particular senses with the *Lesk algorithm* [7]. Synsets in the Word-Net contain definition and illustrative sentences. In the case of polysemous event candidates, we counted how many words from the syntactic environment of the event candidate can be found in the definition and illustrative sentences of the particular WordNet synset (neglecting stop words). The sense containing the highest number of common words was chosen.

WordNet features-1: *UnderEventKinds*: There is an artificial synset in the Hungarian WordNet, which contains mainly events in its hyponym hierarchy. But some of them are not real events and there are events also besides them. This feature indicates whether the given word belongs to the hyponym hierarchy of this synset.

WordNet features-2: *WordNetBoWAverage* and *WordNetBoWMax*: Similar to the Bag of words features, in this case the words belonging to the hyper-nym hierarchy of the candidate were put into a bag of words. *WordNetBoW-MaxSynset*: We selected the synset from the hypernym hierarchy of the candidate that belongs with the highest probability to the hypernym hierarchy of events.

WordNet features-3: *WordNetHypernymSynsetsTrainingSet* (binary): First the synsets of the hypernym hierarchy of event candidates from the training set were collected to a set. Then for each candidate it was marked whether at least one of the synsets from the hypernym hierarchy belongs to this set.

WordNet features-4: *BestEventsHyponym*: First lemmas which were events in the training set with the highest probability rate were collected to a set. Then for each candidate it was indicated whether its lemma is under the hyponym hierarchies of the sets members.

Bag of words features-3: First we selected the best members from the bag of words to a separate set for every case of the Bag of words 1–2 groups, i.e. those members that belong to events with the highest rate probability. Then we indicated, with the following features, whether the given bag of words of the given candidate contains at least one member of the particular set. *BestWordNet-Synsets*: This feature indicates whether the synsets of the candidates hypernym hierarchy is included in the BestWordNetSynsets set. *BestSubTreeLemmas*: It indicates if there is at least one lemma among the lemmas of the candidates sub-tree which is in the BestSubTreeLemmas set. *BestLemmasPathToVerb*: It indicates if there is a lemma among the lemmas between the candidate and the nearest verb in the dependency tree which is in the BestLemmasPathToVerb set. *BestLemmasWindowN*: It indicates if there is a lemma before or after the candidate in a window of N which is in the BestLemmasWindowN set. This was calculated for the cases $N = 3$ and $N = 5$.

List features: *AboveLemmaTemporalList*: We collected frequent temporal expressions to a list (e.g. *előtt* [before], *után* [after], *folyamán* [during]). There are often events under these expressions in the dependency tree. This feature indicates if there is such an expression above the candidate. *VerbAboveAspectualList*: We collected frequent aspectual verbs to a list (e.g. *kezd* [begin], *folytat* [continue]). The nouns under such verbs in the dependency tree are often events. This feature indicates if there is such a verb above the candidate.

Combined features 2 members: For these features two previous features were concatenated. *LemmaAbove+EdgeType*: The eventiveness of a word is often more correctly predicted if the lemma above the candidate and the relation between them are together examined, as opposed to the case if these were examined separately. Similarly, the following features were investigated together: *VerbLemmaAbove+EdgeTypeOBJ*, *VerbLemmaAbove+EdgeTypeSUBJ*, *LemmaAbove+BestWordNetSynsets*, *VerbLemmaAbove + BestWordNetSynsets*.

Combined features 3 members: Similar to the previous ones, in this case three features were concatenated. *LemmaAbove+EdgeType+ BestWordNetSynsets*, *VerbLemmaAbove+EdgeType+BestWordNetSynsets*.

5.2 Additional Methods

The following methods are new because these were not applied in the previous studies of event detection. All of them were useful based on the results, so these can be useful in other NLP tasks.

Using the probabilities of the base features. The features for the candidates were selected using *two main methods. In the first method* we used the base features introduced in the previous section. *In the second method*, instead of the base features, we applied probabilities calculated from the base features from the training set. In the case of each feature instance, we calculated on the basis of the training set how many times it occurred and how many times the candidate was *positive*. Relying on this, the positive-rate was calculated to that feature instance. For example in the case of *Lemma* feature, if the *Lemma = írás* (writing) occurs in 5 cases, and in 3 cases it belongs to a positive candidate, then the probability of 0.6 belongs to it. In this case, we did not give the base feature to the classifier, but instead its probability was given. In the previous example: *Lemma-probability =* 0.6 feature was used. With this method the *size of the classifiers vector space* and thus the *running time were significantly reduced*, compared to the first method. This is useful especially in the development phase. Comparing the two methods, most of the time the *probability method* gave better results and the running time was *70–80 times faster* than with the base features.

Forming groups from the candidates. The classifier can find more easily the rules in a dataset where the members are *similar* than in a dataset which contains diverse members. This is why it is worth grouping the candidates into smaller, similar parts (facilitating the work of the classifier) then summarizing the TP, TN, FP, FN results of the groups. Thus, the candidates were grouped according to two main criteria. First the *candidates were grouped into two parts*: deverbal and non-deverbal nouns since the members of these groups behave differently. The group of deverbal nouns contains events in a bigger rate. The second grouping was performed on the basis of the candidates lemmas. In this case three groups were created. The first group contains lemmas which were usually events in the training set. The second group contains the lemmas of the other candidates from the training set. The third group contains those lemmas of the test set which were not in the training set. *Thus 2*3 = 6 groups were created, and the classification was performed for each group.* For each group separately 10 fold cross validation was used for training and evaluating. Then we summarized the TP, TN, FP, FN results of the groups.

Using the lemmas positive probability for improving the classification result. In the cases when we got weak results (usually due to the low recall), after the classification, we modified the label of candidates *which were usually events in the training set* to positive.

As can be seen from the results, these additional methods improved our results and reduced running time.

5.3   Reducing the Number of Feature Occurrences

The size of the vector space was reduced with the following technique: only those feature occurrences were marked that appeared at least three times in the training set. With this method the running time was significantly reduced, and only the unimportant feature occurrences from the point of view of the classification were left out.

6   Results

For evaluation, the precision (P), recall (R) and F-measure (F) metrics were used.

6.1   Baseline Method

A baseline solution was applied for the examination of our models efficiency. For *baseline method* the deverbal candidates were treated as positive, the others as negative. Its result was: precision: 66.67 recall: 47.57, F-measure: 55.52. According to the following results, *our machine learning model by far outperformed the Baseline method.*

6.2   The Results of Our Model

Our machine learning method achieved the following result on the whole corpus with the given feature set and additional methods with the classifiers (Table 1).

We got better results with the *Decision tree* classifier, therefore only it was used for the following detailed analysis. Without the additional methods we got the following result: precision: 70.32 recall: 60.51, *F-measure: 65.03.* As shown, we could achieve a significant *improvement with the additional methods.* 80 % of the improvement was due to the candidates grouping, while the other part came from correcting

Table 1. Results on the whole corpus (%)

Classifier	Precision	Recall	F-measure
Decision tree	79.25	67.04	**71.94**
Support vector machine	72.43	60.15	**65.27**

the result of classification. When grouping was performed just on according to the first criterion, the model achieved a much better result (F-measure: 84.62) with only deverbal candidates than with only non-deverbal candidates (F-measure: 39.52).

Our model was run separately *on the five sub-corpora*. These results can be found in Table 2.

Table 2. Results on the sub-corpora (%)

Sub-corpus	Precision	Recall	F-measure
Fiction and compositions of pupils	82.36	71.18	**75.24**
Newspaper articles	83.27	72.41	**76.31**
Business and financial news	82.27	71.38	**75.12**
Computer texts	78.83	67.75	**71.57**
Legal texts	75.62	64.59	**68.74**

We got the best results on the *newspaper articles* domain, and the worst on the *legal texts*.

6.3 Results for Ablation Analysis

We examined the efficiency of the particular *feature groups* with an *ablation analysis* for all of the five cases when the target words were not grouped. In this case the particular feature groups were left out from the whole feature set, and we trained on the basis of the features that had remained. The results can be found in Table 3. The figures of the table show how the results changed after leaving out the particular feature group. Negative numbers indicate that the investigated feature group has positive influence on event recognition.

With the contraction of the similar feature groups, we got the following results (Table 4).

As we can see in Tables 3 and 4, almost all feature groups had positive impact to the models performance. The *WordNet* and *Bag of words* features had the best impact, but the *Morphological* and *Dependency tree* features also improved a lot. Both of the Morphological parsers had positive impact. As a sub-group, the WordNet features −2 had the best impact (6.51 %). In this sub-group the WordNet features were applied with a Bag of words model. The List features had no impact. The Combined features with 3 members had negative impact, but the Combined features with 2 members were useful.

Table 3. Results for ablation analysis (%)

Missing features	Difference in F-measure
Surface features	−0.28
Morphological features-1	−2.51
Morphological features-2	−0.52
Morphological features-3	−2.01
Dependency tree features-1	−1.92
Dependency tree features-2	−0.52
Bag of words features-1	−1.34
Bag of words features-2	−2.42
Bag of words features-3	−0.57
WordNet features-1	−0.32
WordNet features-2	−6.51
WordNet features-3	−0.53
WordNet features-4	−0.2
List features	0.0
Combined features 2 members	-0.79
Combined features 3 members	+0.1

Table 4. Results for ablation analysis - contraction (%)

Left out features	Difference in F-measure
Morphological features	−1,63
Bag of words features	−4,0
Dependency tree features	−1,56
WordNet features	−7,7
Combined features	−0,95

6.4 Comparing the Results with the Related Works

For English texts Jeong and Myaeng [6] achieved 71.8 % and Romeo et al. [11] achieved 67 % F-measure. For Italian texts Caselli [3] achieved 69 %, for Spanish texts Peris et al. [10] achieved 59.6 % F-measure. Compared with the related works, our result (F-measure = 71.9 %) is considered good.

7　Discussion, Conclusions

In this paper, we introduced our machine learning approach based upon a rich feature set, which can detect nominal events in Hungarian texts. We tested our methods on 5 domains of the Szeged Corpus, with 10,000 sentences. In our *feature set*, which is based upon a rich feature space, morphological, dependency tree, bag of words, WordNet, list and combined features were used. Beside these feature groups additional methods were applied, which improved our models efficiency and reduced running time. Decision tree and Support Vector Machine (SVM) algorithms were used. In our measurement the Decision tree algorithm outperformed the SVM algorithm. We used the algorithms with the default settings without parameter tuning. The best results were achieved on the newspaper articles and the worst on the legal texts. Its reason is that the newspaper articles contain simpler sentences and the legal texts contain more complicated sentences. The WordNet and Bag of words features had the best impact for the results. It confirms that the WordNet is efficient for semantic tasks. The Bag of words model could well characterize the examined word groups (the words in the candidates sub-tree; the lemmas before and after the candidate in N size window in the sentence; the synsets of the candidates hypernym hierarchy). The elimination of only the "Combined features 3 members" increased the accuracy. May be its ability is in the other feature groups, especially in the "Combined features 2 members". So its presence raised the difficulty for the classifier.

Having evaluated our methods on test databases, our algorithms achieve competitive results as compared to the current English and other language results.

References

1. Bethard, S., Martin, J.H.: Identification of event mentions and their semantic class. In: Proceedings of the 2006 Conference on Empirical Methods in Natural Language Processing, pp. 146–154. Association for Computational Linguistics (2006)
2. Boguraev, B., Ando, R.K.: Effective use of timebank for TimeML analysis. In: Schilder, F., Katz, G., Pustejovsky, J. (eds.) Annotating, Extracting and Reasoning about Time and Events. LNCS, vol. 4795, pp. 41–58. Springer, Heidelberg (2007)
3. Caselli, T., Russo, I., Rubino, F.: Recognizing deverbal events in context. In: Proceedings of CICLing 2011, poster session. Springer (2011)
4. Csendes, D., Csirik, J., Gyimóthy, T.: The szeged corpus: a POS tagged and syntactically annotated hungarian natural language corpus. In: Sojka, P., Kopeček, I., Pala, K. (eds.) TSD 2004. LNCS (LNAI), vol. 3206, pp. 41–47. Springer, Heidelberg (2004)
5. Gorzitze, S., Padó, S.: Corpus-based acquisition of German event- and object-denoting nouns. In: Proceedings of KONVENS 2012 (Main Track: Poster Presentations), pp. 259–263 (2012)
6. Jeong, Y., Myaeng, S.: Using syntactic dependencies and wordnet classes for noun event recognition. In: The 2nd Workhop on Detection, Representation, and Exploitation of Events in the Semantic Web in Conjunction with the 11th International Semantic Web Conference, pp. 41–50 (2012)
7. Jurafsky, D., Martin, J.H.: Speech and Language Processing: An Introduction to Natural Language Processing, Computational Linguistics, and Speech Recognition. Prentice-Hall, Upper Saddle River (2000)

8. Llorens, H., Saquete, E., Navarro-Colorado, B.: TimeML Events recognition and classification: learning CRF models with semantic roles. In: Proceedings of the 23rd International Conference on Computational Linguistics, pp. 725–733. Association for Computational Linguistics (2010)

9. Miháltz, M., Hatvani, Cs., Kuti, J., Szarvas, Gy., Csirik, J., Prószéky, G., Váradi, T.: Methods and results of the Hungarian WordNet project. In: Tanács, A., Csendes, D., Vincze, V., Fellbaum, C., Vossen, P., (eds.) Proceedings of the Fourth Global WordNet Conference (GWC 2008), pp. 311–320. University of Szeged, Szeged (2008)

10. Peris, A., Taulé, M., Boleda, G., Rodriguez, H.: ADN-classifier: automatically assigning denotation types to nominalizations. In: Proceedings of the Seventh LREC Conference, 19-21 May 2010, Valetta, Malta, pp. 1422–1428 (2010)

11. Romeo, L., Lebani, G.E., Bel, N., Lenci, A.: Choosing which to use? A study of distributional models for nominal lexical semantic classification. In: Proceedings of the Ninth International Conference on Language Resources and Evaluation (LREC 2014), pp. 4366–4373 (2014)

12. Saurí, R., Knippen, R., Verhagen, M., Pustejovsky, J.: Evita: a robust event recognizer for QA systems. In: Proceedings of the Conference on Human Language Technology and Empirical Methods in Natural Language Processing, pp. 700–707. Association for Computational Linguistics (2005)

13. Subecz, Z.: Detection and classification of events in hungarian natural language texts. In: Sojka, P., Horák, A., Kopeček, I., Pala, K. (eds.) TSD 2014. LNCS (LNAI), vol. 8655, pp. 68–75. Springer, Heidelberg (2014)

14. Zsibrita, J., Vincze, V., Farkas, R.: magyarlanc: a toolkit for morphological and dependency parsing of Hungarian. In: Proceedings of RANLP 2013, pp. 763–771 (2013)

Extracting Location Names from Unstructured Italian Texts Using Grammar Rules and MapReduce

Christian Napoli[✉], Emiliano Tramontana, and Gabriella Verga

Department of Mathematics and Informatics, University of Catania Viale,
Andrea Doria 6, 95125 Catania, Italy
{napoli,tramontana}@dmi.unict.it

Abstract. Named entity recognition aims at locating elements in a given text and classifying them according to pre-defined categories, such as the names of persons, organisations, locations, quantities, etc. This paper proposes an approach to recognise the location names by extracting them from unstructured Italian language texts. We put forward the use of the framework MapReduce for this task, since it is more robust than a classical analysis when data are unknown and assists at parallelising processing, which is essential for a large amount of data.

Keywords: Mapreduce · Named entity recognition · Hadoop · Information extraction · Italian language

1 Introduction

The problem of named entities recognition can be considered an easy task for humans, however it can not be easily automated. Given the large amount of texts available in electronic form, it is desirable to have an automatic and efficient solution. In this age, big data are becoming the main focus of attention because of the enormous increment of data generation (Marszalek et al. 2015; Wozniak et al. 2016). Named entity recognition can be challenging when huge amounts of data have to be processed to extract knowledge, because existing solutions have not been adapted to the new size and time requirements. Within named entity recognition, the extraction of *location names* from unstructured English texts has been a highly investigated area and several approaches have provided different solutions, e.g. using the support of dictionaries (Chang et al. 2006; Sarawagi 2008), or training data (Nothman et al. 2013). However, most existing approaches are not suitable for unknown place names and less satisfying for languages other than English.

We are interested in the extraction of location names, i.e. proper nouns for places, from texts in Italian. The recognition approach that we are proposing uses the MapReduce paradigm and is based on Italian grammar rules, similarly to the one in (Caruso et al. 2015). Although the latter approach has been proven to have satisfying results in terms of *precision* and *recall*, it has not been adapted for a parallel and distributed environment. Moreover, an automatic tool finding occurrences of the Italian grammar rules on a text could face some robustness issues, due to the varieties of possible constructions encountered in the input texts, especially when the rules are not well separated from the

© Springer International Publishing Switzerland 2016
G. Dregvaite and R. Damasevicius (Eds.): ICIST 2016, CCIS 639, pp. 593–601, 2016.
DOI: 10.1007/978-3-319-46254-7_48

algorithm. In this paper, we use the power of MapReduce paradigm (and the supporting framework) for producing a more robust and efficient tool. MapReduce is a programming model and an associated implementation for processing and generating large data sets (Dean and Ghemawat 2008). According to such a model we have devised a map function that processes a key/value pair extracted from the original text and generates a set of intermediate key/value pairs that express whether the analysed text conforms our rules, then we have built a reduce function that merges all intermediate values associated with the same intermediate key. Furthermore, filtering has been applied to remove false positives. The solution developed according to this paradigm can be automatically parallelised and executed on a large cluster of commodity machines.

The paper is organised as follows. Section 2 introduces the framework MapReduce. Section 3 describes our proposed algorithm based on MapReduce. Section 4 describes the proposed post-processing filters. Section 5 reports the experiments with an analysis of the performances of the proposed solution. Finally, Sect. 6 reports comparisons with the related work and draws our conclusions.

2 MapReduce Paradigm

Hadoop MapReduce is a software framework for easily writing applications that process vast amounts of data (typically multi-terabyte data-sets) in-parallel on large clusters (thousands of nodes) of commodity hardware in a reliable, fault-tolerant manner.

A MapReduce job usually splits the input data-set into independent chunks that are processed by the *map* tasks in a completely parallel manner. The framework sorts the outputs of the maps, which are then given as input to the *reduce* tasks. Typically, both the input and the output of the job are stored in a file-system. The underlying framework takes care of scheduling tasks, monitoring them and re-executes the failed tasks (Dean and Ghemawat 2008; Apache 2016). Therefore, MapReduce gives developers a paradigm to organise their tasks, and each new application has to be adapted to fit MapReduce's main two steps as follows.

- Map is the first task, which takes input data and converts it into a set of data, where individual elements are broken down into tuples (key/value pairs).
- Reduce takes the output from a map task as input and combines those data tuples into a smaller set of tuples. The reduce task is always performed after the map task.

Accordingly, the developer needs to write code similar to the following.

```
map(String key, String value):
        // key: document name
        // value: document contents
        for each word w in value:
                EmitIntermediate(w, "1");
```

```
reduce(String key, Iterator values):
    // key: a word
    // values: a list of counts
    int result = 0;
    for each v in values:
            result += ParseInt(v);
    Emit(AsString(result));
```

The MapReduce framework consists of a single master JobTracker and one slave TaskTracker per cluster node. The master is responsible for resource management, tracking resource consumption/availability and scheduling the jobs component tasks on the slaves, monitoring them and re-executing the failed tasks. TaskTracker slaves execute the tasks as directed by the master and provide task-status information to the master periodically.

3   Proposed Approach for Extracting Named Entities

In order to find the parts of a sentence that are names of places, we organise the processing in several steps: pre-processing, mapping, shuffling, reducing.

During the first step, pre-processing, a text file in Italian language formatted as simple ASCII text is analysed and a triple consisting of (*word, sentence, position*) is obtained for each word in the text. The first element of the triple, *word*, is a word in the text; *sentence* is the position of the sentence in the text; and *position* is the position of the word in the sentence.

E.g a text such as: *"Passeggiando per le vie di Roma. Ho visto il Colosseo. Oggi piove."* (corresponding to the English text "Walking on the streets of Rome. I have seen the Colosseum. Today it rains.") would be split in three sentences each given a numerical id, then each sentence would be split into the composing words. The resulting triples are as follows.

(Passeggiando, 1, 1) (per, 1, 2) (le, 1, 3) (vie, 1, 4) (di, 1, 5) (Roma, 1, 6)
(Ho, 2, 1) (visto, 2, 2) (il, 2, 3) (Colosseo, 2, 4)
(Oggi, 3, 1) (piove, 3, 2)

The numerical ids assigned by this first step to each word on each sentence will be useful after the mapping steps, and will let us properly find the position of words in the text, according to the initial sentences.

The second step is mapping and performs the labelling of each word according to a given category, i.e. it finds the membership category for a word. The categories are as follows.

- Articles (A): a list of all definite Italian articles, e.g. "il (the)" or "la (the)", etc., which consists of seven elements.
- Prepositions (P): a list of definite simple and composite Italian preposition, e.g. "da (from)" or "in (in)", excluding "con (with)" because it is not used when naming places. This lists consists of 43 elements.

- Descriptors (D): a list of Italian adverbs frequently related to a place, e.g. "vicino (near)" or "dietro (inside)". This lists held 20 elements.
- Verbs (V): a subset of Italian verbs related with places, e.g. "abitare (dwell)" or "tornare (go back)". This lists held 22 elements.
- Others (O): all words excluded in the above categories.

Initially, we have manually built the lists of words in the categories A, P, D and V, and such lists are short enough to be easily written once for all. Moreover, lists A and P contain all the possible words, while lists D and V could be enriched with more words, if deemed appropriate, while tuning the proposed tool for larger corpora under analysis. Note that one of the benefits of our approach is that we need not manually classify the several thousand of Italian words to identify all verbs and nouns, and among the latter possible names of places.

For properly processing verbs found in sentences, we have used the Italian version of the stemming algorithm Snowball (Porter 2001) to found stems for verbs in V. Table 1 shows a partial list of words for each of the above categories.

Table 1. List of categories and their characterising words in Italian and English

Article (A)	Preposition (P)	Descriptor (D)	Verb (V)
il (the)	di (of)	verso (towards)	abitare (dwell)
lo (the)	a (to)	vicino (near)	andare (go)
la (the)	da (from)	dietro (behind)	fermare (stop)
i (the)	in (in)	ingresso (entrance)	giungere (arrive)
gli (the)	tra (between)	uscente (outward)	entrare (get in)
le (the)	sugli (on the)	salita (upward)	uscire (get out)

The devised *mapping* function takes as input a pair <word, key> and produces a pair <numid, type> according to the input word:

```
void map(key, word)
    type ← findTypeWord(word);
    emit(numid, type)
```

Parameter *key* is the offset of the word from the beginning of the data file, parameter *numid* contains the pair *sentence id* and *word position* in sentence, *type* is the category of the word, as above defined. Hence, method findTypeWord() reads the input word and returns its category, i.e. either A, P, D, V, or O.

Given the input text as the above three Italian sentences: *"Passeggiando per le vie di Roma. Ho visto il Colosseo. Oggi piove."*, each word is passed as input to the map function that determines a corresponding category. Hence, for this sample text the map function produces the following output.

(1, 1, V) (1, 2, P) (1, 3, A) (1, 4, O) (1, 5, P) (1, 6, O)
(2, 1, O) (2, 2, V) (2, 3, A) (2, 4, O)
(3, 1, O) (3, 2, O)

The third step is shuffling and this orders the results of the mapping, i.e. each found category, according to the sentence id and the word position in the sentence, which are embedded into parameter *numid*.

The corresponding pseudo-code is as follows.

```
void shuffle(numid, type[])
    orderType(type[]);
```

Method orderType() reorders categories according to the original positions of words in the input sentences. I.e. in each sentence, the categories (assigned by the mapping) are chained according to the original position in the sentence. For the given sample text and categories the produced output will be as follows.

```
VPAOPO
OVAO
OO
```

The fourth step is reducing and it identifies the location names. According to the Italian language grammar rules, a location name in a sentence can be found after a preposition (e.g. *"di Roma"* (of Roma)), a verb in V and a preposition in P (e.g. *"andando a Roma"* (going to Roma)), or a descriptor in D and a preposition in P (e.g. *"vicino a Roma"* (near Roma)), etc. Hence, sentences embedding location names conform to one among several patterns. We have listed such patterns by analysing recurrent constructions of Italian sentences and expressed them according to the above sets A, P, D, V. The approach in this paper is based on the search of a pattern in the following list: PO, OPO, VPO, ODPO, POAO, VODAO, PPOAO, VPAO, OVAO. More patterns can be added, once deemed as appropriate for the Italian language, hence enhancing the ability of the approach to analyse sentences.

Therefore, for each input sentence the reducing step checks whether one of the patterns in the list appears and in case a pattern has been found, the word identifying the location name can be read from the input file. The position of the location name is recognised according to the occurring pattern, e.g. for pattern VPO the location name is in the third just after the verb and preposition that have been found.

Patterns PO, OPO and VPO are considered only if they match the beginning part of a sentence. E.g. if a sentence has been mapped as POOPVPO, we can see that pattern PO is at the beginning and at the end of the sentence, then only the beginning part of the sentence will be considered for the matching. This has been found to be more effective when analysing actual sentences.

We have created a function reduce that takes as input two values and returns the location and the type of word. The pseudo-code of this function is as follows.

```
void reduce (numid, type[])
1. find ← compareType(type[], listPattern)
2. if found
3.     name ← readFileOrigin(numid)
4.     emit(name, type[])
5. end if
```

For the above snippet of code, function CompareType() looks for the sequence in the list of previously identified patterns, and it returns true if it matches an existing pattern and false otherwise. Function ReadFileOrigin(), thanks to numid, searches the list of type in the origin text and returns the name that follows it.

Now, let us describe our approach and the results when taking as input the sample sentences shown above. For the first sample text, the input sentence is *Passeggiando per le vie di Roma,* then after having executed the first, second and third step, the output VPAOPO will have been produced. On this output string, the fourth step finds two patterns, i.e. VPAO and OPO, mapping the two parts *Passeggiando per le vie,* and *vie di Roma,* respectively. The first pattern VPAO allows us to identify and extract place name *vie,* and the second pattern OPO let us extract place name *Roma.* Therefore, the place name is given as the word in the sentence corresponding to category O, found in one of the allowed patterns for the Italian language.

Similarly, for the second sentence *Ho visto il Colosseo* the first three steps will give pattern OVAO and this will be recognised as meaningful, since recognised as one of the allowed patterns for the Italian language, then the place *Colosseo* will be identified.

Finally, for the third sentence *Oggi piove* the pattern OO will be found and this will be classified as not meaningful, since not possible for the Italian language, then no place name will be identified.

4   Additional Filtering of Results

With the aim of refining the results we have introduced the following filters that post-process the results given by the above approach. Filter 1 consists in removing from the possible results all words that have length less than three characters. Filter 2 consists of removing from possible results words that are verbs and words with specific suffixes. Filter 3 consists of removing candidates that are common words that cannot be names of places in the Italian language, when used before a preposition or an article. Filter 4 consists of removing words that do not begin with a capital letter. Table 2 shows an example of filtered words.

Table 2.   List of words for post-processing filtering

Filter 1	Filter 2	Filter 3
cui (whose)	avvicinarsi (approaching)	dove (where)
una (a)	pregare (pray)	quello (that)
due (two)	interrogarsi (wondering)	quale (which)
ciò (such)	camminare (walking)	tutto (all)
far (do)	viaggiare (travelling)	altro (else)

5   Experiments

The experiments were performed on three texts, T1, T2 and T3, having different nature. In particular, we have selected a set of dialogues. Parameters for the selected texts are shown in Table 3.

Table 3. Characteristics of the analysed texts

	Sentences	Words	Place names
T1	1293	6181	39
T2	689	3384	19
T3	1654	9108	61

All the analysed texts have been manually labelled for the location names, in order to further compute the number of True Positive (TP), False Positive (FP), True Negative (TN) and False Negative (FN), and in turn *precision, recall, and F1 score*. Table 4 shows the resulting score for the said parameters when analysing the texts using the proposed approach based on MapReduce. Precision is defined as TP/(TP+FP), recall is defined as TP/(TP+FN) and F1 score is the harmonic mean of precision and recall. For the analysed texts, recall values are satisfactory since above 0.68, while the variation on precision is large.

Table 4. Results of the proposed extraction approach

Text	TP	FP	FN	Precision	Recall	F1
T1 Filter 1, 2, 3	36	191	5	0.16	0.88	0.27
T1 Filter 4	35	33	6	0.51	0.85	0.64
T2 Filter 1, 2, 3	13	137	6	0.09	0.68	0.15
T2 Filter 4	13	2	6	0.87	0.68	0.76
T3 Filter 1, 2, 3	56	333	6	0.14	0.90	0.25
T3 Filter 4	55	71	7	0.44	0.89	0.59

Let us note that our approach is robust for long sentences, such as e.g. *"Il processo si sta svolgendo a Milano"* (the trial is taking place in Milano). When processing such a sentence the resulting string of categories will be AOOOVPO, and the identified pattern will be OVPO. As we can see, the initial part of the sentence is discarded, since it is deemed not meaningful.

On the contrary, a previous approach based on automata (Caruso et al. 2015) would find as meaningful patterns A and VP, yielding to the identification of false positives. The main difficulty of the previous approach to filter out such a sentence is related to the handling of the automata at runtime. For analysing a given sentence it considers the current state and given a word can transit to another legit state, while it cannot retain all the previous states it has transited in. The said differences cater for a greater robustness, precision and recall of the results.

6 Conclusions

The previous literature has investigated several approaches for extracting information on texts and among other methods, more recently rule-based methods have been used successfully (Sarawagi 2008). Rules have been properly devised for the category of text to be processed, e.g. advertisements have been a large area of application (Peleato et al. 2001).

Moreover, several supervised approaches, hence semi-automatic, have been proposed (Downey et al. 2007), which are sometimes based on machine learning (Nothman et al. 2013). Word extraction and identification of parts based on grammar rules has been proposed in (Caruso et al. 2014). Approaches using text analyses have been proposed for the semantical characterisation of authors according to neural based methods (Napoli et al. 2014), and for the profiling of users on social network (Fornaia et al. 2015).

This paper has presented a novel approach based on grammar rules to find location names in texts written in Italian language. This work takes a different direction to other previous works, by making it automatic, more robust, easier to develop and to expand, when compared to previous approaches. The MapReduce paradigm has given the possibility to develop a multi-step analysis that can be easily implemented and reused when combining different rules. Moreover, it is prone to be executed in a parallel and distributed environment for enhancing performances. More descriptors and filters can be added to further refine results, i.e. terms such as *"regione"* or *"città"* (region or city) can be used as new rules or as filters on the identified patterns.

The approach proposed here can be applied for other analyses, more general than location name extractions, once given the appropriate mapping and patterns to be found. E.g. person names can be extracted, using similar lists of categories of words, by just adapting the lists of descriptors and verbs, and then given a new set of meaningful patters, derived from the Italian grammar when using names of persons. Similarly, text analyses can be used when taking as input the static code, hence aiming at a semantical analysis of programs, to find properties such as separation of concerns (Tramontana 2013) and to further transform and guide the use of classes (Calvagna and Tramontana 2013; Giunta et al. 2012). Moreover, the proposed approach can be easily employed on cloud resources (Polap et al. 2015; Wozniak et al. 2015) and could be appropriate to process incomplete datasets (Nowak et al. 2015; Nowicki et al. 2016).

Acknowledgements. This work has been partially supported by project PRIME *"Piattaforma di Reasoning Integrata, Multimedia, Esperta"* funded by Regione Sicilia within PO FESR Sicilia 2007/2013 framework, and FIR project *"Organizzazione e trattamento di trascrizioni e testi in scenari di security"*, code 375E90.

References

Apache, Hadoop (2016). http://hadoop.apache.org
Calvagna, A., Tramontana, E.: Delivering dependable reusable components by expressing and enforcing design decisions. In: Proceedings of IEEE International Computer Software and Applications Conference (COMPSAC), Kyoto, Japan, 22–26 July, pp. 493–498 (2013)
Caruso, D., Giunta, R., Messina, D., Pappalardo, G., Tramontana, E.: Rule-based location extraction from Italian unstructured text. In: Proceedings of XVI Workshop From Object to Agents (WOA), 17–19 July, vol. 1382, pp. 46–52 2015
Chang, C.-H., Kayed, M., Girgis, M.R., Shaalan, K.F.: A survey of web information extraction systems. IEEE Trans. Knowl. Data Eng. **18**(10), 1411–1428 (2006)
Dean, J., Ghemawat, S.: Mapreduce: simplified data processing on large clusters. Commun. ACM **51**(1), 107–113 (2008)

Downey, D., Broadhead, M., Etzioni, O.: Locating complex named entities in web text. In: Proceedings of International Joint Conference on Artificial Intelligence (IJCAI), pp. 2733–2739. Morgan Kaufmann Publishers Inc. (2007)

Fornaia, A., Napoli C., Pappalardo, G., Tramontana, E.: An AOP-RBPNN approach to infer user interests and mine contents on social media. Intelligenza Artificiale **9**, 209–219 (2015). IOS Press

Giunta, R., Pappalardo, G., Tramontana, E.: Superimposing roles for design patterns into application classes by means of aspects. In: Proceedings of the ACM Symposium on Applied Computing (SAC), 26–30 March 2012, Trento, Italy, pp. 1866–1868

Marszalek, Z., Wozniak, M., Borowik, G., Wazirali, R., Napoli, C., Pappalardo, G., Tramontana, E.: Benchmark tests on improved merge for big data processing. In: Proceedings of IEEE Asia-Pacific Conference on Computer Aided System Engineering (APCASE), pp. 96–101, July 2015

Napoli, C., Pappalardo, G., Tramontana, E.: An agent-driven semantical identifier using radial basis neural networks and reinforcement learning. In: Proceedings of XV Workshop From Object to Agents (WOA), vol. 1260, 25–26 September 2014

Nothman, J., Ringland, N., Radford, W., Murphy, T., Curran, J.R.: Learning multilingual named entity recognition from Wikipedia. Artif. Intell. **194**, 151–175 (2013). Elsevier

Nowak, B.A., Nowicki, R.K., Woźniak, M., Napoli, C.: Multi-class nearest neighbour classifier for incomplete data handling. In: Rutkowski, L., Korytkowski, M., Scherer, R., Tadeusiewicz, R., Zadeh, L.A., Zurada, J.M. (eds.) Artificial Intelligence and Soft Computing. LNCS, vol. 9119, pp. 469–480. Springer, Heidelberg (2015)

Nowicki, R.K., Nowak, B., Woźniak, M.: Application of rough sets in k nearest neighbours algorithm for classification of incomplete samples. In: Kunifuji, S., Papadopoulos, G.A., Skulimowski, A.M.J., Kacprzyk, J. (eds.) Knowledge, Information and Creativity Support Systems. AISC, vol. 416, pp. 243–257. Springer, Switzerland (2016). doi:10.1007/978-3-319-27478-2_17, ISSN: 2194-5357

Peleato, R.A., Chappelier, J.-C., Rajman, M.: Automated information extraction out of classified advertisements. In: Bouzeghoub, M., Kedad, Z., Métais, E. (eds.) NLDB 2000. LNCS, vol. 1959, p. 203. Springer, Heidelberg (2001)

Połap, D., Woźniak, M., Napoli, C., Tramontana, E.: Real-time cloud-based game management system via cuckoo search algorithm. Int. J. Electron. Telecommun. **61**(4), 333–338 (2015)

Porter, M.F.: Snowball: a language for stemming algorithms (2001). http://snowball.tartarus.org/texts/introduction.html

Sarawagi, S.: Information extraction. Found. Trends Databases **1**(3), 261–377 (2008)

Tramontana, E.: Automatically characterising components with concerns and reducing tangling. In: Proceedings of IEEE International Computer Software and Applications Conference (COMPSAC), Kyoto, Japan, 22–26 July, pp. 499–504 (2013)

Woźniak, M., Marszałek, Z., Gabryel, M., Nowicki, R.K.: Preprocessing large data sets by the use of quick sort algorithm. In: Skulimowski, A.M.J., Kacprzyk, J. (eds.) Knowledge, Information and Creativity Support Systems: Recent Trends, Advances and Solutions. AISC, vol. 364, pp. 111–121. Springer, Switzerland (2016). doi:10.1007/978-3-319-19090-7_9, ISSN: 2194-5357

Wozniak, M., Polap, D., Borowik, G., Napoli, C.: A first attempt to cloud-based user verification in distributed system. In Proceedings of IEEE Asia-Pacific Conference on Computer Aided System Engineering (APCASE), pp. 226–231, July 2015

"Google" Lithuanian Speech Recognition Efficiency Evaluation Research

Donatas Sipavičius[✉] and Rytis Maskeliūnas

Department of Multimedia Engeneering, Kaunas University of Technology,
Studentu St. 50, 51368 Kaunas, Lithuania
donatas.sipavicius@ktu.edu

Abstract. This paper presents "Google" Lithuanian speech recognition efficiency evaluation research. For the experiment it was chosen method that consists of three parts: (1) to process all voice records without adding any noise; (2) process all voice records with several different types of noise, modified so as to get some predefined signal-to-noise ratio (SNR); (3) after one month reprocess all voice records without any additional noise and to assess improvements in the quality of the speech recognition. It was chosen WER metrics for speech recognition quality assessment. Analyzing the results of the experiment it was observed that the greatest impact on the quality of speech recognition has a SNR and speech type (most recognizable is isolated words, the worst - spontaneous speech). Meanwhile, characteristics such as the gender of the speaker, smooth speech, speech speed, speech volume does not make any significant influence on speech recognition quality.

Keywords: "Google" lithuanian speech recognition · Speech recognition · WER (Word Error Rate) · Signal-to-Noise Ratio (SNR)

1 Introduction

In Lithuania keep going speech recognition researches, trying to adapt speech recognition systems to practical challenges. There are number of researches of foreign languages application for the Lithuanian speech recognition area. Authors of project Liepa shared their ideas, that the usage of foreign language based recognizers for Lithuanian speech is often limited vocabulary and economically ineffective [1]. "Google" Lithuanian speech recognizer was released for public use in 2015. "Google" its speech recognition technology now has only an 8 % word error rate (WER) [2].

Using speech recognizers often faced with the problem, that some part of words are recognized incorrectly or not recognized at all. This results in speech recognition quality dependence on the following factors:

- Specifity of recognizing language (e.g., Lithuanian words changing the endings for communications sentence means; changing word ending it gets another meaning);
- Specific terminology specific to a particular application area;
- Speaker dialect, speaking volume, sharpness, various speech disorders;

© Springer International Publishing Switzerland 2016
G. Dregvaite and R. Damasevicius (Eds.): ICIST 2016, CCIS 639, pp. 602–612, 2016.
DOI: 10.1007/978-3-319-46254-7_49

- Background noise level (volume) and its nature (factory, rolling train, shopping center and etc.).

When choosing a speech recognizer must take in account of its characteristics, such as speech type (isolated words, connected words, continuous speech or spontaneous speech must be recognized), size of vocabulary (possible to recognize the number of words), dependence /independence from the speaker (the number of recognizable speakers), communication channels and the environment (resistance to distortion of the communication channel and background noise).

This paper presents "Google" Lithuanian speech recognition efficiency evaluation research. The experiment was accomplished with 63299 voice records, 3318 different phrases. All these voice records have been processed by "Google" speech recognizer at least 18 times (not counting testing of experimental software): 1 time without any additional noise, 16 times with noise (4 different noise types, 4 SNR), 1 time without any additional noise after one month. WER value and the number of voice recordings that have been processed and received speech recognition results were assessed during the experiment.

The paper is structured as follows. The review of related work is presented in second part of the paper. The experimental setup is described in the third part. The fourth part of the paper introduces experimental data and the results of the experiment. The work conclusions are presented in the fifth part of the paper.

2   Related Works

[3] deals with some aspects of development voice user interfaces for several applications (several digits name (0-9); commands for internet browser, text editor and media player control). The experimental investigation showed that 90 % recognition accuracy was achieved in average using adaptation of foreign language speech engine. Detailed analysis showed that most commands are recognized with very high accuracy.

[4] describes development of the Lithuanian voice controlled interface for the medical- pharmaceutical information system. Authors were able to achieve 95 % recognition accuracy acceptable for the practitioners. A phrase recognizer in a medical-pharmaceutical information system achieved 14.5 % average error rate for names of diseases [5]. Proprietary Hybrid approach [6] for Lithuanian medical terms allows achieving a 99.1 % overall speech recognition accuracy. In [7] the best achieved recognition was 98.9 % for 1000 Lithuanian voice commands (diseases, complaints, drugs).

Another Lithuanian voice recognition system of medical- pharmaceutical terms is presented in [8]. Investigations showed that Lithuanian speech recognizer achieves higher accuracy (over 96 % in a speaker independent mode) but the use of the adapted foreign language recognizer allows increase this baseline accuracy even further (over 98 % in a speaker independent mode for 1000 voice commands) [8].

[9] deals with two elements of the artificial intelligence methods—the natural language processing and machine learning to apply to small vocabulary Lithuanian language recognition. The average hybrid operation accuracy reached was 99.24 %,

when the recognizer recognizes voice commands out of 12 known speakers, and was equal to 99.18 %, when it was applied to the unknown speaker.

[10] Same researchers evaluated the use of two recognizers for Lithuanian medical desease digit code corpus and achieved around 96 % accuracy for clean speech. Similar approach to [9] was used in [11, 12]. In the first work the highest accuracy (98.16 %) was obtained when k-Nearest neighbors method was used with 15 nearest neighbors, in the second they have achieved 95 % accuracy by combining 4 different language recognizers.

[13] proposes a method for features quality estimation that does not require recognition experiments and accelerate automatic speech recognition system development. The key component of method is usage of metrics right after front-end features computation. The experimental results show that method is suitable for recognition systems with back-end Euclidean space classifiers.

3 Experimental Setup

"Google" Lithuanian speech recognition efficiency evaluation research method (Fig. 1) consists of three parts:

1. First of all to process all voice records without adding any noise.
2. Process all voice records with several different types of noise, modified so as to get some predefined signal to noise ratios (SNR).
3. "Google" announced its advancements in deep learning, a type of artificial intelligence, for speech recognition [2], so it's appropriate to reprocess all voice records without any additional noise after one month and to assess improvements in the quality of the speech recognition.

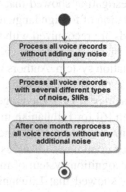

Fig. 1. "Google" speech recognition efficiency evaluation research method

Two methods are needed for processing audio records with "Google" speech recogniton:

1. **Method # 1.** One computer may send many (it depends on thread count) audio records to "Google" speech recognizer at once. Audio format must be FLAC so they

must be properly pre-processed. An audio adapter is unnecessary. We cannot rely only on this solution because the audio processing can be stopped at any time if "Google" disables the active key.

All records which format is FLAC are selected from user defined folder. Then unprocessed audio record is selected and from text file (audio record name and text file name are the same) is read information about audio record (noise type, SNR, sample rate). "Google" speech recognizer is processing received audio record and returns speech recognition result in JSON format. Received speech recognition result and information about noise record, SNR (if noise has been used) are saved in DB. Then speech recognition resuls are processed (decomposed to primary and alternative results, all numerals are transformed into text, calculated WER). Processed audio record and text file are deleted from file system.

2. **Method # 2.** One computer may send only one audio record (audio format does not matter) to "Google" speech recognizer at once. Audio records processing may be accelerated by connecting more computers. Audio adapter is required when processing audio records by this method (experimental software is playing audio record, "Google": speech recognizer is listening for microphone).

When audio records processing runs it automatically opens web site in "Google Chrome" browser and initiates communication component, which initiates webkit-SpeechRecognition component. Then voice record and, if needed, noise record and SNR are selected. WebkitSpeechRecognition component gets message to listen microphone and process sound which is playing. WebkitSpeechRecognition component starts listening sound from microphone while he gets message about audio record playing is finished. If needed noise record is playing at necessary SNR while audio record is playing (noise record and audio record are playing at one time). When audio record is finished, noise record stops playing. WebkitSpeechRecognition component stops listening microphone and is waiting for speech recognition results. "Google" speech recognizer is processing received audio record and returns speech recognition result in JSON format. Received speech recognition result and information about noise record, SNR (if noise has been used) are saved in DB. Then speech recognition resuls are processed (decomposed to primary and alternative results, all numerals are transformed into text, calculated WER).

Necessary environment for realization. Experimental software consists of (Fig. 2):

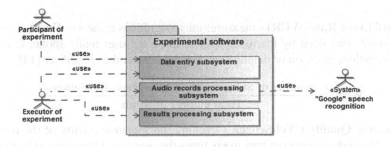

Fig. 2. Decision context diagram

- **Data entry subsystem** – implemented to import existing voice records to DB, to record new voice records, to describe voice records with additional information. Participant of experiment and executor of experiment uses this subsystem. Implemented with ASP.NET for participant of experiment use cases and "Windows Forms" for executor of experiment use cases.
- **Audio records processing subsystem** – responsible for processing audio records. Only executor of experiment uses this subsystem. Detailed information below.
- **Results processing subsystem** – processes the received speech recognition results and presents the aggregated information. Only executor of experiment uses this subsystem. Implemented with "Windows Forms".

Audio records processing subsystem consists of:

1. **Audio records processing (Method # 1)**

- *Audio records preparation for processing* – this process converts all needed voice records to FLAC format, also all voice records combines with all possible noise types modified so as to get some predefined SNRs.
- *Audio records processing* – this process sends many audio records (along with audio format and sample rate) to "Google" speech recognizer at once.

2. **Audio records processing (Method # 2)**

- *Audio records processing* – this process takes voice record from DB, runs browser "Google Chrome" in automatic microphone use state and opens web site with communication component and webkitSpeechRecognition component. Through communication component communicates with webkitSpeechRecognition component and saving speech recognition results. Implemented with "Windows Forms".
- *Communication component* – this component is like intermediary between audio record process and webkitSpeechRecognition component. Implemented with ASP.NET SignalR.
- *webkitSpeechRecognition* – "Google" speech recognition client side component that works in browser "Google Chrome". It processes audio record and returns speech recognition resuls (text).

Metrics. Choosing appropriate metrics to track the quality of the system is critical to success [14]. The common metrics that used to evaluate the quality of the recognizer [14]:

- **Word Error Rate (WER)** – measures misrecognitions at the word level: it compares the words outputted by the recognizer to those the user really spoke. Every error (substitution, insertion or deletion) is counted against the recognizer [14].

$$\text{WER} = \frac{\text{Number of Substitution} + \text{Insertions} + \text{Deletions}}{\text{Total number of words}} \tag{1}$$

- **Semantic Quality (WebScore)** – tracking the semantic quality of the recognizer (WebScore) by measuring how many times the search result as queried by the recognition hypothesis varies from the search result as queried by a human transcription

[14]. A better recognizer has a higher WebScore [14]. The WebScore gives a much clearer picture of what the user experiences when they search by voice [14]. In all research authors tend to focus on optimizing this metric, rather than the more traditional WER metric defined above [14].

- **Perplexity (PPL)** – a measure of the size of the set of words that can be recognized next, given the previously recognized words in the query [14]. This gives a rough measure of the quality of the language model – the lower the perplexity, the better the model is at predicting the next word [14].
- **Out-of-Vocabulary (OOV) Rate** – tracks the percentage of words spoken by the user that are not modeled by our language model [14]. It is important to keep this number as low as possible, because any word spoken by users that is not in vocabulary will ultimately result in a recognition error; furthermore, these recognition errors may also cause errors in surrounding words due to the subsequent poor predictions of the language model and acoustic misalignments. [14].
- **Latency** – is defned as the total time (in seconds) it takes to complete a search request by voice (the time from when the user finishes speaking until the search results appear on the screen) [14]. Many factors contribute to latency as perceived by the user [14]: (a) the time it takes the system to detect end-of-speech, (b) the total time to recognize the spoken query, (c) the time to perform the web query, (d) the time to return the web search results back to the client over the network, and (e) the time it takes to render the search results in the browser of the users phone.

4 Experimental Research

4.1 Experimental Data

An experiment was accomplished with 63299 voice records, the total duration of these records is 86.06 h, average duration per record is 4.89 s. 359 speakers participated in the experiment: male – 111 (30.92 %), female – 248 (69.08 %).

Detailed information about voice records is presented in Tables 1 and 2.

Table 1. Information about voice records

Speech attribute	Yes		No	
	Pcs.	%	Pcs.	%
Smooth speech	61930	97.84	1369	2.16
Speech with accent	1640	2.59	61659	97.41
Fast speech	23773	37.56	39526	62.44
Loud speech	62869	99.32	430	0.68

Table 2. Voice records distribution by type of speech

Isolated words		Connected words		Continuous speech		Spontaneous speech	
Pcs.	%	Pcs.	%	Pcs.	%	Pcs.	%
39349	62.16	35	0.06	23887	37.74	28	0.04

All voice records were processed without noise and with 4 different types of noise (train station, traffic, car driving and white noise), modified so as to get some predefined signal to noise ratios (SNR): 25 dB, 20 dB, 15 dB and 10 dB.

4.2   The Results of the Experiment

Speech recognition results (without noise). After processing all 63299 for the first time (without any noise) for 20784 voice records there was no speech recognition result at all. In this subsection statistic is presented for 42515 voice records (238885 phrases), for which "Google" speech recognition returned results. Average WER for all 42515 voice records is 40.74 % (Table 3). This value is obtained by calculating all voice records with speech recognition results average of WER values. WER standard deviation[1] 37.70 ± 0.30 (± 0.30 value is calculated confidence interval with a 90 % probability that the value is in this range).

Table 3. Speech recognition results by speakers

	Speech recognition results by speakers				
	Average	Best	Average of 3 best speakers	Worst	Average of 3 worst speakers
WER, %	40.74	10.00	14.74	100.00	96.39

Speech recognition results by speaker's gender: female – 39.91 % (WER standard deviation – 38.54 ± 0.36), male – 42.96 % (WER standard deviation – 35.27 ± 0.54).

Speech recognition results by speech attribute are: not smooth speech – 38.71 % (WER standard deviation – 34.91 ± 1.75), smooth speech – 40.79 % (WER standard deviation – 37.77 ± 0.31); speech without accent – 40.56 % (WER standard deviation – 37.76 ± 0.30), speech with accent – 48.39 % (WER standard deviation – 34.25 ± 1.81); fast speech – 42.33 (WER standard deviation – 39.06 ± 0.53), normal speech – 39.90 % (WER standard deviation – 36.95 ± 0.36); quiet speech – 43.59 % (WER standard deviation – 27.96 ± 3.49), loud speech – 40.73 % (WER standard deviation – 37.74 ± 0.30) (Table 4).

Table 4. Speech recognition results by speech type

Speech type	Speech recognition results			
	Number of phrases	Words of phrases	Average WER, %	WER standard deviation
Isolated words	22206	40555	31.55	$43.29 \pm 0,48$
Connected words	12	246	64.55	$30.98 \pm 14,71$
Continuous speech	20297	198084	50.77	$27.09 \pm 0,31$
Spontaneous speech	0	–	–	–

---

[1] The standard deviation is a numerical value used to indicate how widely individuals in a group vary. If individual observations vary greatly from the group mean, the standard deviation is big; and vice versa.

It could be seen that speech type has significant impact on the quality of speech recognition: best speech recognition results are with isolated words, connected words with maximum average WER (12 out of 35 voice records), the worst – spontaneous speech (no of 28 voice records was recognized).

The worst recognized phrases are (average WER is 2.0): penktas (recognized as "tanki test"); išsijunk (recognized as "iš trijų"); sviestas (recognized as "speed test"); lizosoma (recognized as "visos stoma"); taikyk (recognized as "tai kiek"); dešinėn (recognized as "dešimt min"); padidink (recognized as "lady zippy"); šunkelis (recognized as "šunų kelis"); išsijunk (recognized as "iš jų"); bjaurus (recognized as "į eurus"); rnr (recognized as "prie neries"); aštuntas (recognized as "pašto kodas").

Speech recognition results (with noise). In this subsection presented speech recognition results when all 63299 voice records were processed with noise (4 different noise types, 4 different SNRs).

Figure 3 shows how recognized voice records quantity dependends on the noise type and SNR. It could be seen that most of speech recognition results (not necessarily correct) are with SNR at 25 dB (exeption – noise "Car driving" which most of speech recognition results are with SNR at 20 dB).

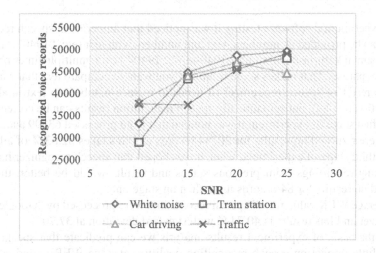

Fig. 3. Recognized voice records quantity dependence on the noise type and SNR

Figure 4 shows how WER dependends on the noise type and SNR. It could be seen that best speech recognition is when SNR = 25 dB (that is with the weakest noise).

"Google" speech recognition assessment of improvements. After processing all 63299 voice records after one month (without noise) for 20868 voice records there was no speech recognition result (84 records more than one month ago). Average WER for 42431 recognized voice records is 40.82 %. It could be seen that average WER is 0.08 % worse than one month ago.

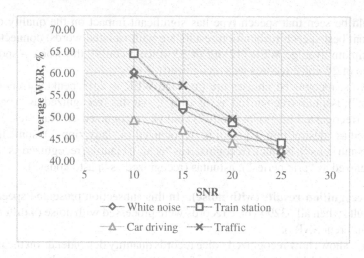

Fig. 4. WER dependence on the noise type and SNR

5   Conclusions and Future Works

After experimental software testing it was noticed that numerals in speech recognition result can be provided as numbers, text and numbers with text (etc. "1940", "tūkstantis devyni šimtai keturiasdešimtieji", "1940-ieji", "1940i") even multiple times processing the same phrase. That makes some trouble if you want to compare text that was spoken and the result of speech recognizer (it needs to replace numbers to text in all speech recognition results), but semantically speech recognition results can be correct.

On first stage of experiment it was noticed that from processed 63299 audio records there were returned no results for 20784 records and this takes 32.83 % of all records. On the third stage of experiment, when it was hoped that speech recognizer has trained processing recordings from previous stages and results would be better, there were returned no results for 84 records more than on stage one.

Average WER value for all speech records that were proceesed by "Google" speech recognizer and has results is 40.74 % with standard deviation at 37.70 %.

On the basis of experiment results analysis we can predicate that speaker gender makes little impact on speech recognition quality – average WER variation between man and woman is 3.05 %. Also for speech recognition quality has little impact smooth speech, speech speed, speech volume (average WER variation between comparable groups varies from 1.49 up to 2.86 %), but speech with accent result is worse by 7.83 %. Big impact for speech recognition has speech type: the best is recognized isolated words and the worst is spontaneous speech.

After completion of speech recognition experiment with 4 different signal to noise ratios (SNR) it was noticed, that best speech recognition is when SNR is 25 dB (with lowest noise level). Most speech recognition results (not including correctness) were returned when SNR was 25 dB (exception – noise "car driving", which has got most results when SNR was 20 dB).

Experimental research results showed that quite often case one of the alternative results is more correct than primary result. This means that speech recognition results could be better if "Google" speech recognizer more precisely estimate which of the results should be final.

A month later after accomplishing processing speech records without noise they were processed repeatedly and the results showed that "Google" speech recognizer recognition quality hasn't got better, because speech recognition results (average WER) got by 0.08 % worse than at initial experiment got value. While "Google" speech recognizer is free we can make assumption that "Google" is seeing speech recognizer drawbacks and speech recognizer will be improved.

Experiment speech records should be the same size in every classified group to increase confidence of experiment results.

References

1. Telksnys, A.L., Navickas, G.: Žmonių ir kompiuterių sąveika šnekant. In: Kompiuterininkų dienos - 2015, ISBN: 9789986343134, pp. 185–193. Žara. Vilnius (2015)
2. Google says its speech recognition technology now has only an 8 % word error rate. http://venturebeat.com/2015/05/28/google-says-its-speech-recognition-technology-now-has-only-an-8-word-error-rate/, 25 Apr. 2016
3. Maskeliunas, R., Ratkevicius, K., Rudzionis, V.: Some aspects of voice user interfaces development for internet and computer control applications. Elektronika ir elektrotechnika 19(2), 53–56 (2013). ISSN 1392-1215
4. Rudzionis, V., Ratkevicius, K., Rudzionis, A., Maskeliunas, R., Raskinis, G.: Voice controlled interface for the medical-pharmaceutical information system. In: Skersys, T., Butleris, R., Butkiene, R. (eds.) ICIST 2012. CCIS, vol. 319, pp. 288–296. Springer, Heidelberg (2012). ISBN: 9783642333071
5. Rudzionis, V., Raskinis, G., Maskeliunas, R., Rudzionis, A., Ratkevicius, K.: Comparative analysis of adapted foreign language and native lithuanian speech recognizers for voice user interface. Elektronika ir elektrotechnika 19(7), 90–93 (2013). ISSN 1392-1215
6. Rudžionis, V., Ratkevičius, K., Rudžionis, A., Raškinis, G., Maskeliunas, R.: Recognition of voice commands using hybrid approach. In: Skersys, T., Butleris, R., Butkiene, R. (eds.) ICIST 2013. CCIS, vol. 403, pp. 249–260. Springer, Heidelberg (2013)
7. Rudzionis, V., Raskinis, G., Maskeliunas, R., Rudzionis, A., Ratkevicius, K., Bartisiute, G.: Web services based hybrid recognizer of lithuanian voice commands. Elektronika ir elektrotechnika 20(9), 50–53 (2014). ISSN 1392-1215
8. Rudžionis, V., Raškinis, G., Ratkevičius, K., Rudžionis, A., Bartišiūtė, G.: Medical – pharmaceutical information system with recognition of Lithuanian voice commands. In: Human language technologies. In: The Baltic Perspective: Proceedings of the 6th International Conference. ISBN: 978161499441, pp. 40–45. IOS Press. Amsterdam (2014)
9. Bartišiūtė, G., Ratkevičius, K., Paškauskaitė, G.: Hybrid recognition technology for isolated voice commands. In: Information Systems Architecture and Technology: Proceedings of 36th International Conference on Information Systems Architecture and Technology – ISAT 2015 – Part IV, ISBN 978-3-319-28565-8, pp. 207–216 (2016)
10. Bartišiūtė, G., Paškauskaitė, G., Ratkevičius, K.: Investigation of disease codes recognition accuracy. In: Proceedings of the 9th International Conference on Electrical and Control Technologies, ECT 2014, pp. 60–63 (2014)

11. Rasymas, T., Rudžionis, V.: Evaluation of methods to combine different speech recognizers. In: Computer Science and Information Systems (FedCSIS), pp. 1043–1047 (2015)
12. Rasymas, T., Rudžionis, V.: Lithuanian digits recognition by using hybrid approach by combining lithuanian google recognizer and some foreign language recognizers. In: Information and Software Technologies, ISBN 978-3-319-24769-4, pp 449–459 (2015)
13. Lileikytė, R., Telksnys, A.L.: Metrics based quality estimation of speech recognition features. Informatica Vilnius, Matematikos ir informatikos institutas **24**(3), 435–446 (2013). ISSN: 0868-4952
14. Schalkwyk, J., Beeferman, D., Beaufays, F., Byrne, B., Chelba, C., Cohen, M., Garret, M., Strope, B.: Google Search by Voice: A case study

Quality and Importance of Wikipedia Articles in Different Languages

Włodzimierz Lewoniewski$^{(\boxtimes)}$, Krzysztof Węcel$^{(\boxtimes)}$, and Witold Abramowicz

Poznań University of Economics and Business,
Al. Niepodległości 10, 61-875 Poznań, Poland
wlodzimierz.lewoniewski@kie.ue.poznan.pl, krzysztof.wecel@ue.poznan.pl

Abstract. This article aims to analyse the importance of the Wikipedia articles in different languages (English, French, Russian, Polish) and the impact of the importance on the quality of articles. Based on the analysis of literature and our own experience we collected measures related to articles, specifying various aspects of quality that will be used to build the models of articles' importance. For each language version, the influential parameters are selected that may allow automatic assessment of the validity of the article. Links between articles in different languages offer opportunities in terms of comparison and verification of the quality of information provided by various Wikipedia communities. Therefore, the model can be used not only for a relative assessment of the content of the whole article, but also for a relative assessment of the quality of data contained in their structural parts, the so-called infoboxes.

Keywords: Wikipedia · DBpedia · Information quality · Data quality · WikiRank · Article importance

JEL Classification: C55 · D8 · L15 · L86

1 Introduction

Currently there are 282 active Wikipedia language editions[1]. The largest is the English version, which has more than 5 million articles. The first ten biggest editions also includes German, French, Russian and Polish.

This online encyclopedia has become one of the most important sources of knowledge throughout the world. In April 2016, the number of visits amounted to 282 million per day in all the language versions[2]. In the ranking of the most popular websites Wikipedia occupies 6th place in the world[3].

Every day increases the number of articles in each language. Articles can be created (edited) also by anonymous users. The authors do not have to formally demonstrate their skills in a specific field. Wikipedia has no central editorial or

---

[1] https://en.wikipedia.org/wiki/List_of_Wikipedias.
[2] https://stats.wikimedia.org/EN/TablesPageViewsMonthly.htm
[3] http://www.alexa.com/topsites

© Springer International Publishing Switzerland 2016
G. Dregvaite and R. Damasevicius (Eds.): ICIST 2016, CCIS 639, pp. 613–624, 2016.
DOI: 10.1007/978-3-319-46254-7_50

group of reviewers who could comprehensive approaches to verify all new and existing products. These and other problems led to criticism of the concept of Wikipedia, in particular pointing out the poor quality of information[4].

Quality issues, however, concern the creators of Wikipedia. Practically every language version of the online encyclopedia have an award system for high quality articles. In the English version of Wikipedia the best articles have name "Featured Article" (FA). Articles that does not fulfill all the criteria FA, but closer to their quality, they can also get slightly lower award "Good Article" (GA).

In order to receive award article must be submitted for nomination by the user. The result of this is carried out discussion and voting takes place, where every user can approve or not to give awards for the specific article and explain their point of view. The criteria and rules for granting awards in each language version may change over time, which in turn may result in loss of award by some articles[5].

In addition to the award, in some language versions the article may receive lower scores. Such an indirect assessment may indicate "maturity " of the article (i.e., in what degree it is close to the best articles). The English version of Wikipedia generally distinguishes 7 quality classes of articles (from the highest): FA, GA, A-class, B-class, C-class, Start, Stub. It is noteworthy that, unlike higher classes FA and GA, the other (lower) grades are received without a community discussion and voting – each user can set the rating by himself on the basis of rules. Some language versions use less-developed grading scale, e.g. in Polish version in addition awarded equivalent FA and GA are also grades[6]: Czwórka, Start, Zalążek (altogether 5 classes).

In Wikipedia there is no generally accepted standard classification of quality articles between different language versions [1]. Some languages use expanded rating scale (EN, RU), others are limited to 2–3 grades (BE, DE). In other words, each language version can have its own classification system of articles quality, but all of them use at least two highest classes - equivalent for FA and GA. However, such articles are very few - on average, in each language version of their share is about 0,07 %. It should also be noted that a large part of the articles is not even evaluated, eg. in Polish edition share of such articles is over 99 %.

In some language there is an importance scale[7] for articles. This feature is used for rating article importance in particular subject (or subjects) and usually marked as Top-, High-, Medium- or Low-importance. It can be expected that the greater the importance of the article, the better its quality. However, it should be taken into account quality class. Figures 1 and 2 show summary table by

---

[4] https://en.wikipedia.org/wiki/Criticism_of_Wikipedia.

[5] For English Wikipedia there is a list of articles that have lost their award - https://en.wikipedia.org/wiki/Wikipedia:Former_featured_articles.

[6] https://pl.wikipedia.org/wiki/Szablon:Stopnie_oceny_jako%C5%9Bci.

[7] https://en.wikipedia.org/wiki/Wikipedia:WikiProject_Wikipedia/Assessment.

Quality	Importance (English Wikipedia)					
	Top	High	Mid	Low	???	Total
FA	854	1 363	1 450	916	185	4 768
⊕ GA	1 543	3 790	8 219	8 996	1 702	24 250
A	12	35	88	36	10	181
B	7 872	16 738	28 602	25 524	11 278	90 014
C	8 927	25 511	56 008	75 987	37 855	204 288
Start	13 117	61 840	259 776	654 384	254 221	1 243 338
Stub	3 027	24 139	190 874	1 594 570	706 921	2 519 531
???	2 130	8 770	28 198	84 995	945 621	1 069 714
Total	37 482	142 186	573 215	2 445 408	1 951 793	5 156 084

Quality	Importance (French Wikipedia)					
	Top	High	Mid	Low	???	Total
FA (AdQ)	410	494	396	211	-	1 511
GA (BA)	382	633	874	654	-	2 543
A	316	399	522	367	6	1 610
B	3 567	6 647	10 148	8 723	221	29 306
Start (BD)	6 355	24 405	71 048	139 354	6 657	247 819
Stub (E)	3 112	19 706	123 515	550 221	91 402	787 956
???	8	70	521	4 249	682 259	687 107
Total	14 150	52 354	207 024	703 779	780 545	1 757 852

Fig. 1. Articles by quality and importance in English (on the left) and French (on the right) Wikipedia. Source: own calculations in May 2016

Quality	Importance (Russian Wikipedia)					
	Top	High	Mid	Low	???	Total
FA (ИС)	79	111	140	13	549	892
★ GA (ХС)	82	224	370	76	1 659	2 411
HqA (ДС)	9	95	446	120	2 304	2 974
I	278	734	649	213	249	2 123
II	621	1 827	4 246	1 285	796	8 775
III	1 144	6 435	19 240	12 887	3 435	43 141
IV	698	4 165	27 717	17 262	8 872	58 714
???	688	3 039	5 213	6 999	1 176 737	1 192 676
Total	3 599	16 630	58 021	38 855	1 194 601	1 311 706

Quality	Importance (Polish Wikipedia)					
	Top	High	Mid	Low	???	Total
FA (AMN)	12	36	19	10	607	684
GA (DA)	18	37	36	27	2 008	2 126
B (Czw)	9	27	62	13	49	160
C (Popr)	9	38	53	15	449	564
Start (Dost)	97	180	518	258	204	1 257
Stub	40	83	323	524	683	1 653
???	304	1 459	1 812	3 159	1 155 318	1 162 052
Total	489	1 860	2 823	4 006	1 159 318	1 168 496

Fig. 2. Articles by quality and importance in Russian (on the left) and Polish (on the right) Wikipedia. Source: own calculations in May 2016

taking quality and importance rating for each assessed article in English, French, Russian and Polish Wikipedia. In contrast to similar statistics at Wikipedia[8], where one article could count to 2 times or more, we took into account only one of the highest quality and importance grade of each article. On it to the reason, for example, the class "A" has only 181 articles, although technically number of such articles - 1593. It is connected with that the vast majority of articles with grade "A" are additionally evaluated as FA or GA. Therefore, in our experiments we will not take into account the class "A".

In the scientific literature we can find studies, which offer different approaches to the automatic evaluation of the quality of Wikipedia articles. Based on the different characteristics of highly-rated (awarded) articles it is possible to evaluate other. Text length, number of references, the number of images and other articles' features can help in the quality assessment.

---

[8] https://en.wikipedia.org/wiki/Wikipedia:Version_1.0_Editorial_Team.

The aim of our research is to answer to the following questions:

- Does article importance affect its quality?
- What parameters can help to assess the importance of the article automatically?
- Is there a difference between importance models in different languages?

Most of the research on models for the quality of Wikipedia articles is focused on the "largest" language – English. In this paper we consider 4 popular languages: English (en), French (fr), Polish (pl), Russian (ru), which have introduced the templates for specifying article's importance. This allows us to build models that will be able to compare articles quality in different languages. Besides, this is the first study in which we have build importance models of the article and we will conduct a comparative analysis of these models in a different languages.

2   Automatic Quality Assessment

Since founding and with the increasing popularity of Wikipedia there are more and more scientific publications on the quality of the information. One of the first studies showed that the measurement of the volume of content can help determine the degree of maturity of the article [2]. Work in this direction show that generally higher quality articles are longer [3], use references in a coherent way, are edited by hundreds of editors and have thousands of editions [4,5].

In addition to quantitative analysis, later research has focused on the qualitative analysis around the content of the article. In one of the works has been used so-called. FOG index readability, which determines the degree accessibility of text [6]. In cases where the volume of contents in articles is similar, better article will have more factual information [7]. Style and variety of words used also affects the quality of the article [8,9]. Wikipedia users can include special templates in an article, indicating gaps in quality. Such annotations can help in assessing the quality of the article [10]. Features related to articles popularity can also be used in assessing the quality of the information they contain [11].

Another works on automatic quality classification of Wikipedia articles taking into account user behavior. There are models that take into account their experience and reputation. Articles quality has a large number of editing and a large number of editors who have a high level of cooperation [12,13]. It is important that in this group of editors was even one user with a high level of experience in content editing in Wikipedia [14]. Particular importance have the reputation of the user who made the first edition of the article [15]. Reputation can be calculated on the basis of "survival" of the text, which user placed [16–18].

In this study, we decided to focus primarily on those aspects that can help improve the quality of the article – so we consider the content of the article and its metadata.

3   Data Selection and Extraction

On the basis of literature [2–4,6,8,10–12,19–22] and our own research we have chosen 85 articles' parameters which will be taken into account when building quality and importance models of Wikipedia articles. These parameters include various areas such as text statistics, parts of speech, readability formulas, similarity of words, the structure of the article, edition history, network parameters, popularity of the article, the characteristics of discussion.

One of the most attractive methods for obtaining data from Wikipedia is API service, which provides easy access to data and metadata of articles using HTTP, via a URL in a variety formats (including XML, JSON). API service works for every language and is available at the address specified by the template: `https://{lang}.wikipedia.org/w/api.php?action={settings}`, where {`lang`} – abbreviation of the language version, {`settings`} – query settings[9]. Possibilities of API used in our specially prepared program WikiAnalyzer, which can get over 50 different parameters of each article.

In Fig. 3 the distribution of variables in articles with different quality class is shown. It is noticeable that the increase in each feature attracts increase in a share of higher-quality articles. We also compared parameters of the articles only from FA-class but of varying importance. Some of them are shown in Fig. 4 in English Wikipedia. Here regularity is also observed: the increase in value of features involves increases in a share of important articles.

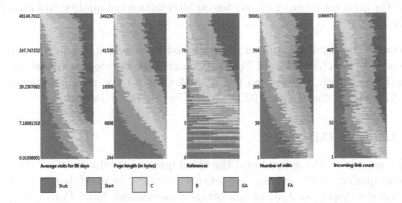

Fig. 3. Distribution of variables in articles with different quality class in English Wikipedia

---

[9] All possible settings in API service can be found on a special page: https://en. wikipedia.org/wiki/Special:ApiSandbox.

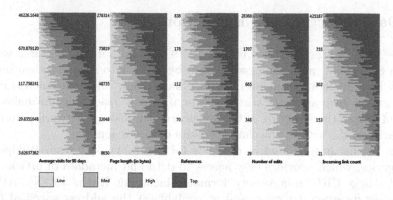

Fig. 4. Distribution of variables in FA articles with different importance in English Wikipedia

3.1 Dataset ENQ

For the answer to the first question raised in the introduction, we decided to make evaluation on articles with certain quality and certain importance of English Wikipedia, because this version:

- is the largest language version
- has the developed system of quality classification of articles
- has the greatest number of articles on intersections of quality and importance (see Fig. 1).

Because the smallest number of articles on intersection of quality and importance is 854 (for class FA and Top-importance) we decided to choose randomly 800 articles of each intersection (without A-class for the reasons described earlier). Altogether, there were 19200 articles in our ENQ dataset.

3.2 Datasets IMP

For the answer to the second and the third question evaluation in articles from different quality with certain importance. From 4 studied language versions the least developed system of importance assessment have Polish Wikipedia. There, the smallest number of Top-important articles was 489. Therefore, we have decided to choose randomly 400 articles from each importance level in each language version to allow the homogeneous distribution of the learning datasets.

4   Evaluation

In many approaches for building models the binary dependent variable was used [7,9,11,22] and the quality was modelled as the probability of belonging to one of the two categories:

- **Complete** articles: FA-class and GA-class
- **Incomplete** articles: all other – developing (which should be further developed) and the unassessed articles.

Our previous research has shown that with such binary forecast variable the precision of 98–100% can be achieved (depending on the language version) [23]. Therefore, we decided to expand the number of alternatives in dependent variable – now each quality class is a separate name of this variable. For example, for our dataset ENQ we have 6 alternatives in dependent variable: FA, GA, B, C, Start, Stub.

Our researches have shown efficiency of Random Forest classifier on similar tasks, therefore in this study we also we use that data mining algorithm with default settings (100 trees, cross-validation with 10 folds) using WEKA software [23].

So, using 85 different articles' parameters as independent variable and quality class as dependent we can reach 60 % precision of classification. After inclusion of additional feature – importance of article – the precision of the model increased to 61 %. Therefore we conclude that inclusion of addition input variable (article importance) can improve the precision of classification.

The confusion matrix for model with quality class and importance level as dependent variables in ENQ dataset are shown in Fig. 5. Tables 1 and 2 show the performance of the classifier. It can be argued that **importance of an article affects its quality**.

Observed	Predicted quality					
quality	FA	⊕ GA	B	C	Start	Stub
FA	2 859	277	52	11	1	0
⊕ GA	575	2 302	207	92	24	0
B	111	417	1 261	853	454	104
C	35	262	856	1251	699	97
Start	8	81	246	609	1 734	522
Stub	1	12	37	97	563	2 490

Observed	Predicted importance			
importance	Top	High	Mid	Low
Top	3 176	900	461	263
High	1 431	1 608	948	813
Mid	618	1 064	1 559	1559
Low	225	507	978	3090

Fig. 5. Confusion matrix - quality (on the left) and importance (on the right). English Wikipedia

Now let's try to answer remaining two research questions. We use our IMP datasets which contains importance level as dependent variable. Using Random Forest as prediction model, we can obtain the most influential features, which affect article importance in each language. In Fig. 6 we show influence of each article parameter in importance model in different language editions of Wikipedia (in scale from 0 to 100, 100 - is the highest influence). As we can see, we have some differences between the models in particular languages. For example for English version the most influential features are: the sum of visits in 30 days, the number of links to article.

Table 1. Classification results per quality class in English Wikipedia using random forest. Source: own study

Quality class	TP Rate	FP Rate	Precision	Recall	F-measure	ROC area
FA	0.893	0.046	0.797	0.893	0.842	0.983
GA	0.719	0.066	0.687	0.719	0.703	0.946
B	0.394	0.087	0.474	0.394	0.43	0.827
C	0.391	0.104	0.429	0.391	0.409	0.827
Start	0.542	0.109	0.499	0.542	0.52	0.859
Stub	0.778	0.045	0.775	0.778	0.777	0.964
Overall	0.62	0.076	0.61	0.62	0.613	0.901

Table 2. Classification results per importance level in English Wikipedia using Random Forest. Source: own study

Importance level	TP Rate	FP Rate	Precision	Recall	F-measure	ROC area
Top	0.662	0.158	0.583	0.662	0.62	0.852
High	0.335	0.172	0.394	0.335	0.362	0.676
Mid	0.325	0.166	0.395	0.325	0.357	0.672
Low	0.644	0.183	0.54	0.644	0.587	0.827
Overall	0.491	0.17	0.478	0.491	0.481	0.757

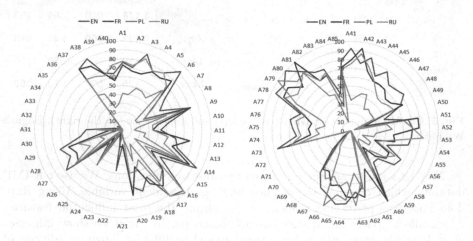

Fig. 6. Influence of article parameters in importance model in different language editions of Wikipedia (description of parameters abbreviations in Table 3). Source: own study.

Table 3. Description of parameters abbreviations used in Fig. 6

Name	Description	Name	Description
A1	Last modified	A44	The number of pictures (all)
A2	Last modified not by the bot	A45	The number of unique pictures 1 lvl
A3	Page length (in bytes)	A46	The number of unique pictures 2 lvl
A4	Informativeness 1	A47	The number of unique pictures 3 lvl
A5	Informativeness 2	A48	The number of unique pictures 4 lvl
A6	Number of edits by anonymous authors for the whole time	A49	The number of unique pictures 5 lvl
A7	Number of edits by anonymous for 12 months	A50	The number of followers
A8	Number of edits by anonymous for 6 months	A51	Number of templates (all)
A9	Number of edits by bots	A52	Number of templates ns10
A10	Number of edits by bots for 12 months	A53	Number of templates ns828
A11	Number of edits by bots for 6 months	A54	The number of unique anonymous for 12 months
A12	Number of edits for 12 months	A55	The number of unique anonymous for 6 months
A13	Number of edits for 6 months	A56	Number of unique authors for 12 months
A14	Number of edits for all time	A57	Number of unique authors for 6 months
A15	Number of edits for all time	A58	Number of unique bots for 12 months
A16	The number of links to the article (all)	A59	Number of unique bots for 6 months
A17	The number of links on the article ns0	A60	Number of unique bots for the all time
A18	The number of links on the article ns1	A61	Unique templates quality gaps
A19	The number of links on the article NS10	A62	Number of unique anonymous authors for the all time
A20	The number of links on the article NS100	A63	The number of language versions
A21	The number of links on the article ns101	A64	Median of non-zero last 30 days
A22	The number of links on the article ns11	A65	The median of visits for 30 days

(*continued*)

Table 3. (*continued*)

Name	Description	Name	Description
A23	The number of links on the article NS12	A66	The median of visits for 90 days
A24	The number of links on the article ns13	A67	Heading 1
A25	The number of links on the article ns14	A68	Heading 2
A26	The number of links on the article NS15	A69	Heading 3
A27	The number of links on the article ns2	A70	Heading 4
A28	The number of links on the article ns3	A71	Heading 5
A29	The number of links on the article ns4	A72	Heading 6
A30	The number of links on the article NS5	A73	Come visit the ost day
A31	The number of links on the article NS6	A74	Ref/Length
A32	The number of links on the article ns7	A75	Ref/number of letters
A33	The number of links on the article ns8	A76	References unique
A34	The number of links on the article ns828	A77	all references
A35	The number of links on the article ns829	A78	Average visits for 30 days
A36	The number of links on the article ns9	A79	Average visits for 90 days
A37	The number of internal links (all)	A80	Total visits for 30 days
A38	The number of good internal links	A81	Total visits for 90 days
A39	The number of broken internal links	A82	Noise1
A40	The number of external links	A83	Noise2
A41	The number of letters	A84	Unique authors for last time
A42	The number of letters without noise 1	A85	Unique authors for all time
A43	The number of letters without noise 2		

5   Conclusions

In this paper we have shown that the importance of the article affects the quality of the information contained in it. In our study we used ca. 80 features of articles and various data mining techniques to come up with a proposal for a quality models. We have also built the importance models for particular language edition of Wikipedia and shown the differences between these models.

The proposed models can help to improve the quality of Wikipedia articles by identifying the best version of a particular article. In consequence, our work can improve the quality of data in DBpedia[10], one of the most famous semantic database, which is enriched by extracting facts from articles of different language versions of Wikipedia. Data mining algorithms allow to determine the significance of the features in models of quality that can later be used to compare articles in different languages. This property is used as the design creation service Wikirank[11], which is used to calculate the so-called relative quality of articles.

References

1. Węcel, K., Lewoniewski, W.: Modelling the quality of attributes in Wikipedia infoboxes. In: Abramowicz, W. (ed.) BIS 2015. LNBIP, vol. 228, pp. 308–320. Springer, Heidelberg (2015)
2. Stvilia, B., Twidale, M.B., Smith, L.C., Gasser, L.: Assessing information quality of a community-based encyclopedia. In: Proceedings of ICIQ, pp. 442–454 (2005)
3. Blumenstock, J.E.: Size matters: word count as a measure of quality on Wikipedia. In: WWW, pp. 1095–1096 (2008)
4. Hu, M., Lim, E.P., Sun, A., Lauw, H.W., Vuong, B.Q.: Measuring article quality in Wikipedia. In: Proceedings of the Sixteenth ACM Conference on Information and Knowledge Management (CIKM 2007), pp. 243–252 (2007)
5. Wöhner, T., Peters, R.: Assessing the quality of Wikipedia articles with lifecycle based metrics. In: Proceedings of the 5th International Symposium on Wikis and Open Collaboration (WikiSym 2009), p. 16 (2009)
6. Dalip, D.H., Gonçalves, M.A., Cristo, M., Calado, P.: Automatic quality assessment of content created collaboratively by web communities: a case study of Wikipedia. In: Proceedings of the 9th ACM/IEEE-CS Joint Conference on Digital Libraries, pp. 295–304 (2009)
7. Lex, E., Voelske, M., Errecalde, M., Ferretti, E., Cagnina, L., Horn, C., Stein, B., Granitzer, M.: Measuring the quality of web content using factual information. In: Proceedings of the 2nd Joint WICOW/AIRWeb Workshop on Web Quality (WebQuality 2012), p. 7 (2012)
8. Lipka, N., Stein, B.: Identifying featured articles in Wikipedia: writing style matters. In: Proceedings of the 19th International Conference on World Wide Web, pp. 1147–1148 (2010)
9. Xu, Y., Luo, T.: Measuring article quality in Wikipedia: lexical clue model. In: IEEE Symposium on Web Society, vol. 19, pp. 141–146 (2011)

---

[10] http://dbpedia.org.
[11] http://wikirank.net.

10. Anderka, M.: Analyzing and predicting quality flaws in user-generated content: the case of Wikipedia. Bauhaus-Universitaet Weimar Germany, Ph.d. (2013)
11. Lewoniewski, W., Węcel, K., Abramowicz, W.: Analiza porównawcza modeli jakości informacji w narodowych wersjach Wikipedii. In: Porębska-Miąc, T., (ed.) Systemy Wspomagania Organizacji (SWO 2015). Wydawnictwo Uniwersytetu Ekonomicznego w Katowicach, pp. 133–154 (2015)
12. Wilkinson, D.M., Huberman, B.A.: Cooperation and quality in Wikipedia. In: Proceedings of the 2007 International Symposium on Wikis (WikiSym 2007), pp. 157–164 (2007)
13. Kittur, A., Kraut, R.E.: Harnessing the wisdom of crowds in Wikipedia. In: Proceedings of the ACM 2008 Conference on Computer Supported Cooperative Work (CSCW 2008), P. 37 (2008)
14. Arazy, O.: Determinants of Wikipedia quality: the roles of global and local contribution inequality. In: Proceedings of the 2010 ACM Conference on Computer Supported Cooperative Work, CSCW 2010. ACM, New York, pp. 233–236 (2010). http://dx.doi.org/10.1145/1718918.1718963
15. Stein, K., Hess, C.: Does it matter who contributes: a study on featured articles in the German Wikipedia. In: Proceedings of the Eighteenth Conference on Hypertext and Hypermedia (HT 2007), pp. 171–174 (2007)
16. Suzuki, Y., Yoshikawa, M.: Mutual evaluation of editors and texts for assessing quality of Wikipedia articles. In: Proceedings of the Eighth Annual International Symposium on Wikis and Open Collaboration (WikiSym 2012), vol. 18: 1–18: 10. ACM, New York (2012)
17. Halfaker, A., Kraut, R., Riedl, J.: A jury of your peers: quality, experience and ownership in Wikipedia. In: WikiSym 2009, pp. 1–10 (2009)
18. Adler, B.T., De Alfaro, L.: A content-driven reputation system for the Wikipedia. In: Proceedings of the 16th International Conference on World Wide Web (WWW 2007), 7(Generic), p. 261 (2007)
19. Lih, A.: Wikipedia as participatory journalism: reliable sources? Metrics for evaluating collaborative media as a news resource. In: 5th International Symposium on Online Journalism, p. 31 (2004)
20. Blumenstock, J.E.: Automatically assessing the quality of Wikipedia articles. Technical report (2008)
21. Dalip, D.H., Gonçalves, M.A., Cristo, M., Calado, P.: Automatic assessment of document quality in web collaborative digital libraries. J. Data Inf. Qual. 2(3), 1–30 (2011)
22. Warncke-wang, M., Cosley, D., Riedl, J.: Tell me more : an actionable quality model for Wikipedia. In: WikiSym 2013, pp. 1–10 (2013)
23. Lewoniewski, W., Węcel, K., Abramowicz, W.: Analiza porównawcza modeli klasyfikacyjnych w kontekście oceny jakości artykułów wikipedii. In: VI Ogólnopolska Konferencja Naukowa. Matematyka i informatyka na usługach ekonomii im. Profesora Zbigniewa Czerwińskiego (2016, in press)

The Logical-Linguistic Model of Fact Extraction from English Texts

Nina Feliksivna Khairova[(✉)], Svetlana Petrasova,
and Ajit Pratap Singh Gautam

National Technical University "Kharkiv Polytechnic Institute", Kharkiv, Ukraine
khairova@kpi.kharkov.ua, svetapetrasova@gmail.com,
apsgautam@gmail.com

Abstract. In this paper we suggest the logical-linguistic model that allows extracting required facts from English sentences. We consider the fact in the form of a triplet: Subject > Predicate > Object with the Predicate representing relations and the Object and Subject pointing out two entities. The logical-linguistic model is based on the use of the grammatical and semantic features of words in English sentences. Basic mathematical characteristic of our model is logical-algebraic equations of the finite predicates algebra. The model was successfully implemented in the system that extracts and identifies some facts from Web-content of a semi-structured and non-structured English text.

Keywords: Logical-linguistic model · Fact extraction · Finite predicates algebra · Triplet · Grammatical features · Syntactic features

1 Introduction

Today the issue of automatic extraction of facts from texts remains open. The common models for facts extraction depend on the degree of a particular text structuring. Similarly to the general classification of the information formalization degree, we can divide text documents into structured (or table data) documents and semi-structured text documents of arbitrary type [1, 2].

Nowadays, there exist quite a lot of the fact extraction methods for processing the structured text data [3–5]. However, there is no technology reliable enough to extract facts from semi-structured and non-structured text documents on the market [6–8].

More than 80 % of information within corporate networks and Internet resources (blogs, forums, mass media etc.) is text information of non-structured and semi-structured nature. Consequently, facts extracted from such information can become an additional powerful source for the different kinds of tasks, for instance, ontology generation from a corpus of a natural language text, development of intelligent question answering systems, business analysis or business intelligence (e.g. predicting expected stock market changes), etc.

Current studies in text mining are mostly based on statistical models using Naïve Bayes method [9–12], Support Vector Machines (SVM) [13], Logistic regression [14] and k-Nearest Neighbors [15, 16]. These methods are used effectively in automated

© Springer International Publishing Switzerland 2016
G. Dregvaite and R. Damasevicius (Eds.): ICIST 2016, CCIS 639, pp. 625–635, 2016.
DOI: 10.1007/978-3-319-46254-7_51

information retrieval systems and automated text classification/categorization systems [8, 13, 17].

On the other hand, the use of statistical methods to extract information and, in particular, to extract facts, is ineffective. There are a few reasons for that: (1) statistical methods treat documents as an unordered "bag of words", which is typical in information retrieval and in text classification problems [18]. Such a simplified representation of text does not exploit natural language processing and loses a lot of knowledge related to the language, i.e. grammar, syntax and semantics. (2) In most cases, when we say about fact extraction, we mean extraction from a sentence rather than from a corpus of texts [19]. This is based on the idea of considering a fact in the form of a triplet: Subject > Predicate > Object with the Predicate representing a verb and the Object and the Subject representing nouns. The noun represents the participant of the action in a sentence [20]. Another cause of the low efficient usage of statistical methods for facts extraction is synonymy and ambiguity of linguistic units. This leads to the frequent appearance of hidden valuable facts in the documents [8] when the Subject, the Object, and the Predicate are represented by different words (sometimes, by different parts of speech). For instance, sentences "The company management sold a part of share", "Management of Apple Inc. sold their share", and "They marketed its" may represent the same fact.

We propose the model which formalizes the semantic meaning of the elements of the triplet by means of defining the syntactic and grammatical characteristics of words in a sentence. The basic idea of this approach is to take into account the morphological and syntactic characteristics of the participants of the sentence to identify facts in the sentence. These characteristics to English are as follows: a particular preposition after a verb, the possessive case of the noun or the pronoun, the location of the noun relative to the verb in the sentence, any form of the verb "to be", the basic form of the verb in the phrase. Whereas, to languages with more complex morphology, for instance, Ukrainian or Russian, such basic characteristics to identify facts in the sentence are morphological cases and syntactic compatibility of collocations.

2   Mathematical Model Description

2.1   Basic Tools of the Finite Predicates Algebra

Basic mathematical means of our model are logical-algebraic equations of the finite predicates algebra [21]. Let U be a universe of elements. The universe U contains various elements of the language system: sentences, phrases, words, grammatical and semantic features, collocations features etc. The universe is finite, as the sets of the elements regarded here are finite and determined. The set $M = \{m_1, ..., m_n\}$ is a subset of grammatical and syntactic features of words in English sentences, and n is a number of system characters. Predicates Pi are defined over Cartesian products $M_1 \times M_2 \times ... \times M_n$. They designate relations between grammatical and semantic features of words by formal tools of the finite predicates algebra [21].

Let us input the system of predicates S. The predicate $P(x) \in S$ equals 1, if the grammatical and semantic features belong to the word that can be the part of a triplet. It means that the word can be the Subject or the Object of the fact in a sentence. The predicate P(x) equals zero otherwise.

Notice, that we use words 'subject' and 'object' in two different ways, i.e. we use 'Subject' and 'Object' with the first upper-case letters to denote the logical sense of the words, and words 'subject' and 'object' with the lower-case letters to denote the grammatical sense of the words.

Variables $x_1, x_2, \ldots, x_n$ are called subject variables and their values are called subjects. The recognition predicate of the subject a by the subject variable xi is the basic one for the algebra of predicates:

$$x_i^a = \begin{cases} 1, \text{if } x_i = a \\ 0, \text{if } x_i \neq a \end{cases} (1 \leq i \leq n), \tag{1}$$

where a is any of the universe elements.

2.2 Main Equations of the Model

We can define the finite set of grammatical and syntactic features of words in English sentences using a few subject variables [22].

The subject variable z defines the syntactic feature of the presence of a preposition in English phrases:

$$P(z) = z^{to} \vee z^{by} \vee z^{with} \vee z^{about} \vee z^{of} \vee z^{on} \vee z^{at} \vee z^{in} \vee z^{out} = 1, \tag{2}$$

where z^{prep} shows the presence of the particular preposition after the predicate of a triplet, $prep = \{to, by, with, about, of, on, at, in\}$ and z^{out} shows the lack of any preposition after the predicate of a triplet.

The subject variable y defines whether there is an apostrophe in the end of the word. In this case, the existence of the apostrophe identifies the possessive case of a subject

$$P(y) = y^{ap} \vee y^{aps} \vee y^{out} = 1, \tag{3}$$

where y^{ap} shows the usage of the apostrophe to identify the possessive case at the end of the word which is a subject; y^{aps} shows the using of the apostrophe with s ('s) to identify of the possessive case at the end of the word which is a subject; y^{out} shows the lack of any apostrophe at the end of the word which is a subject.

The subject variable x defines the position of the noun which names the Object or the Subject of a fact triplet:

$$P(x) = x^f \vee x^l \vee x^{kos} = 1, \tag{4}$$

where x^f shows the position of the noun before finite forms of the verb; x^l shows the position of the noun after a finite verb; x^{kos} shows the position of the noun after the indirect object.

The subject variable m defines whether there is any form of the verb "*to be*" at the phrase:

$$P(m) = m^{is} \vee m^{are} \vee m^{havb} \vee m^{hasb} \vee m^{was} \vee m^{were} \vee m^{out} = 1. \qquad (5)$$

In the equation the superscript of the variable m identifies the form of the verb "*to be*" or the lack of it.

The subject variable p defines the basic forms of the verb in English:

$$P(p) = p^{III} \vee p^{ed} \vee p^{I} \vee p^{ing} \vee p^{II} = 1, \qquad (6)$$

where p^I shows the base form of the verb at the phrase (used as the infinitive form, with or without "*to*"); p^{ed} shows the past form of the verb (used for the past simple tense); p^{III} shows the past participle form (used after auxiliary have and be); p^{II} shows the past form of an irregular verb; p^{ing} shows the $-ing$ form of a verb at the phrase.

We define the semantic roles of a noun via the predicate P, which connects the syntactic feature of the presence of a preposition in the phrase (2), the existence of an apostrophe in the end of the noun (3), the position of the noun in the sentence (4), any form of the verb "*to be*" (5) and the form of the main verb (6):

$$P(x, y, z, m, p) \rightarrow P(x) \wedge P(y) \wedge P(z) \wedge P(m) \wedge P(p)$$

It is obvious that relations between the morphological and syntactic features (subject variables y, m, p, x, z) of the noun do not depend on the particular noun. The predicate P(x, y, z, m, p) equals unity, if the features of sentence words have certain values. In practice the subset of agreed morphological and syntactic features describing facts does not coincide with a Cartesian product over the set of all features.

Let us define the predicate $\gamma(x, y, z, m, p)$ over a Cartesian square S • S:

$$P(x, y, z, m, p) = \gamma_k(x, y, z, m, p) \wedge P(x) \wedge P(y) \wedge P(z) \wedge P(m) \wedge P(p). \qquad (7)$$

The predicate $\gamma_k(x, y, z, m, p)$ equals unity if the concrete morphological and syntactic characteristics of the sentence words express the concrete semantic relations of the concepts in a triple formally and the predicate $\gamma_k(x, y, z, m, p)$ equals zero otherwise. If the conjunction of grammatical categories does not represent any semantic roles and correspondingly any facts, they are excluded from the formula (7) by the predicate $\gamma_k(x, y, z, m, p)$, $k \in [1, h]$, where h is the number of the considered types of facts in the system.

We have considered several different types of facts. The first type of facts is a statement about a Subject which *possesses (acquires, has)* an Object. In English sentences this statement is determined by verbs: *have, purchase, buy, acquire, get, gain, obtain*. We determined the set of the verbs in the database in advance.

Then we can define the semantic relation which denotes the Subject of the fact as the disjunction of conjunctions:

$$\gamma_1(x, y, z, m, p) = z^{out}y^{out}x^f m^{out}p^I \vee z^{out}y^{out}x^f m^{out}p^{II} \vee z^{out}y^{out}x^f m^{out}p^{ed} \vee$$
$$\vee z^{by}y^{out}x^l(p^{ed} \vee p^{III})(m^{is} \vee m^{are} \vee m^{havb} \vee m^{hasb} \vee m^{hadb} \vee m^{was} \vee m^{were}). \tag{8}$$

The Predicate $\gamma_1(x, y, z, m, p)$ defines grammatical and syntactic characteristics of the Subject of the fact. We can also explicitly distinguish the Object via the particular disjunction of conjunctions of the subject variables:

$$\gamma_2(x, y, z, m, p) = z^{out}y^{out}x^l m^{out}p^I \vee z^{out}y^{out}x^l m^{out}p^{II} \vee z^{out}y^{out}x^l m^{out}p^{ed} \vee$$
$$\vee z^{out}y^{out}x^f(p^{ed} \vee p^{III})(m^{is} \vee m^{are} \vee m^{havb} \vee m^{hasb} \vee m^{hudb} \vee m^{was} \vee m^{were}), \tag{9}$$

where the predicate $\gamma_2(x, y, z, m, p)$ defines grammatical and syntactic characteristics of the Object of the fact (Fig. 1).

We distinguish the other group of facts, which are associated with the same verbs. These are the attributes of time, location, mode of action and belonging or possessing.

For instance, we can distinguish the attribute of action time via the predicate

$$\gamma_3(x, y, z, m, p) = z^{on}y^{out}x^{kos} \vee z^{in}y^{out}x^{kos} \vee z^{at}y^{out}x^{kos}(p^{ed} \vee p^{III} \vee p^I \vee$$
$$\vee p^{II} \vee p^{ing})(m^{is} \vee m^{are} \vee m^{havb} \vee m^{hasb} \vee m^{hadb} \vee m^{was} \vee m^{were} \vee m^{out}). \tag{10}$$

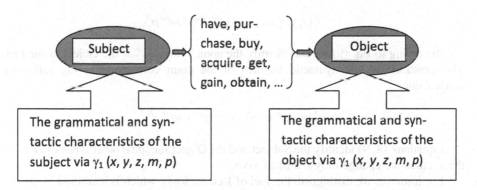

Fig. 1. Identification scheme of the fact of possession. The predicate $\gamma_1(x, y, z, m, p)$ defines grammatical and syntactic characteristics of the Subject of the fact, the predicate $\gamma_2(x, y, z, m, p)$ defines grammatical and syntactic characteristics of the Object of the fact.

The predicate $\gamma_3(x, y, z, m, p)$ shows the disjunction of conjunctions of grammatical and syntactic features of the Object which denotes the time of the fact.

The Object of the attribute of possessing can be distinguished via the predicate

$$\gamma_4(x,y,z,m,p) = z^{out}x^f(y^{ap} \vee y^{aps})(p^{ed} \vee p^{III} \vee p^I \vee p^{II} \vee$$
$$\vee p^{ing})(m^{is} \vee m^{are} \vee m^{havb} \vee m^{hasb} \vee m^{hadb} \vee m^{was} \vee m^{were} \vee m^{out}). \tag{11}$$

The predicate $\gamma_4(x,y,z,m,p)$ shows the relations of grammatical and syntactic features of the Object of the possessing.

Thus, we have introduced the predicates $P(z)$, $P(y)$, $P(x)$, $P(m)$, $P(p)$ identifying the grammatical and syntactic features of words in English sentences via the subject variables and the predicate $P(x, y, z, m, p)$ identifying relations between the morphological and syntactic features. The predicates $\gamma_k(x,y,z,m,p)$, where $k = \overline{1,4}$ eliminate morphological and syntactic characteristics of words irrelevant to the elements of the triplet.

2.3   Examples of-Facts Identification from English Sentences

For instance, let us look at the following sentence:

$$\textit{"The company bought back the business from OTIV"}. \tag{12}$$

We can distinguish the verb "*bought*", which identifies the type of the fact of the acquisition. Then, according to Eq. (8), we can identify the noun "company" as the Subject of the fact. The grammatical and syntactic features of the noun correspond to the following conjunction:

$$\gamma_1'(x,y,z,m,p) = z^{out}y^{out}x^f m^{out}p^{II}.$$

According to Eq. (9) we can identify the noun "*business*" as the Object of the fact. The grammatical and syntactic features of the noun correspond to the following conjunction:

$$\gamma_2'(x,y,z,m,p) = z^{out}y^{out}x^I m^{out}p^{II}.$$

Equations (8, 9) identify the Subject and the Object for some other types of facts. In these cases we change only the main verb.

For instance, we distinguish the fact of lack (or loss), which is identified by the set of the verbs {*sell, market, realize, forfeit, lose*, and some others}; the fact of a displacement, which is identified by the set of such verbs as {*move, relocate, displace, transport, transfer* and some other}.

In the following example, let's analyze the sentence:

$$\textit{"The companies shares were sold by the investor on Tuesday"}. \tag{13}$$

According to Eq. (8) we can identify the noun "*investor*" as the Subject of the fact. The grammatical and syntactic features of the noun correspond to the following conjunction:

$$\gamma_1'' = (x, y, z, m, p) = z^{by}y^{out}x^{J}m^{were}.$$

According to Eq. (9) we can identify the noun "*shares*" as the Object of the fact. The grammatical and syntactic features of the noun correspond to the following conjunction:

$$\gamma_2'' = (x, y, z, m, p) = z^{out}y^{out}x^{f}p^{III}m^{were}.$$

According to Eq. (10) we'll determine the predicate γ_3 as:

$$\gamma_2'' = (x, y, z, m, p) = z^{by}y^{out}x^{f}m^{were}.$$

The predicate provides the time attribute "*Tuesday*" of the fact of the sale at the sentence. If we analyze the sentence (13), according to Eq. (11), we determine the predicate γ_4 as:

$$\gamma_3'' = (x, y, z, m, p) = z^{on}y^{out}x^{kos}m^{were}.$$

The predicate provides the attribute of possessing "*companies*"of the fact of the sale at the sentence (13).

3 Model Implementation

3.1 Web Application

Our model is application that was using PHP, CSS, HTML, Javascript and database MySQL. The application processes a text or several texts. The extracted facts information is displayed in the dialog box. This box we show the Predicate, the Subject, the Object, a temporal attribute, a location attribute, an attribute of possessing and a sentence, from which the fact is extracted (Fig. 2). Furthermore, all normal forms of the terms are displayed.

If the user confirms a fact, it is input in the facts data base. The database schema is organized in the following way: the fields of the tables represent the Subjects and the Objects of the triplet and the name of the table denotes the name of the Predicate. The sentence is input in the DB as metadata, too.

3.2 Performance Evaluation of the Model

We use precision, recall and F_1-score measures in order to evaluate the performance of our logical-linguistic model of fact extraction from English texts. To calculate the coefficients of the program's recall and precision, it's necessary to determine the following parameters:

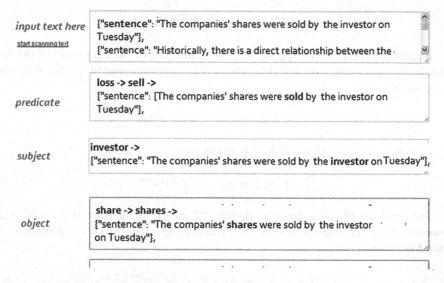

Fig. 2. Result of the facts extraction program. The program extracts a fact from the sentence and displays a predicate, the type of the Predicate, the Subject, the Object, a temporal attribute, a location attribute, an attribute of possessing, normal forms of the terms and the particular sentence.

- n_{yy} is a number of elements identified by the program as facts, which are real correct facts according to an expert;
- n_{yn} is a number of elements identified by the program as facts, which are incorrect facts according to an expert;
- n_{ny} is a number of real facts unidentified by the program.

In this notation, we consider that a fact is identified correctly by the program only if the Predicate, the Subject, and the Object of this fact are identified correctly. If the triplet of the fact is not identified completely (e.g., the Subject and the Predicate are identified correctly and the Object is identified incorrectly) we say that the program doesn't identify the fact. Using parameters listed above, the program's precision and recall are determined by the following formulas:

$$precision = n_{yy}/(n_{yy} + n_{yn}),$$ (14)

$$recall = n_{yy}/(n_{yy} + n_{ny}).$$ (15)

We performed an experiment over 1000 English sentences and around 400 phrases per each of the fact type: (1) the fact of lacking of something by someone, (2) the fact of ownership of something by someone, (3) the fact of transferring of something by someone; and three facts of the presence of the attribute of (4) time, i.e. when the fact of action (1–3) happened; of (5) location, i.e. where the fact of action (1–3) happened; and (6) belonging, i.e. whether the entity or the Object of the fact of actions (1–3) belongs to something or someone. All sentences were specially selected from

Table 1. Experiment results of facts extraction from English sentences.

	Fact of lacking	Fact of owner-ship	Fact of transfer	Fact of attri-bute of time	Fact of attri-bute of location	Fact of attribute of belonging
Recall	0.92	0.91	0.91	0.97	0.96	0.95
Precision	0.81	0.79	0.76	0.90	0.90	0.89
F_1- score	0.86	0.85	0.83	0.93	0.93	0.92

specialized economic web sources, such rating and analytical information agencies as Fitch, Moody's, Standard&Poor's, A.M. Best, Bloomberg, Reuters. The results of the experiment are shown in Table 1.

Overall the average precision of the program is 0.84, the average recall is 0.93 and the average F_1-score = 0.89. Therefore, based on the received results we can conclude that the facts extracted by the program and representing information in compressed form can be successfully used by experts.

4 Conclusions

The main result of this study is the logical-linguistic model of facts extraction from English texts. The model allows extracting several types of facts from different English sentences. The model is built base on distinguishing between types of facts in each sentence (the fact of lacking, the fact of ownership, the fact of transferring, and the fact of the presence of the attribute of time, location, and belonging for the first three fact actions).

Implementation of the model allows experts to automatically extract these facts from different types of texts. The experiments study showed that the use of the model increased the effectiveness of facts extraction from non-structured texts. However, in order to further increases of the effectiveness of the model, we should pay more attention to entities extraction. The problems corresponding to this extraction are co-reference resolution problem, and existence of synonyms and wordy terms problem. Moreover, our future work includes building the logical-linguistic model for the other types of facts, which we could extract from English phrases.

Although, the created application is only the experimental prototype of the web application, in the future, this model will be a part of the subsystem that will be used for information extraction from non-structured English texts.

References

1. Fader, S., Soderland, O.: Etzioni Identifying relations for open information extraction. In: Conference on Empirical Methods in Natural Language Processing. Edinburgh, Scotland, pp. 1535–1545 (2011)

2. Sint, R., Schaffert, S., Stroka, S., Ferstl, R.: Combining unstructured, fully structured and semi-structured information in semantic wikis. In: Proceedings of the 4th Semantic Wiki WorkShop (SemWiki) at the 6th European Semantic Web Conference, ESWC (2009)
3. Crestan, E., Pantel, P.: Web-scale knowledge extraction from semi-structured tables. In: WWW 2010 Proceedings of the 19th International Conference on World Wide Web, pp. 1081–1082 (2010)
4. Gatterbauer, W., Bohunsky, P., Herzog, M., Krupl, B., Pollak, B.: Towards domain-independent information extraction from web tables. In: Proceedings WWW-07, pp. 71–80. Banff, Canada (2007)
5. Wong, Y.W., Widdows, D., Lokovic, T., Nigam, K.: Scalable attribute-value extraction from semi-structured text. In: 2009 IEEE International Conference on Data Mining Workshops, pp. 302–307 (2009)
6. Phillips, W., Riloff, E.: Exploiting strong syntactic heuristics and co-training to learn semantic lexicons. In: Proceedings of the Conference on Empirical Methods in Natural Language Processing (EMNLP) (2002)
7. Jones, R., Ghani, R., Mitchell, T., Riloff, E.: Active learning with multiple view feature sets. In: ECML 2003 Workshop on Adaptive Text Extraction and Mining (2003)
8. Agichtein, E., Gravano, L.: Snowball: extracting relations from large plaintext collections. In: Proceedings of the 5th ACM International Conference on Digital Libraries, pp. 85–94. San Antonio, Texas (2000)
9. Ludovic, L., Gallinari, P.: Bayesian network model for semi-structured document classification. Inf. Proc. Manage. Int. J. Spec. Issue Bayesian Netw. Inf. Retrieval 40, 807–827 (2004)
10. Rish, I.: An empirical study of the naive bayes classifier. In: Proceedings of IJCAI-01 Workshop on Empirical Methods in Artificial Intelligence (2001)
11. Jatana, N., Sharma, K.: Bayesian spam classification: time efficient radix encoded fragmented database approach. In: 2014 International Conference on Computing for Sustainable Global Development (INDIACom), pp. 939–942 (2014)
12. Aiwu, L., Hongying, L.: Utilizing improved bayesian algorithm to identify blog comment spam. In: IEEE Symposium on Robotics and Applications(ISRA), pp. 423–426 (2012)
13. Joachims, T.: Text categorization with support vector machines: learning with many relevant features. In: ECML 1998 Proceedings of the 10th European Conference on Machine Learning, pp. 137–142. Springer-Verlag London, UK (1998)
14. Kleinbaum, D.G., Klein, M., Pryor, E.R.: Logistic Regression: A Self-Learning Text. Springer, New York (2002)
15. Baoli, L., Shiwen, Y., Qin, L.: An improved k-nearest neighbor algorithm for text categorization. In: The 20th International Conference on Computer Processing of Oriental Languages, Shenyang, China (2003)
16. Manne, S., Kotha, S. K., Fatima, S.: Text Categorization with k-nearest neighbor approach . In: Proceedings of the International Conference on Information Systems Design and Intelligent Applications, vol.132, pp. 413–420 (2012)
17. Entezari-Maleki, R., Rezaei, A., Minaei-Bidgoli, B.: Comparison of classification methods based on the type of attributes and sample size. J. Convergence Inf. Technol. (JCIT) 4(3), 94–102 (2009)
18. Mooney, R.J., Bunescu, R.: Mining knowledge from text using information extraction. Newsl. ACM SIGKDD Explor. Newsl. Nat. Lang. Process. Text Min. 7(1), 3–10 (2005)
19. Yahya, M., Whang, E.S., Gupta R., Halevy A.: ReNoun: fact extraction for nominal attributes. In: Proceedings of the Conference on Empirical Methods in Natural Language (EMNLP), pp. 325–335 (2014)

20. Luckicgev, S.: Graphical notations for rule modeling. In: Giurca, A., Gašević, D., Taveter, K. (eds.) Handbook of Research on Emerging Rule-Based Languages and Technologies: Open Solutions and Approaches, Hershey, New York., vol. 1, pp. 76–98 (2009)
21. Bondarenko, M.: Shabanov-Kushnarenko, J. 2007. The intelligence theory. Kharkiv: "SMIT", 576. (In Russian)
22. Khairova, N., Sharonova, N., Gautam, A.P.: Logic-linguistic model of fact generation from text streams of corporate information system. Int. J. Inf. Theor. Appl. **22**(2), 142–152 (2015)

Information Technology Applications: Special Session on Internet-of-Things in Mobility Applications

Analysing of the Voice Communication Channels for Ground Segment of Air Traffic Management System Based on Embedded Cloud Technology

Igor Kabashkin$^{(\boxtimes)}$

Transport and Telecommunication Institute, Riga, Latvia
kiv@tsi.lv

Abstract. Air Traffic Management (ATM) systems represent essential infrastructure that is critical for flight safety. Communication is a key element in the present ATM system. Communication between air traffic controllers and pilots remains a vital part of air traffic control operations, and communication problems can result in hazardous situations. ATM modernization requests for a paradigm shift away from voice towards digital data communications. In the paper the reliability of ATM voice communication system (VCS) on the base of embedded cloud technology is discussed. Mathematical model of the channel reliability in the ATM communication network based on embedded cloud technology in the real conditions of operation is developed. On the base of developed model the boundary value of reliability parameters for automatics of VCS embedded cloud in different failure modes is analyzed.

Keywords: Reliability · Redundancy · Air Traffic Management · Controller · Communication network · Embedded cloud

1 Introduction

Air Traffic Management (ATM) systems represent essential infrastructure that is critical for flight safety. Communication is a key element in the present ATM system. Communication between air traffic controllers and pilots remains a vital part of air traffic control operations, and communication problems can result in hazardous situations. Analysis of aviation accidents has identified that a breakdown in effective human communication has been a causal or contributing factor in the majority of accidents [1].

There are different types of air traffic controllers:

- Tower controllers direct the movement of vehicles on runways and taxiways. Most work from control towers, watching the traffic they control.
- Approach and departure controllers ensure that aircraft traveling within an airport's airspace maintain minimum separation for safety.
- En route controllers monitor aircraft once they leave an airport's airspace.

The modern ATM system has independent direct communication channels (CC) for each controllers operating at different radio frequencies $f_i, i = \overline{1, m}$, where m is number

© Springer International Publishing Switzerland 2016
G. Dregvaite and R. Damasevicius (Eds.): ICIST 2016, CCIS 639, pp. 639–649, 2016.
DOI: 10.1007/978-3-319-46254-7_52

of CC. The amount of the CC is determined by the structure of ATM in the area of a specific airport and provides independent interaction with the aircrafts for all controllers. Technical support of controller-pilot communication carried out by means of radio stations (RS). Interoperability of technical means and controllers in ATM communication network is provided by voice communications system (VCS) which is a state-of-art solution for air traffic control communication. The modern approach to system design focuses on providing high-availability solutions that are based on reliable equipment and on redundancy strategies tailored to customers' needs and requirements.

Currently, the main method of improving the reliability of controller's CC is to duplicate equipment to provide communications on each frequency of interaction ground-to-air channel (Fig. 1). Each of the m controllers communicates with aircraft using the main radio station (MRS) as basic hardware. After the failure of MRS, he switches into a work with the backup (redundant radio station - RRS).

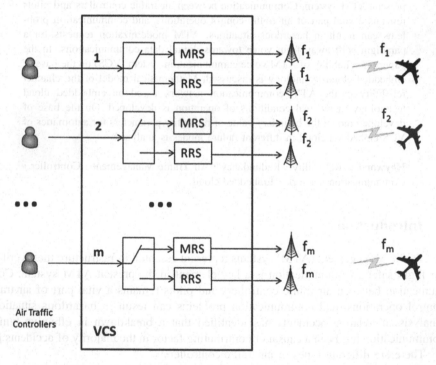

Fig. 1. Redundant communication network of ATM system

Unfortunately the efficiency of used in ATM system fault-tolerance approach is not high. In the paper another method for redundant communication network of ATM system is discussed.

The rest of this paper is organized as follows. In Sect. 2 some important works in the area of reliability with redundancy are reviewed. In Sect. 3 the main definitions and assumptions are presented and a model of ATM communication network reliability on the base of VCS embedded cloud technology is proposed. In Sect. 4 the conclusions are presented.

2 Related Works

The increasing number of flights is a big challenge and it is expected that the current ATM system reaches its capacity limits within the next years in Europe and the US, the world's regions with the highest aircraft densities. Therefore, two major projects have been initiated with the final goal to modernize ATM: SESAR (Single European Sky ATM Research) in Europe [2] and NextGen (Next Generation National Airspace System) in the US. Both projects are globally harmonized under the framework of the International Civil Aviation Organization (ICAO) [3].

For ATM modernization new operational procedures have to be devised. ATM modernization requests for a paradigm shift away from voice towards digital data communications. Increased and more complex information exchange between controllers and pilots demands the use of modern communications technologies. Voice is not capable to efficiently convey the information required for future operational procedures. The need for communication at a domestic and international level for the air traffic management has become perceptible with the potential withdrawal of point-to-point connections from telecommunication providers and the prerequisite for an IP-based network for new and emerging applications.

In this context, the future radio system infrastructure (Fig. 2) will consist of a mix of access technologies, each with its own communication elements at the aircraft side (airborne embedded cloud) and its own ground infrastructure (ground embedded clouds) integrated in common frame of internet of things (IoT).

The embedded cloud is about connecting the edge devices to the IT infrastructure and developing a new genre of applications that can make macro-level decisions about the real-world environment and offer value added services [4].

Voice ATM communications include all voice applications used for the purposes of Air Traffic Management (air-ground communications, co-ordination and transfer, emergency, Search and Rescue, flow management, capacity planning). ATM voice communications covers intra- and inter- centre communications and also ensures the connectivity between the centres and the ground based radio stations on the ground leg of the Air-Ground communications between controllers and pilots (Fig. 2).

The reliability of traditional VCS with duplicated channels is well studied in the literature [5, 6].

One of the methods to increase efficiency of redundancy in the structures with identical elements is the allocation of the common group of reserve elements. The *k-out-of-n* system structure is a very popular type of redundancy in fault tolerant systems. The term *k-out-of-n* system is used to indicate an *n*-component system that works (or is "good") if and only if at least *k* of the *n* components work (or are good). This system is called a *k-out-of-n:G* system. The works [7–9] provide improved versions of the method for reliability evaluation of the *k-out-of-n:G* system. The work

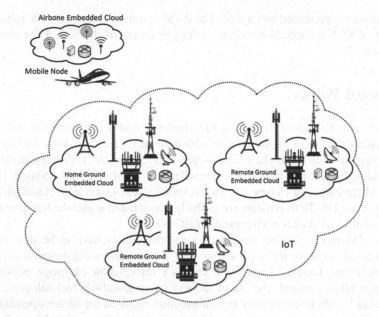

Fig. 2. Modern ATM communication technologies

[10] provides an analysis of the *k-out-of-n:G* system with components whose lifetime distributions are not necessarily exponential.

An *n*-component system that fails if and only if at least *k* of the *n* components fail is called a *k-out-of-n:F* system [11]. The term *k-out-of-n* system is often used to indicate either a G system or an F system or both. The *k-out-of-n* system structure is a very popular type of redundancy in fault-tolerant systems. It finds wide applications in telecommunication systems [5, 12]. This model can be used for analyse of reliability of ATM communication network with *k* controllers and *n* RS provided availability of CC.

In real conditions it is important to know not the reliability of communication network at whole but each selected CC for controller. The channel reliability problem in standby system consisting of independent elements with some units used as a universal component standby pool is investigated in [13].

In this paper we investigate the reliability of selected communication channel with common set of standby radio stations. The ATM voice communication system on the base of embedded cloud technology includes set of human-machine voice interface (VoI), set of main (MRS) and redundant (RRS) radio stations, and set of health and usage monitoring systems (HUMS) for utilize data collection and analysis techniques to help ensure availability of all VCS components (Fig. 3). In such system each of the redundant units can replace any of the failed main units with the appropriate switching of VoI and the tuning of redundant radio station to the frequency of the failed channel.

In such system each of the redundant units can replace any of the failed main units with the appropriate switching of VoI and the tuning of redundant radio station to the frequency of the failed channel. For this technology the reliability of the switching functions in the case of MRS failure in communication channels is becoming a critical factor.

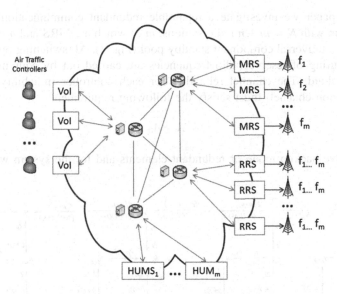

Fig. 3. VCS ground embedded cloud

Let us discuss the dependability of the voice communication channels for above mentioned system in the real conditions of operation with two possible failure modes ("false switching" and "no switching") for automatics of communication network and different number of repair bodies and compare it with traditional one with duplicate radio stations in each channel.

3 Model Formulation and Solution

The following symbols have been used to develop equations for the models:

λ - Failure Rate for MRS and RRS

μ - Repair Rate for MRS and RRS

λ_1 - Failure Rate for automatics of VCS embedded cloud in failure mode "false switching"

λ_2 - Failure Rate for automatics of VCS embedded cloud in failure mode "no switching"

μ_1 - Repair Rate for automatics of VCS embedded cloud in failure mode "false switching"

μ_2 - Repair Rate for automatics of VCS embedded cloud in failure mode "no switching"

m - Number of communication channels and number of MRS

n - Number of RRS in common set of redundant radio stations

l - Number of repair bodies

A - Channel Availability

A_0 - Required Availability of the CC

A_d - Availability of the system with duplicate RS

In this paper we investigate a repairable redundant communication network of ATM system with $N = m + n$ radio stations, m of which are MRS and n radio stations are used as a universal component standby pool (Fig. 3). All switching operations and the restructuring of reserve radio frequencies are carried out by equipment of VCS embedded cloud. The channel reliability for each controller (reliability of selected communication channel) must satisfy the following requirements

$$A \geq A_0 \tag{1}$$

For active backup mode of redundant elements and for the system with $1 \leq l \leq n$

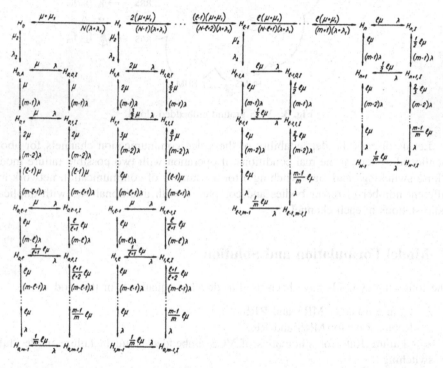

Fig. 4. Markov chain state transition diagram (for $1 \leq l \leq n$)

number of repair bodies the behaviour of the examined system is described by the Markov Chain state transition diagram (Fig. 4), where: H_i – state with i failed RS, but in the selected channel there is a workable RS; H_{iI} – state with $i + 1$ failed RS, in the selected channel there is no a workable RS; $H_{i,A}$ - state with i failed RS, in the selected channel there is a workable RS, there is failure mode "no switching" of automatics of VCS embedded cloud; H_{ij} - state with $i + j$ failed RS, where j is number of failed MRS, i is number of failed RRS, but in the selected channel there is a workable RS; H_{ijI} - state with $i + j + 1$ failed RS, where $j + 1$ is number of failed MRS, i is number of failed RRS, but in the selected channel there is no a workable RS.

On the base of this diagram the system of Chapman–Kolmogorov's equations can be writing in accordance with the general rules [14]. By solving the resulting system of equations, we can obtain an expression for availability of selected communication channel:

$$A = 1 - \sum_{\forall i,j} P_{ijl} = \frac{a_1 + a_2}{a_1 + a_2 + a_3} \tag{2}$$

where

$$a_1 = \sum_{i=0}^{l} \binom{i}{N}\gamma_0 + \frac{N!\gamma_0^n}{m!n!} + \frac{N!l^l}{l!}\sum_{i=l+1}^{n-1} \frac{\omega_0^i}{(N-i)!^{l'}}$$

$$a_2 = \frac{N!l^l\gamma_2}{m!}\left\{\sum_{i=0}^{l}\frac{1}{(N-1)!}\left[\frac{l!\gamma^i}{l^i i!} + \frac{l!\gamma_0^i}{l^l}\sum_{j=1}^{l-i}\binom{j}{m-1}j!\omega! + \omega_0^i\sum_{j=l-i+1}^{m-1}\binom{j}{m-1}j!\omega!\right]\right.$$

$$\left. + \sum_{i=l+1}^{n-1}\frac{\omega_0^i}{(N-i)!}\left[1 + \sum_{j=1}^{m-1}\binom{j}{m-1}j!\omega^j\right] + \frac{\omega_0^n}{\gamma_2 m}\sum_{j=1}^{m-1}\frac{\omega^j}{(m-j-1)!}\right\},$$

$$a_3 = \frac{N!l^l\gamma_2}{l!}\left\{\sum_{i=0}^{l}\frac{1}{(N-i)!}\left[\gamma_0^i\frac{l!}{l^i}\sum_{j=0}^{l-i-1}\binom{j}{m-1}\frac{(j+1)!}{(i+j+1)!}\gamma^{j+1} + \omega_0^i\sum_{j=l-i}^{m-1}\binom{j}{m-1}(j+1)!\omega^{j+1}\right]\right.$$

$$\left. + \sum_{i=l+1}^{n-1}\frac{\omega_0^i}{(N-i)!}\sum_{j=0}^{m-1}\binom{j}{m-1}(j+1)!\omega^{j+1} + \frac{\omega_0^n}{\gamma_2 m}\sum_{j=0}^{m-1}\frac{j+1}{(m-j-1)!}\omega^{j+1}\right\},$$

$$\gamma = \frac{\lambda}{\mu},\omega = \frac{\gamma}{l},\gamma_0 = \frac{\lambda_1+\lambda_2}{\mu+\mu_1},\gamma_2 = \frac{\lambda_2}{\mu_2},\omega_0 = \frac{\gamma_0}{l}.$$

For active backup mode of redundant elements and for the system with $n \leq l \leq N$ number of repair bodies the Markov Chain state transition diagram of the system is shown at the Fig. 5. On the base of this diagram the system of Chapman–Kolmogorov's equations can be writing in accordance with the general rules [14]. By solving the resulting system of equations, we can obtain an expression for availability of selected communication channel in accordance of (2), where

$$a_1 = \frac{N!\gamma_0^n}{m!n!} + \sum_{i=0}^{n-1}\binom{i}{N}\gamma_0^i$$

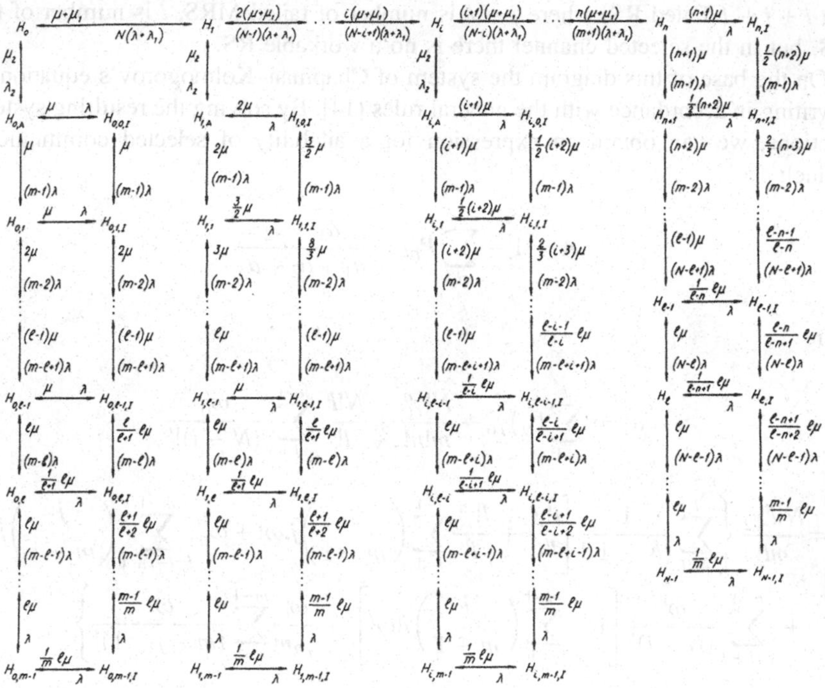

Fig. 5. Markov chain state transition diagram (for $n \leq l \leq N$)

$$a_2 = \sum_{i=0}^{n-1}\binom{i}{N}\left\{\gamma_0^i + i!\gamma_2\left[\gamma_0^i\sum_{j=1}^{l-i}\binom{j}{m-1}\frac{j!}{(i+j)!}\gamma^j + \frac{l^l\omega_0^i}{l!}\sum_{j=l-i+1}^{m-1}\binom{j}{m-1}j!\omega^j\right]\right\}$$
$$+ \frac{\gamma_0^n}{m}\sum_{j=1}^{l-n}(m-j)\binom{m-j}{N}\gamma^j + \frac{N!l^l\omega_0^n}{l!}\sum_{j=1}^{N-l-1}\frac{\omega^{l+j-n}}{(N-l-j-1)!}$$

$$a_3 = \gamma_2\sum_{i=0}^{n-1}\binom{i}{N}i!\left[\gamma_0^i\sum_{j=0}^{l-i-1}\binom{j}{m-1}\frac{(1+j)!}{(i+j+1)!}\gamma^{j+1} + \frac{N!l^l\omega_0^n}{l!}\sum_{j=1}^{N-l-1}\frac{l-n+j+1}{(N-l-j-1)!}\omega^{l+j+1-n}\right]$$

Numerical Example. Let's compare the availability of selected channel in redundant communication network of ATM with two alternatives of VCS architecture. The paradigm shift away from voice (Fig. 1) towards digital data communications (Fig. 2) from reliability point of view will be reasonable if Eq. (1) is valid:

$$A \geq A_0 = A_d \tag{3}$$

where the value of A is determined in accordance with the expression (2), equation for the A_d availability of the system with duplicate RS in each channel was determined in [2].

We can define the boundary value of reliability parameters for automatics of VCS embedded cloud in different failure modes. Let us introduce the following notations and assumptions:

$$\lambda_1 = \alpha\lambda, \ \lambda_2 = \beta\lambda, \ \mu_1 = \mu_2 = \mu.$$

The value of A is determined in accordance with the expression (2), equation for the A_d availability of the system with duplicate RS in each channel was determined in [5]. At the Fig. 6 the boundary value of reliability parameters for automatics of VCS embedded cloud in different failure modes ($\beta = \lambda_2/\lambda$, $\alpha = \lambda_1/\lambda$) shown as function of number m of communication channels with different number n of standby radio stations for $1/\lambda = 10000$ h, $1/\mu = 10$ h and $l = 1$ number of repair bodies.

Condition (3) will be correct if $\beta_r \leq \beta$, where β_r,- real reliability parameter for automatics of VCS embedded cloud in failure mode "no switching", β - boundary value of the same reliability parameter shown at the Fig. 6. Analysis of the curves at Fig. 6 shows that for communication network with proposed model of redundancy the

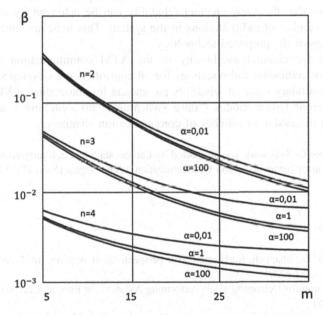

Fig. 6. Markov chain state transition diagram (for $n \leq l \leq N$)

same channel reliability can be achieved by using only two redundant stations. The requirements for reliability parameter for automatics of VCS embedded cloud will be stronger with increasing of number of communication channels.

4 Conclusions

In paper the reliability of ground communication domain of future multichannel communication ATM system integrated in common frame of internet of things is analyzed.

For ground infrastructure the effective dynamic procedure of monitoring and control of common set of redundancy radio stations within the technology of ground embedded clouds is proposed.

The dependability of the voice communication channels for above mentioned system in the real conditions of operation with two possible failure modes ("false switching" and "no switching") for automatics of communication network and different number of repair bodies is discussed.

Mathematical model of the channel reliability of the communication network of Air Traffic Management based on embedded cloud for voice communication system in the real conditions of operation is developed.

Comparative analysis of reliability for proposed system with common set of redundant radio stations and traditional one with duplicate radio stations in each channel shows that the same channel reliability can be achieved by using of much smaller total number of radio stations in the system. This indicates much more hardware efficiency of the proposed technology.

Equations for channel availability of the ATM communication network with common set of redundant radio stations for all controllers are developed. It is shown that there is boundary value of reliability parameters for automatics of VCS embedded cloud in different failure modes ("false switching", "no switching"), and it will be stronger with increasing of number of communication channels.

Acknowledgment. This work was supported by Latvian state research programme project "The Next Generation of Information and Communication Technologies (Next IT)" (2014-2017).

References

1. Wiegmann, D., Shappell, S.: Human error perspectives in aviation. Int. J. Aviation Psychol. 11(4), 341–357 (2001)
2. The Roadmap for Delivering High Performing Aviation for Europe. European ATM Master Plan (2015)
3. ICAO. Aeronautical Telecommunication Network (ATN). Manual for the ATN using IPS Standards and Protocols (Doc 9896). Edition 2.0 (2011)
4. Laukkarinen, T., Suhonen, J., Hännikäinen, M.: An embedded cloud design for internet-of-things. Int. J. Distrib. Sensor Netw. 2013, 13 (2013). Hindawi Publishing Corporation, Article ID 790130
5. Ayers, M.: Telecommunications System Reliability Engineering, Theory, and Practice. Wiley-IEEE Press, Hoboken (2012)
6. Modarres, M., Kaminskiy, M., Krivtsov, V.: Reliability Engineering and Risk Analysis: A Practical Guide (Quality and Reliability), 2nd edn. CRC Press, Boca Raton (2009)

7. Barlow, R., Heidtmann, K.: On the reliability computation of a k-out-of-n system. Microelectron. Reliab. **33**(2), 267–269 (1993). Elsevier
8. Misra, K.: Handbook of Performability Engineering. Springer, London (2008)
9. McGrady, P.: The availability of a k-out-of-n:G network. IEEE Trans. Reliab. **R-34**(5), 451–452 (1985)
10. Liu, H.: Reliability of a load-sharing k-out-of-n: G system: non-iid components with arbitrary distributions. IEEE Trans. Reliab. **47**(3), 279–284 (1998)
11. Rushdi, A.: A switching-algebraic analysis of consecutive-k-out-of-n: F systems. Microelectron. Reliab. **27**(1), 171–174 (1987). Elsevier
12. Chatwattanasiri, N., Coit, D., Wattanapongsakorn, N., Sooktip, T.: Dynamic k-out-of-n system reliability for redundant local area networks. In: 2012 9th International Conference on Electrical Engineering/Electronics, Computer, Telecommunications and Information Technology (ECTI-CON), 16-18 May 2012, pp. 1–4 (2012)
13. Kozlov, B., Ushakov, I.: Reliability Handbook (International Series in Decision Processes). Holt, Rinehart & Winston of Canada Ltd., New York (1970)
14. Rubino, G., Sericola, B.: Markov Chains and Dependability Theory. Cambridge University Press, Cambridge (2014)

Towards a Model-Based Architecture for Road Traffic Management Systems

Florian Rademacher[✉], Mirco Lammert, Marius Khan, and Sabine Sachweh

Department of Computer Science,
University of Applied Sciences and Arts Dortmund, Dortmund, Germany
{florian.rademacher,mirco.lammert,
marius.khan,sabine.sachweh}@fh-dortmund.de

Abstract. The transport domain is expected to substantially profit from the upcoming Internet of Things. Road Traffic Management Systems (RTMSs) constitute Cyber-physical Systems (CPSs) that collect and provide data of traffic events, e.g. for controlling and monitoring purposes. However, CPSs pose challenges like modifiability, heterogeneity and flexibility that are crucial for RTMSs.

In this paper we propose an approach based on the Model-driven Engineering paradigm to address these challenges when implementing and operating RTMSs. Thereby, we specify metamodels for RTMS software components and identify composition relationships between these as well as constructs for runtime modeling. A Domain-specific Language (DSL) based on one of the metamodels might thus reuse elements expressed in a DSL based on another metamodel, while the resulting system of DSLs allows to model various RTMS aspects at both design time and runtime.

Keywords: Road traffic management systems · Metamodel composition · Domain-specific Languages · Language components · Cyber-physical Systems

1 Introduction

In the past decade the vision of a pervasive digitization of the physical world, i.e. the aspiration towards an *Internet of Things* (IoT), stimulated both technology- and application-related computer science research [25]. The technological building blocks of the IoT comprise means for sensing, communication and services, which enable the integration of physical objects into software architectures underlying applications from a variety of domains [1]. Especially the *Transport* domain [10] and its *Intelligent Transportation Systems* (ITSs) [23] are expected to benefit from leveraging IoT key concepts, e.g. the possibility to interrelate isolated roadside sensors for car and cargo recognition.

An ITS constitutes a *Cyber-physical System* (CPS) [13] in that it connects software components and physical processes both influencing each other via feedback loops. However, due to their inherent complexity, the design of CPSs poses

© Springer International Publishing Switzerland 2016
G. Dregvaite and R. Damasevicius (Eds.): ICIST 2016, CCIS 639, pp. 650–662, 2016.
DOI: 10.1007/978-3-319-46254-7_53

several challenges [14]. First, a CPS needs to exhibit a certain degree of *modifiability* to cope with changes. For instance, the vehicle-detection algorithms [24] of an ITS might evolve over time. Second, hardware and software *heterogeneity* is typical for CPSs. In the ITS context, the hardware usually comprises roadside sensors, e.g. inductive loops [20] or end users' mobile phones [15], but also actuators like variable message signs [20]. Additionally, an ITS might receive and provide information leveraging a variety of different software interface technologies and protocols, e.g. REST [15] and DATEX II [6]. Third, *flexibility* in the sense of adaptable functionality and software interfaces, e.g. for the integration of legacy systems, is an important requirement in the ITS domain [22].

In this paper we propose the application of means provided by the *Model-driven Engineering* (MDE) paradigm [21] to design and operate software platforms for *Road Traffic Management Systems* (RTMSs) [20]. An RTMS collects and provides data of traffic events for controlling, monitoring and visualization purposes. It might thus serve as foundation for a more sophisticated ITS. We investigate the capabilities of MDE techniques in ensuring certain degrees of modifiability, heterogeneity and flexibility for the development and operation of RTMS software platforms. To this end, we propose *metamodels* [21] for the description of certain platform components. The metamodels constitute starting points for the subsequent implementation of *Domain-specific Languages* (DSLs) and potential code generators [16]. We furthermore identify those elements of the metamodels available for modeling at runtime and define composition links between metamodels to allow the reuse of certain modeled artifacts.

The paper is organized as follows. Section 2 presents related work. Section 3 describes the RTMS for which metamodels are specified and composed in Sect. 4. Section 5 discusses our approach. Section 6 concludes and presents future work.

2   Related Work

The *Globalization of Modeling Languages* denotes the coordinated use of heterogeneous modeling languages to express different aspects of a system in the way most appropriate for the respective domain [3]. The metamodels specified in Sect. 4 define *abstract syntaxes* tailored to the expression of domain-specific models [21]. Thereby, the composition links between the metamodels ensure language interoperability and reuse both at design time and runtime, while preserving isolated language development to a certain degree [3].

In [17] Mosser et al. discuss the need for composing various modeling languages using the example of an IoT application that allows the creation of monitoring dashboards for sensor data. The authors present the application's architectural components and the assignment of appropriate modeling languages. Additionally, four types of language relationships are identified. However, these are rather coarse-grained as they are not established on the element level of the related metamodels. Furthermore, runtime aspects are not explicitly considered.

CloudML [7] is a modeling language for provisioning, deployment, monitoring and adaptation of multi-cloud systems. It aims to increase the degree of interoperability between heterogeneous techniques and comprises means for design time as well as runtime modeling. At design time, "static" aspects related to provisioning and deployment of cloud systems and artifacts are expressed. Model adaptation is based on model validation and interpretation at runtime. Our approach towards modeling design time and runtime aspects differs in that it promotes the description of static artifacts and adaptation at runtime leveraging possibly different parts of the same metamodels. Furthermore, we rely on code generation at runtime for a better execution performance.

In [12] the composition of a state machine and activity modeling language for expressing barrier detection and barrier motor behavior of a *Railroad Crossing Management System* (RCMS) is shown. Both barrier systems are modeled independently at RCMS design time. The composition is then performed beforehand the system's simulation in terms of coordination constraints between state transition events and activity occurrences. Although this shows the applicability of model composition for CPSs the coordination constraints have to be specified manually between models as they are not formalized in a common metamodel of both modeling languages, which prevents their automatic generation.

3   Architecture of the Road Traffic Management System Under Study

This section introduces the RTMS for whose software components metamodels will be specified in Sect. 4 to achieve modifiability and flexibility at both design time and runtime with regard to the system's inherent heterogeneity. It is created as part of a research project aiming at developing a high-performance roadside sensor technology in combination with cloud-based data processing. Figure 1 shows the system's architecture in the form of a UML deployment diagram. The following paragraphs explain the different device groups and software artifacts.

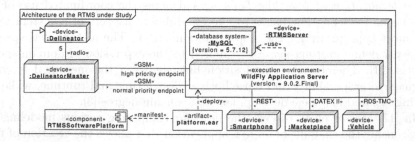

Fig. 1. Deployment diagram of the overall architecture of the RTMS under study

Delineators. The roadside sensor system is based on the *Passive Vehicle Detection* technology proposed in [11]. It relies on IEEE802.15.4 low-power radio modules that are embedded into delineators already existing along the road. A group of six delineators, three on either side of the road, form a *cluster*. Within a cluster, seven radio connections are established, each between two opposite delineators. When a vehicle passes a cluster and the related net of radio connections, variations in the *Received Signal Strength Indicator* (RSSI) are detected in real-time and processed by a pattern recognition algorithm that yields the vehicle's direction, speed and length. The system was originally developed for the detection of wrong way drivers but is currently refined to reliably identify different vehicles types, e.g. cars and trucks, for parking space accounting.

RTMS Server. One delineator within a cluster acts as the *cluster master*. It is responsible for the execution of the pattern recognition algorithm as well as the secured transmission of the gathered raw data and deduced vehicle information to the *RTMS Server* via GSM. Depending on the criticality of the data these are sent to one of two communication endpoints. The *high priority endpoint* receives messages about traffic events that have to be handled immediately, e.g. the detection of wrong way drivers. In contrast, the *normal priority endpoint* processes any other traffic-related information like a car or truck that passed a cluster at the entry or exit of a parking space. For the provisioning of raw data and deduced information the server provides interfaces for various types of external nodes: (i) REST is applied to realize the integration of mobile apps that, e.g., allow truck drivers to find the next available parking space for an overnight stay; (ii) DATEX II interfaces are used to supply raw data and information for traffic-data marketplaces such as the Mobility Data Marketplace[1]; (iii) RDS-TMC enables in-vehicle driver information [9] that, e.g., can be leveraged by navigation systems to communicate congestion status to drivers. All interfaces support push-based data provisioning. REST and RDS-TMC pass high priority delineator messages to clients to immediately warn against wrong way drivers.

RTMS Software Platform. The behavior of the RTMS server is realized by the RTMS software platform based on Java EE. The corresponding RTMSSoftwarePlatform component is deployed to a WildFly application server[2] and uses MySQL[3] as database technology. The platform implements the prioritized communication endpoints for the roadside sensors as well as the algorithms used to deduce further information from gathered raw data. Both raw data and information are presented to platform users via a web-based graphical user interface or provided to external systems leveraging the interface technologies described in the previous paragraph. Figure 2 shows the *sub-components* encapsulated in the deployed RTMSSoftwarePlatform component and their interfaces in UML black box component notation. Table 1 explains the function of each sub-component.

---

[1] http://www.mdm-portal.com.
[2] http://www.wildfly.org.
[3] http://www.mysql.com.

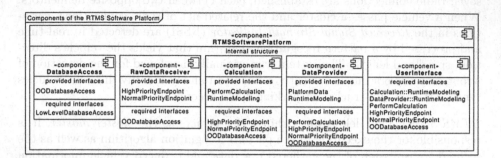

Fig. 2. Sub-components of the RTMS software platform in UML black box notation

Table 1. Functions of RTMS software platform sub-components. Dependencies exist between components that require a provided interface of another component.

ID	Sub-component	Function
C1	DatabaseAccess	Provisioning of object-oriented abstractions for low-level database access means.
C2	RawDataReceiver	Realization of prioritized endpoints for data gathered by delineators. Depends on: C1.
C3	Calculation	Definition of algorithms that transform delineator raw data into information like statistics for a certain parking space. Because an algorithm might also be activated when data is received, the sub-component requires both endpoint interfaces. Depends on: C1, C2.
C4	DataProvider	Provisioning of REST, DATEX II and RDS-TMC interfaces for mobile apps, marketplaces and navigation systems. The activation of an interface might lead to the execution of an algorithm in the Calculation sub-component. Additionally, to be able to push incoming data to external clients, the sub-component requires both endpoint interfaces. Depends on: C1, C2, C3.
C5	UserInterface	Encapsulation of the platform's web-based user interface comprising (i) user management; (ii) means to assign delineator clusters to certain road sections; (iii) a dashboard, which displays aggregated status information of clusters as well as incoming messages like wrong way driver warnings; (iv) detail views for raw data and deduced information. Additionally, the sub-component provides editors for runtime modeling of calculation algorithms and data interfaces. Depends on: C1, C2, C3, C4

4   Identification and Composition of Sub-component Metamodels

In this section we show the composition of metamodels encapsulated within the different sub-components of the RTMSSoftwarePlatform artifact. A metamodel describes the abstract syntax of a modeling language, i.e. the language's concepts and their relationships [8]. The abstract syntax represents the foundation of the language's *concrete syntax* applied by users to express language-specific artifacts.

In Subsect. 4.1 we identify self-contained aspects of the RTMS software platform's sub-components for which we define various metamodels as foundations for aspect-specific modeling languages. As each sub-component might be viewed as its own self-contained domain, e.g. the database domain represented by the DatabaseAccess sub-component, we hereafter call a modeling language deduced from a sub-component metamodel a DSL [16]. In Subsect. 4.2 we show compositional relationships between the metamodels, and thus the DSLs, for the reuse of modeled artifacts between metamodels [17]. We further specify those metamodel elements that are available for runtime modeling to influence certain parts of the platform's behavior.

4.1   Identification of Sub-component Metamodels

Figure 3 shows the identified metamodels of the RTMS software platform per sub-component leveraging UML class diagrams.

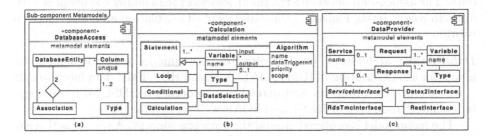

Fig. 3. Identified metamodels of the RTMS sub-components

The RawDataReceiver sub-component does not have a metamodel assigned. That is because the implementation of endpoints for delineator data does not seem to benefit from MDE as it is (i) rather small and simple, i.e. the application of MDE would be oversized, even for documentation purposes; (ii) rather invariant over time, which means a simplified implementation leveraging MDE means like DSLs and repeatable code generation is not necessary. The UserInterface sub-component does not encapsulate a metamodel either, because we do not perceive the resulting restriction of expressiveness as beneficial for user interfaces.

In the following paragraphs we describe each of the identified metamodels.

DatabaseAccess Metamodel. Figure 3a shows the metamodel for the `DatabaseAccess` sub-component. It is used to express the database structure of the RTMS software platform. The main modeling element is `DatabaseEntity`. It represents the object-oriented view of one or more database tables and is equivalent to the Entity concept of the *Java Persistence API* [18]. A `DatabaseEntity` consists of typed `Columns` and `Associations`. A `Column` might be marked as being `unique`. An `Association` is linked with the two database entities involved in the association and, in case the modeled association is unary, one column of the second entity, or, in case the modeled association is binary, one column of each entity.

Calculation Metamodel. The `Calculation` sub-component metamodel, depicted in Fig. 3b, might be used to model `Algorithms`. An algorithm has a high or normal `priority`, a `scope` that narrows its applicability and might be `dataTriggered`, i.e. when an endpoint receives data. A hypothetic algorithm for determining wrong way drivers in a given region would have a high priority, be scoped to wrong way driver data and be data-triggered by the high priority endpoint.

Algorithms exchange data with their invokers via input and output `Variables`. They further consist of a variety of `Statements`. These comprise typical constructs of programming languages, i.e. `Conditionals`, numeric `Calculation` expressions and `Loop` statements. The DSL would also have to provide means for `DataSelection` enabling an algorithm to operate on persisted data. The association between `Statement` and `Variable` allows the usage of variables in conditionals, loops and the assignment of calculation and data selection results.

DataProvider Metamodel. The `DataProvider` metamodel in Fig. 3c defines elements for the description of REST, DATEX II and RDS-TMC data interfaces. It is an excerpt taken from the metamodel that underlies the DSL for technology-independent modeling of REST and SOAP web services in [19].

The metamodel is centered around the `Service` concept. A service is thereby viewed as a black box that might receive a `Request` comprising several variables and produce a `Response` as result. To specify technology-dependent interfaces, one or more `ServiceInterfaces` are assigned to a service. The DSL's code generator produces stub methods for subsequent, onetime service implementation [19]. In the context of the RTMS under study the linkage between a modeled `Algorithm` and `Service`, resulting in the latter being capable of calling the former as executional logic, would be beneficial to propagate calculation results to external clients.

4.2 Composition of Sub-component Metamodels

For metamodel composition we define relationships for sharing instances of selected metamodel elements between sub-components instead of specifying one coherent metamodel. This enables a language developer to maintain a sub-component DSL and its metamodel independently of other sub-components. Each sub-component is thereby treated as a self-contained *language component* [2], which exposes metamodel element instances via well-defined interfaces to be referenced in other sub-component metamodel instances.

Figure 4 shows the compositional relationships between sub-component metamodels as well as information concerning the availability of metamodel elements at design time and runtime.

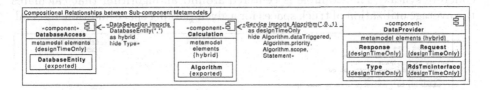

Fig. 4. Compositional relationships between sub-component metamodels and element availability at design time and runtime

Table 2. UML constructs used to describe metamodel element availability, exported concepts and compositional relationships between metamodels

Construct	UML type	Applicable to
{designTimeOnly}	Stereotype	Class/component
Description: Metamodel concepts are available only at design time, i.e. they cannot be used to change the behavior of the RTMS at runtime. When used on a component, this applies to all encapsulated metamodel elements not annotated with {hybrid}		
{hybrid}	Stereotype	Class/component
Description: Metamodel concepts are available both at design time and runtime. When used on a component, this applies to all encapsulated metamodel elements not annotated with {design Time Only}		
{exported}	Stereotype	Class
Description: An instance of the element might be imported to another sub-component metamodel's instance		
Compositional relationship	Annotated dependency	Between components
*Description:*The dependent sub-component DSC imports an **exported** metamodel concept EMC from the independent sub-component ISC by associating it with an internal metamodel concept IMC. The association is described by the dependency annotation, which follows the pattern < IMC > imports < EMC >(m_{IMC}, m_{EMC}) as (hybrid|designTimeOnly) [hide< ISCconcepts >] with m_{IMC} and m_{EMC} being UML multiplicity specifications. The optional **hide** statement might be used to exclude ISC concepts associated with the EMC when mapping the DSC to a concrete syntax		

We express the information related to metamodel composition leveraging annotated UML dependencies and stereotypes. This not only allows us to reuse the existing component diagram in Fig. 3 and enrich it with these constructs by means of existing UML tools, but also provides the basis for the prospective definition of a UML profile targeting metamodel composition [4]. However, due to lack of space, we depict only those metamodel elements that were subsequently extended by stereotypes compared to the component diagram in Fig. 3. The meanings of the employed UML constructs are explained in Table 2.

Listing 1 shows an example of how the metamodel composition affects model-driven RTMS development at design time and its operation at runtime. For this purpose, each sub-component metamodel has been mapped to a specialized concrete syntax. The example is centered around an algorithm that calculates the average utilization of truck spaces for a given parking space and time interval.

```
1   entity ParkingLog {                                               DatabaseEntity
2     col time type Date                                              Column
3     col truckCount type Integer }
4   entity ParkingSpace {
5     col areaName type String unique
6     col truckCapacity type Integer
7     blink log to ParkingLog inverse name space }                    Association (binary)
8
9   algorithm AverageTruckSpaceUtilization(name, beginDate, endDate)   Algorithm
10    local space = select ParkingSpace where areaName = name          Variable, DataSelection
11                                                                     (incl. DatabaseEntity)
12    local log = select space.log where time >= beginDate and time <= endDate
13    local overallTruckCount = 0
14    local lineCount = 0
15    for lineno, line in pairs(log) do                               Loop
16      overallTruckCount = overallTruckCount + line["truckCount"]     Calculation
17      lineCount = lineCount + 1
18    end
19    local averageUtil = overallTruckCount / lineCount
20    return 100 * (averageUtil / space["truckCapacity"])              Algorithm output
21  end
22
23  service GetAverageTruckSpaceUtilization:                           Service
24    receives String name, Date beginDate, Date endDate              Request
25    returns double averageUtilization                               Response
26    invokes AverageTruckSpaceUtilization(name, beginDate, endDate)  Algorithm
27    interface rest method get path "/{name}/averageUtilization" handles "application/json";   RestInterface
```

Listing 1. Usage example of the composed metamodels with concrete syntaxes for `DatabaseAccess` (lines 1 to 7), `Calculation` (lines 9 to 21) and `DataProvider` (lines 23 to 27) metamodels. Italicized lines might be changed at runtime. To show the mapping of abstract to concrete syntaxes, the metamodel concepts used in a line are annotated and underlined at the right side of the listing on their first occurrence.

Lines 1 to 7 define database entities for parking spaces and log entries that represent truck counts deduced from received raw data at certain points in time.

Lines 9 to 21 contain the calculation algorithm. A Lua[4]-dialect with statements enabling data selection from the RTMS database was employed as concrete syntax. Lines 10 and 12 show the effect of composing the `DatabaseAccess` and `Calculation` metamodels as depicted in Fig. 4: Both `DataSelection` statements can refer to the declared database entities. Additionally, the algorithm's behavior might be changed at runtime as the metamodel is `hybrid`.

Lines 23 to 27 show the declaration of a REST interface within the `DataProvider` sub-component. The concrete syntax corresponds to the one described in [19] with an additional `invokes` keyword. It enables the call of a modeled algorithm from a service. Because the `Algorithm` construct was imported as `designTimeOnly` in Fig. 4, the algorithm assignment in line 26 can-

---

[4] https://www.lua.org.

not be changed at runtime. That is to prevent the existence of services that do not encompass any code to execute. In contrast, the assigned service interfaces can be changed at runtime to, for instance, declare an additional DATEX II interface.

5   Discussion

We aim to address the three CPS-related challenges modifiability, heterogeneity and flexibility with the application of metamodels, DSLs and their composition in an RTMS. In the following, we discuss the resulting effects for each challenge.

In general, DSLs introduce modifiability at a higher level of abstraction than general-purpose programming languages [16]. Furthermore, as runtime aspects were considered in the metamodels' composition, RTMS aspects like calculation algorithms and provided data interfaces might be changed at system runtime. However, metamodel composition and consideration of runtime aspects pose additional challenges: (i) Next to the metamodels their relationships have to be managed and it has to be ensured that these are still valid after model evolution; (ii) validation of DSL-based input has to consider existence and applicability of elements modeled in another language, e.g. entities in algorithms; (iii) in the phase of language implementation means have to be provided that allow to identify those parts of a DSL that can be changed at runtime. These challenges might be mitigated using an appropriate language workbench [5].

The metamodel composition follows the heterogeneity between different aspects of the system as it allows to reuse artifacts, e.g. database entities in algorithms, and to model data interfaces at runtime. However, the application of different DSLs for different RTMS parts inherently introduces heterogeneity at the language level. This leads to an increased amount of time a developer has to spent to learn each language. Code generation techniques, e.g. for the deduction of REST interfaces [19], might compensate the resulting cost to a certain degree.

The RTMS flexibility is increased with the application of MDE at runtime. However, to realize runtime modeling, the RTMS has to be extended. First, the sub-components exhibiting runtime modeling capabilities have to provide interfaces for model validation and enactment. Second, the sub-components have to embed a runtime model interpreter, e.g. LuaJ[5] for algorithm execution at runtime. Third, the UserInterface sub-component will have to provide specialized editors for the languages' runtime aspects. This overhead needs to be taken into account when implementing an RTMS leveraging runtime modeling. However, the DSLs and their metamodels' composition are neither specific to a certain RTMS nor the transport domain itself. Instead, an existing implementation of our approach might be reused in other Java-EE-based systems that need to (i) implement sophisticated database structures; (ii) provide flexible algorithms to operate on these; (iii) provide alterable interfaces for data exchange with clients like mobile apps.

---

[5] http://www.luaj.org.

6   Conclusion and Future Work

This paper proposed the application of MDE techniques for developing road traffic management systems. Therefore, we first identified the sub-components of an RTMS software platform (cf. Sect. 3). Next, we created metamodels for each sub-component and composed these leveraging UML stereotypes and dependencies to enable element instance reuse across sub-component borders (cf. Sect. 4). Section 5 discussed the impact of our approach on CPS-related challenges.

In future works we plan to extend the described RTMS architecture with the proposed modeling means. After having finished the implementation of both database and data interface DSL we are currently developing the algorithm DSL. However, while the data interface DSL abstracts from the service technology, the database DSL's applicability is limited to relational databases. Due to the possibly large amount of raw data gathered by the RTMS's delineators along busy roads [23], the usage of non-relational database systems, which are optimized for data-intensive applications, might become necessary. Thus, extending the database DSL and its metamodel with constructs for modeling non-relational data structures could be sensible in the future.

We further plan to create a UML profile that can be used by language developers for modeling compositional relationships between language metamodels based on the constructs listed in Table 2.

Acknowledgements. This research has been partly supported by the Federal Ministry for Economic Affairs and Energy (BMWi), ZIM project "Hochleistungssensorik mit Cloud-basierter Echtzeitdatenverarbeitung für die digitale Straße im urbanen- und Fernverkehr" (funding ID ZF4038201DB5).

References

1. Al-Fuqaha, A., Guizani, M., Mohammadi, M., Aledhari, M., Ayyash, M.: Internet of things: a survey on enabling technologies, protocols, and applications. IEEE Commun. Surv. Tutorials **17**(4), 2347–2376 (2015)
2. Clark, T., Brand, M., Combemale, B., Rumpe, B.: Conceptual model of the globalization for domain-specific languages. In: Cheng, B.H.C., Combemale, B., France, R.B., Jézéquel, J.-M., Rumpe, B. (eds.) Globalizing Domain-Specific Languages. LNCS, vol. 9400, pp. 7–20. Springer, Heidelberg (2015). doi:10.1007/978-3-319-26172-0_2
3. Combemale, B., Deantoni, J., Baudry, B., France, R.B., Jézéquel, J.M., Gray, J.: Globalizing modeling languages. Computer **47**(6), 68–71 (2014)
4. Deantoni, J., Brun, C., Caillaud, B., France, R.B., Karsai, G., Nierstrasz, O., Syriani, E.: Domain globalization: using languages to support technical and social coordination. In: Combemale, B., Jézéquel, J.-M., Rumpe, B. (eds.) Globalizing Domain-Specific Languages. LNCS, vol. 9400, pp. 70–87. Springer, Heidelberg (2015). doi:10.1007/978-3-319-26172-0_5
5. Erdweg, S., Giarrusso, P.G., Rendel, T.: Language composition untangled. In: Sloane, A., Andova, S. (eds.) Proceedings of the 12th Workshop on Language Descriptions, Tools, and Applications (LDTA), pp. 7:1–7:8. ACM (2012)

6. European Committee for Standardization: Intelligent transport systems - datex ii data exchange specifications for traffic management and information - part 1: Context and framework (CEN/TS 16157-1:2011) (2011)
7. Ferry, N., Rossini, A., Chauvel, F., Morin, B., Solberg, A.: Towards model-driven provisioning, deployment, monitoring, and adaptation of multi-cloud systems. In: Proceedings of the 6th International Conference on Cloud Computing, pp. 887–894. IEEE (2013)
8. Fondement, F., Baar, T.: Making metamodels aware of concrete syntax. In: Hartman, A., Kreische, D. (eds.) ECMDA-FA 2005. LNCS, vol. 3748, pp. 190–204. Springer, Heidelberg (2005)
9. Giannopoulos, G.A.: The application of information and communication technologies in transport. Eur. J. Oper. Res. **152**(2), 302–320 (2004)
10. Gubbi, J., Buyya, R., Marusic, S., Palaniswami, M.: Internet of things (IoT): a vision, architectural elements, and future directions. Future Gener. Comput. Syst. **29**(7), 1645–1660 (2013)
11. Haendeler, S., Lewandowski, A., Wietfeld, C.: Passive detection of wrong way drivers on motorways based on low power wireless communications. In: Proceedings of the 79th Vehicular Technology Conference (VTC), pp. 1–5. IEEE (2014)
12. Larsen, M.V., Goknil, A.: Railroad crossing heterogeneous model. In: Proceedings of the 2nd International Workshop on Globalization of Modeling Languages (GEMOC), pp. 4:1–4:6 (2013)
13. Lee, E.A., Seshia, S.A.: Introduction to embedded systems-a cyber-physical systems approach (2011). LeeSeshia.org
14. Malavolta, I., Muccini, H., Sharaf, M.: A preliminary study on architecting cyber-physical systems. In: Proceedings of the 2015 European Conference on Software Architecture Workshops (ECSAW), pp. 20:1–20:6. ACM (2015)
15. Martín-Fernández, F., Caballero-Gil, P., Caballero-Gil, C.: Detection and report of traffic lights violation using sensors and smartphones. In: García-Chamizo, J.M., Fortino, G., Ochoa, S.F. (eds.) UCAmI 2015. LNCS, vol. 9454, pp. 237–248. Springer, Heidelberg (2015). doi:10.1007/978-3-319-26401-1_23
16. Mernik, M., Heering, J., Sloane, A.M.: When and how to develop domain-specific languages. ACM Comput. Surv. (CSUR) **37**(4), 316–344 (2005)
17. Mosser, S., Logre, I., Ferry, N., Collet, P.: From sensors to visualization dashboards: need for language composition. In: Proceedings of the 2nd International Workshop on Globalization of Modeling Languages (GEMOC), pp. 2:1–2:6 (2013)
18. Oracle Inc.: Java persistence api, version 2.1. JSR 338 (2013)
19. Rademacher, F., Peters, M., Sachweh, S.: Design of a domain-specific language based on a technology-independent web service framework. In: Weyns, D., Mirandola, R., Crnkovic, I. (eds.) ECSA 2015. LNCS, vol. 9278, pp. 357–371. Springer, Heidelberg (2015). doi:10.1007/978-3-319-23727-5_29
20. dos Santos Soares, M., Vrancken, J., Wang, Y.: A common architecture to develop road traffic management systems. In: Proceedings of the 16th ITS World Congress and Exhibition on Intelligent Transport Systems and Services (2009)
21. da Silva, A.R.: Model-driven engineering: a survey supported by the unified conceptual model. Comput. Lang. Syst. Struct. **43**, 139–155 (2015)
22. Soares, M.D.S., Vrancken, J., Wang, Y.: Architecture-based development of road traffic management systems. In: Proceedings of the 2010 International Conference on Networking, Sensing and Control (ICNSC), pp. 26–31. IEEE (2010)

23. Sussman, J.S.: Perspectives on intelligent transportation systems. Springer (2008)
24. Wang, R., Zhang, L., Sun, R., Gong, J., Cui, L.: Easitia: a pervasive traffic information acquisition system based on wireless sensor networks. IEEE Trans. Intell. Transp. Syst. **12**(2), 615–621 (2011)
25. Whitmore, A., Agarwal, A., Da Xu, L.: The internet of things - a survey of topics and trends. Inf. Syst. Front. **17**(2), 261–274 (2015)

Ultra Narrow Band Radio Technology in High-Density Built-Up Areas

Radim Kalfus$^{(\boxtimes)}$ and Tomáš Hégr

Department of Telecommunications, Faculty of Electrical Engineering,
Czech Technical University in Prague, Technicka 2, Prague, Czech Republic
{kalfurad,hegrtom1}@fel.cvut.cz

Abstract. The Internet of Things (IoT) is an ever mentioned phenomena which is closely linked to a rapidly growing Low-Power Wide-Area Networks (LPWAN). Although LPWANs are already widely deployed the performance under real-life conditions of the communication system such as Ultra Narrow Band (UNB) radio technology has not been deeply studied yet. Smart City applications of IoT imply low energy consumption, high spectrum efficiency, and comprehensive security hence the range limits are very constrained and must be verified before deployment is started. In this work, authors verify UNB technology called SIGFOX and identify technological constraints. These constraints allow us to formulate a measurement methodology combining range measurements in an urban area to show transmission characteristics of SIGFOX technology. The subsequent evaluation of the technology using reference/commercially available SIGFOX hardware in real urban areas shows the impacts to possible applications of this novel UNB technology.

Keywords: Internet of things · SIGFOX · Ultra narrow band · Methodology

1 Introduction

In 1999, British visionary Kevin Ashton established the term "The Internet of things" as a futuristic world of seamlessly connected devices [5]. In less than twenty years after, the Internet of Things (IoT) is experiencing rapid growth with estimations between 25 and 50 billion connected devices by 2020, with up to 40 Machine-Type Communications (MTC) devices per household [1,11,20]. Although multiple solutions are emerging, the focus on specific services and applications let to the heterogeneity in communication protocols, network technologies and standards [2,17]. Despite the fact that network technologies are different, they all share common objectives: low power consumption, low device cost and a long extended range [11].

Predictions say that smart commercial buildings will have the highest usage of IoT by 2017, with smart homes taking the lead in 2018 [13]. Supported by the Smart Grids Task Force that advises the European Commission on the development and deployment of smart grids, the EU aims to replace at least 80 % of

© Springer International Publishing Switzerland 2016
G. Dregvaite and R. Damasevicius (Eds.): ICIST 2016, CCIS 639, pp. 663–676, 2016.
DOI: 10.1007/978-3-319-46254-7_54

the electricity meters with smart meters by 2020 [8]. Smart Metering, such as smart meters and remote sensors, is currently seen as the first application [12]. Contemporary solutions on the market are mainly represented by traditional cellular technologies that have a higher power consumption, entry cost and low transmission efficiency due to the different nature of Machine to Machine (M2M) communication. M2M sensor applications generally produce a small payload size with bursty nature of the traffic and require wide coverage [15,21]. As ETSI depicts, IoT applications where long-range with low bandwidth and power consumption are not supported by existing technologies, Low Power Wide Area Network (LPWAN) technologies gain their momentum as an alternative to cellular M2M connections [17].

Authors of this paper focus on one of the significant players in LPWANs called SIGFOX marked as the first operator of a dedicated M2M cellular network [1,5,14]. As one of the emerging proprietary technologies, SIGFOX is frequently mentioned as the reference player in IoT but almost no works about real life experiences have been published. As the authors had the privilege to be a part of SIGFOX technology testing in an urban area in the Czech Republic, the paper presents real-life measured data showing variety of impacts to this novel LPWAN technology. By analysing more than 3,700 samples captured over a period of 8 months, during the network roll out, authors try to verify a real-life performance and its constraints.

The paper is structured as follows. In Sect. 2, we present related works and standards. Section 3 details the SIGFOX technology and Sect. 4.1 closes up our experimental setup for stationary and nomadic measurements. In Sects. 4.2 and 4.3, achieved results are presented and we conclude our paper by summary in Sect. 5.

2   Related Works

Most of the related work focuses on IoT competitor LoRa technology. As for example [27], where authors outline the resistance to intentional interference and echo. Experimental studies on coverage limits and attenuation models for LoRa technology [3] concluded measurements to find out a formula for a channel attenuation model. This model was also taken as a ground for stationary measurements in this article. On the other hand, SIGFOX technology is generally described and compared with main competitors in article on lessons learnt from industrial implementations [12], where authors describe an up-link channel structure and access mechanisms.

Standardization work in LPWANs is ingoing, for example within the 3GPP on usage of IoT in licensed spectra LTE-M and EC-GSM [1,21]. Moreover, one of the main initiators in this area is ETSI on open specification of a new standard for Low Throughput Networks (LTN), where one of the main contributors is SIGFOX company [11].

3   SIGFOX at a Glance

3.1   Architecture

SIGFOX, a French technology start-up, was established in 2009. Although the SIGFOX solution is proprietary, the company is also closely cooperating with ETSI on definition of an open LTN standard; thus, we can expect significant intersections [12]. What makes SIGFOX different from other competitors and why it gained momentum on the IoT market is likely a comprehensive business model offered to its customers [9].

The network is based on one-hop star topology and consists of transmitting devices, gateways/base stations and SIGFOX back-end. The network coverage is deployed per each country by chosen partner called SIGFOX Network Operator (SNO). Receiving base stations/gateways operated by SNO are typically placed on Mobile Network Operator's radio towers [16]. These gateways communicate with SIGFOX Cloud platform back-end operated by the SIGFOX company itself. To reach full operational capability, the whole ecosystem has to fulfil only three requirements - coverage from SNO, device/sensor, and a valid device subscription. Subscribers with a yearly subscription fee for each device will be then able to receive messages via web interface, REST API or by a callback mechanism. A general network architecture is depicted in Fig. 1.

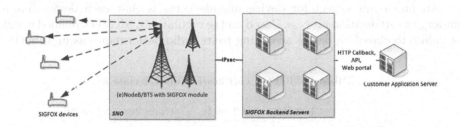

Fig. 1. General network architecture.

3.2   Technology

SIGFOX allows bidirectional communication using Industrial, Scientific and Medical (ISM) radio band, namely frequencies 868 MHz for Europe and 902 MHz for USA. Due to the physical nature of the UNB transmission with random channel frequency hopping, the noise contribution is very low, approx. −150 dBm at 290 K, and the link budget can reach up to 159 dB [19,24].

The protocol exists currently in two versions. The original one where the up-link is using 48 kHz macro channel centered at 868.2 MHz, and the second version using a 192 kHz macro channel centered at 868.13 MHz, that is being deployed since the end of 2014 [25]. The up-link channel bandwidth is 100 Hz with theoretically 480 slots for a 48 kHz macro channel and 1920 slots for a 192 kHz macro channel. Although the authors [12] point that channels 181–219 are reserved and not used in the 48 kHz macro channel. In the Czech Republic, a member country of European Conference of Postal & Telecommunications Administrations (CEPT), used frequencies are a part of spectrum allocations for Short Range Devices (SRDs). Namely for up-link band h1 and for down-link channel band h3 [7].

Since SIGFOX does not employ Listen Before Talk (LBT) nor any sense mechanism to prevent interference among devices operating in the same band (Adaptive Frequency Agility (AFA) technique), duty cycle limitations do not allow to transmit more than 1 % of the time with the maximum of 500 mW (27 dBm) effective radiated power (ERP) for the down-link and maximum power of 25 mW (14 dBm) ERP for the up-link [7,23].

A message emission can take several seconds depending on a required number of repetitions in different subchannels. Typically, the 3-repetition scheme takes approximately 6 s (3 × 1s emission + 3 × 1s gap). Based on expression 1, this leads to a fixed maximum of 140 messages per device per day.

$$n_{max} = \frac{t_d}{t_e} \tag{1}$$

where n_{max} is the maximum number of messages [messages/day], t_d [s] stands for number of seconds per day and t_e is emission time of one message [s].

An important aspect for device manufactures is that each device has to undergo a certification process. Based on the regulations, SIGFOX defined a scale of values to classify a device according to its radio performance as in Table 1.

Table 1. SIGFOX certification up-link classes

	Class 0u	Class 1u	Class 2u	Class 3u
ERP [dBm]	14 > P > 12	12 > P > 7	7 > P > 0	P < 0

One of the main characteristics of UNB is a reduced band occupation; therefore, the noise contribution; is lessened and for a given targeted error probability we can reach much longer distances [19]. SIGFOX technology allows to demodulate an extremely weak received signal −142 dBm [12]. On the other hand, with extended coverage increases the number of devices sharing the same access medium and the medium access control (MAC) protocol gains higher importance. For up-link used modulation technique is Differential Binary Phase-Shift Kying (DBPSK) and for down-link Gaussian Frequency-Shift Keying (GFSK) [4].

A minimization of fading is achieved by the implementation of the Random Frequency Division Multiple Access (R-FDMA) schema. Random frequency hopping in predefined channels that applied on transmitting side devices may use any channel at any time and a receiver must listen on all channels in parallel with the use of signal processing algorithms to retrieve the message [12]. Primarily, due to the contradictory requirements of power limitations while keeping the extended range the technology modulation (G)FSK supports only data rate of 100 bps in up-link and 600 bps in down-link [4].

4 Technology Evaluation

4.1 Experimental Setup

Most of the measurements were done in Prague district in the Czech Republic. Prague with population of approx. 1.2 million inhabitants was a part of the pilot phase which was comprised of three base stations plus one base station in a neighboring region. SNO for the Czech Republic is deploying approximately 350 SIGFOX base stations by the end of 2016 [26]. Thanks to the pilot phase, we could verify the technology in limited roll-out for stationary measurements. Nomadic measurements, i.e. measurements, where the end-device has moved with determined velocity, were carried out in pre-production setup as described later in this paper. The setup for our measurements, which is in principle the same for both nomadic and stationary measurements, is depicted in Fig. 2.

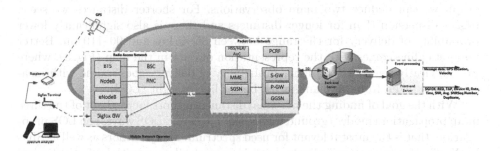

Fig. 2. Diagram of the measurement setup.

Our testing environment consisted of three reference transmitters used during the network roll-out. Devices were equipped with Telecom Design (TD) module that is based on a EFM32/ARM Cortex-M3 micro-controller with a 868 MHz-Band swivel $\frac{1}{2}$ wave antenna. For our measurements, we used TD1208 having a radio chip Si4461 with a receiver sensitivity of −126 dBm with active radio power consumption of 19 mA (for 14 dBm) [10]. All experiments were realized with a device set to ERP = 14 dBm (class 0u) and only in up-link direction. The module is capable of standard communication through AT commands allowing to send custom messages regardless the built-in reference measurement test function. We use this approach later for nomadic measurements, because the TD1208 is not equipped with any GPS module.

A single up-link message is by default sent three times at three distinct channels to increase the probability of reaching at least one base station. The number of repetitions can be even increased or the message can be acknowledged by in down-link channel in case of crucial applications [12].

Since an important factor contributing to the degradation and variability of the link quality is a radio interference, as a mitigation of major external radio interferences, we investigated level of noise in the 868 MHz ISM spectrum before each stationary measurement and during the process as well. We used portable RF Spectrum Analyzer SPECTRAN HF-6060 V4 connected to the computer, with cut-off level set to -100 dBm which is the lowest value possible [6].

4.2 Stationary Measurements

Since the roll-out strategy and radio configuration is largely dependent on the maximum range between transmitter and receiver, in the first set of measurements, we were analysing a relation between distance and reception probability based on messages received by three base stations. Three independent devices were set to send ten messages at each position. This helped to avoid an accidental interference. Measured distances were grouped to show a variation of number of received messages in distance ranges. Additionally, we focused to find the maximum range of the technology.

Figure 4 shows a probability of delivery as a function of distance. From the graph we can deduce two main observations. For shorter distances we see a bigger dispersion than for longer distances and there is also significantly lower probability of delivery for the range between 35–45 km and 90–110 km. Better understanding comes with the representation of data in the map (Fig. 3), where we can clearly see that the higher probability of delivery goes in-line with measurements taken from highlands with better line of sight (LOS).

With the goal of finding the maximal distance authors focused out of the three main propagatiom modes (ground waves, sky waves and LOS waves) on LOS propagation, that is the most relevant for used spectrum. Many authors as well as SIG-FOX official specification indicate, that, in open rural areas with LOS, the typical coverage should be approximately 40 km [4,12,23,24]. Theoretical maximal LOS distance LOS_{MAX} is dependent on the earth's curvature E_R, height of the transmitter H_1 and height of the receiver H_2 as defined in expression 2 [28].

In line with the theoretical expectations, the maximal measured distance of 119.9 km (with success rate 100 % with detection of signal on all four TAPs and with average RSSI $-96, 6$ dBm) was truly achieved from the highest peak of Czech Republic called Sněžka, where the difference between height of transmitter and receiver was the greatest (1258 m).

$$LOS_{MAX} = \frac{\sqrt{2 * H_1 * E_R} + \sqrt{2 * H_2 * E_R}}{1000} \qquad (2)$$

Since the static parameters: Gain of receiving antennas (G_{Rx}) and transmitting power (P_{Tx}) of devices are known, dynamic parameters: Received Signal Strength Indicator (RSSI) and Signal-to-noise-ratio are obtained from SIGFOX back-end, we could apply following formula to calculate Path Loss (PL) [18]:

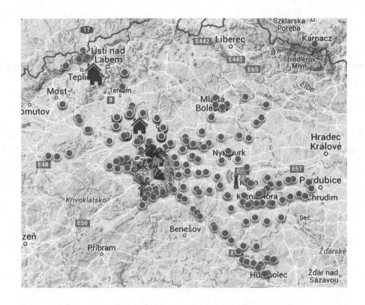

Fig. 3. Stationary measurements carried out in central Bohemia.

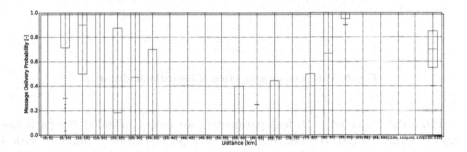

Fig. 4. Probability of delivery as a function of distance

$$PL = |RSSI| + SNR + P_{Tx} + G_{Rx} \qquad (3)$$

Keeping in mind that this formula is defined only for far field distances (d) farther than Fraunhofer distance d_F:

$$d > d_f = \frac{2D^2}{\lambda} \qquad (4)$$

where D is the largest physical linear dimension of the antenna, λ wavelength of the signal, and it must be satisfied $d_f >> D$ and $d_f >> \lambda$

Expected path loss (EPL) was derived using the linear polynomial fit of the logarithmic link distance where B is path loss; n is the path loss exponent; d is the distance; and d_0 is the reference distance, in our case 1 km

$$EPL = B + 10nlog_{10}(\frac{d}{d_0})$$
(5)

As reference free space loss (FSL) values were used obtained from following formula [14]

$$FSL = 20log(\frac{R}{1000}) + 20log(f) + 32,4$$
(6)

The Measured path loss (PL), EPL and FSL as a function of logarithmic distance are depicted in Fig. 5.

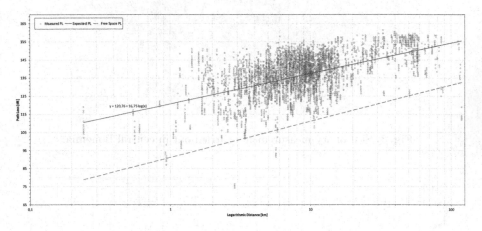

Fig. 5. Path loss as a function of logarithmic distance

From the expected path loss parameters we have concluded the path loss exponent that equals to 1.68. Such value is typically inside a building with a line of sight and it is even lower than the free space value that equals to 2 [22] (Table 2).

Table 2. Results of stationary measurements

Variable	Value
d_{max} [km]	119,9
LOS_{MAX} (for d_{max}) [km]	209.3
d_F [m]	0,984
B [dB]	120,76
n [-]	1,68

4.3 Nomadic Measurements

The term Nomadic measurements stands for measurements carried out during a monitored movement of the terminal. The setup was expanded for a second modem to decrease possible device-selective faults. Both modems were fixed to opposite sides of car roof railings. Modems were set to emit messages alternately to not influence each other during the broadcasting.

The measurements were realized in March, 2016 when the SIGFOX network in Prague (Czech Republic) city was shortly before the production roll out. The network consisted of 21 base stations plus 13 base stations nearby the city border. This is probably not the final state of the construction, and the network will be extended in the region around Prague. Measurements were split in several runs reflecting distinctive urban areas as depicted in Fig. 6.

Fig. 6. Urban area where nomadic measurement runs, indicated by green lines, were carried out. (Color figure online)

The main goal was to verify the expected impact of Doppler effect on the transmission loss rate. The Doppler frequency shift f_D is proportional to the frequency of the electromagnetic wave f [29], and even a relatively low velocity can affect the loss rate at UNB. The Doppler shift is defined as in expression 7.

$$f_D = \frac{v_r f}{c} cos(\alpha) \tag{7}$$

where c is the speed of light [m/s], v_r [m/s] stands for the relative velocity between the terminal and base station, $\alpha \in [0, \pi]$ determines the velocity vector.

The velocity vector angle has a maximum effect on the frequency shift when $\alpha = 0$. In the Table 3 are some examples of real-life speeds expected at regular end-user applications and related frequency shifts. It is obvious that the frequency shift for such UNB technology as SIGFOX could be a real weakness especially if we consider transmission length of a single message.

Table 3. Example Doppler frequency shifts for 868 Mhz

Activity/Limit	Velocity [km/h]	$f_D(\alpha = 0)$ [Hz]	$f_D(\alpha = 45)$ [Hz]	$f_D(\alpha = 90)$ [Hz]
Jogging	10	8,04	4,22	-3,60
Residential zone	30	24,11	12,67	-10,80
In town	50	40,19	21,11	-18,01
In tunnels	70	56,26	29,55	-25,21
Outside town	90	72,33	38,00	-32,41
On highway	130	104,48	54,89	-46,82

Since the area is covered by many base stations, the α between the moving terminal and a particular base station is presumably dissimilar for each case. Moreover, the α can change during the message transmission. Those facts imply that the message is successfully received only in case the Doppler frequency shift aligns with one of the valid channels at least at one of the receiving base stations for the whole time of the transmission. This criterion is most likely more relaxed and the receiver handles also cases when the transmission is not perfectly aligned to the channel center frequency.

As the number of factors affecting the potential loss of message is high and the overall model is complex, we decided in the first attempt for a simple measurement model. The measurement application was basically set to emit a message in regular intervals containing position, velocity and a unique (in the context of this measurement) identification. Simultaneously, the measurement device stored all tracking data and sent messages locally for further analysis. Although velocity and position in messages was not necessary, we followed the idea of an end-user tracking device as one of the potential applications.

The data captured during measurements was compared with the data received via the SIGFOX backend system that forwarded every single received message from the network including all duplicates. In the analysis, we compared data sets and computed message loss-rate for particular travel velocities. Since every broadcasting took several seconds, and it was not possible to keep the velocity constant during all measurements (regular city traffic), we split the data to ranges from 0 to 110 km/h.

The first result describing loss-rate is depicted in Fig. 7. This perspective shows how much the captured samples differ over measurement runs which were carried out in different part of the measurement areas meaning various building density. As one can see, the mean value of the loss-rate is fluctuating around 20 % but it does not evince any trend. However, it is worth to focus on a few particular areas. Slightly higher loss rate for velocities lower than 50 km/h is most probably caused by the fact that those samples were captured in the urban areas with high building density. On the other hand, the loss-rate at higher velocities is in some cases interestingly low, except the ranges (60, 70] and (80, 90] km/h where there was insufficient number of samples. This is most probably caused by several factors. At first, measurements were taken mostly in suburban areas with an improved LOS to base stations. At second, the traffic outside the

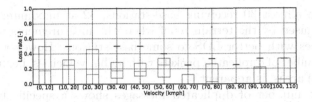

Fig. 7. Message loss-rate for various travel velocities aggregated over measurement runs.

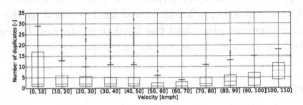

Fig. 8. Number of received duplicate messages aggregated over velocity ranges.

city is more fluent without the need for frequent acceleration. The acceleration is from the perspective of Doppler effect even more problematic, since it causes a continuous frequency shift. The receiving base station may be in such case unable to fix on the particular channel when the frequency changes during the transmission.

The presumption that open space is the originator of the lower loss-rate is supported by the subsequent analysis showing number of received duplicates per single message as is depicted in Fig. 8. As one can see, in extreme cases

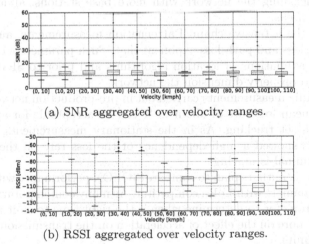

(a) SNR aggregated over velocity ranges.

(b) RSSI aggregated over velocity ranges.

Fig. 9. Radio-related parameters and its dependency on travel velocity.

outliers reach almost 30 receiving base-stations, 32 at maximum. Those cases are mostly caused by the terrain relief where the measurements were taken on elevated places with better LOS to some base-stations. However, the trend of increasing number of duplicated packets with higher velocities, i.e. measurements in open-space areas, is apparent.

While the number of duplicated messages shows a specific behavior with increasing velocity, the radio-related parameters as RSSI and SNR are not as obvious. The results of SNR and RSSI dependencies are shown in Fig. 9. A mean value of both parameters is fluctuating in a relatively narrow zone for most samples. Outliers are in lower velocities most likely caused by the short distance between the measurement place and the local base station. In higher velocities, those are related, as in case above, to the open-space area.

5   Conclusion

The paper presented new UNB technology called SIGFOX and investigations based on 3,700 samples measured before the network commercial launch. Stationary measurements indicate that within limitations of ISM band regulations, the SIGFOX technology can reach an exceptional maximum range. Measurements prove the range limit is strongly dependent on the geographical profile of area. And based on the expectations, the maximal measured distance value of 119.9 Km was achieved from the location with the biggest difference in height of transmitter and receiver antenna and with the potential to reach an even longer distance somewhere where terrain profile would allow us a direct line of sight. Although this is a truly great result in other measurements the loss-rate was strongly dependent on the type of area. In case of high-density built-up areas, the loss increased rapidly above distance of 10 km. This issue will be most likely solved by thickening the network with more base stations, at least in bigger metropolitan areas.

Based on the extensive channel attenuation measurements, authors derived value of path loss and path loss exponent that. Such parameters can be used in the distance estimations of location algorithms and prior to SIGFOX network deployment to properly dimension the network.

The nomadic measurements carried out in pre-production network show that the reached mean loss rate of about 20 % can be acceptable for applications as for example asset tracking. As in the stationary measurements, the nomadic measurements showed a high dependency of the loss rate on the type of area where the terminal is moving.

In the future, authors plan to compare SIGFOX performance with other M2M technologies, namely with LoRa competitor. As many contemporary applications use an accelerometer to determine when is the right time to emit a message, we plan to focus more on the effect of acceleration on the transmission and estimate loss-related limits.

References

1. 3GPP: Cellular system support for ultra-low complexity and low throughput internet of things (ciot) (release 13), tr 45.820 v13.1.0 (2015)
2. 3GPP: Network architecture (release 12), ts 23.002 v12.7.0 (2015)
3. Roivainen, A., Jayasinghe, P., Meinila, J., Hovinen, V., Latva-aho, M.: Vehicle-to-vehicle radio channel characterization in urban environment at 2.3 ghz and 5.25 ghz, pp. 63–67 (2014)
4. a.s., SimpleCellNetworks: Technologie sigfox. http://www.simplecell.eu/pages/technologie_sigfox/
5. Ashton, K.: That internet of things thing. RFiD J. **22**, 97–114 (2009)
6. Baccour, N., et al.: Radio link quality estimation in low-power wireless networks, p. 147 (2013)
7. CEPT: Erc recommendation 70–03. http://www.efis.dk/reports/ReportDownloader?reportid=2
8. Comission, E.: Smart meter rollout. https://ec.europa.eu/energy/en/topics/markets-and-consumers/smart-grids-and-meters
9. Davies, A.: On lpwans: why sigfox and lora are rather different, and the importance of the business model. http://bit.ly/28Nf3qy
10. Design, T., S.A.: Td1208 evaluation board users guide. https://github.com/Telecom-Design/Documentation_TD_RF_Module/raw/master/TD1208
11. ETSI: Low throughput networks (ltn); functional architecture, etsi gs ltn 002 v1.1.1 (2014)
12. Margelis, G., Piechocki, R., Kaleshi, D., Thoma, P.: Low throughput networks for the iot: Lessons learned from industrial implementations, pp. 181–186 (2015)
13. Gartner: Gartner says smart cities will use 1.6 billion connected things in 2016. http://www.gartner.com/newsroom/id/3175418
14. Gomez, C., Paradells, J.: Urban automation networks: current and emerging solutions for sensed data collection and actuation in smart cities. Sensors **9**, 22874–22898 (2015)
15. Poncela, J., Moreno-Roldan, J.M., Aamir, M., Alvi, B.A.: M2m challenges and opportunities in 4g. Wirel. Pers. Commun. **85**, 407–420 (2015)
16. Link Labs, I.: A comprehensive look at low power, wide area networks. http://info.link-labs.com/lpwan
17. Alaya, M.B., Medjiah, S., Monteil, T., Drira, K.: Toward semantic interoperability in onem2m architecture. IEEE Commun. Mag. **53**(12), pp. 35–41 (2015)
18. Meinila, J., et al: Wireless world initiative new radio winner+ (2010). http://projects.celtic-initiative.org/winner+/WINNER+%20Deliverables/D5.3_v1.0.pdf
19. Do, M.-T., Claire Goursaud, J.M.G.: Interference modelling and analysis of random fdma scheme in ultra narrowband networks (2014)
20. Mišić, V., Mišić, J.: Machine-to-machine communications (348) (2014)
21. Ratasuk, R., Mangalvedhe, N., Ghosh, A., Vejlgaard, B.: Narrowband lte-m system for m2m communication 85, pp. 1–5 (2014)
22. Shahin, F.: Zigbee wireless networks and transceivers, p. 364 (2008)
23. SIGFOX: Sigfox, m2m and iot redefined through cost effective and energy optimized connectivity. http://www.SIGFOX.com/static/media/Files/Documentation/SIGFOX_Whitepaper.pdf
24. SIGFOX: Sigfox specifics. http://makers.SIGFOX.com/#about
25. Smierzchalsk, S.: Sigfox technical specification

26. a.s. T-Mobile Czech Republic: T-mobile pokryje českou republiku sítí sigfox pro internet věcí. http://www.t-press.cz/cs/tiskove-materialy/tiskove-zpravy-t-mobile/t-mobile-pokryje-ceskou-republiku-siti-sigfox-pro-internet-veci.html
27. Wendt, T., Volk, F., Mackensen, E.: A benchmark survey of long range (loratm) spread-spectrum-communication at 2.45 ghz for safety applications 16, 1–4 (2015)
28. TI: Achieving optimum radio range (application report swra479) (2015). http://www.ti.com.cn/cn/lit/an/swra479/swra479.pdf
29. Xiong, F., Andro, M.: The effect of doppler frequency shift, frequency offset of the local oscillators, and phase noise on the performance of coherent ofdm receivers (2001)

Change Impact in Product Lines: A Systematic Mapping Study

Christopher Brink[1]([⊠]), Philipp Heisig[2], and Fabian Wackermann[2]

[1] Software Engineering Group, Heinz Nixdorf Institute,
Paderborn University, Paderborn, Germany
christopher.brink@uni-paderborn.de
[2] University of Applied Sciences and Arts Dortmund, Dortmund, Germany
philipp.heisig@fh-dortmund.de

Abstract. A product line (PL) supports and simplifies the development process of (software) systems by reusing assets. As systems are subjected to frequent alterations, the implementation of this changes can be a complex and error-prone task. For this reason a change impact analysis (CIA) systematically identifies locations that are affected by a change. While both approaches (PL and CIA) per se are often discussed in literature, the combination of them is still a challenge. This paper gives a comprehensive overview of literature, which addresses the integration of PL and CIA concepts. Furthermore, we classify our results to outline both, the current research stage as well as gaps. Therefore, we conducted a systematic mapping study incorporating 165 papers. While most of the papers have their background within Software Product Lines (SPLs) (44.2%) or PLs (5.5%), CIA in the combination with Multi Product Lines (2.4%) or Product Families (PFs) (1.8%) is sparsely addressed in literature. The results show that CIA for SPLs has been partially addressed yet, whereas the consideration of different disciplines (PFs) is insufficiently covered.

Keywords: Systematic mapping study · Product family · Product line · Hardware/Software · Embedded systems · Change impact analysis

1 Introduction

Nowadays, companies have to offer their products to a broad range of customers, who expect short time-to-market intervals, customised products and a high quality for a reasonable price, especially in the automotive industry. Product line engineering is a promising way to satisfy this expectations by providing a large range of products through the systematic reuse of assets. In the following a product line (PL) is defined as a context-free family of related products which share a common set of features. Especially within the software engineering domain, software product lines (SPLs) are well established to improve cost, quality, time to

C. Brink—This research has been partially supported by the Federal Ministry of Education and Research, project AMALTHEA4public no. 01IS14029J.

© Springer International Publishing Switzerland 2016
G. Dregvaite and R. Damasevicius (Eds.): ICIST 2016, CCIS 639, pp. 677–694, 2016.
DOI: 10.1007/978-3-319-46254-7_55

market, and productivity during the development of software-intensive systems [11]. A multi product line (MPL) comprises several PLs and is convenient for the configuration of large-scale systems in a distributed manner [6], whereas a product family (PF) is defined as an approach which considers different disciplines like software or hardware within an MPL context.

As software systems are intended to run over a long period of time, they are subjected to frequent alterations, updates, and enhancements like software component evolution [5]. Thereby, changes in a software system can have several reasons like adding new features due to refined requirements [12]. Among changes within software code, the exchange of underlying hardware parts is also a typical issue. Exchanging hardware parts over the lifetime of a product or product family is particular the case for embedded systems [16]. Since an increasing quantity of dependencies in systems can be observed, applying changes is a complex and error-prone process when doing it manually. For this reasons, change impact (CI) as well as change impact analysis (CIA) are approaches to avoid errors and to further support the user during the change process. While CI describes the potential consequences of a change, CIA refers to the identification and analysis of changes as well as estimation of modification needs [2].

Many articles have been published dealing with either a PL context or CI/CIA. However, it seems that there is only a small number of publications that focus on the combination of those two approaches and in particular with considering software and hardware aspects. Since the management of changes within a PL context is a crucial matter, we want to give an overview of the current state of the research field within this systematic mapping study (SMS). Therefore, Sect. 2 gives an overview of related work, while Sect. 3 provides the fundamentals of this SMS including research questions (RQs) to identify research gaps and further knowledge on this topic, a description of the search strategy and a graphical map. Afterwards, Sect. 4 discusses the research questions in combination with the study results, before Sect. 5 concludes our work.

2 Related Work

Within computer science, secondary studies are increasingly used to synthesize information from a wide range of primary studies. Although different kinds of secondary studies exist, only systematic literature reviews (SLRs) and SMSs have a well-defined methodology. While both aim to summarise the current state of a specific research area, they differ in terms of quantity and objectives. According to Kitchenham and Stuart [7], researchers use SLRs to identify, analyse and interpret all available evidence related to a specific research question. As SMSs classify and count contributions within categories rather than analysing publications in detail, they are suitable to give an overview about a specific research area and identify research trends [15].

Since the development of software through the use of SPLs is gaining more and more importance, several secondary studies concerning this topic can be found in literature. In [8], Laguna and Crespo present an SMS which deals with SPL evolution in terms of reengineering legacy systems into SPLs. For this purpose, 74 papers were selected, classified according to dimensions like main focus or contribution type, and analysed towards research trends. An SLR on variability management in SPLs was published by Chen and Babar [3]. Based on inclusion/exclusion criteria, 97 papers have been surveyed with the result that only a few approaches are evaluated using rigorous scientific methods. Mujtaba et al. give another overview on variability in SPLs by means of a research map [13]. Bastos et al. investigate SPL adoption aspects in the context of an SMS [4]. After applying different filters and snowballing, 34 papers were considered and evaluated regarding important aspects that should be noted when adopting SPL approaches.

In contrast to SPLs, secondary studies which address CIA are less frequent. In [9], Lehnert identifies 150 automated and semi-automated impact analysis approaches. Based on taxonomy criteria, each approach is further categorised to outline research questions and opportunities. Li et al. provide an SLR for CIA [10], which focuses mainly on code-based techniques whereby 23 different techniques could be observed. Alam et al. deal in their SLR [1] with the consideration of CIA in business process management and service oriented architecture by evaluating 43 studies.

3 Systematic Mapping

To analyse the given topic we performed an SMS as described by Petersen et al. in [14] and updated in 2015 [15]. Generally an SMS consists of several steps (cf. Fig. 1):

In a first step, the scope is determined by the definition of RQs, which should be answered by the study. Based on the RQs, search strings for the selected search engines are defined and applied. Afterwards, the search results are examined on the basis of exclusion criteria to reduce the set to relevant papers. Following, a classification scheme to range the discovered publications is defined and further used to create a systematic map. Furthermore, we extended the SMS guidelines by Petersen et al. by a subsequent analysis step based on the systematic map.

Fig. 1. Simplified mapping process

3.1 Research Questions

Our research questions are defined as follows:

RQ1: How many studies address change impact analysis including software and hardware aspects in the context of product lines? The goal of this questions is to identify if there are any publications that describe CIA approaches for PFs, which means that among software also hardware should be considered within a CIA.

RQ2: Is change impact analysis in product lines a trending topic? This question should answer whether there is an increased interest in CIA for PLs in recent years.

RQ3: What are the main publication venues for literature regarding change impact analysis in product lines? While we assume that the *Software Product Line Conference* (SPLC) will be one of the main contribution source for our research, it is unclear which other venues are common for publications dealing with CIA in PLs.

3.2 Conducted Search

For our SMS we chosen different search engines to find relevant literature. ACM-DL (dl.acm.org), IEEExplore (ieeexplore.ieee.org/), Springer Link (link.springer.com/) and Science Direct (www.sciencedirect.com) were used as they are well known and common in secondary studies [3]. DBLP (dblp.uni-trier.de/db) and Base (base-search.net) were further included as search engines since they also include articles which are not covered by those well known sources (e.g. open access publications).

Table 1. Search strings

Category	Search strings
Product Line	product line, pl, productline, product families, product variants
Change	change, evolution, agile
Impact	effect, impact, analysis

Several different search strings were used to find articles with related terms or alternative spellings. As CIA is sparsely addressed in literature and leads to only a few search results, we extended our search scope to CI and neglected the analysis part. Therefore, we created three categories which contain different search strings (cf. Table 1). For our search process we combined strings of two or three categories to search terms, whereby the PL category was always used.

Whenever possible the search was restricted to abstract or title scope as otherwise too many irrelevant literature would appear. For example Springer Link found 14471 results for the search term *change impact product line* while the results remained zero when searching within title scope. This problem also appeared with other search engines.

Since some search terms like *change impact product line* produced only few results [26,46,49,78], we applied backward snowballing as described by Wohlin [18] to identify further publications. Afterwards, we used the following exclusion criteria in order to reduce the number of results:

- Non peer reviewed articles
- Articles, which were not published within categories of computer science (computer science articles which use aspects of other fields, e.g. [34], were not excluded)
- Articles not written in English
- Publications before 1996
- Books, because they are likely to summarise existing research
- Grey literature, because of the repeatability of this research
- Articles which were not published in journals or conferences/workshops

Phd theses are included as they likely deal with new topics and have been, if accepted and published, peer reviewed. In total, 165 articles for further analysis were found. According to Petersen et al. [15], we did not look for further sources as a SMS is not merely intended to find all available literature, but rather achieve a good sample through different search engines and search terms.

3.3 Classification

The objective of the mapping process is to show both the kind of contribution and which kind of PLs are addressed while describing CI. Therefore, classification schemes for the type of contribution as well as PL are introduced in the following: To classify the contribution type of each article, different schemes have been proposed in literature. Among others [13], Wieringa et al. propose a classification scheme to divide in articles within contribution categories [17]. However, as shown by Wohlin et al. [19] and stated in [15], this classification scheme leads to different results within similar systematic studies. For this reasons we decided to develop new contribution types based on the key-wording approach in [13]. As shown in Table 2, five different kinds of contributions were found, which are a subset of the categories proposed by Mujtaba et al. [13]. To range the search results into the different categories, we slightly shortened the description and added possible keywords. An overview on the used keywords is given on our website[1].

Table 2. Contribution categories

P Category	Description
0 Towards	Verbal discussion of possible (future) solutions
1 Discussion	Verbal discussion without suggesting a direct solution
2 Approach	Definition of concrete steps for a solution
3 Tooling	Implementation of a concrete solution
4 Case Study	Evaluation through different real-world testing

---

[1] ICIST2016.c-brink.de.

Table 3. Product line categories

P Category	Description
0 No Change Impact (No CI)	No CI or evolution is addressed
1 Single Product (SP)	No PL concept is given but CI is addressed
2 Product Line (PL)	A PL with no further context is given
3 Software Product Line (SPL)	Software is explicitly addressed
4 Multi Product Line (MPL)	Several heterogeneous PLs are comprised
5 Product Families (PF)	Consideration of different system parts within a PL context

In our opinion it is easier to determine whether a publication belongs to a certain category when common keywords are suggested. An iterative key-wording approach to define those keyword is given in [14]. For example in the first iteration keywords like *Model* or *Compositional Approach* appeared, which were later combined to the category *Approach*. To make the mapping process as clear and reproducible as possible we further decided to rank the contribution categories via priorities (P). In case a article could be classified to more than one category, the category with the highest priority was chosen. Due to the fact that *Towards* focusses on verbal discussion of possible solutions, it has the lowest priority. In contrast, *Case Studies* have the highest priority as they likely prove the evidence of concrete approaches and are therefore promising literature to tackle research gaps.

In addition, a PL type is assigned to each article as a second dimension. As we are not aware of any established classification scheme for PLs, we used the key-wording approach to develop PL categories. After some iterations, we finally got five different categories, which have been mainly introduced in Sect. 1. Furthermore, articles that deal with CI but have none underlying PL concept were considered as *Single Products*. While conducting this SMS we observed that some publications do not address any kind of CI or evolution. Since our aim is to provide an overall map of the search results, we decided to add *No Change Impact* as a category for those articles (cf. Table 3). According to the contributions, PL categories are also prioritised: A PF has the highest priority as this category is likely to answer our RQs, whereas *No Change Impact* do not address any facet of change support and consequently has the lowest priority.

3.4 Mapping

Based on the keywords and classification scheme, each article was assigned to a contribution (Table 4) as well as product line (Table 5) category. Due to space limitations, references belonging to the categories *No Change Impact* or *Single Product*, which are not relevant to answer our RQs, have been omitted within this tables. The complete mapping can be found on our website (see Footnote 1).

To make sure that the given description for each category is matched by the article, two researchers independently of each other conducted the assignment.

In case of different matchings, another researcher has been consulted to solve the mismatch. The assignment of the articles into corresponding categories provides the base for a graphical map. In order to visualize the quantity of the publications we chose a bubble chart (cf. Fig. 2), whereby the axis are divided into categories in the order of their priorities. Within the map the x-axis shows the type of contribution while the y-axis reflects the kind of product line. Furthermore, the value in the bubbles represents the number of articles which belong to that point in the map. To emphasize the quantity, the size of every bubble is proportional to the number of articles. Due to lack of space some bubbles overlap other bubble. However, this does not indicate that they share common topics.

Table 4. Mapping into contribution categories

Type	Classified Articles	#
Towards	[66, 71, 78, 95]	4
Discussion	[36, 39, 43, 47, 48, 53, 57, 61, 76, 79, 81, 82, 88, 90, 91, 94, 98, 101]	18
Approach	[20, 21, 23–28, 30–32, 34, 37, 38, 40, 41, 44, 46, 49, 51, 55, 60, 62, 63, 65, 68–70, 73, 77, 80, 83, 85–87, 89, 92, 93, 99, 100, 103–108]	46
Tooling	[35, 42, 52, 58, 84, 102]	6
Case Study	[22, 29, 33, 45, 50, 54, 56, 59, 64, 67, 72, 74, 75, 96, 97]	15

To verify RQ2, a distribution graph based on the publication year of the articles is given in Fig. 3. All classified articles were used except those that were associated with the *Single Product* or *No Change Impact* category. This is due to the fact that this articles would otherwise bias the result, since they do not focus on the examined research area.

Furthermore, an overview of journal and conference distributions (cf. Table 6) is given to support the discussion of RQ3. Thereby, only results with at least three conference publications or journal articles were considered. Again, articles which are associated with the *Single Product* or *No Change Impact* category were excluded.

Table 5. Mapping into product line categories

Type	Classified Articles	#
PL	[22, 41, 46, 63, 68, 93, 99, 101, 105]	9
SPL	[21, 23–29, 31–40, 43–45, 47, 48, 50–61, 64–67, 69–92, 94, 96–98, 102–104, 106–108]	73
MPL	[49, 62, 95, 100]	4
PF	[20, 30, 42]	3

3.5   Further Analysis

To get a closer insight into which approaches consider CIA, we further analysed the seven articles of the category *Product Family* [20,30,42] and *Multi Product Line* [49,62,95,100] in more depth. This should answer whether PFs are addressed and if a contribution to CIA is made. For this purpose the articles were analysed regarding the following five aspects: (1) Is there a **description** of CI/evolution? (2) Is the **problem** of CIA **motivated**? (3) Is CI the **main focus** of the article? (4) Is an **analysis** approach described? (5) Are **hardware and software** considered?

[20] Ahmed and Myers describe the problem of CI as well as propagation in PFs with a focus on partitioning embedded systems. However, they do not directly focus on CIA nor describe an approach for CI in PFs.

[30] Bachmann et al. present a uniform representation of variation in a PF development process. Within their article they discuss changes in variation points of PLs, but do not focus on CIA. Despite the fact that they denote their approach as representation for PFs, they do not cover software and hardware together.

[42] Chen et al. describe a CIA approach for variant product design in a computer-aided design context. Thereby, they show how to analyse changes as well as their impact but they focus on the hardware/product and do not cover hardware and software. Furthermore, PFs are only described as a part of the related work.

[49] Dintzner et al. focus on CI in PL configurations. In their article they introduce an approach for feature CI propagation across feature models by using existing feature configurations. Although they do not cover hardware in conjunction with software, an analysis for SPLs is given.

[62] Hartmann and Trew present an approach for modelling MPLs. Even though their article contains the key-words *change* and *impact*, the focus of the article is neither CIA nor it addresses the problem. Further it does not describe hardware and software mutually.

[95] Schröter et al. propose a technique for combining different SPLs to one MPL by using interfaces for different levels of abstraction. This technique should form the basis for further analysis. Thereby they do neither focus on CIA nor consider hardware and software.

[100] Teixeira et al. propose refinement notions and compositionality properties in order to support modular evolution of MPLs. Therefore, they describe how to perform changes in a systematic manner, but not how to analyse CI. While their article is classified within the *Multi Product Line* category, it does not cover hardware and software jointly.

In summary, two articles [42,49] directly address CIA, while one of them also includes hardware aspects [42]. Furthermore, one publication [100] focuses on the evolution of MPLs, which is a highly related topic. Another article [20] describes the problem of CIA in more detail including hardware and software. Three others [30,62,95] only match the key-words or describe CI but not CIA.

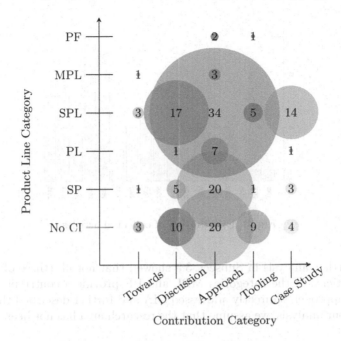

Fig. 2. Mapping of analysed articles

4 Discussion

While performing this SMS, we observed that the automated search using search engines provides a high number of false positives. Those were assigned to the categories *Single Product* (18.2 %) and *No Change Impact* (27.9 %) during the categorization. Furthermore, even after the categorization articles remained which were not relevant for answering the research questions, but contained the defined key-words. This could possibly be avoided by further key-words and more concrete search strings. Nevertheless this could also filter relevant publications.

RQ1: RQ1 addresses the question whether there are any publications, which combine a PL context with CIA. As shown in the bubble chart (cf. Fig. 2) there are articles which address both. However, the bubble chart indicates that articles which deal with MPLs or PFs in combination with CI are very rare, whereas the research field around SPLs is already well covered. Articles for SPLs (44.2 %) are more spread over the contribution categories than any other PL type. SPLs are generally the most common topic in each contribution category except *Tooling*. Only a few publications explicitly address MPLs (2.4 %) or PFs (1.8 %), but there are no case studies for PFs or MPLs. Three out of four MPL articles [49,62,100] were classified as *Approach*, while one MPL article [95] was classified as being *Towards* which is the least frequent category overall. The category *Product Line* was assigned to only a few articles (5.5 %). This could be related to the fact that this category was chosen only if it was unclear whether the approach address software, hardware or both.

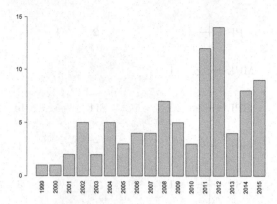

Fig. 3. Distribution of collected articles

Our further analysis in Subsect. 3.5 showed that not all (three of seven) discovered articles of the categories MPL and PF provide a contribution to CIA. Only two approaches directly addressed CIA and further described the problem. Based on our analysis, we assume that the research area has not been sufficiently covered yet.

RQ2: RQ2 asks whether CIA in a PL context is a trending topic. To answer that question we plotted a bar chart of all articles which were classified as MPL, PF, PL and SPL articles (cf. Fig. 3). As described in Subsect. 3.2, we used the publication references of [26, 46, 49, 78] to find further sources. From those articles only [26] and [49] were published in 2014 and 2015, while the other articles were published in 2011.

Due to the search methodology it is not possible to answer the question for the years after these publications were published without any doubt. Most articles with a MPL, PF or SPL context were published between 2011 and 2015. Nevertheless, only seven articles address MPL or PF [20, 30, 42, 49, 62, 95, 100]. An interesting aspect is the fact that three PF and MPL articles were published in 2015 [42, 49, 100]. The other articles were published 2008 and later, whereby [30] has been put out in 2004. This indicates that CI is a current and future research area, especially for a PF or MPL context. Since this mapping study was conducted in the end of 2015, it can be assumed that the number of publications in 2015 might be higher than indicated in this study.

RQ3: Another objective of this research was to find the most popular publication venues for articles regarding CIA in a PL context (*RQ3*). We figured out that a lot of publications were published within the *Software Product Line Conference* (SPLC) (22), *Conference on Software Engineering* (ICSE) (8) and *Journal of Systems and Software* (JSS) (5). Although SPLC and ICSE cover about 18 % of all articles, most of the articles were not submitted within those conference proceedings.

Nevertheless, three out of four articles that were classified as MPL articles were published in the SPLC proceedings [62, 95, 100] and one MPL article [49] appeared

Table 6. Journals and Conferences which appeared 3 times or more

Journal	#
Journal of Systems and Software (JSS)	5
Science of Computer Programming (SCP)	3
Conference	**#**
Int. Software Product Line Conf. (SPLC)	22
Int. Conf. on Software Engineering (ICSE)	8
Working IEEE/IFIP Conf. on Software Architecture (WICSA)	3

within the proceedings of *Int. Conference on Software Reuse*. In contrast, the contribution categories for PFs was comprised of mixed sources [20,30,42], while none of those articles were published at the SPLC. Approximately a quarter of all articles we found were journals, while the venues for CI within a PL context are mixed.

5   Conclusion

Within this paper we conducted an SMS to provide an overview of the current state of the research field for PLs in conjunction with CIA. Further we aim to answer our defined RQs. After applying exclusion criteria, 165 articles remained in our study for further analysis. Each article has been classified in a contribution and PL type to subsequently map them on a graphical map. It became clear that CIA for SPLs has been addressed by several articles, whereas MPLs as well as PFs in combination with CIA are not well covered yet. As shown in Subsect. 3.5, the consideration of hardware in CIA approaches constitutes a research gap. Regarding the year of publication, we further observed that CIA within a PL context is still a relevant research field, whereby in particular CIA for MPLs and PFs seems to be a future topic as most of the articles were published in 2015. The *Software Product Line Conference* is a common venue for publishing articles regarding this topic. Furthermore, the *International Conference on Software Engineering* and the *Journal of Systems and Software* are also quite popular.

Our future work will include a deeper analysis of the identified approaches regarding CIA. Here, all articles of the *PL, SPL, MPL* and *PF* categories will be considered with the objective to develop an approach which supports CIA in a PF context. Therefore, hardware as well as software variants have to be considered.

References

1. Amjad Alam, K., Binti Ahmad, R., Akhtar, M.: Change impact analysis and propagation in service based business process management systems preliminary results from a systematic review. In: 8th Malaysian Software Engineering Conference (2014)

2. Arnold, R.S.: Software Change Impact Analysis. IEEE Computer Society Press, Los Alamitos (1996)
3. Chen, L., Babar, M.A.: A systematic review of evaluation of variability management approaches in software product lines. Inf. Softw. Technol. **53**, 344–362 (2011)
4. Ferreira Bastos, J., Anselmo da Mota Silveira Neto, P., Santana de Almeida, E., Romero de Lemos Meira, S.: Adopting software product lines: a systematic mapping study. In: Conference on Evaluation Assessment in Software Engineering (2011)
5. Godfrey, M., German, D.: The past, present, and future of software evolution. In: Frontiers of Software Maintenance (2008)
6. Holl, G., Grünbacher, P., Rabiser, R.: A systematic review and an expert survey on capabilities supporting multi product lines. Inf. Softw. Technol. **54**, 828–852 (2012)
7. Kitchenham, B., Charters, S.: Guidelines for performing systematic literature reviews in software engineering. Technical report, Keele University and Durham University Joint Report (2007)
8. Laguna, M.A., Crespo, Y.: A systematic mapping study on software product line evolution: from legacy system reengineering to product line refactoring. Sci. Comput. Program. **78**, 1010–1034 (2013)
9. Lehnert, S.: A review of software change impact analysis. Technical report. Ilmenau University of Technology (2011)
10. Li, B., Sun, X., Leung, H., Zhang, S.: A survey of code-based change impact analysis techniques. Softw. Test. Verif. Reliab. **23**, 613–646 (2013)
11. Linden, F.J.v.d., Schmid, K., Rommes, E.: Software Product Lines in Action: The Best Industrial Practice in Product Line Engineering (2007)
12. Mockus, A., Votta, L.: Identifying reasons for software changes using historic databases. In: Proceedings of the International Conference on Software Maintenance (2000)
13. Mujtaba, S., Petersen, K., Feldt, R., Mattsson, M.: Software product line variability: a systematic mapping study. Blekinge Institute of Technology (2008)
14. Petersen, K., Feldt, R., Mujtaba, S., Mattsson, M.: Systematic mapping studies in software engineering. In: 12th International Conference on Evaluation and Assessment in Software Engineering (2008)
15. Petersen, K., Vakkalanka, S., Kuzniarz, L.: Guidelines for conducting systematic mapping studies in software engineering: an update. Inf. Softw. Technol. **64**, 1–18 (2015)
16. Pretschner, A., Broy, M., Kruger, I., Stauner, T.: Software engineering for automotive systems: a roadmap. In: Future of Software Engineering (2007)
17. Wieringa, R., Maiden, N.A.M., Mead, N.R., Rolland, C.: Requirements engineering paper classification and evaluation criteria: a proposal and a discussion. Requir. Eng. **11**, 102–107 (2006)
18. Wohlin, C.: Guidelines for snowballing in systematic literature studies and a replication in software engineering. In: Proceedings of the 18th International Conference on Evaluation and Assessment in Software Engineering (2014)
19. Wohlin, C., Runeson, P., da Mota Silveira Neto, P.A., Engström, E., do Carmo Machado, I., de Almeida, E.S.: On the reliability of mapping studies in software engineering. J. Syst. Softw. **86**, 2594–2610 (2013)

Study References

20. Ahmed, W., Myers, D.: Concept-based partitioning for large multidomain multifunctional embedded systems. ACM Trans. Design Autom. Electr. Syst. **15**(3), 22:1–22:41 (2010). doi:10.1145/1754405.1754407. article no 22

21. Ajila, S., Kaba, B.A.: Using traceability mechanisms to support software product line evolution. In: International Conference on Information Reuse and Integration (2004)

22. Ajila, S.A., Bailetti, A.J., Dumitrescu, R.T.: Experience report on software product line evolution due to market reposition. In: Proceedings of the Workshop on Quantitative Techniques for Software Agile Process (2004)

23. Ajila, S.A., Kaba, A.B.: Evolution support mechanisms for software product line process. J. Syst. Softw. **81**, 1784–1801 (2008)

24. Alves, V., Matos Jr., P., Cole, L., Borba, P., Ramalho, G.L.: Extracting and evolving mobile games product lines. In: Obbink, H., Pohl, K. (eds.) SPLC 2005. LNCS, vol. 3714, pp. 70–81. Springer, Heidelberg (2005)

25. Alves, V., Matos, P., Cole, L., Vasconcelos, A., Borba, P., Ramalho, G.: Extracting and evolving code in product lines with aspect-oriented programming. In: Rashid, A., Aksit, M. (eds.) Transactions on AOSD IV. LNCS, vol. 4640, pp. 117–142. Springer, Heidelberg (2007)

26. Angerer, F.: Variability-aware change impact analysis of multi-language product lines. In: ACM/IEEE International Conference on Automated Software Engineering (2014)

27. Angerer, F., Prähofer, H., Lettner, D., Grimmer, A., Grünbacher, P.: Identifying inactive code in product lines with configuration-aware system dependence graphs. In: 18th International Software Product Line Conference (2014)

28. Araújo, J., Goulão, M., Moreira, A., Simão, I., Amaral, V., Baniassad, E.L.A.: Advanced modularity for building SPL feature models: a model-driven approach. In: Proceedings of the 28th Annual ACM Symposium on Applied Computing (2013)

29. Babar, M.A., Ihme, T., Pikkarainen, M.: An industrial case of exploiting product line architectures in agile software development. In: Proceedings of the 13th International Conference on Software Product Lines (2009)

30. Bachmann, F., Goedicke, M., Leite, J.C.S.P., Nord, R.L., Pohl, K., Ramesh, B., Vilbig, A.: A meta-model for representing variability in product family development. In: van der Linden, F.J. (ed.) PFE 2003. LNCS, vol. 3014, pp. 66–80. Springer, Heidelberg (2004)

31. Baresi, L., Quinton, C.: Dynamically evolving the structural variability of dynamic software product lines. In: 10th IEEE/ACM International Symposium on Software Engineering for Adaptive and Self-Managing Systems (2015)

32. Batista, T.V., Bastarrica, M.C., Soares, S., da Silva, L.F.: A marriage of MDD and early aspects in software product line development. In: Proceedings of the 12th International Conference on Software Product Lines (2008)

33. Batory, D.S., Johnson, C., MacDonald, B., von Heeder, D.: Achieving extensibility through product-lines and domain-specific languages: a case study. ACM Trans. Softw. Eng. Methodol. **11**, 191–214 (2002)

34. Benlarabi, A., Khtira, A., Asri, B.E.: Analyzing trends in software product lines evolution using a cladistics based approach. Information **6**, 550–563 (2015)

35. Beuche, D., Papajewski, H., Schröder-Preikschat, W.: Variability management with feature models. Sci. Comput. Program. **53**, 333–352 (2004)

36. Dannenberg, R.B., Ran, A.: Evolution of software product families. In: van der Linden, F.J. (ed.) IW-SAPF 2000. LNCS, vol. 1951, p. 168. Springer, Heidelberg (2000)
37. Cafeo, B.B.P., Dantas, F., Gurgel, A.C., Guimarães, E.T., Cirilo, E., Garcia, A.F., de Lucena, C.J.P.: Analysing the impact of feature dependency implementation on product line stability: an exploratory study. In: 26th Brazilian Symposium on Software Engineering (2012)
38. Carbon, R., Lindvall, M., Muthig, D., Costa, P.: Integrating product line engineering and agile methods: flexible design up-front vs. incremental design. In: 1st International Workshop on Agile Product Line Engineering (2006)
39. Catal, C.: Barriers to the adoption of software product line engineering. ACM SIGSOFT Softw. Eng. Notes **34**, 1–4 (2009)
40. Cavalcante, E., Almeida, A., Batista, T.V., Cacho, N., Lopes, F., Delicato, F.C., Sena, T.S., Pires, P.F.: Exploiting software product lines to develop cloud computing applications. In: 16th International Software Product Line Conference (2012)
41. Chen, C., Chen, P.: A holistic approach to managing software change impact. J. Syst. Softw. **82**, 2051–2067 (2009)
42. Chen, C., Liao, G., Lin, K.: An attribute-based and object-oriented approach with system implementation for change impact analysis in variant product design. Comput. Aided Des. **62**, 203–217 (2015)
43. Corrêa, C.K.F., de Oliveira, T.C., Werner, C.M.L.: An analysis of change operations to achieve consistency in model-driven software product lines. In: Workshop Proceedings of the 15th International Conference on Software Product Lines (2011)
44. Czarnecki, K., Helsen, S., Eisenecker, U.W.: Staged configuration through specialization and multilevel configuration of feature models. Softw. Process: Improv. Pract. **10**, 143–169 (2005)
45. Díaz, J., Pérez, J., Garbajosa, J.: Agile product-line architecting in practice: A case study in smart grids. Inf. Softw. Technol. **56**(7), 727–748 (2014). Elsevier
46. Díaz, J., Pérez, J., Garbajosa, J., Wolf, A.L.: Change impact analysis in product-line architectures. In: Crnkovic, I., Gruhn, V., Book, M. (eds.) ECSA 2011. LNCS, vol. 6903, pp. 114–129. Springer, Heidelberg (2011)
47. Díaz Fernández, J., Pérez Benedí, J., Yagüe Panadero, A., Garbajosa Sopeña, J.: Tailoring the scrum development process to address agile product line engineering. In: XVI Jornadas de Ingeniería del Software y base de Datos, JISBD (2011)
48. Dintzner, N.: Safe evolution patterns for software product lines. In: 37th IEEE/ACM International Conference on Software Engineering (2015)
49. Dintzner, N., Kulesza, U., van Deursen, A., Pinzger, M.: Evaluating feature change impact on multi-product line configurations using partial information. In: Proceedings of the 14th International Conference on Software Reuse, Software Reuse for Dynamic Systems in the Cloud and Beyond (2015)
50. Dyer, R., Rajan, H., Cai, Y.: An exploratory study of the design impact of language features for aspect-oriented interfaces. In: Proceedings of the 11th International Conference on Aspect-oriented Software Development (2012)
51. Fernández, J.D.: Agile construction and evolution of product-line architectures. Ph.D. thesis, Technical University of Madrid (2012)
52. Ferreira, F., Borba, P., Soares, G., Gheyi, R.: Making software product line evolution safer. In: 6th Brazilian Symposium on Software Components (2012)
53. Ferreira, G.C.S., Gaia, F.N., Figueiredo, E., de Almeida Maia, M.: A comparative study on the use of feature-oriented programming for evolving software product lines. Sci. Comput. Program. **93**, 65–85 (2014)

54. Figueiredo, E., Cacho, N., Sant'Anna, C., Monteiro, M., Kulesza, U., Garcia, A., Soares, S., Ferrari, F.C., Khan, S.S., Filho, F.C., Dantas, F.: Evolving software product lines with aspects: an empirical study on design stability. In: 30th International Conference on Software Engineering (2008)

55. Gaia, F.N., Ferreira, G.C.S., Figueiredo, E., de Almeida Maia, M.: A quantitative assessment of aspectual feature modules for evolving software product lines. In: de Carvalho, F.H., Barbosa, L.S. (eds.) SBLP 2012. LNCS, vol. 7554, pp. 134–149. Springer, Heidelberg (2012)

56. Gaia, F.N., Ferreira, G.C.S., Figueiredo, E., de Almeida Maia, M.: A quantitative and qualitative assessment of aspectual feature modules for evolving software product lines. Sci. Comput. Program **96**, 230–253 (2014)

57. Ganesan, D., Lindvall, M., Ackermann, C., McComas, D., Bartholomew, M.: Verifying architectural design rules of the flight software product line. In: Proceedings of the 13th International Conference on Software Product Lines (2009)

58. Garg, A., Critchlow, M., Chen, P., van der Westhuizen, C., vander Hoek, A.: An environment for managing evolving product line architectures. In: 19th International Conference on Software Maintenance, The Architecture of Existing Systems (2003)

59. Ghanam, Y., Andreychuk, D., Maurer, F.: Reactive variability management in agile software development. In: Agile Conference (2010)

60. Ghanam, Y., Maurer, F.: An iterative model for agile product line engineering. In: Proceedings of the 12th International Conference on Software Product Lines (2008)

61. Hanssen, G.K., Fægri, T.E.: Process fusion: an industrial case study on agile software product line engineering. J. Syst. Softw. **81**, 843–854 (2008)

62. Hartmann, H., Trew, T.: Using feature diagrams with context variability to model multiple product lines for software supply chains. In: Proceedings of the 12th International Conference on Software Product Lines (2008)

63. Heider, W., Rabiser, R., Grünbacher, P., Lettner, D.: Using regression testing to analyze the impact of changes to variability models on products. In: 16th International Software Product Line Conference (2012)

64. Heider, W., Vierhauser, M., Lettner, D., Grünbacher, P.: A case study on the evolution of a component-based product line. In: Joint Working IEEE/IFIP Conference on Software Architecture and European Conference on Software Architecture (2012)

65. Hendrickson, S.A., van der Hoek, A.: Modeling product line architectures through change sets and relationships. In: 29th International Conference on Software Engineering (2007)

66. Holdschick, H.: Challenges in the evolution of model-based software product lines in the automotive domain. In: 4th International Workshop on Feature-Oriented Software Development (2012)

67. Jaring, M., Dannenberg, R.B.: Representing variability in software product lines: a case study. In: Chastek, G.J. (ed.) SPLC 2002. LNCS, vol. 2379, p. 15. Springer, Heidelberg (2002)

68. Jaring, M., Krikhaar, R.L., Bosch, J.: Representing variability in a family of MRI scanners. Softw. Pract. Exper **34**, 69–100 (2004)

69. Käßmeyer, M., Schulze, M., Schurius, M.: A process to support a systematic change impact analysis of variability and safety in automotive functions. In: Proceedings of the 19th International Conference on Software Product Line (2015)

70. Khtira, A., Benlarabi, A., Asri, B.E.: Duplication detection when evolving feature models of software product lines. Information **6**, 592–612 (2015)

71. Kircher, M., Schwanninger, C., Groher, I.: Transitioning to a software product family approach - challenges and best practices. In: Proceedings of the 10th International Conference on Software Product Lines (2006)
72. Krishnan, S., Lutz, R.R., Goseva-Popstojanova, K.: Empirical evaluation of reliability improvement in an evolving software product line. In: Proceedings of the 8th International Working Conference on Mining Software Repositories (2011)
73. Lee, K., Kang, K.C., Kim, M., Park, S.: Combining feature-oriented analysis and aspect-oriented programming for product line asset development. In: Proceedings of the 10th International Conference on Software Product Lines (2006)
74. Lettner, D., Angerer, F., Grünbacher, P., Prähofer, H.: Software evolution in an industrial automation ecosystem: an exploratory study. In: 40th EUROMICRO Conference on Software Engineering and Advanced Applications (2014)
75. Lettner, D., Angerer, F., Prähofer, H., Grünbacher, P.: A case study on software ecosystem characteristics in industrial automation software. In: International Conference on Software and Systems Process (2014)
76. Livengood, S.: Issues in software product line evolution: complex changes in variability models. In: Proceedings of the 2nd International Workshop on Product Line Approaches in Software Engineering (2011)
77. McGregor, J.D., Monteith, J.Y., Zhang, J.: Quantifying value in software product line design. In: Workshop Proceedings of the International Conference on Software Product Lines (2011)
78. Michalik, B., Weyns, D.: Towards a solution for change impact analysis of software product line products. In: 9th Working Conference on Software Architecture (2011)
79. Michalik, B., Weyns, D., Betsbrugge, W.V.: On the problems with evolving egemin's software product line. In: Proceedings of the 2nd International Workshop on Product Line Approaches in Software Engineering (2011)
80. Millo, J., Ramesh, S., Krishna, S.N., Narwane, G.K.: Compositional verification of evolving software product lines. CoRR (2012)
81. Mohan, K., Ramesh, B.: Managing variability with traceability in product and service families. In: Proceedings of the 35th Hawaii International Conference on System Sciences (2002)
82. Mohan, K., Ramesh, B., Sugumaran, V.: Integrating software product line engineering and agile development. IEEE Softw. **27**, 48–55 (2010)
83. Moon, M., Chae, H.S., Nam, T., Yeom, K.: A metamodeling approach to tracing variability between requirements and architecture in software product lines. In: 7th International Conference on Computer and Information Technology (2007)
84. Murashkin, A., Antkiewicz, M., Rayside, D., Czarnecki, K.: Visualization and exploration of optimal variants in product line engineering. In: 17th International Software Product Line Conference (2013)
85. Neves, L., Teixeira, L., Sena, D., Alves, V., Kulesza, U., Borba, P.: Investigating the safe evolution of software product lines. In: Proceedings of the 10th International Conference on Generative Programming and Component Engineering (2011)
86. de Oliveira, T.H.B., Becker, M., Nakagawa, E.Y.: Supporting the analysis of bug prevalence in software product lines with product genealogy. In: 16th International Software Product Line Conference (2012)
87. Paskevicius, P., Damasevicius, R., Štuikys, V.: Change impact analysis of feature models. In: Skersys, T., Butleris, R., Butkiene, R. (eds.) ICIST 2012. CCIS, vol. 319, pp. 108–122. Springer, Heidelberg (2012)

88. Passos, L.T., Czarnecki, K., Apel, S., Wasowski, A., Kästner, C., Guo, J.: Feature-oriented software evolution. In: The 7th International Workshop on Variability Modelling of Software-intensive Systems (2013)
89. Pohl, K., Brandenburg, M., Gülich, A.: Integrating requirement and architecture information: a scenario and meta-model approach. In: Proceedings of the 7th International Workshop on Requirements Engineering (2001)
90. Quinton, C., Rabiser, R., Vierhauser, M., Grünbacher, P., Baresi, L.: Evolution in dynamic software product lines: challenges and perspectives. In: Proceedings of the 19th International Conference on Software Product Line (2015)
91. Riebisch, M., Philippow, I.: Evolution of product lines using traceability. In: Workshop on Engineering Complex Object-Oriented Systems for Evolution (2001)
92. Sabouri, H., Khosravi, R.: Efficient verification of evolving software product lines. Revised Selected Papers of the 4th IPM International Conference on Fundamentals of Software Engineering (2011)
93. Scheidemann, K.D.: Optimizing the selection of representative configurations in verification of evolving product lines of distributed embedded systems. In: Proceedings of the 10th International Conference on Software Product Lines (2006)
94. Schmid, K., Verlage, M.: The economic impact of product line adoption and evolution. IEEE Softw. 19, 50–57 (2002)
95. Schröter, R., Siegmund, N., Thüm, T.: Towards modular analysis of multi product lines. In: 17th International Software Product Line Conference co-located workshops (2013)
96. Sinnema, M., Deelstra, S.: Industrial validation of COVAMOF. J. Syst. Softw. 81, 584–600 (2008)
97. Svahnberg, M., Bosch, J.: Characterizing evolution in product line architectures. In: Proceedings of the International Conference on Software Engineering and Applications (1999)
98. Svahnberg, M., van Gurp, J., Bosch, J.: A taxonomy of variability realization techniques. Softw. Pract. Exper. 35, 705–754 (2005)
99. Taborda, L.J.M.: Planning and managing product line evolution. Revised Papers of the 5th International Workshop on Software Product-Family Engineering (2003)
100. Teixeira, L., Borba, P., Gheyi, R.: Safe evolution of product populations and multi product lines. In: Proceedings of the 19th International Conference on Software Product Line (2015)
101. Tesanovic, A.: Evolving embedded product lines: opportunities for aspects. In: Proceedings of the 6th workshop on Aspects, Components, and Patterns for Infrastructure Software (2007)
102. Thao, C., Munson, E.V.: Flexible support for managing evolving software product lines. In: Proceedings of the 2nd International Workshop on Product Line Approaches in Software Engineering (2011)
103. Thüm, T., Batory, D.S., Kästner, C.: Reasoning about edits to feature models. In: 31st International Conference on Software Engineering (2009)
104. Vianna, A., Pinto, F., Sena, D., Kulesza, U., Coelho, R., Santos, J., Lima, J., Lima, G.: Squid: an extensible infrastructure for analyzing software product line implementations. In: 16th International Software Product Line Conference (2012)
105. Wall, A., Larsson, M., Norström, C.: Towards an impact analysis for component based real-time product line architectures. In: 28th EUROMICRO Conference (2002)

106. Weyns, D., Michalik, B., Helleboogh, A., Boucké, N.: An architectural approach to support online updates of software product lines. In: 9th Working IEEE/IFIP Conference on Software Architecture (2011)
107. White, J., Galindo, J.A., Saxena, T., Dougherty, B., Benavides, D., Schmidt, D.C.: Evolving feature model configurations in software product lines. J. Syst. Softw. **87**, 119–136 (2014)
108. Yazdanshenas, A.R., Moonen, L.: Fine-grained change impact analysis for component-based product families. In: International Conference on Software Maintenance (2012)

Enhancing City Transportation Services Using Cloud Support

Andrea Fornaia, Christian Napoli[(✉)], Giuseppe Pappalardo, and Emiliano Tramontana

Department of Mathematics and Informatics, University of Catania,
Viale Andrea Doria 6, 95125 Catania, Italy
{fornaia, napoli, pappalardo, tramontana}@dmi.unict.it

Abstract. Smart cities will provide enhanced monitoring of crucial infrastructure resources, connectivity to users and advanced information services. Thanks to gathered data the quality of traditional services and infrastructures will be improved, and further services can emerge, such as novel urban transportation services. This paper devises a solution that enforces the cooperation between mobile devices and cloud infrastructures with the aim to bring public transportation where the people need it. Thanks to smart phones, sensing user locations, a request for transportation vehicles can be sent to a cloud-based intelligence, which filters and serves requests according to available transport routes, and their adaptation to user needs. Then, the available transportation vehicles will be timely alerted to operate accordingly.

Keywords: Cloud computing · Mobile users · Workflow · Monitoring · Intelligent assistive services · Smart cities

1 Introduction

We are observing a growing interest in the area of Smart Cities and services providing citizens with means to better organise daily life, and Smart Mobility is one of the most promising topics concerning future city environments (Benevolo et al. 2016). The ultimate goal is providing enhanced urban services, by means of information technology, to obtain a positive impact on the quality of life in urban areas. Major efforts will be devoted to the monitoring of critical infrastructures, the interconnection of physical and social infrastructures, as well as supports to assist physical infrastructures and, of course, citizens (Batty et al. 2012; Chourabi et al. 2012). This paper analyses the scenario of public transportation in urban areas and provides a solution to organise the flow of publicly accessed vehicles according to user requests, i.e. on-demand. Moreover, connectivity to users is enhanced according to the monitored transportation needs. Surely, the communication infrastructure is crucial to ensure the right timing in the planning of routes for the vehicles. The devised solution paves the way for future autonomous unmanned vehicles.

In such a scenario, a user request for a service aiming to find or bring a vehicle closer to her/him has to be taken into account by a defined *workflow*, i.e. a standard flow of execution for the activities related to the offered service (Fornaia et al. 2015).

© Springer International Publishing Switzerland 2016
G. Dregvaite and R. Damasevicius (Eds.): ICIST 2016, CCIS 639, pp. 695–708, 2016.
DOI: 10.1007/978-3-319-46254-7_56

This means executing on the server-side the needed checks for the request at hand, finding the available vehicles, planning the appropriate route for the vehicle, and alerting the requesting users, vehicles and passengers for the adaptation. Of course, route changes will take place only when disruption is minimal, i.e. the other planned stops are satisfied as well as the timing constraints. In a smart environment, such a workflow takes advantage of cloud computing resources and an appropriate processing engine (Erl 2008; Wozniak et al. 2015).

By resorting to cloud-computing, transparent access e.g. to shared services, hardware and data is made possible, thus enabling a high level of *availability* and possibly performances. However, a cloud-based infrastructure can bring about delays for the virtual machine (VM) to be started, services to be allocated, etc. Primary goals for enterprises handling the said urban scenario of on-demand vehicles include: (i) having the minimum amount of disruption to paths of running vehicles, (ii) providing scalability to handle a variable number of requests with high availability, and (iii) minimise the potential delays.

The rest of this paper is structured as follows. Section 2 describes the smart city scenario that we have tackled. Section 3 describes the proposed software components that automatically provide workflow management, and enhance services with monitoring and dependability. Section 4 introduces our strategy for the prediction of transport needs. Section 5 discusses the related work, and Sect. 6 draws our conclusions.

2   Analysed Smart City Transportation Scenario

The proposed novel transport service would be an enhanced bus service, for which seats can be reserved, and the a priori established course can be slightly changed according to user requests and to other configurable settings. Such a bus service would allow citizens to cooperate with the institutions to make the urban transportation properly function, hence users would need to communicate their position and the desired destination for the bus service, as well as the useful timeframe for pick up. The services on a cloud computing system will then reply with a travel solution that satisfies user requests, indicating the best *rendezvous point* for the user to catch the bus.

In our model, a rendezvous point is a possible bus stop, one among many known by the transport operator, that is activated *on-demand* according to actual user requests, hence avoiding the need to serve bus stops when not strictly required, optimising vehicles travel cycles, and reducing energy consumption and CO2 emissions.

Figure 1 shows three possible routes connecting the Itako and Bando cities of the Ibaraki Prefecture, in the Japanese region of Kanto. By sensing actual user requests, the transport operator can determine in advance which of the six potential rendezvous points depicted (two for Bando and one for each of the other cities) will be served, hence planning the course to follow. User requests are gathered before the bus starts going and during its journey, then a server-side component would notify the bus drivers when it would be possible for the bus to change the route in order to serve requested rendezvous points.

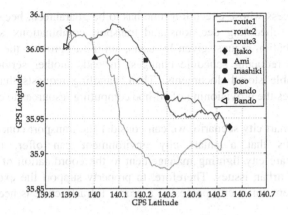

Fig. 1. Adapting routes in a transportation scenario

Choosing the right rendezvous points to satisfy user requests is an important concern: the server-side planning component has to properly manage the trade off between selecting the one nearest to the requesting user and modifying the established bus schedule (even on-the-fly). In Sect. 4 we will see how this schedule management can be assisted by an intelligent system able to predict future transport service requests in a given location.

The proposed solution goes beyond the urban transport scenario, i.e. other smart facilities can take advantage of the said data. The number of citizens wishing to use a transport service would be known for many locations while time goes on during the day. Then, a possible strategy, which can benefit mobile service providers, such as telco operators, is to take advantage of data representing user locations to estimate the mobile cell occupancy and operate needed counteractions.

Figure 2 shows an example of a simplified workflow, dubbed urban on-demand transportation, whereby citizens are able to actively request means of transportation to pass by a suggested place, in a given time-frame, as needed. On the server-side, once a user request has been received, a workflow is available to execute several services (activities), each corresponding to a step that has to be performed. In our reference model for the software system assisting such steps we will have one or more client applications enabling the user to submit a request, and wait for a reply. Hence, e.g. the ask transport vehicle step could be performed using a dedicated smartphone app that lets the user send detailed data such as: GPS position, desired time-frame for pick up, number of passengers.

Services on the server side are processes running, or started, according to the indication given by the workflow description, hence e.g. receive requests is the first step of an ad-hoc workflow, and is a process listening for incoming requests, residing inside a persistent web service, and compute travel solutions is a process started as a second step of the workflow once the previous step has been performed, etc. Since each service needed for a workflow completion in general can have its own preconditions, data and processing requirements, then each service should be handled ad-hoc to provide a proper quality of service. Let us suppose that compute travel solutions is a

CPU-bound process whose execution time has to be guaranteed, because, e.g. it could involve several scheduling decisions and transport combinations, starting from the temporal and location request given by users, aiming to provide the best solution for the users while reducing schedule changes. Instead, another service could simply provide immutable stored documents. Then, handling requests that trigger service execution requires the provisioning of ad-hoc computing resources to ensure the quality of service.

In a wider smart city scenario, we can consider the transport concern as one of the possible services that a smart city environment can offer, ranging from a consumption-aware city lighting management to the coordination of rescue interventions in case of urban issues. Therefore, to properly support the execution and integration of different smart city processes a proper infrastructure is needed.

3   Workflow Management System

A smart city process can be formalised by means of a workflow description and given to a workflow engine that timely starts the composing services in the desired order (Erl 2008; Polap et al. 2015) over a cloud infrastructure. Deploying and executing workflows on a cloud calls for a software architecture providing support for deploying, executing, and monitoring services, while minimising resource waste and standard delays affecting operations typical of this infrastructure (i.e. VM instantiations).

In the scenario depicted above (see Fig. 2), each workflow activity needs a dedicated description to allow proper resource allocations inside the cloud. Table 1 provides each activity with such additional data.

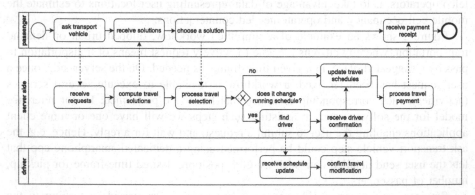

Fig. 2. An example of workflow urban on-demand transportation on a distributed system

In our solution, new workflow instances are started by a request coming from a Web Service (see the following section) and then a Workflow Scheduler finds the related workflow description and prepares resources for the execution of the first workflow activity, e.g. compute travel solutions, starting a dedicated VM with large hardware *flavor* configuration, where a flavour is a set of hardware characteristics for a

Table 1. Characterisation of server side activities for the urban on-demand transportation workflow for cloud resource management

Activity name	Start, end status	Resource type
Receive requests	On, on	No cloud
Compute travel solutions	Off, off	Dedicated, large VM
Process travel selection	Off, off	Dedicated, medium VM
Find driver	Standby, standby	Shared, small VM
Receive driver confirm	Standby, standby	Shared, small VM
Update travel schedules	Standby, standby	Shared, medium VM
Process travel payment	Off, off	Dedicated, medium VM

VM (Jackson 2012). Table 1 shows that each activity is characterised by a start and an end status, together with a description of the cloud resource type: the start status of a service environment (VM), such as already active, waiting for new process submissions (on); to be created and then turned on (off); in a standby state, reducing resource consumption and response time by avoiding the creation of a VM. If we specify that dedicated resources are needed, we will assign a separate VM for task execution, while for shared resources (useful e.g. to handle simple tasks like querying or updating a database or retrieving a document from the object storage) we run a process inside a shared VM. Web applications waiting for user requests (receive requests), and then triggering an actual workflow instantiation are not executed on a cloud.

3.1 Software Infrastructure

In order to support the features outlined above, we propose appropriate software components that enhance services and provide: (i) monitoring of workflow services, (ii) resource management, (iii) high availability.

Figure 3 shows how some of our components cooperate. Workflow Scheduler collects the user requests, determining whether to promptly accept them or not, according to the infrastructure load state. As any other scheduler, it manages a list of pending requests, using priority policies to determine their order, and interacts with other three components: User Manager, Resource Manager and Workflow Repository.

User Manager is responsible for the *AAA* service (Authentication, Authorisation, Accounting) related to user requests and will be asked to check user privileges and roles. Together with the number of requests previously accepted and completed for this user, it determines whether to lower the request priority. Resource Manager provides a high level representation of cloud resource states, holds the scheduling outcomes, and let us know whether a given resource is available in a certain time frame. Workflow Manager handles the descriptions of the workflow recorded inside the Workflow Repository, and is responsible for workflow instantiation and the monitoring of the completion of each inner activity for the requested workflow. It interacts with the Cloud Manager to ask for the execution on the cloud of the services implementing each activity.

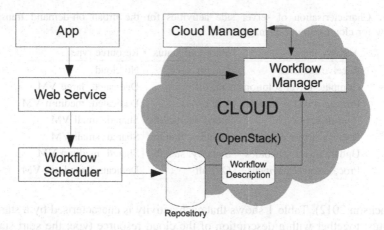

Fig. 3. Client requests served by a web server and a cloud-server

Cloud Manager is a *Facade* for cloud resources, hence providing the means for executing services inside the cloud infrastructure, which is actually managed by a cloud middleware, such as e.g. OpenStack[1]. A `Monitoring Service` gathers data on the completion time of each activity, then accounting information associated with the requesting user will be updated.

3.2   Flow of Operations and Use Case

Figure 3 shows the interactions between the components of the workflow management system for the completion of a workflow execution request. Using, for example, a web interface, the user can submit (either explicitly or not) an instantiation request of a specified workflow registered inside the management system.

This request arrives to `Workflow Scheduler`, that using the information coming from `User Manager` and `Resource Manager` determines whether to accept or reject the workflow execution request. It will then ask the `Workflow Repository` for the description of the requested workflow, providing the required services, resources and the estimated completion time for each of the inner activity. `Workflow Manager` will actually receive the instantiation request of a specified workflow, and starting from the first activity it will be responsible for monitoring the execution state of each activity within the workflow. `Workflow Manager` interacts with the `Cloud Manager` to request the instantiation of the cloud services needed by the current activity, according to the workflow description. We *contextualize* the new VM by loading a text file containing the activity information to which the VM is related to. The most important information required is the *activityID*, that the VM uses to notify the activity completion to `Workflow Manager`, as depicted in Fig. 3. In this way, `Workflow Manager` is informed on the termination of a specific activity of the

---

[1] www.openstack.org.

workflow, and can proceed with the destruction of the dedicated VM (because end state = off), asking also Cloud Manager to delete it. The Workflow Manager can then pass to the next activity described inside the workflow, and so on, until the workflow ends.

4 The WRNN Transport Request Predictor

The proposed management system takes care of the smart urban transport services in terms of number of passengers requesting the service in a certain location or rendezvous point in order to perfect seats allocation strategies and bus routes. In this section we present a module, called Requests Predictor, aiming at predicting the future load of the proposed services in terms of *number of passenger requests in a certain location*. Therefore, the number of requests to be serviced in the future can be easily computed. Prediction is based on the time series of requests, that can be observed and collected by the said management system during workflow execution. By considering the future expected load a fine-tuned management of human and transport resources can be achieved, hence avoiding both over provisioning and overloading.

Without a prediction system, resources are usually managed by considering average values which can be computed over wide-ranging sets, hence are not appropriate for ensuring high quality of the service (Wozniak et al. 2016; Nowicki et al. 2016).

Generally, the benefits of such strategies decrease with the load increase. Moreover, when the amount of passengers overcomes available vehicles, passengers remain unserviced or suffer delays. However, since the amount of required resources (e.g. drivers, vehicles, rendezvous points, etc.) is unknown in advance, this often causes over-provisioning, with negative effects on management and the related cost.

Our experience in the field of neural networks points us towards a novel neural architecture called Wavelet Recurrent Neural Network (WRNN) (Napoli et al. 2014; Napoli et al. 2015). This architecture makes use of the wavelet analysis of a recurrent neural network topology. It has been shown that WRNNs are able to both predict the future evolution of a time series and perform the inverse wavelet transform in a similar way with respect to the Second Generation Wavelet Transform. A WRNN is the basis of our proposed Request Predictor (Napoli et al. 2016). This component predicts over time the amount of incoming passengers and therefore the service workload. The predictions are then used by the management system to allocate vehicles, drivers or other resources.

The predictor is used to model the number of incoming service requests in terms of number of passengers in a certain rendezvous point, and on the other hand it can be used to estimate when the transport will be available to service new passengers. Moreover, the module here presented is able to specialise a neural network to make predictions related to each rendezvous point (see Fig. 4). By specialising a neural network for each point it is possible to obtain a set of predictions that precisely map the status of the smart city-oriented transport services. Doing so it is then possible to provide the system manager with an early alert regarding the occupancy and urgency of several transport lines in order to better schedule and plan the service, allocate new

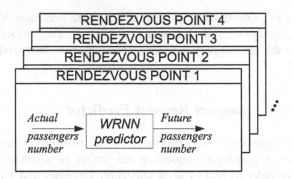

Fig. 4. The adopted WRNN predictor models and predicts the future trends regarding the number of passenger waiting on a rendezvous point. A predictor is specialised for one rendezvous point, hence a set of predictors is used.

vehicles, recall available drivers in service, as well as free resources when unneeded. The WRNN predictor operates with the time series indicating the passenger number at each rendezvous point over time. Firstly, the WRNN predictor transforms the time series in the wavelet domain.

The wavelet transform permits us to reduce data redundancies and obtain a representation that can express the intrinsic structure far more precisely than traditional analysis methods (e.g. Fourier transform). While the wavelet analysis exposes the time-frequency signature of the time series on different scales, the WRNN topology is the perfect complement to model the complexity of non-linear data correlation and perform data prediction on different scales. Thereby, a relatively accurate forecast of the passenger number can be achieved even when load peaks arise. The estimated result is fundamental for a management service that performs human and mechanical resources pre-allocation. The precision of our estimates allows just the right amount of resources to be used avoiding over provisioning. More details on WRNN architecture can be found in (Bonanno et al. 2012; Capizzi et al. 2012; Napoli et al. 2016).

In this paper, we have adopted the Biorthogonal wavelet decomposition (this kind of wavelet family is fully described in (Mallat 2009)), for which symmetrical decomposition and exact reconstruction are possible with finite impulse response (FIR) filters (Rabiner and Gold 1975). The transformed data are fed to the WRNN (see (Williams 1989; Mandic and Chambers 2001)).

The proposed WRNN consists of a Recurrent Neural Network architecture an input layer of 7 neurons, two hidden layers of 8 neurons with a radial basis activation function, a linear output layer with one linear neuron, and two delayed input units as well as two delayed feedback units from the output (see Fig. 5). The neural network is fed with the data constituted by time steps of a time series in the wavelet domain (Napoli et al. 2010; Bonanno et al. 2014a, b) representing the number of passengers requesting a transport services in a given location. Using a discrete time index τ we can call $q^{\mu}(\tau)$ the number of passengers at a time τ for a certain rendezvous point μ. By applying the wavelet transform to the time series $q^{\mu}(\tau)$ we obtain the related representation in the wavelet space.

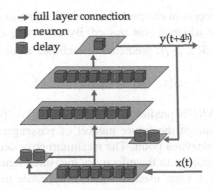

Fig. 5. Devised neural network. Delays and feedback are obtained by using the relative delay lines and operators (D).

$$q^{\mu}(\tau) \xrightarrow{\hat{W}} \left[q^{\mu}_{a_6}(\tau), q^{\mu}_{d_6}(\tau), q^{\mu}_{d_5}(\tau), q^{\mu}_{d_4}(\tau), q^{\mu}_{d_3}(\tau), q^{\mu}_{d_2}(\tau), q^{\mu}_{d_1}(\tau) \right] \tag{1}$$

Since we have used a 5 level transform, we have defined $q^{\mu}(\tau)$ as shown in Eq. 1, where the arrow represent the transform operation, $\hat{W}$ represents the biorthogonal wavelet decomposition and the resulting vectors have the component values on the different decomposition scales (from scale 1 to scale 6, where the letter d indicates the wavelet coefficients and a_6 the residuals on the most gross scale).

For reasons related to the noise signature we were not interested in the last component of the transformed series, therefore we had an input vector $x^{\mu}(\tau)$ in the form shown in Eq. 2.

$$x^{\mu}(\tau) = \left[q^{\mu}_{a_6}(\tau), q^{\mu}_{d_6}(\tau), q^{\mu}_{d_5}(\tau), q^{\mu}_{d_4}(\tau), q^{\mu}_{d_3}(\tau), q^{\mu}_{d_2}(\tau), q^{\mu}_{d_1}(\tau) \right] \tag{2}$$

The overall input set, considering N time steps, can be then represented as a $N \times 7$ matrix where the i-th row represents the i-th time step. Each row of this dataset is given as input value to the 7 input neurons of the proposed WRNN. The properties of this network make it possible, starting from an input at a time step τ_n, to predict the number of requests and throughput at a time step $\tau_n + \sigma$.

$$\tilde{x}^{\mu}(\tau_{n+\sigma}) = \hat{N}_{\mu}[x^{\mu}(\tau_n)] \tag{3}$$

In this way, the WRNN acts like a function $\hat{N}_{\mu}$ as defined by Eq. 3, where σ is the number of time steps of forecast in the future, and the tilde on the symbol $\hat{x}$ indicates that it is a prediction instead of a measurement. The number σ is not specified in the equation since it depends on the sampling frequency of the input and output time series. In our work, the data had a sampling period of 10 min, while we predicted the number of passengers 4 h ahead, therefore with $\sigma = 24$. To model the time series and then to predict their future evolution the neural network is firstly trained with the historical time series, several training epochs are interleaved with the related supervised pruning procedure. When the process in concluded, a network starts to provide forecasts related to a specific service for which it was trained. By collecting each service forecast we obtain a complete map $\tilde{S}(\tau_{n+24})$, predicted beforehand, as defined by Eq. 4.

$$\tilde{S}(\tau_{n+24}) = \{\tilde{x}^\mu(\tau_{n+24}) \forall \mu\}. \tag{4}$$

The results of the WRNN predictor are shown in Fig. 6. The predictor was able to propose an early estimate of the future number of passengers requesting a transport services in a certain rendezvous point. The maximum error occurring in the prediction is two passengers with respect to the effectively measured number. In our experiments the WRNN predictor has been used in order to schedule transportation means and manage an optimized planning of the related human and mechanical resources, and such operations are made possible thanks to predicted number of passengers, due to their availability in advance. Moreover, since each rendezvous point has been associated to a WRNN predictor, the proposed solution is general for any number and kind of transport services as well as for integrated transportation services. Finally due to the cloud technology, the system could be expanded and scaled on demand.

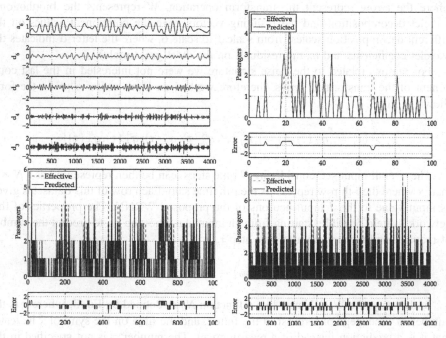

Fig. 6. From left to right and top to bottom: the most gross scales of the wavelet decomposition of the historical time series of passengers for a selected rendezvous point; the predicted and measured throughput, the errors on the throughput predictions, the predicted and measured number of requests, the errors on the requests predictions. The gray dashed lines represent the effective measurements, the overlapping black lines represent the predictions made by the WRNN predictors.

5 Related Works

Future urban environments will gather data from several cheap sensors, using cross-correlation and analytical models to mine valuable and reliable information from a lot of noisy and unreliable heterogeneous sensors. In (Puliafito et al. 2015) authors propose a hierarchical architecture to cope with the heterogeneous nature of sensed data in a World Wide Sensor Network scenario, using a two level data abstraction to uniform exposed information. While this work is focused on how data will have to be collected and organised, our work describes how to drive Smart City processes, that use sensed data, on a Cloud infrastructure, specifically to enhance the transportation service.

Other contributions have covered the interaction between sensors and Cloud services. In (Fazio et al. 2012) authors propose an architecture to assist the integration between IoT devices and federated Cloud providers, focussing on the security concerns that this integration involves, providing an IoT Cloud-based architecture that is able to support self-identification and secure data transfer from self-configuring devices to Cloud providers.

In (Liebig et al. 2016) the authors present a system for individual trip planning that incorporates the current traffic state, gathered by a sensor network positioned in the city environment, and future traffic condition, that is provided by a spatio-temporal random field model leveraging sensed data. They also use a Gaussian process regression to estimate traffic flow in areas with low sensor coverage. This approach not only differs from ours in the model they used to achieve predictions, but also in the motivations and the service point of view. In their approach it is the final user that will adapt his/her trip plan to the one suggested by the proposed system. In our approach it is instead the city environment, i.e. the devised city transportation service, that adapts itself to user requests. Therefore, where they have streets and city points that users have to avoid, according to current and future traffic conditions, we have rendezvous-points, i.e. city locations, that the transportation service vehicles have to reach to serve user requests. On the other hand, our approach can be supported by the service they proposed to make the bus drivers able to choose, among different possibilities, the fastest trip to reach the next rendezvous point to be served.

In (Zhu et al. 2016) the authors propose a public vehicle (PV) system that uses a cloud infrastructure to devise scheduling strategies and paths for PVs based on the demands of passengers. PVs are electric vehicles that can transport more passengers than a taxi and do not have stops or routes like a bus service. The service they propose is different from ours, since we have predefined bus stops (rendezvous-points) which are activated on demand according to user requests, hence adapting the overall trip schedule for the transportation vehicles. Furthermore, in contrast to our approach, they do not make use of a prediction component to assist their scheduling decisions, relying instead on a set of constraint based algorithms to compute the best solution to satisfy user requests.

In (Guitart et al. 2009) an extensive survey of the literature on quality of service, availability and performance for distributed applications has been given. All the approaches in (Guitart et al. 2009) are not intended to be used in combination with cloud resources. Hence, further support is needed as shown in the sections above.

In (Zhang and Qi 2005) the authors use pre-processing stages in order to feed filtered data to neural networks to model time series with both seasonal and trend patterns. Hybrid models are widely used in the literature in order to model phenomena and obtain forecasting software systems for a wide range of purposes, such as e.g. hydro-geological time series and the related risk assessment (Jain and Kumar 2007; Lohani et al. 2012). Other kinds of neural network related approaches have been developed for traffic prediction, e.g. basing on a flexible neural tree and particle swarm optimisation algorithm (Chen et al. 2012).

The novelty of the presented work lies on the pre-processing of the data that, in this system, are transformed to the wavelet domain before they are given to the neural network. Moreover, the neural network itself is able to perform the inverse transform: that is a non trivial feature since it permits us to encapsulate it in a module that can be embedded in more complex systems. In this way the neural architecture is not anymore a stand-alone and separated component, but can be integrated in a software system to internally cooperate with the other components.

6   Conclusions

This paper has proposed a software architecture that gives support when having to deploy, execute, and monitor services that execute on a cloud and according to workflows. A smart city scenario has been put forward for enhanced intelligent services that are related to public transport and can gather useful data to improve the communication infrastructure. The server-side computing architecture, while being independent of specific workflows, has shown to be flexible enough to handle mobile user requests and properly govern the life-time of services executing on a cloud. Moreover, our suggested components realise all the interconnection work needed to let a workflow execute on a cloud infrastructure.

In our solution, a component has been specifically devised to plan the needed transport service ahead of time by modelling incoming requests and analysing them in order to remove noise, while characterising repetitive trends. Then, we can start operations, such as planning vehicles routes and driver shifts, avoiding over-provisioning.

References

Batty, M., Axhausen, K.W., Giannotti, F., Pozdnoukhov, A., Bazzani, A., Wachowicz, M., Ouzounis, G., Portugali, Y.: Smart cities of the future. Eur. Phys. J. Spec. Top. 214(1), 481–518 (2012)

Benevolo, C., Dameri, R.P., D'Auria, B.: Smart mobility in smart city. In: Torre, T., Braccini, A. M., Spinelli, R. (eds.) Empowering Organizations: Enabling Platforms and Artefacts. Lecture Notes in Information Systems and Organisation, vol. 11, pp. 13–28. Springer, Heidelberg (2016)

Bonanno, F., Capizzi, G., Sciuto, G.L., Napoli, C., Pappalardo, G., Tramontana, E.: A novel cloud-distributed toolbox for optimal energy dispatch management from renewables in IGSs by using WRNN predictors and GPU parallel solutions. In: Proceedings of IEEE International Symposium on Power Electronics, Electrical Drives, Automation and Motion (SPEEDAM), Ischia, pp. 1077–1084 (2014). doi:10.1109/SPEEDAM.2014.6872127

Bonanno, F., Capizzi, G., Napoli, C.: Some remarks on the application of RNN and PRNN for the charge-discharge simulation of advanced Lithium-ions battery energy storage. In: Proceedings of IEEE International Symposium on Power Electronics, Electrical Drives, Automation and Motion (SPEEDAM), Sorrento, pp. 941–945 (2012). doi:10.1109/SPEEDAM.2012.6264500

Bonanno, F., Capizzi, G., Coco, S., Napoli, C., Laudani, A., Sciuto, G.L.: Optimal thicknesses determination in a multilayer structure to improve the spp efficiency for photovoltaic devices by an hybrid FEM—cascade neural network based approach. In: Proceedings of IEEE International Symposium on Power Electronics, Electrical Drives, Automation and Motion (SPEEDAM) (2014)

Capizzi, G., Napoli, C., Paternò, L.: An innovative hybrid neuro-wavelet method for reconstruction of missing data in astronomical photometric surveys. In: Rutkowski, L., Korytkowski, M., Scherer, R., Tadeusiewicz, R., Zadeh, L.A., Zurada, J.M. (eds.) ICAISC 2012, Part I. LNCS, vol. 7267, pp. 21–29. Springer, Heidelberg (2012)

Chen, Y., Yang, B., Meng, Q.: Small-time scale network traffic prediction based on flexible neural tree. Appl. Soft Comput. 12(1), 274–279 (2012)

Chourabi, H., Nam, T., Walker, S., Gil-Garcia, J.R., Mellouli, S., Nahon, K., Pardo, T., Scholl, H.J., et al.: Understanding smart cities: an integrative framework. In: Proceedings of 45th Hawaii International Conference on System Science (HICSS), pp. 2289–2297. IEEE (2012)

Erl, T.: SOA Design Patterns. Pearson Education, Boston (2008)

Fazio, M., Paone, M., Puliafito, A., Villari, M.: Heterogeneous sensors become homogeneous things in smart cities. In: Proceedings of International Conference on Innovative Mobile and Internet Services in Ubiquitous Computing (IMIS), pp. 775–780. IEEE (2012)

Fornaia, A., Napoli, C., Pappalardo, G., Tramontana, E.: Using AOP neural networks to infer user behaviours and interests. In: Proceedings of the 16th Workshop From Objects to Agents (WOA), vol. 1382 (2015)

Guitart, J., Torres, J., Ayguadé, E.: A survey on performance management for internet applications. Concurrency Comput. Pract. Exp. 22(1), 68–106 (2009)

Jackson, K.: OpenStack Cloud Computing Cookbook. Packt Publishing Ltd., Birmingham (2012)

Jain, A., Kumar, A.M.: Hybrid neural network models for hydrologic time series forecasting. Appl. Soft Comput. 7(2), 585–592 (2007)

Liebig, T., Piatkowski, N., Bockermann, C., Morik, K.: Dynamic route planning with real-time traffic predictions. Inf. Syst. (2016, in press). doi:10.1016/j.is.2016.01.007, http://www.sciencedirect.com/science/article/pii/S0306437916000181

Lohani, A., Kumar, R., Singh, R.: Hydrological time series modeling: a comparison between adaptive neuro-fuzzy, neural network and autoregressive techniques. J. Hydrol. 442, 23–35 (2012)

Mallat, S.: A Wavelet Tour of Signal Processing: the sparse way. Academic press, Burlington (2009)

Mandic, D.P., Chambers, J.: Recurrent Neural Networks for Prediction: Learning Algorithms, Architectures And Stability. Wiley, New York (2001)

Napoli, C., Bonanno, F., Capizzi, G.: Exploiting solar wind time series correlation with magnetospheric response by using an hybrid neuro-wavelet approach. In: IAU Symposium 274, vol. 6, pp. 156–158. Cambridge University Press (2010). doi:10.1017/S1743921311006806

Napoli, C., Pappalardo, G., Tina, G.M., Tramontana, E.: Cooperative strategy for optimal management of smart grids by wavelet RNNs and cloud computing. IEEE Trans. Neural Netw. Learn. Syst. **27**(8), 1672–1685 (2015)

Napoli, C., Pappalardo, G., Tramontana, E.: Improving files availability for bittorrent using a diffusion model. In: 23rd IEEE International WETICE Conference, pp. 191–196 (2014). doi:10.1109/WETICE.2014.65

Napoli, C., Pappalardo, G., Tramontana, E.: A mathematical model for file fragment diffusion and a neural predictor to manage priority queues over bittorrent. Int. J. Appl. Math. Comput. Sci. **26**(1), 147–160 (2016)

Nowicki, R.K., Nowak, B., Wozniak, M.: Application of rough sets in k nearest neighbours algorithm for classification of incomplete samples. In: Kunifuji, S., Papadopoulos, G.A., Skulimowski, A.M.J., Kacprzyk, J. (eds.) Knowledge, Information and Creativity Support Systems. Advances in Intelligent Systems and Computing (AISC), vol. 416, pp. 243–257. Springer, Heidelberg (2016). doi:10.1007/978-3-319-27478-2_17. ISSN 2194-5357

Polap, D., Wozniak, M., Napoli, C., Tramontana, E.: Real-time cloud-based game management system via cuckoo search algorithm. Int. J. Electron. Telecommun. **61**(4), 333–338 (2015)

Puliafito, A., Celesti, A., Villari, M., Fazio, M.: Towards the integration between IoT and cloud computing: an approach for the secure self-configuration of embedded devices. Int. J. Distrib. Sensor Netw. **11**(12), 268–860 (2015)

Rabiner, L.R., Gold, B.: Theory and Application of Digital Signal Processing. Prentice-Hall, Englewood Cliffs (1975)

Williams, R.J.: A learning algorithm for continually running fully recurrent neural networks. Neural Comput. **1**, 270–280 (1989)

Wozniak, M., Marszalek, Z., Gabryel, M., Nowicki, R.K.: Preprocessing large data sets by the use of quick sort algorithm. In: Skulimowski, A.M.J., Kacprzyk, J. (eds.) Knowledge, Information and Creativity Support Systems: Recent Trends, Advances and Solutions. Advances in Intelligent Systems and Computing (AISC), vol. 364, pp. 111–121. Springer, Heidelberg (2016). doi:10.1007/978-3-319-19090-7_9. ISSN 2194-5357

Wozniak, M., Polap, D., Borowik, G., Napoli, C.: A first attempt to cloud-based user verification in distributed system. In: Proceedings of IEEE Asia-Pacific Conference on Computer Aided System Engineering (APCASE), pp. 226–231, July 2015

Zhang, G., Qi, M.: Neural network forecasting for seasonal and trend time series. Eur. J. Oper. Res. **160**(2), 501–514 (2005)

Zhu, M., Liu, X.-Y., Qiu, M., Shen, R., Shu, W., Wu, M.-Y.: Transfer problem in a cloud-based public vehicle system with sustainable discomfort. Mobile Netw. Appl., 1–11 (2016, in press). doi:10.1007/s11036-016-0675-y

Evaluation of a Mobility Approach to Support Vehicular Applications Using a Realistic Simulation Framework

Nerea Toledo[(✉)], Marivi Higuero, Maider Huarte, and Juanjo Unzilla

University of the Basque Country, Bilbao, Spain
nerea.toledo@ehu.eus

Abstract. The connected vehicle is becoming a reality. Internet access onboard will indeed increase road safety and security thanks to the cooperative networking that it is expected among vehicles, roadside units and the Internet. Moreover, this connectivity will bring innovative driving assistance services and infotainment alike services for end users. This fact is endorsed by standardisation bodies like the ETSI or the 5G-PPP that are actively working on the definition of these innovative services and setting their requirements. The connected vehicle poses technological challenges that need to be addressed. The mobility has to be managed regardless the location of the vehicles to ensure connectivity. At the same time the required security and performance levels for the applications need to be ensured. In this paper, we present a realistic simulation framework to evaluate vehicular applications while the protocol to manage the mobility, NeMHIP, is running underneath. The simulation framework is based on the integration of the OMNeT++, SUMO, VEINS and VsimRTI simulation tools. Obtained results have been compared with the requirements defined by the 5G-PPP automotive white paper, ITU-T Y.1541 and 3GPP TS 22.105 standards with satisfactory results. Thus, we demonstrate that the NeMHIP protocol is suitable because it fulfils the requirements of the applications while it provides an essential mobility service. In addition, this work shows the validity of the simulation framework.

1 Introduction

In a very near future it is foreseeable that onboard Internet access not only for infotainment services but also for road safety assistance services will be a reality. In fact, by 2024 89 % of new cars sold are projected to include both embedded and mobile devices and ensure connectivity [10]. That is, vehicles will be connected to the Internet, to other vehicles, and to roadside units, so vehicles should rely not only on their own sensors but also on other vehicles' devices, and will cooperate with each other. This complex scenario is posing several technological challenges to the underlying communication system that need to be addressed.

From the communications point of view, a vehicle could be regarded as a cluster of mobile nodes that move together as a whole, that is, a mobile network. Vehicles equipped with several devices to measure the state of the engines,

© Springer International Publishing Switzerland 2016
G. Dregvaite and R. Damasevicius (Eds.): ICIST 2016, CCIS 639, pp. 709–721, 2016.
DOI: 10.1007/978-3-319-46254-7_57

machinery, etc. that are requested to provide reports to the control centre of the operation of the vehicle when referring to fleet management services; and end user devices like PDAs, smart phones, laptops, etc. brought in by the travellers are an example of scenarios where a set of nodes comprise a mobile network. Since a vehicle is constantly changing its point of attachment to the Internet one of the key technological elements that it is needed for having efficient vehicular communications is the mobility management protocol. This mobility management solution needs to guarantee the required security and efficiency levels demanded in the vehicular scenario. Consequently, the mobility management protocol we consider in this paper, the NeMHIP protocol, is the most suitable solution because it fulfils the requirements posed by this scenario as demonstrated in [24,25].

The connected vehicle will at the same time enable innovative applications to the automotive scenario to improve road safety and security and offer new services to end users. That is, services like automated overtake, emergency braking or cooperative collision avoidance together with infotainment services that demand high QoS will be possible. In fact, standardisation bodies like the ETSI or the ISO are defining the requirements of these type of services that will also pave the way to the automated driving.

In this paper, we present a simulation framework that integrates different simulation tools to have a realistic environment and evaluate the performance of different vehicular applications. We have compared obtained results with the requirements defined by the 3GPP [7], ITU-T [6] and 5G-PPP [8] standardisation bodies and demonstrate that the NeMHIP protocol is suitable because it fulfils the requirements also in a realistic vehicular simulation framework. At the same time, we show that the developed simulation framework is valid for conducting performance evaluation of vehicular applications.

2   Context

Currently, there is a lot of activity on ITS and vehicular communication standardisation regarding different aspects involved in this type of communications. One of the working areas is the definition of different applications together with their requirements. In fact, the ETSI TR 102 638 standard [11] defines the Basic Set of Applications (BSA) for V2V (Vehicle-to-Vehicle), V2I (Vehicle-to-Infrastructure) and I2V (Infrastructure-to-Vehicle) communications. The standard defines four application classes:

1. *Active road safety.* The goal of these types of applications is to improve road safety by providing driving assistance, with cooperative awareness and/or road hazard warning applications. Example use cases of these applications are intersection collision warning, wrong way driving warning, roadwork warning, etc.
2. *Cooperative traffic efficiency.* Applications from this class are devoted to improve traffic fluidity. Thus, the defined applications are speed management and cooperative navigation, with use cases like regulatory/contextual speed limit notification or traffic information and recommended itinerary.

3. *Cooperative local services.* These type of applications provide on-demand information based on the location of the vehicles and are provided from within the ITS network infrastructure. Common use cases of these type of applications are point of interest notification or media downloading.
4. *Global Internet services.* Applications in this class provide global Internet services on commercial or non-commercial basis. Two different applications are distinguished in this class: (1) community services like fleet management; (2) ITS station life cycle management with services like vehicle software/data provisioning update. That is, these services may include Infotainment, comfort and vehicle or service life cycle management and are acquired from providers in the wider Internet.

In addition, the ETSI TS 102 637-1 [13] defines the functional requirements of the BSA, specifying different flow diagrams for the different use cases of each service class. These requirements are based on the implementation of Cooperative Awareness Message (CAM) and Decentralised Environmental Notification Message (DENM) messages that are defined at the same time in the ETSI EN 302 637-2 [18] and ETSI EN 302 637-3 [19] standards.

On the other hand, security in the ITS context is essential. In fact, the ETSI has published several technical specifications related to security: (1) the ETSI TS 102 940 [14] technical specification where an ITS communication security architecture is defined; (2) a technical specification defining ITS confidentiality services [17], pointing out that there are no mandatory confidentiality services for the application layer, and mentioning that the confidentiality in the network layer is protected using the IPsec ESP protocol; (3) a technical specification defining how to manage trust and privacy [15]; and (4) another specification defining access control [16]. Therefore, the provision of security services is regarded as critical in this scenario.

Regarding the technological strategy to provide communications it is important to take into account that a vehicle is constantly changing its location so its mobility has to be managed in order to have continuous communication without service disruption and to allow reachability to nodes onboard regardless the location of the vehicle. That is, a mobility management protocol is required for vehicular communications. The protocol considered at present by ISO and ETSI standardisation bodies in the definition of a vehicular communication architecture [12,20] for managing mobility is the NEMO BS [26] protocol. However, NEMO BS lacks of the required security support and the efficiency needed in the vehicular communications [9,22]. Because of this, we propose the use of the NeMHIP protocol as an alternative solution to manage securely and efficiently the mobility.

3 The Underlying Mobility Management Protocol: NeMHIP

The NeMHIP protocol is a novel, secure and efficient network mobility management protocol for ITS scenarios which is based on the HIP protocol [21]. HIP is a NeMHIP defines a single security framework for protecting mobility management procedures and data exchanges, by means of the generation of independent and secret keying material in a single procedure.

HIP alike, the NeMHIP protocol consists of three different procedures: (1) the NeMHIP Registration procedure, which has the goal of ensuring the reachability of nodes onboard; (2) the NeMHIP Association Establishment procedure, which has the goal of establishing an association between a node located in the outside network like the Internet, a Correspondent Node (CN), and a node onboard, a Local or Mobile Network Node (LMN, MNN), and of agreeing upon a security context for the exchange of application data securely; (3) the NeMHIP Association Update procedure, which has the goal of maintaining the established associations when a mobility event that involves the change of the IP address takes place, or when rekeying is requested, so, it allows to maintain the communications and the reachability of nodes transparently for user applications. Next, we briefly introduce those procedures. More details can be found in [24,25].

3.1   NeMHIP Registration

The NeMHIP Registration process is aimed at ensuring the reachability of MNNs onboard by registering them in an updated server where their identifiers and locators are stored. In the HIP architecture this server is called a Rendez-Vous server (RVS). As a result of the registration, a mapping between the identifier (HIT) and the locator (IP address) of the HIP node are stored in the RVS.

In the vehicular scenario, it is likely to have all devices switched on simultaneously. Consequently, it is interesting to think on a bulk registration. Figure 1 shows the NeMHIP Registration flow chart. In black, messages that are equal to those defined by the base HIP protocol are shown, while the message in orange ($mI2$) has been specifically designed for the Bulk Registration process.

3.2   NeMHIP Association Establishment

Whenever two HIP-aware nodes want to exchange data for the first time in a secure way, an association establishment signalling exchange takes place. By means of this exchange, both nodes agree upon a security context; that is, they agree upon the algorithms and keys to protect the messages to be exchanged. Consequently, one of the most important procedures when defining a communication protocol between a mobile network and the infrastructure is the end-to-end association establishment. In the same way as for the NeMHIP Registration procedures, the NeMHIP Association Establishment process stems from the HIP association establishment, but new parameters, packet formats and procedures have been introduced to support network mobility scenarios and to provide them with the adequate security and efficiency level.

In this protocol not only end-to-end keying material is agreed but also independent keying between the MR and the CN. That is, in this new approach a security association between the MR and the CN is established to protect

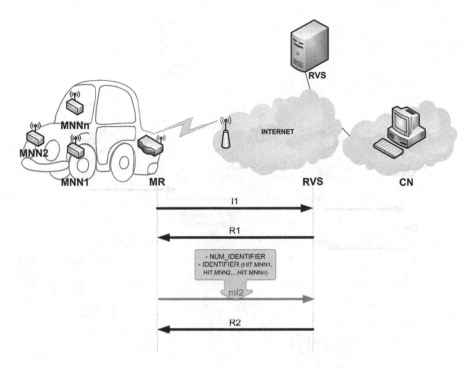

Fig. 1. NeMHIP Registration flow chart

mobility management messages as well as an end-to-end association is established between the MNN and the CN to protect user application data, both by means of a single signalling exchange. During this exchange, the MNN informs the MR about the keying material index that it will use for deriving end-to-end keys. Nevertheless, as the MR does not have knowledge of the keying material agreed upon between the CN and the node inside the moving network, end-to-end integrity and confidentiality are ensured while new end-to-end key generation can be managed by the MR, not revealing to it the keys. Figure 2 shows the NeMHIP Association Establishment flow chart and involved processing in the nodes.

3.3 NeMHIP Association Update

The core of the mobility support of the NeMHIP protocol is the association update process described in this section. Commonly, an established NeMHIP association will be updated when the MR changes its point of attachment to the Internet. This scenario often gives rise to drastically change link characteristics like throughput or delay. These changes may lead to packet reordering and packets falling outside the ESP anti-replay window [23] and therefore, to packet discarding. Consequently, whenever a host changes its locator the NeMHIP SA has to be renewed.

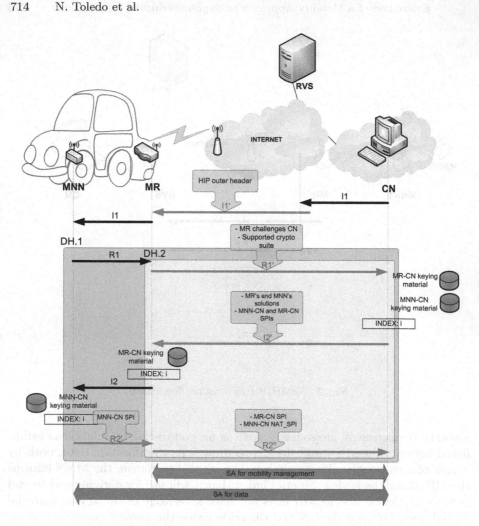

Fig. 2. NeMHIP Association Establishment

Following the same design approach as the other NeMHIP procedures, the NeMHIP Association Update procedure also stems from the HIP update procedure, but new messages and parameters have also been introduced. Figure 3 shows the update signalling exchange caused by the MR.

4 Evaluation Scenario

In this section, the developed simulation framework to evaluate the performance of vehicular applications is described. We have selected the OMNeT++ [3] simulation tool as the communication simulator, the SUMO [2] traffic simulator to simulate the traffic of vehicles, a framework that merges these two simulation

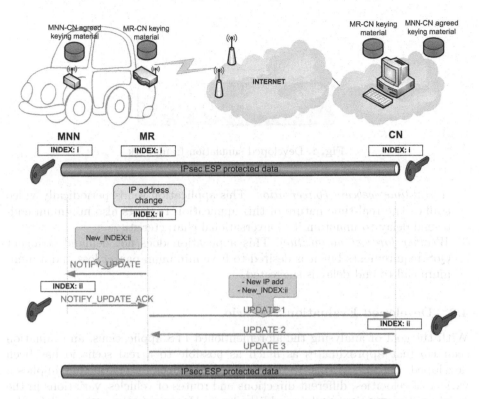

Fig. 3. NeMHIP Association Update caused by the MR

tools named VEINS [4], and the VSimRTI [5] tool to dynamically simulate the vehicular applications. Figure 4 shows the simulation framework.

More precisely, this simulation framework runs on a Ubuntu 12.04 operating system, where we have OMNeT++ 4.4.1, SUMO 0.21.0, VEINS 2.2 and VSimRTI 0.13.4 simulation tools integrated.

4.1   Analysed Vehicular Applications

Although there is a variety of vehicular applications available for vehicular communications, we have selected three different applications because they have different QoS requirements and are expected to be common in the near future. These applications are based on the CAM and DENM messages defined by the ETSI standards [18,19]. We next describe these vehicular applications.

1. *Emergency braking.* The goal of this application is to control the emergency braking of a vehicle. This application sends messages periodically and warns about an emergency braking if necessary. In order to avoid possible accidents, this application demands minimum end-to-end delay. This application sends a notification periodically (every 2 s).

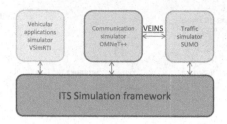

Fig. 4. Developed simulation framework

2. *A real-time webcam conversation.* This application sends periodically video traffic. The real-time nature of this application requests also minimum end-to-end delay to maintain its conversational characteristic.
3. *Weather forecast notification.* This application does not demand stringent QoS requirements but it is desired to have minimum packet loss and a minimum end-to-end delay is suggested.

4.2 Developed Evaluation Scenario

With the goal of analysing the aforementioned ITS applications, an evaluation scenario that approximates as much as possible to a real scenario has been developed. Because of this, we have selected an urban scenario that implies a variety of velocities, different directions and routes of vehicles, variations in the number of connections to be established, etc. More precisely, we have defined a circular route in the city centre that lasts 16 min and with a maximum speed of 50 km/h. For the sake of simplicity and with the goal of analysing the impact of the number of LMNs and the underlying NeMHIP protocol, this study considers a single vehicle. The left side of Fig. 5 shows the route of the vehicle. In order to have a real urban scenario, we have introduced the map of the city of Bilbao (Spain) which is shown in the right side of Fig. 5 provided by the OpenStreetMap tool [1] in the SUMO simulation tool. This way, we can simulate a realistic scenario with real routes that vehicles follow.

 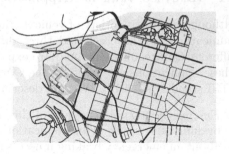

Fig. 5. The route of the vehicle in Bilbao city centre and the map of the city of Bilbao obtained from OpenStreetMap

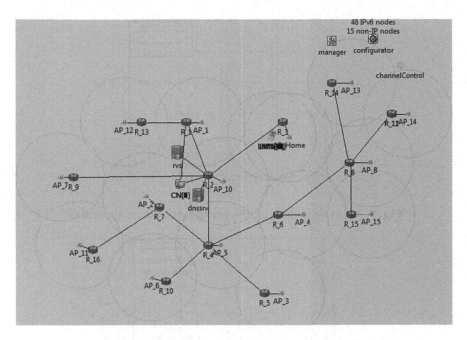

Fig. 6. Network topology defined in OMNeT++

Once the vehicle and its route are defined, it is necessary to configure the OMNeT++ simulator, that is, the communications simulator. More specifically, we have configured a network with 15 WiFi APs, several routers, a DNS server, the mobile network (vehicle), the communication endpoint (CN) and a RVS, and we have placed them as shown in Fig. 6.

5 Results and Discussion

This section shows the obtained results for each of the vehicular applications analysed. In order to evaluate the performance of the applications, we have considered four different scenarios in terms of number of LMNs onboard: 1 LMN, 5 LMNs, 10 LMNs and 20 LMNs. For each of the scenarios we have conducted 30 simulations following the central limit theorem. This way, we obtain the mean value and the limit values for 90%, 95% and 99% confidence intervals. For the three applications (emergency braking, a real-time webcam application and weather forecast notification) we have analysed the mean end-to-end delay of the packets and compare obtained results with the ITU-T and 3GPP standards, which point out that it should be preferably <150 ms and 400 ms at most, as well as with a recent White Paper published by the 5G-PPP where future vehicle communications and enabling technologies are outlined. Figures 7 and 8 show the results obtained for the emergency braking application and for the weather warning application respectively.

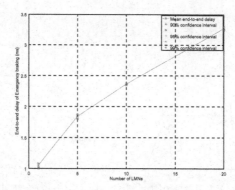

Fig. 7. End-to-end delay of the emergency braking application

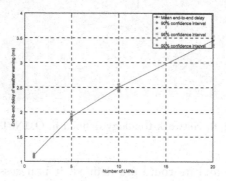

Fig. 8. End-to-end delay of the weather warning application

Obtained results show that with the increase in the number of LMNs the end-to-end delay of the applications increase but it is still less than 4 ms. In the 5G Automotive Vision white paper [8] Key Performance Indicators (KPIs) for vehicle applications are defined. More precisely, although this white paper describes different use cases the emergency braking is not described but other use cases like automated overtake, cooperative collision avoidance or high density platooning are introduced and the defined maximum end-to-end delay is set to 10 ms. Although this value is restrictive due to the nature of the automotive context, we still fulfil the recommendation.

Apart from evaluating *Active Road Safety* type of application by means of the emergency braking and weather notification applications, we have also analysed a *Global Internet Services* type of application, infotainment in this case, by evaluating the end-to-end delay of a real-time webcam conversation. Figure 9 shows obtained results.

As can be regarded, the obtained values for end-to-end delay webcam conversation and also for the other two applications fully satisfy the ITU-T Y.1541 recommendation which points out that the end-to-end delay should be 100 ms at most, and with the 3GPP TS 22.105 which establishes this value in 150 ms.

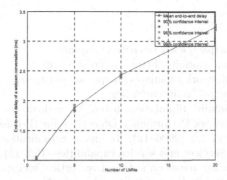

Fig. 9. End-to-end delay of the real time webcam conversation

Consequently, the end-to-end delay can be considered negligible while the impact of the introduction of a novel protocol such as NeMHIP does not involve any additional delay.

6 Conclusions

The connected vehicle is expected to be a reality in the near future. This capacity of being vehicles connected with other vehicles, roadside units or the Internet will increase road safety and security thanks to innovative cooperative applications that will assist driving and offer new services to the users. However, at present this complex scenario poses technological challenges that need to be addressed.

In order to guarantee the demanded safety and security level in the automotive scenario, vehicular applications need to satisfy stringent performance and security requirements.

In this paper we present a realistic simulation framework based on the OMNeT++, SUMO, VEINS and VsimRTI simulation tools to evaluate new vehicular applications. More specifically, we have evaluated an emergency braking application, a weather forecast notification application and a real time webcam conversation application. This way, we have checked a variety of applications each with different QoS demands. Since the vehicle is a moving network, its mobility has to be managed securely and efficiently. Because of this, we have selected the NeMHIP protocol to manage the mobility and include it in our simulation framework as a key enabler of the always connected vehicle.

Obtained results demonstrate that the end-to-end delay of the analysed applications fulfils the ITU-T Y.1541 and 3GPP TS 22.105 recommendations, and even more stringent requirements recently defined in the 5G Automotive Vision white paper by the 5G-PPP. Consequently, we demonstrate that the NeMHIP protocol is suitable because it fulfils the mentioned requirements even in using a realistic simulation framework and that the developed simulation tool is a valid framework for evaluating new vehicular applications.

References

1. OpenStreetMap. https://www.openstreetmap.org/
2. Simulator for Urban Mobility. http://sumo-sim.org/
3. The OMNeT++ Network Simulator. http://omnetpp.org/
4. Veins Simulator. http://veins.car2x.org
5. VSimRT Smart Mobility Simulation. http://www.dcaiti.tu-berlin.de/
6. ITU-T Y.1541. Network Performance Objectives for IP-Based Services (2006)
7. 3GPP TS 22.105 v7.1.0 (2006–12). Technical Specification Group Services and Systems Aspects; Services and service capabilities (Rel. 11) (2013)
8. 5G-PPP: 5g-ppp white paper on automotive vertical sector. Technical report, The 5G Infrastructure Public Private Partnership (2015)
9. Petrescu, A., Olivereau, A., Janneteau, C.: Threats for Basic Network Mobility Support (NEMO threats), January 2004
10. Analysis Mason: Connected cars: worldwide trends, forecasts, and strategies 2014–2024. Technical report (2014)
11. European Telecommunications Standards Institute: ETSI TR 102 638 V1.1.1 (2009–06), Intelligent Transport Systems (ITS); Vehicular Communications; Basic Set of Applications; Definitions. Technical report, ETSI (2009)
12. European Telecommunications Standards Institute: ETSI EN 302 665 (2010). Intelligent Transport Systems (ITS): Communications Architecture. Technical report, ETSI (2010)
13. European Telecommunications Standards Institute: ETSI TS 102 637-1 V1.1.1 (2010–09), Intelligent Transport Systems (ITS); Vehicular Communications; Basic Set of Applications; Definitions; Part 1: Functional Requirements. Technical report, ETSI (2010)
14. European Telecommunications Standards Institute: ETSI TS 102 940 V1.1.1 (2012–06), Intelligent Transport Systems (ITS); Security; ITS communications security architecture and security management. Technical report, ETSI (2012)
15. European Telecommunications Standards Institute: ETSI TS 102 941 V1.1.1 (2012–06), Intelligent Transport Systems (ITS); Security; Trust and Privacy Management. Technical report, ETSI (2012)
16. European Telecommunications Standards Institute: ETSI TS 102 942 V1.1.1 (2012–06), Intelligent Transport Systems (ITS); Security; Access Control. Technical report, ETSI (2012)
17. European Telecommunications Standards Institute: ETSI TS 102 943 V1.1.1 (2012–06), Intelligent Transport Systems (ITS); Security; Confidentiality services. Technical report, ETSI (2012)
18. European Telecommunications Standards Institute: ETSI TS 302 637-2 V1.3.1 (2014–09), Intelligent Transport Systems (ITS); Vehicular Communications; Basic Set of Applications; Part 2: Specification of Cooperative Awareness Basic Service. Technical report, ETSI (2014)
19. European Telecommunications Standards Institute: ETSI TS 302 637-3 V1.2.2 (2014–11), Intelligent Transport Systems (ITS); Vehicular Communications; Basic Set of Applications; Part 3: Specification of Decentralized Environmental Notification Basic Service. Technical report, ETSI (2014)
20. International Standardization for Organization: ISO-21217-CALM-Architecture. Intelligent Transport Systems - Communications access for land mobiles (CALM) - Architecture. Technical report, ISO (2010)

21. Nikander, P., Gurtov, A., Henderson, T.R.: Host Identity Protocol (HIP): connectivity, mobility, multi-homing, security, and privacy over IPv4 and IPv6 networks. IEEE Commun. Surv. Tutorials **12**(2), 186–204 (2010)
22. Jung, S., Zhao, F., Wu, S.F., Kim, H., Sohn, S.: Threat Analysis on NEMO Basic Operations, July 2004
23. Kent, S.: IP Encapsulating Security Payload (ESP). RFC 4303, December 2005
24. Toledo, N., Bonnin, J.M., Higuero, M.: Performance evaluation of user applications in the its scenario: an analytical assessment of the nemhip. J. Netw. Comput. Appl. **36**, 1324–1336 (2013)
25. Toledo, N., Higuero, M., Huarte, M., Matias, J., Jacob, E., Unzilla, J.J.: A proposal to contribute to its standardization activity: a valuable network mobility management approach. Comput. Stand. Interfaces **36**(3), 465–479 (2014)
26. Devarapalli, V., Wakikawa, R., Petrescu, A., Thubert, P.: Network Mobility (NEMO) Basic Support Protocol. RFC 3963, August 2005

An Usable Application for Authentication, Communication and Access Management in the Internet of Things

Matteo Cagnazzo[1]([⊠]), Markus Hertlein[2], and Norbert Pohlmann[1]

[1] Institute for Internet-Security, Gelsenkirchen, Germany
{cagnazzo,pohlmann}@internet-sicherheit.de
[2] XignSys, Gelsenkirchen, Germany
hertlein@xignsys.com
http://www.internet-sicherheit.de, http://www.xignsys.com

Abstract. The following paper introduces a secure and efficient application concept that is capable of authenticating and accessing smart objects. The concept is based on two already developed applications. It describes the used technologies and discusses the outcome and potential downfalls of the idea.

Keywords: Security · Authentication · Communication · Internet of Things

1 Preliminaries

Modern components with connectivity mechanisms need authentication to offer services to the authenticating entity. Especially in the emerging Internet of Things as well as eMobility scenarios this becomes imperative. The requirements to authentication mechanisms are that it should be secure, easy to use and reasonable fast, so that there is no "waiting time" for the user. Nowadays the most common mechanism to authenticate against a service or an object is to use password-based approaches. These are prone to manifold attack-vectors:

- Brute-Force-Attack
- Dictionary-Attack
- Rainbow-Tables
- Keylogging

By choosing unsafe passwords or using the same password for multiple services attacks on the internet become more and more profitable. One alternative is multi-factor authentication which combinates knowledge (username/password), ownership (smartphone) and/or individual biological properties (biometry). Access to a system is therefore granted if and only if the combination of all these challenges return successful. A downfall is that a stolen "root-secret" corrupts

© Springer International Publishing Switzerland 2016
G. Dregvaite and R. Damasevicius (Eds.): ICIST 2016, CCIS 639, pp. 722–731, 2016.
DOI: 10.1007/978-3-319-46254-7_58

a whole system and therefore most problems of password-based authentication are persistent.

Generally identities have different security levels. Depending on the source which is used to verify ones identity, a level of trust can be determined [10].

- Level 1: Data is not verifiable
- Level 2: Verification via Mail
- Level 3: Verification via presence
- Level 4: Verification via official document

Official documents are for example identity cards. These are called primary identity offer the highest level of trust. From those secondary and tertiary-identities are derivable.

One way to depict these different trust levels is via Public-Key-Infrastructure [4].

1.1 Authentication Systems

Todays authentication processes are more dynamic since the interaction of users and machines in the field of the Internet of Things. The classic approaches like password-based authentication or smartcard-based authentication are not able to answer the new challenges developing from the human-machine interaction. On the one hand it is not possible to use password-based authentication for the authentication against a radiator or a coffee brewer due to the need of extra hardware like keyboards or pin-pads. Also the time consuming aspect of using passwords and the user-unfriendly process of managing passwords are not acceptable for small use cases. For high security use cases like the access to production machines a weak one-factor authentication is not applicable. On the other hand strong two-factor authentication methods like smartcard authentication are expensive due to the need of smartcards readers and smartcards or security tokens.

The two examples, the authentication against a radiator and the access to production machines are showing two more demands emerging from the Internet of Things. Unlike authentication systems in the todays Internet, which are mainly working with a level of high or low security, authentication systems in the field of IoT should be able to adjust the security level based on the protection needs of the assets. This so called adaptive authentication is able to increase the usability where possible. Usability is a necessary feature in the field of authentication in IoT, due to the fact that the number of authentication processes will be a multiple of these a user has to perform nowadays. Furthermore the authentication systems have to confluence to an authentication eco-system that works with different technologies in different scenarios and use cases [7].

Summarizing a modern authentication and access management system has to fulfill the following requirements [8]:

- Interoperability
- Adaptive authentication between security and usability
- Reduced complexity and cost-efficient
- Operational in different scenarios and use cases

1.2   Communication Systems

An essential part that becomes even more relevant with further interconnectedness of humans and things is efficient communication. In a system where billion things and humans are interconnected there is no need for redundant and slow communication. Current standardization processes like 5G want to enable tactile user experience through real time communication. To realize that one needs short reaction time and latency (<1ms) [1,12]. Concepts like network-coding try to reduce redundancy in those networks [5].

By analyzing communication behavior of adolescents, one can derive that they are able to pack a lot of information in just a few signs by combining literals, graphics and emoticons. For example the phrase "See you" is reduced to just "cu". The information that is being transmitted is the same but the quantity of used literals is 66 % lower. That is a significant decrease and a lot of behaviors like this are observable in modern lingo. Another example for modern linguistics is the evolution of the "hashtag" or comparable mechanisms to operate as a marker referencing a specific target. Through this tagging, language becomes searchable and it is possible to affiliate values to words by counting mentions or weighing these mentions. One already implemented and tested approach to this is called "TechnoWeb 2.0" but unlike the proposed approach it focuses on "microblogging" of the users and is only focused on user to user interaction [11]. Finally electronic communication is moving from asymmetrical towards symmetrical communication whereby the communicating peers can exchange their information in real-time and see the collaboration of the other peer which increases efficiency and promotes the exchange of information [13].

Modern collaboration tools simplify the mechanism to address someone by just mentioning them in a document and send a notification to them. Efficiency is essential concerning communicating in a business environment, since employees in every level of hierarchy spent a lot of their time communicating. From this stake a lot of time is consumed by e-mails which are inefficient since there is the need for a salutation and valediction in every e-mail alongside arbitrary and reciprocal information until there is unique information being exchanged. Tools that support symmetrical information exchange though make it easier to share unique information, insights, experiences and knowledge in the blink of an eye with colleagues, friends or any other entity. Global communication is a complex system that can be uni- or multi directional, independent of social status, secure or insecure, private or public but in summary it is mostly dependent on protocol-specific human and technical components.

Taking into account the emerging Internet of things it is clearly distinguishable that current communication solutions are not capable of dealing with the increasing number of participants. Not a single platform provides support for communicating with things or has an interface to connect with smart objects. Efficient, smart and secure chat-based communication is the key for the ongoing digitalization.

These key-features are introduced by a novel platform called "Quvert" [3]. This approach will be expanded in this paper to support communication with smart objects in the Internet of things by combining Quvert with XignQR. The support of secure authentication and communication will be addressed and explored in this paper.

2   Used Technologies

Chapter 2 describes the technologies XignQR and Quvert that will be used to create the proposed architecture.

2.1   XignQR

XignQR [9] is an authentication and signature system that fits into a modern authentication eco system. The concept behind XignQR addresses all the requirements mentioned in Chapter 1.1. Therefore the XignQR-System comprises of four actors, shown in Fig. 1:

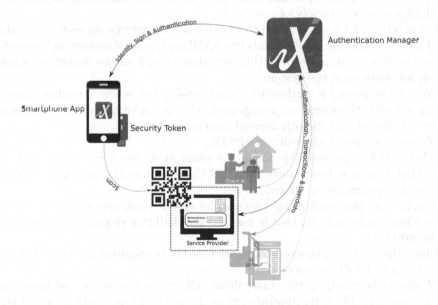

Fig. 1. Interaction of the four Actors

1. Authentication Manager

The authentication manager is the identity provider and broker. It is the main part in the authentication process between an user and a service provider/relying party (3.).

It mediates the authentication result from the user authentication to the service provider. It also enforces the security and trust level of the used digital identity requested by a service provider on server-side. At the beginning of an authentication process the security policy of a service provider and the users self-defined security policy is compared. The policy information are combined and enforced. During an authentication process the authentication manager receives user-behavior from the users personal authentication device (2.) and analyses these data. If anomalies are detected a new factor for authentication is requested through the personal authentication device.

From the users view the authentication manager helps to prevent the loss of privacy. It only delivers the users information to the service provider that are granted through the user.

Another function of the authentication manager is the connection to the public key infrastructure (PKI). Thereby it is responsible for the provisioning of the PKI functionality and its user-management, containing digital certificate enrollment and user pseudonymity.

The PKI, digital certificates and cryptographic protocols are playing a key role in reference of interoperability, adaptive authentication and multi-functional deployment in a variety of use cases.

Besides the PKI a modular protocol stack is necessary for an easy integration. Therefore multiple ID-Protocols like SAML or OpenIDConnect are supported to enable federation between different identity and service providers to build an authentication eco system.

To ensure integrity, authenticity and privacy the whole communication is signed with the users and components elliptic curve private keys and symmetrically encrypted with derived session keys.

2. Personal authentication device (PAD)

The PAD is represented in form of a smartphone and the personalized XignAPP. It acts as user interface, as QR-Code scanner and as token reader for the optional Security Token.

During the personalization process the app is equipped with user specific cryptographic material that is used for the challenge response authentication protocol.

Since there are no passwords or shared secrets transmitted, all the mentioned attacks in 1 will not succeed.

While authenticating, the smartphone collects user behavior and contextual information. These information are analyzed by the authentication manager (1.) to enforce the policies and initiate multiple authentication factors on-demand.

The use of the smartphone as PAD enables the use of many different authentication factors, from classical PIN entries over biometric and

security tokens to new mechanism like photo-authentication or video-chat based authentication.
3. Service Provider/Relying Party
   The service provider is the component the user want to get access to. For example a website or a production machine. The integration is done by one of the many supported ID-protocols. As an entry point for the authentication a QR Code is used. The QR Code contains an ID, static or session-based, representing the service provider, an URL to the authentication manager and a digital signature.
   The authentication process starts with the scan of the QR Code with personalized XignAPP.
4. Security Token (optional)
   A security token can optionally be added to the PAD to increase the security level while increasing the usability through enabling new kinds of multi-factor authentication without interaction.

Authentication flow. The authentication process consists of the following parts:

1. Service Provider requests the QR Code and the user attributes, e. .g. username
2. User scans QR Code with PAD
3. PAD verifies the embedded signature of the QR Code and connects to the authentication manager
4. PKI based mutual authentication between PAD and authentication manager will be executed and the requested attributes will be transmitted encrypted of the established secure channel
5. User sees the information and requested attributes in her app
6. User confirms the authentication by fulfilling the request security level, e.g. PIN or biometry
7. A PKI based challenge response mechanism is executed.
8. Authentication manager transmits the authentication results and user-attributes to the service provider.

2.2 Quvert

Quvert enables fast, reliable, usable and secure business communication based on a chat-system. It introduces mechanisms to conduct legally watertight agreements. It enables a visualizable and configurable knowledge management and other features to develop an internal knowledge big data: Quvert.Knowledge. The foundation of Quvert is a secure, distributed and reliable server based on XMPP and Erlang with various database-schemes (eg. Postgres or CouchDB) available to ensure up to 99,999999999 % service uptime [2]. The mobile and desktop applications have a composed user interface and are easily usable by technological unaffine users. They also provide security in terms that user input can be concealed and all messages are encrypted on transport and application layer before they are being transmitted to the server. The encryption scheme is a modified version of the Axolotl protocol that has already proven that it is capable of securing connections efficiently [6]. The platform is designed in a modular way so every client can specify their needs and Quvert can adapt it to their needs. The whole platform is designed by these principles:

1. Business by design: Inclusion of business processes into a communication platform
2. Compliance by design: Data autonomy and legally watertight archiving
3. Security by design: Usable and economic security from the start of development
4. Privacy by design: Privacy is dealt with during the development process to preserve it
5. Usability by design: Easy and usable for users, low training periods

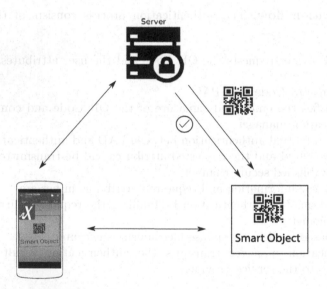

Fig. 2. Schematic view of an authentication

3   Proposed Architecture

To be able to communicate with a Smart Object one needs to authenticate against it. This authentication can be done with a smartphone that scans a QR-code attached to a smart object. After this the schematic authentication process looks like the one in Fig. 2. Every arrow in Fig. 2 is a channel secured with TLS between the endpoints. Furthermore an end-to-end encryption is deployed to verify and establish trustworthy communication over insecure channels. The current mechanism is a Challenge-Response Authentication Mechanism (CRAM).

XignQR offers all the functionality to grant access to a smart object, for example strong authentication and the public key infrastructure that is being used. Quvert serves as the user friendly interface in which XignQR is being embedded. In Fig. 2 XignQR has been personalized to a user in advance by a defined process. Through this personalization XignQR gets meta information and challenges this against the QR-Code. If the challenge-response is successful the user gets access in Quvert to the controls of a smart object. The QR-Code only serves as a trigger for the authentication process and can be replaced by another mechanism for example NFC or indoor geo location.

The QR Code only stores necessary information to identify the Smart Object on the server and a digital signature. After the QR Code is scanned the XignAPP validates the QR Codes signature and requests the information from the Server of the Smart Object. All information are transmitted through the use of attribute certificates. The benefits of the use of attributes certificates is that the information of the Smart Object can be verified towards integrity and authenticity [10]. Now the adaptive authentication mechanism of XignQR will be used. If the authentication point is a non-critical component, like a radiator, the possession of the personalized smartphone suffices to fulfill the authentication process. At critical authentication points like the physical access to industrial facilities or access to production machines the smartphone will prompt the user to enter a pin, use his fingerprint, capture a photo of the user to use biometric authentication mechanisms or a combination of two or more factors. The use of the smartphone as PAD for Smart Objects in the Internet of Things will gain a high level of usability and security. For example a user picture can not only be used for authentication, but also be added to process confirmations as one part of a signature to dedicate the process to the person that is responsible.

XignQR offers bidirectional communication channels through websockets so the smart objects do not have to poll the server. This saves resources in terms of energy which is an essential feature for resource constrained devices.

After a successful authentication process all necessary information are transmitted to the Smart Object. That can be done on a high level with PKI-based attribute certificates or on a low level with a small uni-directional protocol.

On the app-side after a successful authentication the smart object is shown in the user interface Quvert and the user can control it from a mobile device or workstation. A possible control view for a radiator is shown in Fig. 3. This view is an interactive element through which a user can interact with smart objects and communicate with it in a secure way. The control elements in Fig. 3 are only exemplary and can be expanded if Quvert is opened as a desktop application. Most objects with a low trust level will be easily accessible with the smartphone while more complex objects for example production machines will be visualized on a desktop application.

4   Discussion, Outlook and Conclusion

By using this architecture it is possible to authenticate a user with his smartphone against different smart objects by scanning a QR-code attached to it.

Fig. 3. View of userinteraction with a smart object

The platforms that are used for this architecture preconceive data security and privacy so that the possibility of manipulation is still possible but it is very hard to break or fraud the application and it's backend. The scanning of a QR-code is easily feasible by all kinds of users, since it is a intuitive technique. The chat like interface makes the control of smart objects intuitive and flexible as well. A lot of application scenarios are possible for example secure remote maintenance, monitoring, eMobility or distributed testbeds.

Physical and digital restrictions must be considered when combining an Identity Service with a communication platform. Especially if control authentication is granted a holistic contemplation must be done. Every transmission and every endpoint becomes a critical point where security and integrity has to be assured. All of this has to be done in a secure manner without losing the usability of the system. This will soon be a challenging task for the involved researchers. In the future machine-to-machine communication will become the most important topic for digitalized businesses and factories. XignQR is capable of authenticating a machine against another machine and Quvert could operate as a bus system where machines can communicate and push or pull data to specific channels while an administrator has the ability to overview all the machine communication for maintenance or analysis purposes in a tidy and clear interface.

Since XignQR is an authentication and signature system that is able to keep track of the digital processes ensuring integrity and authenticity, the described system is not only able to authenticate and to communicate with and between machines. In combination with the emerging possibilities to create server-side qualified signatures and digital seals, because of the European law eIDAS. Therefore the system can attest the results of digital process or decisions.

Both applications have been tested separately and are currently in the starting phase of a pilot project. Future work will focus on implementation of the proposed framework as well as simulation and testing. Thus the proposed application can be evaluated and further drafted.

All in all the described application could serve as a visionary tool for communicating with smart objects in an efficient and secured way but there is still a lot of research and work to do.

References

1. Andrews, J.G., Buzzi, S., Choi, W., Hanly, S.V., Lozano, A., Soong, A.C.K., Zhang, J.C.: What will 5G be? IEEE J. Sel. Areas Commun. **32**(6), 1065–1082 (2014)
2. Armstrong, J., Virding, R., Wikstrm, C., Williams, M.: Concurrent Programming in ERLANG. Prentice Hall, Hertfordshire (1993)
3. Barchnicki, S.: Eine Antwort auf die Frage nach effizienter Kommunikation von Morgen, IT-Sicherheit (2016)
4. Beutelspacher, A.: Kryptologie. Eine Einfhrung in die Wissenschaft vom Verschlsseln, Verbergen und Verheimlichen; ohne alle Geheimniskrmerei, aber nicht ohne hinterlistigen Schalk, dargestellt zum Nutzen und Ergtzen des allgemeinen Publikums. 7. Auflage. Vieweg, Wiesbaden (2005)
5. Chou, P.A., Wu, Y., Jain, K.: Practical network coding (2003)
6. Frosch, T., Mainka, C., Bader, C., Bergsma, F., Holz, T.: How Secure is TextSecure? (2014)
7. Hertlein, M., Manaras, P., Pohlmann, N.: Die Zeit nach dem Passwort Handhabbare Multifaktor-Authentifizierung fr ein gesundes Eco-System, DuD Datenschutz und Datensicherheit Recht und Sicherheit in Informationsverarbeitung und Kommunikation, Vieweg Verlag (2016)
8. Hertlein, M., Manaras, P., Pohlmann, N.: Abschied vom Passwort Authentifikation fr ein gereiftes Internet, IT-Sicherheit Management und Praxis, DATAKONTEXT-Fachverlag (2015)
9. Hertlein, M., Manaras, P., Pohlmann, N.: Bring your own device for authentication (BYOD4A). The XignSystem. In: Pohlmann, N., Reimer, H., Schneider, W. (eds.) Proceedings of the ISSE Securing Electronic Business Processes Highlights of the Information Security Solutions EuropeConference. Springer, Wiesbaden (2015)
10. Manaras, P.: Konzeption und Implementierung eines Identity Providers auf Basis von FIDO UAF und OpenID Connect Verifikation der Identitt mit der XignTechnologie, Master-thesis (2016)
11. Mörl, S., Heiss, M., Richter, A.: Siemens: Wissensvernetzung mit TechnoWeb 2.0, Schriftenreihe zu Enterprise 2.0-Fallstudien Nr. 09, Andrea Back, Michael Koch, Petra Schubert, Stefan Smolnik (Hrsg.) München/St.Gallen/Koblenz/Frankfurt: Enterprise 2.0 Fallstudien-Netzwerk, February 2011. ISSN 1869-0297
12. Rappaport, T.S., Sun, S., Mayzus, R., Zhao, H., Azar, Y., Wang, K., Wong, G.N., Schulz, J.K., Samimi, M., Gutierrez, F.: Millimeter wave mobile communications for 5G cellular: it will work!. IEEE Access **1**, 335–349 (2013)
13. Zappavigna, M.: Ambient affiliation: a linguistic perspective on Twitter. New Media Soc. **13**(5), 788–806 (2011)

A Case Study on Self-configuring Systems in IoT Based on a Model-Driven Prototyping Approach

Fabian Kneer$^{(\boxtimes)}$ and Erik Kamsties

Dortmund University of Applied Sciences and Arts,
Emil-Figge-Str. 42, 44227 Dortmund, Germany
{fabian.kneer,erik.kamsties}@fh-dortmund.de
http://www.fh-dortmund.de/

Abstract. **[Context and motivation]** In the last years, the development of the Internet of Things (IoT) with self-configuring systems (SCS) became more important. Consequently, many different solutions have been developed. **[Question/problem]** We observed a lack of common benchmarks, in particular for the IoT domain to evaluate and compare solutions. There are very few accessible cases (examples) for SCSs published at all. **[Principal ideas/results]** We propose a case from the IoT domain, smart cities in particular, which comprises of hardware and software components. Starting point is a smart street lighting system with communication between the lamps and passing cars. **[Contribution]** First, in this paper we present our initial results of running a case study with a model-based prototyping framework on the smart street light. The framework includes a software simulation of the street lamp and the events from the passing cars. Second, an engineer can use the case as a benchmark to compare several approaches in order to make a more informed decision which approach to choose.

Keywords: Self-configuring systems · Case studies · Experimentation

1 Introduction

The Internet of Things (IoT) is a global infrastructure for the information society, enabling advanced services by interconnecting (physical and virtual) things based on existing and evolving interoperable information and communication technologies [5]. A *thing* is an object of the physical world (physical things) or the information world (virtual things), which is capable of being identified and integrated into communication networks. A *device* is a piece of equipment with the mandatory capabilities of communication and the optional capabilities of sensing, actuation, data capture, data storage, and data processing. One key concern of systems operating in the IoT is to dynamically adapt to changing environments, due uncertainties during requirements-, design-, and run-time.

A considerable number of concepts for self-configuring systems (SCS) has been developed. From a practitioner's perspective, *open source* implementations

© Springer International Publishing Switzerland 2016
G. Dregvaite and R. Damasevicius (Eds.): ICIST 2016, CCIS 639, pp. 732–741, 2016.
DOI: 10.1007/978-3-319-46254-7_59

of the MAPE feedback loop (IBM [1]) for prototyping purposes are missing. This is a show-stopper in practice, as a practitioner would need to work through research papers in order to build such a prototype. A researcher who is interested in the comparison, extension and/or application of existing solutions to a new domain is in a similar situation.

We suggested a *prototyping and evaluation framework* for self-adaptive systems in [3]. The goal of the framework is to ease the prototyping (and possibly development) of self-configuring systems. For this purpose, the framework offers implementations of selected approaches to SCS based on the MAPE loop (e.g., based on feature models as suggested by Pascual et al. [6]). Another goal of the framework is to ease the evaluation of self-configuring systems, to allow for instance benchmarks between different approaches. For this purpose, we developed a case study drawn from the *smart city* domain. The framework is able to collect data on a subset of the metrics at runtime about overall quality, effort, and cost.

In this paper, a academic case study for *Smart Street Lighting* will be presented as an example of a self-configuring system developed using the abovementioned prototyping framework. The case is based on the real world and is transfered to a model world. In the area of IoT a simple representation of the real world is needed as a base for a simulation to verify and test the requirements and decide between the different used approaches for the implementation of a self-configuring system.

The following section presents an overview of the prototyping framework. Section 3 reports on the construction of the case study and the simulation. Section 4 presents the results and the future work.

2   Overview of the Prototyping Framework

The framework bases on experiences we made with the implementation of a goal-oriented (i*-based) approach to self-adaptive systems [2]. We developed a generalized architecture for prototyping SAS in the spirit of a software product-line (SPL), by an analysis of *commonalities* and *differences* of approaches suggested for SAS. We implemented a feature-orientated approach (Pascual et al. [6]) to validate the initial architecture of the prototyping framework. The details of the implementation, and first experiences are described in the remainder of this section.

Implementation. The framework contains components to implement the different activities of the MAPE loop as well as further functions that are needed to build and run an adaptive system.

Figure 1 shows the concept of the prototyping framework. Fundamentally, we separate *development time* and *runtime* artifacts. The development time artifacts represent additional aspects to be captured in the requirements phase. Runtime artifacts are components required to build the SAS. To easy prototyping, some runtime artifacts are generated from the development time artifacts.

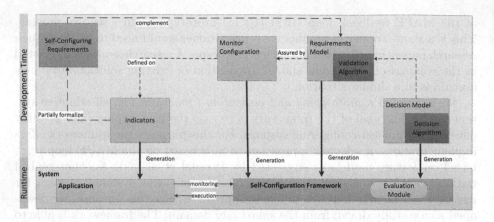

Fig. 1. Prototyping and evaluation framework

The prototyping framework provides a set of components from which can be chosen to develop a self-adaptive system. At the time of writing it contains a feature-oriented approach with utility functions to compute a configuration with a genetic algorithm (see Pascual et al. [6]).

Generator. In order to ease the development of a prototype, a self-adaptive system is partially *generated*. That is, during development time (see upper part of Fig. 1), only the essential information for building the SAS is specified by the user. When using the feature-oriented approach this is: *indicators* (variables of the systems with a type), a *feature model* (different features of the systems and variation points), *ECA rules* (indicator change event, boolean condition, change action on a element, e.g. feature), *utility function* (table with utility values of the different variations of the feature model).

Probes for an application and the whole self-configuring framework (with integrated MAPE loop), see bottom part Fig. 1 can now be *generated* out of a specification. The indicators are used to generate probes for an application. These probes are used by the self-configuring framework to monitor the indicators and check the related ECA rules. The ECA description is used to generate the rules of the ECA rule engine. An application that includes the generated probes can use the self-configuring systems to adapt the behavior to the changing context.

If the specification changes because new elements like indicators, ECA rules, features or utility elements are added or elements are refined for example an ECA rule change, only the generation process is re-triggered and the new prototype can be used for the system which contains the probes. Further details about the generator concept are given in [4].

3   Case Study

Domain. The *Smart City* domain is selected as an instantiation of the Internet of Things. The *Smart Street Lighting* is selected as a subdomain to start with. It is accessible to many readers, it is complex, and comprises many different facets.

Street lights become an important part of smart cities. The lights are extended with new functions beyond the usual function of providing light to a place: the lights are equipped with increasing computing power and communication capabilities like wireless connection, digital street signs, and sensors to measure their environment.

An example for a smart light is provided by the company *Illuminating concepts*[1]. They have designed a flexible wireless solution that is called *Intellistreets*, which includes a energy efficient lighting, audio, digital signage, and more. Figure 2 shows the design of the solution. The light can communicate with other systems and also with humans to help finding a way or send an emergency calls. Also the audio and digital signage can be used for entertainment or announcements.

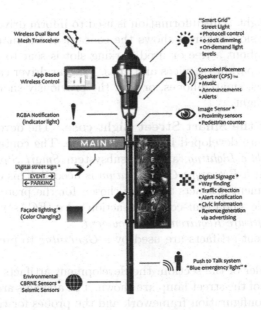

Fig. 2. Intellistreets solution developed by *Illumination concepts* (See Footnote 1).

Further, more companies like *Siemens*[2] are producing parking management systems. The lights have sensors like distance and movement to detect parking

---

[1] www.illuminatingconcepts.com.
[2] www.siemens.com.

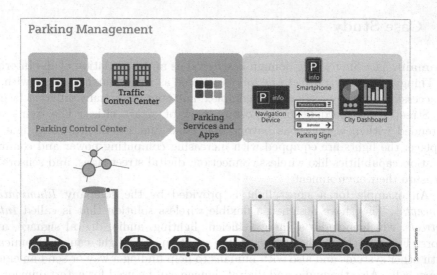

Fig. 3. Smart parking systems developed by *Siemens* (See Footnote 3).

vehicles under a light. This information is used to inform driver who are searching for a parking slot. Figure 3 shows the concept of the management system. The information about a free or used parking slot is sent to the traffic control center and also to parking services and apps. The car driver can be informed by navigation systems, smart phones, or over the previously shown digital signage of a smart street light.

Specification of the Smart Street Light case. The development artifacts of the prototype are developed in a tree structure. The context is *Smart City*, the system is *Public Lighting*, and the subsystem *Smart Street Light*. For the *Smart Street Light* a *Prototype Configuration* is needed. This configuration contains the development artifacts that are chosen for the prototype (e.g. feature model, utility table, and event-condition-action rules (ECAs)). The artifacts are described in a *Software Requirements document*.

The development artifacts are used by a *Generator* to produce source code of a prototype.

In the remainder of the section, the development artifacts that describe the self-configuration of the street lamp are shown. The artifacts are used to generate parts of the self-configuration framework and the probes for the application.

Feature Model. Figure 4 shows the feature model for the street light are shown. The feature model is modeled using the prototyping framework. The different realization strategies are developed as variation points in the model.

The lamp can adapt its luminous color and illumination. The possible values for these parameter are represented as alternative group (Xor-Group) in the feature model. The possible colors are white, blue, and red. The illumination is shown in percent and can variate between 0 %, 20 % and 100 %.

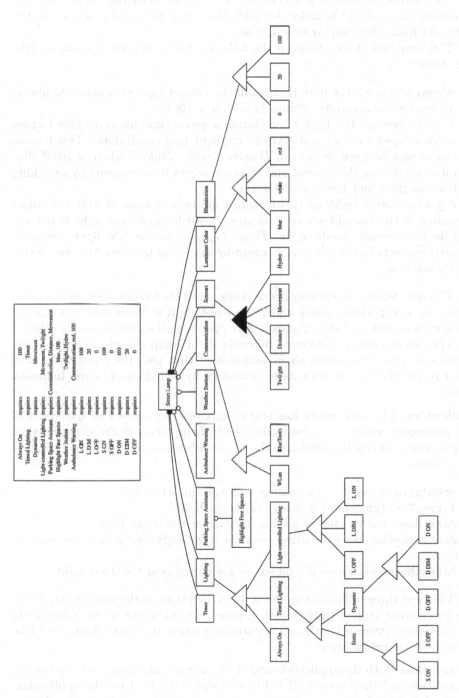

Fig. 4. Feature Model of a Public Street Light. (Color figure online)

The *abstract Sensors* of a street light are *Twilight* to measure light, *Distance* to measure if an object is under the light, *Movement* to react to moves near the light and *Hydro* for weather information.

The lamp can choose between the following three different options to light the street:

- *Always On*: is a error state that results in a street light with maximal illumination. (See constraints: *Always On requires 100*)
- *Timed Lighting*: the light is on during a given time interval. This feature needs a timer to react and activate the light (see constraints). This feature can variate between *Static* and *Dynamic* mode. *Static* leads to a 100 % illumination during the interval and *dynamic* reacts to movements by switching between 20 % and 100 % illumination.
- *Light-controlled Lighting*: this feature requires a *Movement* and a *Twilight* sensor. If the twilight sensor indicates a need for light, the light is put on. Like the dynamic mode of the *Timed Lighting* feature, the light-controlled feature reacts to the movement sensor by switching between 20 % and 100 % illumination.

The next feature is *Parking Space Assistant*. This feature sends information about the free parking spaces under the street light to connected systems like navigation system and also *Highlight Free Spaces* with a blue luminous color.

The last feature is *Ambulance Warning*. If the lamp has an established connection, it gets information about ambulances that pass the street light. The lamp reacts and try to warn its environment by switching to a red luminous color.

Indicators. The case study has status indicator for sensors of the systems, e.g. movement sensor. A boolean value shows if the sensor works as expected or deliver wrong values. In addition to the status indicators, the following indicators are defined:

- `ambulance` shows if an ambulance will pass the street light.
- `detectTwilight` shows a change of the daylight.
- `cars` shows the number of parking cars under the street light.
- `searchingCar` shows if a driver near the street light search for a free parking space.
- `detectMovement` shows if a person or car moves near the street light.

The next three indicators represent the time values of the street light. These are the current system time (`time`), a parameter when the street light should be turned *on* (`turnOnTime`), and a parameter when the street light should be turned *off* (`turnOffTime`).

Simulation. Both the application and the framework are generated as a console application and they need a GUI. Figure 5 shows the GUI for the application. On the left side of the screenshot, the software simulation of the previously presented street light is shown. On the right side, the configurable values are shown.

The first values represent the time indicators (*currentTime*, *turnOffTime*, and *turnOnTime*). The next values represent the status of the sensors. A defect sensor is colored *red*. In this example screen-shot, all sensors are working correctly, which results in green colored sensors. The two buttons with the image of vehicles, can be used to start a moving vehicle (ambulance in the example screen shot). The last configurable values are *parking cars*. Next to the parking symbol are the buttons + and −. Up to three cars can be added to the parking spaces under the street light.

The progress bar and the *Go* button are used to represent and start a scenario. A scenario represents a day of the street light with random events, which are produced during this interval.

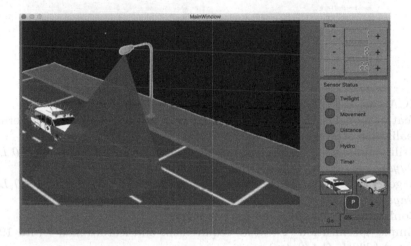

Fig. 5. GUI of the simulated Street Light. (Color figure online)

Figure 6 shows a screenshot of the prototypical GUI for the self-configuring street light. The left table represents the feature model. The *selected* features in the current configuration are colored green and the *deselected* are colored gray. The right table is the utility table. The rows represent a utility element with the utility values and the resource costs.

In the given example, the street light notices a passing ambulance and switches to a configuration with a red light color and maximum illumination.

4   Results and Conclusion

This paper presented an academic case study in which a self-configuring system - a smart street light - was developed using a prototyping framework (developed by the authors in previous work). The case was used to give an impression of the required effort, we provide programming effort data. The development has taken about 3 man-week's and 1500 LoC:

Requirements Monitor for System: 42

#	FeatureModel		#	UtilityTable			
18	Highlight Free Spaces: is selected False		6	L ON	0	0	1
19	Ambulance Warning: is selected True		7	L DIM	0	100	1
20	Weather Station: is selected True		8	L OFF	0	0	1
21	Communication: is selected True		9	D ON	0	0	1
22	WLan: is selected False		10	D DIM	0	100	1
23	BlueTooth: is selected True		11	D OFF	0	0	1
24	Sensors: is selected True		12	S ON	0	200	1
25	Twilight: is selected True		13	S OFF	0	0	1
26	Distance: is selected True		14	WLan	50	20	30
27	Movement: is selected True		15	BlueTooth	25	10	10
28	Hydro: is selected True		16	Parking Space Assistant	50	0	10
29	Luminous Color: is selected True		17	Highlight Free Spaces	0	0	10
30	blue: is selected False		18	Ambulance Warning	0	1000	10
31	white: is selected False		19	0	10	0	1
32	red: is selected True		20	20	20	0	5
33	Illumination: is selected True		21	100	30	0	10
34	0: is selected False		22	red	0	0	1
35	20: is selected False		23	white	10	0	1
36	100: is selected True		24	blue	0	0	1

Fig. 6. GUI of the Feature-based Prototype. (Color figure online)

- ECA's are used for monitoring the system (*400 LoC 3–4 Days*)
- Feature model is used as requirements model and representation of alternative realization strategies (*600 LoC 3–5 days*)
- Utility Table and - function are used to compute a configuration (*200 LoC 3 Days*)
- A genetic algorithm is used to choose the "best" configuration (*100 LoC 2 Days*)
- Configuration example (*150 LoC 1/2 day*)
- Simple Specification (1 textual requirement and feature model with 19 features) (*200 LoC 1/2 day*)

The case itself can be used by a requirements engineer to validate approaches from the area of self-configuration that are integrated in the framework. The case is taken from a subdomain of the smart city domain as an instantiation of the Internet of Things. The case is scalable and can be extended by additional systems or features of the street light, for example, more lights or a public utility system that is connected to the street lights. These extensions could lead to more complex case studies.

The framework for prototyping and evaluation can be used in a number of ways on the given case study:

- to *understand* a particular SCS approach,
- to *optimize* the application of an approach, or
- to *compare* approaches in a particular target environment.

At the time of writing we have developed a software simulation and a prototype of a hardware street light. To enlarge the case, a RC-car is under development, which enriches for instance the parking scenario. Also part of our future work is to build a small street model with up to five street lights, which can be connected to a virtual simulation of a smart city.

It is planed to make the framework and the case study open source and publicly available using GitHub, when it has passed a first validation.

References

1. An architectural blueprint for autonomic computing. Technical report, IBM (2005)
2. Kamsties, E., Kneer, F., Voelter, M., Igel, B., Kolb, B.: Feedback-aware requirements documents for smart devices. In: Salinesi, C., Weerd, I. (eds.) REFSQ 2014. LNCS, vol. 8396, pp. 119–134. Springer, Heidelberg (2014). doi:10.1007/978-3-319-05843-6_10
3. Kneer, F., Kamsties, E.: A framework for prototyping, evaluating self-adaptive systems-a research preview. In: Bjarnason, E. et al. (ed.) REFSQ Workshops, CEUR Workshop Proceedings,vol.1564. CEUR-WS.org (2016)
4. Kneer, F., Kamsties, E.: Model-based generation of a requirements monitor. In: Joint Proceedings of REFSQ- Workshops, Research Method Track, and Poster Track co-located with the 21st International Conference on Requirements Engineering: Foundation for Software Quality (REFSQ 2015), Essen, Germany, pp. 156–170, 23 March 2015
5. Overview of the Internet of things. In: IUT-T Y.2060 (2012)
6. Pascual, G.G., Pinto, M., Fuentes, L.: Run-time adaptation of mobile applications using genetic algorithms. In: Proceedings of the 8th International Symposium on Software Engineering for Adaptive and Self-Managing Systems, SEAMS, San Francisco, CA, USA, pp. 73–82, 20–21 May 2013

Information Technology Applications: Regular Session on Information Technology Applications

Minimization of Numerical Dispersion Errors in 2D Finite Element Models of Short Acoustic Wave Propagation

Andrius Kriščiūnas[1(✉)], Rimantas Barauskas[1], Liudas Mažeika[2], and Tautvydas Fyleris[2]

[1] Faculty of Informatics, Kaunas University of Technology, Kaunas, Lithuania
{andrius.krisciunas,rimantas.barauskas}@ktu.lt
[2] Ultrasound Institute, Kaunas University of Technology, Kaunas, Lithuania
{liudas.mazeika,tautvydas.fieleris}@ktu.lt

Abstract. Numerical dispersion errors are inherent for simulations based on wave propagation models with discrete meshes. The paper presents approach applied to reduce errors of this type in finite element models. High order 2D synthesized finite elements with enhanced convergence properties are obtained by modal synthesis technique. Obtained elements have diagonal mass matrix which enables to employ explicit integration schemes for wave simulation. Waves of more than two times wider frequency can be simulated using model of synthesized elements compared to models assembled of conventional elements. Furthermore, such elements could be used as a template of higher-order element to construct finite element models for all simulation problems of this kind.

Keywords: Finite elements · Wave propagation · Numerical dispersion · Modal synthesis

1 Introduction

The work refers to short-wave simulation finite element (FE) models where the range of investigated wavelengths many times shorter than the characteristic length of the propagation environment. As an example, acoustic waves in solids, hydraulic pressure pulses propagation in large pipeline networks, etc. can be presented as short-wave propagation models. They require huge amount of elements (even "small" models for 2D problems contain $10^6 - 10^7$ elements) and therefore computational resources required for simulation are very large. Generally, the dimensionality of the FE model is reduced as rougher meshes are applied, where measure for roughness of the mesh is the number of elements per characteristic wavelength. Unfortunately, rough meshes tend to increase the simulation errors, which exhibit themselves as severe deterioration of the shapes of propagating wave pulses as the time of simulation increases. In other words, they can be referred to as numerical dispersion and phase velocity errors.

Already in 1980s researchers have noticed different modal convergence features of dynamic models obtained by using lumped and consistent forms of mass matrices [1]. The simplest way to reduce the numerical dispersion of dynamic models is to use the

© Springer International Publishing Switzerland 2016
G. Dregvaite and R. Damasevicius (Eds.): ICIST 2016, CCIS 639, pp. 745–752, 2016.
DOI: 10.1007/978-3-319-46254-7_60

'combined' form of the mass matrix obtained as a weighted superposition of the two traditional forms [2]. However, the models with non-diagonal mass matrix were unable to fully exploit the advantages of explicit time integration schemes. In recent years this problem has been examined more thoroughly. Generally, the results are obtained by using models based on the higher order FE, which could ensure the sufficient accuracy of simulation results within acceptable limits. In [3] equidistant, Lobatto and Cheby-shev nodal positions within a FE were investigated. The positioning of nodes has been demonstrated to be important in case of higher-order FE. In [4] the general template for retrieving characteristic matrices of n-node bar elements based on their reduced diagonal representations has been proposed. In [5] two different formulations based on the modified integration rule for the mass and stiffness matrices and on the averaged mass matrix has been introduced. These techniques with reduced dispersion for linear elastodynamics problems which enable reduce the numerical dispersion for linear FE models has been investigated.

The approach presented in this work is based on synthesized finite elements (SFE). Synthesis of elements is performed by minimizing the penalty-type target function, where the design variables are modal shapes and mode frequencies of elements. The target function evaluates the magnitude of the phase velocity error in terms of the modal frequencies of the sample model consisting of SFE. Originally the method was proposed in [6] for 1D case. In [7] it has been expanded to 2D case. There models consisting of SFE preserve small phase velocity errors in meshes that are 3–5 times rougher than the ones required for conventional lumped mass matrix models. The novelty of this work is that only stiffness matrix of the model is computed by modal synthesis, while the diagonal mass matrix remains unchanged. This enables to use explicit integration schemes for wave simulation. The numerical results obtained during 2D acoustic wave pulse simulation are analyzed.

2   Synthesis of the Finite Element

The finite element model of elastic media in which the propagating acoustic wave is considered is derived from general structural dynamic equation system

$$[M]\{\ddot{U}\} + [K]\{U\} = \{F(t)\} \tag{1}$$

where $[M]$ and $[K]$ are mass and stiffness matrices, $\{U\}$ is the nodal displacement vector and $\{F(t)\}$ is the excitation force vector. Modal frequencies (MF) and modal shapes (MS) of the structure are obtained by solving the eigenvalue problem as

$$([K] - \omega^2[M])\{y\} = \{0\} \tag{2}$$

where ω is modal angular frequency and $\{y\}$ is the modal shape.

For real and symmetric structural matrices $[M]$ and $[K]$ the solutions of (2) equation are obtained as structural modes $\omega_i, \{y_i\}, i = 1, \ldots, n$, where n - is degree of freedom of the structure. The fundamental properties of structural modes provide derivation of [K] matrix in terms of normalized MS and MF as

$$[K] = \left([Y]^T\right)^{-1} \left[diag\left(\omega_1^2, \omega_2^2, \ldots, \omega_n^2\right)\right][Y]^{-1} \qquad (3)$$

where $[Y] = [\{y_1\}, \{y_2\}, \ldots, \{y_n\}]$ is the matrix of MS.

Relationship (3) means that the stiffness matrix of an element, of a substructure or of a structure can be generated by directly referring to their known or desired values of MF and MS. The idea of our approach is to find such modes used for synthesizing an element that the cumulative modal frequency error of the sample domain (SD) assembled of synthesized elements would be as small as possible. The outline of the synthesis procedure is presented in Fig. 1.

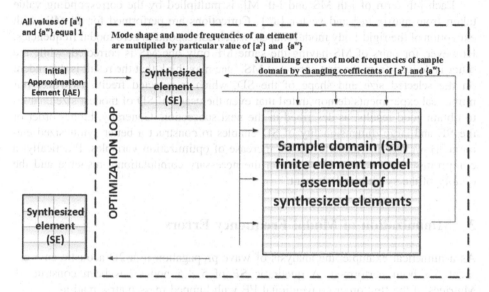

Fig. 1. Outline of the synthesis procedure

In this work structure assembled from conventional square-form elements with lumped mass matrix is used as initial approximation element (IAE). During the optimization loop, MS and MF of synthesized element (SE) were slightly modified in order to ensure that the sample domain assembled of a certain number of synthesized elements provides as many as possible close-to-exact modes. The optimization loop in Fig. 1 is used for the minimization of the target function Ψ, which presents the cumulative error of modal frequencies of the SD as

$$\min_{[a^y],[a^\omega]} \Psi - \sum_{i=1}^{\tilde{N}} \left(\frac{\tilde{\omega}_i - \omega_{i0}}{\omega_{i0}}\right)^2 \qquad (4)$$

where $\{\tilde{\omega}_0, \ldots, \tilde{\omega}_{\tilde{N}}\}$ are the MFs of the SD assembled of SE, $\{\hat{\omega}_{00}, \ldots, \hat{\omega}_{0\tilde{N}}\}$ are close-to-exact MFs of the SD, and $\{a^\omega\}$, $[a^y]$ are the vector and matrix of MF and MS correction coefficients correspondingly, used as optimization variables. The summation of errors is performed over $\tilde{N} \leq N$ modal frequencies of the SD, where N is the number of modes of the SD. The close-to exact modal frequencies have to be computed only once, by using densely meshed FE model or in certain cases they are known analytically.

The correction of modal shapes and modal frequencies is performed as

$$[\tilde{Y}] = [\{y_{11} * a_{11}^y, \ldots, y_{1n} * a_{1n}^y\}, \ldots, \{y_{n1} * a_{n1}^y, \ldots, y_{nn} * a_{nn}^y\}] \qquad (5)$$

$$[\text{diag}(\tilde{\omega}_1^2, \ldots, \tilde{\omega}_n^2)] = [\text{diag}(\omega_1 * a_1^\omega, \ldots, \omega_n * a_n^\omega)] \qquad (6)$$

Each j-th term of i-th MS and i-th MF is multiplied by the corresponding value taken from matrix $[a^y]$ and vector $\{a^\omega\}$. Corrections are performed for all MSs with exception of the rigid-body modal shapes, which correspond to zero modal frequencies. However, for pairs of MS having the same MF only one MS is corrected, while the other is derived from the first corrected MS. One may think that the result is dependent on the selected size and shape of the SD, which is selected freely. However our numerical experiments demonstrated that even the usage of SD of modest size enables to obtain good results, as described in the next subsection. Generally, higher order of the SE and large dimensionality of SD enables to construct a better synthesized element. However, this leads to drastic increase of optimization variables. Practically, a compromise has been sought between the necessary computational resource and the quality of the synthesized element.

3   Minimization of Modal Frequency Errors

As a numerical example, the analysis of wave propagation in a 2D acoustic environment has been performed. A quadratic SE of 5×5 nodes has been constructed. Matrices of the first order conventional FE with lumped mass matrix read as

$$[M^e] = \frac{\rho * S^e}{4}[I] \qquad (7)$$

$$[K^e] = E * S^e[B]^T[B] \qquad (8)$$

where E – Young's modulus, ρ – mass density, S^e – area of the element, $[I]$ and $[B]$ are identity and strain matrices. Stiffness matrix $[K^{IA}]$ of the initial approximation element (IAE), computed by using (3) with modes obtained by solving eigenvalue problem (2) for structure assembled of 16×16 conventional 2×2 nodes finite elements. Mass matrix $[M^{IA}]$ of IAE remains diagonal and is the same as the structural mass matrix assembled of conventional elements. Synthesized element stiffness matrix reads as

$$[K^{SE0}] = \left([\tilde{Y}]^T\right)^{-1}[\text{diag}(\tilde{\omega}_1^2, \tilde{\omega}_2^2, \ldots, \tilde{\omega}_n^2)][\tilde{Y}]^{-1} \qquad (9)$$

where $[\tilde{Y}]$ and $[\text{diag}(\tilde{\omega}_1^2, \tilde{\omega}_2^2, \ldots, \tilde{\omega}_n^2)]$ are the MS and MF obtained after element synthesis, while constants ρ, E, S^e have been assigned the value 1 for the synthesis. The target function included the first 25 % of MF of the sample domain ($\tilde{N} = 0.25 * N$). Close-to-exact MFs of SD used as reference values in the target function have been obtained by solving eigenvalue problem (2) for the structure meshed with 5 times smaller linear dimension of FE. Results of the synthesis in terms of relative modal frequency errors as $\frac{\hat{\omega}_i - \omega_{i0}}{\omega_{i0}}$ are shown in Fig. 2.

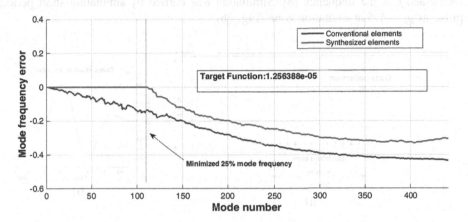

Fig. 2. Modal frequency errors of the sample domain assembled of 25 synthesized elements with minimized cumulative error of 25 % of modal frequencies

From the results of Fig. 2 it can be seen that the synthesis process worked well. First 25 % of MF of the model assembled of synthesized elements was very close-to-exact as was required. The final value of the target function value was $\sum_{i=1}^{\tilde{N}} \left(\frac{\hat{\omega}_i - \omega_{i0}}{\omega_{i0}}\right)^2 \approx 1.2^{-5}$. Elements obtained by the synthesis procedure could be used as a template

$$[K^{SE}] = E * [K^{SE0}] \tag{10}$$

for constructing finite element stiffness matrices for all simulation problems of this kind as a higher-order element stiffness matrix. Mass matrix of the model remains diagonal and is the same as of the structure assembled of conventional elements.

4 Numerical Investigation with Application to 2D Acoustic Wave Propagation

The numerical experiments have been carried out by investigating the wave propagation in water, where 2D rectangular structure model of 0.32 m × 0.24 m was assembled of conventional and synthesized elements using 0.5 mm finite element mesh size (Fig. 3a). Physical constants were $\rho = 995 \, \text{kg/m}^3$ and $E = 2.2 \, \text{GPa}$, the phase velocity of the wave is $v = \sqrt{E/\rho} = 1487 \, \text{m/s}$. The excitation pulse was a sine wave multiplied by a Gaussian window:

$$u(t) = e^{-a(t-b)^2} \sin(2\pi f t) \tag{11}$$

where $a = k_a f \sqrt{-\frac{2 \ln 0.1}{p_s}}$; $b = 2p_s/3f$, p_s is the number of periods, k_a is the asymmetry factor and f is the frequency [8]. Simulation was carried by simulating short period pulse as $p_s = 1.5$ at excitation zone (Fig. 3b).

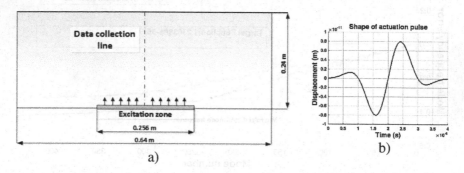

Fig. 3. (a) Geometry of the finite element model (b) excitation pulse shape

Pulse has been actuated for 4 μs at excitation zone and its propagation for 240 μs has been simulated. Figure 4 shows the simulated B-Scan image, where black pattern refers to the amplitude of the pulse along the data collection line at different time moments.

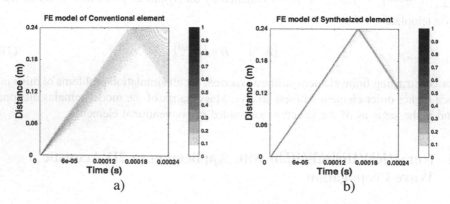

Fig. 4. B-scans of pulse propagation in model assembled of (a) conventional element; (b) synthesized elements

Analysis of the simulation results in Fig. 4 shows that when the pulse is simulated using the model of conventional elements, the numerical distortions grow with time and at the end of simulation the pulse is highly distorted, while in model of SE distortion remains small. Dispersion analysis practically cannot be performed by solving eigenvalue problem (2), because mass and stiffness matrices of the model have size of 616161×616161. In order to estimate the character of the observed dispersion the B-scan data have been converted from space-time domain into phase velocity - frequency domain by using 2D Fourier transform. Obtained images of dispersion curves are presented in Fig. 5 where phase velocity in the images at different frequencies corresponds to the yellow pattern.

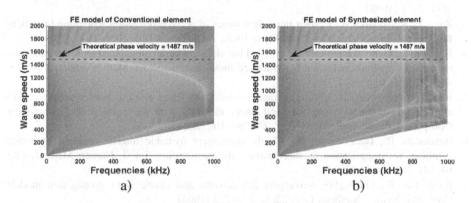

Fig. 5. Dispersion curve of the FE model assembled of (a) conventional elements; (b) synthesized elements (Color figure online)

The comparison of dispersion curves of the models assembled of SE and CE leads to the conclusion that in model of CE phase velocity is close to theoretical till–250 kHz and at higher frequencies phase velocity inaccuracies grow rather quickly (Fig. 5a). On the contrary, the model assembled of SE retains a good accuracy of phase velocity till– 700 kHz (Fig. 5b). This means that models assembled of synthesized elements can be used to simulate the propagation of wave pulses of more than two times wider frequency than the models assembled of conventional elements at the same mesh density.

5 Conclusions

The approach for the reduction of the numerical dispersion in two-dimensional model has been proposed. Fifth order synthesized finite element obtained using modal synthesis technique, where first quarter of mode frequencies of models assembled of synthesized element are close to exact. 2D finite element model of water material has been assembled of conventional and synthesized elements. By investigating driving ultrasonic pulse, numerical dispersion has been compared for models assembled of synthesized and conventional elements. Results show that in models of synthesized elements numerical dispersion is close to zero over more than two times wider frequency range compared against the models assembled of conventional elements at the same mesh density.

References

1. Mullen, R., Belytschko, T.: Dispersion analysis properties of finite element semi-discretizations of the two-dimensional wave equations. Int. J. Numer. Methods Eng. **18**, 1–29 (1982)
2. Daniulaitis, V., Barauskas, R.: Modelling techniques of ultrasonic wave propagation in solids, 1(1), 7–11 (1998)
3. Żak, A., Krawczuk, M.: Certain numerical issues of wave propagation modelling in rods by the spectral finite element method. Finite Elem. Anal. Des. **47**(9), 1036–1046 (2011)
4. Khajavi, R.: General templates for n-noded bar elements based on reduced representations and numerical dispersion reduction by optimized finite elements. Appl. Math. Comput. **233**, 445–462 (2014)
5. Idesman, A., Pham, D.: Finite element modeling of linear elastodynamics problems with explicit time-integration methods and linear elements with the reduced dispersion error. Comput. Methods Appl. Mech. Eng. **271**, 86–108 (2014)
6. Barauskas, R., Barauskiene, R.: Highly convergent dynamic models obtained by modal synthesis with application to short wave pulse propagation. Int. J. Numer. Methods Eng. **61**(14), 2536–2554 (2004)
7. Barauskas, R.: On highly convergent 2D acoustic and elastic wave propagation models. Commun. Numer. Methods Eng. **22**(3), 225–233 (2005)
8. Kažys, R., Mažeika, L., Barauskas, R., Jasiuniene, E., Daniulaitis, V.: Evaluation of diffraction errors in precise pulse-echo measurements of ultrasound velocity in chambers with waveguide. Ultrasonics **40**(1–8), 853–858 (2002)

On Methodology of E-wallet Construction for Partially Off-line Payment System

Jonas Muleravičius$^{(\boxtimes)}$, Eligijus Sakalauskas, and Inga Timofejeva

Department of Applied Mathematics, Kaunas University of Technology,
Studentu Street 50, Kaunas, Lithuania
{jonas.muleravicius,inga.timofejeva}@ktu.edu,
eligijus.sakalauskas@ktu.lt

Abstract. We propose a methodology for the construction of e-wallet with off-line divisible e-cash, with such properties as anonymity against vendor and full traceability from bank. Since this system is fully controlled by bank from the issuance of e-money to e-cash deposit, the prevention of an overpayment and the detection of a dishonest user are provided.

Proposed system prevents the serious drawback of existing anonymous and divisible e-cash systems noticed by Chaum, namely the growth of the amount of information during e-cash transfers among the users. The prevention of this issue is achieved by sacrificing such valuable properties of existing e-cash systems as an honest user's anonymity against bank and off-line deposit.

The proof of the proposed construction's security is provided.

Keywords: Cryptography · E-cash · E-cash system · Homomorphic encryption · Paillier encryption · RSA textbook encryption

1 Introduction

Electronic Cash (E-cash) is the digital analogue of regular money. Hence, in general, it has to satisfy the same properties as the regular money (or as much as possible).

1.1 Overview of Existing E-cash Systems

One of the first e-cash systems, which was based on cut and cut-and-choose approach [23, 24], was introduced by Chaum, Fiat and Naor (CFN) in 1988. The system was not effective since the bank had to store $2k + 3k^2$ bits (where k is bank's secret key) after each Deposit protocol as well as each user's unique identificator Pk for each Withdrawal protocol, while the user had to store $2k + 4k^2$ bits per each e-coin in his e-wallet, and the merchant - $2k + 3k^2$ bits.

In 1993, Stefan Brands and Niels Ferguson [10] introduced two e-cash systems that were significantly more efficient than any other e-cash system created before. Bank had to store $6k$ bits for the public key, Purchaser had to put $12k$ bits in his wallet, while every e-coin in vendor's wallet took up $10k$ bits. This system was more efficient than Chaum's system, firstly, because of the elimination of the cut-and-choose proofs and,

© Springer International Publishing Switzerland 2016
G. Dregvaite and R. Damasevicius (Eds.): ICIST 2016, CCIS 639, pp. 753–765, 2016.
DOI: 10.1007/978-3-319-46254-7_61

secondly, because of the level of indirection added to double-spending detection, after which there was no need for bank to keep cryptographic information about each withdrawal [23].

In the late 1980 s and early 1990 s, cryptographers developed a system of rigorous security definitions to address philosophical notions such as privacy, unforgeability, proof of knowledge, etc. These definitions influenced e-cash research, making it possible to prove statements about the required properties of an e-cash system [3]. In later works [4, 6, 7], properties such as strong or weak exculpability, double spending prevention, untraceability, money divisibility, off-line payment, unlinkability, unforgeability, etc. were considered.

In 2005, Camenisch, Hohenberger, and Lysyanskaya (CHL) introduced Compact E-Cash [11]. The basic idea of this e-cash system was to use a pseudorandom function to generate a sequence of serial numbers from a single seed. The bank had to give the purchaser a blind signature on a secret seed value s. Alice(the purchaser) then had to generate e-coins with serial numbers $F_s(0), F_s(1), \ldots, F_s(W-1)$, where W is the amount of money in purchaser's e-wallet [3, 11]. Bank had to store $3k$ bits after each deposit, purchaser had to store $11k + \log(W)$ bits for the e-money, while vendor had to store $3k$ and $k + \log(W)$ bits. This CHL compact e-cash system was not better than the other e-cash systems, concerning the amount of data needed to store in each user's database, however it was better in a sense that every purchaser could make a payment himself, by using a secret seed value s.

Nevertheless, in 1998, Frankel, Tsiounis and Yung in [26] pointed out that to date, there have been no efficient systems that could offer provable security. They proposed a fair off-line e-cash system, where the trusted third party could revoke the anonymity under a warrant or in the case of specified suspicious activity.

In [22] the first e-cash system based on binary tree approach without the trusted third party was presented, providing both full unlinkability and anonymity, but, as it was noticed in [3], the system was extremely inefficient.

In [19] a transferable e-cash scheme based on CFN e-cash system with the reduced number of communications between the bank and users that fulfilled the computational anonymity property, was presented.

In 2013, Baseri et al., introduced e-cash scheme with five main protocols: initialization, withdrawal, payment, deposit, and the exchange [17]. His main goal was to take advantage of RSA-based method to attach the time to the structure of the signature. However, in [19] it was showed that Baseri's e-cash system has three drawbacks: the scheme cannot satisfy verifiability, unreuseability and unforgeability.

In [20] the construction with more advanced security and anonymity properties of e-cash system was presented, which provided e-cash transferability by capturing issues that were previously overlooked in [5, 10, 11, 17, 23, 27]. In [10] malleable signatures proposed by Chase [21] were used to allow secure and anonymous transferring of coins.

In [15], Chaum and Pedersen for the first time outlined the very significant property, which can be treated as an essential drawback of e-cash systems providing off-line payment, transferability and anonymity. The authors showed that this class of e-cash systems has the following problem – the informational size of e-cash grows after each transaction. This means that it is impossible to construct an electronic money system providing transferability without money growing in size when it is being transferred among the users. Furthermore, the authors proved there that it does not matter whether e-cash system is computationally untraceable or unconditionally untraceable. If e-cash system is based on full purchase anonymity, money divisibility and off-line payment, then the size of the data stored in the user's e-wallet will eventually become overwhelming.

The problem described above is also common for such e-cash systems as the system providing extensions of compact e-cash [3], Ferguson's scheme [6], Hanatani et al. e-cash [16].

In this paper, we concentrate our attention on the main properties of e-cash system overviewed below.

Divisibility. If a coin is not divisible, the purchaser must withdraw a coin whenever he spends it or withdraw many coins of various values and store them in his e-wallet, like with real cash, as proposed in [5]. Divisibility means that if one withdraws a certain amount of money, he can split into as many pieces as he wants with no need of cash return or re-withdrawal from bank at the moment of payment.

Anonymity. It means the user being not identifiable within a set of subjects, namely anonymity set, performing e-cash operations [3, 4].

Anonymity of e-cash can be split into such sections as **Anonymity of Withdrawal**– bank (or else) does not know how much money the subject has in his wallet as well as who is withdrawing money from it; **Anonymity of Payment** – nobody knows subject's payment history; **Anonymity of Deposit** – bank is not able to recognize who is depositing money unless double spending takes place; **Anonymity of Verification** – bank is not able to recognize who is requesting the verification of money.

In general, e-cash can be called *anonymous* if it satisfies the same characteristics as regular cash.

Off-line payment. In [14] a payment scheme is called online if the payment protocol requires the issuer or the acquirer to participate in the payment protocol online. Otherwise, it is called offline, which means there is no need in an additional connection to the bank in a moment of payment.

Transferability. It means that the payee in one payment transaction can spend the received money in a later payment to a third person without contacting the bank between the two transactions.

1.2 Our Proposal

In this paper, we would like to propose a methodology, avoiding the drawback noticed by Chaum in [15], by sacrificing two valuable e-cash properties, namely, anonymity against Bank and off-line deposit option for the Vendor. The latter property can be recovered by introducing tamper resistant observers to e-wallet. However, we will not consider this opportunity in this paper.

In proposed system, Bank (or e-money organization) is able to trace all payment operations of the Purchaser and identify him. Moreover, Bank is acting as Third

Trusted Party – TTP organization issuing e-cash, controlling its circulation and solving conflicts among the users: Purchasers and Vendors. This methodology has several advantages in the case of money laundering and other financial crimes.

Proposed methodology allows to construct e-cash and e-wallet system providing the following options:

1. E-cash placed in e-wallet is divisible.
2. Payments are anonymous against the Vendor and non-anonymous against the Bank, which is reckoned as TTP.
3. Payments are traceable by Bank after its deposit.
4. E-cash amount can be increased/decreased after e-cash income and outcome and its informational size does not grow.
5. All operations are performed without interactive proofs.

According to [26], e-cash system should be (1) provably secure, based on well understood assumptions, (2) efficient and (3) conceptually easy.

We are trying to follow these recommendations in the realization of proposed methodology. The implementation of e-cash in e-wallet system is very transparent and relatively simple since in our case the blinding and linear interpolation of signatures used for double spending prevention is avoided. We use a combination of well-known cryptographic homomorphic functions such as Paillier asymmetric encryption and modified textbook RSA signature schemes and e-cash operations are performed using computations with encrypted data. We have presented a security proof of this combination in random oracle model.

We consider e-cash system consisting of three parties the Bank (**B**), the Purchaser (**P**) and the Vendor (**V**). These parties are interacting by registration, withdrawal, payment and deposit protocols. We also assume that **B** acts as third trusted party for all users and that **B** computational resources are big enough to register all transactions among users for overspending prevention and dishonest user traceability.

E-wallet construction encompasses divisible e-cash implemented in certain mobile device to ensure execution of e-cash circulation protocols, i.e. in device with restricted power and computational resources.

2   Mathematical Background of E-cash Scheme

Proposed e-cash scheme is based on two homomorphic cryptographic schemes, namely, Paillier asymmetric encryption scheme and RSA textbook signature algorithm [1] for signing ciphertext obtained by Paillier encryption. We use the same modulus for both systems.

For key generation, **B** generates two RSA secure Sophie Germain primes p', q' where

$$p = 2p' + 1, \quad q = 2q' + 1 \tag{1}$$

are primes as well. Then RSA modulus n and Euler totient function ϕ are computed

$$n = pq, \quad \phi(n) = 4p'q' = \phi. \tag{2}$$

According to Paillier and RSA algorithms [1], **B** computes his private key PrK and public key PuK in the form

$$PrK = (d, \phi), \quad PuK = (n, e) \tag{3}$$

where $ed \equiv 1 \bmod \phi(n)$ and e is RSA exponent.

The encryption and signing procedures are the following:

Let $m \in \mathbb{Z}_n$ be a message to be encrypted. Then random number $r \in \mathbb{Z}_n^*$ is selected and ciphertext c is computed using Paillier encryption function $Enc_{Pai}()$ in the following way

$$c = Enc_{Pai}(m) = (1+n)^m \cdot r^n \bmod n^2, c \in \mathbb{Z}_{n^2}^*. \tag{4}$$

RSA signature s on c is computed using $Sig_{RSA}()$ function

$$s_c = Sig_{RSA}(c) = c^d \bmod n, s_c \in \mathbb{Z}_n^*.$$

Signature s_c verification on c is performed in an ordinary manner with verification function $Ver_{RSA}()$

$$Ver_{RSA}(s_c, c) = \begin{cases} True, & if\ s_c^e \bmod(n) = c \\ False, & otherwise \end{cases} \tag{5}$$

According to Paillier algorithm, ciphertext c is decrypted with private key ϕ using decryption function $Dec_{Pai}()$ by the formula

$$m = Dec_{Pai}() = (c^{\phi(n)} \bmod(n^2) - 1) \cdot n^{-1} \cdot \phi^{-1} \bmod n, m \in \mathbb{Z}_n \tag{6}$$

Both Paillier encryption and RSA signature have the following homomorphic properties [1]. Let $m = m_1 + m_2$, then

$$Enc_{Pai}(m_1) \cdot Enc_{Pai}(m_2) = Enc_{Pai}((m_1 + m_2) \bmod(n)) = Enc_{Pai}(m) = c, c \in \mathbb{Z}_n^* \tag{7}$$

Let $c = c_1 \cdot c_2$, then

$$Sig_{RSA}(c_1) \cdot Sig_{RSA}(c_2) = Sig_{RSA}((c_1 \cdot c_2) \bmod(n^2)) = Sig_{RSA}(c) = s_c, s_c \in \mathbb{Z}_n^* \tag{8}$$

The security proof of this textbook RSA signature in combination with Paillier encryption is presented in Sect. 6.

3 E-money System

In this section, we present a methodology for e-wallet construction by considering registration, e-cash withdrawal, payment and deposit protocols.

3.1 Registration Protocol

The electronic license is issued by the **B** to **P** during the registration protocol. This protocol is performed once per purchaser, typically when the purchaser opens an account, using secure and authenticated communications between **B** and **P**.

1. **P** appeals to **B** to open his e-cash account for his e-wallet;
2. **B** supplies **P** with his public key $PuK = (n, e)$;
3. **B** assigns an identification Id for **P**, encrypts and signs it by computing $C_{Id} = Enc_{Pai}(Id)$, $S_{Id} = Sig_{RSA}(C_{Id})$;
4. **B** generates random number R, encrypts and signs it by computing $C_R = Enc_{Pai}(R)$ and $S_R = Sig_{RSA}(C_R)$. R represents a random decimal number providing randomness of every transaction.
5. **B** sends to **P** the following registration data D_R using secure and authenticated communication channel;

$$D_R = [n, e, Id, C_{Id}, S_{Id}, R, C_R, S_R] \tag{9}$$

6. **P** forms e-wallet data structure D with the data received from **B**. D structure is represented by a decimal number, satisfying relation

$$D = Id + R + void_1 + void_2, \tag{10}$$

where all decimal positions of added numbers are different and do not intersect, $void_1$ is an empty position for placing maximal amount M of money **B** allows **P** to spend and $void_2$ is an empty position for a decimal number representing e-cash to be paid during payment protocol (Fig. 1).

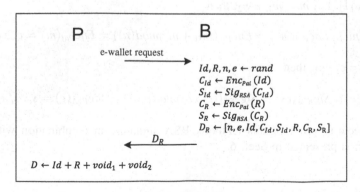

Fig. 1. Registration protocol

3.2 Withdrawal Protocol

After the registration protocol, withdrawal protocol can be executed.

1. **P** sends money request to **B**;
2. **B** defines maximal amount M of e-cash **P** is allowed to spend. **B** encrypts M and signs encrypted value obtaining $C_M = Enc_{Pai}(M)$ and $S_M = Sig_{RSA}(C_M)$. **B** supplies **P** with signed banknotes of several nominal values. For example, we use banknotes with nominal values $m_0 = 0,01€$, $m_{10} = 0,1€$, $m_{100} = 1€$. **B** encrypts banknotes obtaining $c_0 = Enc_{Pai}(m_1)$, $c_{10} = Enc_{Pai}(m_{10})$, $c_{100} = Enc_{Pai}(m_{100})$ and signs encrypted values computing $s_0 = Sig_{RSA}(c_1)$, $s_{10} = Sig_{RSA}(c_{10})$, $s_{100} = Sig_{RSA}(c_{100})$;
3. **B** sends **P** the following withdrawal data

$$D_W = [M, C_M, S_M, m_0, m_{10}, m_{100}, c_0, c_{10}, c_{100}, s_0, s_{10}, s_{100}] \tag{11}$$

E-wallet data D_{E-W} consists of the union of D_R and D_W data, i.e.

$$D_{E-W} = [n, e, Id, C_{Id}, S_{Id}, R, C_R, S_R, M, C_M, S_M, m_0, m_{10}, m_{100}, c_0, c_{10}, c_{100}, s_0, s_{10}, s_{100}] \tag{12}$$

This data is used to form e-cash and perform a payment (Fig. 2).

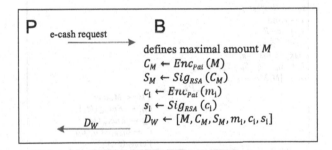

Fig. 2. Withdrawal protocol

3.3 Payment Protocol

Say **P** wants to pay the sum $M_1 < M$ to **V**. **P** takes banknotes m_0, m_{10}, m_{100} and forms the required sum

$$M_1 = a_0 m_0 + a_2 m_{10} + a_3 m_{100} \tag{13}$$

where a_0, a_2, a_3 is a quantity of corresponding banknotes.

1. **P** encrypts M_1, using $PuK = (n)$, obtaining C_{M_1} and then computes S_{M_1} on C_{M_1}

$$Enc_{Pai}(M_1) = C_{M_1}, S_{M_1} = s_0^{a_0} \cdot s_{10}^{a_2} \cdot s_{100}^{a_3} \tag{14}$$

2. **P** randomizes its payment by randomly choosing integer α and computing

$$R_1 = \alpha \cdot R, C_{R_1} = C_R^{\alpha} \tag{15}$$

P computes ciphertext and common signature on $Id_P + \alpha R$

$$C_{IdR_1} = C_{Id} \cdot C_{R_1}, S_1 = S_{Id} \cdot S_R^{\alpha} \cdot S_M \cdot S_{M_1} \tag{16}$$

3. **P** sends **V** the following payment data: $D_P = [M, M_1, C_{IdR_1}, S_1]$.
4. **V** verifies, if $M_1 < M$, and if *Yes*, performs the following computation

$$C_{M_1} = Enc_{Pai}(M_1),\ C_M = Enc_{Pai}(M),\ C_1 = C_{IdR_1} \cdot C_M \cdot C_{M_1} \tag{17}$$

V verifies signature S_1 on C_1 and if $Ver_{RSA}(S_1, C_1) = True$, then e-cash with nominal value M_1 is accepted from **P** (Fig. 3).

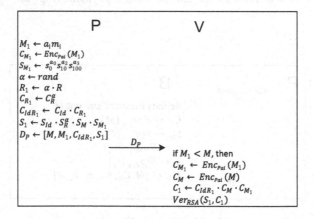

Fig. 3. Payment protocol

3.4 Deposit Protocol

After the payment protocol, **V** sends **B** data $D_D = [M_1, C_1]$ for deposition.

1. **B** decrypts ciphertext $Dec_{Pai}(C_1) = (Id + \alpha \cdot R + M + M_1) = D$;
2. Firstly, **B** checks **P** status according to Id. If it is ok, then **B** confirms e-cash validity to **V**; In this stage, **B** can trace all previous **P**'s payments and if total sum exceeds limited sum M, then overpayment is detected (Fig. 4).

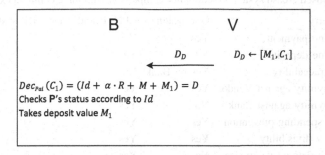

Fig. 4. Deposit protocol

4 E-cash Data Format

In our construction, e-cash is a decimal number $D = (Id + \alpha \cdot R + M + M_1)$ consisting of separated numbers $Id, \alpha \cdot R, M, M_1$, placed in different decimal positions. A certain amount of decimal digits is assigned to all positions in D to represent the values of these numbers. Format of D is shown below, in Table 1.

Table 1. E-cash data format

	Positions in e-cash	Multiplier
Id	10	10^{35}
$\alpha \cdot R$ or R	20	10^{15}
M	9	10^{6}
M_1	6	1

In this table, for Id we provide 10 decimal digits, for random number $\alpha \cdot R$ - 20 decimal digits and so on. For example, for $Id = 1234567890$, $\alpha \cdot R = 10203040506070809011$, $M = 10000$ € and $M_1 = 345$ €, we obtain

$$D = 1234567890 \cdot 10^{35} + 10203040506070809011 \cdot 10^{15} + 10000 \cdot 10^{6} + 345$$

5 Comparison with Several Existing Schemes

The comparison of proposed system with traditional e-cash systems such as CFN [23], Brands [10] and CHL [11] is presented in Table 2.

As we can see from Table 2, we have prevented Chaum's declared drawback [15] of e-cash data growth property, sacrificing off-line deposit and anonymity against bank.

Table 2. Proposed e-cash system functionality comparison with three common existing systems

Property	Our system	CFN, Brand's and CHL systems
Off-line payment	Yes	Yes
Off-line deposit	No	Yes
Full traceability	Yes by Bank	No
Anonymity against Vendor	Yes	Yes
Anonymity against Bank	No	Yes
Over spending prevention	Yes	Yes
Money divisibility	Yes	Yes
E-cash data grows in size	No	Yes

6 Security Proof

Security of proposed e-wallet methodology relies on the security of combination of Paillier encryption scheme and RSA textbook signature scheme. According to our construction, message m is encrypted obtaining ciphertext c which is then signed by RSA, obtaining signature s.

We assume, that Paillier scheme is an indistinguishable encryption under a chosen-plaintext attack if random encryption number r in (4) is chosen as random element in $\mathbb{Z}_n^*$. We assume, that in this case Paillier encryption is performed correctly and we will follow this assumption. Then ciphertext c corresponding to the message m is uniformly distributed in $\mathbb{Z}_{n^2}^*$ if r is uniformly distributed in $\mathbb{Z}_n^*$.

It is known, e.g. in [1], that RSA textbook signature scheme is existentially forgeable under an adaptive chosen message attack.

In [28], authors introduced RSA Full-Domain-Hash (FDH) function, which can be applied for signing with RSA signature scheme. It was shown in [28, 29] that this scheme is provably secure, i.e. existentially unforgeable under adaptive chosen-message attacks in the random oracle model, assuming that inverting RSA is hard, i.e. extracting a root modulo a composite integer, is hard.

Proposition. If Paillier encryption and RSA signature have the same modulus n and message m is in $\mathbb{Z}_n$, then RSA signature $s = Sig_{RSA}(c)$ on ciphertext c is existentially unforgeable under adaptive chosen-message attacks in the random oracle model.

Proof. Firstly, we should show that ciphertext $c = Enc_{Pai}(m)$ obtained by Paillier encryption taken modulo n, is in RSA domain, i.e. $c \bmod n = z\mathbb{Z}_n^*$. It is clear, that $z\mathbb{Z}_n^*$, since $\gcd(h, n) = 1$ if $\gcd(h, n^2) = 1$. Let f be a function of $modn$, i.e. $f(c) = c \bmod n = z$. Hence, the composition $f \circ Enc_{Pai}$ of function f and Enc_{Pai} represents the following mapping

$$f \circ Enc_{Pai} : \mathbb{Z}_n \times \mathbb{Z}_n^* \to \mathbb{Z}_n^*$$

and the range of this composition coincides with RSA domain.

We must show that if Paillier encryption is correct, then for any $m\mathbb{Z}_n$, value z is randomly distributed in $\mathbb{Z}_n^*$ for distinct uniform values of r in (4).

For all z in $\mathbb{Z}_n^*$, the set of elements $f^{-1}(z)$ is $\{z, nz, 2nz, \ldots, (n-1)nz\}$ and consists exactly of n elements. Enc_{Pai} is an isomorphism $\mathbb{Z}_n \times \mathbb{Z}_n^* \to \mathbb{Z}_{n^2}^*$. Since $\mathbb{Z}_{n^2}^*$ has $\phi \cdot n$ elements and $\mathbb{Z}_n^*$ has ϕ elements, where ϕ is defined in (2), the function f is n-to-1 mapping: $\mathbb{Z}_{n^2}^* \to \mathbb{Z}_n^*$ and hence, the composition $f \circ Enc_{Pai}$ can be interpreted as a H-function and as a conditional random oracle if number r in correct Paillier encryption scheme can be treated as random.

This implies that element z as a function of r is strongly universal as defined by Wegman and Carter in [31]. In [30], Vaudenay defines this property as a perfect 1-wise decorrelation. Vaudenay showed, that in this case our scheme is secure against chosen plaintext attack (CPA) and chosen ciphertext attack (CCA) respectively (Theorem 7 in [30]). Then, according to [28, 29], textbook RSA signature on Paillier ciphertext c is existentially unforgeable under adaptive chosen-message attacks in the random oracle model. **End of proof.**

6.1 Anonymity Against Vendor

During the payment protocol, **P** randomizes his *Id* by adding it to a product $\alpha \cdot R$ of two numbers, where α is a random number chosen by **P** and r – random number received from **B**. Hence, **P** hides his *Id* for every payment by choosing different α every time.

6.2 Over Spending Prevention

Overspending prevention is achieved by **B** during deposit protocol. After the decryption of current payment data D, **B** extracts **P**'s *Id* and is able to trace all previous payments of **P** using his database.

7 Discussion and Conclusions

Most of divisible, anonymous, off-line, traceable e-cash systems have a common issue – data grows in size when transferring e-cash. We proposed a methodology, avoiding this drawback and the example of its realization. E-cash placed in e-wallet can be transferred to other users without growing in size. It is achieved by sacrificing such e-cash properties as off-line deposit and anonymity against bank.

We assume that the proposed realization is a step towards the creation of e-cash which would be (1) provably secure based on well understood assumptions, (2) efficient and (3) conceptually easy, which coincides with requirements presented in [26].

In the proposed methodology, bank represents trusted third party – TTP, which is able to trace all users' transactions. It provides us with several benefits in the sense of money laundering and forensic of other financial crimes.

For further research, we intend to improve our scheme by providing it with off-line deposit option.

References

1. Katz, J., Lindell, Y.: Introduction to Modern Cryptography. Chapman and Hall/CRC, Washington (2008)
2. Paillier, P.: Public-key cryptosystems based on composite degree residuosity classes. In: Stern, J. (ed.) EUROCRYPT 1999. LNCS, vol. 1592, pp. 223–238. Springer, Heidelberg (1999). doi:10.1007/3-540-48910-X_16
3. Rosenberg, B.: Handbook of Financial Cryptography and Security. Chapman and Hall/CRC, Washington (2011)
4. Pfitzmann, A., Köhntopp, M.: Anonymity, unobservability, and pseudonymity - a proposal for terminology. In: Federrath, H. (ed.) Designing Privacy Enhancing Technologies. LNCS, vol. 2009, pp. 1–9. Springer, Heidelberg (2001). doi:10.1007/3-540-44702-4_1
5. Okamoto, T.: An efficient divisible electronic cash scheme. In: Coppersmith, D. (ed.) CRYPTO 1995. LNCS, vol. 963, pp. 438–451. Springer, Heidelberg (1995). doi:10.1007/3-540-44750-4_35
6. Eng, T., Okamoto, T.: Single-term divisible electronic coins. In: De Santis, A. (ed.) EUROCRYPT 1994. LNCS, vol. 950, pp. 306–319. Springer, Heidelberg (1995). doi:10.1007/BFb0053446
7. Fan, C., Sun, W.Z., Hau, H.T.: Date Attachable Offline Electronic Cash Scheme, Department of Computer Science and Engineering, National Sun Yat-sen University, Kaohsiung, Taiwan (2014)
8. Pointcheval, D., Sanders, O., Traoré, J.S.: Cut Down the Tree to Achieve Constant Complexity in Divisible E-Cash (2015)
9. Canard, S., Pointcheval, D., Sanders, O., Traoré, J.: Divisible e-cash made practical. In: Katz, J. (ed.) PKC 2015. LNCS, vol. 9020, pp. 77–100. Springer, Heidelberg (2015). doi:10.1007/978-3-662-46447-2_4
10. Brands, S.: An efficient off-line electronic cash system based on the representation problem. Technical Report CS-R9323 1993, Centrum voor Wiskunde en Informatica (1993)
11. Camenisch, J.L., Hohenberger, S., Lysyanskaya, A.: Compact e-cash. In: Cramer, R. (ed.) EUROCRYPT 2005. LNCS, vol. 3494, pp. 302–321. Springer, Heidelberg (2005). doi:10.1007/11426639_18
12. Catalano, D., Gennaro, R., Howgrave-Graham, N.: The bit security of paillier's encryption scheme and its applications. In: Pfitzmann, B. (ed.) EUROCRYPT 2001. LNCS, vol. 2045, pp. 229–243. Springer, Heidelberg (2001). doi:10.1007/3-540-44987-6_15
13. Paillier, P.: Paillier encryption and signature schemes. In: van Tilborg, H. (ed.) Encyclopedia of Cryptography and Security, p. 453. Springer, Heidelberg (2005)
14. Asokan, N., Janson, P.A., Steiner, M., Waidner, M.: The state of the art in electronic payment systems, pp. 28–35 (1997)
15. Chaum, D., Pedersen, T.P.: Transferred cash grows in size. In: Rueppel, R.A. (ed.) EUROCRYPT 1992. LNCS, vol. 658, pp. 390–407. Springer, Heidelberg (1993). doi:10.1007/3-540-47555-9_32
16. Hanatani, Y., Komano, Y., Oht, K., Kunihiro, N.: Provably secure untraceable electronic cash against insider attacks. IEICE Trans. 90-A(5), 980–991 (2007)
17. Baseri, Y., Takhtaei, B., Mohajeri, J.: Secure untraceable off-line electronic cash system. Scientia Iranica 20(3), 637–646 (2013)
18. Wang, F., Chang, C.-C., Lin, C.: Security analysis on "secure untraceable off-line electronic cash system". Int. J. Netw. Secur. 18(3), 454–458 (2016)

19. Canard, S., Gouget, A., Traoré, J.: Improvement of efficiency in (Unconditional) anonymous transferable e-cash. In: Tsudik, G. (ed.) FC 2008. LNCS, vol. 5143, pp. 202–214. Springer, Heidelberg (2008). doi:10.1007/978-3-540-85230-8_19

20. Baldimtsi, F., Chase, M., Fuchsbauer, G., Kohlweiss, M.: Anonymous transferable e-cash. In: Katz, J. (ed.) PKC 2015. LNCS, vol. 9020, pp. 101–124. Springer, Heidelberg (2015). doi:10.1007/978-3-662-46447-2_5

21. Chase, M., Kohlweiss, M., Lysyanskaya, A., Meiklejohn, S.: Malleable signatures: new definitions and delegatable anonymous credentials. In: IEEE Computer Security Foundations Symposium (2014)

22. Canard, S., Gouget, A.: Divisible e-cash systems can be truly anonymous. In: Naor, M. (ed.) EUROCRYPT 2007. LNCS, vol. 4515, pp. 482–497. Springer, Heidelberg (2007). doi:10.1007/978-3-540-72540-4_28

23. Chaum, D., Fiat, A., Naor, M.: Untraceable electronic cash. In: Goldwasser, S. (ed.) CRYPTO 1988. LNCS, vol. 403, pp. 319–327. Springer, Heidelberg (1990). doi:10.1007/0-387-34799-2_25

24. Rabin, M.O.: Digitalized Signatures, in Foundations of Secure Computation. Academic Press, New York (1978)

25. Tsiounis, Y.S.: Efficient electonic cash: new notions and techniques. Ph.D. thesis, Northeastern University, Boston, Massachusetts (1997)

26. Frankel, Y., Tsiounis, Y., Yung, M.: Fair off-line e-cash made easy. In: Ohta, K., Pei, D. (eds.) ASIACRYPT 1998. LNCS, vol. 1514, pp. 257–270. Springer, Heidelberg (1998). doi:10.1007/3-540-49649-1_21

27. Brands, S.: Untraceable off-line cash in wallets with observers. In: Stinson, D.R. (ed.) CRYPTO 1993. LNCS, vol. 773, pp. 302–318. Springer, Heidelberg (1994). doi:10.1007/3-540-48329-2_26

28. Bellare, M., Rogaway, P.: The exact security of digital signatures - how to sign with RSA and rabin. In: Maurer, U.M. (ed.) EUROCRYPT 1996. LNCS, vol. 1070, pp. 399–416. Springer, Heidelberg (1996)

29. Coron, J.-S.: On the exact security of full domain hash. In: Bellare, M. (ed.) CRYPTO 2000. LNCS, vol. 1880, pp. 229–235. Springer, Heidelberg (2000). doi:10.1007/3-540-44598-6_14

30. Vaudenay, S.: Decorrelation: a theory for block cipher security. J. Cryptology 16(4), 249–286 (2003)

31. Wegman, M.N., Carter, J.L.: New hush functions and their use in authentication and set equality. J. Comput. Syst. Sci. 22, 265–279 (1981)

Author Index